The Individual Investor's Guide to

Low-Load Mutual *Funds*®

The American Association of Individual Investors

20th Edition 2001

The American Association of Individual Investors is an independent, not-for-profit corporation formed in 1978 for the purpose of assisting individuals in becoming effective managers of their own assets through programs of education, information, and research.

Previous editions were published under the title "The Individual Investor's Guide to No-Load Mutual Funds"

American Association of Individual Investors
625 North Michigan Avenue
Chicago, Illinois 60611
(312) 280-0170; (800) 428-2244
E-mail: members@aaii.com
Web site: www.aaii.com

ISBN 1-883328-07-1
ISSN: 1079-1841

Data in this guide was provided by Standard & Poor's Micropal and directly from the funds. While the material in this *Guide* cannot be guaranteed to be error free, it has been obtained from sources believed to be reliable.

Preface

Inside the *Guide* are the information and performance statistics you will need to make well-informed decisions on your mutual fund investments. Our goal is to provide pertinent information, organized to minimize your time spent collecting and comparing information on the increasingly large universe of mutual funds.

Information for this *Guide* was gathered from direct contact with funds and from Standard & Poor's Micropal. As always, our objective is full, accurate, and timely disclosure of investment information. The 2001 edition of the *Low-Load Mutual Fund Guide* covers 933 mutual funds.

John Bajkowski oversaw the development of the fund analysis format and supervised the data collection and verification. Jean Henrich and Lauren Schubel provided copy editing and Marika Magnee designed the cover. Alyna M. Johnson served as project editor for the *Guide*.

Chicago
March 2001

John Markese, Ph.D.
President

Table of Contents

How to Use This Guide 1

Selecting a mutual fund, while less time-consuming than investing in individual securities, does require some homework. No one should put money into an investment that is not understood. This does not require a detailed investigation of the fund's investments, but it does require an understanding of the investment objectives and strategies and the possible risks and returns.

This *Guide* is designed to provide you with that understanding. We have kept the chapters brief and to the point, so that individuals new to mutual fund investing will not be overwhelmed with unnecessary details.

Chapters 2 through 5 deal with the basics of investing in mutual funds—diversification; loads; various categories of mutual funds and what they mean; how to read a mutual fund's prospectus and annual report, as well as any other material they send you; and how to evaluate the risk of a mutual fund.

Those who are familiar with mutual funds may want to skip directly to Chapter 6, which describes how the mutual funds were chosen for inclusion in the *Guide*. Chapter 7 is a key to the terms used in the performance tables and the mutual fund data pages, and includes an explanation of how the returns were calculated and what the different risk measures mean.

Chapter 8 presents the performance tables, which include the historical performance of individual funds grouped by category along with corresponding benchmarks. While past performance is no indication of future performance, it may indicate the quality and consistency of fund management. From this section, you should pick out several mutual funds that meet your investment objectives and risk tolerance. These funds can then be examined more closely in the mutual fund data pages.

Chapter 9 contains the individual fund listings. The stock funds are listed alphabetically; their ticker symbol and investment category are indicated at the top of the page after the fund's name. The bond funds are listed separately, following the stock funds. These pages provide 10 years of per share data, performance statistics and risk measures, portfolio information, and shareholder services provided by the fund. Use the telephone numbers and Web addresses provided to contact the funds to request a copy of the prospectus and annual report. Make sure you read the prospectus carefully before investing in any mutual fund.

At the back of the *Guide* is a list of special category funds that includes asset allocation, index, fund of funds, global, sector, socially conscious, and state-specific tax-exempt bond funds. And finally, there is a list of fund changes, including fund name changes, investment category changes, and funds that were dropped from the *Guide*.

Investing in Mutual Funds 2

A mutual fund is an investment company that pools investors' money to invest in securities. An open-end mutual fund continuously issues new shares when investors want to invest in the fund, and it redeems shares when investors want to sell. A mutual fund trades directly with its shareholders, and the share price of the fund represents the market value of the securities that the fund holds.

There are several advantages that mutual funds offer individual investors. They provide:

- Professional investment management usually at a low cost, even for small accounts;
- A diversified group of securities that only a large portfolio can provide;
- Information through prospectuses and annual reports that facilitates comparisons among funds;
- Special services such as check writing, dividend reinvestment plans, telephone switching, and periodic withdrawal and investment plans;
- Account statements that make it easy to track the value of your investment and that ease the paperwork at tax time.

Successful investing takes time and effort, and it requires special knowledge and relevant, up-to-date information. Investors must spend a considerable amount of energy searching for opportunities and monitoring each investment. Professional investment management is relatively cheap with mutual funds. The typical adviser charges about 0.5% annually for managing a fund's assets. For an individual making a $10,000 investment, that comes to only $50 a year.

Of course, mutual fund investing does not preclude investing in securities on your own. One useful strategy would be to invest in mutual funds and individual securities. The mutual funds would ensure your participation in overall market moves and lend diversification to your portfolio, while the individual securities would provide you with the opportunity to apply your specific investment analysis skills.

DIVERSIFICATION

If there is one ingredient to successful investing that is universally agreed upon, it is the benefit of diversification. This is a concept that is backed by a great deal of research, market experience, and common sense. Diversification reduces risk. Risk to investors is frequently defined as volatility of return—in other words, how much an investment's return might vary over a year. Investors prefer returns that are relatively predictable, and thus less volatile. On the other hand, they want returns that are high, but higher returns are accompanied by higher risks. Diversification eliminates some of the risk without reducing potential returns.

Mutual funds, because of their size and the laws governing their operation, provide investors with diversification that might be difficult for an individual to duplicate. This is true not only for common stock funds, but also for bond funds, municipal bond funds, international bond and stock funds—in fact, for almost all mutual funds. Even the sector funds that invest only within one industry offer diversification within that industry. The degree of diversification will vary among funds, but most will provide investors with some amount of diversification.

AVOIDING EXCESSIVE CHARGES

This book is dedicated to no-load and low-load mutual funds. Investors should realize that:

- A load is a sales commission that goes to the seller of the fund shares;
- A load does not go to anyone responsible for managing the fund's assets and does not serve as an incentive for the fund manager to perform better;
- Funds with loads, on average, consistently underperform no-load funds when the load is taken into consideration in performance calculations;
- For every high-performing load fund, there exists a similar no-load or low-load fund that can be purchased more cheaply;
- Loads understate the real commission charged because they reduce the total amount being invested: $10,000 invested in a 6% front-end load fund results in a $600 sales charge and only a $9,400 investment in the fund;
- If the money paid for the load had been working for you, as in a no-load fund, it would have been compounding over your holding period.

The bottom line in any investment is how it performs for you, the investor, and that performance includes consideration of all loads, fees, and expenses. There may be some load funds that will do even better factoring in the load, but you have no way of finding that fund in advance. The only guide you have is historical performance, which is not necessarily an indication of future performance. With a heavily loaded fund, you are starting your investment with a significant loss—the load. Avoid unnecessary charges whenever possible.

SORTING OUT CHARGES

It is best to stick with no-load or low-load funds, but they are becoming more difficult to distinguish from heavily loaded funds. The use of high front-end loads has declined, and funds are now turning to other kinds of charges. Some mutual funds sold by brokerage firms, for example, have lowered their front-end loads to 5%, and others have introduced back-end loads (deferred sales charges), which are sales commissions paid when exiting the fund. In both instances, the load is often accompanied by annual charges.

On the other hand, some no-load funds have found that to compete, they must market themselves much more aggressively. To do so, they have introduced charges of their own.

The result has been the introduction of low loads, redemption fees, and annual charges. Low loads—up to 3%—are sometimes added instead of the annual charges. In addition, some funds have instituted a charge for investing or withdrawing money.

Redemption fees work like back-end loads: You pay a percentage of the value of your fund when you get out. Loads are on the amount you have invested, while redemption fees are calculated against the value of your fund assets. Some funds have sliding scale redemption fees, so that the longer you remain invested, the lower the charge when you leave. Some funds use redemption fees to discourage short-term trading, a policy that is designed to protect longer-term investors. These funds usually have redemption fees that disappear after six months.

Some funds, usually index funds, charge a fee, 1% for example, on all new money invested in the fund. This charge defrays the cost of investing the new money. In effect, the new investment pays its way rather than having the transaction costs charged to investments already in the fund.

Probably the most confusing charge is the annual charge, the 12b-1 plan. The adoption of a 12b-1 plan by a fund permits the adviser to use fund assets to pay for distribution costs, including advertising, distribution of fund literature such as prospectuses and annual reports, and sales commissions paid to brokers. Some funds use 12b-1 plans as masked load charges: They levy very high rates on the fund and use the money to pay brokers to sell the fund. Since the charge is annual and based on the value of the investment, this can result in a total cost to a long-term investor that exceeds a high up-front sales load. A fee table (see Chapter 4: Understanding Mutual Fund Statements) is required in all prospectuses to clarify the impact of a 12b-1 plan and other charges.

The fee table makes the comparison of total expenses among funds easier. Selecting a fund based solely on expenses, including loads and charges, will not give you optimal results, but avoiding funds with high expenses and unnecessary charges is important for long-term performance.

Mutual Fund Categories 3

Mutual funds come in all shapes and sizes; there are over 900 funds covered in this book alone, each with its own characteristics. Many mutual funds, however, have shared investment objectives that generally lead to other characteristics that are similar.

These shared characteristics allow us to divide mutual funds into several broad categories. This chapter defines the mutual fund categories we used for this book. In this guide, the individual fund data pages appear alphabetically (stock funds followed by bond funds); the fund's category is indicated beneath the fund's name.

The table on page 6 summarizes some important characteristics of funds by category. Averages for returns, yield, and risk (see Chapter 7 for definition of these terms) illustrate some of the differences in the categories.

AGGRESSIVE GROWTH FUNDS

The investment objective of aggressive growth funds is maximum capital gains. They invest aggressively in common stocks and tend to stay fully invested over the market cycle. Sometimes, these funds will borrow money to purchase securities, and some may engage in trading stock options or take positions in stock index futures.

Aggressive growth funds typically provide low income distributions. This is because they tend to be fully invested in common stocks and do not earn a significant amount of interest income. In addition, the common stocks they invest in are generally growth-oriented stocks that pay little or no cash dividends.

Many aggressive growth funds concentrate their assets in small firms and particular industries or segments of the market, and their degree of diversification may not be as great as other types of funds. These investment strategies result in increased risk. Thus, they tend to perform better than the overall market during bull markets, but fare worse during bear markets.

In general, long-term investors who need not be concerned with monthly or yearly variation in investment return should be more tolerant of the risks in this class of funds. Because of the extreme volatility of return, however, risk-averse investors with a short-term investment horizon may find that these mutual funds lie well outside their comfort zones. During prolonged market declines, aggressive growth funds can sustain severe declines in net asset value.

Market timing is not a strategy we recommend. Although the transaction costs of switching in and out of no-load mutual funds are near zero, it can create significant tax liabilities. In addition, the ability to consistently time the market correctly, after adjusting for risk, costs, and taxes, has not been demonstrated. However, aggressive growth funds, with their high volatility and fully invested position, do make ideal vehicles for those who believe they know the next market move.

Investment Category	5-Year Annual Return (%)	Bull Market Return (%)	Bear Market Return (%)	Yield (%)	Beta (x)	Average Maturity (yrs)	Standard Deviation (%)
Aggressive Growth	14.6	119.2	-20.6	0.1	1.16	na	32.5
Growth	16.1	49.7	-5.4	0.3	0.94	na	19.5
Growth & Income	14.3	33.5	-0.1	1.8	0.79	na	17.4
International Stock	8.3	90.9	-24.0	0.9	0.79	na	22.7
Balanced	11.4	28.1	-3.2	3.1	0.55	na	11.0
Corporate Bond	5.7	4.1	4.0	7.0	na	7.5	3.3
Corp. High-Yield Bond	5.4	8.0	-8.0	10.8	na	6.5	7.8
Government Bond	5.9	-0.9	7.0	4.9	na	9.1	3.1
Mortgage-Backed Bond	5.9	2.5	6.5	6.3	na	7.0	2.4
General Bond	5.6	2.1	5.8	6.0	na	8.2	3.0
Tax-Exempt Bond	4.9	-1.1	4.2	4.7	na	12.3	3.5
International Bond	5.2	15.5	-0.7	6.6	na	7.4	7.8
Investment Style—Stock Funds							
Large Cap	17.0	60.0	-9.3	0.5	1.00	na	18.8
Growth	18.5	88.2	-19.4	0.1	1.15	na	23.0
Value	16.5	36.3	1.6	0.9	0.86	na	17.4
Mid Cap	14.9	45.8	0.7	0.5	0.85	na	21.2
Growth	15.5	76.8	-15.4	0.2	1.00	na	25.6
Value	14.1	28.2	12.1	0.8	0.71	na	20.0
Small Cap	15.1	101.3	-16.9	0.1	1.05	na	31.1
Growth	16.5	134.3	-24.1	0.1	1.18	na	34.1
Value	11.8	17.8	2.7	0.3	0.65	na	18.4
Growth	17.7	113.4	-22.2	0.1	1.13	na	27.2
Value	14.4	26.2	5.7	1.1	0.76	na	18.1

GROWTH FUNDS

The investment objective of growth funds is to obtain long-term growth of invested capital. Growth funds typically are more stable than aggressive growth funds. Generally, they invest in growth-oriented firms that are more mature and that pay cash dividends.

The degree of concentration of assets is not as severe as with aggressive growth funds. Additionally, these funds may move from effectively fully-invested to larger cash positions during uncertain market environments.

In general, growth fund performance tends to mirror the market during bull and bear markets. Some growth funds have been able to perform relatively well during bear markets because their managers were able to change portfolio composition by a much greater degree or to maintain much higher cash positions than aggressive growth fund managers. However, higher cash positions can also cause the funds to underperform aggressive growth funds during bull markets.

Aggressive investors should consider holding both growth fund shares and aggressive growth fund shares in their overall portfolios. This is an especially appealing strategy for investors who hold aggressive growth mutual funds that invest in small stock growth firms. The portfolios of these funds complement the portfolios of growth funds, leading to greater overall diversification. Aggressive growth funds often concentrate their investments in different industries than growth funds. The combination produces overall returns that will tend to be less volatile than an investment in only aggressive growth funds.

As with aggressive growth funds, these funds can sustain severe declines during prolonged bear markets. Since some portfolio managers of growth funds attempt to time the market over the longer market cycle, using these funds to move in and out of the market for timing purposes may be counter-productive.

GROWTH AND INCOME FUNDS

Growth and income funds generally invest in the common stocks and convertible securities of large, seasoned, well-established, cash-dividend-paying companies. The funds attempt to provide shareholders with significant income along with long-term growth. They generally attempt to avoid excessive fluctuations in return. These funds may have a high concentration of public utility and financial common stocks and sometimes convertible securities in their portfolios. The funds also provide higher income distributions, less variability in return, and greater diversification than growth and aggressive growth funds. Names such as equity-income, income, and total return have been attached to funds that have characteristics of growth and income funds. Because of the high current income offered by these kinds of funds, potential investors should keep the tax consequences in mind.

BALANCED FUNDS

The balanced fund category has become less distinct in recent years, and a significant overlap in fund objectives exists between growth and income funds and balanced funds. In general, the portfolios of balanced funds consist of investments in common stocks and substantial investments in bonds and convertible securities. The range as a percentage of the total portfolio of stocks and bonds is usually stated in the investment objective, and the portfolio manager has the option of allocating the proportions within the range. Some asset allocation funds—funds that have a wide latitude of portfolio composition change—can also be found in the balanced category. Balanced funds are generally less volatile than aggressive growth, growth, and growth and income funds. As with growth and income funds, balanced funds provide a high dividend yield.

BOND FUNDS

Bond mutual funds are attractive to investors because they provide diversification and liquidity, which is not as readily attainable in direct bond investments.

Bond funds have portfolios with a wide range of average maturities. Many funds use their names to characterize their maturity structure. Generally, short term means that the portfolio has a weighted average maturity of less than three years. Intermediate implies an average maturity of three to 10 years, and long term is over 10 years. The longer the maturity, the greater the change in fund value when interest rates change. Longer-term bond funds are riskier than shorter-term funds, and they usually offer higher yields.

Bond funds are principally categorized by the types of bonds they hold. Corporate bond funds invest primarily in investment-grade corporate bonds of various maturities; however, corporate high-yield bond funds provide high income and invest generally in corporate bonds rated below investment grade.

Government bond funds invest in the bonds of the U.S. government and its agencies, while mortgage funds invest primarily in mortgage-backed bonds. General bond funds invest in a mix of government and agency bonds, corporate bonds, and mortgage-backed bonds. Tax-exempt bond funds invest in bonds whose income is exempt from federal income tax. Some tax-exempt funds may invest in bonds whose income is also exempt from the income tax of a specific state.

INTERNATIONAL BOND AND STOCK FUNDS

International funds invest in bonds and stocks of foreign firms and governments. Some funds specialize in regions, such as the Pacific or Europe, and others invest in multiple foreign regions. In addition, some funds—usually termed "global funds"—invest in both foreign and U.S. securities. We have two classifications by type of investment of international funds—international stock funds and international bond funds.

International funds provide investors with added diversification. The most important factor when diversifying a portfolio is selecting investments whose returns are not highly correlated. Within the U.S., investors can diversify by selecting securities of firms in different industries. In the international realm, investors take the diversification process one step further by holding securities of firms in different countries. The more independently these foreign markets move in relation to the U.S. stock market, the greater the diversification benefit will be, and the lower the risk of the total portfolio.

In addition, international funds overcome some of the difficulties investors face in making foreign investments directly. For instance, individuals have to thoroughly understand the foreign brokerage process, be familiar with the various foreign marketplaces and their economies, be aware of currency fluctuation trends, and have access to reliable financial information. This can be a monumental task for the individual investor.

There are some risks unique to investing internationally. In addition to the risk inherent in investing in any security, there is an additional exchange rate risk. The return to a U.S. investor from a foreign security depends on both the security's return in its own currency and the rate at which that currency can be exchanged for U.S. dollars. Another uncertainty is political risk, which includes government restriction, taxation, or even total prohibition of the exchange of one currency into another. Of course, the more the mutual fund is diversified among various countries, the less the risk involved.

OTHER TYPES OF FUNDS

There are many specialized mutual funds that do not have their own categories. Instead, they will be found in one of the various categories mentioned above. These funds are classified by their investment objectives rather than by their investment strategies. For instance, several funds specialize in specific sectors or industries, but one industry-specific fund does not necessarily appear in the same category as another industry-specific sector fund. For example, a technology sector fund would likely appear in the aggressive growth category, while a utility sector fund would be found in the growth and income category. Gold funds are sector funds and, due to their high volatility and low yields, appear in the aggressive growth category. Specialized funds include global funds, small company funds, "socially conscious" funds, index funds, funds investing in funds, and asset allocation funds.

Asset allocation funds, for example, are usually one of two types. Some allocation funds are designed to provide diversification among the various categories of investments and within each investment category. For example, an asset allocation fund may hold minimum percentages in stocks, bonds, cash, and international investments. The second asset allocation strategy used by some funds is to move money around according to what the fund managers believe to be optimal proportions given their expectations for the economy, interest rates, and other market factors. These latter asset allocation funds are market timing funds, distinctly different and with greater risk than the asset allocation funds striving solely for diversification. A careful reading of the investment objective and strategy sections of the prospectus will help you distinguish a diversification-driven asset allocation fund from a market-timing fund.

One other fund type deserves a special mention—the index fund. An example of an index fund is Vanguard's Index Trust 500, categorized as a growth and income fund. This fund is designed to match the Standard & Poor's 500 stock index and does so by investing in all 500 stocks in the S&P 500; the amounts invested in each stock are proportional to the firm's market value representation in the S&P 500. Statistics on index funds are quite useful for comparison with other funds, since indexes represent a widely followed segment of the market. Index funds are available covering most major segments of the bond and stock markets—domestic and international. Because they are unmanaged, they make no research efforts to select particular stocks or bonds, nor do they make timing decisions. They are always 100% invested. This passive management approach makes the cost of managing an index fund relatively low. Lists of specialized funds appear in Appendix A: "Special Types of Funds" at the back of this *Guide*.

Understanding Mutual Fund Statements 4

One of the advantages of mutual fund investing is the wealth of information that mutual funds provide to fund investors and prospective investors. Taken together, the various reports provide investors with vital information concerning financial matters and how the fund is managed, both key elements in the selection process. In fact, mutual fund prospectuses, annual reports, and performance statistics are key sources of information most investors will need in the selection and monitoring process.

To new mutual fund investors, the information may seem overwhelming. However, regulations governing the industry have standardized the reports: Once you know where to look for information, the location will hold true for almost all funds.

There are basically five types of statements produced by the mutual fund: the prospectus; the statement of additional information; annual, semiannual, and quarterly reports; marketing brochures; and account statements. Actually, the second report—the statement of additional information—is part of the prospectus. However, mutual funds are allowed to simplify and streamline the prospectus, if they choose, by dividing it into two parts: a prospectus that all prospective investors must receive if requested, and the statement of additional information—which the fund must send investors if they specifically request it. Some fund families also currently offer an abbreviated profile prospectus.

THE PROSPECTUS

The prospectus is the single most important document produced by the mutual fund, and it is must-reading for investors before investing. Current shareholders must be sent new prospectuses when they are updated, at least once every 14 months.

The prospectus is generally organized into sections, and it must cover specific topics. The cover usually gives a quick synopsis of the fund: investment category, sales or redemption charges, minimum investment, retirement plans available, and address and telephone number. More detailed descriptions are in the body of the prospectus.

Fee Table: All mutual fund prospectuses must include a table near the front that delineates all fees and charges to the investor. The table contains three sections: The first section lists shareholder fees, including all front-end and back-end loads and redemption fees; the second section lists all annual fund operating expenses, including management fees and any 12b-1 charges, as a percentage of net assets; and the third section is an illustration of the total cost of these fees and charges to an investor over time. The illustration assumes an initial investment of $10,000 and a 5% growth rate for the fund, and states the total dollar cost to an investor if shares were redeemed at the end of one year, three years, five years, and 10 years.

Selected Per Share Data and Ratios: One of the most important sections of the prospectus contains the selected per share data and ratios, which provides statistics on income and capital changes per share of the fund. The per share figures are given for the life of the fund or 10 years, whichever is less. Also included are important statistical summaries of investment activities throughout each period. These financial statements are also contained in the annual report.

The Prospectus Fee Table: An Example

The following table describes the fees and expenses that are incurred when you buy, hold or sell shares of the fund. The annual fund operating expenses provided below for the fund do not reflect the effect of any reduction of certain expenses during the period.

Shareholder Fees (paid by the investor directly)

Sales charge (load) on purchases and reinvested distributions	None
Deferred sales charge (load) on redemptions	None
Annual account maintenance fee (for accounts under $2,500)	$12.00

Annual Fund Operating Expenses (paid from fund assets)

Management fee	0.63%
Distribution and Service (12b-1) fee	None
Other Expenses	0.22%
Total annual fund operating expenses	**0.85%**

A portion of the brokerage commissions that the fund pays is used to reduce the fund's expenses. In addition, through arrangements with the fund's transfer agent, credits realized as a result of uninvested cash balances are used to reduce transfer agent expenses. Including this reduction, the total fund operating expenses would have been 0.83%.

This example helps you compare the cost of investing in the fund with the cost of investing in other mutual funds.

Let's say, hypothetically, that the fund's annual return is 5% and that your shareholder fees and the fund's annual operating expenses are exactly as described in the fee table. This example illustrates the effect of fees and expenses, but is not meant to suggest actual or expected fees and expenses or returns, all of which may vary. For every $10,000 you invested, here's how much you would pay in total expenses if you close your account at the end of each time period indicated.

1 year	**$87**
3 years	**$271**
5 years	**$471**
10 years	**$1049**

Source: Fidelity Capital Appreciation Fund prospectus, December 23, 2000.

Selected Per Share Data and Ratios: An Example

	Six Months Ended June 30, 2000*	Vanguard 500 Index Fund Investor Shares Year Ended December 31, 1999	1998	1997	1996	1995
Net Asset Value, Beginning of Period	**$135.33**	**$113.95**	**$ 90.07**	**$69.17**	**$57.60**	**$42.97**
Investment Operations						
Net Investment Income	.65	1.370	1.33	1.31	1.28	1.22
Net Realized and Unrealized Gain (Loss) on Investments	(1.21)	22.415	24.30	21.50	11.82	14.76
Total from Investment Operations	(.56)	23.785	25.63	22.81	13.10	15.98
Distributions						
Dividends from Net Investment Income	(.61)	(1.410)	(1.33)	(1.32)	(1.28)	(1.22)
Distributions from Realized Capital Gains	—	(.995)	(.42)	(.59)	(.25)	(.13)
Total Distributions	(.61)	(2.405)	(1.75)	(1.91)	(1.53)	(1.35)
Net Asset Value, End of Period	**$134.16**	**$135.33**	**$113.95**	**$90.07**	**$69.17**	**$57.60**
Total Return**	**–0.42%**	**21.07%**	**28.62%**	**33.19%**	**22.88%**	**37.45%**
Ratios/Supplemental Data						
Net Assets, End of Period (Millions)	$105,583	$104,652	$74,229	$49,358	$30,332	$17,372
Ratio of Total Expenses to Average Net Assets	0.18%***	0.18%	0.18%	0.19%	0.20%	0.20%
Ratio of Net Investment Income to Average Net Assets	0.97%***	1.13%	1.35%	1.66%	2.04%	2.38%
Turnover Rate†	9%***	6%	6%	5%	5%	4%

*Unaudited.

**Total return figures do not reflect the annual account maintenance fee of $10 applied on balances under $10,000.

***Annualized.

†Turnover rates excluding in-kind redemptions were 7%, 3%, 3%, 3%, 2%, and 2%, respectively.

Source: Vanguard 500 Index supplement to the prospectus, November 1, 2000.

The per share section summarizes the financial activity over the fund's fiscal year, which may or may not correspond to the calendar year, to arrive at the ending net asset value for the fund. The financial activity summarized includes increases in net asset value due to dividend and interest payments received and capital gains from investment activity. Decreases in net asset value are due to capital losses from investment activity, investment expenses, and payouts to fund shareholders in the form of distributions.

Potential investors may want to note the line items in this section. *Investment income* represents the dividends and interest earned by the fund during its fiscal year. *Expenses* reflect such fund costs as the management fee, legal fees, and transfer agent fees. These expenses are given in detail in the statement of operations section of the annual report.

Net investment income is investment income less expenses. This line is important for investors to note because it reflects the level and stability of net income over the time period. A high net investment income would most likely be found in funds that have income, rather than growth, as their investment category. Since net investment income must be distributed to shareholders to avoid direct taxation of the fund, a high net investment income has the potential of translating into a high tax liability for the investor.

Net realized and unrealized gain (loss) on investments is the change in the value of investments that have been sold (realized) during the year or that continue to be held (unrealized) by the fund.

Distributions to fund shareholders are also detailed. These distributions will include dividends from net investment income for the current fiscal period. Tax law requires that income earned must be distributed in the calendar year earned. Also included in distributions will be any realized net capital gains.

The last line in the per share section will be the *net asset value* at the end of the year, which reflects the value of one share of the fund. It is calculated by determining the total assets of the fund and dividing by the number of mutual fund shares outstanding. The figure will change for a variety of reasons, including changes in investment income, expenses, gains, losses, and distributions. Depending upon the source of change, a decline in net asset value may or may not be due to poor performance. For instance, a decline in net asset value may be due to a distribution of net realized gains on securities.

The financial ratios at the bottom of the per share financial data are important indicators of fund performance and strategy. The *expense ratio* relates expenses incurred by the fund to average net assets. These expenses include the investment advisory fee, legal and accounting fees, and 12b-1 charges to the fund; they do not include fund brokerage costs, loads, or redemption fees. A high expense ratio is difficult for a fund manager to overcome and detracts from your investment return. In general, common stock funds have higher expense ratios than bond funds, and smaller funds have higher expense ratios than larger funds. International funds also tend to have higher expense ratios than domestic funds. Index funds usually have the lowest expense ratios. The average expense ratio for common stock funds is 1.00%, international stock funds 1.30%, index stock funds 0.40%, and bond funds (taxable and non-taxable) about 0.60%.

The *ratio of net investment income to average net assets* is very similar to a dividend yield. This, too, should reflect the investment category of the fund. Common stock funds with income as a significant part of their investment objective, such as growth and income funds, would be expected to have the highest ratios and aggressive growth funds would normally have ratios close to 0%. Bond funds would normally have the highest ratios of all funds.

The portfolio *turnover rate* is the lower of purchases or sales divided by average net assets. It reflects how frequently securities are bought and sold by the fund. For purposes of determining the turnover rate for common stock funds, fixed-income securities with a maturity of less than a year are excluded, as are all government securities, short- and long-term. For bond funds, however, long-term U.S. government bonds are included.

Investors should take note of the portfolio turnover rate, because the higher the turnover, the greater the brokerage costs incurred by the fund. Brokerage costs are not reflected in the expense ratio but instead are directly reflected as a decrease in net asset value. In addition, mutual funds with high turnover rates generally have higher capital gains distributions—a potential tax liability. Aggressive growth mutual funds are most likely to have high turnover rates. Some bond funds also have very high portfolio turnover rates. A 100% portfolio turnover rate indicates that the value of the portfolio was completely turned over in a year; a 200% portfolio turnover indicates that the value of the portfolio was completely turned over twice in a year. The portfolio turnover rate for the average mutual fund is around 100% but varies with market conditions and investment category.

Investment Objective/Policy: The investment objective section of the prospectus elaborates on the brief sentence or two from the prospectus cover. In this section, the fund describes the types of investments it will make—whether it is bonds, stocks, convertible securities, options, etc.—along with some general guidelines as to the proportions these securities will represent in the fund's portfolio. The investment objective statement usually indicates whether it will be oriented toward capital gains or income. In this section, the management will also briefly discuss its approach to market timing, risk assumption, and the anticipated level of portfolio turnover. Some prospectuses may indicate any investment restrictions they have placed on the fund, such as purchasing securities on margin, selling short, concentrating in firms or industries, trading foreign securities, and lending securities; this section may also state the allowable proportions in certain investment categories. The restrictions section is usually given in more detail in the statement of additional information.

Fund Management: The fund management section names the investment adviser and gives the advisory fee schedule. Most advisers charge a management fee on a sliding scale that decreases as assets under management increase. Occasionally, some portion of the fund adviser's fees is subject to the fund's performance relative to the market.

Some prospectuses will describe the fund's officers and directors with a short biography of affiliations and relevant experience. For most funds, however, this information is provided in more detail in the statement of additional information. The fund shareholders elect the board of directors; the board of directors selects the fund adviser. The adviser is usually a firm operated by or affiliated with officers of the fund. Information on fund officers and directors is not critical to fund selection. The prospectus also names the portfolio manager of the fund. The portfolio manager is responsible for the day-to-day investment decisions of the fund and is employed by the fund adviser. Who the portfolio manager is and how long the manager has been in the position can be useful in judging historical performance.

Other Important Sections: There are several other sections in a mutual fund prospectus of which investors should be aware. They will appear under various headings, depending upon the prospectus, but they are not difficult to find.

Mutual funds that have 12b-1 plans must describe them in the prospectus. A description of these plans must be prominently and clearly placed in the prospectus, usually in a section titled "Distribution Plan." The distribution plan details the marketing aspects of the fund and how it relates to fund expenses. For instance, advertising, distribution of fund literature, and any arrangements with brokers would be included in the marketing plan; the 12b-1 plan pays for these distribution expenses. The distribution plan section specifies the maximum annual 12b-1 charge that can be made. Funds often charge less than the maximum. The actual charge to the fund of a 12b-1 plan is listed at the front of the prospectus in the fee table.

The *capital stock* section, or *fund share characteristics* section, provides shareholders with a summary of their voting rights, participation in dividends and distributions, and the number of authorized and issued shares of the fund. Often, a separate section will discuss the tax treatment that will apply to fund distributions, which may include dividends, interest, and capital gains.

The *how-to-buy-shares* section gives the minimum initial investment and any subsequent minimums; it will also list load charges or fees. In addition, information on mail, wire, and telephone purchases is provided, along with distribution reinvestment options, automatic exchange, investment and withdrawal plans, and retirement options.

The *how-to-redeem-shares* section discusses telephone, written, and wire redemption options, including automatic withdrawal plans, with a special section on signature guarantees and other documents that may be needed. Also detailed are any fees for reinvestment or redemption. Shareholder services are usually outlined here, with emphasis on exchanges among funds in a family of funds. This will include any fees for exchanging, any limits on the number of exchanges allowed, and any other exchange restrictions.

STATEMENT OF ADDITIONAL INFORMATION

This document elaborates on the prospectus. The investment objectives section is more in-depth, with a list and description of investment restrictions. The management section gives brief biographies of directors and officers, and provides the number of fund shares owned beneficially by the officers and directors named. The investment adviser section, while reiterating the major points made in the prospectus, gives all the expense items and contract provisions of the agreement between the adviser and the fund. If the fund has a

12b-1 plan, further details will likely be in the statement of additional information.

Many times, the statement of additional information will include much more information on the tax consequences of mutual fund distributions and investment. Conditions under which withholding for federal income tax will take place are also provided. The fund's financial statements are incorporated by reference to the annual report to shareholders and generally do not appear in the statement of additional information. Finally, the independent auditors give their opinion on the accuracy of the fund's financial statements.

ANNUAL, SEMIANNUAL, AND QUARTERLY REPORTS

All funds must send their shareholders audited annual and semiannual reports. Mutual funds are allowed to combine their prospectus and annual report; some do this, but many do not.

The annual report describes the fund activities over the past year and provides a listing of all investments of the fund at market value as of the end of the fiscal year. Sometimes the cost basis of each investment is also given. Looking in-depth at the individual securities held by the fund is probably a waste of time. However, it is helpful to be aware of the overall investment categories. For instance, investors should look at the percentage invested in common stocks, bonds, convertible bonds, and any other holdings. In addition, a look at the types of common stocks held and the percentage of fund assets by industry classification gives the investor some indication of how the portfolio will fare in various market environments.

The annual report will also have a balance sheet, listing all assets and liabilities of the fund by general category. This holds little interest for investors.

The statement of operations, similar to an income statement, is of interest only in that the fund expenses are broken down. For most funds, the management fee is by far the largest expense; the expense ratio in the prospectus conveys much more useful information. The statement of changes in net assets is very close to the financial information provided in the prospectus, but the information is not on a per share basis. Per share information will, however, frequently be detailed in the annual report in a separate section. Footnotes to the financial statements elaborate on the entries, but other than any pending litigation against the fund, they are most often routine.

The quarterly or semiannual reports are current accounts of the investment portfolio and provide more timely views of the fund's investments than does the annual report.

MARKETING BROCHURES AND ADVERTISEMENTS

These will generally provide a brief description of the fund. However, the most important bit of information is the telephone number to call and request the fund prospectus and annual report, if you have not received them already.

The rules regarding mutual fund advertising have been tightened and standardized. All mutual funds that use performance figures in their ads must now include one-, five-, and 10-year total return figures. Bond funds that quote yields must use a standardized method for computing yield, and they must include total return figures as well. Finally, any applicable sales commissions must be mentioned in the advertisement.

ACCOUNT STATEMENTS

Mutual funds send out periodic account statements detailing reinvestment of dividend and capital gains distributions, new purchases or redemptions, and any other account activity such as service fees. This statement provides a running account balance by date with share accumulations, an account value to date, and a total of distributions made to date. *These statements are invaluable for tax purposes and should be saved.* The fund will also send out, in January, a Form 1099-DIV for any distributions made in the previous year and a Form 1099-B if any mutual fund shares were sold.

Understanding Risk 5

Risk tolerance refers to the level of volatility of an investment that an investor finds acceptable. The anticipated holding period of an investment is important because it should affect the investor's risk tolerance. Time is a form of diversification; longer holding periods provide greater diversification across different market environments. Investors who anticipate longer holding periods can take on more risk.

The liquidity needs of an investor similarly help define the types of funds that the investor should consider. Liquidity implies preservation of capital, and if liquidity is important, then mutual funds with smaller variations in value should be considered. A liquid mutual fund is one in which withdrawals from the fund can be made at any time with a reasonable certainty that the per share value will not have dropped sharply. Highly volatile aggressive growth funds are the least liquid, and short-term fixed-income funds are the most liquid.

A LOOK AT RISK

Risk is the most difficult concept for many investors to grasp, and yet much of the mutual fund investment decision depends on an understanding of risk. There are many different ways to categorize investment risk and numerous approaches to the measurement of risk. If we can assume that the volatility of the return on your mutual fund investment is the concern you grapple with when you think of risk, the task of making decisions about risk becomes easier.

Questions about how much value a mutual fund is likely to lose in a down market or how certain it is that a fund will be worth a given amount at the end of the year are the same concerns as volatility of return. Changes in the domestic and international economies, interest rates, exchange rates, corporate profits, consumer confidence, and general expectations all combine to move markets up and down, creating volatility, or risk.

Total risk for a mutual fund measures variation in return from all sources. As an example, variation in return for common stocks is caused by factors unique to the firm, industry variables, and conditions affecting all stocks. Market risk refers to the variables such as interest rates, inflation, and the business cycle that affect all stocks to some degree. In well-diversified portfolios of common stock, the firm and industry risk of the various stocks in the portfolio offset each other; thus, these portfolios tend to have lower total risk, and this total risk is usually composed almost entirely of market risk. For less diversified portfolios, funds that hold very few stocks, or sector funds that concentrate investment in one industry, total risk is usually higher and is composed of firm and industry risk in addition to market risk.

Risk levels based upon total risk are given for all funds with 36 months of performance data. The five categories (high, above average, average, below average, and low) serve as a way to compare the risk inherent in common stock funds, international funds, sector funds, bond funds, or any type of mutual fund. Shorter-term bond funds would be expected to have relatively low total risk while some of the concentrated, less-diversified, aggressive common stock funds would likely be ranked in the high total risk category.

The total risk measure will enable you to construct a portfolio of funds that reflects your risk tolerance and the holding period you anticipate for your portfolio. Portfolios for individuals with low risk tolerance and short holding periods should be composed predominantly of funds that are less volatile, with lower total risk. Individuals with high risk tolerances and longer holding periods can form appropriate portfolios by combining mutual funds with higher total risk.

STANDARD DEVIATION

Total risk is measured by the standard deviation statistic, a numerical measure of how much the return on a mutual fund has varied, no matter what the cause, from the historical average return of the fund. Higher standard deviations indicate higher total risk. The category risk rank measures the total risk of a fund to the median total risk for all funds in the same investment category. The rankings for category risk are high, above average, average, below average, and low. Funds ranked above average and high for category risk should produce returns above the average for the investment category.

The risk index indicates the magnitude of the standard deviation for a fund relative to the median standard deviation for funds in the category. A risk index of 1.2, for example, means that the standard deviation for a fund is 20% higher than the median standard deviation for the category.

MARKET RISK

Market risk is a part of total risk but measures only the sensitivity of the fund to movements in the general market. This is valuable information to the individual investor, particularly when combined with use of the total risk and category risk rank measures, to judge how a mutual fund will perform in different market situations. The market risk measure used for common stock funds is beta; for bond funds, average maturity is used.

BETA

Beta is a measure of the relative volatility inherent in a mutual fund investment. This volatility is compared to some measure of the market such as Standard & Poor's index of 500 common stocks. The market's beta is always 1.0 by definition, and a money market fund's beta is always 0. If you hold a mutual fund with a beta of 1.0, it will move, on average, in tandem with the market. If the market is up 10%, the fund will be up, on average, 10%, and if the market drops 10%, the fund will drop, on average, 10%. A mutual fund with a beta of 1.5 is 50% more volatile than the market: If the market is up 10%, the fund will be up, on average, 50% more, or 15%; conversely, if the market is down 10%, the fund, on average, will be down 15%. A negative beta, a rare occurrence, implies that the mutual fund moves in the opposite direction of the market's movement.

The higher the fund's beta, the greater the volatility of the investment in the fund and the less appropriate the fund would be for shorter holding periods or to meet liquidity needs. Remember that beta is a relative measure: A low beta only implies that the fund's movement is not volatile relative to the market. Its return, however, may be quite variable, resulting in high total risk. For instance, industry-specific sector fund moves may not be related to market volatility, but changes in the industry may cause these funds' returns to fluctuate widely. For a well-diversified stock fund, beta is a very useful measure of risk, but for concentrated funds, beta only captures a portion of the variability that the fund may experience. Betas for gold funds, for example, can be very misleading. Gold funds often have relatively low betas, but these funds are extremely volatile. Their volatility stems from factors that do not affect the common stock market as much. In addition, the betas of gold funds sometimes change significantly from year to year.

AVERAGE MATURITY

For all bond funds, the average maturity of the bonds in the portfolio is reported as a market risk measure, rather than beta. The volatility of a bond fund is determined by how the fund reacts primarily to changes in interest rates, although high-yield (junk) bond funds and international bond funds can be affected significantly by factors other than interest rates. When interest rates rise, bond funds fall in value, and conversely, when interest rates fall, bond mutual funds rise in value. The longer the average maturity of the bond fund, the greater will be the variation in the return on the bond fund when interest rates change. Bond mutual fund investors with less risk tolerance and shorter holding periods should seek shorter maturity funds, and longer-term bond fund investors who are more risk tolerant will find funds with longer maturities a better match.

In the case where a bond fund holds mortgage-backed securities, average maturity may not capture the potential for decline in effective maturity when interest rates fall and mortgages are refinanced. Some mortgage funds also use derivatives, highly leveraged financial instruments that derive their value from movements in specific interest rates or indexes, which further complicate an analysis of their risk. Bond funds that hold corporate bonds and municipal bonds also face changing effective maturities when interest rates decline and bond issuers call bonds before maturity.

Which Funds Were Included 6

The funds that appear in *The Individual Investor's Guide to Low-Load Mutual Funds* were selected from the universe of funds. Following are the various screens we used to arrive at the final selection.

SIZE

Funds must appear on the National Association of Securities Dealers mutual fund list found in most major newspapers. Funds are required to have $50 million in assets and three full years of performance statistics to qualify for inclusion in the *Guide*. All funds must be available for investment through contact with the fund directly.

LOADS

The decision as to what constitutes a significant load is difficult, but we took this approach in the *Guide*:

- All funds with front-end loads, back-end loads, or redemption fees of 3% or less were included if the fund did not also have a 12b-1 charge. Funds with redemption fees that disappear after six months that also have 12b-1 charges appear in this *Guide*.
- Funds with 12b-1 plans and no front- or back-end loads were included in the *Guide*; we note, however, if the fund has a 12b-1 plan and what the annual charge is. Investors should carefully assess these plans individually.
- Funds that impose a load that exceeds 3% or increase an existing load above 3% are dropped from the *Guide*.

A Key to Terms and Statistics 7

Most of the information used in the mutual fund data pages and performance tables is provided by Standard & Poor's Micropal, but some may come from mutual fund reports (the prospectus and annual and quarterly reports) and solicitation of information directly from the fund. Any data source has the potential for error, however, and before investing in any mutual fund, the prospectus for the fund should be read and the annual report examined.

When *na* appears in the performance tables or on the mutual fund page, it indicates that the number was not available or does not apply in that particular instance. For example, the 10-year annual return figure would not be available for funds that have been operating less than 10 years. For three-year annual return, category risk, standard deviation, total risk, and beta, funds operating less than three years would not have the number available. We do not compile the bull and bear ratings for funds not operating during the entire bull or bear market period. Dashes (—) are used generally during years when the fund was not in operation or did not have a complete calendar year of operations. All numbers are truncated rather than rounded when necessary, unless noted otherwise in the following descriptions.

The following provides an explanation of the terms we have used in the performance tables and mutual fund data pages. The explanations are listed in the order in which the data and information appear on the mutual fund pages.

Fund Name: The funds are presented alphabetically by fund name.

Ticker: The ticker symbol for each fund is given in parentheses for those investors who may want to access data with their computer or touch-tone phone. The ticker is four letters and is usually followed by an "X," indicating that this is a mutual fund. For example, the Acorn fund ticker symbol is ACRNX.

Investment Category: The fund's investment category is indicated at the top of the page next to the fund's ticker symbol. After evaluating the information and statistics, we placed all mutual funds in exclusive categories by investment category and type of investment. For more complete definitions of the mutual fund investment categories used in the *Guide*, see Chapter 3: "Mutual Fund Categories."

Fund Telephone Number(s) and Internet Address: The management company telephone number and Internet address (if applicable) that investors can call or access to have specific questions answered or to obtain a copy of the prospectus.

Fund Inception Date: The day the fund was made available to the public for purchase.

Performance

Return (%): Return percentages for the periods below.

3yr Annual: Assuming an investment on January 1, 1998, the annual total return if held through December 31, 2000.

5yr Annual: Assuming an investment on January 1, 1996, the annual total return if held through December 31, 2000.

10yr Annual: Assuming an investment on January 1, 1991, the annual total return if held through December 31, 2000.

Bull: This return reflects the fund's performance in the most recent bull market, starting September 1, 1998, and continuing through March 31, 2000.

Bear: This return reflects the fund's performance in the most recent bear market, from April 1, 2000, through November 30, 2000.

Differ from category (+/–): The difference between the return for the fund and average return for all funds in the same investment category for the *3yr Annual, 5yr Annual, 10yr Annual, Bull,* and *Bear* periods. When the difference from category is negative, the fund underperformed the average fund in its investment category for the period by the percent indicated. The rankings, with possibilities of high, above average, average, below average, and low, are relative to all other funds within the same investment category. A rank of high, for example, would indicate that the return is in the highest 20% for that time period of all funds in the investment category.

Standard Deviation: A measure of total risk, expressed as an annual return, that indicates the degree of variation in return experienced relative to the average return for a fund as measured over the last three years. The higher the standard deviation, the greater the total risk of the fund. Standard deviation of any fund can be compared to any other fund. Possibilities are high, above average, average, below average, and low.

Category Risk Index: A numerical measure of relative category risk, the risk index is a ratio of the total risk of the fund to the average total risk of funds in the category as measured over the last three years. Ratios above 1.0 indicate higher than average risk and ratios below 1.0 indicate lower than average risk for the category. The possibilities are high, above average, average, below average, and low.

Beta: A risk measure that relates the fund's volatility of returns to the market. The higher the beta of a fund, the higher the market risk of the fund. The figure is based on monthly returns for 36 months. A beta of 1.0 indicates that the fund's returns will on average be as volatile as the market and move in the same direction; a beta higher than 1.0 indicates that if the market rises or falls, the fund will rise or fall respectively but to a greater degree; a beta of less than 1.0 indicates that if the market rises or falls, the fund will rise or fall to a lesser degree. The S&P 500 index always has a beta of 1.0 because it is the measure we selected to represent the overall stock market. Beta is a meaningful figure of risk only for well-diversified common stock portfolios. For sector funds and other concentrated portfolios, beta is less useful than total risk as a measure of risk. Beta was not calculated for bond funds since they do not react in the same way to the factors that affect the stock market. For bond funds, the average maturity of the bond portfolio is more indicative of market risk, so it is used in place of beta.

Avg Mat: For bond funds, average maturity in years is an indication of market risk. When interest rates rise, bond prices fall, and when interest rates fall, bond prices rise. The longer the average maturity of the bonds held in the portfolio, the greater the sensitivity of the fund to interest rate changes will be, and thus, the greater the risk. The refinancing of mortgages and the calling of outstanding bonds can affect average maturity when interest rates decline. An *na* indicates that the mutual fund did not provide an average maturity figure.

Return (%): This is a total return figure, expressed as a percentage. All distributions were assumed to have been reinvested. Rate of return is calculated on the basis of the calendar year. Return figures do not take into account front-end and back-end loads, redemption fees, or one-time or annual account charges, if any. The 12b-1 charge, as part of the expense ratio, is reflected in the return figure.

Differ from Category (+/–): The difference between the return for the fund and average return for all funds in the same investment category for the time period.

Return, Tax-Adjusted (%): Annual return after adjusting for the maximum federal income tax, currently 39.6% on income and short-term capital gains distributions and 20% on long-term capital gains distributions.

Per Share Data

Dividends, Net Income ($): Per share income distributions for the calendar year. The timing of net income distributions can be found in the prospectus.

Distrib'ns, Cap Gains ($): Per share distributions for the calendar year from realized capital gains after netting out realized losses. The timing of capital gains distributions can be found in the prospectus.

Net Asset Value ($): Calendar year-end net asset value is the sum of all securities held, based on their market value, divided by the number of mutual fund shares outstanding.

Expense Ratio (%): The sum of administrative fees plus adviser management fees and 12b-1 fees divided by the average net asset value of the fund, stated as a percentage. Brokerage costs incurred by the fund are not included in the expense ratio but are instead reflected directly in net asset value. Front-end loads, back-end loads, redemption fees, and account activity charges are not included in this ratio.

Yield (%): The per share annual income distribution made by the fund divided by the sum of the year-ending net asset value plus any capital gains distributions made during the year. This ratio is similar to a dividend yield and would be higher for income-oriented funds and lower for growth-oriented funds. The figure only reflects income; it is not total return. For some funds the yield may be distorted if the fund reports short-term capital gains as income.

Portfolio Turnover (%): A measure of the trading activity of the fund, which is computed by dividing the lesser of purchases or sales for the year by the monthly average value of the securities owned by the fund during the year. Securities with maturities of less than one year are excluded from the calculation. The result is expressed as a percentage, with 100% implying a complete portfolio turnover within one year.

Total Assets (Millions $): Aggregate fund value in millions of dollars at the end of the calendar year.

Portfolio

Portfolio Manager: The name of the portfolio manager(s) and the year when the senior manager(s) began managing the fund are noted, providing additional information useful in evaluating past performance. (Senior managers are listed first.) Funds managed by a committee are so noted. For some funds, a recent change in the portfolio manager(s) may indicate that the long-term annual performance figures and other performance classifications are less meaningful.

Investm't Category: Notes the investment category of the fund. Following this is the geographical distribution, and any special emphasis of the fund. The possible choices in the section include:

Geographical Distribution: Domestic, Foreign

Special Emphasis: Asset Allocation, Index, Sector, and State Specific

Investment Style: Investment style can be categorized by the size of firms the fund invests in as measured by market capitalization and the investment approach employed by the fund, either growth or value or both. The investment style attributed to the fund indicates that the historical performance of the fund most closely follows the style(s) checked (listed below). More than one size may be checked, indicating a blend of size, and growth/value may be checked, indicating a blend of growth and value investment approaches. Style is *only* calculated for equity funds with three or more years of performance data, otherwise this section appears in gray.

Style Categories: Large Cap, Mid Cap, Small Cap, Growth, Grth/Val, Value ('Cap' denotes capitalization, which is market price per share times number of common stock shares outstanding.)

Portfolio: The portfolio composition classifies investments by type and gives the percentage of the total portfolio invested in each. Due to rounding of the percentages and the practice of leverage (borrowing) to buy securities, the portfolio total percentage may not equal 100.0%.

Shareholder Information

Minimum Investment and Minimum IRA Investment: The minimum initial and subsequent investments, by mail, in the fund are detailed. Minimum investment by telephone or by wire may be different. Often, funds will have a lower minimum IRA investment; this is also indicated.

Maximum Fees:

Load: The maximum load is given, if any, and whether the load is front-end or back-end is indicated.

12b-1: If a fund has a 12b-1 plan, the percentage that the fund charges is given.

Other: Redemption fees are given along with the time period, if appropriate.

Services:

IRA: Notes whether the fund offers an individual retirement account option.

Keogh: Notes whether the fund offers a Keogh account option.

Telephone Exchange: Indicates whether telephone exchanges with other funds in the family are permitted.

Check in the prospectus to determine whether the fund allows for an automatic exchange between funds in the family; whether the fund allows for automatic investments through an investor's checking account; and whether the fund allows the automatic and systematic withdrawal of money from the fund. All funds have automatic reinvestment of distributions options.

Fund Performance Rankings

8

When choosing among mutual funds, most investors start with performance statistics: How well have the various mutual funds performed in the past? If past performance alone could perfectly predict future performance, selection would be easy.

What past performance can tell you is how well the fund's management has handled different market environments, how consistent the fund has been, and how well the fund has done relative to its risk level, relative to other similar funds, and relative to the market.

We present performance statistics in several different forms. First, we provide an overall picture, with the average performance of each mutual fund category for the last five years, along with benchmarks for large and small company domestic stocks, international stocks, bonds, and Treasury bills. The top 20 and bottom 20 mutual fund performers for the last year are given as a recent reference of performance. The list changes each year and reflects the cyclical nature of financial markets and the changing success of individual mutual fund managers. Lists of the top 50 mutual funds ranked by annual return over the last 10 years, five years, and three years are given for a long-term perspective on investment performance.

Since the performance of a fund must be judged relative to similar funds, we have also grouped the funds by investment category and ranked them according to their total return performance for the last year. To make the comparison easier, we have also provided other data. The fund's annual returns for the last three years, five years, and 10 years give a longer-term perspective on the performance of the fund; category and total risk ranks are also given to judge performance. (To maintain ranking accuracy, funds are sorted by more decimal points of return than those published in the *Guide*.)

Key to Fund Categories used in Performance Tables

AG-Aggressive Growth	**Bal-**Balanced	**B-MB-**Mortgage-Backed Bond
Grth-Growth	**B-Cor-**Corporate Bond	**B-Gen-**General Bond
GI-Growth & Income	**B-CHY-**Corp. High-Yield Bond	**B-TE-**Tax-Exempt Bond
IntlS-International Stock	**B-Gov-**Government Bond	**IntlB-**International Bond

Total Risk and Return Performance for Different Mutual Fund Categories

Fund Investment Category	Annual Return (%) 2000	1999	1998	1997	1996	5yr	Total Return (%) Bull	Bear	Std Dev (%)	Total Risk
Aggressive Growth	-6.0	57.5	15.1	14.8	18.3	14.6	119.2	-20.6	32.5	abv av
Growth	3.5	18.9	14.3	27.1	22.3	16.1	49.7	-5.4	19.5	av
Growth & Income	5.7	10.8	12.8	26.9	19.7	14.3	33.5	-0.1	17.4	av
International Stock	-19.4	60.7	5.8	1.3	14.5	8.3	90.9	-24.0	22.7	abv av
Balanced	2.0	10.7	13.3	18.8	13.9	11.4	28.1	-3.2	11.0	blw av
Corporate Bond	8.0	1.3	5.9	9.1	5.5	5.7	4.1	4.0	3.3	low
Corporate High-Yield Bond	-6.9	5.6	1.9	14.6	15.7	5.4	8.0	-8.0	7.8	blw av
Government Bond	13.8	-3.0	9.1	9.8	2.1	5.9	-0.9	7.0	3.1	low
Mortgage-Backed Bond	9.9	1.0	6.2	8.5	4.2	5.9	2.5	6.5	2.4	low
General Bond	9.7	0.0	7.3	8.4	3.5	5.6	2.1	5.8	3.0	low
Tax-Exempt Bond	9.4	-2.6	5.6	8.2	3.7	4.9	-1.1	4.2	3.5	low
International Bond	4.5	3.8	3.6	3.9	14.1	5.2	15.5	-0.7	7.8	blw av
Investment Style—Stock Funds										
Large Cap	-4.4	22.4	25.1	29.4	21.3	17.0	60.0	-9.3	18.8	av
Growth	-13.4	35.5	36.9	28.9	20.7	18.5	88.2	-19.4	23.0	abv av
Value	7.2	12.0	13.3	31.1	22.7	16.5	36.3	1.6	17.4	av
Mid Cap	15.3	16.9	7.4	23.2	20.1	14.9	45.8	0.7	21.2	av
Growth	-5.1	36.0	20.3	21.9	18.9	15.5	76.8	-15.4	25.6	abv av
Value	28.8	8.2	-2.0	21.0	21.4	14.1	28.2	12.1	20.0	av
Small Cap	0.2	52.5	4.5	18.1	19.8	15.1	101.3	-16.9	31.1	abv av
Growth	-5.4	71.5	8.8	14.8	17.6	16.5	134.3	-24.1	34.1	high
Value	14.9	4.7	-6.6	26.5	26.2	11.8	17.8	2.7	18.4	av
Growth Average	-9.7	55.0	23.1	20.5	19.0	17.7	113.4	-22.2	27.2	abv av
Value Average	15.1	6.7	4.0	28.0	22.9	14.4	26.2	5.7	18.1	av
Index Comparisons										
S&P 500	-9.0	21.0	28.5	33.3	22.9	18.3	56.2	-11.5	17.7	av
S&P MidCap 400	17.4	14.7	19.1	32.2	19.1	20.4	60.7	-3.1	21.8	abv av
Russell 2000*	-3.0	21.2	-2.5	22.3	16.4	10.3	52.0	-16.5	24.7	abv av
MS EAFE**	-13.9	27.2	20.3	2.0	6.3	7.4	49.0	-16.8	16.0	blw av
MSCI Europe	-8.1	16.2	28.9	24.1	21.5	15.8	32.6	-14.2	16.2	blw av
MSCI Far East	-26.9	62.6	2.5	-26.6	-10.0	-4.3	105.4	-23.5	23.5	abv av

Total Risk and Return Performance for Different Mutual Fund Categories

Fund Investment Category	Annual Return (%) 2000	1999	1998	1997	1996	5yr	Total Return (%) Bull	Bear	Std Dev (%)	Total Risk
Index Comparisons *(cont'd)*										
Lehman Brothers bond indexes										
Corporate	9.3	-1.9	8.5	10.2	3.2	5.8	1.8	5.7	3.8	low
Corporate High Yield	-5.8	2.3	1.8	12.7	11.3	4.2	5.0	-5.4	6.2	low
Government	13.2	-2.2	9.8	9.5	2.7	6.4	0.3	7.4	3.6	low
Mortgage Backed	11.1	1.8	6.9	9.4	5.3	6.9	3.9	7.9	2.4	low
Municipal	11.6	-2.0	6.4	9.1	4.4	5.8	-0.2	5.8	3.5	low
Treasury Bills	6.1	4.8	5.2	5.3	5.3	5.3	6.5	4.1	0.2	low

**Index of small company stocks*
***Europe, Australia, Far East Index*

Total Risk & Return for Domestic Taxable Bond Mutual Funds by Maturity

Maturity Category	Annual Return (%) 2000	1999	1998	1997	1996	5yr	Total Return (%) Bull	Bear	Std Dev (%)	Total Risk
Short-Term Bond Funds	7.7	2.8	6.1	6.3	4.6	5.5	4.6	5.1	1.5	low
Interm-Term Bond Funds	7.1	0.7	6.6	9.6	5.4	5.7	3.0	3.6	3.2	low
Long-Term Bond Funds	15.5	-4.7	9.3	12.8	1.9	6.3	-2.3	6.7	4.0	low

The Top 20 Performers: 2000

Type	Fund Name (Ticker)	Annual Return (%) 2000	3yr	5yr	10yr	Category Risk	Total Risk
Grth	Fidelity Sel Natural Gas (FSNGX)	71.2	23.7	18.5	na	high	high
AG	Fidelity Sel Med Dlvry (FSHCX)	67.8	3.5	8.1	14.3	blw av	high
Grth	Vanguard Specl: Health (VGHCX)	60.5	34.2	30.4	25.4	low	blw av
GI	Galaxy II: Utility (IUTLX)	59.3	18.2	17.0	na	high	abv av
AG	INVESCO Energy/Inv (FSTEX)	58.1	17.4	21.7	11.2	abv av	high
GI	American Gas Index (GASFX)	55.8	16.4	18.8	14.1	av	av
AG	CGM Focus (CGMFX)	53.9	20.0	na	na	blw av	high
Grth	Fidelity Sel Insurance (FSPCX)	53.2	20.1	25.0	22.2	high	high
AG	T Rowe Price Hlth Science (PRHSX)	52.1	26.2	24.9	na	av	high
AG	Fidelity Sel Energy Serv (FSESX)	50.3	9.1	24.1	14.8	high	high
Grth	Fidelity Sel Home Finance (FSVLX)	50.2	3.9	17.4	27.8	high	high
B-Gov	Amer Cent: Target 2020/Inv (BTTTX)	48.0	9.5	9.1	13.4	high	av
B-Gov	Amer Cent: Target 2025/Inv (BTTRX)	42.6	11.1	na	na	high	av
AG	Fidelity Sel Air Trans (FSAIX)	39.7	26.0	21.5	20.2	low	abv av
AG	Warburg Glb Hlth Sci/Cmn (WPHSX)	38.9	25.3	na	na	blw av	high
AG	Wasatch: Micro Cap (WMICX)	37.5	29.5	27.3	na	blw av	abv av
GI	Century Shares (CENSX)	37.4	8.8	17.7	17.2	high	high
GI	Clipper (CFIMX)	37.4	17.0	20.1	19.7	low	blw av
Grth	Wasatch: Core Growth (WGROX)	37.3	18.5	19.8	19.3	abv av	abv av
GI	T Rowe Price Fincl Svc (PRISX)	36.7	15.7	na	na	high	abv av

The Bottom 20 Performers: 2000

Type	Fund Name (Ticker)	Annual Return (%) 2000	3yr	5yr	10yr	Category Risk	Total Risk
AG	ProFunds: UltraOTC/Inv (UOPIX)	-73.7	35.7	na	na	high	high
IntlS	Warburg Japan Sm Co/Cmn (WPJPX)	-71.8	10.8	-2.4	na	high	high
IntlS	Warburg Japan Growth/Cmn (WPJGX)	-68.7	5.0	2.1	na	high	high
IntlS	Matthews Korea (MAKOX)	-52.8	24.3	-14.2	na	high	high
IntlS	Fidelity Japan Smaller Co (FJSCX)	-50.2	30.1	2.9	na	high	high
IntlS	Pilgrim Wldwd Emerg Mkt/A (LEXGX)	-47.0	-7.2	-5.3	2.6	high	high
AG	Janus Inv: Venture (JAVTX)	-45.7	17.0	14.3	16.2	high	high
AG	PBHG Tech & Comm (PBTCX)	-41.0	36.7	32.4	na	high	high
IntlS	Excelsior Pacific-Asia (USPAX)	-40.1	5.9	-2.8	na	abv av	high
IntlS	Scudder Pacific Opport (SCOPX)	-39.1	-2.2	-9.1	na	high	high
IntlS	Montgomery Glbl Commun/R (MNGCX)	-39.1	24.3	19.2	na	high	high
AG	Berger New Generation/Inv (BENGX)	-38.6	22.5	na	na	high	high
AG	Northern Technology (NTCHX)	-38.4	38.2	na	na	high	high
AG	Rydex: OTC/Inv (RYOCX)	-37.9	32.4	32.3	na	abv av	high
IntlS	Gabelli Gl Growth/AAA (GICPX)	-37.4	20.3	22.6	na	abv av	high
AG	Fidelity Sel Telecomm (FSTCX)	-37.4	13.7	14.2	17.8	av	high
IntlS	T Rowe Price Intl: Japan (PRJPX)	-37.2	13.3	0.2	na	abv av	abv av
IntlS	Strong Asia Pacific (SASPX)	-36.9	6.1	-3.3	na	abv av	high
IntlS	Strong Int'l Stk (STISX)	-36.6	4.3	1.0	na	abv av	high
IntlS	Fidelity Japan (FJPNX)	-36.4	20.9	6.9	na	abv av	high

The Top 50 Performers: 10 Years, 1991-2000

Type	Fund Name	Annual Return (%) 10yr	5yr	3yr	2000	Category Risk	Total Risk
AG	Fidelity Sel Electronics (FSELX)	34.0	32.9	37.0	-17.6	high	high
AG	Fidelity Sel Technology (FSPTX)	28.6	28.3	39.7	-32.3	high	high
AG	Fidelity Sel Computers (FDCPX)	28.3	26.3	34.7	-31.1	abv av	high
AG	INVESCO Tech/Inv (FTCHX)	28.3	26.6	35.0	-22.7	high	high
AG	Fidelity Sel Software (FSCSX)	28.2	25.7	30.8	-20.3	abv av	high
AG	Fidelity Sel Brokerage (FSLBX)	27.8	31.9	20.8	27.9	av	high
Grth	Fidelity Sel Home Finance (FSVLX)	27.8	17.4	3.9	50.2	high	high
Grth	Fidelity Sel Financl Serv (FIDSX)	26.8	22.8	14.1	28.5	high	high
AG	Fidelity Sel Develop Comm (FSDCX)	26.7	26.0	37.8	-29.7	high	high
Grth	Vanguard Specl: Health (VGHCX)	25.4	30.4	34.2	60.5	low	blw av
Grth	Fidelity Sel Banking (FSRBX)	25.2	18.7	6.0	18.7	high	high
Grth	INVESCO Financial Svc/Inv (FSFSX)	25.1	22.2	13.1	26.6	high	abv av
AG	T Rowe Price Science & Tech (PRSCX)	24.9	16.9	23.4	-34.1	abv av	high
AG	Fidelity Aggressive Grth (FDEGX)	24.0	23.9	28.4	-27.1	abv av	high
AG	Spectra/N (SPECX)	23.9	20.6	19.7	-32.4	av	high
AG	INVESCO Dynamics/Inv (FIDYX)	23.8	22.8	24.9	-7.7	av	high
AG	RS: Emerging Growth/A (RSEGX)	23.7	31.3	39.4	-25.0	high	high
AG	Fidelity Sel Biotech (FBIOX)	23.3	30.0	45.1	32.7	high	high
Grth	Legg Mason Eq: Value/P (LMVTX)	22.9	27.0	20.3	-7.1	abv av	abv av
Grth	Fidelity Sel Health Care (FSPHX)	22.8	23.2	23.3	36.6	low	av
Grth	Vanguard PRIMECAP (VPMCX)	22.7	24.5	22.8	4.4	abv av	abv av
Grth	INVESCO Leisure/Inv (FLISX)	22.6	22.2	25.5	-7.9	av	abv av
AG	Fidelity Growth Company (FDGRX)	22.3	24.3	28.8	-6.3	av	high
Grth	Fidelity Sel Insurance (FSPCX)	22.2	25.0	20.1	53.2	high	high
AG	Janus Inv: Twenty (JAVLX)	21.9	26.2	24.5	-32.4	blw av	high
AG	PBHG Growth (PBHGX)	21.6	9.6	14.2	-22.9	high	high
Grth	Harbor: Capital Apprec (HACAX)	21.6	21.1	18.2	-17.0	high	abv av
AG	Dreyfus Founders: Dscvry/F (FDISX)	21.3	22.5	26.8	-8.2	abv av	high
AG	Strong Adv Common Stock/Z (STCSX)	21.3	17.1	13.9	-1.2	low	abv av
Grth	Fidelity Contrafund (FCNTX)	21.0	18.1	15.2	-6.8	blw av	av
AG	Kaufmann (KAUFX)	21.0	13.8	12.0	10.8	blw av	high
Grth	Weitz Srs: Value (WVALX)	20.9	25.2	23.1	19.6	low	av
Grth	Mairs & Power Growth (MPGFX)	20.7	19.2	14.0	26.4	low	av
Grth	Brandywine (BRWIX)	20.7	17.9	17.7	7.0	high	abv av
AG	Amer Cent: Ultra/Inv (TWCUX)	20.6	16.4	15.0	-19.9	low	abv av
Grth	Liberty Acorn/Z (ACRNX)	20.5	18.9	15.8	10.0	av	abv av
AG	Fidelity Sel Multimedia (FBMPX)	20.4	14.7	14.6	-23.0	low	abv av
AG	Amer Cent: Giftrust/Inv (TWGTX)	20.3	7.2	10.7	-16.4	high	high
AG	Fidelity Retirement Grth (FDFFX)	20.3	21.1	26.6	1.7	av	high
AG	Fidelity Sel Air Trans (FSAIX)	20.2	21.5	26.0	39.7	low	abv av
AG	Columbia Special (CLSPX)	20.2	18.1	21.8	13.8	blw av	high
Grth	Fidelity Blue Chip Growth (FBGRX)	20.2	17.0	14.4	-10.5	av	abv av
Grth	Longleaf Partners (LLPFX)	20.0	16.9	12.0	20.6	blw av	av
Grth	Muhlenkamp (MUHLX)	19.8	20.0	12.9	25.3	abv av	abv av
GI	Clipper (CFIMX)	19.7	20.1	17.0	37.4	low	blw av
Grth	Warburg Cap App/Cmn (CUCAX)	19.7	23.4	20.8	-5.2	high	abv av
AG	Fidelity OTC Port (FOCPX)	19.6	19.2	21.0	-26.8	abv av	high
Grth	Strong Opportunity/Inv (SOPFX)	19.6	19.5	18.7	8.5	blw av	av
Grth	Fidelity Low Priced Stock (FLPSX)	19.6	15.0	7.8	18.8	low	av
GI	Selected American Shares (SLASX)	19.5	22.3	15.2	9.3	abv av	av

The Top 50 Performers: Five Years, 1996-2000

Type	Fund Name	Annual Return (%) 5yr	10yr	3yr	2000	Category Risk	Total Risk
AG	Firsthand: Tech Value (TVFQX)	40.7	na	47.8	-9.9	high	high
AG	Fidelity Sel Electronics (FSELX)	32.9	34.0	37.0	-17.6	high	high
AG	PBHG Tech & Comm (PBTCX)	32.4	na	36.7	-41.0	high	high
AG	Rydex: OTC/Inv (RYOCX)	32.3	na	32.4	-37.9	abv av	high
AG	Fidelity Sel Brokerage (FSLBX)	31.9	27.8	20.8	27.9	av	high
AG	RS: Emerging Growth/A (RSEGX)	31.3	23.7	39.4	-25.0	high	high
AG	Fidelity New Millennium (FMILX)	30.9	na	35.8	-6.0	high	high
IntlS	INVESCO Telcom/Inv (ISWCX)	30.8	na	36.0	-26.9	high	high
AG	Janus Inv: Olympus (JAOLX)	30.5	na	35.0	-21.6	av	high
Grth	Vanguard Specl: Health (VGHCX)	30.4	25.4	34.2	60.5	low	blw av
AG	Fidelity Sel Biotech (FBIOX)	30.0	23.3	45.1	32.7	high	high
AG	White Oak Growth (WOGSX)	28.9	na	29.4	3.5	blw av	high
AG	Fidelity Sel Technology (FSPTX)	28.3	28.6	39.7	-32.3	high	high
AG	Van Wagoner Emerging Grth (VWEGX)	27.6	na	49.4	-20.9	high	high
AG	Fremont: US Micro Cap (FUSMX)	27.4	na	28.2	-10.6	abv av	high
Grth	PBHG Large Cap Grth (PBHLX)	27.3	na	30.3	1.7	high	high
AG	Wasatch: Micro Cap (WMICX)	27.3	na	29.5	37.5	blw av	abv av
Grth	Legg Mason Eq: Value/P (LMVTX)	27.0	22.9	20.3	-7.1	abv av	abv av
AG	INVESCO Tech/Inv (FTCHX)	26.6	28.3	35.0	-22.7	high	high
AG	Fidelity Sel Computers (FDCPX)	26.3	28.3	34.7	-31.1	abv av	high
AG	Vanguard Capital Opport (VHCOX)	26.3	na	45.5	18.0	blw av	high
AG	Northern Select Equity (NOEQX)	26.3	na	26.1	-3.9	blw av	high
AG	Janus Inv: Twenty (JAVLX)	26.2	21.9	24.5	-32.4	blw av	high
AG	PBHG Select Equity (PBHEX)	26.2	na	32.8	-24.5	high	high
AG	Citizens: Emg Gr/R (WAEGX)	26.1	na	33.5	-0.6	av	high
Grth	Weitz Partners Value (WPVLX)	26.1	na	24.0	21.0	low	av
Grth	Fidelity Mid Cap Stock (FMCSX)	26.1	na	28.6	32.0	high	high
AG	Fidelity Sel Develop Comm (FSDCX)	26.0	26.7	37.8	-29.7	high	high
AG	Janus Inv: Mercury (JAMRX)	25.8	na	33.9	-22.7	blw av	high
AG	Fidelity Sel Software (FSCSX)	25.7	28.2	30.8	-20.3	abv av	high
Grth	Weitz Srs: Value (WVALX)	25.2	20.9	23.1	19.6	low	av
GI	Janus Inv: Growth & Income (JAGIX)	25.1	na	21.7	-11.4	high	abv av
Grth	Fidelity Sel Insurance (FSPCX)	25.0	22.2	20.1	53.2	high	high
AG	T Rowe Price Hlth Science (PRHSX)	24.9	na	26.2	52.1	av	high
AG	Dreyfus Gr & Val: Emg Ldrs (DRELX)	24.7	na	18.0	9.4	blw av	abv av
Grth	Fidelity Export & Multi (FEXPX)	24.7	na	20.7	1.4	av	abv av
AG	RS: Information Age/A (RSIFX)	24.6	na	30.7	-35.0	high	high
IntlS	Fidelity Nordic (FNORX)	24.6	na	23.6	-8.4	abv av	abv av
Grth	Vanguard PRIMECAP (VPMCX)	24.5	22.7	22.8	4.4	abv av	abv av
IntlS	Artisan Int'l (ARTIX)	24.3	na	28.9	-10.5	abv av	high
AG	Fidelity Growth Company (FDGRX)	24.3	22.3	28.8	-6.3	av	high
AG	Fidelity Sel Energy Serv (FSESX)	24.1	14.8	9.1	50.3	high	high
IntlS	Amer Cent: Intl Disc/Inv (TWEGX)	24.0	na	23.9	-14.2	abv av	high
AG	Fidelity Aggressive Grth (FDEGX)	23.9	24.0	28.4	-27.1	abv av	high
Grth	Gabelli Growth (GABGX)	23.6	19.1	19.2	-10.5	abv av	abv av
Grth	Strong Growth (SGROX)	23.4	na	26.3	-9.2	high	high
Grth	Warburg Cap App/Cmn (CUCAX)	23.4	19.7	20.8	-5.2	high	abv av
AG	Van Wagoner Micro-Cap Gr (VWMCX)	23.2	na	41.7	-18.2	high	high
Grth	Fidelity Sel Health Care (FSPHX)	23.2	22.8	23.3	36.6	low	av
Grth	Weitz Srs: Hickory (WEHIX)	23.1	na	14.5	-17.2	abv av	abv av

The Top 50 Performers: Three Years, 1998-2000

Type	Fund Name	Annual Return (%) 3yr	5yr	10yr	2000	Category Risk	Total Risk
AG	Van Wagoner Emerging Grth (VWEGX)	49.4	27.6	na	-20.9	high	high
AG	Firsthand: Tech Value (TVFQX)	47.8	40.7	na	-9.9	high	high
AG	Vanguard Capital Opport (VHCOX)	45.5	26.3	na	18.0	blw av	high
AG	Fidelity Sel Biotech (FBIOX)	45.1	30.0	23.3	32.7	high	high
AG	Brazos Micro Cap Grth/Y (BJMIX)	41.8	na	na	18.8	av	high
AG	Van Wagoner Micro-Cap Gr (VWMCX)	41.7	23.2	na	-18.2	high	high
AG	Fidelity Sel Technology (FSPTX)	39.7	28.3	28.6	-32.3	high	high
AG	RS: Emerging Growth/A (RSEGX)	39.4	31.3	23.7	-25.0	high	high
AG	PBHG Large Cap 20 (PLCPX)	38.4	na	na	-22.0	high	high
AG	Northern Technology (NTCHX)	38.2	na	na	-38.4	high	high
AG	Fidelity Sel Develop Comm (FSDCX)	37.8	26.0	26.7	-29.7	high	high
AG	Fidelity Sel Electronics (FSELX)	37.0	32.9	34.0	-17.6	high	high
AG	Strong Growth 20/Inv (SGRTX)	36.8	na	na	-10.3	abv av	high
AG	PBHG Tech & Comm (PBTCX)	36.7	32.4	na	-41.0	high	high
IntlS	INVESCO Telcom/Inv (ISWCX)	36.0	30.8	na	-26.9	high	high
AG	Fidelity New Millennium (FMILX)	35.8	30.9	na	-6.0	high	high
AG	ProFunds: UltraOTC/Inv (UOPIX)	35.7	na	na	-73.7	high	high
AG	Janus Inv: Olympus (JAOLX)	35.0	30.5	na	-21.6	av	high
AG	INVESCO Tech/Inv (FTCHX)	35.0	26.6	28.3	-22.7	high	high
AG	Fidelity Sel Computers (FDCPX)	34.7	26.3	28.3	-31.1	abv av	high
Grth	Vanguard Specl: Health (VGHCX)	34.2	30.4	25.4	60.5	low	blw av
AG	Janus Inv: Mercury (JAMRX)	33.9	25.8	na	-22.7	blw av	high
AG	Citizens: Emg Gr/R (WAEGX)	33.5	26.1	na	-0.6	av	high
AG	PBHG Select Equity (PBHEX)	32.8	26.2	na	-24.5	high	high
AG	Rydex: OTC/Inv (RYOCX)	32.4	32.3	na	-37.9	abv av	high
IntlS	T Rowe Price Intl: Discvr (PRIDX)	31.6	19.6	12.6	-15.6	abv av	high
AG	Sit Small Cap Growth (SSMGX)	31.2	22.8	na	6.2	abv av	high
AG	Fidelity Sel Software (FSCSX)	30.8	25.7	28.2	-20.3	abv av	high
AG	RS: Information Age/A (RSIFX)	30.7	24.6	na	-35.0	high	high
Grth	PBHG Large Cap Grth (PBHLX)	30.3	27.3	na	1.7	high	high
IntlS	Fidelity Japan Smaller Co (FJSCX)	30.1	2.9	na	-50.2	high	high
AG	Wasatch: Micro Cap (WMICX)	29.5	27.3	na	37.5	blw av	abv av
AG	White Oak Growth (WOGSX)	29.4	28.9	na	3.5	blw av	high
IntlS	Artisan Int'l (ARTIX)	28.9	24.3	na	-10.5	abv av	high
AG	Fidelity Growth Company (FDGRX)	28.8	24.3	22.3	-6.3	av	high
Grth	Fidelity Mid Cap Stock (FMCSX)	28.6	26.1	na	32.0	high	high
AG	RS: Diversifed Growth/A (RSDGX)	28.5	na	na	-26.9	high	high
AG	Fidelity Aggressive Grth (FDEGX)	28.4	23.9	24.0	-27.1	abv av	high
AG	PBHG Mid Cap Value (PBMCX)	28.3	na	na	32.5	low	abv av
AG	Fremont: US Micro Cap (FUSMX)	28.2	27.4	na	-10.6	abv av	high
AG	Berger Select (BESLX)	28.1	na	na	-32.6	abv av	high
AG	Janus Inv: Enterprise (JAENX)	27.2	20.6	na	-30.5	abv av	high
AG	Dreyfus Founders: Dscvry/F (FDISX)	26.8	22.5	21.3	-8.2	abv av	high
AG	Fidelity Retirement Grth (FDFFX)	26.6	21.1	20.3	1.7	av	high
AG	Van Wagoner Mid-Cap Gr (VWMDX)	26.5	16.6	na	-23.2	high	high
Grth	Strong Growth (SGROX)	26.3	23.4	na	-9.2	high	high
AG	T Rowe Price Hlth Science (PRHSX)	26.2	24.9	na	52.1	av	high
IntlS	Wm Blair: Intl Grth/N (WBIGX)	26.2	19.1	na	-8.1	av	abv av
AG	Northern Select Equity (NOEQX)	26.1	26.3	na	-3.9	blw av	high
AG	Fidelity Sel Air Trans (FSAIX)	26.0	21.5	20.2	39.7	low	abv av

Aggressive Growth Funds

Ranked by 2000 Total Returns

Fund Name	Annual Return (%) 2000	3yr	5yr	10yr	Category Risk	Total Risk
Fidelity Sel Med Dlvry (FSHCX)	67.8	3.5	8.1	14.3	blw av	high
INVESCO Energy/Inv (FSTEX)	58.1	17.4	21.7	11.2	abv av	high
CGM Focus (CGMFX)	53.9	20.0	na	na	blw av	high
T Rowe Price Hlth Science (PRHSX)	52.1	26.2	24.9	na	av	high
Fidelity Sel Energy Serv (FSESX)	50.3	9.1	24.1	14.8	high	high
Fidelity Sel Air Trans (FSAIX)	39.7	26.0	21.5	20.2	low	abv av
Warburg Glb Hlth Sci/Cmn (WPHSX)	38.9	25.3	na	na	blw av	high
Wasatch: Micro Cap (WMICX)	37.5	29.5	27.3	na	blw av	abv av
PBHG Small Cap Value (PBSVX)	35.7	17.6	na	na	low	abv av
Schroder Sm Cap Val/Inv (WSCVX)	32.9	9.2	16.4	na	low	abv av
Fidelity Sel Biotech (FBIOX)	32.7	45.1	30.0	23.3	high	high
PBHG Mid Cap Value (PBMCX)	32.5	28.3	na	na	low	abv av
Schroder Cap: US Sm Co/Inv (SCUIX)	31.2	10.4	15.8	na	low	abv av
Prudent Bear (BEARX)	30.4	-12.9	-11.4	na	av	high
Fidelity Sel Brokerage (FSLBX)	27.9	20.8	31.9	27.8	av	high
Wasatch: Ultra Growth (WAMCX)	25.9	22.6	13.7	na	av	high
Oakmark Select/I (OAKLX)	25.8	18.7	na	na	low	abv av
INVESCO Health Sci/Inv (FHLSX)	25.8	21.9	19.0	19.2	blw av	high
SteinRoe Inv: Disc Stock (SRDSX)	20.1	5.6	12.0	14.0	low	abv av
Brazos Micro Cap Grth/Y (BJMIX)	18.8	41.8	na	na	av	high
Vanguard Capital Opport (VHCOX)	18.0	45.5	26.3	na	blw av	high
Wasatch: Small Cap Grth (WAAEX)	16.8	22.2	18.0	19.5	blw av	high
Royce: Micro-Cap/Inv (RYOTX)	16.7	8.6	13.0	na	low	abv av
T Rowe Price Sm Cap Stck (OTCFX)	16.4	8.8	14.9	17.5	low	abv av
Kalmar Growth With Value (KGSCX)	15.7	4.2	na	na	low	abv av
Montgomery US Emg Gr/R (MNMCX)	14.6	13.7	17.3	na	blw av	high
Columbia Special (CLSPX)	13.8	21.8	18.1	20.2	blw av	high
PBHG Strategic Small Co (PSSCX)	11.8	20.1	na	na	abv av	high
Galaxy II: Small Co (ISCIX)	10.9	6.7	12.4	15.4	low	abv av
Kaufmann (KAUFX)	10.8	12.0	13.8	21.0	blw av	high
Dreyfus Gr & Val: Emg Ldrs (DRELX)	9.4	18.0	24.7	na	blw av	abv av
Vanguard Explorer (VEXPX)	9.2	15.7	15.1	18.0	blw av	high
Dreyfus New Leaders (DNLDX)	8.5	12.7	14.9	17.1	low	abv av
Northern Small Cap Value (NOSGX)	8.4	4.5	12.0	na	low	abv av
Rainier: Small/Mid Cap Eq (RIMSX)	7.0	9.0	16.0	na	low	abv av
Sit Small Cap Growth (SSMGX)	6.2	31.2	22.8	na	abv av	high
ABN AMRO: Sm Cap/Cmn (RSMCX)	6.1	4.7	9.7	na	blw av	high
Columbia Small Cap (CMSCX)	5.8	20.8	na	na	av	high
Fidelity Small Cap Sel (FDSCX)	5.7	3.7	10.0	na	low	abv av
Dreyfus Gr & Val: Sm Val (DSCVX)	5.4	6.2	15.1	na	blw av	abv av
Brazos Small Cap Grth/Y (BJSCX)	5.1	17.8	na	na	blw av	high
SSgA: Small Cap (SVSCX)	4.4	0.0	9.7	na	low	abv av
RS: MicroCap Growth/A (RSMGX)	4.4	17.5	na	na	abv av	high
Strong Discovery (STDIX)	3.9	5.4	5.6	13.3	low	abv av
Schwab Cap Tr: Sm Cp Ix/I (SWSMX)	3.7	7.4	12.5	na	low	abv av
White Oak Growth (WOGSX)	3.5	29.4	28.9	na	blw av	high
Navellier: Agg Growth (NPFGX)	3.0	18.8	17.7	na	blw av	high
FTI Small Cap Equity (FTSCX)	3.0	21.5	21.1	na	av	high
NI Numeric Inv Micro Cap (NIMCX)	2.2	16.9	na	na	av	high
Fidelity Retirement Grth (FDFFX)	1.7	26.6	21.1	20.3	av	high
Baron Asset (BARAX)	0.3	6.7	14.7	18.4	blw av	abv av
Galaxy: Growth II/Tr (SEGRX)	0.1	20.0	na	na	av	high

Aggressive Growth Funds

Ranked by 2000 Total Returns

Fund Name	Annual Return (%) 2000	3yr	5yr	10yr	Category Risk	Total Risk
Citizens: Emg Gr/R (WAEGX)	-0.6	33.5	26.1	na	av	high
Amer Cent: Vista/Inv (TWCVX)	-0.9	22.9	12.8	17.4	high	high
Selected Special Shares (SLSSX)	-1.0	12.8	15.3	14.9	low	abv av
Excelsior Small Cap/A (UMLCX)	-1.0	3.9	4.6	na	av	high
Strong Adv Common Stock/Z (STCSX)	-1.2	13.9	17.1	21.3	low	abv av
Artisan Small Cap (ARTSX)	-1.4	0.5	6.8	na	blw av	abv av
T Rowe Price New Horizons (PRNHX)	-1.8	11.3	12.1	18.9	av	high
CGM Capital Development (LOMCX)	-3.7	4.0	12.3	19.3	low	abv av
Northern Select Equity (NOEQX)	-3.9	26.1	26.3	na	blw av	high
SAFECO Growth Opp (SAFGX)	-4.2	0.8	13.5	16.2	blw av	abv av
NI Numeric Inv Grth (NISGX)	-4.3	13.4	na	na	av	high
Sit MidCap Growth (NBNGX)	-4.3	20.3	20.1	19.3	abv av	high
Fidelity Fifty (FFTYX)	-4.5	17.1	18.0	na	low	abv av
WPG Tudor (TUDRX)	-5.1	6.4	9.7	13.4	av	high
Fidelity New Millennium (FMILX)	-6.0	35.8	30.9	na	high	high
Fidelity Technoquant Grth (FTQGX)	-6.1	14.3	na	na	low	abv av
Fidelity Growth Company (FDGRX)	-6.3	28.8	24.3	22.3	av	high
Value Line Specl Situatn (VALSX)	-6.7	25.0	22.6	18.3	av	high
Vanguard Specl: Gold & PM (VGPMX)	-7.3	4.6	-7.0	0.2	abv av	high
Vintage Aggressive Growth (AVAGX)	-7.5	11.5	15.8	na	blw av	abv av
INVESCO Dynamics/Inv (FIDYX)	-7.7	24.9	22.8	23.8	av	high
Dreyfus Founders: Dscvry/F (FDISX)	-8.2	26.8	22.5	21.3	abv av	high
Berger Small Co Grth/Inv (BESCX)	-8.2	24.5	21.2	na	high	high
T Rowe Price Dvsfd Sm Cap (PRDSX)	-8.2	6.6	na	na	av	high
Scudder Gold (SCGDX)	-8.9	-6.1	-8.3	-0.8	abv av	high
Liberty Acorn USA/Z (AUSAX)	-9.0	5.7	na	na	low	abv av
Firsthand: Tech Value (TVFQX)	-9.9	47.8	40.7	na	high	high
Strong Growth 20/Inv (SGRTX)	-10.3	36.8	na	na	abv av	high
Fremont: US Micro Cap (FUSMX)	-10.6	28.2	27.4	na	abv av	high
Oberweis: Emerging Growth (OBEGX)	-10.6	9.8	8.2	16.8	abv av	high
RS: Value + Growth/A (RSVPX)	-11.0	13.3	13.5	na	blw av	high
Marshall: Mid Cap Gr/Inv (MRMSX)	-11.1	18.3	19.6	na	av	high
SteinRoe Inv: Cap Opport (SRFCX)	-11.2	6.9	9.3	17.5	av	high
Schwab MarketMgr: Sm Cp (SWOSX)	-11.3	7.1	na	na	low	abv av
Legg Mason Eq: Special/P (LMASX)	-12.0	13.7	18.2	17.2	blw av	high
Warburg Emerg Grth/Cmn (CUEGX)	-12.0	9.7	11.9	18.0	av	high
INVESCO Small Co Grth/Inv (FIEGX)	-12.1	22.3	19.3	na	abv av	high
INVESCO Gold/Inv (FGLDX)	-12.9	-15.0	-17.4	-7.4	high	high
Harbor: Growth (HAGWX)	-13.0	23.7	20.5	17.9	abv av	high
Value Line Lever Grth Inv (VALLX)	-13.9	16.3	18.9	17.9	low	abv av
Turner: Small Cap Grth (TSCEX)	-14.3	19.8	20.5	na	abv av	high
USAA Inv: Gold (USAGX)	-14.9	-2.7	-10.6	-2.8	high	high
Scudder Development (SCDVX)	-15.9	7.0	7.6	14.2	av	high
Monetta (MONTX)	-15.9	5.0	8.2	11.4	abv av	high
Amer Cent: Giftrust/Inv (TWGTX)	-16.4	10.7	7.2	20.3	high	high
USAA Science & Technology (USSCX)	-16.6	21.5	na	na	blw av	high
Preferred Small Cap (PSMCX)	-16.8	-10.8	2.3	na	av	high
Chesapeake Aggressive Gr (CPGRX)	-17.2	6.1	8.8	na	abv av	high
US Glob Acc: Bonnel Growth (ACBGX)	-17.2	24.0	21.9	na	abv av	high
Westcore: MIDCO Growth (WTMGX)	-17.5	13.2	14.2	17.7	abv av	high
Baron Small Cap (BSCFX)	-17.5	12.9	na	na	blw av	high
Janus Inv: Spl Situations (JASSX)	-17.5	16.3	na	na	blw av	abv av

Aggressive Growth Funds

Ranked by 2000 Total Returns

Fund Name	Annual Return (%) 2000	3yr	5yr	10yr	Category Risk	Total Risk
Fidelity Sel Electronics (FSELX)	-17.6	37.0	32.9	34.0	high	high
Fidelity Sel Gold Port (FSAGX)	-18.0	-6.7	-10.0	-1.0	high	high
Van Wagoner Micro-Cap Gr (VWMCX)	-18.2	41.7	23.2	na	high	high
Berger Growth (BEONX)	-18.8	12.8	13.1	17.9	av	high
Rydex: Nova/Inv (RYNVX)	-19.5	10.4	19.5	na	blw av	high
Marshall: Sm Cap Gr/Inv (MRSCX)	-19.6	3.8	na	na	abv av	high
Excelsior Large Cap Gr (UMLGX)	-19.7	25.5	na	na	blw av	high
Amer Cent: Ultra/Inv (TWCUX)	-19.9	15.0	16.4	20.6	low	abv av
USAA Mutual: Aggr Growth (USAUX)	-19.9	23.1	18.5	19.4	high	high
Fidelity Sel Software (FSCSX)	-20.3	30.8	25.7	28.2	abv av	high
Van Wagoner Emerging Grth (VWEGX)	-20.9	49.4	27.6	na	high	high
PBHG Core Grth (PBCRX)	-21.0	18.7	14.9	na	high	high
Janus Inv: Olympus (JAOLX)	-21.6	35.0	30.5	na	av	high
PBHG Large Cap 20 (PLCPX)	-22.0	38.4	na	na	high	high
Janus Inv: Mercury (JAMRX)	-22.7	33.9	25.8	na	blw av	high
INVESCO Tech/Inv (FTCHX)	-22.7	35.0	26.6	28.3	high	high
PBHG Growth (PBHGX)	-22.9	14.2	9.6	21.6	high	high
Fidelity Sel Multimedia (FBMPX)	-23.0	14.6	14.7	20.4	low	abv av
Van Wagoner Mid-Cap Gr (VWMDX)	-23.2	26.5	16.6	na	high	high
Dreyfus Founders: Md Cp Gr/F (FRSPX)	-23.6	2.1	7.4	13.4	av	high
Amer Cent: Global Gold/Inv (BGEIX)	-23.9	-13.5	-18.1	-6.8	high	high
Fidelity Sel Leisure (FDLSX)	-24.4	11.4	17.2	18.9	low	abv av
PBHG Select Equity (PBHEX)	-24.5	32.8	26.2	na	high	high
RS: Emerging Growth/A (RSEGX)	-25.0	39.4	31.3	23.7	high	high
T Rowe Price Media & Tele (PRMTX)	-25.1	25.0	na	na	av	high
Montgomery Sm Cap/R (MNSCX)	-25.1	2.4	9.5	17.9	abv av	high
PBHG Emerging Grth (PBEGX)	-25.2	4.5	5.2	na	high	high
Fidelity OTC Port (FOCPX)	-26.8	21.0	19.2	19.6	abv av	high
RS: Diversifed Growth/A (RSDGX)	-26.9	28.5	na	na	high	high
Fidelity Aggressive Grth (FDEGX)	-27.1	28.4	23.9	24.0	abv av	high
Markman Aggressive Alloc (MMAGX)	-27.3	11.1	12.7	na	av	high
ProFunds: UltraBull/Inv (ULPIX)	-28.3	9.8	na	na	abv av	high
Fidelity Sel Develop Comm (FSDCX)	-29.7	37.8	26.0	26.7	high	high
Janus Inv: Enterprise (JAENX)	-30.5	27.2	20.6	na	abv av	high
Fidelity Sel Computers (FDCPX)	-31.1	34.7	26.3	28.3	abv av	high
Fidelity Sel Technology (FSPTX)	-32.3	39.7	28.3	28.6	high	high
Janus Inv: Twenty (JAVLX)	-32.4	24.5	26.2	21.9	blw av	high
Spectra/N (SPECX)	-32.4	19.7	20.6	23.9	av	high
Berger Select (BESLX)	-32.6	28.1	na	na	abv av	high
T Rowe Price Science & Tech (PRSCX)	-34.1	23.4	16.9	24.9	abv av	high
Gintel (GINLX)	-34.3	1.9	12.4	11.1	high	high
RS: Information Age/A (RSIFX)	-35.0	30.7	24.6	na	high	high
Fidelity Sel Telecomm (FSTCX)	-37.4	13.7	14.2	17.8	av	high
Rydex: OTC/Inv (RYOCX)	-37.9	32.4	32.3	na	abv av	high
Northern Technology (NTCHX)	-38.4	38.2	na	na	high	high
Berger New Generation/Inv (BENGX)	-38.6	22.5	na	na	high	high
PBHG Tech & Comm (PBTCX)	-41.0	36.7	32.4	na	high	high
Janus Inv: Venture (JAVTX)	-45.7	17.0	14.3	16.2	high	high
ProFunds: UltraOTC/Inv (UOPIX)	-73.7	35.7	na	na	high	high
Aggressive Growth Fund Average	**-6.0**	**16.2**	**14.6**	**15.8**	**—**	**abv av**

Growth Funds

Ranked by 2000 Total Returns

Fund Name	Annual Return (%) 2000	3yr	5yr	10yr	Category Risk	Total Risk
Fidelity Sel Natural Gas (FSNGX)	71.2	23.7	18.5	na	high	high
Vanguard Specl: Health (VGHCX)	60.5	34.2	30.4	25.4	low	blw av
Fidelity Sel Insurance (FSPCX)	53.2	20.1	25.0	22.2	high	high
Fidelity Sel Home Finance (FSVLX)	50.2	3.9	17.4	27.8	high	high
Wasatch: Core Growth (WGROX)	37.3	18.5	19.8	19.3	abv av	abv av
Fidelity Sel Health Care (FSPHX)	36.6	23.3	23.2	22.8	low	av
Vanguard Specl: Energy (VGENX)	36.4	9.4	15.0	12.8	high	high
Vontobel US Value (VUSVX)	35.1	10.0	16.7	17.7	av	abv av
Neuberger Genesis (NBGNX)	32.5	8.6	17.5	18.0	blw av	av
Fidelity Mid Cap Stock (FMCSX)	32.0	28.6	26.1	na	high	high
Fidelity Sel Energy (FSENX)	31.8	14.6	17.1	12.0	high	high
Ariel (ARGFX)	28.7	10.0	17.5	15.1	av	abv av
Fidelity Sel Financl Serv (FIDSX)	28.5	14.1	22.8	26.8	high	high
Meridian (MERDX)	28.2	14.4	14.7	17.4	blw av	av
Dreyfus Gr & Val: Midcp Vl (DMCVX)	27.4	16.0	22.4	na	high	high
Berger Small Cap Val/Inv (BSCVX)	26.8	13.7	na	na	av	abv av
INVESCO Financial Svc/Inv (FSFSX)	26.6	13.1	22.2	25.1	high	abv av
Mairs & Power Growth (MPGFX)	26.4	14.0	19.2	20.7	low	av
Muhlenkamp (MUHLX)	25.3	12.9	20.0	19.8	abv av	abv av
Skyline: Special Equities (SKSEX)	24.2	0.0	12.0	17.7	blw av	av
Loomis Sayles SmCp Vl/Ist (LSSCX)	23.1	6.9	14.9	na	blw av	av
T Rowe Price Mid-Cap Val (TRMCX)	22.7	8.8	na	na	low	av
Victory: Small Co Opp/G (GOGFX)	22.6	4.1	12.1	14.2	blw av	av
Dreyfus Gr & Val: Agg Val (DAGVX)	21.3	13.0	19.5	na	blw av	av
Weitz Partners Value (WPVLX)	21.0	24.0	26.1	na	low	av
Artisan Small Cap Value (ARTVX)	20.8	9.5	na	na	low	av
Third Avenue Value (TAVFX)	20.7	12.2	16.4	18.7	low	av
Longleaf Partners (LLPFX)	20.6	12.0	16.9	20.0	blw av	av
T Rowe Price New Era (PRNEX)	20.3	9.5	12.6	12.0	high	abv av
Sound Shore (SSHFX)	20.1	7.8	17.9	18.2	blw av	av
Sequoia (SEQUX)	20.0	10.6	18.7	19.3	abv av	abv av
T Rowe Price Sm Cap Value (PRSVX)	19.7	1.9	11.0	15.7	low	av
Weitz Srs: Value (WVALX)	19.6	23.1	25.2	20.9	low	av
CA Inv: S&P Mid Cap Index (SPMIX)	19.4	17.5	20.5	na	abv av	abv av
Fidelity Sel Defense (FSDAX)	18.8	11.5	16.4	18.0	abv av	abv av
Fidelity Low Priced Stock (FLPSX)	18.8	7.8	15.0	19.6	low	av
Ariel Appreciation (CAAPX)	18.8	10.9	18.4	15.7	blw av	av
Fidelity Sel Banking (FSRBX)	18.7	6.0	18.7	25.2	high	high
Royce: PA Mutual/Inv (PENNX)	18.3	9.3	12.9	13.9	low	av
Country Growth (CTYGX)	18.2	19.0	19.7	16.2	blw av	av
Oak Value (OAKVX)	18.1	10.8	19.3	na	av	abv av
CRM Small Cap Value/Inv (CRMSX)	18.0	4.7	14.2	na	abv av	abv av
Merger (MERFX)	17.5	13.2	12.2	12.2	low	blw av
LKCM Small Cap Equity (LKSCX)	17.4	8.7	14.7	na	av	abv av
Amer Cent: Heritage/Inv (TWHIX)	17.3	21.0	19.5	17.9	high	high
Vanguard Selected Value (VASVX)	17.3	0.6	na	na	abv av	abv av
Third Avenue Small Cap (TASCX)	17.1	8.2	na	na	blw av	av
Royce: Premier (RYPRX)	17.1	11.7	14.2	na	low	av
Dreyfus Index: Midcap Idx (PESPX)	16.7	16.3	19.6	na	abv av	abv av
Babson Enterprise II (BAETX)	16.6	5.7	15.0	na	av	abv av
Haven (HAVEX)	15.9	12.9	16.8	na	blw av	av

Growth Funds

Ranked by 2000 Total Returns

Fund Name	Annual Return (%) 2000	3yr	5yr	10yr	Category Risk	Total Risk
T Rowe Price Value (TRVLX)	15.7	10.5	17.5	na	blw av	abv av
Lazard: Small Cap/Open (LZCOX)	15.5	3.0	na	na	av	abv av
Tweedy Browne Amer Value (TWEBX)	14.4	8.5	16.8	na	low	av
ICON Leisure & Consumer (ICLEX)	14.3	8.7	na	na	av	abv av
Delafield (DEFIX)	13.9	3.0	10.5	na	abv av	abv av
Yacktman (YACKX)	13.4	-1.7	7.1	na	av	abv av
Longleaf Partners Sm Cap (LLSCX)	12.7	9.7	17.3	16.0	low	av
Scudder Small Co Value/S (SCSUX)	12.7	-2.0	9.7	na	low	av
Strong Value (STVAX)	12.6	8.3	13.3	na	low	blw av
Mutual Discovery/Z (MDISX)	12.5	11.8	16.5	na	low	blw av
Babson Enterprise (BABEX)	12.4	-2.5	8.2	13.8	blw av	av
Neuberger Focus (NBSSX)	12.4	17.0	18.2	18.7	high	high
Fidelity Dividend Growth (FDGFX)	12.2	18.3	22.5	na	low	av
Gabelli Westwood Eqty/AAA (WESWX)	11.9	13.3	18.9	17.5	low	av
Oakmark/I (OAKMX)	11.7	1.2	9.8	na	av	abv av
Babson Shadow Stock (SHSTX)	11.3	4.6	12.1	14.8	low	av
Gabelli Eq: Sm Cp Grth/AAA (GABSX)	11.3	8.3	14.1	na	low	av
Wright Eq: Sel Blue Chip (WSBEX)	10.7	5.4	13.0	12.9	av	abv av
Liberty Acorn/Z (ACRNX)	10.0	15.8	18.9	20.5	av	abv av
Strong Opportunity/Inv (SOPFX)	8.5	18.7	19.5	19.6	blw av	av
Victory: Established Val/G (GETGX)	8.2	10.3	14.5	15.0	blw av	av
Granum Value (GRVFX)	8.1	6.6	na	na	blw av	av
Fidelity Value (FDVLX)	8.1	5.5	10.7	15.6	abv av	abv av
Vanguard Strategic Eqty (VSEQX)	7.4	8.8	15.2	na	av	abv av
T Rowe Price Mid-Cap Grth (RPMGX)	7.4	17.5	19.1	na	abv av	abv av
Excelsior Val & Restrctg (UMBIX)	7.2	18.8	22.9	na	abv av	abv av
Brandywine (BRWIX)	7.0	17.7	17.9	20.7	high	abv av
Brandywine Blue (BLUEX)	6.8	16.4	18.3	na	high	abv av
MSB (MSBFX)	5.6	13.6	18.0	15.9	low	av
Dreyfus Gr & Val: Lrg Val (DLCVX)	5.3	8.5	14.2	na	blw av	av
Hennessy Crnst Grth (HFCGX)	5.3	14.5	na	na	high	high
Vanguard PRIMECAP (VPMCX)	4.4	22.8	24.5	22.7	abv av	abv av
Oakmark Small Cap/I (OAKSX)	4.3	-5.8	10.3	na	av	abv av
US Global Leaders Growth (USGLX)	4.1	14.0	20.7	na	blw av	av
Strong Schafer Value (SCHVX)	3.5	-6.8	5.2	13.1	abv av	abv av
Masters Select Equity (MSEFX)	3.1	14.4	na	na	av	abv av
Alleghany: Chicago G&I/N (CHTIX)	2.0	19.4	22.0	na	blw av	av
Heartland Grp: Value (HRTVX)	2.0	4.1	10.9	18.8	abv av	abv av
Dreyfus Appreciation (DGAGX)	1.8	13.5	18.6	17.2	low	av
PBHG Large Cap Grth (PBHLX)	1.7	30.3	27.3	na	high	high
Fasciano (FASCX)	1.7	4.9	12.2	14.2	low	av
Fidelity Export & Multi (FEXPX)	1.4	20.7	24.7	na	av	abv av
Legg Mason Eq: Am Lead/P (LMALX)	0.5	8.6	15.3	na	blw av	av
First Eagle of Am/Y (FEAFX)	0.3	10.8	17.9	18.8	low	av
T Rowe Price Growth Stock (PRGFX)	0.2	15.9	19.1	17.9	blw av	av
T Rowe Price Spect: Growth (PRSGX)	-0.1	11.2	14.2	15.7	low	av
Neuberger Soc Respv (NBSRX)	-0.4	7.0	12.5	na	blw av	av
Nicholas (NICSX)	-1.4	4.2	13.2	15.2	blw av	av
WPG Large Cap Growth (WPGFX)	-1.6	12.0	19.0	18.0	av	abv av
Neuberger Guardian (NGUAX)	-1.8	2.8	8.6	13.9	abv av	abv av
Nicholas II (NCTWX)	-2.0	2.6	12.0	14.0	blw av	abv av

Growth Funds

Ranked by 2000 Total Returns

Fund Name	Annual Return (%) 2000	3yr	5yr	10yr	Category Risk	Total Risk
Sentry (SNTRX)	-2.2	-1.9	8.4	10.7	low	av
Gabelli Asset (GABAX)	-2.3	13.2	17.8	16.7	low	av
Bramwell Growth (BRGRX)	-2.4	18.1	19.9	na	av	abv av
T Rowe Price Blue Chip Gr (TRBCX)	-2.5	14.6	19.6	na	blw av	av
Vanguard Idx: Sm Cap/Inv (NAESX)	-2.6	5.2	11.4	16.1	high	abv av
Lazard: Equity/Open (LZEOX)	-2.9	5.6	na	na	low	av
Torray (TORYX)	-3.3	9.0	18.0	18.5	av	abv av
Fidelity Disciplined Eqty (FDEQX)	-3.4	12.9	17.1	17.8	low	av
Wayne Hummer Growth (WHGRX)	-3.7	16.0	17.9	15.2	av	abv av
Rainier: Core Equity (RIMEX)	-3.9	13.6	19.3	na	av	abv av
ABN AMRO: Growth/Cmn (RGTCX)	-4.4	11.9	16.2	na	av	abv av
Williamsburg: Gov't St Eqty (GVEQX)	-4.5	11.6	16.6	na	low	av
Warburg Cap App/Cmn (CUCAX)	-5.2	20.8	23.4	19.7	high	abv av
EAI Select Mgr Equity (EASMX)	-5.5	15.2	na	na	blw av	av
Columbia Common Stock (CMSTX)	-5.7	14.3	17.7	na	blw av	av
Papp Stock (LRPSX)	-6.0	11.1	17.3	16.2	av	abv av
RS: Mid Cap Opport/A (RSMOX)	-6.1	17.8	19.9	na	high	high
T Rowe Price Cap Opport (PRCOX)	-6.3	6.2	10.1	na	av	abv av
Fidelity Contrafund (FCNTX)	-6.8	15.2	18.1	21.0	blw av	av
Vintage Equity/S (VEQSX)	-7.0	12.9	17.8	na	av	abv av
Fidelity Stock Selector (FDSSX)	-7.0	10.4	15.2	18.2	av	abv av
Legg Mason Eq: Value/P (LMVTX)	-7.1	20.3	27.0	22.9	abv av	abv av
Fidelity Trend (FTRNX)	-7.1	10.3	11.2	13.9	high	abv av
Northern Growth Equity (NOGEX)	-7.2	15.2	18.5	na	av	abv av
Alleghany: Mntg & Cldwl Gr/N (MCGFX)	-7.3	14.3	21.2	na	blw av	av
Wm Blair: Growth/N (WBGSX)	-7.4	12.1	14.8	17.3	abv av	abv av
Schwab Cap Tr: Analytics (SWANX)	-7.7	14.7	na	na	blw av	av
Babson Growth (BABSX)	-7.8	11.1	16.4	15.5	abv av	abv av
Columbia Growth (CLMBX)	-7.9	14.7	18.2	17.8	abv av	abv av
INVESCO Leisure/Inv (FLISX)	-7.9	25.5	22.2	22.6	av	abv av
Fremont: Growth (FEQFX)	-8.1	7.6	15.0	na	av	abv av
Excelsior Blended Eqty/A (UMEQX)	-8.1	13.2	17.6	18.1	blw av	av
Papp America: Abroad (PAAFX)	-8.6	8.8	16.4	na	abv av	abv av
Nicholas Limited Edition (NCLEX)	-8.6	-3.7	7.6	12.7	av	abv av
Amer Cent: Select/Inv (TWCIX)	-8.7	14.8	19.0	14.5	blw av	av
Capstone Growth (TRDFX)	-9.1	11.2	15.7	13.5	blw av	av
Strong Growth (SGROX)	-9.2	26.3	23.4	na	high	high
Marshall: Lrg Cap G & I/Inv (MASTX)	-9.2	10.5	14.3	na	low	av
Fidelity Magellan (FMAGX)	-9.2	14.5	16.2	18.3	blw av	abv av
Eclipses: Sm Cap Val (EEQFX)	-9.5	-1.2	10.7	13.3	blw av	av
Kobren: Growth (KOGRX)	-9.7	9.2	na	na	blw av	av
SteinRoe Inv: Young Invtr (SRYIX)	-10.0	11.6	18.9	na	high	abv av
Vanguard Tx Mg Cap App (VMCAX)	-10.1	15.3	18.7	na	abv av	abv av
Strong Growth & Inc/Inv (SGRIX)	-10.2	16.4	22.0	na	av	abv av
Scudder Capital Grth/AARP (ACGFX)	-10.3	14.5	19.6	17.2	av	abv av
T Rowe Price New Amer Gr (PRWAX)	-10.5	5.9	11.5	17.0	high	abv av
Fidelity Blue Chip Growth (FBGRX)	-10.5	14.4	17.0	20.2	av	abv av
Bremer Inv: Growth Stock (BSTKX)	-10.5	13.3	na	na	av	abv av
Montgomery Growth/R (MNGFX)	-10.5	3.2	10.4	na	av	abv av
Gabelli Growth (GABGX)	-10.5	19.2	23.6	19.1	abv av	abv av
Weston: New Century Cap (NCCPX)	-10.8	12.7	15.6	15.2	av	abv av

Growth Funds

Ranked by 2000 Total Returns

Fund Name	Annual Return (%) 2000	3yr	5yr	10yr	Category Risk	Total Risk
Amer Cent: Eqty Growth/Inv (BEQGX)	-10.9	9.7	18.0	na	blw av	av
Berger Growth & Income (BEOOX)	-11.2	20.5	19.9	19.3	high	high
Fidelity Sel Retailing (FSRPX)	-11.3	10.7	18.4	19.1	abv av	abv av
SteinRoe Inv: Grth Stock (SRFSX)	-11.3	14.9	19.3	17.7	high	abv av
Neuberger Manhattan (NMANX)	-11.4	15.8	17.1	16.7	high	high
Wright Eq: Major Blue Chip (WQCEX)	-12.4	9.3	15.5	14.8	blw av	av
Vanguard Morgan Growth (VMRGX)	-12.5	12.7	18.2	16.7	abv av	abv av
Dreyfus Premier Third/Z (DRTHX)	-12.9	13.8	18.8	16.0	av	abv av
Strong Lrg Cap Growth (STRFX)	-13.4	22.3	21.0	18.2	high	high
Sit Large Cap Growth (SNIGX)	-13.8	14.4	19.4	16.8	abv av	abv av
SSgA: Matrix Equity (SSMTX)	-14.1	6.4	14.8	na	blw av	av
Fidelity Large Cap Stock (FLCSX)	-14.5	14.9	18.1	na	av	abv av
Amer Cent: Growth/Inv (TWCGX)	-14.7	16.2	18.4	16.6	av	abv av
Janus Inv: Janus (JANSX)	-14.9	20.2	20.6	18.6	abv av	abv av
Northeast Inv Growth (NTHFX)	-14.9	13.5	20.1	16.8	abv av	abv av
Domini Social Equity (DSEFX)	-15.0	11.4	18.0	na	blw av	av
Value Line (VLIFX)	-15.3	8.8	13.9	14.9	abv av	abv av
Vanguard Idx: Ext Mkt/Inv (VEXMX)	-15.5	7.6	13.1	16.1	high	high
Marsico Growth & Income (MGRIX)	-15.8	22.7	na	na	high	high
SAFECO Northwest (SFNWX)	-16.1	10.2	15.0	na	high	high
USAA First Start Growth (UFSGX)	-16.4	12.6	na	na	abv av	abv av
Lindner Large Cap/Inv (LDNRX)	-16.4	-7.8	0.5	7.4	abv av	abv av
Harbor: Capital Apprec (HACAX)	-17.0	18.2	21.1	21.6	high	abv av
Weitz Srs: Hickory (WEHIX)	-17.2	14.5	23.1	na	abv av	abv av
Dreyfus Growth Opport (DREQX)	-17.4	5.7	10.7	11.4	av	abv av
Preferred Growth (PFGRX)	-17.6	17.4	20.4	na	high	abv av
Marsico Focus (MFOCX)	-17.9	24.4	na	na	high	high
Fidelity Capital Apprec (FDCAX)	-18.1	11.7	15.2	15.5	high	high
USAA Mutual: Growth (USAAX)	-19.0	9.1	9.7	12.6	av	abv av
Scudder Large Co Growth/S (SCQGX)	-19.2	13.2	17.9	na	abv av	abv av
Dreyfus Founders: Gr & Inc/F (FRMUX)	-19.5	2.9	10.1	11.9	low	av
Vanguard US Growth (VWUSX)	-20.1	10.9	16.7	16.5	abv av	abv av
TIAA-CREF Growth Equity (TIGEX)	-20.2	12.9	na	na	high	abv av
Citizens: Core Gr/R (WAIDX)	-20.7	12.9	19.0	na	abv av	abv av
Vanguard Idx: Growth/Inv (VIGRX)	-22.2	12.5	19.1	na	abv av	abv av
Vanguard Growth Equity (VGEQX)	-23.1	17.7	20.6	na	high	high
INVESCO Blue Chip Gr/Inv (FLRFX)	-23.9	14.2	18.1	16.6	high	high
Founders: Large Cap Gr (FRGRX)	-27.2	8.1	13.3	17.6	high	high
Reynolds Blue Chip Growth (RBCGX)	-31.8	16.6	21.7	16.3	high	high
Growth Fund Average	**3.5**	**11.0**	**16.1**	**16.8**	**—**	**av**

Growth and Income Funds

Ranked by 2000 Total Returns

Fund Name	Annual Return (%) 2000	3yr	5yr	10yr	Category Risk	Total Risk
Galaxy II: Utility (IUTLX)	59.3	18.2	17.0	na	high	abv av
American Gas Index (GASFX)	55.8	16.4	18.8	14.1	av	av
Century Shares (CENSX)	37.4	8.8	17.7	17.2	high	high
Clipper (CFIMX)	37.4	17.0	20.1	19.7	low	blw av
T Rowe Price Fincl Svc (PRISX)	36.7	15.7	na	na	high	abv av
Fidelity Real Estate Inv (FRESX)	31.3	1.9	11.8	14.0	low	av
Fidelity Sel Food & Agri (FDFAX)	29.8	6.1	12.0	14.7	av	av
CGM Realty (CGMRX)	29.1	1.4	13.7	na	blw av	av
Columbia Real Estate Eqty (CREEX)	28.8	3.2	13.7	na	low	blw av
Strong American Utilities (SAMUX)	27.3	15.5	16.3	na	blw av	av
Amer Cent: Real Estate/Inv (REACX)	27.1	0.6	12.4	na	low	av
Caldwell & Orkin Mrkt Opp (COAGX)	26.6	14.2	19.6	na	low	blw av
Cohen & Steers Realty Shs (CSRSX)	26.6	2.1	12.3	na	blw av	av
Vanguard Specl: REIT Index (VGSIX)	26.3	0.4	na	na	low	blw av
Brazos Real Estate/Y (BJRSX)	25.8	-0.2	na	na	blw av	av
PBHG Large Cap Value (PLCVX)	23.9	23.8	na	na	av	av
Copley (COPLX)	22.4	9.0	11.2	11.6	low	blw av
Amer Cent: Eqty Income/Inv (TWEIX)	21.9	11.1	16.8	na	low	blw av
Stratton Monthly Dvd REIT (STMDX)	20.1	-0.1	4.9	8.1	low	blw av
Royce: Total Return (RYTRX)	19.4	8.3	14.5	na	low	blw av
Fenimore: Value (FAMVX)	19.2	6.3	13.2	15.9	abv av	av
Vanguard Specl: Util Inc (VGSUX)	18.7	11.9	13.0	na	low	blw av
Amer Cent: Value/Inv (TWVLX)	18.2	7.1	14.0	na	high	abv av
Marshall: Mid Cap Val/Inv (MRVEX)	17.2	9.3	12.9	na	high	av
Vanguard Windsor II (VWNFX)	16.8	8.6	16.0	16.8	abv av	av
Dodge & Cox Stock (DODGX)	16.3	13.7	18.2	17.8	av	av
Vanguard Windsor (VWNDX)	15.8	9.2	14.9	16.6	high	abv av
Longleaf Partners Realty (LLREX)	14.7	-3.6	na	na	low	blw av
Scudder Large Co Value (SCDUX)	14.6	9.5	15.7	16.3	av	av
Mutual Beacon/Z (BEGRX)	14.3	10.9	15.2	17.0	low	blw av
Mutual Qualified/Z (MQIFX)	14.2	9.2	14.5	17.0	blw av	av
Mutual Shares/Z (MUTHX)	13.8	9.5	14.9	17.0	blw av	av
Vanguard Equity Income (VEIPX)	13.5	9.9	15.4	15.8	blw av	av
T Rowe Price Equity Inc (PRFDX)	13.1	8.6	14.7	16.3	blw av	av
Gabelli Eq: Eqty Inc/AAA (GABEX)	11.3	11.0	15.6	na	low	blw av
Preferred Value (PFVLX)	10.8	9.7	16.2	na	high	av
USAA Mutual: Income Stock (USISX)	10.8	6.8	12.9	13.6	low	av
T Rowe Price Dividend Gr (PRDGX)	10.0	7.1	15.0	na	low	blw av
Marshall: Equity Inc/Inv (MREIX)	9.7	7.2	13.7	na	blw av	av
Homestead: Value (HOVLX)	9.6	4.7	11.4	13.8	av	av
Selected American Shares (SLASX)	9.3	15.2	22.3	19.5	abv av	av
Warburg Value/Cmn (RBEGX)	9.2	9.1	10.8	13.7	abv av	av
Mercury HW Lrge Cap Val/I (MCPIX)	9.1	3.6	11.3	14.7	high	abv av
Babson Value (BVALX)	9.0	5.3	12.6	16.1	high	abv av
T Rowe Price Growth Inc (PRGIX)	8.9	7.5	14.0	15.7	blw av	av
Fidelity Equity Income (FEQIX)	8.5	9.3	15.5	17.2	av	av
ICAP: Discretionary Equity (ICDEX)	8.3	11.0	17.2	na	blw av	av
ICAP: Equity (ICAEX)	7.8	11.8	17.8	na	av	av
Fidelity Equity Income II (FEQTX)	7.4	11.3	15.7	18.7	blw av	av
Fidelity Convertible Sec (FCVSX)	7.2	21.5	18.7	18.6	high	abv av
Harbor: Value (HAVLX)	7.1	7.2	14.1	14.0	high	av

Growth and Income Funds

Ranked by 2000 Total Returns

Fund Name	Annual Return (%) 2000	3yr	5yr	10yr	Category Risk	Total Risk
Gateway Tr: Gateway (GATEX)	6.6	10.5	10.9	10.1	low	blw av
SteinRoe Inv: Grth & Inc (SRGNX)	6.5	12.1	16.6	16.5	av	av
Northern Income Equity (NOIEX)	6.3	8.5	13.1	na	low	blw av
Vanguard Idx: Value/Inv (VIVAX)	6.0	11.0	16.6	na	abv av	av
Gabelli Mathers (MATRX)	6.0	2.0	1.8	2.4	low	blw av
Eclipses: Mid Cap Val (ECGIX)	5.8	5.3	13.6	na	abv av	av
Vanguard Preferred Stock (VQIIX)	4.7	1.7	5.2	8.2	low	low
Philadelphia (PHILX)	4.7	5.3	12.3	12.0	low	blw av
Vanguard Convertible Sec (VCVSX)	4.2	10.9	12.9	13.8	abv av	av
INVESCO Utilities/Inv (FSTUX)	4.1	15.7	16.8	15.4	blw av	av
Amer Cent: Utilities/Inv (BULIX)	3.9	13.8	15.9	na	low	av
USAA Mutual: Growth & Inc (USGRX)	2.9	7.8	14.2	na	av	av
BS&R Inv: Equity (BREQX)	1.6	13.8	17.4	na	av	av
Neuberger Partners (NPRTX)	0.5	4.8	13.4	15.3	av	av
Westcore: Blue Chip (WTMVX)	0.5	7.5	14.5	15.3	abv av	av
UMB Scout Stock (UMBSX)	0.1	6.8	10.6	11.6	low	blw av
ABN AMRO: Value/Cmn (RVALX)	-0.6	5.1	12.8	na	high	abv av
Aquinas Value (AQEIX)	-1.1	1.7	10.1	na	abv av	av
Strong Adv US Value/Z (SEQIX)	-1.7	11.5	18.4	na	blw av	av
Fidelity Grth & Inc (FGRIX)	-1.9	11.5	16.7	18.9	blw av	av
Scudder Growth and Income/S (SCDGX)	-2.4	3.1	11.8	14.3	blw av	av
Dreyfus Growth & Income (DGRIX)	-3.8	8.2	10.9	na	av	av
Legg Mason Eq: Total Ret/P (LMTRX)	-4.6	-3.8	9.8	13.5	av	av
Pilgrim Corp Leaders/A (LEXCX)	-4.8	5.9	12.3	14.3	blw av	av
Fidelity Freedom 2030 (FFFEX)	-5.0	14.2	na	na	blw av	av
Payden & Rygel Gr & Inc/R (PDOGX)	-5.1	7.9	na	na	blw av	av
INVESCO Value Equity/Inv (FSEQX)	-5.4	3.2	10.7	13.5	blw av	av
SSgA: Growth & Income (SSGWX)	-5.7	15.3	20.7	na	high	av
Scudder Pathway: Growth/S (SPGRX)	-6.2	11.5	na	na	blw av	av
McM Equity Investment (MCMEX)	-6.3	10.0	17.7	na	blw av	av
Janus Inv: Equity Income (JAEIX)	-7.1	21.7	na	na	high	abv av
TIAA-CREF Growth & Income (TIGIX)	-7.3	14.6	na	na	abv av	av
Value Line Convertible (VALCX)	-7.5	7.4	11.7	13.0	abv av	av
Schwab Inv: 1000/I (SNXFX)	-8.2	12.1	17.7	na	abv av	av
CA Inv: S&P 500 Index (SPFIX)	-8.9	12.3	18.2	na	av	av
Vanguard Growth & Income (VQNPX)	-8.9	12.4	18.8	17.6	abv av	av
Vanguard Tx Mg Gr & Inc (VTGIX)	-9.0	12.3	18.3	na	av	av
Vanguard Idx: 500 Idx (VFINX)	-9.0	12.2	18.3	17.3	abv av	av
Galaxy II: Large Co (ILCIX)	-9.0	11.9	17.9	16.9	av	av
Fidelity Spart 500 Index (FSMKX)	-9.1	12.0	18.0	17.1	av	av
SSgA: S&P 500 Index (SVSPX)	-9.2	12.1	18.1	na	abv av	av
Dreyfus Discp Stock (DDSTX)	-9.2	10.7	17.4	17.1	abv av	av
USAA S&P 500 Index (USSPX)	-9.2	12.0	na	na	av	av
T Rowe Price Eq Index 500 (PREIX)	-9.3	11.9	18.0	16.9	abv av	av
Schwab Cap Tr: S&P 500/I (SWPIX)	-9.3	11.8	na	na	av	av
Northern Stock Index (NOSIX)	-9.4	11.6	na	na	abv av	av
Scudder S&P 500 Index/S (SCPIX)	-9.4	11.8	na	na	av	av
Strong Index 500 (SINEX)	-9.5	11.7	na	na	abv av	av
Dreyfus Index: S&P 500 Idx (PEOPX)	-9.5	11.6	17.7	16.8	abv av	av
Amer Cent: Income & Gr/Inv (BIGRX)	-10.5	10.4	17.5	17.7	abv av	av
Vanguard Idx: Tot Stk/Inv (VTSMX)	-10.5	10.9	16.6	na	high	av

Growth and Income Funds

Ranked by 2000 Total Returns

Fund Name	Annual Return (%) 2000	3yr	5yr	10yr	Category Risk	Total Risk
Payden & Rygel Mkt Ret/R (PYMRX)	-10.8	10.0	15.8	na	abv av	av
Fidelity Spart Total Mkt (FSTMX)	-10.9	10.8	na	na	high	av
SAFECO Equity (SAFQX)	-10.9	6.7	13.5	16.8	av	av
Fidelity (FFIDX)	-10.9	13.1	18.0	17.4	high	av
Janus Inv: Growth & Income (JAGIX)	-11.4	21.7	25.1	na	high	abv av
Managers: US Stk Mkt Plus (MGSPX)	-11.7	10.4	17.2	na	abv av	av
Rightime: Fund (RTFDX)	-12.3	7.8	5.9	9.5	blw av	av
Fidelity Sel Utilities Gr (FSUTX)	-13.4	15.9	17.7	15.5	high	av
Dreyfus (DREVX)	-14.2	7.6	9.8	10.5	high	abv av
Flex-fund: Muirfield (FLMFX)	-16.5	7.9	9.5	11.8	blw av	av
Fidelity Utilities (FIUIX)	-20.4	9.0	13.7	13.8	abv av	av
Markman Moderate Alloc (MMMGX)	-29.4	4.1	8.4	na	high	abv av
Growth & Income Fund Average	**5.7**	**8.9**	**14.3**	**14.9**	**—**	**av**

International Stock Funds

Ranked by 2000 Total Returns

Fund Name	Annual Return (%) 2000	3yr	5yr	10yr	Category Risk	Total Risk
Oakmark Intl/I (OAKIX)	12.5	13.4	14.0	na	av	abv av
Tweedy Browne Global Val (TBGVX)	12.3	16.0	18.2	na	low	blw av
Fidelity Canada (FICDX)	12.2	10.3	10.5	9.5	av	abv av
RS: Contrarian/A (RSCOX)	10.2	0.8	-2.5	na	av	abv av
Amer Cent: Global Ntrl/Inv (BGRIX)	5.6	7.7	8.1	na	av	abv av
Vanguard Global Asset All (VHAAX)	4.1	10.2	10.0	na	low	blw av
Mercury HW Intl Val/I (MIVIX)	2.1	10.2	10.8	12.7	low	av
Vanguard Global Equity (VHGEX)	-0.1	11.2	11.1	na	low	av
Schroder Cap: Intl/Inv (SCIEX)	-2.2	13.2	10.5	10.3	low	blw av
Scudder Global/S (SCOBX)	-3.0	10.4	12.4	12.7	low	av
Harbor: Int'l II (HAIIX)	-3.7	10.8	na	na	blw av	abv av
Dreyfus Gr & Val: Intl Val (DIVLX)	-4.0	9.8	9.7	na	low	av
Preferred Int'l (PFIFX)	-4.7	11.8	11.8	na	low	av
Harbor: Int'l (HAINX)	-4.9	9.1	12.5	14.5	low	av
Masters Select Intl (MSILX)	-5.2	22.8	na	na	av	abv av
Fidelity Europe Cap Appr (FECAX)	-5.7	12.3	17.4	na	blw av	abv av
Fidelity Global Balanced (FGBLX)	-5.9	10.8	10.5	na	low	blw av
Fremont: Global (FMAFX)	-6.6	7.9	9.5	10.3	low	blw av
T Rowe Price Intl: Europn (PRESX)	-6.6	12.0	15.6	12.9	low	av
Investec China & HK (ICHKX)	-6.9	9.4	7.0	na	high	high
Vanguard Intl Value (VTRIX)	-7.4	10.4	7.2	7.9	blw av	av
Fidelity Worldwide (FWWFX)	-8.0	8.8	11.4	11.4	blw av	av
Wm Blair: Intl Grth/N (WBIGX)	-8.1	26.2	19.1	na	av	abv av
UMB Scout Worldwide (UMBWX)	-8.1	12.4	14.8	na	low	av
Vanguard Erpn Stock Index (VEURX)	-8.2	11.3	15.7	13.7	low	av
Fidelity Nordic (FNORX)	-8.4	23.6	24.6	na	abv av	abv av
Vanguard World: Intl Grth (VWIGX)	-8.6	10.5	10.0	10.2	low	av
Fidelity Diversified Intl (FDIVX)	-8.9	16.1	16.4	na	blw av	av
Excelsior Pan European (UMPNX)	-9.0	8.2	13.8	na	blw av	abv av
Scudder Greater Europe Gr (SCGEX)	-9.1	16.4	20.7	na	blw av	abv av
Fidelity Europe (FIEUX)	-9.1	9.2	14.9	12.6	blw av	abv av
Northern Intl Growth Eqty (NOIGX)	-9.9	14.6	10.9	na	low	av
Artisan Int'l (ARTIX)	-10.5	28.9	24.3	na	abv av	high
USAA Inv: Int'l (USIFX)	-10.8	6.0	9.1	10.5	low	av
Northern Intl Select Eqty (NINEX)	-10.9	14.0	10.7	na	low	av
T Rowe Price Intl: Lat Am (PRLAX)	-11.1	-2.9	8.2	na	high	high
USAA Inv: World Growth (USAWX)	-11.2	8.6	11.4	na	blw av	av
Fidelity Intl Grth & Inc (FIGRX)	-14.0	13.2	11.8	10.4	blw av	abv av
Amer Cent: Intl Disc/Inv (TWEGX)	-14.2	23.9	24.0	na	abv av	high
1838 Int'l Equity (INTEX)	-14.2	12.5	11.1	na	blw av	av
Schwab MarketMgr: Intl (SWOIX)	-14.4	19.2	na	na	av	abv av
Babson-Stewart Ivory Intl (BAINX)	-14.4	8.2	7.9	9.7	low	av
T Rowe Price Spect: Intl (PSILX)	-14.7	10.1	na	na	low	av
Amer Cent: Intl Gr/Inv (TWIEX)	-15.0	18.4	17.9	na	av	abv av
T Rowe Price Intl: Discvr (PRIDX)	-15.6	31.6	19.6	12.6	abv av	high
Vanguard Tot Itl Stk Idx (VGTSX)	-15.6	8.2	na	na	low	av
Scudder Latin America (SLAFX)	-15.6	-4.4	8.0	na	high	high
Harding Loevner Intl Eqty (HLMIX)	-15.8	11.5	8.9	na	blw av	av
SSgA: Active Int'l (SSAIX)	-16.3	7.9	3.0	na	low	av
Warburg Maj Frgn Mkt/Cmn (WPMFX)	-16.3	16.1	na	na	blw av	abv av
Marshall: Intl Stock/Inv (MRISX)	-16.7	9.8	11.9	na	av	abv av

International Stock Funds

Ranked by 2000 Total Returns

Fund Name	Annual Return (%) 2000	3yr	5yr	10yr	Category Risk	Total Risk
Janus Inv: Worldwide (JAWWX)	-16.8	19.8	21.2	na	av	abv av
T Rowe Price Intl: Stock (PRITX)	-17.0	9.0	9.0	10.3	blw av	av
Fidelity Latin America (FLATX)	-17.4	-7.6	6.4	na	high	high
Fidelity China Region (FHKCX)	-17.5	12.9	9.6	na	high	high
Schwab Intl Index/I (SWINX)	-17.5	8.4	8.3	na	low	av
Wright Eq: Intl Blue Chip (WIBCX)	-18.1	5.5	7.5	8.8	blw av	abv av
Fidelity Overseas (FOSFX)	-18.3	9.6	10.5	9.4	blw av	av
Janus Inv: Overseas (JAOSX)	-18.5	20.6	21.7	na	abv av	high
Legg Mason Gl: Intl Eq/P (LMGEX)	-19.0	1.9	4.6	na	low	av
Scudder Int'l/S (SCINX)	-19.2	14.7	13.3	11.7	blw av	av
BB&K Intl Equity (BBIEX)	-19.2	6.4	7.7	5.9	blw av	av
INVESCO European/Inv (FEURX)	-19.4	13.7	17.0	12.1	abv av	high
Liberty Acorn Internatl/Z (ACINX)	-19.9	18.2	14.8	na	av	abv av
TIAA-CREF Intl Equity (TIINX)	-19.9	14.1	na	na	av	abv av
Dreyfus Emerging Markets (DRFMX)	-20.3	4.5	na	na	abv av	high
Dreyfus Intl Growth (DITFX)	-21.9	6.6	5.3	na	abv av	high
Dreyfus Founders: Wld Gr/F (FWWGX)	-22.1	8.2	9.8	12.8	av	abv av
ABN AMRO: Intl Equity/Cmn (RIEQX)	-22.6	11.2	9.6	na	blw av	av
Columbia Intl Stock (CMISX)	-22.6	11.2	12.3	na	blw av	abv av
Fremont: Intl Growth (FIGFX)	-22.7	10.1	6.6	na	blw av	abv av
Matthews Pacific Tiger (MAPTX)	-23.8	10.6	-0.1	na	high	high
Excelsior Intl (UMINX)	-23.9	8.6	8.4	7.5	blw av	abv av
Gabelli Gl Telecomm/AAA (GABTX)	-24.0	22.6	21.5	na	av	abv av
Neuberger Intl (NBISX)	-24.3	8.6	12.0	na	abv av	high
FTI Intl Equity (FTIEX)	-24.9	6.7	9.2	na	blw av	abv av
Montgomery Global 20/R (MNSFX)	-25.2	5.9	13.1	na	av	abv av
Montgomery Intl Growth/R (MNIGX)	-25.4	6.6	10.0	na	blw av	abv av
Harbor: Int'l Grth (HAIGX)	-25.4	3.4	8.6	na	av	abv av
Dreyfus Global Growth (DSWIX)	-25.5	3.0	6.5	7.1	av	abv av
Vanguard Pacific Stk Idx (VPACX)	-25.7	6.1	-3.9	1.5	av	abv av
T Rowe Price Intl: Em Mk Stk (PRMSX)	-26.3	-0.5	2.1	na	high	high
Sit Intl Growth (SNGRX)	-26.6	9.5	8.7	na	av	abv av
INVESCO Telcom/Inv (ISWCX)	-26.9	36.0	30.8	na	high	high
Japan/S (SJPNX)	-27.2	25.7	8.6	4.8	abv av	high
SteinRoe Inv: Intl (SRITX)	-27.3	2.7	2.5	na	blw av	av
Vanguard Emg Mkt Stk Idx (VEIEX)	-27.5	-1.4	-1.5	na	abv av	high
Loomis Sayles Intl Eq/Ist (LSIEX)	-27.7	14.5	11.9	na	abv av	high
Montgomery Emg Mkts/R (MNEMX)	-29.1	-10.6	-4.9	na	abv av	high
Warburg Intl Eqty/Cmn (CUIEX)	-29.5	4.9	4.1	8.9	av	abv av
Dreyfus Founders: Psport/F (FPSSX)	-29.6	14.0	12.6	na	high	high
Montgomery Glbl Oppor/R (MNGOX)	-29.7	13.6	14.4	na	abv av	high
Scudder Emerg Mkts Grth (SEMGX)	-29.9	-9.9	na	na	av	abv av
SSgA: Emerging Markets (SSEMX)	-29.9	-0.9	0.3	na	abv av	high
Fidelity Southeast Asia (FSEAX)	-30.4	7.8	-3.3	na	high	high
T Rowe Price Intl: Nw Asia (PRASX)	-30.7	7.1	-2.5	5.7	abv av	high
Fidelity Aggressive Intl (FIVFX)	-30.9	7.0	7.6	na	av	abv av
USAA Inv: Emerging Mrkts (USEMX)	-31.9	-8.4	-2.9	na	high	high
Vontobel Intl Equity (VNEPX)	-32.6	4.8	8.0	9.6	av	abv av
Fidelity Emerging Market (FEMKX)	-32.9	-5.6	-11.3	-1.1	abv av	high
Warburg Emerg Mkts/Cmn (WPEMX)	-32.9	-4.1	-5.0	na	high	high
Fidelity Pacific Basin (FPBFX)	-35.3	15.4	4.8	7.0	abv av	high

International Stock Funds

Ranked by 2000 Total Returns

Fund Name	Annual Return (%) 2000	3yr	5yr	10yr	Category Risk	Total Risk
Schroder Cap: Emerging Markets Ist/Inv (SCEIX)	-35.8	-7.9	-4.4	na	abv av	high
Fidelity Japan (FJPNX)	-36.4	20.9	6.9	na	abv av	high
Strong Int'l Stk (STISX)	-36.6	4.3	1.0	na	abv av	high
Strong Asia Pacific (SASPX)	-36.9	6.1	-3.3	na	abv av	high
T Rowe Price Intl: Japan (PRJPX)	-37.2	13.3	0.2	na	abv av	abv av
Gabelli Gl Growth/AAA (GICPX)	-37.4	20.3	22.6	na	abv av	high
Montgomery Glbl Commun/R (MNGCX)	-39.1	24.3	19.2	na	high	high
Scudder Pacific Opport (SCOPX)	-39.1	-2.2	-9.1	na	high	high
Excelsior Pacific-Asia (USPAX)	-40.1	5.9	-2.8	na	abv av	high
Pilgrim Wldwd Emerg Mkt/A (LEXGX)	-47.0	-7.2	-5.3	2.6	high	high
Fidelity Japan Smaller Co (FJSCX)	-50.2	30.1	2.9	na	high	high
Matthews Korea (MAKOX)	-52.8	24.3	-14.2	na	high	high
Warburg Japan Growth/Cmn (WPJGX)	-68.7	5.0	2.1	na	high	high
Warburg Japan Sm Co/Cmn (WPJPX)	-71.8	10.8	-2.4	na	high	high
International Stock Fund Average	**-19.4**	**8.9**	**8.3**	**9.0**	**—**	**abv av**

Balanced Funds

Ranked by 2000 Total Returns

Fund Name	Annual Return (%) 2000	3yr	5yr	10yr	Category Risk	Total Risk
T Rowe Price Cap Apprec (PRWCX)	22.1	11.4	13.4	13.8	blw av	blw av
Oakmark Eqty & Income/I (OAKBX)	19.8	13.2	16.2	na	av	blw av
Vanguard Wellesley Income (VWINX)	16.1	7.5	10.3	11.8	low	blw av
Dodge & Cox Balanced (DODBX)	15.1	11.2	13.8	14.4	av	blw av
USAA Mutual: Income (USAIX)	13.3	5.8	5.9	8.3	low	low
Gabelli Westwood Bal/AAA (WEBAX)	12.6	10.6	14.3	na	blw av	blw av
Vanguard STAR (VGSTX)	10.9	10.1	13.4	13.8	av	blw av
Vanguard Wellington (VWELX)	10.4	8.9	13.0	13.9	av	blw av
Eclipses: Balanced (EBALX)	9.6	5.6	10.4	12.3	blw av	blw av
Vanguard LifeStgy Income (VASIX)	7.9	7.9	9.0	na	low	blw av
Fidelity Puritan (FPURX)	7.7	8.9	12.7	14.6	blw av	blw av
T Rowe Price Spect: Income (RPSIX)	7.4	4.6	6.7	8.9	low	blw av
T Rowe Price Pers Str: Inc (PRSIX)	6.5	7.7	9.9	na	low	blw av
Preferred Asset Allocatn (PFAAX)	6.5	11.4	14.0	na	low	blw av
Fidelity Freedom Income (FFFAX)	6.2	8.1	na	na	low	blw av
Permanent Port: Perm Port (PRPFX)	5.8	3.4	3.5	5.5	low	blw av
Pax World Balanced (PAXWX)	5.6	15.5	16.3	13.0	blw av	blw av
T Rowe Price Pers Str: Bal (TRPBX)	5.6	9.0	11.7	na	blw av	blw av
Alleghany: Chicago Bal/N (CHTAX)	5.4	14.2	15.9	na	abv av	blw av
Fidelity Balanced (FBALX)	5.3	11.2	13.2	12.6	av	blw av
Vanguard Asset Allocation (VAAPX)	4.9	11.4	15.3	15.2	av	blw av
Amer Cent: Stg Al Cnsrv/Inv (TWSCX)	4.8	8.8	na	na	low	blw av
T Rowe Price Pers Str: Gr (TRSGX)	4.6	10.4	13.8	na	abv av	blw av
Fidelity Freedom 2000 (FFFBX)	4.4	10.5	na	na	low	blw av
Aon: Asset Allocation (AONAX)	4.4	8.0	12.8	na	abv av	blw av
INVESCO Equity Income/Inv (FIIIX)	3.8	10.1	14.5	15.3	high	blw av
Fidelity Asset Mgr Income (FASIX)	3.6	6.5	7.9	na	low	blw av
Vanguard LifeStgy Cons Gr (VSCGX)	3.0	8.8	10.6	na	low	blw av
USAA Inv: Crnrst Strategy (USCRX)	2.7	4.2	9.0	10.7	blw av	blw av
Schwab MarketTrack: Cnsrv (SWCGX)	2.7	7.5	9.0	na	low	blw av
Fidelity Asset Mgr (FASMX)	2.6	10.6	13.2	13.4	av	blw av
T Rowe Price Balanced (RPBAX)	2.0	9.2	12.2	12.5	blw av	blw av
Dreyfus Balanced (DRBAX)	1.9	7.2	10.0	na	av	blw av
FBP Contrarian Balanced (FBPBX)	1.0	7.0	11.5	13.4	high	blw av
Alleghany: Mntg & Cldwl Bl/N (MOBAX)	0.9	11.9	15.8	na	abv av	blw av
Dreyfus Life: Gr & Inc/R (DGIRX)	0.9	8.3	12.0	na	low	blw av
Columbia Balanced (CBALX)	0.8	10.9	12.6	na	av	blw av
McM Balanced (MCMBX)	0.7	9.1	13.3	na	blw av	blw av
Fidelity Freedom 2010 (FFFCX)	0.6	12.6	na	na	abv av	blw av
Value Line Asset Alloc (VLAAX)	0.4	14.8	18.3	na	high	abv av
Boston Balanced (BMGFX)	0.3	7.7	12.2	na	av	blw av
Amer Cent: Stg Al Mod/Inv (TWSMX)	0.2	11.3	na	na	abv av	blw av
Vanguard Tx Mg Balanced (VTMFX)	-0.5	10.3	11.9	na	blw av	blw av
Rainier: Balanced (RIMBX)	-0.5	10.3	13.6	na	abv av	blw av
USAA Inv: Growth & Tax (USBLX)	-0.6	6.5	9.3	9.8	blw av	blw av
Vanguard LifeStgy Mod Gr (VSMGX)	-0.9	9.7	12.2	na	blw av	blw av
Schwab MarketTrack: Bal (SWBGX)	-1.0	8.6	10.9	na	blw av	blw av
Montgomery Balanced/R (MNAAX)	-1.3	5.7	9.6	na	av	blw av
Value Line Inc & Grth (VALIX)	-1.6	16.3	17.0	14.1	high	av
INVESCO Balanced/Inv (IMABX)	-1.8	10.3	13.0	na	abv av	blw av
Vanguard Balanced Index (VBINX)	-2.0	9.4	12.8	na	av	blw av

Balanced Funds

Ranked by 2000 Total Returns

Fund Name	Annual Return (%) 2000	3yr	5yr	10yr	Category Risk	Total Risk
Janus Inv: Balanced (JABAX)	-2.1	16.6	17.3	na	high	blw av
SSgA Life Sol: Balanced (SSLBX)	-2.1	7.4	na	na	blw av	blw av
SteinRoe Inv: Balanced (SRFBX)	-2.2	7.1	11.1	12.0	av	blw av
Scudder Balanced/S (SCBAX)	-2.4	10.2	12.9	na	abv av	blw av
Amer Cent: Stg Al Agg/Inv (TWSAX)	-2.5	14.0	na	na	high	av
Scudder Pathway: Balanced (SPBAX)	-2.6	6.9	na	na	av	blw av
Amer Cent: Balanced/Inv (TWBIX)	-2.6	7.6	10.4	11.4	av	blw av
Fidelity Freedom 2020 (FFFDX)	-3.0	13.9	na	na	high	av
Vintage Balanced (AMBFX)	-3.1	9.2	11.8	na	abv av	blw av
Fidelity Asset Mgr Growth (FASGX)	-3.5	9.0	14.0	na	high	av
INVESCO Total Return/Inv (FSFLX)	-3.6	2.5	8.8	11.9	abv av	blw av
Weston: New Century Bal (NCIPX)	-3.7	8.8	11.3	11.6	abv av	blw av
ABN AMRO: Balanced/Cmn (RBTCX)	-4.2	5.1	9.9	na	abv av	blw av
USAA Inv: Balanced Stgy (USBSX)	-4.4	7.2	10.7	na	abv av	blw av
Schwab MarketTrack: Growth (SWHGX)	-4.8	9.3	12.6	na	high	blw av
TIAA-CREF Managed Alloc (TIMAX)	-4.9	11.1	na	na	abv av	blw av
Schwab MarketMgr: Bal (SWOBX)	-5.1	10.6	na	na	high	blw av
Vanguard LifeStgy Grth (VASGX)	-5.4	10.4	13.7	na	high	blw av
SAFECO Div Income (SAFIX)	-6.3	0.2	9.5	12.1	high	av
Strong Balanced (STAAX)	-6.3	9.4	11.0	11.1	high	blw av
USAA Inv: Growth Stgy (USGSX)	-6.8	9.0	11.5	na	high	av
Lindner Asset Alloc/Inv (LDDVX)	-7.5	-0.7	4.4	9.9	abv av	blw av
Dreyfus Founders: Bal/F (FRINX)	-10.4	0.0	6.7	10.8	abv av	blw av
CGM Mutual (LOMMX)	-11.6	4.8	9.0	12.1	high	av
Schwab MarketMgr: Growth (SWOGX)	-11.9	11.2	na	na	high	av
Balanced Fund Average	**2.0**	**8.4**	**11.4**	**11.7**	**—**	**blw av**

Corporate Bond Funds

Ranked by 2000 Total Returns

Fund Name	Annual Return (%) 2000	3yr	5yr	10yr	Category Risk	Total Risk
Vanguard Fxd: Long Tm Corp (VWESX)	11.7	4.6	5.6	9.1	high	blw av
Vanguard Fxd: Interm Corp (VFICX)	10.7	5.6	5.7	na	abv av	blw av
Metropolitan West TR Bd/M (MWTRX)	10.4	7.3	na	na	av	low
SteinRoe Inc: Income (SRINX)	9.8	4.9	5.8	8.2	abv av	low
Amer Cent: Bond/Inv (TWLBX)	9.7	4.5	4.9	7.1	abv av	low
Dreyfus Inv Grd Bd: Sh Inc (DSTIX)	8.9	6.4	6.7	na	blw av	low
Vanguard Fxd: Sh Tm Corp (VFSTX)	8.1	5.9	5.9	6.9	blw av	low
T Rowe Price Corp Income (PRPIX)	7.9	3.0	5.2	na	high	blw av
Strong Corporate Bd/Inv (STCBX)	7.8	4.9	6.3	9.4	high	blw av
Fidelity Short Tm Bond (FSHBX)	7.8	5.7	5.6	6.3	low	low
Janus Inv: Short-Term Bond (JASBX)	7.7	5.7	6.0	na	blw av	low
Metropolitan West Lw Dr/M (MWLDX)	7.5	6.8	na	na	blw av	low
Citizens: Income (WAIMX)	7.2	4.0	5.4	na	av	low
USAA Mutual: Short-Term Bd (USSBX)	7.1	5.3	5.9	na	low	low
SSgA: Yield Plus (SSYPX)	6.6	5.6	5.6	na	low	low
INVESCO Select Income/Inv (FBDSX)	5.1	3.5	5.3	8.4	abv av	low
Janus Inv: Flexible Income (JAFIX)	4.8	4.4	6.3	10.0	av	low
Loomis Sayles Bond/Ist (LSBDX)	4.3	4.5	7.2	na	high	blw av
Corporate Bond Fund Average	**8.0**	**5.0**	**5.7**	**8.1**	**—**	**low**

Corporate High-Yield Funds

Ranked by 2000 Total Returns

Fund Name	Annual Return (%) 2000	3yr	5yr	10yr	Category Risk	Total Risk
Strong Sht Tm HY Bond/Inv (STHBX)	5.0	6.2	na	na	low	low
Janus Inv: High Yield (JAHYX)	2.4	3.0	9.3	na	blw av	blw av
Vanguard Fxd: Hi Yld Corp (VWEHX)	-0.8	2.3	5.6	10.3	low	blw av
Payden & Rygel High Inc/R (PYHRX)	-1.7	2.5	na	na	low	blw av
T Rowe Price High Yield (PRHYX)	-3.2	1.7	6.1	10.1	blw av	blw av
SAFECO High Yld Bd (SAFHX)	-5.4	0.9	5.0	9.1	av	blw av
Northeast Investors Tr (NTHEX)	-6.0	-1.0	5.8	11.3	av	blw av
Scudder High Yield Bond/S (SHBDX)	-6.7	0.2	na	na	av	blw av
Strong Hi Yld Bond/Inv (STHYX)	-7.0	1.0	8.7	na	abv av	blw av
Fidelity Capital & Inc (FAGIX)	-9.4	2.4	6.5	12.2	high	blw av
Nicholas Income (NCINX)	-10.3	-3.4	2.7	7.3	av	blw av
INVESCO High Yield/Inv (FHYPX)	-12.0	-1.2	5.1	8.9	abv av	blw av
Fidelity High Income (SPHIX)	-14.2	-1.1	5.0	12.0	high	blw av
Legg Mason Inc: Hi Yld/P (LMHYX)	-16.5	-3.6	3.5	na	high	blw av
Value Line Aggressive Inc (VAGIX)	-23.6	-7.6	1.5	7.6	high	blw av
Corporate High-Yield Fund Average	**-6.9**	**0.0**	**5.4**	**9.8**	**—**	**blw av**

Government Bond Funds

Ranked by 2000 Total Returns

Fund Name	Annual Return (%) 2000	3yr	5yr	10yr	Category Risk	Total Risk
Amer Cent: Target 2020/Inv (BTTTX)	48.0	9.5	9.1	13.4	high	av
Amer Cent: Target 2025/Inv (BTTRX)	42.6	11.1	na	na	high	av
Amer Cent: Target 2015/Inv (BTFTX)	33.5	9.1	8.4	13.0	high	blw av
Amer Cent: Target 2010/Inv (BTTNX)	28.8	9.0	7.8	11.9	high	blw av
Wasatch-Hoisington: US Trs (WHOSX)	21.9	7.0	8.8	7.9	high	blw av
Amer Cent: Target 2005/Inv (BTFIX)	19.9	8.1	6.8	10.5	high	blw av
Vanguard Admrl: Long Treas (VALGX)	19.8	7.2	6.8	na	high	blw av
Vanguard Fxd: Long Tm Trea (VUSTX)	19.7	7.3	6.8	9.5	high	blw av
Amer Cent: Long Trsy/Inv (BLAGX)	19.4	7.1	6.8	na	high	blw av
T Rowe Price Treas Long (PRULX)	19.1	7.0	6.5	8.7	high	blw av
Dreyfus US Treasury Long (DRGBX)	17.7	6.2	6.1	8.5	abv av	blw av
INVESCO US Gov't Secur/Inv (FBDGX)	14.6	6.0	6.1	7.4	abv av	blw av
Vanguard Admrl: Int Treas (VAITX)	14.1	6.9	6.3	na	abv av	blw av
Vanguard Fxd: Interm Treas (VFITX)	14.0	6.7	6.2	na	abv av	blw av
Aon: Gov't Securities (AGSYX)	13.2	6.1	na	na	abv av	blw av
Galaxy II: US/Ret A (IUTIX)	13.1	6.5	6.2	na	av	low
Dreyfus US Treasury Intm (DRGIX)	12.8	5.4	5.3	7.0	abv av	blw av
Fidelity Spart Gov't Inc (SPGVX)	12.7	6.2	6.0	7.3	av	low
Amer Cent: Intm Trs/Inv (CPTNX)	12.6	6.2	6.2	6.9	abv av	low
Fidelity Gov't Inc (FGOVX)	12.6	6.1	5.8	7.6	av	low
T Rowe Price Treas Interm (PRTIX)	11.6	6.0	5.7	7.0	abv av	blw av
Value Line US Gov't Sec (VALBX)	11.3	5.8	6.1	6.4	av	low
Fidelity Interm Gvt Inc (FSTGX)	10.3	6.0	5.8	6.5	av	low
Warburg Intm Mat Gv/Cmn (CUIGX)	9.8	5.7	5.4	6.9	av	low
Legg Mason Inc: Gov't Int/P (LGINX)	9.6	5.0	5.3	6.4	av	low
Marshall: Gov't Inc/Inv (MRGIX)	9.6	5.4	5.5	na	av	low
Northern US Gov't (NOUGX)	9.4	5.6	5.4	na	av	low
Vanguard Fxd: Sh Tm Fed (VSGBX)	9.1	6.1	5.9	6.5	blw av	low
Sit US Gov't Sec (SNGVX)	9.1	5.6	6.0	6.8	low	low
Schwab Inv: Sh Tm Bd Mkt (SWBDX)	9.1	5.8	5.6	na	blw av	low
Fidelity Instl Sh Int Gvt (FFXSX)	9.0	5.9	5.7	6.4	blw av	low
Vanguard Admrl: Sh Treas (VASTX)	8.9	6.0	5.8	na	blw av	low
Dreyfus Short Int Gov't (DSIGX)	8.9	5.7	5.4	6.6	blw av	low
Payden & Rygel US Gov't/R (PYUSX)	8.8	6.1	5.5	na	blw av	low
Vanguard Fxd: Sh Tm Treas (VFISX)	8.8	5.9	5.7	na	blw av	low
Dreyfus US Treasury Short (DRTSX)	8.7	5.3	5.2	6.3	blw av	low
Preferred Short-Term Gov't (PFSGX)	8.1	5.0	5.2	na	low	low
Montgomery Sht Dur Gvt/R (MNSGX)	8.1	5.9	6.0	na	low	low
Amer Cent: Sht Tm Gov't/Inv (TWUSX)	7.8	5.1	5.1	5.5	blw av	low
AMF Short US Gov't Sec (ASITX)	7.7	5.5	5.3	6.1	low	low
Excelsior Sh Tm Gov't Sec (UMGVX)	7.6	5.3	5.2	na	low	low
Amer Cent: Sht Tm Trsy/Inv (BSTAX)	7.1	5.2	5.1	na	low	low
Permanent Port: Treas Bill (PRTBX)	4.9	4.2	4.2	3.9	low	low
Government Bond Fund Average	**13.8**	**6.2**	**5.9**	**7.6**	**—**	**low**

Mortgage-Backed Funds

Ranked by 2000 Total Returns

Fund Name	Annual Return (%) 2000	3yr	5yr	10yr	Category Risk	Total Risk
USAA Inv: GNMA (USGNX)	12.1	5.3	5.7	na	high	blw av
Vanguard Fxd: GNMA (VFIIX)	11.2	6.2	6.7	7.7	abv av	low
Dreyfus BASIC GNMA (DIGFX)	11.0	6.1	6.5	7.6	high	low
T Rowe Price GNMA (PRGMX)	10.9	5.8	5.9	7.2	high	low
Fidelity Ginnie Mae (FGMNX)	10.7	6.0	6.3	7.1	av	low
Dreyfus GNMA (DRGMX)	10.5	5.2	5.7	6.8	high	low
Amer Cent: GNMA/Inv (BGNMX)	10.5	5.8	6.2	7.4	blw av	low
AMF US Gov't Mortgage Sec (ASMTX)	10.4	5.9	6.0	7.1	av	low
Wright Inc: Current Income (WCIFX)	10.2	5.7	6.0	7.1	abv av	low
Scudder GNMA/AARP (AGNMX)	10.2	5.7	5.9	6.7	av	low
Victory: Fund for Income/G (GGIFX)	9.9	5.9	5.9	7.0	blw av	low
AMF Interm Mortgage Sec (ASCPX)	9.7	5.9	5.8	7.1	blw av	low
AMF Adjust Rate Mortgage (ASARX)	7.1	5.6	5.8	na	low	low
Mortgage-Backed Bond Fund Average	**9.9**	**5.6**	**5.9**	**7.1**	**—**	**low**

General Bond Funds

Ranked by 2000 Total Returns

Fund Name	Annual Return (%) 2000	3yr	5yr	10yr	Category Risk	Total Risk
Vanguard Bd Idx: Long-Term (VBLTX)	16.4	6.3	6.4	na	high	blw av
Vanguard Bd Idx: Interm Tm (VBIIX)	12.7	6.3	6.2	na	high	blw av
Excelsior Managed Income (UMMGX)	12.4	5.9	5.6	7.7	high	low
Fremont: Bond (FBDFX)	11.7	6.6	6.9	na	high	low
TIAA-CREF Bond Plus (TIPBX)	11.6	6.3	na	na	abv av	low
Vanguard Bd Idx: Tot Bd (VBMFX)	11.4	6.2	6.3	7.8	av	low
Strong Gov't Sec/Inv (STVSX)	11.3	5.9	5.9	8.3	av	low
Columbia Fixed Income Sec (CFISX)	11.2	5.8	6.0	7.9	abv av	low
T Rowe Price New Income (PRCIX)	11.1	4.7	5.1	7.0	high	low
Schwab Inv: Tot Bd Mkt Ix (SWLBX)	11.0	6.0	5.7	na	abv av	low
Amer Cent: Premium Bond/Inv (ACBPX)	11.0	5.7	5.7	na	abv av	low
Fidelity Spart Inv Grade (FSIBX)	11.0	6.2	6.1	na	av	low
Northern Fixed Income (NOFIX)	10.9	5.1	5.4	na	high	low
Alleghany: Chicago Bd/N (CHTBX)	10.8	5.9	6.1	na	blw av	low
Fidelity Invest Grade Bd (FBNDX)	10.8	5.8	5.8	8.0	av	low
SSgA: Bond Market (SSBMX)	10.8	5.8	na	na	abv av	low
SteinRoe Inc: Interm Bond (SRBFX)	10.7	6.0	6.3	7.7	av	low
Dodge & Cox Income (DODIX)	10.7	5.8	6.2	8.3	av	low
WPG Tr: Core Bond (WPGVX)	10.6	6.4	6.1	6.1	abv av	low
Excelsior Intm Mgd Inc (UIMIX)	10.6	5.7	5.4	na	abv av	low
ABN AMRO: Fxd Inc/Cmn (RTFTX)	10.6	5.0	5.5	na	av	low
Wright Inc: Total Ret Bd (WTRBX)	10.6	5.2	5.1	7.2	high	blw av
Preferred Fixed Income (PFXIX)	10.5	5.4	5.5	na	abv av	low
1838 Fixed Income (ETFIX)	10.4	5.4	na	na	av	low
Payden & Rygel Inv Qual/R (PYOPX)	10.3	5.2	5.2	na	high	low
Dreyfus A Bonds Plus (DRBDX)	10.2	4.8	5.3	8.0	high	low
Harbor: Bond (HABDX)	10.2	6.3	6.6	8.8	abv av	low

General Bond Funds

Ranked by 2000 Total Returns

Fund Name	Annual Return (%) 2000	3yr	5yr	10yr	Category Risk	Total Risk
Payden & Rygel Tot Ret/R (PYTRX)	10.1	5.3	na	na	high	low
SSgA: Interm (SSINX)	10.0	5.8	5.7	na	blw av	low
Babson Bond Tr: Port L (BABIX)	9.9	5.2	5.5	7.3	abv av	low
McM Interm Fixed Income (MCMNX)	9.8	5.6	5.8	na	av	low
Scudder Income/S (SCSBX)	9.7	4.6	5.2	7.4	abv av	low
Fidelity Interm Bond (FTHRX)	9.7	5.9	5.8	7.1	blw av	low
Vintage Income (AVINX)	9.4	5.1	5.0	na	blw av	low
Bremer Inv: Bond (BBNDX)	9.2	5.1	na	na	blw av	low
UMB Scout Bond (UMBBX)	9.2	5.4	5.4	6.5	blw av	low
Warburg Fixed Inc/Cmn (CUFIX)	9.1	5.1	6.0	7.8	av	low
Vanguard Bd Idx: Short Trm (VBISX)	8.9	6.1	6.0	na	blw av	low
Legg Mason Inc: Inv Grd/P (LMIGX)	8.8	4.8	5.7	7.6	high	low
Marshall: Intm Bond/Inv (MAIBX)	8.7	5.4	5.1	na	blw av	low
Payden & Rygel Sht Bond/R (PYSBX)	8.5	5.8	5.4	na	low	low
T Rowe Price Sht Tm Bond (PRWBX)	8.4	5.6	5.4	5.6	low	low
Homestead: Sht Tm Bond (HOSBX)	7.8	5.7	5.8	na	low	low
Mercury Tot Ret/I (MTOIX)	7.7	4.8	5.9	na	abv av	low
Scudder Sh Term Bd/S (SCSTX)	7.5	4.4	4.6	5.8	low	low
Harbor: Short Duration (HASDX)	7.4	5.8	6.0	na	low	low
Strong Sht Tm Bond/Inv (SSTBX)	7.2	5.4	6.0	7.0	low	low
Payden & Rygel Ltd Mat/R (PYLMX)	7.0	5.6	5.5	na	low	low
Mercury Low Dur/I (MLOIX)	7.0	5.2	5.9	na	low	low
Strong Advantage/Inv (STADX)	6.7	5.5	5.9	6.7	low	low
Vintage Limited Term Bond (AFTRX)	6.7	4.4	4.3	na	blw av	low
Marshall: Short Tm Inc/Inv (MSINX)	6.7	5.3	5.4	na	low	low
Neuberger Ltd Mat Bond (NLMBX)	6.6	4.3	4.8	5.7	low	low
USAA Inv: Income Stgy (USICX)	6.0	6.3	7.2	na	high	blw av
General Bond Fund Average	**9.7**	**5.5**	**5.6**	**7.2**	**—**	**low**

Tax-Exempt Bond Funds

Ranked by 2000 Total Returns

Fund Name	Annual Return (%) 2000	3yr	5yr	10yr	Category Risk	Total Risk
Vanguard CA: Ins Long Tm (VCITX)	19.4	7.2	7.1	8.0	high	blw av
SAFECO CA Tax-Free Inc (SFCAX)	18.7	4.6	5.5	7.5	high	blw av
Excelsior Long-Term Tx Ex (UMLTX)	17.2	4.2	5.1	7.9	high	blw av
Schwab Inv: Lg Tm TF (SWNTX)	15.6	4.3	5.4	na	high	blw av
Dreyfus CA Tax-Exempt Bd (DRCAX)	15.2	5.2	5.4	6.1	high	blw av
Schwab Inv: CA Lg Tm TF Bd (SWCAX)	15.2	4.8	5.7	na	high	blw av
Dreyfus Gen CA Muni Bond (GCABX)	15.1	4.5	5.3	6.9	high	blw av
Amer Cent: CA Long Tm/Inv (BCLTX)	14.9	4.9	5.6	7.3	high	blw av
USAA Tax Ex: NY Bond (USNYX)	14.8	5.1	5.9	7.2	high	blw av
Amer Cent: CA Ins TF/Inv (BCINX)	14.5	5.1	5.6	7.2	high	blw av
USAA Tax Ex: CA Bond (USCBX)	14.3	5.0	6.1	7.2	high	blw av
SAFECO Muni Bond (SFCOX)	14.1	4.3	5.3	7.2	high	blw av
Empire Bldr Tax-Free Bd/Prem (EMTPX)	14.0	4.6	na	na	high	blw av
Dreyfus BASIC Muni Bond (DRMBX)	13.9	4.6	5.8	na	high	blw av
Northern CA Tax-Exempt (NCATX)	13.9	5.1	na	na	high	blw av
Vanguard NY Ins Lg Tm TE (VNYTX)	13.7	5.3	5.7	7.4	high	blw av
Vanguard Muni: Ins Long Tm (VILPX)	13.6	5.4	5.7	7.4	high	blw av
Empire Bldr Tax-Free Bd/Bldr (EMBTX)	13.6	4.3	4.7	6.4	high	blw av
Vanguard Muni: Long-Term (VWLTX)	13.4	5.0	5.7	7.6	high	blw av
Dreyfus Insured Muni Bond (DTBDX)	13.2	4.5	4.8	6.0	high	blw av
Vanguard FL Ins Lg Tm TE (VFLTX)	13.2	5.5	5.9	na	high	blw av
USAA Tax Ex: Virginia Bond (USVAX)	13.1	4.6	5.6	7.0	abv av	blw av
Vanguard OH Ins Lg Tm TE (VOHIX)	12.8	5.1	5.6	7.2	abv av	blw av
USAA State TF: FL TF Inc (UFLTX)	12.8	4.1	5.5	na	high	blw av
Fidelity Spart NY Muni In (FTFMX)	12.8	5.0	5.7	7.3	abv av	blw av
T Rowe Price TF: NY Bond (PRNYX)	12.8	4.5	5.3	7.2	high	blw av
T Rowe Price CA TF: Bond (PRXCX)	12.8	5.1	5.7	7.2	abv av	blw av
Vanguard PA Tx Ex Ins LT (VPAIX)	12.7	5.2	5.6	7.3	abv av	blw av
Amer Cent: Long Tm TF/Inv (TWTLX)	12.7	4.2	5.0	6.7	high	blw av
Amer Cent: CA Hi Yield (BCHYX)	12.7	5.1	6.3	7.6	abv av	blw av
Scudder CA Tax-Free (SCTFX)	12.5	5.0	5.7	7.4	abv av	blw av
Fidelity Spart CA Muni (FCTFX)	12.5	5.2	6.0	7.0	abv av	blw av
Vanguard NJ Ins Lg Tm TE (VNJTX)	12.4	5.3	5.5	7.2	abv av	blw av
SteinRoe Muni: Managed (SRMMX)	12.4	4.6	5.3	6.8	abv av	blw av
CA Inv: CA Tax-Free Income (CFNTX)	12.4	4.8	5.3	7.1	high	blw av
Fidelity Spart Muni Inc (FHIGX)	12.2	5.1	5.8	6.7	av	low
T Rowe Price TF: Income (PRTAX)	12.2	4.5	5.2	7.1	abv av	blw av
Northern Tax-Exempt (NOTEX)	12.2	4.4	4.9	na	abv av	blw av
USAA Tax Ex: Long-Term (USTEX)	12.1	4.1	5.4	6.9	abv av	blw av
Value Line Tx Ex Natl Bd (VLHYX)	12.1	4.0	4.8	6.3	av	low
INVESCO Tax-Free Bond/Inv (FTIFX)	12.0	4.2	4.7	6.5	abv av	low
Dreyfus Gen NY Muni Bond (GNYMX)	11.9	4.3	5.1	7.1	abv av	blw av
T Rowe Price TF: VA Bond (PRVAX)	11.9	4.7	5.4	na	abv av	blw av
Dreyfus Muni Bond (DRTAX)	11.9	3.6	4.5	6.2	high	blw av
T Rowe Price Sum: Muni Inc (PRINX)	11.9	4.4	5.9	na	abv av	blw av
Dreyfus MA Tax-Exempt Bd (DMEBX)	11.8	4.2	5.1	6.6	abv av	blw av
Fidelity Spart MA Muni (FDMMX)	11.8	4.9	5.5	7.1	av	low
Fidelity Spart OH Muni (FOHFX)	11.6	4.7	5.4	6.9	av	low
T Rowe Price TF: GA Bond (GTFBX)	11.6	4.5	5.4	na	abv av	blw av
Scudder NY TF (SCYTX)	11.4	4.6	5.4	7.3	abv av	blw av
T Rowe Price TF: NJ Bond (NJTFX)	11.4	4.3	5.0	na	abv av	blw av

Tax-Exempt Bond Funds

Ranked by 2000 Total Returns

Fund Name	Annual Return (%) 2000	3yr	5yr	10yr	Category Risk	Total Risk
T Rowe Price TF: MD Bond (MDXBX)	11.4	4.6	5.2	6.8	av	low
Dreyfus BASIC Intm Muni (DBIMX)	11.4	5.0	5.7	na	av	low
Fidelity Spart NJ Muni (FNJHX)	11.3	5.1	5.5	6.9	av	low
Dreyfus NJ Mu Bond (DRNJX)	11.2	4.0	4.8	6.5	av	low
Fidelity Spart MI Muni (FMHTX)	11.1	4.6	5.1	6.7	av	low
Dreyfus NY Tax Ex Bond (DRNYX)	11.1	4.4	4.9	6.6	abv av	low
Dreyfus PA Interm Muni Bd (DPABX)	11.0	4.6	5.2	na	av	low
Vanguard CA: Ins Intm TE (VCAIX)	11.0	5.3	5.8	na	blw av	low
Fidelity Spart MD Income (SMDMX)	11.0	4.7	5.4	na	blw av	low
Fidelity Spart PA Muni (FPXTX)	10.9	4.7	5.2	7.2	av	low
Scudder Managed Muni Bd/S (SCMBX)	10.9	4.9	5.6	7.2	av	low
Fidelity Spart CT Muni (FICNX)	10.9	4.7	5.5	6.7	av	low
Dreyfus Gen Muni Bond (GMBDX)	10.9	3.3	4.2	6.6	abv av	low
Scudder MA Tax-Free/S (SCMAX)	10.9	4.8	5.3	7.4	av	low
Fidelity Spart FL Income (FFLIX)	10.8	4.6	5.3	na	av	low
Vanguard Muni: High Yield (VWAHX)	10.7	4.4	5.3	7.5	av	low
Fidelity Spart MN Muni (FIMIX)	10.6	4.4	5.1	6.2	blw av	low
Galaxy: Intm TE Bond/Tr (SETMX)	10.5	4.5	5.3	na	av	low
Galaxy: CT Intm Muni/Tr (SCTEX)	10.1	4.5	5.1	na	av	low
Amer Cent: CA Intm TF/Inv (BCITX)	10.1	4.7	5.2	6.3	blw av	low
Galaxy: MA Intm Muni/Tr (SEMAX)	9.9	4.4	5.1	na	av	low
Amer Cent: FL Intm Muni/Inv (ACBFX)	9.9	5.1	5.4	na	blw av	low
Amer Cent: Intm Tax-Free/Inv (TWTIX)	9.9	4.8	5.1	6.1	blw av	low
USAA Tax Ex: Interm-Term (USATX)	9.8	4.4	5.4	6.8	blw av	low
Columbia OR Muni Bond (CMBFX)	9.8	4.1	4.8	6.1	av	low
Amer Cent: AZ Intm Muni/Inv (BEAMX)	9.7	4.7	4.9	na	blw av	low
Excelsior NY Intm Tx Ex (UMNYX)	9.7	4.5	4.9	5.8	av	low
Dreyfus NY Interm Tx Ex (DRNIX)	9.5	4.3	5.0	6.5	blw av	low
Dreyfus CA Interm Muni Bd (DCIMX)	9.4	4.4	4.8	na	blw av	low
SteinRoe Muni: Interm (SRIMX)	9.4	4.3	4.9	6.2	blw av	low
Excelsior Intm Tax Exmpt (UMITX)	9.4	4.5	5.0	6.4	blw av	low
Fidelity Spart Int Muni (FLTMX)	9.2	4.6	5.2	6.6	blw av	low
Vanguard Muni: Interm Tm (VWITX)	9.2	4.7	5.1	6.8	blw av	low
Marshall: Intm Tax-Free/Inv (MITFX)	9.1	4.1	4.6	na	blw av	low
Scudder High Yld Tax-Free/S (SHYTX)	9.1	4.3	5.8	7.5	blw av	low
Galaxy: FL Muni/Tr (SFTEX)	9.0	4.0	na	na	av	low
T Rowe Price TF: Int (PTIBX)	8.9	4.3	4.8	na	blw av	low
Dreyfus MA Interm Muni Bd (DMAIX)	8.9	4.2	4.7	na	blw av	low
Janus Inv: Federal Tx Ex (JATEX)	8.9	3.1	4.5	na	av	low
Warburg NY Intm Muni/Cmn (CNMBX)	8.9	4.5	4.7	5.9	blw av	low
Fremont: CA Interm Tax-Free (FCATX)	8.7	4.4	4.8	6.0	blw av	low
T Rowe Price Sum: Muni Int (PRSMX)	8.7	4.3	5.2	na	blw av	low
T Rowe Price TF: FL Int (FLTFX)	8.6	4.3	4.6	na	blw av	low
First Hawaii Muni Bond (SURFX)	8.4	3.7	4.4	6.0	low	low
Scudder Medium Tm Tax-Free/S (SCMTX)	8.4	4.2	4.8	6.6	low	low
Sit Tax-Free Income (SNTIX)	8.3	3.3	5.1	6.4	blw av	low
T Rowe Price TF: High Yld (PRFHX)	8.1	2.7	4.6	6.8	av	low
Legg Mason Tax-Free: Int In/P (LTITX)	8.1	4.0	4.3	na	low	low
Sit Minnesota Tax-Free Inc (SMTFX)	8.1	3.3	4.7	na	low	low
Dupree: KY Tax-Free Income (KYTFX)	8.0	3.9	4.7	6.6	av	low
Northern Intm Tax-Exempt (NOITX)	7.9	3.9	4.2	na	low	low

Tax-Exempt Bond Funds

Ranked by 2000 Total Returns

Fund Name	Annual Return (%) 2000	3yr	5yr	10yr	Category Risk	Total Risk
Dreyfus Interm Muni Bond (DITEX)	7.7	3.8	4.5	6.2	low	low
Dreyfus FL Interm Muni Bd (DFLIX)	7.5	3.7	4.1	na	low	low
Dreyfus CT Interm Muni Bd (DCTIX)	7.5	3.8	4.5	na	low	low
Heartland Grp: WI Tax-Free (HRWIX)	7.4	3.0	4.2	na	blw av	low
Schwab Inv: CA Sh Int TF Bd (SWCSX)	7.2	4.2	4.3	na	low	low
Dreyfus NJ Interm Mu Bond (DNJIX)	7.2	3.9	4.4	na	low	low
Amer Cent: CA Ltd TF/Inv (BCSTX)	7.0	4.3	4.4	na	low	low
SteinRoe Muni: High Yield (SRHMX)	7.0	3.3	4.8	6.2	low	low
Excelsior CA Tx Ex Income (UMCAX)	6.9	4.0	na	na	low	low
T Rowe Price TF: Short Int (PRFSX)	6.7	4.2	4.3	5.0	low	low
Schwab Inv: Sh/Int TF (SWITX)	6.6	3.9	4.1	na	low	low
Vanguard Muni: Limited Tm (VMLTX)	6.3	4.2	4.4	5.2	low	low
Fidelity Spart Sh Int Mun (FSTFX)	6.2	4.1	4.3	5.2	low	low
USAA Tax Ex: Short-Term (USSTX)	6.0	4.2	4.5	5.0	low	low
T Rowe Price TF: MD Short (PRMDX)	5.5	3.9	3.8	na	low	low
Dupree: KY Tax-Free Short-Med (KYSMX)	5.4	3.4	3.8	4.6	low	low
Strong Sht Tm Mu Bond/Inv (STSMX)	5.0	3.9	4.6	na	low	low
Dreyfus Short Int Muni Bd (DSIBX)	4.9	3.8	4.1	4.9	low	low
Vanguard Muni: Short-Term (VWSTX)	4.9	3.9	3.9	4.2	low	low
Calvert Tax-Free Rsv: Ltd/A (CTFLX)	4.5	3.7	3.8	4.2	low	low
Strong Sht Tm HY Mu/Inv (SSHMX)	4.2	3.7	na	na	low	low
Strong Muni Advtg (SMUAX)	3.9	3.8	4.2	na	low	low
Strong Muni Bond (SXFIX)	3.3	1.0	3.4	5.9	abv av	blw av
Strong Hi Yld Muni Bd (SHYLX)	-1.4	-0.6	3.2	na	av	low
Tax-Exempt Bond Fund Average	**9.4**	**3.8**	**4.9**	**6.5**	**—**	**low**

International Bond Funds

Ranked by 2000 Total Returns

Fund Name	Annual Return (%) 2000	3yr	5yr	10yr	Category Risk	Total Risk
T Rowe Price Intl: Em Mk Bd (PREMX)	15.2	2.9	11.7	na	high	abv av
Fidelity New Markets Inc (FNMIX)	14.3	6.6	14.8	na	high	high
Payden & Rygel Glbl Fix/R (PYGFX)	13.1	7.9	7.7	na	blw av	low
Scudder Emerg Mkts Inc (SCEMX)	10.0	-2.0	7.4	na	high	high
Warburg Glbl Fxd Inc/Cmn (CGFIX)	7.2	5.2	5.5	7.2	blw av	low
Payden & Rygel Glbl Sht/R (PYGSX)	6.9	5.6	na	na	low	low
Strong Adv Short Dur Bd/Z (STGBX)	6.4	5.4	6.5	na	low	low
Scudder Global Bond/S (SSTGX)	4.3	3.7	2.9	na	av	blw av
Fidelity Intl Bond (FGBDX)	1.4	2.7	2.0	3.5	av	blw av
BB&K Int'l Bd (BBIFX)	1.3	2.5	3.6	5.0	blw av	blw av
Amer Cent: Intl Bond/Inv (BEGBX)	-1.1	1.4	0.8	na	high	blw av
T Rowe Price Intl: Bd (RPIBX)	-3.1	0.8	1.2	6.1	abv av	blw av
Legg Mason Gl: Gl Gov't/P (LMGGX)	-5.0	0.6	1.6	na	av	blw av
International Bond Fund Average	**4.5**	**3.2**	**5.2**	**5.4**	**—**	**blw av**

Individual Fund Listings 9

Stock Funds

1838 Int'l Equity (INTEX)

877-367-1838, 610-293-4300
www.1838ia.com

International Stock

PERFORMANCE — fund inception date: 8/1/95

	3yr Annual	5yr Annual	10yr Annual	Bull	Bear
Return (%)	12.5	11.1	na	62.5	-17.7
Differ from Category (+/-)	3.6 abv av	2.8 abv av	na	-28.4 av	6.3 abv av

Standard Deviation	Category Risk Index	Beta
18.2%—av	0.80—blw av	0.77

	2000	1999	1998	1997	1996	1995	1994	1993	1992	1991
Return (%)	-14.2	41.3	17.5	9.9	8.0	—	—	—	—	—
Differ from Category (+/-)	.5.2	-19.4	11.7	8.6	-6.5	—	—	—	—	—
Return, Tax-Adjusted (%)	-16.0	40.0	14.4	8.6	7.8	—	—	—	—	—

PER SHARE DATA

	2000	1999	1998	1997	1996	1995	1994	1993	1992	1991
Dividends, Net Income ($)	0.00	0.00	0.87	0.00	0.03	—	—	—	—	—
Distrib'ns, Cap Gain ($)	1.53	0.76	0.00	0.66	0.00	—	—	—	—	—
Net Asset Value ($)	12.81	16.76	12.44	11.33	10.93	—	—	—	—	—
Expense Ratio (%)	na	1.09	1.13	1.25	1.25	—	—	—	—	—
Yield (%)	0.00	0.00	6.99	0.00	0.27	—	—	—	—	—
Portfolio Turnover (%)	na	49	167	92	59	—	—	—	—	—
Total Assets (Millions $)	96	106	60	52	46	—	—	—	—	—

PORTFOLIO (as of 6/30/00)

Portfolio Manager: Johannes Van Den Berg - 1995

Investm't Category: International Stock

Domestic	Index
✔ Foreign	Sector
Asset Allocation	State Specific

Investment Style

Large Cap	Mid Cap	Small Cap
Growth	Grth/Val	Value

Portfolio

2.7%	cash	0.0%	corp bonds
97.3%	stocks	0.0%	gov't bonds
0.0%	pref/conv't pref	0.0%	muni bonds
0.0%	conv't bds/wrnts	0.0%	other

SHAREHOLDER INFORMATION

Minimum Investment
Initial: $1,000 — Subsequent: $1

Minimum IRA Investment
Initial: $1 — Subsequent: $1

Maximum Fees
Load: none — 12b-1: none
Other: none

Services
✔ IRA
✔ Keogh
✔ Telephone Exchange

ABN AMRO: Balanced/ Cmn (RBTCX)

800-443-4725, 312-855-3350
www.abnamrofunds-usa.com

Balanced

PERFORMANCE

fund inception date: 1/4/93

	3yr Annual	5yr Annual	10yr Annual	Bull	Bear
Return (%)	5.1	9.9	na	27.8	-5.5
Differ from Category (+/-)	-3.3 low	-1.5 blw av	na	-0.3 av	-2.3 av

Standard Deviation	Category Risk Index	Beta
12.4%—blw av	1.13—abv av	0.68

	2000	1999	1998	1997	1996	1995	1994	1993	1992	1991
Return (%)	-4.2	10.5	9.9	22.0	13.1	21.8	-2.1	—	—	—
Differ from Category (+/-)	-6.2	-0.2	-3.4	3.2	-0.8	-3.7	-0.8	—	—	—
Return, Tax-Adjusted (%)	-6.6	8.3	6.3	20.2	9.7	18.9	-3.2	—	—	—

PER SHARE DATA

	2000	1999	1998	1997	1996	1995	1994	1993	1992	1991
Dividends, Net Income ($)	0.26	0.23	0.26	0.32	0.34	0.39	0.29	—	—	—
Distrib'ns, Cap Gain ($)	0.98	0.84	1.72	0.31	0.79	0.42	0.00	—	—	—
Net Asset Value ($)	10.21	11.96	11.83	12.73	10.98	10.75	9.53	—	—	—
Expense Ratio (%)	na	1.00	1.03	0.93	1.19	1.22	1.34	—	—	—
Yield (%)	2.32	1.79	1.91	2.45	2.88	3.49	3.04	—	—	—
Portfolio Turnover (%)	na	112	84	111	104	85	85	—	—	—
Total Assets (Millions $)	73	83	72	68	54	47	72	—	—	—

PORTFOLIO (as of 6/30/00)

Portfolio Manager: committee - 1999

Investm't Category: Balanced

- ✔ Domestic
- ✔ Foreign
- ✔ Asset Allocation
- Index
- Sector
- State Specific

Investment Style

Large Cap | Mid Cap | Small Cap
Growth | Grth/Val | Value

Portfolio

-1.6%	cash	12.7%	corp bonds
60.2%	stocks	26.3%	gov't bonds
0.0%	pref/conv't pref	0.0%	muni bonds
0.0%	conv't bds/wrnts	2.3%	other

SHAREHOLDER INFORMATION

Minimum Investment
Initial: $2,000 Subsequent: $100

Minimum IRA Investment
Initial: $1,000 Subsequent: $100

Maximum Fees
Load: none 12b-1: none
Other: none

Services
- ✔ IRA
- Keogh
- ✔ Telephone Exchange

ABN AMRO: Growth/Cmn

800-443-4725, 312-855-3350
www.abnamrofunds-usa.com

(RGTCX)

Growth

PERFORMANCE

fund inception date: 1/4/93

	3yr Annual	5yr Annual	10yr Annual	Bull	Bear
Return (%)	11.9	16.2	na	49.2	-13.2
Differ from Category (+/-)	0.9 av	0.1 av	na	-0.5 av	-7.8 blw av

Standard Deviation	Category Risk Index	Beta
20.7%—abv av	1.07—av	1.10

	2000	1999	1998	1997	1996	1995	1994	1993	1992	1991
Return (%)	-4.4	12.8	30.2	23.9	21.6	31.5	-2.0	—	—	—
Differ from Category (+/-)	-7.9	-6.1	15.9	-3.2	-0.7	1.1	-1.8	—	—	—
Return, Tax-Adjusted (%)	-5.6	10.7	27.8	21.3	18.9	27.9	-2.8	—	—	—

PER SHARE DATA

	2000	1999	1998	1997	1996	1995	1994	1993	1992	1991
Dividends, Net Income ($)	0.00	0.00	0.02	0.11	0.17	0.16	0.15	—	—	—
Distrib'ns, Cap Gain ($)	1.10	1.78	1.65	1.46	0.86	1.00	0.11	—	—	—
Net Asset Value ($)	15.59	17.44	17.10	14.57	13.06	11.61	9.73	—	—	—
Expense Ratio (%)	na	1.03	1.06	1.02	1.27	1.31	1.33	—	—	—
Yield (%)	0.00	0.00	0.10	0.68	1.22	1.26	1.52	—	—	—
Portfolio Turnover (%)	na	69	65	62	58	71	68	—	—	—
Total Assets (Millions $)	221	195	177	132	95	78	82	—	—	—

PORTFOLIO (as of 6/30/00)

Portfolio Manager: Paul Becker, Nancy Ellison - 1999

Investm't Category: Growth

✔ Domestic	Index
Foreign	Sector
Asset Allocation	State Specific

Investment Style

✔ Large Cap	Mid Cap	Small Cap
✔ Growth	Grth/Val	Value

Portfolio

2.3%	cash	0.0%	corp bonds
97.7%	stocks	0.0%	gov't bonds
0.0%	pref/conv't pref	0.0%	muni bonds
0.0%	conv't bds/wrnts	0.0%	other

SHAREHOLDER INFORMATION

Minimum Investment
Initial: $2,000 Subsequent: $100

Minimum IRA Investment
Initial: $1,000 Subsequent: $100

Maximum Fees
Load: none 12b-1: none
Other: none

Services
✔ IRA
Keogh
✔ Telephone Exchange

ABN AMRO: Intl Equity/ Cmn (RIEQX)

800-443-4725, 312-855-3350
www.abnamrofunds-usa.com

International Stock

PERFORMANCE

fund inception date: 1/4/93

	3yr Annual	5yr Annual	10yr Annual	Bull	Bear
Return (%)	11.2	9.6	na	69.3	-24.6
Differ from Category (+/-)	2.3 abv av	1.3 av	na	-21.6 av	-0.6 av

Standard Deviation	Category Risk Index	Beta
19.0%—av	0.84—blw av	0.79

	2000	1999	1998	1997	1996	1995	1994	1993	1992	1991
Return (%)	-22.6	41.8	25.4	4.5	10.0	14.0	3.3	—	—	—
Differ from Category (+/-)	-3.2	-18.9	19.6	3.2	-4.5	4.7	6.4	—	—	—
Return, Tax-Adjusted (%)	-23.8	40.0	24.9	2.9	9.6	13.4	3.3	—	—	—

PER SHARE DATA

	2000	1999	1998	1997	1996	1995	1994	1993	1992	1991
Dividends, Net Income ($)	0.00	0.00	0.09	0.07	0.03	0.05	0.00	—	—	—
Distrib'ns, Cap Gain ($)	1.53	1.67	0.18	1.09	0.15	0.20	0.00	—	—	—
Net Asset Value ($)	17.89	25.08	18.97	15.38	15.83	14.56	13.00	—	—	—
Expense Ratio (%)	na	1.31	1.38	1.35	1.61	1.68	2.22	—	—	—
Yield (%)	0.00	0.00	0.46	0.42	0.18	0.33	0.00	—	—	—
Portfolio Turnover (%)	na	31	31	17	9	11	6	—	—	—
Total Assets (Millions $)	157	204	142	85	96	77	41	—	—	—

PORTFOLIO (as of 6/30/00)

Portfolio Manager: committee - 1999

Investm't Category: International Stock

Domestic	Index
✔ Foreign	Sector
Asset Allocation	State Specific

Investment Style

Large Cap	Mid Cap	Small Cap
Growth	Grth/Val	Value

Portfolio

-1.4%	cash	0.0%	corp bonds
101.4%	stocks	0.0%	gov't bonds
0.0%	pref/conv't pref	0.0%	muni bonds
0.0%	conv't bds/wrnts	0.0%	other

SHAREHOLDER INFORMATION

Minimum Investment

Initial: $2,000 Subsequent: $100

Minimum IRA Investment

Initial: $1,000 Subsequent: $100

Maximum Fees

Load: none 12b-1: none

Other: none

Services

✔ IRA

Keogh

✔ Telephone Exchange

ABN AMRO: Sm Cap/ Cmn (RSMCX)

800-443-4725, 312-855-3350
www.abnamrofunds-usa.com

Aggressive Growth

PERFORMANCE — fund inception date: 1/4/93

	3yr Annual	5yr Annual	10yr Annual	Bull	Bear
Return (%)	4.7	9.7	na	46.2	-11.8
Differ from Category (+/-)	-11.5 low	-4.9 blw av	na	-73.0 low	8.8 abv av

Standard Deviation	Category Risk Index	Beta
25.7%—high	0.79—blw av	0.95

	2000	1999	1998	1997	1996	1995	1994	1993	1992	1991
Return (%)	6.1	15.8	-6.5	15.8	19.4	32.1	-6.2	—	—	—
Differ from Category (+/-)	12.1	-41.7	-21.6	1.0	1.1	-2.5	-5.4	—	—	—
Return, Tax-Adjusted (%)	3.8	15.8	-6.8	13.3	15.4	31.5	-6.2	—	—	—

PER SHARE DATA

	2000	1999	1998	1997	1996	1995	1994	1993	1992	1991
Dividends, Net Income ($)	0.00	0.00	0.00	0.00	0.00	0.02	0.02	—	—	—
Distrib'ns, Cap Gain ($)	1.57	0.00	0.22	1.62	1.77	0.15	0.00	—	—	—
Net Asset Value ($)	13.45	14.16	12.22	13.38	13.03	12.46	9.57	—	—	—
Expense Ratio (%)	na	1.19	1.17	1.04	1.30	1.39	1.38	—	—	—
Yield (%)	0.00	0.00	0.00	0.00	0.00	0.15	0.20	—	—	—
Portfolio Turnover (%)	na	167	151	170	158	142	43	—	—	—
Total Assets (Millions $)	65	55	45	42	36	23	31	—	—	—

PORTFOLIO (as of 6/30/00)

Portfolio Manager: Christopher Beck, Gerald Frey - 1999

Investm't Category: Aggressive Growth

✔ Domestic	Index
Foreign	Sector
Asset Allocation	State Specific

Investment Style

Large Cap	Mid Cap	✔ Small Cap
✔ Growth	Grth/Val	Value

Portfolio

-8.7%	cash	0.0%	corp bonds
108.7%	stocks	0.0%	gov't bonds
0.0%	pref/conv't pref	0.0%	muni bonds
0.0%	conv't bds/wrnts	0.0%	other

SHAREHOLDER INFORMATION

Minimum Investment

Initial: $2,000 — Subsequent: $100

Minimum IRA Investment

Initial: $1,000 — Subsequent: $100

Maximum Fees

Load: none — 12b-1: none

Other: none

Services

✔ IRA

Keogh

✔ Telephone Exchange

ABN AMRO: Value/Cmn (RVALX)

800-443-4725, 312-855-3350
www.abnamrofunds-usa.com

Growth & Income

PERFORMANCE

fund inception date: 1/4/93

	3yr Annual	5yr Annual	10yr Annual	Bull	Bear
Return (%)	5.1	12.8	na	33.8	-3.8
Differ from Category (+/-)	-3.8 low	-1.5 blw av	na	0.3 av	-3.7 av

Standard Deviation	Category Risk Index	Beta
19.5%—abv av	1.12—high	0.95

	2000	1999	1998	1997	1996	1995	1994	1993	1992	1991
Return (%)	-0.6	11.1	5.4	30.4	20.4	32.0	0.0	—	—	—
Differ from Category (+/-)	-6.3	0.3	-7.4	3.5	0.7	2.5	0.5	—	—	—
Return, Tax-Adjusted (%)	-2.1	9.3	-1.1	28.9	16.7	29.8	-1.7	—	—	—

PER SHARE DATA

	2000	1999	1998	1997	1996	1995	1994	1993	1992	1991
Dividends, Net Income ($)	0.10	0.13	0.18	0.23	0.28	0.35	0.34	—	—	—
Distrib'ns, Cap Gain ($)	0.82	0.80	5.04	0.48	1.19	0.26	0.16	—	—	—
Net Asset Value ($)	11.68	12.75	12.33	16.51	13.24	12.26	9.79	—	—	—
Expense Ratio (%)	na	1.03	1.05	1.01	1.28	1.33	1.37	—	—	—
Yield (%)	0.80	0.95	1.03	1.35	1.94	2.79	3.41	—	—	—
Portfolio Turnover (%)	na	94	55	79	58	37	38	—	—	—
Total Assets (Millions $)	122	153	161	222	164	131	61	—	—	—

PORTFOLIO (as of 6/30/00)

Portfolio Manager: William Rydell, Mark Sikorski - 1999

Investm't Category: Growth & Income

✔ Domestic — Index
Foreign — Sector
Asset Allocation — State Specific

Investment Style

✔ Large Cap — Mid Cap — Small Cap
Growth — Grth/Val — ✔ Value

Portfolio

-5.5%	cash	0.0%	corp bonds
105.5%	stocks	0.0%	gov't bonds
0.0%	pref/conv't pref	0.0%	muni bonds
0.0%	conv't bds/wrnts	0.0%	other

SHAREHOLDER INFORMATION

Minimum Investment
Initial: $2,000 — Subsequent: $100

Minimum IRA Investment
Initial: $1,000 — Subsequent: $100

Maximum Fees
Load: none — 12b-1: none
Other: none

Services
✔ IRA
Keogh
✔ Telephone Exchange

Alleghany: Chicago Bal/N (CHTAX)

800-992-8151, 312-223-2000
www.alleghanyfunds.com

Balanced

PERFORMANCE — fund inception date: 9/21/95

	3yr Annual	5yr Annual	10yr Annual	Bull	Bear
Return (%)	14.2	15.9	na	38.1	2.2
Differ from Category (+/-)	5.8 high	4.5 high	na	10.0 abv av	5.4 high

Standard Deviation	Category Risk Index	Beta
11.6%—blw av	1.06—abv av	0.62

	2000	1999	1998	1997	1996	1995	1994	1993	1992	1991
Return (%)	5.4	12.8	25.1	20.9	16.5	—	—	—	—	—
Differ from Category (+/-)	3.4	2.1	11.8	2.1	2.6	—	—	—	—	—
Return, Tax-Adjusted (%)	3.0	11.3	22.8	18.3	14.8	—	—	—	—	—

PER SHARE DATA

	2000	1999	1998	1997	1996	1995	1994	1993	1992	1991
Dividends, Net Income ($)	0.29	0.27	0.26	0.28	0.27	—	—	—	—	—
Distrib'ns, Cap Gain ($)	1.00	0.36	0.71	0.67	0.13	—	—	—	—	—
Net Asset Value ($)	12.72	13.31	12.38	10.73	9.70	—	—	—	—	—
Expense Ratio (%)	na	1.06	1.08	1.07	1.00	—	—	—	—	—
Yield (%)	2.11	1.97	1.98	2.45	2.74	—	—	—	—	—
Portfolio Turnover (%)	na	25	40	35	34	—	—	—	—	—
Total Assets (Millions $)	309	303	241	193	162	—	—	—	—	—

PORTFOLIO (as of 6/30/00)

Portfolio Manager: Marthaler, Myszkowski - 1995

Investm't Category: Balanced

✔ Domestic	Index
✔ Foreign	Sector
✔ Asset Allocation	State Specific

Investment Style

Large Cap	Mid Cap	Small Cap
Growth	Grth/Val	Value

Portfolio

2.9%	cash	15.5%	corp bonds
60.9%	stocks	20.7%	gov't bonds
0.0%	pref/conv't pref	0.0%	muni bonds
0.0%	conv't bds/wrnts	0.0%	other

SHAREHOLDER INFORMATION

Minimum Investment
Initial: $2,500 — Subsequent: $50

Minimum IRA Investment
Initial: $500 — Subsequent: $50

Maximum Fees
Load: none — 12b-1: 0.25%
Other: none

Services
✔ IRA
✔ Keogh
✔ Telephone Exchange

Alleghany: Chicago G&I/N (CHTIX)

800-992-8151, 312-223-2000
www.alleghanyfunds.com

Growth

PERFORMANCE

fund inception date: 12/13/93

	3yr Annual	5yr Annual	10yr Annual	Bull	Bear
Return (%)	19.4	22.0	na	68.9	0.0
Differ from Category (+/-)	8.4 high	5.9 high	na	19.2 abv av	5.4 abv av

Standard Deviation	Category Risk Index	Beta
18.8%—av	0.97—blw av	1.00

	2000	1999	1998	1997	1996	1995	1994	1993	1992	1991
Return (%)	2.0	23.2	35.4	26.7	25.4	35.5	0.5	—	—	—
Differ from Category (+/-)	-1.5	4.3	21.1	-0.4	3.1	5.1	0.7	—	—	—
Return, Tax-Adjusted (%)	-0.1	21.5	33.9	24.9	24.3	34.9	0.1	—	—	—

PER SHARE DATA

	2000	1999	1998	1997	1996	1995	1994	1993	1992	1991
Dividends, Net Income ($)	0.00	0.00	0.00	0.06	0.11	0.09	0.08	—	—	—
Distrib'ns, Cap Gain ($)	3.07	2.00	1.43	1.36	0.33	0.07	0.00	—	—	—
Net Asset Value ($)	25.86	28.40	24.74	19.42	16.49	13.52	10.11	—	—	—
Expense Ratio (%)	na	1.06	1.08	1.07	1.00	1.09	1.20	—	—	—
Yield (%)	0.00	0.00	0.00	0.28	0.65	0.66	0.79	—	—	—
Portfolio Turnover (%)	na	29	34	31	25	9	37	—	—	—
Total Assets (Millions $)	514	540	428	289	215	183	12	—	—	—

PORTFOLIO (as of 6/30/00)

Portfolio Manager: Myszkowski, Drake - 1999

Investm't Category: Growth

✔ Domestic　Index
Foreign　Sector
Asset Allocation　State Specific

Investment Style

✔ Large Cap　Mid Cap　Small Cap
Growth　✔ Grth/Val　Value

Portfolio

5.5%	cash	0.0%	corp bonds
94.5%	stocks	0.0%	gov't bonds
0.0%	pref/conv't pref	0.0%	muni bonds
0.0%	conv't bds/wrnts	0.0%	other

SHAREHOLDER INFORMATION

Minimum Investment
Initial: $2,500　Subsequent: $50

Minimum IRA Investment
Initial: $500　Subsequent: $50

Maximum Fees
Load: none　12b-1: 0.25%
Other: none

Services
✔ IRA
✔ Keogh
✔ Telephone Exchange

Alleghany: Mntg & Cldwl Bl/N (MOBAX)

800-992-8151, 312-223-2000
www.alleghanyfunds.com

Balanced

PERFORMANCE

fund inception date: 11/2/94

	3yr Annual	5yr Annual	10yr Annual	Bull	Bear
Return (%)	11.9	15.8	na	36.0	-3.6
Differ from Category (+/-)	3.5 high	4.4 high	na	7.9 abv av	-0.4 av

Standard Deviation	Category Risk Index	Beta
11.8%—blw av	1.07—abv av	0.58

	2000	1999	1998	1997	1996	1995	1994	1993	1992	1991
Return (%)	0.9	12.8	23.0	23.4	20.3	29.3	—	—	—	—
Differ from Category (+/-)	-1.1	2.1	9.7	4.6	6.4	3.8	—	—	—	—
Return, Tax-Adjusted (%)	-0.4	11.2	21.1	22.0	16.7	28.2	—	—	—	—

PER SHARE DATA

	2000	1999	1998	1997	1996	1995	1994	1993	1992	1991
Dividends, Net Income ($)	0.36	0.28	0.26	0.25	0.26	0.26	—	—	—	—
Distrib'ns, Cap Gain ($)	0.62	0.87	0.93	0.38	1.21	0.00	—	—	—	—
Net Asset Value ($)	18.36	19.53	18.36	15.96	13.46	12.44	—	—	—	—
Expense Ratio (%)	na	1.14	1.18	1.25	1.25	1.25	—	—	—	—
Yield (%)	1.89	1.37	1.34	1.52	1.77	2.09	—	—	—	—
Portfolio Turnover (%)	na	34	59	28	43	27	—	—	—	—
Total Assets (Millions $)	159	166	185	89	33	23	—	—	—	—

PORTFOLIO (as of 6/30/00)

Portfolio Manager: Ronald Canakaris - 1994

Investm't Category: Balanced

✔ Domestic	Index
Foreign	Sector
✔ Asset Allocation	State Specific

Investment Style

Large Cap	Mid Cap	Small Cap
Growth	Grth/Val	Value

Portfolio

2.9%	cash	19.9%	corp bonds
60.9%	stocks	16.3%	gov't bonds
0.0%	pref/conv't pref	0.0%	muni bonds
0.0%	conv't bds/wrnts	0.0%	other

SHAREHOLDER INFORMATION

Minimum Investment
Initial: $2,500 Subsequent: $1

Minimum IRA Investment
Initial: $500 Subsequent: $1

Maximum Fees
Load: none 12b-1: 0.25%
Other: none

Services
✔ IRA
Keogh
✔ Telephone Exchange

Alleghany: Mntg & Cldwl Gr/N (MCGFX)

800-992-8151, 312-223-2000
www.alleghanyfunds.com

Growth

PERFORMANCE

fund inception date: 11/2/94

	3yr Annual	5yr Annual	10yr Annual	Bull	Bear
Return (%)	14.3	21.2	na	60.4	-8.8
Differ from Category (+/-)	3.3 abv av	5.1 high	na	10.7 abv av	-3.4 av

Standard Deviation	Category Risk Index	Beta
18.2%—av	0.94—blw av	0.91

	2000	1999	1998	1997	1996	1995	1994	1993	1992	1991
Return (%)	-7.3	22.5	31.8	31.8	32.7	38.6	—	—	—	—
Differ from Category (+/-)	-10.8	3.6	17.5	4.7	10.4	8.2	—	—	—	—
Return, Tax-Adjusted (%)	-9.6	21.3	31.0	31.5	32.4	38.5	—	—	—	—

PER SHARE DATA

	2000	1999	1998	1997	1996	1995	1994	1993	1992	1991
Dividends, Net Income ($)	0.00	0.00	0.00	0.00	0.00	0.02	—	—	—	—
Distrib'ns, Cap Gain ($)	4.07	1.65	0.93	0.21	0.13	0.00	—	—	—	—
Net Asset Value ($)	27.83	34.64	29.65	23.25	17.80	13.52	—	—	—	—
Expense Ratio (%)	na	1.05	1.12	1.23	1.28	1.30	—	—	—	—
Yield (%)	0.00	0.00	0.00	0.00	0.00	0.14	—	—	—	—
Portfolio Turnover (%)	na	31	29	18	26	34	—	—	—	—
Total Assets (Millions $)	1,290	1,735	1,257	548	196	48	—	—	—	—

PORTFOLIO (as of 6/30/00)

Portfolio Manager: Ronald Canakaris - 1994

Investm't Category: Growth

✔ Domestic
Index
Foreign
Sector
Asset Allocation
State Specific

Investment Style

✔ Large Cap
Mid Cap
Small Cap
Growth
✔ Grth/Val
Value

Portfolio

1.6%	cash	0.0%	corp bonds
98.4%	stocks	0.0%	gov't bonds
0.0%	pref/conv't pref	0.0%	muni bonds
0.0%	conv't bds/wrnts	0.0%	other

SHAREHOLDER INFORMATION

Minimum Investment

Initial: $2,500 Subsequent: $1

Minimum IRA Investment

Initial: $500 Subsequent: $1

Maximum Fees

Load: none 12b-1: 0.25%
Other: none

Services

✔ IRA
Keogh
✔ Telephone Exchange

Amer Cent: Balanced/Inv

800-345-2021, 816-531-5575
www.americancentury.com

(TWBIX)

Balanced

PERFORMANCE — fund inception date: 10/20/88

	3yr Annual	5yr Annual	10yr Annual	Bull	Bear
Return (%)	7.6	10.4	11.4	24.4	-6.4
Differ from Category (+/-)	-0.8 blw av	-1.0 blw av	-0.3 av	-3.7 av	-3.2 blw av

Standard Deviation	Category Risk Index	Beta
11.2%—blw av	1.02—av	0.60

	2000	1999	1998	1997	1996	1995	1994	1993	1992	1991
Return (%)	-2.6	10.0	16.2	16.9	12.6	21.3	0.0	7.2	-6.0	46.8
Differ from Category (+/-)	-4.6	-0.7	2.9	-1.9	-1.3	-4.2	1.3	-7.2	-14.4	23.0
Return, Tax-Adjusted (%)	-4.2	6.2	12.9	14.1	9.2	18.2	-1.5	6.2	-6.6	45.8

PER SHARE DATA

	2000	1999	1998	1997	1996	1995	1994	1993	1992	1991
Dividends, Net Income ($)	0.43	0.46	0.42	0.39	0.48	0.48	0.43	0.37	0.34	0.35
Distrib'ns, Cap Gain ($)	0.60	2.54	2.11	1.60	1.38	1.00	0.27	0.00	0.00	0.00
Net Asset Value ($)	15.73	17.22	18.47	18.14	17.26	16.99	15.27	16.00	15.28	16.64
Expense Ratio (%)	na	1.00	1.00	1.00	0.99	1.00	1.00	1.00	1.00	1.00
Yield (%)	2.63	2.32	2.04	1.97	2.57	2.66	2.76	2.31	2.22	2.10
Portfolio Turnover (%)	na	128	102	110	130	85	94	95	100	116
Total Assets (Millions $)	789	950	998	936	878	839	689	683	700	351

PORTFOLIO (as of 6/30/00)

Portfolio Manager: committee - 1998

Investm't Category: Balanced

✔ Domestic	Index
✔ Foreign	Sector
Asset Allocation	State Specific

Investment Style

Large Cap	Mid Cap	Small Cap
Growth	Grth/Val	Value

Portfolio

0.9%	cash	13.5%	corp bonds
59.5%	stocks	24.3%	gov't bonds
0.0%	pref/conv't pref	0.0%	muni bonds
0.0%	conv't bds/wrnts	1.9%	other

SHAREHOLDER INFORMATION

Minimum Investment
Initial: $2,500 — Subsequent: $50

Minimum IRA Investment
Initial: $1,000 — Subsequent: $50

Maximum Fees
Load: none — 12b-1: none
Other: none

Services
✔ IRA
✔ Keogh
✔ Telephone Exchange

Amer Cent: Eqty Growth/ Inv (BEQGX)

800-345-2021, 816-531-5575
www.americancentury.com

Growth

PERFORMANCE — fund inception date: 5/9/91

	3yr Annual	5yr Annual	10yr Annual	Bull	Bear
Return (%)	9.7	18.0	na	53.4	-14.2
Differ from Category (+/-)	-1.3 blw av	1.9 av	na	3.7 av	-8.8 blw av

Standard Deviation	Category Risk Index	Beta
19.0%—av	0.98—blw av	1.05

	2000	1999	1998	1997	1996	1995	1994	1993	1992	1991
Return (%)	-10.9	18.4	25.4	36.0	27.3	34.5	-0.2	11.4	4.1	—
Differ from Category (+/-)	-14.4	-0.5	11.1	8.9	5.0	4.1	0.0	-3.2	-8.5	—
Return, Tax-Adjusted (%)	-12.2	17.7	24.0	32.5	22.9	31.2	-1.7	9.0	3.1	—

PER SHARE DATA

	2000	1999	1998	1997	1996	1995	1994	1993	1992	1991
Dividends, Net Income ($)	0.13	0.18	0.20	0.24	0.26	0.22	0.29	0.23	0.32	—
Distrib'ns, Cap Gain ($)	1.46	0.42	0.87	2.31	1.85	1.01	0.25	0.65	0.02	—
Net Asset Value ($)	21.77	26.23	22.71	19.04	15.96	14.24	11.53	12.12	11.68	—
Expense Ratio (%)	na	0.68	0.69	0.67	0.63	0.75	0.75	0.75	0.75	—
Yield (%)	0.55	0.67	0.84	1.12	1.45	1.44	2.46	1.80	2.73	—
Portfolio Turnover (%)	na	86	89	161	131	125	94	96	114	—
Total Assets (Millions $)	1,906	2,316	2,018	770	274	159	97	96	73	—

PORTFOLIO (as of 6/30/00)

Portfolio Manager: committee - 1991

Investm't Category: Growth

✔ Domestic	Index
Foreign	Sector
Asset Allocation	State Specific

Investment Style

✔ Large Cap	Mid Cap	Small Cap
Growth	✔ Grth/Val	Value

Portfolio

3.4%	cash	0.0%	corp bonds
96.6%	stocks	0.0%	gov't bonds
0.0%	pref/conv't pref	0.0%	muni bonds
0.0%	conv't bds/wrnts	0.0%	other

SHAREHOLDER INFORMATION

Minimum Investment
Initial: $2,500 — Subsequent: $50

Minimum IRA Investment
Initial: $1,000 — Subsequent: $50

Maximum Fees
Load: none — 12b-1: none
Other: none

Services
✔ IRA
✔ Keogh
✔ Telephone Exchange

Amer Cent: Eqty Income/ Inv (TWEIX)

800-345-2021, 816-531-5575
www.americancentury.com

Growth & Income

PERFORMANCE — fund inception date: 8/1/94

	3yr Annual	5yr Annual	10yr Annual	Bull	Bear
Return (%)	11.1	16.8	na	19.3	14.7
Differ from Category (+/-)	2.2 abv av	2.5 abv av	na	-14.2 blw av	14.8 high

Standard Deviation	Category Risk Index	Beta
13.9%—blw av	0.80—low	0.47

	2000	1999	1998	1997	1996	1995	1994	1993	1992	1991
Return (%)	21.9	-0.1	12.9	28.2	23.3	29.6	—	—	—	—
Differ from Category (+/-)	16.2	-10.9	0.1	1.3	3.6	0.1	—	—	—	—
Return, Tax-Adjusted (%)	20.6	-2.9	8.7	22.9	19.4	25.5	—	—	—	—

PER SHARE DATA

	2000	1999	1998	1997	1996	1995	1994	1993	1992	1991
Dividends, Net Income ($)	0.17	0.21	0.21	0.25	0.18	0.19	—	—	—	—
Distrib'ns, Cap Gain ($)	0.00	0.47	0.96	1.16	0.54	0.45	—	—	—	—
Net Asset Value ($)	6.62	5.60	6.31	6.66	6.34	5.76	—	—	—	—
Expense Ratio (%)	1.00	1.00	1.00	1.00	0.98	1.00	—	—	—	—
Yield (%)	2.56	3.45	2.88	3.19	2.61	3.05	—	—	—	—
Portfolio Turnover (%)	141	180	158	159	170	—	—	—	—	—
Total Assets (Millions $)	334	327	326	297	187	96	—	—	—	—

PORTFOLIO (as of 6/30/00)

Portfolio Manager: Phillip Davidson, Scott Moore - 1998

Investm't Category: Growth & Income

✔ Domestic　Index
✔ Foreign　Sector
Asset Allocation　State Specific

Investment Style

Large Cap　✔ Mid Cap　Small Cap
Growth　Grth/Val　✔ Value

Portfolio

1.4%	cash	0.0%	corp bonds
82.0%	stocks	0.0%	gov't bonds
0.0%	pref/conv't pref	0.0%	muni bonds
16.7%	conv't bds/wrnts	0.0%	other

SHAREHOLDER INFORMATION

Minimum Investment
Initial: $2,500　Subsequent: $50

Minimum IRA Investment
Initial: $1,000　Subsequent: $50

Maximum Fees
Load: none　12b-1: none
Other: none

Services
✔ IRA
✔ Keogh
✔ Telephone Exchange

Amer Cent: Giftrust/Inv (TWGTX)

800-345-2021, 816-531-5575
www.americancentury.com

Aggressive Growth

PERFORMANCE — fund inception date: 11/25/83

	3yr Annual	5yr Annual	10yr Annual	Bull	Bear
Return (%)	10.7	7.2	20.3	139.9	-35.2
Differ from Category (+/-)	-5.5 blw av	-7.4 low	4.5 abv av	20.7 abv av	-14.6 blw av

Standard Deviation	Category Risk Index	Beta
44.2%—high	1.36—high	1.38

	2000	1999	1998	1997	1996	1995	1994	1993	1992	1991
Return (%)	-16.4	87.2	-13.0	-1.2	5.7	38.3	13.5	31.4	17.9	84.9
Differ from Category (+/-)	-10.4	29.7	-28.1	-16.0	-12.6	3.7	14.3	6.2	11.0	37.7
Return, Tax-Adjusted (%)	-20.9	87.2	-13.0	-1.8	4.7	35.1	11.7	27.8	15.0	82.4

PER SHARE DATA

	2000	1999	1998	1997	1996	1995	1994	1993	1992	1991
Dividends, Net Income ($)	0.00	0.00	0.00	0.00	0.00	0.00	0.00	0.00	0.00	0.00
Distrib'ns, Cap Gain ($)	8.57	0.00	0.00	0.75	0.78	2.09	1.08	1.91	1.43	0.69
Net Asset Value ($)	23.32	37.92	20.25	23.30	24.39	23.81	18.77	17.53	14.86	13.85
Expense Ratio (%)	na	1.00	1.00	1.00	0.98	0.98	1.00	1.00	1.00	1.00
Yield (%)	0.00	0.00	0.00	0.00	0.00	0.00	0.00	0.00	0.00	0.00
Portfolio Turnover (%)	na	117	147	118	121	105	115	143	134	143
Total Assets (Millions $)	1,423	1,777	920	986	874	603	274	164	97	64

PORTFOLIO (as of 3/31/00)

Portfolio Manager: Boyd, Seitzer, Telford - 1983

Investm't Category: Aggressive Growth

✔ Domestic
✔ Foreign
Asset Allocation
Index
Sector
State Specific

Investment Style

Large Cap / Mid Cap / ✔ Small Cap
✔ Growth / Grth/Val / Value

Portfolio

3.4%	cash	0.0%	corp bonds
96.6%	stocks	0.0%	gov't bonds
0.0%	pref/conv't pref	0.0%	muni bonds
0.0%	conv't bds/wrnts	0.0%	other

SHAREHOLDER INFORMATION

Minimum Investment

Initial: $2,500 — Subsequent: $50

Minimum IRA Investment

Initial: na — Subsequent: na

Maximum Fees

Load: none — 12b-1: none
Other: none

Services

IRA
Keogh
✔ Telephone Exchange

Amer Cent: Global Gold/ Inv (BGEIX)

800-345-2021, 816-531-5575
www.americancentury.com

Aggressive Growth

PERFORMANCE — fund inception date: 8/17/88

	3yr Annual	5yr Annual	10yr Annual	Bull	Bear
Return (%)	-13.5	-18.1	-6.8	31.2	-15.9
Differ from Category (+/-)	-29.7 low	-32.7 low	-22.6 low	-88.0 low	4.7 abv av

Standard Deviation	Category Risk Index	Beta
46.2%—high	1.42—high	0.71

	2000	1999	1998	1997	1996	1995	1994	1993	1992	1991
Return (%)	-23.9	-3.1	-12.1	-41.4	-2.7	9.2	-16.7	81.2	-8.6	-11.2
Differ from Category (+/-)	-17.9	-60.6	-27.2	-56.2	-21.0	-25.4	-15.9	56.0	-15.5	-58.4
Return, Tax-Adjusted (%)	-24.0	-3.4	-12.3	-42.0	-4.2	9.2	-16.7	81.1	-8.6	-11.2

PER SHARE DATA

	2000	1999	1998	1997	1996	1995	1994	1993	1992	1991
Dividends, Net Income ($)	0.02	0.05	0.04	0.09	0.05	0.00	0.02	0.01	0.01	0.01
Distrib'ns, Cap Gain ($)	0.00	0.00	0.00	0.19	0.63	0.00	0.02	0.00	0.00	0.00
Net Asset Value ($)	4.00	5.29	5.52	6.34	11.33	12.37	11.33	13.67	7.55	8.28
Expense Ratio (%)	na	0.68	0.69	0.67	0.62	0.62	0.61	0.72	0.75	0.75
Yield (%)	0.50	0.94	0.72	1.37	0.41	0.00	0.17	0.07	0.13	0.12
Portfolio Turnover (%)	na	53	68	28	45	19	41	28	53	56
Total Assets (Millions $)	132	201	228	249	433	540	570	618	161	124

PORTFOLIO (as of 6/30/00)

Portfolio Manager: committee - 1996

Investm't Category: Aggressive Growth

✔ Domestic ✔ Index
✔ Foreign ✔ Sector
Asset Allocation State Specific

Investment Style

Large Cap Mid Cap Small Cap
Growth Grth/Val Value

Portfolio

1.3%	cash	0.0%	corp bonds
98.7%	stocks	0.0%	gov't bonds
0.0%	pref/conv't pref	0.0%	muni bonds
0.0%	conv't bds/wrnts	0.0%	other

SHAREHOLDER INFORMATION

Minimum Investment
Initial: $2,500 Subsequent: $50

Minimum IRA Investment
Initial: $1,000 Subsequent: $50

Maximum Fees
Load: none 12b-1: none
Other: none

Services
✔ IRA
✔ Keogh
✔ Telephone Exchange

Amer Cent: Global Ntrl/ Inv (BGRIX)

800-345-2021, 816-531-5575
www.americancentury.com

International Stock

PERFORMANCE — fund inception date: 9/15/94

	3yr Annual	5yr Annual	10yr Annual	Bull	Bear
Return (%)	7.7	8.1	na	45.7	-2.8
Differ from Category (+/-)	-1.2 blw av	-0.2 av	na	-45.2 low	21.2 high

Standard Deviation	Category Risk Index	Beta
21.4%—abv av	0.94—av	0.77

	2000	1999	1998	1997	1996	1995	1994	1993	1992	1991
Return (%)	5.6	26.4	-6.3	2.4	15.4	14.4	—	—	—	—
Differ from Category (+/-)	25.0	-34.3	-12.1	1.1	0.9	5.1	—	—	—	—
Return, Tax-Adjusted (%)	4.1	25.5	-6.9	0.8	14.2	13.3	—	—	—	—

PER SHARE DATA

	2000	1999	1998	1997	1996	1995	1994	1993	1992	1991
Dividends, Net Income ($)	0.17	0.17	0.18	0.22	0.16	0.15	—	—	—	—
Distrib'ns, Cap Gain ($)	0.58	0.13	0.00	0.49	0.21	0.16	—	—	—	—
Net Asset Value ($)	12.97	13.06	10.58	11.48	11.91	10.66	—	—	—	—
Expense Ratio (%)	na	0.68	0.69	0.73	0.76	0.76	—	—	—	—
Yield (%)	1.25	1.28	1.70	1.83	1.32	1.38	—	—	—	—
Portfolio Turnover (%)	na	87	76	41	53	39	—	—	—	—
Total Assets (Millions $)	47	52	39	46	66	30	—	—	—	—

PORTFOLIO (as of 6/30/00)

Portfolio Manager: committee - 1996

Investm't Category: International Stock

✔ Domestic — Index
✔ Foreign — Sector
Asset Allocation — State Specific

Investment Style

Large Cap — Mid Cap — Small Cap
Growth — Grth/Val — Value

Portfolio

0.6%	cash	0.0%	corp bonds
99.4%	stocks	0.0%	gov't bonds
0.0%	pref/conv't pref	0.0%	muni bonds
0.0%	conv't bds/wrnts	0.0%	other

SHAREHOLDER INFORMATION

Minimum Investment
Initial: $2,500 — Subsequent: $50

Minimum IRA Investment
Initial: $1,000 — Subsequent: $50

Maximum Fees
Load: none — 12b-1: none
Other: none

Services
✔ IRA
✔ Keogh
✔ Telephone Exchange

Amer Cent: Growth/Inv (TWCGX)

800-345-2021, 816-531-5575
www.americancentury.com

Growth

PERFORMANCE — fund inception date: 10/31/58

	3yr Annual	5yr Annual	10yr Annual	Bull	Bear
Return (%)	16.2	18.4	16.6	74.8	-21.9
Differ from Category (+/-)	5.2 high	2.3 abv av	-0.2 av	25.1 high	-16.5 low

Standard Deviation	Category Risk Index	Beta
20.9%—abv av	1.07—av	1.03

	2000	1999	1998	1997	1996	1995	1994	1993	1992	1991
Return (%)	-14.7	34.6	36.8	29.2	15.0	20.3	-1.4	3.7	-4.2	69.0
Differ from Category (+/-)	-18.2	15.7	22.5	2.1	-7.3	-10.1	-1.2	-10.9	-16.8	31.4
Return, Tax-Adjusted (%)	-16.9	31.5	32.3	25.3	14.2	15.6	-5.5	0.4	-4.5	68.9

PER SHARE DATA

	2000	1999	1998	1997	1996	1995	1994	1993	1992	1991
Dividends, Net Income ($)	0.00	0.00	0.00	0.00	0.18	0.06	0.05	0.05	0.00	0.01
Distrib'ns, Cap Gain ($)	3.57	4.13	5.38	4.16	0.24	3.05	3.22	2.76	0.36	0.00
Net Asset Value ($)	24.00	32.28	27.16	24.01	21.88	19.39	18.74	22.40	24.36	25.83
Expense Ratio (%)	na	1.00	1.00	1.00	1.00	1.00	1.00	1.00	1.00	1.00
Yield (%)	0.00	0.00	0.00	0.00	0.81	0.26	0.22	0.19	0.00	0.03
Portfolio Turnover (%)	na	92	126	75	122	141	100	94	53	69
Total Assets (Millions $)	8,591	9,630	7,092	5,168	4,667	4,849	4,158	4,552	4,853	3,879

PORTFOLIO (as of 6/30/00)

Portfolio Manager: K. Goodwin, G. Woodhams - 1998

Investm't Category: Growth

✔ Domestic	Index
✔ Foreign	Sector
Asset Allocation	State Specific

Investment Style

✔ Large Cap	Mid Cap	Small Cap
✔ Growth	Grth/Val	Value

Portfolio

5.4%	cash	0.0%	corp bonds
94.6%	stocks	0.0%	gov't bonds
0.0%	pref/conv't pref	0.0%	muni bonds
0.0%	conv't bds/wrnts	0.0%	other

SHAREHOLDER INFORMATION

Minimum Investment
Initial: $2,500 — Subsequent: $50

Minimum IRA Investment
Initial: $1,000 — Subsequent: $50

Maximum Fees
Load: none — 12b-1: none
Other: none

Services
✔ IRA
✔ Keogh
✔ Telephone Exchange

Amer Cent: Heritage/Inv (TWHIX)

800-345-2021, 816-531-5575
www.americancentury.com

Growth

PERFORMANCE — fund inception date: 11/10/87

	3yr Annual	5yr Annual	10yr Annual	Bull	Bear
Return (%)	21.0	19.5	17.9	89.0	-7.4
Differ from Category (+/-)	10.0 high	3.4 abv av	1.1 abv av	39.3 high	-2.0 av

Standard Deviation	Category Risk Index	Beta
27.0%—high	1.39—high	0.99

	2000	1999	1998	1997	1996	1995	1994	1993	1992	1991
Return (%)	17.3	51.2	-0.1	19.3	15.3	26.6	-6.3	20.4	10.1	35.9
Differ from Category (+/-)	13.8	32.3	-14.4	-7.8	-7.0	-3.8	-6.1	5.8	-2.5	-1.7
Return, Tax-Adjusted (%)	12.6	48.4	-0.1	14.5	13.2	24.6	-7.8	18.6	7.7	35.4

PER SHARE DATA

	2000	1999	1998	1997	1996	1995	1994	1993	1992	1991
Dividends, Net Income ($)	0.00	0.04	0.02	0.07	0.09	0.04	0.03	0.06	0.09	0.11
Distrib'ns, Cap Gain ($)	3.64	1.48	0.00	2.70	0.70	0.61	0.54	0.50	0.67	0.00
Net Asset Value ($)	14.55	15.64	11.46	11.50	12.07	11.17	9.35	10.61	9.31	9.17
Expense Ratio (%)	na	1.00	1.00	1.00	0.99	1.00	1.00	1.00	1.00	1.00
Yield (%)	0.00	0.23	0.17	0.49	0.70	0.33	0.30	0.54	0.90	1.19
Portfolio Turnover (%)	na	134	148	69	122	121	136	116	119	146
Total Assets (Millions $)	1,749	1,349	1,070	1,277	1,125	1,026	851	724	424	292

PORTFOLIO (as of 6/30/00)

Portfolio Manager: Linda Peterson, Kurt Stalzer - 1998

Investm't Category: Growth

✔ Domestic	Index
✔ Foreign	Sector
Asset Allocation	State Specific

Investment Style

Large Cap	Mid Cap	✔ Small Cap
✔ Growth	Grth/Val	Value

Portfolio

6.0%	cash	0.0%	corp bonds
92.3%	stocks	0.0%	gov't bonds
0.0%	pref/conv't pref	0.0%	muni bonds
1.7%	conv't bds/wrnts	0.0%	other

SHAREHOLDER INFORMATION

Minimum Investment

Initial: $2,500 — Subsequent: $50

Minimum IRA Investment

Initial: $1,000 — Subsequent: $50

Maximum Fees

Load: none — 12b-1: none

Other: none

Services

✔ IRA
✔ Keogh
✔ Telephone Exchange

Amer Cent: Income & Gr/Inv (BIGRX)

800-345-2021, 816-531-5575
www.americancentury.com

Growth & Income

PERFORMANCE

fund inception date: 12/17/90

	3yr Annual	5yr Annual	10yr Annual	Bull	Bear
Return (%)	10.4	17.5	17.7	52.6	-12.2
Differ from Category (+/-)	1.5 av	3.2 abv av	2.8 high	19.1 abv av	-12.1 low

Standard Deviation	Category Risk Index	Beta
18.1%—av	1.04—abv av	1.01

	2000	1999	1998	1997	1996	1995	1994	1993	1992	1991
Return (%)	-10.5	17.9	27.6	34.2	24.1	36.8	-0.5	11.3	7.8	39.0
Differ from Category (+/-)	-16.2	7.1	14.8	7.3	4.4	7.3	0.0	-2.5	-3.8	10.9
Return, Tax-Adjusted (%)	-10.8	17.4	25.9	31.2	20.8	34.0	-2.7	9.7	6.7	37.5

PER SHARE DATA

	2000	1999	1998	1997	1996	1995	1994	1993	1992	1991
Dividends, Net Income ($)	0.28	0.33	0.35	0.34	0.43	0.42	0.43	0.42	0.41	0.48
Distrib'ns, Cap Gain ($)	0.00	0.06	1.29	2.29	1.43	0.75	0.63	0.18	0.03	0.00
Net Asset Value ($)	30.19	34.05	29.25	24.30	20.16	17.81	13.92	15.08	14.11	13.53
Expense Ratio (%)	na	0.68	0.69	0.65	0.62	0.70	0.73	0.75	0.75	0.50
Yield (%)	0.92	0.96	1.14	1.27	1.99	2.26	2.95	2.75	2.89	3.54
Portfolio Turnover (%)	na	58	86	102	92	69	67	31	63	140
Total Assets (Millions $)	5,385	6,346	4,284	1,790	715	372	224	229	140	58

PORTFOLIO (as of 6/30/00)

Portfolio Manager: committee - 1990

Investm't Category: Growth & Income

✔ Domestic — Index
Foreign — Sector
Asset Allocation — State Specific

Investment Style

✔ Large Cap — Mid Cap — Small Cap
Growth — ✔ Grth/Val — Value

Portfolio

1.6%	cash	0.0%	corp bonds
98.4%	stocks	0.0%	gov't bonds
0.0%	pref/conv't pref	0.0%	muni bonds
0.0%	conv't bds/wrnts	0.0%	other

SHAREHOLDER INFORMATION

Minimum Investment

Initial: $2,500 — Subsequent: $50

Minimum IRA Investment

Initial: $1,000 — Subsequent: $50

Maximum Fees

Load: none — 12b-1: none
Other: none

Services

✔ IRA
✔ Keogh
✔ Telephone Exchange

Amer Cent: Intl Disc/Inv (TWEGX)

800-345-2021, 816-531-5575
www.americancentury.com

International Stock

this fund is closed to new investors

PERFORMANCE — fund inception date: 4/1/94

	3yr Annual	5yr Annual	10yr Annual	Bull	Bear
Return (%)	23.9	24.0	na	100.7	-30.9
Differ from Category (+/-)	15.0 high	15.7 high	na	9.8 abv av	-6.9 blw av

Standard Deviation	Category Risk Index	Beta
30.2%—high	1.33—abv av	0.74

	2000	1999	1998	1997	1996	1995	1994	1993	1992	1991
Return (%)	-14.2	88.5	17.8	17.4	31.1	9.8	—	—	—	—
Differ from Category (+/-)	5.2	27.8	12.0	16.1	16.6	0.5	—	—	—	—
Return, Tax-Adjusted (%)	-16.1	86.8	17.7	16.0	29.5	9.5	—	—	—	—

PER SHARE DATA

	2000	1999	1998	1997	1996	1995	1994	1993	1992	1991
Dividends, Net Income ($)	0.00	0.00	0.00	0.02	0.01	0.03	—	—	—	—
Distrib'ns, Cap Gain ($)	1.64	0.80	0.03	0.46	0.32	0.00	—	—	—	—
Net Asset Value ($)	13.09	17.16	9.57	8.15	7.36	5.88	—	—	—	—
Expense Ratio (%)	na	1.55	1.64	1.70	1.88	2.00	—	—	—	—
Yield (%)	0.00	0.00	0.00	0.23	0.13	0.51	—	—	—	—
Portfolio Turnover (%)	na	110	178	146	130	168	—	—	—	—
Total Assets (Millions $)	1,570	1,722	799	622	390	121	—	—	—	—

PORTFOLIO (as of 6/30/00)

Portfolio Manager: committee - 1994

Investm't Category: International Stock

Domestic	Index
✔ Foreign	Sector
Asset Allocation	State Specific

Investment Style

Large Cap	Mid Cap	Small Cap
Growth	Grth/Val	Value

Portfolio

10.6% cash	0.0% corp bonds
89.4% stocks	0.0% gov't bonds
0.0% pref/conv't pref	0.0% muni bonds
0.0% conv't bds/wrnts	0.0% other

SHAREHOLDER INFORMATION

Minimum Investment
Initial: $10,000 Subsequent: $50

Minimum IRA Investment
Initial: $10,000 Subsequent: $50

Maximum Fees
Load: 2.00% redemption 12b-1: none
Other: redemption fee applies for 6 months

Services
✔ IRA
✔ Keogh
✔ Telephone Exchange

Amer Cent: Intl Gr/Inv (TWIEX)

800-345-2021, 816-531-5575
www.americancentury.com

International Stock

PERFORMANCE — fund inception date: 5/9/91

	3yr Annual	5yr Annual	10yr Annual	Bull	Bear
Return (%)	18.4	17.9	na	76.1	-22.8
Differ from Category (+/-)	9.5 high	9.6 high	na	-14.8 av	1.2 av

Standard Deviation	Category Risk Index	Beta
24.5%—abv av	1.08—av	0.72

	2000	1999	1998	1997	1996	1995	1994	1993	1992	1991
Return (%)	-15.0	64.4	19.0	19.7	14.4	11.8	-4.7	42.6	4.8	—
Differ from Category (+/-)	4.4	3.7	13.2	18.4	-0.1	2.5	-1.6	2.4	8.3	—
Return, Tax-Adjusted (%)	-17.3	62.9	18.6	16.4	11.1	11.8	-6.0	40.6	3.7	—

PER SHARE DATA

	2000	1999	1998	1997	1996	1995	1994	1993	1992	1991
Dividends, Net Income ($)	0.00	0.00	0.01	0.02	0.00	0.00	0.00	0.00	0.19	—
Distrib'ns, Cap Gain ($)	1.75	0.69	0.14	1.27	0.91	0.00	0.37	0.40	0.00	—
Net Asset Value ($)	10.93	14.97	9.58	8.19	7.96	7.78	6.96	7.70	5.69	—
Expense Ratio (%)	na	1.27	1.33	1.38	1.65	1.77	1.84	1.90	1.91	—
Yield (%)	0.00	0.00	0.10	0.21	0.00	0.00	0.00	0.00	3.33	—
Portfolio Turnover (%)	na	117	190	163	158	169	242	255	180	—
Total Assets (Millions $)	4,479	4,521	2,640	1,809	1,364	1,258	1,272	944	222	—

PORTFOLIO (as of 6/30/00)

Portfolio Manager: H. Strabo, M. Kopinski - 1994

Investm't Category: International Stock

Domestic	Index
✔ Foreign	Sector
Asset Allocation	State Specific

Investment Style

Large Cap	Mid Cap	Small Cap
Growth	Grth/Val	Value

Portfolio

6.1%	cash	0.0%	corp bonds
93.9%	stocks	0.0%	gov't bonds
0.0%	pref/conv't pref	0.0%	muni bonds
0.0%	conv't bds/wrnts	0.0%	other

SHAREHOLDER INFORMATION

Minimum Investment
Initial: $2,500 Subsequent: $50

Minimum IRA Investment
Initial: $1,000 Subsequent: $50

Maximum Fees
Load: none 12b-1: none
Other: none

Services
✔ IRA
✔ Keogh
✔ Telephone Exchange

Amer Cent: Real Estate/ Inv (REACX)

800-345-2021, 816-531-5575
www.americancentury.com

Growth & Income

PERFORMANCE — fund inception date: 9/19/95

	3yr Annual	5yr Annual	10yr Annual	Bull	Bear
Return (%)	0.6	12.4	na	1.9	17.6
Differ from Category (+/-)	-8.3 low	-1.9 blw av	na	-31.6 low	17.7 high

Standard Deviation	Category Risk Index	Beta
15.0%—av	0.86—low	0.23

	2000	1999	1998	1997	1996	1995	1994	1993	1992	1991
Return (%)	27.1	-2.7	-17.4	25.2	40.8	—	—	—	—	—
Differ from Category (+/-)	21.4	-13.5	-30.2	-1.7	21.1	—	—	—	—	—
Return, Tax-Adjusted (%)	25.0	-4.8	-18.7	23.3	38.3	—	—	—	—	—

PER SHARE DATA

	2000	1999	1998	1997	1996	1995	1994	1993	1992	1991
Dividends, Net Income ($)	0.60	0.69	0.44	0.40	0.45	—	—	—	—	—
Distrib'ns, Cap Gain ($)	0.00	0.00	0.22	0.51	0.29	—	—	—	—	—
Net Asset Value ($)	14.22	11.71	12.77	16.26	13.80	—	—	—	—	—
Expense Ratio (%)	1.20	1.20	1.15	1.17	1.00	—	—	—	—	—
Yield (%)	4.21	5.89	3.38	2.38	3.19	—	—	—	—	—
Portfolio Turnover (%)	102	66	28	69	86	—	—	—	—	—
Total Assets (Millions $)	82	96	121	118	10	—	—	—	—	—

PORTFOLIO (as of 6/30/00)

Portfolio Manager: Redding, Knudson, Mallon - 1995

Investm't Category: Growth & Income

✔ Domestic	Index
Foreign	✔ Sector
Asset Allocation	State Specific

Investment Style

Large Cap	✔ Mid Cap	✔ Small Cap
Growth	Grth/Val	✔ Value

Portfolio

2.2%	cash	0.0%	corp bonds
97.8%	stocks	0.0%	gov't bonds
0.0%	pref/conv't pref	0.0%	muni bonds
0.0%	conv't bds/wrnts	0.0%	other

SHAREHOLDER INFORMATION

Minimum Investment
Initial: $2,500 Subsequent: $50

Minimum IRA Investment
Initial: $1,000 Subsequent: $50

Maximum Fees
Load: none 12b-1: none
Other: none

Services
✔ IRA
Keogh
✔ Telephone Exchange

Amer Cent: Select/Inv

800-345-2021, 816-531-5575
www.americancentury.com

(TWCIX)

Growth

PERFORMANCE — fund inception date: 10/31/58

	3yr Annual	5yr Annual	10yr Annual	Bull	Bear
Return (%)	14.8	19.0	14.5	62.4	-12.8
Differ from Category (+/-)	3.8 abv av	2.9 abv av	-2.3 blw av	12.7 abv av	-7.4 blw av

Standard Deviation	Category Risk Index	Beta
18.3%—av	0.94—blw av	1.00

	2000	1999	1998	1997	1996	1995	1994	1993	1992	1991
Return (%)	-8.7	22.2	35.7	32.1	19.2	22.6	-8.0	14.6	-4.4	31.5
Differ from Category (+/-)	-12.2	3.3	21.4	5.0	-3.1	-7.8	-7.8	0.0	-17.0	-6.1
Return, Tax-Adjusted (%)	-9.7	20.0	30.9	27.7	15.9	18.3	-10.3	10.9	-5.6	29.4

PER SHARE DATA

	2000	1999	1998	1997	1996	1995	1994	1993	1992	1991
Dividends, Net Income ($)	0.00	0.00	0.16	0.19	0.32	0.26	0.28	0.43	0.49	0.65
Distrib'ns, Cap Gain ($)	2.79	5.09	9.78	7.93	3.68	4.65	2.87	4.46	1.32	1.82
Net Asset Value ($)	45.29	52.68	47.39	42.59	38.53	35.62	33.10	39.46	38.72	42.40
Expense Ratio (%)	na	1.00	1.00	1.00	1.00	1.00	1.00	1.00	1.00	1.00
Yield (%)	0.00	0.00	0.27	0.37	0.75	0.64	0.77	0.97	1.22	1.46
Portfolio Turnover (%)	na	130	165	94	105	61	126	82	95	84
Total Assets (Millions $)	6,544	7,674	6,498	5,019	4,060	3,982	3,995	4,939	4,691	4,634

PORTFOLIO (as of 6/30/00)

Portfolio Manager: Jerry Sullivan, Ken Crawford - 1998

Investm't Category: Growth

✔ Domestic	Index
✔ Foreign	Sector
Asset Allocation	State Specific

Investment Style

✔ Large Cap	Mid Cap	Small Cap
✔ Growth	Grth/Val	Value

Portfolio

2.0%	cash	0.0%	corp bonds
96.1%	stocks	0.0%	gov't bonds
0.0%	pref/conv't pref	0.0%	muni bonds
1.9%	conv't bds/wrnts	0.0%	other

SHAREHOLDER INFORMATION

Minimum Investment
Initial: $2,500 Subsequent: $50

Minimum IRA Investment
Initial: $1,000 Subsequent: $50

Maximum Fees
Load: none 12b-1: none
Other: none

Services
✔ IRA
✔ Keogh
✔ Telephone Exchange

Amer Cent: Stg Al Agg/Inv (TWSAX)

800-345-2021, 816-531-5575
www.americancentury.com

Balanced

PERFORMANCE — fund inception date: 2/15/96

	3yr Annual	5yr Annual	10yr Annual	Bull	Bear
Return (%)	14.0	na	na	54.3	-13.1
Differ from Category (+/-)	5.6 high	na	na	26.2 high	-9.9 low

Standard Deviation	Category Risk Index	Beta
15.9%—av	1.45—high	0.72

	2000	1999	1998	1997	1996	1995	1994	1993	1992	1991
Return (%)	-2.5	33.8	13.7	16.2	—	—	—	—	—	—
Differ from Category (+/-)	-4.5	23.1	0.4	-2.6	—	—	—	—	—	—
Return, Tax-Adjusted (%)	-4.8	32.4	12.7	14.8	—	—	—	—	—	—

PER SHARE DATA

	2000	1999	1998	1997	1996	1995	1994	1993	1992	1991
Dividends, Net Income ($)	0.08	0.07	0.07	0.08	—	—	—	—	—	—
Distrib'ns, Cap Gain ($)	0.85	0.31	0.16	0.20	—	—	—	—	—	—
Net Asset Value ($)	7.25	8.42	6.61	6.03	—	—	—	—	—	—
Expense Ratio (%)	na	1.20	1.20	1.20	—	—	—	—	—	—
Yield (%)	0.98	0.80	1.03	1.28	—	—	—	—	—	—
Portfolio Turnover (%)	na	115	134	135	—	—	—	—	—	—
Total Assets (Millions $)	311	216	152	120	—	—	—	—	—	—

PORTFOLIO (as of 6/30/00)

Portfolio Manager: committee - 1996

Investm't Category: Balanced

✔ Domestic — Index
✔ Foreign — Sector
✔ Asset Allocation — State Specific

Investment Style

Large Cap — Mid Cap — Small Cap
Growth — Grth/Val — Value

Portfolio

13.9%	cash	7.2%	corp bonds
69.9%	stocks	8.7%	gov't bonds
0.0%	pref/conv't pref	0.0%	muni bonds
0.0%	conv't bds/wrnts	0.3%	other

SHAREHOLDER INFORMATION

Minimum Investment
Initial: $2,500 — Subsequent: $50

Minimum IRA Investment
Initial: $1,000 — Subsequent: $50

Maximum Fees
Load: none — 12b-1: none
Other: none

Services
✔ IRA
✔ Keogh
✔ Telephone Exchange

Amer Cent: Stg Al Cnsrv/ Inv (TWSCX)

800-345-2021, 816-531-5575
www.americancentury.com

Balanced

PERFORMANCE — fund inception date: 2/15/96

	3yr Annual	5yr Annual	10yr Annual	Bull	Bear
Return (%)	8.8	na	na	21.5	-1.0
Differ from Category (+/-)	0.4 av	na	na	-6.6 blw av	2.2 abv av

Standard Deviation	Category Risk Index	Beta
7.3%—blw av	0.67—low	0.35

	2000	1999	1998	1997	1996	1995	1994	1993	1992	1991
Return (%)	4.8	11.1	10.5	12.8	—	—	—	—	—	—
Differ from Category (+/-)	2.8	0.4	-2.8	-6.0	—	—	—	—	—	—
Return, Tax-Adjusted (%)	2.0	9.2	8.6	10.1	—	—	—	—	—	—

PER SHARE DATA

	2000	1999	1998	1997	1996	1995	1994	1993	1992	1991
Dividends, Net Income ($)	0.17	0.17	0.16	0.18	—	—	—	—	—	—
Distrib'ns, Cap Gain ($)	0.46	0.18	0.17	0.33	—	—	—	—	—	—
Net Asset Value ($)	5.36	5.73	5.50	5.30	—	—	—	—	—	—
Expense Ratio (%)	na	1.00	1.00	1.00	—	—	—	—	—	—
Yield (%)	2.92	2.87	2.82	3.19	—	—	—	—	—	—
Portfolio Turnover (%)	na	105	113	124	—	—	—	—	—	—
Total Assets (Millions $)	167	171	183	161	—	—	—	—	—	—

PORTFOLIO (as of 6/30/00)

Portfolio Manager: committee - 1996

Investm't Category: Balanced

✔ Domestic — Index
✔ Foreign — Sector
✔ Asset Allocation — State Specific

Investment Style

Large Cap — Mid Cap — Small Cap
Growth — Grth/Val — Value

Portfolio

8.8%	cash	14.2%	corp bonds
43.8%	stocks	32.5%	gov't bonds
0.0%	pref/conv't pref	0.0%	muni bonds
0.0%	conv't bds/wrnts	0.7%	other

SHAREHOLDER INFORMATION

Minimum Investment
Initial: $2,500 — Subsequent: $50

Minimum IRA Investment
Initial: $1,000 — Subsequent: $50

Maximum Fees
Load: none — 12b-1: none
Other: none

Services
✔ IRA
✔ Keogh
✔ Telephone Exchange

Amer Cent: Stg Al Mod/ Inv (TWSMX)

800-345-2021, 816-531-5575
www.americancentury.com

Balanced

PERFORMANCE — fund inception date: 2/15/96

	3yr Annual	5yr Annual	10yr Annual	Bull	Bear
Return (%)	11.3	na	na	37.6	-8.0
Differ from Category (+/-)	2.9 high	na	na	9.5 abv av	-4.8 blw av

Standard Deviation	Category Risk Index	Beta
11.6%—blw av	1.06—abv av	0.55

	2000	1999	1998	1997	1996	1995	1994	1993	1992	1991
Return (%)	0.2	22.2	12.7	15.2	—	—	—	—	—	—
Differ from Category (+/-)	-1.8	11.5	-0.6	-3.6	—	—	—	—	—	—
Return, Tax-Adjusted (%)	-2.7	20.8	11.1	13.5	—	—	—	—	—	—

PER SHARE DATA

	2000	1999	1998	1997	1996	1995	1994	1993	1992	1991
Dividends, Net Income ($)	0.13	0.13	0.13	0.13	—	—	—	—	—	—
Distrib'ns, Cap Gain ($)	0.82	0.16	0.20	0.19	—	—	—	—	—	—
Net Asset Value ($)	6.31	7.26	6.21	5.82	—	—	—	—	—	—
Expense Ratio (%)	na	1.10	1.10	1.10	—	—	—	—	—	—
Yield (%)	1.82	1.75	2.02	2.16	—	—	—	—	—	—
Portfolio Turnover (%)	na	107	127	119	—	—	—	—	—	—
Total Assets (Millions $)	444	404	271	215	—	—	—	—	—	—

PORTFOLIO (as of 6/30/00)

Portfolio Manager: committee - 1996

Investm't Category: Balanced

✔ Domestic	Index
✔ Foreign	Sector
✔ Asset Allocation	State Specific

Investment Style

Large Cap	Mid Cap	Small Cap
Growth	Grth/Val	Value

Portfolio

9.2%	cash	10.9%	corp bonds
60.6%	stocks	19.0%	gov't bonds
0.0%	pref/conv't pref	0.0%	muni bonds
0.0%	conv't bds/wrnts	0.4%	other

SHAREHOLDER INFORMATION

Minimum Investment
Initial: $2,500 Subsequent: $50

Minimum IRA Investment
Initial: $1,000 Subsequent: $50

Maximum Fees
Load: none 12b-1: none
Other: none

Services
✔ IRA
✔ Keogh
✔ Telephone Exchange

Amer Cent: Ultra/Inv (TWCUX)

800-345-2021, 816-531-5575
www.americancentury.com

Aggressive Growth

PERFORMANCE — fund inception date: 11/2/81

	3yr Annual	5yr Annual	10yr Annual	Bull	Bear
Return (%)	15.0	16.4	20.6	86.5	-25.8
Differ from Category (+/-)	-1.2 av	1.8 av	4.8 abv av	-32.7 av	-5.2 av

Standard Deviation	Category Risk Index	Beta
24.1%—abv av	0.74—low	1.23

	2000	1999	1998	1997	1996	1995	1994	1993	1992	1991
Return (%)	-19.9	41.4	34.5	23.1	13.8	37.6	-3.6	21.8	1.2	86.4
Differ from Category (+/-)	-13.9	-16.1	19.4	8.3	-4.5	3.0	-2.8	-3.4	-5.7	39.2
Return, Tax-Adjusted (%)	-21.8	40.5	32.2	18.0	11.9	35.7	-4.4	21.8	1.2	86.4

PER SHARE DATA

	2000	1999	1998	1997	1996	1995	1994	1993	1992	1991
Dividends, Net Income ($)	0.00	0.00	0.00	0.01	0.00	0.00	0.00	0.00	0.00	0.00
Distrib'ns, Cap Gain ($)	4.40	1.37	3.12	7.07	1.68	1.29	0.64	0.00	0.00	0.00
Net Asset Value ($)	32.37	45.78	33.41	27.30	28.09	26.11	19.95	21.39	17.56	17.34
Expense Ratio (%)	na	1.00	1.00	1.00	1.00	1.00	1.00	1.00	1.00	1.00
Yield (%)	0.00	0.00	0.00	0.02	0.00	0.00	0.00	0.00	0.00	0.00
Portfolio Turnover (%)	na	42	128	107	87	87	78	53	59	42
Total Assets (Millions $)	33,733	43,192	30,076	22,455	18,418	14,551	9,850	8,362	5,299	2,939

PORTFOLIO (as of 6/30/00)

Portfolio Manager: Stowers, Sykora, Wimberly - 1998

Investm't Category: Aggressive Growth

✔ Domestic — Index
✔ Foreign — Sector
Asset Allocation — State Specific

Investment Style

✔ Large Cap — Mid Cap — Small Cap
✔ Growth — Grth/Val — Value

Portfolio

2.4%	cash	0.0%	corp bonds
97.6%	stocks	0.0%	gov't bonds
0.0%	pref/conv't pref	0.0%	muni bonds
0.0%	conv't bds/wrnts	0.0%	other

SHAREHOLDER INFORMATION

Minimum Investment

Initial: $2,500 — Subsequent: $50

Minimum IRA Investment

Initial: $1,000 — Subsequent: $50

Maximum Fees

Load: none — 12b-1: none
Other: none

Services

✔ IRA
✔ Keogh
✔ Telephone Exchange

Amer Cent: Utilities/Inv

800-345-2021, 816-531-5575
www.americancentury.com

(BULIX)

Growth & Income

PERFORMANCE — fund inception date: 3/1/93

	3yr Annual	5yr Annual	10yr Annual	Bull	Bear
Return (%)	13.8	15.9	na	39.7	-5.4
Differ from Category (+/-)	4.9 high	1.6 abv av	na	6.2 abv av	-5.3 av

Standard Deviation	Category Risk Index	Beta
14.7%—av	0.85—low	0.56

	2000	1999	1998	1997	1996	1995	1994	1993	1992	1991
Return (%)	3.9	11.4	27.4	35.7	4.5	35.2	-10.0	—	—	—
Differ from Category (+/-)	-1.8	0.6	14.6	8.8	-15.2	5.7	-9.5	—	—	—
Return, Tax-Adjusted (%)	0.5	9.4	24.0	32.8	3.0	33.4	-11.6	—	—	—

PER SHARE DATA

	2000	1999	1998	1997	1996	1995	1994	1993	1992	1991
Dividends, Net Income ($)	0.98	0.34	0.37	0.40	0.42	0.38	0.43	—	—	—
Distrib'ns, Cap Gain ($)	0.83	0.92	1.66	0.84	0.00	0.00	0.00	—	—	—
Net Asset Value ($)	15.26	16.46	15.96	14.24	11.51	11.44	8.79	—	—	—
Expense Ratio (%)	na	0.68	0.69	0.72	0.71	0.75	0.75	—	—	—
Yield (%)	6.09	1.95	2.09	2.65	3.64	3.32	4.89	—	—	—
Portfolio Turnover (%)	na	50	98	92	93	68	61	—	—	—
Total Assets (Millions $)	288	319	307	206	144	217	152	—	—	—

PORTFOLIO (as of 6/30/00)

Portfolio Manager: committee - 1996

Investm't Category: Growth & Income

✔ Domestic — Index
Foreign — ✔ Sector
Asset Allocation — State Specific

Investment Style

✔ Large Cap — ✔ Mid Cap — Small Cap
Growth — Grth/Val — ✔ Value

Portfolio

0.8%	cash	0.0%	corp bonds
99.2%	stocks	0.0%	gov't bonds
0.0%	pref/conv't pref	0.0%	muni bonds
0.0%	conv't bds/wrnts	0.0%	other

SHAREHOLDER INFORMATION

Minimum Investment
Initial: $2,500 — Subsequent: $50

Minimum IRA Investment
Initial: $1,000 — Subsequent: $50

Maximum Fees
Load: none — 12b-1: none
Other: none

Services
✔ IRA
✔ Keogh
✔ Telephone Exchange

Amer Cent: Value/Inv (TWVLX)

800-345-2021, 816-531-5575
www.americancentury.com

Growth & Income

PERFORMANCE — fund inception date: 9/1/93

	3yr Annual	5yr Annual	10yr Annual	Bull	Bear
Return (%)	7.1	14.0	na	16.9	14.3
Differ from Category (+/-)	-1.8 blw av	-0.3 av	na	-16.6 blw av	14.4 high

Standard Deviation	Category Risk Index	Beta
19.8%—abv av	1.14—high	0.67

	2000	1999	1998	1997	1996	1995	1994	1993	1992	1991
Return (%)	18.2	-0.7	4.9	26.0	24.2	32.7	3.9	—	—	—
Differ from Category (+/-)	12.5	-11.5	-7.9	-0.9	4.5	3.2	4.4	—	—	—
Return, Tax-Adjusted (%)	17.5	-2.5	1.1	21.6	20.6	28.9	1.4	—	—	—

PER SHARE DATA

	2000	1999	1998	1997	1996	1995	1994	1993	1992	1991
Dividends, Net Income ($)	0.09	0.08	0.08	0.11	0.11	0.13	0.12	—	—	—
Distrib'ns, Cap Gain ($)	0.00	0.41	1.14	1.20	0.60	0.47	0.27	—	—	—
Net Asset Value ($)	6.38	5.49	6.05	6.95	6.59	5.90	4.92	—	—	—
Expense Ratio (%)	1.00	1.00	1.00	1.00	0.97	1.00	1.00	—	—	—
Yield (%)	1.41	1.35	1.11	1.34	1.52	2.04	2.31	—	—	—
Portfolio Turnover (%)	115	130	130	111	145	94	79	—	—	—
Total Assets (Millions $)	1,409	1,605	2,082	2,461	1,548	652	153	—	—	—

PORTFOLIO (as of 6/30/00)

Portfolio Manager: Scott Moore, Phillip Davidson - 1998

Investm't Category: Growth & Income

- ✔ Domestic
- ✔ Foreign
- Asset Allocation
- Index
- Sector
- State Specific

Investment Style

- ✔ Large Cap
- ✔ Mid Cap
- Small Cap
- Growth
- Grth/Val
- ✔ Value

Portfolio

2.1%	cash	0.0%	corp bonds
97.9%	stocks	0.0%	gov't bonds
0.0%	pref/conv't pref	0.0%	muni bonds
0.0%	conv't bds/wrnts	0.0%	other

SHAREHOLDER INFORMATION

Minimum Investment
Initial: $2,500 — Subsequent: $50

Minimum IRA Investment
Initial: $1,000 — Subsequent: $50

Maximum Fees
Load: none — 12b-1: none
Other: none

Services

- ✔ IRA
- ✔ Keogh
- ✔ Telephone Exchange

Amer Cent: Vista/Inv (TWCVX)

800-345-2021, 816-531-5575
www.americancentury.com

Aggressive Growth

PERFORMANCE — fund inception date: 11/25/83

	3yr Annual	5yr Annual	10yr Annual	Bull	Bear
Return (%)	22.9	12.8	17.4	157.5	-27.3
Differ from Category (+/-)	6.7 abv av	-1.8 blw av	1.6 av	38.3 abv av	-6.7 blw av

Standard Deviation	Category Risk Index	Beta
40.6%—high	1.25—high	1.20

	2000	1999	1998	1997	1996	1995	1994	1993	1992	1991
Return (%)	-0.9	119.1	-14.2	-8.6	7.5	46.1	4.6	5.4	-2.1	73.6
Differ from Category (+/-)	5.1	61.6	-29.3	-23.4	-10.8	11.5	5.4	-19.8	-9.0	26.4
Return, Tax-Adjusted (%)	-6.5	117.3	-14.2	-9.7	5.2	43.4	4.5	1.2	-3.5	73.6

PER SHARE DATA

	2000	1999	1998	1997	1996	1995	1994	1993	1992	1991
Dividends, Net Income ($)	0.00	0.00	0.00	0.00	0.00	0.00	0.00	0.00	0.00	0.00
Distrib'ns, Cap Gain ($)	6.32	0.94	0.00	0.80	1.18	1.02	0.02	1.67	0.64	0.00
Net Asset Value ($)	15.33	22.21	10.65	12.42	14.51	14.60	10.72	10.27	11.35	12.28
Expense Ratio (%)	na	1.00	1.00	1.00	0.99	1.00	1.00	1.00	1.00	1.00
Yield (%)	0.00	0.00	0.00	0.00	0.00	0.00	0.00	0.00	0.00	0.00
Portfolio Turnover (%)	na	187	229	96	91	89	111	133	87	92
Total Assets (Millions $)	1,894	1,799	954	1,669	2,236	1,774	820	795	935	766

PORTFOLIO (as of 6/30/00)

Portfolio Manager: Douville, Fogle - 1998

Investm't Category: Aggressive Growth

✔ Domestic | Index
✔ Foreign | Sector
Asset Allocation | State Specific

Investment Style

Large Cap | Mid Cap | ✔ Small Cap
✔ Growth | Grth/Val | Value

Portfolio

3.9% cash | 0.0% corp bonds
96.1% stocks | 0.0% gov't bonds
0.0% pref/conv't pref | 0.0% muni bonds
0.0% conv't bds/wrnts | 0.0% other

SHAREHOLDER INFORMATION

Minimum Investment

Initial: $2,500 | Subsequent: $50

Minimum IRA Investment

Initial: $1,000 | Subsequent: $50

Maximum Fees

Load: none | 12b-1: none
Other: none

Services

✔ IRA
Keogh
✔ Telephone Exchange

American Gas Index

800-622-1386, 301-657-1500

(GASFX)

Growth & Income

PERFORMANCE

fund inception date: 5/10/89

	3yr Annual	5yr Annual	10yr Annual	Bull	Bear
Return (%)	16.4	18.8	14.1	11.8	28.8
Differ from Category (+/-)	7.5 high	4.5 high	-0.8 blw av	-21.7 low	28.9 high

Standard Deviation	Category Risk Index	Beta
17.1%—av	0.99—av	0.24

	2000	1999	1998	1997	1996	1995	1994	1993	1992	1991
Return (%)	55.8	-3.7	5.2	24.1	20.7	30.5	-9.7	16.5	11.4	3.2
Differ from Category (+/-)	50.1	-14.5	-7.6	-2.8	1.0	1.0	-9.2	2.7	-0.2	-24.9
Return, Tax-Adjusted (%)	51.2	-6.3	3.3	22.7	19.3	28.7	-11.1	14.8	9.7	1.8

PER SHARE DATA

	2000	1999	1998	1997	1996	1995	1994	1993	1992	1991
Dividends, Net Income ($)	0.51	0.51	0.50	0.46	0.44	0.46	0.44	0.39	0.41	0.46
Distrib'ns, Cap Gain ($)	2.51	1.41	0.68	0.12	0.00	0.00	0.00	0.06	0.13	0.00
Net Asset Value ($)	20.67	15.37	17.98	18.25	15.22	13.01	10.36	11.96	10.65	10.09
Expense Ratio (%)	0.85	0.85	0.85	0.85	0.85	0.85	0.84	0.85	0.85	0.79
Yield (%)	2.20	3.03	2.67	2.50	2.89	3.53	4.24	3.24	3.80	4.55
Portfolio Turnover (%)	16	10	12	8	10	8	11	21	30	30
Total Assets (Millions $)	291	183	230	245	228	212	176	230	162	145

PORTFOLIO (as of 6/30/00)

Portfolio Manager: committee - 1989

Investm't Category: Growth & Income

✔ Domestic ✔ Index
Foreign ✔ Sector
Asset Allocation State Specific

Investment Style

Large Cap ✔ Mid Cap Small Cap
Growth Grth/Val ✔ Value

Portfolio

4.4%	cash	0.0%	corp bonds
95.6%	stocks	0.0%	gov't bonds
0.0%	pref/conv't pref	0.0%	muni bonds
0.0%	conv't bds/wrnts	0.0%	other

SHAREHOLDER INFORMATION

Minimum Investment

Initial: $2,500 Subsequent: $1

Minimum IRA Investment

Initial: $500 Subsequent: $1

Maximum Fees

Load: none 12b-1: none
Other: none

Services

✔ IRA
✔ Keogh
✔ Telephone Exchange

Aon: Asset Allocation

800-266-3637, 804-281-6049

(AONAX)

Balanced

PERFORMANCE

fund inception date: 3/1/94

	3yr Annual	5yr Annual	10yr Annual	Bull	Bear
Return (%)	8.0	12.8	na	32.6	-2.2
Differ from Category (+/-)	-0.4 av	1.4 abv av	na	4.5 abv av	1.0 av

Standard Deviation	Category Risk Index	Beta
13.1%—blw av	1.20—abv av	0.67

	2000	1999	1998	1997	1996	1995	1994	1993	1992	1991
Return (%)	4.4	14.3	5.5	31.4	10.4	33.7	—	—	—	—
Differ from Category (+/-)	2.4	3.6	-7.8	12.6	-3.5	8.2	—	—	—	—
Return, Tax-Adjusted (%)	1.2	10.8	4.3	29.6	8.6	31.7	—	—	—	—

PER SHARE DATA

	2000	1999	1998	1997	1996	1995	1994	1993	1992	1991
Dividends, Net Income ($)	0.54	0.35	0.48	0.29	0.34	0.24	—	—	—	—
Distrib'ns, Cap Gain ($)	1.52	2.18	0.00	0.55	0.32	0.33	—	—	—	—
Net Asset Value ($)	15.34	16.67	16.84	16.42	13.16	12.55	—	—	—	—
Expense Ratio (%)	na	0.36	0.36	0.56	0.87	0.96	—	—	—	—
Yield (%)	3.20	1.85	2.85	1.70	2.52	1.86	—	—	—	—
Portfolio Turnover (%)	na	46	64	64	120	95	—	—	—	—
Total Assets (Millions $)	177	190	191	166	135	88	—	—	—	—

PORTFOLIO (as of 6/30/00)

Portfolio Manager: John Lagedrost - 1994

Investm't Category: Balanced

✔ Domestic Index
✔ Foreign Sector
✔ Asset Allocation State Specific

Investment Style

Large Cap Mid Cap Small Cap
Growth Grth/Val Value

Portfolio

11.2%	cash	14.9%	corp bonds
71.1%	stocks	0.9%	gov't bonds
0.0%	pref/conv't pref	0.0%	muni bonds
1.9%	conv't bds/wrnts	0.0%	other

SHAREHOLDER INFORMATION

Minimum Investment

Initial: $1,000 Subsequent: $100

Minimum IRA Investment

Initial: $1,000 Subsequent: $100

Maximum Fees

Load: none 12b-1: none

Other: none

Services

✔ IRA
✔ Keogh
✔ Telephone Exchange

Aquinas Value (AQEIX)

800-423-6369, 214-233-6655
www.aquinasfunds.com

Growth & Income

PERFORMANCE — fund inception date: 1/3/94

	3yr Annual	5yr Annual	10yr Annual	Bull	Bear
Return (%)	1.7	10.1	na	24.0	-3.2
Differ from Category (+/-)	-7.2 low	-4.2 low	na	-9.5 blw av	-3.1 av

Standard Deviation	Category Risk Index	Beta
18.1%—av	1.05—abv av	0.79

	2000	1999	1998	1997	1996	1995	1994	1993	1992	1991
Return (%)	-1.1	1.1	5.4	27.8	20.4	35.6	—	—	—	—
Differ from Category (+/-)	-6.8	-9.7	-7.4	0.9	0.7	6.1	—	—	—	—
Return, Tax-Adjusted (%)	-1.8	-2.1	1.7	24.3	17.9	32.6	—	—	—	—

PER SHARE DATA

	2000	1999	1998	1997	1996	1995	1994	1993	1992	1991
Dividends, Net Income ($)	0.16	0.19	0.22	0.26	0.22	0.28	—	—	—	—
Distrib'ns, Cap Gain ($)	0.13	1.79	2.25	1.76	0.74	0.59	—	—	—	—
Net Asset Value ($)	10.91	11.34	13.21	14.89	13.26	11.83	—	—	—	—
Expense Ratio (%)	na	1.38	1.36	1.37	1.40	1.45	—	—	—	—
Yield (%)	1.44	1.44	1.42	1.56	1.57	2.25	—	—	—	—
Portfolio Turnover (%)	na	100	64	42	32	40	—	—	—	—
Total Assets (Millions $)	53	57	64	73	54	42	—	—	—	—

PORTFOLIO (as of 6/30/00)

Portfolio Manager: committee - 1994

Investm't Category: Growth & Income

✔ Domestic — Index
Foreign — Sector
Asset Allocation — State Specific

Investment Style

✔ Large Cap — ✔ Mid Cap — Small Cap
Growth — Grth/Val — ✔ Value

Portfolio

5.1%	cash	0.0%	corp bonds
94.9%	stocks	0.0%	gov't bonds
0.0%	pref/conv't pref	0.0%	muni bonds
0.0%	conv't bds/wrnts	0.0%	other

SHAREHOLDER INFORMATION

Minimum Investment
Initial: $500 — Subsequent: $0

Minimum IRA Investment
Initial: $500 — Subsequent: $0

Maximum Fees
Load: none — 12b-1: none
Other: none

Services
✔ IRA
Keogh
✔ Telephone Exchange

Ariel (ARGFX)

800-292-7435, 312-726-0140
www.arielfunds.com

Growth

PERFORMANCE — fund inception date: 9/29/86

	3yr Annual	5yr Annual	10yr Annual	Bull	Bear
Return (%)	10.0	17.5	15.1	16.9	23.0
Differ from Category (+/-)	-1.0 av	1.4 av	-1.7 blw av	-32.8 low	28.4 high

Standard Deviation	Category Risk Index	Beta
19.4%—abv av	1.00—av	0.66

	2000	1999	1998	1997	1996	1995	1994	1993	1992	1991
Return (%)	28.7	-5.7	9.8	36.4	23.5	18.5	-4.2	8.7	11.7	32.7
Differ from Category (+/-)	25.2	-24.6	-4.5	9.3	1.2	-11.9	-4.0	-5.9	-0.9	-4.9
Return, Tax-Adjusted (%)	24.6	-8.7	7.8	33.9	21.6	13.5	-6.0	6.6	9.0	31.1

PER SHARE DATA

	2000	1999	1998	1997	1996	1995	1994	1993	1992	1991
Dividends, Net Income ($)	0.24	0.07	0.08	0.14	0.00	0.43	0.23	0.29	0.74	0.47
Distrib'ns, Cap Gain ($)	5.75	6.04	3.71	3.57	1.78	4.18	1.70	1.73	1.92	0.79
Net Asset Value ($)	33.61	31.11	39.96	39.88	31.96	27.32	26.98	30.19	29.74	29.10
Expense Ratio (%)	1.24	1.25	1.21	1.25	1.31	1.37	1.25	1.16	1.23	1.25
Yield (%)	0.60	0.18	0.18	0.32	0.00	1.36	0.80	0.90	2.33	1.57
Portfolio Turnover (%)	48	38	22	20	17	16	9	13	19	39
Total Assets (Millions $)	246	205	201	174	120	120	130	225	254	262

PORTFOLIO (as of 6/30/00)

Portfolio Manager: John Rogers - 1986

Investm't Category: Growth

✔ Domestic
Foreign
Asset Allocation
Index
Sector
State Specific

Investment Style

✔ Large Cap ✔ Mid Cap Small Cap
Growth Grth/Val ✔ Value

Portfolio

16.0%	cash	0.0%	corp bonds
84.0%	stocks	0.0%	gov't bonds
0.0%	pref/conv't pref	0.0%	muni bonds
0.0%	conv't bds/wrnts	0.0%	other

SHAREHOLDER INFORMATION

Minimum Investment

Initial: $1,000 Subsequent: $50

Minimum IRA Investment

Initial: $250 Subsequent: $50

Maximum Fees

Load: none 12b-1: 0.25%
Other: none

Services

✔ IRA
✔ Keogh
✔ Telephone Exchange

Ariel Appreciation (CAAPX)

800-292-7435, 312-726-0140
www.arielfunds.com

Growth

PERFORMANCE — fund inception date: 1/15/90

	3yr Annual	5yr Annual	10yr Annual	Bull	Bear
Return (%)	10.9	18.4	15.7	23.8	16.9
Differ from Category (+/-)	-0.1 av	2.3 abv av	-1.1 blw av	-25.9 blw av	22.3 high

Standard Deviation	Category Risk Index	Beta
17.9%—av	0.92—blw av	0.73

	2000	1999	1998	1997	1996	1995	1994	1993	1992	1991
Return (%)	18.8	-3.7	19.5	37.9	23.7	24.1	-8.3	7.9	13.2	33.1
Differ from Category (+/-)	15.3	-22.6	5.2	10.8	1.4	-6.3	-8.1	-6.7	0.6	-4.5
Return, Tax-Adjusted (%)	16.1	-5.5	17.3	35.4	21.8	21.1	-10.1	7.3	13.0	32.7

PER SHARE DATA

	2000	1999	1998	1997	1996	1995	1994	1993	1992	1991
Dividends, Net Income ($)	0.11	0.04	0.03	0.06	0.07	0.19	0.06	0.05	0.08	0.16
Distrib'ns, Cap Gain ($)	3.95	3.15	3.45	3.06	1.36	1.76	1.39	0.34	0.00	0.02
Net Asset Value ($)	32.53	30.97	35.69	32.82	26.07	22.24	19.51	22.89	21.60	19.15
Expense Ratio (%)	1.31	1.26	1.26	1.33	1.36	1.36	1.35	1.37	1.44	1.50
Yield (%)	0.30	0.11	0.07	0.16	0.25	0.79	0.28	0.21	0.37	0.83
Portfolio Turnover (%)	31	24	20	19	26	18	12	56	2	20
Total Assets (Millions $)	323	334	283	204	146	139	128	219	179	90

PORTFOLIO (as of 6/30/00)

Portfolio Manager: Eric McKissack - 1990

Investm't Category: Growth

✔ Domestic — Index
Foreign — Sector
Asset Allocation — State Specific

Investment Style

✔ Large Cap — ✔ Mid Cap — Small Cap
Growth — Grth/Val — ✔ Value

Portfolio

0.6%	cash	0.0%	corp bonds
99.4%	stocks	0.0%	gov't bonds
0.0%	pref/conv't pref	0.0%	muni bonds
0.0%	conv't bds/wrnts	0.0%	other

SHAREHOLDER INFORMATION

Minimum Investment

Initial: $1,000 — Subsequent: $50

Minimum IRA Investment

Initial: $250 — Subsequent: $50

Maximum Fees

Load: none — 12b-1: 0.25%
Other: none

Services

✔ IRA
✔ Keogh
✔ Telephone Exchange

Artisan Int'l (ARTIX)

800-344-1770, 414-390-6100
www.artisanfunds.com

International Stock

PERFORMANCE — fund inception date: 12/28/95

	3yr Annual	5yr Annual	10yr Annual	Bull	Bear
Return (%)	28.9	24.3	na	108.5	-27.5
Differ from Category (+/-)	20.0 high	16.0 high	na	17.6 abv av	-3.5 av

Standard Deviation	Category Risk Index	Beta
27.0%—high	1.19—abv av	0.85

	2000	1999	1998	1997	1996	1995	1994	1993	1992	1991
Return (%)	-10.5	81.2	32.1	3.4	34.3	—	—	—	—	—
Differ from Category (+/-)	8.9	20.5	26.3	2.1	19.8	—	—	—	—	—
Return, Tax-Adjusted (%)	-12.9	80.4	31.6	1.1	33.9	—	—	—	—	—

PER SHARE DATA

	2000	1999	1998	1997	1996	1995	1994	1993	1992	1991
Dividends, Net Income ($)	0.00	0.02	0.03	0.19	0.00	—	—	—	—	—
Distrib'ns, Cap Gain ($)	3.55	0.53	0.24	1.12	0.11	—	—	—	—	—
Net Asset Value ($)	21.90	28.50	16.12	12.46	13.32	—	—	—	—	—
Expense Ratio (%)	1.27	1.38	1.45	1.61	2.50	—	—	—	—	—
Yield (%)	0.00	0.06	0.18	1.39	0.00	—	—	—	—	—
Portfolio Turnover (%)	99	79	109	103	57	—	—	—	—	—
Total Assets (Millions $)	4,438	3,027	612	271	193	—	—	—	—	—

PORTFOLIO (as of 6/30/00)

Portfolio Manager: Mark Yockey - 1995

Investm't Category: International Stock

Domestic	Index
✔ Foreign	Sector
Asset Allocation	State Specific

Investment Style

Large Cap	Mid Cap	Small Cap
Growth	Grth/Val	Value

Portfolio

4.0%	cash	0.0%	corp bonds
96.0%	stocks	0.0%	gov't bonds
0.0%	pref/conv't pref	0.0%	muni bonds
0.0%	conv't bds/wrnts	0.0%	other

SHAREHOLDER INFORMATION

Minimum Investment
Initial: $1,000 Subsequent: $50

Minimum IRA Investment
Initial: $1,000 Subsequent: $50

Maximum Fees
Load: none 12b-1: none
Other: none

Services
✔ IRA
✔ Keogh
✔ Telephone Exchange

Artisan Small Cap (ARTSX)

800-344-1770, 414-390-6100
www.artisanfunds.com

Aggressive Growth

PERFORMANCE — fund inception date: 3/28/95

	3yr Annual	5yr Annual	10yr Annual	Bull	Bear
Return (%)	0.5	6.8	na	38.5	-19.6
Differ from Category (+/-)	-15.7 low	-7.8 low	na	-80.7 low	1.0 av

Standard Deviation	Category Risk Index	Beta
24.7%—abv av	0.76—blw av	0.95

	2000	1999	1998	1997	1996	1995	1994	1993	1992	1991
Return (%)	-1.4	19.1	-13.4	22.6	11.8	—	—	—	—	—
Differ from Category (+/-)	4.6	-38.4	-28.5	7.8	-6.5	—	—	—	—	—
Return, Tax-Adjusted (%)	-2.3	19.1	-14.7	18.8	9.5	—	—	—	—	—

PER SHARE DATA

	2000	1999	1998	1997	1996	1995	1994	1993	1992	1991
Dividends, Net Income ($)	0.00	0.00	0.00	0.00	0.00	—	—	—	—	—
Distrib'ns, Cap Gain ($)	0.66	0.00	0.96	2.57	1.07	—	—	—	—	—
Net Asset Value ($)	12.48	13.30	11.16	14.15	13.64	—	—	—	—	—
Expense Ratio (%)	1.35	1.37	1.33	1.41	1.52	—	—	—	—	—
Yield (%)	0.00	0.00	0.00	0.00	0.00	—	—	—	—	—
Portfolio Turnover (%)	193	155	134	87	105	—	—	—	—	—
Total Assets (Millions $)	146	175	201	291	295	—	—	—	—	—

PORTFOLIO (as of 6/30/00)

Portfolio Manager: C. Ziegler, M. Carlson - 1995

Investm't Category: Aggressive Growth

✔ Domestic — Index
✔ Foreign — Sector
Asset Allocation — State Specific

Investment Style

Large Cap — Mid Cap — ✔ Small Cap
✔ Growth — Grth/Val — Value

Portfolio

2.3%	cash	0.0%	corp bonds
97.7%	stocks	0.0%	gov't bonds
0.0%	pref/conv't pref	0.0%	muni bonds
0.0%	conv't bds/wrnts	0.0%	other

SHAREHOLDER INFORMATION

Minimum Investment
Initial: $1,000 — Subsequent: $50

Minimum IRA Investment
Initial: $1,000 — Subsequent: $50

Maximum Fees
Load: none — 12b-1: none
Other: none

Services
✔ IRA
✔ Keogh
✔ Telephone Exchange

Artisan Small Cap Value (ARTVX)

800-344-1770, 414-390-6100
www.artisanfunds.com

Growth

this fund is closed to new investors

PERFORMANCE

fund inception date: 9/29/97

	3yr Annual	5yr Annual	10yr Annual	Bull	Bear
Return (%)	9.5	na	na	20.7	8.5
Differ from Category (+/-)	-1.5 blw av	na	na	-29.0 low	13.9 high

Standard Deviation	Category Risk Index	Beta
15.3%—av	0.79—low	0.53

	2000	1999	1998	1997	1996	1995	1994	1993	1992	1991
Return (%)	20.8	15.4	-5.7	—	—	—	—	—	—	—
Differ from Category (+/-)	17.3	-3.5	-20.0	—	—	—	—	—	—	—
Return, Tax-Adjusted (%)	19.6	14.5	-6.7	—	—	—	—	—	—	—

PER SHARE DATA

	2000	1999	1998	1997	1996	1995	1994	1993	1992	1991
Dividends, Net Income ($)	0.05	0.02	0.00	—	—	—	—	—	—	—
Distrib'ns, Cap Gain ($)	0.48	0.34	0.53	—	—	—	—	—	—	—
Net Asset Value ($)	11.70	10.16	9.14	—	—	—	—	—	—	—
Expense Ratio (%)	1.35	1.66	1.93	—	—	—	—	—	—	—
Yield (%)	0.41	0.19	0.00	—	—	—	—	—	—	—
Portfolio Turnover (%)	38	49	—	—	—	—	—	—	—	—
Total Assets (Millions $)	300	143	54	—	—	—	—	—	—	—

PORTFOLIO (as of 6/30/00)

Portfolio Manager: S. Satterwhite, J. Kieffrer - 1997

Investm't Category: Growth

✔ Domestic	Index
✔ Foreign	Sector
Asset Allocation	State Specific

Investment Style

Large Cap	Mid Cap	✔ Small Cap
Growth	Grth/Val	✔ Value

Portfolio

5.3%	cash	0.0%	corp bonds
94.7%	stocks	0.0%	gov't bonds
0.0%	pref/conv't pref	0.0%	muni bonds
0.0%	conv't bds/wrnts	0.0%	other

SHAREHOLDER INFORMATION

Minimum Investment
Initial: $1,000 Subsequent: $50

Minimum IRA Investment
Initial: $1,000 Subsequent: $50

Maximum Fees
Load: none 12b-1: none
Other: none

Services
✔ IRA
✔ Keogh
✔ Telephone Exchange

BB&K Intl Equity (BBIEX)

800-882-8383, 650-571-5800
www.bailard.com

International Stock

PERFORMANCE — fund inception date: 9/4/79

	3yr Annual	5yr Annual	10yr Annual	Bull	Bear
Return (%)	6.4	7.7	5.9	51.3	-22.7
Differ from Category (+/-)	-2.5 blw av	-0.6 blw av	-3.1 blw av	-39.6 blw av	1.3 av

Standard Deviation	Category Risk Index	Beta
18.9%—av	0.83—blw av	0.81

	2000	1999	1998	1997	1996	1995	1994	1993	1992	1991
Return (%)	-19.2	33.3	12.0	9.9	9.5	12.4	-12.5	37.8	-11.4	1.8
Differ from Category (+/-)	0.2	-27.4	6.2	8.6	-5.0	3.1	-9.4	-2.4	-7.9	-11.2
Return, Tax-Adjusted (%)	-20.7	30.9	10.1	8.5	7.4	9.3	-12.5	37.8	-11.8	1.2

PER SHARE DATA

	2000	1999	1998	1997	1996	1995	1994	1993	1992	1991
Dividends, Net Income ($)	0.00	0.06	0.06	0.13	0.05	0.06	0.00	0.00	0.08	0.00
Distrib'ns, Cap Gain ($)	0.60	0.64	0.46	0.13	0.36	0.53	0.00	0.00	0.00	0.10
Net Asset Value ($)	5.72	7.84	6.47	6.26	5.94	5.80	5.70	6.52	4.73	5.43
Expense Ratio (%)	1.37	1.49	1.41	1.44	1.54	1.53	1.39	0.68	1.05	1.22
Yield (%)	0.00	0.70	0.86	2.03	0.79	0.94	0.00	0.00	1.69	0.00
Portfolio Turnover (%)	101	85	78	67	103	174	176	131	77	81
Total Assets (Millions $)	138	173	126	132	119	108	148	219	94	148

PORTFOLIO (as of 6/30/00)

Portfolio Manager: Rosemary Macedo - 1995

Investm't Category: International Stock

Domestic	Index
✔ Foreign	Sector
Asset Allocation	State Specific

Investment Style

Large Cap	Mid Cap	Small Cap
Growth	Grth/Val	Value

Portfolio

1.8%	cash	0.0%	corp bonds
98.2%	stocks	0.0%	gov't bonds
0.0%	pref/conv't pref	0.0%	muni bonds
0.0%	conv't bds/wrnts	0.0%	other

SHAREHOLDER INFORMATION

Minimum Investment
Initial: $5,000 — Subsequent: $100

Minimum IRA Investment
Initial: $5,000 — Subsequent: $100

Maximum Fees
Load: none — 12b-1: none
Other: none

Services
✔ IRA
Keogh
✔ Telephone Exchange

BS&R Inv: Equity (BREQX)

800-320-2212, 513-629-2070

Growth & Income

PERFORMANCE — fund inception date: 1/2/91

	3yr Annual	5yr Annual	10yr Annual	Bull	Bear
Return (%)	13.8	17.4	na	56.9	-4.9
Differ from Category (+/-)	4.9 high	3.1 abv av	na	23.4 high	-4.8 av

Standard Deviation	Category Risk Index	Beta
16.9%—av	0.97—av	0.91

	2000	1999	1998	1997	1996	1995	1994	1993	1992	1991
Return (%)	1.6	27.9	13.2	27.2	19.2	27.2	-0.5	10.2	2.4	—
Differ from Category (+/-)	-4.1	17.1	0.4	0.3	-0.5	-2.3	0.0	-3.6	-9.2	—
Return, Tax-Adjusted (%)	-0.5	25.8	11.7	24.6	16.2	25.4	-1.9	9.0	1.3	—

PER SHARE DATA

	2000	1999	1998	1997	1996	1995	1994	1993	1992	1991
Dividends, Net Income ($)	0.02	0.00	0.04	0.05	0.06	0.05	0.06	0.09	0.11	—
Distrib'ns, Cap Gain ($)	2.38	1.90	1.25	1.93	1.42	0.68	0.55	0.37	0.31	—
Net Asset Value ($)	20.14	22.19	18.87	17.86	15.67	14.44	11.94	12.63	11.89	—
Expense Ratio (%)	na	1.15	1.15	1.19	1.45	0.60	0.50	0.50	0.50	—
Yield (%)	0.08	0.00	0.19	0.25	0.35	0.33	0.48	0.69	0.90	—
Portfolio Turnover (%)	na	37	50	49	44	39	57	29	24	—
Total Assets (Millions $)	60	55	42	36	27	24	18	19	16	—

PORTFOLIO (as of 6/30/00)

Portfolio Manager: Gregory Ratte - 1994

Investm't Category: Growth & Income

✔ Domestic	Index
✔ Foreign	Sector
Asset Allocation	State Specific

Investment Style

✔ Large Cap	Mid Cap	Small Cap
Growth	Grth/Val	✔ Value

Portfolio

3.2% cash	0.0% corp bonds
96.8% stocks	0.0% gov't bonds
0.0% pref/conv't pref	0.0% muni bonds
0.0% conv't bds/wrnts	0.0% other

SHAREHOLDER INFORMATION

Minimum Investment
Initial: $1,000 Subsequent: $1

Minimum IRA Investment
Initial: $250 Subsequent: $1

Maximum Fees
Load: none 12b-1: none
Other: none

Services
✔ IRA
✔ Keogh
✔ Telephone Exchange

Babson Enterprise (BABEX)

800-422-2766, 816-751-5900
www.babsonfunds.com

Growth

PERFORMANCE — fund inception date: 12/2/83

	3yr Annual	5yr Annual	10yr Annual	Bull	Bear
Return (%)	-2.5	8.2	13.8	-0.4	-3.7
Differ from Category (+/-)	-13.5 low	-7.9 low	-3.0 low	-50.1 low	1.7 av

Standard Deviation	Category Risk Index	Beta
18.3%—av	0.94—blw av	0.47

	2000	1999	1998	1997	1996	1995	1994	1993	1992	1991
Return (%)	12.4	-7.2	-11.3	32.4	21.2	16.4	2.4	16.2	24.5	43.0
Differ from Category (+/-)	8.9	-26.1	-25.6	5.3	-1.1	-14.0	2.6	1.6	11.9	5.4
Return, Tax-Adjusted (%)	10.5	-8.7	-13.9	29.3	16.4	12.7	-0.5	14.0	19.7	40.7

PER SHARE DATA

	2000	1999	1998	1997	1996	1995	1994	1993	1992	1991
Dividends, Net Income ($)	0.04	0.01	0.05	0.05	0.00	0.11	0.03	0.05	0.08	0.07
Distrib'ns, Cap Gain ($)	1.07	1.05	2.47	2.42	2.66	1.84	1.69	1.10	2.33	0.76
Net Asset Value ($)	12.47	12.11	14.26	19.03	16.31	15.66	15.15	16.51	15.22	14.19
Expense Ratio (%)	1.14	1.11	1.09	1.08	1.08	1.09	1.08	1.09	1.11	1.17
Yield (%)	0.29	0.07	0.29	0.23	0.00	0.62	0.17	0.28	0.45	0.46
Portfolio Turnover (%)	32	12	22	22	24	13	15	17	28	15
Total Assets (Millions $)	101	116	176	217	191	201	190	220	184	133

PORTFOLIO (as of 6/30/00)

Portfolio Manager: Lance James - 1999

Investm't Category: Growth

✔ Domestic
Foreign
Asset Allocation
Index
Sector
State Specific

Investment Style

Large Cap
Mid Cap
✔ Small Cap
Growth
Grth/Val
✔ Value

Portfolio

2.0%	cash	0.0%	corp bonds
98.0%	stocks	0.0%	gov't bonds
0.0%	pref/conv't pref	0.0%	muni bonds
0.0%	conv't bds/wrnts	0.0%	other

SHAREHOLDER INFORMATION

Minimum Investment
Initial: $1,000 — Subsequent: $100

Minimum IRA Investment
Initial: $250 — Subsequent: $50

Maximum Fees
Load: none — 12b-1: none
Other: none

Services
✔ IRA
✔ Keogh
✔ Telephone Exchange

Babson Enterprise II

800-422-2766, 816-751-5900
www.babsonfunds.com

(BAETX)

Growth

PERFORMANCE

fund inception date: 8/5/91

	3yr Annual	5yr Annual	10yr Annual	Bull	Bear
Return (%)	5.7	15.0	na	27.4	3.1
Differ from Category (+/-)	-5.3 blw av	-1.1 blw av	na	-22.3 blw av	8.5 abv av

Standard Deviation	Category Risk Index	Beta
20.3%—abv av	1.04—av	0.84

	2000	1999	1998	1997	1996	1995	1994	1993	1992	1991
Return (%)	16.6	6.1	-4.3	33.2	27.6	19.8	-7.3	19.7	17.2	—
Differ from Category (+/-)	13.1	-12.8	-18.6	6.1	5.3	-10.6	-7.1	5.1	4.6	—
Return, Tax-Adjusted (%)	15.0	5.6	-5.2	31.1	22.8	18.0	-7.4	19.1	17.1	—

PER SHARE DATA

	2000	1999	1998	1997	1996	1995	1994	1993	1992	1991
Dividends, Net Income ($)	0.02	0.01	0.05	0.04	0.11	0.05	0.02	0.00	0.00	—
Distrib'ns, Cap Gain ($)	1.74	0.49	1.07	2.05	2.98	0.94	0.08	0.32	0.03	—
Net Asset Value ($)	25.62	23.59	22.72	24.99	20.37	18.40	16.19	17.60	14.97	—
Expense Ratio (%)	1.27	1.23	1.22	1.28	1.38	1.45	1.50	1.60	1.83	—
Yield (%)	0.07	0.04	0.21	0.14	0.47	0.25	0.12	0.00	0.00	—
Portfolio Turnover (%)	23	14	25	21	30	15	9	18	14	—
Total Assets (Millions $)	52	63	82	87	48	40	36	30	12	—

PORTFOLIO (as of 6/30/00)

Portfolio Manager: Lance James - 1991

Investm't Category: Growth

✔ Domestic — Index
Foreign — Sector
Asset Allocation — State Specific

Investment Style

Large Cap — ✔ Mid Cap — ✔ Small Cap
Growth — Grth/Val — ✔ Value

Portfolio

5.0%	cash	0.0%	corp bonds
95.0%	stocks	0.0%	gov't bonds
0.0%	pref/conv't pref	0.0%	muni bonds
0.0%	conv't bds/wrnts	0.0%	other

SHAREHOLDER INFORMATION

Minimum Investment

Initial: $1,000 — Subsequent: $100

Minimum IRA Investment

Initial: $250 — Subsequent: $50

Maximum Fees

Load: none — 12b-1: none
Other: none

Services

✔ IRA
✔ Keogh
✔ Telephone Exchange

Babson Growth (BABSX)

800-422-2766, 816-751-5900
www.babsonfunds.com

Growth

PERFORMANCE — fund inception date: 4/20/60

	3yr Annual	5yr Annual	10yr Annual	Bull	Bear
Return (%)	11.1	16.4	15.5	52.3	-19.9
Differ from Category (+/-)	0.1 av	0.3 av	-1.3 blw av	2.6 av	-14.5 low

Standard Deviation	Category Risk Index	Beta
22.1%—abv av	1.14—abv av	1.07

	2000	1999	1998	1997	1996	1995	1994	1993	1992	1991
Return (%)	-7.8	12.5	32.2	27.9	21.8	31.4	-0.5	10.2	9.1	26.0
Differ from Category (+/-)	-11.3	-6.4	17.9	0.8	-0.5	1.0	-0.3	-4.4	-3.5	-11.6
Return, Tax-Adjusted (%)	-12.6	10.2	28.7	25.7	17.4	28.9	-2.8	8.3	7.8	25.2

PER SHARE DATA

	2000	1999	1998	1997	1996	1995	1994	1993	1992	1991
Dividends, Net Income ($)	0.00	0.00	0.04	0.09	0.11	0.15	0.20	0.19	0.20	0.21
Distrib'ns, Cap Gain ($)	5.01	2.29	3.05	1.49	2.13	0.85	0.81	0.55	0.32	0.03
Net Asset Value ($)	14.23	20.71	20.64	18.08	15.43	14.66	11.97	13.08	12.58	12.02
Expense Ratio (%)	0.79	0.79	0.80	0.83	0.85	0.85	0.86	0.86	0.86	0.86
Yield (%)	0.00	0.00	0.16	0.45	0.62	0.96	1.56	1.39	1.55	1.74
Portfolio Turnover (%)	62	39	35	20	33	17	10	13	12	22
Total Assets (Millions $)	428	500	512	395	311	271	226	245	244	256

PORTFOLIO (as of 6/30/00)

Portfolio Manager: James Gribbell - 1996

Investm't Category: Growth

✔ Domestic	Index
Foreign	Sector
Asset Allocation	State Specific

Investment Style

✔ Large Cap	✔ Mid Cap	Small Cap
✔ Growth	Grth/Val	Value

Portfolio

4.0%	cash	0.0%	corp bonds
96.0%	stocks	0.0%	gov't bonds
0.0%	pref/conv't pref	0.0%	muni bonds
0.0%	conv't bds/wrnts	0.0%	other

SHAREHOLDER INFORMATION

Minimum Investment

Initial: $1,000 — Subsequent: $100

Minimum IRA Investment

Initial: $250 — Subsequent: $50

Maximum Fees

Load: none — 12b-1: none

Other: none

Services

✔ IRA

✔ Keogh

✔ Telephone Exchange

Babson Shadow Stock

800-422-2766, 816-751-5900
www.babsonfunds.com

(SHSTX)

Growth

PERFORMANCE

fund inception date: 9/10/87

	3yr Annual	5yr Annual	10yr Annual	Bull	Bear
Return (%)	4.6	12.1	14.8	15.8	-0.5
Differ from Category (+/-)	-6.4 low	-4.0 blw av	-2.0 blw av	-33.9 low	4.9 abv av

Standard Deviation	Category Risk Index	Beta
14.8%—av	0.76—low	0.48

	2000	1999	1998	1997	1996	1995	1994	1993	1992	1991
Return (%)	11.3	4.6	-1.4	27.6	21.3	23.6	-4.2	15.2	17.4	39.9
Differ from Category (+/-)	7.8	-14.3	-15.7	0.5	-1.0	-6.8	-4.0	0.6	4.8	2.3
Return, Tax-Adjusted (%)	8.7	2.9	-2.8	23.7	17.5	20.9	-9.3	12.4	17.0	39.5

PER SHARE DATA

	2000	1999	1998	1997	1996	1995	1994	1993	1992	1991
Dividends, Net Income ($)	0.08	0.34	0.06	0.13	0.08	0.10	0.11	0.09	0.08	0.08
Distrib'ns, Cap Gain ($)	1.32	0.31	0.83	1.99	1.35	0.75	2.12	1.02	0.05	0.00
Net Asset Value ($)	11.31	11.46	11.60	12.70	11.70	10.89	9.52	12.32	11.72	10.11
Expense Ratio (%)	1.07	1.10	1.16	1.13	1.14	1.13	1.28	1.25	1.26	1.31
Yield (%)	0.63	2.88	0.48	0.88	0.61	0.85	0.94	0.67	0.67	0.79
Portfolio Turnover (%)	18	21	43	0	25	19	43	15	23	0
Total Assets (Millions $)	40	40	50	49	39	38	33	37	31	24

PORTFOLIO (as of 6/30/00)

Portfolio Manager: Anthony Maramarco - 1999

Investm't Category: Growth

✔ Domestic — Index
Foreign — Sector
Asset Allocation — State Specific

Investment Style

Large Cap — Mid Cap — ✔ Small Cap
Growth — ✔ Grth/Val — Value

Portfolio

11.0%	cash	0.0%	corp bonds
89.0%	stocks	0.0%	gov't bonds
0.0%	pref/conv't pref	0.0%	muni bonds
0.0%	conv't bds/wrnts	0.0%	other

SHAREHOLDER INFORMATION

Minimum Investment
Initial: $1,000 — Subsequent: $100

Minimum IRA Investment
Initial: $250 — Subsequent: $50

Maximum Fees
Load: none — 12b-1: none
Other: none

Services
✔ IRA
✔ Keogh
✔ Telephone Exchange

Babson Value (BVALX)

800-422-2766, 816-751-5900
www.babsonfunds.com

Growth & Income

PERFORMANCE — fund inception date: 12/21/84

	3yr Annual	5yr Annual	10yr Annual	Bull	Bear
Return (%)	5.3	12.6	16.1	20.6	10.3
Differ from Category (+/-)	-3.6 blw av	-1.7 blw av	1.2 av	-12.9 blw av	10.4 abv av

Standard Deviation	Category Risk Index	Beta
20.4%—abv av	1.18—high	0.82

	2000	1999	1998	1997	1996	1995	1994	1993	1992	1991
Return (%)	9.0	1.0	6.0	26.5	22.7	31.7	2.5	22.8	15.3	28.9
Differ from Category (+/-)	3.3	-9.8	-6.8	-0.4	3.0	2.2	3.0	9.0	3.7	0.8
Return, Tax-Adjusted (%)	7.1	-0.2	4.6	25.2	21.5	30.4	1.0	20.6	13.8	27.5

PER SHARE DATA

	2000	1999	1998	1997	1996	1995	1994	1993	1992	1991
Dividends, Net Income ($)	0.91	0.69	0.57	0.50	0.49	0.56	0.47	0.53	0.62	0.71
Distrib'ns, Cap Gain ($)	2.35	1.40	1.97	1.46	0.60	0.34	0.60	0.91	0.32	0.00
Net Asset Value ($)	44.55	44.25	45.88	45.71	37.74	31.68	24.78	25.22	21.75	19.67
Expense Ratio (%)	0.96	0.96	0.98	0.97	0.96	0.98	0.99	1.00	1.01	1.01
Yield (%)	1.94	1.51	1.19	1.05	1.27	1.74	1.85	2.02	2.80	3.60
Portfolio Turnover (%)	18	13	42	17	11	6	14	26	17	31
Total Assets (Millions $)	502	823	1,453	1,421	783	308	121	45	35	27

PORTFOLIO (as of 6/30/00)

Portfolio Manager: Anthony Maramarco - 1999

Investm't Category: Growth & Income

✔ Domestic — Index
Foreign — Sector
Asset Allocation — State Specific

Investment Style

✔ Large Cap — ✔ Mid Cap — Small Cap
Growth — Grth/Val — ✔ Value

Portfolio

3.0%	cash	0.0%	corp bonds
97.0%	stocks	0.0%	gov't bonds
0.0%	pref/conv't pref	0.0%	muni bonds
0.0%	conv't bds/wrnts	0.0%	other

SHAREHOLDER INFORMATION

Minimum Investment
Initial: $1,000 — Subsequent: $100

Minimum IRA Investment
Initial: $250 — Subsequent: $50

Maximum Fees
Load: none — 12b-1: none
Other: none

Services
✔ IRA
✔ Keogh
✔ Telephone Exchange

Babson-Stewart Ivory Intl (BAINX)

800-422-2766, 816-751-5900
www.babsonfunds.com

International Stock

PERFORMANCE — fund inception date: 12/14/87

	3yr Annual	5yr Annual	10yr Annual	Bull	Bear
Return (%)	8.2	7.9	9.7	50.1	-19.7
Differ from Category (+/-)	-0.7 av	-0.4 blw av	0.7 av	-40.8 blw av	4.3 abv av

Standard Deviation	Category Risk Index	Beta
15.7%—av	0.69—low	0.63

	2000	1999	1998	1997	1996	1995	1994	1993	1992	1991
Return (%)	-14.4	31.0	13.2	1.7	13.4	12.5	1.3	33.4	-1.7	15.0
Differ from Category (+/-)	5.0	-29.7	7.4	0.4	-1.1	3.2	4.4	-6.8	1.8	2.0
Return, Tax-Adjusted (%)	-14.7	30.6	12.0	0.5	12.2	11.4	-0.3	32.5	-2.0	14.6

PER SHARE DATA

	2000	1999	1998	1997	1996	1995	1994	1993	1992	1991
Dividends, Net Income ($)	0.00	0.00	0.08	0.07	0.07	0.17	0.04	0.05	0.14	0.11
Distrib'ns, Cap Gain ($)	0.44	0.29	0.82	0.95	0.61	0.36	0.92	0.32	0.02	0.00
Net Asset Value ($)	20.69	24.73	19.11	17.69	18.41	16.85	15.45	16.20	12.43	12.81
Expense Ratio (%)	1.24	1.23	1.16	1.19	1.26	1.30	1.32	1.57	1.58	1.75
Yield (%)	0.00	0.00	0.40	0.37	0.36	0.98	0.24	0.30	1.12	0.85
Portfolio Turnover (%)	47	51	48	40	33	37	60	49	44	52
Total Assets (Millions $)	73	96	96	98	89	71	55	43	20	13

PORTFOLIO (as of 6/30/00)

Portfolio Manager: James Burns - 1999

Investm't Category: International Stock

Domestic — Index
✔ Foreign — Sector
Asset Allocation — State Specific

Investment Style

Large Cap — Mid Cap — Small Cap
Growth — Grth/Val — Value

Portfolio

1.0%	cash	0.0%	corp bonds
99.0%	stocks	0.0%	gov't bonds
0.0%	pref/conv't pref	0.0%	muni bonds
0.0%	conv't bds/wrnts	0.0%	other

SHAREHOLDER INFORMATION

Minimum Investment
Initial: $1,000 — Subsequent: $100

Minimum IRA Investment
Initial: $250 — Subsequent: $50

Maximum Fees
Load: none — 12b-1: none
Other: none

Services
✔ IRA
✔ Keogh
✔ Telephone Exchange

Baron Asset (BARAX)

800-992-2766, 212-583-2100
www.baronfunds.com

Aggressive Growth

PERFORMANCE — fund inception date: 6/12/87

	3yr Annual	5yr Annual	10yr Annual	Bull	Bear
Return (%)	6.7	14.7	18.4	54.4	-15.4
Differ from Category (+/-)	-9.5 blw av	0.1 av	2.6 av	-64.8 blw av	5.2 abv av

Standard Deviation	Category Risk Index	Beta
25.1%—abv av	0.77—blw av	1.21

	2000	1999	1998	1997	1996	1995	1994	1993	1992	1991
Return (%)	0.3	16.2	4.2	33.8	21.9	35.2	7.4	23.4	13.9	34.0
Differ from Category (+/-)	-6.3	-41.3	-10.9	19.0	3.6	0.6	8.2	-1.8	7.0	-13.2
Return, Tax-Adjusted (%)	-1.2	16.2	4.1	33.8	21.8	35.1	6.5	21.9	13.6	33.9

PER SHARE DATA

	2000	1999	1998	1997	1996	1995	1994	1993	1992	1991
Dividends, Net Income ($)	0.00	0.00	0.04	0.00	0.00	0.00	0.00	0.31	0.00	0.03
Distrib'ns, Cap Gain ($)	4.61	0.00	0.00	0.00	0.03	0.03	0.65	0.45	0.16	0.00
Net Asset Value ($)	54.39	58.77	50.54	48.51	36.23	29.74	22.01	21.11	17.73	15.71
Expense Ratio (%)	1.36	1.31	1.32	1.30	1.40	1.50	1.60	1.80	1.70	1.70
Yield (%)	0.00	0.00	0.07	0.00	0.00	0.00	0.00	1.43	0.00	0.19
Portfolio Turnover (%)	2	15	23	13	19	41	55	108	96	143
Total Assets (Millions $)	4,917	6,146	5,672	3,793	1,326	353	87	64	47	46

PORTFOLIO (as of 6/30/00)

Portfolio Manager: Ronald Baron - 1987

Investm't Category: Aggressive Growth

✔ Domestic — Index
✔ Foreign — Sector
Asset Allocation — State Specific

Investment Style

Large Cap — ✔ Mid Cap — Small Cap
Growth — ✔ Grth/Val — Value

Portfolio

0.2%	cash	0.0%	corp bonds
99.8%	stocks	0.0%	gov't bonds
0.0%	pref/conv't pref	0.0%	muni bonds
0.0%	conv't bds/wrnts	0.0%	other

SHAREHOLDER INFORMATION

Minimum Investment
Initial: $2,000 — Subsequent: $1

Minimum IRA Investment
Initial: $2,000 — Subsequent: $1

Maximum Fees
Load: none — 12b-1: 0.25%
Other: none

Services
✔ IRA
Keogh
✔ Telephone Exchange

Baron Small Cap (BSCFX)

800-992-2766, 212-583-2100
www.baronfunds.com

Aggressive Growth

PERFORMANCE

fund inception date: 10/1/97

	3yr Annual	5yr Annual	10yr Annual	Bull	Bear
Return (%)	12.9	na	na	111.5	-22.2
Differ from Category (+/-)	-3.3 av	na	na	-7.7 av	-1.6 av

Standard Deviation	Category Risk Index	Beta
27.3%—high	0.84—blw av	1.14

	2000	1999	1998	1997	1996	1995	1994	1993	1992	1991
Return (%)	-17.5	70.7	2.2	—	—	—	—	—	—	—
Differ from Category (+/-)	-11.5	13.2	-12.9	—	—	—	—	—	—	—
Return, Tax-Adjusted (%)	-17.9	70.7	2.2	—	—	—	—	—	—	—

PER SHARE DATA

	2000	1999	1998	1997	1996	1995	1994	1993	1992	1991
Dividends, Net Income ($)	0.00	0.00	0.00	—	—	—	—	—	—	—
Distrib'ns, Cap Gain ($)	0.37	0.00	0.00	—	—	—	—	—	—	—
Net Asset Value ($)	14.46	18.00	10.54	—	—	—	—	—	—	—
Expense Ratio (%)	1.33	1.34	1.39	—	—	—	—	—	—	—
Yield (%)	0.00	0.00	0.00	—	—	—	—	—	—	—
Portfolio Turnover (%)	53	42	59	—	—	—	—	—	—	—
Total Assets (Millions $)	879	1,088	470	—	—	—	—	—	—	—

PORTFOLIO (as of 6/30/00)

Portfolio Manager: Cliff Greenberg - 1997

Investm't Category: Aggressive Growth

✔ Domestic
✔ Foreign
Asset Allocation
Index
Sector
State Specific

Investment Style

Large Cap
✔ Mid Cap
✔ Small Cap
✔ Growth
Grth/Val
Value

Portfolio

5.0%	cash	0.0%	corp bonds
95.0%	stocks	0.0%	gov't bonds
0.0%	pref/conv't pref	0.0%	muni bonds
0.0%	conv't bds/wrnts	0.0%	other

SHAREHOLDER INFORMATION

Minimum Investment

Initial: $2,000 Subsequent: $1

Minimum IRA Investment

Initial: $2,000 Subsequent: $1

Maximum Fees

Load: none 12b-1: 0.25%
Other: none

Services

✔ IRA
✔ Keogh
✔ Telephone Exchange

Berger Growth (BEONX)

800-333-1001, 303-329-0200
www.bergerfunds.com

Aggressive Growth

PERFORMANCE — fund inception date: 11/10/66

	3yr Annual	5yr Annual	10yr Annual	Bull	Bear
Return (%)	12.8	13.1	17.9	107.4	-33.7
Differ from Category (+/-)	-3.4 av	-1.5 blw av	2.1 av	-11.8 av	-13.1 blw av

Standard Deviation	Category Risk Index	Beta
32.8%—high	1.01—av	1.34

	2000	1999	1998	1997	1996	1995	1994	1993	1992	1991
Return (%)	-18.8	52.3	16.2	13.5	13.7	21.3	-6.6	21.1	8.5	88.8
Differ from Category (+/-)	-12.8	-5.2	1.1	-1.3	-4.6	-13.3	-5.8	-4.1	1.6	41.6
Return, Tax-Adjusted (%)	-21.7	47.3	14.7	5.7	9.4	19.6	-6.6	21.1	8.5	88.1

PER SHARE DATA

	2000	1999	1998	1997	1996	1995	1994	1993	1992	1991
Dividends, Net Income ($)	0.00	0.00	0.00	0.00	0.00	0.00	0.00	0.00	0.00	0.00
Distrib'ns, Cap Gain ($)	2.69	3.58	0.97	6.94	2.77	0.92	0.00	0.00	0.00	0.17
Net Asset Value ($)	12.32	18.53	14.60	13.45	17.83	18.10	15.69	16.81	13.87	12.78
Expense Ratio (%)	1.13	1.36	1.38	1.38	1.42	1.48	1.70	1.69	1.89	2.24
Yield (%)	0.00	0.00	0.00	0.00	0.00	0.00	0.00	0.00	0.00	0.00
Portfolio Turnover (%)	70	274	280	200	122	114	64	74	51	78
Total Assets (Millions $)	1,363	1,816	1,566	1,718	2,003	2,152	2,112	1,648	760	192

PORTFOLIO (as of 6/30/00)

Portfolio Manager: Jay Tracey - 2000

Investm't Category: Aggressive Growth

✔ Domestic	Index
✔ Foreign	Sector
Asset Allocation	State Specific

Investment Style

✔ Large Cap	✔ Mid Cap	✔ Small Cap
✔ Growth	Grth/Val	Value

Portfolio

2.0%	cash	0.0%	corp bonds
98.0%	stocks	0.0%	gov't bonds
0.0%	pref/conv't pref	0.0%	muni bonds
0.0%	conv't bds/wrnts	0.0%	other

SHAREHOLDER INFORMATION

Minimum Investment

Initial: $2,000 — Subsequent: $50

Minimum IRA Investment

Initial: $2,000 — Subsequent: $50

Maximum Fees

Load: none — 12b-1: 0.25%

Other: none

Services

✔ IRA
✔ Keogh
✔ Telephone Exchange

Berger Growth & Income (BEOOX)

800-333-1001, 303-329-0200
www.bergerfunds.com

Growth

PERFORMANCE

fund inception date: 12/12/66

	3yr Annual	5yr Annual	10yr Annual	Bull	Bear
Return (%)	20.5	19.9	19.3	111.4	-25.5
Differ from Category (+/-)	9.5 high	3.8 high	2.5 abv av	61.7 high	-20.1 low

Standard Deviation	Category Risk Index	Beta
26.4%—high	1.36—high	1.10

	2000	1999	1998	1997	1996	1995	1994	1993	1992	1991
Return (%)	-11.2	61.3	22.4	22.7	15.6	23.9	-9.0	23.5	4.8	60.9
Differ from Category (+/-)	-14.7	42.4	8.1	-4.4	-6.7	-6.5	-8.8	8.9	-7.8	23.3
Return, Tax-Adjusted (%)	-13.4	58.0	18.1	18.2	11.5	23.2	-9.4	23.1	4.6	56.5

PER SHARE DATA

	2000	1999	1998	1997	1996	1995	1994	1993	1992	1991
Dividends, Net Income ($)	0.00	0.00	0.03	0.08	0.18	0.18	0.13	0.08	0.04	0.23
Distrib'ns, Cap Gain ($)	2.18	2.17	2.80	2.81	1.63	0.00	0.00	0.00	0.00	0.74
Net Asset Value ($)	14.90	19.29	13.36	13.45	13.30	13.08	10.71	11.92	9.72	9.32
Expense Ratio (%)	1.18	1.35	1.44	1.50	1.56	1.63	1.81	2.10	2.56	2.66
Yield (%)	0.00	0.00	0.18	0.49	1.20	1.37	1.21	0.67	0.41	2.28
Portfolio Turnover (%)	74	173	417	173	112	85	23	62	42	143
Total Assets (Millions $)	533	557	347	340	320	349	368	189	43	7

PORTFOLIO (as of 6/30/00)

Portfolio Manager: Steve Fossel - 2000

Investm't Category: Growth

✔ Domestic — Index
✔ Foreign — Sector
Asset Allocation — State Specific

Investment Style

Large Cap — ✔ Mid Cap — ✔ Small Cap
✔ Growth — Grth/Val — Value

Portfolio

3.0%	cash	0.0%	corp bonds
74.0%	stocks	0.0%	gov't bonds
6.0%	pref/conv't pref	0.0%	muni bonds
17.0%	conv't bds/wrnts	0.0%	other

SHAREHOLDER INFORMATION

Minimum Investment

Initial: $2,000 — Subsequent: $50

Minimum IRA Investment

Initial: $2,000 — Subsequent: $50

Maximum Fees

Load: none — 12b-1: 0.25%
Other: none

Services

✔ IRA
✔ Keogh
✔ Telephone Exchange

Berger New Generation/ Inv (BENGX)

800-333-1001, 303-329-0200
www.bergerfunds.com

Aggressive Growth

PERFORMANCE

fund inception date: 3/29/96

	3yr Annual	5yr Annual	10yr Annual	Bull	Bear
Return (%)	22.5	na	na	265.7	-49.0
Differ from Category (+/-)	6.3 abv av	na	na	146.5 high	-28.4 low

Standard Deviation	Category Risk Index	Beta
46.1%—high	1.42—high	1.55

	2000	1999	1998	1997	1996	1995	1994	1993	1992	1991
Return (%)	-38.6	144.2	23.0	24.2	—	—	—	—	—	—
Differ from Category (+/-)	-32.6	86.7	7.9	9.4	—	—	—	—	—	—
Return, Tax-Adjusted (%)	-41.6	138.5	22.2	24.2	—	—	—	—	—	—

PER SHARE DATA

	2000	1999	1998	1997	1996	1995	1994	1993	1992	1991
Dividends, Net Income ($)	0.00	0.00	0.00	0.00	—	—	—	—	—	—
Distrib'ns, Cap Gain ($)	5.22	4.55	0.50	0.00	—	—	—	—	—	—
Net Asset Value ($)	15.94	34.76	16.14	13.59	—	—	—	—	—	—
Expense Ratio (%)	1.30	1.54	1.72	1.87	—	—	—	—	—	—
Yield (%)	0.00	0.00	0.00	0.00	—	—	—	—	—	—
Portfolio Turnover (%)	149	168	243	184	—	—	—	—	—	—
Total Assets (Millions $)	463	620	147	130	—	—	—	—	—	—

PORTFOLIO (as of 6/30/00)

Portfolio Manager: Mark Sunderhuse - 1999

Investm't Category: Aggressive Growth

✔ Domestic	Index
✔ Foreign	Sector
Asset Allocation	State Specific

Investment Style

Large Cap	Mid Cap	✔ Small Cap
✔ Growth	Grth/Val	Value

Portfolio

0.0%	cash	0.0%	corp bonds
99.0%	stocks	0.0%	gov't bonds
1.0%	pref/conv't pref	0.0%	muni bonds
0.0%	conv't bds/wrnts	0.0%	other

SHAREHOLDER INFORMATION

Minimum Investment

Initial: $2,000 Subsequent: $50

Minimum IRA Investment

Initial: $2,000 Subsequent: $50

Maximum Fees

Load: none 12b-1: 0.25%

Other: none

Services

✔ IRA

✔ Keogh

✔ Telephone Exchange

Berger Select (BESLX)

800-333-1001, 303-329-0200
www.bergerfunds.com

Aggressive Growth

PERFORMANCE

fund inception date: 12/31/97

	3yr Annual	5yr Annual	10yr Annual	Bull	Bear
Return (%)	28.1	na	na	151.7	-41.9
Differ from Category (+/-)	11.9 abv av	na	na	32.5 abv av	-21.3 low

Standard Deviation	Category Risk Index	Beta
39.8%—high	1.23—abv av	1.24

	2000	1999	1998	1997	1996	1995	1994	1993	1992	1991
Return (%)	-32.6	81.6	72.2	—	—	—	—	—	—	—
Differ from Category (+/-)	-26.6	24.1	57.1	—	—	—	—	—	—	—
Return, Tax-Adjusted (%)	-36.7	76.0	70.3	—	—	—	—	—	—	—

PER SHARE DATA

	2000	1999	1998	1997	1996	1995	1994	1993	1992	1991
Dividends, Net Income ($)	0.00	0.02	0.06	—	—	—	—	—	—	—
Distrib'ns, Cap Gain ($)	5.22	4.44	0.83	—	—	—	—	—	—	—
Net Asset Value ($)	11.35	25.00	16.27	—	—	—	—	—	—	—
Expense Ratio (%)	1.23	1.29	1.48	—	—	—	—	—	—	—
Yield (%)	0.00	0.06	0.35	—	—	—	—	—	—	—
Portfolio Turnover (%)	123	696	—	—	—	—	—	—	—	—
Total Assets (Millions $)	63	161	96	—	—	—	—	—	—	—

PORTFOLIO (as of 6/30/00)

Portfolio Manager: committee - 1997

Investm't Category: Aggressive Growth

✔ Domestic
Foreign
Asset Allocation
Index
Sector
State Specific

Investment Style

Large Cap ✔ Mid Cap ✔ Small Cap
✔ Growth Grth/Val Value

Portfolio

1.0%	cash	0.0%	corp bonds
99.0%	stocks	0.0%	gov't bonds
0.0%	pref/conv't pref	0.0%	muni bonds
0.0%	conv't bds/wrnts	0.0%	other

SHAREHOLDER INFORMATION

Minimum Investment

Initial: $2,000 Subsequent: $50

Minimum IRA Investment

Initial: $2,000 Subsequent: $50

Maximum Fees

Load: none 12b-1: 0.25%
Other: none

Services

✔ IRA
✔ Keogh
✔ Telephone Exchange

Berger Small Cap Val/Inv (BSCVX)

800-333-1001, 303-329-0200
www.bergerfunds.com

Growth

this fund is closed to new investors

PERFORMANCE — fund inception date: 2/14/97

	3yr Annual	5yr Annual	10yr Annual	Bull	Bear
Return (%)	13.7	na	na	40.2	10.1
Differ from Category (+/-)	2.7 abv av	na	na	-9.5 av	15.5 high

Standard Deviation	Category Risk Index	Beta
19.5%—abv av	1.00—av	0.78

	2000	1999	1998	1997	1996	1995	1994	1993	1992	1991
Return (%)	26.8	14.3	1.4	—	—	—	—	—	—	—
Differ from Category (+/-)	23.3	-4.6	-12.9	—	—	—	—	—	—	—
Return, Tax-Adjusted (%)	24.7	13.6	0.4	—	—	—	—	—	—	—

PER SHARE DATA

	2000	1999	1998	1997	1996	1995	1994	1993	1992	1991
Dividends, Net Income ($)	0.31	0.20	0.06	—	—	—	—	—	—	—
Distrib'ns, Cap Gain ($)	1.60	0.23	0.80	—	—	—	—	—	—	—
Net Asset Value ($)	25.43	21.64	19.32	—	—	—	—	—	—	—
Expense Ratio (%)	1.19	1.37	1.56	—	—	—	—	—	—	—
Yield (%)	1.14	0.91	0.29	—	—	—	—	—	—	—
Portfolio Turnover (%)	72	66	69	—	—	—	—	—	—	—
Total Assets (Millions $)	887	458	168	—	—	—	—	—	—	—

PORTFOLIO (as of 6/30/00)

Portfolio Manager: Robert Perkins, Thomas Perkins - 1997

Investm't Category: Growth

✔ Domestic — Index
✔ Foreign — Sector
Asset Allocation — State Specific

Investment Style

Large Cap — ✔ Mid Cap — ✔ Small Cap
Growth — Grth/Val — ✔ Value

Portfolio

5.0%	cash	0.0%	corp bonds
91.0%	stocks	4.0%	gov't bonds
0.0%	pref/conv't pref	0.0%	muni bonds
0.0%	conv't bds/wrnts	0.0%	other

SHAREHOLDER INFORMATION

Minimum Investment
Initial: $2,000 — Subsequent: $50

Minimum IRA Investment
Initial: $2,000 — Subsequent: $50

Maximum Fees
Load: none — 12b-1: 0.25%
Other: none

Services
✔ IRA
✔ Keogh
✔ Telephone Exchange

Berger Small Co Grth/Inv (BESCX)

800-333-1001, 303-329-0200
www.bergerfunds.com

Aggressive Growth

PERFORMANCE

fund inception date: 12/30/93

	3yr Annual	5yr Annual	10yr Annual	Bull	Bear
Return (%)	24.5	21.2	na	172.3	-29.3
Differ from Category (+/-)	8.3 abv av	6.6 abv av	na	53.1 abv av	-8.7 blw av

Standard Deviation	Category Risk Index	Beta
42.5%—high	1.31—high	1.40

	2000	1999	1998	1997	1996	1995	1994	1993	1992	1991
Return (%)	-8.2	104.3	3.1	16.1	16.7	33.8	13.7	—	—	—
Differ from Category (+/-)	-2.2	46.8	-12.0	1.3	-1.6	-0.8	14.5	—	—	—
Return, Tax-Adjusted (%)	-11.4	97.5	0.0	13.8	15.3	33.8	13.7	—	—	—

PER SHARE DATA

	2000	1999	1998	1997	1996	1995	1994	1993	1992	1991
Dividends, Net Income ($)	0.00	0.00	0.00	0.00	0.00	0.00	0.00	—	—	—
Distrib'ns, Cap Gain ($)	1.04	1.27	0.69	0.48	0.19	0.00	0.00	—	—	—
Net Asset Value ($)	4.79	6.41	3.78	4.43	4.24	3.80	2.84	—	—	—
Expense Ratio (%)	1.27	1.60	1.48	1.66	1.68	1.89	2.05	—	—	—
Yield (%)	0.00	0.00	0.00	0.00	0.00	0.00	0.00	—	—	—
Portfolio Turnover (%)	92	128	97	111	91	109	—	—	—	—
Total Assets (Millions $)	1,063	1,162	670	784	781	570	291	—	—	—

PORTFOLIO (as of 6/30/00)

Portfolio Manager: Jay Tracey, Mark Sunderhuse - 1998

Investm't Category: Aggressive Growth

✔ Domestic | Index
✔ Foreign | Sector
Asset Allocation | State Specific

Investment Style

Large Cap | Mid Cap | ✔ Small Cap
✔ Growth | Grth/Val | Value

Portfolio

5.0%	cash	0.0%	corp bonds
92.0%	stocks	3.0%	gov't bonds
0.0%	pref/conv't pref	0.0%	muni bonds
0.0%	conv't bds/wrnts	0.0%	other

SHAREHOLDER INFORMATION

Minimum Investment
Initial: $2,000 Subsequent: $50

Minimum IRA Investment
Initial: $2,000 Subsequent: $50

Maximum Fees
Load: none 12b-1: 0.25%
Other: none

Services
✔ IRA
✔ Keogh
✔ Telephone Exchange

Boston Balanced (BMGFX)

617-726-7250

Balanced

PERFORMANCE — fund inception date: 12/1/95

	3yr Annual	5yr Annual	10yr Annual	Bull	Bear
Return (%)	7.7	12.2	na	22.0	-1.9
Differ from Category (+/-)	-0.7 blw av	0.8 av	na	-6.1 blw av	1.3 abv av

Standard Deviation	Category Risk Index	Beta
10.9%—blw av	0.99—av	0.58

	2000	1999	1998	1997	1996	1995	1994	1993	1992	1991
Return (%)	0.3	4.5	19.2	27.0	11.9	—	—	—	—	—
Differ from Category (+/-)	-1.7	-6.2	5.9	8.2	-2.0	—	—	—	—	—
Return, Tax-Adjusted (%)	-2.0	3.2	18.7	25.7	11.9	—	—	—	—	—

PER SHARE DATA

	2000	1999	1998	1997	1996	1995	1994	1993	1992	1991
Dividends, Net Income ($)	0.58	0.53	0.49	0.45	0.00	—	—	—	—	—
Distrib'ns, Cap Gain ($)	2.22	0.76	1.09	0.44	0.00	—	—	—	—	—
Net Asset Value ($)	26.15	28.87	28.86	25.75	20.83	—	—	—	—	—
Expense Ratio (%)	1.09	0.95	1.00	1.00	1.00	—	—	—	—	—
Yield (%)	2.04	1.78	1.63	1.71	0.00	—	—	—	—	—
Portfolio Turnover (%)	28	24	22	30	17	—	—	—	—	—
Total Assets (Millions $)	121	141	138	93	66	—	—	—	—	—

PORTFOLIO (as of 6/30/00)

Portfolio Manager: Domenic Colasacco - 1995

Investm't Category: Balanced

✔ Domestic	Index
✔ Foreign	Sector
✔ Asset Allocation	State Specific

Investment Style

Large Cap	Mid Cap	Small Cap
Growth	Grth/Val	Value

Portfolio

3.5%	cash	8.8%	corp bonds
69.1%	stocks	18.6%	gov't bonds
0.0%	pref/conv't pref	0.0%	muni bonds
0.0%	conv't bds/wrnts	0.0%	other

SHAREHOLDER INFORMATION

Minimum Investment

Initial: $2,000 — Subsequent: $500

Minimum IRA Investment

Initial: $2,000 — Subsequent: $500

Maximum Fees

Load: none — 12b-1: none

Other: none

Services

✔ IRA

Keogh

Telephone Exchange

Bramwell Growth (BRGRX)

800-272-6227, 212-308-0505
www.bramwell.com

Growth

PERFORMANCE

fund inception date: 8/1/94

	3yr Annual	5yr Annual	10yr Annual	Bull	Bear
Return (%)	18.1	19.9	na	65.2	-9.3
Differ from Category (+/-)	7.1 high	3.8 high	na	15.5 abv av	-3.9 av

Standard Deviation	Category Risk Index	Beta
19.9%—abv av	1.03—av	1.04

	2000	1999	1998	1997	1996	1995	1994	1993	1992	1991
Return (%)	-2.4	25.6	34.4	33.6	12.8	32.5	—	—	—	—
Differ from Category (+/-)	-5.9	6.7	20.1	6.5	-9.5	2.1	—	—	—	—
Return, Tax-Adjusted (%)	-3.9	24.5	33.0	32.0	12.2	32.4	—	—	—	—

PER SHARE DATA

	2000	1999	1998	1997	1996	1995	1994	1993	1992	1991
Dividends, Net Income ($)	0.00	0.00	0.00	0.00	0.00	0.00	—	—	—	—
Distrib'ns, Cap Gain ($)	2.22	1.23	1.25	1.17	0.27	0.03	—	—	—	—
Net Asset Value ($)	26.08	28.92	24.12	18.93	15.02	13.55	—	—	—	—
Expense Ratio (%)	1.54	1.58	1.66	1.75	1.75	1.75	—	—	—	—
Yield (%)	0.00	0.00	0.00	0.00	0.00	0.00	—	—	—	—
Portfolio Turnover (%)	25	38	49	82	118	80	—	—	—	—
Total Assets (Millions $)	246	276	248	149	128	137	—	—	—	—

PORTFOLIO (as of 6/30/00)

Portfolio Manager: Elizabeth Bramwell - 1994

Investm't Category: Growth

✔ Domestic — Index
✔ Foreign — Sector
Asset Allocation — State Specific

Investment Style

✔ Large Cap — Mid Cap — Small Cap
✔ Growth — Grth/Val — Value

Portfolio

8.8%	cash	0.0%	corp bonds
91.2%	stocks	0.0%	gov't bonds
0.0%	pref/conv't pref	0.0%	muni bonds
0.0%	conv't bds/wrnts	0.0%	other

SHAREHOLDER INFORMATION

Minimum Investment
Initial: $1,000 — Subsequent: $100

Minimum IRA Investment
Initial: $500 — Subsequent: $100

Maximum Fees
Load: none — 12b-1: 0.25%
Other: none

Services
✔ IRA
Keogh
✔ Telephone Exchange

Brandywine (BRWIX)

800-656-3017, 302-656-6200
www.brandywine.com

Growth

PERFORMANCE — fund inception date: 12/30/85

	3yr Annual	5yr Annual	10yr Annual	Bull	Bear
Return (%)	17.7	17.9	20.7	96.9	-13.3
Differ from Category (+/-)	6.7 high	1.8 av	3.9 high	47.2 high	-7.9 blw av

Standard Deviation	Category Risk Index	Beta
24.7%—abv av	1.27—high	1.04

	2000	1999	1998	1997	1996	1995	1994	1993	1992	1991
Return (%)	7.0	53.4	-0.6	12.0	24.9	35.7	0.0	22.5	15.6	49.1
Differ from Category (+/-)	3.5	34.5	-14.9	-15.1	2.6	5.3	0.2	7.9	3.0	11.5
Return, Tax-Adjusted (%)	-0.5	51.3	-0.9	7.8	23.5	31.1	-1.6	18.9	14.8	44.9

PER SHARE DATA

	2000	1999	1998	1997	1996	1995	1994	1993	1992	1991
Dividends, Net Income ($)	0.00	0.00	0.26	0.00	0.00	0.00	0.00	0.00	0.01	0.12
Distrib'ns, Cap Gain ($)	16.10	3.12	0.07	7.02	1.34	3.84	1.45	2.87	0.54	2.11
Net Asset Value ($)	29.39	42.88	30.28	30.89	33.69	28.08	23.50	24.97	22.74	20.17
Expense Ratio (%)	1.04	1.05	1.04	1.04	1.06	1.07	1.10	1.10	1.10	1.09
Yield (%)	0.00	0.00	0.85	0.00	0.00	0.00	0.00	0.00	0.04	0.53
Portfolio Turnover (%)	244	208	263	192	202	193	190	150	189	188
Total Assets (Millions $)	5,559	5,514	4,890	8,414	6,546	4,210	2,299	1,527	839	623

PORTFOLIO (as of 6/30/00)

Portfolio Manager: committee - 1985

Investm't Category: Growth

- ✔ Domestic
- ✔ Foreign
- Asset Allocation
- Index
- Sector
- State Specific

Investment Style

- Large Cap
- ✔ Mid Cap
- ✔ Small Cap
- ✔ Growth
- Grth/Val
- Value

Portfolio

5.3%	cash	0.0%	corp bonds
94.7%	stocks	0.0%	gov't bonds
0.0%	pref/conv't pref	0.0%	muni bonds
0.0%	conv't bds/wrnts	0.0%	other

SHAREHOLDER INFORMATION

Minimum Investment
Initial: $25,000 Subsequent: $1,000

Minimum IRA Investment
Initial: na Subsequent: na

Maximum Fees
Load: none 12b-1: none
Other: none

Services

- IRA
- Keogh
- ✔ Telephone Exchange

Brandywine Blue (BLUEX)

800-656-3017, 302-656-6200
www.brandywine.com

Growth

PERFORMANCE

fund inception date: 1/10/91

	3yr Annual	5yr Annual	10yr Annual	Bull	Bear
Return (%)	16.4	18.3	na	91.7	-12.6
Differ from Category (+/-)	5.4 high	2.2 abv av	na	42.0 high	-7.2 blw av

Standard Deviation	Category Risk Index	Beta
24.4%—abv av	1.26—high	1.05

	2000	1999	1998	1997	1996	1995	1994	1993	1992	1991
Return (%)	6.8	49.3	-0.9	19.2	23.2	32.3	2.3	27.2	13.1	—
Differ from Category (+/-)	3.3	30.4	-15.2	-7.9	0.9	1.9	2.5	12.6	0.5	—
Return, Tax-Adjusted (%)	0.8	47.6	-1.2	15.3	23.2	30.4	2.1	22.8	13.1	—

PER SHARE DATA

	2000	1999	1998	1997	1996	1995	1994	1993	1992	1991
Dividends, Net Income ($)	0.00	0.00	0.20	0.00	0.00	0.00	0.00	0.00	0.00	—
Distrib'ns, Cap Gain ($)	10.70	2.17	0.13	5.08	0.00	1.10	0.10	2.33	0.00	—
Net Asset Value ($)	27.57	36.24	25.91	26.58	26.47	21.48	17.05	16.77	15.08	—
Expense Ratio (%)	1.07	1.08	1.06	1.08	1.13	1.31	1.80	2.00	2.00	—
Yield (%)	0.00	0.00	0.76	0.00	0.00	0.00	0.00	0.00	0.00	—
Portfolio Turnover (%)	245	228	299	202	196	174	220	144	191	—
Total Assets (Millions $)	392	398	356	589	383	190	32	8	4	—

PORTFOLIO (as of 6/30/00)

Portfolio Manager: committee - 1991

Investm't Category: Growth

✔ Domestic
Foreign
Asset Allocation
Index
Sector
State Specific

Investment Style

Large Cap
✔ Mid Cap
✔ Small Cap
✔ Growth
Grth/Val
Value

Portfolio

4.2%	cash	0.0%	corp bonds
95.9%	stocks	0.0%	gov't bonds
0.0%	pref/conv't pref	0.0%	muni bonds
0.0%	conv't bds/wrnts	0.0%	other

SHAREHOLDER INFORMATION

Minimum Investment

Initial: $100,000 Subsequent: $1,000

Minimum IRA Investment

Initial: $1 Subsequent: $1

Maximum Fees

Load: none 12b-1: none
Other: none

Services

✔ IRA
✔ Keogh
✔ Telephone Exchange

Brazos Micro Cap Grth/Y (BJMIX)

800-426-9157
www.brazosfund.com

Aggressive Growth

PERFORMANCE — fund inception date: 12/30/97

	3yr Annual	5yr Annual	10yr Annual	Bull	Bear
Return (%)	41.8	na	na	128.2	-1.2
Differ from Category (+/-)	25.6 high	na	na	9.0 abv av	19.4 high

Standard Deviation	Category Risk Index	Beta
32.6%—high	1.00—av	1.09

	2000	1999	1998	1997	1996	1995	1994	1993	1992	1991
Return (%)	18.8	80.8	32.8	—	—	—	—	—	—	—
Differ from Category (+/-)	24.8	23.3	17.7	—	—	—	—	—	—	—
Return, Tax-Adjusted (%)	12.7	76.7	32.8	—	—	—	—	—	—	—

PER SHARE DATA

	2000	1999	1998	1997	1996	1995	1994	1993	1992	1991
Dividends, Net Income ($)	0.00	0.00	0.00	—	—	—	—	—	—	—
Distrib'ns, Cap Gain ($)	6.26	2.70	0.00	—	—	—	—	—	—	—
Net Asset Value ($)	18.74	20.86	13.28	—	—	—	—	—	—	—
Expense Ratio (%)	na	1.54	1.60	—	—	—	—	—	—	—
Yield (%)	0.00	0.00	0.00	—	—	—	—	—	—	—
Portfolio Turnover (%)	na	150	—	—	—	—	—	—	—	—
Total Assets (Millions $)	181	148	58	—	—	—	—	—	—	—

PORTFOLIO (as of 6/30/00)

Portfolio Manager: committee - 1997

Investm't Category: Aggressive Growth

✔ Domestic	Index
✔ Foreign	Sector
Asset Allocation	State Specific

Investment Style

Large Cap	Mid Cap	✔ Small Cap
✔ Growth	Grth/Val	Value

Portfolio

18.2%	cash	0.0%	corp bonds
81.8%	stocks	0.0%	gov't bonds
0.0%	pref/conv't pref	0.0%	muni bonds
0.0%	conv't bds/wrnts	0.0%	other

SHAREHOLDER INFORMATION

Minimum Investment
Initial: $50,000 — Subsequent: $1,000

Minimum IRA Investment
Initial: $500 — Subsequent: $100

Maximum Fees
Load: none — 12b-1: none
Other: none

Services
✔ IRA
✔ Keogh
✔ Telephone Exchange

Brazos Real Estate/Y

800-426-9157
www.brazosfund.com

(BJRSX)

Growth & Income

PERFORMANCE

fund inception date: 12/30/96

	3yr Annual	5yr Annual	10yr Annual	Bull	Bear
Return (%)	-0.2	na	na	-0.6	15.3
Differ from Category (+/-)	-9.1 low	na	na	-34.1 low	15.4 high

Standard Deviation	Category Risk Index	Beta
15.3%—av	0.88—blw av	0.22

	2000	1999	1998	1997	1996	1995	1994	1993	1992	1991
Return (%)	25.8	-4.6	-17.3	29.1	—	—	—	—	—	—
Differ from Category (+/-)	20.1	-15.4	-30.1	2.2	—	—	—	—	—	—
Return, Tax-Adjusted (%)	23.5	-6.3	-18.7	25.5	—	—	—	—	—	—

PER SHARE DATA

	2000	1999	1998	1997	1996	1995	1994	1993	1992	1991
Dividends, Net Income ($)	0.46	0.41	0.42	0.36	—	—	—	—	—	—
Distrib'ns, Cap Gain ($)	0.00	0.00	0.00	1.07	—	—	—	—	—	—
Net Asset Value ($)	9.84	8.21	9.03	11.40	—	—	—	—	—	—
Expense Ratio (%)	na	1.19	1.25	1.25	—	—	—	—	—	—
Yield (%)	4.67	4.99	4.65	2.88	—	—	—	—	—	—
Portfolio Turnover (%)	na	100	157	184	—	—	—	—	—	—
Total Assets (Millions $)	196	148	94	59	—	—	—	—	—	—

PORTFOLIO (as of 6/30/00)

Portfolio Manager: committee - 1997

Investm't Category: Growth & Income

✔ Domestic　　Index
✔ Foreign　　✔ Sector
Asset Allocation　　State Specific

Investment Style

Large Cap　　✔ Mid Cap　　✔ Small Cap
Growth　　Grth/Val　　✔ Value

Portfolio

5.5%	cash	0.0%	corp bonds
94.5%	stocks	0.0%	gov't bonds
0.0%	pref/conv't pref	0.0%	muni bonds
0.0%	conv't bds/wrnts	0.0%	other

SHAREHOLDER INFORMATION

Minimum Investment

Initial: $1,000,000　　Subsequent: $1,000

Minimum IRA Investment

Initial: $1,000　　Subsequent: $100

Maximum Fees

Load: 1.00% redemption　　12b-1: none
Other: redemption fee applies for 3 months

Services

✔ IRA
✔ Keogh
✔ Telephone Exchange

Brazos Small Cap Grth/Y

800-426-9157
www.brazosfund.com

(BJSCX)

Aggressive Growth

PERFORMANCE — fund inception date: 12/30/96

	3yr Annual	5yr Annual	10yr Annual	Bull	Bear
Return (%)	17.8	na	na	77.5	-9.2
Differ from Category (+/-)	1.6 av	na	na	-41.7 blw av	11.4 abv av

Standard Deviation	Category Risk Index	Beta
26.8%—high	0.83—blw av	0.99

	2000	1999	1998	1997	1996	1995	1994	1993	1992	1991
Return (%)	5.1	37.0	13.5	54.5	—	—	—	—	—	—
Differ from Category (+/-)	11.1	-20.5	-1.6	39.7	—	—	—	—	—	—
Return, Tax-Adjusted (%)	2.8	36.7	13.5	51.9	—	—	—	—	—	—

PER SHARE DATA

	2000	1999	1998	1997	1996	1995	1994	1993	1992	1991
Dividends, Net Income ($)	0.00	0.00	0.00	0.00	—	—	—	—	—	—
Distrib'ns, Cap Gain ($)	2.40	0.16	0.00	1.26	—	—	—	—	—	—
Net Asset Value ($)	20.50	21.73	15.98	14.07	—	—	—	—	—	—
Expense Ratio (%)	na	1.08	1.21	1.35	—	—	—	—	—	—
Yield (%)	0.00	0.00	0.00	0.00	—	—	—	—	—	—
Portfolio Turnover (%)	na	105	104	147	—	—	—	—	—	—
Total Assets (Millions $)	937	745	382	92	—	—	—	—	—	—

PORTFOLIO (as of 6/30/00)

Portfolio Manager: committee - 1996

Investm't Category: Aggressive Growth

✔ Domestic — Index
✔ Foreign — Sector
Asset Allocation — State Specific

Investment Style

Large Cap — Mid Cap — ✔ Small Cap
✔ Growth — Grth/Val — Value

Portfolio

10.6%	cash	0.0%	corp bonds
89.4%	stocks	0.0%	gov't bonds
0.0%	pref/conv't pref	0.0%	muni bonds
0.0%	conv't bds/wrnts	0.0%	other

SHAREHOLDER INFORMATION

Minimum Investment
Initial: $1,000,000 — Subsequent: $1,000

Minimum IRA Investment
Initial: $1,000 — Subsequent: $100

Maximum Fees
Load: none — 12b-1: none
Other: none

Services
✔ IRA
✔ Keogh
✔ Telephone Exchange

Bremer Inv: Growth Stock (BSTKX)

800-595-5552
www.bremer.com

Growth

PERFORMANCE — fund inception date: 1/27/97

	3yr Annual	5yr Annual	10yr Annual	Bull	Bear
Return (%)	13.3	na	na	71.2	-15.8
Differ from Category (+/-)	2.3 abv av	na	na	21.5 abv av	-10.4 blw av

Standard Deviation	Category Risk Index	Beta
20.5%—abv av	1.05—av	1.11

	2000	1999	1998	1997	1996	1995	1994	1993	1992	1991
Return (%)	-10.5	25.3	29.9	—	—	—	—	—	—	—
Differ from Category (+/-)	-14.0	6.4	15.6	—	—	—	—	—	—	—
Return, Tax-Adjusted (%)	-10.6	24.5	29.7	—	—	—	—	—	—	—

PER SHARE DATA

	2000	1999	1998	1997	1996	1995	1994	1993	1992	1991
Dividends, Net Income ($)	0.00	0.01	0.03	—	—	—	—	—	—	—
Distrib'ns, Cap Gain ($)	0.17	0.56	0.06	—	—	—	—	—	—	—
Net Asset Value ($)	16.66	18.82	15.47	—	—	—	—	—	—	—
Expense Ratio (%)	0.90	0.89	0.91	—	—	—	—	—	—	—
Yield (%)	0.00	0.05	0.19	—	—	—	—	—	—	—
Portfolio Turnover (%)	10	16	13	—	—	—	—	—	—	—
Total Assets (Millions $)	89	91	68	—	—	—	—	—	—	—

PORTFOLIO (as of 6/30/00)

Portfolio Manager: David Erickson - 1997

Investm't Category: Growth

✔ Domestic — Index
✔ Foreign — Sector
Asset Allocation — State Specific

Investment Style

✔ Large Cap — Mid Cap — Small Cap
✔ Growth — Grth/Val — Value

Portfolio

3.3%	cash	0.0%	corp bonds
96.7%	stocks	0.0%	gov't bonds
0.0%	pref/conv't pref	0.0%	muni bonds
0.0%	conv't bds/wrnts	0.0%	other

SHAREHOLDER INFORMATION

Minimum Investment
Initial: $2,000 — Subsequent: $100

Minimum IRA Investment
Initial: $500 — Subsequent: $100

Maximum Fees
Load: none — 12b-1: 0.01%
Other: none

Services
✔ IRA
✔ Keogh
✔ Telephone Exchange

CA Inv: S&P 500 Index

800-225-8778, 415-398-2727
www.caltrust.com

(SPFIX)

Growth & Income

PERFORMANCE — fund inception date: 4/20/92

	3yr Annual	5yr Annual	10yr Annual	Bull	Bear
Return (%)	12.3	18.2	na	56.3	-11.3
Differ from Category (+/-)	3.4 high	3.9 high	na	22.8 high	-11.2 blw av

Standard Deviation	Category Risk Index	Beta
17.5%—av	1.01—av	0.99

	2000	1999	1998	1997	1996	1995	1994	1993	1992	1991
Return (%)	-8.9	21.0	28.7	32.9	22.6	37.1	1.0	9.7	—	—
Differ from Category (+/-)	-14.6	10.2	15.9	6.0	2.9	7.6	1.5	-4.1	—	—
Return, Tax-Adjusted (%)	-9.6	19.3	27.4	31.6	21.0	34.3	-0.2	8.2	—	—

PER SHARE DATA

	2000	1999	1998	1997	1996	1995	1994	1993	1992	1991
Dividends, Net Income ($)	0.34	0.40	0.39	0.33	0.36	0.39	0.32	0.29	—	—
Distrib'ns, Cap Gain ($)	0.41	1.32	0.57	0.38	0.28	0.53	0.03	0.13	—	—
Net Asset Value ($)	26.42	29.81	26.16	21.13	16.46	13.97	10.90	11.15	—	—
Expense Ratio (%)	0.20	0.20	0.20	0.20	0.20	0.20	0.20	0.09	—	—
Yield (%)	1.26	1.28	1.45	1.53	2.15	2.68	2.92	2.57	—	—
Portfolio Turnover (%)	9	9	1	2	1	3	1	8	—	—
Total Assets (Millions $)	146	163	125	79	52	26	14	13	—	—

PORTFOLIO (as of 6/30/00)

Portfolio Manager: Roderick Baldwin - 1992

Investm't Category: Growth & Income

✔ Domestic ✔ Index
Foreign Sector
Asset Allocation State Specific

Investment Style

✔ Large Cap Mid Cap Small Cap
Growth ✔ Grth/Val Value

Portfolio

3.3%	cash	0.0%	corp bonds
96.7%	stocks	0.0%	gov't bonds
0.0%	pref/conv't pref	0.0%	muni bonds
0.0%	conv't bds/wrnts	0.0%	other

SHAREHOLDER INFORMATION

Minimum Investment
Initial: $5,000 Subsequent: $250

Minimum IRA Investment
Initial: $1 Subsequent: $1

Maximum Fees
Load: none 12b-1: none
Other: none

Services
✔ IRA
✔ Keogh
✔ Telephone Exchange

CA Inv: S&P Mid Cap Index (SPMIX)

800-225-8778, 415-398-2727
www.caltrust.com

Growth

PERFORMANCE — fund inception date: 4/20/92

	3yr Annual	5yr Annual	10yr Annual	Bull	Bear
Return (%)	17.5	20.5	na	59.8	-2.7
Differ from Category (+/-)	6.5 high	4.4 high	na	10.1 abv av	2.7 abv av

Standard Deviation	Category Risk Index	Beta
21.6%—abv av	1.11—abv av	1.03

	2000	1999	1998	1997	1996	1995	1994	1993	1992	1991
Return (%)	19.4	14.7	18.4	31.8	18.8	30.5	-3.9	12.8	—	—
Differ from Category (+/-)	15.9	-4.2	4.1	4.7	-3.5	0.1	-3.7	-1.8	—	—
Return, Tax-Adjusted (%)	15.4	9.9	15.1	29.3	16.6	27.8	-5.6	11.4	—	—

PER SHARE DATA

	2000	1999	1998	1997	1996	1995	1994	1993	1992	1991
Dividends, Net Income ($)	0.20	0.18	0.21	0.23	0.22	0.26	0.23	0.23	—	—
Distrib'ns, Cap Gain ($)	2.89	4.01	2.50	1.39	0.73	0.68	0.44	0.24	—	—
Net Asset Value ($)	16.77	16.83	18.55	18.22	15.11	13.53	11.10	12.27	—	—
Expense Ratio (%)	0.40	0.40	0.40	0.40	0.40	0.40	0.40	0.17	—	—
Yield (%)	1.01	0.86	0.99	1.17	1.38	1.82	1.99	1.83	—	—
Portfolio Turnover (%)	46	42	19	18	18	12	15	8	—	—
Total Assets (Millions $)	57	62	56	49	37	27	20	19	—	—

PORTFOLIO (as of 6/30/00)

Portfolio Manager: Roderick Baldwin - 1992

Investm't Category: Growth

✔ Domestic
Foreign
Asset Allocation
✔ Index
Sector
State Specific

Investment Style

Large Cap
✔ Mid Cap
Small Cap
Growth
✔ Grth/Val
Value

Portfolio

8.2%	cash	0.0%	corp bonds
91.8%	stocks	0.0%	gov't bonds
0.0%	pref/conv't pref	0.0%	muni bonds
0.0%	conv't bds/wrnts	0.0%	other

SHAREHOLDER INFORMATION

Minimum Investment

Initial: $5,000 Subsequent: $250

Minimum IRA Investment

Initial: $1 Subsequent: $1

Maximum Fees

Load: none 12b-1: none
Other: none

Services

✔ IRA
✔ Keogh
✔ Telephone Exchange

CGM Capital Development (LOMCX)

800-345-4048, 213-661-3500
cgmfunds.com

Aggressive Growth

this fund is closed to new investors

PERFORMANCE — fund inception date: 6/22/61

	3yr Annual	5yr Annual	10yr Annual	Bull	Bear
Return (%)	4.0	12.3	19.3	47.4	-14.2
Differ from Category (+/-)	-12.2 low	-2.3 blw av	3.5 abv av	-71.8 low	6.4 abv av

Standard Deviation	Category Risk Index	Beta
23.7%—abv av	0.73—low	1.10

	2000	1999	1998	1997	1996	1995	1994	1993	1992	1991
Return (%)	-3.7	7.7	8.4	23.9	28.1	41.0	-22.9	28.6	17.4	99.2
Differ from Category (+/-)	2.3	-49.8	-6.7	9.1	9.8	6.4	-22.1	3.4	10.5	52.0
Return, Tax-Adjusted (%)	-3.8	7.0	5.1	17.6	21.9	38.6	-23.7	20.8	14.2	82.3

PER SHARE DATA

	2000	1999	1998	1997	1996	1995	1994	1993	1992	1991
Dividends, Net Income ($)	0.10	0.11	0.11	0.00	0.07	0.01	0.06	0.06	0.20	0.06
Distrib'ns, Cap Gain ($)	0.00	0.56	4.18	9.07	5.86	1.68	0.71	7.51	2.67	11.07
Net Asset Value ($)	25.12	26.20	24.95	26.96	29.08	27.33	20.58	27.71	27.43	25.80
Expense Ratio (%)	na	1.08	1.07	1.07	0.82	0.85	0.84	0.85	0.86	0.88
Yield (%)	0.39	0.41	0.37	0.00	0.20	0.03	0.28	0.17	0.66	0.16
Portfolio Turnover (%)	na	335	335	230	178	302	146	143	163	272
Total Assets (Millions $)	494	632	703	722	631	521	401	523	394	325

PORTFOLIO (as of 6/30/00)

Portfolio Manager: G. Kenneth Heebner - 1976

Investm't Category: Aggressive Growth

✔ Domestic
Foreign
Asset Allocation
Index
Sector
State Specific

Investment Style

Large Cap ✔ Mid Cap ✔ Small Cap
✔ Growth Grth/Val Value

Portfolio

0.5%	cash	0.0%	corp bonds
99.5%	stocks	0.0%	gov't bonds
0.0%	pref/conv't pref	0.0%	muni bonds
0.0%	conv't bds/wrnts	0.0%	other

SHAREHOLDER INFORMATION

Minimum Investment
Initial: $2,500 Subsequent: $50

Minimum IRA Investment
Initial: $1,000 Subsequent: $50

Maximum Fees
Load: none 12b-1: none
Other: none

Services
✔ IRA
✔ Keogh
✔ Telephone Exchange

CGM Focus (CGMFX)

800-345-4048, 213-661-3500
cgmfunds.com

Aggressive Growth

PERFORMANCE — fund inception date: 9/3/97

	3yr Annual	5yr Annual	10yr Annual	Bull	Bear
Return (%)	20.0	na	na	36.2	43.8
Differ from Category (+/-)	3.8 av	na	na	-83.0 low	64.4 high

Standard Deviation	Category Risk Index	Beta
30.3%—high	0.93—blw av	0.60

	2000	1999	1998	1997	1996	1995	1994	1993	1992	1991
Return (%)	53.9	8.4	3.5	—	—	—	—	—	—	—
Differ from Category (+/-)	59.9	-49.1	-11.6	—	—	—	—	—	—	—
Return, Tax-Adjusted (%)	52.5	8.2	3.5	—	—	—	—	—	—	—

PER SHARE DATA

	2000	1999	1998	1997	1996	1995	1994	1993	1992	1991
Dividends, Net Income ($)	0.36	0.03	0.00	—	—	—	—	—	—	—
Distrib'ns, Cap Gain ($)	0.00	0.00	0.00	—	—	—	—	—	—	—
Net Asset Value ($)	15.80	10.50	9.71	—	—	—	—	—	—	—
Expense Ratio (%)	na	1.21	1.20	—	—	—	—	—	—	—
Yield (%)	2.27	0.28	0.00	—	—	—	—	—	—	—
Portfolio Turnover (%)	na	288	340	—	—	—	—	—	—	—
Total Assets (Millions $)	68	68	110	—	—	—	—	—	—	—

PORTFOLIO (as of 6/30/00)

Portfolio Manager: G. Kenneth Heebner - 1997

Investm't Category: Aggressive Growth

✔ Domestic — Index
✔ Foreign — Sector
Asset Allocation — State Specific

Investment Style

Large Cap — Mid Cap — Small Cap
Growth — Grth/Val — Value

Portfolio

12.8%	cash	0.0%	corp bonds
87.2%	stocks	0.0%	gov't bonds
0.0%	pref/conv't pref	0.0%	muni bonds
0.0%	conv't bds/wrnts	0.0%	other

SHAREHOLDER INFORMATION

Minimum Investment
Initial: $2,500 — Subsequent: $50

Minimum IRA Investment
Initial: $1,000 — Subsequent: $50

Maximum Fees
Load: none — 12b-1: none
Other: none

Services
✔ IRA
✔ Keogh
✔ Telephone Exchange

CGM Mutual (LOMMX)

800-345-4048, 213-661-3500
cgmfunds.com

Balanced

PERFORMANCE — fund inception date: 11/5/29

	3yr Annual	5yr Annual	10yr Annual	Bull	Bear
Return (%)	4.8	9.0	12.1	52.8	-14.0
Differ from Category (+/-)	-3.6 low	-2.4 low	0.4 av	24.7 high	-10.8 low

Standard Deviation	Category Risk Index	Beta
17.9%—av	1.63—high	0.87

	2000	1999	1998	1997	1996	1995	1994	1993	1992	1991
Return (%)	-11.6	20.5	8.2	8.1	23.6	24.3	-9.7	21.8	6.0	40.8
Differ from Category (+/-)	-13.6	9.8	-5.1	-10.7	9.7	-1.2	-8.4	7.4	-2.4	17.0
Return, Tax-Adjusted (%)	-12.6	16.5	6.4	2.2	18.6	22.0	-11.1	18.4	3.4	35.9

PER SHARE DATA

	2000	1999	1998	1997	1996	1995	1994	1993	1992	1991
Dividends, Net Income ($)	0.73	0.84	0.98	0.70	0.74	0.77	1.04	0.85	0.93	0.97
Distrib'ns, Cap Gain ($)	0.00	3.54	0.25	7.78	4.15	0.89	0.00	1.93	1.42	2.64
Net Asset Value ($)	23.38	27.28	26.36	25.52	31.42	29.43	25.05	28.88	26.02	26.80
Expense Ratio (%)	na	1.02	1.02	0.98	0.87	0.93	0.92	0.93	0.93	0.93
Yield (%)	3.12	2.72	3.68	2.10	2.08	2.53	4.15	2.75	3.38	3.29
Portfolio Turnover (%)	na	200	280	386	192	231	173	97	121	201
Total Assets (Millions $)	639	908	940	1,192	1,217	1,154	1,063	947	548	401

PORTFOLIO (as of 6/30/00)

Portfolio Manager: G. Kenneth Heebner - 1981

Investm't Category: Balanced

✔ Domestic	Index
Foreign	Sector
✔ Asset Allocation	State Specific

Investment Style

Large Cap	Mid Cap	Small Cap
Growth	Grth/Val	Value

Portfolio

0.7%	cash	11.5%	corp bonds
70.9%	stocks	14.1%	gov't bonds
0.0%	pref/conv't pref	0.0%	muni bonds
2.8%	conv't bds/wrnts	0.0%	other

SHAREHOLDER INFORMATION

Minimum Investment

Initial: $2,500 — Subsequent: $50

Minimum IRA Investment

Initial: $1,000 — Subsequent: $50

Maximum Fees

Load: none — 12b-1: none

Other: none

Services

✔ IRA
✔ Keogh
✔ Telephone Exchange

CGM Realty (CGMRX)

800-345-4048, 213-661-3500
cgmfunds.com

Growth & Income

PERFORMANCE — fund inception date: 5/13/94

	3yr Annual	5yr Annual	10yr Annual	Bull	Bear
Return (%)	1.4	13.7	na	7.2	19.8
Differ from Category (+/-)	-7.5 low	-0.6 av	na	-26.3 low	19.9 high

Standard Deviation	Category Risk Index	Beta
15.7%—av	0.91—blw av	0.25

	2000	1999	1998	1997	1996	1995	1994	1993	1992	1991
Return (%)	29.1	2.6	-21.1	26.7	44.0	19.7	—	—	—	—
Differ from Category (+/-)	23.4	-8.2	-33.9	-0.2	24.3	-9.8	—	—	—	—
Return, Tax-Adjusted (%)	26.4	-0.1	-22.9	21.9	40.5	16.9	—	—	—	—

PER SHARE DATA

	2000	1999	1998	1997	1996	1995	1994	1993	1992	1991
Dividends, Net Income ($)	0.73	0.81	0.74	0.73	0.67	0.68	—	—	—	—
Distrib'ns, Cap Gain ($)	0.00	0.00	0.00	1.97	0.38	0.00	—	—	—	—
Net Asset Value ($)	13.53	11.08	11.59	15.60	14.50	10.89	—	—	—	—
Expense Ratio (%)	na	1.06	1.04	1.00	1.00	1.00	—	—	—	—
Yield (%)	5.39	7.31	6.38	4.15	4.50	6.24	—	—	—	—
Portfolio Turnover (%)	na	49	86	128	57	85	—	—	—	—
Total Assets (Millions $)	470	371	418	489	161	47	—	—	—	—

PORTFOLIO (as of 6/30/00)

Portfolio Manager: G. Kenneth Heebner - 1994

Investm't Category: Growth & Income

✔ Domestic	Index
Foreign	✔ Sector
Asset Allocation	State Specific

Investment Style

Large Cap	✔ Mid Cap	✔ Small Cap
Growth	Grth/Val	✔ Value

Portfolio

1.2% cash	0.0% corp bonds
98.8% stocks	0.0% gov't bonds
0.0% pref/conv't pref	0.0% muni bonds
0.0% conv't bds/wrnts	0.0% other

SHAREHOLDER INFORMATION

Minimum Investment
Initial: $2,500 Subsequent: $50

Minimum IRA Investment
Initial: $1,000 Subsequent: $50

Maximum Fees
Load: none 12b-1: none
Other: none

Services
✔ IRA
✔ Keogh
✔ Telephone Exchange

CRM Small Cap Value/Inv (CRMSX)

800-276-2883, 212-415-0400
www.crmfunds.com

Growth

PERFORMANCE — fund inception date: 10/2/95

	3yr Annual	5yr Annual	10yr Annual	Bull	Bear
Return (%)	4.7	14.2	na	23.2	9.4
Differ from Category (+/-)	-6.3 low	-1.9 blw av	na	-26.5 blw av	14.8 high

Standard Deviation	Category Risk Index	Beta
20.9%—abv av	1.08—abv av	0.74

	2000	1999	1998	1997	1996	1995	1994	1993	1992	1991
Return (%)	18.0	10.9	-12.2	21.7	38.9	—	—	—	—	—
Differ from Category (+/-)	14.5	-8.0	-26.5	-5.4	16.6	—	—	—	—	—
Return, Tax-Adjusted (%)	16.9	10.9	-12.2	20.4	36.6	—	—	—	—	—

PER SHARE DATA

	2000	1999	1998	1997	1996	1995	1994	1993	1992	1991
Dividends, Net Income ($)	0.02	0.00	0.00	0.00	0.00	—	—	—	—	—
Distrib'ns, Cap Gain ($)	0.81	0.00	0.00	0.85	0.86	—	—	—	—	—
Net Asset Value ($)	17.71	15.76	14.20	16.18	14.02	—	—	—	—	—
Expense Ratio (%)	1.42	1.42	1.38	1.50	1.49	—	—	—	—	—
Yield (%)	0.10	0.00	0.00	0.00	0.00	—	—	—	—	—
Portfolio Turnover (%)	96	64	57	98	111	—	—	—	—	—
Total Assets (Millions $)	77	80	118	163	57	—	—	—	—	—

PORTFOLIO (as of 6/30/00)

Portfolio Manager: committee - 1995

Investm't Category: Growth

✔ Domestic
Foreign
Asset Allocation
Index
Sector
State Specific

Investment Style

Large Cap
Mid Cap
✔ Small Cap
Growth
Grth/Val
✔ Value

Portfolio

2.1%	cash	0.0%	corp bonds
95.6%	stocks	2.3%	gov't bonds
0.0%	pref/conv't pref	0.0%	muni bonds
0.0%	conv't bds/wrnts	0.0%	other

SHAREHOLDER INFORMATION

Minimum Investment

Initial: $10,000 Subsequent: $100

Minimum IRA Investment

Initial: $2,000 Subsequent: $100

Maximum Fees

Load: none 12b-1: none

Other: none

Services

✔ IRA
✔ Keogh
✔ Telephone Exchange

Caldwell & Orkin Mrkt Opp (COAGX)

800-237-7073, 678-533-7850
www.ctrust.com

Growth & Income

this fund is closed to new investors

PERFORMANCE **fund inception date: 3/11/91**

	3yr Annual	5yr Annual	10yr Annual	Bull	Bear
Return (%)	14.2	19.6	na	-2.4	20.1
Differ from Category (+/-)	5.3 high	5.3 high	na	-35.9 low	20.2 high

Standard Deviation	Category Risk Index	Beta
9.6%—blw av	0.55—low	-0.19

	2000	1999	1998	1997	1996	1995	1994	1993	1992	1991
Return (%)	26.6	-3.8	22.4	29.3	27.2	16.5	-0.9	14.9	15.2	—
Differ from Category (+/-)	20.9	-14.6	9.6	2.4	7.5	-13.0	-0.4	1.1	3.6	—
Return, Tax-Adjusted (%)	24.5	-5.2	20.6	27.5	22.2	15.3	-2.2	9.0	13.9	—

PER SHARE DATA

	2000	1999	1998	1997	1996	1995	1994	1993	1992	1991
Dividends, Net Income ($)	0.97	0.05	0.41	0.21	0.50	0.34	0.26	0.04	0.00	—
Distrib'ns, Cap Gain ($)	0.00	1.37	0.74	0.87	1.65	0.00	0.22	2.69	0.51	—
Net Asset Value ($)	22.33	18.43	20.69	17.85	14.65	13.27	11.71	12.31	13.17	—
Expense Ratio (%)	1.40	1.38	1.17	1.26	1.56	1.63	1.21	1.30	1.64	—
Yield (%)	4.34	0.25	1.91	1.12	3.06	2.56	2.17	0.26	0.00	—
Portfolio Turnover (%)	392	378	200	229	222	331	292	223	50	—
Total Assets (Millions $)	243	227	380	141	43	33	35	18	15	—

PORTFOLIO (as of 6/30/00)

Portfolio Manager: Michael Orkin - 1992

Investm't Category: Growth & Income

✔ Domestic Index
Foreign Sector
Asset Allocation State Specific

Investment Style

Large Cap Mid Cap Small Cap
Growth Grth/Val Value

Portfolio

106.1%	cash	0.0%	corp bonds
-6.1%	stocks	0.0%	gov't bonds
0.0%	pref/conv't pref	0.0%	muni bonds
0.0%	conv't bds/wrnts	0.0%	other

SHAREHOLDER INFORMATION

Minimum Investment
Initial: $100,000 Subsequent: $100

Minimum IRA Investment
Initial: $25,000 Subsequent: $100

Maximum Fees
Load: 2.00% redemption 12b-1: none
Other: redemption fee applies for 6 months

Services
✔ IRA
Keogh
✔ Telephone Exchange

Capstone Growth (TRDFX)

800-262-6631, 713-260-9000
www.capstonefinancial.com

Growth

PERFORMANCE — fund inception date: 1/14/52

	3yr Annual	5yr Annual	10yr Annual	Bull	Bear
Return (%)	11.2	15.7	13.5	59.5	-12.3
Differ from Category (+/-)	0.2 av	-0.4 av	-3.3 low	9.8 abv av	-6.9 blw av

Standard Deviation	Category Risk Index	Beta
17.8%—av	0.91—blw av	1.00

	2000	1999	1998	1997	1996	1995	1994	1993	1992	1991
Return (%)	-9.1	22.9	23.3	28.7	17.2	29.1	-7.7	6.1	0.7	34.8
Differ from Category (+/-)	-12.6	4.0	9.0	1.6	-5.1	-1.3	-7.5	-8.5	-11.9	-2.8
Return, Tax-Adjusted (%)	-10.9	21.2	22.0	22.9	11.9	24.2	-8.3	3.7	-0.3	31.2

PER SHARE DATA

	2000	1999	1998	1997	1996	1995	1994	1993	1992	1991
Dividends, Net Income ($)	0.00	0.02	0.12	0.16	0.22	0.17	0.10	0.18	0.20	0.31
Distrib'ns, Cap Gain ($)	1.69	1.28	0.66	3.65	2.28	1.91	0.16	0.94	0.32	1.17
Net Asset Value ($)	15.21	18.63	16.28	13.87	13.74	13.81	12.46	13.81	14.14	14.56
Expense Ratio (%)	na	1.18	1.27	1.25	1.29	1.31	1.28	1.24	1.10	0.97
Yield (%)	0.00	0.10	0.70	0.91	1.37	1.08	0.79	1.22	1.38	1.97
Portfolio Turnover (%)	na	70	93	229	173	119	12	45	22	38
Total Assets (Millions $)	77	91	79	70	60	88	75	102	101	103

PORTFOLIO (as of 3/31/00)

Portfolio Manager: Dan Watson - 1995

Investm't Category: Growth

✔ Domestic — Index
✔ Foreign — Sector
Asset Allocation — State Specific

Investment Style

✔ Large Cap — Mid Cap — Small Cap
Growth — ✔ Grth/Val — Value

Portfolio

0.0%	cash	0.0%	corp bonds
100.0%	stocks	0.0%	gov't bonds
0.0%	pref/conv't pref	0.0%	muni bonds
0.0%	conv't bds/wrnts	0.0%	other

SHAREHOLDER INFORMATION

Minimum Investment

Initial: $200 — Subsequent: $1

Minimum IRA Investment

Initial: $200 — Subsequent: $1

Maximum Fees

Load: none — 12b-1: 0.25%
Other: none

Services

✔ IRA
✔ Keogh
✔ Telephone Exchange

Century Shares (CENSX)

800-321-1928, 617-482-3060
www.centuryfunds.com

Growth & Income

PERFORMANCE — fund inception date: 3/1/28

	3yr Annual	5yr Annual	10yr Annual	Bull	Bear
Return (%)	8.8	17.7	17.2	4.9	27.1
Differ from Category (+/-)	-0.1 av	3.4 high	2.3 high	-28.6 low	27.2 high

Standard Deviation	Category Risk Index	Beta
28.4%—high	1.63—high	0.91

	2000	1999	1998	1997	1996	1995	1994	1993	1992	1991
Return (%)	37.4	-12.3	6.9	50.1	17.1	35.2	-3.9	-0.3	26.9	31.5
Differ from Category (+/-)	31.7	-23.1	-5.9	23.2	-2.6	5.7	-3.4	-14.1	15.3	3.4
Return, Tax-Adjusted (%)	34.7	-14.5	5.3	48.4	15.3	33.2	-5.6	-2.1	25.5	29.6

PER SHARE DATA

	2000	1999	1998	1997	1996	1995	1994	1993	1992	1991
Dividends, Net Income ($)	0.38	0.41	0.40	0.38	0.46	0.41	0.45	0.45	0.42	0.47
Distrib'ns, Cap Gain ($)	3.75	4.30	2.72	1.90	1.11	0.92	0.88	1.10	0.56	0.57
Net Asset Value ($)	42.97	34.32	44.66	44.66	31.30	28.07	21.77	24.04	25.68	21.03
Expense Ratio (%)	na	0.82	0.78	0.82	0.82	1.01	1.01	0.82	0.84	0.95
Yield (%)	0.81	1.06	0.84	0.81	1.41	1.41	1.98	1.78	1.60	2.17
Portfolio Turnover (%)	na	11	6	6	3	3	2	19	5	0
Total Assets (Millions $)	387	309	415	413	270	267	206	233	259	157

PORTFOLIO (as of 6/30/00)

Portfolio Manager: Allan Fulkerson, A. Thorndike - 1999

Investm't Category: Growth & Income

- ✔ Domestic
- Foreign
- Asset Allocation
- Index
- ✔ Sector
- State Specific

Investment Style

- ✔ Large Cap
- ✔ Mid Cap
- Small Cap
- Growth
- Grth/Val
- ✔ Value

Portfolio

1.7%	cash	0.0%	corp bonds
98.3%	stocks	0.0%	gov't bonds
0.0%	pref/conv't pref	0.0%	muni bonds
0.0%	conv't bds/wrnts	0.0%	other

SHAREHOLDER INFORMATION

Minimum Investment
Initial: $1,000 — Subsequent: $50

Minimum IRA Investment
Initial: $1,000 — Subsequent: $50

Maximum Fees
Load: none — 12b-1: none
Other: none

Services

- ✔ IRA
- Keogh
- ✔ Telephone Exchange

Chesapeake Aggressive Gr (CPGRX)

800-430-3863, 252-972-9922
www.fundsrus.com

Aggressive Growth

this fund is closed to new investors

PERFORMANCE — fund inception date: 1/11/93

	3yr Annual	5yr Annual	10yr Annual	Bull	Bear
Return (%)	6.1	8.8	na	94.7	-33.4
Differ from Category (+/-)	-10.1 blw av	-5.8 blw av	na	-24.5 av	-12.8 blw av

Standard Deviation	Category Risk Index	Beta
35.9%—high	1.11—abv av	1.31

	2000	1999	1998	1997	1996	1995	1994	1993	1992	1991
Return (%)	-17.2	49.4	-3.4	15.1	10.8	30.2	7.0	—	—	—
Differ from Category (+/-)	-11.2	-8.1	-18.5	0.3	-7.5	-4.4	7.8	—	—	—
Return, Tax-Adjusted (%)	-21.2	47.3	-3.4	11.8	9.0	27.5	7.0	—	—	—

PER SHARE DATA

	2000	1999	1998	1997	1996	1995	1994	1993	1992	1991
Dividends, Net Income ($)	0.00	0.00	0.00	0.00	0.00	0.00	0.00	—	—	—
Distrib'ns, Cap Gain ($)	4.75	1.81	0.00	2.87	1.06	1.31	0.00	—	—	—
Net Asset Value ($)	14.70	23.24	17.33	17.94	17.84	17.09	14.03	—	—	—
Expense Ratio (%)	1.40	1.39	1.40	1.42	1.42	1.43	1.49	—	—	—
Yield (%)	0.00	0.00	0.00	0.00	0.00	0.00	0.00	—	—	—
Portfolio Turnover (%)	82	110	86	115	110	75	66	—	—	—
Total Assets (Millions $)	200	343	423	558	501	425	235	—	—	—

PORTFOLIO (as of 6/30/00)

Portfolio Manager: Whitfield Gardner, John Lewis - 1993

Investm't Category: Aggressive Growth

✔ Domestic	Index
✔ Foreign	Sector
Asset Allocation	State Specific

Investment Style

Large Cap	Mid Cap	✔ Small Cap
✔ Growth	Grth/Val	Value

Portfolio

1.5%	cash	0.0%	corp bonds
98.5%	stocks	0.0%	gov't bonds
0.0%	pref/conv't pref	0.0%	muni bonds
0.0%	conv't bds/wrnts	0.0%	other

SHAREHOLDER INFORMATION

Minimum Investment
Initial: $25,000 Subsequent: $500

Minimum IRA Investment
Initial: $25,000 Subsequent: $500

Maximum Fees
Load: 3.00% front 12b-1: none
Other: none

Services
✔ IRA
✔ Keogh
✔ Telephone Exchange

Citizens: Core Gr/R (WAIDX)

800-223-7010, 603-436-5152
www.citizensfunds.com

Growth

PERFORMANCE — fund inception date: 3/3/95

	3yr Annual	5yr Annual	10yr Annual	Bull	Bear
Return (%)	12.9	19.0	na	76.7	-22.3
Differ from Category (+/-)	1.9 abv av	2.9 abv av	na	27.0 high	-16.9 low

Standard Deviation	Category Risk Index	Beta
22.2%—abv av	1.14—abv av	1.19

	2000	1999	1998	1997	1996	1995	1994	1993	1992	1991
Return (%)	-20.7	27.4	42.7	34.9	23.0	—	—	—	—	—
Differ from Category (+/-)	-24.2	8.5	28.4	7.8	0.7	—	—	—	—	—
Return, Tax-Adjusted (%)	-21.4	26.0	42.3	33.6	22.6	—	—	—	—	—

PER SHARE DATA

	2000	1999	1998	1997	1996	1995	1994	1993	1992	1991
Dividends, Net Income ($)	0.00	0.00	0.00	0.00	0.05	—	—	—	—	—
Distrib'ns, Cap Gain ($)	1.30	1.79	0.31	0.94	0.09	—	—	—	—	—
Net Asset Value ($)	24.70	32.87	27.24	19.30	15.01	—	—	—	—	—
Expense Ratio (%)	1.49	1.58	1.59	1.59	1.79	—	—	—	—	—
Yield (%)	0.00	0.00	0.00	0.00	0.33	—	—	—	—	—
Portfolio Turnover (%)	20	18	13	18	6	—	—	—	—	—
Total Assets (Millions $)	573	681	437	257	161	—	—	—	—	—

PORTFOLIO (as of 9/30/99)

Portfolio Manager: Sophia Collier - 1995

Investm't Category: Growth

✔ Domestic
Foreign
Asset Allocation
Index
Sector
State Specific

Investment Style

✔ Large Cap
Mid Cap
Small Cap
✔ Growth
Grth/Val
Value

Portfolio

0.3%	cash	0.0%	corp bonds
99.7%	stocks	0.0%	gov't bonds
0.0%	pref/conv't pref	0.0%	muni bonds
0.0%	conv't bds/wrnts	0.0%	other

SHAREHOLDER INFORMATION

Minimum Investment
Initial: $1,000 Subsequent: $1

Minimum IRA Investment
Initial: $250 Subsequent: $1

Maximum Fees
Load: none 12b-1: 0.25%
Other: none

Services
✔ IRA
Keogh
✔ Telephone Exchange

Citizens: Emg Gr/R (WAEGX)

800-223-7010, 603-436-5152
www.citizensfunds.com

Aggressive Growth

PERFORMANCE — fund inception date: 2/8/94

	3yr Annual	5yr Annual	10yr Annual	Bull	Bear
Return (%)	33.5	26.1	na	152.5	-21.4
Differ from Category (+/-)	17.3 high	11.5 high	na	33.3 abv av	-0.8 av

Standard Deviation	Category Risk Index	Beta
32.1%—high	0.99—av	1.32

	2000	1999	1998	1997	1996	1995	1994	1993	1992	1991
Return (%)	-0.6	68.0	42.7	17.6	13.9	40.7	—	—	—	—
Differ from Category (+/-)	5.4	10.5	27.6	2.8	-4.4	6.1	—	—	—	—
Return, Tax-Adjusted (%)	-5.0	63.2	40.2	16.1	11.2	36.4	—	—	—	—

PER SHARE DATA

	2000	1999	1998	1997	1996	1995	1994	1993	1992	1991
Dividends, Net Income ($)	0.00	0.00	0.00	0.00	0.00	0.00	—	—	—	—
Distrib'ns, Cap Gain ($)	6.07	4.56	1.78	1.00	1.24	1.59	—	—	—	—
Net Asset Value ($)	20.36	27.14	19.12	14.70	13.39	12.86	—	—	—	—
Expense Ratio (%)	1.69	1.82	1.96	1.99	2.02	1.90	—	—	—	—
Yield (%)	0.00	0.00	0.00	0.00	0.00	0.00	—	—	—	—
Portfolio Turnover (%)	159	208	245	228	337	231	—	—	—	—
Total Assets (Millions $)	360	221	105	71	52	17	—	—	—	—

PORTFOLIO (as of 12/31/99)

Portfolio Manager: Richard Little - 1994

Investm't Category: Aggressive Growth

✔ Domestic | Index
✔ Foreign | Sector
Asset Allocation | State Specific

Investment Style

Large Cap | ✔ Mid Cap | ✔ Small Cap
✔ Growth | Grth/Val | Value

Portfolio

8.5% cash | 0.0% corp bonds
91.5% stocks | 0.0% gov't bonds
0.0% pref/conv't pref | 0.0% muni bonds
0.0% conv't bds/wrnts | 0.0% other

SHAREHOLDER INFORMATION

Minimum Investment
Initial: $2,500 | Subsequent: $1

Minimum IRA Investment
Initial: $1,000 | Subsequent: $50

Maximum Fees
Load: none | 12b-1: 0.25%
Other: none

Services
✔ IRA
Keogh
✔ Telephone Exchange

Clipper (CFIMX)

800-776-5033, 310-247-3940
www.clipperfund.com

Growth & Income

PERFORMANCE — fund inception date: 2/29/84

	3yr Annual	5yr Annual	10yr Annual	Bull	Bear
Return (%)	17.0	20.1	19.7	16.6	31.4
Differ from Category (+/-)	8.1 high	5.8 high	4.8 high	-16.9 blw av	31.5 high

Standard Deviation	Category Risk Index	Beta
13.7%—blw av	0.79—low	0.36

	2000	1999	1998	1997	1996	1995	1994	1993	1992	1991
Return (%)	37.4	-2.0	19.1	30.4	19.4	45.2	-2.4	11.1	15.9	32.5
Differ from Category (+/-)	31.7	-12.8	6.3	3.5	-0.3	15.7	-1.9	-2.7	4.3	4.4
Return, Tax-Adjusted (%)	33.6	-4.8	14.9	26.6	16.8	41.2	-4.0	6.8	13.5	30.1

PER SHARE DATA

	2000	1999	1998	1997	1996	1995	1994	1993	1992	1991
Dividends, Net Income ($)	1.87	2.24	1.63	1.35	0.83	0.75	0.70	0.75	0.95	1.24
Distrib'ns, Cap Gain ($)	8.38	6.15	12.86	9.83	4.27	5.42	2.00	6.72	3.01	1.91
Net Asset Value ($)	79.25	65.28	75.37	76.86	67.57	60.74	46.09	50.02	51.74	48.10
Expense Ratio (%)	na	1.10	1.06	1.08	1.08	1.12	1.11	1.11	1.12	1.15
Yield (%)	2.13	3.13	1.84	1.55	1.15	1.13	1.45	1.32	1.73	2.47
Portfolio Turnover (%)	na	63	65	31	24	37	45	64	46	42
Total Assets (Millions $)	1,127	960	1,234	824	542	403	247	271	209	161

PORTFOLIO (as of 6/30/00)

Portfolio Manager: committee - 1984

Investm't Category: Growth & Income

✔ Domestic	Index
✔ Foreign	Sector
Asset Allocation	State Specific

Investment Style

✔ Large Cap	✔ Mid Cap	Small Cap
Growth	Grth/Val	✔ Value

Portfolio

23.5% cash	0.0% corp bonds
76.5% stocks	0.0% gov't bonds
0.0% pref/conv't pref	0.0% muni bonds
0.0% conv't bds/wrnts	0.0% other

SHAREHOLDER INFORMATION

Minimum Investment
Initial: $5,000 Subsequent: $1,000

Minimum IRA Investment
Initial: $2,000 Subsequent: $200

Maximum Fees
Load: none 12b-1: none
Other: none

Services
✔ IRA
Keogh
✔ Telephone Exchange

Cohen & Steers Realty Shs (CSRSX)

800-437-9912, 212-832-3232
www.cohenandsteers.com

Growth & Income

PERFORMANCE — fund inception date: 7/1/91

	3yr Annual	5yr Annual	10yr Annual	Bull	Bear
Return (%)	2.1	12.3	na	7.0	17.1
Differ from Category (+/-)	-6.8 low	-2.0 blw av	na	-26.5 low	17.2 high

Standard Deviation	Category Risk Index	Beta
15.7%—av	0.90—blw av	0.22

	2000	1999	1998	1997	1996	1995	1994	1993	1992	1991
Return (%)	26.6	2.6	-18.0	21.1	38.4	11.1	8.3	18.6	20.0	—
Differ from Category (+/-)	20.9	-8.2	-30.8	-5.8	18.7	-18.4	8.8	4.8	8.4	—
Return, Tax-Adjusted (%)	24.1	0.5	-20.0	18.4	35.8	8.8	6.2	14.9	17.6	—

PER SHARE DATA

	2000	1999	1998	1997	1996	1995	1994	1993	1992	1991
Dividends, Net Income ($)	2.24	1.98	1.88	1.88	1.88	1.83	1.66	1.51	1.80	—
Distrib'ns, Cap Gain ($)	0.00	0.00	1.40	2.30	0.55	0.00	0.00	1.68	0.23	—
Net Asset Value ($)	44.26	36.91	37.98	50.18	45.09	34.62	32.90	31.92	29.58	—
Expense Ratio (%)	na	1.06	1.04	1.05	1.08	1.11	1.14	1.18	1.25	—
Yield (%)	5.06	5.36	4.77	3.58	4.11	5.28	5.04	4.49	6.03	—
Portfolio Turnover (%)	na	21	30	40	33	22	39	65	15	—
Total Assets (Millions $)	1,240	1,464	1,933	3,432	2,036	793	458	155	49	—

PORTFOLIO (as of 6/30/00)

Portfolio Manager: Martin Cohen, Robert Steers - 1991

Investm't Category: Growth & Income

✔ Domestic — Index
✔ Foreign — ✔ Sector
Asset Allocation — State Specific

Investment Style

Large Cap — ✔ Mid Cap — ✔ Small Cap
Growth — Grth/Val — ✔ Value

Portfolio

2.8%	cash	0.0%	corp bonds
97.2%	stocks	0.0%	gov't bonds
0.0%	pref/conv't pref	0.0%	muni bonds
0.0%	conv't bds/wrnts	0.0%	other

SHAREHOLDER INFORMATION

Minimum Investment
Initial: $10,000 — Subsequent: $500

Minimum IRA Investment
Initial: na — Subsequent: na

Maximum Fees
Load: none — 12b-1: none
Other: none

Services
IRA
Keogh
✔ Telephone Exchange

Columbia Balanced (CBALX)

800-547-1707, 503-222-3606
www.columbiafunds.com

Balanced

PERFORMANCE — fund inception date: 9/12/91

	3yr Annual	5yr Annual	10yr Annual	Bull	Bear
Return (%)	10.9	12.6	na	31.5	-7.3
Differ from Category (+/-)	2.5 abv av	1.2 abv av	na	3.4 abv av	-4.1 blw av

Standard Deviation	Category Risk Index	Beta
10.7%—blw av	0.98—av	0.57

	2000	1999	1998	1997	1996	1995	1994	1993	1992	1991
Return (%)	0.8	12.6	20.0	18.7	11.8	25.0	0.0	13.6	8.8	—
Differ from Category (+/-)	-1.2	1.9	6.7	-0.1	-2.1	-0.5	1.3	-0.8	0.4	—
Return, Tax-Adjusted (%)	-1.3	10.8	17.0	15.2	8.4	22.1	-1.4	11.2	7.5	—

PER SHARE DATA

	2000	1999	1998	1997	1996	1995	1994	1993	1992	1991
Dividends, Net Income ($)	0.68	0.69	0.73	0.83	0.76	0.73	0.64	0.57	0.57	—
Distrib'ns, Cap Gain ($)	1.34	0.66	1.75	1.83	1.34	0.74	0.00	0.59	0.08	—
Net Asset Value ($)	22.96	24.72	23.17	21.42	20.32	20.08	17.28	17.91	16.80	—
Expense Ratio (%)	na	0.66	0.67	0.68	0.66	0.69	0.72	0.73	0.81	—
Yield (%)	2.79	2.71	2.92	3.56	3.50	3.50	3.70	3.08	3.37	—
Portfolio Turnover (%)	na	133	127	148	133	114	98	107	138	—
Total Assets (Millions $)	1,091	1,040	975	792	672	486	249	186	90	—

PORTFOLIO (as of 6/30/00)

Portfolio Manager: committee - 1998

Investm't Category: Balanced

✔ Domestic	Index
✔ Foreign	Sector
✔ Asset Allocation	State Specific

Investment Style

Large Cap	Mid Cap	Small Cap
Growth	Grth/Val	Value

Portfolio

3.2%	cash	15.9%	corp bonds
59.9%	stocks	15.0%	gov't bonds
0.0%	pref/conv't pref	0.0%	muni bonds
0.0%	conv't bds/wrnts	6.0%	other

SHAREHOLDER INFORMATION

Minimum Investment
Initial: $1,000 Subsequent: $100

Minimum IRA Investment
Initial: $1,000 Subsequent: $100

Maximum Fees
Load: none 12b-1: none
Other: none

Services
✔ IRA
✔ Keogh
✔ Telephone Exchange

Columbia Common Stock (CMSTX)

800-547-1707, 503-222-3606
www.columbiafunds.com

Growth

PERFORMANCE — fund inception date: 9/12/91

	3yr Annual	5yr Annual	10yr Annual	Bull	Bear
Return (%)	14.3	17.7	na	63.1	-16.2
Differ from Category (+/-)	3.3 abv av	1.6 av	na	13.4 abv av	-10.8 blw av

Standard Deviation	Category Risk Index	Beta
18.9%—av	0.97—blw av	1.01

	2000	1999	1998	1997	1996	1995	1994	1993	1992	1991
Return (%)	-5.7	25.7	26.2	25.3	20.8	30.8	2.0	16.4	9.9	—
Differ from Category (+/-)	-9.2	6.8	11.9	-1.8	-1.5	0.4	2.2	1.8	-2.7	—
Return, Tax-Adjusted (%)	-7.7	24.2	23.0	22.8	15.8	28.3	1.0	14.1	8.9	—

PER SHARE DATA

	2000	1999	1998	1997	1996	1995	1994	1993	1992	1991
Dividends, Net Income ($)	0.00	0.04	0.13	0.26	0.23	0.26	0.25	0.21	0.24	—
Distrib'ns, Cap Gain ($)	3.01	1.74	3.26	1.84	2.96	0.95	0.19	0.84	0.17	—
Net Asset Value ($)	24.34	28.90	24.40	22.02	19.26	18.59	15.16	15.29	14.04	—
Expense Ratio (%)	na	0.77	0.80	0.77	0.76	0.79	0.84	0.84	0.86	—
Yield (%)	0.00	0.13	0.46	1.08	1.03	1.33	1.62	1.30	1.68	—
Portfolio Turnover (%)	na	97	140	90	111	49	64	90	68	—
Total Assets (Millions $)	876	959	797	783	536	358	124	100	51	—

PORTFOLIO (as of 6/30/00)

Portfolio Manager: committee - 1998

Investm't Category: Growth

✔ Domestic	Index
✔ Foreign	Sector
Asset Allocation	State Specific

Investment Style

✔ Large Cap	Mid Cap	Small Cap
✔ Growth	Grth/Val	Value

Portfolio

0.9%	cash	0.0%	corp bonds
99.1%	stocks	0.0%	gov't bonds
0.0%	pref/conv't pref	0.0%	muni bonds
0.0%	conv't bds/wrnts	0.0%	other

SHAREHOLDER INFORMATION

Minimum Investment

Initial: $1,000 — Subsequent: $100

Minimum IRA Investment

Initial: $1,000 — Subsequent: $100

Maximum Fees

Load: none — 12b-1: none

Other: none

Services

✔ IRA
✔ Keogh
✔ Telephone Exchange

Columbia Growth (CLMBX)

800-547-1707, 503-222-3606
www.columbiafunds.com

Growth

PERFORMANCE — fund inception date: 6/16/67

	3yr Annual	5yr Annual	10yr Annual	Bull	Bear
Return (%)	14.7	18.2	17.8	64.1	-20.4
Differ from Category (+/-)	3.7 abv av	2.1 abv av	1.0 abv av	14.4 abv av	-15.0 low

Standard Deviation	Category Risk Index	Beta
22.5%—abv av	1.16—abv av	1.15

	2000	1999	1998	1997	1996	1995	1994	1993	1992	1991
Return (%)	-7.9	26.0	30.3	26.3	20.8	32.9	-0.6	13.0	11.8	34.2
Differ from Category (+/-)	-11.4	7.1	16.0	-0.8	-1.5	2.5	-0.4	-1.6	-0.8	-3.4
Return, Tax-Adjusted (%)	-10.0	23.8	28.9	23.2	15.7	29.1	-2.1	9.4	8.3	30.4

PER SHARE DATA

	2000	1999	1998	1997	1996	1995	1994	1993	1992	1991
Dividends, Net Income ($)	0.00	0.00	0.07	0.17	0.17	0.29	0.26	0.18	0.20	0.39
Distrib'ns, Cap Gain ($)	5.26	4.66	2.17	4.32	5.16	2.88	1.11	3.02	2.98	2.44
Net Asset Value ($)	40.07	48.91	42.51	34.34	30.74	29.84	24.84	26.38	26.18	26.26
Expense Ratio (%)	na	0.65	0.68	0.71	0.71	0.77	0.81	0.82	0.86	0.90
Yield (%)	0.00	0.00	0.15	0.43	0.47	0.88	1.00	0.61	0.68	1.35
Portfolio Turnover (%)	na	118	105	95	75	94	79	105	116	164
Total Assets (Millions $)	1,901	2,160	1,753	1,324	1,064	848	591	605	518	431

PORTFOLIO (as of 6/30/00)

Portfolio Manager: Alexander Macmillan - 1992

Investm't Category: Growth

✔ Domestic	Index
Foreign	Sector
Asset Allocation	State Specific

Investment Style

✔ Large Cap	Mid Cap	Small Cap
✔ Growth	Grth/Val	Value

Portfolio

2.1%	cash	0.0%	corp bonds
97.9%	stocks	0.0%	gov't bonds
0.0%	pref/conv't pref	0.0%	muni bonds
0.0%	conv't bds/wrnts	0.0%	other

SHAREHOLDER INFORMATION

Minimum Investment
Initial: $1,000 — Subsequent: $100

Minimum IRA Investment
Initial: $1,000 — Subsequent: $100

Maximum Fees
Load: none — 12b-1: none
Other: none

Services
✔ IRA
✔ Keogh
✔ Telephone Exchange

Columbia Intl Stock (CMISX)

800-547-1707, 503-222-3606
www.columbiafunds.com

International Stock

PERFORMANCE

fund inception date: 9/10/92

	3yr Annual	5yr Annual	10yr Annual	Bull	Bear
Return (%)	11.2	12.3	na	81.3	-25.8
Differ from Category (+/-)	2.3 abv av	4.0 abv av	na	-9.6 av	-1.8 av

Standard Deviation	Category Risk Index	Beta
19.9%—abv av	0.88—blw av	0.71

	2000	1999	1998	1997	1996	1995	1994	1993	1992	1991
Return (%)	-22.6	57.9	12.8	11.4	16.6	5.1	-2.4	33.3	—	—
Differ from Category (+/-)	-3.2	-2.8	7.0	10.1	2.1	-4.2	0.7	-6.9	—	—
Return, Tax-Adjusted (%)	-25.0	55.8	12.8	8.8	13.4	5.1	-2.8	32.4	—	—

PER SHARE DATA

	2000	1999	1998	1997	1996	1995	1994	1993	1992	1991
Dividends, Net Income ($)	0.00	0.00	0.00	0.00	0.23	0.00	0.00	0.00	—	—
Distrib'ns, Cap Gain ($)	2.83	1.59	0.00	1.75	1.14	0.00	0.21	0.31	—	—
Net Asset Value ($)	14.77	22.81	15.45	13.70	13.86	13.07	12.43	12.96	—	—
Expense Ratio (%)	na	1.48	1.56	1.62	1.54	1.52	1.52	1.71	—	—
Yield (%)	0.00	0.00	0.00	0.00	1.53	0.00	0.00	0.00	—	—
Portfolio Turnover (%)	na	94	74	121	129	182	138	144	—	—
Total Assets (Millions $)	171	239	134	146	125	100	118	73	—	—

PORTFOLIO (as of 6/30/00)

Portfolio Manager: James McAlear - 1992

Investm't Category: International Stock

✔ Domestic — Index
✔ Foreign — Sector
Asset Allocation — State Specific

Investment Style

Large Cap — Mid Cap — Small Cap
Growth — Grth/Val — Value

Portfolio

6.2%	cash	0.0%	corp bonds
93.0%	stocks	0.0%	gov't bonds
0.8%	pref/conv't pref	0.0%	muni bonds
0.0%	conv't bds/wrnts	0.0%	other

SHAREHOLDER INFORMATION

Minimum Investment
Initial: $1,000 — Subsequent: $100

Minimum IRA Investment
Initial: $1,000 — Subsequent: $100

Maximum Fees
Load: none — 12b-1: none
Other: none

Services
✔ IRA
✔ Keogh
✔ Telephone Exchange

Columbia Real Estate Eqty (CREEX)

800-547-1707, 503-222-3606
www.columbiafunds.com

Growth & Income

PERFORMANCE — fund inception date: 4/1/94

	3yr Annual	5yr Annual	10yr Annual	Bull	Bear
Return (%)	3.2	13.7	na	2.5	18.0
Differ from Category (+/-)	-5.7 low	-0.6 blw av	na	-31.0 low	18.1 high

Standard Deviation	Category Risk Index	Beta
13.6%—blw av	0.79—low	0.13

	2000	1999	1998	1997	1996	1995	1994	1993	1992	1991
Return (%)	28.8	-2.4	-12.3	24.7	38.2	16.8	—	—	—	—
Differ from Category (+/-)	23.1	-13.2	-25.1	-2.2	18.5	-12.7	—	—	—	—
Return, Tax-Adjusted (%)	26.6	-4.4	-13.8	22.1	34.7	13.8	—	—	—	—

PER SHARE DATA

	2000	1999	1998	1997	1996	1995	1994	1993	1992	1991
Dividends, Net Income ($)	0.80	0.81	0.75	0.79	0.77	0.77	—	—	—	—
Distrib'ns, Cap Gain ($)	0.00	0.00	0.00	0.51	0.49	0.14	—	—	—	—
Net Asset Value ($)	17.89	14.57	15.76	18.80	16.16	12.71	—	—	—	—
Expense Ratio (%)	na	0.99	1.01	1.02	1.06	1.18	—	—	—	—
Yield (%)	4.47	5.55	4.75	4.09	4.62	5.99	—	—	—	—
Portfolio Turnover (%)	na	29	5	33	45	53	—	—	—	—
Total Assets (Millions $)	404	241	164	151	68	21	—	—	—	—

PORTFOLIO (as of 6/30/00)

Portfolio Manager: David Jellison - 1994

Investm't Category: Growth & Income

✔ Domestic	Index
✔ Foreign	✔ Sector
Asset Allocation	State Specific

Investment Style

Large Cap	✔ Mid Cap	✔ Small Cap
Growth	Grth/Val	✔ Value

Portfolio

7.0% cash	0.0% corp bonds
93.0% stocks	0.0% gov't bonds
0.0% pref/conv't pref	0.0% muni bonds
0.0% conv't bds/wrnts	0.0% other

SHAREHOLDER INFORMATION

Minimum Investment
Initial: $1,000 — Subsequent: $100

Minimum IRA Investment
Initial: $1,000 — Subsequent: $100

Maximum Fees
Load: none — 12b-1: none
Other: none

Services
✔ IRA
✔ Keogh
✔ Telephone Exchange

Columbia Small Cap (CMSCX)

800-547-1707, 503-222-3606
www.columbiafunds.com

Aggressive Growth

PERFORMANCE **fund inception date: 10/1/96**

	3yr Annual	5yr Annual	10yr Annual	Bull	Bear
Return (%)	20.8	na	na	104.2	-20.6
Differ from Category (+/-)	4.6 abv av	na	na	-15.0 av	0.0 av

Standard Deviation	Category Risk Index	Beta
33.3%—high	1.03—av	1.10

	2000	1999	1998	1997	1996	1995	1994	1993	1992	1991
Return (%)	5.8	59.1	4.6	34.1	—	—	—	—	—	—
Differ from Category (+/-)	11.8	1.6	-10.5	19.3	—	—	—	—	—	—
Return, Tax-Adjusted (%)	3.5	58.5	4.6	32.9	—	—	—	—	—	—

PER SHARE DATA

	2000	1999	1998	1997	1996	1995	1994	1993	1992	1991
Dividends, Net Income ($)	0.00	0.00	0.00	0.00	—	—	—	—	—	—
Distrib'ns, Cap Gain ($)	3.04	0.48	0.00	0.77	—	—	—	—	—	—
Net Asset Value ($)	25.87	27.26	17.43	16.65	—	—	—	—	—	—
Expense Ratio (%)	na	1.30	1.34	1.46	—	—	—	—	—	—
Yield (%)	0.00	0.00	0.00	0.00	—	—	—	—	—	—
Portfolio Turnover (%)	na	188	157	172	—	—	—	—	—	—
Total Assets (Millions $)	464	290	160	96	—	—	—	—	—	—

PORTFOLIO (as of 6/30/00)

Portfolio Manager: Richard Johnson - 1996

Investm't Category: Aggressive Growth

✔ Domestic
✔ Foreign
Asset Allocation
Index
Sector
State Specific

Investment Style

Large Cap
Mid Cap
✔ Small Cap
✔ Growth
Grth/Val
Value

Portfolio

7.9%	cash	0.0%	corp bonds
92.0%	stocks	0.0%	gov't bonds
0.1%	pref/conv't pref	0.0%	muni bonds
0.0%	conv't bds/wrnts	0.0%	other

SHAREHOLDER INFORMATION

Minimum Investment
Initial: $2,000 Subsequent: $100

Minimum IRA Investment
Initial: $2,000 Subsequent: $100

Maximum Fees
Load: none 12b-1: none
Other: none

Services
✔ IRA
✔ Keogh
✔ Telephone Exchange

Columbia Special (CLSPX)

800-547-1707, 503-222-3606
www.columbiafunds.com

Aggressive Growth

PERFORMANCE — fund inception date: 8/13/85

	3yr Annual	5yr Annual	10yr Annual	Bull	Bear
Return (%)	21.8	18.1	20.2	79.5	-19.2
Differ from Category (+/-)	5.6 abv av	3.5 av	4.4 abv av	-39.7 blw av	1.4 av

Standard Deviation	Category Risk Index	Beta
29.9%—high	0.92—blw av	0.91

	2000	1999	1998	1997	1996	1995	1994	1993	1992	1991
Return (%)	13.8	36.3	16.6	12.6	13.0	29.3	2.2	21.6	13.6	50.4
Differ from Category (+/-)	19.8	-21.2	1.5	-2.2	-5.3	-5.3	3.0	-3.6	6.7	3.2
Return, Tax-Adjusted (%)	8.2	34.3	16.6	10.4	7.2	25.1	0.3	16.6	13.0	48.6

PER SHARE DATA

	2000	1999	1998	1997	1996	1995	1994	1993	1992	1991
Dividends, Net Income ($)	0.00	0.00	0.00	0.00	0.00	0.02	0.07	0.01	0.00	0.00
Distrib'ns, Cap Gain ($)	8.29	2.27	0.00	2.10	4.38	2.71	1.19	3.32	1.04	0.77
Net Asset Value ($)	25.99	29.93	23.62	20.26	19.85	21.44	18.69	19.51	18.79	17.45
Expense Ratio (%)	na	1.09	1.03	0.98	0.94	1.00	1.05	1.12	1.19	1.22
Yield (%)	0.00	0.00	0.00	0.00	0.00	0.08	0.35	0.04	0.00	0.00
Portfolio Turnover (%)	na	135	135	166	150	237	178	154	117	115
Total Assets (Millions $)	1,003	918	969	1,249	1,585	1,384	889	772	470	264

PORTFOLIO (as of 6/30/00)

Portfolio Manager: Richard Johnson - 1998

Investm't Category: Aggressive Growth

✔ Domestic — Index
✔ Foreign — Sector
Asset Allocation — State Specific

Investment Style

Large Cap — Mid Cap — ✔ Small Cap
✔ Growth — Grth/Val — Value

Portfolio

3.4%	cash	0.0%	corp bonds
96.4%	stocks	0.0%	gov't bonds
0.2%	pref/conv't pref	0.0%	muni bonds
0.0%	conv't bds/wrnts	0.0%	other

SHAREHOLDER INFORMATION

Minimum Investment

Initial: $2,000 — Subsequent: $100

Minimum IRA Investment

Initial: $2,000 — Subsequent: $100

Maximum Fees

Load: none — 12b-1: none
Other: none

Services

✔ IRA
✔ Keogh
✔ Telephone Exchange

Copley (COPLX)

508-674-8459

Growth & Income

PERFORMANCE — fund inception date: 1/31/80

	3yr Annual	5yr Annual	10yr Annual	Bull	Bear
Return (%)	9.0	11.2	11.6	7.2	18.7
Differ from Category (+/-)	0.1 av	-3.1 low	-3.3 low	-26.3 low	18.8 high

Standard Deviation	Category Risk Index	Beta
13.4%—blw av	0.77—low	0.26

	2000	1999	1998	1997	1996	1995	1994	1993	1992	1991
Return (%)	22.4	-6.8	13.6	25.0	4.8	26.0	-7.6	10.1	17.6	17.1
Differ from Category (+/-)	16.7	-17.6	0.8	-1.9	-14.9	-3.5	-7.1	-3.7	6.0	-11.0
Return, Tax-Adjusted (%)	22.4	-6.8	13.6	25.0	4.8	26.0	-7.6	10.1	17.6	17.1

PER SHARE DATA

	2000	1999	1998	1997	1996	1995	1994	1993	1992	1991
Dividends, Net Income ($)	0.00	0.00	0.00	0.00	0.00	0.00	0.00	0.00	0.00	0.00
Distrib'ns, Cap Gain ($)	0.00	0.00	0.00	0.00	0.00	0.00	0.00	0.00	0.00	0.00
Net Asset Value ($)	42.26	34.50	37.04	32.58	26.05	24.85	19.71	21.35	19.38	16.47
Expense Ratio (%)	1.06	0.97	0.95	1.00	1.03	1.09	1.51	1.14	1.38	1.50
Yield (%)	0.00	0.00	0.00	0.00	0.00	0.00	0.00	0.00	0.00	0.00
Portfolio Turnover (%)	6	2	43	9	4	31	10	5	7	16
Total Assets (Millions $)	85	81	93	82	75	79	73	80	36	33

PORTFOLIO (as of 6/30/00)

Portfolio Manager: Irving Levine - 1979

Investm't Category: Growth & Income

✔ Domestic — Index
Foreign — Sector
Asset Allocation — State Specific

Investment Style

Large Cap — ✔ Mid Cap — Small Cap
Growth — Grth/Val — ✔ Value

Portfolio

10.0%	cash	0.0%	corp bonds
89.5%	stocks	0.0%	gov't bonds
0.5%	pref/conv't pref	0.0%	muni bonds
0.0%	conv't bds/wrnts	0.0%	other

SHAREHOLDER INFORMATION

Minimum Investment

Initial: $1,000 — Subsequent: $100

Minimum IRA Investment

Initial: $1,000 — Subsequent: $100

Maximum Fees

Load: none — 12b-1: none
Other: none

Services

✔ IRA
✔ Keogh
Telephone Exchange

Country Growth (CTYGX)

800-245-2100, 610-239-4500
www.countryinvestment.com

Growth

PERFORMANCE — fund inception date: 4/21/66

	3yr Annual	5yr Annual	10yr Annual	Bull	Bear
Return (%)	19.0	19.7	16.2	58.8	8.7
Differ from Category (+/-)	8.0 high	3.6 high	-0.6 av	9.1 abv av	14.1 high

Standard Deviation	Category Risk Index	Beta
17.8%—av	0.92—blw av	0.89

	2000	1999	1998	1997	1996	1995	1994	1993	1992	1991
Return (%)	18.2	21.5	17.4	19.7	22.0	31.0	0.2	6.3	2.1	27.8
Differ from Category (+/-)	14.7	2.6	3.1	-7.4	-0.3	0.6	0.4	-8.3	-10.5	-9.8
Return, Tax-Adjusted (%)	12.5	19.3	15.9	17.6	19.7	27.2	-2.6	2.8	-0.3	26.1

PER SHARE DATA

	2000	1999	1998	1997	1996	1995	1994	1993	1992	1991
Dividends, Net Income ($)	0.15	0.16	0.15	0.14	0.19	0.25	0.16	0.22	0.28	0.38
Distrib'ns, Cap Gain ($)	7.02	2.24	1.30	1.68	1.13	1.56	1.43	1.81	1.31	0.49
Net Asset Value ($)	23.58	26.07	23.51	21.34	19.33	17.08	14.45	16.06	17.06	18.32
Expense Ratio (%)	1.13	1.04	1.00	1.16	1.12	1.14	1.24	1.18	0.85	0.82
Yield (%)	0.49	0.56	0.60	0.60	0.92	1.34	1.00	1.23	1.52	2.02
Portfolio Turnover (%)	30	31	33	30	32	31	49	55	45	26
Total Assets (Millions $)	185	187	160	145	92	75	59	64	70	85

PORTFOLIO (as of 3/31/00)

Portfolio Manager: committee - 1998

Investm't Category: Growth

✔ Domestic	Index
Foreign	Sector
Asset Allocation	State Specific

Investment Style

✔ Large Cap	Mid Cap	Small Cap
Growth	✔ Grth/Val	Value

Portfolio

3.7%	cash	0.0%	corp bonds
96.3%	stocks	0.0%	gov't bonds
0.0%	pref/conv't pref	0.0%	muni bonds
0.0%	conv't bds/wrnts	0.0%	other

SHAREHOLDER INFORMATION

Minimum Investment

Initial: $1,000 — Subsequent: $100

Minimum IRA Investment

Initial: $100 — Subsequent: $100

Maximum Fees

Load: none — 12b-1: 0.14%

Other: none

Services

✔ IRA
✔ Keogh
✔ Telephone Exchange

Delafield (DEFIX)

800-221-3079, 212-830-5271
www.delafieldfund.com

Growth

PERFORMANCE — fund inception date: 11/19/93

	3yr Annual	5yr Annual	10yr Annual	Bull	Bear
Return (%)	3.0	10.5	na	22.9	7.6
Differ from Category (+/-)	-8.0 low	-5.6 low	na	-26.8 blw av	13.0 high

Standard Deviation	Category Risk Index	Beta
21.1%—abv av	1.09—abv av	0.73

	2000	1999	1998	1997	1996	1995	1994	1993	1992	1991
Return (%)	13.9	8.3	-11.4	19.6	26.3	27.3	5.5	—	—	—
Differ from Category (+/-)	10.4	-10.6	-25.7	-7.5	4.0	-3.1	5.7	—	—	—
Return, Tax-Adjusted (%)	13.4	8.0	-11.7	17.4	21.6	24.3	4.6	—	—	—

PER SHARE DATA

	2000	1999	1998	1997	1996	1995	1994	1993	1992	1991
Dividends, Net Income ($)	0.07	0.08	0.12	0.20	0.15	0.14	0.10	—	—	—
Distrib'ns, Cap Gain ($)	0.15	0.00	0.00	1.03	1.83	0.89	0.16	—	—	—
Net Asset Value ($)	15.80	14.07	13.06	14.88	13.49	12.26	10.47	—	—	—
Expense Ratio (%)	na	1.25	1.24	1.29	1.29	1.65	1.78	—	—	—
Yield (%)	0.43	0.56	0.91	1.25	0.97	1.06	0.94	—	—	—
Portfolio Turnover (%)	na	105	81	55	75	70	42	—	—	—
Total Assets (Millions $)	93	85	103	146	61	45	10	—	—	—

PORTFOLIO (as of 3/31/00)

Portfolio Manager: D. Delafield, V. Sellecchia - 1993

Investm't Category: Growth

✔ Domestic
✔ Foreign
Asset Allocation
Index
Sector
State Specific

Investment Style

Large Cap ✔ Mid Cap Small Cap
Growth Grth/Val ✔ Value

Portfolio

4.4%	cash	0.0%	corp bonds
95.6%	stocks	0.0%	gov't bonds
0.0%	pref/conv't pref	0.0%	muni bonds
0.0%	conv't bds/wrnts	0.0%	other

SHAREHOLDER INFORMATION

Minimum Investment
Initial: $250,000 Subsequent: $1

Minimum IRA Investment
Initial: $250 Subsequent: $1

Maximum Fees
Load: none 12b-1: none
Other: none

Services
✔ IRA
✔ Keogh
✔ Telephone Exchange

Dodge & Cox Balanced (DODBX)

800-621-3979, 415-981-1710
www.dodgeandcox.com

Balanced

PERFORMANCE — fund inception date: 1/1/31

	3yr Annual	5yr Annual	10yr Annual	Bull	Bear
Return (%)	11.2	13.8	14.4	25.7	7.0
Differ from Category (+/-)	2.8 high	2.4 high	2.7 high	-2.4 av	10.2 high

Standard Deviation	Category Risk Index	Beta
11.1%—blw av	1.01—av	0.45

	2000	1999	1998	1997	1996	1995	1994	1993	1992	1991
Return (%)	15.1	12.0	6.6	21.1	14.7	28.0	1.9	15.9	10.5	20.7
Differ from Category (+/-)	13.1	1.3	-6.7	2.3	0.8	2.5	3.2	1.5	2.1	-3.1
Return, Tax-Adjusted (%)	10.8	9.1	4.1	18.5	12.9	25.5	0.1	13.6	9.1	18.9

PER SHARE DATA

	2000	1999	1998	1997	1996	1995	1994	1993	1992	1991
Dividends, Net Income ($)	2.47	2.22	2.23	2.22	1.99	2.18	1.79	1.67	1.73	1.76
Distrib'ns, Cap Gain ($)	9.22	4.98	3.74	3.27	0.69	0.91	0.33	1.06	0.07	0.29
Net Asset Value ($)	63.42	65.71	65.22	66.78	59.82	54.60	45.21	46.40	42.44	40.09
Expense Ratio (%)	na	0.53	0.54	0.55	0.56	0.58	0.58	0.60	0.63	0.65
Yield (%)	3.40	3.14	3.23	3.16	3.28	3.92	3.93	3.51	4.06	4.35
Portfolio Turnover (%)	na	17	26	32	17	20	20	15	6	10
Total Assets (Millions $)	4,730	5,137	5,700	5,076	3,629	1,800	725	486	268	179

PORTFOLIO (as of 6/30/00)

Portfolio Manager: committee - 1931

Investm't Category: Balanced

✔ Domestic	Index
Foreign	Sector
Asset Allocation	State Specific

Investment Style

Large Cap	Mid Cap	Small Cap
Growth	Grth/Val	Value

Portfolio

1.7%	cash	13.7%	corp bonds
59.7%	stocks	21.6%	gov't bonds
1.8%	pref/conv't pref	0.0%	muni bonds
0.0%	conv't bds/wrnts	1.5%	other

SHAREHOLDER INFORMATION

Minimum Investment

Initial: $2,500 — Subsequent: $100

Minimum IRA Investment

Initial: $1,000 — Subsequent: $100

Maximum Fees

Load: none — 12b-1: none

Other: none

Services

✔ IRA
✔ Keogh
✔ Telephone Exchange

Dodge & Cox Stock (DODGX)

800-621-3979, 415-981-1710
www.dodgeandcox.com

Growth & Income

PERFORMANCE — fund inception date: 12/31/64

	3yr Annual	5yr Annual	10yr Annual	Bull	Bear
Return (%)	13.7	18.2	17.8	42.4	6.8
Differ from Category (+/-)	4.8 high	3.9 high	2.9 high	8.9 abv av	6.9 abv av

Standard Deviation	Category Risk Index	Beta
17.6%—av	1.01—av	0.71

	2000	1999	1998	1997	1996	1995	1994	1993	1992	1991
Return (%)	16.3	20.2	5.3	28.4	22.2	33.3	5.1	18.3	10.8	21.4
Differ from Category (+/-)	10.6	9.4	-7.5	1.5	2.5	3.8	5.6	4.5	-0.8	-6.7
Return, Tax-Adjusted (%)	12.0	18.0	3.0	26.1	20.7	30.9	3.7	15.8	9.9	19.7

PER SHARE DATA

	2000	1999	1998	1997	1996	1995	1994	1993	1992	1991
Dividends, Net Income ($)	2.09	1.48	1.56	1.49	1.29	1.46	1.15	1.04	1.11	1.24
Distrib'ns, Cap Gain ($)	17.10	6.70	7.42	6.09	1.68	2.46	0.89	2.84	0.16	0.87
Net Asset Value ($)	96.67	100.52	90.70	94.57	79.81	67.83	53.94	53.23	48.37	44.85
Expense Ratio (%)	na	0.55	0.57	0.57	0.59	0.61	0.61	0.62	0.64	0.64
Yield (%)	1.83	1.38	1.58	1.48	1.58	2.07	2.09	1.85	2.28	2.71
Portfolio Turnover (%)	na	18	19	19	10	13	7	15	7	5
Total Assets (Millions $)	5,272	4,624	4,400	4,087	2,252	1,227	543	435	335	281

PORTFOLIO (as of 6/30/00)

Portfolio Manager: committee - 1965

Investm't Category: Growth & Income

✔ Domestic
Foreign
Asset Allocation
Index
Sector
State Specific

Investment Style

✔ Large Cap ✔ Mid Cap Small Cap
Growth Grth/Val ✔ Value

Portfolio

7.9%	cash	0.0%	corp bonds
89.4%	stocks	0.0%	gov't bonds
2.7%	pref/conv't pref	0.0%	muni bonds
0.0%	conv't bds/wrnts	0.0%	other

SHAREHOLDER INFORMATION

Minimum Investment
Initial: $2,500 Subsequent: $100

Minimum IRA Investment
Initial: $1,000 Subsequent: $100

Maximum Fees
Load: none 12b-1: none
Other: none

Services
✔ IRA
✔ Keogh
✔ Telephone Exchange

Domini Social Equity (DSEFX)

800-762-6814, 212-217-1100
www.domini.com

Growth

PERFORMANCE — fund inception date: 6/3/91

	3yr Annual	5yr Annual	10yr Annual	Bull	Bear
Return (%)	11.4	18.0	na	62.5	-16.0
Differ from Category (+/-)	0.4 av	1.9 abv av	na	12.8 abv av	-10.6 blw av

Standard Deviation	Category Risk Index	Beta
18.9%—av	0.97—blw av	1.05

	2000	1999	1998	1997	1996	1995	1994	1993	1992	1991
Return (%)	-15.0	22.6	32.9	36.0	21.8	35.1	-0.3	6.5	12.0	—
Differ from Category (+/-)	-18.5	3.7	18.6	8.9	-0.5	4.7	-0.1	-8.1	-0.6	—
Return, Tax-Adjusted (%)	-15.4	22.4	32.5	35.8	21.2	34.4	-1.1	5.8	11.6	—

PER SHARE DATA

	2000	1999	1998	1997	1996	1995	1994	1993	1992	1991
Dividends, Net Income ($)	0.00	0.01	0.01	0.05	0.15	0.15	0.20	0.14	0.12	—
Distrib'ns, Cap Gain ($)	0.98	0.27	0.45	0.03	0.11	0.08	0.08	0.07	0.01	—
Net Asset Value ($)	34.57	41.89	34.40	26.22	19.35	16.11	12.10	12.43	11.87	—
Expense Ratio (%)	0.96	0.98	1.17	0.98	0.98	0.90	0.75	0.75	0.75	—
Yield (%)	0.00	0.02	0.02	0.19	0.77	0.92	1.64	1.12	1.01	—
Portfolio Turnover (%)	9	8	5	1	0	6	8	4	3	—
Total Assets (Millions $)	1,352	1,343	715	282	150	69	33	26	10	—

PORTFOLIO (as of 6/30/00)

Portfolio Manager: committee - 1991

Investm't Category: Growth

✔ Domestic
Foreign
Asset Allocation
Index
Sector
State Specific

Investment Style

✔ Large Cap
Mid Cap
Small Cap
✔ Growth
Grth/Val
Value

Portfolio

0.7%	cash	0.0%	corp bonds
99.3%	stocks	0.0%	gov't bonds
0.0%	pref/conv't pref	0.0%	muni bonds
0.0%	conv't bds/wrnts	0.0%	other

SHAREHOLDER INFORMATION

Minimum Investment
Initial: $1,000 — Subsequent: $50

Minimum IRA Investment
Initial: $250 — Subsequent: $50

Maximum Fees
Load: none — 12b-1: 0.25%
Other: none

Services
✔ IRA
✔ Keogh
✔ Telephone Exchange

Dreyfus (DREVX)

800-645-6561, 516-794-5452
www.dreyfus.com

Growth & Income

PERFORMANCE — fund inception date: 5/24/51

	3yr Annual	5yr Annual	10yr Annual	Bull	Bear
Return (%)	7.6	9.8	10.5	59.2	-15.5
Differ from Category (+/-)	-1.3 blw av	-4.5 low	-4.4 low	25.7 high	-15.4 low

Standard Deviation	Category Risk Index	Beta
19.3%—abv av	1.11—high	1.07

	2000	1999	1998	1997	1996	1995	1994	1993	1992	1991
Return (%)	-14.2	24.0	17.1	10.7	15.8	23.7	-4.2	6.3	5.5	28.0
Differ from Category (+/-)	-19.9	13.2	4.3	-16.2	-3.9	-5.8	-3.7	-7.5	-6.1	-0.1
Return, Tax-Adjusted (%)	-14.5	22.2	16.7	6.8	12.3	13.4	-5.6	3.9	4.2	26.2

PER SHARE DATA

	2000	1999	1998	1997	1996	1995	1994	1993	1992	1991
Dividends, Net Income ($)	0.05	0.06	0.10	0.08	0.08	0.22	0.21	0.32	0.24	0.34
Distrib'ns, Cap Gain ($)	0.15	0.87	0.00	1.91	1.16	4.07	0.39	0.66	0.34	0.28
Net Asset Value ($)	11.20	13.28	11.52	9.93	10.82	10.42	11.93	13.10	13.27	13.14
Expense Ratio (%)	na	0.71	0.73	0.71	0.73	0.74	0.74	0.74	0.74	0.78
Yield (%)	0.44	0.42	0.86	0.67	0.66	1.51	1.70	2.32	1.76	2.53
Portfolio Turnover (%)	na	58	109	201	220	269	27	39	55	80
Total Assets (Millions $)	2,262	2,834	2,591	2,614	2,711	2,654	2,447	2,850	3,174	2,996

PORTFOLIO (as of 6/30/00)

Portfolio Manager: Timothy Ghriskey - 1997

Investm't Category: Growth & Income

✔ Domestic	Index
✔ Foreign	Sector
Asset Allocation	State Specific

Investment Style

✔ Large Cap	Mid Cap	Small Cap
Growth	✔ Grth/Val	Value

Portfolio

0.1%	cash	0.0%	corp bonds
99.9%	stocks	0.0%	gov't bonds
0.0%	pref/conv't pref	0.0%	muni bonds
0.0%	conv't bds/wrnts	0.0%	other

SHAREHOLDER INFORMATION

Minimum Investment
Initial: $2,500 — Subsequent: $100

Minimum IRA Investment
Initial: $750 — Subsequent: $1

Maximum Fees
Load: none — 12b-1: none
Other: none

Services
✔ IRA
✔ Keogh
✔ Telephone Exchange

Dreyfus Appreciation (DGAGX)

800-645-6561, 516-794-5452
www.dreyfus.com

Growth

PERFORMANCE

fund inception date: 1/18/84

	3yr Annual	5yr Annual	10yr Annual	Bull	Bear
Return (%)	13.5	18.6	17.2	39.1	1.0
Differ from Category (+/-)	2.5 abv av	2.5 abv av	0.4 av	-10.6 av	6.4 abv av

Standard Deviation	Category Risk Index	Beta
16.1%—av	0.83—low	0.84

	2000	1999	1998	1997	1996	1995	1994	1993	1992	1991
Return (%)	1.8	9.9	30.8	27.8	25.6	37.8	3.6	0.7	4.6	38.4
Differ from Category (+/-)	-1.7	-9.0	16.5	0.7	3.3	7.4	3.8	-13.9	-8.0	0.8
Return, Tax-Adjusted (%)	0.1	9.5	30.4	27.3	25.1	36.9	2.8	0.0	4.4	37.2

PER SHARE DATA

	2000	1999	1998	1997	1996	1995	1994	1993	1992	1991
Dividends, Net Income ($)	0.28	0.23	0.22	0.26	0.25	0.33	0.27	0.26	0.12	0.20
Distrib'ns, Cap Gain ($)	3.22	0.30	0.07	0.06	0.00	0.02	0.00	0.06	0.07	0.25
Net Asset Value ($)	42.94	45.73	42.07	32.38	25.58	20.55	15.17	14.92	15.15	14.67
Expense Ratio (%)	na	0.88	0.89	0.87	0.91	0.92	0.96	1.07	1.14	1.30
Yield (%)	0.60	0.49	0.52	0.80	0.97	1.60	1.77	1.73	0.78	1.34
Portfolio Turnover (%)	na	11	1	1	4	4	6	9	3	13
Total Assets (Millions $)	3,876	4,750	4,168	1,978	876	460	233	237	208	80

PORTFOLIO (as of 3/31/00)

Portfolio Manager: committee - 1990

Investm't Category: Growth

✔ Domestic	Index
✔ Foreign	Sector
Asset Allocation	State Specific

Investment Style

✔ Large Cap	Mid Cap	Small Cap
Growth	✔ Grth/Val	Value

Portfolio

0.2% cash	0.0% corp bonds
98.9% stocks	0.0% gov't bonds
0.9% pref/conv't pref	0.0% muni bonds
0.0% conv't bds/wrnts	0.0% other

SHAREHOLDER INFORMATION

Minimum Investment
Initial: $2,500 Subsequent: $100

Minimum IRA Investment
Initial: $750 Subsequent: $1

Maximum Fees
Load: none 12b-1: none
Other: none

Services
✔ IRA
✔ Keogh
✔ Telephone Exchange

Dreyfus Balanced (DRBAX)

800-645-6561, 516-794-5452
www.dreyfus.com

Balanced

PERFORMANCE — fund inception date: 9/30/92

	3yr Annual	5yr Annual	10yr Annual	Bull	Bear
Return (%)	7.2	10.0	na	27.7	-3.3
Differ from Category (+/-)	-1.2 blw av	-1.4 blw av	na	-0.4 av	-0.1 av

Standard Deviation	Category Risk Index	Beta
10.8%—blw av	0.99—av	0.57

	2000	1999	1998	1997	1996	1995	1994	1993	1992	1991
Return (%)	1.9	10.2	9.6	17.4	11.6	25.0	3.9	10.8	—	—
Differ from Category (+/-)	-0.1	-0.5	-3.7	-1.4	-2.3	-0.5	5.2	-3.6	—	—
Return, Tax-Adjusted (%)	0.1	7.1	7.1	13.7	9.3	21.7	2.2	9.2	—	—

PER SHARE DATA

	2000	1999	1998	1997	1996	1995	1994	1993	1992	1991
Dividends, Net Income ($)	0.40	0.43	0.48	0.44	0.43	0.57	0.46	0.40	—	—
Distrib'ns, Cap Gain ($)	0.60	1.60	1.07	2.08	0.63	0.75	0.12	0.13	—	—
Net Asset Value ($)	15.07	15.79	16.23	16.27	16.04	15.37	13.39	13.46	—	—
Expense Ratio (%)	0.96	0.94	0.91	0.96	1.00	1.04	0.69	0.23	—	—
Yield (%)	2.55	2.47	2.77	2.39	2.57	3.53	3.40	2.94	—	—
Portfolio Turnover (%)	160	162	177	235	186	72	58	46	—	—
Total Assets (Millions $)	194	193	322	371	292	196	92	59	—	—

PORTFOLIO (as of 6/30/00)

Portfolio Manager: Matthew Kelmon - 1997

Investm't Category: Balanced

✔ Domestic	Index
Foreign	Sector
Asset Allocation	State Specific

Investment Style

Large Cap	Mid Cap	Small Cap
Growth	Grth/Val	Value

Portfolio

-0.3%	cash	19.2%	corp bonds
54.6%	stocks	26.4%	gov't bonds
0.0%	pref/conv't pref	0.0%	muni bonds
0.0%	conv't bds/wrnts	0.0%	other

SHAREHOLDER INFORMATION

Minimum Investment
Initial: $2,500 — Subsequent: $100

Minimum IRA Investment
Initial: $750 — Subsequent: $1

Maximum Fees
Load: none — 12b-1: none
Other: none

Services
✔ IRA
✔ Keogh
✔ Telephone Exchange

Dreyfus Discp Stock (DDSTX)

800-645-6561, 516-794-5452
www.dreyfus.com

Growth & Income

PERFORMANCE

fund inception date: 12/31/87

	3yr Annual	5yr Annual	10yr Annual	Bull	Bear
Return (%)	10.7	17.4	17.1	53.6	-13.3
Differ from Category (+/-)	1.8 av	3.1 abv av	2.2 high	20.1 abv av	-13.2 low

Standard Deviation	Category Risk Index	Beta
18.6%—av	1.07—abv av	1.04

	2000	1999	1998	1997	1996	1995	1994	1993	1992	1991
Return (%)	-9.2	18.2	26.6	31.9	24.8	36.8	-1.0	11.8	7.5	33.6
Differ from Category (+/-)	-14.9	7.4	13.8	5.0	5.1	7.3	-0.5	-2.0	-4.1	5.5
Return, Tax-Adjusted (%)	-10.0	17.3	25.2	29.0	22.1	35.2	-2.3	10.5	5.2	31.9

PER SHARE DATA

	2000	1999	1998	1997	1996	1995	1994	1993	1992	1991
Dividends, Net Income ($)	0.00	0.07	0.22	0.23	0.27	0.31	0.28	0.27	0.26	0.25
Distrib'ns, Cap Gain ($)	1.92	1.39	1.65	3.37	1.77	0.55	0.47	0.39	1.07	0.52
Net Asset Value ($)	36.97	42.76	37.46	31.12	26.40	22.78	17.31	18.26	16.94	17.00
Expense Ratio (%)	na	1.00	0.65	0.90	0.90	0.90	0.90	0.90	0.90	0.90
Yield (%)	0.00	0.15	0.56	0.66	0.95	1.32	1.57	1.44	1.44	1.42
Portfolio Turnover (%)	na	57	37	68	64	60	106	64	84	69
Total Assets (Millions $)	3,184	3,523	2,817	1,645	874	438	219	201	48	31

PORTFOLIO (as of 6/30/00)

Portfolio Manager: Bert Mullins - 1996

Investm't Category: Growth & Income

✔ Domestic — Index
✔ Foreign — Sector
Asset Allocation — State Specific

Investment Style

✔ Large Cap — Mid Cap — Small Cap
Growth — ✔ Grth/Val — Value

Portfolio

1.5%	cash	0.0%	corp bonds
98.5%	stocks	0.0%	gov't bonds
0.0%	pref/conv't pref	0.0%	muni bonds
0.0%	conv't bds/wrnts	0.0%	other

SHAREHOLDER INFORMATION

Minimum Investment

Initial: $2,500 — Subsequent: $100

Minimum IRA Investment

Initial: $750 — Subsequent: $1

Maximum Fees

Load: none — 12b-1: 0.10%
Other: none

Services

✔ IRA
✔ Keogh
✔ Telephone Exchange

Dreyfus Emerging Markets (DRFMX)

800-645-6561, 516-794-5452
www.dreyfus.com

International Stock

PERFORMANCE

fund inception date: 6/28/96

	3yr Annual	5yr Annual	10yr Annual	Bull	Bear
Return (%)	4.5	na	na	118.1	-22.6
Differ from Category (+/-)	-4.4 blw av	na	na	27.2 abv av	1.4 av

Standard Deviation	Category Risk Index	Beta
28.1%—high	1.24—abv av	1.08

	2000	1999	1998	1997	1996	1995	1994	1993	1992	1991
Return (%)	-20.3	74.9	-18.0	-1.5	—	—	—	—	—	—
Differ from Category (+/-)	-0.9	14.2	-23.8	-2.8	—	—	—	—	—	—
Return, Tax-Adjusted (%)	-22.6	72.3	-18.3	-2.2	—	—	—	—	—	—

PER SHARE DATA

	2000	1999	1998	1997	1996	1995	1994	1993	1992	1991
Dividends, Net Income ($)	0.13	0.11	0.09	0.01	—	—	—	—	—	—
Distrib'ns, Cap Gain ($)	1.59	1.01	0.02	0.43	—	—	—	—	—	—
Net Asset Value ($)	10.68	15.50	9.53	11.76	—	—	—	—	—	—
Expense Ratio (%)	1.85	1.88	1.94	na	—	—	—	—	—	—
Yield (%)	1.05	0.66	0.94	0.08	—	—	—	—	—	—
Portfolio Turnover (%)	105	87	87	—	—	—	—	—	—	—
Total Assets (Millions $)	222	190	57	63	—	—	—	—	—	—

PORTFOLIO (as of 6/30/00)

Portfolio Manager: D. Kirk Henry - 1996

Investm't Category: International Stock

Domestic	Index
✔ Foreign	Sector
Asset Allocation	State Specific

Investment Style

Large Cap	Mid Cap	Small Cap
Growth	Grth/Val	Value

Portfolio

7.5%	cash	0.0%	corp bonds
88.9%	stocks	0.0%	gov't bonds
3.6%	pref/conv't pref	0.0%	muni bonds
0.0%	conv't bds/wrnts	0.0%	other

SHAREHOLDER INFORMATION

Minimum Investment
Initial: $2,500 Subsequent: $100

Minimum IRA Investment
Initial: $750 Subsequent: $1

Maximum Fees
Load: 1.00% redemption 12b-1: none
Other: redemption fee applies for 6 months

Services
✔ IRA
Keogh
✔ Telephone Exchange

Dreyfus Founders: Bal/F

800-525-2440, 303-394-4404
www.founders.com

(FRINX)

Balanced

this fund is closed to new investors

PERFORMANCE

fund inception date: 2/19/63

	3yr Annual	5yr Annual	10yr Annual	Bull	Bear
Return (%)	0.0	6.7	10.8	10.5	-16.0
Differ from Category (+/-)	-8.4 low	-4.7 low	-0.9 blw av	-17.6 low	-12.8 low

Standard Deviation	Category Risk Index	Beta
12.5%—blw av	1.14—abv av	0.55

	2000	1999	1998	1997	1996	1995	1994	1993	1992	1991
Return (%)	-10.4	-2.2	13.9	16.9	18.7	29.4	-1.9	21.8	6.0	22.8
Differ from Category (+/-)	-12.4	-12.9	0.6	-1.9	4.8	3.9	-0.6	7.4	-2.4	-1.0
Return, Tax-Adjusted (%)	-10.9	-5.0	12.1	14.4	16.2	24.2	-2.7	17.6	4.6	20.1

PER SHARE DATA

	2000	1999	1998	1997	1996	1995	1994	1993	1992	1991
Dividends, Net Income ($)	0.15	0.31	0.29	0.30	0.26	0.27	0.19	0.20	0.27	0.31
Distrib'ns, Cap Gain ($)	0.01	1.10	0.43	0.73	0.48	1.19	0.00	0.95	0.09	0.33
Net Asset Value ($)	9.22	10.47	12.19	11.35	10.61	9.58	8.56	8.93	8.30	8.19
Expense Ratio (%)	na	0.97	0.99	0.99	1.10	1.24	1.26	1.34	1.88	1.73
Yield (%)	1.62	2.67	2.29	2.48	2.34	2.50	2.21	2.02	3.21	3.63
Portfolio Turnover (%)	na	218	211	203	146	284	258	251	96	133
Total Assets (Millions $)	562	1,057	1,254	937	393	130	95	72	31	18

PORTFOLIO (as of 3/31/00)

Portfolio Manager: Curtis Anderson - 1999

Investm't Category: Balanced

✔ Domestic	Index
✔ Foreign	Sector
Asset Allocation	State Specific

Investment Style

Large Cap	Mid Cap	Small Cap
Growth	Grth/Val	Value

Portfolio

7.2%	cash	0.0%	corp bonds
65.8%	stocks	24.7%	gov't bonds
0.0%	pref/conv't pref	0.0%	muni bonds
0.0%	conv't bds/wrnts	2.3%	other

SHAREHOLDER INFORMATION

Minimum Investment

Initial: $1,000 Subsequent: $100

Minimum IRA Investment

Initial: $500 Subsequent: $100

Maximum Fees

Load: none 12b-1: 0.25%

Other: none

Services

✔ IRA
✔ Keogh
✔ Telephone Exchange

Dreyfus Founders: Dscvry/F (FDISX)

800-525-2440, 303-394-4404
www.founders.com

Aggressive Growth

this fund is closed to new investors

PERFORMANCE

fund inception date: 12/29/89

	3yr Annual	5yr Annual	10yr Annual	Bull	Bear
Return (%)	26.8	22.5	21.3	187.2	-30.9
Differ from Category (+/-)	10.6 abv av	7.9 abv av	5.5 abv av	68.0 high	-10.3 blw av

Standard Deviation	Category Risk Index	Beta
37.1%—high	1.14—abv av	1.41

	2000	1999	1998	1997	1996	1995	1994	1993	1992	1991
Return (%)	-8.2	94.5	14.1	11.9	21.2	31.2	-7.7	10.8	15.1	62.4
Differ from Category (+/-)	-2.2	37.0	-1.0	-2.9	2.9	-3.4	-6.9	-14.4	8.2	15.2
Return, Tax-Adjusted (%)	-9.4	89.4	12.2	8.9	18.6	25.0	-7.7	10.0	14.7	60.7

PER SHARE DATA

	2000	1999	1998	1997	1996	1995	1994	1993	1992	1991
Dividends, Net Income ($)	0.00	0.00	0.00	0.00	0.00	0.00	0.00	0.00	0.06	0.00
Distrib'ns, Cap Gain ($)	2.60	6.15	2.16	3.52	1.99	4.34	0.00	0.51	0.17	0.67
Net Asset Value ($)	34.75	40.86	24.37	23.45	24.22	21.70	19.88	21.55	19.93	17.52
Expense Ratio (%)	na	1.45	1.55	1.52	1.58	1.65	1.67	1.65	1.85	1.77
Yield (%)	0.00	0.00	0.00	0.00	0.00	0.00	0.00	0.00	0.29	0.00
Portfolio Turnover (%)	na	157	121	90	106	99	72	99	111	165
Total Assets (Millions $)	1,035	807	239	247	250	218	187	226	150	47

PORTFOLIO (as of 3/31/00)

Portfolio Manager: Robert Ammann - 1997

Investm't Category: Aggressive Growth

✔ Domestic   Index
✔ Foreign   Sector
Asset Allocation   State Specific

Investment Style

Large Cap   Mid Cap   ✔ Small Cap
✔ Growth   Grth/Val   Value

Portfolio

11.5%	cash	0.0%	corp bonds
88.6%	stocks	0.0%	gov't bonds
0.0%	pref/conv't pref	0.0%	muni bonds
0.0%	conv't bds/wrnts	0.0%	other

SHAREHOLDER INFORMATION

Minimum Investment

Initial: $1,000   Subsequent: $100

Minimum IRA Investment

Initial: $500   Subsequent: $100

Maximum Fees

Load: none   12b-1: 0.25%
Other: none

Services

✔ IRA
✔ Keogh
✔ Telephone Exchange

Dreyfus Founders: Gr & Inc/F (FRMUX)

800-525-2440, 303-394-4404
www.founders.com

Growth

this fund is closed to new investors

PERFORMANCE

fund inception date: 7/5/38

	3yr Annual	5yr Annual	10yr Annual	Bull	Bear
Return (%)	2.9	10.1	11.9	36.5	-23.2
Differ from Category (+/-)	-8.1 low	-6.0 low	-4.9 low	-13.2 blw av	-17.8 low

Standard Deviation	Category Risk Index	Beta
17.7%—av	0.91—low	0.88

	2000	1999	1998	1997	1996	1995	1994	1993	1992	1991
Return (%)	-19.5	15.1	17.7	19.4	24.3	29.0	0.5	14.4	-0.2	28.3
Differ from Category (+/-)	-23.0	-3.8	3.4	-7.7	2.0	-1.4	0.7	-0.2	-12.8	-9.3
Return, Tax-Adjusted (%)	-20.6	12.9	15.0	14.3	19.7	23.1	-1.0	8.5	-2.8	24.6

PER SHARE DATA

	2000	1999	1998	1997	1996	1995	1994	1993	1992	1991
Dividends, Net Income ($)	0.00	0.00	0.10	0.13	0.08	0.08	0.05	0.04	0.08	0.11
Distrib'ns, Cap Gain ($)	0.43	0.78	0.71	1.56	0.98	1.17	0.30	1.38	0.65	0.74
Net Asset Value ($)	5.69	7.61	7.32	6.92	7.23	6.69	6.16	6.49	6.91	7.67
Expense Ratio (%)	na	1.12	1.08	1.09	1.15	1.20	1.21	1.22	1.23	1.10
Yield (%)	0.00	0.00	1.24	1.53	0.97	1.01	0.77	0.50	1.05	1.30
Portfolio Turnover (%)	na	165	259	256	195	233	239	212	103	95
Total Assets (Millions $)	391	538	542	543	535	373	312	307	290	290

PORTFOLIO (as of 3/31/00)

Portfolio Manager: Thomas Arrington - 1998

Investm't Category: Growth

✔ Domestic
✔ Foreign
Asset Allocation
Index
Sector
State Specific

Investment Style

✔ Large Cap
✔ Growth
Mid Cap
Grth/Val
Small Cap
Value

Portfolio

2.5%	cash	0.0%	corp bonds
96.0%	stocks	0.0%	gov't bonds
0.0%	pref/conv't pref	0.0%	muni bonds
0.0%	conv't bds/wrnts	1.6%	other

SHAREHOLDER INFORMATION

Minimum Investment

Initial: $1,000 Subsequent: $100

Minimum IRA Investment

Initial: $500 Subsequent: $100

Maximum Fees

Load: none 12b-1: 0.25%
Other: none

Services

✔ IRA
✔ Keogh
✔ Telephone Exchange

Dreyfus Founders: Md Cp Gr/F (FRSPX)

800-525-2440, 303-394-4404
www.founders.com

Aggressive Growth

this fund is closed to new investors

PERFORMANCE

fund inception date: 9/7/61

	3yr Annual	5yr Annual	10yr Annual	Bull	Bear
Return (%)	2.1	7.4	13.4	80.4	-34.6
Differ from Category (+/-)	-14.1 low	-7.2 low	-2.4 blw av	-38.8 av	-14.0 blw av

Standard Deviation	Category Risk Index	Beta
32.7%—high	1.01—av	1.24

	2000	1999	1998	1997	1996	1995	1994	1993	1992	1991
Return (%)	-23.6	42.2	-1.7	16.4	15.3	25.6	-4.9	16.0	8.2	63.6
Differ from Category (+/-)	-17.6	-15.3	-16.8	1.6	-3.0	-9.0	-4.1	-9.2	1.3	16.4
Return, Tax-Adjusted (%)	-28.7	37.3	-2.0	13.3	13.4	18.6	-5.9	11.2	6.5	60.1

PER SHARE DATA

	2000	1999	1998	1997	1996	1995	1994	1993	1992	1991
Dividends, Net Income ($)	0.00	0.00	0.00	0.00	0.00	0.00	0.00	0.00	0.00	0.04
Distrib'ns, Cap Gain ($)	2.23	1.79	0.13	1.15	0.46	1.75	0.28	1.33	0.45	0.57
Net Asset Value ($)	4.36	8.68	7.44	7.72	7.66	7.05	7.01	7.67	7.76	7.59
Expense Ratio (%)	na	1.40	1.33	1.30	1.34	1.36	1.36	1.33	1.23	1.15
Yield (%)	0.00	0.00	0.00	0.00	0.00	0.00	0.00	0.00	0.00	0.49
Portfolio Turnover (%)	na	186	152	110	186	244	272	285	223	102
Total Assets (Millions $)	165	255	252	320	364	388	300	432	455	224

PORTFOLIO (as of 3/31/00)

Portfolio Manager: Kevin Sonnett - 1999

Investm't Category: Aggressive Growth

✔ Domestic — Index
✔ Foreign — Sector
Asset Allocation — State Specific

Investment Style

Large Cap — ✔ Mid Cap — ✔ Small Cap
✔ Growth — Grth/Val — Value

Portfolio

6.3%	cash	0.0%	corp bonds
93.7%	stocks	0.0%	gov't bonds
0.0%	pref/conv't pref	0.0%	muni bonds
0.0%	conv't bds/wrnts	0.0%	other

SHAREHOLDER INFORMATION

Minimum Investment

Initial: $1,000 — Subsequent: $100

Minimum IRA Investment

Initial: $500 — Subsequent: $100

Maximum Fees

Load: none — 12b-1: 0.25%
Other: none

Services

✔ IRA
✔ Keogh
✔ Telephone Exchange

Dreyfus Founders: Psport/F (FPSSX)

800-525-2440, 303-394-4404
www.founders.com

International Stock

this fund is closed to new investors

PERFORMANCE

fund inception date: 11/16/93

	3yr Annual	5yr Annual	10yr Annual	Bull	Bear
Return (%)	14.0	12.6	na	99.7	-39.9
Differ from Category (+/-)	5.1 abv av	4.3 abv av	na	8.8 abv av	-15.9 low

Standard Deviation	Category Risk Index	Beta
34.4%—high	1.52—high	0.64

	2000	1999	1998	1997	1996	1995	1994	1993	1992	1991
Return (%)	-29.6	87.3	12.4	1.6	20.0	24.3	-10.3	—	—	—
Differ from Category (+/-)	-10.2	26.6	6.6	0.3	5.5	15.0	-7.2	—	—	—
Return, Tax-Adjusted (%)	-31.3	80.8	11.8	0.8	19.7	24.1	-10.3	—	—	—

PER SHARE DATA

	2000	1999	1998	1997	1996	1995	1994	1993	1992	1991
Dividends, Net Income ($)	0.00	0.00	0.01	0.02	0.02	0.03	0.01	—	—	—
Distrib'ns, Cap Gain ($)	1.96	4.82	0.38	0.47	0.08	0.00	0.00	—	—	—
Net Asset Value ($)	14.17	22.92	14.93	13.64	13.91	11.68	9.42	—	—	—
Expense Ratio (%)	na	1.64	1.52	1.53	1.57	1.84	1.88	—	—	—
Yield (%)	0.00	0.00	0.06	0.14	0.14	0.25	0.10	—	—	—
Portfolio Turnover (%)	na	330	34	51	58	37	78	—	—	—
Total Assets (Millions $)	193	261	124	123	179	49	16	—	—	—

PORTFOLIO (as of 3/31/00)

Portfolio Manager: Tracy Stouffer - 1999

Investm't Category: International Stock

Domestic	Index
✔ Foreign	Sector
Asset Allocation	State Specific

Investment Style

Large Cap	Mid Cap	Small Cap
Growth	Grth/Val	Value

Portfolio

5.5% cash	0.0% corp bonds
93.9% stocks	0.0% gov't bonds
0.6% pref/conv't pref	0.0% muni bonds
0.0% conv't bds/wrnts	0.0% other

SHAREHOLDER INFORMATION

Minimum Investment
Initial: $1,000 Subsequent: $100

Minimum IRA Investment
Initial: $500 Subsequent: $100

Maximum Fees
Load: none 12b-1: 0.25%
Other: none

Services
✔ IRA
✔ Keogh
✔ Telephone Exchange

Dreyfus Founders: Wld Gr/F (FWWGX)

800-525-2440, 303-394-4404
www.founders.com

International Stock

this fund is closed to new investors

PERFORMANCE

fund inception date: 12/29/89

	3yr Annual	5yr Annual	10yr Annual	Bull	Bear
Return (%)	8.2	9.8	12.8	67.3	-27.0
Differ from Category (+/-)	-0.7 av	1.5 av	3.8 high	-23.6 av	-3.0 av

Standard Deviation	Category Risk Index	Beta
22.2%—abv av	0.98—av	0.81

	2000	1999	1998	1997	1996	1995	1994	1993	1992	1991
Return (%)	-22.1	48.7	9.6	10.5	13.9	20.6	-2.1	29.8	1.5	34.8
Differ from Category (+/-)	-2.7	-12.0	3.8	9.2	-0.6	11.3	1.0	-10.4	5.0	21.8
Return, Tax-Adjusted (%)	-25.1	42.4	8.5	7.8	12.7	19.3	-2.8	28.9	1.5	34.6

PER SHARE DATA

	2000	1999	1998	1997	1996	1995	1994	1993	1992	1991
Dividends, Net Income ($)	0.00	0.00	0.08	0.03	0.07	0.08	0.00	0.00	0.00	0.03
Distrib'ns, Cap Gain ($)	3.87	6.94	0.94	2.88	0.75	0.65	0.45	0.41	0.00	0.03
Net Asset Value ($)	15.69	25.17	22.06	21.11	21.79	19.87	17.09	17.94	14.13	13.92
Expense Ratio (%)	na	1.53	1.47	1.45	1.53	1.65	1.66	1.80	2.06	1.90
Yield (%)	0.00	0.00	0.34	0.12	0.31	0.38	0.00	0.00	0.00	0.21
Portfolio Turnover (%)	na	157	86	82	72	54	87	117	152	84
Total Assets (Millions $)	211	285	275	308	342	227	104	84	36	20

PORTFOLIO (as of 3/31/00)

Portfolio Manager: Loeffler, Arrington, Chapman - 1999

Investm't Category: International Stock

✔ Domestic | Index
✔ Foreign | Sector
Asset Allocation | State Specific

Investment Style

Large Cap | Mid Cap | Small Cap
Growth | Grth/Val | Value

Portfolio

-0.6%	cash	0.0%	corp bonds
100.0%	stocks	0.0%	gov't bonds
0.7%	pref/conv't pref	0.0%	muni bonds
0.0%	conv't bds/wrnts	0.0%	other

SHAREHOLDER INFORMATION

Minimum Investment

Initial: $1,000 Subsequent: $100

Minimum IRA Investment

Initial: $500 Subsequent: $100

Maximum Fees

Load: none 12b-1: 0.25%
Other: none

Services

✔ IRA
✔ Keogh
✔ Telephone Exchange

Dreyfus Global Growth (DSWIX)

800-645-6561, 516-794-5452
www.dreyfus.com

International Stock

PERFORMANCE

fund inception date: 4/10/87

	3yr Annual	5yr Annual	10yr Annual	Bull	Bear
Return (%)	3.0	6.5	7.1	57.1	-30.1
Differ from Category (+/-)	-5.9 blw av	-1.8 blw av	-1.9 blw av	-33.8 blw av	-6.1 blw av

Standard Deviation	Category Risk Index	Beta
24.2%—abv av	1.07—av	0.84

	2000	1999	1998	1997	1996	1995	1994	1993	1992	1991
Return (%)	-25.5	45.2	1.1	12.2	11.9	12.0	-7.4	21.9	-2.7	17.5
Differ from Category (+/-)	-6.1	-15.5	-4.7	10.9	-2.6	2.7	-4.3	-18.3	0.8	4.5
Return, Tax-Adjusted (%)	-29.5	43.4	0.9	9.6	6.7	12.0	-7.4	21.9	-2.7	17.5

PER SHARE DATA

	2000	1999	1998	1997	1996	1995	1994	1993	1992	1991
Dividends, Net Income ($)	0.00	0.00	0.15	0.10	0.24	0.00	0.00	0.00	0.00	0.00
Distrib'ns, Cap Gain ($)	9.44	3.10	0.00	4.16	6.49	0.00	0.00	0.00	0.00	0.00
Net Asset Value ($)	26.94	47.14	34.77	34.53	34.62	36.97	32.99	35.66	29.24	30.06
Expense Ratio (%)	na	1.41	1.32	1.34	1.39	1.47	1.40	1.50	1.61	1.62
Yield (%)	0.00	0.00	0.43	0.25	0.58	0.00	0.00	0.00	0.00	0.00
Portfolio Turnover (%)	na	256	206	145	163	225	147	187	439	420
Total Assets (Millions $)	59	87	79	89	96	104	134	159	111	54

PORTFOLIO (as of 6/30/00)

Portfolio Manager: Douglas Loeffler - 1999

Investm't Category: International Stock

✔ Domestic — Index
✔ Foreign — Sector
Asset Allocation — State Specific

Investment Style

Large Cap — Mid Cap — Small Cap
Growth — Grth/Val — Value

Portfolio

-11.2%	cash	0.0%	corp bonds
110.4%	stocks	0.0%	gov't bonds
0.8%	pref/conv't pref	0.0%	muni bonds
0.0%	conv't bds/wrnts	0.0%	other

SHAREHOLDER INFORMATION

Minimum Investment
Initial: $2,500 — Subsequent: $100

Minimum IRA Investment
Initial: $750 — Subsequent: $1

Maximum Fees
Load: none — 12b-1: none
Other: none

Services
✔ IRA
✔ Keogh
✔ Telephone Exchange

Dreyfus Gr & Val: Agg Val (DAGVX)

800-645-6561, 516-794-5452
www.dreyfus.com

Growth

PERFORMANCE

fund inception date: 9/29/95

	3yr Annual	5yr Annual	10yr Annual	Bull	Bear
Return (%)	13.0	19.5	na	36.6	4.4
Differ from Category (+/-)	2.0 abv av	3.4 abv av	na	-13.1 blw av	9.8 abv av

Standard Deviation	Category Risk Index	Beta
17.8%—av	0.91—blw av	0.87

	2000	1999	1998	1997	1996	1995	1994	1993	1992	1991
Return (%)	21.3	8.1	9.9	21.5	38.9	—	—	—	—	—
Differ from Category (+/-)	17.8	-10.8	-4.4	-5.6	16.6	—	—	—	—	—
Return, Tax-Adjusted (%)	17.3	5.9	8.9	19.8	35.5	—	—	—	—	—

PER SHARE DATA

	2000	1999	1998	1997	1996	1995	1994	1993	1992	1991
Dividends, Net Income ($)	0.38	0.07	0.04	0.02	0.05	—	—	—	—	—
Distrib'ns, Cap Gain ($)	3.98	2.51	1.05	1.69	1.86	—	—	—	—	—
Net Asset Value ($)	24.50	23.99	24.71	23.50	20.71	—	—	—	—	—
Expense Ratio (%)	1.34	1.29	1.27	1.24	1.17	—	—	—	—	—
Yield (%)	1.33	0.26	0.15	0.07	0.22	—	—	—	—	—
Portfolio Turnover (%)	235	225	170	120	260	—	—	—	—	—
Total Assets (Millions $)	83	64	115	157	33	—	—	—	—	—

PORTFOLIO (as of 6/30/00)

Portfolio Manager: Timothy Ghriskey - 1995

Investm't Category: Growth

✔ Domestic	Index
✔ Foreign	Sector
Asset Allocation	State Specific

Investment Style

✔ Large Cap	✔ Mid Cap	Small Cap
Growth	Grth/Val	✔ Value

Portfolio

5.9% cash	0.0% corp bonds
94.2% stocks	0.0% gov't bonds
0.0% pref/conv't pref	0.0% muni bonds
0.0% conv't bds/wrnts	0.0% other

SHAREHOLDER INFORMATION

Minimum Investment
Initial: $2,500 Subsequent: $100

Minimum IRA Investment
Initial: $750 Subsequent: $1

Maximum Fees
Load: 1.00% redemption 12b-1: none
Other: redemption fee applies for 15 days

Services
✔ IRA
✔ Keogh
✔ Telephone Exchange

Dreyfus Gr & Val: Emg Ldrs (DRELX)

800-645-6561, 516-794-5452
www.dreyfus.com

Aggressive Growth

this fund is closed to new investors

PERFORMANCE

fund inception date: 9/28/95

	3yr Annual	5yr Annual	10yr Annual	Bull	Bear
Return (%)	18.0	24.7	na	82.5	-12.8
Differ from Category (+/-)	1.8 av	10.1 high	na	-36.7 av	7.8 abv av

Standard Deviation	Category Risk Index	Beta
24.5%—abv av	0.75—blw av	0.94

	2000	1999	1998	1997	1996	1995	1994	1993	1992	1991
Return (%)	9.4	38.2	8.5	33.9	37.4	—	—	—	—	—
Differ from Category (+/-)	15.4	-19.3	-6.6	19.1	19.1	—	—	—	—	—
Return, Tax-Adjusted (%)	9.0	38.1	8.4	31.2	34.9	—	—	—	—	—

PER SHARE DATA

	2000	1999	1998	1997	1996	1995	1994	1993	1992	1991
Dividends, Net Income ($)	0.00	0.00	0.00	0.00	0.00	—	—	—	—	—
Distrib'ns, Cap Gain ($)	0.58	0.06	0.04	2.66	1.40	—	—	—	—	—
Net Asset Value ($)	39.59	36.73	26.62	24.57	20.39	—	—	—	—	—
Expense Ratio (%)	1.26	1.38	1.39	1.39	1.16	—	—	—	—	—
Yield (%)	0.00	0.00	0.00	0.00	0.00	—	—	—	—	—
Portfolio Turnover (%)	76	100	199	197	203	—	—	—	—	—
Total Assets (Millions $)	1,248	612	155	129	61	—	—	—	—	—

PORTFOLIO (as of 6/30/00)

Portfolio Manager: Paul Kandel, Hillary Woods - 1996

Investm't Category: Aggressive Growth

✔ Domestic Index
✔ Foreign Sector
Asset Allocation State Specific

Investment Style

Large Cap Mid Cap ✔ Small Cap
✔ Growth Grth/Val Value

Portfolio

4.9%	cash	0.0%	corp bonds
95.1%	stocks	0.0%	gov't bonds
0.0%	pref/conv't pref	0.0%	muni bonds
0.0%	conv't bds/wrnts	0.0%	other

SHAREHOLDER INFORMATION

Minimum Investment
Initial: $2,500 Subsequent: $100

Minimum IRA Investment
Initial: $750 Subsequent: $1

Maximum Fees
Load: 1.00% redemption 12b-1: none
Other: redemption fee applies for 15 days

Services
✔ IRA
✔ Keogh
✔ Telephone Exchange

Dreyfus Gr & Val: Intl Val (DIVLX)

800-645-6561, 516-794-5452
www.dreyfus.com

International Stock

PERFORMANCE

fund inception date: 9/29/95

	3yr Annual	5yr Annual	10yr Annual	Bull	Bear
Return (%)	9.8	9.7	na	39.2	-4.6
Differ from Category (+/-)	0.9 av	1.4 av	na	-51.7 low	19.4 high

Standard Deviation	Category Risk Index	Beta
15.2%—av	0.67—low	0.57

	2000	1999	1998	1997	1996	1995	1994	1993	1992	1991
Return (%)	-4.0	25.7	9.9	9.0	10.3	—	—	—	—	—
Differ from Category (+/-)	15.4	-35.0	4.1	7.7	-4.2	—	—	—	—	—
Return, Tax-Adjusted (%)	-5.3	24.3	8.5	8.2	9.7	—	—	—	—	—

PER SHARE DATA

	2000	1999	1998	1997	1996	1995	1994	1993	1992	1991
Dividends, Net Income ($)	0.10	0.11	0.14	0.08	0.10	—	—	—	—	—
Distrib'ns, Cap Gain ($)	1.05	0.79	0.74	0.39	0.13	—	—	—	—	—
Net Asset Value ($)	16.14	18.07	15.14	14.60	13.82	—	—	—	—	—
Expense Ratio (%)	1.40	1.40	1.44	1.49	1.39	—	—	—	—	—
Yield (%)	0.58	0.58	0.88	0.53	0.71	—	—	—	—	—
Portfolio Turnover (%)	37	30	34	25	19	—	—	—	—	—
Total Assets (Millions $)	366	320	179	114	41	—	—	—	—	—

PORTFOLIO (as of 6/30/00)

Portfolio Manager: Sandor Cseh - 1995

Investm't Category: International Stock

Domestic	Index
✔ Foreign	Sector
Asset Allocation	State Specific

Investment Style

Large Cap	Mid Cap	Small Cap
Growth	Grth/Val	Value

Portfolio

3.9% cash	0.0% corp bonds
96.1% stocks	0.0% gov't bonds
0.0% pref/conv't pref	0.0% muni bonds
0.0% conv't bds/wrnts	0.0% other

SHAREHOLDER INFORMATION

Minimum Investment
Initial: $2,500 Subsequent: $100

Minimum IRA Investment
Initial: $750 Subsequent: $1

Maximum Fees
Load: 1.00% redemption 12b-1: none
Other: redemption fee applies for 15 days

Services
✔ IRA
✔ Keogh
✔ Telephone Exchange

Dreyfus Gr & Val: Lrg Val (DLCVX)

800-645-6561, 516-794-5452
www.dreyfus.com

Growth

PERFORMANCE

fund inception date: 12/29/93

	3yr Annual	5yr Annual	10yr Annual	Bull	Bear
Return (%)	8.5	14.2	na	33.6	-1.6
Differ from Category (+/-)	-2.5 blw av	-1.9 blw av	na	-16.1 blw av	3.8 abv av

Standard Deviation	Category Risk Index	Beta
17.8%—av	0.91—blw av	0.89

	2000	1999	1998	1997	1996	1995	1994	1993	1992	1991
Return (%)	5.3	6.5	13.7	15.9	31.4	43.0	-1.0	—	—	—
Differ from Category (+/-)	1.8	-12.4	-0.6	-11.2	9.1	12.6	-0.8	—	—	—
Return, Tax-Adjusted (%)	4.0	3.7	13.5	14.6	29.2	37.6	-2.0	—	—	—

PER SHARE DATA

	2000	1999	1998	1997	1996	1995	1994	1993	1992	1991
Dividends, Net Income ($)	0.12	0.13	0.09	0.05	0.11	0.21	0.32	—	—	—
Distrib'ns, Cap Gain ($)	1.10	2.91	0.00	1.05	0.98	2.00	0.00	—	—	—
Net Asset Value ($)	21.32	21.43	23.01	20.31	18.46	14.88	11.97	—	—	—
Expense Ratio (%)	na	1.25	1.24	1.22	1.25	0.83	—	—	—	—
Yield (%)	0.53	0.53	0.39	0.23	0.56	1.24	2.67	—	—	—
Portfolio Turnover (%)	na	141	156	110	186	143	48	—	—	—
Total Assets (Millions $)	89	115	142	165	51	7	5	—	—	—

PORTFOLIO (as of 6/30/00)

Portfolio Manager: Timothy Ghriskey - 1995

Investm't Category: Growth

✔ Domestic | Index
✔ Foreign | Sector
Asset Allocation | State Specific

Investment Style

✔ Large Cap | Mid Cap | Small Cap
Growth | Grth/Val | ✔ Value

Portfolio

4.9% cash | 0.0% corp bonds
95.1% stocks | 0.0% gov't bonds
0.0% pref/conv't pref | 0.0% muni bonds
0.0% conv't bds/wrnts | 0.0% other

SHAREHOLDER INFORMATION

Minimum Investment

Initial: $2,500 | Subsequent: $100

Minimum IRA Investment

Initial: $750 | Subsequent: $1

Maximum Fees

Load: 1.00% redemption | 12b-1: none
Other: redemption fee applies for 15 days

Services

✔ IRA
✔ Keogh
✔ Telephone Exchange

Dreyfus Gr & Val: Midcp VI (DMCVX)

800-645-6561, 516-794-5452
www.dreyfus.com

Growth

PERFORMANCE

fund inception date: 9/29/95

	3yr Annual	5yr Annual	10yr Annual	Bull	Bear
Return (%)	16.0	22.4	na	63.5	5.5
Differ from Category (+/-)	5.0 high	6.3 high	na	13.8 abv av	10.9 abv av

Standard Deviation	Category Risk Index	Beta
27.3%—high	1.40—high	1.26

	2000	1999	1998	1997	1996	1995	1994	1993	1992	1991
Return (%)	27.4	28.0	-4.2	27.9	37.3	—	—	—	—	—
Differ from Category (+/-)	23.9	9.1	-18.5	0.8	15.0	—	—	—	—	—
Return, Tax-Adjusted (%)	24.3	26.6	-5.9	26.6	33.5	—	—	—	—	—

PER SHARE DATA

	2000	1999	1998	1997	1996	1995	1994	1993	1992	1991
Dividends, Net Income ($)	0.00	0.00	0.00	0.00	0.04	—	—	—	—	—
Distrib'ns, Cap Gain ($)	3.28	1.24	1.78	1.04	1.75	—	—	—	—	—
Net Asset Value ($)	23.94	21.46	17.80	20.52	16.83	—	—	—	—	—
Expense Ratio (%)	1.27	1.34	1.29	1.25	1.18	—	—	—	—	—
Yield (%)	0.00	0.00	0.00	0.00	0.21	—	—	—	—	—
Portfolio Turnover (%)	242	257	168	154	267	—	—	—	—	—
Total Assets (Millions $)	254	85	94	123	8	—	—	—	—	—

PORTFOLIO (as of 6/30/00)

Portfolio Manager: Peter Higgins - 1995

Investm't Category: Growth

✔ Domestic | Index
✔ Foreign | Sector
Asset Allocation | State Specific

Investment Style

Large Cap | ✔ Mid Cap | Small Cap
Growth | Grth/Val | ✔ Value

Portfolio

0.6% cash | 0.0% corp bonds
99.4% stocks | 0.0% gov't bonds
0.0% pref/conv't pref | 0.0% muni bonds
0.0% conv't bds/wrnts | 0.0% other

SHAREHOLDER INFORMATION

Minimum Investment
Initial: $2,500 | Subsequent: $100

Minimum IRA Investment
Initial: $750 | Subsequent: $1

Maximum Fees
Load: 1.00% redemption | 12b-1: none
Other: redemption fee applies for 15 days

Services
✔ IRA
✔ Keogh
✔ Telephone Exchange

Dreyfus Gr & Val: Sm Val (DSCVX)

800-645-6561, 516-794-5452
www.dreyfus.com

Aggressive Growth

this fund is closed to new investors

PERFORMANCE — fund inception date: 12/29/93

	3yr Annual	5yr Annual	10yr Annual	Bull	Bear
Return (%)	6.2	15.1	na	53.5	-12.7
Differ from Category (+/-)	-10.0 blw av	0.5 av	na	-65.7 blw av	7.9 abv av

Standard Deviation	Category Risk Index	Beta
25.2%—abv av	0.78—blw av	1.10

	2000	1999	1998	1997	1996	1995	1994	1993	1992	1991
Return (%)	5.4	21.2	-6.2	25.9	34.1	36.1	-1.5	—	—	—
Differ from Category (+/-)	11.4	-36.3	-21.3	11.1	15.8	1.5	-0.7	—	—	—
Return, Tax-Adjusted (%)	3.9	19.7	-6.2	25.4	29.9	33.2	-3.7	—	—	—

PER SHARE DATA

	2000	1999	1998	1997	1996	1995	1994	1993	1992	1991
Dividends, Net Income ($)	0.00	0.00	0.00	0.01	0.04	0.09	0.33	—	—	—
Distrib'ns, Cap Gain ($)	1.61	1.40	0.00	0.38	2.09	1.01	0.53	—	—	—
Net Asset Value ($)	21.90	22.44	19.75	21.07	17.04	14.33	11.35	—	—	—
Expense Ratio (%)	na	1.23	1.21	1.23	1.27	0.84	—	—	—	—
Yield (%)	0.00	0.00	0.00	0.04	0.20	0.58	2.77	—	—	—
Portfolio Turnover (%)	na	170	132	76	183	161	219	—	—	—
Total Assets (Millions $)	253	304	327	402	23	7	5	—	—	—

PORTFOLIO (as of 6/30/00)

Portfolio Manager: Peter Higgins - 1997

Investm't Category: Aggressive Growth

✔ Domestic — Index
✔ Foreign — Sector
Asset Allocation — State Specific

Investment Style

Large Cap — Mid Cap — ✔ Small Cap
Growth — Grth/Val — ✔ Value

Portfolio

-0.1%	cash	0.0%	corp bonds
100.1%	stocks	0.0%	gov't bonds
0.0%	pref/conv't pref	0.0%	muni bonds
0.0%	conv't bds/wrnts	0.0%	other

SHAREHOLDER INFORMATION

Minimum Investment

Initial: $2,500 — Subsequent: $100

Minimum IRA Investment

Initial: $750 — Subsequent: $1

Maximum Fees

Load: 1.00% redemption — 12b-1: none

Other: redemption fee applies for 15 days

Services

✔ IRA
✔ Keogh
✔ Telephone Exchange

Dreyfus Growth & Income (DGRIX)

800-645-6561, 516-794-5452
www.dreyfus.com

Growth & Income

PERFORMANCE — fund inception date: 12/31/91

	3yr Annual	5yr Annual	10yr Annual	Bull	Bear
Return (%)	8.2	10.9	na	48.0	-10.1
Differ from Category (+/-)	-0.7 av	-3.4 low	na	14.5 abv av	-10.0 blw av

Standard Deviation	Category Risk Index	Beta
17.3%—av	1.00—av	0.92

	2000	1999	1998	1997	1996	1995	1994	1993	1992	1991
Return (%)	-3.8	16.8	12.8	15.9	14.4	25.0	-5.1	18.5	20.1	—
Differ from Category (+/-)	-9.5	6.0	0.0	-11.0	-5.3	-4.5	-4.6	4.7	8.5	—
Return, Tax-Adjusted (%)	-5.1	14.2	11.1	11.8	9.6	22.9	-6.1	17.4	19.4	—

PER SHARE DATA

	2000	1999	1998	1997	1996	1995	1994	1993	1992	1991
Dividends, Net Income ($)	0.04	0.08	0.17	0.30	0.34	0.44	0.36	0.35	0.27	—
Distrib'ns, Cap Gain ($)	1.26	2.20	1.12	3.09	2.65	0.50	0.16	0.04	0.00	—
Net Asset Value ($)	17.15	19.24	18.49	17.60	18.16	18.55	15.63	17.04	14.73	—
Expense Ratio (%)	0.96	1.03	1.10	1.01	1.02	1.05	1.14	1.24	1.02	—
Yield (%)	0.21	0.37	0.86	1.44	1.63	2.30	2.27	2.04	1.83	—
Portfolio Turnover (%)	54	96	101	129	131	132	97	85	127	—
Total Assets (Millions $)	1,349	1,628	1,777	1,943	2,008	1,860	1,621	1,277	134	—

PORTFOLIO (as of 6/30/00)

Portfolio Manager: Douglas Ramos - 1997

Investm't Category: Growth & Income

✔ Domestic — Index
✔ Foreign — Sector
Asset Allocation — State Specific

Investment Style

✔ Large Cap — Mid Cap — Small Cap
Growth — Grth/Val — ✔ Value

Portfolio

3.4%	cash	0.0%	corp bonds
96.6%	stocks	0.0%	gov't bonds
0.0%	pref/conv't pref	0.0%	muni bonds
0.0%	conv't bds/wrnts	0.0%	other

SHAREHOLDER INFORMATION

Minimum Investment
Initial: $2,500 — Subsequent: $100

Minimum IRA Investment
Initial: $750 — Subsequent: $1

Maximum Fees
Load: none — 12b-1: none
Other: none

Services
✔ IRA
✔ Keogh
✔ Telephone Exchange

Dreyfus Growth Opport (DREQX)

800-645-6561, 516-794-5452
www.dreyfus.com

Growth

PERFORMANCE

fund inception date: 2/4/72

	3yr Annual	5yr Annual	10yr Annual	Bull	Bear
Return (%)	5.7	10.7	11.4	61.5	-19.8
Differ from Category (+/-)	-5.3 blw av	-5.4 low	-5.4 low	11.8 abv av	-14.4 low

Standard Deviation	Category Risk Index	Beta
19.6%—abv av	1.01—av	1.08

	2000	1999	1998	1997	1996	1995	1994	1993	1992	1991
Return (%)	-17.4	23.3	16.1	15.0	22.2	28.3	-6.3	1.7	-4.1	51.4
Differ from Category (+/-)	-20.9	4.4	1.8	-12.1	-0.1	-2.1	-6.1	-12.9	-16.7	13.8
Return, Tax-Adjusted (%)	-18.2	21.0	14.8	11.8	17.9	23.3	-11.3	-3.8	-4.1	50.9

PER SHARE DATA

	2000	1999	1998	1997	1996	1995	1994	1993	1992	1991
Dividends, Net Income ($)	0.00	0.00	0.07	0.06	0.08	0.12	0.08	0.00	0.02	0.13
Distrib'ns, Cap Gain ($)	0.48	1.17	0.46	1.43	1.28	1.27	1.84	2.60	0.00	0.00
Net Asset Value ($)	9.21	11.70	10.59	9.60	9.71	9.09	8.18	10.74	13.14	13.73
Expense Ratio (%)	1.03	1.04	1.06	1.06	1.04	1.10	1.09	1.00	0.95	0.98
Yield (%)	0.00	0.00	0.63	0.54	0.72	1.15	0.79	0.00	0.15	0.94
Portfolio Turnover (%)	86	162	112	137	268	242	194	90	57	147
Total Assets (Millions $)	379	506	469	499	464	408	365	485	635	704

PORTFOLIO (as of 6/30/00)

Portfolio Manager: Timothy Ghriskey - 1996

Investm't Category: Growth

✔ Domestic
✔ Foreign
Asset Allocation
Index
Sector
State Specific

Investment Style

✔ Large Cap
✔ Growth
Mid Cap
Grth/Val
Small Cap
Value

Portfolio

3.0%	cash	0.0%	corp bonds
97.0%	stocks	0.0%	gov't bonds
0.0%	pref/conv't pref	0.0%	muni bonds
0.0%	conv't bds/wrnts	0.0%	other

SHAREHOLDER INFORMATION

Minimum Investment

Initial: $2,500 Subsequent: $100

Minimum IRA Investment

Initial: $750 Subsequent: $1

Maximum Fees

Load: none 12b-1: none
Other: none

Services

✔ IRA
✔ Keogh
✔ Telephone Exchange

Dreyfus Index: Midcap Idx

800-645-6561, 516-794-5452
www.dreyfus.com

(PESPX)

Growth

PERFORMANCE — fund inception date: 6/19/91

	3yr Annual	5yr Annual	10yr Annual	Bull	Bear
Return (%)	16.3	19.6	na	59.3	-3.4
Differ from Category (+/-)	5.3 high	3.5 high	na	9.6 abv av	2.0 av

Standard Deviation	Category Risk Index	Beta
21.7%—abv av	1.12—abv av	1.02

	2000	1999	1998	1997	1996	1995	1994	1993	1992	1991
Return (%)	16.7	14.0	18.4	31.5	18.5	30.3	-3.9	13.5	11.9	—
Differ from Category (+/-)	13.2	-4.9	4.1	4.4	-3.8	-0.1	-3.7	-1.1	-0.7	—
Return, Tax-Adjusted (%)	13.2	9.8	13.2	29.2	16.4	27.9	-5.7	11.8	10.8	—

PER SHARE DATA

	2000	1999	1998	1997	1996	1995	1994	1993	1992	1991
Dividends, Net Income ($)	0.21	0.20	0.31	0.23	0.27	0.30	0.28	0.27	0.26	—
Distrib'ns, Cap Gain ($)	3.38	4.46	6.02	1.98	0.99	0.87	0.75	0.55	0.25	—
Net Asset Value ($)	22.03	21.94	23.58	25.64	21.24	19.00	15.48	17.19	15.87	—
Expense Ratio (%)	na	0.50	0.50	0.50	0.50	0.50	0.40	0.09	0.00	—
Yield (%)	0.82	0.75	1.04	0.83	1.21	1.50	1.72	1.52	1.61	—
Portfolio Turnover (%)	na	50	67	20	14	20	19	16	16	—
Total Assets (Millions $)	456	322	272	257	184	128	74	74	48	—

PORTFOLIO (as of 6/30/00)

Portfolio Manager: committee - 1995

Investm't Category: Growth

✔ Domestic ✔ Index
Foreign Sector
Asset Allocation State Specific

Investment Style

Large Cap ✔ Mid Cap Small Cap
Growth ✔ Grth/Val Value

Portfolio

3.0%	cash	0.0%	corp bonds
97.0%	stocks	0.0%	gov't bonds
0.0%	pref/conv't pref	0.0%	muni bonds
0.0%	conv't bds/wrnts	0.0%	other

SHAREHOLDER INFORMATION

Minimum Investment
Initial: $2,500 Subsequent: $100

Minimum IRA Investment
Initial: $750 Subsequent: $1

Maximum Fees
Load: 1.00% redemption 12b-1: none
Other: redemption fee applies for 6 months

Services
✔ IRA
✔ Keogh
✔ Telephone Exchange

Dreyfus Index: S&P 500 Idx (PEOPX)

800-645-6561, 516-794-5452
www.dreyfus.com

Growth & Income

PERFORMANCE — fund inception date: 1/2/90

	3yr Annual	5yr Annual	10yr Annual	Bull	Bear
Return (%)	11.6	17.7	16.8	55.1	-11.8
Differ from Category (+/-)	2.7 abv av	3.4 abv av	1.9 abv av	21.6 abv av	-11.7 low

Standard Deviation	Category Risk Index	Beta
17.6%—av	1.02—abv av	1.00

	2000	1999	1998	1997	1996	1995	1994	1993	1992	1991
Return (%)	-9.5	20.2	28.0	32.6	22.3	36.7	0.6	9.5	7.7	29.8
Differ from Category (+/-)	-15.2	9.4	15.2	5.7	2.6	7.2	1.1	-4.3	-3.9	1.7
Return, Tax-Adjusted (%)	-9.7	19.5	27.5	31.6	20.5	35.4	-2.7	7.5	6.8	28.7

PER SHARE DATA

	2000	1999	1998	1997	1996	1995	1994	1993	1992	1991
Dividends, Net Income ($)	0.31	0.32	0.36	0.30	0.37	0.32	0.41	0.31	0.40	0.38
Distrib'ns, Cap Gain ($)	0.00	0.51	0.00	0.45	0.66	0.21	1.33	0.66	0.03	0.00
Net Asset Value ($)	38.49	42.91	36.39	28.70	22.22	19.00	14.29	15.93	15.43	14.73
Expense Ratio (%)	na	0.50	0.50	0.50	0.57	0.55	0.61	0.39	0.00	0.00
Yield (%)	0.80	0.73	0.98	1.02	1.61	1.66	2.62	1.86	2.58	2.57
Portfolio Turnover (%)	na	9	7	2	5	3	18	3	3	1
Total Assets (Millions $)	2,885	3,056	2,153	1,430	653	378	209	276	97	76

PORTFOLIO (as of 6/30/00)

Portfolio Manager: committee - 1995

Investm't Category: Growth & Income

✔ Domestic ✔ Index
Foreign Sector
Asset Allocation State Specific

Investment Style

✔ Large Cap Mid Cap Small Cap
Growth ✔ Grth/Val Value

Portfolio

1.6%	cash	0.0%	corp bonds
98.4%	stocks	0.0%	gov't bonds
0.0%	pref/conv't pref	0.0%	muni bonds
0.0%	conv't bds/wrnts	0.0%	other

SHAREHOLDER INFORMATION

Minimum Investment
Initial: $2,500 Subsequent: $100

Minimum IRA Investment
Initial: $750 Subsequent: $1

Maximum Fees
Load: 1.00% redemption 12b-1: none
Other: redemption fee applies for 6 months

Services
✔ IRA
✔ Keogh
✔ Telephone Exchange

Dreyfus Intl Growth (DITFX)

800-645-6561, 516-794-5452
www.dreyfus.com

International Stock

PERFORMANCE — fund inception date: 6/29/93

	3yr Annual	5yr Annual	10yr Annual	Bull	Bear
Return (%)	6.6	5.3	na	56.3	-27.7
Differ from Category (+/-)	-2.3 blw av	-3.0 blw av	na	-34.6 blw av	-3.7 blw av

Standard Deviation	Category Risk Index	Beta
25.2%—high	1.11—abv av	0.70

	2000	1999	1998	1997	1996	1995	1994	1993	1992	1991
Return (%)	-21.9	53.1	1.6	-1.4	8.4	0.7	-5.4	—	—	—
Differ from Category (+/-)	-2.5	-7.6	-4.2	-2.7	-6.1	-8.6	-2.3	—	—	—
Return, Tax-Adjusted (%)	-26.6	52.9	0.9	-3.9	6.8	0.7	-5.9	—	—	—

PER SHARE DATA

	2000	1999	1998	1997	1996	1995	1994	1993	1992	1991
Dividends, Net Income ($)	0.00	0.00	0.00	0.01	0.11	0.00	0.03	—	—	—
Distrib'ns, Cap Gain ($)	4.50	0.08	0.40	1.90	0.62	0.00	0.25	—	—	—
Net Asset Value ($)	10.48	19.12	12.55	12.76	14.85	14.38	14.28	—	—	—
Expense Ratio (%)	1.98	2.01	1.92	1.98	2.04	1.92	1.71	—	—	—
Yield (%)	0.00	0.00	0.00	0.06	0.71	0.00	0.20	—	—	—
Portfolio Turnover (%)	236	232	167	158	96	40	51	—	—	—
Total Assets (Millions $)	48	69	57	77	91	107	160	—	—	—

PORTFOLIO (as of 6/30/00)

Portfolio Manager: Douglas Loeffler - 1999

Investm't Category: International Stock

Domestic	Index
✔ Foreign	Sector
Asset Allocation	State Specific

Investment Style

Large Cap	Mid Cap	Small Cap
Growth	Grth/Val	Value

Portfolio

-6.1%	cash	0.0%	corp bonds
105.0%	stocks	0.0%	gov't bonds
1.1%	pref/conv't pref	0.0%	muni bonds
0.0%	conv't bds/wrnts	0.0%	other

SHAREHOLDER INFORMATION

Minimum Investment
Initial: $2,500 — Subsequent: $100

Minimum IRA Investment
Initial: $750 — Subsequent: $1

Maximum Fees
Load: 1.00% redemption — 12b-1: 0.50%
Other: redemption fee applies for 6 months

Services
✔ IRA
✔ Keogh
✔ Telephone Exchange

Dreyfus Life: Gr & Inc/R

800-782-6620, 516-794-5452
www.dreyfus.com

(DGIRX)

Balanced

PERFORMANCE — fund inception date: 3/31/95

	3yr Annual	5yr Annual	10yr Annual	Bull	Bear
Return (%)	8.3	12.0	na	24.4	-1.8
Differ from Category (+/-)	-0.1 av	0.6 av	na	-3.7 av	1.4 abv av

Standard Deviation	Category Risk Index	Beta
7.3%—blw av	0.67—low	0.38

	2000	1999	1998	1997	1996	1995	1994	1993	1992	1991
Return (%)	0.9	7.0	17.7	20.5	15.2	—	—	—	—	—
Differ from Category (+/-)	-1.1	-3.7	4.4	1.7	1.3	—	—	—	—	—
Return, Tax-Adjusted (%)	-1.1	4.2	15.5	15.8	13.6	—	—	—	—	—

PER SHARE DATA

	2000	1999	1998	1997	1996	1995	1994	1993	1992	1991
Dividends, Net Income ($)	0.76	0.61	0.63	0.63	0.34	—	—	—	—	—
Distrib'ns, Cap Gain ($)	0.23	1.18	0.45	2.34	0.30	—	—	—	—	—
Net Asset Value ($)	15.91	16.77	17.38	15.71	15.51	—	—	—	—	—
Expense Ratio (%)	0.86	0.84	0.84	0.78	0.75	—	—	—	—	—
Yield (%)	4.70	3.39	3.53	3.49	2.15	—	—	—	—	—
Portfolio Turnover (%)	87	142	76	107	122	—	—	—	—	—
Total Assets (Millions $)	199	213	209	173	132	—	—	—	—	—

PORTFOLIO (as of 6/30/00)

Portfolio Manager: Steven Falci - 1995

Investm't Category: Balanced

✔ Domestic — Index
✔ Foreign — Sector
✔ Asset Allocation — State Specific

Investment Style

Large Cap — Mid Cap — Small Cap
Growth — Grth/Val — Value

Portfolio

13.7%	cash	28.0%	corp bonds
22.9%	stocks	35.5%	gov't bonds
0.0%	pref/conv't pref	0.0%	muni bonds
0.0%	conv't bds/wrnts	0.0%	other

SHAREHOLDER INFORMATION

Minimum Investment
Initial: $2,500 — Subsequent: $100

Minimum IRA Investment
Initial: $750 — Subsequent: $1

Maximum Fees
Load: none — 12b-1: none
Other: none

Services
✔ IRA
✔ Keogh
✔ Telephone Exchange

Dreyfus New Leaders (DNLDX)

800-645-6561, 516-794-5452
www.dreyfus.com

Aggressive Growth

PERFORMANCE — fund inception date: 1/29/85

	3yr Annual	5yr Annual	10yr Annual	Bull	Bear
Return (%)	12.7	14.9	17.1	61.3	-11.8
Differ from Category (+/-)	-3.5 blw av	0.3 av	1.3 blw av	-57.9 blw av	8.8 abv av

Standard Deviation	Category Risk Index	Beta
22.9%—abv av	0.71—low	0.96

	2000	1999	1998	1997	1996	1995	1994	1993	1992	1991
Return (%)	8.5	37.4	-3.9	19.5	17.3	29.7	-0.1	17.0	9.4	45.3
Differ from Category (+/-)	14.5	-20.1	-19.0	4.7	-1.0	-4.9	0.7	-8.2	2.5	-1.9
Return, Tax-Adjusted (%)	4.8	34.5	-4.4	17.4	15.0	26.8	-2.3	14.0	6.7	41.8

PER SHARE DATA

	2000	1999	1998	1997	1996	1995	1994	1993	1992	1991
Dividends, Net Income ($)	0.00	0.00	0.00	0.00	0.00	0.07	0.07	0.07	0.14	0.22
Distrib'ns, Cap Gain ($)	9.16	5.93	1.16	4.24	3.07	3.10	2.60	3.34	2.93	2.74
Net Asset Value ($)	45.52	50.67	41.31	44.35	40.74	37.39	31.33	34.13	32.17	32.29
Expense Ratio (%)	na	1.13	1.14	1.12	1.17	1.19	1.16	1.22	1.21	1.29
Yield (%)	0.00	0.00	0.00	0.00	0.00	0.17	0.20	0.18	0.39	0.62
Portfolio Turnover (%)	na	95	107	82	102	108	94	127	119	108
Total Assets (Millions $)	643	676	691	866	795	608	392	338	232	194

PORTFOLIO (as of 6/30/00)

Portfolio Manager: Hilary Woods, Paul Kandel - 1996

Investm't Category: Aggressive Growth

✔ Domestic — Index
✔ Foreign — Sector
Asset Allocation — State Specific

Investment Style

Large Cap — Mid Cap — ✔ Small Cap
✔ Growth — Grth/Val — Value

Portfolio

5.7%	cash	0.0%	corp bonds
94.2%	stocks	0.0%	gov't bonds
0.1%	pref/conv't pref	0.0%	muni bonds
0.0%	conv't bds/wrnts	0.0%	other

SHAREHOLDER INFORMATION

Minimum Investment
Initial: $2,500 — Subsequent: $100

Minimum IRA Investment
Initial: $750 — Subsequent: $1

Maximum Fees
Load: 1.00% redemption — 12b-1: none
Other: redemption fee applies for 6 months

Services
✔ IRA
✔ Keogh
✔ Telephone Exchange

Dreyfus Premier Third/Z (DRTHX)

800-554-4611, 516-794-5452
www.dreyfus.com

Growth

PERFORMANCE — fund inception date: 3/29/72

	3yr Annual	5yr Annual	10yr Annual	Bull	Bear
Return (%)	13.8	18.8	16.0	73.3	-14.4
Differ from Category (+/-)	2.8 abv av	2.7 abv av	-0.8 av	23.6 abv av	-9.0 blw av

Standard Deviation	Category Risk Index	Beta
19.4%—abv av	1.00—av	1.05

	2000	1999	1998	1997	1996	1995	1994	1993	1992	1991
Return (%)	-12.9	30.1	30.1	29.3	24.3	35.8	-7.4	5.2	1.9	38.0
Differ from Category (+/-)	-16.4	11.2	15.8	2.2	2.0	5.4	-7.2	-9.4	-10.7	0.4
Return, Tax-Adjusted (%)	-14.2	27.9	27.5	27.1	19.4	33.1	-11.0	2.9	1.5	36.6

PER SHARE DATA

	2000	1999	1998	1997	1996	1995	1994	1993	1992	1991
Dividends, Net Income ($)	0.08	0.00	0.00	0.02	0.02	0.04	0.06	0.04	0.04	0.08
Distrib'ns, Cap Gain ($)	0.84	1.34	1.33	0.90	1.39	0.57	1.00	0.61	0.05	0.22
Net Asset Value ($)	11.79	14.55	12.28	10.51	8.82	8.24	6.53	8.26	8.48	8.42
Expense Ratio (%)	0.96	0.96	0.97	1.03	1.11	1.12	1.17	1.11	1.08	1.04
Yield (%)	0.63	0.00	0.00	0.17	0.19	0.45	0.79	0.45	0.46	0.92
Portfolio Turnover (%)	60	75	70	66	92	133	71	67	48	73
Total Assets (Millions $)	1,188	1,397	1,048	804	562	419	348	463	529	360

PORTFOLIO (as of 6/30/00)

Portfolio Manager: Maceo Sloan, Paul Hilton - 1994

Investm't Category: Growth

✔ Domestic | Index
Foreign | Sector
Asset Allocation | State Specific

Investment Style

✔ Large Cap | Mid Cap | Small Cap
✔ Growth | Grth/Val | Value

Portfolio

-0.2%	cash	0.0%	corp bonds
100.2%	stocks	0.0%	gov't bonds
0.0%	pref/conv't pref	0.0%	muni bonds
0.0%	conv't bds/wrnts	0.0%	other

SHAREHOLDER INFORMATION

Minimum Investment
Initial: $1,000 — Subsequent: $100

Minimum IRA Investment
Initial: $750 — Subsequent: $1

Maximum Fees
Load: none — 12b-1: none
Other: none

Services
✔ IRA
✔ Keogh
✔ Telephone Exchange

EAI Select Mgr Equity

203-855-2200
www.eval-assoc.com

(EASMX)

Growth

PERFORMANCE — fund inception date: 1/2/96

	3yr Annual	5yr Annual	10yr Annual	Bull	Bear
Return (%)	15.2	na	na	68.1	-13.6
Differ from Category (+/-)	4.2 abv av	na	na	18.4 abv av	-8.2 blw av

Standard Deviation	Category Risk Index	Beta
18.9%—av	0.97—blw av	1.02

	2000	1999	1998	1997	1996	1995	1994	1993	1992	1991
Return (%)	-5.5	30.9	23.7	29.2	—	—	—	—	—	—
Differ from Category (+/-)	-9.0	12.0	9.4	2.1	—	—	—	—	—	—
Return, Tax-Adjusted (%)	-8.2	26.3	20.7	20.7	—	—	—	—	—	—

PER SHARE DATA

	2000	1999	1998	1997	1996	1995	1994	1993	1992	1991
Dividends, Net Income ($)	0.00	0.00	0.02	0.08	—	—	—	—	—	—
Distrib'ns, Cap Gain ($)	1.51	2.32	1.37	4.43	—	—	—	—	—	—
Net Asset Value ($)	9.02	11.13	10.29	9.44	—	—	—	—	—	—
Expense Ratio (%)	na	1.15	1.15	1.15	—	—	—	—	—	—
Yield (%)	0.00	0.00	0.17	0.57	—	—	—	—	—	—
Portfolio Turnover (%)	na	82	63	78	—	—	—	—	—	—
Total Assets (Millions $)	62	55	55	52	—	—	—	—	—	—

PORTFOLIO (as of 6/30/00)

Portfolio Manager: Keith Stransky - 1996

Investm't Category: Growth

✔ Domestic | Index
Foreign | Sector
Asset Allocation | State Specific

Investment Style

✔ Large Cap | Mid Cap | Small Cap
✔ Growth | Grth/Val | Value

Portfolio

4.5%	cash	0.0%	corp bonds
95.5%	stocks	0.0%	gov't bonds
0.0%	pref/conv't pref	0.0%	muni bonds
0.0%	conv't bds/wrnts	0.0%	other

SHAREHOLDER INFORMATION

Minimum Investment

Initial: $50,000 — Subsequent: $1,000

Minimum IRA Investment

Initial: na — Subsequent: na

Maximum Fees

Load: none — 12b-1: none
Other: none

Services

IRA
Keogh
Telephone Exchange

Eclipses: Balanced (EBALX)

800-872-2710, 212-696-4130
www.towneley.com

Balanced

PERFORMANCE — fund inception date: 5/1/89

	3yr Annual	5yr Annual	10yr Annual	Bull	Bear
Return (%)	5.6	10.4	12.3	9.8	8.2
Differ from Category (+/-)	-2.8 low	-1.0 blw av	0.6 abv av	-18.3 low	11.4 high

Standard Deviation	Category Risk Index	Beta
10.4%—blw av	0.95—blw av	0.46

	2000	1999	1998	1997	1996	1995	1994	1993	1992	1991
Return (%)	9.6	-0.3	8.0	23.3	12.9	23.0	0.0	17.0	12.0	20.9
Differ from Category (+/-)	7.6	-11.0	-5.3	4.5	-1.0	-2.5	1.3	2.6	3.6	-2.9
Return, Tax-Adjusted (%)	8.5	-2.4	5.1	19.2	9.4	20.6	-1.6	13.8	9.1	19.4

PER SHARE DATA

	2000	1999	1998	1997	1996	1995	1994	1993	1992	1991
Dividends, Net Income ($)	0.54	0.58	0.61	0.66	0.77	0.64	0.55	0.63	0.73	0.71
Distrib'ns, Cap Gain ($)	0.00	1.16	1.92	2.98	1.43	0.56	0.31	1.04	0.93	0.00
Net Asset Value ($)	20.82	19.53	21.37	22.15	21.00	20.59	17.75	18.63	17.37	17.02
Expense Ratio (%)	na	0.94	0.87	0.84	0.80	0.80	0.80	0.69	0.52	0.66
Yield (%)	2.59	2.80	2.61	2.62	3.43	3.02	3.04	3.20	3.98	4.17
Portfolio Turnover (%)	na	33	69	46	71	74	94	65	95	101
Total Assets (Millions $)	63	77	128	88	83	85	27	21	14	10

PORTFOLIO (as of 6/30/00)

Portfolio Manager: Wesley McCain, Joan Sabella - 1989

Investm't Category: Balanced

✔ Domestic	Index
✔ Foreign	Sector
Asset Allocation	State Specific

Investment Style

Large Cap	Mid Cap	Small Cap
Growth	Grth/Val	Value

Portfolio

4.3%	cash	32.3%	corp bonds
56.9%	stocks	0.0%	gov't bonds
0.0%	pref/conv't pref	0.0%	muni bonds
0.0%	conv't bds/wrnts	6.4%	other

SHAREHOLDER INFORMATION

Minimum Investment
Initial: $1,000 Subsequent: $1

Minimum IRA Investment
Initial: $1,000 Subsequent: $1

Maximum Fees
Load: none 12b-1: none
Other: none

Services
✔ IRA
Keogh
✔ Telephone Exchange

Eclipses: Mid Cap Val (ECGIX)

800-872-2710, 212-696-4130
www.towneley.com

Growth & Income

PERFORMANCE — fund inception date: 12/27/94

	3yr Annual	5yr Annual	10yr Annual	Bull	Bear
Return (%)	5.3	13.6	na	16.6	6.3
Differ from Category (+/-)	-3.6 blw av	-0.7 blw av	na	-16.9 blw av	6.4 abv av

Standard Deviation	Category Risk Index	Beta
18.1%—av	1.05—abv av	0.85

	2000	1999	1998	1997	1996	1995	1994	1993	1992	1991
Return (%)	5.8	0.0	10.3	32.4	22.4	26.8	—	—	—	—
Differ from Category (+/-)	0.1	-10.8	-2.5	5.5	2.7	-2.7	—	—	—	—
Return, Tax-Adjusted (%)	5.6	-1.9	8.1	32.2	18.6	25.6	—	—	—	—

PER SHARE DATA

	2000	1999	1998	1997	1996	1995	1994	1993	1992	1991
Dividends, Net Income ($)	0.05	0.10	0.05	0.03	0.22	0.10	—	—	—	—
Distrib'ns, Cap Gain ($)	0.00	1.53	1.78	0.07	1.35	0.26	—	—	—	—
Net Asset Value ($)	16.93	16.06	17.73	17.76	13.49	12.31	—	—	—	—
Expense Ratio (%)	na	1.05	0.98	0.94	0.90	1.00	—	—	—	—
Yield (%)	0.29	0.56	0.25	0.16	1.48	0.79	—	—	—	—
Portfolio Turnover (%)	na	50	80	51	102	63	—	—	—	—
Total Assets (Millions $)	62	83	125	110	9	8	—	—	—	—

PORTFOLIO (as of 6/30/00)

Portfolio Manager: Wesley McCain, Kathy O'Connor - 1994

Investm't Category: Growth & Income

✔ Domestic　Index
✔ Foreign　Sector
Asset Allocation　State Specific

Investment Style

✔ Large Cap　✔ Mid Cap　Small Cap
Growth　Grth/Val　✔ Value

Portfolio

2.8%	cash	0.0%	corp bonds
97.2%	stocks	0.0%	gov't bonds
0.0%	pref/conv't pref	0.0%	muni bonds
0.0%	conv't bds/wrnts	0.0%	other

SHAREHOLDER INFORMATION

Minimum Investment
Initial: $1,000　Subsequent: $1

Minimum IRA Investment
Initial: $1,000　Subsequent: $1

Maximum Fees
Load: none　12b-1: none
Other: none

Services
✔ IRA
Keogh
✔ Telephone Exchange

Eclipses: Sm Cap Val

800-872-2710, 212-696-4130
www.towneley.com

(EEQFX)

Growth

PERFORMANCE — fund inception date: 1/12/87

	3yr Annual	5yr Annual	10yr Annual	Bull	Bear
Return (%)	-1.2	10.7	13.3	22.5	-13.6
Differ from Category (+/-)	-12.2 low	-5.4 low	-3.5 low	-27.2 low	-8.2 blw av

Standard Deviation	Category Risk Index	Beta
18.8%—av	0.97—blw av	0.85

	2000	1999	1998	1997	1996	1995	1994	1993	1992	1991
Return (%)	-9.5	3.0	3.3	33.3	29.8	19.5	-4.6	17.0	19.3	31.1
Differ from Category (+/-)	-13.0	-15.9	-11.0	6.2	7.5	-10.9	-4.4	2.4	6.7	-6.5
Return, Tax-Adjusted (%)	-9.5	2.1	-0.4	27.6	21.2	18.0	-6.4	12.5	17.3	30.5

PER SHARE DATA

	2000	1999	1998	1997	1996	1995	1994	1993	1992	1991
Dividends, Net Income ($)	0.00	0.00	0.00	0.14	0.13	0.06	0.02	0.07	0.15	0.16
Distrib'ns, Cap Gain ($)	0.00	0.51	2.67	3.51	3.98	0.51	0.86	2.02	0.65	0.00
Net Asset Value ($)	10.64	11.76	11.93	14.19	13.47	13.56	11.83	13.35	13.20	11.73
Expense Ratio (%)	na	1.18	1.14	1.14	1.15	1.14	1.12	1.12	1.15	1.18
Yield (%)	0.00	0.00	0.00	0.79	0.74	0.42	0.15	0.45	1.08	1.36
Portfolio Turnover (%)	na	56	73	55	82	74	92	101	111	119
Total Assets (Millions $)	156	250	199	192	170	174	195	197	163	148

PORTFOLIO (as of 6/30/00)

Portfolio Manager: Wesley McCain, Kathy O'Connor - 1987

Investm't Category: Growth

✔ Domestic	Index
✔ Foreign	Sector
Asset Allocation	State Specific

Investment Style

Large Cap	Mid Cap	✔ Small Cap
Growth	Grth/Val	✔ Value

Portfolio

4.1% cash	0.0% corp bonds
95.9% stocks	0.0% gov't bonds
0.0% pref/conv't pref	0.0% muni bonds
0.0% conv't bds/wrnts	0.0% other

SHAREHOLDER INFORMATION

Minimum Investment
Initial: $1,000 Subsequent: $1

Minimum IRA Investment
Initial: $1,000 Subsequent: $1

Maximum Fees
Load: none 12b-1: none
Other: none

Services
✔ IRA
Keogh
✔ Telephone Exchange

Excelsior Blended Eqty/A (UMEQX)

800-446-1012
www.excelsiorfunds.com

Growth

PERFORMANCE — fund inception date: 4/24/85

	3yr Annual	5yr Annual	10yr Annual	Bull	Bear
Return (%)	13.2	17.6	18.1	59.7	-13.2
Differ from Category (+/-)	2.2 abv av	1.5 av	1.3 abv av	10.0 abv av	-7.8 blw av

Standard Deviation	Category Risk Index	Beta
18.9%—av	0.97—blw av	1.05

	2000	1999	1998	1997	1996	1995	1994	1993	1992	1991
Return (%)	-8.1	22.6	28.8	29.7	19.8	28.9	0.1	16.3	16.6	34.4
Differ from Category (+/-)	-11.6	3.7	14.5	2.6	-2.5	-1.5	0.3	1.7	4.0	-3.2
Return, Tax-Adjusted (%)	-8.6	21.8	28.3	27.7	18.1	25.5	-0.6	15.0	15.5	33.8

PER SHARE DATA

	2000	1999	1998	1997	1996	1995	1994	1993	1992	1991
Dividends, Net Income ($)	0.01	0.06	0.12	0.16	0.13	0.11	0.03	0.07	0.09	0.21
Distrib'ns, Cap Gain ($)	1.33	1.38	0.49	2.28	1.16	2.19	0.47	0.73	0.50	0.00
Net Asset Value ($)	42.51	47.70	40.13	31.66	26.30	23.07	19.82	20.31	18.21	16.16
Expense Ratio (%)	0.97	0.95	0.99	1.01	1.05	1.05	1.14	1.08	1.15	1.23
Yield (%)	0.02	0.12	0.29	0.47	0.47	0.43	0.14	0.33	0.48	1.29
Portfolio Turnover (%)	24	20	28	39	27	23	17	24	20	41
Total Assets (Millions $)	921	892	664	542	307	172	115	120	96	61

PORTFOLIO (as of 6/30/00)

Portfolio Manager: Leigh Weiss, Bruce Tavel - 1997

Investm't Category: Growth

✔ Domestic	Index
Foreign	Sector
Asset Allocation	State Specific

Investment Style

✔ Large Cap	Mid Cap	Small Cap
✔ Growth	Grth/Val	Value

Portfolio

0.3%	cash	0.0%	corp bonds
99.7%	stocks	0.0%	gov't bonds
0.0%	pref/conv't pref	0.0%	muni bonds
0.0%	conv't bds/wrnts	0.0%	other

SHAREHOLDER INFORMATION

Minimum Investment

Initial: $500 — Subsequent: $50

Minimum IRA Investment

Initial: $250 — Subsequent: $50

Maximum Fees

Load: none — 12b-1: none

Other: none

Services

✔ IRA
✔ Keogh
✔ Telephone Exchange

Excelsior Intl (UMINX)

800-446-1012
www.excelsiorfunds.com

International Stock

PERFORMANCE

fund inception date: 7/21/87

	3yr Annual	5yr Annual	10yr Annual	Bull	Bear
Return (%)	8.6	8.4	7.5	73.9	-27.0
Differ from Category (+/-)	-0.3 av	0.1 av	-1.5 blw av	-17.0 av	-3.0 av

Standard Deviation	Category Risk Index	Beta
21.3%—abv av	0.94—blw av	0.79

	2000	1999	1998	1997	1996	1995	1994	1993	1992	1991
Return (%)	-23.9	56.2	7.8	9.2	7.2	7.2	-2.0	36.5	-9.3	5.9
Differ from Category (+/-)	-4.5	-4.5	2.0	7.9	-7.3	-2.1	1.1	-3.7	-5.8	-7.1
Return, Tax-Adjusted (%)	-24.7	56.1	7.5	8.2	6.3	6.6	-3.2	35.8	-9.3	5.5

PER SHARE DATA

	2000	1999	1998	1997	1996	1995	1994	1993	1992	1991
Dividends, Net Income ($)	0.12	0.00	0.06	0.05	0.10	0.09	0.10	0.14	0.01	0.10
Distrib'ns, Cap Gain ($)	0.59	0.04	0.00	0.43	0.19	0.06	0.32	0.00	0.00	0.00
Net Asset Value ($)	14.08	19.42	12.46	11.61	11.07	10.60	10.03	10.67	7.93	8.76
Expense Ratio (%)	1.40	1.42	1.44	1.43	1.40	1.47	1.53	1.50	1.52	1.61
Yield (%)	0.81	0.00	0.48	0.41	0.88	0.84	0.96	1.31	0.12	1.14
Portfolio Turnover (%)	25	50	37	116	38	66	64	31	32	47
Total Assets (Millions $)	395	373	230	177	105	86	63	49	34	45

PORTFOLIO (as of 6/30/00)

Portfolio Manager: Rosemary Sager - 1996

Investm't Category: International Stock

Domestic	Index
✔ Foreign	Sector
Asset Allocation	State Specific

Investment Style

Large Cap	Mid Cap	Small Cap
Growth	Grth/Val	Value

Portfolio

4.3%	cash	0.0%	corp bonds
95.5%	stocks	0.0%	gov't bonds
0.0%	pref/conv't pref	0.0%	muni bonds
0.2%	conv't bds/wrnts	0.0%	other

SHAREHOLDER INFORMATION

Minimum Investment
Initial: $500 Subsequent: $50

Minimum IRA Investment
Initial: $250 Subsequent: $50

Maximum Fees
Load: 2.00% redemption 12b-1: none
Other: redemption fee applies for 1 month

Services
✔ IRA
✔ Keogh
✔ Telephone Exchange

Excelsior Large Cap Gr (UMLGX)

800-446-1012
www.excelsiorfunds.com

Aggressive Growth

PERFORMANCE — fund inception date: 10/1/97

	3yr Annual	5yr Annual	10yr Annual	Bull	Bear
Return (%)	25.5	na	na	127.1	-24.5
Differ from Category (+/-)	9.3 abv av	na	na	7.9 abv av	-3.9 av

Standard Deviation	Category Risk Index	Beta
29.0%—high	0.90—blw av	1.50

	2000	1999	1998	1997	1996	1995	1994	1993	1992	1991
Return (%)	-19.7	47.4	67.0	—	—	—	—	—	—	—
Differ from Category (+/-)	-13.7	-10.1	51.9	—	—	—	—	—	—	—
Return, Tax-Adjusted (%)	-19.7	47.4	67.0	—	—	—	—	—	—	—

PER SHARE DATA

	2000	1999	1998	1997	1996	1995	1994	1993	1992	1991
Dividends, Net Income ($)	0.00	0.00	0.00	—	—	—	—	—	—	—
Distrib'ns, Cap Gain ($)	0.00	0.00	0.00	—	—	—	—	—	—	—
Net Asset Value ($)	14.04	17.49	11.86	—	—	—	—	—	—	—
Expense Ratio (%)	1.01	1.04	1.05	—	—	—	—	—	—	—
Yield (%)	0.00	0.00	0.00	—	—	—	—	—	—	—
Portfolio Turnover (%)	20	4	12	—	—	—	—	—	—	—
Total Assets (Millions $)	437	396	146	—	—	—	—	—	—	—

PORTFOLIO (as of 6/30/00)

Portfolio Manager: committee - 1997

Investm't Category: Aggressive Growth

✔ Domestic — Index
✔ Foreign — Sector
Asset Allocation — State Specific

Investment Style

✔ Large Cap — Mid Cap — Small Cap
✔ Growth — Grth/Val — Value

Portfolio

4.6%	cash	0.0%	corp bonds
95.4%	stocks	0.0%	gov't bonds
0.0%	pref/conv't pref	0.0%	muni bonds
0.0%	conv't bds/wrnts	0.0%	other

SHAREHOLDER INFORMATION

Minimum Investment

Initial: $500 — Subsequent: $50

Minimum IRA Investment

Initial: $250 — Subsequent: $50

Maximum Fees

Load: none — 12b-1: none
Other: none

Services

✔ IRA
✔ Keogh
✔ Telephone Exchange

Excelsior Pacific-Asia (USPAX)

800-446-1012
www.excelsiorfunds.com

International Stock

PERFORMANCE — fund inception date: 12/31/92

	3yr Annual	5yr Annual	10yr Annual	Bull	Bear
Return (%)	5.9	-2.8	na	177.5	-35.4
Differ from Category (+/-)	-3.0 blw av	-11.1 low	na	86.6 high	-11.4 low

Standard Deviation	Category Risk Index	Beta
29.6%—high	1.30—abv av	1.04

	2000	1999	1998	1997	1996	1995	1994	1993	1992	1991
Return (%)	-40.1	102.1	-1.7	-32.1	7.2	8.5	-14.6	66.3	—	—
Differ from Category (+/-)	-20.7	41.4	-7.5	-33.4	-7.3	-0.8	-11.5	26.1	—	—
Return, Tax-Adjusted (%)	-41.2	102.1	-2.8	-32.3	6.4	8.0	-17.5	64.5	—	—

PER SHARE DATA

	2000	1999	1998	1997	1996	1995	1994	1993	1992	1991
Dividends, Net Income ($)	0.35	0.00	0.19	0.06	0.07	0.10	0.25	0.11	—	—
Distrib'ns, Cap Gain ($)	0.00	0.00	0.00	0.00	0.15	0.01	0.83	0.27	—	—
Net Asset Value ($)	7.04	12.35	6.11	6.45	9.60	9.17	8.56	11.22	—	—
Expense Ratio (%)	1.49	1.55	1.48	1.45	1.43	1.47	1.53	1.67	—	—
Yield (%)	4.97	0.00	3.10	0.93	0.71	1.08	2.66	0.95	—	—
Portfolio Turnover (%)	105	78	52	126	29	69	68	1	—	—
Total Assets (Millions $)	56	88	27	41	86	60	49	48	—	—

PORTFOLIO (as of 6/30/00)

Portfolio Manager: David Linehan - 1998

Investm't Category: International Stock

Domestic	Index
✔ Foreign	Sector
Asset Allocation	State Specific

Investment Style

Large Cap	Mid Cap	Small Cap
Growth	Grth/Val	Value

Portfolio

3.2%	cash	0.0%	corp bonds
96.2%	stocks	0.0%	gov't bonds
0.0%	pref/conv't pref	0.0%	muni bonds
0.6%	conv't bds/wrnts	0.0%	other

SHAREHOLDER INFORMATION

Minimum Investment
Initial: $500 — Subsequent: $50

Minimum IRA Investment
Initial: $250 — Subsequent: $50

Maximum Fees
Load: 2.00% redemption — 12b-1: none
Other: redemption fee applies for 1 month

Services
✔ IRA
✔ Keogh
✔ Telephone Exchange

Excelsior Pan European (UMPNX)

800-446-1012
www.excelsiorfunds.com

International Stock

PERFORMANCE — fund inception date: 12/31/92

	3yr Annual	5yr Annual	10yr Annual	Bull	Bear
Return (%)	8.2	13.8	na	30.4	-23.3
Differ from Category (+/-)	-0.7 av	5.5 abv av	na	-60.5 low	0.7 av

Standard Deviation	Category Risk Index	Beta
19.6%—abv av	0.86—blw av	0.61

	2000	1999	1998	1997	1996	1995	1994	1993	1992	1991
Return (%)	-9.0	24.6	11.7	24.2	21.6	14.8	0.0	17.2	—	—
Differ from Category (+/-)	10.4	-36.1	5.9	22.9	7.1	5.5	3.1	-23.0	—	—
Return, Tax-Adjusted (%)	-10.8	22.5	10.8	22.6	20.3	13.1	-0.6	16.9	—	—

PER SHARE DATA

	2000	1999	1998	1997	1996	1995	1994	1993	1992	1991
Dividends, Net Income ($)	0.02	0.00	0.00	0.00	0.09	0.09	0.08	0.04	—	—
Distrib'ns, Cap Gain ($)	1.31	1.30	0.48	0.80	0.27	0.35	0.09	0.00	—	—
Net Asset Value ($)	11.79	14.32	12.73	11.84	10.18	8.70	7.98	8.16	—	—
Expense Ratio (%)	1.43	1.43	1.43	1.45	1.46	1.51	1.61	1.67	—	—
Yield (%)	0.15	0.00	0.00	0.00	0.86	0.99	0.99	0.49	—	—
Portfolio Turnover (%)	46	46	40	82	42	47	30	9	—	—
Total Assets (Millions $)	145	157	185	168	75	43	39	27	—	—

PORTFOLIO (as of 6/30/00)

Portfolio Manager: Rosemary Sagar, Leonard Geiger - 1996

Investm't Category: International Stock

Domestic	Index
✔ Foreign	Sector
Asset Allocation	State Specific

Investment Style

Large Cap	Mid Cap	Small Cap
Growth	Grth/Val	Value

Portfolio

3.1%	cash	0.0%	corp bonds
96.9%	stocks	0.0%	gov't bonds
0.0%	pref/conv't pref	0.0%	muni bonds
0.0%	conv't bds/wrnts	0.0%	other

SHAREHOLDER INFORMATION

Minimum Investment
Initial: $500 Subsequent: $50

Minimum IRA Investment
Initial: $250 Subsequent: $50

Maximum Fees
Load: 2.00% redemption 12b-1: none
Other: redemption fee applies for 1 month

Services
✔ IRA
✔ Keogh
✔ Telephone Exchange

Excelsior Small Cap/A (UMLCX)

800-466-1012
www.excelsiorfunds.com

Aggressive Growth

PERFORMANCE — fund inception date: 12/31/92

	3yr Annual	5yr Annual	10yr Annual	Bull	Bear
Return (%)	3.9	4.6	na	66.5	-24.9
Differ from Category (+/-)	-12.3 low	-10.0 low	na	-52.7 blw av	-4.3 av

Standard Deviation	Category Risk Index	Beta
32.4%—high	1.00—av	1.01

	2000	1999	1998	1997	1996	1995	1994	1993	1992	1991
Return (%)	-1.0	29.7	-12.3	14.2	-2.3	22.8	5.2	27.9	—	—
Differ from Category (+/-)	5.0	-27.8	-27.4	-0.6	-20.6	-11.8	6.0	2.7	—	—
Return, Tax-Adjusted (%)	-2.6	29.7	-12.4	14.2	-3.6	20.6	4.6	27.5	—	—

PER SHARE DATA

	2000	1999	1998	1997	1996	1995	1994	1993	1992	1991
Dividends, Net Income ($)	0.06	0.00	0.00	0.00	0.00	0.00	0.00	0.00	—	—
Distrib'ns, Cap Gain ($)	0.91	0.00	0.11	0.00	0.49	0.69	0.17	0.09	—	—
Net Asset Value ($)	11.38	12.53	9.66	11.17	9.78	10.47	9.14	8.86	—	—
Expense Ratio (%)	0.92	0.94	0.94	0.94	0.90	0.96	0.95	0.99	—	—
Yield (%)	0.48	0.00	0.00	0.00	0.00	0.00	0.00	0.00	—	—
Portfolio Turnover (%)	134	115	73	55	38	42	20	4	—	—
Total Assets (Millions $)	107	63	46	65	70	73	41	15	—	—

PORTFOLIO (as of 6/30/00)

Portfolio Manager: T. Pettee, M. Doyle, T. Herget - 1998

Investm't Category: Aggressive Growth

✔ Domestic
Foreign
Asset Allocation
Index
Sector
State Specific

Investment Style

Large Cap
Mid Cap
✔ Small Cap
✔ Growth
Grth/Val
Value

Portfolio

30.3% cash	0.0% corp bonds
69.7% stocks	0.0% gov't bonds
0.0% pref/conv't pref	0.0% muni bonds
0.0% conv't bds/wrnts	0.0% other

SHAREHOLDER INFORMATION

Minimum Investment
Initial: $500 Subsequent: $50

Minimum IRA Investment
Initial: $250 Subsequent: $50

Maximum Fees
Load: none 12b-1: none
Other: none

Services
✔ IRA
✔ Keogh
✔ Telephone Exchange

Excelsior Val & Restrctg (UMBIX)

800-446-1012
www.excelsiorfunds.com

Growth

PERFORMANCE — fund inception date: 12/31/92

	3yr Annual	5yr Annual	10yr Annual	Bull	Bear
Return (%)	18.8	22.9	na	77.1	-6.7
Differ from Category (+/-)	7.8 high	6.8 high	na	27.4 high	-1.3 av

Standard Deviation	Category Risk Index	Beta
22.4%—abv av	1.15—abv av	1.11

	2000	1999	1998	1997	1996	1995	1994	1993	1992	1991
Return (%)	7.2	41.9	10.3	33.5	25.0	38.8	2.5	39.9	—	—
Differ from Category (+/-)	3.7	23.0	-4.0	6.4	2.7	8.4	2.7	25.3	—	—
Return, Tax-Adjusted (%)	6.4	41.7	9.9	32.9	23.6	37.7	1.9	39.4	—	—

PER SHARE DATA

	2000	1999	1998	1997	1996	1995	1994	1993	1992	1991
Dividends, Net Income ($)	0.59	0.08	0.11	0.09	0.12	0.09	0.06	0.07	—	—
Distrib'ns, Cap Gain ($)	0.00	0.00	0.13	0.27	0.47	0.23	0.11	0.01	—	—
Net Asset Value ($)	33.82	32.14	22.71	20.82	15.87	13.20	9.76	9.69	—	—
Expense Ratio (%)	0.90	0.93	0.89	0.91	0.91	0.98	0.99	0.99	—	—
Yield (%)	1.74	0.24	0.48	0.42	0.73	0.67	0.60	0.72	—	—
Portfolio Turnover (%)	20	43	30	62	56	82	75	9	—	—
Total Assets (Millions $)	1,577	964	597	230	111	57	25	7	—	—

PORTFOLIO (as of 6/30/00)

Portfolio Manager: David Williams - 1992

Investm't Category: Growth

✔ Domestic   Index
✔ Foreign   Sector
Asset Allocation   State Specific

Investment Style

✔ Large Cap   Mid Cap   Small Cap
Growth   Grth/Val   ✔ Value

Portfolio

2.4%	cash	0.0%	corp bonds
97.0%	stocks	0.0%	gov't bonds
0.5%	pref/conv't pref	0.0%	muni bonds
0.0%	conv't bds/wrnts	0.0%	other

SHAREHOLDER INFORMATION

Minimum Investment
Initial: $500   Subsequent: $50

Minimum IRA Investment
Initial: $250   Subsequent: $50

Maximum Fees
Load: none   12b-1: none
Other: none

Services
✔ IRA
✔ Keogh
✔ Telephone Exchange

FBP Contrarian Balanced

800-443-4249, 800-327-9375

(FBPBX)

Balanced

PERFORMANCE — fund inception date: 7/3/89

	3yr Annual	5yr Annual	10yr Annual	Bull	Bear
Return (%)	7.0	11.5	13.4	25.3	1.6
Differ from Category (+/-)	-1.4 blw av	0.1 av	1.7 abv av	-2.8 av	4.8 abv av

Standard Deviation	Category Risk Index	Beta
13.2%—blw av	1.20—high	0.64

	2000	1999	1998	1997	1996	1995	1994	1993	1992	1991
Return (%)	1.0	4.9	15.4	20.6	16.5	25.6	1.8	9.9	13.9	27.3
Differ from Category (+/-)	-1.0	-5.8	2.1	1.8	2.6	0.1	3.1	-4.5	5.5	3.5
Return, Tax-Adjusted (%)	-0.6	2.6	13.8	18.5	14.4	23.3	0.1	8.7	12.9	25.9

PER SHARE DATA

	2000	1999	1998	1997	1996	1995	1994	1993	1992	1991
Dividends, Net Income ($)	0.44	0.38	0.39	0.42	0.41	0.42	0.36	0.31	0.34	0.38
Distrib'ns, Cap Gain ($)	0.66	1.48	0.64	0.76	0.48	0.38	0.25	0.06	0.00	0.00
Net Asset Value ($)	17.63	18.58	19.52	17.87	15.83	14.39	12.13	12.52	11.74	10.62
Expense Ratio (%)	1.02	1.04	1.04	1.08	1.17	1.17	1.25	1.31	1.35	1.40
Yield (%)	2.40	1.89	1.93	2.25	2.51	2.84	2.90	2.46	2.89	3.57
Portfolio Turnover (%)	31	25	21	24	17	14	28	27	14	13
Total Assets (Millions $)	51	64	60	50	41	34	24	20	13	7

PORTFOLIO (as of 6/30/00)

Portfolio Manager: John Bruce - 1989

Investm't Category: Balanced

✔ Domestic	Index
Foreign	Sector
Asset Allocation	State Specific

Investment Style

Large Cap	Mid Cap	Small Cap
Growth	Grth/Val	Value

Portfolio

0.9%	cash	14.9%	corp bonds
68.5%	stocks	15.7%	gov't bonds
0.0%	pref/conv't pref	0.0%	muni bonds
0.0%	conv't bds/wrnts	0.0%	other

SHAREHOLDER INFORMATION

Minimum Investment

Initial: $25,000 — Subsequent: $100

Minimum IRA Investment

Initial: $1,000 — Subsequent: $300

Maximum Fees

Load: none — 12b-1: none

Other: none

Services

✔ IRA

✔ Keogh

✔ Telephone Exchange

FTI Intl Equity (FTIEX)

888-343-8242, 412-288-1900
www.ftifunds.com

International Stock

PERFORMANCE

fund inception date: 12/22/95

	3yr Annual	5yr Annual	10yr Annual	Bull	Bear
Return (%)	6.7	9.2	na	54.1	-29.0
Differ from Category (+/-)	-2.2 blw av	0.9 av	na	-36.8 blw av	-5.0 blw av

Standard Deviation	Category Risk Index	Beta
21.3%—abv av	0.94—blw av	0.77

	2000	1999	1998	1997	1996	1995	1994	1993	1992	1991
Return (%)	-24.9	43.8	12.8	13.3	12.7	—	—	—	—	—
Differ from Category (+/-)	-5.5	-16.9	7.0	12.0	-1.8	—	—	—	—	—
Return, Tax-Adjusted (%)	-24.9	42.5	12.6	12.9	12.0	—	—	—	—	—

PER SHARE DATA

	2000	1999	1998	1997	1996	1995	1994	1993	1992	1991
Dividends, Net Income ($)	0.02	0.00	0.04	0.11	0.17	—	—	—	—	—
Distrib'ns, Cap Gain ($)	0.00	0.86	0.00	0.00	0.00	—	—	—	—	—
Net Asset Value ($)	14.41	19.24	14.02	12.46	11.10	—	—	—	—	—
Expense Ratio (%)	na	1.20	1.39	1.60	1.68	—	—	—	—	—
Yield (%)	0.13	0.00	0.28	0.88	1.53	—	—	—	—	—
Portfolio Turnover (%)	na	72	68	55	29	—	—	—	—	—
Total Assets (Millions $)	94	92	73	43	12	—	—	—	—	—

PORTFOLIO (as of 9/30/00)

Portfolio Manager: S. Coco, W. Yun, J. Rosenthal - 1995

Investm't Category: International Stock

Domestic	Index
✔ Foreign	Sector
Asset Allocation	State Specific

Investment Style

Large Cap	Mid Cap	Small Cap
Growth	Grth/Val	Value

Portfolio

9.8%	cash	0.0%	corp bonds
90.2%	stocks	0.0%	gov't bonds
0.0%	pref/conv't pref	0.0%	muni bonds
0.0%	conv't bds/wrnts	0.0%	other

SHAREHOLDER INFORMATION

Minimum Investment

Initial: $1,000 Subsequent: $1

Minimum IRA Investment

Initial: $1,000 Subsequent: $1

Maximum Fees

Load: none 12b-1: none

Other: none

Services

✔ IRA

Keogh

✔ Telephone Exchange

FTI Small Cap Equity (FTSCX)

888-343-8242, 412-288-1900
www.ftifunds.com

Aggressive Growth

PERFORMANCE — fund inception date: 12/22/95

	3yr Annual	5yr Annual	10yr Annual	Bull	Bear
Return (%)	21.5	21.1	na	128.4	-18.9
Differ from Category (+/-)	5.3 abv av	6.5 abv av	na	9.2 abv av	1.7 av

Standard Deviation	Category Risk Index	Beta
31.9%—high	0.98—av	1.17

	2000	1999	1998	1997	1996	1995	1994	1993	1992	1991
Return (%)	3.0	69.3	3.0	17.7	23.4	—	—	—	—	—
Differ from Category (+/-)	9.0	11.8	-12.1	2.9	5.1	—	—	—	—	—
Return, Tax-Adjusted (%)	3.0	66.6	3.0	17.1	23.4	—	—	—	—	—

PER SHARE DATA

	2000	1999	1998	1997	1996	1995	1994	1993	1992	1991
Dividends, Net Income ($)	0.00	0.00	0.00	0.00	0.00	—	—	—	—	—
Distrib'ns, Cap Gain ($)	0.00	1.90	0.00	0.34	0.00	—	—	—	—	—
Net Asset Value ($)	23.32	22.63	14.60	14.17	12.34	—	—	—	—	—
Expense Ratio (%)	na	1.44	1.50	1.50	—	—	—	—	—	—
Yield (%)	0.00	0.00	0.00	0.00	0.00	—	—	—	—	—
Portfolio Turnover (%)	na	130	158	111	—	—	—	—	—	—
Total Assets (Millions $)	109	86	52	42	20	—	—	—	—	—

PORTFOLIO (as of 9/30/00)

Portfolio Manager: Karen Fang - 2000

Investm't Category: Aggressive Growth

✔ Domestic | Index
✔ Foreign | Sector
Asset Allocation | State Specific

Investment Style

Large Cap | Mid Cap | ✔ Small Cap
✔ Growth | Grth/Val | Value

Portfolio

6.9%	cash	0.0%	corp bonds
93.1%	stocks	0.0%	gov't bonds
0.0%	pref/conv't pref	0.0%	muni bonds
0.0%	conv't bds/wrnts	0.0%	other

SHAREHOLDER INFORMATION

Minimum Investment
Initial: $1,000 Subsequent: $1

Minimum IRA Investment
Initial: $1,000 Subsequent: $1

Maximum Fees
Load: none 12b-1: none
Other: none

Services
✔ IRA
Keogh
✔ Telephone Exchange

Fasciano (FASCX)

800-982-3533, 312-444-6050
www.fascianofunds.com

Growth

PERFORMANCE fund inception date: 11/10/88

	3yr Annual	5yr Annual	10yr Annual	Bull	Bear
Return (%)	4.9	12.2	14.2	20.1	-1.5
Differ from Category (+/-)	-6.1 low	-3.9 blw av	-2.6 blw av	-29.6 low	3.9 abv av

Standard Deviation	Category Risk Index	Beta
15.9%—av	0.82—low	0.70

	2000	1999	1998	1997	1996	1995	1994	1993	1992	1991
Return (%)	1.7	6.1	7.1	21.5	26.5	31.1	3.6	8.0	7.6	35.0
Differ from Category (+/-)	-1.8	-12.8	-7.2	-5.6	4.2	0.7	3.8	-6.6	-5.0	-2.6
Return, Tax-Adjusted (%)	1.3	5.6	6.2	20.3	25.5	28.9	1.7	6.3	6.8	34.1

PER SHARE DATA

	2000	1999	1998	1997	1996	1995	1994	1993	1992	1991
Dividends, Net Income ($)	0.29	0.39	0.03	0.00	0.33	0.00	0.00	0.00	0.00	0.01
Distrib'ns, Cap Gain ($)	0.00	0.00	1.25	1.49	0.26	1.34	1.14	1.00	0.46	0.36
Net Asset Value ($)	32.98	32.72	31.19	30.31	26.20	21.18	17.18	17.68	17.29	16.49
Expense Ratio (%)	1.20	1.20	1.30	1.40	1.50	1.70	1.70	1.70	1.70	1.90
Yield (%)	0.87	1.19	0.09	0.00	1.24	0.00	0.00	0.00	0.00	0.05
Portfolio Turnover (%)	29	19	49	41	45	37	99	43	29	7
Total Assets (Millions $)	228	398	233	55	33	24	17	17	13	9

PORTFOLIO (as of 3/31/00)

Portfolio Manager: Michael Fasciano - 1988

Investm't Category: Growth

✔ Domestic	Index
Foreign	Sector
Asset Allocation	State Specific

Investment Style

Large Cap	✔ Mid Cap	✔ Small Cap
Growth	Grth/Val	✔ Value

Portfolio

0.8%	cash	0.0%	corp bonds
99.2%	stocks	0.0%	gov't bonds
0.0%	pref/conv't pref	0.0%	muni bonds
0.0%	conv't bds/wrnts	0.0%	other

SHAREHOLDER INFORMATION

Minimum Investment
Initial: $1,000 Subsequent: $100

Minimum IRA Investment
Initial: $1,000 Subsequent: $100

Maximum Fees
Load: none 12b-1: none
Other: none

Services
✔ IRA
✔ Keogh
Telephone Exchange

Fenimore: Value (FAMVX)

800-932-3271, 518-234-7400
www.famfunds.com

Growth & Income

PERFORMANCE — fund inception date: 10/31/86

	3yr Annual	5yr Annual	10yr Annual	Bull	Bear
Return (%)	6.3	13.2	15.9	12.3	10.8
Differ from Category (+/-)	-2.6 blw av	-1.1 blw av	1.0 av	-21.2 low	10.9 high

Standard Deviation	Category Risk Index	Beta
18.1%—av	1.04—abv av	0.68

	2000	1999	1998	1997	1996	1995	1994	1993	1992	1991
Return (%)	19.2	-4.8	6.1	39.0	11.2	19.7	6.8	0.2	25.0	47.6
Differ from Category (+/-)	13.5	-15.6	-6.7	12.1	-8.5	-9.8	7.3	-13.6	13.4	19.5
Return, Tax-Adjusted (%)	16.1	-5.7	4.0	38.1	10.2	18.8	5.7	0.0	24.0	45.5

PER SHARE DATA

	2000	1999	1998	1997	1996	1995	1994	1993	1992	1991
Dividends, Net Income ($)	0.36	0.29	0.20	0.07	0.17	0.20	0.12	0.09	0.10	0.08
Distrib'ns, Cap Gain ($)	4.02	1.09	3.25	1.05	0.62	0.39	0.62	0.04	0.48	0.81
Net Asset Value ($)	32.70	31.35	34.44	35.76	26.53	24.58	21.04	20.40	20.50	16.87
Expense Ratio (%)	na	1.23	1.19	1.24	1.27	1.37	1.39	1.39	1.50	1.49
Yield (%)	0.98	0.89	0.53	0.19	0.62	0.80	0.55	0.44	0.47	0.45
Portfolio Turnover (%)	na	16	16	9	12	3	2	5	10	14
Total Assets (Millions $)	336	373	376	331	253	266	210	220	44	13

PORTFOLIO (as of 6/30/00)

Portfolio Manager: Thomas Putnam, John Fox - 1986

Investm't Category: Growth & Income

✔ Domestic — Index
Foreign — Sector
Asset Allocation — State Specific

Investment Style

Large Cap — ✔ Mid Cap — Small Cap
Growth — Grth/Val — ✔ Value

Portfolio

17.9%	cash	0.0%	corp bonds
82.1%	stocks	0.0%	gov't bonds
0.0%	pref/conv't pref	0.0%	muni bonds
0.0%	conv't bds/wrnts	0.0%	other

SHAREHOLDER INFORMATION

Minimum Investment
Initial: $2,000 — Subsequent: $50

Minimum IRA Investment
Initial: $100 — Subsequent: $50

Maximum Fees
Load: none — 12b-1: none
Other: none

Services
✔ IRA
✔ Keogh
Telephone Exchange

Fidelity (FFIDX)

800-544-8888, 801-534-1910
www.fidelity.com

Growth & Income

PERFORMANCE — fund inception date: 12/31/30

	3yr Annual	5yr Annual	10yr Annual	Bull	Bear
Return (%)	13.1	18.0	17.4	60.5	-15.8
Differ from Category (+/-)	4.2 high	3.7 high	2.5 high	27.0 high	-15.7 low

Standard Deviation	Category Risk Index	Beta
18.8%—av	1.09—high	0.99

	2000	1999	1998	1997	1996	1995	1994	1993	1992	1991
Return (%)	-10.9	24.2	31.0	32.0	19.8	32.8	2.5	18.3	8.4	24.1
Differ from Category (+/-)	-16.6	13.4	18.2	5.1	0.1	3.3	3.0	4.5	-3.2	-4.0
Return, Tax-Adjusted (%)	-13.5	22.6	29.3	29.5	16.8	29.7	0.4	13.6	6.7	21.1

PER SHARE DATA

	2000	1999	1998	1997	1996	1995	1994	1993	1992	1991
Dividends, Net Income ($)	0.23	0.29	0.30	0.32	0.37	0.42	0.33	0.44	0.48	0.50
Distrib'ns, Cap Gain ($)	5.20	2.21	1.81	2.35	1.82	1.40	0.94	2.55	0.58	1.15
Net Asset Value ($)	32.76	42.61	36.69	29.81	24.70	22.61	18.48	19.27	18.94	18.46
Expense Ratio (%)	0.56	0.55	0.56	0.59	0.60	0.64	0.65	0.66	0.67	0.68
Yield (%)	0.60	0.64	0.77	0.99	1.39	1.74	1.69	2.01	2.45	2.54
Portfolio Turnover (%)	113	71	65	107	150	157	207	261	151	267
Total Assets (Millions $)	14,905	16,114	10,563	6,529	4,450	3,213	1,886	1,546	1,351	1,309

PORTFOLIO (as of 6/30/00)

Portfolio Manager: Nick Thakore - 2000

Investm't Category: Growth & Income

- ✔ Domestic
- ✔ Foreign
- Asset Allocation
- Index
- Sector
- State Specific

Investment Style

- ✔ Large Cap
- ✔ Growth
- Mid Cap
- Grth/Val
- Small Cap
- Value

Portfolio

3.9%	cash	0.0%	corp bonds
95.1%	stocks	0.0%	gov't bonds
0.0%	pref/conv't pref	0.0%	muni bonds
1.0%	conv't bds/wrnts	0.0%	other

SHAREHOLDER INFORMATION

Minimum Investment
Initial: $2,500 Subsequent: $250

Minimum IRA Investment
Initial: $500 Subsequent: $250

Maximum Fees
Load: none 12b-1: none
Other: none

Services
- ✔ IRA
- ✔ Keogh
- ✔ Telephone Exchange

Fidelity Aggressive Grth (FDEGX)

800-544-8888, 801-534-1910
www.fidelity.com

Aggressive Growth

PERFORMANCE — fund inception date: 12/28/90

	3yr Annual	5yr Annual	10yr Annual	Bull	Bear
Return (%)	28.4	23.9	24.0	188.2	-39.6
Differ from Category (+/-)	12.2 high	9.3 abv av	8.2 high	69.0 high	-19.0 low

Standard Deviation	Category Risk Index	Beta
37.3%—high	1.15—abv av	1.52

	2000	1999	1998	1997	1996	1995	1994	1993	1992	1991
Return (%)	-27.1	103.5	42.9	19.4	15.7	35.9	-0.1	19.8	8.3	67.0
Differ from Category (+/-)	-21.1	46.0	27.8	4.6	-2.6	1.3	0.7	-5.4	1.4	19.8
Return, Tax-Adjusted (%)	-29.6	101.0	41.1	14.6	14.9	34.5	-0.6	14.1	8.0	65.9

PER SHARE DATA

	2000	1999	1998	1997	1996	1995	1994	1993	1992	1991
Dividends, Net Income ($)	0.00	0.00	0.00	0.00	0.00	0.00	0.00	0.00	0.02	0.00
Distrib'ns, Cap Gain ($)	7.58	3.92	2.08	6.00	0.60	0.80	0.31	3.57	0.14	0.39
Net Asset Value ($)	36.17	59.63	31.69	23.75	25.19	22.32	16.99	17.33	17.58	16.38
Expense Ratio (%)	na	0.97	1.08	1.09	1.09	1.10	1.02	1.19	1.09	1.31
Yield (%)	0.00	0.00	0.00	0.00	0.00	0.00	0.00	0.00	0.11	0.00
Portfolio Turnover (%)	na	186	199	212	105	97	180	332	531	326
Total Assets (Millions $)	14,638	15,199	2,897	1,981	1,854	1,249	635	652	642	724

PORTFOLIO (as of 6/30/00)

Portfolio Manager: Robert Bertelson - 2000

Investm't Category: Aggressive Growth

✔ Domestic — Index
✔ Foreign — Sector
Asset Allocation — State Specific

Investment Style

✔ Large Cap — ✔ Mid Cap — ✔ Small Cap
✔ Growth — Grth/Val — Value

Portfolio

3.1%	cash	0.0%	corp bonds
96.9%	stocks	0.0%	gov't bonds
0.0%	pref/conv't pref	0.0%	muni bonds
0.0%	conv't bds/wrnts	0.0%	other

SHAREHOLDER INFORMATION

Minimum Investment

Initial: $2,500 — Subsequent: $250

Minimum IRA Investment

Initial: $500 — Subsequent: $250

Maximum Fees

Load: 1.50% redemption — 12b-1: none

Other: redemption fee applies for 3 months

Services

✔ IRA
✔ Keogh
✔ Telephone Exchange

Fidelity Aggressive Intl (FIVFX)

800-544-6666, 801-534-1910
www.fidelity.com

International Stock

PERFORMANCE — fund inception date: 11/1/94

	3yr Annual	5yr Annual	10yr Annual	Bull	Bear
Return (%)	7.0	7.6	na	88.7	-29.8
Differ from Category (+/-)	-1.9 blw av	-0.7 blw av	na	-2.2 abv av	-5.8 blw av

Standard Deviation	Category Risk Index	Beta
24.2%—abv av	1.07—av	0.96

	2000	1999	1998	1997	1996	1995	1994	1993	1992	1991
Return (%)	-30.9	58.8	11.7	7.8	9.5	13.9	—	—	—	—
Differ from Category (+/-)	-11.5	-1.9	5.9	6.5	-5.0	4.6	—	—	—	—
Return, Tax-Adjusted (%)	-31.6	57.2	11.5	7.1	8.5	13.0	—	—	—	—

PER SHARE DATA

	2000	1999	1998	1997	1996	1995	1994	1993	1992	1991
Dividends, Net Income ($)	0.02	0.08	0.05	0.06	0.10	0.01	—	—	—	—
Distrib'ns, Cap Gain ($)	0.70	0.90	0.00	0.28	0.22	0.30	—	—	—	—
Net Asset Value ($)	13.31	20.31	13.48	12.11	11.55	10.84	—	—	—	—
Expense Ratio (%)	1.16	1.14	1.21	1.28	1.26	1.72	—	—	—	—
Yield (%)	0.14	0.37	0.37	0.48	0.84	0.08	—	—	—	—
Portfolio Turnover (%)	344	173	137	86	71	109	—	—	—	—
Total Assets (Millions $)	388	697	435	390	267	72	—	—	—	—

PORTFOLIO (as of 6/30/00)

Portfolio Manager: Kevin McCarey - 1999

Investm't Category: International Stock

Domestic	Index
✔ Foreign	Sector
Asset Allocation	State Specific

Investment Style

Large Cap	Mid Cap	Small Cap
Growth	Grth/Val	Value

Portfolio

5.9%	cash	0.0%	corp bonds
94.1%	stocks	0.0%	gov't bonds
0.0%	pref/conv't pref	0.0%	muni bonds
0.0%	conv't bds/wrnts	0.0%	other

SHAREHOLDER INFORMATION

Minimum Investment
Initial: $2,500 — Subsequent: $250

Minimum IRA Investment
Initial: $500 — Subsequent: $250

Maximum Fees
Load: 0.01% redemption — 12b-1: none
Other: redemption fee applies for 1 month

Services
✔ IRA
✔ Keogh
✔ Telephone Exchange

Fidelity Asset Mgr (FASMX)

800-544-8544, 801-534-1910
www.fidelity.com

Balanced

PERFORMANCE — fund inception date: 12/28/88

	3yr Annual	5yr Annual	10yr Annual	Bull	Bear
Return (%)	10.6	13.2	13.4	35.1	-3.5
Differ from Category (+/-)	2.2 abv av	1.8 abv av	1.7 abv av	7.0 abv av	-0.3 av

Standard Deviation	Category Risk Index	Beta
11.4%—blw av	1.04—av	0.60

	2000	1999	1998	1997	1996	1995	1994	1993	1992	1991
Return (%)	2.6	13.5	16.0	22.2	12.7	18.1	-6.6	23.2	12.7	23.6
Differ from Category (+/-)	0.6	2.8	2.7	3.4	-1.2	-7.4	-5.3	8.8	4.3	-0.2
Return, Tax-Adjusted (%)	-0.3	11.3	11.2	19.3	9.8	16.7	-7.9	20.5	11.0	21.0

PER SHARE DATA

	2000	1999	1998	1997	1996	1995	1994	1993	1992	1991
Dividends, Net Income ($)	0.71	0.56	0.60	0.61	0.62	0.46	0.40	0.59	0.48	0.45
Distrib'ns, Cap Gain ($)	1.34	0.74	3.15	1.11	0.75	0.00	0.17	0.43	0.19	0.50
Net Asset Value ($)	16.82	18.38	17.39	18.35	16.47	15.85	13.83	15.40	13.37	12.46
Expense Ratio (%)	0.73	0.73	0.74	0.79	0.93	0.97	1.04	1.09	1.17	1.17
Yield (%)	3.90	2.92	2.92	3.13	3.60	2.90	2.85	3.72	3.53	3.47
Portfolio Turnover (%)	109	104	136	79	131	137	109	98	134	134
Total Assets (Millions $)	12,782	13,253	12,879	12,098	10,971	11,165	11,075	9,094	3,407	1,016

PORTFOLIO (as of 6/30/00)

Portfolio Manager: Richard Habermann - 2000

Investm't Category: Balanced

✔ Domestic — Index
✔ Foreign — Sector
✔ Asset Allocation — State Specific

Investment Style

Large Cap — Mid Cap — Small Cap
Growth — Grth/Val — Value

Portfolio

10.7%	cash	13.3%	corp bonds
54.6%	stocks	20.4%	gov't bonds
0.0%	pref/conv't pref	0.0%	muni bonds
0.0%	conv't bds/wrnts	1.0%	other

SHAREHOLDER INFORMATION

Minimum Investment
Initial: $2,500 — Subsequent: $250

Minimum IRA Investment
Initial: $500 — Subsequent: $250

Maximum Fees
Load: none — 12b-1: none
Other: none

Services
✔ IRA
✔ Keogh
✔ Telephone Exchange

Fidelity Asset Mgr Growth (FASGX)

800-544-8544, 801-534-1910
www.fidelity.com

Balanced

PERFORMANCE fund inception date: 12/30/91

	3yr Annual	5yr Annual	10yr Annual	Bull	Bear
Return (%)	9.0	14.0	na	38.5	-7.6
Differ from Category (+/-)	0.6 av	2.6 high	na	10.4 abv av	-4.4 blw av

Standard Deviation	Category Risk Index	Beta
14.3%—av	1.31—high	0.75

	2000	1999	1998	1997	1996	1995	1994	1993	1992	1991
Return (%)	-3.5	13.9	18.0	26.4	17.5	19.9	-7.3	26.3	19.0	—
Differ from Category (+/-)	-5.5	3.2	4.7	7.6	3.6	-5.6	-6.0	11.9	10.6	—
Return, Tax-Adjusted (%)	-7.0	11.7	14.3	23.2	14.4	19.1	-8.1	24.7	18.3	—

PER SHARE DATA

	2000	1999	1998	1997	1996	1995	1994	1993	1992	1991
Dividends, Net Income ($)	0.46	0.45	0.35	0.40	0.43	0.23	0.19	0.09	0.15	—
Distrib'ns, Cap Gain ($)	2.56	1.10	2.68	1.75	1.07	0.00	0.17	0.51	0.08	—
Net Asset Value ($)	15.91	19.67	18.68	18.48	16.35	15.17	12.84	14.25	11.77	—
Expense Ratio (%)	0.80	0.80	0.80	0.87	1.01	1.03	1.15	1.19	1.64	—
Yield (%)	2.49	2.16	1.63	1.97	2.46	1.51	1.46	0.60	1.26	—
Portfolio Turnover (%)	197	101	150	70	138	119	104	97	693	—
Total Assets (Millions $)	4,780	5,490	5,119	4,662	3,377	2,894	2,852	1,795	242	—

PORTFOLIO (as of 6/30/00)

Portfolio Manager: Richard Habermann - 1996

Investm't Category: Balanced

✔ Domestic	Index
✔ Foreign	Sector
✔ Asset Allocation	State Specific

Investment Style

Large Cap	Mid Cap	Small Cap
Growth	Grth/Val	Value

Portfolio

4.6%	cash	12.3%	corp bonds
75.6%	stocks	6.8%	gov't bonds
0.0%	pref/conv't pref	0.0%	muni bonds
0.0%	conv't bds/wrnts	0.7%	other

SHAREHOLDER INFORMATION

Minimum Investment
Initial: $2,500 Subsequent: $250

Minimum IRA Investment
Initial: $500 Subsequent: $250

Maximum Fees
Load: none 12b-1: none
Other: none

Services
✔ IRA
✔ Keogh
✔ Telephone Exchange

Fidelity Asset Mgr Income (FASIX)

800-544-8544, 801-534-1910
www.fidelity.com

Balanced

PERFORMANCE

fund inception date: 10/1/92

	3yr Annual	5yr Annual	10yr Annual	Bull	Bear
Return (%)	6.5	7.9	na	13.3	0.3
Differ from Category (+/-)	-1.9 blw av	-3.5 low	na	-14.8 low	3.5 abv av

Standard Deviation	Category Risk Index	Beta
4.5%—blw av	0.42—low	0.21

	2000	1999	1998	1997	1996	1995	1994	1993	1992	1991
Return (%)	3.6	5.7	10.3	12.4	7.8	16.6	-1.3	15.3	—	—
Differ from Category (+/-)	1.6	-5.0	-3.0	-6.4	-6.1	-8.9	0.0	0.9	—	—
Return, Tax-Adjusted (%)	1.0	3.3	7.6	10.0	5.0	14.5	-3.0	13.1	—	—

PER SHARE DATA

	2000	1999	1998	1997	1996	1995	1994	1993	1992	1991
Dividends, Net Income ($)	0.66	0.61	0.55	0.55	0.61	0.53	0.49	0.49	—	—
Distrib'ns, Cap Gain ($)	0.22	0.21	0.53	0.29	0.26	0.00	0.00	0.08	—	—
Net Asset Value ($)	11.73	12.18	12.32	12.18	11.61	11.60	10.42	11.06	—	—
Expense Ratio (%)	0.65	0.67	0.69	0.77	0.80	0.79	0.71	0.65	—	—
Yield (%)	5.52	4.92	4.28	4.41	5.13	4.56	4.70	4.39	—	—
Portfolio Turnover (%)	140	121	156	112	148	157	83	47	—	—
Total Assets (Millions $)	796	888	940	687	588	600	476	292	—	—

PORTFOLIO (as of 6/30/00)

Portfolio Manager: Richard Habermann - 1996

Investm't Category: Balanced

✔ Domestic	Index
✔ Foreign	Sector
✔ Asset Allocation	State Specific

Investment Style

Large Cap	Mid Cap	Small Cap
Growth	Grth/Val	Value

Portfolio

24.1%	cash	18.8%	corp bonds
21.2%	stocks	34.5%	gov't bonds
0.0%	pref/conv't pref	0.0%	muni bonds
0.0%	conv't bds/wrnts	1.4%	other

SHAREHOLDER INFORMATION

Minimum Investment

Initial: $2,500 Subsequent: $250

Minimum IRA Investment

Initial: $500 Subsequent: $250

Maximum Fees

Load: none 12b-1: none

Other: none

Services

✔ IRA
✔ Keogh
✔ Telephone Exchange

Fidelity Balanced (FBALX)

800-544-8544, 801-534-1910
www.fidelity.com

Balanced

PERFORMANCE

fund inception date: 11/6/86

	3yr Annual	5yr Annual	10yr Annual	Bull	Bear
Return (%)	11.2	13.2	12.6	29.7	0.1
Differ from Category (+/-)	2.8 high	1.8 abv av	0.9 abv av	1.6 av	3.3 abv av

Standard Deviation	Category Risk Index	Beta
10.6%—blw av	0.97—av	0.55

	2000	1999	1998	1997	1996	1995	1994	1993	1992	1991
Return (%)	5.3	8.8	20.2	23.4	9.3	14.9	-5.3	19.2	7.9	26.7
Differ from Category (+/-)	3.3	-1.9	6.9	4.6	-4.6	-10.6	-4.0	4.8	-0.5	2.9
Return, Tax-Adjusted (%)	3.4	5.2	17.3	19.7	7.3	13.0	-6.4	15.8	5.4	23.7

PER SHARE DATA

	2000	1999	1998	1997	1996	1995	1994	1993	1992	1991
Dividends, Net Income ($)	0.48	0.46	0.46	0.56	0.65	0.57	0.40	0.60	0.66	0.60
Distrib'ns, Cap Gain ($)	0.49	1.98	1.27	1.46	0.00	0.00	0.00	0.64	0.36	0.45
Net Asset Value ($)	15.19	15.36	16.36	15.27	14.08	13.52	12.29	13.39	12.29	12.35
Expense Ratio (%)	0.67	0.65	0.67	0.74	0.79	0.90	1.01	0.93	0.96	0.98
Yield (%)	3.06	2.65	2.60	3.34	4.61	4.21	3.25	4.27	5.21	4.68
Portfolio Turnover (%)	139	157	135	70	247	269	157	162	242	238
Total Assets (Millions $)	5,914	6,122	5,316	4,283	3,919	4,880	4,999	4,684	1,761	725

PORTFOLIO (as of 6/30/00)

Portfolio Manager: Robert Ewing - 2000

Investm't Category: Balanced

✔ Domestic	Index
Foreign	Sector
✔ Asset Allocation	State Specific

Investment Style

Large Cap	Mid Cap	Small Cap
Growth	Grth/Val	Value

Portfolio

7.2%	cash	8.0%	corp bonds
55.7%	stocks	28.4%	gov't bonds
0.0%	pref/conv't pref	0.0%	muni bonds
0.0%	conv't bds/wrnts	0.7%	other

SHAREHOLDER INFORMATION

Minimum Investment

Initial: $2,500 Subsequent: $250

Minimum IRA Investment

Initial: $500 Subsequent: $250

Maximum Fees

Load: none 12b-1: none

Other: none

Services

✔ IRA

✔ Keogh

✔ Telephone Exchange

Fidelity Blue Chip Growth (FBGRX)

800-544-8544, 801-534-1910
www.fidelity.com

Growth

PERFORMANCE

fund inception date: 12/31/87

	3yr Annual	5yr Annual	10yr Annual	Bull	Bear
Return (%)	14.4	17.0	20.2	64.7	-15.2
Differ from Category (+/-)	3.4 abv av	0.9 av	3.4 high	15.0 abv av	-9.8 blw av

Standard Deviation	Category Risk Index	Beta
19.5%—abv av	1.00—av	1.03

	2000	1999	1998	1997	1996	1995	1994	1993	1992	1991
Return (%)	-10.5	24.2	34.7	27.0	15.3	28.3	9.8	24.5	6.1	54.8
Differ from Category (+/-)	-14.0	5.3	20.4	-0.1	-7.0	-2.1	10.0	9.9	-6.5	17.2
Return, Tax-Adjusted (%)	-11.3	23.2	33.5	25.6	12.8	25.4	9.1	19.4	5.1	54.6

PER SHARE DATA

	2000	1999	1998	1997	1996	1995	1994	1993	1992	1991
Dividends, Net Income ($)	0.00	0.14	0.10	0.26	0.28	0.12	0.00	0.01	0.14	0.08
Distrib'ns, Cap Gain ($)	2.52	2.07	2.06	1.75	2.25	2.47	0.58	4.12	0.62	0.00
Net Asset Value ($)	51.53	60.11	50.39	39.46	32.69	30.77	25.95	24.17	22.83	22.25
Expense Ratio (%)	0.88	0.70	0.70	0.78	0.95	1.02	1.22	1.25	1.27	1.26
Yield (%)	0.00	0.22	0.19	0.63	0.80	0.36	0.00	0.03	0.59	0.35
Portfolio Turnover (%)	40	38	49	51	206	182	271	319	71	99
Total Assets (Millions $)	26,720	27,876	19,904	13,428	9,569	7,801	3,287	1,094	565	390

PORTFOLIO (as of 6/30/00)

Portfolio Manager: John McDowell - 1996

Investm't Category: Growth

✔ Domestic | Index
✔ Foreign | Sector
Asset Allocation | State Specific

Investment Style

✔ Large Cap | Mid Cap | Small Cap
✔ Growth | Grth/Val | Value

Portfolio

2.4%	cash	0.0%	corp bonds
97.6%	stocks	0.0%	gov't bonds
0.0%	pref/conv't pref	0.0%	muni bonds
0.0%	conv't bds/wrnts	0.0%	other

SHAREHOLDER INFORMATION

Minimum Investment

Initial: $2,500 Subsequent: $250

Minimum IRA Investment

Initial: $500 Subsequent: $250

Maximum Fees

Load: none 12b-1: none
Other: none

Services

✔ IRA
✔ Keogh
✔ Telephone Exchange

Fidelity Canada (FICDX)

800-544-8888, 801-534-1910
www.fidelity.com

International Stock

PERFORMANCE

fund inception date: 11/17/87

	3yr Annual	5yr Annual	10yr Annual	Bull	Bear
Return (%)	10.3	10.5	9.5	65.1	-6.9
Differ from Category (+/-)	1.4 av	2.2 abv av	0.5 av	-25.8 av	17.1 high

Standard Deviation	Category Risk Index	Beta
24.3%—abv av	1.07—av	1.05

	2000	1999	1998	1997	1996	1995	1994	1993	1992	1991
Return (%)	12.2	40.5	-14.9	6.1	15.9	19.3	-11.9	25.4	-2.8	17.6
Differ from Category (+/-)	31.6	-20.2	-20.7	4.8	1.4	10.0	-8.8	-14.8	0.7	4.6
Return, Tax-Adjusted (%)	10.1	40.4	-15.0	3.6	9.3	19.1	-11.9	25.3	-2.8	15.6

PER SHARE DATA

	2000	1999	1998	1997	1996	1995	1994	1993	1992	1991
Dividends, Net Income ($)	1.04	0.03	0.07	0.05	0.13	0.08	0.01	0.00	0.02	0.00
Distrib'ns, Cap Gain ($)	0.00	0.00	0.00	2.08	4.29	0.00	0.00	0.04	0.00	0.92
Net Asset Value ($)	21.02	19.63	13.99	16.53	17.62	19.02	16.00	18.19	14.53	14.98
Expense Ratio (%)	na	1.06	0.80	0.92	0.98	1.15	1.57	2.00	2.00	2.01
Yield (%)	4.94	0.15	0.50	0.26	0.59	0.42	0.06	0.00	0.13	0.00
Portfolio Turnover (%)	na	286	215	139	139	83	59	131	55	68
Total Assets (Millions $)	145	57	47	87	129	174	332	109	26	22

PORTFOLIO (as of 6/30/00)

Portfolio Manager: Stephen Binder - 1999

Investm't Category: International Stock

Domestic	Index
✔ Foreign	Sector
Asset Allocation	State Specific

Investment Style

Large Cap	Mid Cap	Small Cap
Growth	Grth/Val	Value

Portfolio

7.5%	cash	0.0%	corp bonds
92.5%	stocks	0.0%	gov't bonds
0.0%	pref/conv't pref	0.0%	muni bonds
0.0%	conv't bds/wrnts	0.0%	other

SHAREHOLDER INFORMATION

Minimum Investment
Initial: $2,500 Subsequent: $250

Minimum IRA Investment
Initial: $500 Subsequent: $250

Maximum Fees
Load: 3.00% front 12b-1: none
Other: 1.50% redemption fee for 3 months

Services
✔ IRA
✔ Keogh
✔ Telephone Exchange

Fidelity Capital Apprec (FDCAX)

800-544-8888, 801-534-1910
www.fidelity.com

Growth

PERFORMANCE

fund inception date: 11/26/86

	3yr Annual	5yr Annual	10yr Annual	Bull	Bear
Return (%)	11.7	15.2	15.5	95.2	-27.9
Differ from Category (+/-)	0.7 av	-0.9 blw av	-1.3 blw av	45.5 high	-22.5 low

Standard Deviation	Category Risk Index	Beta
25.9%—high	1.33—high	1.22

	2000	1999	1998	1997	1996	1995	1994	1993	1992	1991
Return (%)	-18.1	45.8	16.9	26.5	15.1	18.7	2.5	33.4	16.3	9.9
Differ from Category (+/-)	-21.6	26.9	2.6	-0.6	-7.2	-11.7	2.7	18.8	3.7	-27.7
Return, Tax-Adjusted (%)	-19.7	43.4	16.2	23.0	12.2	15.8	-0.9	30.9	14.4	4.2

PER SHARE DATA

	2000	1999	1998	1997	1996	1995	1994	1993	1992	1991
Dividends, Net Income ($)	0.15	0.57	0.10	0.08	0.12	0.40	0.17	0.10	0.18	0.62
Distrib'ns, Cap Gain ($)	2.13	1.49	0.45	2.85	1.54	1.00	1.85	1.06	0.60	2.13
Net Asset Value ($)	22.23	29.87	22.07	19.38	17.64	16.78	15.31	16.92	13.57	12.34
Expense Ratio (%)	0.83	0.65	0.67	0.66	0.80	1.07	1.17	0.86	0.71	0.83
Yield (%)	0.61	1.81	0.44	0.35	0.62	2.24	0.99	0.55	1.27	4.28
Portfolio Turnover (%)	85	78	121	176	205	93	124	120	99	72
Total Assets (Millions $)	2,570	3,686	2,602	2,109	1,642	1,669	1,623	1,428	988	992

PORTFOLIO (as of 6/30/00)

Portfolio Manager: Harry Lange - 1996

Investm't Category: Growth

✔ Domestic | Index
✔ Foreign | Sector
Asset Allocation | State Specific

Investment Style

Large Cap | ✔ Mid Cap | Small Cap
✔ Growth | Grth/Val | Value

Portfolio

3.8%	cash	0.0%	corp bonds
96.2%	stocks	0.0%	gov't bonds
0.0%	pref/conv't pref	0.0%	muni bonds
0.0%	conv't bds/wrnts	0.0%	other

SHAREHOLDER INFORMATION

Minimum Investment
Initial: $2,500 | Subsequent: $250

Minimum IRA Investment
Initial: $500 | Subsequent: $250

Maximum Fees
Load: none | 12b-1: none
Other: none

Services
✔ IRA
✔ Keogh
✔ Telephone Exchange

Fidelity China Region (FHKCX)

800-544-8888, 801-534-1910
www.fidelity.com

International Stock

PERFORMANCE — fund inception date: 11/1/95

	3yr Annual	5yr Annual	10yr Annual	Bull	Bear
Return (%)	12.9	9.6	na	151.4	-26.8
Differ from Category (+/-)	4.0 abv av	1.3 av	na	60.5 high	-2.8 av

Standard Deviation	Category Risk Index	Beta
33.4%—high	1.47—high	1.14

	2000	1999	1998	1997	1996	1995	1994	1993	1992	1991
Return (%)	-17.5	84.9	-5.3	-22.0	40.9	—	—	—	—	—
Differ from Category (+/-)	1.9	24.2	-11.1	-23.3	26.4	—	—	—	—	—
Return, Tax-Adjusted (%)	-18.6	84.2	-6.4	-22.1	40.1	—	—	—	—	—

PER SHARE DATA

	2000	1999	1998	1997	1996	1995	1994	1993	1992	1991
Dividends, Net Income ($)	0.56	0.17	0.32	0.06	0.14	—	—	—	—	—
Distrib'ns, Cap Gain ($)	0.00	0.00	0.00	0.00	0.08	—	—	—	—	—
Net Asset Value ($)	14.70	18.51	10.11	11.02	14.21	—	—	—	—	—
Expense Ratio (%)	na	1.32	1.40	1.31	1.62	—	—	—	—	—
Yield (%)	3.80	0.91	3.16	0.54	0.97	—	—	—	—	—
Portfolio Turnover (%)	na	84	109	174	118	—	—	—	—	—
Total Assets (Millions $)	169	273	133	180	197	—	—	—	—	—

PORTFOLIO (as of 6/30/00)

Portfolio Manager: Joseph Tse - 1995

Investm't Category: International Stock

Domestic — Index
✔ Foreign — Sector
Asset Allocation — State Specific

Investment Style

Large Cap — Mid Cap — Small Cap
Growth — Grth/Val — Value

Portfolio

4.7%	cash	0.0%	corp bonds
95.3%	stocks	0.0%	gov't bonds
0.0%	pref/conv't pref	0.0%	muni bonds
0.0%	conv't bds/wrnts	0.0%	other

SHAREHOLDER INFORMATION

Minimum Investment
Initial: $2,500 — Subsequent: $250

Minimum IRA Investment
Initial: $500 — Subsequent: $250

Maximum Fees
Load: 3.00% front — 12b-1: none
Other: 1.50% redemption fee for 3 months

Services
✔ IRA
✔ Keogh
✔ Telephone Exchange

Fidelity Contrafund (FCNTX)

800-544-8888, 801-534-1910
www.fidelity.com

Growth

PERFORMANCE

fund inception date: 5/17/67

	3yr Annual	5yr Annual	10yr Annual	Bull	Bear
Return (%)	15.2	18.1	21.0	64.0	-14.6
Differ from Category (+/-)	4.2 abv av	2.0 abv av	4.2 high	14.3 abv av	-9.2 blw av

Standard Deviation	Category Risk Index	Beta
18.1%—av	0.93—blw av	0.90

	2000	1999	1998	1997	1996	1995	1994	1993	1992	1991
Return (%)	-6.8	25.0	31.5	22.9	21.9	36.2	-1.1	21.4	15.8	54.9
Differ from Category (+/-)	-10.3	6.1	17.2	-4.2	-0.4	5.8	-0.9	6.8	3.2	17.3
Return, Tax-Adjusted (%)	-9.1	21.2	29.4	20.4	18.9	33.1	-1.2	18.8	13.4	52.9

PER SHARE DATA

	2000	1999	1998	1997	1996	1995	1994	1993	1992	1991
Dividends, Net Income ($)	0.24	0.28	0.30	0.35	0.38	0.09	0.00	0.18	0.20	0.11
Distrib'ns, Cap Gain ($)	6.62	10.22	4.22	4.56	3.45	3.13	0.22	2.25	1.92	1.06
Net Asset Value ($)	49.17	60.02	56.81	46.63	42.15	38.02	30.28	30.84	27.47	25.60
Expense Ratio (%)	na	0.65	0.65	0.67	0.79	0.97	1.03	1.06	0.87	0.89
Yield (%)	0.43	0.39	0.49	0.68	0.83	0.21	0.00	0.54	0.68	0.41
Portfolio Turnover (%)	na	177	197	144	159	210	235	255	297	217
Total Assets (Millions $)	39,241	46,927	38,821	30,808	23,797	14,831	8,682	6,193	1,974	1,002

PORTFOLIO (as of 6/30/00)

Portfolio Manager: William Danoff - 1990

Investm't Category: Growth

✔ Domestic	Index
✔ Foreign	Sector
Asset Allocation	State Specific

Investment Style

✔ Large Cap	✔ Mid Cap	Small Cap
✔ Growth	Grth/Val	Value

Portfolio

6.6%	cash	0.0%	corp bonds
90.9%	stocks	2.5%	gov't bonds
0.0%	pref/conv't pref	0.0%	muni bonds
0.0%	conv't bds/wrnts	0.0%	other

SHAREHOLDER INFORMATION

Minimum Investment

Initial: $2,500 Subsequent: $250

Minimum IRA Investment

Initial: $500 Subsequent: $250

Maximum Fees

Load: 3.00% front 12b-1: none

Other: none

Services

✔ IRA

✔ Keogh

✔ Telephone Exchange

Fidelity Convertible Sec (FCVSX)

800-544-8888, 801-534-1910
www.fidelity.com

Growth & Income

PERFORMANCE — fund inception date: 1/5/87

	3yr Annual	5yr Annual	10yr Annual	Bull	Bear
Return (%)	21.5	18.7	18.6	72.4	-10.1
Differ from Category (+/-)	12.6 high	4.4 high	3.7 high	38.9 high	-10.0 blw av

Standard Deviation	Category Risk Index	Beta
22.5%—abv av	1.30—high	0.89

	2000	1999	1998	1997	1996	1995	1994	1993	1992	1991
Return (%)	7.2	44.0	16.2	14.4	15.0	19.3	-1.7	17.7	22.0	38.7
Differ from Category (+/-)	1.5	33.2	3.4	-12.5	-4.7	-10.2	-1.2	3.9	10.4	10.6
Return, Tax-Adjusted (%)	2.3	41.1	13.4	10.8	11.6	15.9	-3.6	13.8	19.6	35.8

PER SHARE DATA

	2000	1999	1998	1997	1996	1995	1994	1993	1992	1991
Dividends, Net Income ($)	0.69	0.58	0.62	0.70	0.77	0.76	0.80	0.73	0.67	0.64
Distrib'ns, Cap Gain ($)	4.57	1.50	1.16	1.77	0.89	0.76	0.00	1.09	0.40	0.37
Net Asset Value ($)	20.78	24.28	18.49	17.51	17.56	16.77	15.36	16.45	15.55	13.67
Expense Ratio (%)	na	0.82	0.79	0.73	0.85	0.71	0.85	0.92	0.96	1.17
Yield (%)	2.72	2.24	3.15	3.63	4.17	4.33	5.20	4.16	4.20	4.55
Portfolio Turnover (%)	na	246	223	212	175	219	318	312	258	152
Total Assets (Millions $)	1,844	1,422	1,035	1,002	1,119	1,045	891	1,063	485	133

PORTFOLIO (as of 6/30/00)

Portfolio Manager: Beso Sikharulidze - 1999

Investm't Category: Growth & Income

✔ Domestic — Index
✔ Foreign — Sector
Asset Allocation — State Specific

Investment Style

Large Cap — Mid Cap — ✔ Small Cap
✔ Growth — Grth/Val — Value

Portfolio

8.6%	cash	0.4%	corp bonds
0.0%	stocks	0.0%	gov't bonds
8.4%	pref/conv't pref	0.0%	muni bonds
82.6%	conv't bds/wrnts	0.0%	other

SHAREHOLDER INFORMATION

Minimum Investment
Initial: $2,500 — Subsequent: $250

Minimum IRA Investment
Initial: $500 — Subsequent: $250

Maximum Fees
Load: none — 12b-1: none
Other: none

Services
✔ IRA
✔ Keogh
✔ Telephone Exchange

Fidelity Disciplined Eqty (FDEQX)

800-544-8888, 801-534-1910
www.fidelity.com

Growth

PERFORMANCE

fund inception date: 12/28/88

	3yr Annual	5yr Annual	10yr Annual	Bull	Bear
Return (%)	12.9	17.1	17.8	55.3	-10.1
Differ from Category (+/-)	1.9 av	1.0 av	1.0 abv av	5.6 av	-4.7 av

Standard Deviation	Category Risk Index	Beta
17.7%—av	0.91—low	0.96

	2000	1999	1998	1997	1996	1995	1994	1993	1992	1991
Return (%)	-3.4	22.4	21.8	33.3	15.1	29.0	3.0	13.9	13.2	36.0
Differ from Category (+/-)	-6.9	3.5	7.5	6.2	-7.2	-1.4	3.2	-0.7	0.6	-1.6
Return, Tax-Adjusted (%)	-5.9	18.6	20.0	29.8	12.6	24.8	1.6	11.7	11.1	32.6

PER SHARE DATA

	2000	1999	1998	1997	1996	1995	1994	1993	1992	1991
Dividends, Net Income ($)	0.16	0.27	0.22	0.25	0.23	0.30	0.25	0.21	0.19	0.23
Distrib'ns, Cap Gain ($)	3.57	4.90	1.82	3.30	1.49	2.23	0.52	1.04	0.99	1.32
Net Asset Value ($)	25.82	30.51	29.32	25.86	22.04	20.64	17.94	18.18	17.07	16.14
Expense Ratio (%)	0.79	0.62	0.64	0.69	0.81	0.92	1.05	1.09	1.16	1.19
Yield (%)	0.54	0.76	0.70	0.85	0.97	1.31	1.35	1.09	1.05	1.31
Portfolio Turnover (%)	118	113	125	127	297	222	143	279	255	210
Total Assets (Millions $)	3,322	3,613	3,145	2,557	2,099	2,145	1,160	795	452	175

PORTFOLIO (as of 6/30/00)

Portfolio Manager: Steven Snider - 2000

Investm't Category: Growth

✔ Domestic	Index
✔ Foreign	Sector
Asset Allocation	State Specific

Investment Style

✔ Large Cap	Mid Cap	Small Cap
✔ Growth	Grth/Val	Value

Portfolio

3.0%	cash	0.0%	corp bonds
97.0%	stocks	0.0%	gov't bonds
0.0%	pref/conv't pref	0.0%	muni bonds
0.0%	conv't bds/wrnts	0.0%	other

SHAREHOLDER INFORMATION

Minimum Investment

Initial: $2,500 Subsequent: $250

Minimum IRA Investment

Initial: $500 Subsequent: $250

Maximum Fees

Load: none 12b-1: none

Other: none

Services

✔ IRA
✔ Keogh
✔ Telephone Exchange

Fidelity Diversified Intl (FDIVX)

800-544-6666, 801-534-1910
www.fidelity.com

International Stock

PERFORMANCE — fund inception date: 12/30/91

	3yr Annual	5yr Annual	10yr Annual	Bull	Bear
Return (%)	16.1	16.4	na	72.0	-12.9
Differ from Category (+/-)	7.2 high	8.1 high	na	-18.9 av	11.1 high

Standard Deviation	Category Risk Index	Beta
18.0%—av	0.79—blw av	0.70

	2000	1999	1998	1997	1996	1995	1994	1993	1992	1991
Return (%)	-8.9	50.6	14.3	13.7	20.0	17.9	1.0	36.6	-13.8	—
Differ from Category (+/-)	10.5	-10.1	8.5	12.4	5.5	8.6	4.1	-3.6	-10.3	—
Return, Tax-Adjusted (%)	-10.3	49.2	13.1	12.6	18.7	16.1	0.0	36.2	-14.1	—

PER SHARE DATA

	2000	1999	1998	1997	1996	1995	1994	1993	1992	1991
Dividends, Net Income ($)	0.55	0.25	0.23	0.19	0.15	0.22	0.03	0.01	0.10	—
Distrib'ns, Cap Gain ($)	0.81	0.70	0.47	0.41	0.36	0.41	0.39	0.10	0.00	—
Net Asset Value ($)	21.94	25.62	17.72	16.13	14.71	12.69	11.30	11.60	8.57	—
Expense Ratio (%)	1.12	1.18	1.19	1.23	1.27	1.10	1.25	1.47	2.00	—
Yield (%)	2.41	0.94	1.26	1.14	0.99	1.67	0.25	0.08	1.16	—
Portfolio Turnover (%)	94	73	95	81	94	111	89	56	56	—
Total Assets (Millions $)	6,169	4,908	2,156	1,536	754	340	306	238	37	—

PORTFOLIO (as of 6/30/00)

Portfolio Manager: Gregory Fraser - 1991

Investm't Category: International Stock

Domestic	Index
✔ Foreign	Sector
Asset Allocation	State Specific

Investment Style

Large Cap	Mid Cap	Small Cap
Growth	Grth/Val	Value

Portfolio

8.4%	cash	0.0%	corp bonds
91.5%	stocks	0.0%	gov't bonds
0.0%	pref/conv't pref	0.0%	muni bonds
0.0%	conv't bds/wrnts	0.1%	other

SHAREHOLDER INFORMATION

Minimum Investment
Initial: $2,500 Subsequent: $250

Minimum IRA Investment
Initial: $500 Subsequent: $250

Maximum Fees
Load: 0.01% redemption 12b-1: none
Other: redemption fee applies for 1 month

Services
✔ IRA
✔ Keogh
✔ Telephone Exchange

Fidelity Dividend Growth (FDGFX)

800-544-8544, 801-534-1910
www.fidelity.com

Growth

PERFORMANCE — fund inception date: 4/28/93

	3yr Annual	5yr Annual	10yr Annual	Bull	Bear
Return (%)	18.3	22.5	na	40.8	7.8
Differ from Category (+/-)	7.3 high	6.4 high	na	-8.9 av	13.2 high

Standard Deviation	Category Risk Index	Beta
16.5%—av	0.85—low	0.86

	2000	1999	1998	1997	1996	1995	1994	1993	1992	1991
Return (%)	12.2	8.8	35.8	27.8	30.1	37.5	4.2	—	—	—
Differ from Category (+/-)	8.7	-10.1	21.5	0.7	7.8	7.1	4.4	—	—	—
Return, Tax-Adjusted (%)	10.2	7.1	33.6	25.3	29.2	34.7	3.6	—	—	—

PER SHARE DATA

	2000	1999	1998	1997	1996	1995	1994	1993	1992	1991
Dividends, Net Income ($)	0.18	0.14	0.13	0.15	0.09	0.09	0.01	—	—	—
Distrib'ns, Cap Gain ($)	2.40	2.14	2.19	2.19	0.37	1.07	0.24	—	—	—
Net Asset Value ($)	29.96	28.99	28.73	23.27	20.09	15.84	12.37	—	—	—
Expense Ratio (%)	0.77	0.84	0.86	0.92	0.99	1.19	1.40	—	—	—
Yield (%)	0.55	0.44	0.42	0.58	0.43	0.53	0.07	—	—	—
Portfolio Turnover (%)	86	104	109	141	129	162	291	—	—	—
Total Assets (Millions $)	11,303	12,623	10,368	4,480	2,345	528	102	—	—	—

PORTFOLIO (as of 6/30/00)

Portfolio Manager: Charles Mangum - 1997

Investm't Category: Growth

✔ Domestic — Index
Foreign — Sector
Asset Allocation — State Specific

Investment Style

✔ Large Cap — Mid Cap — Small Cap
Growth — Grth/Val — ✔ Value

Portfolio

3.8%	cash	0.0%	corp bonds
95.8%	stocks	0.0%	gov't bonds
0.0%	pref/conv't pref	0.0%	muni bonds
0.4%	conv't bds/wrnts	0.0%	other

SHAREHOLDER INFORMATION

Minimum Investment

Initial: $2,500 — Subsequent: $250

Minimum IRA Investment

Initial: $500 — Subsequent: $250

Maximum Fees

Load: none — 12b-1: none
Other: none

Services

✔ IRA
✔ Keogh
✔ Telephone Exchange

Fidelity Emerging Market (FEMKX)

800-544-8888, 801-534-1910
www.fidelity.com

International Stock

PERFORMANCE

fund inception date: 11/1/90

	3yr Annual	5yr Annual	10yr Annual	Bull	Bear
Return (%)	-5.6	-11.3	-1.1	112.7	-35.3
Differ from Category (+/-)	-14.5 low	-19.6 low	-10.1 low	21.8 abv av	-11.3 low

Standard Deviation	Category Risk Index	Beta
32.3%—high	1.43—abv av	1.36

	2000	1999	1998	1997	1996	1995	1994	1993	1992	1991
Return (%)	-32.9	70.4	-26.5	-40.7	9.9	-3.1	-17.9	81.7	5.8	6.7
Differ from Category (+/-)	-13.5	9.7	-32.3	-42.0	-4.6	-12.4	-14.8	41.5	9.3	-6.3
Return, Tax-Adjusted (%)	-32.9	70.4	-26.5	-41.2	9.2	-3.7	-17.9	81.5	5.1	6.0

PER SHARE DATA

	2000	1999	1998	1997	1996	1995	1994	1993	1992	1991
Dividends, Net Income ($)	0.03	0.00	0.00	0.23	0.25	0.27	0.04	0.05	0.08	0.08
Distrib'ns, Cap Gain ($)	0.00	0.00	0.00	0.00	0.00	0.00	0.00	0.00	0.15	0.14
Net Asset Value ($)	8.03	12.02	7.05	9.60	16.62	15.34	16.13	19.70	10.87	10.49
Expense Ratio (%)	na	1.42	1.56	1.35	1.29	1.41	1.52	1.91	2.60	2.60
Yield (%)	0.37	0.00	0.00	2.39	1.50	1.76	0.24	0.25	0.72	0.75
Portfolio Turnover (%)	na	94	87	69	77	74	107	57	159	45
Total Assets (Millions $)	270	554	270	446	1,161	1,085	1,508	1,908	14	6

PORTFOLIO (as of 6/30/00)

Portfolio Manager: Patricia Satterthwaite - 2000

Investm't Category: International Stock

Domestic	Index
✔ Foreign	Sector
Asset Allocation	State Specific

Investment Style

Large Cap	Mid Cap	Small Cap
Growth	Grth/Val	Value

Portfolio

0.5%	cash	0.0%	corp bonds
99.4%	stocks	0.0%	gov't bonds
0.0%	pref/conv't pref	0.0%	muni bonds
0.1%	conv't bds/wrnts	0.0%	other

SHAREHOLDER INFORMATION

Minimum Investment

Initial: $2,500 Subsequent: $250

Minimum IRA Investment

Initial: $500 Subsequent: $250

Maximum Fees

Load: 3.00% front 12b-1: none

Other: 1.50% redemption fee for 3 months

Services

✔ IRA
✔ Keogh
✔ Telephone Exchange

Fidelity Equity Income (FEQIX)

800-544-8888, 801-534-1910
www.fidelity.com

Growth & Income

PERFORMANCE

fund inception date: 5/16/66

	3yr Annual	5yr Annual	10yr Annual	Bull	Bear
Return (%)	9.3	15.5	17.2	31.6	6.7
Differ from Category (+/-)	0.4 av	1.2 av	2.3 high	-1.9 av	6.8 abv av

Standard Deviation	Category Risk Index	Beta
17.3%—av	1.00—av	0.80

	2000	1999	1998	1997	1996	1995	1994	1993	1992	1991
Return (%)	8.5	7.1	12.5	29.9	21.0	31.8	0.2	21.3	14.6	29.4
Differ from Category (+/-)	2.8	-3.7	-0.3	3.0	1.3	2.3	0.7	7.5	3.0	1.3
Return, Tax-Adjusted (%)	6.6	4.6	10.9	28.0	18.5	29.3	-2.7	19.6	13.3	27.6

PER SHARE DATA

	2000	1999	1998	1997	1996	1995	1994	1993	1992	1991
Dividends, Net Income ($)	0.87	0.81	0.85	0.96	1.02	0.96	0.98	1.15	1.08	1.20
Distrib'ns, Cap Gain ($)	3.32	5.14	2.39	2.04	1.84	1.36	2.22	0.12	0.00	0.00
Net Asset Value ($)	53.43	53.48	55.55	52.41	42.83	37.93	30.70	33.84	29.01	26.31
Expense Ratio (%)	0.67	0.67	0.67	0.66	0.67	0.69	0.66	0.67	0.68	0.70
Yield (%)	1.53	1.38	1.46	1.76	2.28	2.44	2.97	3.38	3.72	4.56
Portfolio Turnover (%)	26	30	23	30	39	50	70	84	111	107
Total Assets (Millions $)	21,432	22,828	23,707	21,177	14,258	10,492	7,412	6,641	4,977	4,413

PORTFOLIO (as of 6/30/00)

Portfolio Manager: Stephen Petersen - 1993

Investm't Category: Growth & Income

✔ Domestic — Index
Foreign — Sector
Asset Allocation — State Specific

Investment Style

✔ Large Cap — Mid Cap — Small Cap
Growth — Grth/Val — ✔ Value

Portfolio

2.6%	cash	0.0%	corp bonds
91.8%	stocks	0.0%	gov't bonds
0.0%	pref/conv't pref	0.0%	muni bonds
5.2%	conv't bds/wrnts	0.4%	other

SHAREHOLDER INFORMATION

Minimum Investment
Initial: $2,500 — Subsequent: $250

Minimum IRA Investment
Initial: $500 — Subsequent: $250

Maximum Fees
Load: none — 12b-1: none
Other: none

Services
✔ IRA
✔ Keogh
✔ Telephone Exchange

Fidelity Equity Income II (FEQTX)

800-544-8888, 801-534-1910
www.fidelity.com

Growth & Income

PERFORMANCE

fund inception date: 8/21/90

	3yr Annual	5yr Annual	10yr Annual	Bull	Bear
Return (%)	11.3	15.7	18.7	31.3	2.3
Differ from Category (+/-)	2.4 abv av	1.4 abv av	3.8 high	-2.2 av	2.4 av

Standard Deviation	Category Risk Index	Beta
15.9%—av	0.92—blw av	0.78

	2000	1999	1998	1997	1996	1995	1994	1993	1992	1991
Return (%)	7.4	4.3	22.9	27.1	18.7	26.3	3.1	18.8	19.0	45.1
Differ from Category (+/-)	1.7	-6.5	10.1	0.2	-1.0	-3.2	3.6	5.0	7.4	17.0
Return, Tax-Adjusted (%)	3.1	1.4	20.4	24.1	16.2	24.6	0.9	16.4	17.4	43.6

PER SHARE DATA

	2000	1999	1998	1997	1996	1995	1994	1993	1992	1991
Dividends, Net Income ($)	0.42	0.36	0.33	0.43	0.51	0.37	0.39	0.45	0.38	0.34
Distrib'ns, Cap Gain ($)	4.98	3.50	2.65	2.63	1.14	0.55	0.88	0.73	0.36	0.17
Net Asset Value ($)	23.86	27.37	30.01	27.01	23.75	21.43	17.72	18.41	16.51	14.52
Expense Ratio (%)	na	0.66	0.66	0.68	0.72	0.78	0.81	0.88	1.01	1.52
Yield (%)	1.45	1.16	1.01	1.45	2.04	1.68	2.09	2.35	2.25	2.31
Portfolio Turnover (%)	na	71	62	77	46	51	75	55	89	206
Total Assets (Millions $)	13,408	17,579	19,453	16,977	15,238	11,977	7,697	5,021	2,180	370

PORTFOLIO (as of 6/30/00)

Portfolio Manager: Stephen Dufour - 2000

Investm't Category: Growth & Income

✔ Domestic | Index
✔ Foreign | Sector
Asset Allocation | State Specific

Investment Style

✔ Large Cap | Mid Cap | Small Cap
Growth | Grth/Val | ✔ Value

Portfolio

10.7%	cash	0.0%	corp bonds
85.3%	stocks	0.0%	gov't bonds
0.0%	pref/conv't pref	0.0%	muni bonds
4.0%	conv't bds/wrnts	0.0%	other

SHAREHOLDER INFORMATION

Minimum Investment

Initial: $2,500 Subsequent: $250

Minimum IRA Investment

Initial: $500 Subsequent: $250

Maximum Fees

Load: none 12b-1: none
Other: none

Services

✔ IRA
✔ Keogh
✔ Telephone Exchange

Fidelity Europe (FIEUX)

800-544-8888, 801-534-1910
www.fidelity.com

International Stock

PERFORMANCE

fund inception date: 10/1/86

	3yr Annual	5yr Annual	10yr Annual	Bull	Bear
Return (%)	9.2	14.9	12.6	37.1	-20.2
Differ from Category (+/-)	0.3 av	6.6 high	3.6 abv av	-53.8 low	3.8 abv av

Standard Deviation	Category Risk Index	Beta
19.2%—abv av	0.85—blw av	0.82

	2000	1999	1998	1997	1996	1995	1994	1993	1992	1991
Return (%)	-9.1	18.6	20.7	22.8	25.6	18.8	6.2	27.1	-2.5	4.1
Differ from Category (+/-)	10.3	-42.1	14.9	21.5	11.1	9.5	9.3	-13.1	1.0	-8.9
Return, Tax-Adjusted (%)	-11.4	17.2	18.8	20.4	23.0	17.4	5.6	26.8	-3.0	3.0

PER SHARE DATA

	2000	1999	1998	1997	1996	1995	1994	1993	1992	1991
Dividends, Net Income ($)	0.12	0.18	0.28	0.39	0.24	0.12	0.20	0.08	0.29	0.51
Distrib'ns, Cap Gain ($)	4.09	1.94	2.25	2.35	1.73	0.81	0.11	0.00	0.00	0.00
Net Asset Value ($)	29.77	37.47	33.48	29.94	26.61	22.82	20.00	19.12	15.10	15.79
Expense Ratio (%)	na	0.89	1.09	1.18	1.27	1.16	1.35	1.25	1.22	1.31
Yield (%)	0.35	0.45	0.78	1.20	0.84	0.50	0.99	0.41	1.92	3.22
Portfolio Turnover (%)	na	106	114	57	45	44	49	76	95	80
Total Assets (Millions $)	1,318	1,477	1,622	951	773	500	478	494	437	291

PORTFOLIO (as of 6/30/00)

Portfolio Manager: Thierry Serero - 1998

Investm't Category: International Stock

Domestic	Index
✔ Foreign	Sector
Asset Allocation	State Specific

Investment Style

Large Cap	Mid Cap	Small Cap
Growth	Grth/Val	Value

Portfolio

3.8%	cash	0.0%	corp bonds
95.3%	stocks	0.0%	gov't bonds
0.0%	pref/conv't pref	0.0%	muni bonds
0.5%	conv't bds/wrnts	0.4%	other

SHAREHOLDER INFORMATION

Minimum Investment

Initial: $2,500 Subsequent: $250

Minimum IRA Investment

Initial: $500 Subsequent: $250

Maximum Fees

Load: 1.00% redemption 12b-1: none

Other: redemption fee applies for 3 months

Services

✔ IRA

✔ Keogh

✔ Telephone Exchange

Fidelity Europe Cap Appr (FECAX)

800-544-8888, 801-534-1910
www.fidelity.com

International Stock

PERFORMANCE — fund inception date: 12/21/93

	3yr Annual	5yr Annual	10yr Annual	Bull	Bear
Return (%)	12.3	17.4	na	42.4	-13.4
Differ from Category (+/-)	3.4 abv av	9.1 high	na	-48.5 low	10.6 high

Standard Deviation	Category Risk Index	Beta
19.4%—abv av	0.86—blw av	0.72

	2000	1999	1998	1997	1996	1995	1994	1993	1992	1991
Return (%)	-5.7	23.7	21.6	24.9	25.8	14.6	6.8	—	—	—
Differ from Category (+/-)	13.7	-37.0	15.8	23.6	11.3	5.3	9.9	—	—	—
Return, Tax-Adjusted (%)	-6.7	22.8	21.6	21.3	22.0	13.7	6.8	—	—	—

PER SHARE DATA

	2000	1999	1998	1997	1996	1995	1994	1993	1992	1991
Dividends, Net Income ($)	0.11	0.13	0.00	0.16	0.23	0.23	0.00	—	—	—
Distrib'ns, Cap Gain ($)	0.87	0.47	0.00	2.09	1.29	0.00	0.00	—	—	—
Net Asset Value ($)	19.19	21.46	17.86	14.68	13.59	12.06	10.72	—	—	—
Expense Ratio (%)	na	0.97	1.08	1.07	2.00	1.36	1.54	—	—	—
Yield (%)	0.54	0.59	0.00	0.95	1.54	1.90	0.00	—	—	—
Portfolio Turnover (%)	na	150	179	189	1	138	317	—	—	—
Total Assets (Millions $)	587	710	689	371	189	180	291	—	—	—

PORTFOLIO (as of 6/30/00)

Portfolio Manager: Ian Hart - 2000

Investm't Category: International Stock

Domestic	Index
✔ Foreign	Sector
Asset Allocation	State Specific

Investment Style

Large Cap	Mid Cap	Small Cap
Growth	Grth/Val	Value

Portfolio

7.8%	cash	0.0%	corp bonds
92.2%	stocks	0.0%	gov't bonds
0.0%	pref/conv't pref	0.0%	muni bonds
0.0%	conv't bds/wrnts	0.0%	other

SHAREHOLDER INFORMATION

Minimum Investment
Initial: $2,500 Subsequent: $250

Minimum IRA Investment
Initial: $500 Subsequent: $250

Maximum Fees
Load: 1.00% redemption 12b-1: none
Other: redemption fee applies for 3 months

Services
✔ IRA
✔ Keogh
✔ Telephone Exchange

Fidelity Export & Multi (FEXPX)

800-544-8888, 801-534-1910
www.fidelity.com

Growth

PERFORMANCE

fund inception date: 10/4/94

	3yr Annual	5yr Annual	10yr Annual	Bull	Bear
Return (%)	20.7	24.7	na	83.9	-2.9
Differ from Category (+/-)	9.7 high	8.6 high	na	34.2 high	2.5 av

Standard Deviation	Category Risk Index	Beta
20.2%—abv av	1.04—av	0.95

	2000	1999	1998	1997	1996	1995	1994	1993	1992	1991
Return (%)	1.4	41.8	22.4	23.6	38.6	32.2	—	—	—	—
Differ from Category (+/-)	-2.1	22.9	8.1	-3.5	16.3	1.8	—	—	—	—
Return, Tax-Adjusted (%)	-3.5	36.8	21.4	19.0	36.7	29.9	—	—	—	—

PER SHARE DATA

	2000	1999	1998	1997	1996	1995	1994	1993	1992	1991
Dividends, Net Income ($)	0.10	0.05	0.00	0.00	0.00	0.00	—	—	—	—
Distrib'ns, Cap Gain ($)	5.21	4.80	0.77	3.79	0.86	0.84	—	—	—	—
Net Asset Value ($)	16.88	21.97	19.88	17.02	16.75	12.72	—	—	—	—
Expense Ratio (%)	0.86	0.86	0.93	0.98	1.03	1.22	—	—	—	—
Yield (%)	0.45	0.18	0.00	0.00	0.00	0.00	—	—	—	—
Portfolio Turnover (%)	380	265	281	429	313	245	—	—	—	—
Total Assets (Millions $)	488	514	411	465	397	382	—	—	—	—

PORTFOLIO (as of 6/30/00)

Portfolio Manager: Douglas Chase - 2000

Investm't Category: Growth

✔ Domestic	Index
✔ Foreign	Sector
Asset Allocation	State Specific

Investment Style

✔ Large Cap	✔ Mid Cap	Small Cap
✔ Growth	Grth/Val	Value

Portfolio

3.7%	cash	0.0%	corp bonds
96.3%	stocks	0.0%	gov't bonds
0.0%	pref/conv't pref	0.0%	muni bonds
0.0%	conv't bds/wrnts	0.0%	other

SHAREHOLDER INFORMATION

Minimum Investment

Initial: $2,500 Subsequent: $250

Minimum IRA Investment

Initial: $500 Subsequent: $250

Maximum Fees

Load: 0.75% redemption 12b-1: none

Other: redemption fee applies for 1 month

Services

✔ IRA

✔ Keogh

✔ Telephone Exchange

Fidelity Fifty (FFTYX)

800-544-8888, 801-534-1910
www.fidelity.com

Aggressive Growth

PERFORMANCE — fund inception date: 9/20/93

	3yr Annual	5yr Annual	10yr Annual	Bull	Bear
Return (%)	17.1	18.0	na	92.9	-18.1
Differ from Category (+/-)	0.9 av	3.4 av	na	-26.3 av	2.5 abv av

Standard Deviation	Category Risk Index	Beta
24.3%—abv av	0.75—low	0.99

	2000	1999	1998	1997	1996	1995	1994	1993	1992	1991
Return (%)	-4.5	45.7	15.5	23.0	15.9	32.1	3.9	—	—	—
Differ from Category (+/-)	1.5	-11.8	0.4	8.2	-2.4	-2.5	4.7	—	—	—
Return, Tax-Adjusted (%)	-7.4	43.9	14.5	20.0	13.8	28.4	3.5	—	—	—

PER SHARE DATA

	2000	1999	1998	1997	1996	1995	1994	1993	1992	1991
Dividends, Net Income ($)	0.25	0.03	0.02	0.05	0.09	0.13	0.02	—	—	—
Distrib'ns, Cap Gain ($)	2.90	1.43	0.67	2.00	0.83	1.24	0.10	—	—	—
Net Asset Value ($)	18.50	22.81	16.86	15.22	14.04	12.97	10.88	—	—	—
Expense Ratio (%)	0.88	0.79	0.77	0.84	0.99	1.19	1.58	—	—	—
Yield (%)	1.16	0.12	0.11	0.29	0.60	0.91	0.18	—	—	—
Portfolio Turnover (%)	295	316	121	131	152	180	320	—	—	—
Total Assets (Millions $)	400	609	178	174	147	155	60	—	—	—

PORTFOLIO (as of 6/30/00)

Portfolio Manager: John Muresianu - 1999

Investm't Category: Aggressive Growth

✔ Domestic
Index
✔ Foreign
Sector
Asset Allocation
State Specific

Investment Style

✔ Large Cap
Mid Cap
Small Cap
Growth
✔ Grth/Val
Value

Portfolio

3.1%	cash	0.0%	corp bonds
96.9%	stocks	0.0%	gov't bonds
0.0%	pref/conv't pref	0.0%	muni bonds
0.0%	conv't bds/wrnts	0.0%	other

SHAREHOLDER INFORMATION

Minimum Investment

Initial: $2,500 Subsequent: $250

Minimum IRA Investment

Initial: $500 Subsequent: $250

Maximum Fees

Load: 0.75% redemption 12b-1: none

Other: redemption fee applies for 1 month

Services

✔ IRA
✔ Keogh
✔ Telephone Exchange

Fidelity Freedom 2000

800-544-8544, 801-534-1910
www.fidelity.com

(FFFBX)

Balanced

PERFORMANCE — fund inception date: 10/17/96

	3yr Annual	5yr Annual	10yr Annual	Bull	Bear
Return (%)	10.5	na	na	26.4	-0.7
Differ from Category (+/-)	2.1 abv av	na	na	-1.7 av	2.5 abv av

Standard Deviation	Category Risk Index	Beta
7.4%—blw av	0.67—low	0.38

	2000	1999	1998	1997	1996	1995	1994	1993	1992	1991
Return (%)	4.4	12.1	15.2	15.2	—	—	—	—	—	—
Differ from Category (+/-)	2.4	1.4	1.9	-3.6	—	—	—	—	—	—
Return, Tax-Adjusted (%)	0.8	9.9	13.4	13.6	—	—	—	—	—	—

PER SHARE DATA

	2000	1999	1998	1997	1996	1995	1994	1993	1992	1991
Dividends, Net Income ($)	0.61	0.52	0.40	0.33	—	—	—	—	—	—
Distrib'ns, Cap Gain ($)	1.13	0.29	0.21	0.12	—	—	—	—	—	—
Net Asset Value ($)	11.81	12.99	12.33	11.24	—	—	—	—	—	—
Expense Ratio (%)	0.08	0.07	0.08	0.08	—	—	—	—	—	—
Yield (%)	4.71	3.91	3.18	2.90	—	—	—	—	—	—
Portfolio Turnover (%)	37	27	24	19	—	—	—	—	—	—
Total Assets (Millions $)	682	714	502	81	—	—	—	—	—	—

PORTFOLIO (as of 6/30/00)

Portfolio Manager: Ren Cheng, Scott Stewart - 1996

Investm't Category: Balanced

✔ Domestic — Index
✔ Foreign — Sector
Asset Allocation — State Specific

Investment Style

Large Cap — Mid Cap — Small Cap
Growth — Grth/Val — Value

Portfolio

0.0%	cash	0.0%	corp bonds
0.0%	stocks	0.0%	gov't bonds
0.0%	pref/conv't pref	0.0%	muni bonds
0.0%	conv't bds/wrnts	100.0%	other

SHAREHOLDER INFORMATION

Minimum Investment

Initial: $2,500 — Subsequent: $250

Minimum IRA Investment

Initial: $500 — Subsequent: $250

Maximum Fees

Load: none — 12b-1: none
Other: none

Services

✔ IRA
✔ Keogh
✔ Telephone Exchange

Fidelity Freedom 2010 (FFFCX)

800-544-8544, 801-534-1910
www.fidelity.com

Balanced

PERFORMANCE

fund inception date: 10/17/96

	3yr Annual	5yr Annual	10yr Annual	Bull	Bear
Return (%)	12.6	na	na	41.4	-5.4
Differ from Category (+/-)	4.2 high	na	na	13.3 high	-2.2 av

Standard Deviation	Category Risk Index	Beta
11.5%—blw av	1.05—abv av	0.60

	2000	1999	1998	1997	1996	1995	1994	1993	1992	1991
Return (%)	0.6	19.0	19.3	19.3	—	—	—	—	—	—
Differ from Category (+/-)	-1.4	8.3	6.0	0.5	—	—	—	—	—	—
Return, Tax-Adjusted (%)	-1.5	16.9	17.6	17.6	—	—	—	—	—	—

PER SHARE DATA

	2000	1999	1998	1997	1996	1995	1994	1993	1992	1991
Dividends, Net Income ($)	0.46	0.49	0.35	0.37	—	—	—	—	—	—
Distrib'ns, Cap Gain ($)	0.67	0.42	0.28	0.09	—	—	—	—	—	—
Net Asset Value ($)	13.84	14.87	13.30	11.69	—	—	—	—	—	—
Expense Ratio (%)	0.08	0.07	0.08	0.08	—	—	—	—	—	—
Yield (%)	3.17	3.20	2.57	3.14	—	—	—	—	—	—
Portfolio Turnover (%)	33	27	20	3	—	—	—	—	—	—
Total Assets (Millions $)	2,287	1,643	914	123	—	—	—	—	—	—

PORTFOLIO (as of 6/30/00)

Portfolio Manager: Ren Cheng, Scott Stewart - 1996

Investm't Category: Balanced

✔ Domestic	Index
✔ Foreign	Sector
Asset Allocation	State Specific

Investment Style

Large Cap	Mid Cap	Small Cap
Growth	Grth/Val	Value

Portfolio

0.0%	cash	0.0%	corp bonds
0.0%	stocks	0.0%	gov't bonds
0.0%	pref/conv't pref	0.0%	muni bonds
0.0%	conv't bds/wrnts	100.0%	other

SHAREHOLDER INFORMATION

Minimum Investment
Initial: $2,500 Subsequent: $250

Minimum IRA Investment
Initial: $500 Subsequent: $250

Maximum Fees
Load: none 12b-1: none
Other: none

Services
✔ IRA
✔ Keogh
✔ Telephone Exchange

Fidelity Freedom 2020

800-544-8544, 801-534-1910
www.fidelity.com

(FFFDX)

Balanced

PERFORMANCE — fund inception date: 10/17/96

	3yr Annual	5yr Annual	10yr Annual	Bull	Bear
Return (%)	13.9	na	na	54.5	-9.7
Differ from Category (+/-)	5.5 high	na	na	26.4 high	-6.5 low

Standard Deviation	Category Risk Index	Beta
14.9%—av	1.36—high	0.77

	2000	1999	1998	1997	1996	1995	1994	1993	1992	1991
Return (%)	-3.0	25.3	21.6	21.2	—	—	—	—	—	—
Differ from Category (+/-)	-5.0	14.6	8.3	2.4	—	—	—	—	—	—
Return, Tax-Adjusted (%)	-5.1	23.2	20.2	19.6	—	—	—	—	—	—

PER SHARE DATA

	2000	1999	1998	1997	1996	1995	1994	1993	1992	1991
Dividends, Net Income ($)	0.39	0.45	0.28	0.34	—	—	—	—	—	—
Distrib'ns, Cap Gain ($)	0.96	0.57	0.27	0.13	—	—	—	—	—	—
Net Asset Value ($)	14.56	16.38	13.95	11.93	—	—	—	—	—	—
Expense Ratio (%)	0.08	0.07	0.08	0.08	—	—	—	—	—	—
Yield (%)	2.51	2.65	1.96	2.81	—	—	—	—	—	—
Portfolio Turnover (%)	28	18	15	21	—	—	—	—	—	—
Total Assets (Millions $)	1,886	1,559	859	84	—	—	—	—	—	—

PORTFOLIO (as of 6/30/00)

Portfolio Manager: Ren Cheng, Scott Stewart - 1996

Investm't Category: Balanced

✔ Domestic   Index
✔ Foreign   Sector
Asset Allocation   State Specific

Investment Style

Large Cap   Mid Cap   Small Cap
Growth   Grth/Val   Value

Portfolio

0.0%	cash	0.0%	corp bonds
0.0%	stocks	0.0%	gov't bonds
0.0%	pref/conv't pref	0.0%	muni bonds
0.0%	conv't bds/wrnts	100.0%	other

SHAREHOLDER INFORMATION

Minimum Investment
Initial: $2,500   Subsequent: $250

Minimum IRA Investment
Initial: $500   Subsequent: $250

Maximum Fees
Load: none   12b-1: none
Other: none

Services
✔ IRA
✔ Keogh
✔ Telephone Exchange

Fidelity Freedom 2030

800-544-8544, 801-534-1910
www.fidelity.com

(FFFEX)

Growth & Income

PERFORMANCE — fund inception date: 10/17/96

	3yr Annual	5yr Annual	10yr Annual	Bull	Bear
Return (%)	14.2	na	na	60.3	-11.8
Differ from Category (+/-)	5.3 high	na	na	26.8 high	-11.7 low

Standard Deviation	Category Risk Index	Beta
16.3%—av	0.94—blw av	0.84

	2000	1999	1998	1997	1996	1995	1994	1993	1992	1991
Return (%)	-5.0	28.4	22.1	21.3	—	—	—	—	—	—
Differ from Category (+/-)	-10.7	17.6	9.3	-5.6	—	—	—	—	—	—
Return, Tax-Adjusted (%)	-6.6	26.5	20.5	19.8	—	—	—	—	—	—

PER SHARE DATA

	2000	1999	1998	1997	1996	1995	1994	1993	1992	1991
Dividends, Net Income ($)	0.34	0.41	0.24	0.31	—	—	—	—	—	—
Distrib'ns, Cap Gain ($)	0.71	0.48	0.48	0.12	—	—	—	—	—	—
Net Asset Value ($)	15.00	16.88	13.89	11.99	—	—	—	—	—	—
Expense Ratio (%)	0.08	0.07	0.08	0.08	—	—	—	—	—	—
Yield (%)	2.16	2.36	1.67	2.55	—	—	—	—	—	—
Portfolio Turnover (%)	26	16	34	19	—	—	—	—	—	—
Total Assets (Millions $)	1,269	787	282	57	—	—	—	—	—	—

PORTFOLIO (as of 6/30/00)

Portfolio Manager: Ren Cheng, Scott Stewart - 1996

Investm't Category: Growth & Income

✔ Domestic	Index
✔ Foreign	Sector
Asset Allocation	State Specific

Investment Style

✔ Large Cap	✔ Mid Cap	Small Cap
✔ Growth	Grth/Val	Value

Portfolio

0.0%	cash	0.0%	corp bonds
0.0%	stocks	0.0%	gov't bonds
0.0%	pref/conv't pref	0.0%	muni bonds
0.0%	conv't bds/wrnts	100.0%	other

SHAREHOLDER INFORMATION

Minimum Investment
Initial: $2,500 Subsequent: $250

Minimum IRA Investment
Initial: $500 Subsequent: $250

Maximum Fees
Load: none 12b-1: none
Other: none

Services
✔ IRA
✔ Keogh
✔ Telephone Exchange

Fidelity Freedom Income (FFFAX)

800-544-8544, 801-534-1910
www.fidelity.com

Balanced

PERFORMANCE — fund inception date: 10/17/96

	3yr Annual	5yr Annual	10yr Annual	Bull	Bear
Return (%)	8.1	na	na	15.2	1.9
Differ from Category (+/-)	-0.3 av	na	na	-12.9 blw av	5.1 abv av

Standard Deviation	Category Risk Index	Beta
3.9%—blw av	0.36—low	0.19

	2000	1999	1998	1997	1996	1995	1994	1993	1992	1991
Return (%)	6.2	7.1	11.1	10.9	—	—	—	—	—	—
Differ from Category (+/-)	4.2	-3.6	-2.2	-7.9	—	—	—	—	—	—
Return, Tax-Adjusted (%)	3.6	5.0	9.1	8.8	—	—	—	—	—	—

PER SHARE DATA

	2000	1999	1998	1997	1996	1995	1994	1993	1992	1991
Dividends, Net Income ($)	0.59	0.51	0.47	0.48	—	—	—	—	—	—
Distrib'ns, Cap Gain ($)	0.26	0.12	0.12	0.06	—	—	—	—	—	—
Net Asset Value ($)	11.17	11.33	11.18	10.62	—	—	—	—	—	—
Expense Ratio (%)	0.08	0.07	0.08	0.08	—	—	—	—	—	—
Yield (%)	5.16	4.45	4.15	4.49	—	—	—	—	—	—
Portfolio Turnover (%)	37	29	33	32	—	—	—	—	—	—
Total Assets (Millions $)	410	292	180	29	—	—	—	—	—	—

PORTFOLIO (as of 6/30/00)

Portfolio Manager: Ren Cheng, Scott Stewart - 1996

Investm't Category: Balanced

✔ Domestic
Foreign
Asset Allocation
Index
Sector
State Specific

Investment Style

Large Cap
Mid Cap
Small Cap
Growth
Grth/Val
Value

Portfolio

0.0%	cash	0.0%	corp bonds
0.0%	stocks	0.0%	gov't bonds
0.0%	pref/conv't pref	0.0%	muni bonds
0.0%	conv't bds/wrnts	100.0%	other

SHAREHOLDER INFORMATION

Minimum Investment
Initial: $2,500 Subsequent: $250

Minimum IRA Investment
Initial: $500 Subsequent: $250

Maximum Fees
Load: none 12b-1: none
Other: none

Services
✔ IRA
✔ Keogh
✔ Telephone Exchange

Fidelity Global Balanced (FGBLX)

800-544-6666, 801-534-1910
www.fidelity.com

International Stock

PERFORMANCE — fund inception date: 2/1/93

	3yr Annual	5yr Annual	10yr Annual	Bull	Bear
Return (%)	10.8	10.5	na	43.0	-10.6
Differ from Category (+/-)	1.9 abv av	2.2 abv av	na	-47.9 low	13.4 high

Standard Deviation	Category Risk Index	Beta
12.2%—blw av	0.54—low	0.60

	2000	1999	1998	1997	1996	1995	1994	1993	1992	1991
Return (%)	-5.9	23.0	17.7	12.5	7.7	11.5	-11.4	—	—	—
Differ from Category (+/-)	13.5	-37.7	11.9	11.2	-6.8	2.2	-8.3	—	—	—
Return, Tax-Adjusted (%)	-7.7	21.9	16.9	11.3	6.3	11.3	-11.7	—	—	—

PER SHARE DATA

	2000	1999	1998	1997	1996	1995	1994	1993	1992	1991
Dividends, Net Income ($)	0.32	0.32	0.28	0.40	0.45	0.05	0.10	—	—	—
Distrib'ns, Cap Gain ($)	1.24	0.25	0.00	0.00	0.00	0.00	0.00	—	—	—
Net Asset Value ($)	17.43	20.20	16.92	14.63	13.36	12.84	11.56	—	—	—
Expense Ratio (%)	1.25	1.19	1.37	1.49	1.36	1.33	1.67	—	—	—
Yield (%)	1.71	1.56	1.65	2.73	3.36	0.38	0.86	—	—	—
Portfolio Turnover (%)	62	80	81	57	189	242	226	—	—	—
Total Assets (Millions $)	101	106	94	68	77	121	236	—	—	—

PORTFOLIO (as of 6/30/00)

Portfolio Manager: Richard Mace - 1996

Investm't Category: International Stock

✔ Domestic	Index
✔ Foreign	Sector
✔ Asset Allocation	State Specific

Investment Style

Large Cap	Mid Cap	Small Cap
Growth	Grth/Val	Value

Portfolio

9.7%	cash	0.0%	corp bonds
62.9%	stocks	27.4%	gov't bonds
0.0%	pref/conv't pref	0.0%	muni bonds
0.0%	conv't bds/wrnts	0.0%	other

SHAREHOLDER INFORMATION

Minimum Investment
Initial: $2,500 Subsequent: $250

Minimum IRA Investment
Initial: $500 Subsequent: $250

Maximum Fees
Load: 0.01% redemption 12b-1: none
Other: redemption fee applies for 1 month

Services
✔ IRA
✔ Keogh
✔ Telephone Exchange

Fidelity Growth Company (FDGRX)

800-544-8888, 801-534-1910
www.fidelity.com

Aggressive Growth

PERFORMANCE — fund inception date: 1/17/83

	3yr Annual	5yr Annual	10yr Annual	Bull	Bear
Return (%)	28.8	24.3	22.3	139.6	-24.4
Differ from Category (+/-)	12.6 high	9.7 abv av	6.5 high	20.4 abv av	-3.8 av

Standard Deviation	Category Risk Index	Beta
31.5%—high	0.97—av	0.98

	2000	1999	1998	1997	1996	1995	1994	1993	1992	1991
Return (%)	-6.3	79.4	27.2	18.9	16.8	39.6	-2.2	16.1	7.9	48.3
Differ from Category (+/-)	-0.3	21.9	12.1	4.1	-1.5	5.0	-1.4	-9.1	1.0	1.1
Return, Tax-Adjusted (%)	-8.0	76.9	25.3	16.5	15.2	37.7	-3.3	13.0	6.2	45.7

PER SHARE DATA

	2000	1999	1998	1997	1996	1995	1994	1993	1992	1991
Dividends, Net Income ($)	0.00	0.00	0.09	0.22	0.28	0.16	0.22	0.07	0.09	0.08
Distrib'ns, Cap Gain ($)	7.50	6.29	3.73	4.35	1.60	1.57	0.92	2.92	1.48	1.73
Net Asset Value ($)	71.43	84.30	51.02	43.32	40.46	36.29	27.26	29.06	27.64	27.09
Expense Ratio (%)	na	0.74	0.65	0.71	0.85	0.94	1.05	1.07	1.09	1.07
Yield (%)	0.00	0.00	0.16	0.46	0.66	0.42	0.78	0.21	0.30	0.27
Portfolio Turnover (%)	na	86	76	93	78	119	135	159	250	174
Total Assets (Millions $)	29,145	24,337	11,440	10,509	9,272	6,278	2,993	2,542	1,815	1,376

PORTFOLIO (as of 6/30/00)

Portfolio Manager: Steven Wymer - 1997

Investm't Category: Aggressive Growth

✔ Domestic	Index
✔ Foreign	Sector
Asset Allocation	State Specific

Investment Style

Large Cap	✔ Mid Cap	✔ Small Cap
✔ Growth	Grth/Val	Value

Portfolio

2.2% cash	0.0% corp bonds
97.8% stocks	0.0% gov't bonds
0.0% pref/conv't pref	0.0% muni bonds
0.0% conv't bds/wrnts	0.0% other

SHAREHOLDER INFORMATION

Minimum Investment
Initial: $2,500 Subsequent: $250

Minimum IRA Investment
Initial: $500 Subsequent: $250

Maximum Fees
Load: none 12b-1: none
Other: none

Services
✔ IRA
✔ Keogh
✔ Telephone Exchange

Fidelity Grth & Inc (FGRIX)

800-544-8544, 801-534-1910
www.fidelity.com

Growth & Income

PERFORMANCE — fund inception date: 12/30/85

	3yr Annual	5yr Annual	10yr Annual	Bull	Bear
Return (%)	11.5	16.7	18.9	42.1	-3.3
Differ from Category (+/-)	2.6 abv av	2.4 abv av	4.0 high	8.6 abv av	-3.2 av

Standard Deviation	Category Risk Index	Beta
15.2%—av	0.88—blw av	0.84

	2000	1999	1998	1997	1996	1995	1994	1993	1992	1991
Return (%)	-1.9	10.4	28.3	30.1	20.0	35.3	2.2	19.5	11.5	41.8
Differ from Category (+/-)	-7.6	-0.4	15.5	3.2	0.3	5.8	2.7	5.7	-0.1	13.7
Return, Tax-Adjusted (%)	-3.8	8.7	26.7	28.6	18.1	33.2	0.0	17.3	7.3	39.8

PER SHARE DATA

	2000	1999	1998	1997	1996	1995	1994	1993	1992	1991
Dividends, Net Income ($)	0.37	0.39	0.39	0.43	0.46	0.48	0.40	0.52	0.57	0.38
Distrib'ns, Cap Gain ($)	3.91	2.90	2.16	1.36	1.12	0.90	1.24	0.77	2.40	0.64
Net Asset Value ($)	42.10	47.16	45.84	38.10	30.73	27.05	21.09	22.22	19.71	20.49
Expense Ratio (%)	0.67	0.66	0.68	0.71	0.74	0.77	0.82	0.83	0.86	0.87
Yield (%)	0.80	0.77	0.81	1.08	1.44	1.71	1.79	2.26	2.57	1.79
Portfolio Turnover (%)	41	35	32	38	41	67	92	87	221	215
Total Assets (Millions $)	39,761	48,528	48,639	36,656	23,896	14,818	9,344	7,684	4,842	3,355

PORTFOLIO (as of 6/30/00)

Portfolio Manager: Steven Kaye - 1993

Investm't Category: Growth & Income

✔ Domestic	Index
✔ Foreign	Sector
Asset Allocation	State Specific

Investment Style

✔ Large Cap	Mid Cap	Small Cap
Growth	✔ Grth/Val	Value

Portfolio

4.4% cash	0.0% corp bonds
95.0% stocks	0.0% gov't bonds
0.0% pref/conv't pref	0.0% muni bonds
0.6% conv't bds/wrnts	0.0% other

SHAREHOLDER INFORMATION

Minimum Investment

Initial: $2,500 — Subsequent: $250

Minimum IRA Investment

Initial: $500 — Subsequent: $250

Maximum Fees

Load: none — 12b-1: none

Other: none

Services

✔ IRA
✔ Keogh
✔ Telephone Exchange

Fidelity Intl Grth & Inc (FIGRX)

800-544-6666, 801-534-1910
www.fidelity.com

International Stock

PERFORMANCE — fund inception date: 12/29/86

	3yr Annual	5yr Annual	10yr Annual	Bull	Bear
Return (%)	13.2	11.8	10.4	77.5	-16.9
Differ from Category (+/-)	4.3 abv av	3.5 abv av	1.4 abv av	-13.4 av	7.1 abv av

Standard Deviation	Category Risk Index	Beta
19.5%—abv av	0.86—blw av	0.77

	2000	1999	1998	1997	1996	1995	1994	1993	1992	1991
Return (%)	-14.0	53.7	9.9	7.1	12.6	12.2	-2.8	35.0	-3.3	8.0
Differ from Category (+/-)	5.4	-7.0	4.1	5.8	-1.9	2.9	0.3	-5.2	0.2	-5.0
Return, Tax-Adjusted (%)	-16.4	51.6	9.0	5.4	11.3	10.7	-3.6	34.7	-4.0	7.5

PER SHARE DATA

	2000	1999	1998	1997	1996	1995	1994	1993	1992	1991
Dividends, Net Income ($)	0.51	0.33	0.09	0.37	0.29	0.60	0.00	0.06	0.32	0.17
Distrib'ns, Cap Gain ($)	2.66	1.50	0.63	0.88	0.37	0.00	0.53	0.05	0.00	0.00
Net Asset Value ($)	22.72	30.10	20.91	19.70	19.55	17.95	16.53	17.57	13.09	13.87
Expense Ratio (%)	1.05	1.10	1.13	1.15	1.14	1.17	1.21	1.52	1.62	1.89
Yield (%)	2.00	1.04	0.41	1.79	1.45	3.34	0.00	0.34	2.44	1.22
Portfolio Turnover (%)	104	94	143	70	95	131	173	24	76	117
Total Assets (Millions $)	1,172	1,395	870	1,030	1,080	941	1,272	1,068	65	58

PORTFOLIO (as of 6/30/00)

Portfolio Manager: William Bower - 1998

Investm't Category: International Stock

✔ Domestic — Index
✔ Foreign — Sector
Asset Allocation — State Specific

Investment Style

Large Cap — Mid Cap — Small Cap
Growth — Grth/Val — Value

Portfolio

9.0%	cash	0.0%	corp bonds
90.7%	stocks	0.0%	gov't bonds
0.0%	pref/conv't pref	0.0%	muni bonds
0.0%	conv't bds/wrnts	0.3%	other

SHAREHOLDER INFORMATION

Minimum Investment
Initial: $2,500 — Subsequent: $250

Minimum IRA Investment
Initial: $500 — Subsequent: $250

Maximum Fees
Load: 0.01% redemption — 12b-1: none
Other: redemption fee applies for 1 month

Services
✔ IRA
Keogh
✔ Telephone Exchange

Fidelity Japan (FJPNX)

800-544-8888, 801-534-1910
www.fidelity.com

International Stock

PERFORMANCE — fund inception date: 9/15/92

	3yr Annual	5yr Annual	10yr Annual	Bull	Bear
Return (%)	20.9	6.9	na	203.7	-26.0
Differ from Category (+/-)	12.0 high	-1.4 blw av	na	112.8 high	-2.0 av

Standard Deviation	Category Risk Index	Beta
27.7%—high	1.22—abv av	0.75

	2000	1999	1998	1997	1996	1995	1994	1993	1992	1991
Return (%)	-36.4	146.0	13.0	-10.7	-11.1	-2.1	16.4	20.4	—	—
Differ from Category (+/-)	-17.0	85.3	7.2	-12.0	-25.6	-11.4	19.5	-19.8	—	—
Return, Tax-Adjusted (%)	-39.3	144.3	12.8	-11.3	-11.1	-2.1	15.5	19.3	—	—

PER SHARE DATA

	2000	1999	1998	1997	1996	1995	1994	1993	1992	1991
Dividends, Net Income ($)	0.00	0.46	0.03	0.18	0.01	0.00	0.00	0.00	—	—
Distrib'ns, Cap Gain ($)	4.07	0.00	0.00	0.00	0.00	0.00	0.36	0.39	—	—
Net Asset Value ($)	13.75	27.28	11.30	10.02	11.42	12.87	13.15	11.61	—	—
Expense Ratio (%)	na	1.23	1.48	1.40	1.14	1.15	1.42	1.71	—	—
Yield (%)	0.00	1.68	0.26	1.79	0.08	0.00	0.00	0.00	—	—
Portfolio Turnover (%)	na	79	62	70	83	86	153	257	—	—
Total Assets (Millions $)	586	1,242	312	215	255	378	389	96	—	—

PORTFOLIO (as of 6/30/00)

Portfolio Manager: Yoko Ishibashi - 2000

Investm't Category: International Stock

Domestic	Index
✔ Foreign	Sector
Asset Allocation	State Specific

Investment Style

Large Cap	Mid Cap	Small Cap
Growth	Grth/Val	Value

Portfolio

5.5%	cash	0.0%	corp bonds
94.5%	stocks	0.0%	gov't bonds
0.0%	pref/conv't pref	0.0%	muni bonds
0.0%	conv't bds/wrnts	0.0%	other

SHAREHOLDER INFORMATION

Minimum Investment
Initial: $2,500 Subsequent: $250

Minimum IRA Investment
Initial: $500 Subsequent: $250

Maximum Fees
Load: 3.00% front 12b-1: none
Other: 1.50% redemption fee for 3 months

Services
✔ IRA
✔ Keogh
✔ Telephone Exchange

Fidelity Japan Smaller Co (FJSCX)

800-544-8888, 801-534-1910
www.fidelity.com

International Stock

PERFORMANCE — fund inception date: 11/1/95

	3yr Annual	5yr Annual	10yr Annual	Bull	Bear
Return (%)	30.1	2.9	na	349.0	-40.7
Differ from Category (+/-)	21.2 high	-5.4 blw av	na	258.1 high	-16.7 low

Standard Deviation	Category Risk Index	Beta
37.7%—high	1.66—high	0.75

	2000	1999	1998	1997	1996	1995	1994	1993	1992	1991
Return (%)	-50.2	237.4	31.1	-30.3	-24.5	—	—	—	—	—
Differ from Category (+/-)	-30.8	176.7	25.3	-31.6	-39.0	—	—	—	—	—
Return, Tax-Adjusted (%)	-53.8	236.5	31.1	-30.3	-24.6	—	—	—	—	—

PER SHARE DATA

	2000	1999	1998	1997	1996	1995	1994	1993	1992	1991
Dividends, Net Income ($)	0.00	0.15	0.00	0.01	0.00	—	—	—	—	—
Distrib'ns, Cap Gain ($)	4.46	0.00	0.00	0.00	0.04	—	—	—	—	—
Net Asset Value ($)	7.98	24.27	7.24	5.52	7.94	—	—	—	—	—
Expense Ratio (%)	na	1.07	1.23	1.34	1.34	—	—	—	—	—
Yield (%)	0.00	0.61	0.00	0.18	0.00	—	—	—	—	—
Portfolio Turnover (%)	na	39	39	101	66	—	—	—	—	—
Total Assets (Millions $)	510	2,113	129	76	78	—	—	—	—	—

PORTFOLIO (as of 6/30/00)

Portfolio Manager: Kenichi Mizushita - 1996

Investm't Category: International Stock

Domestic	Index
✔ Foreign	Sector
Asset Allocation	State Specific

Investment Style

Large Cap	Mid Cap	Small Cap
Growth	Grth/Val	Value

Portfolio

1.6%	cash	0.0%	corp bonds
98.4%	stocks	0.0%	gov't bonds
0.0%	pref/conv't pref	0.0%	muni bonds
0.0%	conv't bds/wrnts	0.0%	other

SHAREHOLDER INFORMATION

Minimum Investment
Initial: $2,500 Subsequent: $250

Minimum IRA Investment
Initial: $500 Subsequent: $250

Maximum Fees
Load: 3.00% front 12b-1: none
Other: 1.50% redemption fee for 3 months

Services
✔ IRA
✔ Keogh
✔ Telephone Exchange

Fidelity Large Cap Stock (FLCSX)

800-544-8888, 801-534-1910
www.fidelity.com

Growth

PERFORMANCE — fund inception date: 6/22/95

	3yr Annual	5yr Annual	10yr Annual	Bull	Bear
Return (%)	14.9	18.1	na	74.7	-18.5
Differ from Category (+/-)	3.9 abv av	2.0 abv av	na	25.0 high	-13.1 low

Standard Deviation	Category Risk Index	Beta
19.9%—abv av	1.02—av	1.00

	2000	1999	1998	1997	1996	1995	1994	1993	1992	1991
Return (%)	-14.5	30.1	36.4	24.7	21.5	—	—	—	—	—
Differ from Category (+/-)	-18.0	11.2	22.1	-2.4	-0.8	—	—	—	—	—
Return, Tax-Adjusted (%)	-15.2	29.5	33.2	22.7	19.2	—	—	—	—	—

PER SHARE DATA

	2000	1999	1998	1997	1996	1995	1994	1993	1992	1991
Dividends, Net Income ($)	0.01	0.04	0.02	0.06	0.05	—	—	—	—	—
Distrib'ns, Cap Gain ($)	0.79	0.43	2.23	1.07	0.80	—	—	—	—	—
Net Asset Value ($)	17.75	21.57	16.98	14.41	12.51	—	—	—	—	—
Expense Ratio (%)	0.89	0.90	0.84	0.99	1.30	—	—	—	—	—
Yield (%)	0.05	0.18	0.10	0.38	0.37	—	—	—	—	—
Portfolio Turnover (%)	99	100	159	110	155	—	—	—	—	—
Total Assets (Millions $)	874	1,082	316	139	111	—	—	—	—	—

PORTFOLIO (as of 6/30/00)

Portfolio Manager: Karen Firestone - 1998

Investm't Category: Growth

✔ Domestic	Index
✔ Foreign	Sector
Asset Allocation	State Specific

Investment Style

✔ Large Cap	Mid Cap	Small Cap
✔ Growth	Grth/Val	Value

Portfolio

2.4%	cash	0.0%	corp bonds
97.6%	stocks	0.0%	gov't bonds
0.0%	pref/conv't pref	0.0%	muni bonds
0.0%	conv't bds/wrnts	0.0%	other

SHAREHOLDER INFORMATION

Minimum Investment
Initial: $2,500 — Subsequent: $250

Minimum IRA Investment
Initial: $500 — Subsequent: $250

Maximum Fees
Load: none — 12b-1: none
Other: none

Services
✔ IRA
✔ Keogh
✔ Telephone Exchange

Fidelity Latin America (FLATX)

800-544-8888, 801-534-1910
www.fidelity.com

International Stock

PERFORMANCE — fund inception date: 4/19/93

	3yr Annual	5yr Annual	10yr Annual	Bull	Bear
Return (%)	-7.6	6.4	na	83.5	-26.9
Differ from Category (+/-)	-16.5 low	-1.9 blw av	na	-7.4 av	-2.9 av

Standard Deviation	Category Risk Index	Beta
38.8%—high	1.71—high	1.42

	2000	1999	1998	1997	1996	1995	1994	1993	1992	1991
Return (%)	-17.4	54.9	-38.3	32.8	30.7	-16.4	-23.1	—	—	—
Differ from Category (+/-)	2.0	-5.8	-44.1	31.5	16.2	-25.7	-20.0	—	—	—
Return, Tax-Adjusted (%)	-17.5	54.3	-38.8	32.1	29.8	-16.7	-23.1	—	—	—

PER SHARE DATA

	2000	1999	1998	1997	1996	1995	1994	1993	1992	1991
Dividends, Net Income ($)	0.07	0.14	0.25	0.20	0.23	0.12	0.00	—	—	—
Distrib'ns, Cap Gain ($)	0.00	0.00	0.00	0.00	0.00	0.00	0.00	—	—	—
Net Asset Value ($)	13.06	15.91	10.37	17.22	13.11	10.21	12.37	—	—	—
Expense Ratio (%)	na	1.30	1.33	1.29	1.32	1.41	1.48	—	—	—
Yield (%)	0.53	0.87	2.41	1.16	1.75	1.17	0.00	—	—	—
Portfolio Turnover (%)	na	49	31	64	70	69	77	—	—	—
Total Assets (Millions $)	255	409	306	860	535	473	616	—	—	—

PORTFOLIO (as of 6/30/00)

Portfolio Manager: Patricia Satterthwaite - 1993

Investm't Category: International Stock

Domestic	Index
✔ Foreign	Sector
Asset Allocation	State Specific

Investment Style

Large Cap	Mid Cap	Small Cap
Growth	Grth/Val	Value

Portfolio

3.0%	cash	0.0%	corp bonds
97.0%	stocks	0.0%	gov't bonds
0.0%	pref/conv't pref	0.0%	muni bonds
0.0%	conv't bds/wrnts	0.0%	other

SHAREHOLDER INFORMATION

Minimum Investment
Initial: $2,500 Subsequent: $250

Minimum IRA Investment
Initial: $500 Subsequent: $250

Maximum Fees
Load: 3.00% front 12b-1: none
Other: 1.50% redemption fee for 3 months

Services
✔ IRA
✔ Keogh
✔ Telephone Exchange

Fidelity Low Priced Stock (FLPSX)

800-544-8544, 801-534-1910
www.fidelity.com

Growth

PERFORMANCE

fund inception date: 12/27/89

	3yr Annual	5yr Annual	10yr Annual	Bull	Bear
Return (%)	7.8	15.0	19.6	21.7	6.3
Differ from Category (+/-)	-3.2 blw av	-1.1 blw av	2.8 high	-28.0 low	11.7 abv av

Standard Deviation	Category Risk Index	Beta
14.9%—av	0.76—low	0.60

	2000	1999	1998	1997	1996	1995	1994	1993	1992	1991
Return (%)	18.8	5.0	0.5	26.7	26.8	24.8	4.8	20.2	28.9	46.2
Differ from Category (+/-)	15.3	-13.9	-13.8	-0.4	4.5	-5.6	5.0	5.6	16.3	8.6
Return, Tax-Adjusted (%)	15.4	3.6	-1.3	24.7	23.7	22.0	1.2	16.9	27.1	43.9

PER SHARE DATA

	2000	1999	1998	1997	1996	1995	1994	1993	1992	1991
Dividends, Net Income ($)	0.16	0.15	0.20	0.28	0.24	0.23	0.09	0.16	0.10	0.15
Distrib'ns, Cap Gain ($)	3.43	1.19	1.94	1.58	1.66	1.24	2.05	1.62	0.69	0.60
Net Asset Value ($)	23.12	22.64	22.85	25.13	21.35	18.50	16.00	17.30	15.96	13.05
Expense Ratio (%)	0.81	1.08	0.95	1.01	1.04	1.11	1.13	1.12	1.20	1.36
Yield (%)	0.60	0.62	0.80	1.04	1.04	1.16	0.49	0.84	0.60	1.09
Portfolio Turnover (%)	15	24	47	45	79	65	54	47	82	84
Total Assets (Millions $)	6,363	6,646	9,194	10,691	5,664	3,349	2,354	2,060	2,306	375

PORTFOLIO (as of 6/30/00)

Portfolio Manager: Joel Tillinghast - 1989

Investm't Category: Growth

✔ Domestic	Index
✔ Foreign	Sector
Asset Allocation	State Specific

Investment Style

Large Cap	Mid Cap	✔ Small Cap
Growth	Grth/Val	✔ Value

Portfolio

4.5%	cash	0.0%	corp bonds
95.5%	stocks	0.0%	gov't bonds
0.0%	pref/conv't pref	0.0%	muni bonds
0.0%	conv't bds/wrnts	0.0%	other

SHAREHOLDER INFORMATION

Minimum Investment

Initial: $2,500 Subsequent: $250

Minimum IRA Investment

Initial: $500 Subsequent: $250

Maximum Fees

Load: 3.00% front 12b-1: none

Other: 1.50% redemption fee for 3 months

Services

✔ IRA

✔ Keogh

✔ Telephone Exchange

Fidelity Magellan (FMAGX)

800-544-8888, 801-534-1910
www.fidelity.com

Growth

this fund is closed to new investors

PERFORMANCE — fund inception date: 5/2/63

	3yr Annual	5yr Annual	10yr Annual	Bull	Bear
Return (%)	14.5	16.2	18.3	67.3	-14.2
Differ from Category (+/-)	3.5 abv av	0.1 av	1.5 abv av	17.6 abv av	-8.8 blw av

Standard Deviation	Category Risk Index	Beta
19.1%—abv av	0.98—blw av	1.06

	2000	1999	1998	1997	1996	1995	1994	1993	1992	1991
Return (%)	-9.2	24.0	33.6	26.5	11.6	36.8	-1.8	24.6	7.0	41.0
Differ from Category (+/-)	-12.7	5.1	19.3	-0.6	-10.7	6.4	-1.6	10.0	-5.6	3.4
Return, Tax-Adjusted (%)	-9.9	21.8	32.2	24.5	6.9	34.4	-2.9	21.2	2.8	37.4

PER SHARE DATA

	2000	1999	1998	1997	1996	1995	1994	1993	1992	1991
Dividends, Net Income ($)	0.27	0.73	0.67	1.25	1.10	0.59	0.13	0.75	1.25	1.30
Distrib'ns, Cap Gain ($)	4.69	11.39	5.15	5.21	12.85	4.69	2.64	6.50	8.82	5.43
Net Asset Value ($)	119.30	136.63	120.82	95.27	80.65	85.98	66.80	70.85	63.01	68.61
Expense Ratio (%)	0.74	0.60	0.61	0.64	0.92	0.96	0.99	1.00	1.05	1.06
Yield (%)	0.21	0.49	0.53	1.24	1.17	0.65	0.18	0.96	1.74	1.75
Portfolio Turnover (%)	28	37	34	67	155	120	132	155	172	135
Total Assets (Millions $)	92,588	105,938	83,552	63,766	53,988	53,702	36,441	31,705	22,268	19,257

PORTFOLIO (as of 6/30/00)

Portfolio Manager: Robert Stansky - 1996

Investm't Category: Growth

✔ Domestic — Index
✔ Foreign — Sector
Asset Allocation — State Specific

Investment Style

✔ Large Cap — Mid Cap — Small Cap
✔ Growth — Grth/Val — Value

Portfolio

1.4%	cash	0.0%	corp bonds
98.6%	stocks	0.0%	gov't bonds
0.0%	pref/conv't pref	0.0%	muni bonds
0.0%	conv't bds/wrnts	0.0%	other

SHAREHOLDER INFORMATION

Minimum Investment

Initial: $2,500 — Subsequent: $250

Minimum IRA Investment

Initial: $500 — Subsequent: $250

Maximum Fees

Load: 3.00% front — 12b-1: none
Other: none

Services

✔ IRA
✔ Keogh
✔ Telephone Exchange

Fidelity Mid Cap Stock (FMCSX)

800-544-8888, 801-534-1910
www.fidelity.com

Growth

PERFORMANCE — fund inception date: 3/29/94

	3yr Annual	5yr Annual	10yr Annual	Bull	Bear
Return (%)	28.6	26.1	na	81.0	-0.4
Differ from Category (+/-)	17.6 high	10.0 high	na	31.3 high	5.0 abv av

Standard Deviation	Category Risk Index	Beta
27.2%—high	1.40—high	0.84

	2000	1999	1998	1997	1996	1995	1994	1993	1992	1991
Return (%)	32.0	39.8	15.1	27.0	18.1	33.9	—	—	—	—
Differ from Category (+/-)	28.5	20.9	0.8	-0.1	-4.2	3.5	—	—	—	—
Return, Tax-Adjusted (%)	29.5	36.8	13.5	24.5	15.3	31.7	—	—	—	—

PER SHARE DATA

	2000	1999	1998	1997	1996	1995	1994	1993	1992	1991
Dividends, Net Income ($)	0.10	0.01	0.00	0.01	0.03	0.06	—	—	—	—
Distrib'ns, Cap Gain ($)	2.50	2.59	1.28	1.77	1.26	0.74	—	—	—	—
Net Asset Value ($)	26.06	21.87	17.88	16.69	14.64	13.50	—	—	—	—
Expense Ratio (%)	0.86	0.74	0.86	0.96	1.00	1.63	—	—	—	—
Yield (%)	0.35	0.04	0.00	0.05	0.18	0.42	—	—	—	—
Portfolio Turnover (%)	205	121	132	155	179	190	—	—	—	—
Total Assets (Millions $)	6,194	2,286	1,784	1,763	1,695	1,150	—	—	—	—

PORTFOLIO (as of 6/30/00)

Portfolio Manager: David Felman - 1999

Investm't Category: Growth

✔ Domestic	Index
✔ Foreign	Sector
Asset Allocation	State Specific

Investment Style

Large Cap	✔ Mid Cap	✔ Small Cap
✔ Growth	Grth/Val	Value

Portfolio

9.2%	cash	0.0%	corp bonds
90.8%	stocks	0.0%	gov't bonds
0.0%	pref/conv't pref	0.0%	muni bonds
0.0%	conv't bds/wrnts	0.0%	other

SHAREHOLDER INFORMATION

Minimum Investment
Initial: $2,500 — Subsequent: $250

Minimum IRA Investment
Initial: $500 — Subsequent: $250

Maximum Fees
Load: none — 12b-1: none
Other: none

Services
✔ IRA
✔ Keogh
✔ Telephone Exchange

Fidelity New Millennium (FMILX)

800-544-8888, 801-534-1910
www.fidelity.com

Aggressive Growth

this fund is closed to new investors

PERFORMANCE

fund inception date: 12/28/92

	3yr Annual	5yr Annual	10yr Annual	Bull	Bear
Return (%)	35.8	30.9	na	207.4	-25.6
Differ from Category (+/-)	19.6 high	16.3 high	na	88.2 high	-5.0 av

Standard Deviation	Category Risk Index	Beta
40.4%—high	1.25—high	1.54

	2000	1999	1998	1997	1996	1995	1994	1993	1992	1991
Return (%)	-6.0	108.7	27.6	24.6	23.1	52.1	0.8	24.6	—	—
Differ from Category (+/-)	0.0	51.2	12.5	9.8	4.8	17.5	1.6	-0.6	—	—
Return, Tax-Adjusted (%)	-10.2	103.8	25.8	21.7	22.1	48.8	0.1	23.8	—	—

PER SHARE DATA

	2000	1999	1998	1997	1996	1995	1994	1993	1992	1991
Dividends, Net Income ($)	0.00	0.00	0.00	0.00	0.00	0.00	0.00	0.01	—	—
Distrib'ns, Cap Gain ($)	10.11	6.37	1.94	2.89	0.60	1.40	0.28	0.25	—	—
Net Asset Value ($)	34.33	47.46	26.27	22.19	20.25	16.96	12.11	12.30	—	—
Expense Ratio (%)	na	0.93	0.86	0.99	1.07	1.27	1.29	1.32	—	—
Yield (%)	0.00	0.00	0.00	0.00	0.00	0.00	0.00	0.07	—	—
Portfolio Turnover (%)	na	116	121	142	158	169	199	204	—	—
Total Assets (Millions $)	3,372	3,772	1,683	1,564	1,252	594	319	276	—	—

PORTFOLIO (as of 6/30/00)

Portfolio Manager: Neal Miller - 1992

Investm't Category: Aggressive Growth

✔ Domestic | Index
✔ Foreign | Sector
Asset Allocation | State Specific

Investment Style

Large Cap | Mid Cap | ✔ Small Cap
✔ Growth | Grth/Val | Value

Portfolio

4.4% cash | 0.0% corp bonds
95.6% stocks | 0.0% gov't bonds
0.0% pref/conv't pref | 0.0% muni bonds
0.0% conv't bds/wrnts | 0.0% other

SHAREHOLDER INFORMATION

Minimum Investment
Initial: $2,500 | Subsequent: $250

Minimum IRA Investment
Initial: $500 | Subsequent: $250

Maximum Fees
Load: 3.00% front | 12b-1: none
Other: none

Services
✔ IRA
✔ Keogh
✔ Telephone Exchange

Fidelity Nordic (FNORX)

800-544-8888, 801-534-1910
www.fidelity.com

International Stock

PERFORMANCE

fund inception date: 11/1/95

	3yr Annual	5yr Annual	10yr Annual	Bull	Bear
Return (%)	23.6	24.6	na	89.1	-23.7
Differ from Category (+/-)	14.7 high	16.3 high	na	-1.8 abv av	0.3 av

Standard Deviation	Category Risk Index	Beta
24.8%—abv av	1.09—abv av	0.96

	2000	1999	1998	1997	1996	1995	1994	1993	1992	1991
Return (%)	-8.4	59.5	29.5	12.1	41.6	—	—	—	—	—
Differ from Category (+/-)	11.0	-1.2	23.7	10.8	27.1	—	—	—	—	—
Return, Tax-Adjusted (%)	-8.5	58.8	29.5	10.1	41.1	—	—	—	—	—

PER SHARE DATA

	2000	1999	1998	1997	1996	1995	1994	1993	1992	1991
Dividends, Net Income ($)	0.03	0.06	0.00	0.07	0.05	—	—	—	—	—
Distrib'ns, Cap Gain ($)	0.22	0.45	0.00	1.18	0.10	—	—	—	—	—
Net Asset Value ($)	26.13	28.83	18.42	14.22	13.80	—	—	—	—	—
Expense Ratio (%)	na	1.23	1.35	1.42	2.00	—	—	—	—	—
Yield (%)	0.11	0.20	0.00	0.45	0.35	—	—	—	—	—
Portfolio Turnover (%)	na	70	69	74	35	—	—	—	—	—
Total Assets (Millions $)	181	168	109	64	43	—	—	—	—	—

PORTFOLIO (as of 6/30/00)

Portfolio Manager: Trygve Toraasen - 1998

Investm't Category: International Stock

Domestic	Index
✔ Foreign	Sector
Asset Allocation	State Specific

Investment Style

Large Cap	Mid Cap	Small Cap
Growth	Grth/Val	Value

Portfolio

4.4%	cash	0.0%	corp bonds
95.6%	stocks	0.0%	gov't bonds
0.0%	pref/conv't pref	0.0%	muni bonds
0.0%	conv't bds/wrnts	0.0%	other

SHAREHOLDER INFORMATION

Minimum Investment

Initial: $2,500 Subsequent: $250

Minimum IRA Investment

Initial: $500 Subsequent: $100

Maximum Fees

Load: 3.00% front 12b-1: none

Other: 1.50% redemption fee for 3 months

Services

✔ IRA
✔ Keogh
✔ Telephone Exchange

Fidelity OTC Port (FOCPX)

800-544-8544, 801-534-1910
www.fidelity.com

Aggressive Growth

PERFORMANCE

fund inception date: 12/31/84

	3yr Annual	5yr Annual	10yr Annual	Bull	Bear
Return (%)	21.0	19.2	19.6	153.6	-33.3
Differ from Category (+/-)	4.8 abv av	4.6 abv av	3.8 abv av	34.4 abv av	-12.7 blw av

Standard Deviation	Category Risk Index	Beta
36.0%—high	1.11—abv av	1.46

	2000	1999	1998	1997	1996	1995	1994	1993	1992	1991
Return (%)	-26.8	72.5	40.3	9.9	23.7	38.2	-2.6	8.3	14.9	49.1
Differ from Category (+/-)	-20.8	15.0	25.2	-4.9	5.4	3.6	-1.8	-16.9	8.0	1.9
Return, Tax-Adjusted (%)	-30.5	69.9	38.8	8.3	19.6	36.0	-2.9	4.4	12.0	45.1

PER SHARE DATA

	2000	1999	1998	1997	1996	1995	1994	1993	1992	1991
Dividends, Net Income ($)	0.00	0.00	0.00	0.00	0.08	0.02	0.21	0.10	0.25	0.12
Distrib'ns, Cap Gain ($)	12.66	5.51	2.38	2.52	4.32	1.80	0.00	3.42	2.24	2.51
Net Asset Value ($)	41.05	67.97	43.63	33.45	32.71	30.33	23.27	24.14	25.65	24.78
Expense Ratio (%)	0.76	0.74	0.75	0.84	0.82	0.81	0.88	1.08	1.17	1.29
Yield (%)	0.00	0.00	0.00	0.00	0.21	0.06	0.90	0.36	0.89	0.43
Portfolio Turnover (%)	196	117	125	147	133	62	222	213	245	198
Total Assets (Millions $)	11,652	11,705	5,476	3,858	3,387	2,350	1,381	1,343	1,256	1,070

PORTFOLIO (as of 6/30/00)

Portfolio Manager: Jason Weiner - 2000

Investm't Category: Aggressive Growth

✔ Domestic — Index
Foreign — Sector
Asset Allocation — State Specific

Investment Style

Large Cap — ✔ Mid Cap — ✔ Small Cap
✔ Growth — Grth/Val — Value

Portfolio

6.3%	cash	0.0%	corp bonds
93.7%	stocks	0.0%	gov't bonds
0.0%	pref/conv't pref	0.0%	muni bonds
0.0%	conv't bds/wrnts	0.0%	other

SHAREHOLDER INFORMATION

Minimum Investment

Initial: $2,500 — Subsequent: $250

Minimum IRA Investment

Initial: $500 — Subsequent: $250

Maximum Fees

Load: none — 12b-1: none
Other: none

Services

✔ IRA
✔ Keogh
✔ Telephone Exchange

Fidelity Overseas (FOSFX)

800-544-6666, 801-534-1910
www.fidelity.com

International Stock

PERFORMANCE — fund inception date: 12/4/84

	3yr Annual	5yr Annual	10yr Annual	Bull	Bear
Return (%)	9.6	10.5	9.4	68.3	-19.2
Differ from Category (+/-)	0.7 av	2.2 abv av	0.4 av	-22.6 av	4.8 abv av

Standard Deviation	Category Risk Index	Beta
18.9%—av	0.84—blw av	0.83

	2000	1999	1998	1997	1996	1995	1994	1993	1992	1991
Return (%)	-18.3	42.8	12.8	10.9	13.0	9.0	1.2	40.0	-11.4	8.6
Differ from Category (+/-)	1.1	-17.9	7.0	9.6	-1.5	-0.3	4.3	-0.2	-7.9	-4.4
Return, Tax-Adjusted (%)	-20.7	40.8	12.2	9.5	10.9	8.1	0.7	39.1	-14.1	6.7

PER SHARE DATA

	2000	1999	1998	1997	1996	1995	1994	1993	1992	1991
Dividends, Net Income ($)	0.86	0.44	0.20	0.34	0.37	0.34	0.00	0.43	0.37	0.44
Distrib'ns, Cap Gain ($)	4.12	2.64	0.51	1.34	1.63	0.35	0.47	0.00	2.10	1.16
Net Asset Value ($)	34.37	48.01	35.98	32.54	30.84	29.07	27.30	27.43	19.90	25.26
Expense Ratio (%)	1.16	1.23	1.24	1.20	1.12	1.08	1.24	1.27	1.52	1.53
Yield (%)	2.23	0.86	0.54	1.00	1.13	1.15	0.00	1.56	1.68	1.66
Portfolio Turnover (%)	132	85	69	68	82	47	49	64	122	132
Total Assets (Millions $)	4,657	5,403	3,846	3,704	3,247	2,409	2,194	1,519	780	958

PORTFOLIO (as of 6/30/00)

Portfolio Manager: Richard Mace - 1996

Investm't Category: International Stock

Domestic	Index
✔ Foreign	Sector
Asset Allocation	State Specific

Investment Style

Large Cap	Mid Cap	Small Cap
Growth	Grth/Val	Value

Portfolio

7.6%	cash	0.0%	corp bonds
92.4%	stocks	0.0%	gov't bonds
0.0%	pref/conv't pref	0.0%	muni bonds
0.0%	conv't bds/wrnts	0.0%	other

SHAREHOLDER INFORMATION

Minimum Investment
Initial: $2,500 Subsequent: $250

Minimum IRA Investment
Initial: $500 Subsequent: $250

Maximum Fees
Load: 0.01% redemption 12b-1: none
Other: redemption fee applies for 1 month

Services
✔ IRA
✔ Keogh
✔ Telephone Exchange

Fidelity Pacific Basin (FPBFX)

800-544-8888, 801-534-1910
www.fidelity.com

International Stock

PERFORMANCE — fund inception date: 10/1/86

	3yr Annual	5yr Annual	10yr Annual	Bull	Bear
Return (%)	15.4	4.8	7.0	175.6	-29.2
Differ from Category (+/-)	6.5 high	-3.5 blw av	-2.0 blw av	84.7 high	-5.2 blw av

Standard Deviation	Category Risk Index	Beta
25.4%—high	1.12—abv av	0.85

	2000	1999	1998	1997	1996	1995	1994	1993	1992	1991
Return (%)	-35.3	119.6	8.2	-15.0	-2.7	-6.1	-2.8	63.9	-7.6	12.5
Differ from Category (+/-)	-15.9	58.9	2.4	-16.3	-17.2	-15.4	0.3	23.7	-4.1	-0.5
Return, Tax-Adjusted (%)	-37.0	118.8	8.1	-15.6	-2.9	-6.1	-5.8	62.8	-7.8	12.5

PER SHARE DATA

	2000	1999	1998	1997	1996	1995	1994	1993	1992	1991
Dividends, Net Income ($)	1.12	0.26	0.02	0.25	0.08	0.00	0.02	0.13	0.11	0.00
Distrib'ns, Cap Gain ($)	0.23	0.00	0.00	0.00	0.00	0.00	2.02	0.27	0.00	0.00
Net Asset Value ($)	17.29	28.74	13.22	12.23	14.70	15.20	16.19	18.80	11.74	12.83
Expense Ratio (%)	na	1.36	1.72	1.31	1.24	1.36	1.54	1.59	1.84	1.88
Yield (%)	6.39	0.90	0.15	2.04	0.54	0.00	0.10	0.68	0.93	0.00
Portfolio Turnover (%)	na	101	57	42	85	50	88	77	105	143
Total Assets (Millions $)	477	989	227	213	446	469	475	526	113	93

PORTFOLIO (as of 6/30/00)

Portfolio Manager: William Kennedy - 1998

Investm't Category: International Stock

Domestic	Index
✔ Foreign	Sector
Asset Allocation	State Specific

Investment Style

Large Cap	Mid Cap	Small Cap
Growth	Grth/Val	Value

Portfolio

4.8% cash	0.0% corp bonds
95.2% stocks	0.0% gov't bonds
0.0% pref/conv't pref	0.0% muni bonds
0.0% conv't bds/wrnts	0.0% other

SHAREHOLDER INFORMATION

Minimum Investment
Initial: $2,500 Subsequent: $250

Minimum IRA Investment
Initial: $500 Subsequent: $100

Maximum Fees
Load: 3.00% front 12b-1: none
Other: 0.15% redemption fee for 3 months

Services
✔ IRA
✔ Keogh
✔ Telephone Exchange

Fidelity Puritan (FPURX)

800-544-8544, 801-534-1910
www.fidelity.com

Balanced

PERFORMANCE

fund inception date: 4/16/47

	3yr Annual	5yr Annual	10yr Annual	Bull	Bear
Return (%)	8.9	12.7	14.6	20.2	4.2
Differ from Category (+/-)	0.5 av	1.3 abv av	2.9 high	-7.9 blw av	7.4 high

Standard Deviation	Category Risk Index	Beta
10.1%—blw av	0.92—blw av	0.51

	2000	1999	1998	1997	1996	1995	1994	1993	1992	1991
Return (%)	7.7	2.8	16.5	22.3	15.1	21.4	1.7	21.4	15.4	24.4
Differ from Category (+/-)	5.7	-7.9	3.2	3.5	1.2	-4.1	3.0	7.0	7.0	0.6
Return, Tax-Adjusted (%)	5.3	0.5	13.5	19.6	11.1	19.2	-0.9	16.8	12.2	22.3

PER SHARE DATA

	2000	1999	1998	1997	1996	1995	1994	1993	1992	1991
Dividends, Net Income ($)	0.61	0.64	0.67	0.68	0.62	0.49	0.54	0.72	0.82	0.80
Distrib'ns, Cap Gain ($)	1.01	0.97	1.56	0.96	1.54	0.44	0.71	1.36	0.69	0.00
Net Asset Value ($)	18.83	19.03	20.07	19.38	17.24	17.01	14.81	15.75	14.74	14.14
Expense Ratio (%)	0.64	0.63	0.63	0.66	0.72	0.77	0.79	0.74	0.64	0.66
Yield (%)	3.07	3.20	3.09	3.34	3.30	2.80	3.47	4.20	5.31	5.65
Portfolio Turnover (%)	62	80	84	80	139	76	74	76	102	108
Total Assets (Millions $)	20,720	24,370	25,682	22,821	18,501	15,628	11,769	8,988	5,912	5,108

PORTFOLIO (as of 6/30/00)

Portfolio Manager: Stephen Petersen - 2000

Investm't Category: Balanced

- ✔ Domestic
- ✔ Foreign
- Asset Allocation
- Index
- Sector
- State Specific

Investment Style

Large Cap	Mid Cap	Small Cap
Growth	Grth/Val	Value

Portfolio

2.4%	cash	10.9%	corp bonds
62.9%	stocks	23.2%	gov't bonds
0.0%	pref/conv't pref	0.0%	muni bonds
0.0%	conv't bds/wrnts	0.6%	other

SHAREHOLDER INFORMATION

Minimum Investment

Initial: $2,500 Subsequent: $250

Minimum IRA Investment

Initial: $500 Subsequent: $250

Maximum Fees

Load: none 12b-1: none

Other: none

Services

- ✔ IRA
- ✔ Keogh
- ✔ Telephone Exchange

Fidelity Real Estate Inv

800-544-8888, 801-534-1910
www.fidelity.com

(FRESX)

Growth & Income

PERFORMANCE — fund inception date: 11/14/86

	3yr Annual	5yr Annual	10yr Annual	Bull	Bear
Return (%)	1.9	11.8	14.0	2.0	19.8
Differ from Category (+/-)	-7.0 low	-2.5 blw av	-0.9 blw av	-31.5 low	19.9 high

Standard Deviation	Category Risk Index	Beta
14.7%—av	0.85—low	0.19

	2000	1999	1998	1997	1996	1995	1994	1993	1992	1991
Return (%)	31.3	-0.9	-18.6	21.3	36.2	10.9	2.0	12.5	19.5	39.1
Differ from Category (+/-)	25.6	-11.7	-31.4	-5.6	16.5	-18.6	2.5	-1.3	7.9	11.0
Return, Tax-Adjusted (%)	29.3	-2.6	-20.4	18.9	34.1	8.7	0.1	10.6	18.2	37.2

PER SHARE DATA

	2000	1999	1998	1997	1996	1995	1994	1993	1992	1991
Dividends, Net Income ($)	0.73	0.69	0.77	0.79	0.72	0.71	0.63	0.60	0.43	0.49
Distrib'ns, Cap Gain ($)	0.00	0.00	0.41	0.56	0.00	0.00	0.00	0.00	0.00	0.00
Net Asset Value ($)	18.50	14.70	15.54	20.45	18.03	13.88	13.20	13.57	12.60	10.94
Expense Ratio (%)	0.88	0.89	0.84	0.90	0.95	1.03	1.13	1.16	1.24	1.47
Yield (%)	3.94	4.69	4.82	3.76	3.99	5.11	4.77	4.42	3.41	4.47
Portfolio Turnover (%)	32	28	76	55	85	75	110	82	84	49
Total Assets (Millions $)	942	724	1,239	2,480	1,721	708	555	424	150	62

PORTFOLIO (as of 6/30/00)

Portfolio Manager: Steve Buller - 1998

Investm't Category: Growth & Income

✔ Domestic　　Index
Foreign　　✔ Sector
Asset Allocation　　State Specific

Investment Style

Large Cap　　✔ Mid Cap　　✔ Small Cap
Growth　　Grth/Val　　✔ Value

Portfolio

7.3%	cash	0.0%	corp bonds
92.7%	stocks	0.0%	gov't bonds
0.0%	pref/conv't pref	0.0%	muni bonds
0.0%	conv't bds/wrnts	0.0%	other

SHAREHOLDER INFORMATION

Minimum Investment
Initial: $2,500　　Subsequent: $250

Minimum IRA Investment
Initial: $500　　Subsequent: $250

Maximum Fees
Load: 0.75% redemption　　12b-1: none
Other: redemption fee applies for 3 months

Services
✔ IRA
✔ Keogh
✔ Telephone Exchange

Fidelity Retirement Grth (FDFFX)

800-544-8888, 801-534-1910
www.fidelity.com

Aggressive Growth

PERFORMANCE

fund inception date: 3/24/83

	3yr Annual	5yr Annual	10yr Annual	Bull	Bear
Return (%)	26.6	21.1	20.3	95.6	-19.0
Differ from Category (+/-)	10.4 abv av	6.5 abv av	4.5 abv av	-23.6 av	1.6 av

Standard Deviation	Category Risk Index	Beta
32.8%—high	1.01—av	1.14

	2000	1999	1998	1997	1996	1995	1994	1993	1992	1991
Return (%)	1.7	47.0	35.8	18.5	8.3	24.2	0.0	22.1	10.5	45.5
Differ from Category (+/-)	7.7	-10.5	20.7	3.7	-10.0	-10.4	0.8	-3.1	3.6	-1.7
Return, Tax-Adjusted (%)	-1.6	43.3	32.9	14.2	4.4	20.6	-3.0	18.7	4.8	42.8

PER SHARE DATA

	2000	1999	1998	1997	1996	1995	1994	1993	1992	1991
Dividends, Net Income ($)	0.08	0.05	0.14	0.13	0.26	0.35	0.22	0.14	0.16	0.20
Distrib'ns, Cap Gain ($)	4.19	3.66	2.13	3.41	2.15	1.58	1.68	1.75	3.53	1.04
Net Asset Value ($)	22.01	25.85	20.51	16.85	17.29	18.19	16.24	18.14	16.44	18.23
Expense Ratio (%)	na	0.58	0.62	0.64	0.70	1.03	1.07	1.05	1.02	0.83
Yield (%)	0.30	0.16	0.61	0.64	1.33	1.77	1.22	0.70	0.80	1.03
Portfolio Turnover (%)	na	310	266	205	230	54	72	101	138	119
Total Assets (Millions $)	7,928	7,268	4,946	3,932	4,045	4,071	3,184	2,848	2,222	1,835

PORTFOLIO (as of 6/30/00)

Portfolio Manager: Fergus Shiel - 1996

Investm't Category: Aggressive Growth

✔ Domestic	Index
✔ Foreign	Sector
Asset Allocation	State Specific

Investment Style

Large Cap	Mid Cap	✔ Small Cap
✔ Growth	Grth/Val	Value

Portfolio

3.1%	cash	0.0%	corp bonds
96.9%	stocks	0.0%	gov't bonds
0.0%	pref/conv't pref	0.0%	muni bonds
0.0%	conv't bds/wrnts	0.0%	other

SHAREHOLDER INFORMATION

Minimum Investment
Initial: $2,500 Subsequent: $250

Minimum IRA Investment
Initial: $500 Subsequent: $250

Maximum Fees
Load: none 12b-1: none
Other: none

Services
✔ IRA
✔ Keogh
✔ Telephone Exchange

Fidelity Sel Air Trans (FSAIX)

800-544-8888, 801-534-1910
www.fidelity.com

Aggressive Growth

PERFORMANCE — fund inception date: 12/16/85

	3yr Annual	5yr Annual	10yr Annual	Bull	Bear
Return (%)	26.0	21.5	20.2	56.5	28.9
Differ from Category (+/-)	9.8 abv av	6.9 abv av	4.4 abv av	-62.7 blw av	49.5 high

Standard Deviation	Category Risk Index	Beta
23.9%—abv av	0.74—low	1.01

	2000	1999	1998	1997	1996	1995	1994	1993	1992	1991
Return (%)	39.7	34.6	6.4	31.1	1.2	59.5	-21.7	30.8	6.5	37.0
Differ from Category (+/-)	45.7	-22.9	-8.7	16.3	-17.1	24.9	-20.9	5.6	-0.4	-10.2
Return, Tax-Adjusted (%)	37.2	31.5	6.2	29.6	0.8	58.4	-23.4	30.2	5.7	36.2

PER SHARE DATA

	2000	1999	1998	1997	1996	1995	1994	1993	1992	1991
Dividends, Net Income ($)	0.00	0.00	0.00	0.00	0.00	0.00	0.00	0.00	0.00	0.00
Distrib'ns, Cap Gain ($)	3.68	3.88	0.21	1.43	0.27	0.46	1.09	0.27	0.36	0.25
Net Asset Value ($)	37.24	29.88	25.30	23.95	19.41	19.40	12.43	17.09	13.27	12.81
Expense Ratio (%)	1.40	1.35	1.93	1.89	1.41	2.50	2.31	2.48	2.51	2.48
Yield (%)	0.00	0.00	0.00	0.00	0.00	0.00	0.00	0.00	0.00	0.00
Portfolio Turnover (%)	252	260	294	469	504	200	171	96	261	106
Total Assets (Millions $)	66	40	57	61	150	94	7	15	10	5

PORTFOLIO (as of 6/30/00)

Portfolio Manager: Jeffrey Feingold - 2000

Investm't Category: Aggressive Growth

✔ Domestic | Index
✔ Foreign | ✔ Sector
Asset Allocation | State Specific

Investment Style

✔ Large Cap | Mid Cap | Small Cap
Growth | Grth/Val | ✔ Value

Portfolio

8.1% cash | 0.0% corp bonds
91.9% stocks | 0.0% gov't bonds
0.0% pref/conv't pref | 0.0% muni bonds
0.0% conv't bds/wrnts | 0.0% other

SHAREHOLDER INFORMATION

Minimum Investment
Initial: $2,500 | Subsequent: $250

Minimum IRA Investment
Initial: $500 | Subsequent: $250

Maximum Fees
Load: 3.00% front | 12b-1: none
Other: 0.75% redemption fee for 1 month

Services
✔ IRA
✔ Keogh
✔ Telephone Exchange

Fidelity Sel Banking (FSRBX)

800-544-8888, 801-534-1910
www.fidelity.com

Growth

PERFORMANCE

fund inception date: 6/30/86

	3yr Annual	5yr Annual	10yr Annual	Bull	Bear
Return (%)	6.0	18.7	25.2	16.0	11.9
Differ from Category (+/-)	-5.0 blw av	2.6 abv av	8.4 high	-33.7 low	17.3 high

Standard Deviation	Category Risk Index	Beta
27.7%—high	1.42—high	1.03

	2000	1999	1998	1997	1996	1995	1994	1993	1992	1991
Return (%)	18.7	-10.1	11.8	45.5	35.8	46.7	0.2	11.1	48.5	65.7
Differ from Category (+/-)	15.2	-29.0	-2.5	18.4	13.5	16.3	0.4	-3.5	35.9	28.1
Return, Tax-Adjusted (%)	16.3	-13.9	10.2	44.2	33.6	44.8	-2.0	5.1	46.6	63.4

PER SHARE DATA

	2000	1999	1998	1997	1996	1995	1994	1993	1992	1991
Dividends, Net Income ($)	0.59	0.36	0.28	0.28	0.27	0.25	0.26	0.15	0.11	0.15
Distrib'ns, Cap Gain ($)	2.48	7.44	2.66	1.23	1.40	0.72	1.01	3.92	0.81	0.53
Net Asset Value ($)	33.56	31.50	42.87	41.05	29.29	22.94	16.28	17.49	19.44	13.75
Expense Ratio (%)	1.19	1.16	1.25	1.46	1.40	1.56	1.60	1.49	1.77	2.51
Yield (%)	1.63	0.92	0.61	0.66	0.87	1.05	1.50	0.70	0.54	1.05
Portfolio Turnover (%)	94	22	25	43	103	106	74	63	89	110
Total Assets (Millions $)	423	514	1,178	1,351	510	322	108	113	238	36

PORTFOLIO (as of 6/30/00)

Portfolio Manager: Samuel Peters - 2000

Investm't Category: Growth

✔ Domestic — Index
✔ Foreign — ✔ Sector
Asset Allocation — State Specific

Investment Style

✔ Large Cap — ✔ Mid Cap — Small Cap
Growth — Grth/Val — ✔ Value

Portfolio

7.1%	cash	0.0%	corp bonds
92.9%	stocks	0.0%	gov't bonds
0.0%	pref/conv't pref	0.0%	muni bonds
0.0%	conv't bds/wrnts	0.0%	other

SHAREHOLDER INFORMATION

Minimum Investment

Initial: $2,500 — Subsequent: $250

Minimum IRA Investment

Initial: $500 — Subsequent: $100

Maximum Fees

Load: 3.00% front — 12b-1: none
Other: 0.75% redemption fee for 1 month

Services

✔ IRA
Keogh
✔ Telephone Exchange

Fidelity Sel Biotech (FBIOX)

800-544-8888, 801-534-1910
www.fidelity.com

Aggressive Growth

PERFORMANCE — fund inception date: 12/16/85

	3yr Annual	5yr Annual	10yr Annual	Bull	Bear
Return (%)	45.1	30.0	23.3	161.6	9.3
Differ from Category (+/-)	28.9 high	15.4 high	7.5 high	42.4 abv av	29.9 high

Standard Deviation	Category Risk Index	Beta
44.8%—high	1.38—high	0.60

	2000	1999	1998	1997	1996	1995	1994	1993	1992	1991
Return (%)	32.7	77.7	29.7	15.2	5.5	49.1	-18.1	0.7	-10.3	99.0
Differ from Category (+/-)	38.7	20.2	14.6	0.4	-12.8	14.5	-17.3	-24.5	-17.2	51.8
Return, Tax-Adjusted (%)	32.0	76.2	28.4	12.3	2.2	48.9	-18.1	0.7	-13.2	95.4

PER SHARE DATA

	2000	1999	1998	1997	1996	1995	1994	1993	1992	1991
Dividends, Net Income ($)	0.00	0.00	0.00	0.00	0.03	0.07	0.00	0.00	0.00	0.02
Distrib'ns, Cap Gain ($)	2.11	2.82	2.09	4.71	4.06	0.00	0.00	0.00	3.89	2.52
Net Asset Value ($)	86.80	67.13	39.77	32.54	32.51	34.83	23.41	28.61	28.41	36.42
Expense Ratio (%)	1.15	1.30	1.49	1.57	1.43	1.59	1.61	1.50	1.50	1.63
Yield (%)	0.00	0.00	0.00	0.00	0.08	0.20	0.00	0.00	0.00	0.05
Portfolio Turnover (%)	72	86	162	41	67	77	51	79	160	166
Total Assets (Millions $)	4,117	1,622	704	551	635	846	396	557	799	1,146

PORTFOLIO (as of 6/30/00)

Portfolio Manager: Brian Younger - 2000

Investm't Category: Aggressive Growth

✔ Domestic   Index
✔ Foreign   ✔ Sector
Asset Allocation   State Specific

Investment Style

Large Cap   Mid Cap   ✔ Small Cap
✔ Growth   Grth/Val   Value

Portfolio

9.7%	cash	0.0%	corp bonds
90.3%	stocks	0.0%	gov't bonds
0.0%	pref/conv't pref	0.0%	muni bonds
0.0%	conv't bds/wrnts	0.0%	other

SHAREHOLDER INFORMATION

Minimum Investment
Initial: $2,500   Subsequent: $250

Minimum IRA Investment
Initial: $500   Subsequent: $250

Maximum Fees
Load: 3.00% front   12b-1: none
Other: 0.75% redemption fee for 1 month

Services
✔ IRA
✔ Keogh
✔ Telephone Exchange

Fidelity Sel Brokerage (FSLBX)

800-544-8888, 801-534-1910
www.fidelity.com

Aggressive Growth

PERFORMANCE — fund inception date: 7/29/85

	3yr Annual	5yr Annual	10yr Annual	Bull	Bear
Return (%)	20.8	31.9	27.8	55.3	1.8
Differ from Category (+/-)	4.6 abv av	17.3 high	12.0 high	-63.9 blw av	22.4 high

Standard Deviation	Category Risk Index	Beta
31.3%—high	0.97—av	1.46

	2000	1999	1998	1997	1996	1995	1994	1993	1992	1991
Return (%)	27.9	30.6	5.6	62.3	39.6	23.5	-17.2	49.3	5.1	82.2
Differ from Category (+/-)	33.9	-26.9	-9.5	47.5	21.3	-11.1	-16.4	24.1	-1.8	35.0
Return, Tax-Adjusted (%)	25.1	28.9	5.3	61.6	38.4	20.7	-17.2	46.1	5.1	82.1

PER SHARE DATA

	2000	1999	1998	1997	1996	1995	1994	1993	1992	1991
Dividends, Net Income ($)	0.00	0.05	0.01	0.09	0.06	0.04	0.00	0.01	0.00	0.01
Distrib'ns, Cap Gain ($)	6.49	3.13	0.52	0.61	0.65	1.44	0.00	1.47	0.00	0.00
Net Asset Value ($)	53.14	46.83	38.47	36.86	23.17	17.18	15.14	18.30	13.34	12.69
Expense Ratio (%)	1.28	1.24	1.33	1.94	1.61	2.54	1.77	2.21	2.17	2.50
Yield (%)	0.00	0.10	0.02	0.24	0.25	0.21	0.00	0.05	0.00	0.07
Portfolio Turnover (%)	47	59	100	16	166	139	295	111	254	62
Total Assets (Millions $)	589	468	550	647	111	26	21	94	20	29

PORTFOLIO (as of 6/30/00)

Portfolio Manager: Jennifer Nettesheim - 2000

Investm't Category: Aggressive Growth

✔ Domestic — Index
✔ Foreign — ✔ Sector
Asset Allocation — State Specific

Investment Style

✔ Large Cap — Mid Cap — Small Cap
Growth — Grth/Val — ✔ Value

Portfolio

7.1%	cash	0.0%	corp bonds
92.9%	stocks	0.0%	gov't bonds
0.0%	pref/conv't pref	0.0%	muni bonds
0.0%	conv't bds/wrnts	0.0%	other

SHAREHOLDER INFORMATION

Minimum Investment

Initial: $2,500 — Subsequent: $250

Minimum IRA Investment

Initial: $500 — Subsequent: $250

Maximum Fees

Load: 3.00% front — 12b-1: none
Other: 0.75% redemption fee for 1 month

Services

✔ IRA
✔ Keogh
✔ Telephone Exchange

Fidelity Sel Computers (FDCPX)

800-544-8888, 801-534-1910
www.fidelity.com

Aggressive Growth

PERFORMANCE — fund inception date: 7/29/85

	3yr Annual	5yr Annual	10yr Annual	Bull	Bear
Return (%)	34.7	26.3	28.3	201.2	-41.0
Differ from Category (+/-)	18.5 high	11.7 high	12.5 high	82.0 high	-20.4 low

Standard Deviation	Category Risk Index	Beta
39.9%—high	1.23—abv av	1.51

	2000	1999	1998	1997	1996	1995	1994	1993	1992	1991
Return (%)	-31.1	81.1	96.3	0.1	31.6	51.8	20.4	28.8	21.9	30.7
Differ from Category (+/-)	-25.1	23.6	81.2	-14.7	13.3	17.2	21.2	3.6	15.0	-16.5
Return, Tax-Adjusted (%)	-35.2	76.6	96.3	-5.4	29.8	46.4	20.4	26.3	21.9	29.5

PER SHARE DATA

	2000	1999	1998	1997	1996	1995	1994	1993	1992	1991
Dividends, Net Income ($)	0.00	0.00	0.00	0.00	0.00	0.00	0.00	0.00	0.00	0.27
Distrib'ns, Cap Gain ($)	21.79	14.92	0.00	13.39	2.47	5.61	0.00	1.80	0.00	0.22
Net Asset Value ($)	52.33	104.51	67.71	34.48	48.68	38.99	29.33	24.35	20.44	16.76
Expense Ratio (%)	1.05	1.23	1.40	1.48	1.38	1.69	1.89	1.81	2.17	2.26
Yield (%)	0.00	0.00	0.00	0.00	0.00	0.00	0.00	0.00	0.00	1.59
Portfolio Turnover (%)	129	133	333	255	129	189	145	254	568	695
Total Assets (Millions $)	2,163	3,205	1,514	569	664	499	175	61	56	20

PORTFOLIO (as of 6/30/00)

Portfolio Manager: Lawrence Rakers - 2000

Investm't Category: Aggressive Growth

✔ Domestic — Index
✔ Foreign — ✔ Sector
Asset Allocation — State Specific

Investment Style

✔ Large Cap — ✔ Mid Cap — Small Cap
✔ Growth — Grth/Val — Value

Portfolio

5.2%	cash	0.0%	corp bonds
94.8%	stocks	0.0%	gov't bonds
0.0%	pref/conv't pref	0.0%	muni bonds
0.0%	conv't bds/wrnts	0.0%	other

SHAREHOLDER INFORMATION

Minimum Investment

Initial: $2,500 — Subsequent: $250

Minimum IRA Investment

Initial: $500 — Subsequent: $250

Maximum Fees

Load: 3.00% front — 12b-1: none
Other: 0.75% redemption fee for 1 month

Services

✔ IRA
✔ Keogh
✔ Telephone Exchange

Fidelity Sel Defense (FSDAX)

800-544-8888, 801-534-1910
www.fidelity.com

Growth

PERFORMANCE — fund inception date: 5/8/84

	3yr Annual	5yr Annual	10yr Annual	Bull	Bear
Return (%)	11.5	16.4	18.0	34.3	11.2
Differ from Category (+/-)	0.5 av	0.3 av	1.2 abv av	-15.4 blw av	16.6 high

Standard Deviation	Category Risk Index	Beta
21.9%—abv av	1.13—abv av	0.99

	2000	1999	1998	1997	1996	1995	1994	1993	1992	1991
Return (%)	18.8	11.8	4.3	23.5	25.0	47.3	1.7	28.8	0.0	26.9
Differ from Category (+/-)	15.3	-7.1	-10.0	-3.6	2.7	16.9	1.9	14.2	-12.6	-10.7
Return, Tax-Adjusted (%)	17.8	11.4	4.3	21.4	22.5	44.5	1.2	27.3	0.0	26.7

PER SHARE DATA

	2000	1999	1998	1997	1996	1995	1994	1993	1992	1991
Dividends, Net Income ($)	0.02	0.00	0.00	0.00	0.00	0.00	0.00	0.10	0.00	0.06
Distrib'ns, Cap Gain ($)	1.81	0.59	0.00	3.04	2.17	1.82	0.27	0.62	0.00	0.00
Net Asset Value ($)	42.68	37.56	34.16	32.74	29.12	25.15	18.32	18.27	14.75	14.75
Expense Ratio (%)	1.59	1.42	1.77	1.84	1.75	2.49	2.53	2.48	2.46	2.49
Yield (%)	0.04	0.00	0.00	0.00	0.00	0.00	0.00	0.52	0.00	0.40
Portfolio Turnover (%)	146	221	311	219	267	146	324	87	32	162
Total Assets (Millions $)	49	27	33	49	39	27	3	2	1	1

PORTFOLIO (as of 6/30/00)

Portfolio Manager: Jeffrey Feingold - 1998

Investm't Category: Growth

✔ Domestic　　Index
✔ Foreign　　✔ Sector
Asset Allocation　　State Specific

Investment Style

✔ Large Cap　✔ Mid Cap　Small Cap
Growth　Grth/Val　✔ Value

Portfolio

7.4%	cash	0.0%	corp bonds
92.6%	stocks	0.0%	gov't bonds
0.0%	pref/conv't pref	0.0%	muni bonds
0.0%	conv't bds/wrnts	0.0%	other

SHAREHOLDER INFORMATION

Minimum Investment

Initial: $2,500　　Subsequent: $250

Minimum IRA Investment

Initial: $500　　Subsequent: $250

Maximum Fees

Load: 3.00% front　　12b-1: none
Other: 0.75% redemption fee for 1 month

Services

✔ IRA
✔ Keogh
✔ Telephone Exchange

Fidelity Sel Develop Comm (FSDCX)

800-544-8888, 801-534-1910
www.fidelity.com

Aggressive Growth

PERFORMANCE — fund inception date: 6/29/90

	3yr Annual	5yr Annual	10yr Annual	Bull	Bear
Return (%)	37.8	26.0	26.7	277.9	-41.2
Differ from Category (+/-)	21.6 high	11.4 high	10.9 high	158.7 high	-20.6 low

Standard Deviation	Category Risk Index	Beta
44.3%—high	1.37—high	1.68

	2000	1999	1998	1997	1996	1995	1994	1993	1992	1991
Return (%)	-29.7	122.4	67.6	6.0	14.5	17.3	15.1	31.7	17.2	61.3
Differ from Category (+/-)	-23.7	64.9	52.5	-8.8	-3.8	-17.3	15.9	6.5	10.3	14.1
Return, Tax-Adjusted (%)	-34.6	120.3	67.5	1.9	14.5	10.3	12.6	29.1	17.1	58.8

PER SHARE DATA

	2000	1999	1998	1997	1996	1995	1994	1993	1992	1991
Dividends, Net Income ($)	0.00	0.00	0.00	0.00	0.00	0.00	0.00	0.00	0.00	0.00
Distrib'ns, Cap Gain ($)	15.45	3.07	0.07	4.35	0.00	5.00	1.67	1.47	0.03	0.79
Net Asset Value ($)	29.59	62.88	30.08	18.00	21.26	18.56	20.24	19.24	15.91	13.60
Expense Ratio (%)	1.11	1.34	1.61	1.64	1.51	1.56	1.56	1.88	2.50	2.50
Yield (%)	0.00	0.00	0.00	0.00	0.00	0.00	0.00	0.00	0.00	0.00
Portfolio Turnover (%)	112	299	383	202	249	266	280	77	25	469
Total Assets (Millions $)	1,850	2,260	445	203	275	296	276	245	70	19

PORTFOLIO (as of 6/30/00)

Portfolio Manager: Rajiv Kaul - 2000

Investm't Category: Aggressive Growth

✔ Domestic　Index
✔ Foreign　✔ Sector
Asset Allocation　State Specific

Investment Style

Large Cap　✔ Mid Cap　✔ Small Cap
✔ Growth　Grth/Val　Value

Portfolio

4.5%	cash	0.0%	corp bonds
95.5%	stocks	0.0%	gov't bonds
0.0%	pref/conv't pref	0.0%	muni bonds
0.0%	conv't bds/wrnts	0.0%	other

SHAREHOLDER INFORMATION

Minimum Investment

Initial: $2,500　Subsequent: $250

Minimum IRA Investment

Initial: $500　Subsequent: $250

Maximum Fees

Load: 3.00% front　12b-1: none
Other: 0.75% redemption fee for 1 month

Services

✔ IRA
✔ Keogh
✔ Telephone Exchange

Fidelity Sel Electronics (FSELX)

800-544-8888, 801-534-1910
www.fidelity.com

Aggressive Growth

PERFORMANCE — fund inception date: 7/29/85

	3yr Annual	5yr Annual	10yr Annual	Bull	Bear
Return (%)	37.0	32.9	34.0	266.8	-42.9
Differ from Category (+/-)	20.8 high	18.3 high	18.2 high	147.6 high	-22.3 low

Standard Deviation	Category Risk Index	Beta
44.4%—high	1.37—high	1.71

	2000	1999	1998	1997	1996	1995	1994	1993	1992	1991
Return (%)	-17.6	106.6	51.1	13.7	41.7	68.9	17.1	32.0	27.4	35.2
Differ from Category (+/-)	-11.6	49.1	36.0	-1.1	23.4	34.3	17.9	6.8	20.5	-12.0
Return, Tax-Adjusted (%)	-21.8	103.7	51.1	8.1	41.7	60.9	17.1	26.5	27.4	35.2

PER SHARE DATA

	2000	1999	1998	1997	1996	1995	1994	1993	1992	1991
Dividends, Net Income ($)	0.00	0.00	0.00	0.00	0.00	0.00	0.00	0.00	0.00	0.00
Distrib'ns, Cap Gain ($)	18.68	6.62	0.00	10.20	0.00	5.25	0.00	2.75	0.00	0.00
Net Asset Value ($)	57.78	88.88	46.56	30.81	36.48	25.74	18.49	15.78	14.12	11.08
Expense Ratio (%)	0.98	1.15	1.18	1.33	1.22	1.71	1.67	1.69	2.16	2.26
Yield (%)	0.00	0.00	0.00	0.00	0.00	0.00	0.00	0.00	0.00	0.00
Portfolio Turnover (%)	125	160	435	341	366	205	163	293	299	268
Total Assets (Millions $)	6,494	6,781	2,722	2,301	1,565	892	156	45	53	10

PORTFOLIO (as of 6/30/00)

Portfolio Manager: Brian Hanson - 2000

Investm't Category: Aggressive Growth

✔ Domestic　　Index
✔ Foreign　　✔ Sector
Asset Allocation　　State Specific

Investment Style

✔ Large Cap　　✔ Mid Cap　　✔ Small Cap
✔ Growth　　Grth/Val　　Value

Portfolio

7.3% cash　　0.0% corp bonds
92.7% stocks　　0.0% gov't bonds
0.0% pref/conv't pref　　0.0% muni bonds
0.0% conv't bds/wrnts　　0.0% other

SHAREHOLDER INFORMATION

Minimum Investment

Initial: $2,500　　Subsequent: $250

Minimum IRA Investment

Initial: $500　　Subsequent: $250

Maximum Fees

Load: 3.00% front　　12b-1: none
Other: 0.75% redemption fee for 1 month

Services

✔ IRA
✔ Keogh
✔ Telephone Exchange

Fidelity Sel Energy (FSENX)

800-544-8888, 801-534-1910
www.fidelity.com

Growth

PERFORMANCE

fund inception date: 7/14/81

	3yr Annual	5yr Annual	10yr Annual	Bull	Bear
Return (%)	14.6	17.1	12.0	49.2	1.4
Differ from Category (+/-)	3.6 abv av	1.0 av	-4.8 low	-0.5 av	6.8 abv av

Standard Deviation	Category Risk Index	Beta
28.4%—high	1.46—high	0.84

	2000	1999	1998	1997	1996	1995	1994	1993	1992	1991
Return (%)	31.8	34.2	-14.7	10.2	32.4	21.3	0.4	19.1	-2.3	0.0
Differ from Category (+/-)	28.3	15.3	-29.0	-16.9	10.1	-9.1	0.6	4.5	-14.9	-37.6
Return, Tax-Adjusted (%)	29.0	33.6	-15.1	6.5	30.1	20.3	-0.7	17.9	-2.8	-0.3

PER SHARE DATA

	2000	1999	1998	1997	1996	1995	1994	1993	1992	1991
Dividends, Net Income ($)	0.14	0.09	0.01	0.09	0.13	0.11	0.11	0.03	0.27	0.16
Distrib'ns, Cap Gain ($)	2.97	0.29	0.41	4.09	1.31	0.36	0.51	0.57	0.00	0.02
Net Asset Value ($)	27.29	23.35	17.70	21.15	23.21	18.77	15.87	16.43	14.32	14.95
Expense Ratio (%)	1.25	1.42	1.58	1.57	1.63	1.85	1.66	1.71	1.78	1.79
Yield (%)	0.46	0.38	0.05	0.35	0.53	0.57	0.67	0.17	1.88	1.06
Portfolio Turnover (%)	124	138	115	87	97	106	157	72	81	61
Total Assets (Millions $)	241	193	122	158	239	131	96	82	68	72

PORTFOLIO (as of 6/30/00)

Portfolio Manager: Scott Offen - 1999

Investm't Category: Growth

✔ Domestic
Index
✔ Foreign
✔ Sector
Asset Allocation
State Specific

Investment Style

Large Cap
✔ Mid Cap
Small Cap
Growth
Grth/Val
✔ Value

Portfolio

4.9%	cash	0.0%	corp bonds
94.7%	stocks	0.0%	gov't bonds
0.0%	pref/conv't pref	0.0%	muni bonds
0.4%	conv't bds/wrnts	0.0%	other

SHAREHOLDER INFORMATION

Minimum Investment

Initial: $2,500 Subsequent: $250

Minimum IRA Investment

Initial: $500 Subsequent: $250

Maximum Fees

Load: 3.00% front 12b-1: none
Other: 0.75% redemption fee for 1 month

Services

✔ IRA
✔ Keogh
✔ Telephone Exchange

Fidelity Sel Energy Serv (FSESX)

800-544-8888, 801-534-1910
www.fidelity.com

Aggressive Growth

PERFORMANCE

fund inception date: 12/16/85

	3yr Annual	5yr Annual	10yr Annual	Bull	Bear
Return (%)	9.1	24.1	14.8	86.4	-15.4
Differ from Category (+/-)	-7.1 blw av	9.5 abv av	-1.0 blw av	-32.8 av	5.2 abv av

Standard Deviation	Category Risk Index	Beta
51.4%—high	1.58—high	1.39

	2000	1999	1998	1997	1996	1995	1994	1993	1992	1991
Return (%)	50.3	72.1	-49.7	51.8	49.0	40.8	0.4	20.9	3.4	-23.4
Differ from Category (+/-)	56.3	14.6	-64.8	37.0	30.7	6.2	1.2	-4.3	-3.5	-70.6
Return, Tax-Adjusted (%)	50.3	72.1	-50.8	50.0	47.5	39.4	-0.8	20.6	3.4	-23.4

PER SHARE DATA

	2000	1999	1998	1997	1996	1995	1994	1993	1992	1991
Dividends, Net Income ($)	0.00	0.00	0.00	0.00	0.01	0.04	0.02	0.05	0.00	0.00
Distrib'ns, Cap Gain ($)	0.00	0.00	1.71	1.85	0.78	0.48	0.48	0.00	0.00	0.00
Net Asset Value ($)	37.45	24.91	14.47	30.45	21.73	15.16	11.14	11.61	9.64	9.32
Expense Ratio (%)	1.23	1.35	1.25	1.47	1.58	1.79	1.65	1.76	2.07	1.82
Yield (%)	0.00	0.00	0.00	0.00	0.04	0.25	0.17	0.43	0.00	0.00
Portfolio Turnover (%)	69	75	78	167	223	209	137	236	89	62
Total Assets (Millions $)	623	618	394	1,133	562	254	50	40	35	28

PORTFOLIO (as of 6/30/00)

Portfolio Manager: Nicholas Tiller - 2000

Investm't Category: Aggressive Growth

✔ Domestic　　Index
✔ Foreign　　✔ Sector
Asset Allocation　　State Specific

Investment Style

Large Cap　　✔ Mid Cap　　✔ Small Cap
Growth　　Grth/Val　　✔ Value

Portfolio

4.6%	cash	0.0%	corp bonds
95.4%	stocks	0.0%	gov't bonds
0.0%	pref/conv't pref	0.0%	muni bonds
0.0%	conv't bds/wrnts	0.0%	other

SHAREHOLDER INFORMATION

Minimum Investment
Initial: $2,500　　Subsequent: $250

Minimum IRA Investment
Initial: $500　　Subsequent: $250

Maximum Fees
Load: 3.00% front　　12b-1: none
Other: 0.75% redemption fee for 1 month

Services
✔ IRA
Keogh
✔ Telephone Exchange

Fidelity Sel Financl Serv (FIDSX)

800-544-8888, 801-534-1910
www.fidelity.com

Growth

PERFORMANCE

fund inception date: 12/10/81

	3yr Annual	5yr Annual	10yr Annual	Bull	Bear
Return (%)	14.1	22.8	26.8	26.3	17.4
Differ from Category (+/-)	3.1 abv av	6.7 high	10.0 high	-23.4 blw av	22.8 high

Standard Deviation	Category Risk Index	Beta
25.2%—high	1.30—high	1.05

	2000	1999	1998	1997	1996	1995	1994	1993	1992	1991
Return (%)	28.5	1.5	14.1	41.9	32.1	47.3	-3.6	17.5	42.8	61.6
Differ from Category (+/-)	25.0	-17.4	-0.2	14.8	9.8	16.9	-3.4	2.9	30.2	24.0
Return, Tax-Adjusted (%)	27.4	0.2	11.7	38.8	29.6	46.3	-6.3	13.1	39.8	61.1

PER SHARE DATA

	2000	1999	1998	1997	1996	1995	1994	1993	1992	1991
Dividends, Net Income ($)	0.80	0.64	0.19	0.64	0.63	0.37	0.59	0.20	0.51	0.35
Distrib'ns, Cap Gain ($)	3.45	5.09	10.81	10.51	4.56	0.91	4.13	7.32	3.38	0.00
Net Asset Value ($)	116.54	94.52	98.63	95.98	76.59	62.24	43.12	49.79	48.83	37.14
Expense Ratio (%)	1.17	1.18	1.31	1.45	1.41	1.54	1.63	1.54	1.85	2.49
Yield (%)	0.66	0.64	0.17	0.60	0.77	0.58	1.24	0.35	0.97	0.94
Portfolio Turnover (%)	57	60	84	80	125	107	93	100	164	237
Total Assets (Millions $)	555	435	597	548	337	251	94	126	132	53

PORTFOLIO (as of 6/30/00)

Portfolio Manager: James Catudal - 2000

Investm't Category: Growth

✔ Domestic
Index
✔ Foreign
✔ Sector
Asset Allocation
State Specific

Investment Style

✔ Large Cap
Mid Cap
Small Cap
Growth
Grth/Val
✔ Value

Portfolio

5.8%	cash	0.0%	corp bonds
94.2%	stocks	0.0%	gov't bonds
0.0%	pref/conv't pref	0.0%	muni bonds
0.0%	conv't bds/wrnts	0.0%	other

SHAREHOLDER INFORMATION

Minimum Investment

Initial: $2,500 Subsequent: $250

Minimum IRA Investment

Initial: $500 Subsequent: $250

Maximum Fees

Load: 3.00% front 12b-1: none

Other: 0.75% redemption fee for 1 month

Services

✔ IRA
✔ Keogh
✔ Telephone Exchange

Fidelity Sel Food & Agri (FDFAX)

800-544-8888, 801-534-1910
www.fidelity.com

Growth & Income

PERFORMANCE

fund inception date: 7/29/85

	3yr Annual	5yr Annual	10yr Annual	Bull	Bear
Return (%)	6.1	12.0	14.7	-1.9	30.9
Differ from Category (+/-)	-2.8 blw av	-2.3 blw av	-0.2 av	-35.4 low	31.0 high

Standard Deviation	Category Risk Index	Beta
16.5%—av	0.95—av	0.41

	2000	1999	1998	1997	1996	1995	1994	1993	1992	1991
Return (%)	29.8	-20.4	15.6	30.3	13.3	36.6	6.0	8.8	6.0	34.0
Differ from Category (+/-)	24.1	-31.2	2.8	3.4	-6.4	7.1	6.5	-5.0	-5.6	5.9
Return, Tax-Adjusted (%)	29.4	-21.5	13.1	27.5	11.0	34.3	4.2	5.8	4.4	32.0

PER SHARE DATA

	2000	1999	1998	1997	1996	1995	1994	1993	1992	1991
Dividends, Net Income ($)	0.36	0.42	0.16	0.37	0.24	0.20	0.08	1.33	0.10	0.11
Distrib'ns, Cap Gain ($)	0.00	2.00	5.47	4.95	2.77	2.20	1.85	1.43	1.57	1.59
Net Asset Value ($)	47.64	36.98	49.37	47.87	41.41	39.28	30.60	30.75	30.93	30.86
Expense Ratio (%)	1.29	1.29	1.49	1.52	1.42	1.68	1.64	1.67	1.83	2.22
Yield (%)	0.75	1.07	0.29	0.70	0.54	0.48	0.24	4.13	0.30	0.33
Portfolio Turnover (%)	38	68	74	91	124	126	96	515	63	124
Total Assets (Millions $)	151	109	233	309	252	240	85	173	117	122

PORTFOLIO (as of 6/30/00)

Portfolio Manager: Matthew Fruhan - 1999

Investm't Category: Growth & Income

✔ Domestic
Index
✔ Foreign
✔ Sector
Asset Allocation
State Specific

Investment Style

✔ Large Cap
✔ Mid Cap
Small Cap
Growth
Grth/Val
✔ Value

Portfolio

7.4%	cash	0.0%	corp bonds
92.6%	stocks	0.0%	gov't bonds
0.0%	pref/conv't pref	0.0%	muni bonds
0.0%	conv't bds/wrnts	0.0%	other

SHAREHOLDER INFORMATION

Minimum Investment
Initial: $2,500 Subsequent: $250

Minimum IRA Investment
Initial: $500 Subsequent: $250

Maximum Fees
Load: 3.00% front 12b-1: none
Other: 0.75% redemption fee for 1 month

Services
✔ IRA
✔ Keogh
✔ Telephone Exchange

Fidelity Sel Gold Port (FSAGX)

800-544-8888, 801-534-1910
www.fidelity.com

Aggressive Growth

PERFORMANCE

fund inception date: 12/16/85

	3yr Annual	5yr Annual	10yr Annual	Bull	Bear
Return (%)	-6.7	-10.0	-1.0	67.3	-12.6
Differ from Category (+/-)	-22.9 low	-24.6 low	-16.8 low	-51.9 blw av	8.0 abv av

Standard Deviation	Category Risk Index	Beta
46.3%—high	1.43—high	0.88

	2000	1999	1998	1997	1996	1995	1994	1993	1992	1991
Return (%)	-18.0	8.3	-8.6	-39.3	19.9	11.2	-15.4	78.6	-3.0	-6.1
Differ from Category (+/-)	-12.0	-49.2	-23.7	-54.1	1.6	-23.4	-14.6	53.4	-9.9	-53.3
Return, Tax-Adjusted (%)	-18.1	8.3	-8.6	-40.2	19.2	11.2	-15.4	78.6	-3.0	-6.1

PER SHARE DATA

	2000	1999	1998	1997	1996	1995	1994	1993	1992	1991
Dividends, Net Income ($)	0.07	0.00	0.00	0.00	0.00	0.00	0.00	0.00	0.00	0.00
Distrib'ns, Cap Gain ($)	0.00	0.00	0.00	1.29	0.50	0.00	0.00	0.00	0.00	0.00
Net Asset Value ($)	12.04	14.78	13.64	14.93	26.04	22.14	19.91	23.55	13.18	13.60
Expense Ratio (%)	1.41	1.54	1.55	1.44	1.39	1.41	1.49	1.59	1.75	1.75
Yield (%)	0.58	0.00	0.00	0.00	0.00	0.00	0.00	0.00	0.00	0.00
Portfolio Turnover (%)	71	59	89	63	56	34	39	30	40	38
Total Assets (Millions $)	212	200	201	211	354	313	314	365	155	153

PORTFOLIO (as of 6/30/00)

Portfolio Manager: Niel Marotta - 2000

Investm't Category: Aggressive Growth

✔ Domestic
✔ Foreign
Asset Allocation
Index
✔ Sector
State Specific

Investment Style

Large Cap Growth
Mid Cap Grth/Val
Small Cap Value

Portfolio

8.9%	cash	0.0%	corp bonds
91.1%	stocks	0.0%	gov't bonds
0.0%	pref/conv't pref	0.0%	muni bonds
0.0%	conv't bds/wrnts	0.0%	other

SHAREHOLDER INFORMATION

Minimum Investment

Initial: $2,500 Subsequent: $250

Minimum IRA Investment

Initial: $500 Subsequent: $250

Maximum Fees

Load: 3.00% front 12b-1: none

Other: 0.75% redemption fee for 1 month

Services

✔ IRA
✔ Keogh
✔ Telephone Exchange

Fidelity Sel Health Care (FSPHX)

800-544-8888, 801-534-1910
www.fidelity.com

Growth

PERFORMANCE

fund inception date: 7/14/81

	3yr Annual	5yr Annual	10yr Annual	Bull	Bear
Return (%)	23.3	23.2	22.8	22.9	28.5
Differ from Category (+/-)	12.3 high	7.1 high	6.0 high	-26.8 low	33.9 high

Standard Deviation	Category Risk Index	Beta
16.3%—av	0.84—low	0.41

	2000	1999	1998	1997	1996	1995	1994	1993	1992	1991
Return (%)	36.6	-2.8	41.2	31.1	15.4	45.8	21.4	2.4	-17.4	83.6
Differ from Category (+/-)	33.1	-21.7	26.9	4.0	-6.9	15.4	21.6	-12.2	-30.0	46.0
Return, Tax-Adjusted (%)	33.5	-3.9	39.9	26.6	10.5	43.5	18.4	2.3	-20.2	78.7

PER SHARE DATA

	2000	1999	1998	1997	1996	1995	1994	1993	1992	1991
Dividends, Net Income ($)	0.24	0.08	0.19	0.25	0.65	0.59	0.62	0.07	0.16	0.34
Distrib'ns, Cap Gain ($)	18.63	7.85	6.17	20.73	15.95	4.92	5.74	0.00	8.51	8.81
Net Asset Value ($)	150.13	124.82	136.77	101.87	95.40	97.57	70.80	63.62	62.19	85.95
Expense Ratio (%)	1.05	1.05	1.18	1.33	1.30	1.68	1.64	1.46	1.44	1.53
Yield (%)	0.14	0.06	0.13	0.20	0.58	0.57	0.81	0.11	0.22	0.35
Portfolio Turnover (%)	70	66	79	59	54	126	96	112	154	159
Total Assets (Millions $)	2,989	2,427	3,032	1,631	1,242	1,448	796	573	755	1,169

PORTFOLIO (as of 6/30/00)

Portfolio Manager: Yolanda McGettigan - 2000

Investm't Category: Growth

✔ Domestic	Index
✔ Foreign	✔ Sector
Asset Allocation	State Specific

Investment Style

✔ Large Cap	Mid Cap	Small Cap
✔ Growth	Grth/Val	Value

Portfolio

11.4% cash	0.0% corp bonds
88.6% stocks	0.0% gov't bonds
0.0% pref/conv't pref	0.0% muni bonds
0.0% conv't bds/wrnts	0.0% other

SHAREHOLDER INFORMATION

Minimum Investment
Initial: $2,500 Subsequent: $250

Minimum IRA Investment
Initial: $500 Subsequent: $250

Maximum Fees
Load: 3.00% front 12b-1: none
Other: 0.75% redemption fee for 1 month

Services
✔ IRA
✔ Keogh
✔ Telephone Exchange

Fidelity Sel Home Finance (FSVLX)

800-544-8888, 801-534-1910
www.fidelity.com

Growth

PERFORMANCE

fund inception date: 12/16/85

	3yr Annual	5yr Annual	10yr Annual	Bull	Bear
Return (%)	3.9	17.4	27.8	-0.3	37.6
Differ from Category (+/-)	-7.1 low	1.3 av	11.0 high	-50.0 low	43.0 high

Standard Deviation	Category Risk Index	Beta
27.5%—high	1.41—high	0.79

	2000	1999	1998	1997	1996	1995	1994	1993	1992	1991
Return (%)	50.2	-12.3	-14.8	45.7	36.8	53.4	2.6	27.2	57.8	64.6
Differ from Category (+/-)	46.7	-31.2	-29.1	18.6	14.5	23.0	2.8	12.6	45.2	27.0
Return, Tax-Adjusted (%)	49.8	-12.7	-15.3	42.5	34.5	52.0	-1.7	25.2	57.1	64.0

PER SHARE DATA

	2000	1999	1998	1997	1996	1995	1994	1993	1992	1991
Dividends, Net Income ($)	0.26	0.19	0.07	0.29	0.32	0.19	0.12	0.01	0.01	0.14
Distrib'ns, Cap Gain ($)	0.07	0.69	1.38	5.84	2.16	0.73	3.60	1.40	0.28	0.00
Net Asset Value ($)	55.33	37.09	43.28	52.09	40.79	31.82	21.33	24.44	20.35	13.09
Expense Ratio (%)	1.37	1.18	1.21	1.38	1.32	1.45	1.58	1.55	2.08	2.50
Yield (%)	0.46	0.50	0.15	0.50	0.74	0.58	0.48	0.03	0.04	1.06
Portfolio Turnover (%)	91	18	54	78	81	124	95	61	134	159
Total Assets (Millions $)	362	332	990	1,663	794	586	130	159	216	9

PORTFOLIO (as of 6/30/00)

Portfolio Manager: Victor Thay - 1999

Investm't Category: Growth

✔ Domestic　　Index
✔ Foreign　　✔ Sector
Asset Allocation　　State Specific

Investment Style

✔ Large Cap　　✔ Mid Cap　　Small Cap
Growth　　Grth/Val　　✔ Value

Portfolio

7.2%	cash	0.0%	corp bonds
92.8%	stocks	0.0%	gov't bonds
0.0%	pref/conv't pref	0.0%	muni bonds
0.0%	conv't bds/wrnts	0.0%	other

SHAREHOLDER INFORMATION

Minimum Investment

Initial: $2,500　　Subsequent: $250

Minimum IRA Investment

Initial: $500　　Subsequent: $250

Maximum Fees

Load: 3.00% front　　12b-1: none
Other: 0.75% redemption fee for 1 month

Services

✔ IRA
✔ Keogh
✔ Telephone Exchange

Fidelity Sel Insurance

800-544-8888, 801-534-1910
www.fidelity.com

(FSPCX)

Growth

PERFORMANCE — fund inception date: 12/16/85

	3yr Annual	5yr Annual	10yr Annual	Bull	Bear
Return (%)	20.1	25.0	22.2	17.0	41.4
Differ from Category (+/-)	9.1 high	8.9 high	5.4 high	-32.7 low	46.8 high

Standard Deviation	Category Risk Index	Beta
26.4%—high	1.36—high	0.89

	2000	1999	1998	1997	1996	1995	1994	1993	1992	1991
Return (%)	53.2	-6.0	20.3	42.4	23.7	34.8	-0.3	8.1	22.4	36.6
Differ from Category (+/-)	49.7	-24.9	6.0	15.3	1.4	4.4	-0.1	-6.5	9.8	-1.0
Return, Tax-Adjusted (%)	52.6	-9.0	18.2	40.0	22.0	33.6	-0.3	5.3	19.7	36.0

PER SHARE DATA

	2000	1999	1998	1997	1996	1995	1994	1993	1992	1991
Dividends, Net Income ($)	0.12	0.00	0.00	0.00	0.03	0.07	0.00	0.01	0.03	0.26
Distrib'ns, Cap Gain ($)	0.65	6.60	3.98	3.54	1.45	0.72	0.00	1.96	1.71	0.00
Net Asset Value ($)	51.75	34.30	43.30	39.49	30.67	26.10	19.96	20.03	20.33	18.30
Expense Ratio (%)	1.36	1.31	1.45	1.82	1.74	2.34	1.93	2.49	2.47	2.49
Yield (%)	0.22	0.00	0.00	0.00	0.09	0.26	0.00	0.04	0.13	1.42
Portfolio Turnover (%)	107	72	157	142	164	265	101	81	112	98
Total Assets (Millions $)	173	46	100	111	35	32	10	18	22	4

PORTFOLIO (as of 6/30/00)

Portfolio Manager: Fontana Forrest - 2000

Investm't Category: Growth

✔ Domestic — Index
✔ Foreign — ✔ Sector
Asset Allocation — State Specific

Investment Style

✔ Large Cap — ✔ Mid Cap — Small Cap
Growth — Grth/Val — ✔ Value

Portfolio

6.3%	cash	0.0%	corp bonds
93.7%	stocks	0.0%	gov't bonds
0.0%	pref/conv't pref	0.0%	muni bonds
0.0%	conv't bds/wrnts	0.0%	other

SHAREHOLDER INFORMATION

Minimum Investment

Initial: $2,500 — Subsequent: $250

Minimum IRA Investment

Initial: $500 — Subsequent: $250

Maximum Fees

Load: 3.00% front — 12b-1: none
Other: 0.75% redemption fee for 1 month

Services

✔ IRA
✔ Keogh
✔ Telephone Exchange

Fidelity Sel Leisure (FDLSX)

800-544-8888, 801-534-1910
www.fidelity.com

Aggressive Growth

PERFORMANCE

fund inception date: 5/8/84

	3yr Annual	5yr Annual	10yr Annual	Bull	Bear
Return (%)	11.4	17.2	18.9	82.5	-24.6
Differ from Category (+/-)	-4.8 blw av	2.6 av	3.1 av	-36.7 av	-4.0 av

Standard Deviation	Category Risk Index	Beta
22.2%—abv av	0.69—low	1.13

	2000	1999	1998	1997	1996	1995	1994	1993	1992	1991
Return (%)	-24.4	32.8	37.9	41.2	13.4	26.9	-6.7	39.5	16.2	32.9
Differ from Category (+/-)	-18.4	-24.7	22.8	26.4	-4.9	-7.7	-5.9	14.3	9.3	-14.3
Return, Tax-Adjusted (%)	-26.5	30.6	36.7	38.3	11.5	23.0	-9.1	36.8	16.2	32.9

PER SHARE DATA

	2000	1999	1998	1997	1996	1995	1994	1993	1992	1991
Dividends, Net Income ($)	0.00	0.00	0.00	0.00	0.00	0.00	0.00	0.00	0.00	0.00
Distrib'ns, Cap Gain ($)	9.92	8.15	3.44	6.46	2.83	5.32	3.93	3.26	0.00	0.00
Net Asset Value ($)	61.45	91.54	75.44	57.55	46.06	43.18	38.27	45.22	35.09	30.19
Expense Ratio (%)	1.12	1.24	1.44	1.56	1.63	1.62	1.53	1.90	2.21	2.27
Yield (%)	0.00	0.00	0.00	0.00	0.00	0.00	0.00	0.00	0.00	0.00
Portfolio Turnover (%)	120	107	209	127	141	103	170	109	45	75
Total Assets (Millions $)	213	387	315	229	107	78	61	117	41	38

PORTFOLIO (as of 6/30/00)

Portfolio Manager: Michael Tarlowe - 2000

Investm't Category: Aggressive Growth

✔ Domestic
Index
✔ Foreign
✔ Sector
Asset Allocation
State Specific

Investment Style

✔ Large Cap
Mid Cap
Small Cap
✔ Growth
Grth/Val
Value

Portfolio

9.0%	cash	0.0%	corp bonds
91.0%	stocks	0.0%	gov't bonds
0.0%	pref/conv't pref	0.0%	muni bonds
0.0%	conv't bds/wrnts	0.0%	other

SHAREHOLDER INFORMATION

Minimum Investment

Initial: $2,500 Subsequent: $250

Minimum IRA Investment

Initial: $500 Subsequent: $250

Maximum Fees

Load: 3.00% front 12b-1: none

Other: 0.75% redemption fee for 1 month

Services

✔ IRA
✔ Keogh
✔ Telephone Exchange

Fidelity Sel Med Dlvry (FSHCX)

800-544-8888, 801-534-1910
www.fidelity.com

Aggressive Growth

PERFORMANCE — fund inception date: 6/30/86

	3yr Annual	5yr Annual	10yr Annual	Bull	Bear
Return (%)	3.5	8.1	14.3	-17.3	65.3
Differ from Category (+/-)	-12.7 low	-6.5 low	-1.5 blw av	-136.5 low	85.9 high

Standard Deviation	Category Risk Index	Beta
25.5%—high	0.79—blw av	0.60

	2000	1999	1998	1997	1996	1995	1994	1993	1992	1991
Return (%)	67.8	-29.5	-6.1	20.1	11.0	32.2	19.8	5.5	-13.1	77.8
Differ from Category (+/-)	73.8	-87.0	-21.2	5.3	-7.3	-2.4	20.6	-19.7	-20.0	30.6
Return, Tax-Adjusted (%)	67.8	-29.5	-7.1	16.1	7.4	29.7	18.3	5.5	-15.0	75.2

PER SHARE DATA

	2000	1999	1998	1997	1996	1995	1994	1993	1992	1991
Dividends, Net Income ($)	0.00	0.00	0.00	0.00	0.00	0.00	0.07	0.00	0.00	0.00
Distrib'ns, Cap Gain ($)	0.00	0.00	1.34	5.23	3.45	1.91	0.88	0.00	1.55	1.24
Net Asset Value ($)	27.59	16.44	23.35	26.05	26.42	26.96	21.87	19.10	18.10	22.76
Expense Ratio (%)	1.67	1.37	1.57	1.57	1.62	1.45	1.79	1.77	1.69	1.94
Yield (%)	0.00	0.00	0.00	0.00	0.00	0.00	0.30	0.00	0.00	0.00
Portfolio Turnover (%)	154	67	109	78	132	123	164	155	181	165
Total Assets (Millions $)	251	50	146	141	182	203	247	150	197	200

PORTFOLIO (as of 6/30/00)

Portfolio Manager: Sanjeev Makan - 2000

Investm't Category: Aggressive Growth

✔ Domestic | Index
✔ Foreign | ✔ Sector
Asset Allocation | State Specific

Investment Style

Large Cap | ✔ Mid Cap | Small Cap
Growth | Grth/Val | ✔ Value

Portfolio

4.6%	cash	0.0%	corp bonds
95.4%	stocks	0.0%	gov't bonds
0.0%	pref/conv't pref	0.0%	muni bonds
0.0%	conv't bds/wrnts	0.0%	other

SHAREHOLDER INFORMATION

Minimum Investment

Initial: $2,500 — Subsequent: $250

Minimum IRA Investment

Initial: $500 — Subsequent: $250

Maximum Fees

Load: 3.00% front — 12b-1: none

Other: 0.75% redemption fee for 1 month

Services

✔ IRA
Keogh
✔ Telephone Exchange

Fidelity Sel Multimedia (FBMPX)

800-544-8888, 801-534-1910
www.fidelity.com

Aggressive Growth

PERFORMANCE

fund inception date: 6/30/86

	3yr Annual	5yr Annual	10yr Annual	Bull	Bear
Return (%)	14.6	14.7	20.4	91.4	-24.9
Differ from Category (+/-)	-1.6 av	0.1 av	4.6 abv av	-27.8 av	-4.3 av

Standard Deviation	Category Risk Index	Beta
21.5%—abv av	0.66—low	1.06

	2000	1999	1998	1997	1996	1995	1994	1993	1992	1991
Return (%)	-23.0	44.1	35.6	30.9	1.0	33.7	3.9	38.0	21.4	37.8
Differ from Category (+/-)	-17.0	-13.4	20.5	16.1	-17.3	-0.9	4.7	12.8	14.5	-9.4
Return, Tax-Adjusted (%)	-24.4	43.3	34.2	29.7	-0.1	30.7	0.1	36.9	20.9	37.8

PER SHARE DATA

	2000	1999	1998	1997	1996	1995	1994	1993	1992	1991
Dividends, Net Income ($)	0.00	0.00	0.00	0.00	0.00	0.02	0.00	0.00	0.00	0.00
Distrib'ns, Cap Gain ($)	4.16	1.57	2.19	1.52	1.07	2.19	3.21	0.65	0.23	0.00
Net Asset Value ($)	39.32	56.05	40.09	31.44	25.37	26.15	21.23	23.84	17.82	14.86
Expense Ratio (%)	1.17	1.33	1.75	1.60	1.54	2.03	1.63	2.49	2.49	2.53
Yield (%)	0.00	0.00	0.00	0.00	0.00	0.07	0.00	0.00	0.00	0.00
Portfolio Turnover (%)	76	109	219	99	223	107	340	70	111	150
Total Assets (Millions $)	166	252	135	70	72	89	26	65	16	5

PORTFOLIO (as of 6/30/00)

Portfolio Manager: Michael Tarlowe - 2000

Investm't Category: Aggressive Growth

✔ Domestic　Index
✔ Foreign　✔ Sector
Asset Allocation　State Specific

Investment Style

✔ Large Cap　✔ Mid Cap　Small Cap
✔ Growth　Grth/Val　Value

Portfolio

12.5% cash　0.0% corp bonds
87.5% stocks　0.0% gov't bonds
0.0% pref/conv't pref　0.0% muni bonds
0.0% conv't bds/wrnts　0.0% other

SHAREHOLDER INFORMATION

Minimum Investment

Initial: $2,500　Subsequent: $250

Minimum IRA Investment

Initial: $500　Subsequent: $250

Maximum Fees

Load: 3.00% front　12b-1: none
Other: 0.75% redemption fee for 1 month

Services

✔ IRA
✔ Keogh
✔ Telephone Exchange

Fidelity Sel Natural Gas (FSNGX)

800-544-8888, 801-534-1910
www.fidelity.com

Growth

PERFORMANCE — fund inception date: 4/21/93

	3yr Annual	5yr Annual	10yr Annual	Bull	Bear
Return (%)	23.7	18.5	na	46.3	17.3
Differ from Category (+/-)	12.7 high	2.4 abv av	na	-3.4 av	22.7 high

Standard Deviation	Category Risk Index	Beta
30.7%—high	1.58—high	0.78

	2000	1999	1998	1997	1996	1995	1994	1993	1992	1991
Return (%)	71.2	26.1	-12.3	-8.0	34.3	30.3	-6.8	—	—	—
Differ from Category (+/-)	67.7	7.2	-26.6	-35.1	12.0	-0.1	-6.6	—	—	—
Return, Tax-Adjusted (%)	70.6	25.7	-12.5	-8.4	33.5	30.0	-6.8	—	—	—

PER SHARE DATA

	2000	1999	1998	1997	1996	1995	1994	1993	1992	1991
Dividends, Net Income ($)	0.04	0.09	0.10	0.00	0.01	0.05	0.02	—	—	—
Distrib'ns, Cap Gain ($)	0.30	0.00	0.00	0.33	0.29	0.00	0.00	—	—	—
Net Asset Value ($)	24.31	14.43	11.52	13.27	14.84	11.29	8.70	—	—	—
Expense Ratio (%)	1.39	1.52	1.82	1.70	1.67	1.66	1.93	—	—	—
Yield (%)	0.16	0.62	0.86	0.00	0.06	0.44	0.22	—	—	—
Portfolio Turnover (%)	85	107	118	283	79	177	44	—	—	—
Total Assets (Millions $)	331	52	43	69	153	85	79	—	—	—

PORTFOLIO (as of 6/30/00)

Portfolio Manager: Christian Zann - 1999

Investm't Category: Growth

✔ Domestic
Index
✔ Foreign
✔ Sector
Asset Allocation
State Specific

Investment Style

Large Cap
✔ Mid Cap
Small Cap
Growth
Grth/Val
✔ Value

Portfolio

6.4%	cash	0.0%	corp bonds
93.6%	stocks	0.0%	gov't bonds
0.0%	pref/conv't pref	0.0%	muni bonds
0.0%	conv't bds/wrnts	0.0%	other

SHAREHOLDER INFORMATION

Minimum Investment

Initial: $2,500 Subsequent: $250

Minimum IRA Investment

Initial: $500 Subsequent: $250

Maximum Fees

Load: 3.00% front 12b-1: none

Other: 0.75% redemption fee for 1 month

Services

✔ IRA
Keogh
✔ Telephone Exchange

Fidelity Sel Retailing (FSRPX)

800-544-8888, 801-534-1910
www.fidelity.com

Growth

PERFORMANCE — fund inception date: 12/16/85

	3yr Annual	5yr Annual	10yr Annual	Bull	Bear
Return (%)	10.7	18.4	19.1	42.5	-13.3
Differ from Category (+/-)	-0.3 av	2.3 abv av	2.3 abv av	-7.2 av	-7.9 blw av

Standard Deviation	Category Risk Index	Beta
21.3%—abv av	1.09—abv av	0.94

	2000	1999	1998	1997	1996	1995	1994	1993	1992	1991
Return (%)	-11.3	5.1	45.7	41.7	20.8	11.9	-5.0	13.0	22.0	68.1
Differ from Category (+/-)	-14.8	-13.8	31.4	14.6	-1.5	-18.5	-4.8	-1.6	9.4	30.5
Return, Tax-Adjusted (%)	-13.7	1.9	45.3	41.3	20.7	11.9	-5.0	10.0	20.4	67.0

PER SHARE DATA

	2000	1999	1998	1997	1996	1995	1994	1993	1992	1991
Dividends, Net Income ($)	0.00	0.00	0.00	0.00	0.00	0.00	0.00	0.00	0.00	0.00
Distrib'ns, Cap Gain ($)	7.18	10.13	0.69	0.51	0.08	0.00	0.00	2.63	1.17	0.50
Net Asset Value ($)	44.71	57.99	64.83	45.06	32.24	26.74	23.88	25.14	24.64	21.28
Expense Ratio (%)	1.20	1.22	1.63	1.45	1.92	1.96	1.83	1.77	1.87	2.54
Yield (%)	0.00	0.00	0.00	0.00	0.00	0.00	0.00	0.00	0.00	0.00
Portfolio Turnover (%)	88	165	308	278	235	481	154	171	205	115
Total Assets (Millions $)	69	129	362	191	157	39	35	60	93	29

PORTFOLIO (as of 6/30/00)

Portfolio Manager: Steven Calhoun - 1999

Investm't Category: Growth

✔ Domestic   Index
✔ Foreign   ✔ Sector
Asset Allocation   State Specific

Investment Style

✔ Large Cap   Mid Cap   Small Cap
Growth   ✔ Grth/Val   Value

Portfolio

5.9%	cash	0.0%	corp bonds
94.1%	stocks	0.0%	gov't bonds
0.0%	pref/conv't pref	0.0%	muni bonds
0.0%	conv't bds/wrnts	0.0%	other

SHAREHOLDER INFORMATION

Minimum Investment

Initial: $2,500   Subsequent: $250

Minimum IRA Investment

Initial: $500   Subsequent: $250

Maximum Fees

Load: 3.00% front   12b-1: none
Other: 0.75% redemption fee for 1 month

Services

✔ IRA
✔ Keogh
✔ Telephone Exchange

Fidelity Sel Software (FSCSX)

800-544-8888, 801-534-1910
www.fidelity.com

Aggressive Growth

PERFORMANCE — fund inception date: 7/29/85

	3yr Annual	5yr Annual	10yr Annual	Bull	Bear
Return (%)	30.8	25.7	28.2	188.9	-22.4
Differ from Category (+/-)	14.6 high	11.1 high	12.4 high	69.7 high	-1.8 av

Standard Deviation	Category Risk Index	Beta
39.7%—high	1.22—abv av	1.52

	2000	1999	1998	1997	1996	1995	1994	1993	1992	1991
Return (%)	-20.3	93.1	45.7	15.0	21.7	46.0	0.3	32.7	35.5	45.8
Differ from Category (+/-)	-14.3	35.6	30.6	0.2	3.4	11.4	1.1	7.5	28.6	-1.4
Return, Tax-Adjusted (%)	-26.7	90.7	45.0	11.6	19.0	41.2	0.0	25.8	35.5	41.2

PER SHARE DATA

	2000	1999	1998	1997	1996	1995	1994	1993	1992	1991
Dividends, Net Income ($)	0.00	0.00	0.00	0.00	0.00	0.00	0.00	0.00	0.00	0.00
Distrib'ns, Cap Gain ($)	31.32	6.33	1.32	6.61	3.31	4.60	0.33	6.48	0.00	2.50
Net Asset Value ($)	51.51	96.86	54.72	38.58	39.62	35.46	27.29	27.55	26.43	19.50
Expense Ratio (%)	1.11	1.27	1.44	1.51	1.47	1.50	1.57	1.64	1.98	2.50
Yield (%)	0.00	0.00	0.00	0.00	0.00	0.00	0.00	0.00	0.00	0.00
Portfolio Turnover (%)	59	72	145	279	183	164	376	402	348	326
Total Assets (Millions $)	1,102	1,412	656	426	401	351	211	164	143	20

PORTFOLIO (as of 6/30/00)

Portfolio Manager: Telis Bertsekas - 2000

Investm't Category: Aggressive Growth

✔ Domestic
Index
✔ Foreign
✔ Sector
Asset Allocation
State Specific

Investment Style

✔ Large Cap
✔ Mid Cap
✔ Small Cap
✔ Growth
Grth/Val
Value

Portfolio

9.6%	cash	0.0%	corp bonds
90.4%	stocks	0.0%	gov't bonds
0.0%	pref/conv't pref	0.0%	muni bonds
0.0%	conv't bds/wrnts	0.0%	other

SHAREHOLDER INFORMATION

Minimum Investment
Initial: $2,500 Subsequent: $250

Minimum IRA Investment
Initial: $500 Subsequent: $250

Maximum Fees
Load: 3.00% front 12b-1: none
Other: 0.75% redemption fee for 1 month

Services
✔ IRA
✔ Keogh
✔ Telephone Exchange

Fidelity Sel Technology (FSPTX)

800-544-8888, 801-534-1910
www.fidelity.com

Aggressive Growth

PERFORMANCE — fund inception date: 7/14/81

	3yr Annual	5yr Annual	10yr Annual	Bull	Bear
Return (%)	39.7	28.3	28.6	297.3	-43.4
Differ from Category (+/-)	23.5 high	13.7 high	12.8 high	178.1 high	-22.8 low

Standard Deviation	Category Risk Index	Beta
45.5%—high	1.40—high	1.72

	2000	1999	1998	1997	1996	1995	1994	1993	1992	1991
Return (%)	-32.3	131.7	74.1	10.3	15.8	43.8	11.1	28.6	8.7	58.9
Differ from Category (+/-)	-26.3	74.2	59.0	-4.5	-2.5	9.2	11.9	3.4	1.8	11.7
Return, Tax-Adjusted (%)	-35.0	126.6	74.1	4.6	13.7	38.3	10.0	25.3	6.4	58.6

PER SHARE DATA

	2000	1999	1998	1997	1996	1995	1994	1993	1992	1991
Dividends, Net Income ($)	0.00	0.00	0.00	0.00	0.00	0.00	0.00	0.13	0.00	0.16
Distrib'ns, Cap Gain ($)	20.73	19.80	0.00	15.69	3.68	8.05	1.50	3.70	2.75	0.00
Net Asset Value ($)	88.72	152.39	78.86	45.28	55.68	51.31	41.36	38.73	33.79	33.92
Expense Ratio (%)	1.04	1.20	1.38	1.49	1.39	1.56	1.54	1.64	1.72	1.83
Yield (%)	0.00	0.00	0.00	0.00	0.00	0.00	0.00	0.30	0.00	0.47
Portfolio Turnover (%)	210	339	556	549	112	102	213	259	353	442
Total Assets (Millions $)	4,595	5,208	1,061	526	491	400	227	229	130	124

PORTFOLIO (as of 6/30/00)

Portfolio Manager: Lawrence Rakers - 2000

Investm't Category: Aggressive Growth

✔ Domestic — Index
✔ Foreign — ✔ Sector
Asset Allocation — State Specific

Investment Style

Large Cap — ✔ Mid Cap — ✔ Small Cap
✔ Growth — Grth/Val — Value

Portfolio

5.6%	cash	0.0%	corp bonds
94.4%	stocks	0.0%	gov't bonds
0.0%	pref/conv't pref	0.0%	muni bonds
0.0%	conv't bds/wrnts	0.0%	other

SHAREHOLDER INFORMATION

Minimum Investment
Initial: $2,500 — Subsequent: $250

Minimum IRA Investment
Initial: $500 — Subsequent: $250

Maximum Fees
Load: 3.00% front — 12b-1: none
Other: 0.75% redemption fee for 1 month

Services
✔ IRA
✔ Keogh
✔ Telephone Exchange

Fidelity Sel Telecomm (FSTCX)

800-544-8888, 801-534-1910
www.fidelity.com

Aggressive Growth

PERFORMANCE

fund inception date: 7/29/85

	3yr Annual	5yr Annual	10yr Annual	Bull	Bear
Return (%)	13.7	14.2	17.8	131.3	-45.1
Differ from Category (+/-)	-2.5 av	-0.4 av	2.0 av	12.1 abv av	-24.5 low

Standard Deviation	Category Risk Index	Beta
31.6%—high	0.97—av	1.41

	2000	1999	1998	1997	1996	1995	1994	1993	1992	1991
Return (%)	-37.4	66.5	41.0	25.8	5.3	29.6	4.3	29.7	15.3	30.8
Differ from Category (+/-)	-31.4	9.0	25.9	11.0	-13.0	-5.0	5.1	4.5	8.4	-16.4
Return, Tax-Adjusted (%)	-39.4	63.0	39.6	22.6	1.4	27.1	2.9	25.8	14.6	30.4

PER SHARE DATA

	2000	1999	1998	1997	1996	1995	1994	1993	1992	1991
Dividends, Net Income ($)	0.00	0.00	0.00	0.00	0.27	0.39	0.53	0.20	0.18	0.28
Distrib'ns, Cap Gain ($)	9.04	10.48	2.96	6.44	5.87	2.75	1.07	4.18	0.48	0.00
Net Asset Value ($)	50.31	88.70	60.36	45.13	41.16	45.21	37.48	37.54	32.51	28.79
Expense Ratio (%)	1.09	1.25	1.51	1.54	1.52	1.55	1.53	1.74	1.90	1.97
Yield (%)	0.00	0.00	0.00	0.00	0.57	0.81	1.37	0.47	0.54	0.97
Portfolio Turnover (%)	173	150	157	175	89	107	241	115	20	262
Total Assets (Millions $)	936	1,595	810	441	437	451	363	414	111	68

PORTFOLIO (as of 6/30/00)

Portfolio Manager: Tim Cohen - 2000

Investm't Category: Aggressive Growth

✔ Domestic
✔ Foreign
Asset Allocation
Index
✔ Sector
State Specific

Investment Style

✔ Large Cap
✔ Mid Cap
Small Cap
✔ Growth
Grth/Val
Value

Portfolio

4.7%	cash	0.0%	corp bonds
95.3%	stocks	0.0%	gov't bonds
0.0%	pref/conv't pref	0.0%	muni bonds
0.0%	conv't bds/wrnts	0.0%	other

SHAREHOLDER INFORMATION

Minimum Investment

Initial: $2,500 Subsequent: $250

Minimum IRA Investment

Initial: $500 Subsequent: $250

Maximum Fees

Load: 3.00% front 12b-1: none

Other: 0.75% redemption fee for 1 month

Services

✔ IRA
✔ Keogh
✔ Telephone Exchange

Fidelity Sel Utilities Gr (FSUTX)

800-544-8888, 801-534-1910
www.fidelity.com

Growth & Income

PERFORMANCE — fund inception date: 12/10/81

	3yr Annual	5yr Annual	10yr Annual	Bull	Bear
Return (%)	15.9	17.7	15.5	70.2	-23.2
Differ from Category (+/-)	7.0 high	3.4 high	0.6 av	36.7 high	-23.1 low

Standard Deviation	Category Risk Index	Beta
19.0%—av	1.09—high	0.83

	2000	1999	1998	1997	1996	1995	1994	1993	1992	1991
Return (%)	-13.4	25.9	43.1	30.3	11.4	34.3	-7.4	12.5	10.5	21.0
Differ from Category (+/-)	-19.1	15.1	30.3	3.4	-8.3	4.8	-6.9	-1.3	-1.1	-7.1
Return, Tax-Adjusted (%)	-16.0	22.5	39.6	26.4	8.4	33.2	-9.0	7.7	8.1	18.4

PER SHARE DATA

	2000	1999	1998	1997	1996	1995	1994	1993	1992	1991
Dividends, Net Income ($)	1.97	0.42	0.25	0.58	0.70	0.84	1.05	1.13	1.33	1.69
Distrib'ns, Cap Gain ($)	4.85	9.30	7.93	7.30	3.54	0.00	0.67	4.94	1.70	1.19
Net Asset Value ($)	50.80	66.10	60.94	48.88	43.90	43.59	33.08	37.58	38.80	38.01
Expense Ratio (%)	1.04	1.16	1.33	1.47	1.38	1.42	1.35	1.42	1.51	1.65
Yield (%)	3.53	0.55	0.36	1.03	1.47	1.92	3.11	2.65	3.28	4.31
Portfolio Turnover (%)	93	113	78	31	65	24	61	34	45	45
Total Assets (Millions $)	568	626	504	358	255	312	202	275	247	264

PORTFOLIO (as of 6/30/00)

Portfolio Manager: John Roth - 1999

Investm't Category: Growth & Income

✔ Domestic — Index
✔ Foreign — ✔ Sector
Asset Allocation — State Specific

Investment Style

✔ Large Cap — ✔ Mid Cap — Small Cap
Growth — ✔ Grth/Val — Value

Portfolio

6.9%	cash	0.0%	corp bonds
93.1%	stocks	0.0%	gov't bonds
0.0%	pref/conv't pref	0.0%	muni bonds
0.0%	conv't bds/wrnts	0.0%	other

SHAREHOLDER INFORMATION

Minimum Investment
Initial: $2,500 — Subsequent: $250

Minimum IRA Investment
Initial: $500 — Subsequent: $250

Maximum Fees
Load: 3.00% front — 12b-1: none
Other: 0.75% redemption fee for 1 month

Services
✔ IRA
✔ Keogh
✔ Telephone Exchange

Fidelity Small Cap Sel (FDSCX)

800-544-8888, 801-534-1910
www.fidelity.com

Aggressive Growth

PERFORMANCE — fund inception date: 6/28/93

	3yr Annual	5yr Annual	10yr Annual	Bull	Bear
Return (%)	3.7	10.0	na	35.0	-14.0
Differ from Category (+/-)	-12.5 low	-4.6 blw av	na	-84.2 low	6.6 abv av

Standard Deviation	Category Risk Index	Beta
23.1%—abv av	0.71—low	0.93

	2000	1999	1998	1997	1996	1995	1994	1993	1992	1991
Return (%)	5.7	14.1	-7.3	27.2	13.6	26.6	-3.3	—	—	—
Differ from Category (+/-)	11.7	-43.4	-22.4	12.4	-4.7	-8.0	-2.5	—	—	—
Return, Tax-Adjusted (%)	4.7	13.8	-8.1	25.1	12.4	24.2	-3.3	—	—	—

PER SHARE DATA

	2000	1999	1998	1997	1996	1995	1994	1993	1992	1991
Dividends, Net Income ($)	0.03	0.09	0.03	0.13	0.01	0.08	0.01	—	—	—
Distrib'ns, Cap Gain ($)	0.74	0.00	0.62	1.14	0.51	0.77	0.00	—	—	—
Net Asset Value ($)	16.23	16.09	14.19	15.93	13.56	12.39	10.45	—	—	—
Expense Ratio (%)	0.88	0.85	0.97	0.90	0.99	0.97	1.20	—	—	—
Yield (%)	0.17	0.55	0.20	0.76	0.07	0.60	0.09	—	—	—
Portfolio Turnover (%)	122	96	88	176	192	182	210	—	—	—
Total Assets (Millions $)	625	612	747	824	538	438	664	—	—	—

PORTFOLIO (as of 6/30/00)

Portfolio Manager: Tim Krochuck - 2000

Investm't Category: Aggressive Growth

✔ Domestic — Index
✔ Foreign — Sector
Asset Allocation — State Specific

Investment Style

Large Cap — Mid Cap — ✔ Small Cap
Growth — ✔ Grth/Val — Value

Portfolio

8.0% cash — 0.0% corp bonds
92.0% stocks — 0.0% gov't bonds
0.0% pref/conv't pref — 0.0% muni bonds
0.0% conv't bds/wrnts — 0.0% other

SHAREHOLDER INFORMATION

Minimum Investment
Initial: $2,500 — Subsequent: $250

Minimum IRA Investment
Initial: $500 — Subsequent: $250

Maximum Fees
Load: 1.50% redemption — 12b-1: none
Other: redemption fee applies for 3 months

Services
✔ IRA
✔ Keogh
✔ Telephone Exchange

Fidelity Southeast Asia (FSEAX)

800-544-8888, 801-534-1910
www.fidelity.com

International Stock

PERFORMANCE — fund inception date: 4/19/93

	3yr Annual	5yr Annual	10yr Annual	Bull	Bear
Return (%)	7.8	-3.3	na	168.5	-36.4
Differ from Category (+/-)	-1.1 blw av	-11.6 low	na	77.6 high	-12.4 low

Standard Deviation	Category Risk Index	Beta
33.8%—high	1.49—high	1.23

	2000	1999	1998	1997	1996	1995	1994	1993	1992	1991
Return (%)	-30.4	91.5	-5.7	-38.8	10.1	12.1	-21.7	—	—	—
Differ from Category (+/-)	-11.0	30.8	-11.5	-40.1	-4.4	2.8	-18.6	—	—	—
Return, Tax-Adjusted (%)	-30.4	91.4	-5.7	-38.9	8.8	11.3	-21.7	—	—	—

PER SHARE DATA

	2000	1999	1998	1997	1996	1995	1994	1993	1992	1991
Dividends, Net Income ($)	0.00	0.02	0.02	0.05	0.17	0.23	0.00	—	—	—
Distrib'ns, Cap Gain ($)	0.00	0.00	0.00	0.00	0.40	0.00	0.00	—	—	—
Net Asset Value ($)	11.43	16.43	8.59	9.14	15.03	14.17	12.84	—	—	—
Expense Ratio (%)	na	1.43	1.79	1.32	1.12	1.15	1.47	—	—	—
Yield (%)	0.00	0.12	0.23	0.54	1.10	1.62	0.00	—	—	—
Portfolio Turnover (%)	na	93	95	141	102	90	157	—	—	—
Total Assets (Millions $)	280	502	235	263	762	684	660	—	—	—

PORTFOLIO (as of 6/30/00)

Portfolio Manager: Allan Liu - 1993

Investm't Category: International Stock

Domestic	Index
✔ Foreign	Sector
Asset Allocation	State Specific

Investment Style

Large Cap	Mid Cap	Small Cap
Growth	Grth/Val	Value

Portfolio

4.3% cash	0.0% corp bonds
95.7% stocks	0.0% gov't bonds
0.0% pref/conv't pref	0.0% muni bonds
0.0% conv't bds/wrnts	0.0% other

SHAREHOLDER INFORMATION

Minimum Investment
Initial: $2,500 Subsequent: $250

Minimum IRA Investment
Initial: $500 Subsequent: $100

Maximum Fees
Load: 3.00% front 12b-1: none
Other: 1.50% redemption fee for 3 months

Services
✔ IRA
✔ Keogh
✔ Telephone Exchange

Fidelity Spart 500 Index (FSMKX)

800-544-8888, 801-534-1910
www.fidelity.com

Growth & Income

PERFORMANCE — fund inception date: 3/6/90

	3yr Annual	5yr Annual	10yr Annual	Bull	Bear
Return (%)	12.0	18.0	17.1	55.8	-11.5
Differ from Category (+/-)	3.1 abv av	3.7 high	2.2 abv av	22.3 high	-11.4 blw av

Standard Deviation	Category Risk Index	Beta
17.6%—av	1.01—av	1.00

	2000	1999	1998	1997	1996	1995	1994	1993	1992	1991
Return (%)	-9.1	20.6	28.4	33.0	22.5	36.9	1.0	9.6	7.3	30.3
Differ from Category (+/-)	-14.8	9.8	15.6	6.1	2.8	7.4	1.5	-4.2	-4.3	2.2
Return, Tax-Adjusted (%)	-9.4	19.8	27.4	31.7	21.0	35.4	0.0	8.4	6.4	29.1

PER SHARE DATA

	2000	1999	1998	1997	1996	1995	1994	1993	1992	1991
Dividends, Net Income ($)	0.97	1.19	0.79	0.97	0.91	0.96	0.80	0.80	0.81	0.83
Distrib'ns, Cap Gain ($)	0.00	0.70	1.68	1.38	1.05	0.37	0.00	0.18	0.00	0.07
Net Asset Value ($)	90.76	100.89	85.29	68.50	53.42	45.32	34.15	34.60	32.49	31.07
Expense Ratio (%)	0.19	0.19	0.19	0.44	0.45	0.45	0.45	0.44	0.35	0.28
Yield (%)	1.06	1.17	0.90	1.38	1.67	2.10	2.34	2.30	2.49	2.66
Portfolio Turnover (%)	8	4	6	6	5	2	3	0	1	1
Total Assets (Millions $)	9,464	10,437	7,149	3,869	1,597	689	306	299	283	202

PORTFOLIO (as of 6/30/00)

Portfolio Manager: Jennifer Farrelly - 1994

Investm't Category: Growth & Income

✔ Domestic ✔ Index
Foreign Sector
Asset Allocation State Specific

Investment Style

✔ Large Cap Mid Cap Small Cap
Growth ✔ Grth/Val Value

Portfolio

0.0%	cash	0.0%	corp bonds
100.0%	stocks	0.0%	gov't bonds
0.0%	pref/conv't pref	0.0%	muni bonds
0.0%	conv't bds/wrnts	0.0%	other

SHAREHOLDER INFORMATION

Minimum Investment

Initial: $10,000 Subsequent: $1,000

Minimum IRA Investment

Initial: $500 Subsequent: $250

Maximum Fees

Load: 0.50% redemption 12b-1: none
Other: redemption fee applies for 3 months

Services

✔ IRA
✔ Keogh
✔ Telephone Exchange

Fidelity Spart Total Mkt (FSTMX)

800-544-8888, 801-534-1910
www.fidelity.com

Growth & Income

PERFORMANCE — fund inception date: 11/5/97

	3yr Annual	5yr Annual	10yr Annual	Bull	Bear
Return (%)	10.8	na	na	60.5	-15.8
Differ from Category (+/-)	1.9 abv av	na	na	27.0 high	-15.7 low

Standard Deviation	Category Risk Index	Beta
18.7%—av	1.08—high	1.02

	2000	1999	1998	1997	1996	1995	1994	1993	1992	1991
Return (%)	-10.9	23.2	24.0	—	—	—	—	—	—	—
Differ from Category (+/-)	-16.6	12.4	11.2	—	—	—	—	—	—	—
Return, Tax-Adjusted (%)	-11.3	22.7	23.4	—	—	—	—	—	—	—

PER SHARE DATA

	2000	1999	1998	1997	1996	1995	1994	1993	1992	1991
Dividends, Net Income ($)	0.30	0.29	0.23	—	—	—	—	—	—	—
Distrib'ns, Cap Gain ($)	0.18	0.19	0.28	—	—	—	—	—	—	—
Net Asset Value ($)	33.50	38.13	31.36	—	—	—	—	—	—	—
Expense Ratio (%)	0.25	0.27	0.25	—	—	—	—	—	—	—
Yield (%)	0.89	0.75	0.72	—	—	—	—	—	—	—
Portfolio Turnover (%)	11	4	7	—	—	—	—	—	—	—
Total Assets (Millions $)	1,015	755	166	—	—	—	—	—	—	—

PORTFOLIO (as of 6/30/00)

Portfolio Manager: committee - 1997

Investm't Category: Growth & Income

✔ Domestic ✔ Index
Foreign Sector
Asset Allocation State Specific

Investment Style

✔ Large Cap Mid Cap Small Cap
Growth ✔ Grth/Val Value

Portfolio

0.0%	cash	0.0%	corp bonds
100.0%	stocks	0.0%	gov't bonds
0.0%	pref/conv't pref	0.0%	muni bonds
0.0%	conv't bds/wrnts	0.0%	other

SHAREHOLDER INFORMATION

Minimum Investment

Initial: $15,000 Subsequent: $1,000

Minimum IRA Investment

Initial: $15,000 Subsequent: $1,000

Maximum Fees

Load: 0.50% redemption 12b-1: none
Other: redemption fee applies for 3 months

Services

✔ IRA
✔ Keogh
✔ Telephone Exchange

Fidelity Stock Selector

800-544-8888, 801-534-1910
www.fidelity.com

(FDSSX)

Growth

PERFORMANCE — fund inception date: 9/28/90

	3yr Annual	5yr Annual	10yr Annual	Bull	Bear
Return (%)	10.4	15.2	18.2	58.0	-11.8
Differ from Category (+/-)	-0.6 av	-0.9 blw av	1.4 abv av	8.3 abv av	-6.4 blw av

Standard Deviation	Category Risk Index	Beta
19.4%—abv av	1.00—av	1.02

	2000	1999	1998	1997	1996	1995	1994	1993	1992	1991
Return (%)	-7.0	26.2	14.6	28.8	17.1	36.4	0.7	13.9	15.4	45.9
Differ from Category (+/-)	-10.5	7.3	0.3	1.7	-5.2	6.0	0.9	-0.7	2.8	8.3
Return, Tax-Adjusted (%)	-10.2	23.3	12.7	25.4	14.2	32.7	-0.8	11.6	14.6	44.4

PER SHARE DATA

	2000	1999	1998	1997	1996	1995	1994	1993	1992	1991
Dividends, Net Income ($)	0.13	0.12	0.30	0.33	0.23	0.20	0.15	0.24	0.10	0.08
Distrib'ns, Cap Gain ($)	4.94	3.84	1.93	3.32	1.92	2.08	0.81	1.06	0.32	0.47
Net Asset Value ($)	24.84	32.00	28.71	27.13	23.85	22.19	17.91	18.75	17.61	15.63
Expense Ratio (%)	0.56	0.59	0.64	0.74	0.84	0.97	1.09	1.10	1.22	1.43
Yield (%)	0.43	0.33	0.97	1.08	0.89	0.82	0.80	1.21	0.55	0.49
Portfolio Turnover (%)	164	106	122	117	247	238	187	192	268	317
Total Assets (Millions $)	1,466	1,801	1,747	1,895	1,601	1,262	786	624	353	126

PORTFOLIO (as of 6/30/00)

Portfolio Manager: Bobby Kuo - 2000

Investm't Category: Growth

✔ Domestic   Index
✔ Foreign   Sector
Asset Allocation   State Specific

Investment Style

✔ Large Cap   ✔ Mid Cap   Small Cap
✔ Growth   Grth/Val   Value

Portfolio

4.4%	cash	0.0%	corp bonds
95.6%	stocks	0.0%	gov't bonds
0.0%	pref/conv't pref	0.0%	muni bonds
0.0%	conv't bds/wrnts	0.0%	other

SHAREHOLDER INFORMATION

Minimum Investment
Initial: $2,500   Subsequent: $250

Minimum IRA Investment
Initial: $500   Subsequent: $250

Maximum Fees
Load: none   12b-1: none
Other: none

Services
✔ IRA
✔ Keogh
✔ Telephone Exchange

Fidelity Technoquant Grth (FTQGX)

800-544-6666, 801-534-1910
www.fidelity.com

Aggressive Growth

PERFORMANCE — fund inception date: 11/12/96

	3yr Annual	5yr Annual	10yr Annual	Bull	Bear
Return (%)	14.3	na	na	71.5	-15.5
Differ from Category (+/-)	-1.9 av	na	na	-47.7 blw av	5.1 abv av

Standard Deviation	Category Risk Index	Beta
21.1%—abv av	0.65—low	1.02

	2000	1999	1998	1997	1996	1995	1994	1993	1992	1991
Return (%)	-6.1	34.7	18.0	17.9	—	—	—	—	—	—
Differ from Category (+/-)	-0.1	-22.8	2.9	3.1	—	—	—	—	—	—
Return, Tax-Adjusted (%)	-7.7	31.6	17.5	16.7	—	—	—	—	—	—

PER SHARE DATA

	2000	1999	1998	1997	1996	1995	1994	1993	1992	1991
Dividends, Net Income ($)	0.02	0.04	0.02	0.00	—	—	—	—	—	—
Distrib'ns, Cap Gain ($)	1.25	1.99	0.24	0.61	—	—	—	—	—	—
Net Asset Value ($)	13.61	15.82	13.37	11.56	—	—	—	—	—	—
Expense Ratio (%)	1.02	0.86	0.88	1.24	—	—	—	—	—	—
Yield (%)	0.13	0.22	0.14	0.00	—	—	—	—	—	—
Portfolio Turnover (%)	94	128	334	—	—	—	—	—	—	—
Total Assets (Millions $)	65	61	50	82	—	—	—	—	—	—

PORTFOLIO (as of 6/30/00)

Portfolio Manager: Tim Krochuck - 1996

Investm't Category: Aggressive Growth

✔ Domestic — Index
✔ Foreign — Sector
Asset Allocation — State Specific

Investment Style

✔ Large Cap — ✔ Mid Cap — Small Cap
✔ Growth — Grth/Val — Value

Portfolio

5.2%	cash	0.0%	corp bonds
94.8%	stocks	0.0%	gov't bonds
0.0%	pref/conv't pref	0.0%	muni bonds
0.0%	conv't bds/wrnts	0.0%	other

SHAREHOLDER INFORMATION

Minimum Investment
Initial: $2,500 — Subsequent: $250

Minimum IRA Investment
Initial: $500 — Subsequent: $250

Maximum Fees
Load: 0.75% redemption — 12b-1: none
Other: redemption fee applies for 1 month

Services
✔ IRA
✔ Keogh
✔ Telephone Exchange

Fidelity Trend (FTRNX)

800-544-8888, 801-534-1910
www.fidelity.com

Growth

PERFORMANCE — fund inception date: 6/16/58

	3yr Annual	5yr Annual	10yr Annual	Bull	Bear
Return (%)	10.3	11.2	13.9	82.0	-13.7
Differ from Category (+/-)	-0.7 av	-4.9 low	-2.9 blw av	32.3 high	-8.3 blw av

Standard Deviation	Category Risk Index	Beta
25.1%—abv av	1.29—high	1.20

	2000	1999	1998	1997	1996	1995	1994	1993	1992	1991
Return (%)	-7.1	40.8	2.7	8.5	16.9	22.1	-6.6	19.1	16.7	36.2
Differ from Category (+/-)	-10.6	21.9	-11.6	-18.6	-5.4	-8.3	-6.4	4.5	4.1	-1.4
Return, Tax-Adjusted (%)	-10.2	38.4	2.7	5.9	14.4	16.6	-8.5	16.2	14.6	34.5

PER SHARE DATA

	2000	1999	1998	1997	1996	1995	1994	1993	1992	1991
Dividends, Net Income ($)	0.69	0.20	0.00	0.05	0.45	0.39	0.16	0.27	0.44	0.48
Distrib'ns, Cap Gain ($)	9.85	6.15	0.00	7.19	4.02	9.29	3.89	5.06	3.23	1.79
Net Asset Value ($)	56.41	71.72	55.60	54.10	56.81	52.48	50.99	59.08	54.20	49.63
Expense Ratio (%)	na	0.58	0.62	0.59	0.64	0.89	1.04	0.92	0.56	0.53
Yield (%)	1.04	0.25	0.00	0.08	0.73	0.63	0.29	0.42	0.76	0.93
Portfolio Turnover (%)	na	309	348	334	142	146	29	50	47	57
Total Assets (Millions $)	1,245	1,533	1,198	1,428	1,333	1,274	1,193	1,393	1,115	900

PORTFOLIO (as of 6/30/00)

Portfolio Manager: Ramin Arani - 2000

Investm't Category: Growth

✔ Domestic — Index
✔ Foreign — Sector
Asset Allocation — State Specific

Investment Style

Large Cap — ✔ Mid Cap — ✔ Small Cap
✔ Growth — Grth/Val — Value

Portfolio

1.0%	cash	0.0%	corp bonds
99.0%	stocks	0.0%	gov't bonds
0.0%	pref/conv't pref	0.0%	muni bonds
0.0%	conv't bds/wrnts	0.0%	other

SHAREHOLDER INFORMATION

Minimum Investment
Initial: $2,500 — Subsequent: $250

Minimum IRA Investment
Initial: $500 — Subsequent: $250

Maximum Fees
Load: none — 12b-1: none
Other: none

Services
✔ IRA
✔ Keogh
✔ Telephone Exchange

Fidelity Utilities (FIUIX)

800-544-8888, 801-534-1910
www.fidelity.com

Growth & Income

PERFORMANCE — fund inception date: 11/27/87

	3yr Annual	5yr Annual	10yr Annual	Bull	Bear
Return (%)	9.0	13.7	13.8	64.3	-27.3
Differ from Category (+/-)	0.1 av	-0.6 blw av	-1.1 blw av	30.8 high	-27.2 low

Standard Deviation	Category Risk Index	Beta
18.4%—av	1.06—abv av	0.82

	2000	1999	1998	1997	1996	1995	1994	1993	1992	1991
Return (%)	-20.4	26.7	28.5	31.5	11.4	30.6	-5.2	15.6	10.9	21.1
Differ from Category (+/-)	-26.1	15.9	15.7	4.6	-8.3	1.1	-4.7	1.8	-0.7	-7.0
Return, Tax-Adjusted (%)	-24.2	23.7	26.4	27.8	9.2	28.3	-8.0	13.6	8.7	19.0

PER SHARE DATA

	2000	1999	1998	1997	1996	1995	1994	1993	1992	1991
Dividends, Net Income ($)	0.09	0.18	0.35	0.44	0.48	0.54	0.54	0.52	0.60	0.63
Distrib'ns, Cap Gain ($)	4.73	3.05	1.29	2.20	0.54	0.28	0.80	0.22	0.38	0.18
Net Asset Value ($)	16.09	25.77	23.18	19.46	16.91	16.16	13.06	15.18	13.79	13.38
Expense Ratio (%)	0.80	0.85	0.81	0.81	0.77	0.87	0.86	0.87	0.95	0.94
Yield (%)	0.43	0.62	1.43	2.03	2.75	3.28	3.89	3.37	4.23	4.64
Portfolio Turnover (%)	50	55	57	56	98	98	47	73	39	43
Total Assets (Millions $)	2,269	2,884	2,128	1,708	1,267	1,510	1,079	1,456	962	620

PORTFOLIO (as of 6/30/00)

Portfolio Manager: Tim Cohen - 2000

Investm't Category: Growth & Income

✔ Domestic
Index
✔ Foreign
✔ Sector
Asset Allocation
State Specific

Investment Style

✔ Large Cap
✔ Mid Cap
Small Cap
Growth
✔ Grth/Val
Value

Portfolio

9.6% cash
90.4% stocks
0.0% pref/conv't pref
0.0% conv't bds/wrnts
0.0% corp bonds
0.0% gov't bonds
0.0% muni bonds
0.0% other

SHAREHOLDER INFORMATION

Minimum Investment

Initial: $2,500 Subsequent: $250

Minimum IRA Investment

Initial: $500 Subsequent: $250

Maximum Fees

Load: none 12b-1: none
Other: none

Services

✔ IRA
✔ Keogh
✔ Telephone Exchange

Fidelity Value (FDVLX)

800-544-8544, 801-534-1910
www.fidelity.com

Growth

PERFORMANCE

fund inception date: 12/1/78

	3yr Annual	5yr Annual	10yr Annual	Bull	Bear
Return (%)	5.5	10.7	15.6	26.2	4.0
Differ from Category (+/-)	-5.5 low	-5.4 low	-1.2 blw av	-23.5 blw av	9.4 abv av

Standard Deviation	Category Risk Index	Beta
21.7%—abv av	1.12—abv av	0.77

	2000	1999	1998	1997	1996	1995	1994	1993	1992	1991
Return (%)	8.1	8.5	0.1	21.0	16.8	27.1	7.6	22.9	21.1	26.1
Differ from Category (+/-)	4.6	-10.4	-14.2	-6.1	-5.5	-3.3	7.8	8.3	8.5	-11.5
Return, Tax-Adjusted (%)	7.2	5.4	-2.9	17.5	13.0	25.4	5.8	20.3	20.7	25.0

PER SHARE DATA

	2000	1999	1998	1997	1996	1995	1994	1993	1992	1991
Dividends, Net Income ($)	0.95	0.73	0.55	0.48	0.53	0.48	0.17	0.34	0.23	0.85
Distrib'ns, Cap Gain ($)	0.00	5.62	7.15	7.95	5.92	1.73	2.28	2.80	0.15	0.00
Net Asset Value ($)	46.35	43.81	46.35	54.04	51.54	49.64	40.81	40.23	35.35	29.50
Expense Ratio (%)	0.48	0.54	0.61	0.66	0.88	1.01	1.08	1.11	1.00	0.98
Yield (%)	2.04	1.47	1.02	0.77	0.92	0.93	0.39	0.79	0.64	2.88
Portfolio Turnover (%)	48	50	36	56	112	113	112	117	81	137
Total Assets (Millions $)	3,202	4,383	5,522	7,913	7,080	5,745	3,720	1,716	667	123

PORTFOLIO (as of 6/30/00)

Portfolio Manager: Richard Fentin - 1996

Investm't Category: Growth

✔ Domestic — Index
✔ Foreign — Sector
Asset Allocation — State Specific

Investment Style

✔ Large Cap — ✔ Mid Cap — Small Cap
Growth — Grth/Val — ✔ Value

Portfolio

4.9%	cash	0.0%	corp bonds
94.0%	stocks	0.0%	gov't bonds
0.0%	pref/conv't pref	0.0%	muni bonds
1.1%	conv't bds/wrnts	0.0%	other

SHAREHOLDER INFORMATION

Minimum Investment

Initial: $2,500 — Subsequent: $250

Minimum IRA Investment

Initial: $500 — Subsequent: $250

Maximum Fees

Load: none — 12b-1: none
Other: none

Services

✔ IRA
✔ Keogh
✔ Telephone Exchange

Fidelity Worldwide (FWWFX)

800-544-6666, 801-534-1910
www.fidelity.com

International Stock

PERFORMANCE — fund inception date: 5/30/90

	3yr Annual	5yr Annual	10yr Annual	Bull	Bear
Return (%)	8.8	11.4	11.4	49.9	-11.5
Differ from Category (+/-)	-0.1 av	3.1 abv av	2.4 abv av	-41.0 blw av	12.5 high

Standard Deviation	Category Risk Index	Beta
17.6%—av	0.78—blw av	0.82

	2000	1999	1998	1997	1996	1995	1994	1993	1992	1991
Return (%)	-8.0	30.7	7.1	12.0	18.7	7.1	2.9	36.5	6.2	7.8
Differ from Category (+/-)	11.4	-30.0	1.3	10.7	4.2	-2.2	6.0	-3.7	9.7	-5.2
Return, Tax-Adjusted (%)	-11.0	28.6	6.2	10.2	17.4	6.6	1.2	35.6	5.3	7.4

PER SHARE DATA

	2000	1999	1998	1997	1996	1995	1994	1993	1992	1991
Dividends, Net Income ($)	0.40	0.10	0.10	0.11	0.17	0.15	0.07	0.10	0.26	0.10
Distrib'ns, Cap Gain ($)	2.25	1.52	0.44	1.16	0.38	0.00	0.66	0.15	0.00	0.00
Net Asset Value ($)	15.63	19.90	16.53	15.95	15.39	13.44	12.68	13.03	9.73	9.41
Expense Ratio (%)	1.04	1.07	1.12	1.16	1.18	1.17	1.32	1.40	1.51	1.69
Yield (%)	2.23	0.46	0.58	0.64	1.07	1.11	0.52	0.75	2.67	1.06
Portfolio Turnover (%)	235	164	100	85	49	49	69	57	130	129
Total Assets (Millions $)	925	1,125	1,013	1,145	925	654	703	339	98	100

PORTFOLIO (as of 6/30/00)

Portfolio Manager: Penelope Dobkin - 1990

Investm't Category: International Stock

✔ Domestic — Index
✔ Foreign — Sector
Asset Allocation — State Specific

Investment Style

Large Cap — Mid Cap — Small Cap
Growth — Grth/Val — Value

Portfolio

7.1%	cash	0.0%	corp bonds
92.9%	stocks	0.0%	gov't bonds
0.0%	pref/conv't pref	0.0%	muni bonds
0.0%	conv't bds/wrnts	0.0%	other

SHAREHOLDER INFORMATION

Minimum Investment
Initial: $2,500 — Subsequent: $250

Minimum IRA Investment
Initial: $500 — Subsequent: $250

Maximum Fees
Load: 0.01% redemption — 12b-1: none
Other: redemption fee applies for 1 month

Services
✔ IRA
✔ Keogh
✔ Telephone Exchange

First Eagle of Am/Y (FEAFX)

800-482-5667, 212-698-3000
www.firsteaglefunds.com

Growth

PERFORMANCE — fund inception date: 4/10/87

	3yr Annual	5yr Annual	10yr Annual	Bull	Bear
Return (%)	10.8	17.9	18.8	40.0	-0.5
Differ from Category (+/-)	-0.2 av	1.8 av	2.0 abv av	-9.7 av	4.9 abv av

Standard Deviation	Category Risk Index	Beta
16.9%—av	0.87—low	0.81

	2000	1999	1998	1997	1996	1995	1994	1993	1992	1991
Return (%)	0.3	12.0	20.9	29.4	29.3	36.3	-2.5	23.8	24.3	20.9
Differ from Category (+/-)	-3.2	-6.9	6.6	2.3	7.0	5.9	-2.3	9.2	11.7	-16.7
Return, Tax-Adjusted (%)	0.1	8.9	18.9	24.9	24.1	35.5	-6.2	20.4	21.5	18.6

PER SHARE DATA

	2000	1999	1998	1997	1996	1995	1994	1993	1992	1991
Dividends, Net Income ($)	0.00	0.00	0.00	0.00	0.00	0.00	0.00	0.00	0.00	0.08
Distrib'ns, Cap Gain ($)	0.14	3.29	1.84	4.10	3.13	0.35	2.00	1.62	1.17	0.74
Net Asset Value ($)	20.47	20.56	21.43	19.33	18.30	16.96	12.70	15.04	13.48	11.85
Expense Ratio (%)	1.40	1.40	1.50	1.70	1.80	0.90	1.90	2.90	3.00	2.00
Yield (%)	0.00	0.00	0.00	0.00	0.00	0.00	0.00	0.00	0.00	0.63
Portfolio Turnover (%)	55	89	83	98	93	44	125	141	145	92
Total Assets (Millions $)	368	528	456	268	171	132	105	108	85	74

PORTFOLIO (as of 6/30/00)

Portfolio Manager: Harold Levy, David Cohen - 1987

Investm't Category: Growth

✔ Domestic — Index
✔ Foreign — Sector
Asset Allocation — State Specific

Investment Style

✔ Large Cap — Mid Cap — Small Cap
Growth — Grth/Val — ✔ Value

Portfolio

4.4%	cash	0.0%	corp bonds
95.6%	stocks	0.0%	gov't bonds
0.0%	pref/conv't pref	0.0%	muni bonds
0.0%	conv't bds/wrnts	0.0%	other

SHAREHOLDER INFORMATION

Minimum Investment
Initial: $1,000 — Subsequent: $100

Minimum IRA Investment
Initial: $500 — Subsequent: $1

Maximum Fees
Load: none — 12b-1: none
Other: none

Services

✔ IRA
✔ Keogh
✔ Telephone Exchange

Firsthand: Tech Value

888-883-3863, 408-294-2200
www.firsthandfunds.com

(TVFQX)

Aggressive Growth

PERFORMANCE — fund inception date: 5/20/94

	3yr Annual	5yr Annual	10yr Annual	Bull	Bear
Return (%)	47.8	40.7	na	370.0	-40.1
Differ from Category (+/-)	31.6 high	26.1 high	na	250.8 high	-19.5 low

Standard Deviation	Category Risk Index	Beta
49.7%—high	1.53—high	1.64

	2000	1999	1998	1997	1996	1995	1994	1993	1992	1991
Return (%)	-9.9	190.4	23.7	6.4	60.5	61.1	—	—	—	—
Differ from Category (+/-)	-3.9	132.9	8.6	-8.4	42.2	26.5	—	—	—	—
Return, Tax-Adjusted (%)	-11.6	188.7	23.7	4.7	56.0	60.1	—	—	—	—

PER SHARE DATA

	2000	1999	1998	1997	1996	1995	1994	1993	1992	1991
Dividends, Net Income ($)	0.00	0.00	0.00	0.00	0.00	0.00	—	—	—	—
Distrib'ns, Cap Gain ($)	7.86	2.72	0.00	2.23	2.90	0.40	—	—	—	—
Net Asset Value ($)	74.33	90.52	32.24	26.06	26.66	18.44	—	—	—	—
Expense Ratio (%)	na	1.91	1.95	1.93	1.81	1.98	—	—	—	—
Yield (%)	0.00	0.00	0.00	0.00	0.00	0.00	—	—	—	—
Portfolio Turnover (%)	na	41	126	101	43	45	—	—	—	—
Total Assets (Millions $)	2,904	1,355	178	194	35	2	—	—	—	—

PORTFOLIO (as of 6/30/00)

Portfolio Manager: Kevin Landis - 1994

Investm't Category: Aggressive Growth

✔ Domestic — Index
✔ Foreign — ✔ Sector
Asset Allocation — State Specific

Investment Style

Large Cap — Mid Cap — ✔ Small Cap
✔ Growth — Grth/Val — Value

Portfolio

10.9%	cash	0.0%	corp bonds
89.1%	stocks	0.0%	gov't bonds
0.0%	pref/conv't pref	0.0%	muni bonds
0.0%	conv't bds/wrnts	0.0%	other

SHAREHOLDER INFORMATION

Minimum Investment

Initial: $10,000 — Subsequent: $50

Minimum IRA Investment

Initial: $2,000 — Subsequent: $50

Maximum Fees

Load: 2.00% redemption — 12b-1: none
Other: redemption fee applies for 6 months

Services

✔ IRA
✔ Keogh
✔ Telephone Exchange

Flex-fund: Muirfield (FLMFX)

800-325-3539, 614-766-7000
www.flexfunds.com

Growth & Income

PERFORMANCE

fund inception date: 8/10/88

	3yr Annual	5yr Annual	10yr Annual	Bull	Bear
Return (%)	7.9	9.5	11.8	46.5	-20.2
Differ from Category (+/-)	-1.0 blw av	-4.8 low	-3.1 low	13.0 abv av	-20.1 low

Standard Deviation	Category Risk Index	Beta
15.1%—av	0.87—blw av	0.54

	2000	1999	1998	1997	1996	1995	1994	1993	1992	1991
Return (%)	-16.5	15.2	30.6	18.5	5.7	25.8	2.7	8.0	6.9	29.8
Differ from Category (+/-)	-22.2	4.4	17.8	-8.4	-14.0	-3.7	3.2	-5.8	-4.7	1.7
Return, Tax-Adjusted (%)	-18.1	10.5	29.6	14.4	2.6	20.6	1.6	0.8	4.3	28.1

PER SHARE DATA

	2000	1999	1998	1997	1996	1995	1994	1993	1992	1991
Dividends, Net Income ($)	0.19	0.09	0.10	0.10	0.09	0.05	0.13	0.65	0.06	0.27
Distrib'ns, Cap Gain ($)	0.14	1.45	0.07	0.90	0.50	0.92	0.02	0.67	0.52	0.00
Net Asset Value ($)	4.95	6.32	6.95	5.47	5.47	5.73	5.34	5.36	6.25	6.43
Expense Ratio (%)	na	1.21	1.24	1.29	1.19	1.27	1.22	1.26	1.40	1.50
Yield (%)	3.73	1.15	1.42	1.56	1.50	0.75	2.42	10.77	0.88	4.19
Portfolio Turnover (%)	na	787	128	395	297	186	168	280	324	107
Total Assets (Millions $)	104	155	123	111	106	93	81	64	62	43

PORTFOLIO (as of 6/30/00)

Portfolio Manager: Robert Meeder - 1988

Investm't Category: Growth & Income

✔ Domestic	Index
Foreign	Sector
✔ Asset Allocation	State Specific

Investment Style

✔ Large Cap	✔ Mid Cap	Small Cap
✔ Growth	Grth/Val	Value

Portfolio

59.4%	cash	0.0%	corp bonds
29.3%	stocks	0.0%	gov't bonds
0.0%	pref/conv't pref	0.0%	muni bonds
0.0%	conv't bds/wrnts	11.3%	other

SHAREHOLDER INFORMATION

Minimum Investment
Initial: $2,500 Subsequent: $100

Minimum IRA Investment
Initial: $500 Subsequent: $100

Maximum Fees
Load: none 12b-1: 0.16%
Other: none

Services
✔ IRA
✔ Keogh
✔ Telephone Exchange

Founders: Large Cap Gr (FRGRX)

800-525-2440, 303-394-4404
www.founders.com

Growth

this fund is closed to new investors

PERFORMANCE — fund inception date: 4/3/63

	3yr Annual	5yr Annual	10yr Annual	Bull	Bear
Return (%)	8.1	13.3	17.6	78.8	-32.6
Differ from Category (+/-)	-2.9 blw av	-2.8 blw av	0.8 av	29.1 high	-27.2 low

Standard Deviation	Category Risk Index	Beta
26.0%—high	1.33—high	1.16

	2000	1999	1998	1997	1996	1995	1994	1993	1992	1991
Return (%)	-27.2	39.0	25.0	26.5	16.5	45.5	-3.3	25.5	4.3	47.3
Differ from Category (+/-)	-30.7	20.1	10.7	-0.6	-5.8	15.1	-3.1	10.9	-8.3	9.7
Return, Tax-Adjusted (%)	-30.0	34.9	23.6	22.9	14.0	40.3	-4.0	23.2	1.4	44.1

PER SHARE DATA

	2000	1999	1998	1997	1996	1995	1994	1993	1992	1991
Dividends, Net Income ($)	0.00	0.00	0.01	0.06	0.01	0.01	0.00	0.00	0.11	0.06
Distrib'ns, Cap Gain ($)	3.41	4.17	1.13	2.68	1.30	2.13	0.33	0.84	1.04	0.87
Net Asset Value ($)	14.03	23.87	20.41	17.28	15.87	14.77	11.63	12.38	10.54	11.22
Expense Ratio (%)	na	1.08	1.08	1.10	1.19	1.32	1.33	1.32	1.54	1.45
Yield (%)	0.00	0.00	0.04	0.30	0.05	0.05	0.00	0.00	0.94	0.49
Portfolio Turnover (%)	na	117	143	189	134	134	172	131	216	161
Total Assets (Millions $)	2,278	3,325	2,377	1,758	1,032	651	310	343	145	139

PORTFOLIO (as of 3/31/00)

Portfolio Manager: Thomas Arrington, Scott Chapman - 1998

Investm't Category: Growth

✔ Domestic	Index
✔ Foreign	Sector
Asset Allocation	State Specific

Investment Style

✔ Large Cap	Mid Cap	Small Cap
✔ Growth	Grth/Val	Value

Portfolio

3.6% cash	0.0% corp bonds
96.4% stocks	0.0% gov't bonds
0.0% pref/conv't pref	0.0% muni bonds
0.0% conv't bds/wrnts	0.0% other

SHAREHOLDER INFORMATION

Minimum Investment
Initial: $1,000 — Subsequent: $100

Minimum IRA Investment
Initial: $500 — Subsequent: $100

Maximum Fees
Load: none — 12b-1: 0.25%
Other: none

Services
✔ IRA
✔ Keogh
✔ Telephone Exchange

Fremont: Global (FMAFX)

800-548-4539, 415-284-8900
www.fremontfunds.com

International Stock

PERFORMANCE — fund inception date: 11/18/88

	3yr Annual	5yr Annual	10yr Annual	Bull	Bear
Return (%)	7.9	9.5	10.3	41.9	-11.9
Differ from Category (+/-)	-1.0 blw av	1.2 av	1.3 abv av	-49.0 low	12.1 high

Standard Deviation	Category Risk Index	Beta
12.9%—blw av	0.57—low	0.62

	2000	1999	1998	1997	1996	1995	1994	1993	1992	1991
Return (%)	-6.6	22.3	10.0	9.9	13.9	19.2	-4.1	19.5	5.2	18.6
Differ from Category (+/-)	12.8	-38.4	4.2	8.6	-0.6	9.9	-1.0	-20.7	8.7	5.6
Return, Tax-Adjusted (%)	-9.7	19.0	7.7	7.6	8.9	16.4	-4.7	18.2	3.7	17.4

PER SHARE DATA

	2000	1999	1998	1997	1996	1995	1994	1993	1992	1991
Dividends, Net Income ($)	0.61	0.49	0.31	0.47	0.49	0.49	0.13	0.33	0.43	0.36
Distrib'ns, Cap Gain ($)	1.22	1.30	0.97	0.60	1.80	0.57	0.13	0.06	0.15	0.03
Net Asset Value ($)	12.50	15.30	14.11	14.04	13.77	14.16	12.79	13.62	11.74	11.74
Expense Ratio (%)	na	0.86	0.85	0.85	0.87	0.89	0.95	0.99	1.09	1.12
Yield (%)	4.44	2.95	2.05	3.21	3.14	3.32	1.00	2.41	3.61	3.05
Portfolio Turnover (%)	na	113	75	48	71	70	52	40	50	81
Total Assets (Millions $)	734	772	646	661	596	502	438	214	109	85

PORTFOLIO (as of 6/30/00)

Portfolio Manager: committee - 1988

Investm't Category: International Stock

✔ Domestic — Index
✔ Foreign — Sector
✔ Asset Allocation — State Specific

Investment Style

Large Cap — Mid Cap — Small Cap
Growth — Grth/Val — Value

Portfolio

6.7%	cash	27.9%	corp bonds
65.4%	stocks	0.0%	gov't bonds
0.0%	pref/conv't pref	0.0%	muni bonds
0.0%	conv't bds/wrnts	0.0%	other

SHAREHOLDER INFORMATION

Minimum Investment
Initial: $2,000 — Subsequent: $100

Minimum IRA Investment
Initial: $1,000 — Subsequent: $100

Maximum Fees
Load: none — 12b-1: none
Other: none

Services
✔ IRA
✔ Keogh
✔ Telephone Exchange

Fremont: Growth (FEQFX)

800-548-4539, 415-284-8900
www.fremontfunds.com

Growth

PERFORMANCE — fund inception date: 8/14/92

	3yr Annual	5yr Annual	10yr Annual	Bull	Bear
Return (%)	7.6	15.0	na	54.7	-10.9
Differ from Category (+/-)	-3.4 blw av	-1.1 blw av	na	5.0 av	-5.5 av

Standard Deviation	Category Risk Index	Beta
19.3%—abv av	0.99—av	1.06

	2000	1999	1998	1997	1996	1995	1994	1993	1992	1991
Return (%)	-8.1	17.1	15.8	28.9	25.0	33.6	0.4	6.4	—	—
Differ from Category (+/-)	-11.6	-1.8	1.5	1.8	2.7	3.2	0.6	-8.2	—	—
Return, Tax-Adjusted (%)	-9.5	14.5	12.5	27.1	18.1	31.3	-2.6	5.8	—	—

PER SHARE DATA

	2000	1999	1998	1997	1996	1995	1994	1993	1992	1991
Dividends, Net Income ($)	0.10	0.12	0.20	0.16	0.13	0.07	0.22	0.16	—	—
Distrib'ns, Cap Gain ($)	0.99	1.73	2.14	0.82	2.95	0.70	0.90	0.00	—	—
Net Asset Value ($)	13.56	15.95	15.35	15.43	12.76	12.73	10.11	11.18	—	—
Expense Ratio (%)	na	0.82	0.82	0.85	0.92	1.08	0.94	0.87	—	—
Yield (%)	0.68	0.67	1.14	0.98	0.82	0.52	1.99	1.43	—	—
Portfolio Turnover (%)	na	80	111	48	129	91	55	44	—	—
Total Assets (Millions $)	113	149	164	155	96	66	23	42	—	—

PORTFOLIO (as of 6/30/00)

Portfolio Manager: K. Copa, D. McNeil, P. Landini - 1995

Investm't Category: Growth

✔ Domestic   Index
✔ Foreign   Sector
Asset Allocation   State Specific

Investment Style

✔ Large Cap   Mid Cap   Small Cap
Growth   ✔ Grth/Val   Value

Portfolio

4.7%	cash	0.0%	corp bonds
95.3%	stocks	0.0%	gov't bonds
0.0%	pref/conv't pref	0.0%	muni bonds
0.0%	conv't bds/wrnts	0.0%	other

SHAREHOLDER INFORMATION

Minimum Investment
Initial: $2,000   Subsequent: $100

Minimum IRA Investment
Initial: $1,000   Subsequent: $100

Maximum Fees
Load: none   12b-1: none
Other: none

Services
✔ IRA
✔ Keogh
✔ Telephone Exchange

Fremont: Intl Growth (FIGFX)

800-548-4539, 415-284-8900
www.fremontfunds.com

International Stock

PERFORMANCE — fund inception date: 3/1/94

	3yr Annual	5yr Annual	10yr Annual	Bull	Bear
Return (%)	10.1	6.6	na	83.4	-25.6
Differ from Category (+/-)	1.2 av	-1.7 blw av	na	-7.5 av	-1.6 av

Standard Deviation	Category Risk Index	Beta
19.3%—abv av	0.85—blw av	0.84

	2000	1999	1998	1997	1996	1995	1994	1993	1992	1991
Return (%)	-22.7	57.3	9.8	-8.3	13.0	7.2	—	—	—	—
Differ from Category (+/-)	-3.3	-3.4	4.0	-9.6	-1.5	-2.1	—	—	—	—
Return, Tax-Adjusted (%)	-23.9	56.2	8.0	-8.4	12.9	6.8	—	—	—	—

PER SHARE DATA

	2000	1999	1998	1997	1996	1995	1994	1993	1992	1991
Dividends, Net Income ($)	0.00	0.02	0.00	0.00	0.00	0.08	—	—	—	—
Distrib'ns, Cap Gain ($)	0.98	0.51	0.90	0.10	0.03	0.00	—	—	—	—
Net Asset Value ($)	10.84	15.28	10.10	10.06	11.10	9.85	—	—	—	—
Expense Ratio (%)	na	1.50	1.50	1.50	1.50	1.50	—	—	—	—
Yield (%)	0.00	0.12	0.00	0.00	0.00	0.81	—	—	—	—
Portfolio Turnover (%)	na	76	106	95	74	32	—	—	—	—
Total Assets (Millions $)	68	76	44	36	38	34	—	—	—	—

PORTFOLIO (as of 6/30/00)

Portfolio Manager: committee - 1998

Investm't Category: International Stock

Domestic	Index
✔ Foreign	Sector
Asset Allocation	State Specific

Investment Style

Large Cap	Mid Cap	Small Cap
Growth	Grth/Val	Value

Portfolio

4.4%	cash	0.0%	corp bonds
95.6%	stocks	0.0%	gov't bonds
0.0%	pref/conv't pref	0.0%	muni bonds
0.0%	conv't bds/wrnts	0.0%	other

SHAREHOLDER INFORMATION

Minimum Investment
Initial: $2,000 Subsequent: $100

Minimum IRA Investment
Initial: $1,000 Subsequent: $100

Maximum Fees
Load: none 12b-1: 0.25%
Other: none

Services
✔ IRA
✔ Keogh
✔ Telephone Exchange

Fremont: US Micro Cap (FUSMX)

800-548-4539, 415-284-8900
www.fremontfunds.com

Aggressive Growth

this fund is closed to new investors

PERFORMANCE — fund inception date: 6/30/94

	3yr Annual	5yr Annual	10yr Annual	Bull	Bear
Return (%)	28.2	27.4	na	238.8	-27.4
Differ from Category (+/-)	12.0 high	12.8 high	na	119.6 high	-6.8 blw av

Standard Deviation	Category Risk Index	Beta
38.1%—high	1.17—abv av	1.13

	2000	1999	1998	1997	1996	1995	1994	1993	1992	1991
Return (%)	-10.6	129.5	2.8	6.9	48.7	54.0	—	—	—	—
Differ from Category (+/-)	-4.6	72.0	-12.3	-7.9	30.4	19.4	—	—	—	—
Return, Tax-Adjusted (%)	-15.3	123.8	2.8	4.3	47.0	52.6	—	—	—	—

PER SHARE DATA

	2000	1999	1998	1997	1996	1995	1994	1993	1992	1991
Dividends, Net Income ($)	0.02	0.00	0.00	0.00	0.00	0.00	—	—	—	—
Distrib'ns, Cap Gain ($)	9.23	5.85	0.00	2.76	0.91	0.50	—	—	—	—
Net Asset Value ($)	26.87	39.35	20.86	20.28	21.50	15.10	—	—	—	—
Expense Ratio (%)	na	1.82	1.94	1.88	1.96	2.04	—	—	—	—
Yield (%)	0.05	0.00	0.00	0.00	0.00	0.00	—	—	—	—
Portfolio Turnover (%)	na	164	170	125	81	144	—	—	—	—
Total Assets (Millions $)	663	574	164	166	142	9	—	—	—	—

PORTFOLIO (as of 6/30/00)

Portfolio Manager: Robert Kern - 1994

Investm't Category: Aggressive Growth

✔ Domestic Index
✔ Foreign Sector
Asset Allocation State Specific

Investment Style

Large Cap Mid Cap ✔ Small Cap
✔ Growth Grth/Val Value

Portfolio

29.4%	cash	0.0%	corp bonds
70.6%	stocks	0.0%	gov't bonds
0.0%	pref/conv't pref	0.0%	muni bonds
0.0%	conv't bds/wrnts	0.0%	other

SHAREHOLDER INFORMATION

Minimum Investment
Initial: $2,000 Subsequent: $100

Minimum IRA Investment
Initial: $1,000 Subsequent: $100

Maximum Fees
Load: none 12b-1: none
Other: none

Services
✔ IRA
✔ Keogh
✔ Telephone Exchange

Gabelli Asset (GABAX)

800-422-3554, 914-921-5100
www.gabelli.com

Growth

PERFORMANCE — fund inception date: 3/3/86

	3yr Annual	5yr Annual	10yr Annual	Bull	Bear
Return (%)	13.2	17.8	16.7	57.9	-5.5
Differ from Category (+/-)	2.2 abv av	1.7 av	-0.1 av	8.2 av	-0.1 av

Standard Deviation	Category Risk Index	Beta
15.3%—av	0.79—low	0.80

	2000	1999	1998	1997	1996	1995	1994	1993	1992	1991
Return (%)	-2.3	28.4	15.8	38.0	13.3	24.9	-0.1	21.8	14.8	18.1
Differ from Category (+/-)	-5.8	9.5	1.5	10.9	-9.0	-5.5	0.1	7.2	2.2	-19.5
Return, Tax-Adjusted (%)	-5.3	25.7	14.9	34.4	10.2	22.2	-1.4	20.4	13.5	17.1

PER SHARE DATA

	2000	1999	1998	1997	1996	1995	1994	1993	1992	1991
Dividends, Net Income ($)	0.30	0.00	0.01	0.07	0.15	0.25	0.26	0.16	0.25	0.38
Distrib'ns, Cap Gain ($)	5.57	4.63	1.40	4.54	2.61	1.74	0.79	0.75	0.50	0.12
Net Asset Value ($)	33.90	40.84	35.47	31.85	26.42	25.75	22.21	23.30	19.88	17.96
Expense Ratio (%)	na	1.37	1.36	1.37	1.34	1.33	1.28	1.31	1.31	1.30
Yield (%)	0.76	0.00	0.02	0.19	0.51	0.90	1.13	0.66	1.22	2.10
Portfolio Turnover (%)	na	32	21	22	14	26	18	16	14	20
Total Assets (Millions $)	1,894	1,993	1,593	1,334	1,081	1,090	940	948	631	485

PORTFOLIO (as of 6/30/00)

Portfolio Manager: Mario Gabelli - 1986

Investm't Category: Growth

✔ Domestic	Index
✔ Foreign	Sector
Asset Allocation	State Specific

Investment Style

✔ Large Cap	Mid Cap	Small Cap
Growth	Grth/Val	✔ Value

Portfolio

8.8%	cash	0.0%	corp bonds
91.1%	stocks	0.0%	gov't bonds
0.1%	pref/conv't pref	0.0%	muni bonds
0.0%	conv't bds/wrnts	0.0%	other

SHAREHOLDER INFORMATION

Minimum Investment
Initial: $1,000 Subsequent: $1

Minimum IRA Investment
Initial: $250 Subsequent: $1

Maximum Fees
Load: none 12b-1: 0.25%
Other: none

Services
✔ IRA
Keogh
✔ Telephone Exchange

Gabelli Eq: Eqty Inc/AAA (GABEX)

800-422-3554, 914-921-5100
www.gabelli.com

Growth & Income

PERFORMANCE — fund inception date: 1/1/92

	3yr Annual	5yr Annual	10yr Annual	Bull	Bear
Return (%)	11.0	15.6	na	28.8	5.7
Differ from Category (+/-)	2.1 abv av	1.3 av	na	-4.7 av	5.8 abv av

Standard Deviation	Category Risk Index	Beta
12.9%—blw av	0.74—low	0.57

	2000	1999	1998	1997	1996	1995	1994	1993	1992	1991
Return (%)	11.3	9.3	12.6	27.8	17.8	28.3	1.0	17.8	—	—
Differ from Category (+/-)	5.6	-1.5	-0.2	0.9	-1.9	-1.2	1.5	4.0	—	—
Return, Tax-Adjusted (%)	7.5	6.1	10.6	24.6	15.4	25.6	-1.6	14.9	—	—

PER SHARE DATA

	2000	1999	1998	1997	1996	1995	1994	1993	1992	1991
Dividends, Net Income ($)	0.47	0.23	0.14	0.27	0.26	0.29	0.31	0.28	—	—
Distrib'ns, Cap Gain ($)	2.07	2.14	1.27	1.67	0.70	0.60	0.65	0.68	—	—
Net Asset Value ($)	14.91	15.80	16.70	16.12	14.16	12.84	10.72	11.57	—	—
Expense Ratio (%)	1.66	1.32	1.27	1.78	1.93	1.83	1.81	1.78	—	—
Yield (%)	2.76	1.28	0.77	1.51	1.74	2.15	2.72	2.28	—	—
Portfolio Turnover (%)	33	39	35	43	20	30	20	76	—	—
Total Assets (Millions $)	89	88	87	76	60	56	48	54	—	—

PORTFOLIO (as of 6/30/00)

Portfolio Manager: Mario Gabelli - 1992

Investm't Category: Growth & Income

✔ Domestic — Index
✔ Foreign — Sector
Asset Allocation — State Specific

Investment Style

✔ Large Cap — ✔ Mid Cap — Small Cap
Growth — Grth/Val — ✔ Value

Portfolio

4.3%	cash	5.0%	corp bonds
87.2%	stocks	0.0%	gov't bonds
3.5%	pref/conv't pref	0.0%	muni bonds
0.0%	conv't bds/wrnts	0.0%	other

SHAREHOLDER INFORMATION

Minimum Investment
Initial: $1,000 — Subsequent: $1

Minimum IRA Investment
Initial: $250 — Subsequent: $1

Maximum Fees
Load: none — 12b-1: 0.25%
Other: none

Services
✔ IRA
Keogh
✔ Telephone Exchange

Gabelli Eq: Sm Cp Grth/ AAA (GABSX)

800-422-3554, 914-921-5100
www.gabelli.com

Growth

PERFORMANCE — fund inception date: 10/22/91

	3yr Annual	5yr Annual	10yr Annual	Bull	Bear
Return (%)	8.3	14.1	na	31.5	1.5
Differ from Category (+/-)	-2.7 blw av	-2.0 blw av	na	-18.2 blw av	6.9 abv av

Standard Deviation	Category Risk Index	Beta
16.3%—av	0.84—low	0.69

	2000	1999	1998	1997	1996	1995	1994	1993	1992	1991
Return (%)	11.3	14.2	0.0	36.4	11.8	25.1	-2.8	22.7	20.2	—
Differ from Category (+/-)	7.8	-4.7	-14.3	9.3	-10.5	-5.3	-2.6	8.1	7.6	—
Return, Tax-Adjusted (%)	6.8	11.8	-0.4	32.4	8.5	22.7	-4.4	21.8	19.7	—

PER SHARE DATA

	2000	1999	1998	1997	1996	1995	1994	1993	1992	1991
Dividends, Net Income ($)	0.05	0.00	0.00	0.00	0.00	0.00	0.00	0.00	0.02	—
Distrib'ns, Cap Gain ($)	4.72	2.46	0.53	3.66	2.16	1.34	1.03	0.42	0.16	—
Net Asset Value ($)	18.71	21.43	21.01	21.58	18.53	18.50	15.85	17.38	14.50	—
Expense Ratio (%)	1.49	1.56	1.44	1.62	1.58	1.54	1.54	1.64	1.97	—
Yield (%)	0.21	0.00	0.00	0.00	0.00	0.00	0.00	0.00	0.13	—
Portfolio Turnover (%)	47	24	20	14	11	17	18	13	—	—
Total Assets (Millions $)	356	338	321	292	216	228	196	214	123	—

PORTFOLIO (as of 6/30/00)

Portfolio Manager: Mario Gabelli - 1991

Investm't Category: Growth

✔ Domestic	Index
✔ Foreign	Sector
Asset Allocation	State Specific

Investment Style

Large Cap	Mid Cap	✔ Small Cap
Growth	Grth/Val	✔ Value

Portfolio

6.5%	cash	0.0%	corp bonds
93.2%	stocks	0.0%	gov't bonds
0.3%	pref/conv't pref	0.0%	muni bonds
0.0%	conv't bds/wrnts	0.0%	other

SHAREHOLDER INFORMATION

Minimum Investment

Initial: $1,000 — Subsequent: $1

Minimum IRA Investment

Initial: $250 — Subsequent: $1

Maximum Fees

Load: none — 12b-1: 0.25%

Other: none

Services

✔ IRA

Keogh

✔ Telephone Exchange

Gabelli Gl Growth/AAA (GICPX)

800-422-3554, 914-921-5100
www.gabelli.com

International Stock

PERFORMANCE — fund inception date: 2/7/94

	3yr Annual	5yr Annual	10yr Annual	Bull	Bear
Return (%)	20.3	22.6	na	174.5	-38.1
Differ from Category (+/-)	11.4 high	14.3 high	na	83.6 high	-14.1 low

Standard Deviation	Category Risk Index	Beta
27.7%—high	1.22—abv av	1.06

	2000	1999	1998	1997	1996	1995	1994	1993	1992	1991
Return (%)	-37.4	116.0	28.9	41.7	12.5	17.8	—	—	—	—
Differ from Category (+/-)	-18.0	55.3	23.1	40.4	-2.0	8.5	—	—	—	—
Return, Tax-Adjusted (%)	-38.3	114.2	26.8	37.6	9.0	16.8	—	—	—	—

PER SHARE DATA

	2000	1999	1998	1997	1996	1995	1994	1993	1992	1991
Dividends, Net Income ($)	0.00	0.00	0.11	0.00	0.00	0.00	—	—	—	—
Distrib'ns, Cap Gain ($)	1.59	1.46	1.27	2.37	1.43	0.36	—	—	—	—
Net Asset Value ($)	20.37	35.17	16.99	14.28	11.75	11.72	—	—	—	—
Expense Ratio (%)	na	1.58	1.66	1.78	2.06	2.47	—	—	—	—
Yield (%)	0.00	0.00	0.60	0.00	0.00	0.00	—	—	—	—
Portfolio Turnover (%)	na	63	105	68	47	33	—	—	—	—
Total Assets (Millions $)	302	445	73	40	31	31	—	—	—	—

PORTFOLIO (as of 6/30/00)

Portfolio Manager: Marc Gabelli - 1994

Investm't Category: International Stock

✔ Domestic	Index
✔ Foreign	Sector
Asset Allocation	State Specific

Investment Style

Large Cap	Mid Cap	Small Cap
Growth	Grth/Val	Value

Portfolio

5.0%	cash	0.0%	corp bonds
94.2%	stocks	0.0%	gov't bonds
0.8%	pref/conv't pref	0.0%	muni bonds
0.0%	conv't bds/wrnts	0.0%	other

SHAREHOLDER INFORMATION

Minimum Investment
Initial: $1,000 Subsequent: $1

Minimum IRA Investment
Initial: $250 Subsequent: $1

Maximum Fees
Load: none 12b-1: 0.25%
Other: none

Services
✔ IRA
Keogh
✔ Telephone Exchange

Gabelli Gl Telecomm/AAA (GABTX)

800-422-3554, 914-921-5100
www.gabelli.com

International Stock

PERFORMANCE

fund inception date: 11/1/93

	3yr Annual	5yr Annual	10yr Annual	Bull	Bear
Return (%)	22.6	21.5	na	129.6	-26.8
Differ from Category (+/-)	13.7 high	13.2 high	na	38.7 high	-2.8 av

Standard Deviation	Category Risk Index	Beta
21.5%—abv av	0.95—av	0.95

	2000	1999	1998	1997	1996	1995	1994	1993	1992	1991
Return (%)	-24.0	80.2	34.7	31.8	8.9	16.1	-3.6	—	—	—
Differ from Category (+/-)	-4.6	19.5	28.9	30.5	-5.6	6.8	-0.5	—	—	—
Return, Tax-Adjusted (%)	-26.5	76.6	32.7	29.0	6.7	15.5	-3.9	—	—	—

PER SHARE DATA

	2000	1999	1998	1997	1996	1995	1994	1993	1992	1991
Dividends, Net Income ($)	0.63	0.04	0.01	0.00	0.04	0.06	0.06	—	—	—
Distrib'ns, Cap Gain ($)	2.15	2.89	1.29	1.55	0.79	0.11	0.03	—	—	—
Net Asset Value ($)	17.63	26.95	16.62	13.32	11.28	11.12	9.73	—	—	—
Expense Ratio (%)	na	1.48	1.60	1.78	1.72	1.75	1.80	—	—	—
Yield (%)	3.18	0.13	0.05	0.00	0.33	0.53	0.61	—	—	—
Portfolio Turnover (%)	na	60	20	9	7	24	14	—	—	—
Total Assets (Millions $)	348	459	170	117	108	122	137	—	—	—

PORTFOLIO (as of 6/30/00)

Portfolio Manager: Mario Gabelli - 1993

Investm't Category: International Stock

✔ Domestic
Index
✔ Foreign
✔ Sector
Asset Allocation
State Specific

Investment Style

Large Cap
Mid Cap
Small Cap
Growth
Grth/Val
Value

Portfolio

17.0%	cash	0.3%	corp bonds
82.3%	stocks	0.0%	gov't bonds
0.4%	pref/conv't pref	0.0%	muni bonds
0.0%	conv't bds/wrnts	0.0%	other

SHAREHOLDER INFORMATION

Minimum Investment

Initial: $1,000 Subsequent: $1

Minimum IRA Investment

Initial: $250 Subsequent: $1

Maximum Fees

Load: none 12b-1: 0.25%
Other: none

Services

✔ IRA
Keogh
✔ Telephone Exchange

Gabelli Growth (GABGX)

800-422-3554, 914-921-5100
www.gabelli.com

Growth

PERFORMANCE — fund inception date: 4/10/87

	3yr Annual	5yr Annual	10yr Annual	Bull	Bear
Return (%)	19.2	23.6	19.1	102.4	-17.4
Differ from Category (+/-)	8.2 high	7.5 high	2.3 abv av	52.7 high	-12.0 blw av

Standard Deviation	Category Risk Index	Beta
21.1%—abv av	1.08—abv av	1.13

	2000	1999	1998	1997	1996	1995	1994	1993	1992	1991
Return (%)	-10.5	46.2	29.7	42.6	19.4	32.6	-3.3	11.2	4.4	34.3
Differ from Category (+/-)	-14.0	27.3	15.4	15.5	-2.9	2.2	-3.1	-3.4	-8.2	-3.3
Return, Tax-Adjusted (%)	-12.1	43.2	28.4	37.8	16.4	26.9	-6.6	10.1	3.5	33.3

PER SHARE DATA

	2000	1999	1998	1997	1996	1995	1994	1993	1992	1991
Dividends, Net Income ($)	0.00	0.00	0.00	0.00	0.02	0.05	0.08	0.09	0.08	0.15
Distrib'ns, Cap Gain ($)	3.84	5.16	1.74	5.78	2.30	3.90	2.70	0.67	0.56	0.41
Net Asset Value ($)	37.79	46.51	35.40	28.63	24.14	22.16	19.69	23.26	21.59	21.28
Expense Ratio (%)	na	1.37	1.41	1.43	1.43	1.41	1.36	1.41	1.41	1.45
Yield (%)	0.00	0.00	0.00	0.00	0.07	0.19	0.35	0.37	0.36	0.69
Portfolio Turnover (%)	na	52	40	83	88	140	40	80	46	50
Total Assets (Millions $)	3,849	3,155	1,864	951	623	526	426	695	624	420

PORTFOLIO (as of 6/30/00)

Portfolio Manager: Howard Ward - 1995

Investm't Category: Growth

✔ Domestic　Index
✔ Foreign　Sector
Asset Allocation　State Specific

Investment Style

✔ Large Cap　Mid Cap　Small Cap
✔ Growth　Grth/Val　Value

Portfolio

0.6%	cash	0.0%	corp bonds
99.4%	stocks	0.0%	gov't bonds
0.0%	pref/conv't pref	0.0%	muni bonds
0.0%	conv't bds/wrnts	0.0%	other

SHAREHOLDER INFORMATION

Minimum Investment
Initial: $1,000　Subsequent: $1

Minimum IRA Investment
Initial: $250　Subsequent: $1

Maximum Fees
Load: none　12b-1: 0.25%
Other: none

Services
✔ IRA
Keogh
✔ Telephone Exchange

Gabelli Mathers (MATRX)

800-422-3554, 914-921-5100
www.gabelli.com

Growth & Income

PERFORMANCE — fund inception date: 8/19/65

	3yr Annual	5yr Annual	10yr Annual	Bull	Bear
Return (%)	2.0	1.8	2.4	3.4	0.9
Differ from Category (+/-)	-6.9 low	-12.5 low	-12.5 low	-30.1 low	1.0 av

Standard Deviation	Category Risk Index	Beta
3.8%—blw av	0.22—low	-0.04

	2000	1999	1998	1997	1996	1995	1994	1993	1992	1991
Return (%)	6.0	5.7	-5.2	3.0	0.0	7.0	-5.8	2.1	3.1	9.4
Differ from Category (+/-)	0.3	-5.1	-18.0	-23.9	-19.7	-22.5	-5.3	-11.7	-8.5	-18.7
Return, Tax-Adjusted (%)	4.7	4.1	-7.1	1.1	-1.3	4.8	-7.5	1.4	2.0	6.8

PER SHARE DATA

	2000	1999	1998	1997	1996	1995	1994	1993	1992	1991
Dividends, Net Income ($)	0.12	0.46	0.65	0.61	0.47	0.71	0.67	0.23	0.50	0.74
Distrib'ns, Cap Gain ($)	0.49	0.00	0.00	0.00	0.00	0.03	0.00	0.00	0.00	0.55
Net Asset Value ($)	12.05	11.94	11.73	13.06	13.27	13.75	13.55	15.11	15.02	15.06
Expense Ratio (%)	na	1.24	1.16	1.07	1.03	0.98	0.93	0.89	0.88	0.94
Yield (%)	0.95	3.85	5.54	4.67	3.54	5.15	4.94	1.52	3.32	4.74
Portfolio Turnover (%)	na	922	67	50	38	58	211	136	212	80
Total Assets (Millions $)	98	104	108	138	171	232	293	435	554	516

PORTFOLIO (as of 9/30/99)

Portfolio Manager: Henry Van Der Eb - 1975

Investm't Category: Growth & Income

✔ Domestic	Index
✔ Foreign	Sector
Asset Allocation	State Specific

Investment Style

Large Cap	Mid Cap	Small Cap
Growth	Grth/Val	Value

Portfolio

101.5%	cash	0.0%	corp bonds
-1.5%	stocks	0.0%	gov't bonds
0.0%	pref/conv't pref	0.0%	muni bonds
0.0%	conv't bds/wrnts	0.0%	other

SHAREHOLDER INFORMATION

Minimum Investment

Initial: $1,000 Subsequent: $1

Minimum IRA Investment

Initial: $1,000 Subsequent: $1

Maximum Fees

Load: none 12b-1: 0.25%

Other: none

Services

✔ IRA

Keogh

Telephone Exchange

Gabelli Westwood Bal/AAA (WEBAX)

800-422-3554, 914-921-5100
www.gabelli.com

Balanced

PERFORMANCE — fund inception date: 10/1/91

	3yr Annual	5yr Annual	10yr Annual	Bull	Bear
Return (%)	10.6	14.3	na	23.0	3.2
Differ from Category (+/-)	2.2 abv av	2.9 high	na	-5.1 blw av	6.4 high

Standard Deviation	Category Risk Index	Beta
9.8%—blw av	0.90—blw av	0.46

	2000	1999	1998	1997	1996	1995	1994	1993	1992	1991
Return (%)	12.6	7.7	11.5	22.4	18.1	31.1	0.0	16.8	5.8	—
Differ from Category (+/-)	10.6	-3.0	-1.8	3.6	4.2	5.6	1.3	2.4	-2.6	—
Return, Tax-Adjusted (%)	9.7	5.5	10.4	20.1	15.2	29.4	-0.9	4.2	2.5	—

PER SHARE DATA

	2000	1999	1998	1997	1996	1995	1994	1993	1992	1991
Dividends, Net Income ($)	0.28	0.25	0.24	0.26	0.22	0.20	0.18	0.19	0.24	—
Distrib'ns, Cap Gain ($)	1.10	0.81	0.12	0.56	0.58	0.13	0.00	4.18	0.95	—
Net Asset Value ($)	11.62	11.71	11.88	11.00	9.68	8.89	7.05	7.23	9.96	—
Expense Ratio (%)	1.19	1.20	1.20	1.28	1.32	1.35	1.68	1.82	1.44	—
Yield (%)	2.20	1.99	2.00	2.24	2.14	2.21	2.55	1.66	2.19	—
Portfolio Turnover (%)	65	86	77	110	111	133	168	192	178	—
Total Assets (Millions $)	138	160	141	80	30	9	3	1	4	—

PORTFOLIO (as of 6/30/00)

Portfolio Manager: Susan Byrne, Patricia Fraze - 1991

Investm't Category: Balanced

✔ Domestic
✔ Foreign
✔ Asset Allocation
Index
Sector
State Specific

Investment Style

Large Cap, Mid Cap, Small Cap
Growth, Grth/Val, Value

Portfolio

1.4%	cash	10.4%	corp bonds
59.5%	stocks	18.7%	gov't bonds
0.0%	pref/conv't pref	6.3%	muni bonds
0.0%	conv't bds/wrnts	3.7%	other

SHAREHOLDER INFORMATION

Minimum Investment
Initial: $1,000 — Subsequent: $1

Minimum IRA Investment
Initial: $250 — Subsequent: $1

Maximum Fees
Load: none — 12b-1: 0.25%
Other: none

Services
✔ IRA
Keogh
✔ Telephone Exchange

Gabelli Westwood Eqty/AAA (WESWX)

800-422-3554, 914-921-5100
www.gabelli.com

Growth

PERFORMANCE — fund inception date: 1/2/87

	3yr Annual	5yr Annual	10yr Annual	Bull	Bear
Return (%)	13.3	18.9	17.5	38.7	1.6
Differ from Category (+/-)	2.3 abv av	2.8 abv av	0.7 av	-11.0 av	7.0 abv av

Standard Deviation	Category Risk Index	Beta
15.4%—av	0.79—low	0.75

	2000	1999	1998	1997	1996	1995	1994	1993	1992	1991
Return (%)	11.9	14.6	13.5	29.0	26.7	36.8	2.2	17.1	6.4	21.1
Differ from Category (+/-)	8.4	-4.3	-0.8	1.9	4.4	6.4	2.4	2.5	-6.2	-16.5
Return, Tax-Adjusted (%)	9.3	12.1	12.7	27.6	22.7	33.6	0.7	1.0	-6.1	19.5

PER SHARE DATA

	2000	1999	1998	1997	1996	1995	1994	1993	1992	1991
Dividends, Net Income ($)	0.01	0.02	0.06	0.06	0.06	0.05	0.06	0.00	0.59	0.50
Distrib'ns, Cap Gain ($)	1.30	1.18	0.22	0.37	0.83	0.51	0.20	5.15	5.90	0.14
Net Asset Value ($)	10.11	10.27	10.05	9.11	7.41	6.55	5.21	5.35	8.98	14.58
Expense Ratio (%)	1.48	1.49	1.47	1.53	1.50	1.61	0.71	1.95	1.40	1.29
Yield (%)	0.08	0.17	0.58	0.63	0.72	0.70	1.10	0.00	3.96	3.39
Portfolio Turnover (%)	91	67	77	61	106	107	137	102	75	143
Total Assets (Millions $)	211	169	199	150	38	16	9	4	13	47

PORTFOLIO (as of 6/30/00)

Portfolio Manager: Susan Byrne, Kellie Stark - 1987

Investm't Category: Growth

✔ Domestic — Index
✔ Foreign — Sector
Asset Allocation — State Specific

Investment Style

✔ Large Cap — Mid Cap — Small Cap
Growth — Grth/Val — ✔ Value

Portfolio

2.2%	cash	0.0%	corp bonds
97.8%	stocks	0.0%	gov't bonds
0.0%	pref/conv't pref	0.0%	muni bonds
0.0%	conv't bds/wrnts	0.0%	other

SHAREHOLDER INFORMATION

Minimum Investment
Initial: $1,000 — Subsequent: $1

Minimum IRA Investment
Initial: $250 — Subsequent: $1

Maximum Fees
Load: none — 12b-1: 0.25%
Other: none

Services
✔ IRA
Keogh
✔ Telephone Exchange

Galaxy II: Large Co (ILCIX)

877-289-4252, 508-871-9908
www.galaxyfunds.com

Growth & Income

PERFORMANCE

fund inception date: 10/1/90

	3yr Annual	5yr Annual	10yr Annual	Bull	Bear
Return (%)	11.9	17.9	16.9	55.3	-11.4
Differ from Category (+/-)	3.0 abv av	3.6 high	2.0 abv av	21.8 abv av	-11.3 blw av

Standard Deviation	Category Risk Index	Beta
17.6%—av	1.01—av	0.99

	2000	1999	1998	1997	1996	1995	1994	1993	1992	1991
Return (%)	-9.0	20.4	28.0	32.8	22.5	37.0	0.9	9.6	7.0	29.0
Differ from Category (+/-)	-14.7	9.6	15.2	5.9	2.8	7.5	1.4	-4.2	-4.6	0.9
Return, Tax-Adjusted (%)	-11.1	19.6	27.2	30.8	21.0	35.3	-0.6	8.5	6.2	28.1

PER SHARE DATA

	2000	1999	1998	1997	1996	1995	1994	1993	1992	1991
Dividends, Net Income ($)	0.25	0.33	0.35	0.44	0.38	0.38	0.36	0.35	0.32	0.31
Distrib'ns, Cap Gain ($)	3.96	0.68	0.39	1.36	0.42	0.34	0.33	0.02	0.00	0.00
Net Asset Value ($)	33.29	41.32	35.17	28.07	22.52	19.05	14.46	15.02	14.06	13.45
Expense Ratio (%)	0.47	0.47	0.40	0.40	0.40	0.40	0.40	0.40	0.40	0.40
Yield (%)	0.67	0.78	0.98	1.49	1.65	1.95	2.43	2.32	2.27	2.30
Portfolio Turnover (%)	12	3	3	11	5	7	3	0	0	0
Total Assets (Millions $)	962	1,047	747	547	352	214	137	149	124	65

PORTFOLIO (as of 6/30/00)

Portfolio Manager: Jay Evans - 1998

Investm't Category: Growth & Income

✔ Domestic | ✔ Index
Foreign | Sector
Asset Allocation | State Specific

Investment Style

✔ Large Cap | Mid Cap | Small Cap
Growth | ✔ Grth/Val | Value

Portfolio

1.4%	cash	0.0%	corp bonds
98.7%	stocks	0.0%	gov't bonds
0.0%	pref/conv't pref	0.0%	muni bonds
0.0%	conv't bds/wrnts	0.0%	other

SHAREHOLDER INFORMATION

Minimum Investment
Initial: $2,500 Subsequent: $100

Minimum IRA Investment
Initial: $500 Subsequent: $100

Maximum Fees
Load: none 12b-1: none
Other: none

Services
✔ IRA
✔ Keogh
✔ Telephone Exchange

Galaxy II: Small Co (ISCIX)

877-289-4252, 508-871-9908
www.galaxyfunds.com

Aggressive Growth

PERFORMANCE — fund inception date: 10/1/90

	3yr Annual	5yr Annual	10yr Annual	Bull	Bear
Return (%)	6.7	12.4	15.4	39.0	-6.5
Differ from Category (+/-)	-9.5 blw av	-2.2 blw av	-0.4 blw av	-80.2 low	14.1 high

Standard Deviation	Category Risk Index	Beta
22.9%—abv av	0.71—low	0.86

	2000	1999	1998	1997	1996	1995	1994	1993	1992	1991
Return (%)	10.9	11.6	-1.7	23.5	19.6	33.1	-3.6	11.3	12.2	45.4
Differ from Category (+/-)	16.9	-45.9	-16.8	8.7	1.3	-1.5	-2.8	-13.9	5.3	-1.8
Return, Tax-Adjusted (%)	8.0	9.4	-3.4	14.8	17.0	31.6	-5.4	10.2	11.6	44.6

PER SHARE DATA

	2000	1999	1998	1997	1996	1995	1994	1993	1992	1991
Dividends, Net Income ($)	0.04	0.08	0.08	0.32	0.33	0.37	0.26	0.24	0.23	0.21
Distrib'ns, Cap Gain ($)	2.32	1.61	1.48	9.49	1.46	0.33	0.83	0.32	0.05	0.06
Net Asset Value ($)	16.18	16.84	16.73	18.73	23.38	21.08	16.38	18.16	16.84	15.27
Expense Ratio (%)	0.41	0.40	0.40	0.40	0.40	0.40	0.40	0.40	0.40	0.40
Yield (%)	0.21	0.43	0.43	1.13	1.32	1.72	1.51	1.29	1.36	1.36
Portfolio Turnover (%)	36	22	99	8	14	10	17	4	6	1
Total Assets (Millions $)	249	273	310	379	326	276	230	263	181	67

PORTFOLIO (as of 6/30/00)

Portfolio Manager: Jay Evans - 1998

Investm't Category: Aggressive Growth

✔ Domestic
✔ Index
Foreign
Sector
Asset Allocation
State Specific

Investment Style

Large Cap
Mid Cap
✔ Small Cap
Growth
✔ Grth/Val
Value

Portfolio

2.4% cash
97.6% stocks
0.0% pref/conv't pref
0.0% conv't bds/wrnts
0.0% corp bonds
0.0% gov't bonds
0.0% muni bonds
0.0% other

SHAREHOLDER INFORMATION

Minimum Investment

Initial: $2,500 Subsequent: $100

Minimum IRA Investment

Initial: $500 Subsequent: $100

Maximum Fees

Load: none 12b-1: none
Other: none

Services

✔ IRA
✔ Keogh
✔ Telephone Exchange

Galaxy II: Utility (IUTLX)

877-289-4252, 508-871-9908
www.galaxyfunds.com

Growth & Income

PERFORMANCE

fund inception date: 1/5/93

	3yr Annual	5yr Annual	10yr Annual	Bull	Bear
Return (%)	18.2	17.0	na	0.6	34.5
Differ from Category (+/-)	9.3 high	2.7 abv av	na	-32.9 low	34.6 high

Standard Deviation	Category Risk Index	Beta
19.1%—abv av	1.10—high	0.04

	2000	1999	1998	1997	1996	1995	1994	1993	1992	1991
Return (%)	59.3	-9.4	14.7	28.5	3.4	37.0	-8.6	—	—	—
Differ from Category (+/-)	53.6	-20.2	1.9	1.6	-16.3	7.5	-8.1	—	—	—
Return, Tax-Adjusted (%)	55.3	-11.3	12.6	25.1	0.7	35.4	-10.6	—	—	—

PER SHARE DATA

	2000	1999	1998	1997	1996	1995	1994	1993	1992	1991
Dividends, Net Income ($)	0.45	0.51	0.62	0.54	0.44	0.36	0.58	—	—	—
Distrib'ns, Cap Gain ($)	1.57	0.44	0.14	0.90	0.55	0.00	0.00	—	—	—
Net Asset Value ($)	17.66	12.48	14.84	13.64	11.88	12.50	9.43	—	—	—
Expense Ratio (%)	0.40	0.40	0.40	0.40	0.40	0.40	0.40	—	—	—
Yield (%)	2.34	3.94	4.13	3.71	3.53	2.88	6.15	—	—	—
Portfolio Turnover (%)	19	8	72	170	12	5	19	—	—	—
Total Assets (Millions $)	75	49	61	55	50	58	53	—	—	—

PORTFOLIO (as of 6/30/00)

Portfolio Manager: Jay Evans - 1998

Investm't Category: Growth & Income

✔ Domestic	✔ Index
Foreign	✔ Sector
Asset Allocation	State Specific

Investment Style

Large Cap	Mid Cap	Small Cap
Growth	Grth/Val	Value

Portfolio

0.6% cash	0.0% corp bonds
99.4% stocks	0.0% gov't bonds
0.0% pref/conv't pref	0.0% muni bonds
0.0% conv't bds/wrnts	0.0% other

SHAREHOLDER INFORMATION

Minimum Investment
Initial: $2,500 Subsequent: $100

Minimum IRA Investment
Initial: $500 Subsequent: $100

Maximum Fees
Load: none 12b-1: none
Other: none

Services
✔ IRA
✔ Keogh
✔ Telephone Exchange

Galaxy: Growth II/Tr (SEGRX)

877-289-4252, 508-871-9908
www.1784funds.com

Aggressive Growth

PERFORMANCE — fund inception date: 3/28/96

	3yr Annual	5yr Annual	10yr Annual	Bull	Bear
Return (%)	20.0	na	na	129.0	-18.9
Differ from Category (+/-)	3.8 av	na	na	9.8 abv av	1.7 abv av

Standard Deviation	Category Risk Index	Beta
33.4%—high	1.03—av	1.11

	2000	1999	1998	1997	1996	1995	1994	1993	1992	1991
Return (%)	0.1	70.4	1.3	13.9	—	—	—	—	—	—
Differ from Category (+/-)	6.1	12.9	-13.8	-0.9	—	—	—	—	—	—
Return, Tax-Adjusted (%)	-8.1	68.4	0.7	12.5	—	—	—	—	—	—

PER SHARE DATA

	2000	1999	1998	1997	1996	1995	1994	1993	1992	1991
Dividends, Net Income ($)	0.00	0.00	0.00	0.00	—	—	—	—	—	—
Distrib'ns, Cap Gain ($)	8.08	1.19	0.37	0.80	—	—	—	—	—	—
Net Asset Value ($)	11.97	19.51	12.28	12.53	—	—	—	—	—	—
Expense Ratio (%)	0.88	0.93	0.91	0.77	—	—	—	—	—	—
Yield (%)	0.00	0.00	0.00	0.00	—	—	—	—	—	—
Portfolio Turnover (%)	79	61	48	57	—	—	—	—	—	—
Total Assets (Millions $)	76	302	203	294	—	—	—	—	—	—

PORTFOLIO (as of 3/31/00)

Portfolio Manager: Ted Ober, Eugene Takach - 1996

Investm't Category: Aggressive Growth

✔ Domestic
✔ Foreign
Asset Allocation
Index
Sector
State Specific

Investment Style

Large Cap
✔ Mid Cap
Small Cap
✔ Growth
Grth/Val
Value

Portfolio

20.0%	cash	0.0%	corp bonds
80.0%	stocks	0.0%	gov't bonds
0.0%	pref/conv't pref	0.0%	muni bonds
0.0%	conv't bds/wrnts	0.0%	other

SHAREHOLDER INFORMATION

Minimum Investment
Initial: $1,000 — Subsequent: $100

Minimum IRA Investment
Initial: $250 — Subsequent: $100

Maximum Fees
Load: none — 12b-1: 0.25%
Other: none

Services
✔ IRA
Keogh
✔ Telephone Exchange

Gateway Tr: Gateway (GATEX)

800-354-6339, 513-248-2700
www.gatewayfund.com

Growth & Income

PERFORMANCE

fund inception date: 12/7/77

	3yr Annual	5yr Annual	10yr Annual	Bull	Bear
Return (%)	10.5	10.9	10.1	24.5	2.4
Differ from Category (+/-)	1.6 av	-3.4 low	-4.8 low	-9.0 blw av	2.5 av

Standard Deviation	Category Risk Index	Beta
5.4%—blw av	0.31—low	0.27

	2000	1999	1998	1997	1996	1995	1994	1993	1992	1991
Return (%)	6.6	12.9	12.2	12.3	10.5	11.0	5.5	7.4	5.1	17.7
Differ from Category (+/-)	0.9	2.1	-0.6	-14.6	-9.2	-18.5	6.0	-6.4	-6.5	-10.4
Return, Tax-Adjusted (%)	4.5	12.7	11.9	10.0	10.0	10.3	3.1	5.7	4.1	15.9

PER SHARE DATA

	2000	1999	1998	1997	1996	1995	1994	1993	1992	1991
Dividends, Net Income ($)	0.07	0.07	0.12	0.17	0.20	0.26	0.27	0.29	0.28	0.30
Distrib'ns, Cap Gain ($)	2.23	0.00	0.01	1.72	0.00	0.00	0.97	0.51	0.23	0.51
Net Asset Value ($)	22.92	23.67	21.02	18.85	18.48	16.91	15.48	15.85	15.51	15.24
Expense Ratio (%)	na	0.98	0.99	1.07	1.14	1.22	1.21	1.11	1.11	1.22
Yield (%)	0.27	0.29	0.57	0.82	1.08	1.53	1.64	1.77	1.77	1.90
Portfolio Turnover (%)	na	11	12	82	17	0	4	17	15	31
Total Assets (Millions $)	1,591	922	464	254	194	176	164	207	212	81

PORTFOLIO (as of 6/30/00)

Portfolio Manager: J. Patrick Rogers - 1994

Investm't Category: Growth & Income

✔ Domestic	Index
Foreign	Sector
Asset Allocation	State Specific

Investment Style

✔ Large Cap	Mid Cap	Small Cap
Growth	✔ Grth/Val	Value

Portfolio

4.4% cash	0.0% corp bonds
98.2% stocks	0.0% gov't bonds
0.0% pref/conv't pref	0.0% muni bonds
0.0% conv't bds/wrnts	-2.6% other

SHAREHOLDER INFORMATION

Minimum Investment
Initial: $1,000 Subsequent: $100

Minimum IRA Investment
Initial: $500 Subsequent: $100

Maximum Fees
Load: none 12b-1: 0.31%
Other: none

Services
✔ IRA
✔ Keogh
✔ Telephone Exchange

Gintel (GINLX)

800-243-5808, 203-622-6400
www.gintel.net

Aggressive Growth

PERFORMANCE — fund inception date: 6/10/81

	3yr Annual	5yr Annual	10yr Annual	Bull	Bear
Return (%)	1.9	12.4	11.1	149.5	-31.9
Differ from Category (+/-)	-14.3 low	-2.2 blw av	-4.7 low	30.3 abv av	-11.3 blw av

Standard Deviation	Category Risk Index	Beta
41.7%—high	1.28—high	1.16

	2000	1999	1998	1997	1996	1995	1994	1993	1992	1991
Return (%)	-34.3	81.5	-10.9	29.2	31.0	30.9	-16.4	2.0	24.6	15.5
Differ from Category (+/-)	-28.3	24.0	-26.0	14.4	12.7	-3.7	-15.6	-23.2	17.7	-31.7
Return, Tax-Adjusted (%)	-39.9	81.5	-13.7	27.2	27.0	28.8	-16.7	-1.1	24.4	12.4

PER SHARE DATA

	2000	1999	1998	1997	1996	1995	1994	1993	1992	1991
Dividends, Net Income ($)	0.00	0.00	0.11	0.16	0.34	0.00	0.04	0.51	0.12	1.19
Distrib'ns, Cap Gain ($)	8.37	0.00	2.89	1.41	1.68	0.93	0.11	1.13	0.23	0.06
Net Asset Value ($)	13.65	29.37	16.18	21.78	18.10	15.37	12.46	15.11	16.45	13.48
Expense Ratio (%)	na	1.90	1.70	1.80	1.80	2.30	2.40	2.20	1.70	1.40
Yield (%)	0.00	0.00	0.57	0.68	1.71	0.00	0.31	3.14	0.71	8.76
Portfolio Turnover (%)	na	95	52	52	64	58	69	50	56	66
Total Assets (Millions $)	124	221	144	180	147	96	88	136	164	77

PORTFOLIO (as of 6/30/00)

Portfolio Manager: Robert Gintel - 1981

Investm't Category: Aggressive Growth

✔ Domestic   Index
✔ Foreign   Sector
Asset Allocation   State Specific

Investment Style

Large Cap   Mid Cap   ✔ Small Cap
✔ Growth   Grth/Val   Value

Portfolio

20.7%	cash	0.0%	corp bonds
79.4%	stocks	0.0%	gov't bonds
0.0%	pref/conv't pref	0.0%	muni bonds
0.0%	conv't bds/wrnts	0.0%	other

SHAREHOLDER INFORMATION

Minimum Investment

Initial: $5,000   Subsequent: $1

Minimum IRA Investment

Initial: $2,000   Subsequent: $1

Maximum Fees

Load: 2.00% redemption   12b-1: none
Other: redemption fee applies for 1 month

Services

✔ IRA
Keogh
✔ Telephone Exchange

Granum Value (GRVFX)

888-547-2686, 414-287-3851
www.granum.com

Growth

PERFORMANCE — fund inception date: 5/1/97

	3yr Annual	5yr Annual	10yr Annual	Bull	Bear
Return (%)	6.6	na	na	38.9	-2.4
Differ from Category (+/-)	-4.4 blw av	na	na	-10.8 av	3.0 abv av

Standard Deviation	Category Risk Index	Beta
18.3%—av	0.94—blw av	0.85

	2000	1999	1998	1997	1996	1995	1994	1993	1992	1991
Return (%)	8.1	10.7	1.3	—	—	—	—	—	—	—
Differ from Category (+/-)	-4.6	-8.2	-13.0	—	—	—	—	—	—	—
Return, Tax-Adjusted (%)	8.1	10.4	1.1	—	—	—	—	—	—	—

PER SHARE DATA

	2000	1999	1998	1997	1996	1995	1994	1993	1992	1991
Dividends, Net Income ($)	0.00	0.13	0.07	—	—	—	—	—	—	—
Distrib'ns, Cap Gain ($)	0.00	0.00	0.00	—	—	—	—	—	—	—
Net Asset Value ($)	29.16	26.97	24.48	—	—	—	—	—	—	—
Expense Ratio (%)	na	1.59	1.88	—	—	—	—	—	—	—
Yield (%)	0.00	0.48	0.28	—	—	—	—	—	—	—
Portfolio Turnover (%)	na	18	3	—	—	—	—	—	—	—
Total Assets (Millions $)	114	128	133	—	—	—	—	—	—	—

PORTFOLIO (as of 3/31/00)

Portfolio Manager: committee - 1997

Investm't Category: Growth

✔ Domestic — Index
✔ Foreign — Sector
Asset Allocation — State Specific

Investment Style

Large Cap — ✔ Mid Cap — Small Cap
Growth — Grth/Val — ✔ Value

Portfolio

1.4%	cash	0.0%	corp bonds
98.4%	stocks	0.0%	gov't bonds
0.0%	pref/conv't pref	0.0%	muni bonds
0.2%	conv't bds/wrnts	0.0%	other

SHAREHOLDER INFORMATION

Minimum Investment

Initial: $5,000 — Subsequent: $1,000

Minimum IRA Investment

Initial: $5,000 — Subsequent: $1,000

Maximum Fees

Load: none — 12b-1: 0.75%
Other: none

Services

✔ IRA
✔ Keogh
✔ Telephone Exchange

Harbor: Capital Apprec (HACAX)

800-422-1050, 419-247-2477
www.harborfund.com

Growth

PERFORMANCE — fund inception date: 12/29/87

	3yr Annual	5yr Annual	10yr Annual	Bull	Bear
Return (%)	18.2	21.1	21.6	101.3	-27.3
Differ from Category (+/-)	7.2 high	5.0 high	4.8 high	51.6 high	-21.9 low

Standard Deviation	Category Risk Index	Beta
25.2%—abv av	1.29—high	1.26

	2000	1999	1998	1997	1996	1995	1994	1993	1992	1991
Return (%)	-17.0	45.8	36.8	31.4	19.8	37.8	3.3	12.1	9.9	54.7
Differ from Category (+/-)	-20.5	26.9	22.5	4.3	-2.5	7.4	3.5	-2.5	-2.7	17.1
Return, Tax-Adjusted (%)	-19.4	43.3	35.1	27.6	18.7	37.2	2.9	10.0	6.3	52.1

PER SHARE DATA

	2000	1999	1998	1997	1996	1995	1994	1993	1992	1991
Dividends, Net Income ($)	0.00	0.00	0.06	0.06	0.02	0.02	0.03	0.03	0.01	0.04
Distrib'ns, Cap Gain ($)	6.17	4.60	2.27	4.85	0.85	0.31	0.17	1.12	2.03	0.97
Net Asset Value ($)	35.58	50.65	37.99	29.47	26.33	22.69	16.71	16.37	15.65	16.11
Expense Ratio (%)	na	0.66	0.68	0.70	0.75	0.75	0.81	0.86	0.91	0.89
Yield (%)	0.00	0.00	0.14	0.17	0.07	0.08	0.17	0.17	0.05	0.23
Portfolio Turnover (%)	na	68	69	72	73	48	72	93	69	90
Total Assets (Millions $)	7,842	7,947	4,696	2,906	1,681	989	239	149	105	90

PORTFOLIO (as of 6/30/00)

Portfolio Manager: Spiros Segalas - 1990

Investm't Category: Growth

✔ Domestic
Foreign
Asset Allocation
Index
Sector
State Specific

Investment Style

✔ Large Cap
✔ Growth
Mid Cap
Grth/Val
Small Cap
Value

Portfolio

3.4% cash
96.6% stocks
0.0% pref/conv't pref
0.0% conv't bds/wrnts
0.0% corp bonds
0.0% gov't bonds
0.0% muni bonds
0.0% other

SHAREHOLDER INFORMATION

Minimum Investment
Initial: $1,000 Subsequent: $100

Minimum IRA Investment
Initial: $500 Subsequent: $100

Maximum Fees
Load: none 12b-1: none
Other: none

Services
✔ IRA
✔ Keogh
✔ Telephone Exchange

Harbor: Growth (HAGWX)

800-422-1050, 419-247-2477
www.harborfund.com

Aggressive Growth

PERFORMANCE

fund inception date: 11/19/86

	3yr Annual	5yr Annual	10yr Annual	Bull	Bear
Return (%)	23.7	20.5	17.9	172.2	-32.0
Differ from Category (+/-)	7.5 abv av	5.9 abv av	2.1 av	53.0 abv av	-11.4 blw av

Standard Deviation	Category Risk Index	Beta
36.2%—high	1.12—abv av	1.18

	2000	1999	1998	1997	1996	1995	1994	1993	1992	1991
Return (%)	-13.0	95.3	11.3	20.8	11.0	38.1	-11.4	18.3	-6.3	50.4
Differ from Category (+/-)	-7.0	37.8	-3.8	6.0	-7.3	3.5	-10.6	-6.9	-13.2	3.2
Return, Tax-Adjusted (%)	-14.3	93.4	9.5	17.0	3.1	33.7	-12.0	18.2	-9.0	44.4

PER SHARE DATA

	2000	1999	1998	1997	1996	1995	1994	1993	1992	1991
Dividends, Net Income ($)	0.00	0.00	0.00	0.00	0.00	0.00	0.00	0.01	0.00	0.04
Distrib'ns, Cap Gain ($)	1.55	1.19	1.07	2.28	4.10	1.85	0.32	0.00	1.36	2.30
Net Asset Value ($)	18.47	23.24	12.55	12.27	12.17	14.65	11.97	13.88	11.74	14.02
Expense Ratio (%)	na	0.90	1.00	1.12	0.92	0.94	0.93	0.90	0.90	0.91
Yield (%)	0.00	0.00	0.00	0.00	0.00	0.00	0.00	0.07	0.00	0.24
Portfolio Turnover (%)	na	13	23	147	87	75	115	170	83	98
Total Assets (Millions $)	216	215	104	109	111	136	134	192	202	216

PORTFOLIO (as of 6/30/00)

Portfolio Manager: Peter Welles - 1997

Investm't Category: Aggressive Growth

✔ Domestic — Index
Foreign — Sector
Asset Allocation — State Specific

Investment Style

Large Cap — Mid Cap — ✔ Small Cap
✔ Growth — Grth/Val — Value

Portfolio

14.0%	cash	0.0%	corp bonds
85.3%	stocks	0.0%	gov't bonds
0.0%	pref/conv't pref	0.0%	muni bonds
0.7%	conv't bds/wrnts	0.0%	other

SHAREHOLDER INFORMATION

Minimum Investment

Initial: $1,000 — Subsequent: $100

Minimum IRA Investment

Initial: $500 — Subsequent: $100

Maximum Fees

Load: none — 12b-1: none
Other: none

Services

✔ IRA
✔ Keogh
✔ Telephone Exchange

Harbor: Int'l (HAINX)

800-422-1050, 419-247-2477
www.harborfund.com

International Stock

PERFORMANCE — fund inception date: 12/29/87

	3yr Annual	5yr Annual	10yr Annual	Bull	Bear
Return (%)	9.1	12.5	14.5	40.4	-7.4
Differ from Category (+/-)	0.2 av	4.2 abv av	5.5 high	-50.5 low	16.6 high

Standard Deviation	Category Risk Index	Beta
16.6%—av	0.73—low	0.68

	2000	1999	1998	1997	1996	1995	1994	1993	1992	1991
Return (%)	-4.9	23.8	10.3	15.4	20.1	16.0	5.4	45.4	0.0	21.3
Differ from Category (+/-)	14.5	-36.9	4.5	14.1	5.6	6.7	8.5	5.2	3.5	8.3
Return, Tax-Adjusted (%)	-7.3	21.5	8.3	14.3	18.7	15.2	3.9	44.9	-0.6	20.8

PER SHARE DATA

	2000	1999	1998	1997	1996	1995	1994	1993	1992	1991
Dividends, Net Income ($)	0.70	0.64	0.57	0.40	0.41	0.40	0.24	0.21	0.21	0.21
Distrib'ns, Cap Gain ($)	3.79	2.85	2.30	0.89	0.79	0.12	0.93	0.00	0.17	0.00
Net Asset Value ($)	35.09	41.86	36.72	35.86	32.20	27.84	24.45	24.32	16.87	17.28
Expense Ratio (%)	na	0.92	0.94	0.97	0.99	1.10	1.10	1.20	1.28	1.35
Yield (%)	1.80	1.43	1.46	1.08	1.24	1.43	0.94	0.86	1.23	1.21
Portfolio Turnover (%)	na	1	13	6	9	17	28	15	25	19
Total Assets (Millions $)	4,667	5,842	5,373	5,276	4,318	3,460	2,953	2,537	728	220

PORTFOLIO (as of 6/30/00)

Portfolio Manager: Hakan Castegren - 1987

Investm't Category: International Stock

Domestic	Index
✔ Foreign	Sector
Asset Allocation	State Specific

Investment Style

Large Cap	Mid Cap	Small Cap
Growth	Grth/Val	Value

Portfolio

2.4%	cash	0.7%	corp bonds
96.9%	stocks	0.0%	gov't bonds
0.0%	pref/conv't pref	0.0%	muni bonds
0.0%	conv't bds/wrnts	0.0%	other

SHAREHOLDER INFORMATION

Minimum Investment
Initial: $1,000 Subsequent: $100

Minimum IRA Investment
Initial: $500 Subsequent: $100

Maximum Fees
Load: none 12b-1: none
Other: none

Services
✔ IRA
✔ Keogh
✔ Telephone Exchange

Harbor: Int'l Grth (HAIGX)

800-422-1050, 419-247-2477
www.harborfund.com

International Stock

PERFORMANCE

fund inception date: 11/1/93

	3yr Annual	5yr Annual	10yr Annual	Bull	Bear
Return (%)	3.4	8.6	na	40.6	-30.3
Differ from Category (+/-)	-5.5 blw av	0.3 av	na	-50.3 low	-6.3 blw av

Standard Deviation	Category Risk Index	Beta
21.5%—abv av	0.95—av	0.75

	2000	1999	1998	1997	1996	1995	1994	1993	1992	1991
Return (%)	-25.4	20.1	23.4	3.5	32.0	24.2	-7.7	—	—	—
Differ from Category (+/-)	-6.0	-40.6	17.6	2.2	17.5	14.9	-4.6	—	—	—
Return, Tax-Adjusted (%)	-27.0	18.4	22.7	2.4	30.9	23.7	-7.9	—	—	—

PER SHARE DATA

	2000	1999	1998	1997	1996	1995	1994	1993	1992	1991
Dividends, Net Income ($)	0.00	0.13	0.11	0.12	0.07	0.12	0.06	—	—	—
Distrib'ns, Cap Gain ($)	1.82	1.37	0.27	0.59	0.36	0.00	0.00	—	—	—
Net Asset Value ($)	14.37	21.86	19.49	16.09	16.24	12.64	10.27	—	—	—
Expense Ratio (%)	na	0.91	0.96	1.02	1.10	1.28	1.32	—	—	—
Yield (%)	0.00	0.55	0.55	0.71	0.42	0.94	0.58	—	—	—
Portfolio Turnover (%)	na	48	85	76	55	56	41	—	—	—
Total Assets (Millions $)	1,058	1,672	1,323	943	645	147	69	—	—	—

PORTFOLIO (as of 6/30/00)

Portfolio Manager: Howard Moss, Blair Boyer - 1993

Investm't Category: International Stock

Domestic	Index
✔ Foreign	Sector
Asset Allocation	State Specific

Investment Style

Large Cap	Mid Cap	Small Cap
Growth	Grth/Val	Value

Portfolio

4.3% cash	0.0% corp bonds
95.7% stocks	0.0% gov't bonds
0.0% pref/conv't pref	0.0% muni bonds
0.0% conv't bds/wrnts	0.0% other

SHAREHOLDER INFORMATION

Minimum Investment
Initial: $1,000 Subsequent: $100

Minimum IRA Investment
Initial: $500 Subsequent: $100

Maximum Fees
Load: none 12b-1: none
Other: none

Services
✔ IRA
✔ Keogh
✔ Telephone Exchange

Harbor: Int'l II (HAIIX)

800-422-1050, 419-247-2477
www.harborfund.com

International Stock

PERFORMANCE — fund inception date: 6/3/96

	3yr Annual	5yr Annual	10yr Annual	Bull	Bear
Return (%)	10.8	na	na	55.2	-12.2
Differ from Category (+/-)	1.9 abv av	na	na	-35.7 blw av	11.8 high

Standard Deviation	Category Risk Index	Beta
21.4%—abv av	0.94—blw av	0.83

	2000	1999	1998	1997	1996	1995	1994	1993	1992	1991
Return (%)	-3.7	30.8	7.9	9.7	—	—	—	—	—	—
Differ from Category (+/-)	15.7	-29.9	2.1	8.4	—	—	—	—	—	—
Return, Tax-Adjusted (%)	-5.0	29.2	7.3	8.4	—	—	—	—	—	—

PER SHARE DATA

	2000	1999	1998	1997	1996	1995	1994	1993	1992	1991
Dividends, Net Income ($)	0.14	0.16	0.15	0.09	—	—	—	—	—	—
Distrib'ns, Cap Gain ($)	0.74	0.61	0.00	0.53	—	—	—	—	—	—
Net Asset Value ($)	13.67	15.16	12.21	11.45	—	—	—	—	—	—
Expense Ratio (%)	na	0.92	1.15	0.98	—	—	—	—	—	—
Yield (%)	0.97	1.01	1.22	0.75	—	—	—	—	—	—
Portfolio Turnover (%)	na	51	70	58	—	—	—	—	—	—
Total Assets (Millions $)	116	128	130	130	—	—	—	—	—	—

PORTFOLIO (as of 6/30/00)

Portfolio Manager: James LaTorre - 1996

Investm't Category: International Stock

- Domestic
- ✔ Foreign
- Asset Allocation
- Index
- Sector
- State Specific

Investment Style

Large Cap Mid Cap Small Cap
Growth Grth/Val Value

Portfolio

6.5%	cash	0.0%	corp bonds
93.5%	stocks	0.0%	gov't bonds
0.0%	pref/conv't pref	0.0%	muni bonds
0.0%	conv't bds/wrnts	0.0%	other

SHAREHOLDER INFORMATION

Minimum Investment
Initial: $1,000 Subsequent: $100

Minimum IRA Investment
Initial: $500 Subsequent: $100

Maximum Fees
Load: none 12b-1: none
Other: none

Services
- ✔ IRA
- ✔ Keogh
- ✔ Telephone Exchange

Harbor: Value (HAVLX)

800-422-1050, 419-247-2477
www.harborfund.com

Growth & Income

PERFORMANCE — fund inception date: 12/29/87

	3yr Annual	5yr Annual	10yr Annual	Bull	Bear
Return (%)	7.2	14.1	14.0	29.4	2.0
Differ from Category (+/-)	-1.7 blw av	-0.2 av	-0.9 blw av	-4.1 av	2.1 av

Standard Deviation	Category Risk Index	Beta
18.9%—av	1.09—high	0.82

	2000	1999	1998	1997	1996	1995	1994	1993	1992	1991
Return (%)	7.1	7.5	6.9	31.2	20.0	35.3	0.6	8.3	7.4	21.2
Differ from Category (+/-)	1.4	-3.3	-5.9	4.3	0.3	5.8	1.1	-5.5	-4.2	-6.9
Return, Tax-Adjusted (%)	6.0	4.6	4.0	25.2	14.9	30.9	-2.6	5.1	6.2	19.1

PER SHARE DATA

	2000	1999	1998	1997	1996	1995	1994	1993	1992	1991
Dividends, Net Income ($)	0.27	0.25	0.27	0.32	0.40	0.40	0.35	0.32	0.37	0.46
Distrib'ns, Cap Gain ($)	0.18	1.57	1.62	3.74	2.00	1.26	1.06	1.09	0.14	0.34
Net Asset Value ($)	14.03	13.55	14.34	15.20	14.79	14.34	11.88	13.21	13.50	13.06
Expense Ratio (%)	na	0.76	0.79	0.83	0.83	0.99	1.04	0.88	0.84	0.93
Yield (%)	1.90	1.65	1.69	1.68	2.38	2.56	2.70	2.23	2.71	3.43
Portfolio Turnover (%)	na	110	113	145	132	129	150	50	20	33
Total Assets (Millions $)	134	155	176	174	116	91	56	59	66	42

PORTFOLIO (as of 6/30/00)

Portfolio Manager: David Tierney, Gregory DePrince - 1993

Investm't Category: Growth & Income

✔ Domestic
Foreign
Asset Allocation
Index
Sector
State Specific

Investment Style

✔ Large Cap ✔ Mid Cap Small Cap
Growth Grth/Val ✔ Value

Portfolio

3.4%	cash	0.0%	corp bonds
96.6%	stocks	0.0%	gov't bonds
0.0%	pref/conv't pref	0.0%	muni bonds
0.0%	conv't bds/wrnts	0.0%	other

SHAREHOLDER INFORMATION

Minimum Investment
Initial: $1,000 Subsequent: $100

Minimum IRA Investment
Initial: $500 Subsequent: $100

Maximum Fees
Load: none 12b-1: none
Other: none

Services
✔ IRA
✔ Keogh
✔ Telephone Exchange

Harding Loevner Intl Eqty (HLMIX)

877-435-8105, 212-332-5210
www.hardingloevner.com

International Stock

PERFORMANCE — fund inception date: 5/11/94

	3yr Annual	5yr Annual	10yr Annual	Bull	Bear
Return (%)	11.5	8.9	na	73.9	-16.0
Differ from Category (+/-)	2.6 abv av	0.6 av	na	-17.0 av	8.0 abv av

Standard Deviation	Category Risk Index	Beta
18.8%—av	0.83—blw av	0.77

	2000	1999	1998	1997	1996	1995	1994	1993	1992	1991
Return (%)	-15.8	49.7	10.1	-4.2	15.4	11.9	—	—	—	—
Differ from Category (+/-)	3.6	-11.0	4.3	-5.5	0.9	2.6	—	—	—	—
Return, Tax-Adjusted (%)	-17.0	48.2	9.4	-4.6	14.7	11.4	—	—	—	—

PER SHARE DATA

	2000	1999	1998	1997	1996	1995	1994	1993	1992	1991
Dividends, Net Income ($)	0.00	0.22	0.18	0.10	0.11	0.10	—	—	—	—
Distrib'ns, Cap Gain ($)	1.14	0.50	0.01	0.06	0.10	0.00	—	—	—	—
Net Asset Value ($)	13.99	17.98	12.49	11.51	12.20	10.77	—	—	—	—
Expense Ratio (%)	na	1.00	1.00	1.00	1.00	0.99	—	—	—	—
Yield (%)	0.00	1.19	1.44	0.86	0.89	0.92	—	—	—	—
Portfolio Turnover (%)	na	35	33	31	17	28	—	—	—	—
Total Assets (Millions $)	338	369	479	402	285	67	—	—	—	—

PORTFOLIO (as of 6/30/00)

Portfolio Manager: Simon Halllett - 1994

Investm't Category: International Stock

Domestic	Index
✔ Foreign	Sector
Asset Allocation	State Specific

Investment Style

Large Cap	Mid Cap	Small Cap
Growth	Grth/Val	Value

Portfolio

3.2%	cash	0.0%	corp bonds
95.4%	stocks	0.0%	gov't bonds
0.0%	pref/conv't pref	0.0%	muni bonds
0.0%	conv't bds/wrnts	1.4%	other

SHAREHOLDER INFORMATION

Minimum Investment
Initial: $100,000 Subsequent: $1

Minimum IRA Investment
Initial: $100,000 Subsequent: $1

Maximum Fees
Load: none 12b-1: none
Other: none

Services
✔ IRA
Keogh
✔ Telephone Exchange

Haven (HAVEX)

800-850-7163, 212-953-2322
www.havencapital.com

Growth

PERFORMANCE — fund inception date: 6/22/94

	3yr Annual	5yr Annual	10yr Annual	Bull	Bear
Return (%)	12.9	16.8	na	47.2	2.7
Differ from Category (+/-)	1.9 av	0.7 av	na	-2.5 av	8.1 abv av

Standard Deviation	Category Risk Index	Beta
19.1%—av	0.98—blw av	0.93

	2000	1999	1998	1997	1996	1995	1994	1993	1992	1991
Return (%)	15.9	18.2	5.0	18.8	27.3	26.8	—	—	—	—
Differ from Category (+/-)	12.4	-0.7	-9.3	-8.3	5.0	-3.6	—	—	—	—
Return, Tax-Adjusted (%)	12.7	16.8	2.7	16.2	23.8	24.2	—	—	—	—

PER SHARE DATA

	2000	1999	1998	1997	1996	1995	1994	1993	1992	1991
Dividends, Net Income ($)	0.05	0.04	0.06	0.10	0.06	0.14	—	—	—	—
Distrib'ns, Cap Gain ($)	2.33	0.85	1.48	1.51	1.35	0.69	—	—	—	—
Net Asset Value ($)	15.20	15.19	13.61	14.46	13.53	11.74	—	—	—	—
Expense Ratio (%)	na	1.34	1.26	1.33	1.59	1.53	—	—	—	—
Yield (%)	0.28	0.24	0.39	0.62	0.40	1.12	—	—	—	—
Portfolio Turnover (%)	na	31	59	57	67	77	—	—	—	—
Total Assets (Millions $)	85	73	79	80	69	55	—	—	—	—

PORTFOLIO (as of 3/31/00)

Portfolio Manager: Colin Ferenbach, Denis Turko - 1994

Investm't Category: Growth

✔ Domestic	Index
✔ Foreign	Sector
Asset Allocation	State Specific

Investment Style

✔ Large Cap	✔ Mid Cap	Small Cap
Growth	Grth/Val	✔ Value

Portfolio

4.5% cash	0.0% corp bonds
95.5% stocks	0.0% gov't bonds
0.0% pref/conv't pref	0.0% muni bonds
0.0% conv't bds/wrnts	0.0% other

SHAREHOLDER INFORMATION

Minimum Investment
Initial: $2,500 — Subsequent: $100

Minimum IRA Investment
Initial: $2,000 — Subsequent: $100

Maximum Fees
Load: none — 12b-1: 0.20%
Other: none

Services
✔ IRA
Keogh
Telephone Exchange

Heartland Grp: Value

800-432-7856, 414-289-7000
www.heartlandfunds.com

(HRTVX)

Growth

PERFORMANCE

fund inception date: 12/28/84

	3yr Annual	5yr Annual	10yr Annual	Bull	Bear
Return (%)	4.1	10.9	18.8	36.8	-2.4
Differ from Category (+/-)	-6.9 low	-5.2 low	2.0 abv av	-12.9 blw av	3.0 abv av

Standard Deviation	Category Risk Index	Beta
20.9%—abv av	1.07—abv av	0.71

	2000	1999	1998	1997	1996	1995	1994	1993	1992	1991
Return (%)	2.0	25.0	-11.4	23.1	20.9	29.8	1.7	18.7	42.4	49.3
Differ from Category (+/-)	-1.5	6.1	-25.7	-4.0	-1.4	-0.6	1.9	4.1	29.8	11.7
Return, Tax-Adjusted (%)	-0.2	24.9	-11.8	19.8	18.7	27.8	0.6	17.3	38.0	47.2

PER SHARE DATA

	2000	1999	1998	1997	1996	1995	1994	1993	1992	1991
Dividends, Net Income ($)	0.00	0.00	0.11	0.17	0.06	0.13	0.00	0.00	0.00	0.00
Distrib'ns, Cap Gain ($)	4.03	0.09	0.57	4.86	2.07	1.39	0.87	1.02	2.47	0.84
Net Asset Value ($)	32.98	36.50	29.29	33.87	31.65	27.95	22.72	23.22	20.41	16.06
Expense Ratio (%)	na	1.34	1.15	1.12	1.23	1.12	1.39	1.51	1.48	1.69
Yield (%)	0.00	0.00	0.36	0.43	0.17	0.44	0.00	0.00	0.00	0.00
Portfolio Turnover (%)	na	23	36	55	31	25	35	51	76	79
Total Assets (Millions $)	897	1,195	1,545	2,126	1,627	1,190	338	186	43	29

PORTFOLIO (as of 6/30/00)

Portfolio Manager: William Nasgovitz, Eric Miller - 1984

Investm't Category: Growth

✔ Domestic　　Index
✔ Foreign　　Sector
Asset Allocation　　State Specific

Investment Style

Large Cap　　Mid Cap　　✔ Small Cap
Growth　　Grth/Val　　✔ Value

Portfolio

1.4%	cash	0.0%	corp bonds
98.6%	stocks	0.0%	gov't bonds
0.0%	pref/conv't pref	0.0%	muni bonds
0.0%	conv't bds/wrnts	0.0%	other

SHAREHOLDER INFORMATION

Minimum Investment

Initial: $5,000　　Subsequent: $100

Minimum IRA Investment

Initial: $500　　Subsequent: $100

Maximum Fees

Load: none　　12b-1: 0.25%
Other: none

Services

✔ IRA
✔ Keogh
✔ Telephone Exchange

Hennessy Crnst Grth

800-261-6950, 415-899-1555
www.oshaughnessyfunds.com

(HFCGX)

Growth

PERFORMANCE — fund inception date: 11/1/96

	3yr Annual	5yr Annual	10yr Annual	Bull	Bear
Return (%)	14.5	na	na	78.1	-8.0
Differ from Category (+/-)	3.5 abv av	na	na	28.4 high	-2.6 av

Standard Deviation	Category Risk Index	Beta
27.9%—high	1.43—high	1.37

	2000	1999	1998	1997	1996	1995	1994	1993	1992	1991
Return (%)	5.3	37.7	3.6	31.3	—	—	—	—	—	—
Differ from Category (+/-)	1.8	18.8	-10.7	4.2	—	—	—	—	—	—
Return, Tax-Adjusted (%)	1.0	37.7	3.6	27.7	—	—	—	—	—	—

PER SHARE DATA

	2000	1999	1998	1997	1996	1995	1994	1993	1992	1991
Dividends, Net Income ($)	0.00	0.00	0.00	0.00	—	—	—	—	—	—
Distrib'ns, Cap Gain ($)	3.50	0.00	0.00	1.78	—	—	—	—	—	—
Net Asset Value ($)	13.85	16.32	11.85	11.43	—	—	—	—	—	—
Expense Ratio (%)	1.18	1.15	1.16	1.56	—	—	—	—	—	—
Yield (%)	0.00	0.00	0.00	0.00	—	—	—	—	—	—
Portfolio Turnover (%)	95	125	119	—	—	—	—	—	—	—
Total Assets (Millions $)	153	157	116	54	—	—	—	—	—	—

PORTFOLIO (as of 6/30/00)

Portfolio Manager: J. O'Shaughnessy, N. Hennessey - 2000

Investm't Category: Growth

✔ Domestic
Foreign
Asset Allocation
Index
Sector
State Specific

Investment Style

✔ Large Cap
✔ Mid Cap
Small Cap
✔ Growth
Grth/Val
Value

Portfolio

-0.3%	cash	0.0%	corp bonds
100.3%	stocks	0.0%	gov't bonds
0.0%	pref/conv't pref	0.0%	muni bonds
0.0%	conv't bds/wrnts	0.0%	other

SHAREHOLDER INFORMATION

Minimum Investment
Initial: $2,500 Subsequent: $250

Minimum IRA Investment
Initial: $250 Subsequent: $250

Maximum Fees
Load: 1.50% redemption 12b-1: none
Other: redemption fee applies for 3 months

Services
✔ IRA
✔ Keogh
✔ Telephone Exchange

Homestead: Value (HOVLX)

800-258-3030, 703-907-6039
www.nreca.org/homestead

Growth & Income

PERFORMANCE

fund inception date: 11/19/90

	3yr Annual	5yr Annual	10yr Annual	Bull	Bear
Return (%)	4.7	11.4	13.8	12.3	1.4
Differ from Category (+/-)	-4.2 low	-2.9 low	-1.1 blw av	-21.2 low	1.5 av

Standard Deviation	Category Risk Index	Beta
17.6%—av	1.01—av	0.67

	2000	1999	1998	1997	1996	1995	1994	1993	1992	1991
Return (%)	9.6	-3.2	8.3	26.6	17.9	33.7	2.4	18.8	11.6	17.1
Differ from Category (+/-)	3.9	-14.0	-4.5	-0.3	-1.8	4.2	2.9	5.0	0.0	-11.0
Return, Tax-Adjusted (%)	8.9	-5.1	7.1	25.2	16.5	31.6	1.4	17.9	10.7	15.9

PER SHARE DATA

	2000	1999	1998	1997	1996	1995	1994	1993	1992	1991
Dividends, Net Income ($)	0.38	0.41	0.39	0.36	0.38	0.40	0.28	0.22	0.24	0.38
Distrib'ns, Cap Gain ($)	0.00	1.73	0.72	0.71	0.35	0.52	0.11	0.07	0.07	0.01
Net Asset Value ($)	25.38	23.53	26.50	25.50	20.99	18.44	14.50	14.54	12.49	11.48
Expense Ratio (%)	na	0.74	0.72	0.79	0.73	0.97	1.15	1.25	1.25	1.25
Yield (%)	1.49	1.62	1.43	1.37	1.78	2.10	1.91	1.50	1.91	3.30
Portfolio Turnover (%)	na	17	10	6	5	10	4	2	5	26
Total Assets (Millions $)	313	375	434	366	232	141	90	52	19	10

PORTFOLIO (as of 6/30/00)

Portfolio Manager: Peter Morris, Stuart Teach - 1990

Investm't Category: Growth & Income

✔ Domestic
Foreign
Asset Allocation
Index
Sector
State Specific

Investment Style

✔ Large Cap
✔ Mid Cap
Small Cap
Growth
Grth/Val
✔ Value

Portfolio

1.7%	cash	0.0%	corp bonds
98.0%	stocks	0.0%	gov't bonds
0.3%	pref/conv't pref	0.0%	muni bonds
0.0%	conv't bds/wrnts	0.0%	other

SHAREHOLDER INFORMATION

Minimum Investment

Initial: $500 Subsequent: $1

Minimum IRA Investment

Initial: $200 Subsequent: $1

Maximum Fees

Load: none 12b-1: none
Other: none

Services

✔ IRA
✔ Keogh
✔ Telephone Exchange

ICAP: Discretionary Equity (ICDEX)

888-221-4227
www.icapfunds.com

Growth & Income

PERFORMANCE — fund inception date: 1/3/95

	3yr Annual	5yr Annual	10yr Annual	Bull	Bear
Return (%)	11.0	17.2	na	36.1	1.7
Differ from Category (+/-)	2.1 abv av	2.9 abv av	na	2.6 av	1.8 av

Standard Deviation	Category Risk Index	Beta
16.0%—av	0.92—blw av	0.75

	2000	1999	1998	1997	1996	1995	1994	1993	1992	1991
Return (%)	8.3	14.8	10.1	28.6	25.5	—	—	—	—	—
Differ from Category (+/-)	2.6	4.0	-2.7	1.7	5.8	—	—	—	—	—
Return, Tax-Adjusted (%)	4.6	12.6	8.8	23.2	22.7	—	—	—	—	—

PER SHARE DATA

	2000	1999	1998	1997	1996	1995	1994	1993	1992	1991
Dividends, Net Income ($)	0.41	0.45	0.51	0.48	0.35	—	—	—	—	—
Distrib'ns, Cap Gain ($)	5.29	2.58	0.89	6.99	1.96	—	—	—	—	—
Net Asset Value ($)	30.51	33.69	32.01	30.34	29.55	—	—	—	—	—
Expense Ratio (%)	na	0.80	0.80	0.80	0.80	—	—	—	—	—
Yield (%)	1.14	1.24	1.55	1.28	1.11	—	—	—	—	—
Portfolio Turnover (%)	na	137	129	131	138	—	—	—	—	—
Total Assets (Millions $)	142	222	205	157	110	—	—	—	—	—

PORTFOLIO (as of 6/30/00)

Portfolio Manager: committee - 1995

Investm't Category: Growth & Income

✔ Domestic — Index
✔ Foreign — Sector
Asset Allocation — State Specific

Investment Style

✔ Large Cap — Mid Cap — Small Cap
Growth — Grth/Val — ✔ Value

Portfolio

4.0%	cash	0.0%	corp bonds
96.0%	stocks	0.0%	gov't bonds
0.0%	pref/conv't pref	0.0%	muni bonds
0.0%	conv't bds/wrnts	0.0%	other

SHAREHOLDER INFORMATION

Minimum Investment
Initial: $10,000 — Subsequent: $1,000

Minimum IRA Investment
Initial: $10,000 — Subsequent: $1,000

Maximum Fees
Load: none — 12b-1: none
Other: none

Services
✔ IRA
✔ Keogh
✔ Telephone Exchange

ICAP: Equity (ICAEX)

888-221-4227
www.icapfunds.com

Growth & Income

PERFORMANCE — fund inception date: 1/3/95

	3yr Annual	5yr Annual	10yr Annual	Bull	Bear
Return (%)	11.8	17.8	na	41.2	1.3
Differ from Category (+/-)	2.9 abv av	3.5 high	na	7.7 abv av	1.4 av

Standard Deviation	Category Risk Index	Beta
17.0%—av	0.98—av	0.81

	2000	1999	1998	1997	1996	1995	1994	1993	1992	1991
Return (%)	7.8	16.2	11.4	29.0	26.2	—	—	—	—	—
Differ from Category (+/-)	2.1	5.4	-1.4	2.1	6.5	—	—	—	—	—
Return, Tax-Adjusted (%)	6.2	15.0	10.8	25.5	24.2	—	—	—	—	—

PER SHARE DATA

	2000	1999	1998	1997	1996	1995	1994	1993	1992	1991
Dividends, Net Income ($)	0.48	0.51	0.49	0.37	0.29	—	—	—	—	—
Distrib'ns, Cap Gain ($)	2.34	1.24	0.00	4.59	1.37	—	—	—	—	—
Net Asset Value ($)	43.66	43.14	38.63	35.12	31.16	—	—	—	—	—
Expense Ratio (%)	na	0.80	0.80	0.80	0.80	—	—	—	—	—
Yield (%)	1.04	1.14	1.26	0.93	0.89	—	—	—	—	—
Portfolio Turnover (%)	na	118	133	121	125	—	—	—	—	—
Total Assets (Millions $)	1,017	959	717	371	149	—	—	—	—	—

PORTFOLIO (as of 6/30/00)

Portfolio Manager: committee - 1995

Investm't Category: Growth & Income

✔ Domestic — Index
✔ Foreign — Sector
Asset Allocation — State Specific

Investment Style

✔ Large Cap — Mid Cap — Small Cap
Growth — Grth/Val — ✔ Value

Portfolio

1.1%	cash	0.0%	corp bonds
98.9%	stocks	0.0%	gov't bonds
0.0%	pref/conv't pref	0.0%	muni bonds
0.0%	conv't bds/wrnts	0.0%	other

SHAREHOLDER INFORMATION

Minimum Investment

Initial: $10,000 — Subsequent: $1,000

Minimum IRA Investment

Initial: $10,000 — Subsequent: $1,000

Maximum Fees

Load: none — 12b-1: none
Other: none

Services

✔ IRA
✔ Keogh
✔ Telephone Exchange

ICON Leisure & Consumer (ICLEX)

888-389-4266, 817-251-6700

Growth

PERFORMANCE

fund inception date: 5/12/97

	3yr Annual	5yr Annual	10yr Annual	Bull	Bear
Return (%)	8.7	na	na	23.4	11.6
Differ from Category (+/-)	-2.3 blw av	na	na	-26.3 blw av	17.0 high

Standard Deviation	Category Risk Index	Beta
19.1%—abv av	0.98—av	0.71

	2000	1999	1998	1997	1996	1995	1994	1993	1992	1991
Return (%)	14.3	-4.5	17.8	—	—	—	—	—	—	—
Differ from Category (+/-)	10.8	-23.4	3.5	—	—	—	—	—	—	—
Return, Tax-Adjusted (%)	14.2	-9.5	14.8	—	—	—	—	—	—	—

PER SHARE DATA

	2000	1999	1998	1997	1996	1995	1994	1993	1992	1991
Dividends, Net Income ($)	0.00	0.00	0.26	—	—	—	—	—	—	—
Distrib'ns, Cap Gain ($)	0.02	3.07	1.18	—	—	—	—	—	—	—
Net Asset Value ($)	9.59	8.41	12.09	—	—	—	—	—	—	—
Expense Ratio (%)	1.51	1.38	1.30	—	—	—	—	—	—	—
Yield (%)	0.00	0.00	1.95	—	—	—	—	—	—	—
Portfolio Turnover (%)	24	49	34	—	—	—	—	—	—	—
Total Assets (Millions $)	62	28	42	—	—	—	—	—	—	—

PORTFOLIO (as of 6/30/00)

Portfolio Manager: Craig Callahan - 1999

Investm't Category: Growth

✔ Domestic
Foreign
Asset Allocation
Index
✔ Sector
State Specific

Investment Style

✔ Large Cap
✔ Mid Cap
Small Cap
Growth
Grth/Val
✔ Value

Portfolio

2.2% cash
97.8% stocks
0.0% pref/conv't pref
0.0% conv't bds/wrnts
0.0% corp bonds
0.0% gov't bonds
0.0% muni bonds
0.0% other

SHAREHOLDER INFORMATION

Minimum Investment

Initial: $1,000 Subsequent: $100

Minimum IRA Investment

Initial: $1,000 Subsequent: $100

Maximum Fees

Load: none 12b-1: none
Other: none

Services

✔ IRA
✔ Keogh
✔ Telephone Exchange

INVESCO Balanced/Inv (IMABX)

800-525-8085, 303-930-6300
www.invesco.com

Balanced

PERFORMANCE — fund inception date: 12/1/93

	3yr Annual	5yr Annual	10yr Annual	Bull	Bear
Return (%)	10.3	13.0	na	38.0	-6.0
Differ from Category (+/-)	1.9 abv av	1.6 abv av	na	9.9 abv av	-2.8 blw av

Standard Deviation	Category Risk Index	Beta
12.1%—blw av	1.11—abv av	0.65

	2000	1999	1998	1997	1996	1995	1994	1993	1992	1991
Return (%)	-1.8	16.8	17.3	19.5	14.6	36.4	7.7	—	—	—
Differ from Category (+/-)	-3.8	6.1	4.0	0.7	0.7	10.9	9.0	—	—	—
Return, Tax-Adjusted (%)	-2.8	15.3	15.6	16.1	11.5	33.0	6.8	—	—	—

PER SHARE DATA

	2000	1999	1998	1997	1996	1995	1994	1993	1992	1991
Dividends, Net Income ($)	0.36	0.33	0.26	0.35	0.39	0.30	0.05	—	—	—
Distrib'ns, Cap Gain ($)	0.25	0.52	0.66	1.63	0.87	0.84	0.24	—	—	—
Net Asset Value ($)	16.86	17.80	16.01	14.48	13.82	13.19	10.54	—	—	—
Expense Ratio (%)	1.15	1.21	1.22	1.29	1.29	1.25	1.25	—	—	—
Yield (%)	2.10	1.80	1.55	2.17	2.65	2.13	0.46	—	—	—
Portfolio Turnover (%)	89	100	108	155	259	255	61	—	—	—
Total Assets (Millions $)	970	487	260	167	134	87	12	—	—	—

PORTFOLIO (as of 6/30/00)

Portfolio Manager: Jerry Paul, Charles Mayer - 1994

Investm't Category: Balanced

✔ Domestic — Index
Foreign — Sector
Asset Allocation — State Specific

Investment Style

Large Cap — Mid Cap — Small Cap
Growth — Grth/Val — Value

Portfolio

3.0%	cash	21.2%	corp bonds
65.8%	stocks	9.0%	gov't bonds
1.1%	pref/conv't pref	0.0%	muni bonds
0.0%	conv't bds/wrnts	0.0%	other

SHAREHOLDER INFORMATION

Minimum Investment
Initial: $1,000 — Subsequent: $50

Minimum IRA Investment
Initial: $250 — Subsequent: $50

Maximum Fees
Load: none — 12b-1: 0.25%
Other: none

Services
✔ IRA
Keogh
✔ Telephone Exchange

INVESCO Blue Chip Gr/Inv (FLRFX)

800-525-8085, 303-930-6300
www.invesco.com

Growth

PERFORMANCE

fund inception date: 11/25/35

	3yr Annual	5yr Annual	10yr Annual	Bull	Bear
Return (%)	14.2	18.1	16.6	88.2	-25.8
Differ from Category (+/-)	3.2 abv av	2.0 abv av	-0.2 av	38.5 high	-20.4 low

Standard Deviation	Category Risk Index	Beta
29.3%—high	1.50—high	1.29

	2000	1999	1998	1997	1996	1995	1994	1993	1992	1991
Return (%)	-23.9	38.4	41.7	27.2	20.9	29.5	-8.8	17.9	2.9	42.1
Differ from Category (+/-)	-27.4	19.5	27.4	0.1	-1.4	-0.9	-8.6	3.3	-9.7	4.5
Return, Tax-Adjusted (%)	-26.5	36.0	39.5	21.0	16.4	23.8	-11.5	15.2	0.0	38.5

PER SHARE DATA

	2000	1999	1998	1997	1996	1995	1994	1993	1992	1991
Dividends, Net Income ($)	0.00	0.00	0.02	0.00	0.02	0.05	0.03	0.03	0.04	0.07
Distrib'ns, Cap Gain ($)	1.07	0.76	0.50	1.60	0.76	0.84	0.50	0.44	0.54	0.47
Net Asset Value ($)	5.15	8.11	6.46	4.96	5.19	4.95	4.52	5.54	5.12	5.59
Expense Ratio (%)	1.02	1.03	1.04	1.07	1.05	1.06	1.03	1.04	1.04	1.00
Yield (%)	0.00	0.00	0.28	0.00	0.33	0.86	0.59	0.50	0.70	1.15
Portfolio Turnover (%)	168	134	153	286	207	111	63	77	77	69
Total Assets (Millions $)	1,711	1,637	1,220	753	651	535	444	510	449	455

PORTFOLIO (as of 6/30/00)

Portfolio Manager: Trent May - 1996

Investm't Category: Growth

✔ Domestic	Index
Foreign	Sector
Asset Allocation	State Specific

Investment Style

✔ Large Cap	Mid Cap	Small Cap
✔ Growth	Grth/Val	Value

Portfolio

1.7% cash	0.0% corp bonds
98.3% stocks	0.0% gov't bonds
0.0% pref/conv't pref	0.0% muni bonds
0.0% conv't bds/wrnts	0.0% other

SHAREHOLDER INFORMATION

Minimum Investment
Initial: $1,000 Subsequent: $50

Minimum IRA Investment
Initial: $250 Subsequent: $50

Maximum Fees
Load: none 12b-1: 0.25%
Other: none

Services
✔ IRA
✔ Keogh
✔ Telephone Exchange

INVESCO Dynamics/Inv (FIDYX)

800-525-8085, 303-930-6300
www.invesco.com

Aggressive Growth

PERFORMANCE — fund inception date: 9/15/67

	3yr Annual	5yr Annual	10yr Annual	Bull	Bear
Return (%)	24.9	22.8	23.8	132.1	-24.1
Differ from Category (+/-)	8.7 abv av	8.2 abv av	8.0 high	12.9 abv av	-3.5 av

Standard Deviation	Category Risk Index	Beta
32.7%—high	1.01—av	1.24

	2000	1999	1998	1997	1996	1995	1994	1993	1992	1991
Return (%)	-7.7	71.7	23.2	24.0	15.6	37.5	-1.9	19.1	13.1	67.0
Differ from Category (+/-)	-1.7	14.2	8.1	9.2	-2.7	2.9	-1.1	-6.1	6.2	19.8
Return, Tax-Adjusted (%)	-7.7	70.3	21.3	20.9	12.4	32.7	-6.8	17.1	12.3	62.2

PER SHARE DATA

	2000	1999	1998	1997	1996	1995	1994	1993	1992	1991
Dividends, Net Income ($)	0.00	0.00	0.00	0.00	0.01	0.03	0.00	0.00	0.00	0.00
Distrib'ns, Cap Gain ($)	0.07	1.04	1.30	1.94	1.36	1.70	2.29	0.80	0.28	1.20
Net Asset Value ($)	23.77	25.86	15.75	13.96	12.89	12.34	10.24	12.83	11.50	10.47
Expense Ratio (%)	0.89	1.03	1.08	1.16	1.14	1.20	1.17	1.20	1.18	1.15
Yield (%)	0.00	0.00	0.00	0.00	0.07	0.21	0.00	0.00	0.00	0.00
Portfolio Turnover (%)	75	23	178	204	196	176	169	144	174	243
Total Assets (Millions $)	7,548	4,609	1,549	1,120	856	624	338	319	273	141

PORTFOLIO (as of 6/30/00)

Portfolio Manager: Timothy Miller, Thomas Wald - 1993

Investm't Category: Aggressive Growth

✔ Domestic — Index
✔ Foreign — Sector
Asset Allocation — State Specific

Investment Style

Large Cap — Mid Cap — ✔ Small Cap
✔ Growth — Grth/Val — Value

Portfolio

7.0%	cash	0.0%	corp bonds
93.1%	stocks	0.0%	gov't bonds
0.0%	pref/conv't pref	0.0%	muni bonds
0.0%	conv't bds/wrnts	0.0%	other

SHAREHOLDER INFORMATION

Minimum Investment
Initial: $1,000 — Subsequent: $50

Minimum IRA Investment
Initial: $250 — Subsequent: $50

Maximum Fees
Load: none — 12b-1: 0.25%
Other: none

Services
✔ IRA
✔ Keogh
✔ Telephone Exchange

INVESCO Energy/Inv (FSTEX)

800-525-8085, 303-930-6300
www.invesco.com

Aggressive Growth

PERFORMANCE

fund inception date: 1/19/84

	3yr Annual	5yr Annual	10yr Annual	Bull	Bear
Return (%)	17.4	21.7	11.2	56.1	4.5
Differ from Category (+/-)	1.2 av	7.1 abv av	-4.6 low	-63.1 blw av	25.1 high

Standard Deviation	Category Risk Index	Beta
37.2%—high	1.15—abv av	0.98

	2000	1999	1998	1997	1996	1995	1994	1993	1992	1991
Return (%)	58.1	41.8	-27.8	19.0	38.8	19.7	-7.2	16.7	-13.2	-3.4
Differ from Category (+/-)	64.1	-15.7	-42.9	4.2	20.5	-14.9	-6.4	-8.5	-20.1	-50.6
Return, Tax-Adjusted (%)	56.1	41.8	-27.8	14.6	35.7	19.3	-7.3	16.2	-13.2	-3.7

PER SHARE DATA

	2000	1999	1998	1997	1996	1995	1994	1993	1992	1991
Dividends, Net Income ($)	0.00	0.00	0.01	0.06	0.03	0.09	0.05	0.10	0.02	0.11
Distrib'ns, Cap Gain ($)	1.43	0.00	0.00	3.03	1.21	0.00	0.00	0.00	0.00	0.00
Net Asset Value ($)	20.88	14.33	10.10	14.01	14.46	11.36	9.57	10.37	8.97	10.36
Expense Ratio (%)	1.60	1.68	1.58	1.21	1.30	1.53	1.35	1.18	1.73	1.69
Yield (%)	0.00	0.00	0.09	0.35	0.19	0.79	0.52	0.96	0.22	1.06
Portfolio Turnover (%)	109	279	192	249	392	300	123	190	370	337
Total Assets (Millions $)	374	170	105	212	233	98	46	49	12	10

PORTFOLIO (as of 6/30/00)

Portfolio Manager: John Segner - 1997

Investm't Category: Aggressive Growth

✔ Domestic Index
✔ Foreign ✔ Sector
Asset Allocation State Specific

Investment Style

Large Cap ✔ Mid Cap ✔ Small Cap
Growth Grth/Val ✔ Value

Portfolio

4.0%	cash	0.0%	corp bonds
96.0%	stocks	0.0%	gov't bonds
0.0%	pref/conv't pref	0.0%	muni bonds
0.0%	conv't bds/wrnts	0.0%	other

SHAREHOLDER INFORMATION

Minimum Investment

Initial: $1,000 Subsequent: $50

Minimum IRA Investment

Initial: $250 Subsequent: $50

Maximum Fees

Load: none 12b-1: 0.25%
Other: none

Services

✔ IRA
✔ Keogh
✔ Telephone Exchange

INVESCO Equity Income/Inv (FIIIX)

800-525-8085, 303-930-6300
www.invesco.com

Balanced

PERFORMANCE — fund inception date: 2/1/60

	3yr Annual	5yr Annual	10yr Annual	Bull	Bear
Return (%)	10.1	14.5	15.3	33.8	-4.3
Differ from Category (+/-)	1.7 abv av	3.1 high	3.6 high	5.7 abv av	-1.1 av

Standard Deviation	Category Risk Index	Beta
13.6%—blw av	1.24—high	0.72

	2000	1999	1998	1997	1996	1995	1994	1993	1992	1991
Return (%)	3.8	12.8	14.1	26.4	16.7	27.3	-3.8	16.6	0.9	46.2
Differ from Category (+/-)	1.8	2.1	0.8	7.6	2.8	1.8	-2.5	2.2	-7.5	22.4
Return, Tax-Adjusted (%)	1.7	10.1	11.1	22.8	13.3	25.1	-6.4	13.7	-0.7	43.5

PER SHARE DATA

	2000	1999	1998	1997	1996	1995	1994	1993	1992	1991
Dividends, Net Income ($)	0.19	0.26	0.36	0.36	0.39	0.40	0.41	0.43	0.29	0.31
Distrib'ns, Cap Gain ($)	1.22	1.45	1.51	1.66	0.95	0.23	0.53	0.54	0.38	0.46
Net Asset Value ($)	14.36	15.25	15.06	14.91	13.46	12.72	10.52	11.93	11.10	11.70
Expense Ratio (%)	0.93	0.90	0.90	0.95	0.93	0.94	0.92	0.96	0.98	0.94
Yield (%)	1.21	1.55	2.17	2.17	2.70	3.08	3.71	3.44	2.52	2.54
Portfolio Turnover (%)	50	47	58	47	63	54	56	121	119	104
Total Assets (Millions $)	4,124	4,712	4,927	4,858	4,281	4,256	3,695	3,905	2,751	1,596

PORTFOLIO (as of 6/30/00)

Portfolio Manager: Charles Mayer - 2000

Investm't Category: Balanced

✔ Domestic — Index
✔ Foreign — Sector
✔ Asset Allocation — State Specific

Investment Style

Large Cap — Mid Cap — Small Cap
Growth — Grth/Val — Value

Portfolio

5.9%	cash	12.1%	corp bonds
81.0%	stocks	0.2%	gov't bonds
0.7%	pref/conv't pref	0.0%	muni bonds
0.0%	conv't bds/wrnts	0.0%	other

SHAREHOLDER INFORMATION

Minimum Investment
Initial: $1,000 — Subsequent: $50

Minimum IRA Investment
Initial: $250 — Subsequent: $50

Maximum Fees
Load: none — 12b-1: 0.25%
Other: none

Services
✔ IRA
✔ Keogh
✔ Telephone Exchange

INVESCO European/Inv

800-525-8085, 303-930-6300
www.invesco.com

(FEURX)

International Stock

PERFORMANCE — fund inception date: 6/2/86

	3yr Annual	5yr Annual	10yr Annual	Bull	Bear
Return (%)	13.7	17.0	12.1	47.7	-34.7
Differ from Category (+/-)	4.8 abv av	8.7 high	3.1 abv av	-43.2 blw av	-10.7 low

Standard Deviation	Category Risk Index	Beta
27.9%—high	1.23—abv av	0.74

	2000	1999	1998	1997	1996	1995	1994	1993	1992	1991
Return (%)	-19.4	37.5	32.9	15.1	29.6	19.1	-3.0	24.5	-7.6	8.0
Differ from Category (+/-)	0.0	-23.2	27.1	13.8	15.1	9.8	0.1	-15.7	-4.1	-5.0
Return, Tax-Adjusted (%)	-20.6	37.0	30.5	10.7	27.0	15.5	-3.4	24.0	-8.1	6.9

PER SHARE DATA

	2000	1999	1998	1997	1996	1995	1994	1993	1992	1991
Dividends, Net Income ($)	0.00	0.00	0.03	0.09	0.05	0.24	0.15	0.13	0.19	0.36
Distrib'ns, Cap Gain ($)	1.47	0.44	1.69	3.27	1.13	1.21	0.00	0.00	0.00	0.00
Net Asset Value ($)	17.80	24.04	17.87	14.82	15.86	13.19	12.29	12.83	10.41	11.49
Expense Ratio (%)	1.33	1.56	1.34	1.25	1.36	0.70	1.20	1.28	1.29	1.43
Yield (%)	0.00	0.00	0.15	0.49	0.29	1.66	1.22	1.01	1.82	3.13
Portfolio Turnover (%)	84	90	102	90	91	42	70	44	87	61
Total Assets (Millions $)	736	742	770	331	326	221	245	308	124	79

PORTFOLIO (as of 6/30/00)

Portfolio Manager: committee - 1990

Investm't Category: International Stock

Domestic — Index
✔ Foreign — Sector
Asset Allocation — State Specific

Investment Style

Large Cap — Mid Cap — Small Cap
Growth — Grth/Val — Value

Portfolio

3.7%	cash	0.0%	corp bonds
93.7%	stocks	0.0%	gov't bonds
2.5%	pref/conv't pref	0.0%	muni bonds
0.0%	conv't bds/wrnts	0.0%	other

SHAREHOLDER INFORMATION

Minimum Investment
Initial: $1,000 — Subsequent: $50

Minimum IRA Investment
Initial: $250 — Subsequent: $50

Maximum Fees
Load: 2.00% redemption — 12b-1: 0.25%
Other: redemption fee applies for 3 months

Services
✔ IRA
✔ Keogh
✔ Telephone Exchange

INVESCO Financial Svc/Inv (FSFSX)

800-525-8085, 303-930-6300
www.invesco.com

Growth

PERFORMANCE — fund inception date: 6/2/86

	3yr Annual	5yr Annual	10yr Annual	Bull	Bear
Return (%)	13.1	22.2	25.1	23.3	12.6
Differ from Category (+/-)	2.1 abv av	6.1 high	8.3 high	-26.4 blw av	18.0 high

Standard Deviation	Category Risk Index	Beta
24.9%—abv av	1.28—high	1.05

	2000	1999	1998	1997	1996	1995	1994	1993	1992	1991
Return (%)	26.6	0.7	13.4	44.7	30.2	39.8	-5.8	18.4	26.7	73.9
Differ from Category (+/-)	23.1	-18.2	-0.9	17.6	7.9	9.4	-5.6	3.8	14.1	36.3
Return, Tax-Adjusted (%)	25.5	-1.2	11.4	40.9	26.2	36.8	-6.6	10.9	24.5	73.1

PER SHARE DATA

	2000	1999	1998	1997	1996	1995	1994	1993	1992	1991
Dividends, Net Income ($)	0.08	0.08	0.24	0.24	0.53	0.28	0.34	0.21	0.18	0.11
Distrib'ns, Cap Gain ($)	1.22	2.64	2.23	3.69	1.93	1.14	0.00	4.30	0.90	0.10
Net Asset Value ($)	32.29	26.62	29.18	28.11	22.22	19.02	14.64	15.91	17.24	14.57
Expense Ratio (%)	1.29	1.26	1.05	0.99	1.11	1.26	1.18	1.03	1.07	1.13
Yield (%)	0.23	0.27	0.76	0.75	2.19	1.38	2.32	1.03	0.99	0.74
Portfolio Turnover (%)	38	83	52	96	141	171	88	236	208	249
Total Assets (Millions $)	1,347	1,123	1,522	1,307	622	432	236	339	246	90

PORTFOLIO (as of 6/30/00)

Portfolio Manager: Jeffery Morris - 1997

Investm't Category: Growth

✔ Domestic — Index
✔ Foreign — ✔ Sector
Asset Allocation — State Specific

Investment Style

✔ Large Cap — Mid Cap — Small Cap
Growth — Grth/Val — ✔ Value

Portfolio

7.4%	cash	0.0%	corp bonds
92.6%	stocks	0.0%	gov't bonds
0.0%	pref/conv't pref	0.0%	muni bonds
0.0%	conv't bds/wrnts	0.0%	other

SHAREHOLDER INFORMATION

Minimum Investment

Initial: $1,000 — Subsequent: $50

Minimum IRA Investment

Initial: $250 — Subsequent: $50

Maximum Fees

Load: none — 12b-1: 0.25%
Other: none

Services

✔ IRA
✔ Keogh
✔ Telephone Exchange

INVESCO Gold/Inv (FGLDX)

800-525-8085, 303-930-6300
www.invesco.com

Aggressive Growth

PERFORMANCE — fund inception date: 1/19/84

	3yr Annual	5yr Annual	10yr Annual	Bull	Bear
Return (%)	-15.0	-17.4	-7.4	26.4	-16.2
Differ from Category (+/-)	-31.2 low	-32.0 low	-23.2 low	-92.8 low	4.4 abv av

Standard Deviation	Category Risk Index	Beta
40.9%—high	1.26—high	0.75

	2000	1999	1998	1997	1996	1995	1994	1993	1992	1991
Return (%)	-12.9	-8.9	-22.5	-55.4	40.6	12.7	-27.8	72.6	-8.2	-7.1
Differ from Category (+/-)	-6.9	-66.4	-37.6	-70.2	22.3	-21.9	-27.0	47.4	-15.1	-54.3
Return, Tax-Adjusted (%)	-13.5	-8.9	-22.5	-55.6	25.1	12.7	-27.8	72.6	-8.2	-7.1

PER SHARE DATA

	2000	1999	1998	1997	1996	1995	1994	1993	1992	1991
Dividends, Net Income ($)	0.03	0.00	0.00	0.03	2.14	0.00	0.00	0.00	0.00	0.00
Distrib'ns, Cap Gain ($)	0.00	0.00	0.00	0.00	0.00	0.00	0.00	0.00	0.00	0.00
Net Asset Value ($)	1.46	1.72	1.89	2.44	5.56	5.48	4.87	6.75	3.91	4.26
Expense Ratio (%)	2.08	2.20	1.90	1.47	1.22	1.32	1.07	1.03	1.41	1.47
Yield (%)	2.05	0.00	0.00	1.22	38.48	0.00	0.00	0.00	0.00	0.00
Portfolio Turnover (%)	37	141	133	148	155	72	97	142	101	43
Total Assets (Millions $)	64	95	99	127	229	163	222	315	55	35

PORTFOLIO (as of 6/30/00)

Portfolio Manager: John Segner - 1999

Investm't Category: Aggressive Growth

✔ Domestic
✔ Foreign
Asset Allocation
Index
✔ Sector
State Specific

Investment Style

Large Cap — Mid Cap — Small Cap
Growth — Grth/Val — Value

Portfolio

7.2%	cash	0.0%	corp bonds
75.0%	stocks	0.0%	gov't bonds
5.8%	pref/conv't pref	0.0%	muni bonds
0.0%	conv't bds/wrnts	12.1%	other

SHAREHOLDER INFORMATION

Minimum Investment
Initial: $1,000 — Subsequent: $50

Minimum IRA Investment
Initial: $250 — Subsequent: $50

Maximum Fees
Load: none — 12b-1: 0.25%
Other: none

Services
✔ IRA
✔ Keogh
✔ Telephone Exchange

INVESCO Health Sci/Inv

800-525-8085, 303-930-6300
www.invesco.com

(FHLSX)

Aggressive Growth

PERFORMANCE — fund inception date: 1/19/84

	3yr Annual	5yr Annual	10yr Annual	Bull	Bear
Return (%)	21.9	19.0	19.2	29.4	16.9
Differ from Category (+/-)	5.7 abv av	4.4 abv av	3.4 abv av	-89.8 low	37.5 high

Standard Deviation	Category Risk Index	Beta
30.0%—high	0.92—blw av	0.38

	2000	1999	1998	1997	1996	1995	1994	1993	1992	1991
Return (%)	25.8	0.5	43.3	18.4	11.4	58.8	0.9	-8.4	-13.7	91.7
Differ from Category (+/-)	31.8	-57.0	28.2	3.6	-6.9	24.2	1.7	-33.6	-20.6	44.5
Return, Tax-Adjusted (%)	22.4	-1.6	39.6	14.6	6.7	55.6	0.9	-8.4	-14.0	87.7

PER SHARE DATA

	2000	1999	1998	1997	1996	1995	1994	1993	1992	1991
Dividends, Net Income ($)	0.00	0.28	0.12	0.18	0.07	0.00	0.00	0.00	0.10	0.10
Distrib'ns, Cap Gain ($)	9.10	6.08	8.85	8.80	8.59	4.00	0.00	0.00	0.44	3.47
Net Asset Value ($)	59.37	54.89	61.04	49.18	49.36	52.35	35.47	35.14	38.38	45.17
Expense Ratio (%)	1.18	1.22	1.12	1.08	0.98	1.15	1.19	1.16	1.00	1.03
Yield (%)	0.00	0.45	0.17	0.31	0.12	0.00	0.00	0.00	0.25	0.20
Portfolio Turnover (%)	107	127	92	143	90	107	80	87	91	100
Total Assets (Millions $)	1,989	1,518	1,567	945	936	1,040	488	566	792	1,069

PORTFOLIO (as of 6/30/00)

Portfolio Manager: John Schroer - 1994

Investm't Category: Aggressive Growth

✔ Domestic — Index
✔ Foreign — ✔ Sector
Asset Allocation — State Specific

Investment Style

Large Cap — Mid Cap — ✔ Small Cap
✔ Growth — Grth/Val — Value

Portfolio

8.8%	cash	0.0%	corp bonds
90.9%	stocks	0.0%	gov't bonds
0.3%	pref/conv't pref	0.0%	muni bonds
0.0%	conv't bds/wrnts	0.0%	other

SHAREHOLDER INFORMATION

Minimum Investment
Initial: $1,000 — Subsequent: $50

Minimum IRA Investment
Initial: $250 — Subsequent: $50

Maximum Fees
Load: none — 12b-1: 0.25%
Other: none

Services
✔ IRA
✔ Keogh
✔ Telephone Exchange

INVESCO Leisure/Inv (FLISX)

800-525-8085, 303-930-6300
www.invesco.com

Growth

PERFORMANCE

fund inception date: 1/19/84

	3yr Annual	5yr Annual	10yr Annual	Bull	Bear
Return (%)	25.5	22.2	22.6	118.1	-11.3
Differ from Category (+/-)	14.5 high	6.1 high	5.8 high	68.4 high	-5.9 blw av

Standard Deviation	Category Risk Index	Beta
20.8%—abv av	1.07—av	1.04

	2000	1999	1998	1997	1996	1995	1994	1993	1992	1991
Return (%)	-7.9	65.5	29.7	26.4	9.0	15.7	-4.9	35.7	23.4	52.7
Differ from Category (+/-)	-11.4	46.6	15.4	-0.7	-13.3	-14.7	-4.7	21.1	10.8	15.1
Return, Tax-Adjusted (%)	-10.8	63.4	28.2	23.7	8.0	11.4	-5.9	32.8	21.6	47.7

PER SHARE DATA

	2000	1999	1998	1997	1996	1995	1994	1993	1992	1991
Dividends, Net Income ($)	0.00	0.00	0.00	0.01	0.04	0.08	0.00	0.00	0.00	0.00
Distrib'ns, Cap Gain ($)	6.94	3.22	1.90	2.97	0.63	3.14	0.91	1.89	0.98	2.12
Net Asset Value ($)	36.52	47.59	30.93	25.43	22.58	21.33	21.21	23.28	18.55	15.94
Expense Ratio (%)	1.28	1.44	1.41	1.41	1.30	1.29	1.17	1.14	1.51	1.86
Yield (%)	0.00	0.00	0.00	0.03	0.17	0.32	0.00	0.00	0.00	0.00
Portfolio Turnover (%)	23	35	31	25	56	119	116	116	148	122
Total Assets (Millions $)	539	556	276	222	237	262	262	304	79	17

PORTFOLIO (as of 6/30/00)

Portfolio Manager: Mark Greenberg - 1996

Investm't Category: Growth

✔ Domestic — Index
✔ Foreign — ✔ Sector
Asset Allocation — State Specific

Investment Style

✔ Large Cap — Mid Cap — Small Cap
✔ Growth — Grth/Val — Value

Portfolio

4.3%	cash	0.0%	corp bonds
94.7%	stocks	0.0%	gov't bonds
1.0%	pref/conv't pref	0.0%	muni bonds
0.0%	conv't bds/wrnts	0.0%	other

SHAREHOLDER INFORMATION

Minimum Investment
Initial: $1,000 — Subsequent: $50

Minimum IRA Investment
Initial: $250 — Subsequent: $50

Maximum Fees
Load: none — 12b-1: 0.25%
Other: none

Services
✔ IRA
✔ Keogh
✔ Telephone Exchange

INVESCO Small Co Grth/Inv (FIEGX)

800-525-8085, 303-930-6300
www.invesco.com

Aggressive Growth

this fund is closed to new investors

PERFORMANCE

fund inception date: 1/2/92

	3yr Annual	5yr Annual	10yr Annual	Bull	Bear
Return (%)	22.3	19.3	na	155.6	-28.0
Differ from Category (+/-)	6.1 abv av	4.7 abv av	na	36.4 abv av	-7.4 blw av

Standard Deviation	Category Risk Index	Beta
37.6%—high	1.16—abv av	1.29

	2000	1999	1998	1997	1996	1995	1994	1993	1992	1991
Return (%)	-12.1	81.6	14.8	18.3	11.6	30.0	-3.7	23.3	25.7	—
Differ from Category (+/-)	-6.1	24.1	-0.3	3.5	-6.7	-4.6	-2.9	-1.9	18.8	—
Return, Tax-Adjusted (%)	-13.0	78.1	12.7	12.8	10.3	29.3	-9.4	23.3	25.7	—

PER SHARE DATA

	2000	1999	1998	1997	1996	1995	1994	1993	1992	1991
Dividends, Net Income ($)	0.00	0.00	0.00	0.00	0.00	0.04	0.00	0.00	0.00	—
Distrib'ns, Cap Gain ($)	0.92	1.98	1.17	3.42	0.53	0.17	2.48	0.00	0.00	—
Net Asset Value ($)	15.35	18.62	11.58	11.21	12.52	11.69	9.17	12.11	9.82	—
Expense Ratio (%)	1.20	1.50	1.48	1.52	1.48	1.49	1.37	1.54	1.93	—
Yield (%)	0.00	0.00	0.00	0.00	0.00	0.33	0.00	0.00	0.00	—
Portfolio Turnover (%)	186	41	158	216	221	228	196	153	50	—
Total Assets (Millions $)	1,336	846	316	313	267	212	179	223	123	—

PORTFOLIO (as of 6/30/00)

Portfolio Manager: Cowell, May, Miller - 1996

Investm't Category: Aggressive Growth

✔ Domestic	Index
✔ Foreign	Sector
Asset Allocation	State Specific

Investment Style

Large Cap	Mid Cap	✔ Small Cap
✔ Growth	Grth/Val	Value

Portfolio

10.3% cash	0.0% corp bonds
89.7% stocks	0.0% gov't bonds
0.0% pref/conv't pref	0.0% muni bonds
0.0% conv't bds/wrnts	0.0% other

SHAREHOLDER INFORMATION

Minimum Investment
Initial: $1,000 Subsequent: $50

Minimum IRA Investment
Initial: $250 Subsequent: $50

Maximum Fees
Load: none 12b-1: 0.25%
Other: none

Services
✔ IRA
✔ Keogh
✔ Telephone Exchange

INVESCO Tech/Inv (FTCHX)

800-525-8085, 303-930-6300
www.invesco.com

Aggressive Growth

PERFORMANCE — fund inception date: 1/19/84

	3yr Annual	5yr Annual	10yr Annual	Bull	Bear
Return (%)	35.0	26.6	28.3	239.9	-38.5
Differ from Category (+/-)	18.8 high	12.0 high	12.5 high	120.7 high	-17.9 low

Standard Deviation	Category Risk Index	Beta
43.4%—high	1.34—high	1.42

	2000	1999	1998	1997	1996	1995	1994	1993	1992	1991
Return (%)	-22.7	144.9	30.1	8.8	21.7	45.7	5.2	15.0	18.8	76.8
Differ from Category (+/-)	-16.7	87.4	15.0	-6.0	3.4	11.1	6.0	-10.2	11.9	29.6
Return, Tax-Adjusted (%)	-23.3	142.6	30.1	4.4	17.2	38.8	4.2	11.1	18.8	67.9

PER SHARE DATA

	2000	1999	1998	1997	1996	1995	1994	1993	1992	1991
Dividends, Net Income ($)	0.00	0.00	0.00	0.13	0.07	0.00	0.00	0.00	0.00	0.00
Distrib'ns, Cap Gain ($)	2.63	3.91	0.00	6.45	4.49	5.85	0.79	3.22	0.00	4.38
Net Asset Value ($)	59.77	80.79	34.99	26.89	30.99	29.19	24.04	23.59	23.31	19.62
Expense Ratio (%)	0.88	1.20	1.17	1.05	1.08	1.12	1.17	1.13	1.12	1.19
Yield (%)	0.00	0.00	0.00	0.38	0.19	0.00	0.00	0.00	0.00	0.00
Portfolio Turnover (%)	28	143	178	237	168	191	145	184	169	307
Total Assets (Millions $)	3,547	3,376	1,147	1,021	838	576	310	253	256	106

PORTFOLIO (as of 6/30/00)

Portfolio Manager: William Keithler - 1999

Investm't Category: Aggressive Growth

✔ Domestic — Index
✔ Foreign — ✔ Sector
Asset Allocation — State Specific

Investment Style

Large Cap — Mid Cap — ✔ Small Cap
✔ Growth — Grth/Val — Value

Portfolio

6.6%	cash	0.0%	corp bonds
93.3%	stocks	0.0%	gov't bonds
0.2%	pref/conv't pref	0.0%	muni bonds
0.0%	conv't bds/wrnts	0.0%	other

SHAREHOLDER INFORMATION

Minimum Investment
Initial: $1,000 — Subsequent: $50

Minimum IRA Investment
Initial: $250 — Subsequent: $50

Maximum Fees
Load: none — 12b-1: 0.25%
Other: none

Services
✔ IRA
✔ Keogh
✔ Telephone Exchange

INVESCO Telcom/Inv (ISWCX)

800-525-8085, 303-930-6300
www.invesco.com

International Stock

PERFORMANCE

fund inception date: 8/1/94

	3yr Annual	5yr Annual	10yr Annual	Bull	Bear
Return (%)	36.0	30.8	na	254.3	-41.1
Differ from Category (+/-)	27.1 high	22.5 high	na	163.4 high	-17.1 low

Standard Deviation	Category Risk Index	Beta
39.4%—high	1.74—high	1.61

	2000	1999	1998	1997	1996	1995	1994	1993	1992	1991
Return (%)	-26.9	144.2	40.9	30.2	16.8	27.3	—	—	—	—
Differ from Category (+/-)	-7.5	83.5	35.1	28.9	2.3	18.0	—	—	—	—
Return, Tax-Adjusted (%)	-27.4	144.0	40.4	28.3	13.9	23.3	—	—	—	—

PER SHARE DATA

	2000	1999	1998	1997	1996	1995	1994	1993	1992	1991
Dividends, Net Income ($)	0.00	0.00	0.00	0.05	0.13	0.16	—	—	—	—
Distrib'ns, Cap Gain ($)	1.46	0.14	0.37	1.04	1.01	1.24	—	—	—	—
Net Asset Value ($)	36.28	51.63	21.21	15.34	12.63	11.83	—	—	—	—
Expense Ratio (%)	0.99	1.24	1.32	1.69	1.66	2.00	—	—	—	—
Yield (%)	0.00	0.00	0.00	0.30	0.95	1.22	—	—	—	—
Portfolio Turnover (%)	24	62	55	96	157	193	—	—	—	—
Total Assets (Millions $)	2,432	2,372	323	83	54	31	—	—	—	—

PORTFOLIO (as of 6/30/00)

Portfolio Manager: Brian Hayward - 1997

Investm't Category: International Stock

✔ Domestic
✔ Foreign
Asset Allocation
Index
✔ Sector
State Specific

Investment Style

Large Cap | Mid Cap | Small Cap
Growth | Grth/Val | Value

Portfolio

6.9%	cash	0.3%	corp bonds
92.3%	stocks	0.0%	gov't bonds
0.5%	pref/conv't pref	0.0%	muni bonds
0.0%	conv't bds/wrnts	0.0%	other

SHAREHOLDER INFORMATION

Minimum Investment
Initial: $1,000 Subsequent: $50

Minimum IRA Investment
Initial: $250 Subsequent: $50

Maximum Fees
Load: none 12b-1: 0.25%
Other: none

Services
✔ IRA
✔ Keogh
✔ Telephone Exchange

INVESCO Total Return/Inv (FSFLX)

800-525-8085, 303-930-6300
www.invesco.com

Balanced

PERFORMANCE — fund inception date: 9/22/87

	3yr Annual	5yr Annual	10yr Annual	Bull	Bear
Return (%)	2.5	8.8	11.9	13.5	-3.2
Differ from Category (+/-)	-5.9 low	-2.6 low	0.2 av	-14.6 low	0.0 av

Standard Deviation	Category Risk Index	Beta
11.4%—blw av	1.04—abv av	0.53

	2000	1999	1998	1997	1996	1995	1994	1993	1992	1991
Return (%)	-3.6	-1.3	13.6	25.0	13.0	28.6	2.5	12.3	9.8	24.9
Differ from Category (+/-)	-5.6	-12.0	0.3	6.2	-0.9	3.1	3.8	-2.1	1.4	1.1
Return, Tax-Adjusted (%)	-5.0	-3.0	11.9	23.4	11.4	26.8	1.2	10.1	8.2	22.2

PER SHARE DATA

	2000	1999	1998	1997	1996	1995	1994	1993	1992	1991
Dividends, Net Income ($)	0.74	0.81	0.79	0.74	0.82	0.73	0.56	0.69	0.65	0.71
Distrib'ns, Cap Gain ($)	0.69	1.16	0.82	0.47	0.08	0.12	0.04	0.32	0.18	0.55
Net Asset Value ($)	26.43	28.96	31.36	29.09	24.30	22.34	18.10	18.26	17.18	16.43
Expense Ratio (%)	1.00	0.83	0.79	0.86	0.89	0.95	0.96	0.93	0.88	0.92
Yield (%)	2.72	2.68	2.45	2.50	3.36	3.25	3.08	3.71	3.74	4.18
Portfolio Turnover (%)	49	7	17	4	10	30	12	19	13	49
Total Assets (Millions $)	1,837	2,934	3,040	2,160	1,227	768	293	240	137	82

PORTFOLIO (as of 6/30/00)

Portfolio Manager: Charles Mayer - 2000

Investm't Category: Balanced

✔ Domestic — Index
✔ Foreign — Sector
✔ Asset Allocation — State Specific

Investment Style

Large Cap	Mid Cap	Small Cap
Growth	Grth/Val	Value

Portfolio

6.7%	cash	12.8%	corp bonds
61.6%	stocks	16.8%	gov't bonds
0.0%	pref/conv't pref	0.0%	muni bonds
0.0%	conv't bds/wrnts	2.2%	other

SHAREHOLDER INFORMATION

Minimum Investment
Initial: $1,000 — Subsequent: $50

Minimum IRA Investment
Initial: $250 — Subsequent: $50

Maximum Fees
Load: none — 12b-1: 0.25%
Other: none

Services
✔ IRA
✔ Keogh
✔ Telephone Exchange

INVESCO Utilities/Inv (FSTUX)

800-525-8085, 303-930-6300
www.invesco.com

Growth & Income

PERFORMANCE — fund inception date: 6/2/86

	3yr Annual	5yr Annual	10yr Annual	Bull	Bear
Return (%)	15.7	16.8	15.4	50.1	-15.2
Differ from Category (+/-)	6.8 high	2.5 abv av	0.5 av	16.6 abv av	-15.1 low

Standard Deviation	Category Risk Index	Beta
16.0%—av	0.92—blw av	0.61

	2000	1999	1998	1997	1996	1995	1994	1993	1992	1991
Return (%)	4.1	19.8	24.3	24.3	12.7	25.2	-9.9	21.2	10.7	27.9
Differ from Category (+/-)	-1.6	9.0	11.5	-2.6	-7.0	-4.3	-9.4	7.4	-0.9	-0.2
Return, Tax-Adjusted (%)	2.7	17.9	23.1	22.6	9.3	23.4	-11.0	14.9	7.9	26.6

PER SHARE DATA

	2000	1999	1998	1997	1996	1995	1994	1993	1992	1991
Dividends, Net Income ($)	0.13	0.16	0.27	0.32	0.34	0.41	0.31	0.26	0.25	0.34
Distrib'ns, Cap Gain ($)	0.99	1.21	0.21	0.29	0.87	0.00	0.00	2.00	0.77	0.00
Net Asset Value ($)	17.49	17.96	16.21	13.47	11.38	11.21	9.32	10.68	10.69	10.64
Expense Ratio (%)	1.24	1.26	1.29	1.22	1.17	1.18	1.13	1.06	1.13	1.21
Yield (%)	0.70	0.83	1.64	2.32	2.77	3.65	3.32	2.05	2.18	3.19
Portfolio Turnover (%)	18	32	47	55	141	185	180	202	226	151
Total Assets (Millions $)	237	212	193	212	157	150	122	174	108	85

PORTFOLIO (as of 6/30/00)

Portfolio Manager: Brian Hayward - 1997

Investm't Category: Growth & Income

✔ Domestic — Index
Foreign — ✔ Sector
Asset Allocation — State Specific

Investment Style

Large Cap — ✔ Mid Cap — ✔ Small Cap
Growth — Grth/Val — ✔ Value

Portfolio

9.2%	cash	0.0%	corp bonds
90.8%	stocks	0.0%	gov't bonds
0.0%	pref/conv't pref	0.0%	muni bonds
0.0%	conv't bds/wrnts	0.0%	other

SHAREHOLDER INFORMATION

Minimum Investment
Initial: $1,000 — Subsequent: $50

Minimum IRA Investment
Initial: $250 — Subsequent: $50

Maximum Fees
Load: none — 12b-1: 0.25%
Other: none

Services
✔ IRA
✔ Keogh
✔ Telephone Exchange

INVESCO Value Equity/Inv (FSEQX)

800-525-8085, 303-930-6300
www.invesco.com

Growth & Income

PERFORMANCE — fund inception date: 5/16/86

	3yr Annual	5yr Annual	10yr Annual	Bull	Bear
Return (%)	3.2	10.7	13.5	25.5	-5.0
Differ from Category (+/-)	-5.7 low	-3.6 low	-1.4 blw av	-8.0 blw av	-4.9 av

Standard Deviation	Category Risk Index	Beta
16.2%—av	0.93—blw av	0.84

	2000	1999	1998	1997	1996	1995	1994	1993	1992	1991
Return (%)	-5.4	1.1	15.0	27.9	18.4	30.6	4.0	10.4	4.9	35.8
Differ from Category (+/-)	-11.1	-9.7	2.2	1.0	-1.3	1.1	4.5	-3.4	-6.7	7.7
Return, Tax-Adjusted (%)	-8.3	-0.8	13.0	25.6	16.8	29.0	1.4	8.1	4.0	31.2

PER SHARE DATA

	2000	1999	1998	1997	1996	1995	1994	1993	1992	1991
Dividends, Net Income ($)	0.09	0.16	0.24	0.23	0.43	0.39	0.30	0.36	0.34	0.39
Distrib'ns, Cap Gain ($)	3.81	2.50	2.31	2.19	0.56	0.37	1.17	0.87	0.12	1.84
Net Asset Value ($)	21.49	26.99	29.41	27.88	23.74	20.90	16.63	17.41	16.91	16.57
Expense Ratio (%)	1.31	1.27	1.15	1.04	1.01	0.97	1.01	1.00	0.91	0.98
Yield (%)	0.35	0.54	0.75	0.76	1.76	1.83	1.68	1.96	1.99	2.11
Portfolio Turnover (%)	67	22	48	37	27	34	53	35	37	64
Total Assets (Millions $)	275	324	432	379	251	174	108	108	78	39

PORTFOLIO (as of 6/30/00)

Portfolio Manager: Charles Mayer - 2000

Investm't Category: Growth & Income

✔ Domestic — Index
✔ Foreign — Sector
Asset Allocation — State Specific

Investment Style

✔ Large Cap — Mid Cap — Small Cap
Growth — Grth/Val — ✔ Value

Portfolio

1.3%	cash	0.0%	corp bonds
98.7%	stocks	0.0%	gov't bonds
0.0%	pref/conv't pref	0.0%	muni bonds
0.0%	conv't bds/wrnts	0.0%	other

SHAREHOLDER INFORMATION

Minimum Investment
Initial: $1,000 — Subsequent: $50

Minimum IRA Investment
Initial: $250 — Subsequent: $50

Maximum Fees
Load: none — 12b-1: 0.25%
Other: none

Services
✔ IRA
✔ Keogh
✔ Telephone Exchange

Investec China & HK (ICHKX)

800-915-6565, 818-795-0039
www.investecfunds.com

International Stock

PERFORMANCE — fund inception date: 6/30/94

	3yr Annual	5yr Annual	10yr Annual	Bull	Bear
Return (%)	9.4	7.0	na	136.5	-17.4
Differ from Category (+/-)	0.5 av	-1.3 blw av	na	45.6 high	6.6 abv av

Standard Deviation	Category Risk Index	Beta
35.3%—high	1.56—high	1.10

	2000	1999	1998	1997	1996	1995	1994	1993	1992	1991
Return (%)	-6.9	66.2	-15.2	-20.2	34.3	20.4	—	—	—	—
Differ from Category (+/-)	12.5	5.5	-21.0	-21.5	19.8	11.1	—	—	—	—
Return, Tax-Adjusted (%)	-8.3	65.2	-15.6	-21.8	33.0	19.8	—	—	—	—

PER SHARE DATA

	2000	1999	1998	1997	1996	1995	1994	1993	1992	1991
Dividends, Net Income ($)	0.66	0.25	0.14	0.19	0.19	0.13	—	—	—	—
Distrib'ns, Cap Gain ($)	0.00	0.00	0.00	1.09	0.35	0.03	—	—	—	—
Net Asset Value ($)	15.75	17.65	10.77	12.91	17.71	13.64	—	—	—	—
Expense Ratio (%)	na	1.86	1.89	1.70	1.96	1.98	—	—	—	—
Yield (%)	4.19	1.41	1.29	1.35	1.05	0.95	—	—	—	—
Portfolio Turnover (%)	na	29	86	53	30	10	—	—	—	—
Total Assets (Millions $)	112	161	147	242	308	55	—	—	—	—

PORTFOLIO (as of 6/30/00)

Portfolio Manager: Edmond Harris, Adrian Fu - 1994

Investm't Category: International Stock

Domestic	Index
✔ Foreign	Sector
Asset Allocation	State Specific

Investment Style

Large Cap	Mid Cap	Small Cap
Growth	Grth/Val	Value

Portfolio

-0.1% cash	0.0% corp bonds
100.1% stocks	0.0% gov't bonds
0.0% pref/conv't pref	0.0% muni bonds
0.0% conv't bds/wrnts	0.0% other

SHAREHOLDER INFORMATION

Minimum Investment
Initial: $2,500 Subsequent: $250

Minimum IRA Investment
Initial: $1,000 Subsequent: $250

Maximum Fees
Load: 1.00% redemption 12b-1: none
Other: redemption fee applies for 1 month

Services
✔ IRA
Keogh
✔ Telephone Exchange

Janus Inv: Balanced (JABAX)

800-525-8983, 303-333-3863
www.janus.com

Balanced

PERFORMANCE

fund inception date: 9/1/92

	3yr Annual	5yr Annual	10yr Annual	Bull	Bear
Return (%)	16.6	17.3	na	56.0	-8.1
Differ from Category (+/-)	8.2 high	5.9 high	na	27.9 high	-4.9 low

Standard Deviation	Category Risk Index	Beta
14.2%—blw av	1.30—high	0.69

	2000	1999	1998	1997	1996	1995	1994	1993	1992	1991
Return (%)	-2.1	23.5	31.1	21.8	15.3	27.3	0.0	10.5	—	—
Differ from Category (+/-)	-4.1	12.8	17.8	3.0	1.4	1.8	1.3	-3.9	—	—
Return, Tax-Adjusted (%)	-4.0	22.2	30.0	18.7	11.6	23.6	-1.8	9.7	—	—

PER SHARE DATA

	2000	1999	1998	1997	1996	1995	1994	1993	1992	1991
Dividends, Net Income ($)	0.63	0.45	0.35	0.35	0.31	1.06	0.56	0.22	—	—
Distrib'ns, Cap Gain ($)	1.02	0.31	0.10	1.48	1.34	0.00	0.00	0.00	—	—
Net Asset Value ($)	21.24	23.39	19.61	15.33	14.14	13.72	11.63	12.19	—	—
Expense Ratio (%)	na	0.91	1.01	1.10	1.21	1.35	1.42	1.70	—	—
Yield (%)	2.83	1.89	1.77	2.08	2.00	7.72	4.81	1.80	—	—
Portfolio Turnover (%)	na	64	73	139	151	185	167	131	—	—
Total Assets (Millions $)	4,638	3,420	1,136	389	219	138	93	77	—	—

PORTFOLIO (as of 6/30/00)

Portfolio Manager: Karen Reidy - 1999

Investm't Category: Balanced

✔ Domestic
Foreign
Asset Allocation
Index
Sector
State Specific

Investment Style

Large Cap
Mid Cap
Small Cap
Growth
Grth/Val
Value

Portfolio

9.8% cash
40.9% stocks
4.4% pref/conv't pref
2.2% conv't bds/wrnts
25.3% corp bonds
17.5% gov't bonds
0.0% muni bonds
0.0% other

SHAREHOLDER INFORMATION

Minimum Investment
Initial: $2,500
Subsequent: $100

Minimum IRA Investment
Initial: $500
Subsequent: $100

Maximum Fees
Load: none
12b-1: none
Other: none

Services
✔ IRA
✔ Keogh
✔ Telephone Exchange

Janus Inv: Enterprise (JAENX)

800-525-8983, 303-333-3863
www.janus.com

Aggressive Growth

PERFORMANCE — fund inception date: 9/1/92

	3yr Annual	5yr Annual	10yr Annual	Bull	Bear
Return (%)	27.2	20.6	na	227.0	-39.8
Differ from Category (+/-)	11.0 abv av	6.0 abv av	na	107.8 high	-19.2 low

Standard Deviation	Category Risk Index	Beta
38.9%—high	1.20—abv av	1.37

	2000	1999	1998	1997	1996	1995	1994	1993	1992	1991
Return (%)	-30.5	121.8	33.7	10.8	11.6	27.2	8.9	15.6	—	—
Differ from Category (+/-)	-24.5	64.3	18.6	-4.0	-6.7	-7.4	9.7	-9.6	—	—
Return, Tax-Adjusted (%)	-30.5	118.7	30.8	9.4	10.3	24.1	7.5	14.8	—	—

PER SHARE DATA

	2000	1999	1998	1997	1996	1995	1994	1993	1992	1991
Dividends, Net Income ($)	0.00	2.22	0.00	0.00	0.00	1.63	0.51	0.01	—	—
Distrib'ns, Cap Gain ($)	0.00	1.10	4.30	1.96	1.27	0.16	0.37	0.54	—	—
Net Asset Value ($)	53.27	76.67	36.22	30.48	29.34	27.44	22.98	21.92	—	—
Expense Ratio (%)	na	0.95	1.06	1.04	1.12	1.26	1.25	1.36	—	—
Yield (%)	0.00	2.85	0.00	0.00	0.00	5.90	2.18	0.04	—	—
Portfolio Turnover (%)	na	98	134	111	93	194	193	201	—	—
Total Assets (Millions $)	6,116	4,434	728	573	721	498	354	258	—	—

PORTFOLIO (as of 6/30/00)

Portfolio Manager: James Goff - 1992

Investm't Category: Aggressive Growth

✔ Domestic — Index
✔ Foreign — Sector
Asset Allocation — State Specific

Investment Style

Large Cap — Mid Cap — ✔ Small Cap
✔ Growth — Grth/Val — Value

Portfolio

0.5%	cash	0.0%	corp bonds
99.0%	stocks	0.0%	gov't bonds
0.0%	pref/conv't pref	0.0%	muni bonds
0.5%	conv't bds/wrnts	0.0%	other

SHAREHOLDER INFORMATION

Minimum Investment
Initial: $2,500 — Subsequent: $100

Minimum IRA Investment
Initial: $500 — Subsequent: $100

Maximum Fees
Load: none — 12b-1: none
Other: none

Services
✔ IRA
✔ Keogh
✔ Telephone Exchange

Janus Inv: Equity Income

800-525-8983, 303-333-3863
www.janus.com

(JAEIX)

Growth & Income

PERFORMANCE — fund inception date: 6/28/96

	3yr Annual	5yr Annual	10yr Annual	Bull	Bear
Return (%)	21.7	na	na	90.4	-14.7
Differ from Category (+/-)	12.8 high	na	na	56.9 high	-14.6 low

Standard Deviation	Category Risk Index	Beta
20.3%—abv av	1.17—high	1.01

	2000	1999	1998	1997	1996	1995	1994	1993	1992	1991
Return (%)	-7.1	38.5	40.3	31.0	—	—	—	—	—	—
Differ from Category (+/-)	-12.8	27.7	27.5	4.1	—	—	—	—	—	—
Return, Tax-Adjusted (%)	-9.3	37.5	39.8	29.1	—	—	—	—	—	—

PER SHARE DATA

	2000	1999	1998	1997	1996	1995	1994	1993	1992	1991
Dividends, Net Income ($)	0.16	0.15	0.05	0.06	—	—	—	—	—	—
Distrib'ns, Cap Gain ($)	2.53	0.57	0.21	0.88	—	—	—	—	—	—
Net Asset Value ($)	20.63	25.14	18.72	13.54	—	—	—	—	—	—
Expense Ratio (%)	na	1.01	1.18	1.45	—	—	—	—	—	—
Yield (%)	0.69	0.58	0.26	0.41	—	—	—	—	—	—
Portfolio Turnover (%)	na	81	101	180	—	—	—	—	—	—
Total Assets (Millions $)	944	948	349	88	—	—	—	—	—	—

PORTFOLIO (as of 6/30/00)

Portfolio Manager: Karen Reidy - 1999

Investm't Category: Growth & Income

✔ Domestic
Foreign
Asset Allocation
Index
Sector
State Specific

Investment Style

✔ Large Cap
Mid Cap
Small Cap
✔ Growth
Grth/Val
Value

Portfolio

13.9% cash
70.4% stocks
8.0% pref/conv't pref
5.3% conv't bds/wrnts
2.5% corp bonds
0.0% gov't bonds
0.0% muni bonds
0.0% other

SHAREHOLDER INFORMATION

Minimum Investment
Initial: $2,500 Subsequent: $100

Minimum IRA Investment
Initial: $500 Subsequent: $100

Maximum Fees
Load: none 12b-1: none
Other: none

Services
✔ IRA
✔ Keogh
✔ Telephone Exchange

Janus Inv: Growth & Income (JAGIX)

800-525-8983, 303-333-3863
www.janus.com

Growth & Income

PERFORMANCE

fund inception date: 5/15/91

	3yr Annual	5yr Annual	10yr Annual	Bull	Bear
Return (%)	21.7	25.1	na	96.9	-19.5
Differ from Category (+/-)	12.8 high	10.8 high	na	63.4 high	-19.4 low

Standard Deviation	Category Risk Index	Beta
21.0%—abv av	1.21—high	1.00

	2000	1999	1998	1997	1996	1995	1994	1993	1992	1991
Return (%)	-11.4	51.1	34.8	34.6	26.0	36.3	-4.8	6.6	5.3	—
Differ from Category (+/-)	-17.1	40.3	22.0	7.7	6.3	6.8	-4.3	-7.2	-6.3	—
Return, Tax-Adjusted (%)	-12.3	49.6	32.9	31.9	22.6	30.9	-5.0	5.5	4.9	—

PER SHARE DATA

	2000	1999	1998	1997	1996	1995	1994	1993	1992	1991
Dividends, Net Income ($)	0.23	0.13	0.07	0.07	0.11	1.01	0.09	0.16	0.15	—
Distrib'ns, Cap Gain ($)	1.61	1.79	2.01	2.37	1.86	1.23	0.00	0.33	0.00	—
Net Asset Value ($)	35.35	41.94	29.10	23.15	19.05	16.67	13.88	14.69	14.24	—
Expense Ratio (%)	na	0.90	0.94	0.96	1.03	1.19	1.22	1.28	1.52	—
Yield (%)	0.62	0.29	0.22	0.27	0.52	5.64	0.64	1.06	1.05	—
Portfolio Turnover (%)	na	43	95	127	153	195	123	138	120	—
Total Assets (Millions $)	8,363	7,492	3,504	2,004	1,100	632	456	513	310	—

PORTFOLIO (as of 6/30/00)

Portfolio Manager: David Corkins - 1997

Investm't Category: Growth & Income

✔ Domestic — Index
✔ Foreign — Sector
Asset Allocation — State Specific

Investment Style

✔ Large Cap — Mid Cap — Small Cap
✔ Growth — Grth/Val — Value

Portfolio

17.1% cash — 1.1% corp bonds
76.7% stocks — 0.0% gov't bonds
2.4% pref/conv't pref — 0.0% muni bonds
2.7% conv't bds/wrnts — 0.0% other

SHAREHOLDER INFORMATION

Minimum Investment

Initial: $2,500 — Subsequent: $100

Minimum IRA Investment

Initial: $500 — Subsequent: $100

Maximum Fees

Load: none — 12b-1: none
Other: none

Services

✔ IRA
✔ Keogh
✔ Telephone Exchange

Janus Inv: Janus (JANSX)

800-525-8983, 303-333-3863
www.janus.com

Growth

this fund is closed to new investors

PERFORMANCE — fund inception date: 2/5/70

	3yr Annual	5yr Annual	10yr Annual	Bull	Bear
Return (%)	20.2	20.6	18.6	102.2	-22.0
Differ from Category (+/-)	9.2 high	4.5 high	1.8 abv av	52.5 high	-16.6 low

Standard Deviation	Category Risk Index	Beta
23.4%—abv av	1.20—abv av	1.14

	2000	1999	1998	1997	1996	1995	1994	1993	1992	1991
Return (%)	-14.9	47.1	38.8	22.7	19.6	29.4	-1.1	10.9	6.8	42.7
Differ from Category (+/-)	-18.4	28.2	24.5	-4.4	-2.7	-1.0	-0.9	-3.7	-5.8	5.1
Return, Tax-Adjusted (%)	-16.8	43.8	38.0	18.4	15.7	27.0	-1.6	8.6	4.9	40.4

PER SHARE DATA

	2000	1999	1998	1997	1996	1995	1994	1993	1992	1991
Dividends, Net Income ($)	0.00	0.34	0.08	0.23	0.20	0.77	0.00	0.38	0.29	0.18
Distrib'ns, Cap Gain ($)	4.39	4.87	0.82	4.74	2.91	0.49	0.38	0.94	0.90	0.90
Net Asset Value ($)	33.29	44.05	33.65	24.90	24.45	23.04	18.78	19.39	18.68	18.60
Expense Ratio (%)	na	0.84	0.86	0.86	0.85	0.87	0.91	0.92	0.97	0.98
Yield (%)	0.00	0.69	0.23	0.77	0.73	3.27	0.00	1.86	1.48	0.92
Portfolio Turnover (%)	na	63	70	132	104	118	139	127	153	132
Total Assets (Millions $)	40,080	42,330	25,490	19,200	15,890	12,466	9,400	9,199	5,831	2,992

PORTFOLIO (as of 6/30/00)

Portfolio Manager: Blaine Rollins - 1999

Investm't Category: Growth

✔ Domestic — Index
✔ Foreign — Sector
Asset Allocation — State Specific

Investment Style

✔ Large Cap — Mid Cap — Small Cap
✔ Growth — Grth/Val — Value

Portfolio

7.4%	cash	0.0%	corp bonds
92.1%	stocks	0.0%	gov't bonds
0.0%	pref/conv't pref	0.0%	muni bonds
0.5%	conv't bds/wrnts	0.0%	other

SHAREHOLDER INFORMATION

Minimum Investment
Initial: $2,500 — Subsequent: $100

Minimum IRA Investment
Initial: $500 — Subsequent: $100

Maximum Fees
Load: none — 12b-1: none
Other: none

Services
✔ IRA
✔ Keogh
✔ Telephone Exchange

Janus Inv: Mercury (JAMRX)

800-525-8983, 303-333-3863
www.janus.com

Aggressive Growth

PERFORMANCE

fund inception date: 5/3/93

	3yr Annual	5yr Annual	10yr Annual	Bull	Bear
Return (%)	33.9	25.8	na	186.3	-31.3
Differ from Category (+/-)	17.7 high	11.2 high	na	67.1 high	-10.7 blw av

Standard Deviation	Category Risk Index	Beta
29.5%—high	0.91—blw av	1.26

	2000	1999	1998	1997	1996	1995	1994	1993	1992	1991
Return (%)	-22.7	96.2	58.4	11.8	17.6	33.0	15.8	—	—	—
Differ from Category (+/-)	-16.7	38.7	43.3	-3.0	-0.7	-1.6	16.6	—	—	—
Return, Tax-Adjusted (%)	-24.7	91.7	55.9	9.4	13.4	27.2	15.0	—	—	—

PER SHARE DATA

	2000	1999	1998	1997	1996	1995	1994	1993	1992	1991
Dividends, Net Income ($)	0.02	2.10	0.00	0.04	0.07	1.75	0.16	—	—	—
Distrib'ns, Cap Gain ($)	4.41	1.16	2.01	1.90	2.28	0.30	0.10	—	—	—
Net Asset Value ($)	29.67	43.81	24.11	16.50	16.52	16.04	13.61	—	—	—
Expense Ratio (%)	na	0.91	0.94	0.96	1.00	1.14	1.33	—	—	—
Yield (%)	0.05	4.66	0.00	0.21	0.37	10.70	1.16	—	—	—
Portfolio Turnover (%)	na	89	105	157	177	201	283	—	—	—
Total Assets (Millions $)	13,619	13,543	3,111	1,911	2,061	1,596	690	—	—	—

PORTFOLIO (as of 6/30/00)

Portfolio Manager: Warren Lammert - 1993

Investm't Category: Aggressive Growth

✔ Domestic
✔ Foreign
Asset Allocation
Index
Sector
State Specific

Investment Style

✔ Large Cap
✔ Mid Cap
Small Cap
✔ Growth
Grth/Val
Value

Portfolio

15.2% cash
84.8% stocks
0.0% pref/conv't pref
0.0% conv't bds/wrnts
0.0% corp bonds
0.0% gov't bonds
0.0% muni bonds
0.0% other

SHAREHOLDER INFORMATION

Minimum Investment
Initial: $2,500 Subsequent: $100

Minimum IRA Investment
Initial: $500 Subsequent: $100

Maximum Fees
Load: none 12b-1: none
Other: none

Services
✔ IRA
✔ Keogh
✔ Telephone Exchange

Janus Inv: Olympus (JAOLX)

800-525-8983, 303-333-3863
www.janus.com

Aggressive Growth

this fund is closed to new investors

PERFORMANCE — fund inception date: 12/29/95

	3yr Annual	5yr Annual	10yr Annual	Bull	Bear
Return (%)	35.0	30.5	na	187.9	-28.9
Differ from Category (+/-)	18.8 high	15.9 high	na	68.7 high	-8.3 blw av

Standard Deviation	Category Risk Index	Beta
32.2%—high	0.99—av	1.16

	2000	1999	1998	1997	1996	1995	1994	1993	1992	1991
Return (%)	-21.6	100.1	56.9	26.7	21.7	—	—	—	—	—
Differ from Category (+/-)	-15.6	42.6	41.8	11.9	3.4	—	—	—	—	—
Return, Tax-Adjusted (%)	-21.9	98.5	56.8	25.6	21.3	—	—	—	—	—

PER SHARE DATA

	2000	1999	1998	1997	1996	1995	1994	1993	1992	1991
Dividends, Net Income ($)	0.23	0.39	0.01	0.03	0.12	—	—	—	—	—
Distrib'ns, Cap Gain ($)	0.38	1.39	0.00	0.70	0.00	—	—	—	—	—
Net Asset Value ($)	41.15	53.26	27.58	17.58	14.48	—	—	—	—	—
Expense Ratio (%)	na	0.93	0.98	1.03	1.17	—	—	—	—	—
Yield (%)	0.55	0.71	0.03	0.16	0.82	—	—	—	—	—
Portfolio Turnover (%)	na	91	123	244	303	—	—	—	—	—
Total Assets (Millions $)	6,359	6,174	1,288	629	412	—	—	—	—	—

PORTFOLIO (as of 6/30/00)

Portfolio Manager: Claire Young - 1997

Investm't Category: Aggressive Growth

✔ Domestic — Index
✔ Foreign — Sector
Asset Allocation — State Specific

Investment Style

✔ Large Cap — ✔ Mid Cap — Small Cap
✔ Growth — Grth/Val — Value

Portfolio

21.4%	cash	1.2%	corp bonds
75.6%	stocks	0.0%	gov't bonds
0.6%	pref/conv't pref	0.0%	muni bonds
1.2%	conv't bds/wrnts	0.0%	other

SHAREHOLDER INFORMATION

Minimum Investment
Initial: $2,500 — Subsequent: $100

Minimum IRA Investment
Initial: $500 — Subsequent: $100

Maximum Fees
Load: none — 12b-1: none
Other: none

Services
✔ IRA
✔ Keogh
✔ Telephone Exchange

Janus Inv: Overseas (JAOSX)

800-525-8983, 303-333-3863
www.janus.com

International Stock

this fund is closed to new investors

PERFORMANCE

fund inception date: 5/2/94

	3yr Annual	5yr Annual	10yr Annual	Bull	Bear
Return (%)	20.6	21.7	na	103.0	-29.5
Differ from Category (+/-)	11.7 high	13.4 high	na	12.1 abv av	-5.5 blw av

Standard Deviation	Category Risk Index	Beta
28.3%—high	1.25—abv av	0.78

	2000	1999	1998	1997	1996	1995	1994	1993	1992	1991
Return (%)	-18.5	86.0	16.0	18.2	28.8	22.0	—	—	—	—
Differ from Category (+/-)	0.9	25.3	10.2	16.9	14.3	12.7	—	—	—	—
Return, Tax-Adjusted (%)	-20.6	85.8	15.7	17.3	28.0	21.2	—	—	—	—

PER SHARE DATA

	2000	1999	1998	1997	1996	1995	1994	1993	1992	1991
Dividends, Net Income ($)	0.19	0.00	0.09	0.09	0.04	0.16	—	—	—	—
Distrib'ns, Cap Gain ($)	3.65	0.14	0.00	0.50	0.25	0.05	—	—	—	—
Net Asset Value ($)	26.54	37.20	20.08	17.39	15.22	12.05	—	—	—	—
Expense Ratio (%)	na	0.91	0.94	1.01	1.23	1.73	—	—	—	—
Yield (%)	0.62	0.00	0.44	0.50	0.25	1.32	—	—	—	—
Portfolio Turnover (%)	na	92	105	72	71	188	—	—	—	—
Total Assets (Millions $)	8,292	8,765	4,329	3,240	955	129	—	—	—	—

PORTFOLIO (as of 6/30/00)

Portfolio Manager: Helen Hayes, Laurence Chang - 1994

Investm't Category: International Stock

Domestic	Index
✔ Foreign	Sector
Asset Allocation	State Specific

Investment Style

Large Cap	Mid Cap	Small Cap
Growth	Grth/Val	Value

Portfolio

8.9%	cash	0.0%	corp bonds
88.7%	stocks	0.0%	gov't bonds
2.4%	pref/conv't pref	0.0%	muni bonds
0.0%	conv't bds/wrnts	0.0%	other

SHAREHOLDER INFORMATION

Minimum Investment

Initial: $2,500 Subsequent: $100

Minimum IRA Investment

Initial: $500 Subsequent: $100

Maximum Fees

Load: none 12b-1: none

Other: none

Services

✔ IRA
✔ Keogh
✔ Telephone Exchange

Janus Inv: Spl Situations (JASSX)

800-525-8983, 303-333-3863
www.janus.com

Aggressive Growth

PERFORMANCE — fund inception date: 12/31/96

	3yr Annual	5yr Annual	10yr Annual	Bull	Bear
Return (%)	16.3	na	na	104.0	-30.5
Differ from Category (+/-)	0.1 av	na	na	-15.2 av	-9.9 blw av

Standard Deviation	Category Risk Index	Beta
24.9%—abv av	0.77—blw av	1.19

	2000	1999	1998	1997	1996	1995	1994	1993	1992	1991
Return (%)	-17.5	52.4	25.3	46.0	—	—	—	—	—	—
Differ from Category (+/-)	-11.5	-5.1	10.2	31.2	—	—	—	—	—	—
Return, Tax-Adjusted (%)	-18.6	46.4	25.2	44.7	—	—	—	—	—	—

PER SHARE DATA

	2000	1999	1998	1997	1996	1995	1994	1993	1992	1991
Dividends, Net Income ($)	0.00	1.90	0.00	0.00	—	—	—	—	—	—
Distrib'ns, Cap Gain ($)	1.31	1.39	0.04	0.65	—	—	—	—	—	—
Net Asset Value ($)	17.69	23.05	17.41	13.93	—	—	—	—	—	—
Expense Ratio (%)	na	0.98	1.05	1.18	—	—	—	—	—	—
Yield (%)	0.00	7.77	0.00	0.00	—	—	—	—	—	—
Portfolio Turnover (%)	na	104	117	—	—	—	—	—	—	—
Total Assets (Millions $)	1,431	1,420	893	389	—	—	—	—	—	—

PORTFOLIO (as of 6/30/00)

Portfolio Manager: David Decker - 1996

Investm't Category: Aggressive Growth

✔ Domestic — Index
✔ Foreign — Sector
Asset Allocation — State Specific

Investment Style

✔ Large Cap — ✔ Mid Cap — ✔ Small Cap
✔ Growth — Grth/Val — Value

Portfolio

3.9%	cash	0.0%	corp bonds
96.1%	stocks	0.0%	gov't bonds
0.0%	pref/conv't pref	0.0%	muni bonds
0.1%	conv't bds/wrnts	0.0%	other

SHAREHOLDER INFORMATION

Minimum Investment
Initial: $2,500 — Subsequent: $100

Minimum IRA Investment
Initial: $500 — Subsequent: $100

Maximum Fees
Load: none — 12b-1: none
Other: none

Services
✔ IRA
✔ Keogh
✔ Telephone Exchange

Janus Inv: Twenty (JAVLX)

800-525-8983, 303-333-3863
www.janus.com

Aggressive Growth

this fund is closed to new investors

PERFORMANCE — fund inception date: 4/26/85

	3yr Annual	5yr Annual	10yr Annual	Bull	Bear
Return (%)	24.5	26.2	21.9	136.7	-31.7
Differ from Category (+/-)	8.3 abv av	11.6 high	6.1 high	17.5 abv av	-11.1 blw av

Standard Deviation	Category Risk Index	Beta
29.1%—high	0.90—blw av	1.29

	2000	1999	1998	1997	1996	1995	1994	1993	1992	1991
Return (%)	-32.4	64.9	73.3	29.6	27.8	36.2	-6.7	3.4	1.9	69.2
Differ from Category (+/-)	-26.4	7.4	58.2	14.8	9.5	1.6	-5.9	-21.8	-5.0	22.0
Return, Tax-Adjusted (%)	-32.8	63.2	72.9	26.2	21.7	28.5	-6.7	2.4	1.4	68.3

PER SHARE DATA

	2000	1999	1998	1997	1996	1995	1994	1993	1992	1991
Dividends, Net Income ($)	0.00	0.18	0.13	0.09	0.18	2.27	0.06	0.25	0.18	0.02
Distrib'ns, Cap Gain ($)	1.75	4.07	0.30	4.46	5.31	2.98	0.00	0.45	0.19	0.42
Net Asset Value ($)	54.80	83.43	53.30	30.99	27.47	25.67	22.71	24.42	24.29	24.19
Expense Ratio (%)	na	0.87	0.90	0.91	0.92	1.00	1.02	1.05	1.01	1.07
Yield (%)	0.00	0.20	0.24	0.25	0.54	7.92	0.26	1.00	0.73	0.08
Portfolio Turnover (%)	na	40	54	123	137	147	102	99	83	163
Total Assets (Millions $)	26,193	36,909	15,787	6,003	4,070	3,057	2,504	3,575	3,137	1,348

PORTFOLIO (as of 6/30/00)

Portfolio Manager: Scott Schoelzel - 1997

Investm't Category: Aggressive Growth

✔ Domestic　　Index
✔ Foreign　　Sector
Asset Allocation　　State Specific

Investment Style

✔ Large Cap　　Mid Cap　　Small Cap
✔ Growth　　Grth/Val　　Value

Portfolio

6.4%	cash	1.2%	corp bonds
92.4%	stocks	0.0%	gov't bonds
0.0%	pref/conv't pref	0.0%	muni bonds
0.0%	conv't bds/wrnts	0.0%	other

SHAREHOLDER INFORMATION

Minimum Investment
Initial: $2,500　　Subsequent: $100

Minimum IRA Investment
Initial: $500　　Subsequent: $50

Maximum Fees
Load: none　　12b-1: none
Other: none

Services
✔ IRA
✔ Keogh
✔ Telephone Exchange

Janus Inv: Venture (JAVTX)

800-525-8983, 303-333-3863
www.janus.com

Aggressive Growth

this fund is closed to new investors

PERFORMANCE — fund inception date: 4/26/85

	3yr Annual	5yr Annual	10yr Annual	Bull	Bear
Return (%)	17.0	14.3	16.2	233.9	-48.0
Differ from Category (+/-)	0.8 av	-0.3 av	0.4 blw av	114.7 high	-27.4 low

Standard Deviation	Category Risk Index	Beta
44.1%—high	1.36—high	1.47

	2000	1999	1998	1997	1996	1995	1994	1993	1992	1991
Return (%)	-45.7	140.7	22.6	13.0	8.0	26.4	5.4	9.0	7.4	47.8
Differ from Category (+/-)	-39.7	83.2	7.5	-1.8	-10.3	-8.2	6.2	-16.2	0.5	0.6
Return, Tax-Adjusted (%)	-48.3	133.7	20.8	9.4	5.2	21.2	3.7	6.1	6.2	44.8

PER SHARE DATA

	2000	1999	1998	1997	1996	1995	1994	1993	1992	1991
Dividends, Net Income ($)	0.00	5.71	0.00	0.07	0.00	3.60	0.02	0.52	1.16	0.24
Distrib'ns, Cap Gain ($)	16.37	8.54	4.40	9.29	5.27	3.85	2.83	4.36	0.71	3.43
Net Asset Value ($)	49.94	121.67	57.14	50.26	53.06	54.10	48.68	48.88	49.30	47.63
Expense Ratio (%)	na	0.92	0.93	0.92	0.88	0.92	0.96	0.97	1.00	1.04
Yield (%)	0.00	4.38	0.00	0.11	0.00	6.21	0.03	0.97	2.31	0.47
Portfolio Turnover (%)	na	104	90	146	136	113	114	139	166	167
Total Assets (Millions $)	1,458	2,876	1,246	1,234	1,705	1,790	1,496	1,778	1,706	1,464

PORTFOLIO (as of 3/31/00)

Portfolio Manager: W. Bales, J. Coleman - 1997

Investm't Category: Aggressive Growth

✔ Domestic — Index
✔ Foreign — Sector
Asset Allocation — State Specific

Investment Style

Large Cap — Mid Cap — ✔ Small Cap
✔ Growth — Grth/Val — Value

Portfolio

3.9%	cash	0.0%	corp bonds
96.2%	stocks	0.0%	gov't bonds
0.0%	pref/conv't pref	0.0%	muni bonds
0.0%	conv't bds/wrnts	0.0%	other

SHAREHOLDER INFORMATION

Minimum Investment
Initial: $2,500 — Subsequent: $100

Minimum IRA Investment
Initial: $500 — Subsequent: $50

Maximum Fees
Load: none — 12b-1: none
Other: none

Services
✔ IRA
✔ Keogh
✔ Telephone Exchange

Janus Inv: Worldwide (JAWWX)

800-525-8983, 303-333-3863
www.janus.com

International Stock

this fund is closed to new investors

PERFORMANCE — fund inception date: 5/15/91

	3yr Annual	5yr Annual	10yr Annual	Bull	Bear
Return (%)	19.8	21.2	na	91.2	-25.1
Differ from Category (+/-)	10.9 high	12.9 high	na	0.3 abv av	-1.1 av

Standard Deviation	Category Risk Index	Beta
22.7%—abv av	1.00—av	0.83

	2000	1999	1998	1997	1996	1995	1994	1993	1992	1991
Return (%)	-16.8	64.3	25.8	20.4	26.4	21.8	3.6	28.4	9.0	—
Differ from Category (+/-)	2.6	3.6	20.0	19.1	11.9	12.5	6.7	-11.8	12.5	—
Return, Tax-Adjusted (%)	-18.7	63.7	25.6	18.6	24.1	20.1	1.6	27.3	8.6	—

PER SHARE DATA

	2000	1999	1998	1997	1996	1995	1994	1993	1992	1991
Dividends, Net Income ($)	0.41	0.02	0.19	0.19	0.15	0.26	0.53	0.27	0.22	—
Distrib'ns, Cap Gain ($)	6.50	1.28	0.00	2.59	2.04	1.06	1.00	0.37	0.00	—
Net Asset Value ($)	56.86	76.43	47.36	37.78	33.69	28.40	24.39	25.03	20.00	—
Expense Ratio (%)	na	0.88	0.90	0.95	1.01	1.24	1.12	1.32	1.73	—
Yield (%)	0.64	0.02	0.40	0.47	0.41	0.88	2.08	1.06	1.09	—
Portfolio Turnover (%)	na	68	86	79	80	142	158	124	147	—
Total Assets (Millions $)	33,953	33,802	16,322	10,567	5,046	1,975	1,542	935	208	—

PORTFOLIO (as of 6/30/00)

Portfolio Manager: Helen Hayes, Laurence Chang - 1991

Investm't Category: International Stock

✔ Domestic — Index
✔ Foreign — Sector
Asset Allocation — State Specific

Investment Style

Large Cap — Mid Cap — Small Cap
Growth — Grth/Val — Value

Portfolio

9.5%	cash	0.0%	corp bonds
89.5%	stocks	0.0%	gov't bonds
1.0%	pref/conv't pref	0.0%	muni bonds
0.0%	conv't bds/wrnts	0.0%	other

SHAREHOLDER INFORMATION

Minimum Investment
Initial: $2,500 — Subsequent: $100

Minimum IRA Investment
Initial: $500 — Subsequent: $100

Maximum Fees
Load: none — 12b-1: none
Other: none

Services
✔ IRA
✔ Keogh
✔ Telephone Exchange

Japan/S (SJPNX)

800-535-2726, 312-781-1121
www.scudder.com

International Stock

PERFORMANCE — fund inception date: 3/30/62

	3yr Annual	5yr Annual	10yr Annual	Bull	Bear
Return (%)	25.7	8.6	4.8	170.9	-26.4
Differ from Category (+/-)	16.8 high	0.3 av	-4.2 low	80.0 high	-2.4 av

Standard Deviation	Category Risk Index	Beta
25.7%—high	1.14—abv av	0.79

	2000	1999	1998	1997	1996	1995	1994	1993	1992	1991
Return (%)	-27.2	119.8	24.2	-14.3	-10.9	-9.0	10.0	23.6	-16.7	3.1
Differ from Category (+/-)	-7.8	59.1	18.4	-15.6	-25.4	-18.3	13.1	-16.6	-13.2	-9.9
Return, Tax-Adjusted (%)	-30.8	115.1	23.7	-16.0	-11.2	-9.2	7.6	21.1	-16.7	2.0

PER SHARE DATA

	2000	1999	1998	1997	1996	1995	1994	1993	1992	1991
Dividends, Net Income ($)	0.58	0.08	0.07	0.36	0.08	0.00	0.00	0.28	0.00	0.00
Distrib'ns, Cap Gain ($)	1.82	1.77	0.00	0.00	0.00	0.11	0.85	0.39	0.00	0.41
Net Asset Value ($)	9.99	16.41	8.33	6.77	8.33	9.44	10.51	10.33	8.90	10.69
Expense Ratio (%)	na	0.98	1.26	1.21	1.16	1.27	1.08	1.25	1.42	1.26
Yield (%)	4.91	0.44	0.84	5.31	0.96	0.00	0.00	2.61	0.00	0.00
Portfolio Turnover (%)	na	114	90	96	72	66	74	81	47	46
Total Assets (Millions $)	624	1,089	348	270	383	550	585	471	409	334

PORTFOLIO (as of 6/30/00)

Portfolio Manager: Seung Kwak, Elizabeth Allan - 1989

Investm't Category: International Stock

Domestic	Index
✔ Foreign	Sector
Asset Allocation	State Specific

Investment Style

Large Cap	Mid Cap	Small Cap
Growth	Grth/Val	Value

Portfolio

4.5%	cash	0.0%	corp bonds
95.5%	stocks	0.0%	gov't bonds
0.0%	pref/conv't pref	0.0%	muni bonds
0.0%	conv't bds/wrnts	0.0%	other

SHAREHOLDER INFORMATION

Minimum Investment
Initial: $2,500 — Subsequent: $100

Minimum IRA Investment
Initial: $1,000 — Subsequent: $100

Maximum Fees
Load: none — 12b-1: none
Other: none

Services
✔ IRA
✔ Keogh
✔ Telephone Exchange

Kalmar Growth With Value (KGSCX)

800-282-2319, 302-658-7575
www.kalmarinvestments.com

Aggressive Growth

PERFORMANCE — fund inception date: 4/11/97

	3yr Annual	5yr Annual	10yr Annual	Bull	Bear
Return (%)	4.2	na	na	29.4	-7.2
Differ from Category (+/-)	-12.0 low	na	na	-89.8 low	13.4 high

Standard Deviation	Category Risk Index	Beta
23.9%—abv av	0.74—low	0.96

	2000	1999	1998	1997	1996	1995	1994	1993	1992	1991
Return (%)	15.7	6.0	-7.6	—	—	—	—	—	—	—
Differ from Category (+/-)	21.7	-51.5	-22.7	—	—	—	—	—	—	—
Return, Tax-Adjusted (%)	11.8	6.0	-7.6	—	—	—	—	—	—	—

PER SHARE DATA

	2000	1999	1998	1997	1996	1995	1994	1993	1992	1991
Dividends, Net Income ($)	0.00	0.00	0.00	—	—	—	—	—	—	—
Distrib'ns, Cap Gain ($)	2.58	0.00	0.00	—	—	—	—	—	—	—
Net Asset Value ($)	12.95	13.41	12.65	—	—	—	—	—	—	—
Expense Ratio (%)	na	1.25	1.24	—	—	—	—	—	—	—
Yield (%)	0.00	0.00	0.00	—	—	—	—	—	—	—
Portfolio Turnover (%)	na	52	27	—	—	—	—	—	—	—
Total Assets (Millions $)	197	195	237	—	—	—	—	—	—	—

PORTFOLIO (as of 3/31/00)

Portfolio Manager: committee - 1997

Investm't Category: Aggressive Growth

✔ Domestic — Index
✔ Foreign — Sector
Asset Allocation — State Specific

Investment Style

Large Cap — Mid Cap — ✔ Small Cap
Growth — ✔ Grth/Val — Value

Portfolio

1.6%	cash	0.0%	corp bonds
98.4%	stocks	0.0%	gov't bonds
0.0%	pref/conv't pref	0.0%	muni bonds
0.0%	conv't bds/wrnts	0.0%	other

SHAREHOLDER INFORMATION

Minimum Investment
Initial: $10,000 — Subsequent: $1,000

Minimum IRA Investment
Initial: $1,000 — Subsequent: $1

Maximum Fees
Load: none — 12b-1: none
Other: none

Services
✔ IRA
Keogh
Telephone Exchange

Kaufmann (KAUFX)

800-237-0132, 212-922-0123
www.kaufmann.com

Aggressive Growth

PERFORMANCE — fund inception date: 2/21/86

	3yr Annual	5yr Annual	10yr Annual	Bull	Bear
Return (%)	12.0	13.8	21.0	57.2	-14.1
Differ from Category (+/-)	-4.2 blw av	-0.8 av	5.2 abv av	-62.0 blw av	6.5 abv av

Standard Deviation	Category Risk Index	Beta
29.5%—high	0.91—blw av	0.91

	2000	1999	1998	1997	1996	1995	1994	1993	1992	1991
Return (%)	10.8	26.0	0.7	12.5	20.9	36.8	8.9	18.1	11.3	79.4
Differ from Category (+/-)	16.8	-31.5	-14.4	-2.3	2.6	2.2	9.7	-7.1	4.4	32.2
Return, Tax-Adjusted (%)	3.3	22.5	-1.3	11.8	19.4	36.1	8.9	17.8	11.3	77.9

PER SHARE DATA

	2000	1999	1998	1997	1996	1995	1994	1993	1992	1991
Dividends, Net Income ($)	0.00	0.00	0.00	0.00	0.00	0.00	0.00	0.00	0.00	0.00
Distrib'ns, Cap Gain ($)	2.23	0.98	0.66	0.20	0.26	0.09	0.00	0.03	0.00	0.08
Net Asset Value ($)	4.43	5.95	5.68	6.37	5.84	5.05	3.76	3.45	2.95	2.65
Expense Ratio (%)	na	1.94	1.95	1.88	1.93	2.24	2.29	2.53	2.94	3.64
Yield (%)	0.00	0.00	0.00	0.00	0.00	0.00	0.00	0.00	0.00	0.00
Portfolio Turnover (%)	na	78	59	65	72	60	47	55	51	128
Total Assets (Millions $)	3,185	3,481	4,631	6,010	5,200	3,159	1,583	965	313	140

PORTFOLIO (as of 6/30/00)

Portfolio Manager: Hans Utsch, Lawrence Auriana - 1986

Investm't Category: Aggressive Growth

✔ Domestic — Index
✔ Foreign — Sector
Asset Allocation — State Specific

Investment Style

Large Cap — Mid Cap — ✔ Small Cap
✔ Growth — Grth/Val — Value

Portfolio

14.4%	cash	0.0%	corp bonds
80.5%	stocks	0.0%	gov't bonds
0.0%	pref/conv't pref	0.0%	muni bonds
1.1%	conv't bds/wrnts	4.0%	other

SHAREHOLDER INFORMATION

Minimum Investment
Initial: $1,500 — Subsequent: $100

Minimum IRA Investment
Initial: $500 — Subsequent: $1

Maximum Fees
Load: 0.20% redemption — 12b-1: 0.36%
Other: redemption fee applies for 15 days

Services
✔ IRA
✔ Keogh
✔ Telephone Exchange

Kobren: Growth (KOGRX)

800-456-2736
www.kobren.com

Growth

PERFORMANCE — fund inception date: 12/16/96

	3yr Annual	5yr Annual	10yr Annual	Bull	Bear
Return (%)	9.2	na	na	53.7	-16.1
Differ from Category (+/-)	-1.8 blw av	na	na	4.0 av	-10.7 blw av

Standard Deviation	Category Risk Index	Beta
18.2%—av	0.93—blw av	0.82

	2000	1999	1998	1997	1996	1995	1994	1993	1992	1991
Return (%)	-9.7	29.7	11.4	15.1	—	—	—	—	—	—
Differ from Category (+/-)	-13.2	10.8	-2.9	-12.0	—	—	—	—	—	—
Return, Tax-Adjusted (%)	-11.9	28.1	10.8	14.0	—	—	—	—	—	—

PER SHARE DATA

	2000	1999	1998	1997	1996	1995	1994	1993	1992	1991
Dividends, Net Income ($)	0.18	0.09	0.02	0.26	—	—	—	—	—	—
Distrib'ns, Cap Gain ($)	1.34	0.82	0.26	0.00	—	—	—	—	—	—
Net Asset Value ($)	12.32	15.34	12.54	11.51	—	—	—	—	—	—
Expense Ratio (%)	na	1.07	0.91	0.89	—	—	—	—	—	—
Yield (%)	1.31	0.55	0.15	2.25	—	—	—	—	—	—
Portfolio Turnover (%)	na	66	62	43	—	—	—	—	—	—
Total Assets (Millions $)	61	69	63	61	—	—	—	—	—	—

PORTFOLIO (as of 6/30/00)

Portfolio Manager: Eric Kobren - 1996

Investm't Category: Growth

✔ Domestic
✔ Foreign
Asset Allocation
Index
Sector
State Specific

Investment Style

Large Cap ✔ Mid Cap ✔ Small Cap
✔ Growth Grth/Val Value

Portfolio

2.7%	cash	0.0%	corp bonds
97.3%	stocks	0.0%	gov't bonds
0.0%	pref/conv't pref	0.0%	muni bonds
0.0%	conv't bds/wrnts	0.0%	other

SHAREHOLDER INFORMATION

Minimum Investment

Initial: $2,500 Subsequent: $500

Minimum IRA Investment

Initial: $2,000 Subsequent: $500

Maximum Fees

Load: none 12b-1: none
Other: none

Services

✔ IRA
✔ Keogh
✔ Telephone Exchange

LKCM Small Cap Equity (LKSCX)

800-688-5526, 617-557-8785
www.lkcm.com

Growth

PERFORMANCE

fund inception date: 7/14/94

	3yr Annual	5yr Annual	10yr Annual	Bull	Bear
Return (%)	8.7	14.7	na	37.3	-4.9
Differ from Category (+/-)	-2.3 blw av	-1.4 blw av	na	-12.4 blw av	0.5 av

Standard Deviation	Category Risk Index	Beta
19.7%—abv av	1.01—av	0.67

	2000	1999	1998	1997	1996	1995	1994	1993	1992	1991
Return (%)	17.4	16.8	-6.2	23.0	25.6	33.2	—	—	—	—
Differ from Category (+/-)	13.9	-2.1	-20.5	-4.1	3.3	2.8	—	—	—	—
Return, Tax-Adjusted (%)	12.6	16.4	-6.3	19.5	23.6	32.6	—	—	—	—

PER SHARE DATA

	2000	1999	1998	1997	1996	1995	1994	1993	1992	1991
Dividends, Net Income ($)	0.04	0.02	0.06	0.07	0.06	0.14	—	—	—	—
Distrib'ns, Cap Gain ($)	4.19	0.25	0.04	2.64	0.87	0.00	—	—	—	—
Net Asset Value ($)	17.00	18.08	15.72	16.89	16.20	13.84	—	—	—	—
Expense Ratio (%)	na	0.90	0.91	0.95	1.00	1.00	—	—	—	—
Yield (%)	0.18	0.10	0.38	0.35	0.35	1.01	—	—	—	—
Portfolio Turnover (%)	na	48	35	34	66	—	—	—	—	—
Total Assets (Millions $)	192	230	246	255	199	122	—	—	—	—

PORTFOLIO (as of 6/30/00)

Portfolio Manager: J. King - 1994

Investm't Category: Growth

✔ Domestic — Index
✔ Foreign — Sector
Asset Allocation — State Specific

Investment Style

Large Cap — Mid Cap — ✔ Small Cap
Growth — ✔ Grth/Val — Value

Portfolio

15.5%	cash	0.0%	corp bonds
82.2%	stocks	0.0%	gov't bonds
0.1%	pref/conv't pref	0.0%	muni bonds
2.2%	conv't bds/wrnts	0.0%	other

SHAREHOLDER INFORMATION

Minimum Investment
Initial: $10,000 — Subsequent: $1,000

Minimum IRA Investment
Initial: $10,000 — Subsequent: $1,000

Maximum Fees
Load: none — 12b-1: none
Other: none

Services
✔ IRA
✔ Keogh
✔ Telephone Exchange

Lazard: Equity/Open (LZEOX)

800-823-6300, 212-632-6000
www.lazardnet.com

Growth

PERFORMANCE — fund inception date: 2/5/97

	3yr Annual	5yr Annual	10yr Annual	Bull	Bear
Return (%)	5.6	na	na	31.2	-5.5
Differ from Category (+/-)	-5.4 low	na	na	-18.5 blw av	-0.1 av

Standard Deviation	Category Risk Index	Beta
17.4%—av	0.90—low	0.90

	2000	1999	1998	1997	1996	1995	1994	1993	1992	1991
Return (%)	-2.9	3.9	16.9	—	—	—	—	—	—	—
Differ from Category (+/-)	-6.4	-15.0	2.6	—	—	—	—	—	—	—
Return, Tax-Adjusted (%)	-6.5	2.2	15.1	—	—	—	—	—	—	—

PER SHARE DATA

	2000	1999	1998	1997	1996	1995	1994	1993	1992	1991
Dividends, Net Income ($)	0.16	0.22	0.20	—	—	—	—	—	—	—
Distrib'ns, Cap Gain ($)	3.51	1.32	1.35	—	—	—	—	—	—	—
Net Asset Value ($)	16.70	21.05	21.76	—	—	—	—	—	—	—
Expense Ratio (%)	na	1.10	1.12	—	—	—	—	—	—	—
Yield (%)	0.79	0.98	0.86	—	—	—	—	—	—	—
Portfolio Turnover (%)	na	62	76	—	—	—	—	—	—	—
Total Assets (Millions $)	64	122	117	—	—	—	—	—	—	—

PORTFOLIO (as of 6/30/00)

Portfolio Manager: H. Gullquist, E. Alexanderson - 1999

Investm't Category: Growth

✔ Domestic — Index
✔ Foreign — Sector
Asset Allocation — State Specific

Investment Style

✔ Large Cap — Mid Cap — Small Cap
Growth — Grth/Val — ✔ Value

Portfolio

3.2%	cash	0.0%	corp bonds
96.8%	stocks	0.0%	gov't bonds
0.0%	pref/conv't pref	0.0%	muni bonds
0.0%	conv't bds/wrnts	0.0%	other

SHAREHOLDER INFORMATION

Minimum Investment
Initial: $10,000 — Subsequent: $1

Minimum IRA Investment
Initial: $10,000 — Subsequent: $1

Maximum Fees
Load: none — 12b-1: 0.25%
Other: none

Services
✔ IRA
✔ Keogh
✔ Telephone Exchange

Lazard: Small Cap/Open (LZCOX)

800-823-6300, 212-632-6000
www.lazardnet.com

Growth

PERFORMANCE — fund inception date: 1/30/97

	3yr Annual	5yr Annual	10yr Annual	Bull	Bear
Return (%)	3.0	na	na	25.9	2.1
Differ from Category (+/-)	-8.0 low	na	na	-23.8 blw av	7.5 abv av

Standard Deviation	Category Risk Index	Beta
20.3%—abv av	1.04—av	0.82

	2000	1999	1998	1997	1996	1995	1994	1993	1992	1991
Return (%)	15.5	1.4	-6.6	—	—	—	—	—	—	—
Differ from Category (+/-)	12.0	-17.5	-20.9	—	—	—	—	—	—	—
Return, Tax-Adjusted (%)	14.1	0.1	-8.1	—	—	—	—	—	—	—

PER SHARE DATA

	2000	1999	1998	1997	1996	1995	1994	1993	1992	1991
Dividends, Net Income ($)	0.15	0.07	0.31	—	—	—	—	—	—	—
Distrib'ns, Cap Gain ($)	0.80	0.97	0.96	—	—	—	—	—	—	—
Net Asset Value ($)	18.04	16.51	17.35	—	—	—	—	—	—	—
Expense Ratio (%)	na	1.09	1.09	—	—	—	—	—	—	—
Yield (%)	0.79	0.40	1.69	—	—	—	—	—	—	—
Portfolio Turnover (%)	na	50	46	—	—	—	—	—	—	—
Total Assets (Millions $)	61	85	93	—	—	—	—	—	—	—

PORTFOLIO (as of 6/30/00)

Portfolio Manager: H. Gullquist, E. Alexanderson - 1997

Investm't Category: Growth

✔ Domestic	Index
✔ Foreign	Sector
Asset Allocation	State Specific

Investment Style

Large Cap	✔ Mid Cap	✔ Small Cap
Growth	Grth/Val	✔ Value

Portfolio

3.3%	cash	0.0%	corp bonds
96.7%	stocks	0.0%	gov't bonds
0.0%	pref/conv't pref	0.0%	muni bonds
0.0%	conv't bds/wrnts	0.0%	other

SHAREHOLDER INFORMATION

Minimum Investment
Initial: $10,000 — Subsequent: $1

Minimum IRA Investment
Initial: $10,000 — Subsequent: $1

Maximum Fees
Load: none — 12b-1: 0.25%
Other: none

Services
✔ IRA
✔ Keogh
✔ Telephone Exchange

Legg Mason Eq: Am Lead/P (LMALX)

800-822-5544, 410-539-0000
www.leggmason.com

Growth

PERFORMANCE — fund inception date: 9/1/93

	3yr Annual	5yr Annual	10yr Annual	Bull	Bear
Return (%)	8.6	15.3	na	37.7	0.0
Differ from Category (+/-)	-2.4 blw av	-0.8 av	na	-12.0 blw av	5.4 abv av

Standard Deviation	Category Risk Index	Beta
18.8%—av	0.97—blw av	0.97

	2000	1999	1998	1997	1996	1995	1994	1993	1992	1991
Return (%)	0.5	5.2	21.3	23.7	28.3	22.9	-4.1	—	—	—
Differ from Category (+/-)	-3.0	-13.7	7.0	-3.4	6.0	-7.5	-3.9	—	—	—
Return, Tax-Adjusted (%)	0.3	4.8	20.4	21.1	27.0	22.4	-4.5	—	—	—

PER SHARE DATA

	2000	1999	1998	1997	1996	1995	1994	1993	1992	1991
Dividends, Net Income ($)	0.00	0.00	0.00	0.00	0.02	0.10	0.11	—	—	—
Distrib'ns, Cap Gain ($)	0.10	0.36	0.71	1.84	0.47	0.00	0.00	—	—	—
Net Asset Value ($)	19.12	19.13	18.50	15.90	14.40	11.61	9.53	—	—	—
Expense Ratio (%)	1.90	1.93	1.95	1.95	1.95	1.95	1.95	—	—	—
Yield (%)	0.00	0.00	0.00	0.00	0.13	0.86	1.15	—	—	—
Portfolio Turnover (%)	43	47	51	55	43	30	21	—	—	—
Total Assets (Millions $)	271	328	238	171	90	71	56	—	—	—

PORTFOLIO (as of 6/30/00)

Portfolio Manager: David Nelson - 1998

Investm't Category: Growth

✔ Domestic | Index
✔ Foreign | Sector
Asset Allocation | State Specific

Investment Style

✔ Large Cap | Mid Cap | Small Cap
Growth | ✔ Grth/Val | Value

Portfolio

1.9% cash
98.1% stocks
0.0% pref/conv't pref
0.0% conv't bds/wrnts
0.0% corp bonds
0.0% gov't bonds
0.0% muni bonds
0.0% other

SHAREHOLDER INFORMATION

Minimum Investment
Initial: $1,000 Subsequent: $100

Minimum IRA Investment
Initial: $1,000 Subsequent: $100

Maximum Fees
Load: none 12b-1: 1.00%
Other: none

Services
✔ IRA
✔ Keogh
✔ Telephone Exchange

Legg Mason Eq: Special/P (LMASX)

800-822-5544, 410-539-0000
www.leggmason.com

Aggressive Growth

PERFORMANCE

fund inception date: 12/30/85

	3yr Annual	5yr Annual	10yr Annual	Bull	Bear
Return (%)	13.7	18.2	17.2	107.3	-14.6
Differ from Category (+/-)	-2.5 av	3.6 abv av	1.4 av	-11.9 av	6.0 abv av

Standard Deviation	Category Risk Index	Beta
25.6%—high	0.79—blw av	1.19

	2000	1999	1998	1997	1996	1995	1994	1993	1992	1991
Return (%)	-12.0	35.5	23.3	22.1	28.6	22.5	-13.0	24.1	15.3	39.4
Differ from Category (+/-)	-6.0	-22.0	8.2	7.3	10.3	-12.1	-12.2	-1.1	8.4	-7.8
Return, Tax-Adjusted (%)	-12.7	31.1	21.6	21.0	26.8	21.7	-13.2	23.8	13.2	39.1

PER SHARE DATA

	2000	1999	1998	1997	1996	1995	1994	1993	1992	1991
Dividends, Net Income ($)	0.00	0.00	0.00	0.00	0.00	0.03	0.00	0.03	0.11	0.03
Distrib'ns, Cap Gain ($)	1.51	8.04	2.65	1.49	1.41	0.44	0.23	0.14	1.10	0.08
Net Asset Value ($)	33.94	40.15	36.70	32.27	27.83	22.81	19.03	22.14	17.98	16.78
Expense Ratio (%)	1.80	1.84	1.86	1.92	1.96	1.93	1.94	2.00	2.10	2.30
Yield (%)	0.00	0.00	0.00	0.00	0.00	0.12	0.00	0.13	0.57	0.17
Portfolio Turnover (%)	29	47	29	29	36	27	16	32	57	76
Total Assets (Millions $)	2,222	2,587	1,730	1,366	964	713	605	510	287	163

PORTFOLIO (as of 6/30/00)

Portfolio Manager: William Miller, Lisa Rapuano - 1999

Investm't Category: Aggressive Growth

✔ Domestic — Index
✔ Foreign — Sector
Asset Allocation — State Specific

Investment Style

Large Cap — ✔ Mid Cap — ✔ Small Cap
✔ Growth — Grth/Val — Value

Portfolio

4.6%	cash	0.0%	corp bonds
93.0%	stocks	0.0%	gov't bonds
0.0%	pref/conv't pref	0.0%	muni bonds
2.4%	conv't bds/wrnts	0.0%	other

SHAREHOLDER INFORMATION

Minimum Investment
Initial: $1,000 — Subsequent: $100

Minimum IRA Investment
Initial: $1,000 — Subsequent: $100

Maximum Fees
Load: none — 12b-1: 1.00%
Other: none

Services
✔ IRA
✔ Keogh
✔ Telephone Exchange

Legg Mason Eq: Total Ret/P (LMTRX)

800-822-5544, 410-539-0000
www.leggmason.com

Growth & Income

PERFORMANCE

fund inception date: 11/21/85

	3yr Annual	5yr Annual	10yr Annual	Bull	Bear
Return (%)	-3.8	9.8	13.5	8.7	-3.0
Differ from Category (+/-)	-12.7 low	-4.5 low	-1.4 low	-24.8 low	-2.9 av

Standard Deviation	Category Risk Index	Beta
17.4%—av	1.00—av	0.77

	2000	1999	1998	1997	1996	1995	1994	1993	1992	1991
Return (%)	-4.6	-6.5	-0.3	37.5	31.1	30.3	-7.1	14.0	14.3	40.4
Differ from Category (+/-)	-10.3	-17.3	-13.1	10.6	11.4	0.8	-6.6	0.2	2.7	12.3
Return, Tax-Adjusted (%)	-5.3	-8.2	-1.9	34.5	29.0	28.6	-9.1	12.0	13.5	39.7

PER SHARE DATA

	2000	1999	1998	1997	1996	1995	1994	1993	1992	1991
Dividends, Net Income ($)	0.12	0.30	0.38	0.39	0.42	0.51	0.29	0.41	0.30	0.18
Distrib'ns, Cap Gain ($)	0.43	1.31	1.20	2.03	0.55	0.00	0.60	0.34	0.00	0.00
Net Asset Value ($)	17.36	18.75	21.64	23.31	19.01	15.29	12.15	14.00	12.98	11.64
Expense Ratio (%)	1.89	1.87	1.88	1.93	1.95	1.93	1.94	1.95	2.30	2.50
Yield (%)	0.67	1.49	1.66	1.53	2.14	3.33	2.27	2.85	2.31	1.54
Portfolio Turnover (%)	85	44	20	38	34	61	46	40	38	62
Total Assets (Millions $)	309	444	635	598	344	242	193	175	110	40

PORTFOLIO (as of 6/30/00)

Portfolio Manager: Nancy Dennin - 1992

Investm't Category: Growth & Income

✔ Domestic
✔ Foreign
Asset Allocation
Index
Sector
State Specific

Investment Style

✔ Large Cap
Mid Cap
Small Cap
Growth
Grth/Val
✔ Value

Portfolio

6.0%	cash	0.0%	corp bonds
91.6%	stocks	0.0%	gov't bonds
0.0%	pref/conv't pref	0.0%	muni bonds
2.4%	conv't bds/wrnts	0.0%	other

SHAREHOLDER INFORMATION

Minimum Investment

Initial: $1,000 Subsequent: $100

Minimum IRA Investment

Initial: $1,000 Subsequent: $100

Maximum Fees

Load: none 12b-1: 1.00%
Other: none

Services

✔ IRA
✔ Keogh
✔ Telephone Exchange

Legg Mason Eq: Value/P (LMVTX)

800-822-5544, 410-539-0000
www.leggmason.com

Growth

PERFORMANCE

fund inception date: 4/16/82

	3yr Annual	5yr Annual	10yr Annual	Bull	Bear
Return (%)	20.3	27.0	22.9	83.9	-9.1
Differ from Category (+/-)	9.3 high	10.9 high	6.1 high	34.2 high	-3.7 av

Standard Deviation	Category Risk Index	Beta
23.6%—abv av	1.21—abv av	1.23

	2000	1999	1998	1997	1996	1995	1994	1993	1992	1991
Return (%)	-7.1	26.7	48.0	37.0	38.4	40.7	1.3	11.2	11.4	34.7
Differ from Category (+/-)	-10.6	7.8	33.7	9.9	16.1	10.3	1.5	-3.4	-1.2	-2.9
Return, Tax-Adjusted (%)	-10.9	25.9	47.3	35.5	36.4	38.5	1.1	10.4	11.0	34.4

PER SHARE DATA

	2000	1999	1998	1997	1996	1995	1994	1993	1992	1991
Dividends, Net Income ($)	0.00	0.00	0.00	0.03	0.16	0.17	0.05	0.23	0.16	0.22
Distrib'ns, Cap Gain ($)	14.47	2.46	1.40	2.32	1.53	1.24	0.04	0.15	0.00	0.00
Net Asset Value ($)	55.44	75.27	61.58	42.74	32.99	25.19	19.04	18.87	17.32	15.70
Expense Ratio (%)	1.68	1.69	1.73	1.77	1.82	1.81	1.82	1.86	1.90	1.90
Yield (%)	0.00	0.00	0.00	0.06	0.46	0.64	0.26	1.20	0.92	1.40
Portfolio Turnover (%)	19	19	12	10	20	20	25	21	39	39
Total Assets (Millions $)	10,734	12,540	7,507	3,683	1,978	1,340	967	914	842	747

PORTFOLIO (as of 6/30/00)

Portfolio Manager: William Miller - 1990

Investm't Category: Growth

✔ Domestic	Index
✔ Foreign	Sector
Asset Allocation	State Specific

Investment Style

✔ Large Cap	Mid Cap	Small Cap
Growth	✔ Grth/Val	Value

Portfolio

2.8%	cash	0.0%	corp bonds
97.2%	stocks	0.0%	gov't bonds
0.0%	pref/conv't pref	0.0%	muni bonds
0.0%	conv't bds/wrnts	0.0%	other

SHAREHOLDER INFORMATION

Minimum Investment
Initial: $1,000 Subsequent: $100

Minimum IRA Investment
Initial: $1,000 Subsequent: $100

Maximum Fees
Load: none 12b-1: 0.25%
Other: none

Services
✔ IRA
✔ Keogh
✔ Telephone Exchange

Legg Mason Gl: Intl Eq/P (LMGEX)

800-822-5544, 410-539-0000
www.leggmason.com

International Stock

PERFORMANCE

fund inception date: 2/17/95

	3yr Annual	5yr Annual	10yr Annual	Bull	Bear
Return (%)	1.9	4.6	na	29.8	-19.7
Differ from Category (+/-)	-7.0 low	-3.7 blw av	na	-61.1 low	4.3 abv av

Standard Deviation	Category Risk Index	Beta
17.1%—av	0.75—low	0.71

	2000	1999	1998	1997	1996	1995	1994	1993	1992	1991
Return (%)	-19.0	20.5	8.4	1.6	16.5	—	—	—	—	—
Differ from Category (+/-)	0.4	-40.2	2.6	0.3	2.0	—	—	—	—	—
Return, Tax-Adjusted (%)	-19.2	18.9	7.9	0.6	15.5	—	—	—	—	—

PER SHARE DATA

	2000	1999	1998	1997	1996	1995	1994	1993	1992	1991
Dividends, Net Income ($)	0.00	0.05	0.13	0.08	0.04	—	—	—	—	—
Distrib'ns, Cap Gain ($)	0.18	0.86	0.00	0.44	0.32	—	—	—	—	—
Net Asset Value ($)	11.35	14.23	12.64	11.78	12.10	—	—	—	—	—
Expense Ratio (%)	na	2.13	2.14	2.17	2.25	—	—	—	—	—
Yield (%)	0.00	0.33	1.02	0.65	0.32	—	—	—	—	—
Portfolio Turnover (%)	na	148	72	59	83	—	—	—	—	—
Total Assets (Millions $)	182	295	258	228	167	—	—	—	—	—

PORTFOLIO (as of 6/30/00)

Portfolio Manager: Charles Lovejoy - 1995

Investm't Category: International Stock

Domestic	Index
✔ Foreign	Sector
Asset Allocation	State Specific

Investment Style

Large Cap	Mid Cap	Small Cap
Growth	Grth/Val	Value

Portfolio

1.0% cash	0.0% corp bonds
99.1% stocks	0.0% gov't bonds
0.0% pref/conv't pref	0.0% muni bonds
0.0% conv't bds/wrnts	0.0% other

SHAREHOLDER INFORMATION

Minimum Investment
Initial: $1,000 Subsequent: $100

Minimum IRA Investment
Initial: $1,000 Subsequent: $100

Maximum Fees
Load: none 12b-1: 1.00%
Other: none

Services
✔ IRA
✔ Keogh
✔ Telephone Exchange

Liberty Acorn Internatl/Z (ACINX)

800-922-6769, 312-634-9200
www.wanger.com

International Stock

PERFORMANCE

fund inception date: 9/23/92

	3yr Annual	5yr Annual	10yr Annual	Bull	Bear
Return (%)	18.2	14.8	na	95.4	-30.0
Differ from Category (+/-)	9.3 high	6.5 high	na	4.5 abv av	-6.0 blw av

Standard Deviation	Category Risk Index	Beta
23.7%—abv av	1.05—av	0.68

	2000	1999	1998	1997	1996	1995	1994	1993	1992	1991
Return (%)	-19.9	79.1	15.4	0.1	20.6	8.9	-3.7	49.1	—	—
Differ from Category (+/-)	-0.5	18.4	9.6	-1.2	6.1	-0.4	-0.6	8.9	—	—
Return, Tax-Adjusted (%)	-22.9	77.1	14.7	-1.5	19.8	8.8	-3.8	49.1	—	—

PER SHARE DATA

	2000	1999	1998	1997	1996	1995	1994	1993	1992	1991
Dividends, Net Income ($)	0.66	0.22	0.15	0.38	0.12	0.00	0.01	0.00	—	—
Distrib'ns, Cap Gain ($)	4.10	1.55	0.27	0.90	0.28	0.01	0.09	0.00	—	—
Net Asset Value ($)	23.86	35.33	20.82	18.39	19.61	16.59	15.24	15.94	—	—
Expense Ratio (%)	na	1.11	1.12	1.19	1.17	1.20	1.20	1.20	—	—
Yield (%)	2.36	0.59	0.71	1.96	0.60	0.00	0.06	0.00	—	—
Portfolio Turnover (%)	na	46	37	39	34	26	20	19	—	—
Total Assets (Millions $)	2,441	2,868	1,726	1,628	1,771	1,276	1,364	906	—	—

PORTFOLIO (as of 6/30/00)

Portfolio Manager: committee - 1995

Investm't Category: International Stock

Domestic	Index
✔ Foreign	Sector
Asset Allocation	State Specific

Investment Style

Large Cap	Mid Cap	Small Cap
Growth	Grth/Val	Value

Portfolio

11.5% cash	0.0% corp bonds
88.5% stocks	0.0% gov't bonds
0.0% pref/conv't pref	0.0% muni bonds
0.0% conv't bds/wrnts	0.0% other

SHAREHOLDER INFORMATION

Minimum Investment
Initial: $1,000 Subsequent: $100

Minimum IRA Investment
Initial: $1,000 Subsequent: $100

Maximum Fees
Load: none 12b-1: none
Other: none

Services
✔ IRA
✔ Keogh
✔ Telephone Exchange

Liberty Acorn USA/Z

800-922-6769, 312-634-9200
www.wanger.com

(AUSAX)

Aggressive Growth

PERFORMANCE — fund inception date: 9/4/96

	3yr Annual	5yr Annual	10yr Annual	Bull	Bear
Return (%)	5.7	na	na	43.9	-16.1
Differ from Category (+/-)	-10.5 blw av	na	na	-75.3 low	4.5 abv av

Standard Deviation	Category Risk Index	Beta
20.0%—abv av	0.62—low	0.79

	2000	1999	1998	1997	1996	1995	1994	1993	1992	1991
Return (%)	-9.0	23.0	5.7	31.8	—	—	—	—	—	—
Differ from Category (+/-)	-3.0	-34.5	-9.4	17.0	—	—	—	—	—	—
Return, Tax-Adjusted (%)	-9.3	21.1	4.2	31.3	—	—	—	—	—	—

PER SHARE DATA

	2000	1999	1998	1997	1996	1995	1994	1993	1992	1991
Dividends, Net Income ($)	0.00	0.00	0.00	0.00	—	—	—	—	—	—
Distrib'ns, Cap Gain ($)	0.32	1.37	1.12	0.24	—	—	—	—	—	—
Net Asset Value ($)	14.90	16.75	14.80	15.12	—	—	—	—	—	—
Expense Ratio (%)	na	1.15	1.20	1.35	—	—	—	—	—	—
Yield (%)	0.00	0.00	0.00	0.00	—	—	—	—	—	—
Portfolio Turnover (%)	na	49	42	33	—	—	—	—	—	—
Total Assets (Millions $)	220	371	281	184	—	—	—	—	—	—

PORTFOLIO (as of 6/30/00)

Portfolio Manager: committee - 1996

Investm't Category: Aggressive Growth

✔ Domestic	Index
Foreign	Sector
Asset Allocation	State Specific

Investment Style

Large Cap	Mid Cap	✔ Small Cap
Growth	✔ Grth/Val	Value

Portfolio

7.9%	cash	0.0%	corp bonds
92.1%	stocks	0.0%	gov't bonds
0.0%	pref/conv't pref	0.0%	muni bonds
0.0%	conv't bds/wrnts	0.0%	other

SHAREHOLDER INFORMATION

Minimum Investment
Initial: $1,000 — Subsequent: $100

Minimum IRA Investment
Initial: $1,000 — Subsequent: $100

Maximum Fees
Load: none — 12b-1: none
Other: none

Services
✔ IRA
✔ Keogh
✔ Telephone Exchange

Liberty Acorn/Z (ACRNX)

800-922-6769, 312-634-9200
www.wanger.com

Growth

PERFORMANCE

fund inception date: 6/10/70

	3yr Annual	5yr Annual	10yr Annual	Bull	Bear
Return (%)	15.8	18.9	20.5	64.1	-0.7
Differ from Category (+/-)	4.8 abv av	2.8 abv av	3.7 high	14.4 abv av	4.7 abv av

Standard Deviation	Category Risk Index	Beta
19.7%—abv av	1.01—av	0.75

	2000	1999	1998	1997	1996	1995	1994	1993	1992	1991
Return (%)	10.0	33.3	6.0	24.9	22.5	20.8	-7.4	32.3	24.2	47.3
Differ from Category (+/-)	6.5	14.4	-8.3	-2.2	0.2	-9.6	-7.2	17.7	11.6	9.7
Return, Tax-Adjusted (%)	6.6	28.8	4.6	22.3	19.1	18.0	-8.8	31.9	22.7	46.1

PER SHARE DATA

	2000	1999	1998	1997	1996	1995	1994	1993	1992	1991
Dividends, Net Income ($)	0.11	0.09	0.03	0.16	0.11	0.09	0.11	0.06	0.14	0.10
Distrib'ns, Cap Gain ($)	2.86	3.54	1.06	1.61	1.47	1.08	0.56	0.59	0.35	0.15
Net Asset Value ($)	17.21	18.53	16.85	16.99	15.04	13.60	12.24	13.95	11.06	9.32
Expense Ratio (%)	na	0.85	0.84	0.56	0.57	0.57	0.62	0.65	0.67	0.72
Yield (%)	0.54	0.40	0.16	0.86	0.66	0.61	0.85	0.41	1.20	1.07
Portfolio Turnover (%)	na	34	24	32	33	29	18	20	25	25
Total Assets (Millions $)	3,623	3,920	3,584	3,687	2,853	2,399	1,982	2,034	1,449	1,150

PORTFOLIO (as of 6/30/00)

Portfolio Manager: committee - 1970

Investm't Category: Growth

✔ Domestic	Index
✔ Foreign	Sector
Asset Allocation	State Specific

Investment Style

Large Cap	✔ Mid Cap	✔ Small Cap
Growth	✔ Grth/Val	Value

Portfolio

7.2% cash	0.0% corp bonds
92.8% stocks	0.0% gov't bonds
0.0% pref/conv't pref	0.0% muni bonds
0.0% conv't bds/wrnts	0.0% other

SHAREHOLDER INFORMATION

Minimum Investment

Initial: $1,000 Subsequent: $100

Minimum IRA Investment

Initial: $1,000 Subsequent: $100

Maximum Fees

Load: none 12b-1: none

Other: none

Services

✔ IRA

✔ Keogh

✔ Telephone Exchange

Lindner Asset Alloc/Inv

800-995-7777, 314-727-5305
www.lindnerfunds.com

(LDDVX)

Balanced

PERFORMANCE — fund inception date: 6/22/76

	3yr Annual	5yr Annual	10yr Annual	Bull	Bear
Return (%)	-0.7	4.4	9.9	12.6	-8.0
Differ from Category (+/-)	-9.1 low	-7.0 low	-1.8 blw av	-15.5 low	-4.8 blw av

Standard Deviation	Category Risk Index	Beta
11.7%—blw av	1.07—abv av	0.47

	2000	1999	1998	1997	1996	1995	1994	1993	1992	1991
Return (%)	-7.5	10.0	-4.0	13.9	11.5	21.5	-3.3	14.9	21.1	27.3
Differ from Category (+/-)	-9.5	-0.7	-17.3	-4.9	-2.4	-4.0	-2.0	0.5	12.7	3.5
Return, Tax-Adjusted (%)	-8.6	7.1	-7.2	9.6	8.1	18.2	-6.6	11.6	18.4	24.1

PER SHARE DATA

	2000	1999	1998	1997	1996	1995	1994	1993	1992	1991
Dividends, Net Income ($)	0.69	1.67	1.96	1.68	1.72	1.83	1.90	1.74	1.86	1.99
Distrib'ns, Cap Gain ($)	0.00	0.00	0.50	2.48	0.78	0.23	0.57	0.58	0.10	0.00
Net Asset Value ($)	21.56	24.06	23.53	26.99	27.50	26.96	23.97	27.32	25.84	23.06
Expense Ratio (%)	0.73	0.66	0.61	0.60	0.60	0.61	0.64	0.74	0.80	0.87
Yield (%)	3.20	6.94	8.15	5.70	6.08	6.73	7.74	6.23	7.17	8.62
Portfolio Turnover (%)	124	31	28	40	30	29	43	13	24	3
Total Assets (Millions $)	371	642	1,163	1,800	2,281	2,088	1,605	1,374	711	234

PORTFOLIO (as of 6/30/00)

Portfolio Manager: M. Finn, J. Fotta, G. Barnes - 2000

Investm't Category: Balanced

✔ Domestic	Index
Foreign	Sector
Asset Allocation	State Specific

Investment Style

Large Cap	Mid Cap	Small Cap
Growth	Grth/Val	Value

Portfolio

0.1%	cash	6.1%	corp bonds
48.6%	stocks	43.2%	gov't bonds
1.7%	pref/conv't pref	0.0%	muni bonds
0.3%	conv't bds/wrnts	0.0%	other

SHAREHOLDER INFORMATION

Minimum Investment
Initial: $2,000 Subsequent: $100

Minimum IRA Investment
Initial: $250 Subsequent: $100

Maximum Fees
Load: 2.00% redemption 12b-1: none
Other: redemption fee applies for 2 months

Services
✔ IRA
✔ Keogh
✔ Telephone Exchange

Lindner Large Cap/Inv (LDNRX)

800-995-7777, 314-727-5305
www.lindnerfunds.com

Growth

PERFORMANCE

fund inception date: 9/30/69

	3yr Annual	5yr Annual	10yr Annual	Bull	Bear
Return (%)	-7.8	0.5	7.4	24.7	-24.6
Differ from Category (+/-)	-18.8 low	-15.6 low	-9.4 low	-25.0 blw av	-19.2 low

Standard Deviation	Category Risk Index	Beta
21.2%—abv av	1.09—abv av	0.93

	2000	1999	1998	1997	1996	1995	1994	1993	1992	1991
Return (%)	-16.4	11.3	-15.8	8.6	21.0	19.8	-0.6	19.8	12.7	23.4
Differ from Category (+/-)	-19.9	-7.6	-30.1	-18.5	-1.3	-10.6	-0.4	5.2	0.1	-14.2
Return, Tax-Adjusted (%)	-18.5	9.6	-18.7	5.2	16.5	17.1	-3.3	18.1	11.6	22.0

PER SHARE DATA

	2000	1999	1998	1997	1996	1995	1994	1993	1992	1991
Dividends, Net Income ($)	0.10	0.23	0.32	0.33	0.39	0.46	0.33	0.45	0.52	0.66
Distrib'ns, Cap Gain ($)	1.59	0.87	2.73	3.47	3.10	1.34	1.84	0.53	0.15	0.00
Net Asset Value ($)	12.32	16.84	16.15	22.85	24.60	23.23	20.89	23.22	20.22	18.55
Expense Ratio (%)	0.82	0.57	0.44	0.44	0.63	0.54	0.65	0.80	0.80	0.83
Yield (%)	0.71	1.29	1.69	1.25	1.40	1.87	1.45	1.89	2.55	3.55
Portfolio Turnover (%)	129	53	44	36	39	24	37	18	11	13
Total Assets (Millions $)	253	402	617	1,300	1,495	1,407	1,503	1,469	1,073	836

PORTFOLIO (as of 6/30/00)

Portfolio Manager: M. Finn, J. Fotta - 2000

Investm't Category: Growth

✔ Domestic
✔ Foreign
Asset Allocation
Index
Sector
State Specific

Investment Style

Large Cap
Growth
✔ Mid Cap
✔ Grth/Val
✔ Small Cap
Value

Portfolio

-7.5%	cash	0.0%	corp bonds
91.3%	stocks	16.2%	gov't bonds
0.0%	pref/conv't pref	0.0%	muni bonds
0.0%	conv't bds/wrnts	0.0%	other

SHAREHOLDER INFORMATION

Minimum Investment
Initial: $2,000 Subsequent: $100

Minimum IRA Investment
Initial: $250 Subsequent: $100

Maximum Fees
Load: 2.00% redemption 12b-1: none
Other: redemption fee applies for 2 months

Services
✔ IRA
✔ Keogh
✔ Telephone Exchange

Longleaf Partners (LLPFX)

800-445-9469, 901-818-5100
www.longleafpartners.com

Growth

PERFORMANCE — fund inception date: 3/24/87

	3yr Annual	5yr Annual	10yr Annual	Bull	Bear
Return (%)	12.0	16.9	20.0	17.4	21.4
Differ from Category (+/-)	1.0 av	0.8 av	3.2 high	-32.3 low	26.8 high

Standard Deviation	Category Risk Index	Beta
18.5%—av	0.95—blw av	0.63

	2000	1999	1998	1997	1996	1995	1994	1993	1992	1991
Return (%)	20.6	2.1	14.2	28.2	21.0	27.4	8.9	22.2	20.4	39.1
Differ from Category (+/-)	17.1	-16.8	-0.1	1.1	-1.3	-3.0	9.1	7.6	7.8	1.5
Return, Tax-Adjusted (%)	18.6	-1.8	10.1	25.1	17.1	26.1	6.6	20.1	17.5	36.8

PER SHARE DATA

	2000	1999	1998	1997	1996	1995	1994	1993	1992	1991
Dividends, Net Income ($)	0.15	0.28	0.24	0.21	0.38	0.24	0.16	0.09	0.07	0.05
Distrib'ns, Cap Gain ($)	1.71	4.23	4.81	3.11	2.38	0.44	1.13	0.95	1.29	0.78
Net Asset Value ($)	22.71	20.49	24.39	25.98	22.85	21.15	17.13	16.92	14.70	13.34
Expense Ratio (%)	na	0.92	0.93	0.94	0.95	1.06	1.17	1.26	1.29	1.30
Yield (%)	0.61	1.13	0.82	0.72	1.50	1.11	0.87	0.50	0.43	0.35
Portfolio Turnover (%)	na	50	43	38	33	12	27	19	29	45
Total Assets (Millions $)	3,558	3,630	3,687	2,605	2,300	1,876	753	397	243	177

PORTFOLIO (as of 6/30/00)

Portfolio Manager: Hawkins, Cates, Buford - 1987

Investm't Category: Growth

✔ Domestic　　Index
✔ Foreign　　Sector
Asset Allocation　　State Specific

Investment Style

✔ Large Cap　　Mid Cap　　Small Cap
Growth　　Grth/Val　　✔ Value

Portfolio

2.8% cash　　0.0% corp bonds
96.3% stocks　　0.0% gov't bonds
0.0% pref/conv't pref　　0.0% muni bonds
0.0% conv't bds/wrnts　　0.9% other

SHAREHOLDER INFORMATION

Minimum Investment
Initial: $10,000　　Subsequent: $1

Minimum IRA Investment
Initial: $10,000　　Subsequent: $1

Maximum Fees
Load: none　　12b-1: none
Other: none

Services
✔ IRA
✔ Keogh
✔ Telephone Exchange

Longleaf Partners Realty (LLREX)

800-445-9469, 901-818-5100
www.longleafpartners.com

Growth & Income

PERFORMANCE — fund inception date: 1/2/96

	3yr Annual	5yr Annual	10yr Annual	Bull	Bear
Return (%)	-3.6	na	na	-3.6	14.8
Differ from Category (+/-)	-12.5 low	na	na	-37.1 low	14.9 high

Standard Deviation	Category Risk Index	Beta
14.3%—blw av	0.83—low	0.41

	2000	1999	1998	1997	1996	1995	1994	1993	1992	1991
Return (%)	14.7	-10.4	-12.9	29.7	—	—	—	—	—	—
Differ from Category (+/-)	9.0	-21.2	-25.7	2.8	—	—	—	—	—	—
Return, Tax-Adjusted (%)	13.3	-11.2	-14.1	28.4	—	—	—	—	—	—

PER SHARE DATA

	2000	1999	1998	1997	1996	1995	1994	1993	1992	1991
Dividends, Net Income ($)	0.43	0.33	0.54	0.13	—	—	—	—	—	—
Distrib'ns, Cap Gain ($)	0.00	0.00	0.00	0.64	—	—	—	—	—	—
Net Asset Value ($)	14.13	12.69	14.55	17.35	—	—	—	—	—	—
Expense Ratio (%)	na	1.17	1.17	1.20	—	—	—	—	—	—
Yield (%)	3.04	2.60	3.71	0.72	—	—	—	—	—	—
Portfolio Turnover (%)	na	22	21	28	—	—	—	—	—	—
Total Assets (Millions $)	602	641	776	737	—	—	—	—	—	—

PORTFOLIO (as of 6/30/00)

Portfolio Manager: Hawkins, Cates, Fitzpatrick - 1996

Investm't Category: Growth & Income

✔ Domestic
Index
✔ Foreign
✔ Sector
Asset Allocation
State Specific

Investment Style

Large Cap
✔ Mid Cap
✔ Small Cap
Growth
Grth/Val
✔ Value

Portfolio

2.3%	cash	0.0%	corp bonds
96.8%	stocks	0.0%	gov't bonds
0.0%	pref/conv't pref	0.0%	muni bonds
0.0%	conv't bds/wrnts	0.9%	other

SHAREHOLDER INFORMATION

Minimum Investment
Initial: $10,000 Subsequent: $1

Minimum IRA Investment
Initial: $10,000 Subsequent: $1

Maximum Fees
Load: none 12b-1: none
Other: none

Services
✔ IRA
✔ Keogh
✔ Telephone Exchange

Longleaf Partners Sm Cap (LLSCX)

800-445-9469, 901-818-5100
www.longleafpartners.com

Growth

this fund is closed to new investors

PERFORMANCE

fund inception date: 12/28/88

	3yr Annual	5yr Annual	10yr Annual	Bull	Bear
Return (%)	9.7	17.3	16.0	16.3	6.8
Differ from Category (+/-)	-1.3 blw av	1.2 av	-0.8 av	-33.4 low	12.2 abv av

Standard Deviation	Category Risk Index	Beta
15.7%—av	0.81—low	0.53

	2000	1999	1998	1997	1996	1995	1994	1993	1992	1991
Return (%)	12.7	4.0	12.7	29.0	30.6	18.5	3.7	19.8	6.8	26.2
Differ from Category (+/-)	9.2	-14.9	-1.6	1.9	8.3	-11.9	3.9	5.2	-5.8	-11.4
Return, Tax-Adjusted (%)	12.5	1.5	9.9	27.8	28.6	15.7	2.2	19.4	6.8	25.9

PER SHARE DATA

	2000	1999	1998	1997	1996	1995	1994	1993	1992	1991
Dividends, Net Income ($)	0.04	0.07	0.16	0.18	0.02	0.11	0.00	0.00	0.00	0.06
Distrib'ns, Cap Gain ($)	0.11	2.54	2.77	0.68	1.00	1.16	0.70	0.16	0.00	0.00
Net Asset Value ($)	22.62	20.20	21.95	22.18	17.86	14.46	13.28	13.49	11.40	10.67
Expense Ratio (%)	na	0.97	1.01	1.09	1.23	1.32	1.38	1.45	1.45	1.43
Yield (%)	0.17	0.30	0.64	0.78	0.10	0.70	0.00	0.00	0.00	0.56
Portfolio Turnover (%)	na	47	52	16	27	32	19	14	26	65
Total Assets (Millions $)	1,295	1,431	1,350	915	252	135	99	85	62	60

PORTFOLIO (as of 6/30/00)

Portfolio Manager: Hawkins, Cates, Buford - 1988

Investm't Category: Growth

✔ Domestic	Index
✔ Foreign	Sector
Asset Allocation	State Specific

Investment Style

Large Cap	✔ Mid Cap	✔ Small Cap
Growth	Grth/Val	✔ Value

Portfolio

7.8% cash	0.0% corp bonds
91.8% stocks	0.0% gov't bonds
0.0% pref/conv't pref	0.0% muni bonds
0.0% conv't bds/wrnts	0.4% other

SHAREHOLDER INFORMATION

Minimum Investment

Initial: $10,000 Subsequent: $1

Minimum IRA Investment

Initial: $10,000 Subsequent: $1

Maximum Fees

Load: none 12b-1: none
Other: none

Services

✔ IRA
Keogh
✔ Telephone Exchange

Loomis Sayles Intl Eq/Ist (LSIEX)

800-633-3330, 617-482-2450
www.loomissayles.com

International Stock

PERFORMANCE

fund inception date: 5/10/91

	3yr Annual	5yr Annual	10yr Annual	Bull	Bear
Return (%)	14.5	11.9	na	112.4	-33.2
Differ from Category (+/-)	5.6 abv av	3.6 abv av	na	21.5 abv av	-9.2 blw av

Standard Deviation	Category Risk Index	Beta
28.7%—high	1.27—abv av	0.69

	2000	1999	1998	1997	1996	1995	1994	1993	1992	1991
Return (%)	-27.7	90.2	9.3	-0.9	18.3	8.7	-1.7	38.5	-5.0	—
Differ from Category (+/-)	-8.3	29.5	3.5	-2.2	3.8	-0.6	1.4	-1.7	-1.5	—
Return, Tax-Adjusted (%)	-28.3	88.2	8.5	-3.8	16.7	6.2	-4.1	37.0	-5.2	—

PER SHARE DATA

	2000	1999	1998	1997	1996	1995	1994	1993	1992	1991
Dividends, Net Income ($)	0.00	0.08	0.13	0.19	0.08	0.14	0.14	0.10	0.09	—
Distrib'ns, Cap Gain ($)	0.71	0.99	0.19	1.55	0.53	0.82	0.92	0.35	0.01	—
Net Asset Value ($)	14.80	21.48	12.02	11.30	13.16	11.65	11.61	12.90	9.64	—
Expense Ratio (%)	1.00	1.00	1.00	1.00	1.42	1.45	1.46	1.50	1.50	—
Yield (%)	0.00	0.35	1.06	1.47	0.58	1.12	1.11	0.75	0.93	—
Portfolio Turnover (%)	226	207	96	119	151	126	116	128	101	—
Total Assets (Millions $)	90	134	76	82	90	79	71	56	15	—

PORTFOLIO (as of 6/30/00)

Portfolio Manager: Muromcew, Tribolet, Menon - 1999

Investm't Category: International Stock

Domestic	Index
✔ Foreign	Sector
Asset Allocation	State Specific

Investment Style

Large Cap	Mid Cap	Small Cap
Growth	Grth/Val	Value

Portfolio

2.0%	cash	0.0%	corp bonds
96.8%	stocks	0.0%	gov't bonds
1.2%	pref/conv't pref	0.0%	muni bonds
0.0%	conv't bds/wrnts	0.0%	other

SHAREHOLDER INFORMATION

Minimum Investment

Initial: $250,000 Subsequent: $50

Minimum IRA Investment

Initial: $5,000 Subsequent: $50

Maximum Fees

Load: none 12b-1: none

Other: none

Services

✔ IRA
✔ Keogh
✔ Telephone Exchange

Loomis Sayles SmCp Vl/Ist (LSSCX)

800-633-3330, 617-482-2450
www.loomissayles.com

Growth

PERFORMANCE

fund inception date: 5/13/91

	3yr Annual	5yr Annual	10yr Annual	Bull	Bear
Return (%)	6.9	14.9	na	24.4	3.9
Differ from Category (+/-)	-4.1 blw av	-1.2 blw av	na	-25.3 blw av	9.3 abv av

Standard Deviation	Category Risk Index	Beta
18.4%—av	0.95—blw av	0.75

	2000	1999	1998	1997	1996	1995	1994	1993	1992	1991
Return (%)	23.1	0.3	-1.0	25.9	30.3	32.1	-8.3	24.6	13.1	—
Differ from Category (+/-)	19.6	-18.6	-15.3	-1.2	8.0	1.7	-8.1	10.0	0.5	—
Return, Tax-Adjusted (%)	21.4	-0.2	-1.3	22.0	25.6	28.5	-8.4	20.4	10.3	—

PER SHARE DATA

	2000	1999	1998	1997	1996	1995	1994	1993	1992	1991
Dividends, Net Income ($)	0.20	0.14	0.12	0.14	0.10	0.04	0.00	0.00	0.00	—
Distrib'ns, Cap Gain ($)	1.08	0.26	0.13	3.05	2.41	1.58	0.10	1.90	1.22	—
Net Asset Value ($)	20.54	17.78	18.14	18.62	17.39	15.33	12.85	14.13	12.88	—
Expense Ratio (%)	0.93	0.90	0.92	0.94	1.19	1.28	1.27	1.35	1.50	—
Yield (%)	0.92	0.77	0.65	0.64	0.50	0.23	0.00	0.00	0.00	—
Portfolio Turnover (%)	1,020	113	78	94	73	105	87	106	109	—
Total Assets (Millions $)	212	300	346	245	163	90	74	67	39	—

PORTFOLIO (as of 6/30/00)

Portfolio Manager: Joseph Gatz, Daniel Thelan - 2000

Investm't Category: Growth

✔ Domestic	Index
Foreign	Sector
Asset Allocation	State Specific

Investment Style

Large Cap	Mid Cap	✔ Small Cap
Growth	Grth/Val	✔ Value

Portfolio

4.8% cash	0.0% corp bonds
95.2% stocks	0.0% gov't bonds
0.0% pref/conv't pref	0.0% muni bonds
0.0% conv't bds/wrnts	0.0% other

SHAREHOLDER INFORMATION

Minimum Investment
Initial: $250,000 Subsequent: $50

Minimum IRA Investment
Initial: $5,000 Subsequent: $50

Maximum Fees
Load: none 12b-1: none
Other: none

Services
✔ IRA
✔ Keogh
✔ Telephone Exchange

MSB (MSBFX)

800-661-3938, 212-573-9354

Growth

PERFORMANCE

fund inception date: 12/31/64

	3yr Annual	5yr Annual	10yr Annual	Bull	Bear
Return (%)	13.6	18.0	15.9	37.0	7.3
Differ from Category (+/-)	2.6 abv av	1.9 abv av	-0.9 blw av	-12.7 blw av	12.7 high

Standard Deviation	Category Risk Index	Beta
16.6%—av	0.85—low	0.72

	2000	1999	1998	1997	1996	1995	1994	1993	1992	1991
Return (%)	5.6	5.7	31.4	28.8	21.1	24.9	-1.6	20.6	10.6	16.9
Differ from Category (+/-)	2.1	-13.2	17.1	1.7	-1.2	-5.5	-1.4	6.0	-2.0	-20.7
Return, Tax-Adjusted (%)	4.1	4.2	29.3	27.2	17.1	18.5	-7.1	16.6	9.5	12.3

PER SHARE DATA

	2000	1999	1998	1997	1996	1995	1994	1993	1992	1991
Dividends, Net Income ($)	0.00	0.00	0.00	0.07	0.13	0.08	0.45	0.30	0.28	0.21
Distrib'ns, Cap Gain ($)	1.53	1.59	1.79	0.96	1.75	2.93	2.67	1.79	0.22	2.11
Net Asset Value ($)	20.73	21.09	21.49	17.73	14.60	13.64	13.39	16.79	15.67	14.62
Expense Ratio (%)	na	1.24	1.32	1.41	1.41	1.68	1.28	1.12	1.13	1.86
Yield (%)	0.00	0.00	0.00	0.37	0.79	0.48	2.80	1.61	1.76	1.25
Portfolio Turnover (%)	na	22	32	23	45	29	62	26	13	17
Total Assets (Millions $)	62	67	65	49	37	28	35	45	40	41

PORTFOLIO (as of 6/30/00)

Portfolio Manager: Mark Trautman, John McCabe - 1993

Investm't Category: Growth

✔ Domestic | Index
Foreign | Sector
Asset Allocation | State Specific

Investment Style

✔ Large Cap | Mid Cap | Small Cap
Growth | Grth/Val | ✔ Value

Portfolio

2.1%	cash	0.0%	corp bonds
97.9%	stocks	0.0%	gov't bonds
0.0%	pref/conv't pref	0.0%	muni bonds
0.0%	conv't bds/wrnts	0.0%	other

SHAREHOLDER INFORMATION

Minimum Investment

Initial: $250 | Subsequent: $50

Minimum IRA Investment

Initial: $50 | Subsequent: $50

Maximum Fees

Load: none | 12b-1: none
Other: none

Services

✔ IRA
Keogh
✔ Telephone Exchange

Mairs & Power Growth

800-304-7404, 651-222-8478

(MPGFX)

Growth

PERFORMANCE — fund inception date: 11/7/58

	3yr Annual	5yr Annual	10yr Annual	Bull	Bear
Return (%)	14.0	19.2	20.7	32.1	18.0
Differ from Category (+/-)	3.0 abv av	3.1 abv av	3.9 high	-17.6 blw av	23.4 high

Standard Deviation	Category Risk Index	Beta
16.1%—av	0.83—low	0.62

	2000	1999	1998	1997	1996	1995	1994	1993	1992	1991
Return (%)	26.4	7.1	9.3	28.6	26.4	49.3	5.6	12.8	7.8	42.0
Differ from Category (+/-)	22.9	-11.8	-5.0	1.5	4.1	18.9	5.8	-1.8	-4.8	4.4
Return, Tax-Adjusted (%)	23.8	5.5	8.6	27.5	25.2	47.6	4.2	11.3	6.5	39.8

PER SHARE DATA

	2000	1999	1998	1997	1996	1995	1994	1993	1992	1991
Dividends, Net Income ($)	1.09	0.93	0.72	1.00	0.75	0.56	0.65	0.43	0.40	0.39
Distrib'ns, Cap Gain ($)	9.64	5.48	1.36	1.69	1.35	1.51	0.98	1.22	1.16	1.58
Net Asset Value ($)	106.82	92.91	92.68	86.67	69.48	56.64	39.37	38.84	35.91	34.78
Expense Ratio (%)	na	0.79	0.82	0.84	0.89	0.99	0.99	0.98	1.00	1.09
Yield (%)	0.93	0.94	0.76	1.13	1.05	0.96	1.61	1.07	1.07	1.07
Portfolio Turnover (%)	na	5	2	5	3	4	5	4	4	5
Total Assets (Millions $)	548	546	580	412	150	70	41	39	34	31

PORTFOLIO (as of 3/31/00)

Portfolio Manager: George Mairs, William Frels - 1980

Investm't Category: Growth

- ✔ Domestic
- Foreign
- Asset Allocation
- Index
- Sector
- State Specific

Investment Style

- ✔ Large Cap
- ✔ Mid Cap
- Small Cap
- Growth
- Grth/Val
- ✔ Value

Portfolio

1.4%	cash	0.0%	corp bonds
98.6%	stocks	0.0%	gov't bonds
0.0%	pref/conv't pref	0.0%	muni bonds
0.0%	conv't bds/wrnts	0.0%	other

SHAREHOLDER INFORMATION

Minimum Investment

Initial: $2,500 Subsequent: $100

Minimum IRA Investment

Initial: $1,000 Subsequent: $100

Maximum Fees

Load: none 12b-1: none

Other: none

Services

- ✔ IRA
- Keogh
- Telephone Exchange

Managers: US Stk Mkt Plus (MGSPX)

800-835-3879, 919-967-7221
www.smithbreeden.com

Growth & Income

PERFORMANCE — fund inception date: 7/1/92

	3yr Annual	5yr Annual	10yr Annual	Bull	Bear
Return (%)	10.4	17.2	na	54.9	-12.4
Differ from Category (+/-)	1.5 av	2.9 abv av	na	21.4 abv av	-12.3 low

Standard Deviation	Category Risk Index	Beta
17.6%—av	1.02—abv av	0.99

	2000	1999	1998	1997	1996	1995	1994	1993	1992	1991
Return (%)	-11.7	20.6	26.4	32.2	24.3	36.7	1.8	13.2	—	—
Differ from Category (+/-)	-17.4	9.8	13.6	5.3	4.6	7.2	2.3	-0.6	—	—
Return, Tax-Adjusted (%)	-14.4	15.9	22.4	29.1	18.6	30.2	-1.5	9.9	—	—

PER SHARE DATA

	2000	1999	1998	1997	1996	1995	1994	1993	1992	1991
Dividends, Net Income ($)	0.58	0.84	0.53	0.63	0.60	0.61	0.56	0.45	—	—
Distrib'ns, Cap Gain ($)	1.05	2.04	1.90	0.64	1.52	1.48	0.52	0.63	—	—
Net Asset Value ($)	12.86	16.23	16.04	14.86	12.25	11.70	10.15	11.09	—	—
Expense Ratio (%)	0.88	0.88	0.88	0.88	0.90	0.90	0.90	0.57	—	—
Yield (%)	4.16	4.59	2.95	4.06	4.35	4.62	5.24	3.83	—	—
Portfolio Turnover (%)	442	527	424	182	107	120	119	—	—	—
Total Assets (Millions $)	145	224	169	86	8	3	1	1	—	—

PORTFOLIO (as of 6/30/00)

Portfolio Manager: John Sprow - 1992

Investm't Category: Growth & Income

✔ Domestic
Foreign
Asset Allocation
Index
Sector
State Specific

Investment Style

✔ Large Cap
Mid Cap
Small Cap
Growth
✔ Grth/Val
Value

Portfolio

-6.8%	cash	0.0%	corp bonds
0.0%	stocks	89.2%	gov't bonds
4.9%	pref/conv't pref	0.0%	muni bonds
0.0%	conv't bds/wrnts	12.7%	other

SHAREHOLDER INFORMATION

Minimum Investment

Initial: $2,000 Subsequent: $100

Minimum IRA Investment

Initial: $500 Subsequent: $100

Maximum Fees

Load: none 12b-1: none
Other: none

Services

✔ IRA
Keogh
✔ Telephone Exchange

Markman Aggressive Alloc (MMAGX)

800-707-2771, 612-920-4848
www.markman.com

Aggressive Growth

PERFORMANCE — fund inception date: 1/26/95

	3yr Annual	5yr Annual	10yr Annual	Bull	Bear
Return (%)	11.1	12.7	na	112.6	-32.6
Differ from Category (+/-)	-5.1 blw av	-1.9 blw av	na	-6.6 abv av	-12.0 blw av

Standard Deviation	Category Risk Index	Beta
30.6%—high	0.94—av	1.28

	2000	1999	1998	1997	1996	1995	1994	1993	1992	1991
Return (%)	-27.3	49.8	26.1	18.9	11.7	—	—	—	—	—
Differ from Category (+/-)	-21.3	-7.7	11.0	4.1	-6.6	—	—	—	—	—
Return, Tax-Adjusted (%)	-27.3	47.5	26.0	15.6	9.4	—	—	—	—	—

PER SHARE DATA

	2000	1999	1998	1997	1996	1995	1994	1993	1992	1991
Dividends, Net Income ($)	0.00	0.00	0.00	0.19	0.15	—	—	—	—	—
Distrib'ns, Cap Gain ($)	0.00	1.79	0.06	1.64	0.75	—	—	—	—	—
Net Asset Value ($)	16.13	22.20	16.01	12.74	12.26	—	—	—	—	—
Expense Ratio (%)	na	0.95	0.95	0.95	0.95	—	—	—	—	—
Yield (%)	0.00	0.00	0.00	1.32	1.15	—	—	—	—	—
Portfolio Turnover (%)	na	56	101	141	340	—	—	—	—	—
Total Assets (Millions $)	112	136	91	84	84	—	—	—	—	—

PORTFOLIO (as of 6/30/00)

Portfolio Manager: Robert Markman - 1995

Investm't Category: Aggressive Growth

✔ Domestic — Index
✔ Foreign — Sector
Asset Allocation — State Specific

Investment Style

✔ Large Cap — ✔ Mid Cap — ✔ Small Cap
✔ Growth — Grth/Val — Value

Portfolio

0.0%	cash	0.0%	corp bonds
0.0%	stocks	0.0%	gov't bonds
0.0%	pref/conv't pref	0.0%	muni bonds
0.0%	conv't bds/wrnts	100.0%	other

SHAREHOLDER INFORMATION

Minimum Investment
Initial: $25,000 — Subsequent: $500

Minimum IRA Investment
Initial: $25,000 — Subsequent: $500

Maximum Fees
Load: none — 12b-1: none
Other: none

Services
✔ IRA
✔ Keogh
✔ Telephone Exchange

Markman Moderate Alloc (MMMGX)

800-707-2771, 612-920-4848
www.markman.com

Growth & Income

PERFORMANCE — fund inception date: 1/26/95

	3yr Annual	5yr Annual	10yr Annual	Bull	Bear
Return (%)	4.1	8.4	na	70.1	-26.9
Differ from Category (+/-)	-4.8 low	-5.9 low	na	36.6 high	-26.8 low

Standard Deviation	Category Risk Index	Beta
23.1%—abv av	1.33—high	0.90

	2000	1999	1998	1997	1996	1995	1994	1993	1992	1991
Return (%)	-29.4	35.4	18.3	19.3	11.1	—	—	—	—	—
Differ from Category (+/-)	-35.1	24.6	5.5	-7.6	-8.6	—	—	—	—	—
Return, Tax-Adjusted (%)	-29.6	32.9	16.8	15.3	8.1	—	—	—	—	—

PER SHARE DATA

	2000	1999	1998	1997	1996	1995	1994	1993	1992	1991
Dividends, Net Income ($)	0.10	0.28	0.16	0.47	0.31	—	—	—	—	—
Distrib'ns, Cap Gain ($)	0.00	1.11	0.57	1.34	0.76	—	—	—	—	—
Net Asset Value ($)	11.67	16.69	13.35	11.90	11.49	—	—	—	—	—
Expense Ratio (%)	na	0.95	0.95	0.95	0.95	—	—	—	—	—
Yield (%)	0.85	1.57	1.14	3.54	2.53	—	—	—	—	—
Portfolio Turnover (%)	na	68	117	82	280	—	—	—	—	—
Total Assets (Millions $)	66	100	83	86	78	—	—	—	—	—

PORTFOLIO (as of 6/30/00)

Portfolio Manager: Robert Markman - 1995

Investm't Category: Growth & Income

✔ Domestic　Index
✔ Foreign　Sector
✔ Asset Allocation　State Specific

Investment Style

✔ Large Cap　✔ Mid Cap　✔ Small Cap
✔ Growth　Grth/Val　Value

Portfolio

1.5%	cash	0.0%	corp bonds
0.0%	stocks	0.0%	gov't bonds
0.0%	pref/conv't pref	0.0%	muni bonds
0.0%	conv't bds/wrnts	98.5%	other

SHAREHOLDER INFORMATION

Minimum Investment
Initial: $25,000　Subsequent: $500

Minimum IRA Investment
Initial: $25,000　Subsequent: $500

Maximum Fees
Load: none　12b-1: none
Other: none

Services
✔ IRA
✔ Keogh
✔ Telephone Exchange

Marshall: Equity Inc/Inv (MREIX)

800-236-8554, 412-288-1900
www.marshallfunds.com

Growth & Income

PERFORMANCE — fund inception date: 9/30/93

	3yr Annual	5yr Annual	10yr Annual	Bull	Bear
Return (%)	7.2	13.7	na	22.6	8.0
Differ from Category (+/-)	-1.7 blw av	-0.6 av	na	-10.9 blw av	8.1 abv av

Standard Deviation	Category Risk Index	Beta
16.2%—av	0.93—blw av	0.64

	2000	1999	1998	1997	1996	1995	1994	1993	1992	1991
Return (%)	9.7	1.6	10.4	27.5	21.1	34.2	-1.6	—	—	—
Differ from Category (+/-)	4.0	-9.2	-2.4	0.6	1.4	4.7	-1.1	—	—	—
Return, Tax-Adjusted (%)	9.0	-0.7	8.2	24.6	18.0	32.1	-2.8	—	—	—

PER SHARE DATA

	2000	1999	1998	1997	1996	1995	1994	1993	1992	1991
Dividends, Net Income ($)	0.20	0.27	0.31	0.33	0.34	0.34	0.31	—	—	—
Distrib'ns, Cap Gain ($)	0.10	1.35	1.03	1.27	0.85	0.20	0.00	—	—	—
Net Asset Value ($)	15.61	14.52	15.89	15.62	13.55	12.20	9.53	—	—	—
Expense Ratio (%)	1.16	1.17	1.17	1.22	0.98	1.01	1.01	—	—	—
Yield (%)	1.27	1.70	1.83	1.95	2.36	2.74	3.25	—	—	—
Portfolio Turnover (%)	98	72	69	61	60	43	—	—	—	—
Total Assets (Millions $)	428	497	537	526	231	132	60	—	—	—

PORTFOLIO (as of 9/30/00)

Portfolio Manager: Bruce Hutson - 1993

Investm't Category: Growth & Income

✔ Domestic | Index
Foreign | Sector
Asset Allocation | State Specific

Investment Style

✔ Large Cap | Mid Cap | Small Cap
Growth | Grth/Val | ✔ Value

Portfolio

1.3% cash | 0.0% corp bonds
98.7% stocks | 0.0% gov't bonds
0.0% pref/conv't pref | 0.0% muni bonds
0.0% conv't bds/wrnts | 0.0% other

SHAREHOLDER INFORMATION

Minimum Investment

Initial: $1,000 | Subsequent: $50

Minimum IRA Investment

Initial: $1,000 | Subsequent: $50

Maximum Fees

Load: none | 12b-1: none
Other: none

Services

✔ IRA
Keogh
✔ Telephone Exchange

Marshall: Intl Stock/Inv (MRISX)

800-236-8554, 412-288-1900
www.marshallfunds.com

International Stock

PERFORMANCE — fund inception date: 9/1/94

	3yr Annual	5yr Annual	10yr Annual	Bull	Bear
Return (%)	9.8	11.9	na	73.8	-20.3
Differ from Category (+/-)	0.9 av	3.6 abv av	na	-17.1 av	3.7 abv av

Standard Deviation	Category Risk Index	Beta
23.4%—abv av	1.03—av	0.83

	2000	1999	1998	1997	1996	1995	1994	1993	1992	1991
Return (%)	-16.7	54.4	3.2	10.8	19.6	11.5	—	—	—	—
Differ from Category (+/-)	2.7	-6.3	-2.6	9.5	5.1	2.2	—	—	—	—
Return, Tax-Adjusted (%)	-18.4	51.7	2.4	9.6	18.3	10.5	—	—	—	—

PER SHARE DATA

	2000	1999	1998	1997	1996	1995	1994	1993	1992	1991
Dividends, Net Income ($)	0.00	0.16	0.25	0.21	0.26	0.22	—	—	—	—
Distrib'ns, Cap Gain ($)	1.61	1.35	0.00	0.28	0.09	0.02	—	—	—	—
Net Asset Value ($)	13.47	18.14	12.74	12.58	11.80	10.16	—	—	—	—
Expense Ratio (%)	1.50	1.50	1.49	1.59	1.35	1.54	—	—	—	—
Yield (%)	0.00	0.82	1.96	1.63	2.18	2.16	—	—	—	—
Portfolio Turnover (%)	225	182	91	26	26	61	—	—	—	—
Total Assets (Millions $)	308	328	235	225	169	104	—	—	—	—

PORTFOLIO (as of 9/30/00)

Portfolio Manager: Dan Jaworski - 1999

Investm't Category: International Stock

Domestic	Index
✔ Foreign	Sector
Asset Allocation	State Specific

Investment Style

Large Cap	Mid Cap	Small Cap
Growth	Grth/Val	Value

Portfolio

10.7% cash	0.0% corp bonds
89.3% stocks	0.0% gov't bonds
0.0% pref/conv't pref	0.0% muni bonds
0.0% conv't bds/wrnts	0.0% other

SHAREHOLDER INFORMATION

Minimum Investment

Initial: $1,000 Subsequent: $50

Minimum IRA Investment

Initial: $1,000 Subsequent: $50

Maximum Fees

Load: none 12b-1: none

Other: none

Services

✔ IRA

Keogh

✔ Telephone Exchange

Marshall: Lrg Cap G & I/Inv (MASTX)

800-236-8554, 412-288-1900
www.marshallfunds.com

Growth

PERFORMANCE — fund inception date: 11/20/92

	3yr Annual	5yr Annual	10yr Annual	Bull	Bear
Return (%)	10.5	14.3	na	53.2	-9.9
Differ from Category (+/-)	-0.5 av	-1.8 blw av	na	3.5 av	-4.5 av

Standard Deviation	Category Risk Index	Beta
17.2%—av	0.88—low	0.96

	2000	1999	1998	1997	1996	1995	1994	1993	1992	1991
Return (%)	-9.2	18.0	26.1	26.2	14.6	33.1	-5.7	1.1	—	—
Differ from Category (+/-)	-12.7	-0.9	11.8	-0.9	-7.7	2.7	-5.5	-13.5	—	—
Return, Tax-Adjusted (%)	-10.0	16.7	24.8	23.8	9.6	30.7	-5.9	0.6	—	—

PER SHARE DATA

	2000	1999	1998	1997	1996	1995	1994	1993	1992	1991
Dividends, Net Income ($)	0.01	0.03	0.05	0.09	0.15	0.10	0.07	0.11	—	—
Distrib'ns, Cap Gain ($)	0.80	0.98	0.77	1.18	1.94	0.66	0.00	0.00	—	—
Net Asset Value ($)	15.73	18.22	16.34	13.63	11.81	12.11	9.68	10.35	—	—
Expense Ratio (%)	1.18	1.20	1.21	1.23	0.97	0.94	0.99	0.94	—	—
Yield (%)	0.06	0.15	0.29	0.60	1.09	0.78	0.72	1.06	—	—
Portfolio Turnover (%)	71	32	33	43	147	98	86	98	—	—
Total Assets (Millions $)	439	462	360	288	236	273	226	265	—	—

PORTFOLIO (as of 9/30/00)

Portfolio Manager: William O'Connor - 1996

Investm't Category: Growth

✔ Domestic | Index
Foreign | Sector
Asset Allocation | State Specific

Investment Style

✔ Large Cap | Mid Cap | Small Cap
Growth | ✔ Grth/Val | Value

Portfolio

8.3%	cash	0.0%	corp bonds
91.7%	stocks	0.0%	gov't bonds
0.0%	pref/conv't pref	0.0%	muni bonds
0.0%	conv't bds/wrnts	0.0%	other

SHAREHOLDER INFORMATION

Minimum Investment

Initial: $1,000 — Subsequent: $50

Minimum IRA Investment

Initial: $1,000 — Subsequent: $50

Maximum Fees

Load: none — 12b-1: none
Other: none

Services

✔ IRA
Keogh
✔ Telephone Exchange

Marshall: Mid Cap Gr/Inv (MRMSX)

800-236-8554, 412-288-1900
www.marshallfunds.com

Aggressive Growth

PERFORMANCE — fund inception date: 9/30/93

	3yr Annual	5yr Annual	10yr Annual	Bull	Bear
Return (%)	18.3	19.6	na	121.7	-32.2
Differ from Category (+/-)	2.1 av	5.0 abv av	na	2.5 abv av	-11.6 blw av

Standard Deviation	Category Risk Index	Beta
33.1%—high	1.02—av	1.34

	2000	1999	1998	1997	1996	1995	1994	1993	1992	1991
Return (%)	-11.1	61.1	15.7	22.7	20.6	33.7	-5.6	—	—	—
Differ from Category (+/-)	-5.1	3.6	0.6	7.9	2.3	-0.9	-4.8	—	—	—
Return, Tax-Adjusted (%)	-15.4	58.9	14.5	19.9	17.7	31.0	-5.6	—	—	—

PER SHARE DATA

	2000	1999	1998	1997	1996	1995	1994	1993	1992	1991
Dividends, Net Income ($)	0.00	0.00	0.00	0.00	0.00	0.00	0.00	—	—	—
Distrib'ns, Cap Gain ($)	4.97	1.69	0.81	1.81	1.21	0.91	0.00	—	—	—
Net Asset Value ($)	15.57	23.06	15.50	14.21	13.10	11.84	9.55	—	—	—
Expense Ratio (%)	1.18	1.21	1.23	1.24	1.01	1.01	1.01	—	—	—
Yield (%)	0.00	0.00	0.00	0.00	0.00	0.00	0.00	—	—	—
Portfolio Turnover (%)	108	173	167	211	189	157	113	—	—	—
Total Assets (Millions $)	374	423	262	216	161	108	69	—	—	—

PORTFOLIO (as of 9/30/00)

Portfolio Manager: C. Bohlen, M. Groblewski - 2000

Investm't Category: Aggressive Growth

✔ Domestic — Index
Foreign — Sector
Asset Allocation — State Specific

Investment Style

Large Cap — ✔ Mid Cap — ✔ Small Cap
✔ Growth — Grth/Val — Value

Portfolio

7.8%	cash	0.0%	corp bonds
92.3%	stocks	0.0%	gov't bonds
0.0%	pref/conv't pref	0.0%	muni bonds
0.0%	conv't bds/wrnts	0.0%	other

SHAREHOLDER INFORMATION

Minimum Investment
Initial: $1,000 — Subsequent: $50

Minimum IRA Investment
Initial: $1,000 — Subsequent: $50

Maximum Fees
Load: none — 12b-1: none
Other: none

Services
✔ IRA
Keogh
✔ Telephone Exchange

Marshall: Mid Cap Val/Inv (MRVEX)

800-236-8560, 412-288-1900
www.marshallfunds.com

Growth & Income

PERFORMANCE

fund inception date: 9/30/93

	3yr Annual	5yr Annual	10yr Annual	Bull	Bear
Return (%)	9.3	12.9	na	25.3	10.1
Differ from Category (+/-)	0.4 av	-1.4 blw av	na	-8.2 blw av	10.2 abv av

Standard Deviation	Category Risk Index	Beta
18.7%—av	1.07—high	0.71

	2000	1999	1998	1997	1996	1995	1994	1993	1992	1991
Return (%)	17.2	6.1	5.1	23.3	13.9	25.3	2.0	—	—	—
Differ from Category (+/-)	11.5	-4.7	-7.7	-3.6	-5.8	-4.2	2.5	—	—	—
Return, Tax-Adjusted (%)	15.5	3.3	3.0	19.3	8.7	22.0	1.1	—	—	—

PER SHARE DATA

	2000	1999	1998	1997	1996	1995	1994	1993	1992	1991
Dividends, Net Income ($)	0.07	0.08	0.14	0.12	0.18	0.21	0.15	—	—	—
Distrib'ns, Cap Gain ($)	0.69	1.37	0.93	1.94	1.88	0.87	0.11	—	—	—
Net Asset Value ($)	11.16	10.22	11.08	11.57	11.09	11.59	10.13	—	—	—
Expense Ratio (%)	1.33	1.25	1.25	1.23	0.98	0.96	1.00	—	—	—
Yield (%)	0.59	0.69	1.16	0.88	1.38	1.68	1.46	—	—	—
Portfolio Turnover (%)	94	90	59	55	67	78	39	—	—	—
Total Assets (Millions $)	103	116	144	184	175	204	195	—	—	—

PORTFOLIO (as of 9/30/00)

Portfolio Manager: Matthew Fahey, John Potter - 1993

Investm't Category: Growth & Income

✔ Domestic	Index
Foreign	Sector
Asset Allocation	State Specific

Investment Style

Large Cap	✔ Mid Cap	Small Cap
Growth	Grth/Val	✔ Value

Portfolio

6.2%	cash	0.0%	corp bonds
93.8%	stocks	0.0%	gov't bonds
0.0%	pref/conv't pref	0.0%	muni bonds
0.0%	conv't bds/wrnts	0.0%	other

SHAREHOLDER INFORMATION

Minimum Investment
Initial: $1,000 Subsequent: $50

Minimum IRA Investment
Initial: $1,000 Subsequent: $50

Maximum Fees
Load: none 12b-1: none
Other: none

Services
✔ IRA
✔ Keogh
✔ Telephone Exchange

Marshall: Sm Cap Gr/Inv (MRSCX)

800-236-8554, 412-288-1900
www.marshallfunds.com

Aggressive Growth

PERFORMANCE

fund inception date: 9/4/96

	3yr Annual	5yr Annual	10yr Annual	Bull	Bear
Return (%)	3.8	na	na	80.9	-37.8
Differ from Category (+/-)	-12.4 low	na	na	-38.3 av	-17.2 low

Standard Deviation	Category Risk Index	Beta
35.6%—high	1.10—abv av	1.24

	2000	1999	1998	1997	1996	1995	1994	1993	1992	1991
Return (%)	-19.6	34.7	3.4	23.1	—	—	—	—	—	—
Differ from Category (+/-)	-13.6	-22.8	-11.7	8.3	—	—	—	—	—	—
Return, Tax-Adjusted (%)	-21.4	34.0	3.3	22.2	—	—	—	—	—	—

PER SHARE DATA

	2000	1999	1998	1997	1996	1995	1994	1993	1992	1991
Dividends, Net Income ($)	0.00	0.00	0.00	0.00	—	—	—	—	—	—
Distrib'ns, Cap Gain ($)	1.62	0.41	0.02	0.48	—	—	—	—	—	—
Net Asset Value ($)	12.25	17.27	13.16	12.75	—	—	—	—	—	—
Expense Ratio (%)	1.59	1.59	1.60	1.80	—	—	—	—	—	—
Yield (%)	0.00	0.00	0.00	0.00	—	—	—	—	—	—
Portfolio Turnover (%)	105	219	139	—	—	—	—	—	—	—
Total Assets (Millions $)	106	143	111	70	—	—	—	—	—	—

PORTFOLIO (as of 9/30/00)

Portfolio Manager: C. Bohlen, M. Groblewski - 2000

Investm't Category: Aggressive Growth

✔ Domestic
Foreign
Asset Allocation
Index
Sector
State Specific

Investment Style

Large Cap
Mid Cap
✔ Small Cap
✔ Growth
Grth/Val
Value

Portfolio

11.1%	cash	0.0%	corp bonds
88.9%	stocks	0.0%	gov't bonds
0.0%	pref/conv't pref	0.0%	muni bonds
0.0%	conv't bds/wrnts	0.0%	other

SHAREHOLDER INFORMATION

Minimum Investment

Initial: $1,000 Subsequent: $50

Minimum IRA Investment

Initial: $1,000 Subsequent: $50

Maximum Fees

Load: none 12b-1: none
Other: none

Services

✔ IRA
Keogh
✔ Telephone Exchange

Marsico Focus (MFOCX)

888-860-8686
www.marsico.com

Growth

PERFORMANCE — fund inception date: 12/31/97

	3yr Annual	5yr Annual	10yr Annual	Bull	Bear
Return (%)	24.4	na	na	103.5	-21.7
Differ from Category (+/-)	13.4 high	na	na	53.8 high	-16.3 low

Standard Deviation	Category Risk Index	Beta
27.0%—high	1.39—high	1.15

	2000	1999	1998	1997	1996	1995	1994	1993	1992	1991
Return (%)	-17.9	55.2	51.3	—	—	—	—	—	—	—
Differ from Category (+/-)	-21.4	36.3	37.0	—	—	—	—	—	—	—
Return, Tax-Adjusted (%)	-19.5	55.1	51.3	—	—	—	—	—	—	—

PER SHARE DATA

	2000	1999	1998	1997	1996	1995	1994	1993	1992	1991
Dividends, Net Income ($)	0.00	0.00	0.00	—	—	—	—	—	—	—
Distrib'ns, Cap Gain ($)	1.96	0.03	0.00	—	—	—	—	—	—	—
Net Asset Value ($)	17.23	23.45	15.13	—	—	—	—	—	—	—
Expense Ratio (%)	1.27	1.31	1.56	—	—	—	—	—	—	—
Yield (%)	0.00	0.00	0.00	—	—	—	—	—	—	—
Portfolio Turnover (%)	176	173	170	—	—	—	—	—	—	—
Total Assets (Millions $)	2,298	3,256	1,204	—	—	—	—	—	—	—

PORTFOLIO (as of 6/30/00)

Portfolio Manager: Thomas Marsico - 1997

Investm't Category: Growth

✔ Domestic — Index
✔ Foreign — Sector
Asset Allocation — State Specific

Investment Style

Large Cap — ✔ Mid Cap — Small Cap
✔ Growth — Grth/Val — Value

Portfolio

4.0%	cash	0.0%	corp bonds
96.0%	stocks	0.0%	gov't bonds
0.0%	pref/conv't pref	0.0%	muni bonds
0.0%	conv't bds/wrnts	0.0%	other

SHAREHOLDER INFORMATION

Minimum Investment
Initial: $2,500 — Subsequent: $100

Minimum IRA Investment
Initial: $1,000 — Subsequent: $100

Maximum Fees
Load: none — 12b-1: 0.25%
Other: none

Services
✔ IRA
✔ Keogh
✔ Telephone Exchange

Marsico Growth & Income (MGRIX)

888-860-8686
www.marsico.com

Growth

PERFORMANCE — fund inception date: 12/31/97

	3yr Annual	5yr Annual	10yr Annual	Bull	Bear
Return (%)	22.7	na	na	102.6	-22.0
Differ from Category (+/-)	11.7 high	na	na	52.9 high	-16.6 low

Standard Deviation	Category Risk Index	Beta
25.5%—high	1.31—high	1.13

	2000	1999	1998	1997	1996	1995	1994	1993	1992	1991
Return (%)	-15.8	53.3	43.4	—	—	—	—	—	—	—
Differ from Category (+/-)	-19.3	34.4	29.1	—	—	—	—	—	—	—
Return, Tax-Adjusted (%)	-16.4	53.1	43.4	—	—	—	—	—	—	—

PER SHARE DATA

	2000	1999	1998	1997	1996	1995	1994	1993	1992	1991
Dividends, Net Income ($)	0.00	0.00	0.00	—	—	—	—	—	—	—
Distrib'ns, Cap Gain ($)	0.70	0.11	0.00	—	—	—	—	—	—	—
Net Asset Value ($)	17.67	21.86	14.34	—	—	—	—	—	—	—
Expense Ratio (%)	1.30	1.43	1.78	—	—	—	—	—	—	—
Yield (%)	0.00	0.00	0.00	—	—	—	—	—	—	—
Portfolio Turnover (%)	137	137	141	—	—	—	—	—	—	—
Total Assets (Millions $)	805	1,048	373	—	—	—	—	—	—	—

PORTFOLIO (as of 6/30/00)

Portfolio Manager: Thomas Marsico - 1997

Investm't Category: Growth

✔ Domestic | Index
✔ Foreign | Sector
Asset Allocation | State Specific

Investment Style

Large Cap | ✔ Mid Cap | Small Cap
✔ Growth | Grth/Val | Value

Portfolio

0.3%	cash	0.2%	corp bonds
99.5%	stocks	0.0%	gov't bonds
0.0%	pref/conv't pref	0.0%	muni bonds
0.0%	conv't bds/wrnts	0.0%	other

SHAREHOLDER INFORMATION

Minimum Investment
Initial: $2,500 | Subsequent: $100

Minimum IRA Investment
Initial: $1,000 | Subsequent: $100

Maximum Fees
Load: none | 12b-1: 0.25%
Other: none

Services
✔ IRA
✔ Keogh
✔ Telephone Exchange

Masters Select Equity (MSEFX)

800-656-8864, 510-254-8999
www.mastersselect.com

Growth

PERFORMANCE — fund inception date: 12/31/96

	3yr Annual	5yr Annual	10yr Annual	Bull	Bear
Return (%)	14.4	na	na	58.2	-9.4
Differ from Category (+/-)	3.4 abv av	na	na	8.5 abv av	-4.0 av

Standard Deviation	Category Risk Index	Beta
19.7%—abv av	1.01—av	1.02

	2000	1999	1998	1997	1996	1995	1994	1993	1992	1991
Return (%)	3.1	26.4	14.8	29.1	—	—	—	—	—	—
Differ from Category (+/-)	-0.4	7.5	0.5	2.0	—	—	—	—	—	—
Return, Tax-Adjusted (%)	0.6	22.4	14.7	26.8	—	—	—	—	—	—

PER SHARE DATA

	2000	1999	1998	1997	1996	1995	1994	1993	1992	1991
Dividends, Net Income ($)	0.00	0.01	0.02	0.03	—	—	—	—	—	—
Distrib'ns, Cap Gain ($)	1.76	2.68	0.00	1.05	—	—	—	—	—	—
Net Asset Value ($)	12.98	14.38	13.57	11.84	—	—	—	—	—	—
Expense Ratio (%)	na	1.26	1.38	1.47	—	—	—	—	—	—
Yield (%)	0.00	0.05	0.14	0.23	—	—	—	—	—	—
Portfolio Turnover (%)	na	116	135	145	—	—	—	—	—	—
Total Assets (Millions $)	447	448	405	296	—	—	—	—	—	—

PORTFOLIO (as of 6/30/00)

Portfolio Manager: committee - 1996

Investm't Category: Growth

✔ Domestic	Index
✔ Foreign	Sector
Asset Allocation	State Specific

Investment Style

✔ Large Cap	Mid Cap	Small Cap
Growth	✔ Grth/Val	Value

Portfolio

6.9% cash	0.0% corp bonds
93.1% stocks	0.0% gov't bonds
0.0% pref/conv't pref	0.0% muni bonds
0.0% conv't bds/wrnts	0.0% other

SHAREHOLDER INFORMATION

Minimum Investment

Initial: $5,000 Subsequent: $250

Minimum IRA Investment

Initial: $1,000 Subsequent: $250

Maximum Fees

Load: 2.00% redemption 12b-1: none

Other: redemption fee applies for 6 months

Services

✔ IRA

✔ Keogh

✔ Telephone Exchange

Masters Select Intl (MSILX)

800-656-8864, 510-254-8999
www.mastersselect.com

International Stock

PERFORMANCE — fund inception date: 12/1/97

	3yr Annual	5yr Annual	10yr Annual	Bull	Bear
Return (%)	22.8	na	na	105.5	-18.9
Differ from Category (+/-)	13.9 high	na	na	14.6 abv av	5.1 abv av

Standard Deviation	Category Risk Index	Beta
22.7%—abv av	1.00—av	0.82

	2000	1999	1998	1997	1996	1995	1994	1993	1992	1991
Return (%)	-5.2	75.0	11.7	—	—	—	—	—	—	—
Differ from Category (+/-)	14.2	14.3	5.9	—	—	—	—	—	—	—
Return, Tax-Adjusted (%)	-7.7	74.1	11.3	—	—	—	—	—	—	—

PER SHARE DATA

	2000	1999	1998	1997	1996	1995	1994	1993	1992	1991
Dividends, Net Income ($)	0.00	0.03	0.08	—	—	—	—	—	—	—
Distrib'ns, Cap Gain ($)	2.34	0.38	0.00	—	—	—	—	—	—	—
Net Asset Value ($)	15.31	18.67	10.95	—	—	—	—	—	—	—
Expense Ratio (%)	na	1.29	1.55	—	—	—	—	—	—	—
Yield (%)	0.00	0.15	0.73	—	—	—	—	—	—	—
Portfolio Turnover (%)	na	100	73	—	—	—	—	—	—	—
Total Assets (Millions $)	272	218	95	—	—	—	—	—	—	—

PORTFOLIO (as of 6/30/00)

Portfolio Manager: committee - 1997

Investm't Category: International Stock

Domestic	Index
✔ Foreign	Sector
Asset Allocation	State Specific

Investment Style

Large Cap	Mid Cap	Small Cap
Growth	Grth/Val	Value

Portfolio

8.6%	cash	0.0%	corp bonds
91.4%	stocks	0.0%	gov't bonds
0.0%	pref/conv't pref	0.0%	muni bonds
0.0%	conv't bds/wrnts	0.0%	other

SHAREHOLDER INFORMATION

Minimum Investment

Initial: $5,000 Subsequent: $250

Minimum IRA Investment

Initial: $1,000 Subsequent: $250

Maximum Fees

Load: 2.00% redemption 12b-1: none

Other: redemption fee applies for 6 months

Services

✔ IRA

✔ Keogh

✔ Telephone Exchange

Matthews Korea (MAKOX)

800-789-2742
www.matthewsfunds.com

International Stock

PERFORMANCE — fund inception date: 1/3/95

	3yr Annual	5yr Annual	10yr Annual	Bull	Bear
Return (%)	24.3	-14.2	na	318.0	-38.7
Differ from Category (+/-)	15.4 high	-22.5 low	na	227.1 high	-14.7 low

Standard Deviation	Category Risk Index	Beta
59.3%—high	2.61—high	1.59

	2000	1999	1998	1997	1996	1995	1994	1993	1992	1991
Return (%)	-52.8	108.0	96.1	-64.7	-31.7	—	—	—	—	—
Differ from Category (+/-)	-33.4	47.3	90.3	-66.0	-46.2	—	—	—	—	—
Return, Tax-Adjusted (%)	-56.7	103.7	96.1	-64.7	-31.7	—	—	—	—	—

PER SHARE DATA

	2000	1999	1998	1997	1996	1995	1994	1993	1992	1991
Dividends, Net Income ($)	0.00	0.00	0.00	0.00	0.00	—	—	—	—	—
Distrib'ns, Cap Gain ($)	1.49	0.87	0.00	0.00	0.00	—	—	—	—	—
Net Asset Value ($)	2.24	7.63	4.08	2.08	5.90	—	—	—	—	—
Expense Ratio (%)	1.75	1.77	2.06	2.50	2.23	—	—	—	—	—
Yield (%)	0.00	0.00	0.00	0.00	0.00	—	—	—	—	—
Portfolio Turnover (%)	47	57	94	112	139	—	—	—	—	—
Total Assets (Millions $)	83	212	131	25	2	—	—	—	—	—

PORTFOLIO (as of 3/31/00)

Portfolio Manager: G. Paul Matthews, Mark Headley - 1995

Investm't Category: International Stock

Domestic	Index
✔ Foreign	Sector
Asset Allocation	State Specific

Investment Style

Large Cap	Mid Cap	Small Cap
Growth	Grth/Val	Value

Portfolio

0.6%	cash	0.0%	corp bonds
97.1%	stocks	0.0%	gov't bonds
0.0%	pref/conv't pref	0.0%	muni bonds
2.3%	conv't bds/wrnts	0.0%	other

SHAREHOLDER INFORMATION

Minimum Investment
Initial: $2,500 Subsequent: $250

Minimum IRA Investment
Initial: $500 Subsequent: $50

Maximum Fees
Load: 2.00% redemption 12b-1: none
Other: redemption fee applies for 3 months

Services
✔ IRA
Keogh
✔ Telephone Exchange

Matthews Pacific Tiger (MAPTX)

800-789-2742
www.matthewsfunds.com

International Stock

PERFORMANCE — fund inception date: 9/12/94

	3yr Annual	5yr Annual	10yr Annual	Bull	Bear
Return (%)	10.6	-0.1	na	207.5	-30.3
Differ from Category (+/-)	1.7 abv av	-8.4 low	na	116.6 high	-6.3 blw av

Standard Deviation	Category Risk Index	Beta
37.9%—high	1.67—high	1.42

	2000	1999	1998	1997	1996	1995	1994	1993	1992	1991
Return (%)	-23.8	83.0	-2.8	-40.8	24.1	3.0	—	—	—	—
Differ from Category (+/-)	-4.4	22.3	-8.6	-42.1	9.6	-6.3	—	—	—	—
Return, Tax-Adjusted (%)	-26.4	81.9	-3.0	-40.8	24.1	3.0	—	—	—	—

PER SHARE DATA

	2000	1999	1998	1997	1996	1995	1994	1993	1992	1991
Dividends, Net Income ($)	0.41	0.18	0.01	0.00	0.00	0.00	—	—	—	—
Distrib'ns, Cap Gain ($)	0.84	0.00	0.06	0.02	0.00	0.00	—	—	—	—
Net Asset Value ($)	8.20	12.32	6.84	7.15	12.12	9.76	—	—	—	—
Expense Ratio (%)	1.81	1.90	1.90	1.90	1.90	2.17	—	—	—	—
Yield (%)	4.53	1.46	0.14	0.00	0.00	0.00	—	—	—	—
Portfolio Turnover (%)	52	98	73	71	125	—	—	—	—	—
Total Assets (Millions $)	84	119	51	37	32	3	—	—	—	—

PORTFOLIO (as of 3/31/00)

Portfolio Manager: Headley, Matthews, Foster - 1994

Investm't Category: International Stock

Domestic	Index
✔ Foreign	Sector
Asset Allocation	State Specific

Investment Style

Large Cap	Mid Cap	Small Cap
Growth	Grth/Val	Value

Portfolio

0.8%	cash	0.0%	corp bonds
96.9%	stocks	0.0%	gov't bonds
0.0%	pref/conv't pref	0.0%	muni bonds
2.3%	conv't bds/wrnts	0.0%	other

SHAREHOLDER INFORMATION

Minimum Investment
Initial: $2,500 Subsequent: $250

Minimum IRA Investment
Initial: $500 Subsequent: $50

Maximum Fees
Load: 2.00% redemption 12b-1: none
Other: redemption fee applies for 3 months

Services
✔ IRA
Keogh
✔ Telephone Exchange

McM Balanced (MCMBX)

800-788-9485, 415-616-9320
www.mcmfunds.com

Balanced

PERFORMANCE

fund inception date: 7/14/94

	3yr Annual	5yr Annual	10yr Annual	Bull	Bear
Return (%)	9.1	13.3	na	25.7	-2.4
Differ from Category (+/-)	0.7 av	1.9 abv av	na	-2.4 av	0.8 av

Standard Deviation	Category Risk Index	Beta
9.8%—blw av	0.89—blw av	0.53

	2000	1999	1998	1997	1996	1995	1994	1993	1992	1991
Return (%)	0.7	7.0	20.6	23.6	16.2	28.7	—	—	—	—
Differ from Category (+/-)	-1.3	-3.7	7.3	4.8	2.3	3.2	—	—	—	—
Return, Tax-Adjusted (%)	-1.0	5.6	19.3	22.3	14.9	26.8	—	—	—	—

PER SHARE DATA

	2000	1999	1998	1997	1996	1995	1994	1993	1992	1991
Dividends, Net Income ($)	0.54	0.52	0.48	0.45	0.39	0.39	—	—	—	—
Distrib'ns, Cap Gain ($)	0.70	0.29	0.07	0.00	0.00	0.09	—	—	—	—
Net Asset Value ($)	18.80	19.91	19.38	16.57	13.79	12.23	—	—	—	—
Expense Ratio (%)	0.60	0.60	0.60	0.60	0.60	0.60	—	—	—	—
Yield (%)	2.76	2.57	2.46	2.71	2.82	3.16	—	—	—	—
Portfolio Turnover (%)	22	18	20	32	26	81	—	—	—	—
Total Assets (Millions $)	179	176	114	64	23	5	—	—	—	—

PORTFOLIO (as of 6/30/00)

Portfolio Manager: committee - 1994

Investm't Category: Balanced

✔ Domestic	Index
✔ Foreign	Sector
Asset Allocation	State Specific

Investment Style

Large Cap	Mid Cap	Small Cap
Growth	Grth/Val	Value

Portfolio

3.4%	cash	10.0%	corp bonds
61.0%	stocks	25.6%	gov't bonds
0.0%	pref/conv't pref	0.0%	muni bonds
0.0%	conv't bds/wrnts	0.0%	other

SHAREHOLDER INFORMATION

Minimum Investment
Initial: $5,000 — Subsequent: $250

Minimum IRA Investment
Initial: $5,000 — Subsequent: $250

Maximum Fees
Load: none — 12b-1: none
Other: none

Services
✔ IRA
✔ Keogh
✔ Telephone Exchange

McM Equity Investment (MCMEX)

800-788-9485, 415-616-9320
www.mcmfunds.com

Growth & Income

PERFORMANCE — fund inception date: 7/14/94

	3yr Annual	5yr Annual	10yr Annual	Bull	Bear
Return (%)	10.0	17.7	na	42.5	-8.6
Differ from Category (+/-)	1.1 av	3.4 abv av	na	9.0 abv av	-8.5 blw av

Standard Deviation	Category Risk Index	Beta
16.1%—av	0.93—blw av	0.89

	2000	1999	1998	1997	1996	1995	1994	1993	1992	1991
Return (%)	-6.3	11.5	27.7	33.8	26.8	35.9	—	—	—	—
Differ from Category (+/-)	-12.0	0.7	14.9	6.9	7.1	6.4	—	—	—	—
Return, Tax-Adjusted (%)	-7.7	10.8	27.1	33.2	26.1	35.0	—	—	—	—

PER SHARE DATA

	2000	1999	1998	1997	1996	1995	1994	1993	1992	1991
Dividends, Net Income ($)	0.20	0.23	0.22	0.23	0.22	0.20	—	—	—	—
Distrib'ns, Cap Gain ($)	1.75	0.49	0.14	0.04	0.00	0.03	—	—	—	—
Net Asset Value ($)	26.33	30.22	27.77	22.05	16.70	13.37	—	—	—	—
Expense Ratio (%)	0.68	0.66	0.75	0.75	0.75	0.75	—	—	—	—
Yield (%)	0.71	0.74	0.78	1.04	1.31	1.49	—	—	—	—
Portfolio Turnover (%)	13	4	0	0	1	2	—	—	—	—
Total Assets (Millions $)	261	238	171	91	39	7	—	—	—	—

PORTFOLIO (as of 6/30/00)

Portfolio Manager: committee - 1994

Investm't Category: Growth & Income

✔ Domestic — Index
Foreign — Sector
Asset Allocation — State Specific

Investment Style

✔ Large Cap — Mid Cap — Small Cap
Growth — ✔ Grth/Val — Value

Portfolio

1.2%	cash	0.0%	corp bonds
98.8%	stocks	0.0%	gov't bonds
0.0%	pref/conv't pref	0.0%	muni bonds
0.0%	conv't bds/wrnts	0.0%	other

SHAREHOLDER INFORMATION

Minimum Investment
Initial: $5,000 — Subsequent: $250

Minimum IRA Investment
Initial: $5,000 — Subsequent: $250

Maximum Fees
Load: none — 12b-1: none
Other: none

Services
✔ IRA
✔ Keogh
✔ Telephone Exchange

Mercury HW Intl Val/I

800-236-4479, 609-282-2800
www.mercuryfunds.com

(MIVIX)

International Stock

PERFORMANCE — fund inception date: 10/1/90

	3yr Annual	5yr Annual	10yr Annual	Bull	Bear
Return (%)	10.2	10.8	12.7	36.7	-3.2
Differ from Category (+/-)	1.3 av	2.5 abv av	3.7 high	-54.2 low	20.8 high

Standard Deviation	Category Risk Index	Beta
15.7%—av	0.69—low	0.58

	2000	1999	1998	1997	1996	1995	1994	1993	1992	1991
Return (%)	2.1	23.4	6.4	5.3	18.2	19.8	-2.9	45.7	-2.6	20.3
Differ from Category (+/-)	21.5	-37.3	0.6	4.0	3.7	10.5	0.2	5.5	0.9	7.3
Return, Tax-Adjusted (%)	0.0	20.8	5.2	4.0	17.1	18.5	-4.2	45.3	-3.7	16.1

PER SHARE DATA

	2000	1999	1998	1997	1996	1995	1994	1993	1992	1991
Dividends, Net Income ($)	0.50	0.75	0.49	0.71	0.38	0.40	0.31	0.00	0.21	0.50
Distrib'ns, Cap Gain ($)	1.80	1.50	0.33	0.00	0.16	0.18	0.45	0.15	0.31	1.29
Net Asset Value ($)	24.58	26.40	23.28	22.67	22.19	19.25	16.58	17.88	12.37	13.23
Expense Ratio (%)	na	0.95	0.89	1.00	1.00	1.00	1.00	1.00	1.00	1.00
Yield (%)	1.89	2.68	2.07	3.13	1.70	2.05	1.82	0.00	1.65	3.44
Portfolio Turnover (%)	na	41	20	18	12	24	23	24	88	224
Total Assets (Millions $)	1,203	1,432	1,409	1,041	521	97	27	10	4	1

PORTFOLIO (as of 3/31/00)

Portfolio Manager: Ketterer, Hartford, Chambers - 1990

Investm't Category: International Stock

Domestic	Index
✔ Foreign	Sector
Asset Allocation	State Specific

Investment Style

Large Cap	Mid Cap	Small Cap
Growth	Grth/Val	Value

Portfolio

0.0%	cash	0.0%	corp bonds
100.0%	stocks	0.0%	gov't bonds
0.0%	pref/conv't pref	0.0%	muni bonds
0.0%	conv't bds/wrnts	0.0%	other

SHAREHOLDER INFORMATION

Minimum Investment
Initial: $10,000 — Subsequent: $1

Minimum IRA Investment
Initial: $10,000 — Subsequent: $1

Maximum Fees
Load: none — 12b-1: none
Other: none

Services
✔ IRA
✔ Keogh
✔ Telephone Exchange

Mercury HW Lrge Cap Val/I (MCPIX)

800-236-4479, 609-282-2800
www.mercuryfunds.com

Growth & Income

PERFORMANCE — fund inception date: 6/24/87

	3yr Annual	5yr Annual	10yr Annual	Bull	Bear
Return (%)	3.6	11.3	14.7	13.4	10.8
Differ from Category (+/-)	-5.3 low	-3.0 low	-0.2 av	-20.1 low	10.9 abv av

Standard Deviation	Category Risk Index	Beta
19.1%—abv av	1.10—high	0.66

	2000	1999	1998	1997	1996	1995	1994	1993	1992	1991
Return (%)	9.1	-2.3	4.3	31.1	17.3	34.4	-3.4	15.7	13.9	34.6
Differ from Category (+/-)	3.4	-13.1	-8.5	4.2	-2.4	4.9	-2.9	1.9	2.3	6.5
Return, Tax-Adjusted (%)	8.0	-6.2	0.7	26.6	13.2	31.0	-5.1	13.4	12.3	33.3

PER SHARE DATA

	2000	1999	1998	1997	1996	1995	1994	1993	1992	1991
Dividends, Net Income ($)	0.37	0.41	0.41	0.47	0.57	0.47	0.44	0.45	0.45	0.41
Distrib'ns, Cap Gain ($)	0.00	2.80	2.88	3.25	1.81	1.06	0.36	0.53	0.23	0.00
Net Asset Value ($)	15.50	14.59	18.31	20.75	18.75	18.04	14.61	15.97	14.66	13.48
Expense Ratio (%)	na	0.91	0.87	0.88	0.98	1.00	1.00	1.00	1.00	1.00
Yield (%)	2.38	2.35	1.93	1.95	2.77	2.46	2.93	2.72	3.02	3.04
Portfolio Turnover (%)	na	18	23	44	24	50	36	25	32	39
Total Assets (Millions $)	49	113	162	196	203	162	106	82	65	78

PORTFOLIO (as of 3/31/00)

Portfolio Manager: Gail Bardin, Sheldon Lieberman - 1994

Investm't Category: Growth & Income

✔ Domestic
Index
✔ Foreign
Sector
Asset Allocation
State Specific

Investment Style

✔ Large Cap
✔ Mid Cap
Small Cap
Growth
Grth/Val
✔ Value

Portfolio

0.0%	cash	0.0%	corp bonds
100.0%	stocks	0.0%	gov't bonds
0.0%	pref/conv't pref	0.0%	muni bonds
0.0%	conv't bds/wrnts	0.0%	other

SHAREHOLDER INFORMATION

Minimum Investment

Initial: $10,000 — Subsequent: $1

Minimum IRA Investment

Initial: $10,000 — Subsequent: $1

Maximum Fees

Load: none — 12b-1: none
Other: none

Services

✔ IRA
✔ Keogh
✔ Telephone Exchange

Merger (MERFX)

800-343-8959, 914-741-5600

Growth

this fund is closed to new investors

PERFORMANCE

fund inception date: 7/20/82

	3yr Annual	5yr Annual	10yr Annual	Bull	Bear
Return (%)	13.2	12.2	12.2	24.9	11.9
Differ from Category (+/-)	2.2 abv av	-3.9 blw av	-4.6 low	-24.8 blw av	17.3 high

Standard Deviation	Category Risk Index	Beta
4.8%—blw av	0.25—low	0.12

	2000	1999	1998	1997	1996	1995	1994	1993	1992	1991
Return (%)	17.5	17.3	5.3	11.6	9.9	14.1	7.1	17.6	5.3	16.8
Differ from Category (+/-)	14.0	-1.6	-9.0	-15.5	-12.4	-16.3	7.3	3.0	-7.3	-20.8
Return, Tax-Adjusted (%)	14.9	15.4	3.1	9.3	6.9	12.1	5.5	15.0	3.8	14.9

PER SHARE DATA

	2000	1999	1998	1997	1996	1995	1994	1993	1992	1991
Dividends, Net Income ($)	0.13	0.07	0.22	0.02	0.18	0.07	0.00	0.00	0.00	0.03
Distrib'ns, Cap Gain ($)	1.64	1.14	1.09	1.57	1.23	0.82	0.70	1.09	0.63	0.67
Net Asset Value ($)	15.52	14.72	13.58	14.15	14.11	14.13	13.17	12.96	11.95	11.95
Expense Ratio (%)	1.34	1.38	1.33	1.36	1.36	1.39	1.58	2.19	2.75	3.05
Yield (%)	0.75	0.44	1.49	0.12	1.17	0.46	0.00	0.00	0.00	0.23
Portfolio Turnover (%)	419	386	355	271	405	418	390	186	231	311
Total Assets (Millions $)	1,150	635	346	435	473	245	171	27	11	10

PORTFOLIO (as of 6/30/00)

Portfolio Manager: Fred Green, Bonnie Smith - 1989

Investm't Category: Growth

✔ Domestic	Index
Foreign	Sector
Asset Allocation	State Specific

Investment Style

Large Cap	✔ Mid Cap	Small Cap
✔ Growth	Grth/Val	Value

Portfolio

45.5%	cash	0.0%	corp bonds
54.6%	stocks	0.0%	gov't bonds
0.0%	pref/conv't pref	0.0%	muni bonds
0.0%	conv't bds/wrnts	-0.1%	other

SHAREHOLDER INFORMATION

Minimum Investment

Initial: $2,000 Subsequent: $1

Minimum IRA Investment

Initial: $2,000 Subsequent: $1

Maximum Fees

Load: none 12b-1: 0.19%

Other: none

Services

✔ IRA

✔ Keogh

Telephone Exchange

Meridian (MERDX)

800-446-6662, 415-461-6237

Growth

PERFORMANCE — fund inception date: 8/2/84

	3yr Annual	5yr Annual	10yr Annual	Bull	Bear
Return (%)	14.4	14.7	17.4	37.5	4.4
Differ from Category (+/-)	3.4 abv av	-1.4 blw av	0.6 av	-12.2 blw av	9.8 abv av

Standard Deviation	Category Risk Index	Beta
18.7%—av	0.96—blw av	0.79

	2000	1999	1998	1997	1996	1995	1994	1993	1992	1991
Return (%)	28.2	13.3	3.0	19.2	11.1	22.4	0.5	13.0	15.5	56.8
Differ from Category (+/-)	24.7	-5.6	-11.3	-7.9	-11.2	-8.0	0.7	-1.6	2.9	19.2
Return, Tax-Adjusted (%)	22.9	11.5	-1.4	15.5	8.0	21.3	-0.5	12.4	14.6	53.3

PER SHARE DATA

	2000	1999	1998	1997	1996	1995	1994	1993	1992	1991
Dividends, Net Income ($)	2.43	0.15	0.14	0.31	0.36	0.30	0.17	0.02	0.03	0.09
Distrib'ns, Cap Gain ($)	1.85	1.78	6.50	4.81	2.75	0.53	0.70	0.43	0.56	1.69
Net Asset Value ($)	28.06	25.40	24.29	30.73	30.08	29.90	25.12	25.87	23.29	20.75
Expense Ratio (%)	1.09	1.01	0.95	0.96	0.96	1.06	1.22	1.47	1.75	1.68
Yield (%)	8.12	0.55	0.45	0.87	1.09	0.98	0.65	0.07	0.12	0.40
Portfolio Turnover (%)	28	51	38	37	34	29	43	61	61	85
Total Assets (Millions $)	140	138	230	332	377	395	256	160	34	16

PORTFOLIO (as of 6/30/00)

Portfolio Manager: Richard Aster - 1984

Investm't Category: Growth

✔ Domestic — Index
Foreign — Sector
Asset Allocation — State Specific

Investment Style

Large Cap — ✔ Mid Cap — ✔ Small Cap
Growth — Grth/Val — ✔ Value

Portfolio

8.6%	cash	0.0%	corp bonds
91.4%	stocks	0.0%	gov't bonds
0.0%	pref/conv't pref	0.0%	muni bonds
0.0%	conv't bds/wrnts	0.0%	other

SHAREHOLDER INFORMATION

Minimum Investment
Initial: $1,000 — Subsequent: $50

Minimum IRA Investment
Initial: $1,000 — Subsequent: $50

Maximum Fees
Load: none — 12b-1: none
Other: none

Services
✔ IRA
✔ Keogh
✔ Telephone Exchange

Monetta (MONTX)

800-666-3882, 630-462-9800
www.monetta.com

Aggressive Growth

PERFORMANCE — fund inception date: 5/6/86

	3yr Annual	5yr Annual	10yr Annual	Bull	Bear
Return (%)	5.0	8.2	11.4	92.3	-34.7
Differ from Category (+/-)	-11.2 blw av	-6.4 blw av	-4.4 low	-26.9 av	-14.1 blw av

Standard Deviation	Category Risk Index	Beta
40.2%—high	1.24—abv av	1.15

	2000	1999	1998	1997	1996	1995	1994	1993	1992	1991
Return (%)	-15.9	51.8	-9.0	26.1	1.6	28.0	-6.2	0.4	5.4	55.8
Differ from Category (+/-)	-9.9	-5.7	-24.1	11.3	-16.7	-6.6	-5.4	-24.8	-1.5	8.6
Return, Tax-Adjusted (%)	-22.0	51.8	-9.7	22.6	1.6	22.1	-6.3	-0.5	4.3	52.3

PER SHARE DATA

	2000	1999	1998	1997	1996	1995	1994	1993	1992	1991
Dividends, Net Income ($)	0.00	0.00	0.00	0.00	0.00	0.02	0.05	0.00	0.02	0.05
Distrib'ns, Cap Gain ($)	7.00	0.00	0.65	2.75	0.00	3.00	0.00	0.53	0.57	1.30
Net Asset Value ($)	11.78	22.71	14.96	17.27	15.84	15.59	14.52	15.54	15.99	15.73
Expense Ratio (%)	na	1.45	1.36	1.48	1.38	1.40	1.35	1.38	1.45	1.42
Yield (%)	0.00	0.00	0.00	0.00	0.00	0.10	0.34	0.00	0.12	0.29
Portfolio Turnover (%)	na	210	107	97	204	148	191	227	127	154
Total Assets (Millions $)	96	135	124	163	211	362	364	524	408	56

PORTFOLIO (as of 6/30/00)

Portfolio Manager: committee - 1986

Investm't Category: Aggressive Growth

✔ Domestic — Index
Foreign — Sector
Asset Allocation — State Specific

Investment Style

Large Cap — Mid Cap — ✔ Small Cap
✔ Growth — Grth/Val — Value

Portfolio

0.9%	cash	0.0%	corp bonds
99.1%	stocks	0.0%	gov't bonds
0.0%	pref/conv't pref	0.0%	muni bonds
0.0%	conv't bds/wrnts	0.0%	other

SHAREHOLDER INFORMATION

Minimum Investment

Initial: $250 — Subsequent: $1

Minimum IRA Investment

Initial: $250 — Subsequent: $1

Maximum Fees

Load: none — 12b-1: none
Other: none

Services

✔ IRA
✔ Keogh
✔ Telephone Exchange

Montgomery Balanced/R (MNAAX)

800-572-3863, 415-248-6000
www.montgomeryfunds.com

Balanced

PERFORMANCE

fund inception date: 3/31/94

	3yr Annual	5yr Annual	10yr Annual	Bull	Bear
Return (%)	5.7	9.6	na	23.3	-6.1
Differ from Category (+/-)	-2.7 blw av	-1.8 blw av	na	-4.8 blw av	-2.9 blw av

Standard Deviation	Category Risk Index	Beta
10.7%—blw av	0.98—av	0.52

	2000	1999	1998	1997	1996	1995	1994	1993	1992	1991
Return (%)	-1.3	12.8	6.1	19.0	12.8	32.6	—	—	—	—
Differ from Category (+/-)	-3.3	2.1	-7.2	0.2	-1.1	7.1	—	—	—	—
Return, Tax-Adjusted (%)	-5.1	11.4	0.6	13.4	9.3	30.8	—	—	—	—

PER SHARE DATA

	2000	1999	1998	1997	1996	1995	1994	1993	1992	1991
Dividends, Net Income ($)	0.93	0.29	0.93	1.63	0.39	0.25	—	—	—	—
Distrib'ns, Cap Gain ($)	1.27	0.44	3.09	1.82	1.66	0.55	—	—	—	—
Net Asset Value ($)	13.82	16.24	15.06	18.01	18.09	17.86	—	—	—	—
Expense Ratio (%)	0.13	0.25	0.25	1.31	1.30	1.31	—	—	—	—
Yield (%)	6.16	1.73	5.12	8.21	1.97	1.35	—	—	—	—
Portfolio Turnover (%)	35	36	84	168	225	96	—	—	—	—
Total Assets (Millions $)	51	69	107	136	141	120	—	—	—	—

PORTFOLIO (as of 6/30/00)

Portfolio Manager: committee - 2000

Investm't Category: Balanced

✔ Domestic — Index
Foreign — Sector
✔ Asset Allocation — State Specific

Investment Style

Large Cap — Mid Cap — Small Cap
Growth — Grth/Val — Value

Portfolio

-1.8%	cash	0.0%	corp bonds
0.0%	stocks	0.0%	gov't bonds
0.0%	pref/conv't pref	0.0%	muni bonds
0.0%	conv't bds/wrnts	101.8%	other

SHAREHOLDER INFORMATION

Minimum Investment
Initial: $1,000 — Subsequent: $100

Minimum IRA Investment
Initial: $1,000 — Subsequent: $100

Maximum Fees
Load: none — 12b-1: none
Other: none

Services
✔ IRA
Keogh
✔ Telephone Exchange

Montgomery Emg Mkts/R (MNEMX)

800-572-3863, 415-248-6000
www.montgomeryfunds.com

International Stock

PERFORMANCE — fund inception date: 3/2/92

	3yr Annual	5yr Annual	10yr Annual	Bull	Bear
Return (%)	-10.6	-4.9	na	81.3	-34.2
Differ from Category (+/-)	-19.5 low	-13.2 low	na	-9.6 av	-10.2 low

Standard Deviation	Category Risk Index	Beta
32.2%—high	1.42—abv av	1.23

	2000	1999	1998	1997	1996	1995	1994	1993	1992	1991
Return (%)	-29.1	63.1	-38.2	-3.1	12.3	-9.0	-7.5	58.6	—	—
Differ from Category (+/-)	-9.7	2.4	-44.0	-4.4	-2.2	-18.3	-4.4	18.4	—	—
Return, Tax-Adjusted (%)	-29.1	63.1	-38.2	-4.0	12.1	-9.0	-8.9	57.8	—	—

PER SHARE DATA

	2000	1999	1998	1997	1996	1995	1994	1993	1992	1991
Dividends, Net Income ($)	0.00	0.00	0.00	0.15	0.06	0.00	0.00	0.01	—	—
Distrib'ns, Cap Gain ($)	0.00	0.00	0.00	0.33	0.00	0.00	0.79	0.25	—	—
Net Asset Value ($)	9.23	13.02	7.98	12.93	13.87	12.41	13.65	15.58	—	—
Expense Ratio (%)	1.90	2.05	1.60	1.67	1.72	1.80	1.85	1.90	—	—
Yield (%)	0.00	0.00	0.00	1.13	0.43	0.00	0.00	0.06	—	—
Portfolio Turnover (%)	113	86	96	83	109	92	63	21	—	—
Total Assets (Millions $)	186	369	338	988	912	855	878	610	—	—

PORTFOLIO (as of 6/30/00)

Portfolio Manager: Jimenez, Chiang - 1992

Investm't Category: International Stock

Domestic	Index
✔ Foreign	Sector
Asset Allocation	State Specific

Investment Style

Large Cap	Mid Cap	Small Cap
Growth	Grth/Val	Value

Portfolio

18.5% cash	0.0% corp bonds
80.9% stocks	0.0% gov't bonds
0.6% pref/conv't pref	0.0% muni bonds
0.0% conv't bds/wrnts	0.0% other

SHAREHOLDER INFORMATION

Minimum Investment
Initial: $1,000 — Subsequent: $100

Minimum IRA Investment
Initial: $1,000 — Subsequent: $100

Maximum Fees
Load: none — 12b-1: none
Other: none

Services
✔ IRA
Keogh
✔ Telephone Exchange

Montgomery Glbl Commun/R (MNGCX)

800-572-3863, 415-248-6000
www.montgomeryfunds.com

International Stock

PERFORMANCE — fund inception date: 6/1/93

	3yr Annual	5yr Annual	10yr Annual	Bull	Bear
Return (%)	24.3	19.2	na	166.9	-47.3
Differ from Category (+/-)	15.4 high	10.9 high	na	76.0 high	-23.3 low

Standard Deviation	Category Risk Index	Beta
36.2%—high	1.60—high	1.44

	2000	1999	1998	1997	1996	1995	1994	1993	1992	1991
Return (%)	-39.1	104.0	54.9	15.8	8.0	16.8	-13.4	—	—	—
Differ from Category (+/-)	-19.7	43.3	49.1	14.5	-6.5	7.5	-10.3	—	—	—
Return, Tax-Adjusted (%)	-42.5	98.1	51.6	11.3	6.4	16.8	-13.4	—	—	—

PER SHARE DATA

	2000	1999	1998	1997	1996	1995	1994	1993	1992	1991
Dividends, Net Income ($)	0.00	0.00	0.00	0.00	0.00	0.00	0.00	—	—	—
Distrib'ns, Cap Gain ($)	6.34	6.25	2.50	3.75	0.90	0.00	0.03	—	—	—
Net Asset Value ($)	16.79	36.85	21.41	15.57	16.74	16.34	13.98	—	—	—
Expense Ratio (%)	1.47	1.69	1.90	1.91	1.90	1.91	1.94	—	—	—
Yield (%)	0.00	0.00	0.00	0.00	0.00	0.00	0.00	—	—	—
Portfolio Turnover (%)	186	146	79	75	103	50	29	—	—	—
Total Assets (Millions $)	283	598	282	135	165	219	216	—	—	—

PORTFOLIO (as of 6/30/00)

Portfolio Manager: Oscar Castro, Stephen Parlett - 1993

Investm't Category: International Stock

✔ Domestic
Index
✔ Foreign
✔ Sector
Asset Allocation
State Specific

Investment Style

Large Cap · Mid Cap · Small Cap
Growth · Grth/Val · Value

Portfolio

5.9%	cash	0.0%	corp bonds
91.1%	stocks	0.0%	gov't bonds
3.1%	pref/conv't pref	0.0%	muni bonds
0.0%	conv't bds/wrnts	0.0%	other

SHAREHOLDER INFORMATION

Minimum Investment
Initial: $1,000 Subsequent: $100

Minimum IRA Investment
Initial: $1,000 Subsequent: $100

Maximum Fees
Load: none 12b-1: none
Other: none

Services
✔ IRA
✔ Keogh
✔ Telephone Exchange

Montgomery Glbl Oppor/R (MNGOX)

800-572-3863, 415-248-6000
www.montgomeryfunds.com

International Stock

PERFORMANCE — fund inception date: 9/30/93

	3yr Annual	5yr Annual	10yr Annual	Bull	Bear
Return (%)	13.6	14.4	na	91.9	-37.8
Differ from Category (+/-)	4.7 abv av	6.1 high	na	1.0 abv av	-13.8 low

Standard Deviation	Category Risk Index	Beta
26.9%—high	1.19—abv av	1.09

	2000	1999	1998	1997	1996	1995	1994	1993	1992	1991
Return (%)	-29.7	57.5	32.7	11.0	20.1	17.2	-8.4	—	—	—
Differ from Category (+/-)	-10.3	-3.2	26.9	9.7	5.6	7.9	-5.3	—	—	—
Return, Tax-Adjusted (%)	-30.6	55.5	29.1	6.3	18.5	16.9	-9.3	—	—	—

PER SHARE DATA

	2000	1999	1998	1997	1996	1995	1994	1993	1992	1991
Dividends, Net Income ($)	0.00	0.00	0.21	0.00	0.00	0.07	0.00	—	—	—
Distrib'ns, Cap Gain ($)	1.16	1.65	2.20	3.85	0.82	0.00	0.49	—	—	—
Net Asset Value ($)	16.18	24.67	16.79	14.63	16.73	14.62	12.53	—	—	—
Expense Ratio (%)	1.90	2.01	1.90	1.90	1.90	1.91	1.90	—	—	—
Yield (%)	0.00	0.00	1.10	0.00	0.00	0.47	0.00	—	—	—
Portfolio Turnover (%)	203	172	135	117	163	119	—	—	—	—
Total Assets (Millions $)	62	90	54	22	29	16	13	—	—	—

PORTFOLIO (as of 6/30/00)

Portfolio Manager: John Boich, Oscar Castro - 1993

Investm't Category: International Stock

✔ Domestic — Index
✔ Foreign — Sector
Asset Allocation — State Specific

Investment Style

Large Cap — Mid Cap — Small Cap
Growth — Grth/Val — Value

Portfolio

6.3%	cash	0.0%	corp bonds
91.8%	stocks	0.0%	gov't bonds
1.9%	pref/conv't pref	0.0%	muni bonds
0.0%	conv't bds/wrnts	0.0%	other

SHAREHOLDER INFORMATION

Minimum Investment
Initial: $1,000 — Subsequent: $100

Minimum IRA Investment
Initial: $1,000 — Subsequent: $100

Maximum Fees
Load: none — 12b-1: none
Other: none

Services
✔ IRA
Keogh
✔ Telephone Exchange

Montgomery Global 20/R (MNSFX)

800-572-3863, 415-248-6000
www.montgomeryfunds.com

International Stock

PERFORMANCE

fund inception date: 10/2/95

	3yr Annual	5yr Annual	10yr Annual	Bull	Bear
Return (%)	5.9	13.1	na	77.5	-31.4
Differ from Category (+/-)	-3.0 blw av	4.8 abv av	na	-13.4 av	-7.4 blw av

Standard Deviation	Category Risk Index	Beta
22.3%—abv av	0.98—av	1.00

	2000	1999	1998	1997	1996	1995	1994	1993	1992	1991
Return (%)	-25.2	45.2	9.3	29.2	20.4	—	—	—	—	—
Differ from Category (+/-)	-5.8	-15.5	3.5	27.9	5.9	—	—	—	—	—
Return, Tax-Adjusted (%)	-28.4	41.9	7.4	26.8	19.1	—	—	—	—	—

PER SHARE DATA

	2000	1999	1998	1997	1996	1995	1994	1993	1992	1991
Dividends, Net Income ($)	0.00	0.00	0.34	0.00	0.01	—	—	—	—	—
Distrib'ns, Cap Gain ($)	3.95	3.10	1.04	1.85	0.60	—	—	—	—	—
Net Asset Value ($)	14.31	24.39	19.13	18.83	16.03	—	—	—	—	—
Expense Ratio (%)	1.80	1.76	1.80	1.82	1.80	—	—	—	—	—
Yield (%)	0.00	0.00	1.68	0.00	0.06	—	—	—	—	—
Portfolio Turnover (%)	181	115	151	157	—	—	—	—	—	—
Total Assets (Millions $)	79	141	176	230	89	—	—	—	—	—

PORTFOLIO (as of 6/30/00)

Portfolio Manager: John Boich, Oscar Castro - 2000

Investm't Category: International Stock

✔ Domestic
✔ Foreign
Asset Allocation
Index
Sector
State Specific

Investment Style

Large Cap | Mid Cap | Small Cap
Growth | Grth/Val | Value

Portfolio

4.0%	cash	0.0%	corp bonds
96.0%	stocks	0.0%	gov't bonds
0.0%	pref/conv't pref	0.0%	muni bonds
0.0%	conv't bds/wrnts	0.0%	other

SHAREHOLDER INFORMATION

Minimum Investment
Initial: $1,000 Subsequent: $100

Minimum IRA Investment
Initial: $1,000 Subsequent: $100

Maximum Fees
Load: none 12b-1: none
Other: none

Services
✔ IRA
Keogh
✔ Telephone Exchange

Montgomery Growth/R (MNGFX)

800-572-3863, 415-248-6000
www.montgomeryfunds.com

Growth

PERFORMANCE

fund inception date: 9/30/93

	3yr Annual	5yr Annual	10yr Annual	Bull	Bear
Return (%)	3.2	10.4	na	44.3	-14.8
Differ from Category (+/-)	-7.8 low	-5.7 low	na	-5.4 av	-9.4 blw av

Standard Deviation	Category Risk Index	Beta
20.0%—abv av	1.03—av	1.01

	2000	1999	1998	1997	1996	1995	1994	1993	1992	1991
Return (%)	-10.5	20.5	2.1	24.1	20.2	23.6	20.9	—	—	—
Differ from Category (+/-)	-14.0	1.6	-12.2	-3.0	-2.1	-6.8	21.1	—	—	—
Return, Tax-Adjusted (%)	-12.8	17.2	0.5	20.9	15.8	20.6	20.5	—	—	—

PER SHARE DATA

	2000	1999	1998	1997	1996	1995	1994	1993	1992	1991
Dividends, Net Income ($)	0.00	0.17	0.09	0.14	0.15	0.16	0.07	—	—	—
Distrib'ns, Cap Gain ($)	2.52	3.00	1.56	2.92	2.76	1.53	0.07	—	—	—
Net Asset Value ($)	16.78	21.46	20.62	21.89	20.15	19.20	16.93	—	—	—
Expense Ratio (%)	1.46	1.38	1.19	1.27	1.35	1.50	1.49	—	—	—
Yield (%)	0.00	0.69	0.40	0.56	0.65	0.77	0.41	—	—	—
Portfolio Turnover (%)	79	39	53	61	118	128	110	—	—	—
Total Assets (Millions $)	333	572	1,047	1,364	994	859	592	—	—	—

PORTFOLIO (as of 6/30/00)

Portfolio Manager: Andrew Pratt - 1993

Investm't Category: Growth

✔ Domestic — Index
Foreign — Sector
Asset Allocation — State Specific

Investment Style

✔ Large Cap — Mid Cap — Small Cap
Growth — Grth/Val — ✔ Value

Portfolio

4.7% cash — 0.0% corp bonds
95.3% stocks — 0.0% gov't bonds
0.0% pref/conv't pref — 0.0% muni bonds
0.0% conv't bds/wrnts — 0.0% other

SHAREHOLDER INFORMATION

Minimum Investment

Initial: $1,000 — Subsequent: $100

Minimum IRA Investment

Initial: $1,000 — Subsequent: $100

Maximum Fees

Load: none — 12b-1: none
Other: none

Services

✔ IRA
Keogh
✔ Telephone Exchange

Montgomery Intl Growth/R (MNIGX)

800-572-3863, 415-248-6000
www.montgomeryfunds.com

International Stock

PERFORMANCE

fund inception date: 7/3/95

	3yr Annual	5yr Annual	10yr Annual	Bull	Bear
Return (%)	6.6	10.0	na	48.1	-29.5
Differ from Category (+/-)	-2.3 blw av	1.7 av	na	-42.8 blw av	-5.5 blw av

Standard Deviation	Category Risk Index	Beta
21.0%—abv av	0.93—blw av	0.87

	2000	1999	1998	1997	1996	1995	1994	1993	1992	1991
Return (%)	-25.4	26.2	28.6	10.1	20.9	—	—	—	—	—
Differ from Category (+/-)	-6.0	-34.5	22.8	8.8	6.4	—	—	—	—	—
Return, Tax-Adjusted (%)	-26.9	25.7	28.4	8.5	17.4	—	—	—	—	—

PER SHARE DATA

	2000	1999	1998	1997	1996	1995	1994	1993	1992	1991
Dividends, Net Income ($)	0.00	0.00	0.00	0.02	0.00	—	—	—	—	—
Distrib'ns, Cap Gain ($)	1.78	0.39	0.09	1.06	1.67	—	—	—	—	—
Net Asset Value ($)	15.68	23.43	18.89	14.76	14.40	—	—	—	—	—
Expense Ratio (%)	1.65	1.66	1.65	0.00	0.00	—	—	—	—	—
Yield (%)	0.00	0.00	0.00	0.12	0.00	—	—	—	—	—
Portfolio Turnover (%)	207	150	127	95	238	—	—	—	—	—
Total Assets (Millions $)	87	255	200	31	25	—	—	—	—	—

PORTFOLIO (as of 3/31/00)

Portfolio Manager: John Boich, Oscar Castro - 1995

Investm't Category: International Stock

Domestic	Index
✔ Foreign	Sector
Asset Allocation	State Specific

Investment Style

Large Cap	Mid Cap	Small Cap
Growth	Grth/Val	Value

Portfolio

-15.5% cash	0.0% corp bonds
112.9% stocks	0.0% gov't bonds
2.6% pref/conv't pref	0.0% muni bonds
0.0% conv't bds/wrnts	0.0% other

SHAREHOLDER INFORMATION

Minimum Investment

Initial: $1,000 Subsequent: $100

Minimum IRA Investment

Initial: $1,000 Subsequent: $100

Maximum Fees

Load: none 12b-1: none

Other: none

Services

✔ IRA

Keogh

✔ Telephone Exchange

Montgomery Sm Cap/R (MNSCX)

800-572-3863, 415-248-6000
www.montgomeryfunds.com

Aggressive Growth

PERFORMANCE — fund inception date: 7/13/90

	3yr Annual	5yr Annual	10yr Annual	Bull	Bear
Return (%)	2.4	9.5	17.9	104.4	-34.5
Differ from Category (+/-)	-13.8 low	-5.1 blw av	2.1 av	-14.8 av	-13.9 blw av

Standard Deviation	Category Risk Index	Beta
36.5%—high	1.13—abv av	1.41

	2000	1999	1998	1997	1996	1995	1994	1993	1992	1991
Return (%)	-25.1	55.8	-7.9	23.8	18.6	35.1	-9.9	24.3	9.5	98.7
Differ from Category (+/-)	-19.1	-1.7	-23.0	9.0	0.3	0.5	-9.1	-0.9	2.6	51.5
Return, Tax-Adjusted (%)	-30.0	55.8	-10.7	20.5	13.5	31.7	-11.4	21.5	9.5	88.1

PER SHARE DATA

	2000	1999	1998	1997	1996	1995	1994	1993	1992	1991
Dividends, Net Income ($)	0.00	0.00	0.00	0.00	0.00	0.00	0.00	0.00	0.00	0.00
Distrib'ns, Cap Gain ($)	5.78	0.00	2.76	2.96	3.28	1.78	0.97	1.51	0.00	3.52
Net Asset Value ($)	11.98	23.48	15.07	19.64	18.40	18.28	14.96	17.67	15.54	14.18
Expense Ratio (%)	1.35	1.32	1.24	1.20	1.24	1.37	1.35	1.40	1.50	1.45
Yield (%)	0.00	0.00	0.00	0.00	0.00	0.00	0.00	0.00	0.00	0.00
Portfolio Turnover (%)	93	71	68	58	80	85	95	130	81	194
Total Assets (Millions $)	74	136	145	207	220	236	202	259	207	74

PORTFOLIO (as of 6/30/00)

Portfolio Manager: Larocco, Philpott, Reed, Roberts - 1990

Investm't Category: Aggressive Growth

✔ Domestic　Index
Foreign　Sector
Asset Allocation　State Specific

Investment Style

Large Cap　Mid Cap　✔ Small Cap
✔ Growth　Grth/Val　Value

Portfolio

1.0%	cash	0.0%	corp bonds
99.1%	stocks	0.0%	gov't bonds
0.0%	pref/conv't pref	0.0%	muni bonds
0.0%	conv't bds/wrnts	0.0%	other

SHAREHOLDER INFORMATION

Minimum Investment

Initial: $1,000　Subsequent: $100

Minimum IRA Investment

Initial: $1,000　Subsequent: $100

Maximum Fees

Load: none　12b-1: none
Other: none

Services

✔ IRA
Keogh
✔ Telephone Exchange

Montgomery US Emg Gr/R (MNMCX)

800-572-3863, 415-248-6000
www.montgomeryfunds.com

Aggressive Growth

PERFORMANCE

fund inception date: 12/30/94

	3yr Annual	5yr Annual	10yr Annual	Bull	Bear
Return (%)	13.7	17.3	na	50.5	-7.9
Differ from Category (+/-)	-2.5 av	2.7 av	na	-68.7 blw av	12.7 abv av

Standard Deviation	Category Risk Index	Beta
26.6%—high	0.82—blw av	1.05

	2000	1999	1998	1997	1996	1995	1994	1993	1992	1991
Return (%)	14.6	18.8	7.9	27.0	19.1	28.6	—	—	—	—
Differ from Category (+/-)	20.6	-38.7	-7.2	12.2	0.8	-6.0	—	—	—	—
Return, Tax-Adjusted (%)	6.8	16.2	6.7	25.6	16.8	28.1	—	—	—	—

PER SHARE DATA

	2000	1999	1998	1997	1996	1995	1994	1993	1992	1991
Dividends, Net Income ($)	0.00	0.00	0.00	0.00	0.00	0.08	—	—	—	—
Distrib'ns, Cap Gain ($)	8.43	2.67	1.12	1.13	1.22	0.06	—	—	—	—
Net Asset Value ($)	16.55	21.66	20.70	20.31	16.91	15.28	—	—	—	—
Expense Ratio (%)	1.50	1.66	1.56	1.71	1.75	1.75	—	—	—	—
Yield (%)	0.00	0.00	0.00	0.00	0.00	0.52	—	—	—	—
Portfolio Turnover (%)	63	76	23	79	88	44	—	—	—	—
Total Assets (Millions $)	183	301	410	368	298	272	—	—	—	—

PORTFOLIO (as of 6/30/00)

Portfolio Manager: K. Peters - 1994

Investm't Category: Aggressive Growth

✔ Domestic
✔ Foreign
Asset Allocation
Index
Sector
State Specific

Investment Style

Large Cap
Mid Cap
✔ Small Cap
✔ Growth
Grth/Val
Value

Portfolio

4.8% cash	0.0% corp bonds
95.2% stocks	0.0% gov't bonds
0.0% pref/conv't pref	0.0% muni bonds
0.0% conv't bds/wrnts	0.0% other

SHAREHOLDER INFORMATION

Minimum Investment

Initial: $1,000 Subsequent: $100

Minimum IRA Investment

Initial: $1,000 Subsequent: $100

Maximum Fees

Load: none 12b-1: none
Other: none

Services

✔ IRA
Keogh
✔ Telephone Exchange

Muhlenkamp (MUHLX)

800-860-3863, 724-935-5520
www.muhlenkamp.com

Growth

PERFORMANCE — fund inception date: 11/18/88

	3yr Annual	5yr Annual	10yr Annual	Bull	Bear
Return (%)	12.9	20.0	19.8	27.8	-3.3
Differ from Category (+/-)	1.9 av	3.9 high	3.0 high	-21.9 blw av	2.1 av

Standard Deviation	Category Risk Index	Beta
22.2%—abv av	1.14—abv av	0.91

	2000	1999	1998	1997	1996	1995	1994	1993	1992	1991
Return (%)	25.3	11.3	3.2	33.2	29.9	32.9	-7.1	18.1	15.8	45.3
Differ from Category (+/-)	21.8	-7.6	-11.1	6.1	7.6	2.5	-6.9	3.5	3.2	7.7
Return, Tax-Adjusted (%)	24.1	10.8	3.1	33.0	29.6	32.1	-7.7	17.8	15.4	44.8

PER SHARE DATA

	2000	1999	1998	1997	1996	1995	1994	1993	1992	1991
Dividends, Net Income ($)	0.00	0.00	0.07	0.12	0.11	0.21	0.10	0.09	0.14	0.14
Distrib'ns, Cap Gain ($)	2.33	0.80	0.00	0.00	0.00	0.11	0.25	0.00	0.00	0.00
Net Asset Value ($)	48.98	41.11	37.65	36.55	27.52	21.26	16.23	17.86	15.20	13.25
Expense Ratio (%)	na	1.35	1.32	1.33	1.55	1.40	1.57	1.30	1.41	1.71
Yield (%)	0.00	0.00	0.18	0.32	0.39	0.98	0.60	0.50	0.92	1.05
Portfolio Turnover (%)	na	14	27	13	16	22	25	14	20	52
Total Assets (Millions $)	227	176	195	125	41	23	16	12	4	1

PORTFOLIO (as of 6/30/00)

Portfolio Manager: Ronald Muhlenkamp - 1988

Investm't Category: Growth

✔ Domestic	Index
Foreign	Sector
Asset Allocation	State Specific

Investment Style

Large Cap	✔ Mid Cap	✔ Small Cap
Growth	✔ Grth/Val	Value

Portfolio

9.8%	cash	0.8%	corp bonds
90.2%	stocks	0.0%	gov't bonds
0.0%	pref/conv't pref	0.0%	muni bonds
0.0%	conv't bds/wrnts	-0.8%	other

SHAREHOLDER INFORMATION

Minimum Investment
Initial: $1,500 — Subsequent: $50

Minimum IRA Investment
Initial: $1 — Subsequent: $1

Maximum Fees
Load: none — 12b-1: none
Other: none

Services
✔ IRA
✔ Keogh
Telephone Exchange

Mutual Beacon/Z (BEGRX)

800-342-5236, 412-312-2000
www.franklintempleton.com

Growth & Income

this fund is closed to new investors

PERFORMANCE

fund inception date: 6/11/62

	3yr Annual	5yr Annual	10yr Annual	Bull	Bear
Return (%)	10.9	15.2	17.0	28.7	4.8
Differ from Category (+/-)	2.0 abv av	0.9 av	2.1 abv av	-4.8 av	4.9 abv av

Standard Deviation	Category Risk Index	Beta
14.2%—blw av	0.82—low	0.63

	2000	1999	1998	1997	1996	1995	1994	1993	1992	1991
Return (%)	14.3	16.7	2.3	22.9	21.1	25.8	5.6	22.9	22.9	17.5
Differ from Category (+/-)	8.6	5.9	-10.5	-4.0	1.4	-3.7	6.1	9.1	11.3	-10.6
Return, Tax-Adjusted (%)	10.3	14.1	-0.1	21.7	17.2	22.7	3.8	20.4	20.9	15.9

PER SHARE DATA

	2000	1999	1998	1997	1996	1995	1994	1993	1992	1991
Dividends, Net Income ($)	0.43	0.26	0.45	0.54	0.35	0.28	0.15	0.12	0.15	0.25
Distrib'ns, Cap Gain ($)	1.86	1.18	0.87	1.26	1.13	0.73	0.45	0.60	0.36	0.11
Net Asset Value ($)	13.38	13.84	13.12	14.12	12.98	11.98	10.34	10.36	9.03	7.79
Expense Ratio (%)	na	0.78	0.76	0.74	0.73	0.71	0.75	0.73	0.81	0.85
Yield (%)	2.82	1.73	3.21	3.51	2.50	2.20	1.35	1.12	1.63	3.12
Portfolio Turnover (%)	na	67	65	54	66	73	70	52	58	57
Total Assets (Millions $)	2,950	3,218	4,039	5,684	4,950	3,566	2,056	1,060	533	399

PORTFOLIO (as of 6/30/00)

Portfolio Manager: Sondike, Winters, Langerman - 1985

Investm't Category: Growth & Income

✔ Domestic	Index
✔ Foreign	Sector
Asset Allocation	State Specific

Investment Style

✔ Large Cap	Mid Cap	Small Cap
Growth	Grth/Val	✔ Value

Portfolio

10.0% cash	0.0% corp bonds
83.0% stocks	0.0% gov't bonds
0.0% pref/conv't pref	0.0% muni bonds
0.0% conv't bds/wrnts	7.0% other

SHAREHOLDER INFORMATION

Minimum Investment

Initial: $1,000 Subsequent: $50

Minimum IRA Investment

Initial: $250 Subsequent: $50

Maximum Fees

Load: none 12b-1: none

Other: none

Services

✔ IRA

Keogh

Telephone Exchange

Mutual Discovery/Z (MDISX)

800-342-5236, 412-312-2000
www.franklintempleton.com

Growth

this fund is closed to new investors

PERFORMANCE — fund inception date: 1/4/93

	3yr Annual	5yr Annual	10yr Annual	Bull	Bear
Return (%)	11.8	16.5	na	31.7	2.0
Differ from Category (+/-)	0.8 av	0.4 av	na	-18.0 blw av	7.4 abv av

Standard Deviation	Category Risk Index	Beta
12.9%—blw av	0.66—low	0.50

	2000	1999	1998	1997	1996	1995	1994	1993	1992	1991
Return (%)	12.5	26.7	-1.9	22.9	24.9	28.6	3.6	—	—	—
Differ from Category (+/-)	9.0	7.8	-16.2	-4.2	2.6	-1.8	3.8	—	—	—
Return, Tax-Adjusted (%)	7.5	25.3	-3.7	19.4	21.5	26.3	1.3	—	—	—

PER SHARE DATA

	2000	1999	1998	1997	1996	1995	1994	1993	1992	1991
Dividends, Net Income ($)	0.62	0.41	0.48	0.81	0.31	0.14	0.16	—	—	—
Distrib'ns, Cap Gain ($)	4.04	0.32	0.81	1.36	1.40	0.82	0.81	—	—	—
Net Asset Value ($)	18.93	21.10	17.27	18.89	17.18	15.16	12.55	—	—	—
Expense Ratio (%)	na	1.05	1.00	0.98	0.96	0.98	0.99	—	—	—
Yield (%)	2.69	1.91	2.65	4.00	1.66	0.87	1.19	—	—	—
Portfolio Turnover (%)	na	87	83	58	80	73	72	—	—	—
Total Assets (Millions $)	1,989	2,038	2,523	3,878	2,974	1,368	725	—	—	—

PORTFOLIO (as of 6/30/00)

Portfolio Manager: Winters, Langerman - 1993

Investm't Category: Growth

✔ Domestic	Index
✔ Foreign	Sector
Asset Allocation	State Specific

Investment Style

✔ Large Cap	✔ Mid Cap	Small Cap
Growth	Grth/Val	✔ Value

Portfolio

20.0%	cash	0.0%	corp bonds
75.0%	stocks	0.0%	gov't bonds
0.0%	pref/conv't pref	0.0%	muni bonds
0.0%	conv't bds/wrnts	5.0%	other

SHAREHOLDER INFORMATION

Minimum Investment
Initial: $1,000 Subsequent: $50

Minimum IRA Investment
Initial: $250 Subsequent: $50

Maximum Fees
Load: none 12b-1: none
Other: none

Services
✔ IRA
Keogh
Telephone Exchange

Mutual Qualified/Z (MQIFX)

800-342-5236, 412-312-2000
www.franklintempleton.com

Growth & Income

this fund is closed to new investors

PERFORMANCE

fund inception date: 9/29/80

	3yr Annual	5yr Annual	10yr Annual	Bull	Bear
Return (%)	9.2	14.5	17.0	27.5	6.1
Differ from Category (+/-)	0.3 av	0.2 av	2.1 abv av	-6.0 av	6.2 abv av

Standard Deviation	Category Risk Index	Beta
15.4%—av	0.89—blw av	0.67

	2000	1999	1998	1997	1996	1995	1994	1993	1992	1991
Return (%)	14.2	13.6	0.5	24.9	21.1	26.5	5.7	22.7	22.6	21.1
Differ from Category (+/-)	8.5	2.8	-12.3	-2.0	1.4	-3.0	6.2	8.9	11.0	-7.0
Return, Tax-Adjusted (%)	10.5	11.1	-1.9	23.2	17.5	22.1	3.5	19.1	20.5	19.4

PER SHARE DATA

	2000	1999	1998	1997	1996	1995	1994	1993	1992	1991
Dividends, Net Income ($)	0.55	0.29	0.45	0.64	0.43	0.32	0.21	0.18	0.24	0.33
Distrib'ns, Cap Gain ($)	1.97	1.48	1.33	1.40	1.29	1.63	0.71	1.28	0.51	0.18
Net Asset Value ($)	16.61	16.91	16.46	18.18	16.23	14.87	13.34	13.50	12.22	10.59
Expense Ratio (%)	na	0.77	0.76	0.75	0.75	0.71	0.73	0.78	0.82	0.87
Yield (%)	2.96	1.57	2.52	3.26	2.48	1.96	1.53	1.25	1.92	3.10
Portfolio Turnover (%)	na	59	66	52	65	75	67	56	47	52
Total Assets (Millions $)	2,830	3,153	3,962	5,239	4,999	2,999	1,788	1,539	1,251	1,111

PORTFOLIO (as of 6/30/00)

Portfolio Manager: Garea, Diamond, Langerman - 1980

Investm't Category: Growth & Income

✔ Domestic　Index
✔ Foreign　Sector
Asset Allocation　State Specific

Investment Style

✔ Large Cap　✔ Mid Cap　Small Cap
Growth　Grth/Val　✔ Value

Portfolio

9.0%	cash	0.0%	corp bonds
84.0%	stocks	0.0%	gov't bonds
0.0%	pref/conv't pref	0.0%	muni bonds
0.0%	conv't bds/wrnts	7.0%	other

SHAREHOLDER INFORMATION

Minimum Investment
Initial: $1,000　Subsequent: $50

Minimum IRA Investment
Initial: $250　Subsequent: $50

Maximum Fees
Load: none　12b-1: none
Other: none

Services
✔ IRA
Keogh
Telephone Exchange

Mutual Shares/Z (MUTHX)

800-342-5236, 412-312-2000
www.franklintempleton.com

Growth & Income

this fund is closed to new investors

PERFORMANCE

fund inception date: 7/1/49

	3yr Annual	5yr Annual	10yr Annual	Bull	Bear
Return (%)	9.5	14.9	17.0	29.5	5.3
Differ from Category (+/-)	0.6 av	0.6 av	2.1 abv av	-4.0 av	5.4 abv av

Standard Deviation	Category Risk Index	Beta
15.1%—av	0.87—blw av	0.68

	2000	1999	1998	1997	1996	1995	1994	1993	1992	1991
Return (%)	13.8	15.0	0.4	26.3	20.7	29.1	4.5	20.9	21.3	20.9
Differ from Category (+/-)	8.1	4.2	-12.4	-0.6	1.0	-0.4	5.0	7.1	9.7	-7.2
Return, Tax-Adjusted (%)	9.9	12.5	-1.7	25.7	16.7	23.5	2.2	17.7	19.1	18.9

PER SHARE DATA

	2000	1999	1998	1997	1996	1995	1994	1993	1992	1991
Dividends, Net Income ($)	0.70	0.41	0.53	0.54	0.49	0.38	0.26	0.27	0.31	0.40
Distrib'ns, Cap Gain ($)	2.50	1.57	1.29	1.58	1.73	2.56	0.91	1.26	0.63	0.32
Net Asset Value ($)	19.79	20.43	19.54	21.29	18.57	17.29	15.74	16.19	14.67	12.90
Expense Ratio (%)	na	0.75	0.73	0.72	0.70	0.70	0.72	0.74	0.78	0.82
Yield (%)	3.14	1.86	2.54	2.36	2.44	1.94	1.60	1.58	2.07	3.02
Portfolio Turnover (%)	na	66	69	49	58	79	66	48	41	48
Total Assets (Millions $)	5,160	5,573	6,289	7,917	6,107	5,224	3,745	3,527	2,915	2,642

PORTFOLIO (as of 6/30/00)

Portfolio Manager: Sondike, Potto, Langerman - 1985

Investm't Category: Growth & Income

✔ Domestic — Index
✔ Foreign — Sector
Asset Allocation — State Specific

Investment Style

✔ Large Cap — Mid Cap — Small Cap
Growth — Grth/Val — ✔ Value

Portfolio

12.0%	cash	0.0%	corp bonds
82.0%	stocks	0.0%	gov't bonds
0.0%	pref/conv't pref	0.0%	muni bonds
0.0%	conv't bds/wrnts	6.0%	other

SHAREHOLDER INFORMATION

Minimum Investment

Initial: $1,000 — Subsequent: $50

Minimum IRA Investment

Initial: $250 — Subsequent: $50

Maximum Fees

Load: none — 12b-1: none
Other: none

Services

✔ IRA
Keogh
Telephone Exchange

NI Numeric Inv Grth (NISGX)

800-686-3742, 617-577-1166
www.numeric.com

Aggressive Growth

PERFORMANCE

fund inception date: 5/31/96

	3yr Annual	5yr Annual	10yr Annual	Bull	Bear
Return (%)	13.4	na	na	102.3	-28.1
Differ from Category (+/-)	-2.8 av	na	na	-16.9 av	-7.5 blw av

Standard Deviation	Category Risk Index	Beta
34.1%—high	1.05—av	1.29

	2000	1999	1998	1997	1996	1995	1994	1993	1992	1991
Return (%)	-4.3	49.4	2.2	15.6	—	—	—	—	—	—
Differ from Category (+/-)	1.7	-8.1	-12.9	0.8	—	—	—	—	—	—
Return, Tax-Adjusted (%)	-11.0	48.8	2.2	11.8	—	—	—	—	—	—

PER SHARE DATA

	2000	1999	1998	1997	1996	1995	1994	1993	1992	1991
Dividends, Net Income ($)	0.00	0.00	0.00	0.00	—	—	—	—	—	—
Distrib'ns, Cap Gain ($)	6.52	0.36	0.00	2.49	—	—	—	—	—	—
Net Asset Value ($)	12.81	19.23	13.19	12.91	—	—	—	—	—	—
Expense Ratio (%)	1.00	1.00	1.00	1.00	—	—	—	—	—	—
Yield (%)	0.00	0.00	0.00	0.00	—	—	—	—	—	—
Portfolio Turnover (%)	228	309	338	266	—	—	—	—	—	—
Total Assets (Millions $)	49	74	98	116	—	—	—	—	—	—

PORTFOLIO (as of 6/30/00)

Portfolio Manager: committee - 1996

Investm't Category: Aggressive Growth

✔ Domestic
Foreign
Asset Allocation
Index
Sector
State Specific

Investment Style

Large Cap
Mid Cap
✔ Small Cap
✔ Growth
Grth/Val
Value

Portfolio

0.0%	cash	0.0%	corp bonds
97.0%	stocks	0.0%	gov't bonds
0.0%	pref/conv't pref	0.0%	muni bonds
0.0%	conv't bds/wrnts	3.0%	other

SHAREHOLDER INFORMATION

Minimum Investment
Initial: $3,000 Subsequent: $100

Minimum IRA Investment
Initial: $1,000 Subsequent: $100

Maximum Fees
Load: none 12b-1: none
Other: none

Services
✔ IRA
✔ Keogh
✔ Telephone Exchange

NI Numeric Inv Micro Cap (NIMCX)

800-686-3742, 617-577-1166
www.numeric.com

Aggressive Growth

this fund is closed to new investors

PERFORMANCE — fund inception date: 5/31/96

	3yr Annual	5yr Annual	10yr Annual	Bull	Bear
Return (%)	16.9	na	na	95.7	-20.6
Differ from Category (+/-)	0.7 av	na	na	-23.5 av	0.0 av

Standard Deviation	Category Risk Index	Beta
31.6%—high	0.98—av	1.24

	2000	1999	1998	1997	1996	1995	1994	1993	1992	1991
Return (%)	2.2	34.4	16.2	30.8	—	—	—	—	—	—
Differ from Category (+/-)	-8.2	-23.1	1.1	16.0	—	—	—	—	—	—
Return, Tax-Adjusted (%)	-3.2	29.2	14.8	27.0	—	—	—	—	—	—

PER SHARE DATA

	2000	1999	1998	1997	1996	1995	1994	1993	1992	1991
Dividends, Net Income ($)	0.00	0.00	0.00	0.00	—	—	—	—	—	—
Distrib'ns, Cap Gain ($)	4.61	4.33	1.02	2.64	—	—	—	—	—	—
Net Asset Value ($)	13.24	17.05	16.82	15.68	—	—	—	—	—	—
Expense Ratio (%)	1.00	1.00	1.00	1.00	—	—	—	—	—	—
Yield (%)	0.00	0.00	0.00	0.00	—	—	—	—	—	—
Portfolio Turnover (%)	297	316	408	233	—	—	—	—	—	—
Total Assets (Millions $)	101	117	129	131	—	—	—	—	—	—

PORTFOLIO (as of 6/30/00)

Portfolio Manager: committee - 1996

Investm't Category: Aggressive Growth

✔ Domestic
Foreign
Asset Allocation
Index
Sector
State Specific

Investment Style

Large Cap
Mid Cap
✔ Small Cap
✔ Growth
Grth/Val
Value

Portfolio

0.0% cash	0.0% corp bonds
93.5% stocks	0.0% gov't bonds
0.0% pref/conv't pref	0.0% muni bonds
0.0% conv't bds/wrnts	6.5% other

SHAREHOLDER INFORMATION

Minimum Investment
Initial: $3,000 Subsequent: $100

Minimum IRA Investment
Initial: $1,000 Subsequent: $100

Maximum Fees
Load: none 12b-1: none
Other: none

Services
✔ IRA
✔ Keogh
✔ Telephone Exchange

Navellier: Agg Growth (NPFGX)

800-887-8671, 775-785-2300
www.navellier.com

Aggressive Growth

PERFORMANCE

fund inception date: 12/28/95

	3yr Annual	5yr Annual	10yr Annual	Bull	Bear
Return (%)	18.8	17.7	na	102.5	-6.7
Differ from Category (+/-)	2.6 av	3.1 av	na	-16.7 av	13.9 high

Standard Deviation	Category Risk Index	Beta
27.4%—high	0.85—blw av	1.04

	2000	1999	1998	1997	1996	1995	1994	1993	1992	1991
Return (%)	3.0	46.1	11.5	9.7	22.6	—	—	—	—	—
Differ from Category (+/-)	9.0	-11.4	-3.6	-5.1	4.3	—	—	—	—	—
Return, Tax-Adjusted (%)	-0.3	42.5	11.5	9.4	22.6	—	—	—	—	—

PER SHARE DATA

	2000	1999	1998	1997	1996	1995	1994	1993	1992	1991
Dividends, Net Income ($)	0.00	0.00	0.00	0.00	0.00	—	—	—	—	—
Distrib'ns, Cap Gain ($)	3.19	2.60	0.00	0.15	0.00	—	—	—	—	—
Net Asset Value ($)	16.22	19.01	14.82	13.29	12.25	—	—	—	—	—
Expense Ratio (%)	na	1.49	1.68	2.00	2.00	—	—	—	—	—
Yield (%)	0.00	0.00	0.00	0.00	0.00	—	—	—	—	—
Portfolio Turnover (%)	na	702	237	247	169	—	—	—	—	—
Total Assets (Millions $)	83	87	80	101	95	—	—	—	—	—

PORTFOLIO (as of 6/30/00)

Portfolio Manager: Louis Navellier, Alan Alpers - 1995

Investm't Category: Aggressive Growth

✔ Domestic	Index
Foreign	Sector
Asset Allocation	State Specific

Investment Style

Large Cap	✔ Mid Cap	✔ Small Cap
✔ Growth	Grth/Val	Value

Portfolio

9.3% cash	0.0% corp bonds
90.7% stocks	0.0% gov't bonds
0.0% pref/conv't pref	0.0% muni bonds
0.0% conv't bds/wrnts	0.0% other

SHAREHOLDER INFORMATION

Minimum Investment

Initial: $2,000 Subsequent: $100

Minimum IRA Investment

Initial: $500 Subsequent: $100

Maximum Fees

Load: none 12b-1: 0.25%

Other: none

Services

✔ IRA

✔ Keogh

Telephone Exchange

Neuberger Focus (NBSSX)

800-877-9700, 212-476-8800
www.nbfunds.com

Growth

PERFORMANCE

fund inception date: 10/19/55

	3yr Annual	5yr Annual	10yr Annual	Bull	Bear
Return (%)	17.0	18.2	18.7	69.9	-10.6
Differ from Category (+/-)	6.0 high	2.1 abv av	1.9 abv av	20.2 abv av	-5.2 av

Standard Deviation	Category Risk Index	Beta
29.4%—high	1.51—high	1.47

	2000	1999	1998	1997	1996	1995	1994	1993	1992	1991
Return (%)	12.4	26.0	13.2	24.1	16.2	36.1	0.8	16.3	21.0	24.6
Differ from Category (+/-)	8.9	7.1	-1.1	-3.0	-6.1	5.7	1.0	1.7	8.4	-13.0
Return, Tax-Adjusted (%)	10.2	22.9	11.9	20.8	14.4	34.1	-1.3	13.6	17.5	22.5

PER SHARE DATA

	2000	1999	1998	1997	1996	1995	1994	1993	1992	1991
Dividends, Net Income ($)	0.00	0.01	0.09	0.06	0.22	0.11	0.20	0.25	0.28	0.36
Distrib'ns, Cap Gain ($)	4.23	5.31	1.97	4.93	1.43	1.35	1.48	1.70	2.13	0.87
Net Asset Value ($)	39.40	39.10	35.40	33.08	30.82	27.93	21.58	23.06	21.50	19.97
Expense Ratio (%)	0.85	0.85	0.84	0.86	0.89	0.87	0.85	0.92	0.91	0.93
Yield (%)	0.00	0.02	0.24	0.15	0.68	0.37	0.86	1.00	1.18	1.72
Portfolio Turnover (%)	55	57	64	63	39	36	52	52	77	60
Total Assets (Millions $)	1,557	1,548	1,418	1,368	1,178	1,027	603	591	497	421

PORTFOLIO (as of 6/30/00)

Portfolio Manager: Kent Simons - 1988

Investm't Category: Growth

✔ Domestic | Index
✔ Foreign | Sector
Asset Allocation | State Specific

Investment Style

✔ Large Cap | Mid Cap | Small Cap
Growth | ✔ Grth/Val | Value

Portfolio

2.7%	cash	0.0%	corp bonds
97.3%	stocks	0.0%	gov't bonds
0.0%	pref/conv't pref	0.0%	muni bonds
0.0%	conv't bds/wrnts	0.0%	other

SHAREHOLDER INFORMATION

Minimum Investment

Initial: $1,000 Subsequent: $100

Minimum IRA Investment

Initial: $250 Subsequent: $100

Maximum Fees

Load: none 12b-1: none
Other: none

Services

✔ IRA
✔ Keogh
✔ Telephone Exchange

Neuberger Genesis (NBGNX)

800-877-9700, 212-476-8800
www.nbfunds.com

Growth

PERFORMANCE

fund inception date: 9/27/88

	3yr Annual	5yr Annual	10yr Annual	Bull	Bear
Return (%)	8.6	17.5	18.0	24.4	9.0
Differ from Category (+/-)	-2.4 blw av	1.4 av	1.2 abv av	-25.3 blw av	14.4 high

Standard Deviation	Category Risk Index	Beta
18.0%—av	0.93—blw av	0.66

	2000	1999	1998	1997	1996	1995	1994	1993	1992	1991
Return (%)	32.5	4.0	-6.9	34.8	29.8	27.3	-1.8	13.8	15.6	41.5
Differ from Category (+/-)	29.0	-14.9	-21.2	7.7	7.5	-3.1	-1.6	-0.8	3.0	3.9
Return, Tax-Adjusted (%)	31.1	3.7	-7.6	34.4	29.3	25.3	-2.8	11.0	15.6	40.9

PER SHARE DATA

	2000	1999	1998	1997	1996	1995	1994	1993	1992	1991
Dividends, Net Income ($)	0.00	0.08	0.12	0.00	0.00	0.00	0.00	0.01	0.00	0.01
Distrib'ns, Cap Gain ($)	1.04	0.00	0.34	0.19	0.15	0.55	0.31	0.75	0.00	0.09
Net Asset Value ($)	18.67	14.94	14.44	16.03	12.03	9.38	7.80	8.26	7.92	6.85
Expense Ratio (%)	1.21	1.17	1.10	1.16	1.28	1.35	1.36	1.65	2.00	2.00
Yield (%)	0.00	0.53	0.81	0.00	0.00	0.00	0.00	0.11	0.00	0.14
Portfolio Turnover (%)	38	33	18	18	21	37	63	54	23	46
Total Assets (Millions $)	753	735	1,194	1,246	298	118	108	124	87	42

PORTFOLIO (as of 6/30/00)

Portfolio Manager: Judith Vale, Robert D'Alelio - 1994

Investm't Category: Growth

✔ Domestic | Index
✔ Foreign | Sector
Asset Allocation | State Specific

Investment Style

Large Cap | ✔ Mid Cap | ✔ Small Cap
Growth | Grth/Val | ✔ Value

Portfolio

5.9%	cash	0.0%	corp bonds
94.1%	stocks	0.0%	gov't bonds
0.0%	pref/conv't pref	0.0%	muni bonds
0.0%	conv't bds/wrnts	0.0%	other

SHAREHOLDER INFORMATION

Minimum Investment

Initial: $1,000 Subsequent: $100

Minimum IRA Investment

Initial: $250 Subsequent: $100

Maximum Fees

Load: none 12b-1: none
Other: none

Services

✔ IRA
✔ Keogh
✔ Telephone Exchange

Neuberger Guardian

800-877-9700, 212-476-8800
www.nbfunds.com

(NGUAX)

Growth

PERFORMANCE

fund inception date: 6/1/50

	3yr Annual	5yr Annual	10yr Annual	Bull	Bear
Return (%)	2.8	8.6	13.9	34.5	-8.9
Differ from Category (+/-)	-8.2 low	-7.5 low	-2.9 blw av	-15.2 blw av	-3.5 av

Standard Deviation	Category Risk Index	Beta
23.3%—abv av	1.20—abv av	1.20

	2000	1999	1998	1997	1996	1995	1994	1993	1992	1991
Return (%)	-1.8	8.4	2.3	17.9	17.8	32.1	0.6	14.4	19.0	34.3
Differ from Category (+/-)	-5.3	-10.5	-12.0	-9.2	-4.5	1.7	0.8	-0.2	6.4	-3.3
Return, Tax-Adjusted (%)	-5.4	3.1	-0.9	14.5	15.8	30.3	-0.2	13.9	17.2	31.3

PER SHARE DATA

	2000	1999	1998	1997	1996	1995	1994	1993	1992	1991
Dividends, Net Income ($)	0.12	0.19	0.15	0.18	0.27	0.28	0.25	0.30	0.25	0.31
Distrib'ns, Cap Gain ($)	3.10	5.48	3.91	4.00	1.24	0.76	0.23	0.40	0.66	0.90
Net Asset Value ($)	14.84	18.50	22.42	25.90	25.63	23.03	18.23	18.60	16.87	14.97
Expense Ratio (%)	0.84	0.82	0.79	0.80	0.82	0.80	0.80	0.81	0.82	0.84
Yield (%)	0.66	0.79	0.56	0.60	1.00	1.17	1.35	1.57	1.46	1.99
Portfolio Turnover (%)	83	73	60	50	37	26	24	27	41	59
Total Assets (Millions $)	2,262	3,131	4,394	5,987	5,473	4,389	2,423	1,973	1,038	682

PORTFOLIO (as of 6/30/00)

Portfolio Manager: Kevin Risen, Rick White - 1996

Investm't Category: Growth

✔ Domestic	Index
✔ Foreign	Sector
Asset Allocation	State Specific

Investment Style

✔ Large Cap	Mid Cap	Small Cap
Growth	Grth/Val	✔ Value

Portfolio

3.8%	cash	0.0%	corp bonds
93.2%	stocks	0.0%	gov't bonds
3.0%	pref/conv't pref	0.0%	muni bonds
0.0%	conv't bds/wrnts	0.0%	other

SHAREHOLDER INFORMATION

Minimum Investment
Initial: $1,000 Subsequent: $100

Minimum IRA Investment
Initial: $250 Subsequent: $100

Maximum Fees
Load: none 12b-1: none
Other: none

Services
✔ IRA
✔ Keogh
✔ Telephone Exchange

Neuberger Intl (NBISX)

800-877-9700, 212-476-8800
www.nbfunds.com

International Stock

PERFORMANCE

fund inception date: 6/15/94

	3yr Annual	5yr Annual	10yr Annual	Bull	Bear
Return (%)	8.6	12.0	na	77.3	-27.5
Differ from Category (+/-)	-0.3 av	3.7 abv av	na	-13.6 av	-3.5 av

Standard Deviation	Category Risk Index	Beta
25.3%—high	1.12—abv av	0.80

	2000	1999	1998	1997	1996	1995	1994	1993	1992	1991
Return (%)	-24.3	65.8	2.3	11.2	23.6	7.8	—	—	—	—
Differ from Category (+/-)	-4.9	5.1	-3.5	9.9	9.1	-1.5	—	—	—	—
Return, Tax-Adjusted (%)	-27.8	65.4	2.2	10.9	23.5	7.6	—	—	—	—

PER SHARE DATA

	2000	1999	1998	1997	1996	1995	1994	1993	1992	1991
Dividends, Net Income ($)	0.00	0.01	0.00	0.00	0.02	0.04	—	—	—	—
Distrib'ns, Cap Gain ($)	4.32	0.21	0.01	0.14	0.00	0.00	—	—	—	—
Net Asset Value ($)	14.04	24.31	14.80	14.47	13.14	10.64	—	—	—	—
Expense Ratio (%)	1.43	1.61	1.62	1.70	1.70	1.70	—	—	—	—
Yield (%)	0.00	0.04	0.00	0.00	0.15	0.37	—	—	—	—
Portfolio Turnover (%)	80	94	46	37	45	41	—	—	—	—
Total Assets (Millions $)	140	191	127	111	73	33	—	—	—	—

PORTFOLIO (as of 6/30/00)

Portfolio Manager: Valerie Chang, Benjamin Segal - 1997

Investm't Category: International Stock

Domestic | Index
✔ Foreign | Sector
Asset Allocation | State Specific

Investment Style

Large Cap | Mid Cap | Small Cap
Growth | Grth/Val | Value

Portfolio

7.0% cash | 0.0% corp bonds
91.2% stocks | 0.0% gov't bonds
1.8% pref/conv't pref | 0.0% muni bonds
0.0% conv't bds/wrnts | 0.0% other

SHAREHOLDER INFORMATION

Minimum Investment
Initial: $1,000 | Subsequent: $100

Minimum IRA Investment
Initial: $250 | Subsequent: $100

Maximum Fees
Load: none | 12b-1: none
Other: none

Services
✔ IRA
✔ Keogh
✔ Telephone Exchange

Neuberger Manhattan (NMANX)

800-877-9700, 212-476-8800
www.nbfunds.com

Growth

PERFORMANCE — fund inception date: 2/15/66

	3yr Annual	5yr Annual	10yr Annual	Bull	Bear
Return (%)	15.8	17.1	16.7	105.0	-33.3
Differ from Category (+/-)	4.8 abv av	1.0 av	-0.1 av	55.3 high	-27.9 low

Standard Deviation	Category Risk Index	Beta
37.8%—high	1.94—high	1.37

	2000	1999	1998	1997	1996	1995	1994	1993	1992	1991
Return (%)	-11.4	50.7	16.3	29.2	9.8	31.0	-3.6	10.0	17.7	30.8
Differ from Category (+/-)	-14.9	31.8	2.0	2.1	-12.5	0.6	-3.4	-4.6	5.1	-6.8
Return, Tax-Adjusted (%)	-17.8	48.6	14.7	22.6	5.9	28.3	-5.3	5.1	13.5	29.2

PER SHARE DATA

	2000	1999	1998	1997	1996	1995	1994	1993	1992	1991
Dividends, Net Income ($)	0.00	0.00	0.00	0.00	0.00	0.00	0.01	0.02	0.05	0.11
Distrib'ns, Cap Gain ($)	5.36	1.20	0.83	3.84	1.66	0.96	0.70	2.06	1.68	0.40
Net Asset Value ($)	9.54	16.69	11.95	11.01	11.68	12.14	10.00	11.11	11.99	11.65
Expense Ratio (%)	0.92	1.00	0.94	0.98	0.98	0.98	0.96	1.04	1.07	1.09
Yield (%)	0.00	0.00	0.00	0.00	0.00	0.00	0.09	0.15	0.36	0.91
Portfolio Turnover (%)	105	115	90	89	53	44	50	76	83	78
Total Assets (Millions $)	749	822	627	571	531	594	462	524	514	463

PORTFOLIO (as of 6/30/00)

Portfolio Manager: Jennifer Silver, Brooke Cobb - 1997

Investm't Category: Growth

✔ Domestic	Index
✔ Foreign	Sector
Asset Allocation	State Specific

Investment Style

Large Cap	✔ Mid Cap	✔ Small Cap
✔ Growth	Grth/Val	Value

Portfolio

2.7%	cash	0.0%	corp bonds
97.3%	stocks	0.0%	gov't bonds
0.0%	pref/conv't pref	0.0%	muni bonds
0.0%	conv't bds/wrnts	0.0%	other

SHAREHOLDER INFORMATION

Minimum Investment
Initial: $1,000 — Subsequent: $100

Minimum IRA Investment
Initial: $250 — Subsequent: $100

Maximum Fees
Load: none — 12b-1: none
Other: none

Services
✔ IRA
✔ Keogh
✔ Telephone Exchange

Neuberger Partners (NPRTX)

800-877-9700, 212-476-8800
www.nbfunds.com

Growth & Income

PERFORMANCE

fund inception date: 7/16/68

	3yr Annual	5yr Annual	10yr Annual	Bull	Bear
Return (%)	4.8	13.4	15.3	31.1	-5.3
Differ from Category (+/-)	-4.1 low	-0.9 blw av	0.4 av	-2.4 av	-5.2 av

Standard Deviation	Category Risk Index	Beta
17.4%—av	1.00—av	0.88

	2000	1999	1998	1997	1996	1995	1994	1993	1992	1991
Return (%)	0.5	7.7	6.2	29.2	26.4	35.2	-1.8	16.4	17.5	22.3
Differ from Category (+/-)	-5.2	-3.1	-6.6	2.3	6.7	5.7	-1.3	2.6	5.9	-5.8
Return, Tax-Adjusted (%)	-1.3	4.8	4.3	24.2	22.7	30.6	-4.1	13.0	14.4	20.2

PER SHARE DATA

	2000	1999	1998	1997	1996	1995	1994	1993	1992	1991
Dividends, Net Income ($)	0.17	0.29	0.00	0.19	0.22	0.20	0.11	0.11	0.19	0.34
Distrib'ns, Cap Gain ($)	1.93	3.10	2.41	5.84	2.61	2.70	1.60	2.20	1.79	0.78
Net Asset Value ($)	21.93	24.00	25.50	26.30	25.19	22.14	18.52	20.62	19.69	18.44
Expense Ratio (%)	0.84	0.82	0.80	0.81	0.84	0.83	0.81	0.86	0.86	0.88
Yield (%)	0.71	1.07	0.00	0.59	0.79	0.80	0.54	0.48	0.88	1.76
Portfolio Turnover (%)	95	132	109	77	96	98	75	82	97	161
Total Assets (Millions $)	1,922	2,667	3,249	3,230	2,218	1,656	1,245	1,127	974	889

PORTFOLIO (as of 6/30/00)

Portfolio Manager: R. Gendelman, S. Mullick - 1990

Investm't Category: Growth & Income

✔ Domestic
✔ Foreign
Asset Allocation
Index
Sector
State Specific

Investment Style

✔ Large Cap
Growth
Mid Cap
Grth/Val
Small Cap
✔ Value

Portfolio

1.2%	cash	0.0%	corp bonds
96.1%	stocks	0.0%	gov't bonds
2.7%	pref/conv't pref	0.0%	muni bonds
0.0%	conv't bds/wrnts	0.0%	other

SHAREHOLDER INFORMATION

Minimum Investment

Initial: $1,000 Subsequent: $100

Minimum IRA Investment

Initial: $250 Subsequent: $100

Maximum Fees

Load: none 12b-1: none
Other: none

Services

✔ IRA
✔ Keogh
✔ Telephone Exchange

Neuberger Soc Respv (NBSRX)

800-877-9700, 212-476-8800
www.nbfunds.com

Growth

PERFORMANCE — fund inception date: 3/15/94

	3yr Annual	5yr Annual	10yr Annual	Bull	Bear
Return (%)	7.0	12.5	na	37.5	-4.4
Differ from Category (+/-)	-4.0 blw av	-3.6 blw av	na	-12.2 blw av	1.0 av

Standard Deviation	Category Risk Index	Beta
18.3%—av	0.94—blw av	0.93

	2000	1999	1998	1997	1996	1995	1994	1993	1992	1991
Return (%)	-0.4	7.0	15.0	24.4	18.4	38.9	—	—	—	—
Differ from Category (+/-)	-3.9	-11.9	0.7	-2.7	-3.9	8.5	—	—	—	—
Return, Tax-Adjusted (%)	-0.4	6.0	13.8	23.7	17.4	37.9	—	—	—	—

PER SHARE DATA

	2000	1999	1998	1997	1996	1995	1994	1993	1992	1991
Dividends, Net Income ($)	0.00	0.02	0.07	0.03	0.03	0.02	—	—	—	—
Distrib'ns, Cap Gain ($)	0.00	0.87	0.88	0.40	0.42	0.31	—	—	—	—
Net Asset Value ($)	20.39	20.48	20.00	18.24	15.02	13.05	—	—	—	—
Expense Ratio (%)	1.12	1.10	1.10	1.48	1.50	1.51	—	—	—	—
Yield (%)	0.00	0.09	0.33	0.16	0.19	0.14	—	—	—	—
Portfolio Turnover (%)	76	53	47	51	53	58	—	—	—	—
Total Assets (Millions $)	94	119	106	71	42	11	—	—	—	—

PORTFOLIO (as of 6/30/00)

Portfolio Manager: Janet Prindle - 1994

Investm't Category: Growth

✔ Domestic | Index
✔ Foreign | Sector
Asset Allocation | State Specific

Investment Style

✔ Large Cap | Mid Cap | Small Cap
Growth | Grth/Val | ✔ Value

Portfolio

2.1% cash | 0.0% corp bonds
97.9% stocks | 0.0% gov't bonds
0.0% pref/conv't pref | 0.0% muni bonds
0.0% conv't bds/wrnts | 0.0% other

SHAREHOLDER INFORMATION

Minimum Investment

Initial: $1,000 | Subsequent: $100

Minimum IRA Investment

Initial: $250 | Subsequent: $100

Maximum Fees

Load: none | 12b-1: none
Other: none

Services

✔ IRA
✔ Keogh
✔ Telephone Exchange

Nicholas (NICSX)

800-227-5987, 414-272-6133
www.nicholasfunds.com

Growth

PERFORMANCE

fund inception date: 7/14/69

	3yr Annual	5yr Annual	10yr Annual	Bull	Bear
Return (%)	4.2	13.2	15.2	26.6	-7.1
Differ from Category (+/-)	-6.8 low	-2.9 blw av	-1.6 blw av	-23.1 blw av	-1.7 av

Standard Deviation	Category Risk Index	Beta
17.8%—av	0.92—blw av	0.92

	2000	1999	1998	1997	1996	1995	1994	1993	1992	1991
Return (%)	-1.4	1.7	13.1	37.0	19.7	35.3	-2.8	5.8	12.6	41.9
Differ from Category (+/-)	-4.9	-17.2	-1.2	9.9	-2.6	4.9	-2.6	-8.8	0.0	4.3
Return, Tax-Adjusted (%)	-6.2	0.1	10.8	35.0	16.9	32.4	-5.0	4.6	11.0	40.6

PER SHARE DATA

	2000	1999	1998	1997	1996	1995	1994	1993	1992	1991
Dividends, Net Income ($)	0.19	0.31	0.58	0.33	0.56	0.62	0.70	0.81	0.71	0.67
Distrib'ns, Cap Gain ($)	19.25	5.94	8.27	5.82	5.17	4.03	3.31	1.04	2.01	0.82
Net Asset Value ($)	61.45	81.15	85.82	83.80	65.94	60.03	48.03	53.64	52.47	49.17
Expense Ratio (%)	0.73	0.71	0.71	0.72	0.74	0.77	0.78	0.76	0.78	0.81
Yield (%)	0.23	0.35	0.61	0.36	0.78	0.96	1.36	1.48	1.30	1.34
Portfolio Turnover (%)	39	25	17	15	26	29	33	10	15	22
Total Assets (Millions $)	4,082	5,154	5,823	5,257	3,984	3,505	2,820	3,179	2,772	2,103

PORTFOLIO (as of 6/30/00)

Portfolio Manager: Albert Nicholas, David Nicholas - 1969

Investm't Category: Growth

✔ Domestic | Index
Foreign | Sector
Asset Allocation | State Specific

Investment Style

✔ Large Cap | ✔ Mid Cap | Small Cap
Growth | Grth/Val | ✔ Value

Portfolio

3.3%	cash	0.0%	corp bonds
96.7%	stocks	0.0%	gov't bonds
0.0%	pref/conv't pref	0.0%	muni bonds
0.0%	conv't bds/wrnts	0.0%	other

SHAREHOLDER INFORMATION

Minimum Investment

Initial: $500 Subsequent: $100

Minimum IRA Investment

Initial: $500 Subsequent: $100

Maximum Fees

Load: none 12b-1: none
Other: none

Services

✔ IRA
✔ Keogh
✔ Telephone Exchange

Nicholas II (NCTWX)

800-227-5987, 414-272-6133
www.nicholasfunds.com

Growth

PERFORMANCE — fund inception date: 10/17/83

	3yr Annual	5yr Annual	10yr Annual	Bull	Bear
Return (%)	2.6	12.0	14.0	24.0	-4.3
Differ from Category (+/-)	-8.4 low	-4.1 blw av	-2.8 blw av	-25.7 blw av	1.1 av

Standard Deviation	Category Risk Index	Beta
19.1%—abv av	0.98—blw av	0.95

	2000	1999	1998	1997	1996	1995	1994	1993	1992	1991
Return (%)	-2.0	1.1	9.2	37.0	19.3	28.5	1.0	6.4	9.3	39.5
Differ from Category (+/-)	-5.5	-17.8	-5.1	9.9	-3.0	-1.9	1.2	-8.2	-3.3	1.9
Return, Tax-Adjusted (%)	-9.2	0.8	6.8	33.5	16.0	25.3	-1.3	4.5	8.1	38.4

PER SHARE DATA

	2000	1999	1998	1997	1996	1995	1994	1993	1992	1991
Dividends, Net Income ($)	0.00	0.01	0.13	0.06	0.22	0.27	0.31	0.27	0.23	0.24
Distrib'ns, Cap Gain ($)	13.12	0.47	4.00	5.24	3.02	2.40	1.79	1.40	0.80	0.40
Net Asset Value ($)	21.34	35.96	36.03	36.94	30.99	28.73	24.46	26.32	26.32	25.02
Expense Ratio (%)	0.62	0.61	0.59	0.61	0.62	0.66	0.67	0.67	0.66	0.70
Yield (%)	0.00	0.02	0.32	0.14	0.64	0.86	1.18	0.97	0.84	0.94
Portfolio Turnover (%)	65	21	20	30	24	19	17	27	11	12
Total Assets (Millions $)	703	940	1,109	1,024	784	693	603	703	742	557

PORTFOLIO (as of 6/30/00)

Portfolio Manager: David Nicholas - 1993

Investm't Category: Growth

✔ Domestic	Index
Foreign	Sector
Asset Allocation	State Specific

Investment Style

✔ Large Cap	✔ Mid Cap	Small Cap
Growth	Grth/Val	✔ Value

Portfolio

3.6% cash	0.0% corp bonds
96.4% stocks	0.0% gov't bonds
0.0% pref/conv't pref	0.0% muni bonds
0.0% conv't bds/wrnts	0.0% other

SHAREHOLDER INFORMATION

Minimum Investment

Initial: $500 Subsequent: $100

Minimum IRA Investment

Initial: $500 Subsequent: $100

Maximum Fees

Load: none 12b-1: none

Other: none

Services

✔ IRA

✔ Keogh

✔ Telephone Exchange

Nicholas Limited Edition (NCLEX)

800-227-5987, 414-272-6133
www.nicholasfunds.com

Growth

PERFORMANCE — fund inception date: 5/18/87

	3yr Annual	5yr Annual	10yr Annual	Bull	Bear
Return (%)	-3.7	7.6	12.7	20.7	-17.2
Differ from Category (+/-)	-14.7 low	-8.5 low	-4.1 low	-29.0 low	-11.8 blw av

Standard Deviation	Category Risk Index	Beta
20.8%—abv av	1.07—av	0.90

	2000	1999	1998	1997	1996	1995	1994	1993	1992	1991
Return (%)	-8.6	-4.0	1.6	33.0	21.8	30.1	-3.0	9.0	16.7	43.2
Differ from Category (+/-)	-12.1	-22.9	-12.7	5.9	-0.5	-0.3	-2.8	-5.6	4.1	5.6
Return, Tax-Adjusted (%)	-13.7	-4.5	0.5	30.6	17.6	24.9	-4.5	6.3	15.1	42.3

PER SHARE DATA

	2000	1999	1998	1997	1996	1995	1994	1993	1992	1991
Dividends, Net Income ($)	0.21	0.05	0.01	0.00	0.52	0.30	0.10	0.08	0.08	0.12
Distrib'ns, Cap Gain ($)	5.37	0.54	1.24	2.48	2.09	2.71	0.90	1.67	0.82	0.24
Net Asset Value ($)	15.16	22.61	24.20	25.07	20.74	19.22	17.09	18.68	18.77	16.86
Expense Ratio (%)	na	0.87	0.85	0.86	0.86	0.90	0.90	0.88	0.92	0.94
Yield (%)	1.02	0.21	0.03	0.00	2.27	1.36	0.55	0.39	0.40	0.70
Portfolio Turnover (%)	na	36	30	37	32	35	16	24	24	13
Total Assets (Millions $)	194	278	367	328	232	169	142	180	190	175

PORTFOLIO (as of 6/30/00)

Portfolio Manager: David Nicholas - 1993

Investm't Category: Growth

✔ Domestic | Index
Foreign | Sector
Asset Allocation | State Specific

Investment Style

Large Cap | ✔ Mid Cap | ✔ Small Cap
Growth | ✔ Grth/Val | Value

Portfolio

9.5%	cash	0.0%	corp bonds
90.5%	stocks	0.0%	gov't bonds
0.0%	pref/conv't pref	0.0%	muni bonds
0.0%	conv't bds/wrnts	0.0%	other

SHAREHOLDER INFORMATION

Minimum Investment
Initial: $2,000 Subsequent: $100

Minimum IRA Investment
Initial: $2,000 Subsequent: $100

Maximum Fees
Load: none 12b-1: none
Other: none

Services
✔ IRA
✔ Keogh
✔ Telephone Exchange

Northeast Inv Growth

800-225-6704, 617-523-3588
www.northeastinvestors.com

(NTHFX)

Growth

PERFORMANCE — fund inception date: 10/27/80

	3yr Annual	5yr Annual	10yr Annual	Bull	Bear
Return (%)	13.5	20.1	16.8	73.4	-19.4
Differ from Category (+/-)	2.5 abv av	4.0 high	0.0 av	23.7 abv av	-14.0 low

Standard Deviation	Category Risk Index	Beta
22.6%—abv av	1.16—abv av	1.20

	2000	1999	1998	1997	1996	1995	1994	1993	1992	1991
Return (%)	-14.9	29.1	33.3	37.2	24.6	36.4	0.0	2.3	-0.7	36.9
Differ from Category (+/-)	-18.4	10.2	19.0	10.1	2.3	6.0	0.2	-12.3	-13.3	-0.7
Return, Tax-Adjusted (%)	-16.4	28.7	32.4	36.7	21.8	34.5	-0.8	-2.2	-2.3	35.7

PER SHARE DATA

	2000	1999	1998	1997	1996	1995	1994	1993	1992	1991
Dividends, Net Income ($)	0.00	0.01	0.05	0.05	0.07	0.07	0.06	0.06	0.06	0.12
Distrib'ns, Cap Gain ($)	2.05	0.30	0.54	0.76	0.98	0.44	0.16	1.48	0.52	0.18
Net Asset Value ($)	20.23	26.08	20.47	15.84	12.15	10.59	8.13	8.37	9.70	10.37
Expense Ratio (%)	na	0.85	0.83	0.97	1.21	1.54	1.53	1.45	1.42	1.50
Yield (%)	0.00	0.03	0.23	0.30	0.40	0.63	0.76	0.64	0.65	1.13
Portfolio Turnover (%)	na	31	33	16	25	26	25	35	29	16
Total Assets (Millions $)	276	356	210	108	60	48	35	38	42	40

PORTFOLIO (as of 6/30/00)

Portfolio Manager: William Oates - 1980

Investm't Category: Growth

✔ Domestic	Index
Foreign	Sector
Asset Allocation	State Specific

Investment Style

✔ Large Cap	Mid Cap	Small Cap
✔ Growth	Grth/Val	Value

Portfolio

0.0%	cash	0.0%	corp bonds
100.0%	stocks	0.0%	gov't bonds
0.0%	pref/conv't pref	0.0%	muni bonds
0.0%	conv't bds/wrnts	0.0%	other

SHAREHOLDER INFORMATION

Minimum Investment
Initial: $1,000 — Subsequent: $1

Minimum IRA Investment
Initial: $500 — Subsequent: $1

Maximum Fees
Load: none — 12b-1: none
Other: none

Services
✔ IRA
✔ Keogh
✔ Telephone Exchange

Northern Growth Equity (NOGEX)

800-595-9111
www.northernfunds.com

Growth

PERFORMANCE — fund inception date: 4/4/94

	3yr Annual	5yr Annual	10yr Annual	Bull	Bear
Return (%)	15.2	18.5	na	65.8	-15.1
Differ from Category (+/-)	4.2 abv av	2.4 abv av	na	16.1 abv av	-9.7 blw av

Standard Deviation	Category Risk Index	Beta
20.1%—abv av	1.03—av	1.09

	2000	1999	1998	1997	1996	1995	1994	1993	1992	1991
Return (%)	-7.2	23.8	33.1	30.1	17.8	26.1	—	—	—	—
Differ from Category (+/-)	-10.7	4.9	18.8	3.0	-4.5	-4.3	—	—	—	—
Return, Tax-Adjusted (%)	-9.7	21.8	31.6	27.6	16.0	25.6	—	—	—	—

PER SHARE DATA

	2000	1999	1998	1997	1996	1995	1994	1993	1992	1991
Dividends, Net Income ($)	0.00	0.01	0.02	0.05	0.06	0.08	—	—	—	—
Distrib'ns, Cap Gain ($)	3.03	2.00	1.18	1.66	0.71	0.04	—	—	—	—
Net Asset Value ($)	18.72	23.48	20.80	16.54	14.11	12.62	—	—	—	—
Expense Ratio (%)	1.00	1.00	1.00	1.00	1.00	1.00	—	—	—	—
Yield (%)	0.00	0.03	0.09	0.27	0.40	0.63	—	—	—	—
Portfolio Turnover (%)	88	49	73	67	73	82	—	—	—	—
Total Assets (Millions $)	1,147	1,270	594	422	289	192	—	—	—	—

PORTFOLIO (as of 6/30/00)

Portfolio Manager: John Zielenski, Jon Brorson - 1998

Investm't Category: Growth

✔ Domestic — Index
✔ Foreign — Sector
Asset Allocation — State Specific

Investment Style

✔ Large Cap — Mid Cap — Small Cap
✔ Growth — Grth/Val — Value

Portfolio

0.1%	cash	0.0%	corp bonds
99.9%	stocks	0.0%	gov't bonds
0.0%	pref/conv't pref	0.0%	muni bonds
0.0%	conv't bds/wrnts	0.0%	other

SHAREHOLDER INFORMATION

Minimum Investment
Initial: $2,500 — Subsequent: $50

Minimum IRA Investment
Initial: $500 — Subsequent: $50

Maximum Fees
Load: none — 12b-1: none
Other: none

Services
✔ IRA
✔ Keogh
✔ Telephone Exchange

Northern Income Equity (NOIEX)

800-595-9111
www.northernfunds.com

Growth & Income

PERFORMANCE — fund inception date: 4/4/94

	3yr Annual	5yr Annual	10yr Annual	Bull	Bear
Return (%)	8.5	13.1	na	24.6	-8.3
Differ from Category (+/-)	-0.4 av	-1.2 blw av	na	-8.9 blw av	-8.2 blw av

Standard Deviation	Category Risk Index	Beta
12.4%—blw av	0.71—low	0.59

	2000	1999	1998	1997	1996	1995	1994	1993	1992	1991
Return (%)	6.3	9.9	9.2	20.8	19.9	19.0	—	—	—	—
Differ from Category (+/-)	0.6	-0.9	-3.6	-6.1	0.2	-10.5	—	—	—	—
Return, Tax-Adjusted (%)	2.4	8.1	6.6	17.6	15.9	17.7	—	—	—	—

PER SHARE DATA

	2000	1999	1998	1997	1996	1995	1994	1993	1992	1991
Dividends, Net Income ($)	0.39	0.30	0.48	0.43	0.41	0.31	—	—	—	—
Distrib'ns, Cap Gain ($)	1.78	0.50	0.65	1.03	0.97	0.00	—	—	—	—
Net Asset Value ($)	11.71	13.10	12.69	12.69	11.77	11.00	—	—	—	—
Expense Ratio (%)	1.00	1.00	1.00	1.00	1.00	1.00	—	—	—	—
Yield (%)	2.89	2.20	3.59	3.13	3.21	2.81	—	—	—	—
Portfolio Turnover (%)	125	79	81	72	67	45	—	—	—	—
Total Assets (Millions $)	179	228	119	103	71	48	—	—	—	—

PORTFOLIO (as of 6/30/00)

Portfolio Manager: Theodore Southworth - 1995

Investm't Category: Growth & Income

✔ Domestic | Index
✔ Foreign | Sector
Asset Allocation | State Specific

Investment Style

✔ Large Cap | ✔ Mid Cap | Small Cap
Growth | ✔ Grth/Val | Value

Portfolio

9.4% cash | 0.0% corp bonds
50.6% stocks | 0.0% gov't bonds
0.0% pref/conv't pref | 0.0% muni bonds
40.1% conv't bds/wrnts | 0.0% other

SHAREHOLDER INFORMATION

Minimum Investment

Initial: $2,500 | Subsequent: $50

Minimum IRA Investment

Initial: $500 | Subsequent: $50

Maximum Fees

Load: none | 12b-1: none
Other: none

Services

✔ IRA
✔ Keogh
✔ Telephone Exchange

Northern Intl Growth Eqty (NOIGX)

800-595-9111
www.northernfunds.com

International Stock

PERFORMANCE — fund inception date: 4/4/94

	3yr Annual	5yr Annual	10yr Annual	Bull	Bear
Return (%)	14.6	10.9	na	56.0	-13.0
Differ from Category (+/-)	5.7 abv av	2.6 abv av	na	-34.9 blw av	11.0 high

Standard Deviation	Category Risk Index	Beta
15.3%—av	0.67—low	0.65

	2000	1999	1998	1997	1996	1995	1994	1993	1992	1991
Return (%)	-9.9	35.1	23.9	6.3	5.0	2.0	—	—	—	—
Differ from Category (+/-)	9.5	-25.6	18.1	5.0	-9.5	-7.3	—	—	—	—
Return, Tax-Adjusted (%)	-12.3	31.6	22.5	5.0	3.7	1.2	—	—	—	—

PER SHARE DATA

	2000	1999	1998	1997	1996	1995	1994	1993	1992	1991
Dividends, Net Income ($)	0.03	0.20	0.12	0.16	0.06	0.19	—	—	—	—
Distrib'ns, Cap Gain ($)	1.68	1.68	0.46	0.29	0.37	0.00	—	—	—	—
Net Asset Value ($)	11.10	14.28	12.10	10.24	10.07	10.02	—	—	—	—
Expense Ratio (%)	1.25	1.25	1.25	1.25	1.25	1.25	—	—	—	—
Yield (%)	0.23	1.25	0.95	1.51	0.57	1.89	—	—	—	—
Portfolio Turnover (%)	155	177	145	190	217	158	—	—	—	—
Total Assets (Millions $)	603	603	206	163	179	161	—	—	—	—

PORTFOLIO (as of 6/30/00)

Portfolio Manager: Robert LaFleur, Andrew Parry - 1994

Investm't Category: International Stock

Domestic	Index
✔ Foreign	Sector
Asset Allocation	State Specific

Investment Style

Large Cap	Mid Cap	Small Cap
Growth	Grth/Val	Value

Portfolio

7.2%	cash	0.0%	corp bonds
92.8%	stocks	0.0%	gov't bonds
0.0%	pref/conv't pref	0.0%	muni bonds
0.0%	conv't bds/wrnts	0.0%	other

SHAREHOLDER INFORMATION

Minimum Investment
Initial: $2,500 Subsequent: $50

Minimum IRA Investment
Initial: $500 Subsequent: $50

Maximum Fees
Load: none 12b-1: none
Other: none

Services
✔ IRA
✔ Keogh
✔ Telephone Exchange

Northern Intl Select Eqty (NINEX)

800-595-9111
www.northernfunds.com

International Stock

PERFORMANCE — fund inception date: 4/5/94

	3yr Annual	5yr Annual	10yr Annual	Bull	Bear
Return (%)	14.0	10.7	na	57.3	-12.7
Differ from Category (+/-)	5.1 abv av	2.4 abv av	na	-33.6 blw av	11.3 high

Standard Deviation	Category Risk Index	Beta
15.2%—av	0.67—low	0.67

	2000	1999	1998	1997	1996	1995	1994	1993	1992	1991
Return (%)	-10.9	36.1	22.2	9.1	2.8	-0.8	—	—	—	—
Differ from Category (+/-)	8.5	-24.6	16.4	7.8	-11.7	-10.1	—	—	—	—
Return, Tax-Adjusted (%)	-14.6	31.9	21.0	8.1	2.3	-0.9	—	—	—	—

PER SHARE DATA

	2000	1999	1998	1997	1996	1995	1994	1993	1992	1991
Dividends, Net Income ($)	0.25	0.26	0.00	0.25	0.06	0.04	—	—	—	—
Distrib'ns, Cap Gain ($)	2.27	2.08	0.65	0.00	0.08	0.00	—	—	—	—
Net Asset Value ($)	10.53	14.74	12.65	10.89	10.22	10.08	—	—	—	—
Expense Ratio (%)	1.25	1.25	1.25	1.25	1.25	1.25	—	—	—	—
Yield (%)	1.95	1.54	0.00	2.29	0.58	0.39	—	—	—	—
Portfolio Turnover (%)	145	168	98	97	177	97	—	—	—	—
Total Assets (Millions $)	206	215	124	104	109	80	—	—	—	—

PORTFOLIO (as of 6/30/00)

Portfolio Manager: Robert LaFleur, Andrew Parry - 1994

Investm't Category: International Stock

Domestic	Index
✔ Foreign	Sector
Asset Allocation	State Specific

Investment Style

Large Cap	Mid Cap	Small Cap
Growth	Grth/Val	Value

Portfolio

6.0%	cash	0.0%	corp bonds
94.0%	stocks	0.0%	gov't bonds
0.0%	pref/conv't pref	0.0%	muni bonds
0.0%	conv't bds/wrnts	0.0%	other

SHAREHOLDER INFORMATION

Minimum Investment
Initial: $2,500 — Subsequent: $50

Minimum IRA Investment
Initial: $500 — Subsequent: $50

Maximum Fees
Load: none — 12b-1: none
Other: none

Services
✔ IRA
✔ Keogh
✔ Telephone Exchange

Northern Select Equity (NOEQX)

800-595-9111
www.northernfunds.com

Aggressive Growth

PERFORMANCE — fund inception date: 4/6/94

	3yr Annual	5yr Annual	10yr Annual	Bull	Bear
Return (%)	26.1	26.3	na	110.2	-15.9
Differ from Category (+/-)	9.9 abv av	11.7 high	na	-9.0 av	4.7 abv av

Standard Deviation	Category Risk Index	Beta
26.4%—high	0.81—blw av	1.02

	2000	1999	1998	1997	1996	1995	1994	1993	1992	1991
Return (%)	-3.9	54.5	35.1	31.8	21.5	28.9	—	—	—	—
Differ from Category (+/-)	2.1	-3.0	20.0	17.0	3.2	-5.7	—	—	—	—
Return, Tax-Adjusted (%)	-6.3	53.4	33.6	28.7	20.1	27.8	—	—	—	—

PER SHARE DATA

	2000	1999	1998	1997	1996	1995	1994	1993	1992	1991
Dividends, Net Income ($)	0.00	0.00	0.01	0.02	0.01	0.02	—	—	—	—
Distrib'ns, Cap Gain ($)	3.96	1.11	1.21	2.20	0.61	0.36	—	—	—	—
Net Asset Value ($)	26.84	32.28	21.70	16.98	14.65	12.57	—	—	—	—
Expense Ratio (%)	1.00	1.00	1.00	1.00	1.00	1.00	—	—	—	—
Yield (%)	0.00	0.00	0.04	0.10	0.06	0.15	—	—	—	—
Portfolio Turnover (%)	153	87	148	72	138	49	—	—	—	—
Total Assets (Millions $)	521	389	164	104	54	27	—	—	—	—

PORTFOLIO (as of 6/30/00)

Portfolio Manager: Robert Streed - 1994

Investm't Category: Aggressive Growth

✔ Domestic
✔ Foreign
Asset Allocation
Index
Sector
State Specific

Investment Style

Large Cap
✔ Mid Cap
Small Cap
✔ Growth
Grth/Val
Value

Portfolio

0.8%	cash	0.0%	corp bonds
99.2%	stocks	0.0%	gov't bonds
0.0%	pref/conv't pref	0.0%	muni bonds
0.0%	conv't bds/wrnts	0.0%	other

SHAREHOLDER INFORMATION

Minimum Investment

Initial: $2,500 Subsequent: $50

Minimum IRA Investment

Initial: $500 Subsequent: $50

Maximum Fees

Load: none 12b-1: none
Other: none

Services

✔ IRA
✔ Keogh
✔ Telephone Exchange

Northern Small Cap Value (NOSGX)

800-595-9111
www.northernfunds.com

Aggressive Growth

PERFORMANCE — fund inception date: 4/4/94

	3yr Annual	5yr Annual	10yr Annual	Bull	Bear
Return (%)	4.5	12.0	na	30.5	-5.5
Differ from Category (+/-)	-11.7 low	-2.6 blw av	na	-88.7 low	15.1 high

Standard Deviation	Category Risk Index	Beta
21.8%—abv av	0.67—low	0.70

	2000	1999	1998	1997	1996	1995	1994	1993	1992	1991
Return (%)	8.4	12.0	-5.9	29.8	18.9	22.5	—	—	—	—
Differ from Category (+/-)	14.4	-45.5	-21.0	15.0	0.6	-12.1	—	—	—	—
Return, Tax-Adjusted (%)	1.6	10.0	-6.6	28.6	17.0	20.3	—	—	—	—

PER SHARE DATA

	2000	1999	1998	1997	1996	1995	1994	1993	1992	1991
Dividends, Net Income ($)	0.05	0.11	0.01	0.03	0.05	0.06	—	—	—	—
Distrib'ns, Cap Gain ($)	4.66	1.13	0.53	0.68	0.65	0.66	—	—	—	—
Net Asset Value ($)	10.15	14.10	13.78	15.26	12.33	10.97	—	—	—	—
Expense Ratio (%)	1.00	1.00	1.00	1.00	1.00	1.00	—	—	—	—
Yield (%)	0.33	0.72	0.06	0.18	0.38	0.51	—	—	—	—
Portfolio Turnover (%)	18	18	18	18	47	82	—	—	—	—
Total Assets (Millions $)	153	239	314	336	193	142	—	—	—	—

PORTFOLIO (as of 6/30/00)

Portfolio Manager: Susan French - 1994

Investm't Category: Aggressive Growth

✔ Domestic
Index
✔ Foreign
Sector
Asset Allocation
State Specific

Investment Style

Large Cap
Mid Cap
✔ Small Cap
Growth
✔ Grth/Val
Value

Portfolio

0.0%	cash	0.0%	corp bonds
100.0%	stocks	0.0%	gov't bonds
0.0%	pref/conv't pref	0.0%	muni bonds
0.0%	conv't bds/wrnts	0.0%	other

SHAREHOLDER INFORMATION

Minimum Investment

Initial: $2,500 Subsequent: $50

Minimum IRA Investment

Initial: $500 Subsequent: $50

Maximum Fees

Load: none 12b-1: none
Other: none

Services

✔ IRA
✔ Keogh
✔ Telephone Exchange

Northern Stock Index (NOSIX)

800-595-9111
www.northernfunds.com

Growth & Income

PERFORMANCE — fund inception date: 10/7/96

	3yr Annual	5yr Annual	10yr Annual	Bull	Bear
Return (%)	11.6	na	na	55.1	-11.9
Differ from Category (+/-)	2.7 abv av	na	na	21.6 abv av	-11.8 low

Standard Deviation	Category Risk Index	Beta
17.6%—av	1.02—abv av	1.00

	2000	1999	1998	1997	1996	1995	1994	1993	1992	1991
Return (%)	-9.4	20.3	27.9	32.6	—	—	—	—	—	—
Differ from Category (+/-)	-15.1	9.5	15.1	5.7	—	—	—	—	—	—
Return, Tax-Adjusted (%)	-10.9	19.8	27.1	31.1	—	—	—	—	—	—

PER SHARE DATA

	2000	1999	1998	1997	1996	1995	1994	1993	1992	1991
Dividends, Net Income ($)	0.12	0.14	0.16	0.14	—	—	—	—	—	—
Distrib'ns, Cap Gain ($)	1.26	0.09	0.16	0.51	—	—	—	—	—	—
Net Asset Value ($)	16.39	19.70	16.59	13.24	—	—	—	—	—	—
Expense Ratio (%)	0.55	0.55	0.55	1.00	—	—	—	—	—	—
Yield (%)	0.67	0.70	0.95	1.01	—	—	—	—	—	—
Portfolio Turnover (%)	12	2	32	67	—	—	—	—	—	—
Total Assets (Millions $)	481	538	141	66	—	—	—	—	—	—

PORTFOLIO (as of 6/30/00)

Portfolio Manager: Lucy Quintana Johnston - 1998

Investm't Category: Growth & Income

✔ Domestic ✔ Index
Foreign Sector
Asset Allocation State Specific

Investment Style

✔ Large Cap Mid Cap Small Cap
Growth ✔ Grth/Val Value

Portfolio

0.8%	cash	0.0%	corp bonds
99.3%	stocks	0.0%	gov't bonds
0.0%	pref/conv't pref	0.0%	muni bonds
0.0%	conv't bds/wrnts	0.0%	other

SHAREHOLDER INFORMATION

Minimum Investment
Initial: $2,500 Subsequent: $50

Minimum IRA Investment
Initial: $500 Subsequent: $50

Maximum Fees
Load: none 12b-1: none
Other: none

Services
✔ IRA
✔ Keogh
✔ Telephone Exchange

Northern Technology (NTCHX)

800-595-9111
www.northernfunds.com

Aggressive Growth

PERFORMANCE — fund inception date: 4/1/96

	3yr Annual	5yr Annual	10yr Annual	Bull	Bear
Return (%)	38.2	na	na	315.5	-49.4
Differ from Category (+/-)	22.0 high	na	na	196.3 high	-28.8 low

Standard Deviation	Category Risk Index	Beta
49.0%—high	1.51—high	1.69

	2000	1999	1998	1997	1996	1995	1994	1993	1992	1991
Return (%)	-38.4	134.5	82.9	16.7	—	—	—	—	—	—
Differ from Category (+/-)	-32.4	77.0	67.8	1.9	—	—	—	—	—	—
Return, Tax-Adjusted (%)	-43.2	130.0	81.9	15.3	—	—	—	—	—	—

PER SHARE DATA

	2000	1999	1998	1997	1996	1995	1994	1993	1992	1991
Dividends, Net Income ($)	0.00	0.00	0.00	0.00	—	—	—	—	—	—
Distrib'ns, Cap Gain ($)	12.50	5.73	0.67	0.90	—	—	—	—	—	—
Net Asset Value ($)	19.03	51.76	25.58	14.35	—	—	—	—	—	—
Expense Ratio (%)	1.25	1.23	1.25	1.25	—	—	—	—	—	—
Yield (%)	0.00	0.00	0.00	0.00	—	—	—	—	—	—
Portfolio Turnover (%)	156	61	74	67	—	—	—	—	—	—
Total Assets (Millions $)	1,448	1,809	227	80	—	—	—	—	—	—

PORTFOLIO (as of 6/30/00)

Portfolio Manager: Gilbert, Leo, Eggly - 1996

Investm't Category: Aggressive Growth

✔ Domestic
Index
✔ Foreign
✔ Sector
Asset Allocation
State Specific

Investment Style

Large Cap
✔ Mid Cap
✔ Small Cap
✔ Growth
Grth/Val
Value

Portfolio

3.2%	cash	0.0%	corp bonds
96.8%	stocks	0.0%	gov't bonds
0.0%	pref/conv't pref	0.0%	muni bonds
0.0%	conv't bds/wrnts	0.0%	other

SHAREHOLDER INFORMATION

Minimum Investment

Initial: $2,500 Subsequent: $50

Minimum IRA Investment

Initial: $500 Subsequent: $50

Maximum Fees

Load: none 12b-1: none
Other: none

Services

✔ IRA
✔ Keogh
✔ Telephone Exchange

Oak Value (OAKVX)

800-622-2474, 800-282-5706
www.oakvaluefund.com

Growth

PERFORMANCE — fund inception date: 1/11/93

	3yr Annual	5yr Annual	10yr Annual	Bull	Bear
Return (%)	10.8	19.3	na	19.0	15.2
Differ from Category (+/-)	-0.2 av	3.2 abv av	na	-30.7 low	20.6 high

Standard Deviation	Category Risk Index	Beta
19.7%—abv av	1.01—av	0.83

	2000	1999	1998	1997	1996	1995	1994	1993	1992	1991
Return (%)	18.1	-3.1	18.9	37.7	28.9	28.8	-1.5	—	—	—
Differ from Category (+/-)	14.6	-22.0	4.6	10.6	6.6	-1.6	-1.3	—	—	—
Return, Tax-Adjusted (%)	17.6	-3.8	18.5	36.7	27.6	28.5	-3.3	—	—	—

PER SHARE DATA

	2000	1999	1998	1997	1996	1995	1994	1993	1992	1991
Dividends, Net Income ($)	0.02	0.07	0.09	0.00	0.00	0.00	0.00	—	—	—
Distrib'ns, Cap Gain ($)	0.54	0.90	0.19	0.81	0.63	0.09	0.81	—	—	—
Net Asset Value ($)	29.49	25.52	27.29	23.19	17.49	14.06	10.99	—	—	—
Expense Ratio (%)	1.13	1.10	1.22	1.59	1.90	1.89	1.89	—	—	—
Yield (%)	0.06	0.26	0.32	0.00	0.00	0.00	0.00	—	—	—
Portfolio Turnover (%)	22	38	15	22	58	103	91	—	—	—
Total Assets (Millions $)	304	394	562	139	31	13	7	—	—	—

PORTFOLIO (as of 3/31/00)

Portfolio Manager: David Carr, George Brumley - 1993

Investm't Category: Growth

✔ Domestic	Index
✔ Foreign	Sector
Asset Allocation	State Specific

Investment Style

✔ Large Cap	Mid Cap	Small Cap
Growth	Grth/Val	✔ Value

Portfolio

4.8%	cash	0.0%	corp bonds
95.2%	stocks	0.0%	gov't bonds
0.0%	pref/conv't pref	0.0%	muni bonds
0.0%	conv't bds/wrnts	0.0%	other

SHAREHOLDER INFORMATION

Minimum Investment
Initial: $2,500 Subsequent: $100

Minimum IRA Investment
Initial: $1,000 Subsequent: $100

Maximum Fees
Load: none 12b-1: none
Other: none

Services
✔ IRA
✔ Keogh
✔ Telephone Exchange

Oakmark Eqty & Income/I (OAKBX)

800-625-6275, 312-621-0600
www.oakmark.com

Balanced

PERFORMANCE — fund inception date: 11/1/95

	3yr Annual	5yr Annual	10yr Annual	Bull	Bear
Return (%)	13.2	16.2	na	26.5	9.7
Differ from Category (+/-)	4.8 high	4.8 high	na	-1.6 av	12.9 high

Standard Deviation	Category Risk Index	Beta
10.9%—blw av	0.99—av	0.41

	2000	1999	1998	1997	1996	1995	1994	1993	1992	1991
Return (%)	19.8	7.8	12.3	26.5	15.2	—	—	—	—	—
Differ from Category (+/-)	17.8	-2.9	-1.0	7.7	1.3	—	—	—	—	—
Return, Tax-Adjusted (%)	17.7	4.8	11.4	24.7	14.3	—	—	—	—	—

PER SHARE DATA

	2000	1999	1998	1997	1996	1995	1994	1993	1992	1991
Dividends, Net Income ($)	0.24	0.45	0.21	0.23	0.12	—	—	—	—	—
Distrib'ns, Cap Gain ($)	1.00	1.36	0.20	0.58	0.13	—	—	—	—	—
Net Asset Value ($)	15.96	14.40	15.03	13.76	11.55	—	—	—	—	—
Expense Ratio (%)	1.24	1.18	1.31	1.50	2.50	—	—	—	—	—
Yield (%)	1.41	2.85	1.37	1.60	1.02	—	—	—	—	—
Portfolio Turnover (%)	87	81	46	na	66	—	—	—	—	—
Total Assets (Millions $)	56	57	66	40	14	—	—	—	—	—

PORTFOLIO (as of 3/31/00)

Portfolio Manager: Clyde McGregor - 1995

Investm't Category: Balanced

✔ Domestic — Index
Foreign — Sector
Asset Allocation — State Specific

Investment Style

Large Cap — Mid Cap — Small Cap
Growth — Grth/Val — Value

Portfolio

4.4%	cash	3.6%	corp bonds
58.5%	stocks	25.0%	gov't bonds
8.5%	pref/conv't pref	0.0%	muni bonds
0.0%	conv't bds/wrnts	0.0%	other

SHAREHOLDER INFORMATION

Minimum Investment
Initial: $1,000 — Subsequent: $100

Minimum IRA Investment
Initial: $1,000 — Subsequent: $100

Maximum Fees
Load: none — 12b-1: none
Other: none

Services
✔ IRA
✔ Keogh
✔ Telephone Exchange

Oakmark Intl/I (OAKIX)

800-625-6275, 312-621-0600
www.oakmark.com

International Stock

PERFORMANCE — fund inception date: 9/30/92

	3yr Annual	5yr Annual	10yr Annual	Bull	Bear
Return (%)	13.4	14.0	na	55.2	4.8
Differ from Category (+/-)	4.5 abv av	5.7 high	na	-35.7 blw av	28.8 high

Standard Deviation	Category Risk Index	Beta
21.6%—abv av	0.95—av	0.77

	2000	1999	1998	1997	1996	1995	1994	1993	1992	1991
Return (%)	12.5	39.4	-6.9	3.3	28.0	8.3	-9.0	53.5	—	—
Differ from Category (+/-)	31.9	-21.3	-12.7	2.0	13.5	-1.0	-5.9	13.3	—	—
Return, Tax-Adjusted (%)	10.4	37.6	-8.8	-1.7	27.4	5.9	-10.9	52.7	—	—

PER SHARE DATA

	2000	1999	1998	1997	1996	1995	1994	1993	1992	1991
Dividends, Net Income ($)	0.50	0.48	0.24	0.57	0.16	0.00	0.00	0.08	—	—
Distrib'ns, Cap Gain ($)	0.50	0.00	0.77	2.86	0.00	1.04	1.05	0.15	—	—
Net Asset Value ($)	15.46	14.70	10.91	12.83	15.68	12.38	12.41	14.79	—	—
Expense Ratio (%)	1.30	1.29	1.32	1.26	1.32	1.40	1.37	1.26	—	—
Yield (%)	3.13	3.26	2.05	3.63	1.02	0.00	0.00	0.53	—	—
Portfolio Turnover (%)	64	54	43	61	42	27	55	21	—	—
Total Assets (Millions $)	741	827	740	1,237	1,232	785	1,079	1,108	—	—

PORTFOLIO (as of 3/31/00)

Portfolio Manager: David Herro, Michael Welsh - 1992

Investm't Category: International Stock

Domestic	Index
✔ Foreign	Sector
Asset Allocation	State Specific

Investment Style

Large Cap	Mid Cap	Small Cap
Growth	Grth/Val	Value

Portfolio

5.2% cash	0.0% corp bonds
94.8% stocks	0.0% gov't bonds
0.0% pref/conv't pref	0.0% muni bonds
0.0% conv't bds/wrnts	0.0% other

SHAREHOLDER INFORMATION

Minimum Investment
Initial: $1,000 Subsequent: $100

Minimum IRA Investment
Initial: $1,000 Subsequent: $100

Maximum Fees
Load: 2.00% redemption 12b-1: none
Other: redemption fee applies for 3 months

Services
✔ IRA
✔ Keogh
✔ Telephone Exchange

Oakmark Select/I (OAKLX)

800-625-6275, 312-621-0600
www.oakmark.com

Aggressive Growth

PERFORMANCE

fund inception date: 11/1/96

	3yr Annual	5yr Annual	10yr Annual	Bull	Bear
Return (%)	18.7	na	na	50.9	10.5
Differ from Category (+/-)	2.5 av	na	na	-68.3 blw av	31.1 high

Standard Deviation	Category Risk Index	Beta
22.2%—abv av	0.68—low	0.99

	2000	1999	1998	1997	1996	1995	1994	1993	1992	1991
Return (%)	25.8	14.4	16.2	55.0	—	—	—	—	—	—
Differ from Category (+/-)	31.8	-43.1	1.1	40.2	—	—	—	—	—	—
Return, Tax-Adjusted (%)	24.1	10.2	15.2	54.7	—	—	—	—	—	—

PER SHARE DATA

	2000	1999	1998	1997	1996	1995	1994	1993	1992	1991
Dividends, Net Income ($)	0.08	0.19	0.04	0.00	—	—	—	—	—	—
Distrib'ns, Cap Gain ($)	1.36	3.71	0.71	0.16	—	—	—	—	—	—
Net Asset Value ($)	21.65	18.42	19.54	17.52	—	—	—	—	—	—
Expense Ratio (%)	1.17	1.16	1.22	1.12	—	—	—	—	—	—
Yield (%)	0.34	0.85	0.19	0.00	—	—	—	—	—	—
Portfolio Turnover (%)	69	67	56	—	—	—	—	—	—	—
Total Assets (Millions $)	1,863	1,581	1,390	981	—	—	—	—	—	—

PORTFOLIO (as of 3/31/00)

Portfolio Manager: William Nygren - 1996

Investm't Category: Aggressive Growth

✔ Domestic	Index
✔ Foreign	Sector
Asset Allocation	State Specific

Investment Style

✔ Large Cap	Mid Cap	Small Cap
Growth	Grth/Val	✔ Value

Portfolio

7.8% cash	0.0% corp bonds
92.2% stocks	0.0% gov't bonds
0.0% pref/conv't pref	0.0% muni bonds
0.0% conv't bds/wrnts	0.0% other

SHAREHOLDER INFORMATION

Minimum Investment
Initial: $1,000 Subsequent: $100

Minimum IRA Investment
Initial: $1,000 Subsequent: $100

Maximum Fees
Load: 2.00% redemption 12b-1: none
Other: redemption fee applies for 3 months

Services
✔ IRA
✔ Keogh
✔ Telephone Exchange

Oakmark Small Cap/I

800-625-6275, 312-621-0600
www.oakmark.com

(OAKSX)

Growth

PERFORMANCE — fund inception date: 11/1/95

	3yr Annual	5yr Annual	10yr Annual	Bull	Bear
Return (%)	-5.8	10.3	na	8.5	3.0
Differ from Category (+/-)	-16.8 low	-5.8 low	na	-41.2 low	8.4 abv av

Standard Deviation	Category Risk Index	Beta
19.2%—abv av	0.99—av	0.76

	2000	1999	1998	1997	1996	1995	1994	1993	1992	1991
Return (%)	4.3	-7.9	-13.1	40.5	39.7	—	—	—	—	—
Differ from Category (+/-)	0.8	-26.8	-27.4	13.4	17.4	—	—	—	—	—
Return, Tax-Adjusted (%)	3.5	-7.9	-15.2	39.3	39.7	—	—	—	—	—

PER SHARE DATA

	2000	1999	1998	1997	1996	1995	1994	1993	1992	1991
Dividends, Net Income ($)	0.00	0.00	0.00	0.00	0.00	—	—	—	—	—
Distrib'ns, Cap Gain ($)	0.51	0.00	2.10	0.84	0.00	—	—	—	—	—
Net Asset Value ($)	13.69	13.60	14.77	19.42	14.44	—	—	—	—	—
Expense Ratio (%)	1.50	1.48	1.45	1.37	1.61	—	—	—	—	—
Yield (%)	0.00	0.00	0.00	0.00	0.00	—	—	—	—	—
Portfolio Turnover (%)	28	68	34	26	23	—	—	—	—	—
Total Assets (Millions $)	231	336	703	1,492	360	—	—	—	—	—

PORTFOLIO (as of 3/31/00)

Portfolio Manager: Clyde McGregor, James Benson - 1995

Investm't Category: Growth

✔ Domestic	Index
✔ Foreign	Sector
Asset Allocation	State Specific

Investment Style

Large Cap	✔ Mid Cap	✔ Small Cap
Growth	Grth/Val	✔ Value

Portfolio

9.1%	cash	0.0%	corp bonds
91.0%	stocks	0.0%	gov't bonds
0.0%	pref/conv't pref	0.0%	muni bonds
0.0%	conv't bds/wrnts	-0.1%	other

SHAREHOLDER INFORMATION

Minimum Investment
Initial: $1,000 — Subsequent: $100

Minimum IRA Investment
Initial: $1,000 — Subsequent: $100

Maximum Fees
Load: 2.00% redemption — 12b-1: none
Other: redemption fee applies for 3 months

Services
✔ IRA
✔ Keogh
✔ Telephone Exchange

Oakmark/I (OAKMX)

800-625-6275, 312-621-0600
www.oakmark.com

Growth

PERFORMANCE

fund inception date: 8/5/91

	3yr Annual	5yr Annual	10yr Annual	Bull	Bear
Return (%)	1.2	9.8	na	4.4	14.6
Differ from Category (+/-)	-9.8 low	-6.3 low	na	-45.3 low	20.0 high

Standard Deviation	Category Risk Index	Beta
19.4%—abv av	1.00—av	0.66

	2000	1999	1998	1997	1996	1995	1994	1993	1992	1991
Return (%)	11.7	-10.4	3.7	32.5	16.2	34.4	3.3	30.5	48.8	—
Differ from Category (+/-)	8.2	-29.3	-10.6	5.4	-6.1	4.0	3.5	15.9	36.2	—
Return, Tax-Adjusted (%)	11.1	-13.3	0.4	30.8	13.9	32.8	1.2	28.8	48.2	—

PER SHARE DATA

	2000	1999	1998	1997	1996	1995	1994	1993	1992	1991
Dividends, Net Income ($)	0.38	0.26	0.43	0.39	0.34	0.28	0.23	0.23	0.03	—
Distrib'ns, Cap Gain ($)	0.00	4.73	5.62	1.97	1.86	0.84	1.46	0.77	0.21	—
Net Asset Value ($)	29.99	27.20	35.82	40.41	32.35	29.75	22.97	23.93	19.13	—
Expense Ratio (%)	1.21	1.11	1.08	1.08	1.18	1.17	1.22	1.32	1.70	—
Yield (%)	1.26	0.81	1.03	0.92	0.99	0.91	0.94	0.93	0.15	—
Portfolio Turnover (%)	50	13	43	17	23	18	29	18	34	—
Total Assets (Millions $)	2,116	3,368	7,320	7,301	4,194	3,301	1,626	1,214	328	—

PORTFOLIO (as of 3/31/00)

Portfolio Manager: Bill Nygren, Kevin Grant - 2000

Investm't Category: Growth

✔ Domestic — Index
✔ Foreign — Sector
Asset Allocation — State Specific

Investment Style

✔ Large Cap — ✔ Mid Cap — Small Cap
Growth — Grth/Val — ✔ Value

Portfolio

9.3%	cash	0.0%	corp bonds
90.7%	stocks	0.0%	gov't bonds
0.0%	pref/conv't pref	0.0%	muni bonds
0.0%	conv't bds/wrnts	0.0%	other

SHAREHOLDER INFORMATION

Minimum Investment
Initial: $1,000 — Subsequent: $100

Minimum IRA Investment
Initial: $1,000 — Subsequent: $100

Maximum Fees
Load: none — 12b-1: none
Other: none

Services
✔ IRA
✔ Keogh
✔ Telephone Exchange

Oberweis: Emerging Growth (OBEGX)

800-323-6166, 630-801-6000
www.oberweisfunds.com

Aggressive Growth

PERFORMANCE

fund inception date: 1/7/87

	3yr Annual	5yr Annual	10yr Annual	Bull	Bear
Return (%)	9.8	8.2	16.8	123.4	-31.0
Differ from Category (+/-)	-6.4 blw av	-6.4 low	1.0 blw av	4.2 abv av	-10.4 blw av

Standard Deviation	Category Risk Index	Beta
38.9%—high	1.20—abv av	1.40

	2000	1999	1998	1997	1996	1995	1994	1993	1992	1991
Return (%)	-10.6	53.1	-3.1	-8.5	22.4	42.5	-3.5	9.7	13.7	87.0
Differ from Category (+/-)	-4.6	-4.4	-18.2	-23.3	4.1	7.9	-2.7	-15.5	6.8	39.8
Return, Tax-Adjusted (%)	-17.8	53.1	-3.9	-11.3	19.8	40.6	-3.5	8.7	13.7	77.1

PER SHARE DATA

	2000	1999	1998	1997	1996	1995	1994	1993	1992	1991
Dividends, Net Income ($)	0.00	0.00	0.00	0.00	0.00	0.00	0.00	0.00	0.00	0.00
Distrib'ns, Cap Gain ($)	13.10	0.00	1.15	4.64	2.64	1.42	0.00	0.74	0.00	4.27
Net Asset Value ($)	21.19	36.15	23.60	25.71	32.86	29.09	21.41	22.19	20.90	18.38
Expense Ratio (%)	na	1.59	1.55	1.44	1.48	1.75	1.78	1.80	1.99	2.13
Yield (%)	0.00	0.00	0.00	0.00	0.00	0.00	0.00	0.00	0.00	0.00
Portfolio Turnover (%)	na	63	49	75	64	79	66	70	63	114
Total Assets (Millions $)	86	105	93	140	185	134	90	101	53	19

PORTFOLIO (as of 6/30/00)

Portfolio Manager: James Oberweis - 1987

Investm't Category: Aggressive Growth

✔ Domestic	Index
Foreign	Sector
Asset Allocation	State Specific

Investment Style

Large Cap	Mid Cap	✔ Small Cap
✔ Growth	Grth/Val	Value

Portfolio

-0.6%	cash	0.0%	corp bonds
100.6%	stocks	0.0%	gov't bonds
0.0%	pref/conv't pref	0.0%	muni bonds
0.0%	conv't bds/wrnts	0.0%	other

SHAREHOLDER INFORMATION

Minimum Investment
Initial: $1,000 Subsequent: $100

Minimum IRA Investment
Initial: $500 Subsequent: $100

Maximum Fees
Load: none 12b-1: 0.25%
Other: none

Services
✔ IRA
✔ Keogh
✔ Telephone Exchange

PBHG Core Grth (PBCRX)

800-433-0051, 610-647-4100
www.pbhgfunds.com

Aggressive Growth

PERFORMANCE — fund inception date: 12/29/95

	3yr Annual	5yr Annual	10yr Annual	Bull	Bear
Return (%)	18.7	14.9	na	162.9	-37.8
Differ from Category (+/-)	2.5 av	0.3 av	na	43.7 abv av	-17.2 low

Standard Deviation	Category Risk Index	Beta
47.7%—high	1.47—high	1.44

	2000	1999	1998	1997	1996	1995	1994	1993	1992	1991
Return (%)	-21.0	97.5	7.4	-9.7	32.8	—	—	—	—	—
Differ from Category (+/-)	-15.0	40.0	-7.7	-24.5	14.5	—	—	—	—	—
Return, Tax-Adjusted (%)	-23.1	97.5	7.4	-9.7	32.8	—	—	—	—	—

PER SHARE DATA

	2000	1999	1998	1997	1996	1995	1994	1993	1992	1991
Dividends, Net Income ($)	0.00	0.00	0.00	0.00	0.00	—	—	—	—	—
Distrib'ns, Cap Gain ($)	2.75	0.00	0.00	0.00	0.00	—	—	—	—	—
Net Asset Value ($)	17.70	25.45	12.88	11.99	13.28	—	—	—	—	—
Expense Ratio (%)	1.33	1.45	1.35	1.36	1.50	—	—	—	—	—
Yield (%)	0.00	0.00	0.00	0.00	0.00	—	—	—	—	—
Portfolio Turnover (%)	312	120	72	46	—	—	—	—	—	—
Total Assets (Millions $)	104	133	105	192	455	—	—	—	—	—

PORTFOLIO (as of 6/30/00)

Portfolio Manager: Jeffrey Wrona - 1999

Investm't Category: Aggressive Growth

✔ Domestic	Index
✔ Foreign	Sector
Asset Allocation	State Specific

Investment Style

Large Cap	Mid Cap	✔ Small Cap
✔ Growth	Grth/Val	Value

Portfolio

12.0%	cash	0.0%	corp bonds
88.0%	stocks	0.0%	gov't bonds
0.0%	pref/conv't pref	0.0%	muni bonds
0.0%	conv't bds/wrnts	0.0%	other

SHAREHOLDER INFORMATION

Minimum Investment

Initial: $2,500 — Subsequent: $1

Minimum IRA Investment

Initial: $2,000 — Subsequent: $1

Maximum Fees

Load: none — 12b-1: none

Other: none

Services

✔ IRA
✔ Keogh
✔ Telephone Exchange

PBHG Emerging Grth

800-433-0051, 610-647-4100
www.pbhgfunds.com

(PBEGX)

Aggressive Growth

PERFORMANCE — fund inception date: 6/14/93

	3yr Annual	5yr Annual	10yr Annual	Bull	Bear
Return (%)	4.5	5.2	na	96.1	-39.0
Differ from Category (+/-)	-11.7 low	-9.4 low	na	-23.1 av	-18.4 low

Standard Deviation	Category Risk Index	Beta
43.1%—high	1.33—high	1.24

	2000	1999	1998	1997	1996	1995	1994	1993	1992	1991
Return (%)	-25.2	48.3	3.0	-3.6	17.0	48.4	23.7	—	—	—
Differ from Category (+/-)	-19.2	-9.2	-12.1	-18.4	-1.3	13.8	24.5	—	—	—
Return, Tax-Adjusted (%)	-26.4	47.3	2.9	-3.6	15.9	46.5	23.6	—	—	—

PER SHARE DATA

	2000	1999	1998	1997	1996	1995	1994	1993	1992	1991
Dividends, Net Income ($)	0.00	0.00	0.00	0.00	0.00	0.00	0.00	—	—	—
Distrib'ns, Cap Gain ($)	2.12	1.16	0.08	0.00	0.82	0.98	0.03	—	—	—
Net Asset Value ($)	23.74	34.25	23.95	23.34	24.23	21.39	15.10	—	—	—
Expense Ratio (%)	1.24	1.34	1.27	1.28	1.47	1.50	1.45	—	—	—
Yield (%)	0.00	0.00	0.00	0.00	0.00	0.00	0.00	—	—	—
Portfolio Turnover (%)	141	101	95	47	97	27	95	—	—	—
Total Assets (Millions $)	758	953	1,043	1,516	1,518	635	177	—	—	—

PORTFOLIO (as of 6/30/00)

Portfolio Manager: Erin Piner - 2000

Investm't Category: Aggressive Growth

✔ Domestic — Index
✔ Foreign — Sector
Asset Allocation — State Specific

Investment Style

Large Cap — Mid Cap — ✔ Small Cap
✔ Growth — Grth/Val — Value

Portfolio

7.8%	cash	0.0%	corp bonds
92.2%	stocks	0.0%	gov't bonds
0.0%	pref/conv't pref	0.0%	muni bonds
0.0%	conv't bds/wrnts	0.0%	other

SHAREHOLDER INFORMATION

Minimum Investment
Initial: $2,500 — Subsequent: $1

Minimum IRA Investment
Initial: $2,000 — Subsequent: $1

Maximum Fees
Load: none — 12b-1: none
Other: none

Services
✔ IRA
Keogh
✔ Telephone Exchange

PBHG Growth (PBHGX)

800-433-0051, 610-647-4100
www.pbhgfunds.com

Aggressive Growth

PERFORMANCE — fund inception date: 12/19/85

	3yr Annual	5yr Annual	10yr Annual	Bull	Bear
Return (%)	14.2	9.6	21.6	164.2	-39.2
Differ from Category (+/-)	-2.0 av	-5.0 blw av	5.8 high	45.0 abv av	-18.6 low

Standard Deviation	Category Risk Index	Beta
45.8%—high	1.41—high	1.45

	2000	1999	1998	1997	1996	1995	1994	1993	1992	1991
Return (%)	-22.9	92.4	0.5	-3.3	9.8	50.3	4.7	46.7	28.3	51.6
Differ from Category (+/-)	-16.9	34.9	-14.6	-18.1	-8.5	15.7	5.5	21.5	21.4	4.4
Return, Tax-Adjusted (%)	-25.5	91.1	0.5	-3.3	9.8	50.3	4.6	45.9	21.7	43.8

PER SHARE DATA

	2000	1999	1998	1997	1996	1995	1994	1993	1992	1991
Dividends, Net Income ($)	0.00	0.00	0.00	0.00	0.00	0.00	0.00	0.19	0.00	0.00
Distrib'ns, Cap Gain ($)	6.26	1.59	0.00	0.00	0.00	0.00	0.01	0.00	2.45	2.43
Net Asset Value ($)	31.10	47.38	25.54	25.39	26.27	23.92	15.91	15.20	10.50	10.53
Expense Ratio (%)	1.23	1.32	1.26	1.25	1.48	1.50	1.55	2.39	1.52	1.50
Yield (%)	0.00	0.00	0.00	0.00	0.00	0.00	0.00	1.25	0.00	0.00
Portfolio Turnover (%)	107	80	94	64	45	118	94	209	114	228
Total Assets (Millions $)	3,940	4,370	3,939	5,464	5,931	2,028	745	121	2	8

PORTFOLIO (as of 6/30/00)

Portfolio Manager: Gary Pilgrim - 1985

Investm't Category: Aggressive Growth

✔ Domestic	Index
✔ Foreign	Sector
Asset Allocation	State Specific

Investment Style

Large Cap	Mid Cap	✔ Small Cap
✔ Growth	Grth/Val	Value

Portfolio

9.8%	cash	0.0%	corp bonds
90.2%	stocks	0.0%	gov't bonds
0.0%	pref/conv't pref	0.0%	muni bonds
0.0%	conv't bds/wrnts	0.0%	other

SHAREHOLDER INFORMATION

Minimum Investment

Initial: $2,500 — Subsequent: $1

Minimum IRA Investment

Initial: $2,000 — Subsequent: $1

Maximum Fees

Load: none — 12b-1: none

Other: none

Services

✔ IRA
✔ Keogh
✔ Telephone Exchange

PBHG Large Cap 20 (PLCPX)

800-433-0051, 610-647-4100
www.pbhgfunds.com

Aggressive Growth

PERFORMANCE — fund inception date: 11/29/96

	3yr Annual	5yr Annual	10yr Annual	Bull	Bear
Return (%)	38.4	na	na	207.0	-33.2
Differ from Category (+/-)	22.2 high	na	na	87.8 high	-12.6 blw av

Standard Deviation	Category Risk Index	Beta
41.0%—high	1.26—high	1.57

	2000	1999	1998	1997	1996	1995	1994	1993	1992	1991
Return (%)	-22.0	102.9	67.8	32.9	—	—	—	—	—	—
Differ from Category (+/-)	-16.0	45.4	52.7	18.1	—	—	—	—	—	—
Return, Tax-Adjusted (%)	-24.3	97.5	67.4	32.9	—	—	—	—	—	—

PER SHARE DATA

	2000	1999	1998	1997	1996	1995	1994	1993	1992	1991
Dividends, Net Income ($)	0.00	0.00	0.00	0.00	—	—	—	—	—	—
Distrib'ns, Cap Gain ($)	4.37	5.77	0.21	0.00	—	—	—	—	—	—
Net Asset Value ($)	25.20	37.17	21.69	13.07	—	—	—	—	—	—
Expense Ratio (%)	1.23	1.27	1.41	1.50	—	—	—	—	—	—
Yield (%)	0.00	0.00	0.00	0.00	—	—	—	—	—	—
Portfolio Turnover (%)	147	76	98	—	—	—	—	—	—	—
Total Assets (Millions $)	807	790	545	116	—	—	—	—	—	—

PORTFOLIO (as of 6/30/00)

Portfolio Manager: Michael Sutton - 1999

Investm't Category: Aggressive Growth

✔ Domestic	Index
✔ Foreign	Sector
Asset Allocation	State Specific

Investment Style

✔ Large Cap	Mid Cap	Small Cap
✔ Growth	Grth/Val	Value

Portfolio

9.6%	cash	0.0%	corp bonds
90.4%	stocks	0.0%	gov't bonds
0.0%	pref/conv't pref	0.0%	muni bonds
0.0%	conv't bds/wrnts	0.0%	other

SHAREHOLDER INFORMATION

Minimum Investment

Initial: $2,500 — Subsequent: $1

Minimum IRA Investment

Initial: $2,000 — Subsequent: $1

Maximum Fees

Load: none — 12b-1: none

Other: none

Services

✔ IRA
✔ Keogh
✔ Telephone Exchange

PBHG Large Cap Grth (PBHLX)

800-433-0051, 610-647-4100
www.pbhgfunds.com

Growth

PERFORMANCE — fund inception date: 4/5/95

	3yr Annual	5yr Annual	10yr Annual	Bull	Bear
Return (%)	30.3	27.3	na	120.7	-20.2
Differ from Category (+/-)	19.3 high	11.2 high	na	71.0 high	-14.8 low

Standard Deviation	Category Risk Index	Beta
35.5%—high	1.82—high	1.22

	2000	1999	1998	1997	1996	1995	1994	1993	1992	1991
Return (%)	1.7	67.0	30.4	22.3	23.3	—	—	—	—	—
Differ from Category (+/-)	-1.8	48.1	16.1	-4.8	1.0	—	—	—	—	—
Return, Tax-Adjusted (%)	0.0	60.8	28.8	22.0	23.2	—	—	—	—	—

PER SHARE DATA

	2000	1999	1998	1997	1996	1995	1994	1993	1992	1991
Dividends, Net Income ($)	0.00	0.00	0.00	0.00	0.00	—	—	—	—	—
Distrib'ns, Cap Gain ($)	2.69	7.28	1.48	0.19	0.01	—	—	—	—	—
Net Asset Value ($)	29.10	30.99	23.59	19.36	15.99	—	—	—	—	—
Expense Ratio (%)	1.17	1.25	1.22	1.23	1.50	—	—	—	—	—
Yield (%)	0.00	0.00	0.00	0.00	0.00	—	—	—	—	—
Portfolio Turnover (%)	184	46	46	51	117	—	—	—	—	—
Total Assets (Millions $)	393	174	150	141	154	—	—	—	—	—

PORTFOLIO (as of 6/30/00)

Portfolio Manager: Michael Sutton - 1999

Investm't Category: Growth

✔ Domestic — Index
✔ Foreign — Sector
Asset Allocation — State Specific

Investment Style

Large Cap — ✔ Mid Cap — ✔ Small Cap
✔ Growth — Grth/Val — Value

Portfolio

11.5%	cash	0.0%	corp bonds
88.5%	stocks	0.0%	gov't bonds
0.0%	pref/conv't pref	0.0%	muni bonds
0.0%	conv't bds/wrnts	0.0%	other

SHAREHOLDER INFORMATION

Minimum Investment
Initial: $2,500 — Subsequent: $1

Minimum IRA Investment
Initial: $2,000 — Subsequent: $1

Maximum Fees
Load: none — 12b-1: none
Other: none

Services
✔ IRA
✔ Keogh
✔ Telephone Exchange

PBHG Large Cap Value (PLCVX)

800-433-0051, 610-647-4100
www.pbhgfunds.com

Growth & Income

PERFORMANCE — fund inception date: 12/31/96

	3yr Annual	5yr Annual	10yr Annual	Bull	Bear
Return (%)	23.8	na	na	56.1	13.7
Differ from Category (+/-)	14.9 high	na	na	22.6 high	13.8 high

Standard Deviation	Category Risk Index	Beta
17.2%—av	0.99—av	0.73

	2000	1999	1998	1997	1996	1995	1994	1993	1992	1991
Return (%)	23.9	13.5	34.7	25.5	—	—	—	—	—	—
Differ from Category (+/-)	18.2	2.7	21.9	-1.4	—	—	—	—	—	—
Return, Tax-Adjusted (%)	22.9	7.4	31.6	23.4	—	—	—	—	—	—

PER SHARE DATA

	2000	1999	1998	1997	1996	1995	1994	1993	1992	1991
Dividends, Net Income ($)	0.08	0.08	0.09	0.06	—	—	—	—	—	—
Distrib'ns, Cap Gain ($)	0.40	4.03	1.59	0.89	—	—	—	—	—	—
Net Asset Value ($)	13.88	11.61	13.82	11.59	—	—	—	—	—	—
Expense Ratio (%)	1.11	1.01	1.17	1.50	—	—	—	—	—	—
Yield (%)	0.56	0.51	0.58	0.48	—	—	—	—	—	—
Portfolio Turnover (%)	1,018	568	403	—	—	—	—	—	—	—
Total Assets (Millions $)	111	32	94	70	—	—	—	—	—	—

PORTFOLIO (as of 6/30/00)

Portfolio Manager: Ray McCaffrey - 1999

Investm't Category: Growth & Income

✔ Domestic	Index
✔ Foreign	Sector
Asset Allocation	State Specific

Investment Style

✔ Large Cap	✔ Mid Cap	Small Cap
Growth	Grth/Val	✔ Value

Portfolio

16.6%	cash	0.0%	corp bonds
83.4%	stocks	0.0%	gov't bonds
0.0%	pref/conv't pref	0.0%	muni bonds
0.0%	conv't bds/wrnts	0.0%	other

SHAREHOLDER INFORMATION

Minimum Investment
Initial: $2,500 — Subsequent: $1

Minimum IRA Investment
Initial: $2,000 — Subsequent: $1

Maximum Fees
Load: none — 12b-1: none
Other: none

Services
✔ IRA
✔ Keogh
✔ Telephone Exchange

PBHG Mid Cap Value

800-433-0051, 610-647-4100
www.pbhgfunds.com

(PBMCX)

Aggressive Growth

PERFORMANCE — fund inception date: 4/30/97

	3yr Annual	5yr Annual	10yr Annual	Bull	Bear
Return (%)	28.3	na	na	76.8	6.8
Differ from Category (+/-)	12.1 high	na	na	-42.4 blw av	27.4 high

Standard Deviation	Category Risk Index	Beta
21.7%—abv av	0.67—low	1.00

	2000	1999	1998	1997	1996	1995	1994	1993	1992	1991
Return (%)	32.5	24.8	27.8	—	—	—	—	—	—	—
Differ from Category (+/-)	38.5	-32.7	12.7	—	—	—	—	—	—	—
Return, Tax-Adjusted (%)	29.9	16.2	26.1	—	—	—	—	—	—	—

PER SHARE DATA

	2000	1999	1998	1997	1996	1995	1994	1993	1992	1991
Dividends, Net Income ($)	0.09	0.00	0.00	—	—	—	—	—	—	—
Distrib'ns, Cap Gain ($)	1.36	6.71	1.13	—	—	—	—	—	—	—
Net Asset Value ($)	14.77	12.26	15.64	—	—	—	—	—	—	—
Expense Ratio (%)	1.44	1.33	1.47	—	—	—	—	—	—	—
Yield (%)	0.55	0.00	0.00	—	—	—	—	—	—	—
Portfolio Turnover (%)	742	732	399	—	—	—	—	—	—	—
Total Assets (Millions $)	126	34	112	—	—	—	—	—	—	—

PORTFOLIO (as of 6/30/00)

Portfolio Manager: Jerome Heppelmann - 1999

Investm't Category: Aggressive Growth

- ✔ Domestic
- ✔ Foreign
- Asset Allocation
- Index
- Sector
- State Specific

Investment Style

- Large Cap
- ✔ Mid Cap
- Small Cap
- Growth
- Grth/Val
- ✔ Value

Portfolio

9.7%	cash	0.0%	corp bonds
90.3%	stocks	0.0%	gov't bonds
0.0%	pref/conv't pref	0.0%	muni bonds
0.0%	conv't bds/wrnts	0.0%	other

SHAREHOLDER INFORMATION

Minimum Investment
Initial: $2,500 Subsequent: $1

Minimum IRA Investment
Initial: $2,000 Subsequent: $1

Maximum Fees
Load: none 12b-1: none
Other: none

Services

- ✔ IRA
- ✔ Keogh
- ✔ Telephone Exchange

PBHG Select Equity (PBHEX)

800-433-0051, 610-647-4100
www.pbhgfunds.com

Aggressive Growth

PERFORMANCE

fund inception date: 4/5/95

	3yr Annual	5yr Annual	10yr Annual	Bull	Bear
Return (%)	32.8	26.2	na	243.1	-43.4
Differ from Category (+/-)	16.6 high	11.6 high	na	123.9 high	-22.8 low

Standard Deviation	Category Risk Index	Beta
60.3%—high	1.86—high	1.63

	2000	1999	1998	1997	1996	1995	1994	1993	1992	1991
Return (%)	-24.5	160.8	19.0	6.8	27.9	—	—	—	—	—
Differ from Category (+/-)	-18.5	103.3	3.9	-8.0	9.6	—	—	—	—	—
Return, Tax-Adjusted (%)	-25.3	155.5	19.0	6.8	27.5	—	—	—	—	—

PER SHARE DATA

	2000	1999	1998	1997	1996	1995	1994	1993	1992	1991
Dividends, Net Income ($)	0.00	0.00	0.00	0.00	0.00	—	—	—	—	—
Distrib'ns, Cap Gain ($)	2.44	6.49	0.00	0.00	0.20	—	—	—	—	—
Net Asset Value ($)	41.23	57.22	24.91	20.93	19.59	—	—	—	—	—
Expense Ratio (%)	1.18	1.34	1.35	1.26	1.50	—	—	—	—	—
Yield (%)	0.00	0.00	0.00	0.00	0.00	—	—	—	—	—
Portfolio Turnover (%)	200	56	72	71	206	—	—	—	—	—
Total Assets (Millions $)	1,182	624	289	348	580	—	—	—	—	—

PORTFOLIO (as of 6/30/00)

Portfolio Manager: Michael Sutton - 2000

Investm't Category: Aggressive Growth

✔ Domestic
✔ Foreign
Asset Allocation
Index
Sector
State Specific

Investment Style

Large Cap
Mid Cap
✔ Small Cap
✔ Growth
Grth/Val
Value

Portfolio

12.7% cash
87.3% stocks
0.0% pref/conv't pref
0.0% conv't bds/wrnts
0.0% corp bonds
0.0% gov't bonds
0.0% muni bonds
0.0% other

SHAREHOLDER INFORMATION

Minimum Investment

Initial: $2,500 Subsequent: $1

Minimum IRA Investment

Initial: $2,000 Subsequent: $1

Maximum Fees

Load: none 12b-1: none
Other: none

Services

✔ IRA
✔ Keogh
✔ Telephone Exchange

PBHG Small Cap Value (PBSVX)

800-433-0051, 610-647-4100
www.pbhgfunds.com

Aggressive Growth

PERFORMANCE — fund inception date: 4/30/97

	3yr Annual	5yr Annual	10yr Annual	Bull	Bear
Return (%)	17.6	na	na	51.8	-0.9
Differ from Category (+/-)	1.4 av	na	na	-67.4 blw av	19.7 high

Standard Deviation	Category Risk Index	Beta
24.3%—abv av	0.75—low	0.88

	2000	1999	1998	1997	1996	1995	1994	1993	1992	1991
Return (%)	35.7	18.6	1.2	—	—	—	—	—	—	—
Differ from Category (+/-)	41.7	-38.9	-13.9	—	—	—	—	—	—	—
Return, Tax-Adjusted (%)	34.0	18.6	0.0	—	—	—	—	—	—	—

PER SHARE DATA

	2000	1999	1998	1997	1996	1995	1994	1993	1992	1991
Dividends, Net Income ($)	0.03	0.00	0.00	—	—	—	—	—	—	—
Distrib'ns, Cap Gain ($)	1.25	0.00	0.85	—	—	—	—	—	—	—
Net Asset Value ($)	19.67	15.47	13.04	—	—	—	—	—	—	—
Expense Ratio (%)	1.50	1.48	1.49	—	—	—	—	—	—	—
Yield (%)	0.14	0.00	0.00	—	—	—	—	—	—	—
Portfolio Turnover (%)	352	273	263	—	—	—	—	—	—	—
Total Assets (Millions $)	197	70	104	—	—	—	—	—	—	—

PORTFOLIO (as of 6/30/00)

Portfolio Manager: Jerome Heppelmann - 1999

Investm't Category: Aggressive Growth

✔ Domestic | Index
✔ Foreign | Sector
Asset Allocation | State Specific

Investment Style

Large Cap | Mid Cap | ✔ Small Cap
✔ Growth | Grth/Val | Value

Portfolio

17.4% cash | 0.0% corp bonds
82.6% stocks | 0.0% gov't bonds
0.0% pref/conv't pref | 0.0% muni bonds
0.0% conv't bds/wrnts | 0.0% other

SHAREHOLDER INFORMATION

Minimum Investment
Initial: $2,500 Subsequent: $1

Minimum IRA Investment
Initial: $2,000 Subsequent: $1

Maximum Fees
Load: none 12b-1: none
Other: none

Services
✔ IRA
✔ Keogh
✔ Telephone Exchange

PBHG Strategic Small Co (PSSCX)

800-433-0051, 610-647-4100
www.pbhgfunds.com

Aggressive Growth

PERFORMANCE — fund inception date: 12/31/96

	3yr Annual	5yr Annual	10yr Annual	Bull	Bear
Return (%)	20.1	na	na	105.8	-16.7
Differ from Category (+/-)	3.9 abv av	na	na	-13.4 av	3.9 abv av

Standard Deviation	Category Risk Index	Beta
35.6%—high	1.10—abv av	1.15

	2000	1999	1998	1997	1996	1995	1994	1993	1992	1991
Return (%)	11.8	51.7	2.1	25.6	—	—	—	—	—	—
Differ from Category (+/-)	17.8	-5.8	-13.0	10.8	—	—	—	—	—	—
Return, Tax-Adjusted (%)	8.5	49.5	1.3	23.8	—	—	—	—	—	—

PER SHARE DATA

	2000	1999	1998	1997	1996	1995	1994	1993	1992	1991
Dividends, Net Income ($)	0.00	0.00	0.00	0.00	—	—	—	—	—	—
Distrib'ns, Cap Gain ($)	2.59	1.24	0.46	0.87	—	—	—	—	—	—
Net Asset Value ($)	15.24	15.91	11.41	11.67	—	—	—	—	—	—
Expense Ratio (%)	1.50	1.50	1.45	1.50	—	—	—	—	—	—
Yield (%)	0.00	0.00	0.00	0.00	—	—	—	—	—	—
Portfolio Turnover (%)	240	140	215	—	—	—	—	—	—	—
Total Assets (Millions $)	77	59	69	117	—	—	—	—	—	—

PORTFOLIO (as of 6/30/00)

Portfolio Manager: J. Smith, J. Heppelmann - 1997

Investm't Category: Aggressive Growth

✔ Domestic — Index
✔ Foreign — Sector
Asset Allocation — State Specific

Investment Style

Large Cap — Mid Cap — ✔ Small Cap
✔ Growth — Grth/Val — Value

Portfolio

14.7%	cash	0.0%	corp bonds
85.3%	stocks	0.0%	gov't bonds
0.0%	pref/conv't pref	0.0%	muni bonds
0.0%	conv't bds/wrnts	0.0%	other

SHAREHOLDER INFORMATION

Minimum Investment
Initial: $5,000 — Subsequent: $1

Minimum IRA Investment
Initial: $2,000 — Subsequent: $1

Maximum Fees
Load: none — 12b-1: none
Other: none

Services
✔ IRA
✔ Keogh
✔ Telephone Exchange

PBHG Tech & Comm (PBTCX)

800-433-0051, 610-647-4100
www.pbhgfunds.com

Aggressive Growth

PERFORMANCE

fund inception date: 9/29/95

	3yr Annual	5yr Annual	10yr Annual	Bull	Bear
Return (%)	36.7	32.4	na	401.1	-52.8
Differ from Category (+/-)	20.5 high	17.8 high	na	281.9 high	-32.2 low

Standard Deviation	Category Risk Index	Beta
61.6%—high	1.90—high	1.79

	2000	1999	1998	1997	1996	1995	1994	1993	1992	1991
Return (%)	-41.0	243.8	25.9	3.3	54.4	—	—	—	—	—
Differ from Category (+/-)	-35.0	186.3	10.8	-11.5	36.1	—	—	—	—	—
Return, Tax-Adjusted (%)	-43.6	239.2	25.5	2.3	53.5	—	—	—	—	—

PER SHARE DATA

	2000	1999	1998	1997	1996	1995	1994	1993	1992	1991
Dividends, Net Income ($)	0.00	0.00	0.00	0.00	0.00	—	—	—	—	—
Distrib'ns, Cap Gain ($)	8.85	4.86	0.29	0.85	0.35	—	—	—	—	—
Net Asset Value ($)	34.43	68.06	21.45	17.28	17.56	—	—	—	—	—
Expense Ratio (%)	1.19	1.34	1.30	1.33	1.50	—	—	—	—	—
Yield (%)	0.00	0.00	0.00	0.00	0.00	—	—	—	—	—
Portfolio Turnover (%)	362	276	259	289	—	—	—	—	—	—
Total Assets (Millions $)	1,637	1,626	396	550	562	—	—	—	—	—

PORTFOLIO (as of 6/30/00)

Portfolio Manager: Jeffrey Wrona - 1998

Investm't Category: Aggressive Growth

✔ Domestic — Index
✔ Foreign — ✔ Sector
Asset Allocation — State Specific

Investment Style

Large Cap — Mid Cap — ✔ Small Cap
✔ Growth — Grth/Val — Value

Portfolio

5.1%	cash	0.0%	corp bonds
94.9%	stocks	0.0%	gov't bonds
0.0%	pref/conv't pref	0.0%	muni bonds
0.0%	conv't bds/wrnts	0.0%	other

SHAREHOLDER INFORMATION

Minimum Investment
Initial: $2,500 — Subsequent: $1

Minimum IRA Investment
Initial: $2,000 — Subsequent: $1

Maximum Fees
Load: none — 12b-1: none
Other: none

Services
✔ IRA
✔ Keogh
✔ Telephone Exchange

Papp America: Abroad (PAAFX)

800-421-4004, 602-956-1115
www.roypapp.com

Growth

PERFORMANCE

fund inception date: 12/6/91

	3yr Annual	5yr Annual	10yr Annual	Bull	Bear
Return (%)	8.8	16.4	na	52.8	-18.1
Differ from Category (+/-)	-2.2 blw av	0.3 av	na	3.1 av	-12.7 low

Standard Deviation	Category Risk Index	Beta
21.8%—abv av	1.12—abv av	1.10

	2000	1999	1998	1997	1996	1995	1994	1993	1992	1991
Return (%)	-8.6	13.9	23.8	29.9	27.6	37.0	7.7	0.0	7.3	—
Differ from Category (+/-)	-12.1	-5.0	9.5	2.8	5.3	6.6	7.9	-14.6	-5.3	—
Return, Tax-Adjusted (%)	-11.4	13.0	23.7	29.7	26.1	36.2	7.3	-0.5	6.9	—

PER SHARE DATA

	2000	1999	1998	1997	1996	1995	1994	1993	1992	1991
Dividends, Net Income ($)	0.00	0.00	0.03	0.01	0.00	0.04	0.09	0.09	0.09	—
Distrib'ns, Cap Gain ($)	5.09	1.38	0.00	0.12	0.84	0.25	0.00	0.11	0.02	—
Net Asset Value ($)	27.75	35.25	32.13	25.98	20.11	16.47	12.24	11.45	11.67	—
Expense Ratio (%)	na	1.07	1.08	1.11	1.25	1.22	1.25	1.25	1.25	—
Yield (%)	0.00	0.00	0.09	0.03	0.00	0.23	0.73	0.77	0.76	—
Portfolio Turnover (%)	na	5	24	4	12	26	16	8	16	—
Total Assets (Millions $)	177	242	342	288	29	15	11	10	5	—

PORTFOLIO (as of 6/30/00)

Portfolio Manager: L. Roy Papp, Rosellen Papp - 1991

Investm't Category: Growth

✔ Domestic	Index
Foreign	Sector
Asset Allocation	State Specific

Investment Style

✔ Large Cap	Mid Cap	Small Cap
✔ Growth	Grth/Val	Value

Portfolio

0.5%	cash	0.0%	corp bonds
99.5%	stocks	0.0%	gov't bonds
0.0%	pref/conv't pref	0.0%	muni bonds
0.0%	conv't bds/wrnts	0.0%	other

SHAREHOLDER INFORMATION

Minimum Investment
Initial: $5,000 Subsequent: $1,000

Minimum IRA Investment
Initial: $1,000 Subsequent: $1,000

Maximum Fees
Load: none 12b-1: none
Other: none

Services
✔ IRA
Keogh
Telephone Exchange

Papp Stock (LRPSX)

800-421-4004, 602-956-1115
www.roypapp.com

Growth

PERFORMANCE — fund inception date: 11/29/89

	3yr Annual	5yr Annual	10yr Annual	Bull	Bear
Return (%)	11.1	17.3	16.2	49.9	-10.4
Differ from Category (+/-)	0.1 av	1.2 av	-0.6 av	0.2 av	-5.0 av

Standard Deviation	Category Risk Index	Beta
19.8%—abv av	1.02—av	1.03

	2000	1999	1998	1997	1996	1995	1994	1993	1992	1991
Return (%)	-6.0	14.9	26.9	33.1	21.8	32.9	-1.4	1.6	13.5	33.8
Differ from Category (+/-)	-9.5	-4.0	12.6	6.0	-0.5	2.5	-1.2	-13.0	0.9	-3.8
Return, Tax-Adjusted (%)	-7.3	14.4	26.3	32.7	20.7	32.5	-1.7	1.0	12.8	32.4

PER SHARE DATA

	2000	1999	1998	1997	1996	1995	1994	1993	1992	1991
Dividends, Net Income ($)	0.00	0.00	0.45	0.00	0.00	0.07	0.13	0.13	0.13	0.13
Distrib'ns, Cap Gain ($)	2.76	0.76	0.00	0.43	0.75	0.07	0.00	0.09	0.16	0.34
Net Asset Value ($)	37.09	42.20	37.36	29.78	22.70	19.29	14.63	14.98	14.96	13.45
Expense Ratio (%)	na	1.09	1.10	1.12	1.16	1.20	1.19	1.25	1.25	1.25
Yield (%)	0.00	0.00	1.20	0.00	0.00	0.36	0.88	0.86	0.85	0.94
Portfolio Turnover (%)	na	6	9	6	14	8	20	15	11	4
Total Assets (Millions $)	102	105	98	79	53	44	36	39	22	13

PORTFOLIO (as of 6/30/00)

Portfolio Manager: L. Roy Papp, Rosellen Papp - 1989

Investm't Category: Growth

✔ Domestic	Index
Foreign	Sector
Asset Allocation	State Specific

Investment Style

✔ Large Cap	Mid Cap	Small Cap
✔ Growth	Grth/Val	Value

Portfolio

0.2% cash	0.0% corp bonds
99.8% stocks	0.0% gov't bonds
0.0% pref/conv't pref	0.0% muni bonds
0.0% conv't bds/wrnts	0.0% other

SHAREHOLDER INFORMATION

Minimum Investment
Initial: $5,000 Subsequent: $1,000

Minimum IRA Investment
Initial: $1,000 Subsequent: $1,000

Maximum Fees
Load: none 12b-1: none
Other: none

Services
✔ IRA
✔ Keogh
Telephone Exchange

Pax World Balanced (PAXWX)

800-767-1729, 212-830-5220
www.paxfund.com

Balanced

PERFORMANCE — fund inception date: 8/10/71

	3yr Annual	5yr Annual	10yr Annual	Bull	Bear
Return (%)	15.5	16.3	13.0	40.7	-2.6
Differ from Category (+/-)	7.1 high	4.9 high	1.3 abv av	12.6 high	0.6 av

Standard Deviation	Category Risk Index	Beta
9.8%—blw av	0.90—blw av	0.45

	2000	1999	1998	1997	1996	1995	1994	1993	1992	1991
Return (%)	5.6	17.2	24.6	25.1	10.3	29.1	2.6	-1.0	0.6	20.7
Differ from Category (+/-)	3.6	6.5	11.3	6.3	-3.6	3.6	3.9	-15.4	-7.8	-3.1
Return, Tax-Adjusted (%)	3.2	15.0	22.6	21.9	7.4	26.4	1.1	-2.5	-1.0	16.9

PER SHARE DATA

	2000	1999	1998	1997	1996	1995	1994	1993	1992	1991
Dividends, Net Income ($)	0.52	0.45	0.46	0.50	0.55	0.79	0.50	0.50	0.67	0.76
Distrib'ns, Cap Gain ($)	1.75	1.41	0.88	1.65	0.89	0.14	0.00	0.07	0.13	1.04
Net Asset Value ($)	22.41	23.40	21.64	18.52	16.56	16.33	13.39	13.55	14.27	14.99
Expense Ratio (%)	na	0.89	0.95	0.91	0.89	1.00	0.98	0.94	1.00	1.20
Yield (%)	2.15	1.81	2.04	2.47	3.15	4.79	3.73	3.67	4.65	4.74
Portfolio Turnover (%)	na	21	28	13	34	28	25	22	17	26
Total Assets (Millions $)	1,187	1,072	837	628	518	476	388	464	468	270

PORTFOLIO (as of 6/30/00)

Portfolio Manager: Christopher Brown, Robert Colin - 1998

Investm't Category: Balanced

✔ Domestic	Index
Foreign	Sector
Asset Allocation	State Specific

Investment Style

Large Cap	Mid Cap	Small Cap
Growth	Grth/Val	Value

Portfolio

7.5%	cash	1.3%	corp bonds
62.3%	stocks	27.8%	gov't bonds
1.3%	pref/conv't pref	0.0%	muni bonds
0.0%	conv't bds/wrnts	0.0%	other

SHAREHOLDER INFORMATION

Minimum Investment

Initial: $250 Subsequent: $50

Minimum IRA Investment

Initial: $250 Subsequent: $50

Maximum Fees

Load: none 12b-1: 0.19%

Other: none

Services

✔ IRA

Keogh

Telephone Exchange

Payden & Rygel Gr & Inc/R (PDOGX)

800-572-9336, 213-625-1900
www.payden.com

Growth & Income

PERFORMANCE — fund inception date: 11/1/96

	3yr Annual	5yr Annual	10yr Annual	Bull	Bear
Return (%)	7.9	na	na	35.8	-7.5
Differ from Category (+/-)	-1.0 av	na	na	2.3 av	-7.4 blw av

Standard Deviation	Category Risk Index	Beta
16.3%—av	0.94—blw av	0.83

	2000	1999	1998	1997	1996	1995	1994	1993	1992	1991
Return (%)	-5.1	12.3	18.1	26.9	—	—	—	—	—	—
Differ from Category (+/-)	-10.8	1.5	5.3	0.0	—	—	—	—	—	—
Return, Tax-Adjusted (%)	-9.4	11.1	16.9	26.1	—	—	—	—	—	—

PER SHARE DATA

	2000	1999	1998	1997	1996	1995	1994	1993	1992	1991
Dividends, Net Income ($)	0.18	0.18	0.21	0.19	—	—	—	—	—	—
Distrib'ns, Cap Gain ($)	3.16	0.51	0.33	0.00	—	—	—	—	—	—
Net Asset Value ($)	12.12	16.24	15.10	13.26	—	—	—	—	—	—
Expense Ratio (%)	na	0.75	0.54	0.54	—	—	—	—	—	—
Yield (%)	1.17	1.07	1.36	1.43	—	—	—	—	—	—
Portfolio Turnover (%)	na	5	10	—	—	—	—	—	—	—
Total Assets (Millions $)	93	253	265	188	—	—	—	—	—	—

PORTFOLIO (as of 6/30/00)

Portfolio Manager: committee - 1996

Investm't Category: Growth & Income

✔ Domestic — Index
Foreign — Sector
Asset Allocation — State Specific

Investment Style

✔ Large Cap — Mid Cap — Small Cap
Growth — Grth/Val — ✔ Value

Portfolio

3.8%	cash	0.0%	corp bonds
96.2%	stocks	0.0%	gov't bonds
0.0%	pref/conv't pref	0.0%	muni bonds
0.0%	conv't bds/wrnts	0.0%	other

SHAREHOLDER INFORMATION

Minimum Investment
Initial: $5,000 — Subsequent: $1,000

Minimum IRA Investment
Initial: $2,000 — Subsequent: $1,000

Maximum Fees
Load: none — 12b-1: none
Other: none

Services
✔ IRA
Keogh
✔ Telephone Exchange

Payden & Rygel Mkt Ret/R (PYMRX)

800-572-9336, 213-625-1900
www.payden.com

Growth & Income

PERFORMANCE

fund inception date: 12/1/95

	3yr Annual	5yr Annual	10yr Annual	Bull	Bear
Return (%)	10.0	15.8	na	53.0	-11.8
Differ from Category (+/-)	1.1 av	1.5 abv av	na	19.5 abv av	-11.7 low

Standard Deviation	Category Risk Index	Beta
17.9%—av	1.03—abv av	1.00

	2000	1999	1998	1997	1996	1995	1994	1993	1992	1991
Return (%)	-10.8	18.0	26.4	33.3	17.3	—	—	—	—	—
Differ from Category (+/-)	-16.5	7.2	13.6	6.4	-2.4	—	—	—	—	—
Return, Tax-Adjusted (%)	-13.1	13.6	22.8	28.7	13.8	—	—	—	—	—

PER SHARE DATA

	2000	1999	1998	1997	1996	1995	1994	1993	1992	1991
Dividends, Net Income ($)	0.84	0.76	0.73	0.64	0.56	—	—	—	—	—
Distrib'ns, Cap Gain ($)	0.00	1.54	0.73	1.22	0.44	—	—	—	—	—
Net Asset Value ($)	11.92	14.26	14.15	12.42	10.82	—	—	—	—	—
Expense Ratio (%)	na	0.45	0.45	0.45	0.00	—	—	—	—	—
Yield (%)	7.04	4.81	4.90	4.69	4.97	—	—	—	—	—
Portfolio Turnover (%)	na	113	48	140	—	—	—	—	—	—
Total Assets (Millions $)	54	91	51	24	6	—	—	—	—	—

PORTFOLIO (as of 6/30/00)

Portfolio Manager: committee - 1995

Investm't Category: Growth & Income

✔ Domestic | Index
Foreign | Sector
Asset Allocation | State Specific

Investment Style

✔ Large Cap | Mid Cap | Small Cap
Growth | ✔ Grth/Val | Value

Portfolio

25.0%	cash	50.0%	corp bonds
0.0%	stocks	25.0%	gov't bonds
0.0%	pref/conv't pref	0.0%	muni bonds
0.0%	conv't bds/wrnts	0.0%	other

SHAREHOLDER INFORMATION

Minimum Investment

Initial: $5,000 Subsequent: $1,000

Minimum IRA Investment

Initial: $2,000 Subsequent: $1,000

Maximum Fees

Load: none 12b-1: none
Other: none

Services

✔ IRA
Keogh
✔ Telephone Exchange

Permanent Port: Perm Port (PRPFX)

800-531-5142, 512-453-7558

Balanced

PERFORMANCE

fund inception date: 12/1/82

	3yr Annual	5yr Annual	10yr Annual	Bull	Bear
Return (%)	3.4	3.5	5.5	9.0	-2.0
Differ from Category (+/-)	-5.0 low	-7.9 low	-6.2 low	-19.1 low	1.2 abv av

Standard Deviation	Category Risk Index	Beta
7.6%—blw av	0.69—low	0.23

	2000	1999	1998	1997	1996	1995	1994	1993	1992	1991
Return (%)	5.8	1.1	3.4	5.6	1.6	15.4	-2.8	15.5	2.5	8.0
Differ from Category (+/-)	3.8	-9.6	-9.9	-13.2	-12.3	-10.1	-1.5	1.1	-5.9	-15.8
Return, Tax-Adjusted (%)	4.8	-0.3	2.3	4.4	0.5	14.4	-3.3	14.8	1.9	6.0

PER SHARE DATA

	2000	1999	1998	1997	1996	1995	1994	1993	1992	1991
Dividends, Net Income ($)	0.16	0.29	0.20	0.34	0.42	0.38	0.22	0.24	0.29	0.91
Distrib'ns, Cap Gain ($)	0.52	0.77	0.64	0.36	0.09	0.00	0.00	0.00	0.00	0.00
Net Asset Value ($)	18.16	17.81	18.68	18.87	18.53	18.73	16.55	17.27	15.16	15.07
Expense Ratio (%)	1.47	1.43	1.91	1.49	1.35	1.32	1.21	1.25	1.27	1.36
Yield (%)	0.85	1.56	1.03	1.76	2.25	2.02	1.32	1.38	1.91	6.03
Portfolio Turnover (%)	23	14	7	12	10	31	49	70	8	32
Total Assets (Millions $)	52	58	66	70	74	75	72	83	65	71

PORTFOLIO (as of 6/30/00)

Portfolio Manager: Terry Coxon - 1982

Investm't Category: Balanced

✔ Domestic — Index
✔ Foreign — Sector
✔ Asset Allocation — State Specific

Investment Style

Large Cap — Mid Cap — Small Cap
Growth — Grth/Val — Value

Portfolio

6.4%	cash	0.0%	corp bonds
29.1%	stocks	34.1%	gov't bonds
0.0%	pref/conv't pref	0.0%	muni bonds
2.2%	conv't bds/wrnts	28.2%	other

SHAREHOLDER INFORMATION

Minimum Investment
Initial: $1,000 — Subsequent: $100

Minimum IRA Investment
Initial: $1,000 — Subsequent: $100

Maximum Fees
Load: none — 12b-1: none
Other: none

Services
✔ IRA
✔ Keogh
✔ Telephone Exchange

Philadelphia (PHILX)

800-749-9933, 561-395-2155

Growth & Income

PERFORMANCE

fund inception date: 1/1/29

	3yr Annual	5yr Annual	10yr Annual	Bull	Bear
Return (%)	5.3	12.3	12.0	14.9	2.9
Differ from Category (+/-)	-3.6 blw av	-2.0 blw av	-2.9 low	-18.6 blw av	3.0 abv av

Standard Deviation	Category Risk Index	Beta
13.4%—blw av	0.77—low	0.52

	2000	1999	1998	1997	1996	1995	1994	1993	1992	1991
Return (%)	4.7	1.7	9.8	35.9	12.7	27.3	-8.5	18.2	19.7	5.7
Differ from Category (+/-)	-1.0	-9.1	-3.0	9.0	-7.0	-2.2	-8.0	4.4	8.1	-22.4
Return, Tax-Adjusted (%)	2.5	-0.3	5.1	33.3	11.9	22.9	-9.0	14.6	18.9	5.1

PER SHARE DATA

	2000	1999	1998	1997	1996	1995	1994	1993	1992	1991
Dividends, Net Income ($)	0.14	0.06	0.13	0.10	0.12	0.13	0.09	0.13	0.08	0.09
Distrib'ns, Cap Gain ($)	0.56	0.77	1.98	0.81	0.03	0.79	0.02	0.66	0.07	0.00
Net Asset Value ($)	7.51	7.85	8.53	9.67	7.82	7.08	6.29	7.01	6.61	5.66
Expense Ratio (%)	na	1.55	1.53	1.53	1.56	1.72	1.67	1.60	1.79	1.61
Yield (%)	1.73	0.69	1.23	0.95	1.52	1.65	1.42	1.69	1.19	1.59
Portfolio Turnover (%)	na	81	37	17	14	59	28	24	39	49
Total Assets (Millions $)	96	105	117	116	95	91	80	94	87	84

PORTFOLIO (as of 6/30/00)

Portfolio Manager: Donald Baxter - 1987

Investm't Category: Growth & Income

✔ Domestic | Index
✔ Foreign | Sector
Asset Allocation | State Specific

Investment Style

✔ Large Cap | Mid Cap | Small Cap
Growth | Grth/Val | ✔ Value

Portfolio

43.4%	cash	0.0%	corp bonds
49.9%	stocks	6.7%	gov't bonds
0.0%	pref/conv't pref	0.0%	muni bonds
0.0%	conv't bds/wrnts	0.0%	other

SHAREHOLDER INFORMATION

Minimum Investment

Initial: $1,000 | Subsequent: $1

Minimum IRA Investment

Initial: $1,000 | Subsequent: $1

Maximum Fees

Load: none | 12b-1: 0.26%
Other: none

Services

✔ IRA
✔ Keogh
Telephone Exchange

Pilgrim Corp Leaders/A (LEXCX)

800-992-0180, 480-477-3000
www.pilgrimfunds.com

Growth & Income

PERFORMANCE — fund inception date: 3/3/41

	3yr Annual	5yr Annual	10yr Annual	Bull	Bear
Return (%)	5.9	12.3	14.3	29.8	0.4
Differ from Category (+/-)	-3.0 blw av	-2.0 blw av	-0.6 blw av	-3.7 av	0.5 av

Standard Deviation	Category Risk Index	Beta
15.2%—av	0.87—blw av	0.66

	2000	1999	1998	1997	1996	1995	1994	1993	1992	1991
Return (%)	-4.8	13.6	9.9	23.0	22.4	39.2	-0.7	17.5	9.6	19.4
Differ from Category (+/-)	-10.5	2.8	-2.9	-3.9	2.7	9.7	-0.2	3.7	-2.0	-8.7
Return, Tax-Adjusted (%)	-7.4	12.2	8.7	16.8	20.5	36.2	-5.7	14.7	7.2	16.4

PER SHARE DATA

	2000	1999	1998	1997	1996	1995	1994	1993	1992	1991
Dividends, Net Income ($)	1.17	0.54	0.22	0.27	0.53	0.70	0.44	0.64	0.35	0.96
Distrib'ns, Cap Gain ($)	0.00	0.00	0.43	4.43	0.18	0.13	1.66	0.22	0.59	0.06
Net Asset Value ($)	15.28	17.30	15.70	14.88	16.05	13.74	10.51	12.78	11.62	11.52
Expense Ratio (%)	na	0.61	0.65	0.62	0.63	0.58	0.62	0.57	0.60	0.67
Yield (%)	7.65	3.12	1.36	1.39	3.26	5.04	3.61	4.92	2.86	8.29
Portfolio Turnover (%)	—	—	—	—	—	—	—	—	—	—
Total Assets (Millions $)	340	454	482	526	391	247	156	147	105	98

PORTFOLIO (as of 6/30/00)

Portfolio Manager: Lawrence Kantor - 1988

Investm't Category: Growth & Income

✔ Domestic — Index
✔ Foreign — Sector
Asset Allocation — State Specific

Investment Style

✔ Large Cap — Mid Cap — Small Cap
Growth — Grth/Val — ✔ Value

Portfolio

0.2%	cash	0.0%	corp bonds
99.8%	stocks	0.0%	gov't bonds
0.0%	pref/conv't pref	0.0%	muni bonds
0.0%	conv't bds/wrnts	0.0%	other

SHAREHOLDER INFORMATION

Minimum Investment
Initial: $1,000 — Subsequent: $50

Minimum IRA Investment
Initial: $1,000 — Subsequent: $50

Maximum Fees
Load: none — 12b-1: none
Other: none

Services
✔ IRA
✔ Keogh
✔ Telephone Exchange

Pilgrim Wldwd Emerg Mkt/A (LEXGX)

800-992-0180, 480-477-3000
www.pilgrimfunds.com

International Stock

PERFORMANCE — fund inception date: 1/22/69

	3yr Annual	5yr Annual	10yr Annual	Bull	Bear
Return (%)	-7.2	-5.3	2.6	144.0	-54.7
Differ from Category (+/-)	-16.1 low	-13.6 low	-6.4 low	53.1 high	-30.7 low

Standard Deviation	Category Risk Index	Beta
41.4%—high	1.83—high	1.24

	2000	1999	1998	1997	1996	1995	1994	1993	1992	1991
Return (%)	-47.0	113.1	-29.2	-11.4	7.3	-5.9	-13.8	63.3	3.7	24.1
Differ from Category (+/-)	-27.6	52.4	-35.0	-12.7	-7.2	-15.2	-10.7	23.1	7.2	11.1
Return, Tax-Adjusted (%)	-47.0	112.9	-29.5	-11.4	7.3	-6.1	-14.9	62.7	1.4	18.8

PER SHARE DATA

	2000	1999	1998	1997	1996	1995	1994	1993	1992	1991
Dividends, Net Income ($)	0.00	0.03	0.08	0.00	0.00	0.08	0.00	0.00	0.11	0.11
Distrib'ns, Cap Gain ($)	0.00	0.00	0.00	0.00	0.00	0.00	0.56	0.17	0.60	1.48
Net Asset Value ($)	7.99	15.10	7.11	10.18	11.49	10.70	11.47	13.96	8.66	9.03
Expense Ratio (%)	na	2.00	1.85	1.82	1.76	1.72	1.65	1.64	1.89	1.97
Yield (%)	0.00	0.19	1.12	0.00	0.00	0.74	0.00	0.00	1.18	1.04
Portfolio Turnover (%)	na	184	107	112	86	77	79	38	91	112
Total Assets (Millions $)	70	153	67	137	256	260	288	227	30	24

PORTFOLIO (as of 6/30/00)

Portfolio Manager: Richard Saler, Phillip Schwartz - 2000

Investm't Category: International Stock

Domestic	Index
✔ Foreign	Sector
Asset Allocation	State Specific

Investment Style

Large Cap	Mid Cap	Small Cap
Growth	Grth/Val	Value

Portfolio

17.9%	cash	0.0%	corp bonds
82.1%	stocks	0.0%	gov't bonds
0.0%	pref/conv't pref	0.0%	muni bonds
0.0%	conv't bds/wrnts	0.0%	other

SHAREHOLDER INFORMATION

Minimum Investment
Initial: $1,000 Subsequent: $100

Minimum IRA Investment
Initial: $250 Subsequent: $100

Maximum Fees
Load: none 12b-1: 0.25%
Other: none

Services
✔ IRA
✔ Keogh
✔ Telephone Exchange

Preferred Asset Allocatn (PFAAX)

800-662-4769, 309-675-5123
www.preferredgroup.com

Balanced

PERFORMANCE — fund inception date: 7/1/92

	3yr Annual	5yr Annual	10yr Annual	Bull	Bear
Return (%)	11.4	14.0	na	23.4	-1.2
Differ from Category (+/-)	3.0 high	2.6 high	na	-4.7 blw av	2.0 abv av

Standard Deviation	Category Risk Index	Beta
8.9%—blw av	0.82—low	0.45

	2000	1999	1998	1997	1996	1995	1994	1993	1992	1991
Return (%)	6.5	2.1	27.0	21.0	15.0	32.8	-2.5	10.5	—	—
Differ from Category (+/-)	4.5	-8.6	13.7	2.2	1.1	7.3	-1.2	-3.9	—	—
Return, Tax-Adjusted (%)	2.5	0.5	24.3	17.5	12.5	29.1	-3.8	8.7	—	—

PER SHARE DATA

	2000	1999	1998	1997	1996	1995	1994	1993	1992	1991
Dividends, Net Income ($)	0.60	0.48	0.45	0.46	0.41	0.39	0.33	0.31	—	—
Distrib'ns, Cap Gain ($)	2.01	0.36	1.01	1.38	0.52	0.81	0.08	0.21	—	—
Net Asset Value ($)	14.53	16.11	16.61	14.28	13.37	12.45	10.32	11.02	—	—
Expense Ratio (%)	0.89	0.89	0.92	0.99	1.04	1.11	1.25	1.27	—	—
Yield (%)	3.62	2.91	2.55	2.93	2.95	2.94	3.17	2.76	—	—
Portfolio Turnover (%)	32	5	27	27	38	18	24	34	—	—
Total Assets (Millions $)	208	221	210	138	107	82	61	53	—	—

PORTFOLIO (as of 6/30/00)

Portfolio Manager: Thomas Hazuka, Ed Peters - 1992

Investm't Category: Balanced

✔ Domestic — Index
✔ Foreign — Sector
✔ Asset Allocation — State Specific

Investment Style

Large Cap — Mid Cap — Small Cap
Growth — Grth/Val — Value

Portfolio

13.9%	cash	0.0%	corp bonds
31.1%	stocks	55.1%	gov't bonds
0.0%	pref/conv't pref	0.0%	muni bonds
0.0%	conv't bds/wrnts	0.0%	other

SHAREHOLDER INFORMATION

Minimum Investment
Initial: $1,000 — Subsequent: $50

Minimum IRA Investment
Initial: $250 — Subsequent: $50

Maximum Fees
Load: none — 12b-1: none
Other: none

Services
✔ IRA
✔ Keogh
✔ Telephone Exchange

Preferred Growth (PFGRX)

800-662-4769, 309-675-5123
www.preferredgroup.com

Growth

PERFORMANCE

fund inception date: 7/1/92

	3yr Annual	5yr Annual	10yr Annual	Bull	Bear
Return (%)	17.4	20.4	na	98.7	-27.5
Differ from Category (+/-)	6.4 high	4.3 high	na	49.0 high	-22.1 low

Standard Deviation	Category Risk Index	Beta
25.0%—abv av	1.28—high	1.24

	2000	1999	1998	1997	1996	1995	1994	1993	1992	1991
Return (%)	-17.6	44.8	35.8	31.9	18.7	28.3	-1.1	16.0	—	—
Differ from Category (+/-)	-21.1	25.9	21.5	4.8	-3.6	-2.1	-0.9	1.4	—	—
Return, Tax-Adjusted (%)	-22.1	41.6	30.3	26.8	13.9	27.2	-1.2	16.0	—	—

PER SHARE DATA

	2000	1999	1998	1997	1996	1995	1994	1993	1992	1991
Dividends, Net Income ($)	0.00	0.00	0.00	0.00	0.00	0.00	0.02	0.00	—	—
Distrib'ns, Cap Gain ($)	5.83	3.09	4.95	4.37	2.86	0.53	0.05	0.00	—	—
Net Asset Value ($)	15.05	25.43	19.76	18.23	17.23	16.90	13.59	13.82	—	—
Expense Ratio (%)	0.83	0.83	0.84	0.84	0.86	0.87	0.91	1.00	—	—
Yield (%)	0.00	0.00	0.00	0.00	0.00	0.00	0.14	0.00	—	—
Portfolio Turnover (%)	72	74	70	58	75	55	51	58	—	—
Total Assets (Millions $)	663	822	555	448	381	390	241	143	—	—

PORTFOLIO (as of 6/30/00)

Portfolio Manager: Kathleen McCarraghen - 1999

Investm't Category: Growth

✔ Domestic	Index
✔ Foreign	Sector
Asset Allocation	State Specific

Investment Style

✔ Large Cap	Mid Cap	Small Cap
✔ Growth	Grth/Val	Value

Portfolio

1.7%	cash	0.0%	corp bonds
98.3%	stocks	0.0%	gov't bonds
0.0%	pref/conv't pref	0.0%	muni bonds
0.0%	conv't bds/wrnts	0.0%	other

SHAREHOLDER INFORMATION

Minimum Investment
Initial: $1,000 Subsequent: $50

Minimum IRA Investment
Initial: $250 Subsequent: $50

Maximum Fees
Load: none 12b-1: none
Other: none

Services
✔ IRA
✔ Keogh
✔ Telephone Exchange

Preferred Int'l (PFIFX)

800-662-4769, 309-675-5123
www.preferredgroup.com

International Stock

PERFORMANCE — fund inception date: 7/1/92

	3yr Annual	5yr Annual	10yr Annual	Bull	Bear
Return (%)	11.8	11.8	na	45.0	-3.5
Differ from Category (+/-)	2.9 abv av	3.5 abv av	na	-45.9 low	20.5 high

Standard Deviation	Category Risk Index	Beta
16.1%—av	0.71—low	0.63

	2000	1999	1998	1997	1996	1995	1994	1993	1992	1991
Return (%)	-4.7	32.8	10.5	6.8	17.2	9.9	0.6	41.5	—	—
Differ from Category (+/-)	14.7	-27.9	4.7	5.5	2.7	0.6	3.7	1.3	—	—
Return, Tax-Adjusted (%)	-8.4	31.3	9.3	5.1	15.5	9.3	0.0	41.0	—	—

PER SHARE DATA

	2000	1999	1998	1997	1996	1995	1994	1993	1992	1991
Dividends, Net Income ($)	0.34	0.23	0.16	0.24	0.34	0.16	0.12	0.07	—	—
Distrib'ns, Cap Gain ($)	2.90	0.63	0.47	0.71	0.25	0.01	0.11	0.05	—	—
Net Asset Value ($)	14.72	18.95	14.95	14.10	14.10	12.55	11.58	11.75	—	—
Expense Ratio (%)	1.20	1.20	1.22	1.25	1.31	1.32	1.38	1.60	—	—
Yield (%)	1.92	1.17	1.03	1.62	2.36	1.27	1.02	0.59	—	—
Portfolio Turnover (%)	28	15	17	13	19	29	27	16	—	—
Total Assets (Millions $)	309	376	275	241	209	136	107	65	—	—

PORTFOLIO (as of 6/30/00)

Portfolio Manager: Peter Spano - 1992

Investm't Category: International Stock

Domestic	Index
✔ Foreign	Sector
Asset Allocation	State Specific

Investment Style

Large Cap	Mid Cap	Small Cap
Growth	Grth/Val	Value

Portfolio

2.3%	cash	0.0%	corp bonds
97.8%	stocks	0.0%	gov't bonds
0.0%	pref/conv't pref	0.0%	muni bonds
0.0%	conv't bds/wrnts	0.0%	other

SHAREHOLDER INFORMATION

Minimum Investment
Initial: $1,000 — Subsequent: $50

Minimum IRA Investment
Initial: $250 — Subsequent: $50

Maximum Fees
Load: none — 12b-1: none
Other: none

Services
✔ IRA
✔ Keogh
✔ Telephone Exchange

Preferred Small Cap (PSMCX)

800-662-4769, 309-675-5123
www.preferredgroup.com

Aggressive Growth

PERFORMANCE — fund inception date: 11/1/95

	3yr Annual	5yr Annual	10yr Annual	Bull	Bear
Return (%)	-10.8	2.3	na	4.9	-33.7
Differ from Category (+/-)	-27.0 low	-12.3 low	na	-114.3 low	-13.1 blw av

Standard Deviation	Category Risk Index	Beta
33.6%—high	1.04—av	0.87

	2000	1999	1998	1997	1996	1995	1994	1993	1992	1991
Return (%)	-16.8	-10.6	-4.7	31.8	20.4	—	—	—	—	—
Differ from Category (+/-)	-10.8	-68.1	-19.8	17.0	2.1	—	—	—	—	—
Return, Tax-Adjusted (%)	-16.8	-10.6	-5.5	28.6	19.9	—	—	—	—	—

PER SHARE DATA

	2000	1999	1998	1997	1996	1995	1994	1993	1992	1991
Dividends, Net Income ($)	0.00	0.02	0.01	0.08	0.02	—	—	—	—	—
Distrib'ns, Cap Gain ($)	0.00	0.00	0.56	1.82	0.15	—	—	—	—	—
Net Asset Value ($)	9.75	11.72	13.14	14.45	12.45	—	—	—	—	—
Expense Ratio (%)	1.11	0.92	0.90	0.88	0.88	—	—	—	—	—
Yield (%)	0.00	0.17	0.07	0.49	0.15	—	—	—	—	—
Portfolio Turnover (%)	236	121	105	104	—	—	—	—	—	—
Total Assets (Millions $)	82	96	124	121	68	—	—	—	—	—

PORTFOLIO (as of 3/31/00)

Portfolio Manager: Bill McVail - 2000

Investm't Category: Aggressive Growth

✔ Domestic — Index
✔ Foreign — Sector
Asset Allocation — State Specific

Investment Style

Large Cap — Mid Cap — ✔ Small Cap
✔ Growth — Grth/Val — Value

Portfolio

3.5%	cash	0.0%	corp bonds
96.5%	stocks	0.0%	gov't bonds
0.0%	pref/conv't pref	0.0%	muni bonds
0.0%	conv't bds/wrnts	0.0%	other

SHAREHOLDER INFORMATION

Minimum Investment
Initial: $1,000 — Subsequent: $50

Minimum IRA Investment
Initial: $250 — Subsequent: $50

Maximum Fees
Load: none — 12b-1: none
Other: none

Services
✔ IRA
✔ Keogh
✔ Telephone Exchange

Preferred Value (PFVLX)

800-662-4769, 309-675-5123
www.preferredgroup.com

Growth & Income

PERFORMANCE — fund inception date: 7/1/92

	3yr Annual	5yr Annual	10yr Annual	Bull	Bear
Return (%)	9.7	16.2	na	26.6	2.1
Differ from Category (+/-)	0.8 av	1.9 abv av	na	-6.9 av	2.2 av

Standard Deviation	Category Risk Index	Beta
18.7%—av	1.08—high	0.87

	2000	1999	1998	1997	1996	1995	1994	1993	1992	1991
Return (%)	10.8	4.1	14.3	28.0	25.2	37.7	0.4	8.8	—	—
Differ from Category (+/-)	5.1	-6.7	1.5	1.1	5.5	8.2	0.9	-5.0	—	—
Return, Tax-Adjusted (%)	8.1	1.2	12.9	27.5	23.5	36.2	-0.6	7.9	—	—

PER SHARE DATA

	2000	1999	1998	1997	1996	1995	1994	1993	1992	1991
Dividends, Net Income ($)	0.15	0.17	0.26	0.21	0.20	0.20	0.20	0.16	—	—
Distrib'ns, Cap Gain ($)	2.68	3.25	1.04	0.00	0.60	0.29	0.14	0.11	—	—
Net Asset Value ($)	21.81	22.33	24.81	22.85	18.02	15.02	11.27	11.56	—	—
Expense Ratio (%)	0.86	0.84	0.84	0.85	0.85	0.89	0.93	0.96	—	—
Yield (%)	0.61	0.66	1.00	0.91	1.07	1.30	1.75	1.37	—	—
Portfolio Turnover (%)	7	23	10	7	17	29	11	17	—	—
Total Assets (Millions $)	359	383	393	342	307	229	148	123	—	—

PORTFOLIO (as of 3/31/00)

Portfolio Manager: John Lindenthal - 1992

Investm't Category: Growth & Income

✔ Domestic — Index
✔ Foreign — Sector
Asset Allocation — State Specific

Investment Style

✔ Large Cap — Mid Cap — Small Cap
Growth — Grth/Val — ✔ Value

Portfolio

1.0%	cash	0.0%	corp bonds
99.0%	stocks	0.0%	gov't bonds
0.0%	pref/conv't pref	0.0%	muni bonds
0.0%	conv't bds/wrnts	0.0%	other

SHAREHOLDER INFORMATION

Minimum Investment
Initial: $1,000 — Subsequent: $50

Minimum IRA Investment
Initial: $250 — Subsequent: $50

Maximum Fees
Load: none — 12b-1: none
Other: none

Services
✔ IRA
✔ Keogh
✔ Telephone Exchange

ProFunds: UltraBull/Inv (ULPIX)

888-776-3637, 301-657-1970
www.profunds.com

Aggressive Growth

PERFORMANCE — fund inception date: 11/28/97

	3yr Annual	5yr Annual	10yr Annual	Bull	Bear
Return (%)	9.8	na	na	105.1	-29.1
Differ from Category (+/-)	-6.4 blw av	na	na	-14.1 av	-8.5 blw av

Standard Deviation	Category Risk Index	Beta
34.9%—high	1.07—abv av	1.97

	2000	1999	1998	1997	1996	1995	1994	1993	1992	1991
Return (%)	-28.3	29.5	42.9	—	—	—	—	—	—	—
Differ from Category (+/-)	-22.3	-28.0	27.8	—	—	—	—	—	—	—
Return, Tax-Adjusted (%)	-28.4	29.3	42.8	—	—	—	—	—	—	—

PER SHARE DATA

	2000	1999	1998	1997	1996	1995	1994	1993	1992	1991
Dividends, Net Income ($)	0.04	0.03	0.01	—	—	—	—	—	—	—
Distrib'ns, Cap Gain ($)	0.06	0.10	0.00	—	—	—	—	—	—	—
Net Asset Value ($)	16.86	23.67	18.36	—	—	—	—	—	—	—
Expense Ratio (%)	na	1.34	1.50	—	—	—	—	—	—	—
Yield (%)	0.23	0.08	0.06	—	—	—	—	—	—	—
Portfolio Turnover (%)	na	764	—	—	—	—	—	—	—	—
Total Assets (Millions $)	98	174	90	—	—	—	—	—	—	—

PORTFOLIO (as of 3/31/00)

Portfolio Manager: committee - 1997

Investm't Category: Aggressive Growth

✔ Domestic | Index
Foreign | Sector
Asset Allocation | State Specific

Investment Style

✔ Large Cap | Mid Cap | Small Cap
Growth | ✔ Grth/Val | Value

Portfolio

13.9%	cash	0.0%	corp bonds
71.6%	stocks	14.5%	gov't bonds
0.0%	pref/conv't pref	0.0%	muni bonds
0.0%	conv't bds/wrnts	0.0%	other

SHAREHOLDER INFORMATION

Minimum Investment

Initial: $15,000 Subsequent: $100

Minimum IRA Investment

Initial: $15,000 Subsequent: $100

Maximum Fees

Load: none 12b-1: none
Other: none

Services

✔ IRA
✔ Keogh
✔ Telephone Exchange

ProFunds: UltraOTC/Inv (UOPIX)

888-776-3637, 301-657-1970
www.profunds.com

Aggressive Growth

PERFORMANCE — fund inception date: 12/1/97

	3yr Annual	5yr Annual	10yr Annual	Bull	Bear
Return (%)	35.7	na	na	699.6	-75.5
Differ from Category (+/-)	19.5 high	na	na	580.4 high	-54.9 low

Standard Deviation	Category Risk Index	Beta
80.7%—high	2.48—high	3.28

	2000	1999	1998	1997	1996	1995	1994	1993	1992	1991
Return (%)	-73.7	233.2	185.3	—	—	—	—	—	—	—
Differ from Category (+/-)	-67.7	175.7	170.2	—	—	—	—	—	—	—
Return, Tax-Adjusted (%)	-74.4	232.8	185.3	—	—	—	—	—	—	—

PER SHARE DATA

	2000	1999	1998	1997	1996	1995	1994	1993	1992	1991
Dividends, Net Income ($)	0.00	0.00	0.00	—	—	—	—	—	—	—
Distrib'ns, Cap Gain ($)	3.54	0.46	0.00	—	—	—	—	—	—	—
Net Asset Value ($)	22.82	98.88	29.81	—	—	—	—	—	—	—
Expense Ratio (%)	na	1.31	1.47	—	—	—	—	—	—	—
Yield (%)	0.00	0.00	0.00	—	—	—	—	—	—	—
Portfolio Turnover (%)	na	670	156	—	—	—	—	—	—	—
Total Assets (Millions $)	495	1,191	239	—	—	—	—	—	—	—

PORTFOLIO (as of 3/31/00)

Portfolio Manager: William Seale - 1997

Investm't Category: Aggressive Growth

✔ Domestic	Index
Foreign	Sector
Asset Allocation	State Specific

Investment Style

✔ Large Cap	Mid Cap	Small Cap
✔ Growth	Grth/Val	Value

Portfolio

19.1%	cash	0.0%	corp bonds
59.8%	stocks	21.2%	gov't bonds
0.0%	pref/conv't pref	0.0%	muni bonds
0.0%	conv't bds/wrnts	0.0%	other

SHAREHOLDER INFORMATION

Minimum Investment
Initial: $15,000 Subsequent: $100

Minimum IRA Investment
Initial: $15,000 Subsequent: $100

Maximum Fees
Load: none 12b-1: none
Other: none

Services
✔ IRA
✔ Keogh
✔ Telephone Exchange

Prudent Bear (BEARX)

800-711-1848, 888-778-2327
www.prudentbear.com

Aggressive Growth

PERFORMANCE — fund inception date: 12/28/95

	3yr Annual	5yr Annual	10yr Annual	Bull	Bear
Return (%)	-12.9	-11.4	na	-48.4	36.3
Differ from Category (+/-)	-29.1 low	-26.0 low	na	-167.6 low	56.9 high

Standard Deviation	Category Risk Index	Beta
31.0%—high	0.96—av	-1.60

	2000	1999	1998	1997	1996	1995	1994	1993	1992	1991
Return (%)	30.4	-23.3	-34.0	-4.3	-13.6	—	—	—	—	—
Differ from Category (+/-)	36.4	-80.8	-49.1	-19.1	-31.9	—	—	—	—	—
Return, Tax-Adjusted (%)	27.9	-24.4	-34.9	-5.3	-14.1	—	—	—	—	—

PER SHARE DATA

	2000	1999	1998	1997	1996	1995	1994	1993	1992	1991
Dividends, Net Income ($)	0.23	0.14	0.19	0.23	0.15	—	—	—	—	—
Distrib'ns, Cap Gain ($)	0.00	0.00	0.00	0.00	0.00	—	—	—	—	—
Net Asset Value ($)	4.58	3.69	5.00	7.88	8.48	—	—	—	—	—
Expense Ratio (%)	1.71	1.97	2.08	2.59	2.75	—	—	—	—	—
Yield (%)	5.02	3.79	3.80	2.91	1.76	—	—	—	—	—
Portfolio Turnover (%)	221	536	480	413	91	—	—	—	—	—
Total Assets (Millions $)	178	147	110	62	10	—	—	—	—	—

PORTFOLIO (as of 3/31/00)

Portfolio Manager: David Tice - 1995

Investm't Category: Aggressive Growth

✔ Domestic
✔ Foreign
Asset Allocation
Index
Sector
State Specific

Investment Style

✔ Large Cap
Growth
Mid Cap
✔ Grth/Val
Small Cap
Value

Portfolio

56.4%	cash	0.0%	corp bonds
-29.1%	stocks	67.3%	gov't bonds
1.8%	pref/conv't pref	0.0%	muni bonds
0.5%	conv't bds/wrnts	3.2%	other

SHAREHOLDER INFORMATION

Minimum Investment

Initial: $2,000 — Subsequent: $100

Minimum IRA Investment

Initial: $1,000 — Subsequent: $100

Maximum Fees

Load: none — 12b-1: 0.25%
Other: none

Services

✔ IRA
✔ Keogh
Telephone Exchange

RS: Contrarian/A (RSCOX)

800-766-3863, 415-591-2700
www.rsim.com

International Stock

PERFORMANCE — fund inception date: 6/30/93

	3yr Annual	5yr Annual	10yr Annual	Bull	Bear
Return (%)	0.8	-2.5	na	50.1	7.2
Differ from Category (+/-)	-8.1 low	-10.8 low	na	-40.8 blw av	31.2 high

Standard Deviation	Category Risk Index	Beta
23.0%—abv av	1.01—av	0.78

	2000	1999	1998	1997	1996	1995	1994	1993	1992	1991
Return (%)	10.2	38.3	-32.6	-29.5	21.6	30.8	-5.5	—	—	—
Differ from Category (+/-)	29.6	-22.4	-38.4	-30.8	7.1	21.5	-2.4	—	—	—
Return, Tax-Adjusted (%)	10.2	38.3	-33.5	-29.6	21.2	30.8	-6.1	—	—	—

PER SHARE DATA

	2000	1999	1998	1997	1996	1995	1994	1993	1992	1991
Dividends, Net Income ($)	0.00	0.00	0.00	0.04	0.00	0.00	0.00	—	—	—
Distrib'ns, Cap Gain ($)	0.00	0.00	0.57	0.02	0.19	0.00	0.25	—	—	—
Net Asset Value ($)	11.02	10.00	7.23	11.61	16.57	13.78	10.53	—	—	—
Expense Ratio (%)	na	2.17	2.83	2.48	2.46	2.46	2.22	—	—	—
Yield (%)	0.00	0.00	0.00	0.34	0.00	0.00	0.00	—	—	—
Portfolio Turnover (%)	na	86	39	36	44	79	—	—	—	—
Total Assets (Millions $)	89	115	126	402	1,063	508	485	—	—	—

PORTFOLIO (as of 6/30/00)

Portfolio Manager: committee - 1993

Investm't Category: International Stock

✔ Domestic — Index
✔ Foreign — Sector
Asset Allocation — State Specific

Investment Style

Large Cap — Mid Cap — Small Cap
Growth — Grth/Val — Value

Portfolio

9.6%	cash	0.0%	corp bonds
88.7%	stocks	0.0%	gov't bonds
1.1%	pref/conv't pref	0.0%	muni bonds
0.7%	conv't bds/wrnts	0.0%	other

SHAREHOLDER INFORMATION

Minimum Investment
Initial: $5,000 — Subsequent: $100

Minimum IRA Investment
Initial: $1,000 — Subsequent: $1

Maximum Fees
Load: none — 12b-1: 0.25%
Other: none

Services
✔ IRA
Keogh
✔ Telephone Exchange

RS: Diversifed Growth/A (RSDGX)

800-766-3863, 415-591-2700
www.rsim.com

Aggressive Growth

PERFORMANCE

fund inception date: 8/1/96

	3yr Annual	5yr Annual	10yr Annual	Bull	Bear
Return (%)	28.5	na	na	242.6	-47.3
Differ from Category (+/-)	12.3 high	na	na	123.4 high	-26.7 low

Standard Deviation	Category Risk Index	Beta
40.6%—high	1.25—high	1.38

	2000	1999	1998	1997	1996	1995	1994	1993	1992	1991
Return (%)	-26.9	150.2	16.2	29.5	—	—	—	—	—	—
Differ from Category (+/-)	-20.9	92.7	1.1	14.7	—	—	—	—	—	—
Return, Tax-Adjusted (%)	-27.6	143.3	15.6	26.3	—	—	—	—	—	—

PER SHARE DATA

	2000	1999	1998	1997	1996	1995	1994	1993	1992	1991
Dividends, Net Income ($)	0.00	0.00	0.00	0.00	—	—	—	—	—	—
Distrib'ns, Cap Gain ($)	1.22	5.48	0.38	1.93	—	—	—	—	—	—
Net Asset Value ($)	22.83	32.99	15.89	14.04	—	—	—	—	—	—
Expense Ratio (%)	na	1.84	1.89	1.94	—	—	—	—	—	—
Yield (%)	0.00	0.00	0.00	0.00	—	—	—	—	—	—
Portfolio Turnover (%)	na	473	403	370	—	—	—	—	—	—
Total Assets (Millions $)	498	304	69	79	—	—	—	—	—	—

PORTFOLIO (as of 6/30/00)

Portfolio Manager: John Seabern, John Wallace - 1996

Investm't Category: Aggressive Growth

✔ Domestic	Index
Foreign	Sector
Asset Allocation	State Specific

Investment Style

Large Cap	Mid Cap	✔ Small Cap
✔ Growth	Grth/Val	Value

Portfolio

0.0% cash	0.2% corp bonds
99.6% stocks	0.0% gov't bonds
0.2% pref/conv't pref	0.0% muni bonds
0.1% conv't bds/wrnts	0.0% other

SHAREHOLDER INFORMATION

Minimum Investment
Initial: $5,000 Subsequent: $100

Minimum IRA Investment
Initial: $1,000 Subsequent: $1

Maximum Fees
Load: none 12b-1: 0.25%
Other: none

Services
✔ IRA
Keogh
✔ Telephone Exchange

RS: Emerging Growth/A (RSEGX)

800-766-3863, 415-591-2700
www.rsim.com

Aggressive Growth

this fund is closed to new investors

PERFORMANCE — fund inception date: 11/30/87

	3yr Annual	5yr Annual	10yr Annual	Bull	Bear
Return (%)	39.4	31.3	23.7	317.0	-40.2
Differ from Category (+/-)	23.2 high	16.7 high	7.9 high	197.8 high	-19.6 low

Standard Deviation	Category Risk Index	Beta
49.4%—high	1.52—high	1.58

	2000	1999	1998	1997	1996	1995	1994	1993	1992	1991
Return (%)	-25.0	182.5	28.0	18.5	21.5	20.3	7.9	7.2	-2.4	58.5
Differ from Category (+/-)	-19.0	125.0	12.9	3.7	3.2	-14.3	8.7	-18.0	-9.3	11.3
Return, Tax-Adjusted (%)	-25.4	179.6	27.0	13.4	16.8	17.7	4.6	7.2	-2.8	56.3

PER SHARE DATA

	2000	1999	1998	1997	1996	1995	1994	1993	1992	1991
Dividends, Net Income ($)	0.00	0.00	0.00	0.00	0.00	0.00	0.00	0.00	0.20	0.00
Distrib'ns, Cap Gain ($)	1.44	3.31	0.87	5.02	3.19	1.58	2.10	0.00	0.07	0.90
Net Asset Value ($)	44.01	60.67	22.95	18.71	20.07	19.21	17.32	17.98	16.77	17.48
Expense Ratio (%)	na	1.51	1.47	1.50	1.60	1.56	1.60	1.54	1.49	1.59
Yield (%)	0.00	0.00	0.00	0.00	0.00	0.00	0.00	0.00	1.18	0.00
Portfolio Turnover (%)	na	177	291	462	270	280	274	43	124	147
Total Assets (Millions $)	3,812	3,577	394	248	210	158	176	169	277	141

PORTFOLIO (as of 6/30/00)

Portfolio Manager: James Callinan - 1996

Investm't Category: Aggressive Growth

✔ Domestic	Index
Foreign	Sector
Asset Allocation	State Specific

Investment Style

Large Cap	Mid Cap	✔ Small Cap
✔ Growth	Grth/Val	Value

Portfolio

6.7%	cash	0.0%	corp bonds
93.3%	stocks	0.0%	gov't bonds
0.0%	pref/conv't pref	0.0%	muni bonds
0.0%	conv't bds/wrnts	0.0%	other

SHAREHOLDER INFORMATION

Minimum Investment
Initial: $5,000 Subsequent: $100

Minimum IRA Investment
Initial: $1,000 Subsequent: $1

Maximum Fees
Load: none 12b-1: 0.25%
Other: none

Services
✔ IRA
Keogh
✔ Telephone Exchange

RS: Information Age/A (RSIFX)

800-766-3863, 415-591-2700
www.rsim.com

Aggressive Growth

PERFORMANCE

fund inception date: 11/15/95

	3yr Annual	5yr Annual	10yr Annual	Bull	Bear
Return (%)	30.7	24.6	na	278.6	-41.5
Differ from Category (+/-)	14.5 high	10.0 high	na	159.4 high	-20.9 low

Standard Deviation	Category Risk Index	Beta
42.1%—high	1.30—high	1.79

	2000	1999	1998	1997	1996	1995	1994	1993	1992	1991
Return (%)	-35.0	126.2	52.2	6.1	26.7	—	—	—	—	—
Differ from Category (+/-)	-29.0	68.7	37.1	-8.7	8.4	—	—	—	—	—
Return, Tax-Adjusted (%)	-37.4	121.8	52.2	4.6	25.5	—	—	—	—	—

PER SHARE DATA

	2000	1999	1998	1997	1996	1995	1994	1993	1992	1991
Dividends, Net Income ($)	0.00	0.00	0.00	0.43	0.27	—	—	—	—	—
Distrib'ns, Cap Gain ($)	4.32	3.88	0.00	0.00	0.00	—	—	—	—	—
Net Asset Value ($)	19.01	35.79	17.96	11.80	11.51	—	—	—	—	—
Expense Ratio (%)	na	1.68	1.74	1.82	2.03	—	—	—	—	—
Yield (%)	0.00	0.00	0.00	3.64	2.34	—	—	—	—	—
Portfolio Turnover (%)	na	182	224	369	452	—	—	—	—	—
Total Assets (Millions $)	228	354	157	118	106	—	—	—	—	—

PORTFOLIO (as of 6/30/00)

Portfolio Manager: Roderick Berry, Ronald Elijah - 1995

Investm't Category: Aggressive Growth

✔ Domestic
Index
✔ Foreign
✔ Sector
Asset Allocation
State Specific

Investment Style

✔ Large Cap
✔ Mid Cap
✔ Small Cap
✔ Growth
Grth/Val
Value

Portfolio

0.8%	cash	0.0%	corp bonds
99.2%	stocks	0.0%	gov't bonds
0.0%	pref/conv't pref	0.0%	muni bonds
0.0%	conv't bds/wrnts	0.0%	other

SHAREHOLDER INFORMATION

Minimum Investment

Initial: $5,000 Subsequent: $100

Minimum IRA Investment

Initial: $1,000 Subsequent: $1

Maximum Fees

Load: none 12b-1: 0.25%
Other: none

Services

✔ IRA
Keogh
✔ Telephone Exchange

RS: MicroCap Growth/A (RSMGX)

800-766-3863, 415-591-2700
www.rsim.com

Aggressive Growth

PERFORMANCE

fund inception date: 8/15/96

	3yr Annual	5yr Annual	10yr Annual	Bull	Bear
Return (%)	17.5	na	na	109.1	-27.2
Differ from Category (+/-)	1.3 av	na	na	-10.1 av	-6.6 av

Standard Deviation	Category Risk Index	Beta
37.5%—high	1.16—abv av	1.23

	2000	1999	1998	1997	1996	1995	1994	1993	1992	1991
Return (%)	4.4	56.6	-0.6	30.4	—	—	—	—	—	—
Differ from Category (+/-)	10.4	-0.9	-15.7	15.6	—	—	—	—	—	—
Return, Tax-Adjusted (%)	2.1	56.6	-0.6	30.4	—	—	—	—	—	—

PER SHARE DATA

	2000	1999	1998	1997	1996	1995	1994	1993	1992	1991
Dividends, Net Income ($)	0.00	0.00	0.00	0.00	—	—	—	—	—	—
Distrib'ns, Cap Gain ($)	2.55	0.00	0.00	0.00	—	—	—	—	—	—
Net Asset Value ($)	20.69	22.34	14.26	14.35	—	—	—	—	—	—
Expense Ratio (%)	na	1.92	1.91	1.95	—	—	—	—	—	—
Yield (%)	0.00	0.00	0.00	0.00	—	—	—	—	—	—
Portfolio Turnover (%)	na	90	108	170	—	—	—	—	—	—
Total Assets (Millions $)	101	103	93	103	—	—	—	—	—	—

PORTFOLIO (as of 6/30/00)

Portfolio Manager: David Evans, Rainerio Reyes - 1996

Investm't Category: Aggressive Growth

✔ Domestic | Index
✔ Foreign | Sector
Asset Allocation | State Specific

Investment Style

Large Cap | Mid Cap | ✔ Small Cap
✔ Growth | Grth/Val | Value

Portfolio

10.7%	cash	0.0%	corp bonds
89.3%	stocks	0.0%	gov't bonds
0.0%	pref/conv't pref	0.0%	muni bonds
0.0%	conv't bds/wrnts	0.0%	other

SHAREHOLDER INFORMATION

Minimum Investment
Initial: $5,000 — Subsequent: $100

Minimum IRA Investment
Initial: $1,000 — Subsequent: $1

Maximum Fees
Load: none — 12b-1: 0.25%
Other: none

Services
✔ IRA
Keogh
✔ Telephone Exchange

RS: Mid Cap Opport/A

800-766-3863, 415-591-2700
www.rsim.com

(RSMOX)

Growth

PERFORMANCE — fund inception date: 7/12/95

	3yr Annual	5yr Annual	10yr Annual	Bull	Bear
Return (%)	17.8	19.9	na	102.4	-25.1
Differ from Category (+/-)	6.8 high	3.8 high	na	52.7 high	-19.7 low

Standard Deviation	Category Risk Index	Beta
27.3%—high	1.40—high	1.09

	2000	1999	1998	1997	1996	1995	1994	1993	1992	1991
Return (%)	-6.1	56.1	11.7	22.3	24.1	—	—	—	—	—
Differ from Category (+/-)	-9.6	37.2	-2.6	-4.8	1.8	—	—	—	—	—
Return, Tax-Adjusted (%)	-10.0	48.7	10.0	17.7	22.9	—	—	—	—	—

PER SHARE DATA

	2000	1999	1998	1997	1996	1995	1994	1993	1992	1991
Dividends, Net Income ($)	0.01	0.04	0.19	0.03	0.34	—	—	—	—	—
Distrib'ns, Cap Gain ($)	3.13	5.05	0.77	3.03	0.00	—	—	—	—	—
Net Asset Value ($)	11.66	15.92	14.04	13.51	13.62	—	—	—	—	—
Expense Ratio (%)	na	1.59	1.30	1.30	1.71	—	—	—	—	—
Yield (%)	0.06	0.19	1.28	0.18	2.49	—	—	—	—	—
Portfolio Turnover (%)	na	408	212	236	212	—	—	—	—	—
Total Assets (Millions $)	194	226	183	298	309	—	—	—	—	—

PORTFOLIO (as of 6/30/00)

Portfolio Manager: John Wallace - 1995

Investm't Category: Growth

✔ Domestic	Index
✔ Foreign	Sector
Asset Allocation	State Specific

Investment Style

Large Cap	✔ Mid Cap	✔ Small Cap
✔ Growth	Grth/Val	Value

Portfolio

5.4%	cash	0.0%	corp bonds
90.8%	stocks	0.0%	gov't bonds
0.0%	pref/conv't pref	0.0%	muni bonds
3.8%	conv't bds/wrnts	0.0%	other

SHAREHOLDER INFORMATION

Minimum Investment
Initial: $5,000 Subsequent: $100

Minimum IRA Investment
Initial: $1,000 Subsequent: $1

Maximum Fees
Load: none 12b-1: 0.25%
Other: none

Services
✔ IRA
Keogh
✔ Telephone Exchange

RS: Value + Growth/A (RSVPX)

800-766-3863, 415-591-2700
www.rsim.com

Aggressive Growth

PERFORMANCE — fund inception date: 5/12/92

	3yr Annual	5yr Annual	10yr Annual	Bull	Bear
Return (%)	13.3	13.5	na	74.1	-25.4
Differ from Category (+/-)	-2.9 av	-1.1 blw av	na	-45.1 blw av	-4.8 av

Standard Deviation	Category Risk Index	Beta
25.7%—high	0.79—blw av	1.23

	2000	1999	1998	1997	1996	1995	1994	1993	1992	1991
Return (%)	-11.0	28.4	27.4	13.8	14.0	42.6	23.1	21.5	—	—
Differ from Category (+/-)	-5.0	-29.1	12.3	-1.0	-4.3	8.0	23.9	-3.7	—	—
Return, Tax-Adjusted (%)	-12.5	26.3	24.5	10.1	11.8	42.6	22.6	20.6	—	—

PER SHARE DATA

	2000	1999	1998	1997	1996	1995	1994	1993	1992	1991
Dividends, Net Income ($)	0.00	0.00	0.00	0.00	0.00	0.00	0.00	0.00	—	—
Distrib'ns, Cap Gain ($)	2.33	2.65	3.33	4.42	1.73	0.00	0.19	0.32	—	—
Net Asset Value ($)	24.62	30.43	25.92	23.18	24.15	22.66	15.88	13.06	—	—
Expense Ratio (%)	na	1.59	1.46	1.44	1.51	1.68	1.55	1.33	—	—
Yield (%)	0.00	0.00	0.00	0.00	0.00	0.00	0.00	0.00	—	—
Portfolio Turnover (%)	na	80	190	228	221	232	250	210	—	—
Total Assets (Millions $)	476	673	678	756	643	1,144	132	23	—	—

PORTFOLIO (as of 6/30/00)

Portfolio Manager: Ronald Elijah - 1992

Investm't Category: Aggressive Growth

- ✔ Domestic
- Foreign
- Asset Allocation
- Index
- Sector
- State Specific

Investment Style

- ✔ Large Cap
- ✔ Growth
- Mid Cap
- Grth/Val
- Small Cap
- Value

Portfolio

0.1% cash	0.0% corp bonds
99.9% stocks	0.0% gov't bonds
0.0% pref/conv't pref	0.0% muni bonds
0.0% conv't bds/wrnts	0.0% other

SHAREHOLDER INFORMATION

Minimum Investment
Initial: $5,000 — Subsequent: $100

Minimum IRA Investment
Initial: $1,000 — Subsequent: $1

Maximum Fees
Load: none — 12b-1: 0.25%
Other: none

Services

- ✔ IRA
- Keogh
- ✔ Telephone Exchange

Rainier: Balanced (RIMBX)

800-248-6314, 206-464-0400
www.rainierfunds.com

Balanced

PERFORMANCE — fund inception date: 5/10/94

	3yr Annual	5yr Annual	10yr Annual	Bull	Bear
Return (%)	10.3	13.6	na	41.5	-4.9
Differ from Category (+/-)	1.9 abv av	2.2 abv av	na	13.4 high	-1.7 av

Standard Deviation	Category Risk Index	Beta
12.8%—blw av	1.17—abv av	0.69

	2000	1999	1998	1997	1996	1995	1994	1993	1992	1991
Return (%)	-0.5	16.9	15.4	23.9	14.0	33.1	—	—	—	—
Differ from Category (+/-)	-2.5	6.2	2.1	5.1	0.1	7.6	—	—	—	—
Return, Tax-Adjusted (%)	-1.5	15.2	13.5	19.6	10.9	28.9	—	—	—	—

PER SHARE DATA

	2000	1999	1998	1997	1996	1995	1994	1993	1992	1991
Dividends, Net Income ($)	0.23	0.27	0.26	0.36	0.36	0.37	—	—	—	—
Distrib'ns, Cap Gain ($)	0.52	0.79	0.92	2.44	1.05	1.25	—	—	—	—
Net Asset Value ($)	17.35	18.20	16.54	15.42	14.75	14.24	—	—	—	—
Expense Ratio (%)	1.19	1.19	1.19	1.40	1.19	1.19	—	—	—	—
Yield (%)	1.28	1.42	1.48	2.01	2.27	2.38	—	—	—	—
Portfolio Turnover (%)	67	108	102	130	114	152	—	—	—	—
Total Assets (Millions $)	122	106	98	60	38	27	—	—	—	—

PORTFOLIO (as of 6/30/00)

Portfolio Manager: committee - 1994

Investm't Category: Balanced

✔ Domestic — Index
Foreign — Sector
✔ Asset Allocation — State Specific

Investment Style

Large Cap — Mid Cap — Small Cap
Growth — Grth/Val — Value

Portfolio

16.9%	cash	17.6%	corp bonds
58.5%	stocks	7.0%	gov't bonds
0.0%	pref/conv't pref	0.0%	muni bonds
0.0%	conv't bds/wrnts	0.0%	other

SHAREHOLDER INFORMATION

Minimum Investment
Initial: $25,000 — Subsequent: $1,000

Minimum IRA Investment
Initial: $25,000 — Subsequent: $1,000

Maximum Fees
Load: none — 12b-1: 0.25%
Other: none

Services
✔ IRA
✔ Keogh
✔ Telephone Exchange

Rainier: Core Equity

800-248-6314, 206-464-0400
www.rainierfunds.com

(RIMEX)

Growth

PERFORMANCE

fund inception date: 5/10/94

	3yr Annual	5yr Annual	10yr Annual	Bull	Bear
Return (%)	13.6	19.3	na	70.1	-10.6
Differ from Category (+/-)	2.6 abv av	3.2 abv av	na	20.4 abv av	-5.2 av

Standard Deviation	Category Risk Index	Beta
20.1%—abv av	1.03—av	1.08

	2000	1999	1998	1997	1996	1995	1994	1993	1992	1991
Return (%)	-3.9	26.6	20.6	33.8	23.2	47.1	—	—	—	—
Differ from Category (+/-)	-7.4	7.7	6.3	6.7	0.9	16.7	—	—	—	—
Return, Tax-Adjusted (%)	-5.5	25.2	19.3	30.2	20.4	43.4	—	—	—	—

PER SHARE DATA

	2000	1999	1998	1997	1996	1995	1994	1993	1992	1991
Dividends, Net Income ($)	0.00	0.00	0.06	0.07	0.13	0.11	—	—	—	—
Distrib'ns, Cap Gain ($)	2.48	1.67	1.26	3.15	1.42	1.43	—	—	—	—
Net Asset Value ($)	26.02	29.69	24.86	21.79	18.73	16.55	—	—	—	—
Expense Ratio (%)	1.11	1.13	1.14	1.22	1.29	1.29	—	—	—	—
Yield (%)	0.00	0.00	0.22	0.28	0.64	0.61	—	—	—	—
Portfolio Turnover (%)	82	132	119	146	138	133	—	—	—	—
Total Assets (Millions $)	864	957	878	497	220	70	—	—	—	—

PORTFOLIO (as of 6/30/00)

Portfolio Manager: committee - 1994

Investm't Category: Growth

✔ Domestic
Foreign
Asset Allocation
Index
Sector
State Specific

Investment Style

✔ Large Cap ✔ Mid Cap Small Cap
✔ Growth Grth/Val Value

Portfolio

1.1%	cash	0.0%	corp bonds
98.9%	stocks	0.0%	gov't bonds
0.0%	pref/conv't pref	0.0%	muni bonds
0.0%	conv't bds/wrnts	0.0%	other

SHAREHOLDER INFORMATION

Minimum Investment

Initial: $25,000 Subsequent: $1,000

Minimum IRA Investment

Initial: $25,000 Subsequent: $1,000

Maximum Fees

Load: none 12b-1: 0.25%
Other: none

Services

✔ IRA
✔ Keogh
✔ Telephone Exchange

Rainier: Small/Mid Cap Eq (RIMSX)

800-248-6314, 206-464-0400
www.rainierfunds.com

Aggressive Growth

PERFORMANCE

fund inception date: 5/10/94

	3yr Annual	5yr Annual	10yr Annual	Bull	Bear
Return (%)	9.0	16.0	na	52.2	-12.3
Differ from Category (+/-)	-7.2 blw av	1.4 av	na	-67.0 blw av	8.3 abv av

Standard Deviation	Category Risk Index	Beta
24.2%—abv av	0.75—low	1.06

	2000	1999	1998	1997	1996	1995	1994	1993	1992	1991
Return (%)	7.0	17.6	2.9	32.2	22.5	47.4	—	—	—	—
Differ from Category (+/-)	13.0	-39.9	-12.2	17.4	4.2	12.8	—	—	—	—
Return, Tax-Adjusted (%)	4.0	17.6	2.1	29.7	19.4	44.5	—	—	—	—

PER SHARE DATA

	2000	1999	1998	1997	1996	1995	1994	1993	1992	1991
Dividends, Net Income ($)	0.00	0.00	0.00	0.00	0.05	0.06	—	—	—	—
Distrib'ns, Cap Gain ($)	3.87	0.00	0.84	2.31	1.77	1.15	—	—	—	—
Net Asset Value ($)	23.92	26.11	22.19	22.45	18.78	16.94	—	—	—	—
Expense Ratio (%)	1.25	1.25	1.26	1.40	1.48	1.48	—	—	—	—
Yield (%)	0.00	0.00	0.00	0.00	0.24	0.33	—	—	—	—
Portfolio Turnover (%)	199	143	107	130	151	152	—	—	—	—
Total Assets (Millions $)	400	439	541	353	124	53	—	—	—	—

PORTFOLIO (as of 6/30/00)

Portfolio Manager: committee - 1994

Investm't Category: Aggressive Growth

✔ Domestic | Index
Foreign | Sector
Asset Allocation | State Specific

Investment Style

Large Cap | ✔ Mid Cap | ✔ Small Cap
Growth | ✔ Grth/Val | Value

Portfolio

1.6%	cash	0.0%	corp bonds
98.4%	stocks	0.0%	gov't bonds
0.0%	pref/conv't pref	0.0%	muni bonds
0.0%	conv't bds/wrnts	0.0%	other

SHAREHOLDER INFORMATION

Minimum Investment
Initial: $25,000 | Subsequent: $1,000

Minimum IRA Investment
Initial: $25,000 | Subsequent: $1,000

Maximum Fees
Load: none | 12b-1: 0.25%
Other: none

Services
✔ IRA
✔ Keogh
✔ Telephone Exchange

Reynolds Blue Chip Growth (RBCGX)

800-773-9665, 415-461-7860
www.reynoldsfunds.com

Growth

PERFORMANCE

fund inception date: 8/12/88

	3yr Annual	5yr Annual	10yr Annual	Bull	Bear
Return (%)	16.6	21.7	16.3	116.2	-33.2
Differ from Category (+/-)	5.6 high	5.6 high	-0.5 av	66.5 high	-27.8 low

Standard Deviation	Category Risk Index	Beta
27.5%—high	1.41—high	1.30

	2000	1999	1998	1997	1996	1995	1994	1993	1992	1991
Return (%)	-31.8	50.9	54.1	31.4	28.2	32.9	-0.5	-5.2	0.1	35.8
Differ from Category (+/-)	-35.3	32.0	39.8	4.3	5.9	2.5	-0.3	-19.8	-12.5	-1.8
Return, Tax-Adjusted (%)	-31.8	50.9	53.6	31.0	27.7	32.7	-0.9	-5.5	0.0	35.5

PER SHARE DATA

	2000	1999	1998	1997	1996	1995	1994	1993	1992	1991
Dividends, Net Income ($)	0.00	0.00	0.00	0.00	0.00	0.03	0.06	0.13	0.08	0.09
Distrib'ns, Cap Gain ($)	0.00	0.00	0.64	0.37	0.34	0.02	0.16	0.00	0.00	0.00
Net Asset Value ($)	49.14	72.07	47.74	31.50	24.27	19.22	14.50	14.82	15.78	15.85
Expense Ratio (%)	1.30	1.50	1.40	1.47	1.50	1.50	1.50	1.40	1.50	1.70
Yield (%)	0.00	0.00	0.00	0.00	0.00	0.15	0.40	0.87	0.50	0.56
Portfolio Turnover (%)	17	6	35	25	21	49	43	38	0	1
Total Assets (Millions $)	435	589	171	60	34	31	23	37	44	34

PORTFOLIO (as of 6/30/00)

Portfolio Manager: Frederick Reynolds - 1988

Investm't Category: Growth

✔ Domestic | Index
Foreign | Sector
Asset Allocation | State Specific

Investment Style

✔ Large Cap | Mid Cap | Small Cap
✔ Growth | Grth/Val | Value

Portfolio

0.2% cash | 0.0% corp bonds
99.8% stocks | 0.0% gov't bonds
0.0% pref/conv't pref | 0.0% muni bonds
0.0% conv't bds/wrnts | 0.0% other

SHAREHOLDER INFORMATION

Minimum Investment

Initial: $1,000 | Subsequent: $100

Minimum IRA Investment

Initial: $1,000 | Subsequent: $100

Maximum Fees

Load: none | 12b-1: 0.25%
Other: none

Services

✔ IRA
✔ Keogh
✔ Telephone Exchange

Rightime: Fund (RTFDX)

215-887-8111

Growth & Income

PERFORMANCE

fund inception date: 9/17/85

	3yr Annual	5yr Annual	10yr Annual	Bull	Bear
Return (%)	7.8	5.9	9.5	30.1	-15.0
Differ from Category (+/-)	-1.1 blw av	-8.4 low	-5.4 low	-3.4 av	-14.9 low

Standard Deviation	Category Risk Index	Beta
15.4%—av	0.89—blw av	0.45

	2000	1999	1998	1997	1996	1995	1994	1993	1992	1991
Return (%)	-12.3	9.8	30.4	-2.1	8.5	26.8	0.8	8.0	3.6	30.1
Differ from Category (+/-)	-18.0	-1.0	17.6	-29.0	-11.2	-2.7	1.3	-5.8	-8.0	2.0
Return, Tax-Adjusted (%)	-12.3	6.7	26.8	-2.6	2.0	24.9	-3.3	6.5	1.6	25.7

PER SHARE DATA

	2000	1999	1998	1997	1996	1995	1994	1993	1992	1991
Dividends, Net Income ($)	0.03	0.69	0.40	0.40	0.42	0.73	0.43	0.00	0.05	0.17
Distrib'ns, Cap Gain ($)	0.00	3.98	4.57	0.00	7.95	0.94	4.62	1.72	2.38	4.68
Net Asset Value ($)	29.33	33.48	34.86	30.57	31.67	37.07	30.53	35.32	34.29	35.43
Expense Ratio (%)	na	2.51	2.53	2.45	2.45	2.50	2.51	2.52	2.56	2.67
Yield (%)	0.10	1.84	1.01	1.30	1.06	1.92	1.22	0.00	0.13	0.42
Portfolio Turnover (%)	na	106	117	62	15	9	11	2	73	136
Total Assets (Millions $)	85	123	122	120	168	162	143	166	179	173

PORTFOLIO (as of 6/30/00)

Portfolio Manager: David Rights - 1987

Investm't Category: Growth & Income

✔ Domestic
Foreign
Asset Allocation
Index
Sector
State Specific

Investment Style

Large Cap
✔ Mid Cap
✔ Small Cap
✔ Growth
Grth/Val
Value

Portfolio

51.0% cash
0.0% stocks
0.0% pref/conv't pref
0.0% conv't bds/wrnts
0.0% corp bonds
0.0% gov't bonds
0.0% muni bonds
49.0% other

SHAREHOLDER INFORMATION

Minimum Investment

Initial: $1,000 Subsequent: $25

Minimum IRA Investment

Initial: $1,000 Subsequent: $25

Maximum Fees

Load: none 12b-1: 0.75%
Other: none

Services

✔ IRA
✔ Keogh
✔ Telephone Exchange

Royce: Micro-Cap/Inv

800-221-4268, 212-486-1445
www.roycefunds.com

(RYOTX)

Aggressive Growth

PERFORMANCE

fund inception date: 12/31/91

	3yr Annual	5yr Annual	10yr Annual	Bull	Bear
Return (%)	8.6	13.0	na	32.5	0.3
Differ from Category (+/-)	-7.6 blw av	-1.6 blw av	na	-86.7 low	20.9 high

Standard Deviation	Category Risk Index	Beta
19.1%—abv av	0.59—low	0.60

	2000	1999	1998	1997	1996	1995	1994	1993	1992	1991
Return (%)	16.7	13.6	-3.3	24.6	15.5	19.0	3.5	23.6	29.4	—
Differ from Category (+/-)	22.7	-43.9	-18.4	9.8	-2.8	-15.6	4.3	-1.6	22.5	—
Return, Tax-Adjusted (%)	14.0	13.1	-4.3	22.7	13.4	18.2	2.5	20.0	25.8	—

PER SHARE DATA

	2000	1999	1998	1997	1996	1995	1994	1993	1992	1991
Dividends, Net Income ($)	0.00	0.00	0.00	0.00	0.00	0.00	0.00	0.00	0.00	—
Distrib'ns, Cap Gain ($)	1.28	0.20	0.50	0.75	0.54	0.18	0.22	0.74	0.64	—
Net Asset Value ($)	9.78	9.50	8.55	9.40	8.14	7.53	6.48	6.47	5.83	—
Expense Ratio (%)	na	1.35	1.49	1.50	1.79	1.94	1.99	1.99	1.69	—
Yield (%)	0.00	0.00	0.00	0.00	0.00	0.00	0.00	0.00	0.00	—
Portfolio Turnover (%)	na	102	56	38	70	25	54	116	171	—
Total Assets (Millions $)	132	111	165	199	141	97	26	10	3	—

PORTFOLIO (as of 6/30/00)

Portfolio Manager: Charles Royce - 1991

Investm't Category: Aggressive Growth

✔ Domestic
✔ Foreign
Asset Allocation
Index
Sector
State Specific

Investment Style

Large Cap
Mid Cap
✔ Small Cap
Growth
✔ Grth/Val
Value

Portfolio

6.7% cash
93.3% stocks
0.0% pref/conv't pref
0.0% conv't bds/wrnts
0.0% corp bonds
0.0% gov't bonds
0.0% muni bonds
0.0% other

SHAREHOLDER INFORMATION

Minimum Investment

Initial: $2,000 Subsequent: $50

Minimum IRA Investment

Initial: $500 Subsequent: $50

Maximum Fees

Load: 1.00% redemption 12b-1: none
Other: redemption fee applies for 12 months

Services

✔ IRA
✔ Keogh
✔ Telephone Exchange

Royce: PA Mutual/Inv

(PENNX)

800-221-4268, 212-486-1445
www.roycefunds.com

Growth

PERFORMANCE

fund inception date: 10/3/68

	3yr Annual	5yr Annual	10yr Annual	Bull	Bear
Return (%)	9.3	12.9	13.9	21.7	6.1
Differ from Category (+/-)	-1.7 blw av	-3.2 blw av	-2.9 blw av	-28.0 low	11.5 abv av

Standard Deviation	Category Risk Index	Beta
15.0%—av	0.77—low	0.52

	2000	1999	1998	1997	1996	1995	1994	1993	1992	1991
Return (%)	18.3	5.9	4.1	24.9	12.8	18.7	-0.7	11.2	16.1	31.8
Differ from Category (+/-)	14.8	-13.0	-10.2	-2.2	-9.5	-11.7	-0.5	-3.4	3.5	-5.8
Return, Tax-Adjusted (%)	13.6	4.4	2.0	21.7	7.0	14.4	-3.6	8.9	14.2	30.1

PER SHARE DATA

	2000	1999	1998	1997	1996	1995	1994	1993	1992	1991
Dividends, Net Income ($)	0.05	0.04	0.05	0.06	0.11	0.11	0.11	0.11	0.10	0.12
Distrib'ns, Cap Gain ($)	1.59	0.45	0.71	0.99	1.44	0.97	0.73	0.48	0.37	0.21
Net Asset Value ($)	6.88	7.28	7.35	7.82	7.11	7.71	7.41	8.31	8.00	7.29
Expense Ratio (%)	na	1.04	1.01	1.05	0.99	0.97	0.98	0.98	0.91	0.95
Yield (%)	0.59	0.51	0.62	0.68	1.28	1.26	1.35	1.25	1.19	1.60
Portfolio Turnover (%)	na	21	29	18	29	10	17	24	22	29
Total Assets (Millions $)	354	371	466	507	456	637	771	1,022	1,102	789

PORTFOLIO (as of 6/30/00)

Portfolio Manager: Charles Royce - 1968

Investm't Category: Growth

✔ Domestic | Index
Foreign | Sector
Asset Allocation | State Specific

Investment Style

Large Cap | Mid Cap | ✔ Small Cap
Growth | Grth/Val | ✔ Value

Portfolio

5.7%	cash	0.0%	corp bonds
94.3%	stocks	0.0%	gov't bonds
0.0%	pref/conv't pref	0.0%	muni bonds
0.0%	conv't bds/wrnts	0.0%	other

SHAREHOLDER INFORMATION

Minimum Investment

Initial: $2,000 Subsequent: $50

Minimum IRA Investment

Initial: $500 Subsequent: $50

Maximum Fees

Load: 1.00% redemption 12b-1: none

Other: redemption fee applies for 12 months

Services

✔ IRA
✔ Keogh
✔ Telephone Exchange

Royce: Premier (RYPRX)

800-221-4268, 212-486-1445
www.roycefunds.com

Growth

PERFORMANCE — fund inception date: 12/31/91

	3yr Annual	5yr Annual	10yr Annual	Bull	Bear
Return (%)	11.7	14.2	na	31.7	3.9
Differ from Category (+/-)	0.7 av	-1.9 blw av	na	-18.0 blw av	9.3 abv av

Standard Deviation	Category Risk Index	Beta
16.8%—av	0.86—low	0.63

	2000	1999	1998	1997	1996	1995	1994	1993	1992	1991
Return (%)	17.1	11.4	6.7	18.4	18.1	17.8	3.2	19.0	15.8	—
Differ from Category (+/-)	13.6	-7.5	-7.6	-8.7	-4.2	-12.6	3.4	4.4	3.2	—
Return, Tax-Adjusted (%)	14.3	10.0	6.2	16.8	15.6	15.4	2.4	18.1	14.2	—

PER SHARE DATA

	2000	1999	1998	1997	1996	1995	1994	1993	1992	1991
Dividends, Net Income ($)	0.03	0.01	0.05	0.08	0.10	0.09	0.05	0.02	0.02	—
Distrib'ns, Cap Gain ($)	1.27	0.58	0.09	0.46	0.49	0.41	0.09	0.14	0.25	—
Net Asset Value ($)	9.83	9.56	9.14	8.70	7.81	7.12	6.48	6.41	5.52	—
Expense Ratio (%)	na	1.35	1.23	1.24	1.25	1.29	1.38	1.50	1.77	—
Yield (%)	0.27	0.09	0.54	0.87	1.20	1.19	0.76	0.30	0.34	—
Portfolio Turnover (%)	na	70	46	18	34	39	38	85	116	—
Total Assets (Millions $)	610	567	571	533	316	302	202	47	2	—

PORTFOLIO (as of 6/30/00)

Portfolio Manager: Charles Royce - 1991

Investm't Category: Growth

✔ Domestic
Index
✔ Foreign
Sector
Asset Allocation
State Specific

Investment Style

Large Cap
Mid Cap
✔ Small Cap
Growth
Grth/Val
✔ Value

Portfolio

8.7%	cash	0.0%	corp bonds
91.3%	stocks	0.0%	gov't bonds
0.0%	pref/conv't pref	0.0%	muni bonds
0.0%	conv't bds/wrnts	0.0%	other

SHAREHOLDER INFORMATION

Minimum Investment

Initial: $2,000 Subsequent: $1

Minimum IRA Investment

Initial: $500 Subsequent: $1

Maximum Fees

Load: 1.00% redemption 12b-1: none

Other: redemption fee applies for 12 months

Services

✔ IRA
✔ Keogh
✔ Telephone Exchange

Royce: Total Return (RYTRX)

800-221-4268, 212-486-1445
www.roycefunds.com

Growth & Income

PERFORMANCE — fund inception date: 12/15/93

	3yr Annual	5yr Annual	10yr Annual	Bull	Bear
Return (%)	8.3	14.5	na	15.2	9.7
Differ from Category (+/-)	-0.6 av	0.2 av	na	-18.3 blw av	9.8 abv av

Standard Deviation	Category Risk Index	Beta
12.4%—blw av	0.72—low	0.43

	2000	1999	1998	1997	1996	1995	1994	1993	1992	1991
Return (%)	19.4	1.5	4.7	23.6	25.5	26.8	5.2	—	—	—
Differ from Category (+/-)	13.7	-9.3	-8.1	-3.3	5.8	-2.7	5.7	—	—	—
Return, Tax-Adjusted (%)	16.9	-0.2	3.4	22.4	20.8	22.5	4.3	—	—	—

PER SHARE DATA

	2000	1999	1998	1997	1996	1995	1994	1993	1992	1991
Dividends, Net Income ($)	0.15	0.16	0.15	0.11	0.16	0.13	0.02	—	—	—
Distrib'ns, Cap Gain ($)	0.57	0.35	0.16	0.14	0.73	0.60	0.12	—	—	—
Net Asset Value ($)	7.77	7.15	7.56	7.52	6.29	5.76	5.12	—	—	—
Expense Ratio (%)	na	1.25	1.25	1.25	1.25	1.67	1.96	—	—	—
Yield (%)	1.79	2.13	1.94	1.43	2.27	2.04	0.38	—	—	—
Portfolio Turnover (%)	na	39	66	26	111	68	88	—	—	—
Total Assets (Millions $)	263	249	244	120	6	2	1	—	—	—

PORTFOLIO (as of 6/30/00)

Portfolio Manager: Charles Royce - 1993

Investm't Category: Growth & Income

✔ Domestic	Index
✔ Foreign	Sector
Asset Allocation	State Specific

Investment Style

Large Cap	Mid Cap	✔ Small Cap
Growth	Grth/Val	✔ Value

Portfolio

0.5% cash	0.0% corp bonds
99.5% stocks	0.0% gov't bonds
0.0% pref/conv't pref	0.0% muni bonds
0.0% conv't bds/wrnts	0.0% other

SHAREHOLDER INFORMATION

Minimum Investment
Initial: $2,000 Subsequent: $50

Minimum IRA Investment
Initial: $500 Subsequent: $50

Maximum Fees
Load: 1.00% redemption 12b-1: none
Other: redemption fee applies for 12 months

Services
✔ IRA
✔ Keogh
✔ Telephone Exchange

Rydex: Nova/Inv (RYNVX)

800-820-0888, 301-296-5100
www.rydexfunds.com

Aggressive Growth

PERFORMANCE — fund inception date: 7/12/93

	3yr Annual	5yr Annual	10yr Annual	Bull	Bear
Return (%)	10.4	19.5	na	77.3	-21.0
Differ from Category (+/-)	-5.8 blw av	4.9 abv av	na	-41.9 blw av	-0.4 av

Standard Deviation	Category Risk Index	Beta
26.3%—high	0.81—blw av	1.49

	2000	1999	1998	1997	1996	1995	1994	1993	1992	1991
Return (%)	-19.5	24.0	35.1	42.3	27.2	50.4	-4.7	—	—	—
Differ from Category (+/-)	-13.5	-33.5	20.0	27.5	8.9	15.8	-3.9	—	—	—
Return, Tax-Adjusted (%)	-19.5	23.9	34.4	42.2	26.6	47.6	-5.3	—	—	—

PER SHARE DATA

	2000	1999	1998	1997	1996	1995	1994	1993	1992	1991
Dividends, Net Income ($)	0.00	0.02	0.41	0.00	0.00	0.23	0.08	—	—	—
Distrib'ns, Cap Gain ($)	0.00	0.00	0.00	0.05	0.25	0.64	0.12	—	—	—
Net Asset Value ($)	33.13	41.19	33.23	24.93	17.55	13.98	9.99	—	—	—
Expense Ratio (%)	1.18	1.19	1.11	1.16	1.31	1.43	1.74	—	—	—
Yield (%)	0.00	0.04	1.23	0.00	0.00	1.57	0.79	—	—	—
Portfolio Turnover (%)	311	445	0	0	0	0	0	—	—	—
Total Assets (Millions $)	328	652	941	776	360	222	58	—	—	—

PORTFOLIO (as of 6/30/00)

Portfolio Manager: Thomas Michael - 1994

Investm't Category: Aggressive Growth

✔ Domestic — Index
Foreign — Sector
Asset Allocation — State Specific

Investment Style

✔ Large Cap — Mid Cap — Small Cap
Growth — ✔ Grth/Val — Value

Portfolio

0.0%	cash	0.0%	corp bonds
100.0%	stocks	0.0%	gov't bonds
0.0%	pref/conv't pref	0.0%	muni bonds
0.0%	conv't bds/wrnts	0.0%	other

SHAREHOLDER INFORMATION

Minimum Investment
Initial: $25,000 — Subsequent: $1

Minimum IRA Investment
Initial: $25,000 — Subsequent: $1

Maximum Fees
Load: none — 12b-1: none
Other: none

Services
✔ IRA
✔ Keogh
✔ Telephone Exchange

Rydex: OTC/Inv (RYOCX)

800-820-0888, 301-296-5100
www.rydexfunds.com

Aggressive Growth

PERFORMANCE

fund inception date: 2/14/94

	3yr Annual	5yr Annual	10yr Annual	Bull	Bear
Return (%)	32.4	32.3	na	221.2	-43.6
Differ from Category (+/-)	16.2 high	17.7 high	na	102.0 high	-23.0 low

Standard Deviation	Category Risk Index	Beta
39.3%—high	1.21—abv av	1.63

	2000	1999	1998	1997	1996	1995	1994	1993	1992	1991
Return (%)	-37.9	100.6	86.4	21.8	43.4	44.2	—	—	—	—
Differ from Category (+/-)	-31.9	43.1	71.3	7.0	25.1	9.6	—	—	—	—
Return, Tax-Adjusted (%)	-37.9	100.3	86.1	21.6	43.2	41.7	—	—	—	—

PER SHARE DATA

	2000	1999	1998	1997	1996	1995	1994	1993	1992	1991
Dividends, Net Income ($)	0.00	0.00	0.00	0.00	0.01	0.02	—	—	—	—
Distrib'ns, Cap Gain ($)	0.17	0.15	0.09	0.03	0.00	0.25	—	—	—	—
Net Asset Value ($)	16.91	27.45	13.78	7.45	6.14	4.29	—	—	—	—
Expense Ratio (%)	1.15	1.15	1.13	1.27	1.33	1.41	—	—	—	—
Yield (%)	0.00	0.00	0.00	0.00	0.21	0.51	—	—	—	—
Portfolio Turnover (%)	385	773	971	1,140	2,578	2,241	—	—	—	—
Total Assets (Millions $)	1,899	3,010	1,109	206	174	30	—	—	—	—

PORTFOLIO (as of 6/30/00)

Portfolio Manager: Michael Byrum - 1997

Investm't Category: Aggressive Growth

✔ Domestic
Foreign
Asset Allocation
✔ Index
Sector
State Specific

Investment Style

✔ Large Cap ✔ Mid Cap ✔ Small Cap
✔ Growth Grth/Val Value

Portfolio

0.0%	cash	0.0%	corp bonds
100.0%	stocks	0.0%	gov't bonds
0.0%	pref/conv't pref	0.0%	muni bonds
0.0%	conv't bds/wrnts	0.0%	other

SHAREHOLDER INFORMATION

Minimum Investment

Initial: $25,000 Subsequent: $1

Minimum IRA Investment

Initial: $25,000 Subsequent: $1

Maximum Fees

Load: none 12b-1: none
Other: none

Services

✔ IRA
✔ Keogh
✔ Telephone Exchange

SAFECO Div Income

800-624-5711, 206-545-7319
www.safecofunds.com

(SAFIX)

Balanced

PERFORMANCE **fund inception date: 10/1/69**

	3yr Annual	5yr Annual	10yr Annual	Bull	Bear
Return (%)	0.2	9.5	12.1	18.0	-7.0
Differ from Category (+/-)	-8.2 low	-1.9 blw av	0.4 av	-10.1 blw av	-3.8 blw av

Standard Deviation	Category Risk Index	Beta
16.2%—av	1.48—high	0.82

	2000	1999	1998	1997	1996	1995	1994	1993	1992	1991
Return (%)	-6.3	1.1	6.3	26.4	23.9	30.3	-1.0	12.5	11.4	23.2
Differ from Category (+/-)	-8.3	-9.6	-7.0	7.6	10.0	4.8	0.3	-1.9	3.0	-0.6
Return, Tax-Adjusted (%)	-6.9	-0.4	4.1	23.1	19.1	26.7	-3.1	10.6	9.7	21.2

PER SHARE DATA

	2000	1999	1998	1997	1996	1995	1994	1993	1992	1991
Dividends, Net Income ($)	0.38	0.50	0.64	0.65	0.67	0.82	0.80	0.78	0.78	0.80
Distrib'ns, Cap Gain ($)	0.00	0.82	1.27	2.10	2.38	0.91	0.23	0.00	0.04	0.05
Net Asset Value ($)	20.58	22.39	23.47	23.89	21.13	19.70	16.54	17.77	16.50	15.58
Expense Ratio (%)	na	0.99	0.82	0.89	0.89	0.87	0.86	0.90	0.90	0.93
Yield (%)	1.84	2.15	2.58	2.50	2.84	3.97	4.77	4.38	4.71	5.11
Portfolio Turnover (%)	na	42	46	82	37	31	19	20	20	22
Total Assets (Millions $)	212	293	373	371	281	226	180	200	185	181

PORTFOLIO (as of 6/30/00)

Portfolio Manager: Thomas Rath - 1996

Investm't Category: Balanced

✔ Domestic | Index
Foreign | Sector
Asset Allocation | State Specific

Investment Style

Large Cap | Mid Cap | Small Cap
Growth | Grth/Val | Value

Portfolio

0.6%	cash	0.0%	corp bonds
94.3%	stocks	0.0%	gov't bonds
5.1%	pref/conv't pref	0.0%	muni bonds
0.0%	conv't bds/wrnts	0.0%	other

SHAREHOLDER INFORMATION

Minimum Investment
Initial: $1,000 Subsequent: $100

Minimum IRA Investment
Initial: $250 Subsequent: $100

Maximum Fees
Load: none 12b-1: none
Other: none

Services
✔ IRA
✔ Keogh
✔ Telephone Exchange

SAFECO Equity (SAFQX)

800-624-5711, 206-545-7319
www.safecofunds.com

Growth & Income

PERFORMANCE — fund inception date: 3/14/32

	3yr Annual	5yr Annual	10yr Annual	Bull	Bear
Return (%)	6.7	13.5	16.8	39.0	-10.1
Differ from Category (+/-)	-2.2 blw av	-0.8 blw av	1.9 abv av	5.5 abv av	-10.0 blw av

Standard Deviation	Category Risk Index	Beta
16.8%—av	0.97—av	0.89

	2000	1999	1998	1997	1996	1995	1994	1993	1992	1991
Return (%)	-10.9	9.3	24.9	24.2	25.0	25.2	9.9	30.9	9.2	27.9
Differ from Category (+/-)	-16.6	-1.5	12.1	-2.7	5.3	-4.3	10.4	17.1	-2.4	-0.2
Return, Tax-Adjusted (%)	-11.6	7.9	23.5	22.6	20.4	21.3	7.9	28.1	7.5	25.2

PER SHARE DATA

	2000	1999	1998	1997	1996	1995	1994	1993	1992	1991
Dividends, Net Income ($)	0.13	0.17	0.21	0.22	0.25	0.34	0.26	0.17	0.13	0.17
Distrib'ns, Cap Gain ($)	0.61	1.22	0.92	0.83	2.14	1.40	0.53	0.81	0.48	0.67
Net Asset Value ($)	20.65	24.02	23.25	19.54	16.60	15.33	13.68	13.18	10.87	10.59
Expense Ratio (%)	na	0.83	0.74	0.78	0.78	0.84	0.85	0.94	0.96	0.98
Yield (%)	0.61	0.67	0.86	1.08	1.33	2.03	1.82	1.21	1.14	1.50
Portfolio Turnover (%)	na	34	33	34	59	56	33	37	40	45
Total Assets (Millions $)	1,443	2,047	2,024	1,438	821	604	449	193	84	75

PORTFOLIO (as of 3/31/00)

Portfolio Manager: Richard Meagley - 1995

Investm't Category: Growth & Income

✔ Domestic — Index
Foreign — Sector
Asset Allocation — State Specific

Investment Style

✔ Large Cap — Mid Cap — Small Cap
Growth — Grth/Val — ✔ Value

Portfolio

2.6%	cash	0.0%	corp bonds
97.4%	stocks	0.0%	gov't bonds
0.0%	pref/conv't pref	0.0%	muni bonds
0.0%	conv't bds/wrnts	0.0%	other

SHAREHOLDER INFORMATION

Minimum Investment
Initial: $1,000 — Subsequent: $100

Minimum IRA Investment
Initial: $250 — Subsequent: $100

Maximum Fees
Load: none — 12b-1: none
Other: none

Services
✔ IRA
✔ Keogh
✔ Telephone Exchange

SAFECO Growth Opp (SAFGX)

800-624-5711, 206-545-7319
www.safecofunds.com

Aggressive Growth

PERFORMANCE — fund inception date: 1/18/68

	3yr Annual	5yr Annual	10yr Annual	Bull	Bear
Return (%)	0.8	13.5	16.2	27.3	-15.7
Differ from Category (+/-)	-15.4 low	-1.1 blw av	0.4 blw av	-91.9 low	4.9 abv av

Standard Deviation	Category Risk Index	Beta
25.0%—abv av	0.77—blw av	1.14

	2000	1999	1998	1997	1996	1995	1994	1993	1992	1991
Return (%)	-4.2	2.6	4.3	49.9	22.8	26.1	-1.6	22.1	-3.0	62.6
Differ from Category (+/-)	1.8	-54.9	-10.8	35.1	4.5	-8.5	-0.8	-3.1	-9.9	15.4
Return, Tax-Adjusted (%)	-4.2	2.6	3.6	46.3	18.2	16.9	-4.6	20.9	-3.9	59.8

PER SHARE DATA

	2000	1999	1998	1997	1996	1995	1994	1993	1992	1991
Dividends, Net Income ($)	0.00	0.00	0.00	0.00	0.00	0.06	0.00	0.00	0.00	0.04
Distrib'ns, Cap Gain ($)	0.00	0.00	0.73	2.99	2.66	5.67	2.15	0.70	0.61	1.14
Net Asset Value ($)	22.30	23.30	22.70	22.45	16.97	16.20	17.55	20.06	17.00	18.31
Expense Ratio (%)	na	1.23	0.77	0.99	0.99	0.98	0.95	0.91	0.91	0.90
Yield (%)	0.00	0.00	0.00	0.00	0.00	0.27	0.00	0.00	0.00	0.20
Portfolio Turnover (%)	na	38	54	82	82	110	71	57	85	50
Total Assets (Millions $)	623	815	1,394	561	192	181	150	163	171	172

PORTFOLIO (as of 6/30/00)

Portfolio Manager: Thomas Maguire - 1989

Investm't Category: Aggressive Growth

✔ Domestic
Foreign
Asset Allocation
Index
Sector
State Specific

Investment Style

Large Cap
✔ Mid Cap
✔ Small Cap
✔ Growth
Grth/Val
Value

Portfolio

3.5% cash
96.4% stocks
0.0% pref/conv't pref
0.1% conv't bds/wrnts
0.0% corp bonds
0.0% gov't bonds
0.0% muni bonds
0.0% other

SHAREHOLDER INFORMATION

Minimum Investment

Initial: $1,000 — Subsequent: $100

Minimum IRA Investment

Initial: $250 — Subsequent: $100

Maximum Fees

Load: none — 12b-1: none
Other: none

Services

✔ IRA
✔ Keogh
✔ Telephone Exchange

SAFECO Northwest (SFNWX)

800-624-5711, 206-545-7319
www.safecofunds.com

Growth

PERFORMANCE — fund inception date: 2/7/91

	3yr Annual	5yr Annual	10yr Annual	Bull	Bear
Return (%)	10.2	15.0	na	97.4	-26.2
Differ from Category (+/-)	-0.8 av	-1.1 blw av	na	47.7 high	-20.8 low

Standard Deviation	Category Risk Index	Beta
25.9%—high	1.33—high	1.11

	2000	1999	1998	1997	1996	1995	1994	1993	1992	1991
Return (%)	-16.1	54.2	3.4	31.1	15.0	20.1	-1.5	1.0	14.0	—
Differ from Category (+/-)	-19.6	35.3	-10.9	4.0	-7.3	-10.3	-1.3	-13.6	1.4	—
Return, Tax-Adjusted (%)	-16.1	51.9	3.1	29.4	11.7	17.9	-1.8	0.3	13.0	—

PER SHARE DATA

	2000	1999	1998	1997	1996	1995	1994	1993	1992	1991
Dividends, Net Income ($)	0.00	0.00	0.00	0.00	0.00	0.04	0.03	0.03	0.06	—
Distrib'ns, Cap Gain ($)	0.00	2.01	0.18	1.13	1.60	0.87	0.10	0.23	0.31	—
Net Asset Value ($)	21.25	25.33	17.73	17.31	14.07	13.66	12.12	12.45	12.59	—
Expense Ratio (%)	na	1.10	1.12	1.25	1.25	1.09	1.06	1.11	1.11	—
Yield (%)	0.00	0.00	0.00	0.00	0.00	0.27	0.24	0.23	0.46	—
Portfolio Turnover (%)	na	49	50	55	67	19	18	14	33	—
Total Assets (Millions $)	109	90	63	63	43	38	34	39	40	—

PORTFOLIO (as of 3/31/00)

Portfolio Manager: Bill Whitlow - 1997

Investm't Category: Growth

✔ Domestic
Foreign
Asset Allocation
Index
Sector
State Specific

Investment Style

✔ Large Cap
✔ Mid Cap
✔ Small Cap
✔ Growth
Grth/Val
Value

Portfolio

0.6% cash
99.4% stocks
0.0% pref/conv't pref
0.0% conv't bds/wrnts
0.0% corp bonds
0.0% gov't bonds
0.0% muni bonds
0.0% other

SHAREHOLDER INFORMATION

Minimum Investment

Initial: $1,000 Subsequent: $100

Minimum IRA Investment

Initial: $250 Subsequent: $100

Maximum Fees

Load: none 12b-1: none
Other: none

Services

✔ IRA
✔ Keogh
✔ Telephone Exchange

SSgA Life Sol: Balanced

800-647-7327, 206-572-9500
www.ssgafunds.com

(SSLBX)

Balanced

PERFORMANCE — fund inception date: 7/1/97

	3yr Annual	5yr Annual	10yr Annual	Bull	Bear
Return (%)	7.4	na	na	29.2	-6.6
Differ from Category (+/-)	-1.0 blw av	na	na	1.1 av	-3.4 blw av

Standard Deviation	Category Risk Index	Beta
10.3%—blw av	0.94—blw av	0.55

	2000	1999	1998	1997	1996	1995	1994	1993	1992	1991
Return (%)	-2.1	12.7	12.3	—	—	—	—	—	—	—
Differ from Category (+/-)	-4.1	2.0	-1.0	—	—	—	—	—	—	—
Return, Tax-Adjusted (%)	-7.1	10.0	9.3	—	—	—	—	—	—	—

PER SHARE DATA

	2000	1999	1998	1997	1996	1995	1994	1993	1992	1991
Dividends, Net Income ($)	1.00	0.69	0.61	—	—	—	—	—	—	—
Distrib'ns, Cap Gain ($)	1.57	0.40	0.75	—	—	—	—	—	—	—
Net Asset Value ($)	11.07	13.96	13.42	—	—	—	—	—	—	—
Expense Ratio (%)	0.24	0.28	0.36	—	—	—	—	—	—	—
Yield (%)	7.91	4.80	4.30	—	—	—	—	—	—	—
Portfolio Turnover (%)	42	51	101	—	—	—	—	—	—	—
Total Assets (Millions $)	80	129	103	—	—	—	—	—	—	—

PORTFOLIO (as of 3/31/00)

Portfolio Manager: Heydon Traub - 1997

Investm't Category: Balanced

✔ Domestic — Index
✔ Foreign — Sector
Asset Allocation — State Specific

Investment Style

Large Cap — Mid Cap — Small Cap
Growth — Grth/Val — Value

Portfolio

0.0%	cash	0.0%	corp bonds
0.0%	stocks	0.0%	gov't bonds
0.0%	pref/conv't pref	0.0%	muni bonds
0.0%	conv't bds/wrnts	100.0%	other

SHAREHOLDER INFORMATION

Minimum Investment
Initial: $1,000 — Subsequent: $100

Minimum IRA Investment
Initial: $250 — Subsequent: $100

Maximum Fees
Load: none — 12b-1: 0.15%
Other: none

Services
✔ IRA
✔ Keogh
✔ Telephone Exchange

SSgA: Active Int'l (SSAIX)

800-647-7327, 253-572-9500
www.ssgafunds.com

International Stock

PERFORMANCE — fund inception date: 3/7/95

	3yr Annual	5yr Annual	10yr Annual	Bull	Bear
Return (%)	7.9	3.0	na	49.3	-18.7
Differ from Category (+/-)	-1.0 blw av	-5.3 blw av	na	-41.6 blw av	5.3 abv av

Standard Deviation	Category Risk Index	Beta
16.6%—av	0.73—low	0.70

	2000	1999	1998	1997	1996	1995	1994	1993	1992	1991
Return (%)	-16.3	32.5	13.5	-10.0	2.6	—	—	—	—	—
Differ from Category (+/-)	3.1	-28.2	7.7	-11.3	-11.9	—	—	—	—	—
Return, Tax-Adjusted (%)	-18.3	31.9	10.3	-11.4	2.3	—	—	—	—	—

PER SHARE DATA

	2000	1999	1998	1997	1996	1995	1994	1993	1992	1991
Dividends, Net Income ($)	0.00	0.12	0.38	0.14	0.04	—	—	—	—	—
Distrib'ns, Cap Gain ($)	1.26	0.00	0.69	0.49	0.05	—	—	—	—	—
Net Asset Value ($)	8.79	12.06	9.21	9.17	10.84	—	—	—	—	—
Expense Ratio (%)	1.00	1.00	1.00	1.00	1.00	—	—	—	—	—
Yield (%)	0.00	0.99	3.83	1.44	0.36	—	—	—	—	—
Portfolio Turnover (%)	64	62	74	48	22	—	—	—	—	—
Total Assets (Millions $)	88	119	97	142	67	—	—	—	—	—

PORTFOLIO (as of 3/31/00)

Portfolio Manager: Geoff Benarick - 1995

Investm't Category: International Stock

Domestic	Index
✔ Foreign	Sector
Asset Allocation	State Specific

Investment Style

Large Cap	Mid Cap	Small Cap
Growth	Grth/Val	Value

Portfolio

0.0%	cash	0.0%	corp bonds
100.0%	stocks	0.0%	gov't bonds
0.0%	pref/conv't pref	0.0%	muni bonds
0.0%	conv't bds/wrnts	0.0%	other

SHAREHOLDER INFORMATION

Minimum Investment
Initial: $1,000 Subsequent: $100

Minimum IRA Investment
Initial: $250 Subsequent: $100

Maximum Fees
Load: none 12b-1: 0.08%
Other: none

Services
✔ IRA
Keogh
✔ Telephone Exchange

SSgA: Emerging Markets (SSEMX)

800-647-7327, 523-798-9500
www.ssgafunds.com

International Stock

PERFORMANCE — fund inception date: 3/1/94

	3yr Annual	5yr Annual	10yr Annual	Bull	Bear
Return (%)	-0.9	0.3	na	105.9	-33.2
Differ from Category (+/-)	-9.8 low	-8.0 blw av	na	15.0 abv av	-9.2 blw av

Standard Deviation	Category Risk Index	Beta
28.2%—high	1.25—abv av	1.17

	2000	1999	1998	1997	1996	1995	1994	1993	1992	1991
Return (%)	-29.9	64.8	-15.9	-8.8	14.8	-7.8	—	—	—	—
Differ from Category (+/-)	-10.5	4.1	-21.7	-10.1	0.3	-17.1	—	—	—	—
Return, Tax-Adjusted (%)	-30.0	63.6	-17.0	-9.7	14.2	-8.4	—	—	—	—

PER SHARE DATA

	2000	1999	1998	1997	1996	1995	1994	1993	1992	1991
Dividends, Net Income ($)	0.06	0.23	0.27	0.15	0.10	0.11	—	—	—	—
Distrib'ns, Cap Gain ($)	0.00	0.00	0.00	0.25	0.05	0.10	—	—	—	—
Net Asset Value ($)	8.81	12.67	7.86	9.69	10.98	9.70	—	—	—	—
Expense Ratio (%)	1.25	1.25	1.25	1.25	1.28	1.50	—	—	—	—
Yield (%)	0.68	1.81	3.43	1.50	0.90	1.12	—	—	—	—
Portfolio Turnover (%)	55	39	38	15	4	20	—	—	—	—
Total Assets (Millions $)	320	414	236	254	148	80	—	—	—	—

PORTFOLIO (as of 3/31/00)

Portfolio Manager: Brad Aham - 1997

Investm't Category: International Stock

✔ Domestic — Index
✔ Foreign — Sector
Asset Allocation — State Specific

Investment Style

Large Cap — Mid Cap — Small Cap
Growth — Grth/Val — Value

Portfolio

0.0%	cash	0.0%	corp bonds
100.0%	stocks	0.0%	gov't bonds
0.0%	pref/conv't pref	0.0%	muni bonds
0.0%	conv't bds/wrnts	0.0%	other

SHAREHOLDER INFORMATION

Minimum Investment
Initial: $1,000 — Subsequent: $100

Minimum IRA Investment
Initial: $250 — Subsequent: $100

Maximum Fees
Load: none — 12b-1: 0.12%
Other: none

Services
✔ IRA
Keogh
✔ Telephone Exchange

SSgA: Growth & Income (SSGWX)

800-647-7327, 253-572-9500
www.ssgafunds.com

Growth & Income

PERFORMANCE — fund inception date: 9/1/93

	3yr Annual	5yr Annual	10yr Annual	Bull	Bear
Return (%)	15.3	20.7	na	62.1	-9.5
Differ from Category (+/-)	6.4 high	6.4 high	na	28.6 high	-9.4 blw av

Standard Deviation	Category Risk Index	Beta
18.7%—av	1.08—high	1.03

	2000	1999	1998	1997	1996	1995	1994	1993	1992	1991
Return (%)	-5.7	20.8	34.7	37.6	21.4	28.6	-0.2	—	—	—
Differ from Category (+/-)	-11.4	10.0	21.9	10.7	1.7	-0.9	0.3	—	—	—
Return, Tax-Adjusted (%)	-6.7	19.6	31.8	34.8	19.9	27.8	-0.8	—	—	—

PER SHARE DATA

	2000	1999	1998	1997	1996	1995	1994	1993	1992	1991
Dividends, Net Income ($)	0.05	0.07	0.10	0.09	0.14	0.17	0.17	—	—	—
Distrib'ns, Cap Gain ($)	1.19	1.07	2.35	1.80	0.44	0.04	0.00	—	—	—
Net Asset Value ($)	21.95	24.52	21.39	18.07	14.54	12.49	9.89	—	—	—
Expense Ratio (%)	1.10	1.03	0.95	0.95	0.95	0.95	0.95	—	—	—
Yield (%)	0.21	0.27	0.42	0.45	0.93	1.35	1.71	—	—	—
Portfolio Turnover (%)	49	72	66	29	38	39	36	—	—	—
Total Assets (Millions $)	459	409	204	80	71	49	26	—	—	—

PORTFOLIO (as of 3/31/00)

Portfolio Manager: Emerson Tuttle - 1993

Investm't Category: Growth & Income

✔ Domestic — Index
Foreign — Sector
Asset Allocation — State Specific

Investment Style

✔ Large Cap — Mid Cap — Small Cap
Growth — ✔ Grth/Val — Value

Portfolio

0.0%	cash	0.0%	corp bonds
100.0%	stocks	0.0%	gov't bonds
0.0%	pref/conv't pref	0.0%	muni bonds
0.0%	conv't bds/wrnts	0.0%	other

SHAREHOLDER INFORMATION

Minimum Investment
Initial: $1,000 — Subsequent: $100

Minimum IRA Investment
Initial: $250 — Subsequent: $100

Maximum Fees
Load: none — 12b-1: 0.15%
Other: none

Services
✔ IRA
Keogh
✔ Telephone Exchange

SSgA: Matrix Equity (SSMTX)

800-647-7327, 253-572-9500
www.ssgafunds.com

Growth

PERFORMANCE — fund inception date: 5/4/92

	3yr Annual	5yr Annual	10yr Annual	Bull	Bear
Return (%)	6.4	14.8	na	46.9	-15.2
Differ from Category (+/-)	-4.6 blw av	-1.3 blw av	na	-2.8 av	-9.8 blw av

Standard Deviation	Category Risk Index	Beta
19.0%—av	0.98—blw av	1.05

	2000	1999	1998	1997	1996	1995	1994	1993	1992	1991
Return (%)	-14.1	15.3	21.7	34.2	23.6	28.1	-0.3	16.2	—	—
Differ from Category (+/-)	-17.6	-3.6	7.4	7.1	1.3	-2.3	-0.1	1.6	—	—
Return, Tax-Adjusted (%)	-19.5	12.2	18.2	29.5	20.4	23.7	-1.2	15.0	—	—

PER SHARE DATA

	2000	1999	1998	1997	1996	1995	1994	1993	1992	1991
Dividends, Net Income ($)	0.04	0.06	0.12	0.20	0.24	0.25	0.26	0.18	—	—
Distrib'ns, Cap Gain ($)	4.39	2.45	2.57	3.00	1.13	1.43	0.05	0.18	—	—
Net Asset Value ($)	10.07	16.51	16.83	16.47	14.73	13.08	11.56	11.93	—	—
Expense Ratio (%)	0.91	0.78	0.69	0.58	0.66	0.68	0.58	0.60	—	—
Yield (%)	0.27	0.31	0.61	1.02	1.51	1.72	2.23	1.48	—	—
Portfolio Turnover (%)	149	130	133	117	150	129	127	58	—	—
Total Assets (Millions $)	341	592	566	470	314	211	138	89	—	—

PORTFOLIO (as of 3/31/00)

Portfolio Manager: Theodore Gekas - 1992

Investm't Category: Growth

✔ Domestic — Index
Foreign — Sector
Asset Allocation — State Specific

Investment Style

✔ Large Cap — Mid Cap — Small Cap
Growth — ✔ Grth/Val — Value

Portfolio

0.0% cash — 0.0% corp bonds
100.0% stocks — 0.0% gov't bonds
0.0% pref/conv't pref — 0.0% muni bonds
0.0% conv't bds/wrnts — 0.0% other

SHAREHOLDER INFORMATION

Minimum Investment
Initial: $1,000 — Subsequent: $100

Minimum IRA Investment
Initial: $250 — Subsequent: $100

Maximum Fees
Load: none — 12b-1: 0.13%
Other: none

Services
✔ IRA
Keogh
✔ Telephone Exchange

SSgA: S&P 500 Index (SVSPX)

800-647-7327, 253-572-9500
www.ssgafunds.com

Growth & Income

PERFORMANCE

fund inception date: 12/30/92

	3yr Annual	5yr Annual	10yr Annual	Bull	Bear
Return (%)	12.1	18.1	na	56.0	-11.6
Differ from Category (+/-)	3.2 abv av	3.8 high	na	22.5 high	-11.5 blw av

Standard Deviation	Category Risk Index	Beta
17.6%—av	1.02—abv av	1.00

	2000	1999	1998	1997	1996	1995	1994	1993	1992	1991
Return (%)	-9.2	20.8	28.4	33.1	22.6	37.0	1.3	9.6	—	—
Differ from Category (+/-)	-14.9	10.0	15.6	6.2	2.9	7.5	1.8	-4.2	—	—
Return, Tax-Adjusted (%)	-10.5	19.6	25.3	31.4	20.3	34.7	0.1	8.5	—	—

PER SHARE DATA

	2000	1999	1998	1997	1996	1995	1994	1993	1992	1991
Dividends, Net Income ($)	0.26	0.27	0.30	0.29	0.31	0.31	0.29	0.19	—	—
Distrib'ns, Cap Gain ($)	1.17	0.72	2.42	0.71	0.67	0.39	0.02	0.12	—	—
Net Asset Value ($)	21.82	25.53	22.09	19.66	15.57	13.55	10.44	10.63	—	—
Expense Ratio (%)	0.18	0.18	0.17	0.16	0.18	0.19	0.15	0.15	—	—
Yield (%)	1.13	1.02	1.22	1.42	1.90	2.22	2.77	1.76	—	—
Portfolio Turnover (%)	16	13	26	7	28	38	7	48	—	—
Total Assets (Millions $)	2,651	2,986	2,250	1,452	860	532	302	309	—	—

PORTFOLIO (as of 3/31/00)

Portfolio Manager: James May - 1995

Investm't Category: Growth & Income

✔ Domestic
Foreign
Asset Allocation
✔ Index
Sector
State Specific

Investment Style

✔ Large Cap
Mid Cap
Small Cap
Growth
✔ Grth/Val
Value

Portfolio

0.0% cash
100.0% stocks
0.0% pref/conv't pref
0.0% conv't bds/wrnts
0.0% corp bonds
0.0% gov't bonds
0.0% muni bonds
0.0% other

SHAREHOLDER INFORMATION

Minimum Investment

Initial: $1,000 Subsequent: $100

Minimum IRA Investment

Initial: $250 Subsequent: $100

Maximum Fees

Load: none 12b-1: 0.09%
Other: none

Services

✔ IRA
Keogh
✔ Telephone Exchange

SSgA: Small Cap (SVSCX)

800-647-7327, 253-572-9500
www.ssgafunds.com

Aggressive Growth

this fund is closed to new investors

PERFORMANCE — fund inception date: 7/1/92

	3yr Annual	5yr Annual	10yr Annual	Bull	Bear
Return (%)	0.0	9.7	na	26.1	-7.8
Differ from Category (+/-)	-16.2 low	-4.9 blw av	na	-93.1 low	12.8 high

Standard Deviation	Category Risk Index	Beta
23.4%—abv av	0.72—low	0.96

	2000	1999	1998	1997	1996	1995	1994	1993	1992	1991
Return (%)	4.4	3.5	-7.5	23.6	28.7	41.8	-0.9	12.9	—	—
Differ from Category (+/-)	10.4	-54.0	-22.6	8.8	10.4	7.2	-0.1	-12.3	—	—
Return, Tax-Adjusted (%)	4.4	3.4	-7.5	21.7	26.3	41.1	-3.1	10.6	—	—

PER SHARE DATA

	2000	1999	1998	1997	1996	1995	1994	1993	1992	1991
Dividends, Net Income ($)	0.00	0.01	0.02	0.04	0.03	0.05	0.23	0.22	—	—
Distrib'ns, Cap Gain ($)	0.00	0.00	0.00	1.59	1.22	0.19	0.63	0.60	—	—
Net Asset Value ($)	20.99	20.09	19.41	21.02	18.30	15.25	10.94	11.92	—	—
Expense Ratio (%)	1.07	1.07	1.04	1.00	1.00	0.97	0.30	0.25	—	—
Yield (%)	0.00	0.04	0.10	0.17	0.15	0.32	1.98	1.75	—	—
Portfolio Turnover (%)	156	110	86	143	76	193	45	81	—	—
Total Assets (Millions $)	250	351	453	281	76	29	4	37	—	—

PORTFOLIO (as of 3/31/00)

Portfolio Manager: Jeff Adams - 1994

Investm't Category: Aggressive Growth

✔ Domestic
Foreign
Asset Allocation
Index
Sector
State Specific

Investment Style

Large Cap
Growth
Mid Cap
✔ Grth/Val
✔ Small Cap
Value

Portfolio

0.0%	cash	0.0%	corp bonds
100.0%	stocks	0.0%	gov't bonds
0.0%	pref/conv't pref	0.0%	muni bonds
0.0%	conv't bds/wrnts	0.0%	other

SHAREHOLDER INFORMATION

Minimum Investment
Initial: $1,000 — Subsequent: $100

Minimum IRA Investment
Initial: $250 — Subsequent: $100

Maximum Fees
Load: none — 12b-1: 0.19%
Other: none

Services
✔ IRA
Keogh
✔ Telephone Exchange

Schroder Cap: Emerging Markets Ist/Inv (SCEIX)

800-464-3108, 212-641-3900

International Stock

PERFORMANCE

fund inception date: 3/31/95

	3yr Annual	5yr Annual	10yr Annual	Bull	Bear
Return (%)	-7.9	-4.4	na	97.3	-37.2
Differ from Category (+/-)	-16.8 low	-12.7 low	na	6.4 abv av	-13.2 low

Standard Deviation	Category Risk Index	Beta
29.7%—high	1.31—abv av	1.26

	2000	1999	1998	1997	1996	1995	1994	1993	1992	1991
Return (%)	-35.8	62.6	-25.2	-5.2	7.9	—	—	—	—	—
Differ from Category (+/-)	-16.4	1.9	-31.0	-6.5	-6.6	—	—	—	—	—
Return, Tax-Adjusted (%)	-35.8	61.9	-25.3	-5.3	7.9	—	—	—	—	—

PER SHARE DATA

	2000	1999	1998	1997	1996	1995	1994	1993	1992	1991
Dividends, Net Income ($)	0.01	0.13	0.03	0.03	0.00	—	—	—	—	—
Distrib'ns, Cap Gain ($)	0.00	0.00	0.00	0.00	0.00	—	—	—	—	—
Net Asset Value ($)	8.38	13.08	8.13	10.93	11.57	—	—	—	—	—
Expense Ratio (%)	na	1.27	1.36	1.41	1.60	—	—	—	—	—
Yield (%)	0.11	0.99	0.36	0.27	0.00	—	—	—	—	—
Portfolio Turnover (%)	na	77	67	43	103	—	—	—	—	—
Total Assets (Millions $)	80	266	115	177	175	—	—	—	—	—

PORTFOLIO (as of 3/31/99)

Portfolio Manager: Troiano, Crighton, Bridgeman - 1995

Investm't Category: International Stock

Domestic	Index
✔ Foreign	Sector
Asset Allocation	State Specific

Investment Style

Large Cap	Mid Cap	Small Cap
Growth	Grth/Val	Value

Portfolio

2.9%	cash	0.0%	corp bonds
90.0%	stocks	0.0%	gov't bonds
6.7%	pref/conv't pref	0.0%	muni bonds
0.4%	conv't bds/wrnts	0.0%	other

SHAREHOLDER INFORMATION

Minimum Investment

Initial: $1,000,000 Subsequent: $1

Minimum IRA Investment

Initial: $1 Subsequent: $1

Maximum Fees

Load: 0.50% redemption 12b-1: none

Other: redemption fee applies for 15 days

Services

✔ IRA

✔ Keogh

✔ Telephone Exchange

Schroder Cap: Intl/Inv

800-464-3108, 212-641-3900

(SCIEX)

International Stock

PERFORMANCE **fund inception date: 12/20/85**

	3yr Annual	5yr Annual	10yr Annual	Bull	Bear
Return (%)	13.2	10.5	10.3	43.6	-10.0
Differ from Category (+/-)	4.3 abv av	2.2 abv av	1.3 av	-47.3 low	14.0 high

Standard Deviation	Category Risk Index	Beta
13.8%—blw av	0.61—low	0.49

	2000	1999	1998	1997	1996	1995	1994	1993	1992	1991
Return (%)	-2.2	30.9	13.5	3.3	9.9	11.5	-0.2	45.7	-4.0	4.5
Differ from Category (+/-)	17.2	-29.8	7.7	2.0	-4.6	2.2	2.9	5.5	-0.5	-8.5
Return, Tax-Adjusted (%)	-10.4	28.5	9.1	0.8	5.0	7.2	-3.4	45.5	-4.2	3.9

PER SHARE DATA

	2000	1999	1998	1997	1996	1995	1994	1993	1992	1991
Dividends, Net Income ($)	0.30	0.07	0.18	0.29	0.45	0.47	0.00	0.07	0.11	0.23
Distrib'ns, Cap Gain ($)	6.87	1.60	3.17	1.55	2.62	2.31	2.54	0.00	0.00	0.05
Net Asset Value ($)	10.17	18.01	15.10	16.28	17.57	18.86	19.44	21.94	15.11	15.86
Expense Ratio (%)	na	0.99	0.99	0.99	0.99	0.99	0.90	0.91	0.93	1.07
Yield (%)	1.76	0.35	0.98	1.62	2.22	2.22	0.00	0.31	0.72	1.44
Portfolio Turnover (%)	na	85	53	36	56	17	25	56	49	51
Total Assets (Millions $)	99	156	127	174	188	205	174	358	172	115

PORTFOLIO (as of 3/31/99)

Portfolio Manager: Michael Perelstein - 1997

Investm't Category: International Stock

Domestic	Index
✔ Foreign	Sector
Asset Allocation	State Specific

Investment Style

Large Cap	Mid Cap	Small Cap
Growth	Grth/Val	Value

Portfolio

11.0% cash	0.0% corp bonds
89.0% stocks	0.0% gov't bonds
0.0% pref/conv't pref	0.0% muni bonds
0.0% conv't bds/wrnts	0.0% other

SHAREHOLDER INFORMATION

Minimum Investment
Initial: $10,000 Subsequent: $1,000

Minimum IRA Investment
Initial: $2,000 Subsequent: $250

Maximum Fees
Load: none 12b-1: none
Other: none

Services
✔ IRA
✔ Keogh
✔ Telephone Exchange

Schroder Cap: US Sm Co/Inv (SCUIX)

800-464-3108, 212-641-3900

Aggressive Growth

PERFORMANCE

fund inception date: 8/5/93

	3yr Annual	5yr Annual	10yr Annual	Bull	Bear
Return (%)	10.4	15.8	na	29.8	0.1
Differ from Category (+/-)	-5.8 blw av	1.2 av	na	-89.4 low	20.7 high

Standard Deviation	Category Risk Index	Beta
21.2%—abv av	0.65—low	0.87

	2000	1999	1998	1997	1996	1995	1994	1993	1992	1991
Return (%)	31.2	13.1	-9.2	26.8	22.2	49.0	4.4	—	—	—
Differ from Category (+/-)	37.2	-44.4	-24.3	12.0	3.9	14.4	5.2	—	—	—
Return, Tax-Adjusted (%)	26.6	13.1	-9.2	24.7	11.1	44.1	3.3	—	—	—

PER SHARE DATA

	2000	1999	1998	1997	1996	1995	1994	1993	1992	1991
Dividends, Net Income ($)	0.00	0.00	0.00	0.00	0.00	0.00	0.00	—	—	—
Distrib'ns, Cap Gain ($)	3.29	0.00	0.02	1.26	5.82	1.94	0.40	—	—	—
Net Asset Value ($)	15.34	14.33	12.67	13.99	12.05	14.69	11.20	—	—	—
Expense Ratio (%)	na	1.35	1.37	1.49	1.49	1.49	1.45	—	—	—
Yield (%)	0.00	0.00	0.00	0.00	0.00	0.00	0.00	—	—	—
Portfolio Turnover (%)	na	52	55	34	59	93	71	—	—	—
Total Assets (Millions $)	51	45	52	42	13	16	13	—	—	—

PORTFOLIO (as of 3/31/99)

Portfolio Manager: Ira Unschuld - 1998

Investm't Category: Aggressive Growth

✔ Domestic | Index
✔ Foreign | Sector
Asset Allocation | State Specific

Investment Style

Large Cap | Mid Cap | ✔ Small Cap
Growth | Grth/Val | ✔ Value

Portfolio

5.2% cash | 0.0% corp bonds
94.9% stocks | 0.0% gov't bonds
0.0% pref/conv't pref | 0.0% muni bonds
0.0% conv't bds/wrnts | 0.0% other

SHAREHOLDER INFORMATION

Minimum Investment

Initial: $10,000 Subsequent: $1,000

Minimum IRA Investment

Initial: $2,000 Subsequent: $250

Maximum Fees

Load: none 12b-1: none
Other: none

Services

✔ IRA
✔ Keogh
✔ Telephone Exchange

Schroder Sm Cap Val/Inv (WSCVX)

800-464-3108, 212-492-6000

Aggressive Growth

PERFORMANCE

fund inception date: 2/16/94

	3yr Annual	5yr Annual	10yr Annual	Bull	Bear
Return (%)	9.2	16.4	na	29.0	2.5
Differ from Category (+/-)	-7.0 blw av	1.8 av	na	-90.2 low	23.1 high

Standard Deviation	Category Risk Index	Beta
23.5%—abv av	0.72—low	0.89

	2000	1999	1998	1997	1996	1995	1994	1993	1992	1991
Return (%)	32.9	4.8	-6.3	32.3	23.9	23.3	—	—	—	—
Differ from Category (+/-)	38.9	-52.7	-21.4	17.5	5.6	-11.3	—	—	—	—
Return, Tax-Adjusted (%)	27.8	3.9	-6.6	28.2	20.8	23.3	—	—	—	—

PER SHARE DATA

	2000	1999	1998	1997	1996	1995	1994	1993	1992	1991
Dividends, Net Income ($)	0.00	0.00	0.00	0.00	0.00	0.00	—	—	—	—
Distrib'ns, Cap Gain ($)	3.44	0.57	0.23	2.68	1.26	0.00	—	—	—	—
Net Asset Value ($)	14.35	13.61	13.57	14.75	13.23	11.70	—	—	—	—
Expense Ratio (%)	na	1.50	1.28	1.32	1.43	1.56	—	—	—	—
Yield (%)	0.00	0.00	0.00	0.00	0.00	0.00	—	—	—	—
Portfolio Turnover (%)	na	101	34	77	81	45	—	—	—	—
Total Assets (Millions $)	51	60	71	94	62	50	—	—	—	—

PORTFOLIO (as of 6/30/00)

Portfolio Manager: Nancy Tooke - 1994

Investm't Category: Aggressive Growth

✔ Domestic
Index
✔ Foreign
Sector
Asset Allocation
State Specific

Investment Style

Large Cap
✔ Mid Cap
✔ Small Cap
Growth
Grth/Val
✔ Value

Portfolio

1.4% cash
0.0% corp bonds
98.6% stocks
0.0% gov't bonds
0.0% pref/conv't pref
0.0% muni bonds
0.0% conv't bds/wrnts
0.0% other

SHAREHOLDER INFORMATION

Minimum Investment

Initial: $10,000
Subsequent: $1,000

Minimum IRA Investment

Initial: $2,000
Subsequent: $250

Maximum Fees

Load: none
12b-1: none
Other: none

Services

✔ IRA
✔ Keogh
✔ Telephone Exchange

Schwab Cap Tr: Analytics (SWANX)

800-435-4000, 800-266-5623
www.schwab.com

Growth

PERFORMANCE

fund inception date: 7/1/96

	3yr Annual	5yr Annual	10yr Annual	Bull	Bear
Return (%)	14.7	na	na	68.1	-16.0
Differ from Category (+/-)	3.7 abv av	na	na	18.4 abv av	-10.6 blw av

Standard Deviation	Category Risk Index	Beta
18.9%—av	0.97—blw av	1.03

	2000	1999	1998	1997	1996	1995	1994	1993	1992	1991
Return (%)	-7.7	27.7	28.0	31.6	—	—	—	—	—	—
Differ from Category (+/-)	-11.2	8.8	13.7	4.5	—	—	—	—	—	—
Return, Tax-Adjusted (%)	-9.3	25.8	26.8	28.7	—	—	—	—	—	—

PER SHARE DATA

	2000	1999	1998	1997	1996	1995	1994	1993	1992	1991
Dividends, Net Income ($)	0.07	0.04	0.08	0.12	—	—	—	—	—	—
Distrib'ns, Cap Gain ($)	1.44	1.46	0.57	1.33	—	—	—	—	—	—
Net Asset Value ($)	16.17	19.19	16.22	13.19	—	—	—	—	—	—
Expense Ratio (%)	na	0.75	0.75	0.74	—	—	—	—	—	—
Yield (%)	0.39	0.19	0.47	0.82	—	—	—	—	—	—
Portfolio Turnover (%)	na	99	115	120	—	—	—	—	—	—
Total Assets (Millions $)	317	361	218	159	—	—	—	—	—	—

PORTFOLIO (as of 6/30/00)

Portfolio Manager: Geri Hom, Praveen Gottipalli - 1996

Investm't Category: Growth

✔ Domestic
Foreign
Asset Allocation
Index
Sector
State Specific

Investment Style

✔ Large Cap
Mid Cap
Small Cap
✔ Growth
Grth/Val
Value

Portfolio

2.3%	cash	0.0%	corp bonds
97.7%	stocks	0.0%	gov't bonds
0.0%	pref/conv't pref	0.0%	muni bonds
0.0%	conv't bds/wrnts	0.0%	other

SHAREHOLDER INFORMATION

Minimum Investment

Initial: $2,500 Subsequent: $500

Minimum IRA Investment

Initial: $1,000 Subsequent: $250

Maximum Fees

Load: none 12b-1: none
Other: none

Services

✔ IRA
✔ Keogh
✔ Telephone Exchange

Schwab Cap Tr: S&P 500/I (SWPIX)

800-435-4000, 800-266-5623
www.schwab.com

Growth & Income

PERFORMANCE

fund inception date: 5/1/96

	3yr Annual	5yr Annual	10yr Annual	Bull	Bear
Return (%)	11.8	na	na	55.3	-11.7
Differ from Category (+/-)	2.9 abv av	na	na	21.8 abv av	-11.6 blw av

Standard Deviation	Category Risk Index	Beta
17.6%—av	1.01—av	0.99

	2000	1999	1998	1997	1996	1995	1994	1993	1992	1991
Return (%)	-9.3	20.5	28.0	32.4	—	—	—	—	—	—
Differ from Category (+/-)	-15.0	9.7	15.2	5.5	—	—	—	—	—	—
Return, Tax-Adjusted (%)	-9.5	20.0	27.6	31.9	—	—	—	—	—	—

PER SHARE DATA

	2000	1999	1998	1997	1996	1995	1994	1993	1992	1991
Dividends, Net Income ($)	0.17	0.18	0.15	0.12	—	—	—	—	—	—
Distrib'ns, Cap Gain ($)	0.00	0.06	0.00	0.00	—	—	—	—	—	—
Net Asset Value ($)	20.33	22.61	18.96	14.93	—	—	—	—	—	—
Expense Ratio (%)	na	0.35	0.35	0.38	—	—	—	—	—	—
Yield (%)	0.83	0.79	0.79	0.80	—	—	—	—	—	—
Portfolio Turnover (%)	na	3	1	3	—	—	—	—	—	—
Total Assets (Millions $)	3,363	3,443	2,297	1,032	—	—	—	—	—	—

PORTFOLIO (as of 6/30/00)

Portfolio Manager: Geri Hom - 1996

Investm't Category: Growth & Income

✔ Domestic
Foreign
Asset Allocation
✔ Index
Sector
State Specific

Investment Style

✔ Large Cap
Mid Cap
Small Cap
Growth
✔ Grth/Val
Value

Portfolio

0.3% cash
99.7% stocks
0.0% pref/conv't pref
0.0% conv't bds/wrnts
0.0% corp bonds
0.0% gov't bonds
0.0% muni bonds
0.0% other

SHAREHOLDER INFORMATION

Minimum Investment

Initial: $2,500 Subsequent: $500

Minimum IRA Investment

Initial: $500 Subsequent: $100

Maximum Fees

Load: none 12b-1: none
Other: none

Services

✔ IRA
Keogh
✔ Telephone Exchange

Schwab Cap Tr: Sm Cp Ix/I (SWSMX)

800-435-4000, 800-266-5623
www.schwab.com

Aggressive Growth

PERFORMANCE

fund inception date: 12/3/93

	3yr Annual	5yr Annual	10yr Annual	Bull	Bear
Return (%)	7.4	12.5	na	55.3	-10.5
Differ from Category (+/-)	-8.8 blw av	-2.1 blw av	na	-63.9 blw av	10.1 abv av

Standard Deviation	Category Risk Index	Beta
23.5%—abv av	0.72—low	0.92

	2000	1999	1998	1997	1996	1995	1994	1993	1992	1991
Return (%)	3.7	24.1	-3.5	25.6	15.4	27.6	-3.0	—	—	—
Differ from Category (+/-)	9.7	-33.4	-18.6	10.8	-2.9	-7.0	-2.2	—	—	—
Return, Tax-Adjusted (%)	1.2	24.0	-4.5	25.4	15.2	27.3	-3.1	—	—	—

PER SHARE DATA

	2000	1999	1998	1997	1996	1995	1994	1993	1992	1991
Dividends, Net Income ($)	0.08	0.03	0.05	0.06	0.06	0.06	0.05	—	—	—
Distrib'ns, Cap Gain ($)	2.30	0.00	0.86	0.00	0.00	0.00	0.00	—	—	—
Net Asset Value ($)	18.36	20.14	16.25	17.87	14.27	12.41	9.77	—	—	—
Expense Ratio (%)	na	0.49	0.49	0.52	0.59	0.68	0.67	—	—	—
Yield (%)	0.38	0.14	0.29	0.33	0.42	0.48	0.51	—	—	—
Portfolio Turnover (%)	na	41	40	23	23	24	16	—	—	—
Total Assets (Millions $)	739	551	548	427	232	138	70	—	—	—

PORTFOLIO (as of 6/30/00)

Portfolio Manager: Geri Hom - 1995

Investm't Category: Aggressive Growth

✔ Domestic
Foreign
Asset Allocation
✔ Index
Sector
State Specific

Investment Style

Large Cap
Mid Cap
✔ Small Cap
✔ Growth
Grth/Val
Value

Portfolio

0.4% cash
99.6% stocks
0.0% pref/conv't pref
0.0% conv't bds/wrnts
0.0% corp bonds
0.0% gov't bonds
0.0% muni bonds
0.0% other

SHAREHOLDER INFORMATION

Minimum Investment

Initial: $2,500 Subsequent: $500

Minimum IRA Investment

Initial: $500 Subsequent: $100

Maximum Fees

Load: 0.50% redemption 12b-1: none
Other: redemption fee applies for 6 months

Services

✔ IRA
✔ Keogh
✔ Telephone Exchange

Schwab Intl Index/I (SWINX)

800-435-4000, 800-266-5623
www.schwab.com

International Stock

PERFORMANCE

fund inception date: 9/9/93

	3yr Annual	5yr Annual	10yr Annual	Bull	Bear
Return (%)	8.4	8.3	na	54.0	-18.2
Differ from Category (+/-)	-0.5 av	0.0 av	na	-36.9 blw av	5.8 abv av

Standard Deviation	Category Risk Index	Beta
16.3%—av	0.72—low	0.74

	2000	1999	1998	1997	1996	1995	1994	1993	1992	1991
Return (%)	-17.5	33.6	15.8	7.3	9.1	14.2	3.8	—	—	—
Differ from Category (+/-)	1.9	-27.1	10.0	6.0	-5.4	4.9	6.9	—	—	—
Return, Tax-Adjusted (%)	-17.9	33.2	15.4	6.8	8.5	13.7	3.3	—	—	—

PER SHARE DATA

	2000	1999	1998	1997	1996	1995	1994	1993	1992	1991
Dividends, Net Income ($)	0.24	0.15	0.13	0.15	0.16	0.12	0.11	—	—	—
Distrib'ns, Cap Gain ($)	0.00	0.00	0.00	0.00	0.00	0.00	0.00	—	—	—
Net Asset Value ($)	16.43	20.24	15.27	13.30	12.54	11.65	10.31	—	—	—
Expense Ratio (%)	na	0.41	0.46	0.61	0.69	0.85	0.90	—	—	—
Yield (%)	1.46	0.74	0.85	1.12	1.27	1.03	1.06	—	—	—
Portfolio Turnover (%)	na	5	6	13	0	0	6	—	—	—
Total Assets (Millions $)	619	543	468	325	259	195	138	—	—	—

PORTFOLIO (as of 6/30/00)

Portfolio Manager: Geri Hom - 1995

Investm't Category: International Stock

Domestic	✔ Index
✔ Foreign	Sector
Asset Allocation	State Specific

Investment Style

Large Cap	Mid Cap	Small Cap
Growth	Grth/Val	Value

Portfolio

1.7%	cash	0.0%	corp bonds
98.3%	stocks	0.0%	gov't bonds
0.1%	pref/conv't pref	0.0%	muni bonds
0.0%	conv't bds/wrnts	0.0%	other

SHAREHOLDER INFORMATION

Minimum Investment
Initial: $2,500 Subsequent: $500

Minimum IRA Investment
Initial: $500 Subsequent: $100

Maximum Fees
Load: 0.75% redemption 12b-1: none
Other: redemption fee applies for 6 months

Services
✔ IRA
✔ Keogh
✔ Telephone Exchange

Schwab Inv: 1000/I (SNXFX)

800-435-4000, 800-266-5623
www.schwab.com

Growth & Income

PERFORMANCE

fund inception date: 4/2/91

	3yr Annual	5yr Annual	10yr Annual	Bull	Bear
Return (%)	12.1	17.7	na	57.0	-12.4
Differ from Category (+/-)	3.2 high	3.4 high	na	23.5 high	-12.3 low

Standard Deviation	Category Risk Index	Beta
17.9%—av	1.03—abv av	1.01

	2000	1999	1998	1997	1996	1995	1994	1993	1992	1991
Return (%)	-8.2	21.0	27.1	31.9	21.5	36.6	-0.1	9.6	8.5	—
Differ from Category (+/-)	-13.9	10.2	14.3	5.0	1.8	7.1	0.4	-4.2	-3.1	—
Return, Tax-Adjusted (%)	-8.4	20.7	26.7	31.3	20.9	35.8	-0.9	8.7	7.8	—

PER SHARE DATA

	2000	1999	1998	1997	1996	1995	1994	1993	1992	1991
Dividends, Net Income ($)	0.23	0.25	0.25	0.26	0.25	0.23	0.26	0.25	0.24	—
Distrib'ns, Cap Gain ($)	0.00	0.00	0.00	0.00	0.00	0.00	0.00	0.00	0.00	—
Net Asset Value ($)	36.73	40.28	33.51	26.56	20.34	16.94	12.57	12.85	11.96	—
Expense Ratio (%)	na	0.46	0.46	0.46	0.49	0.54	0.51	0.45	0.35	—
Yield (%)	0.62	0.62	0.74	0.97	1.22	1.35	2.06	1.94	2.00	—
Portfolio Turnover (%)	na	3	2	0	2	2	3	1	1	—
Total Assets (Millions $)	4,669	5,311	4,184	2,823	1,908	1,063	553	529	370	—

PORTFOLIO (as of 6/30/00)

Portfolio Manager: Geri Hom - 1995

Investm't Category: Growth & Income

✔ Domestic
Foreign
Asset Allocation
✔ Index
Sector
State Specific

Investment Style

✔ Large Cap
Mid Cap
Small Cap
Growth
✔ Grth/Val
Value

Portfolio

0.1% cash
99.9% stocks
0.0% pref/conv't pref
0.0% conv't bds/wrnts
0.0% corp bonds
0.0% gov't bonds
0.0% muni bonds
0.0% other

SHAREHOLDER INFORMATION

Minimum Investment

Initial: $2,500 Subsequent: $500

Minimum IRA Investment

Initial: $500 Subsequent: $100

Maximum Fees

Load: 0.50% redemption 12b-1: none
Other: redemption fee applies for 6 months

Services

✔ IRA
✔ Keogh
✔ Telephone Exchange

Schwab MarketMgr: Bal

800-435-4000, 800-266-5623
www.schwab.com

(SWOBX)

Balanced

PERFORMANCE — fund inception date: 11/18/96

	3yr Annual	5yr Annual	10yr Annual	Bull	Bear
Return (%)	10.6	na	na	44.5	-10.8
Differ from Category (+/-)	2.2 abv av	na	na	16.4 high	-7.6 low

Standard Deviation	Category Risk Index	Beta
13.2%—blw av	1.20—high	0.58

	2000	1999	1998	1997	1996	1995	1994	1993	1992	1991
Return (%)	-5.1	25.7	13.5	16.5	—	—	—	—	—	—
Differ from Category (+/-)	-7.1	15.0	0.2	-2.3	—	—	—	—	—	—
Return, Tax-Adjusted (%)	-8.2	22.4	12.4	14.7	—	—	—	—	—	—

PER SHARE DATA

	2000	1999	1998	1997	1996	1995	1994	1993	1992	1991
Dividends, Net Income ($)	0.52	0.35	0.30	0.34	—	—	—	—	—	—
Distrib'ns, Cap Gain ($)	1.11	1.28	0.00	0.21	—	—	—	—	—	—
Net Asset Value ($)	11.37	13.70	12.20	11.01	—	—	—	—	—	—
Expense Ratio (%)	na	0.50	0.50	0.50	—	—	—	—	—	—
Yield (%)	4.16	2.33	2.45	3.03	—	—	—	—	—	—
Portfolio Turnover (%)	na	244	353	—	—	—	—	—	—	—
Total Assets (Millions $)	144	140	101	68	—	—	—	—	—	—

PORTFOLIO (as of 6/30/00)

Portfolio Manager: Jeffrey Mortimer - 2000

Investm't Category: Balanced

✔ Domestic — Index
✔ Foreign — Sector
✔ Asset Allocation — State Specific

Investment Style

Large Cap — Mid Cap — Small Cap
Growth — Grth/Val — Value

Portfolio

3.7%	cash	0.0%	corp bonds
0.0%	stocks	0.0%	gov't bonds
0.0%	pref/conv't pref	0.0%	muni bonds
0.0%	conv't bds/wrnts	96.3%	other

SHAREHOLDER INFORMATION

Minimum Investment
Initial: $1,000 — Subsequent: $500

Minimum IRA Investment
Initial: $500 — Subsequent: $250

Maximum Fees
Load: none — 12b-1: none
Other: none

Services
✔ IRA
✔ Keogh
✔ Telephone Exchange

Schwab MarketMgr: Growth (SWOGX)

800-435-4000, 800-266-5623
www.schwab.com

Balanced

PERFORMANCE

fund inception date: 11/18/96

	3yr Annual	5yr Annual	10yr Annual	Bull	Bear
Return (%)	11.2	na	na	60.0	-17.5
Differ from Category (+/-)	2.8 high	na	na	31.9 high	-14.3 low

Standard Deviation	Category Risk Index	Beta
17.8%—av	1.62—high	0.75

	2000	1999	1998	1997	1996	1995	1994	1993	1992	1991
Return (%)	-11.9	35.6	15.1	18.3	—	—	—	—	—	—
Differ from Category (+/-)	-13.9	24.9	1.8	-0.5	—	—	—	—	—	—
Return, Tax-Adjusted (%)	-14.9	31.7	13.9	16.5	—	—	—	—	—	—

PER SHARE DATA

	2000	1999	1998	1997	1996	1995	1994	1993	1992	1991
Dividends, Net Income ($)	0.45	0.32	0.20	0.29	—	—	—	—	—	—
Distrib'ns, Cap Gain ($)	1.39	1.77	0.23	0.30	—	—	—	—	—	—
Net Asset Value ($)	11.12	14.72	12.41	11.16	—	—	—	—	—	—
Expense Ratio (%)	na	0.50	0.50	0.50	—	—	—	—	—	—
Yield (%)	3.59	1.94	1.58	2.53	—	—	—	—	—	—
Portfolio Turnover (%)	na	284	384	—	—	—	—	—	—	—
Total Assets (Millions $)	226	218	167	132	—	—	—	—	—	—

PORTFOLIO (as of 6/30/00)

Portfolio Manager: Jeffrey Mortimer - 2000

Investm't Category: Balanced

✔ Domestic
✔ Foreign
✔ Asset Allocation
Index
Sector
State Specific

Investment Style

Large Cap | Mid Cap | Small Cap
Growth | Grth/Val | Value

Portfolio

13.0%	cash	0.0%	corp bonds
0.0%	stocks	0.0%	gov't bonds
0.0%	pref/conv't pref	0.0%	muni bonds
0.0%	conv't bds/wrnts	87.0%	other

SHAREHOLDER INFORMATION

Minimum Investment
Initial: $1,000 Subsequent: $500

Minimum IRA Investment
Initial: $500 Subsequent: $250

Maximum Fees
Load: none 12b-1: none
Other: none

Services
✔ IRA
✔ Keogh
✔ Telephone Exchange

Schwab MarketMgr: Intl (SWOIX)

800-435-4000, 800-266-5623
www.schwab.com

International Stock

PERFORMANCE

fund inception date: 10/16/96

	3yr Annual	5yr Annual	10yr Annual	Bull	Bear
Return (%)	19.2	na	na	87.2	-22.7
Differ from Category (+/-)	10.3 high	na	na	-3.7 abv av	1.3 av

Standard Deviation	Category Risk Index	Beta
22.9%—abv av	1.01—av	0.69

	2000	1999	1998	1997	1996	1995	1994	1993	1992	1991
Return (%)	-14.4	74.8	13.2	6.8	—	—	—	—	—	—
Differ from Category (+/-)	5.0	14.1	7.4	5.5	—	—	—	—	—	—
Return, Tax-Adjusted (%)	-16.9	69.8	12.6	4.9	—	—	—	—	—	—

PER SHARE DATA

	2000	1999	1998	1997	1996	1995	1994	1993	1992	1991
Dividends, Net Income ($)	0.76	0.49	0.13	0.33	—	—	—	—	—	—
Distrib'ns, Cap Gain ($)	0.78	1.83	0.00	0.30	—	—	—	—	—	—
Net Asset Value ($)	13.50	17.60	11.41	10.19	—	—	—	—	—	—
Expense Ratio (%)	na	0.50	0.50	0.50	—	—	—	—	—	—
Yield (%)	5.32	2.52	1.13	3.14	—	—	—	—	—	—
Portfolio Turnover (%)	na	249	236	179	—	—	—	—	—	—
Total Assets (Millions $)	265	155	78	76	—	—	—	—	—	—

PORTFOLIO (as of 6/30/00)

Portfolio Manager: Jeffrey Mortimer - 2000

Investm't Category: International Stock

Domestic	Index
✔ Foreign	Sector
Asset Allocation	State Specific

Investment Style

Large Cap	Mid Cap	Small Cap
Growth	Grth/Val	Value

Portfolio

4.6% cash	0.0% corp bonds
0.0% stocks	0.0% gov't bonds
0.0% pref/conv't pref	0.0% muni bonds
0.0% conv't bds/wrnts	95.4% other

SHAREHOLDER INFORMATION

Minimum Investment
Initial: $2,500 Subsequent: $500

Minimum IRA Investment
Initial: $1,000 Subsequent: $250

Maximum Fees
Load: none 12b-1: none
Other: none

Services
✔ IRA
✔ Keogh
✔ Telephone Exchange

Schwab MarketMgr: Sm Cp (SWOSX)

800-435-4000, 800-266-5623
www.schwab.com

Aggressive Growth

PERFORMANCE

fund inception date: 9/16/97

	3yr Annual	5yr Annual	10yr Annual	Bull	Bear
Return (%)	7.1	na	na	65.8	-21.8
Differ from Category (+/-)	-9.1 blw av	na	na	-53.4 blw av	-1.2 av

Standard Deviation	Category Risk Index	Beta
24.4%—abv av	0.75—low	0.94

	2000	1999	1998	1997	1996	1995	1994	1993	1992	1991
Return (%)	-11.3	37.8	0.6	—	—	—	—	—	—	—
Differ from Category (+/-)	-5.3	-19.7	-14.5	—	—	—	—	—	—	—
Return, Tax-Adjusted (%)	-14.1	35.9	0.4	—	—	—	—	—	—	—

PER SHARE DATA

	2000	1999	1998	1997	1996	1995	1994	1993	1992	1991
Dividends, Net Income ($)	0.55	0.45	0.04	—	—	—	—	—	—	—
Distrib'ns, Cap Gain ($)	0.71	0.00	0.00	—	—	—	—	—	—	—
Net Asset Value ($)	10.09	12.80	9.62	—	—	—	—	—	—	—
Expense Ratio (%)	na	0.50	0.50	—	—	—	—	—	—	—
Yield (%)	5.09	3.51	0.41	—	—	—	—	—	—	—
Portfolio Turnover (%)	na	145	166	—	—	—	—	—	—	—
Total Assets (Millions $)	138	149	137	—	—	—	—	—	—	—

PORTFOLIO (as of 6/30/00)

Portfolio Manager: Jeffrey Mortimer - 2000

Investm't Category: Aggressive Growth

✔ Domestic | Index
✔ Foreign | Sector
Asset Allocation | State Specific

Investment Style

Large Cap | Mid Cap | ✔ Small Cap
✔ Growth | Grth/Val | Value

Portfolio

4.5% cash | 0.0% corp bonds
0.0% stocks | 0.0% gov't bonds
0.0% pref/conv't pref | 0.0% muni bonds
0.0% conv't bds/wrnts | 95.5% other

SHAREHOLDER INFORMATION

Minimum Investment

Initial: $2,500 | Subsequent: $500

Minimum IRA Investment

Initial: $1,000 | Subsequent: $250

Maximum Fees

Load: none | 12b-1: none
Other: none

Services

✔ IRA
✔ Keogh
✔ Telephone Exchange

Schwab MarketTrack: Bal (SWBGX)

800-435-4000, 800-266-5623
www.schwab.com

Balanced

PERFORMANCE — fund inception date: 11/17/95

	3yr Annual	5yr Annual	10yr Annual	Bull	Bear
Return (%)	8.6	10.9	na	31.3	-5.6
Differ from Category (+/-)	0.2 av	-0.5 av	na	3.2 av	-2.4 av

Standard Deviation	Category Risk Index	Beta
10.2%—blw av	0.93—blw av	0.54

	2000	1999	1998	1997	1996	1995	1994	1993	1992	1991
Return (%)	-1.0	13.9	13.6	17.7	11.1	—	—	—	—	—
Differ from Category (+/-)	-3.0	3.2	0.3	-1.1	-2.8	—	—	—	—	—
Return, Tax-Adjusted (%)	-2.3	12.9	12.4	16.3	10.2	—	—	—	—	—

PER SHARE DATA

	2000	1999	1998	1997	1996	1995	1994	1993	1992	1991
Dividends, Net Income ($)	0.49	0.28	0.33	0.23	0.23	—	—	—	—	—
Distrib'ns, Cap Gain ($)	0.10	0.08	0.07	0.31	0.00	—	—	—	—	—
Net Asset Value ($)	14.70	15.46	13.89	12.58	11.15	—	—	—	—	—
Expense Ratio (%)	na	0.58	0.59	0.78	0.89	—	—	—	—	—
Yield (%)	3.31	1.80	2.36	1.78	2.06	—	—	—	—	—
Portfolio Turnover (%)	na	7	32	104	44	—	—	—	—	—
Total Assets (Millions $)	491	436	297	162	97	—	—	—	—	—

PORTFOLIO (as of 6/30/00)

Portfolio Manager: Geri Hom, Kimon Daifotis - 1995

Investm't Category: Balanced

✔ Domestic	Index
✔ Foreign	Sector
✔ Asset Allocation	State Specific

Investment Style

Large Cap	Mid Cap	Small Cap
Growth	Grth/Val	Value

Portfolio

5.0%	cash	0.0%	corp bonds
17.1%	stocks	0.0%	gov't bonds
0.0%	pref/conv't pref	0.0%	muni bonds
0.0%	conv't bds/wrnts	77.9%	other

SHAREHOLDER INFORMATION

Minimum Investment
Initial: $1,000 — Subsequent: $500

Minimum IRA Investment
Initial: $500 — Subsequent: $250

Maximum Fees
Load: none — 12b-1: none
Other: none

Services
✔ IRA
✔ Keogh
✔ Telephone Exchange

Schwab MarketTrack: Cnsrv (SWCGX)

800-435-4000, 800-266-5623
www.schwab.com

Balanced

PERFORMANCE

fund inception date: 11/17/95

	3yr Annual	5yr Annual	10yr Annual	Bull	Bear
Return (%)	7.5	9.0	na	20.5	-1.7
Differ from Category (+/-)	-0.9 blw av	-2.4 blw av	na	-7.6 blw av	1.5 abv av

Standard Deviation	Category Risk Index	Beta
7.0%—blw av	0.64—low	0.36

	2000	1999	1998	1997	1996	1995	1994	1993	1992	1991
Return (%)	2.7	8.6	11.5	14.7	8.1	—	—	—	—	—
Differ from Category (+/-)	0.7	-2.1	-1.8	-4.1	-5.8	—	—	—	—	—
Return, Tax-Adjusted (%)	0.9	7.4	9.9	13.0	6.7	—	—	—	—	—

PER SHARE DATA

	2000	1999	1998	1997	1996	1995	1994	1993	1992	1991
Dividends, Net Income ($)	0.55	0.36	0.43	0.33	0.35	—	—	—	—	—
Distrib'ns, Cap Gain ($)	0.08	0.02	0.06	0.23	0.00	—	—	—	—	—
Net Asset Value ($)	12.83	13.12	12.45	11.63	10.66	—	—	—	—	—
Expense Ratio (%)	na	0.57	0.58	0.81	0.89	—	—	—	—	—
Yield (%)	4.26	2.73	3.43	2.78	3.28	—	—	—	—	—
Portfolio Turnover (%)	na	8	58	104	—	—	—	—	—	—
Total Assets (Millions $)	191	177	126	46	23	—	—	—	—	—

PORTFOLIO (as of 6/30/00)

Portfolio Manager: Geri Hom, Kimon Daifotis - 1995

Investm't Category: Balanced

✔ Domestic — Index
✔ Foreign — Sector
Asset Allocation — State Specific

Investment Style

Large Cap — Mid Cap — Small Cap
Growth — Grth/Val — Value

Portfolio

5.1%	cash	0.0%	corp bonds
10.1%	stocks	0.0%	gov't bonds
0.0%	pref/conv't pref	0.0%	muni bonds
0.0%	conv't bds/wrnts	84.8%	other

SHAREHOLDER INFORMATION

Minimum Investment
Initial: $1,000 — Subsequent: $500

Minimum IRA Investment
Initial: $500 — Subsequent: $250

Maximum Fees
Load: none — 12b-1: none
Other: none

Services
✔ IRA
✔ Keogh
✔ Telephone Exchange

Schwab MarketTrack: Growth (SWHGX)

800-435-4000, 800-266-5623
www.schwab.com

Balanced

PERFORMANCE — fund inception date: 11/17/95

	3yr Annual	5yr Annual	10yr Annual	Bull	Bear
Return (%)	9.3	12.6	na	42.7	-9.4
Differ from Category (+/-)	0.9 abv av	1.2 abv av	na	14.6 high	-6.2 low

Standard Deviation	Category Risk Index	Beta
13.5%—blw av	1.24—high	0.72

	2000	1999	1998	1997	1996	1995	1994	1993	1992	1991
Return (%)	-4.8	19.3	15.1	21.0	14.4	—	—	—	—	—
Differ from Category (+/-)	-6.8	8.6	1.8	2.2	0.5	—	—	—	—	—
Return, Tax-Adjusted (%)	-5.8	18.6	14.4	19.4	13.6	—	—	—	—	—

PER SHARE DATA

	2000	1999	1998	1997	1996	1995	1994	1993	1992	1991
Dividends, Net Income ($)	0.43	0.18	0.22	0.15	0.19	—	—	—	—	—
Distrib'ns, Cap Gain ($)	0.09	0.12	0.02	0.61	0.00	—	—	—	—	—
Net Asset Value ($)	16.15	17.53	14.95	13.20	11.56	—	—	—	—	—
Expense Ratio (%)	na	0.58	0.60	0.75	0.89	—	—	—	—	—
Yield (%)	2.64	1.01	1.46	1.08	1.64	—	—	—	—	—
Portfolio Turnover (%)	na	7	14	113	46	—	—	—	—	—
Total Assets (Millions $)	538	492	311	183	112	—	—	—	—	—

PORTFOLIO (as of 6/30/00)

Portfolio Manager: Geri Hom, Kimon Daifotis - 1995

Investm't Category: Balanced

✔ Domestic
✔ Foreign
✔ Asset Allocation
Index
Sector
State Specific

Investment Style

Large Cap	Mid Cap	Small Cap
Growth	Grth/Val	Value

Portfolio

4.9%	cash	0.0%	corp bonds
22.0%	stocks	0.0%	gov't bonds
0.0%	pref/conv't pref	0.0%	muni bonds
0.0%	conv't bds/wrnts	73.1%	other

SHAREHOLDER INFORMATION

Minimum Investment
Initial: $1,000 Subsequent: $500

Minimum IRA Investment
Initial: $500 Subsequent: $250

Maximum Fees
Load: none 12b-1: none
Other: none

Services
✔ IRA
✔ Keogh
✔ Telephone Exchange

Scudder Balanced/S (SCBAX)

800-225-2470, 312-781-1121
www.scudder.com

Balanced

PERFORMANCE

fund inception date: 1/4/93

	3yr Annual	5yr Annual	10yr Annual	Bull	Bear
Return (%)	10.2	12.9	na	35.0	-5.2
Differ from Category (+/-)	1.8 abv av	1.5 abv av	na	6.9 abv av	-2.0 av

Standard Deviation	Category Risk Index	Beta
11.9%—blw av	1.09—abv av	0.64

	2000	1999	1998	1997	1996	1995	1994	1993	1992	1991
Return (%)	-2.4	13.4	21.0	22.7	11.5	26.4	-2.3	—	—	—
Differ from Category (+/-)	-4.4	2.7	7.7	3.9	-2.4	0.9	-1.0	—	—	—
Return, Tax-Adjusted (%)	-4.0	12.7	18.9	20.8	8.9	24.7	-3.2	—	—	—

PER SHARE DATA

	2000	1999	1998	1997	1996	1995	1994	1993	1992	1991
Dividends, Net Income ($)	0.36	0.32	0.36	0.36	0.34	0.32	0.30	—	—	—
Distrib'ns, Cap Gain ($)	1.04	0.01	1.01	0.67	0.79	0.24	0.00	—	—	—
Net Asset Value ($)	19.25	21.15	18.96	16.85	14.60	14.12	11.63	—	—	—
Expense Ratio (%)	na	1.29	1.29	1.02	1.00	1.00	1.00	—	—	—
Yield (%)	1.77	1.51	1.80	2.05	2.20	2.22	2.57	—	—	—
Portfolio Turnover (%)	na	102	75	43	69	114	105	—	—	—
Total Assets (Millions $)	514	573	261	158	112	90	66	—	—	—

PORTFOLIO (as of 6/30/00)

Portfolio Manager: Langbaum, McCormick, Cessine - 1999

Investm't Category: Balanced

✔ Domestic
✔ Foreign
Asset Allocation
Index
Sector
State Specific

Investment Style

Large Cap
Mid Cap
Small Cap
Growth
Grth/Val
Value

Portfolio

3.9%	cash	6.2%	corp bonds
63.0%	stocks	25.6%	gov't bonds
0.0%	pref/conv't pref	0.0%	muni bonds
0.0%	conv't bds/wrnts	1.3%	other

SHAREHOLDER INFORMATION

Minimum Investment
Initial: $2,500 Subsequent: $100

Minimum IRA Investment
Initial: $1,000 Subsequent: $50

Maximum Fees
Load: none 12b-1: none
Other: none

Services
✔ IRA
✔ Keogh
✔ Telephone Exchange

Scudder Capital Grth/ AARP (ACGFX)

800-253-2277, 617-295-1000
aarp.scudder.com

Growth

PERFORMANCE

fund inception date: 11/30/84

	3yr Annual	5yr Annual	10yr Annual	Bull	Bear
Return (%)	14.5	19.6	17.2	77.9	-12.8
Differ from Category (+/-)	3.5 abv av	3.5 abv av	0.4 av	28.2 high	-7.4 blw av

Standard Deviation	Category Risk Index	Beta
20.4%—abv av	1.05—av	1.10

	2000	1999	1998	1997	1996	1995	1994	1993	1992	1991
Return (%)	-10.3	35.4	23.7	35.0	20.6	30.5	-10.0	15.9	4.7	40.5
Differ from Category (+/-)	-13.8	16.5	9.4	7.9	-1.7	0.1	-9.8	1.3	-7.9	2.9
Return, Tax-Adjusted (%)	-12.4	33.5	21.0	32.6	17.2	29.5	-10.5	13.3	3.5	39.0

PER SHARE DATA

	2000	1999	1998	1997	1996	1995	1994	1993	1992	1991
Dividends, Net Income ($)	0.00	0.03	0.24	0.31	0.41	0.39	0.01	0.05	0.14	0.23
Distrib'ns, Cap Gain ($)	7.71	5.40	6.55	4.30	3.99	0.51	0.64	2.90	1.21	0.94
Net Asset Value ($)	57.37	72.55	57.63	52.11	42.07	38.46	30.15	34.24	32.09	31.94
Expense Ratio (%)	0.90	0.91	0.87	0.92	0.90	0.95	0.97	1.05	1.13	1.17
Yield (%)	0.00	0.03	0.37	0.54	0.89	1.00	0.03	0.13	0.42	0.69
Portfolio Turnover (%)	79	68	53	39	64	98	79	100	89	100
Total Assets (Millions $)	2,143	2,238	1,550	1,217	877	709	631	682	491	284

PORTFOLIO (as of 6/30/00)

Portfolio Manager: William Gadsen - 1994

Investm't Category: Growth

✔ Domestic — Index
✔ Foreign — Sector
Asset Allocation — State Specific

Investment Style

✔ Large Cap — Mid Cap — Small Cap
✔ Growth — Grth/Val — Value

Portfolio

2.4%	cash	0.0%	corp bonds
97.6%	stocks	0.0%	gov't bonds
0.0%	pref/conv't pref	0.0%	muni bonds
0.0%	conv't bds/wrnts	0.0%	other

SHAREHOLDER INFORMATION

Minimum Investment
Initial: $1,000 — Subsequent: $50

Minimum IRA Investment
Initial: $500 — Subsequent: $1

Maximum Fees
Load: none — 12b-1: none
Other: none

Services
✔ IRA
✔ Keogh
✔ Telephone Exchange

Scudder Development (SCDVX)

800-225-2471, 312-781-1121
www.scudder.com

Aggressive Growth

PERFORMANCE

fund inception date: 1/18/71

	3yr Annual	5yr Annual	10yr Annual	Bull	Bear
Return (%)	7.0	7.6	14.2	81.2	-30.6
Differ from Category (+/-)	-9.2 blw av	-7.0 low	-1.6 blw av	-38.0 av	-10.0 blw av

Standard Deviation	Category Risk Index	Beta
34.0%—high	1.05—av	1.26

	2000	1999	1998	1997	1996	1995	1994	1993	1992	1991
Return (%)	-15.9	35.0	8.0	6.9	10.0	50.6	-5.3	8.8	-1.8	71.8
Differ from Category (+/-)	-9.9	-22.5	-7.1	-7.9	-8.3	16.0	-4.5	-16.4	-8.7	24.6
Return, Tax-Adjusted (%)	-18.5	31.5	6.0	4.9	6.8	46.6	-7.0	6.2	-3.1	70.5

PER SHARE DATA

	2000	1999	1998	1997	1996	1995	1994	1993	1992	1991
Dividends, Net Income ($)	0.00	0.00	0.00	0.00	0.00	0.00	0.00	0.00	0.00	0.00
Distrib'ns, Cap Gain ($)	5.85	6.50	3.75	3.88	4.48	4.20	2.12	3.07	1.70	0.96
Net Asset Value ($)	31.16	43.90	37.66	38.55	39.79	40.12	29.54	33.51	33.62	36.23
Expense Ratio (%)	1.40	1.52	1.41	1.36	1.24	1.32	1.27	1.30	1.30	1.29
Yield (%)	0.00	0.00	0.00	0.00	0.00	0.00	0.00	0.00	0.00	0.00
Portfolio Turnover (%)	100	3	52	52	58	41	48	49	54	71
Total Assets (Millions $)	602	837	782	862	971	877	601	765	923	892

PORTFOLIO (as of 6/30/00)

Portfolio Manager: committee - 1999

Investm't Category: Aggressive Growth

✔ Domestic　　Index
✔ Foreign　　Sector
Asset Allocation　　State Specific

Investment Style

Large Cap　　Mid Cap　　✔ Small Cap
✔ Growth　　Grth/Val　　Value

Portfolio

5.3%	cash	0.0%	corp bonds
94.7%	stocks	0.0%	gov't bonds
0.0%	pref/conv't pref	0.0%	muni bonds
0.0%	conv't bds/wrnts	0.0%	other

SHAREHOLDER INFORMATION

Minimum Investment

Initial: $2,500　　Subsequent: $100

Minimum IRA Investment

Initial: $1,000　　Subsequent: $50

Maximum Fees

Load: none　　12b-1: none
Other: none

Services

✔ IRA
✔ Keogh
✔ Telephone Exchange

Scudder Emerg Mkts Grth (SEMGX)

800-225-2470, 312-781-1121
www.scudder.com

International Stock

PERFORMANCE — fund inception date: 5/1/96

	3yr Annual	5yr Annual	10yr Annual	Bull	Bear
Return (%)	-9.9	na	na	47.0	-34.2
Differ from Category (+/-)	-18.8 low	na	na	-43.9 blw av	-10.2 blw av

Standard Deviation	Category Risk Index	Beta
23.8%—abv av	1.05—av	0.98

	2000	1999	1998	1997	1996	1995	1994	1993	1992	1991
Return (%)	-29.9	38.0	-24.4	3.5	—	—	—	—	—	—
Differ from Category (+/-)	-10.5	-22.7	-30.2	2.2	—	—	—	—	—	—
Return, Tax-Adjusted (%)	-29.9	38.0	-24.4	3.3	—	—	—	—	—	—

PER SHARE DATA

	2000	1999	1998	1997	1996	1995	1994	1993	1992	1991
Dividends, Net Income ($)	0.00	0.00	0.03	0.06	—	—	—	—	—	—
Distrib'ns, Cap Gain ($)	0.00	0.00	0.00	0.00	—	—	—	—	—	—
Net Asset Value ($)	10.37	14.80	10.72	14.23	—	—	—	—	—	—
Expense Ratio (%)	na	2.25	2.16	2.00	—	—	—	—	—	—
Yield (%)	0.00	0.00	0.27	0.42	—	—	—	—	—	—
Portfolio Turnover (%)	na	63	44	62	—	—	—	—	—	—
Total Assets (Millions $)	63	121	117	205	—	—	—	—	—	—

PORTFOLIO (as of 6/30/00)

Portfolio Manager: Cornell, DeSimone, Kenney - 1996

Investm't Category: International Stock

Domestic	Index
✔ Foreign	Sector
Asset Allocation	State Specific

Investment Style

Large Cap	Mid Cap	Small Cap
Growth	Grth/Val	Value

Portfolio

9.1%	cash	0.0%	corp bonds
90.9%	stocks	0.0%	gov't bonds
0.0%	pref/conv't pref	0.0%	muni bonds
0.0%	conv't bds/wrnts	0.0%	other

SHAREHOLDER INFORMATION

Minimum Investment
Initial: $2,500 Subsequent: $100

Minimum IRA Investment
Initial: $1,000 Subsequent: $50

Maximum Fees
Load: 2.00% redemption 12b-1: none
Other: redemption fee applies for 12 months

Services
✔ IRA
✔ Keogh
✔ Telephone Exchange

Scudder Global/S (SCOBX)

800-225-2471, 312-781-1121
www.scudder.com

International Stock

PERFORMANCE fund inception date: 7/23/86

	3yr Annual	5yr Annual	10yr Annual	Bull	Bear
Return (%)	10.4	12.4	12.7	41.0	-9.9
Differ from Category (+/-)	1.5 av	4.1 abv av	3.7 high	-49.9 low	14.1 high

Standard Deviation	Category Risk Index	Beta
15.1%—av	0.67—low	0.72

	2000	1999	1998	1997	1996	1995	1994	1993	1992	1991
Return (%)	-3.0	23.4	12.5	17.2	13.6	20.5	-4.2	31.1	4.4	17.0
Differ from Category (+/-)	16.4	-37.3	6.7	15.9	-0.9	11.2	-1.1	-9.1	7.9	4.0
Return, Tax-Adjusted (%)	-5.4	20.4	9.9	12.8	11.6	19.0	-4.7	30.2	3.6	15.3

PER SHARE DATA

	2000	1999	1998	1997	1996	1995	1994	1993	1992	1991
Dividends, Net Income ($)	0.24	0.19	0.54	0.88	0.28	0.25	0.11	0.23	0.16	0.31
Distrib'ns, Cap Gain ($)	3.40	3.91	2.60	4.58	1.53	0.84	0.34	0.26	0.34	0.66
Net Asset Value ($)	26.72	31.22	28.68	28.28	28.80	27.01	23.33	24.80	19.31	18.96
Expense Ratio (%)	1.33	1.36	1.34	1.37	1.34	1.38	1.45	1.48	1.59	1.70
Yield (%)	0.79	0.54	1.72	2.67	0.92	0.89	0.46	0.91	0.81	1.58
Portfolio Turnover (%)	60	28	51	40	29	44	59	64	45	85
Total Assets (Millions $)	1,340	1,692	1,613	1,570	1,409	1,271	1,117	963	400	298

PORTFOLIO (as of 6/30/00)

Portfolio Manager: W. Holzer, N. Bratt - 1986

Investm't Category: International Stock

✔ Domestic	Index
✔ Foreign	Sector
Asset Allocation	State Specific

Investment Style

Large Cap	Mid Cap	Small Cap
Growth	Grth/Val	Value

Portfolio

3.2%	cash	3.9%	corp bonds
92.9%	stocks	0.0%	gov't bonds
0.0%	pref/conv't pref	0.0%	muni bonds
0.0%	conv't bds/wrnts	0.0%	other

SHAREHOLDER INFORMATION

Minimum Investment
Initial: $2,500 Subsequent: $100

Minimum IRA Investment
Initial: $1,000 Subsequent: $50

Maximum Fees
Load: none 12b-1: none
Other: none

Services
✔ IRA
✔ Keogh
✔ Telephone Exchange

Scudder Gold (SCGDX)

800-225-2470, 312-781-1121
www.scudder.com

Aggressive Growth

PERFORMANCE

fund inception date: 8/12/88

	3yr Annual	5yr Annual	10yr Annual	Bull	Bear
Return (%)	-6.1	-8.3	-0.8	40.7	-2.7
Differ from Category (+/-)	-22.3 low	-22.9 low	-16.6 low	-78.5 low	17.9 high

Standard Deviation	Category Risk Index	Beta
35.4%—high	1.09—abv av	0.76

	2000	1999	1998	1997	1996	1995	1994	1993	1992	1991
Return (%)	-8.9	9.0	-16.7	-40.8	32.1	13.1	-7.3	59.3	-9.0	-6.9
Differ from Category (+/-)	-2.9	-48.5	-31.8	-55.6	13.8	-21.5	-6.5	34.1	-15.9	-54.1
Return, Tax-Adjusted (%)	-8.9	8.4	-16.7	-41.2	23.2	7.9	-8.9	58.1	-9.0	-6.9

PER SHARE DATA

	2000	1999	1998	1997	1996	1995	1994	1993	1992	1991
Dividends, Net Income ($)	0.01	0.08	0.00	0.14	2.39	1.08	0.24	0.24	0.00	0.00
Distrib'ns, Cap Gain ($)	0.00	0.00	0.00	0.00	0.26	0.63	0.46	0.00	0.00	0.00
Net Asset Value ($)	5.99	6.60	6.13	7.36	12.68	11.53	11.71	13.35	8.55	9.40
Expense Ratio (%)	na	2.01	2.13	1.60	1.50	1.65	1.69	2.17	2.54	2.54
Yield (%)	0.16	1.21	0.00	1.90	18.46	8.88	1.97	1.79	0.00	0.00
Portfolio Turnover (%)	na	91	157	38	29	42	50	59	58	71
Total Assets (Millions $)	85	111	108	124	184	117	129	110	31	22

PORTFOLIO (as of 6/30/00)

Portfolio Manager: Joann Barry, Robert Hardiman - 1999

Investm't Category: Aggressive Growth

✔ Domestic — Index
✔ Foreign — ✔ Sector
Asset Allocation — State Specific

Investment Style

Large Cap — Mid Cap — Small Cap
Growth — Grth/Val — Value

Portfolio

6.5%	cash	0.0%	corp bonds
93.5%	stocks	0.0%	gov't bonds
0.0%	pref/conv't pref	0.0%	muni bonds
0.0%	conv't bds/wrnts	0.0%	other

SHAREHOLDER INFORMATION

Minimum Investment

Initial: $2,500 — Subsequent: $100

Minimum IRA Investment

Initial: $1,000 — Subsequent: $50

Maximum Fees

Load: none — 12b-1: none
Other: none

Services

✔ IRA
✔ Keogh
✔ Telephone Exchange

Scudder Greater Europe Gr (SCGEX)

800-225-2470, 312-781-1121
www.scudder.com

International Stock

PERFORMANCE — fund inception date: 10/10/94

	3yr Annual	5yr Annual	10yr Annual	Bull	Bear
Return (%)	16.4	20.7	na	43.5	-20.1
Differ from Category (+/-)	7.5 high	12.4 high	na	-47.4 low	3.9 abv av

Standard Deviation	Category Risk Index	Beta
21.1%—abv av	0.93—blw av	0.58

	2000	1999	1998	1997	1996	1995	1994	1993	1992	1991
Return (%)	-9.1	34.5	29.2	23.9	30.8	23.6	—	—	—	—
Differ from Category (+/-)	10.3	-26.2	23.4	22.6	16.3	14.3	—	—	—	—
Return, Tax-Adjusted (%)	-9.7	34.3	29.0	21.2	30.3	22.9	—	—	—	—

PER SHARE DATA

	2000	1999	1998	1997	1996	1995	1994	1993	1992	1991
Dividends, Net Income ($)	0.01	0.08	0.06	0.54	0.06	0.10	—	—	—	—
Distrib'ns, Cap Gain ($)	1.20	0.10	0.00	1.30	0.14	0.14	—	—	—	—
Net Asset Value ($)	31.05	35.52	26.53	20.58	18.08	13.97	—	—	—	—
Expense Ratio (%)	na	1.46	1.48	1.66	1.50	1.50	—	—	—	—
Yield (%)	0.03	0.22	0.22	2.46	0.32	0.70	—	—	—	—
Portfolio Turnover (%)	na	83	93	88	39	28	—	—	—	—
Total Assets (Millions $)	1,278	1,341	1,267	228	150	43	—	—	—	—

PORTFOLIO (as of 6/30/00)

Portfolio Manager: Carol Franklin - 1994

Investm't Category: International Stock

Domestic	Index
✔ Foreign	Sector
Asset Allocation	State Specific

Investment Style

Large Cap	Mid Cap	Small Cap
Growth	Grth/Val	Value

Portfolio

4.6%	cash	0.5%	corp bonds
94.9%	stocks	0.0%	gov't bonds
0.0%	pref/conv't pref	0.0%	muni bonds
0.0%	conv't bds/wrnts	0.0%	other

SHAREHOLDER INFORMATION

Minimum Investment
Initial: $2,500 Subsequent: $100

Minimum IRA Investment
Initial: $1,000 Subsequent: $50

Maximum Fees
Load: none 12b-1: none
Other: none

Services
✔ IRA
✔ Keogh
✔ Telephone Exchange

Scudder Growth and Income/S (SCDGX)

800-225-2470, 312-781-1121
www.scudder.com

Growth & Income

PERFORMANCE — fund inception date: 11/13/84

	3yr Annual	5yr Annual	10yr Annual	Bull	Bear
Return (%)	3.1	11.8	14.3	22.3	-4.2
Differ from Category (+/-)	-5.8 low	-2.5 blw av	-0.6 blw av	-11.2 blw av	-4.1 av

Standard Deviation	Category Risk Index	Beta
15.5%—av	0.89—blw av	0.76

	2000	1999	1998	1997	1996	1995	1994	1993	1992	1991
Return (%)	-2.4	6.1	6.0	30.3	22.1	31.1	2.5	15.5	9.5	28.1
Differ from Category (+/-)	-8.1	-4.7	-6.8	3.4	2.4	1.6	3.0	1.7	-2.1	0.0
Return, Tax-Adjusted (%)	-3.9	4.8	3.5	27.4	19.7	28.9	-0.1	12.6	7.5	26.7

PER SHARE DATA

	2000	1999	1998	1997	1996	1995	1994	1993	1992	1991
Dividends, Net Income ($)	0.15	0.51	0.61	0.58	0.57	0.55	0.50	0.45	0.52	0.55
Distrib'ns, Cap Gain ($)	1.76	0.70	2.08	2.20	0.86	0.48	0.90	1.01	0.50	0.00
Net Asset Value ($)	24.15	26.69	26.31	27.33	23.23	20.23	16.27	17.24	16.20	15.76
Expense Ratio (%)	na	0.55	0.74	0.76	0.78	0.85	0.86	0.86	0.94	0.97
Yield (%)	0.57	1.86	2.14	1.96	2.36	2.65	2.91	2.46	3.11	3.48
Portfolio Turnover (%)	na	65	41	22	26	34	42	36	28	45
Total Assets (Millions $)	5,440	6,762	7,633	6,832	4,200	3,067	1,994	1,631	1,168	723

PORTFOLIO (as of 6/30/00)

Portfolio Manager: Kathleen Millard, Gregory Adams - 1991

Investm't Category: Growth & Income

✔ Domestic	Index
✔ Foreign	Sector
Asset Allocation	State Specific

Investment Style

✔ Large Cap	Mid Cap	Small Cap
Growth	Grth/Val	✔ Value

Portfolio

1.9%	cash	0.0%	corp bonds
98.1%	stocks	0.0%	gov't bonds
0.0%	pref/conv't pref	0.0%	muni bonds
0.0%	conv't bds/wrnts	0.0%	other

SHAREHOLDER INFORMATION

Minimum Investment
Initial: $2,500 Subsequent: $100

Minimum IRA Investment
Initial: $1,000 Subsequent: $50

Maximum Fees
Load: none 12b-1: none
Other: none

Services
✔ IRA
✔ Keogh
✔ Telephone Exchange

Scudder Int'l/S (SCINX)

800-225-2470, 312-781-1121
www.scudder.com

International Stock

PERFORMANCE — fund inception date: 6/14/54

	3yr Annual	5yr Annual	10yr Annual	Bull	Bear
Return (%)	14.7	13.3	11.7	76.0	-21.0
Differ from Category (+/-)	5.8 high	5.0 abv av	2.7 abv av	-14.9 av	3.0 abv av

Standard Deviation	Category Risk Index	Beta
18.9%—av	0.83—blw av	0.72

	2000	1999	1998	1997	1996	1995	1994	1993	1992	1991
Return (%)	-19.2	57.8	18.6	7.9	14.5	12.2	-2.9	36.5	-2.6	11.7
Differ from Category (+/-)	0.2	-2.9	12.8	6.6	0.0	2.9	0.2	-3.7	0.9	-1.3
Return, Tax-Adjusted (%)	-21.2	55.7	16.1	5.4	12.5	10.9	-4.4	35.7	-4.0	11.3

PER SHARE DATA

	2000	1999	1998	1997	1996	1995	1994	1993	1992	1991
Dividends, Net Income ($)	0.05	0.13	0.00	0.25	1.28	0.40	0.00	0.39	0.83	0.00
Distrib'ns, Cap Gain ($)	7.01	4.82	5.56	5.35	1.19	1.18	2.42	0.38	0.86	0.40
Net Asset Value ($)	50.31	70.74	48.70	45.75	47.56	43.72	40.37	44.10	32.93	35.53
Expense Ratio (%)	na	1.21	1.18	1.15	1.14	1.19	1.21	1.26	1.30	1.24
Yield (%)	0.08	0.17	0.00	0.48	2.62	0.89	0.00	0.87	2.45	0.00
Portfolio Turnover (%)	na	81	55	35	45	46	39	29	50	70
Total Assets (Millions $)	4,286	5,064	2,945	2,617	2,644	2,352	2,271	2,069	1,048	965

PORTFOLIO (as of 6/30/00)

Portfolio Manager: Cheng, Franklin, Bratt - 1993

Investm't Category: International Stock

Domestic	Index
✔ Foreign	Sector
Asset Allocation	State Specific

Investment Style

Large Cap	Mid Cap	Small Cap
Growth	Grth/Val	Value

Portfolio

3.4%	cash	0.0%	corp bonds
96.6%	stocks	0.0%	gov't bonds
0.0%	pref/conv't pref	0.0%	muni bonds
0.0%	conv't bds/wrnts	0.0%	other

SHAREHOLDER INFORMATION

Minimum Investment
Initial: $2,500 Subsequent: $100

Minimum IRA Investment
Initial: $1,000 Subsequent: $50

Maximum Fees
Load: none 12b-1: none
Other: none

Services
✔ IRA
✔ Keogh
✔ Telephone Exchange

Scudder Large Co Growth/S (SCQGX)

800-225-2470, 312-781-1121
www.scudder.com

Growth

PERFORMANCE

fund inception date: 5/20/91

	3yr Annual	5yr Annual	10yr Annual	Bull	Bear
Return (%)	13.2	17.9	na	78.7	-24.5
Differ from Category (+/-)	2.2 abv av	1.8 av	na	29.0 high	-19.1 low

Standard Deviation	Category Risk Index	Beta
22.7%—abv av	1.17—abv av	1.15

	2000	1999	1998	1997	1996	1995	1994	1993	1992	1991
Return (%)	-19.2	35.0	33.2	32.7	18.2	32.4	-1.3	0.0	6.6	—
Differ from Category (+/-)	-22.7	16.1	18.9	5.6	-4.1	2.0	-1.1	-14.6	-6.0	—
Return, Tax-Adjusted (%)	-19.6	34.6	31.8	31.2	15.5	30.8	-3.5	-0.5	6.5	—

PER SHARE DATA

	2000	1999	1998	1997	1996	1995	1994	1993	1992	1991
Dividends, Net Income ($)	0.00	0.00	0.00	0.00	0.00	0.14	0.15	0.07	0.02	—
Distrib'ns, Cap Gain ($)	1.03	0.59	1.71	1.46	1.77	0.60	1.09	0.23	0.00	—
Net Asset Value ($)	33.11	42.27	31.76	25.12	20.04	18.43	14.47	15.92	16.23	—
Expense Ratio (%)	1.21	1.23	1.19	1.21	1.07	1.24	1.25	1.20	1.25	—
Yield (%)	0.00	0.00	0.00	0.00	0.00	0.73	0.96	0.43	0.12	—
Portfolio Turnover (%)	56	62	54	67	68	101	119	111	27	—
Total Assets (Millions $)	1,220	1,154	626	307	217	185	112	123	130	—

PORTFOLIO (as of 6/30/00)

Portfolio Manager: Valerie Malter, George Fraise - 1997

Investm't Category: Growth

✔ Domestic	Index
✔ Foreign	Sector
Asset Allocation	State Specific

Investment Style

✔ Large Cap	Mid Cap	Small Cap
✔ Growth	Grth/Val	Value

Portfolio

4.7% cash	0.0% corp bonds
95.3% stocks	0.0% gov't bonds
0.0% pref/conv't pref	0.0% muni bonds
0.0% conv't bds/wrnts	0.0% other

SHAREHOLDER INFORMATION

Minimum Investment
Initial: $2,500 Subsequent: $100

Minimum IRA Investment
Initial: $1,000 Subsequent: $50

Maximum Fees
Load: none 12b-1: none
Other: none

Services
✔ IRA
✔ Keogh
✔ Telephone Exchange

Scudder Large Co Value (SCDUX)

800-225-2470, 312-781-1121
www.scudder.com

Growth & Income

PERFORMANCE

fund inception date: 6/26/56

	3yr Annual	5yr Annual	10yr Annual	Bull	Bear
Return (%)	9.5	15.7	16.3	26.6	8.7
Differ from Category (+/-)	0.6 av	1.4 abv av	1.4 av	-6.9 av	8.8 abv av

Standard Deviation	Category Risk Index	Beta
17.3%—av	1.00—av	0.77

	2000	1999	1998	1997	1996	1995	1994	1993	1992	1991
Return (%)	14.6	4.6	9.4	32.5	19.5	31.6	-9.8	20.0	7.0	42.9
Differ from Category (+/-)	8.9	-6.2	-3.4	5.6	-0.2	2.1	-9.3	6.2	-4.6	14.8
Return, Tax-Adjusted (%)	12.0	2.9	7.5	30.3	15.8	26.1	-10.7	16.3	5.0	40.5

PER SHARE DATA

	2000	1999	1998	1997	1996	1995	1994	1993	1992	1991
Dividends, Net Income ($)	0.32	0.39	0.18	0.24	0.16	0.08	0.00	0.00	0.10	0.22
Distrib'ns, Cap Gain ($)	2.81	1.45	2.10	1.86	2.48	3.50	0.72	2.62	1.25	0.98
Net Asset Value ($)	27.72	26.91	27.49	27.17	22.11	20.67	18.43	21.26	19.91	19.86
Expense Ratio (%)	0.94	0.87	0.88	0.93	0.92	0.98	0.97	0.96	0.98	1.04
Yield (%)	1.04	1.37	0.60	0.82	0.65	0.33	0.00	0.00	0.47	1.05
Portfolio Turnover (%)	46	35	39	43	150	153	75	92	92	93
Total Assets (Millions $)	2,272	2,338	2,355	2,230	1,774	1,565	1,291	1,427	1,244	1,152

PORTFOLIO (as of 6/30/00)

Portfolio Manager: committee - 1995

Investm't Category: Growth & Income

✔ Domestic	Index
✔ Foreign	Sector
Asset Allocation	State Specific

Investment Style

✔ Large Cap	Mid Cap	Small Cap
Growth	Grth/Val	✔ Value

Portfolio

3.4%	cash	0.0%	corp bonds
96.6%	stocks	0.0%	gov't bonds
0.0%	pref/conv't pref	0.0%	muni bonds
0.0%	conv't bds/wrnts	0.0%	other

SHAREHOLDER INFORMATION

Minimum Investment

Initial: $2,500 Subsequent: $100

Minimum IRA Investment

Initial: $1,000 Subsequent: $50

Maximum Fees

Load: none 12b-1: none

Other: none

Services

✔ IRA

✔ Keogh

✔ Telephone Exchange

Scudder Latin America (SLAFX)

800-225-2470, 312-781-1121
www.scudder.com

International Stock

PERFORMANCE — fund inception date: 12/8/92

	3yr Annual	5yr Annual	10yr Annual	Bull	Bear
Return (%)	-4.4	8.0	na	72.6	-21.8
Differ from Category (+/-)	-13.3 low	-0.3 blw av	na	-18.3 av	2.2 abv av

Standard Deviation	Category Risk Index	Beta
35.7%—high	1.57—high	1.28

	2000	1999	1998	1997	1996	1995	1994	1993	1992	1991
Return (%)	-15.6	47.1	-29.7	31.2	28.3	-9.8	-9.4	74.3	—	—
Differ from Category (+/-)	3.8	-13.6	-35.5	29.9	13.8	-19.1	-6.3	34.1	—	—
Return, Tax-Adjusted (%)	-17.0	46.9	-30.7	29.6	27.6	-10.1	-10.3	74.0	—	—

PER SHARE DATA

	2000	1999	1998	1997	1996	1995	1994	1993	1992	1991
Dividends, Net Income ($)	0.18	0.05	0.37	0.25	0.26	0.15	0.00	0.05	—	—
Distrib'ns, Cap Gain ($)	1.49	0.00	0.64	1.14	0.00	0.00	0.73	0.05	—	—
Net Asset Value ($)	20.26	26.04	17.73	26.67	21.40	16.88	18.88	21.68	—	—
Expense Ratio (%)	na	1.96	1.87	1.89	1.96	2.14	2.01	2.00	—	—
Yield (%)	0.82	0.19	2.01	0.89	1.21	0.88	0.00	0.23	—	—
Portfolio Turnover (%)	na	48	44	41	22	33	22	5	—	—
Total Assets (Millions $)	380	577	462	962	636	514	649	409	—	—

PORTFOLIO (as of 6/30/00)

Portfolio Manager: Edmund Games - 1992

Investm't Category: International Stock

Domestic	Index
✔ Foreign	Sector
Asset Allocation	State Specific

Investment Style

Large Cap	Mid Cap	Small Cap
Growth	Grth/Val	Value

Portfolio

5.1%	cash	0.0%	corp bonds
94.9%	stocks	0.0%	gov't bonds
0.0%	pref/conv't pref	0.0%	muni bonds
0.0%	conv't bds/wrnts	0.0%	other

SHAREHOLDER INFORMATION

Minimum Investment
Initial: $2,500 — Subsequent: $100

Minimum IRA Investment
Initial: $1,000 — Subsequent: $50

Maximum Fees
Load: none — 12b-1: none
Other: none

Services
✔ IRA
✔ Keogh
✔ Telephone Exchange

Scudder Pacific Opport (SCOPX)

800-225-2470, 312-781-1121
www.scudder.com

International Stock

PERFORMANCE — fund inception date: 12/8/92

	3yr Annual	5yr Annual	10yr Annual	Bull	Bear
Return (%)	-2.2	-9.1	na	124.5	-44.0
Differ from Category (+/-)	-11.1 low	-17.4 low	na	33.6 high	-20.0 low

Standard Deviation	Category Risk Index	Beta
32.6%—high	1.44—high	1.16

	2000	1999	1998	1997	1996	1995	1994	1993	1992	1991
Return (%)	-39.1	75.6	-12.6	-37.7	6.4	1.2	-17.1	60.0	—	—
Differ from Category (+/-)	-19.7	14.9	-18.4	-39.0	-8.1	-8.1	-14.0	19.8	—	—
Return, Tax-Adjusted (%)	-39.1	75.6	-12.6	-38.4	6.3	0.9	-17.2	59.7	—	—

PER SHARE DATA

	2000	1999	1998	1997	1996	1995	1994	1993	1992	1991
Dividends, Net Income ($)	0.00	0.00	0.02	0.30	0.01	0.10	0.09	0.08	—	—
Distrib'ns, Cap Gain ($)	0.00	0.00	0.00	0.00	0.00	0.00	0.00	0.01	—	—
Net Asset Value ($)	9.47	15.56	8.86	10.17	16.82	15.81	15.71	19.07	—	—
Expense Ratio (%)	na	2.35	2.46	1.94	1.75	1.80	1.81	1.75	—	—
Yield (%)	0.00	0.00	0.22	2.94	0.05	0.63	0.57	0.41	—	—
Portfolio Turnover (%)	na	122	141	97	95	43	38	10	—	—
Total Assets (Millions $)	96	188	110	127	344	377	422	453	—	—

PORTFOLIO (as of 6/30/00)

Portfolio Manager: Tien Yu Sieh - 1999

Investm't Category: International Stock

Domestic	Index
✔ Foreign	Sector
Asset Allocation	State Specific

Investment Style

Large Cap	Mid Cap	Small Cap
Growth	Grth/Val	Value

Portfolio

2.6%	cash	0.0%	corp bonds
97.4%	stocks	0.0%	gov't bonds
0.0%	pref/conv't pref	0.0%	muni bonds
0.0%	conv't bds/wrnts	0.0%	other

SHAREHOLDER INFORMATION

Minimum Investment
Initial: $2,500 Subsequent: $100

Minimum IRA Investment
Initial: $1,000 Subsequent: $50

Maximum Fees
Load: 2.00% redemption 12b-1: none
Other: redemption fee applies for 12 months

Services
✔ IRA
✔ Keogh
✔ Telephone Exchange

Scudder Pathway: Balanced (SPBAX)

800-225-2470, 312-781-1121
www.scudder.com

Balanced

PERFORMANCE — fund inception date: 11/26/96

	3yr Annual	5yr Annual	10yr Annual	Bull	Bear
Return (%)	6.9	na	na	32.4	-5.8
Differ from Category (+/-)	-1.5 blw av	na	na	4.3 abv av	-2.6 blw av

Standard Deviation	Category Risk Index	Beta
11.3%—blw av	1.03—av	0.59

	2000	1999	1998	1997	1996	1995	1994	1993	1992	1991
Return (%)	-2.6	16.6	7.6	13.3	—	—	—	—	—	—
Differ from Category (+/-)	-4.6	5.9	-5.7	-5.5	—	—	—	—	—	—
Return, Tax-Adjusted (%)	-5.5	14.0	5.7	11.6	—	—	—	—	—	—

PER SHARE DATA

	2000	1999	1998	1997	1996	1995	1994	1993	1992	1991
Dividends, Net Income ($)	0.45	0.48	0.40	0.38	—	—	—	—	—	—
Distrib'ns, Cap Gain ($)	1.18	0.69	0.42	0.21	—	—	—	—	—	—
Net Asset Value ($)	12.04	14.03	13.06	12.91	—	—	—	—	—	—
Expense Ratio (%)	na	1.03	0.00	0.00	—	—	—	—	—	—
Yield (%)	3.40	3.26	2.96	2.89	—	—	—	—	—	—
Portfolio Turnover (%)	na	24	28	—	—	—	—	—	—	—
Total Assets (Millions $)	244	270	242	207	—	—	—	—	—	—

PORTFOLIO (as of 6/30/00)

Portfolio Manager: Benjamin Thorndike - 1996

Investm't Category: Balanced

✔ Domestic — Index
✔ Foreign — Sector
✔ Asset Allocation — State Specific

Investment Style

Large Cap — Mid Cap — Small Cap
Growth — Grth/Val — Value

Portfolio

0.8%	cash	0.0%	corp bonds
0.0%	stocks	0.0%	gov't bonds
0.0%	pref/conv't pref	0.0%	muni bonds
0.0%	conv't bds/wrnts	99.2%	other

SHAREHOLDER INFORMATION

Minimum Investment
Initial: $2,500 — Subsequent: $100

Minimum IRA Investment
Initial: $1,000 — Subsequent: $50

Maximum Fees
Load: none — 12b-1: none
Other: none

Services
✔ IRA
✔ Keogh
✔ Telephone Exchange

Scudder Pathway: Growth/S (SPGRX)

800-225-2470, 312-781-1121
www.scudder.com

Growth & Income

PERFORMANCE

fund inception date: 11/26/96

	3yr Annual	5yr Annual	10yr Annual	Bull	Bear
Return (%)	11.5	na	na	61.1	-11.2
Differ from Category (+/-)	2.6 abv av	na	na	27.6 high	-11.1 blw av

Standard Deviation	Category Risk Index	Beta
16.4%—av	0.95—blw av	0.83

	2000	1999	1998	1997	1996	1995	1994	1993	1992	1991
Return (%)	-6.2	35.2	9.5	14.9	—	—	—	—	—	—
Differ from Category (+/-)	-11.9	24.4	-3.3	-12.0	—	—	—	—	—	—
Return, Tax-Adjusted (%)	-8.8	33.1	8.2	13.7	—	—	—	—	—	—

PER SHARE DATA

	2000	1999	1998	1997	1996	1995	1994	1993	1992	1991
Dividends, Net Income ($)	0.36	0.29	0.20	0.21	—	—	—	—	—	—
Distrib'ns, Cap Gain ($)	1.64	0.88	0.43	0.26	—	—	—	—	—	—
Net Asset Value ($)	14.55	17.58	13.87	13.23	—	—	—	—	—	—
Expense Ratio (%)	na	1.18	0.00	0.00	—	—	—	—	—	—
Yield (%)	2.22	1.57	1.39	1.55	—	—	—	—	—	—
Portfolio Turnover (%)	na	28	23	—	—	—	—	—	—	—
Total Assets (Millions $)	116	125	76	50	—	—	—	—	—	—

PORTFOLIO (as of 6/30/00)

Portfolio Manager: Benjamin Thorndike - 1996

Investm't Category: Growth & Income

✔ Domestic | Index
✔ Foreign | Sector
Asset Allocation | State Specific

Investment Style

✔ Large Cap | Mid Cap | Small Cap
Growth | ✔ Grth/Val | Value

Portfolio

4.6%	cash	0.0%	corp bonds
0.0%	stocks	0.0%	gov't bonds
0.0%	pref/conv't pref	0.0%	muni bonds
0.0%	conv't bds/wrnts	95.4%	other

SHAREHOLDER INFORMATION

Minimum Investment

Initial: $2,500 Subsequent: $100

Minimum IRA Investment

Initial: $1,000 Subsequent: $50

Maximum Fees

Load: none 12b-1: none
Other: none

Services

✔ IRA
✔ Keogh
✔ Telephone Exchange

Scudder S&P 500 Index/S (SCPIX)

800-225-2471, 312-781-1121
www.scudder.com

Growth & Income

PERFORMANCE — fund inception date: 8/29/97

	3yr Annual	5yr Annual	10yr Annual	Bull	Bear
Return (%)	11.8	na	na	55.3	-11.8
Differ from Category (+/-)	2.9 abv av	na	na	21.8 abv av	-11.7 blw av

Standard Deviation	Category Risk Index	Beta
17.6%—av	1.01—av	0.99

	2000	1999	1998	1997	1996	1995	1994	1993	1992	1991
Return (%)	-9.4	20.3	28.2	—	—	—	—	—	—	—
Differ from Category (+/-)	-15.1	9.5	15.4	—	—	—	—	—	—	—
Return, Tax-Adjusted (%)	-9.7	19.8	27.7	—	—	—	—	—	—	—

PER SHARE DATA

	2000	1999	1998	1997	1996	1995	1994	1993	1992	1991
Dividends, Net Income ($)	0.15	0.17	0.14	—	—	—	—	—	—	—
Distrib'ns, Cap Gain ($)	0.00	0.00	0.00	—	—	—	—	—	—	—
Net Asset Value ($)	17.60	19.60	16.44	—	—	—	—	—	—	—
Expense Ratio (%)	na	0.40	0.40	—	—	—	—	—	—	—
Yield (%)	0.85	0.86	0.85	—	—	—	—	—	—	—
Portfolio Turnover (%)	na	13	4	—	—	—	—	—	—	—
Total Assets (Millions $)	369	328	125	—	—	—	—	—	—	—

PORTFOLIO (as of 6/30/00)

Portfolio Manager: Frank Salerno - 1997

Investm't Category: Growth & Income

✔ Domestic
✔ Index
✔ Foreign
Sector
Asset Allocation
State Specific

Investment Style

✔ Large Cap
Mid Cap
Small Cap
Growth
✔ Grth/Val
Value

Portfolio

5.3%	cash	0.0%	corp bonds
94.7%	stocks	0.0%	gov't bonds
0.0%	pref/conv't pref	0.0%	muni bonds
0.0%	conv't bds/wrnts	0.0%	other

SHAREHOLDER INFORMATION

Minimum Investment

Initial: $2,500 Subsequent: $100

Minimum IRA Investment

Initial: $1,000 Subsequent: $50

Maximum Fees

Load: none 12b-1: none
Other: none

Services

✔ IRA
✔ Keogh
✔ Telephone Exchange

Scudder Small Co Value/S (SCSUX)

800-225-2470, 312-781-1121
www.scudder.com

Growth

PERFORMANCE — fund inception date: 10/6/95

	3yr Annual	5yr Annual	10yr Annual	Bull	Bear
Return (%)	-2.0	9.7	na	-1.7	7.4
Differ from Category (+/-)	-13.0 low	-6.4 low	na	-51.4 low	12.8 high

Standard Deviation	Category Risk Index	Beta
17.0%—av	0.87—low	0.56

	2000	1999	1998	1997	1996	1995	1994	1993	1992	1991
Return (%)	12.7	-11.8	-5.5	37.0	23.8	—	—	—	—	—
Differ from Category (+/-)	9.2	-30.7	-19.8	9.9	1.5	—	—	—	—	—
Return, Tax-Adjusted (%)	12.6	-11.8	-5.7	36.5	23.7	—	—	—	—	—

PER SHARE DATA

	2000	1999	1998	1997	1996	1995	1994	1993	1992	1991
Dividends, Net Income ($)	0.02	0.02	0.04	0.02	0.03	—	—	—	—	—
Distrib'ns, Cap Gain ($)	0.00	0.00	0.13	0.30	0.00	—	—	—	—	—
Net Asset Value ($)	19.32	17.16	19.49	20.83	15.44	—	—	—	—	—
Expense Ratio (%)	1.32	1.32	1.63	1.50	1.50	—	—	—	—	—
Yield (%)	0.10	0.11	0.20	0.09	0.19	—	—	—	—	—
Portfolio Turnover (%)	29	33	22	43	4	—	—	—	—	—
Total Assets (Millions $)	163	223	279	211	56	—	—	—	—	—

PORTFOLIO (as of 6/30/00)

Portfolio Manager: J. Eysenbach, C. Young - 1995

Investm't Category: Growth

✔ Domestic	Index
Foreign	Sector
Asset Allocation	State Specific

Investment Style

Large Cap	Mid Cap	✔ Small Cap
Growth	Grth/Val	✔ Value

Portfolio

2.6%	cash	0.0%	corp bonds
97.4%	stocks	0.0%	gov't bonds
0.0%	pref/conv't pref	0.0%	muni bonds
0.0%	conv't bds/wrnts	0.0%	other

SHAREHOLDER INFORMATION

Minimum Investment
Initial: $2,500 Subsequent: $100

Minimum IRA Investment
Initial: $1,000 Subsequent: $50

Maximum Fees
Load: 1.00% redemption 12b-1: none
Other: redemption fee applies for 12 months

Services
✔ IRA
✔ Keogh
✔ Telephone Exchange

Selected American Shares (SLASX)

800-243-1575, 505-820-3101
www.selectedfunds.com

Growth & Income

PERFORMANCE — fund inception date: 1/30/33

	3yr Annual	5yr Annual	10yr Annual	Bull	Bear
Return (%)	15.2	22.3	19.5	53.7	-5.4
Differ from Category (+/-)	6.3 high	8.0 high	4.6 high	20.2 abv av	-5.3 blw av

Standard Deviation	Category Risk Index	Beta
18.4%—av	1.06—abv av	0.96

	2000	1999	1998	1997	1996	1995	1994	1993	1992	1991
Return (%)	9.3	20.3	16.2	37.2	30.7	38.0	-3.2	5.4	5.8	46.2
Differ from Category (+/-)	3.6	9.5	3.4	10.3	11.0	8.5	-2.7	-8.4	-5.8	18.1
Return, Tax-Adjusted (%)	7.2	19.1	15.7	34.9	28.2	37.0	-5.3	-0.4	2.1	45.6

PER SHARE DATA

	2000	1999	1998	1997	1996	1995	1994	1993	1992	1991
Dividends, Net Income ($)	0.13	0.15	0.15	0.20	0.18	0.22	0.22	0.26	0.19	0.24
Distrib'ns, Cap Gain ($)	3.46	1.44	0.26	2.02	1.30	0.15	0.82	3.22	2.19	0.00
Net Asset Value ($)	35.33	35.80	31.16	27.18	21.53	17.68	13.09	14.60	17.13	18.43
Expense Ratio (%)	na	0.93	0.94	0.96	1.03	1.16	1.26	1.01	1.17	1.19
Yield (%)	0.33	0.40	0.47	0.68	0.78	1.23	1.58	1.45	0.98	1.30
Portfolio Turnover (%)	na	21	20	26	29	27	23	79	50	21
Total Assets (Millions $)	4,794	3,703	2,905	2,218	1,378	924	502	451	587	711

PORTFOLIO (as of 6/30/00)

Portfolio Manager: Christopher Davis, Ken Feinberg - 1997

Investm't Category: Growth & Income

✔ Domestic	Index
Foreign	Sector
Asset Allocation	State Specific

Investment Style

✔ Large Cap	Mid Cap	Small Cap
Growth	Grth/Val	✔ Value

Portfolio

9.0%	cash	0.0%	corp bonds
89.6%	stocks	0.0%	gov't bonds
1.4%	pref/conv't pref	0.0%	muni bonds
0.0%	conv't bds/wrnts	0.0%	other

SHAREHOLDER INFORMATION

Minimum Investment
Initial: $1,000 — Subsequent: $25

Minimum IRA Investment
Initial: $250 — Subsequent: $25

Maximum Fees
Load: none — 12b-1: 0.25%
Other: none

Services
✔ IRA
✔ Keogh
✔ Telephone Exchange

Selected Special Shares (SLSSX)

800-243-1575, 505-820-3101
www.selectedfunds.com

Aggressive Growth

PERFORMANCE — fund inception date: 5/1/39

	3yr Annual	5yr Annual	10yr Annual	Bull	Bear
Return (%)	12.8	15.3	14.9	55.7	-12.2
Differ from Category (+/-)	-3.4 av	0.7 av	-0.9 blw av	-63.5 blw av	8.4 abv av

Standard Deviation	Category Risk Index	Beta
21.9%—abv av	0.67—low	1.11

	2000	1999	1998	1997	1996	1995	1994	1993	1992	1991
Return (%)	-1.0	16.8	24.5	26.9	11.8	34.2	-2.5	10.8	8.4	25.5
Differ from Category (+/-)	5.0	-40.7	9.4	12.1	-6.5	-0.4	-1.7	-14.4	1.5	-21.7
Return, Tax-Adjusted (%)	-3.7	15.4	22.4	25.7	8.7	30.2	-3.7	7.3	6.7	21.9

PER SHARE DATA

	2000	1999	1998	1997	1996	1995	1994	1993	1992	1991
Dividends, Net Income ($)	0.00	0.00	0.00	0.00	0.00	0.00	0.00	0.00	0.06	0.50
Distrib'ns, Cap Gain ($)	2.24	0.97	1.32	0.62	1.18	1.26	0.93	1.30	0.54	0.61
Net Asset Value ($)	13.68	16.17	14.76	13.03	10.89	10.80	9.02	10.21	10.41	10.17
Expense Ratio (%)	na	1.17	1.25	1.28	1.33	1.56	1.41	1.24	1.41	1.39
Yield (%)	0.00	0.00	0.00	0.00	0.00	0.00	0.00	0.00	0.54	4.59
Portfolio Turnover (%)	na	44	41	51	98	127	99	100	41	74
Total Assets (Millions $)	80	106	93	74	62	59	45	53	57	60

PORTFOLIO (as of 6/30/00)

Portfolio Manager: Elizabeth Bramwell - 1997

Investm't Category: Aggressive Growth

✔ Domestic — Index
Foreign — Sector
Asset Allocation — State Specific

Investment Style

✔ Large Cap — ✔ Mid Cap — Small Cap
✔ Growth — Grth/Val — Value

Portfolio

16.0%	cash	0.0%	corp bonds
84.0%	stocks	0.0%	gov't bonds
0.0%	pref/conv't pref	0.0%	muni bonds
0.0%	conv't bds/wrnts	0.0%	other

SHAREHOLDER INFORMATION

Minimum Investment
Initial: $1,000 — Subsequent: $25

Minimum IRA Investment
Initial: $250 — Subsequent: $25

Maximum Fees
Load: none — 12b-1: 0.25%
Other: none

Services
✔ IRA
✔ Keogh
✔ Telephone Exchange

Sentry (SNTRX)

800-533-7827, 715-346-7048
www.sentry.com

Growth

PERFORMANCE — fund inception date: 5/22/70

	3yr Annual	5yr Annual	10yr Annual	Bull	Bear
Return (%)	-1.9	8.4	10.7	14.3	-8.9
Differ from Category (+/-)	-12.9 low	-7.7 low	-6.1 low	-35.4 low	-3.5 av

Standard Deviation	Category Risk Index	Beta
17.2%—av	0.88—low	0.81

	2000	1999	1998	1997	1996	1995	1994	1993	1992	1991
Return (%)	-2.2	-9.3	6.4	29.9	22.8	27.7	-1.1	5.9	7.4	28.8
Differ from Category (+/-)	-5.7	-28.2	-7.9	2.8	0.5	-2.7	-0.9	-8.7	-5.2	-8.8
Return, Tax-Adjusted (%)	-5.9	-12.2	4.2	25.5	20.8	24.9	-2.9	3.5	6.1	25.3

PER SHARE DATA

	2000	1999	1998	1997	1996	1995	1994	1993	1992	1991
Dividends, Net Income ($)	0.08	0.16	0.13	0.11	0.16	0.18	0.17	0.21	0.26	0.38
Distrib'ns, Cap Gain ($)	2.63	2.59	1.97	3.85	0.91	1.11	0.76	0.98	0.36	1.14
Net Asset Value ($)	11.79	14.81	19.46	20.39	18.84	16.24	13.75	14.85	15.15	14.68
Expense Ratio (%)	na	0.84	0.83	0.83	0.84	0.86	0.86	0.87	0.88	0.84
Yield (%)	0.55	0.91	0.60	0.45	0.81	1.03	1.17	1.32	1.67	2.40
Portfolio Turnover (%)	na	24	29	40	28	26	16	22	13	3
Total Assets (Millions $)	74	93	121	120	105	88	75	76	72	64

PORTFOLIO (as of 9/30/99)

Portfolio Manager: Keith Ringberg - 1977

Investm't Category: Growth

✔ Domestic
Foreign
Asset Allocation
Index
Sector
State Specific

Investment Style

✔ Large Cap
✔ Mid Cap
Small Cap
Growth
Grth/Val
✔ Value

Portfolio

4.9% cash
95.1% stocks
0.0% pref/conv't pref
0.0% conv't bds/wrnts
0.0% corp bonds
0.0% gov't bonds
0.0% muni bonds
0.0% other

SHAREHOLDER INFORMATION

Minimum Investment
Initial: $500 Subsequent: $50

Minimum IRA Investment
Initial: $500 Subsequent: $50

Maximum Fees
Load: none 12b-1: none
Other: none

Services
✔ IRA
✔ Keogh
Telephone Exchange

Sequoia (SEQUX)

800-686-6884, 212-832-5280
www.sequoiafund.com

Growth

this fund is closed to new investors

PERFORMANCE — fund inception date: 7/20/70

	3yr Annual	5yr Annual	10yr Annual	Bull	Bear
Return (%)	10.6	18.7	19.3	6.7	12.9
Differ from Category (+/-)	-0.4 av	2.6 abv av	2.5 high	-43.0 low	18.3 high

Standard Deviation	Category Risk Index	Beta
22.6%—abv av	1.16—abv av	0.77

	2000	1999	1998	1997	1996	1995	1994	1993	1992	1991
Return (%)	20.0	-16.5	35.2	43.2	21.7	41.3	3.3	10.7	9.3	40.0
Differ from Category (+/-)	16.5	-35.4	20.9	16.1	-0.6	10.9	3.5	-3.9	-3.3	2.4
Return, Tax-Adjusted (%)	15.0	-17.5	33.8	42.9	18.4	41.0	2.6	6.6	8.4	36.6

PER SHARE DATA

	2000	1999	1998	1997	1996	1995	1994	1993	1992	1991
Dividends, Net Income ($)	1.66	0.85	0.37	0.11	6.47	0.39	0.41	0.65	0.93	1.36
Distrib'ns, Cap Gain ($)	28.51	6.58	8.02	0.88	0.00	0.00	0.66	7.19	0.62	3.58
Net Asset Value ($)	122.09	127.27	160.70	125.63	88.44	78.13	55.59	54.84	56.66	53.31
Expense Ratio (%)	na	1.00	1.00	1.00	1.00	1.00	1.00	1.00	1.00	1.00
Yield (%)	1.10	0.63	0.21	0.08	7.31	0.49	0.72	1.04	1.62	2.39
Portfolio Turnover (%)	na	12	21	8	23	15	32	24	28	36
Total Assets (Millions $)	3,944	3,897	5,001	3,672	2,581	2,185	1,548	1,512	1,389	1,251

PORTFOLIO (as of 6/30/00)

Portfolio Manager: W. Ruane, R. Cunniff, R. Goldfarb - 1970

Investm't Category: Growth

✔ Domestic	Index
✔ Foreign	Sector
Asset Allocation	State Specific

Investment Style

✔ Large Cap	✔ Mid Cap	Small Cap
Growth	Grth/Val	✔ Value

Portfolio

34.3% cash	0.0% corp bonds
65.7% stocks	0.0% gov't bonds
0.0% pref/conv't pref	0.0% muni bonds
0.0% conv't bds/wrnts	0.0% other

SHAREHOLDER INFORMATION

Minimum Investment
Initial: $1,000 — Subsequent: $50

Minimum IRA Investment
Initial: na — Subsequent: na

Maximum Fees
Load: none — 12b-1: none
Other: none

Services
IRA
✔ Keogh
Telephone Exchange

Sit Intl Growth (SNGRX)

800-332-5580, 612-334-5888
www.sitfunds.com

International Stock

PERFORMANCE — fund inception date: 11/1/91

	3yr Annual	5yr Annual	10yr Annual	Bull	Bear
Return (%)	9.5	8.7	na	73.6	-31.2
Differ from Category (+/-)	0.6 av	0.4 av	na	-17.3 av	-7.2 blw av

Standard Deviation	Category Risk Index	Beta
21.8%—abv av	0.96—av	0.80

	2000	1999	1998	1997	1996	1995	1994	1993	1992	1991
Return (%)	-26.6	50.7	18.9	4.8	10.3	9.3	-2.9	48.3	2.6	—
Differ from Category (+/-)	-7.2	-10.0	13.1	3.5	-4.2	0.0	0.2	8.1	6.1	—
Return, Tax-Adjusted (%)	-26.9	48.8	17.4	3.7	9.5	7.5	-3.4	47.8	2.5	—

PER SHARE DATA

	2000	1999	1998	1997	1996	1995	1994	1993	1992	1991
Dividends, Net Income ($)	0.00	0.22	0.05	0.19	0.01	0.08	0.03	0.09	0.02	—
Distrib'ns, Cap Gain ($)	0.51	1.28	1.08	0.50	0.41	0.84	0.26	0.05	0.00	—
Net Asset Value ($)	18.73	26.20	18.45	16.53	16.45	15.31	14.88	15.66	10.66	—
Expense Ratio (%)	1.50	1.50	1.50	1.50	1.50	1.50	1.65	1.85	1.85	—
Yield (%)	0.00	0.80	0.25	1.11	0.05	0.49	0.19	0.57	0.18	—
Portfolio Turnover (%)	30	45	43	41	38	40	42	52	19	—
Total Assets (Millions $)	148	136	96	90	87	73	65	64	26	—

PORTFOLIO (as of 6/30/00)

Portfolio Manager: E. Sit, P. Mitchelson, R. Sit - 1991

Investm't Category: International Stock

Domestic	Index
✔ Foreign	Sector
Asset Allocation	State Specific

Investment Style

Large Cap	Mid Cap	Small Cap
Growth	Grth/Val	Value

Portfolio

10.1% cash	0.0% corp bonds
89.9% stocks	0.0% gov't bonds
0.0% pref/conv't pref	0.0% muni bonds
0.0% conv't bds/wrnts	0.0% other

SHAREHOLDER INFORMATION

Minimum Investment
Initial: $2,000 Subsequent: $100

Minimum IRA Investment
Initial: $1 Subsequent: $1

Maximum Fees
Load: none 12b-1: none
Other: none

Services
✔ IRA
✔ Keogh
✔ Telephone Exchange

Sit Large Cap Growth (SNIGX)

800-332-5580, 612-334-5888
www.sitfunds.com

Growth

PERFORMANCE — fund inception date: 10/19/81

	3yr Annual	5yr Annual	10yr Annual	Bull	Bear
Return (%)	14.4	19.4	16.8	73.9	-20.3
Differ from Category (+/-)	3.4 abv av	3.3 abv av	0.0 av	24.2 abv av	-14.9 low

Standard Deviation	Category Risk Index	Beta
21.8%—abv av	1.12—abv av	1.13

	2000	1999	1998	1997	1996	1995	1994	1993	1992	1991
Return (%)	-13.8	33.4	30.5	31.6	23.0	31.6	2.8	3.1	4.9	32.7
Differ from Category (+/-)	-17.3	14.5	16.2	4.5	0.7	1.2	3.0	-11.5	-7.7	-4.9
Return, Tax-Adjusted (%)	-15.4	32.0	28.8	29.0	20.6	28.9	1.0	1.1	3.8	31.1

PER SHARE DATA

	2000	1999	1998	1997	1996	1995	1994	1993	1992	1991
Dividends, Net Income ($)	0.00	0.00	0.00	0.06	0.04	0.05	0.09	0.27	0.38	0.52
Distrib'ns, Cap Gain ($)	5.02	3.40	3.40	4.17	2.41	2.24	1.40	1.38	0.54	0.54
Net Asset Value ($)	48.14	61.20	48.64	40.04	33.68	29.39	24.09	24.92	25.79	25.49
Expense Ratio (%)	1.00	1.00	1.00	1.00	1.00	1.00	1.10	1.42	1.50	1.50
Yield (%)	0.00	0.00	0.00	0.13	0.11	0.15	0.35	1.02	1.44	1.99
Portfolio Turnover (%)	48	70	43	32	49	67	73	47	73	70
Total Assets (Millions $)	148	164	119	81	57	46	36	37	37	30

PORTFOLIO (as of 6/30/00)

Portfolio Manager: E. Sit, P. Mitcheslon, R. Sit - 1981

Investm't Category: Growth

✔ Domestic　Index
Foreign　Sector
Asset Allocation　State Specific

Investment Style

✔ Large Cap　Mid Cap　Small Cap
✔ Growth　Grth/Val　Value

Portfolio

2.4% cash　0.0% corp bonds
97.6% stocks　0.0% gov't bonds
0.0% pref/conv't pref　0.0% muni bonds
0.0% conv't bds/wrnts　0.0% other

SHAREHOLDER INFORMATION

Minimum Investment
Initial: $2,000　Subsequent: $100

Minimum IRA Investment
Initial: $1　Subsequent: $1

Maximum Fees
Load: none　12b-1: none
Other: none

Services
✔ IRA
✔ Keogh
✔ Telephone Exchange

Sit MidCap Growth (NBNGX)

800-332-5580, 612-334-5888
www.sitfunds.com

Aggressive Growth

PERFORMANCE — fund inception date: 10/19/81

	3yr Annual	5yr Annual	10yr Annual	Bull	Bear
Return (%)	20.3	20.1	19.3	117.3	-26.8
Differ from Category (+/-)	4.1 abv av	5.5 abv av	3.5 abv av	-1.9 abv av	-6.2 av

Standard Deviation	Category Risk Index	Beta
34.4%—high	1.06—abv av	1.22

	2000	1999	1998	1997	1996	1995	1994	1993	1992	1991
Return (%)	-4.3	70.6	6.8	17.6	21.8	33.6	-0.4	8.5	-2.1	65.4
Differ from Category (+/-)	1.7	13.1	-8.3	2.8	3.5	-1.0	0.4	-16.7	-9.0	18.2
Return, Tax-Adjusted (%)	-8.2	68.7	3.3	14.7	16.5	30.0	-2.7	8.3	-2.2	65.0

PER SHARE DATA

	2000	1999	1998	1997	1996	1995	1994	1993	1992	1991
Dividends, Net Income ($)	0.00	0.00	0.00	0.00	0.00	0.00	0.00	0.01	0.05	0.06
Distrib'ns, Cap Gain ($)	4.06	1.22	2.54	2.01	2.62	1.45	1.04	0.29	0.02	0.04
Net Asset Value ($)	16.03	20.69	12.94	14.69	14.27	13.86	11.51	12.66	11.96	12.29
Expense Ratio (%)	1.00	1.00	1.00	0.92	0.77	0.83	0.82	0.80	0.83	1.03
Yield (%)	0.00	0.00	0.00	0.00	0.00	0.00	0.00	0.07	0.37	0.44
Portfolio Turnover (%)	62	68	52	38	50	75	46	45	25	37
Total Assets (Millions $)	454	510	363	382	375	377	303	332	334	208

PORTFOLIO (as of 6/30/00)

Portfolio Manager: E. Sit, P. Mitchelson, R. Sit - 1981

Investm't Category: Aggressive Growth

✔ Domestic　Index
Foreign　Sector
Asset Allocation　State Specific

Investment Style

Large Cap　✔ Mid Cap　✔ Small Cap
✔ Growth　Grth/Val　Value

Portfolio

6.2%	cash	0.0%	corp bonds
93.2%	stocks	0.0%	gov't bonds
0.0%	pref/conv't pref	0.0%	muni bonds
0.6%	conv't bds/wrnts	0.0%	other

SHAREHOLDER INFORMATION

Minimum Investment
Initial: $2,000　Subsequent: $100

Minimum IRA Investment
Initial: $1　Subsequent: $1

Maximum Fees
Load: none　12b-1: none
Other: none

Services
✔ IRA
✔ Keogh
✔ Telephone Exchange

Sit Small Cap Growth (SSMGX)

800-332-5580, 612-334-5888
www.sitfunds.com

Aggressive Growth

PERFORMANCE — fund inception date: 7/1/94

	3yr Annual	5yr Annual	10yr Annual	Bull	Bear
Return (%)	31.2	22.8	na	173.1	-21.7
Differ from Category (+/-)	15.0 high	8.2 abv av	na	53.9 abv av	-1.1 av

Standard Deviation	Category Risk Index	Beta
39.0%—high	1.20—abv av	1.18

	2000	1999	1998	1997	1996	1995	1994	1993	1992	1991
Return (%)	6.2	108.6	1.9	7.6	14.9	52.1	—	—	—	—
Differ from Category (+/-)	12.2	51.1	-13.2	-7.2	-3.4	17.5	—	—	—	—
Return, Tax-Adjusted (%)	5.8	108.6	-1.3	6.8	13.5	51.7	—	—	—	—

PER SHARE DATA

	2000	1999	1998	1997	1996	1995	1994	1993	1992	1991
Dividends, Net Income ($)	0.00	0.00	0.00	0.00	0.00	0.00	—	—	—	—
Distrib'ns, Cap Gain ($)	0.58	0.00	3.08	0.67	0.80	0.14	—	—	—	—
Net Asset Value ($)	35.16	33.61	16.11	19.13	18.43	16.74	—	—	—	—
Expense Ratio (%)	1.50	1.50	1.50	1.50	1.50	1.50	—	—	—	—
Yield (%)	0.00	0.00	0.00	0.00	0.00	0.00	—	—	—	—
Portfolio Turnover (%)	39	71	79	58	69	49	—	—	—	—
Total Assets (Millions $)	246	102	47	66	57	31	—	—	—	—

PORTFOLIO (as of 6/30/00)

Portfolio Manager: E. Sit, P. Mitchelson, R. Sit - 1994

Investm't Category: Aggressive Growth

✔ Domestic　　Index
Foreign　　Sector
Asset Allocation　　State Specific

Investment Style

Large Cap　　Mid Cap　　✔ Small Cap
✔ Growth　　Grth/Val　　Value

Portfolio

16.2%	cash	0.0%	corp bonds
83.8%	stocks	0.0%	gov't bonds
0.0%	pref/conv't pref	0.0%	muni bonds
0.0%	conv't bds/wrnts	0.0%	other

SHAREHOLDER INFORMATION

Minimum Investment
Initial: $2,000　　Subsequent: $100

Minimum IRA Investment
Initial: $1　　Subsequent: $1

Maximum Fees
Load: none　　12b-1: none
Other: none

Services
✔ IRA
✔ Keogh
✔ Telephone Exchange

Skyline: Special Equities (SKSEX)

800-828-2759, 312-595-6035

Growth

PERFORMANCE

fund inception date: 4/23/87

	3yr Annual	5yr Annual	10yr Annual	Bull	Bear
Return (%)	0.0	12.0	17.7	-1.8	7.6
Differ from Category (+/-)	-11.0 low	-4.1 blw av	0.9 abv av	-51.5 low	13.0 high

Standard Deviation	Category Risk Index	Beta
18.3%—av	0.94—blw av	0.67

	2000	1999	1998	1997	1996	1995	1994	1993	1992	1991
Return (%)	24.2	-13.2	-7.1	35.4	30.3	13.8	-1.1	22.8	42.4	47.3
Differ from Category (+/-)	20.7	-32.1	-21.4	8.3	8.0	-16.6	-0.9	8.2	29.8	9.7
Return, Tax-Adjusted (%)	24.2	-14.4	-7.3	32.2	24.2	12.0	-4.1	17.6	40.4	40.7

PER SHARE DATA

	2000	1999	1998	1997	1996	1995	1994	1993	1992	1991
Dividends, Net Income ($)	0.00	0.00	0.00	0.00	0.00	0.00	0.00	0.00	0.00	0.01
Distrib'ns, Cap Gain ($)	0.00	1.23	0.32	2.89	3.61	1.00	1.93	3.14	0.90	2.39
Net Asset Value ($)	19.75	15.90	19.78	21.66	18.16	16.79	15.64	17.83	17.12	12.67
Expense Ratio (%)	na	1.48	1.47	1.48	1.51	1.51	1.49	1.48	1.51	1.55
Yield (%)	0.00	0.00	0.00	0.00	0.00	0.00	0.00	0.00	0.00	0.06
Portfolio Turnover (%)	na	81	68	62	130	71	82	104	87	104
Total Assets (Millions $)	252	222	445	466	218	175	202	227	172	37

PORTFOLIO (as of 3/31/00)

Portfolio Manager: William Dutton - 1987

Investm't Category: Growth

✔ Domestic — Index
Foreign — Sector
Asset Allocation — State Specific

Investment Style

Large Cap — ✔ Mid Cap — ✔ Small Cap
Growth — Grth/Val — ✔ Value

Portfolio

1.3%	cash	0.0%	corp bonds
98.7%	stocks	0.0%	gov't bonds
0.0%	pref/conv't pref	0.0%	muni bonds
0.0%	conv't bds/wrnts	0.0%	other

SHAREHOLDER INFORMATION

Minimum Investment

Initial: $1,000 — Subsequent: $100

Minimum IRA Investment

Initial: $1,000 — Subsequent: $100

Maximum Fees

Load: none — 12b-1: none
Other: none

Services

✔ IRA
✔ Keogh
✔ Telephone Exchange

Sound Shore (SSHFX)

800-551-1980, 800-754-8758
www.soundshorefund.com

Growth

PERFORMANCE — fund inception date: 5/3/85

	3yr Annual	5yr Annual	10yr Annual	Bull	Bear
Return (%)	7.8	17.9	18.2	20.3	6.5
Differ from Category (+/-)	-3.2 blw av	1.8 av	1.4 abv av	-29.4 low	11.9 abv av

Standard Deviation	Category Risk Index	Beta
17.9%—av	0.92—blw av	0.78

	2000	1999	1998	1997	1996	1995	1994	1993	1992	1991
Return (%)	20.1	0.0	4.4	36.4	33.2	29.8	0.2	11.9	21.1	32.2
Differ from Category (+/-)	16.6	-18.9	-9.9	9.3	10.9	-0.6	0.4	-2.7	8.5	-5.4
Return, Tax-Adjusted (%)	18.8	-0.2	4.1	35.3	29.3	26.2	-1.7	8.9	17.1	31.2

PER SHARE DATA

	2000	1999	1998	1997	1996	1995	1994	1993	1992	1991
Dividends, Net Income ($)	0.14	0.16	0.20	0.12	0.12	0.21	0.21	0.14	0.17	0.28
Distrib'ns, Cap Gain ($)	1.56	0.00	0.00	0.88	2.35	1.67	0.86	1.53	1.95	0.09
Net Asset Value ($)	33.70	29.47	29.62	28.57	21.71	18.16	15.46	16.50	16.24	15.17
Expense Ratio (%)	na	0.98	0.99	1.08	1.15	1.17	1.22	1.27	1.37	1.30
Yield (%)	0.39	0.54	0.67	0.40	0.49	1.05	1.28	0.77	0.93	1.83
Portfolio Turnover (%)	na	41	44	53	69	53	75	90	88	100
Total Assets (Millions $)	1,016	1,183	1,964	1,303	131	67	56	58	35	31

PORTFOLIO (as of 6/30/00)

Portfolio Manager: Kane, Burn - 1985

Investm't Category: Growth

✔ Domestic
Foreign
Asset Allocation
Index
Sector
State Specific

Investment Style

✔ Large Cap
✔ Mid Cap
Small Cap
Growth
Grth/Val
✔ Value

Portfolio

4.5% cash
95.5% stocks
0.0% pref/conv't pref
0.0% conv't bds/wrnts
0.0% corp bonds
0.0% gov't bonds
0.0% muni bonds
0.0% other

SHAREHOLDER INFORMATION

Minimum Investment

Initial: $10,000 Subsequent: $1

Minimum IRA Investment

Initial: $2,000 Subsequent: $1

Maximum Fees

Load: none 12b-1: none
Other: none

Services

✔ IRA
✔ Keogh
✔ Telephone Exchange

Spectra/N (SPECX)

800-711-6141, 212-806-8800
www.spectrafund.com

Aggressive Growth

PERFORMANCE — fund inception date: 7/28/69

	3yr Annual	5yr Annual	10yr Annual	Bull	Bear
Return (%)	19.7	20.6	23.9	151.8	-39.1
Differ from Category (+/-)	3.5 av	6.0 abv av	8.1 high	32.6 abv av	-18.5 low

Standard Deviation	Category Risk Index	Beta
33.1%—high	1.02—av	1.32

	2000	1999	1998	1997	1996	1995	1994	1993	1992	1991
Return (%)	-32.4	71.9	47.9	24.6	19.4	47.6	3.6	27.5	8.4	57.2
Differ from Category (+/-)	-26.4	14.4	32.8	9.8	1.1	13.0	4.4	2.3	1.5	10.0
Return, Tax-Adjusted (%)	-33.3	71.1	47.7	24.4	19.4	23.4	-6.1	18.6	4.8	51.3

PER SHARE DATA

	2000	1999	1998	1997	1996	1995	1994	1993	1992	1991
Dividends, Net Income ($)	0.00	0.00	0.00	0.00	0.00	2.77	1.53	1.43	0.77	1.00
Distrib'ns, Cap Gain ($)	0.62	0.93	0.04	0.05	0.00	0.00	0.00	0.00	0.00	0.00
Net Asset Value ($)	8.46	13.44	8.40	5.71	4.62	3.87	4.54	6.21	6.35	6.83
Expense Ratio (%)	na	1.85	1.96	2.12	2.55	3.76	2.59	2.57	2.14	2.74
Yield (%)	0.00	0.00	0.00	0.00	0.00	71.63	33.79	22.98	12.17	14.64
Portfolio Turnover (%)	na	102	190	133	197	207	116	100	63	78
Total Assets (Millions $)	739	750	271	96	17	2	3	4	4	5

PORTFOLIO (as of 6/30/00)

Portfolio Manager: David Alger, Seilai Khoo - 1974

Investm't Category: Aggressive Growth
✔ Domestic — Index
✔ Foreign — Sector
Asset Allocation — State Specific

Investment Style
✔ Large Cap — ✔ Mid Cap — Small Cap
✔ Growth — Grth/Val — Value

Portfolio

7.2%	cash	0.0%	corp bonds
91.3%	stocks	0.0%	gov't bonds
1.5%	pref/conv't pref	0.0%	muni bonds
0.0%	conv't bds/wrnts	0.0%	other

SHAREHOLDER INFORMATION

Minimum Investment
Initial: $1,000 — Subsequent: $100

Minimum IRA Investment
Initial: $250 — Subsequent: $100

Maximum Fees
Load: none — 12b-1: none
Other: none

Services
✔ IRA
✔ Keogh
✔ Telephone Exchange

SteinRoe Inv: Balanced (SRFBX)

800-338-2550, 312-368-7800
www.steinroe.com

Balanced

PERFORMANCE

fund inception date: 8/25/49

	3yr Annual	5yr Annual	10yr Annual	Bull	Bear
Return (%)	7.1	11.1	12.0	30.6	-6.9
Differ from Category (+/-)	-1.3 blw av	-0.3 av	0.3 av	2.5 av	-3.7 blw av

Standard Deviation	Category Risk Index	Beta
10.9%—blw av	1.00—av	0.59

	2000	1999	1998	1997	1996	1995	1994	1993	1992	1991
Return (%)	-2.2	12.2	12.1	17.4	17.0	22.6	-4.1	12.3	7.8	29.5
Differ from Category (+/-)	-4.2	1.5	-1.2	-1.4	3.1	-2.9	-2.8	-2.1	-0.6	5.7
Return, Tax-Adjusted (%)	-3.9	9.6	9.6	14.8	13.3	19.8	-6.1	9.6	4.5	26.8

PER SHARE DATA

	2000	1999	1998	1997	1996	1995	1994	1993	1992	1991
Dividends, Net Income ($)	0.66	0.91	0.90	0.88	0.99	1.17	1.18	1.22	1.29	1.32
Distrib'ns, Cap Gain ($)	1.52	2.30	2.07	1.99	2.26	0.70	0.27	0.71	1.66	0.61
Net Asset Value ($)	29.66	32.54	31.98	31.31	29.18	27.80	24.30	26.85	25.69	26.62
Expense Ratio (%)	na	1.14	1.03	1.05	1.05	0.87	0.83	0.81	0.85	0.87
Yield (%)	2.11	2.61	2.64	2.64	3.14	4.10	4.80	4.42	4.71	4.84
Portfolio Turnover (%)	na	41	61	15	87	45	29	53	59	71
Total Assets (Millions $)	219	246	269	278	257	227	215	226	180	156

PORTFOLIO (as of 9/30/99)

Portfolio Manager: committee - 1996

Investm't Category: Balanced

✔ Domestic
✔ Foreign
✔ Asset Allocation
Index
Sector
State Specific

Investment Style

Large Cap, Mid Cap, Small Cap
Growth, Grth/Val, Value

Portfolio

12.0%	cash	10.7%	corp bonds
53.1%	stocks	23.2%	gov't bonds
1.1%	pref/conv't pref	0.0%	muni bonds
0.0%	conv't bds/wrnts	0.0%	other

SHAREHOLDER INFORMATION

Minimum Investment
Initial: $2,500 Subsequent: $100

Minimum IRA Investment
Initial: $500 Subsequent: $50

Maximum Fees
Load: none 12b-1: none
Other: none

Services
✔ IRA
✔ Keogh
✔ Telephone Exchange

SteinRoe Inv: Cap Opport (SRFCX)

800-338-2550, 312-368-7800
www.steinroe.com

Aggressive Growth

PERFORMANCE — fund inception date: 3/31/69

	3yr Annual	5yr Annual	10yr Annual	Bull	Bear
Return (%)	6.9	9.3	17.5	74.1	-26.0
Differ from Category (+/-)	-9.3 blw av	-5.3 blw av	1.7 av	-45.1 blw av	-5.4 av

Standard Deviation	Category Risk Index	Beta
31.2%—high	0.96—av	1.20

	2000	1999	1998	1997	1996	1995	1994	1993	1992	1991
Return (%)	-11.2	40.3	-1.6	6.1	20.3	50.7	0.0	27.5	2.4	62.7
Differ from Category (+/-)	-5.2	-17.2	-16.7	-8.7	2.0	16.1	0.8	2.3	-4.5	15.5
Return, Tax-Adjusted (%)	-14.2	37.5	-1.6	6.1	20.3	49.8	0.0	27.4	2.3	62.3

PER SHARE DATA

	2000	1999	1998	1997	1996	1995	1994	1993	1992	1991
Dividends, Net Income ($)	0.00	0.00	0.00	0.00	0.00	0.01	0.01	0.01	0.04	0.08
Distrib'ns, Cap Gain ($)	5.53	3.98	0.00	0.00	0.00	0.99	0.00	0.00	0.00	0.00
Net Asset Value ($)	27.16	36.56	29.36	29.84	28.11	23.35	16.18	16.20	12.71	12.45
Expense Ratio (%)	na	1.19	1.20	1.17	1.22	1.05	0.97	1.06	1.06	1.18
Yield (%)	0.00	0.00	0.00	0.00	0.00	0.04	0.06	0.03	0.31	0.76
Portfolio Turnover (%)	na	88	45	35	22	60	46	55	46	53
Total Assets (Millions $)	422	534	726	1,012	1,423	332	172	166	129	152

PORTFOLIO (as of 9/30/99)

Portfolio Manager: David Brady, Steve Hayward - 1999

Investm't Category: Aggressive Growth

✔ Domestic — Index
✔ Foreign — Sector
Asset Allocation — State Specific

Investment Style

Large Cap — Mid Cap — ✔ Small Cap
✔ Growth — Grth/Val — Value

Portfolio

7.3%	cash	0.0%	corp bonds
92.7%	stocks	0.0%	gov't bonds
0.0%	pref/conv't pref	0.0%	muni bonds
0.0%	conv't bds/wrnts	0.0%	other

SHAREHOLDER INFORMATION

Minimum Investment
Initial: $2,500 — Subsequent: $100

Minimum IRA Investment
Initial: $500 — Subsequent: $50

Maximum Fees
Load: none — 12b-1: none
Other: none

Services
✔ IRA
✔ Keogh
✔ Telephone Exchange

SteinRoe Inv: Disc Stock (SRDSX)

800-338-2550, 312-368-7800
www.steinroe.com

Aggressive Growth

PERFORMANCE

fund inception date: 5/22/68

	3yr Annual	5yr Annual	10yr Annual	Bull	Bear
Return (%)	5.6	12.0	14.0	22.5	3.0
Differ from Category (+/-)	-10.6 blw av	-2.6 blw av	-1.8 blw av	-96.7 low	23.6 high

Standard Deviation	Category Risk Index	Beta
19.9%—abv av	0.61—low	0.80

	2000	1999	1998	1997	1996	1995	1994	1993	1992	1991
Return (%)	20.1	10.5	-11.2	25.9	18.8	18.7	-3.3	20.4	14.0	34.0
Differ from Category (+/-)	26.1	-47.0	-26.3	11.1	0.5	-15.9	-2.5	-4.8	7.1	-13.2
Return, Tax-Adjusted (%)	18.2	5.5	-14.4	23.3	16.3	16.0	-5.0	17.7	12.1	32.7

PER SHARE DATA

	2000	1999	1998	1997	1996	1995	1994	1993	1992	1991
Dividends, Net Income ($)	0.07	0.11	0.11	0.00	0.00	0.10	0.14	0.21	0.18	0.36
Distrib'ns, Cap Gain ($)	1.56	5.00	4.56	3.32	2.10	1.91	1.31	1.77	1.16	0.30
Net Asset Value ($)	19.96	18.06	21.19	29.36	26.01	23.72	21.72	24.00	21.63	20.16
Expense Ratio (%)	na	1.16	1.13	1.14	1.18	1.02	0.96	0.97	0.99	1.04
Yield (%)	0.32	0.47	0.42	0.00	0.00	0.39	0.60	0.81	0.78	1.75
Portfolio Turnover (%)	na	47	46	7	32	41	58	42	40	50
Total Assets (Millions $)	469	546	862	1,267	1,149	1,133	1,167	1,167	718	590

PORTFOLIO (as of 9/30/99)

Portfolio Manager: committee - 1997

Investm't Category: Aggressive Growth

✔ Domestic — Index
✔ Foreign — Sector
Asset Allocation — State Specific

Investment Style

Large Cap — ✔ Mid Cap — Small Cap
Growth — Grth/Val — ✔ Value

Portfolio

10.1%	cash	0.0%	corp bonds
88.9%	stocks	0.0%	gov't bonds
0.0%	pref/conv't pref	0.0%	muni bonds
1.0%	conv't bds/wrnts	0.0%	other

SHAREHOLDER INFORMATION

Minimum Investment

Initial: $2,500 — Subsequent: $100

Minimum IRA Investment

Initial: $500 — Subsequent: $50

Maximum Fees

Load: none — 12b-1: none
Other: none

Services

✔ IRA
✔ Keogh
✔ Telephone Exchange

SteinRoe Inv: Grth & Inc (SRGNX)

800-338-2550, 312-368-7800
www.steinroe.com

Growth & Income

PERFORMANCE — fund inception date: 3/24/87

	3yr Annual	5yr Annual	10yr Annual	Bull	Bear
Return (%)	12.1	16.6	16.5	34.8	3.1
Differ from Category (+/-)	3.2 high	2.3 abv av	1.6 abv av	1.3 av	3.2 abv av

Standard Deviation	Category Risk Index	Beta
16.7%—av	0.96—av	0.83

	2000	1999	1998	1997	1996	1995	1994	1993	1992	1991
Return (%)	6.5	10.7	19.5	25.7	21.8	30.1	-0.1	12.8	10.0	32.4
Differ from Category (+/-)	0.8	-0.1	6.7	-1.2	2.1	0.6	0.4	-1.0	-1.6	4.3
Return, Tax-Adjusted (%)	2.0	9.6	18.7	24.1	20.0	26.3	-1.7	10.9	8.0	30.7

PER SHARE DATA

	2000	1999	1998	1997	1996	1995	1994	1993	1992	1991
Dividends, Net Income ($)	0.09	0.09	0.24	0.27	0.27	0.28	0.18	0.16	0.16	0.23
Distrib'ns, Cap Gain ($)	5.92	1.15	0.37	0.96	0.64	1.43	0.59	0.70	0.75	0.35
Net Asset Value ($)	22.98	27.44	25.96	22.28	18.73	16.17	13.78	14.58	13.71	13.32
Expense Ratio (%)	na	1.06	1.07	1.13	1.18	0.96	0.90	0.88	0.97	1.00
Yield (%)	0.31	0.31	0.91	1.16	1.39	1.59	1.25	1.04	1.10	1.68
Portfolio Turnover (%)	na	7	11	2	13	70	85	50	40	48
Total Assets (Millions $)	302	388	418	340	241	151	121	108	77	62

PORTFOLIO (as of 9/30/99)

Portfolio Manager: H. Hirschhorn, S. Schermerhorn - 2000

Investm't Category: Growth & Income

✔ Domestic — Index
✔ Foreign — Sector
Asset Allocation — State Specific

Investment Style

✔ Large Cap — Mid Cap — Small Cap
Growth — Grth/Val — ✔ Value

Portfolio

8.8%	cash	0.0%	corp bonds
91.2%	stocks	0.0%	gov't bonds
0.0%	pref/conv't pref	0.0%	muni bonds
0.0%	conv't bds/wrnts	0.0%	other

SHAREHOLDER INFORMATION

Minimum Investment
Initial: $2,500 — Subsequent: $100

Minimum IRA Investment
Initial: $500 — Subsequent: $50

Maximum Fees
Load: none — 12b-1: none
Other: none

Services
✔ IRA
✔ Keogh
✔ Telephone Exchange

SteinRoe Inv: Grth Stock (SRFSX)

800-338-2550, 312-368-7800
www.steinroe.com

Growth

this fund is closed to new investors

PERFORMANCE

fund inception date: 7/1/58

	3yr Annual	5yr Annual	10yr Annual	Bull	Bear
Return (%)	14.9	19.3	17.7	77.4	-25.9
Differ from Category (+/-)	3.9 abv av	3.2 abv av	0.9 abv av	27.7 high	-20.5 low

Standard Deviation	Category Risk Index	Beta
23.9%—abv av	1.23—high	1.13

	2000	1999	1998	1997	1996	1995	1994	1993	1992	1991
Return (%)	-11.3	36.6	25.5	31.6	20.9	35.6	-3.7	2.8	8.2	46.0
Differ from Category (+/-)	-14.8	17.7	11.2	4.5	-1.4	5.2	-3.5	-11.8	-4.4	8.4
Return, Tax-Adjusted (%)	-14.1	35.0	25.5	30.0	18.2	32.2	-7.3	0.6	6.9	43.7

PER SHARE DATA

	2000	1999	1998	1997	1996	1995	1994	1993	1992	1991
Dividends, Net Income ($)	0.00	0.00	0.00	0.00	0.07	0.09	0.14	0.15	0.15	0.27
Distrib'ns, Cap Gain ($)	7.97	3.43	0.00	2.15	2.23	2.33	3.01	1.73	0.94	1.17
Net Asset Value ($)	41.27	55.39	43.31	34.50	27.90	25.05	20.29	24.39	25.59	24.67
Expense Ratio (%)	na	0.97	1.03	1.07	1.08	0.99	0.94	0.93	0.92	0.79
Yield (%)	0.00	0.00	0.00	0.00	0.23	0.32	0.60	0.57	0.56	1.04
Portfolio Turnover (%)	na	57	39	5	39	36	27	29	23	34
Total Assets (Millions $)	856	1,023	760	623	443	375	302	369	426	344

PORTFOLIO (as of 9/30/99)

Portfolio Manager: Erik Gustafson - 1997

Investm't Category: Growth

✔ Domestic   Index
✔ Foreign   Sector
Asset Allocation   State Specific

Investment Style

✔ Large Cap   Mid Cap   Small Cap
✔ Growth   Grth/Val   Value

Portfolio

4.5%	cash	0.0%	corp bonds
95.5%	stocks	0.0%	gov't bonds
0.0%	pref/conv't pref	0.0%	muni bonds
0.0%	conv't bds/wrnts	0.0%	other

SHAREHOLDER INFORMATION

Minimum Investment

Initial: $2,500   Subsequent: $100

Minimum IRA Investment

Initial: $500   Subsequent: $50

Maximum Fees

Load: none   12b-1: none
Other: none

Services

✔ IRA
✔ Keogh
✔ Telephone Exchange

SteinRoe Inv: Intl (SRITX)

800-338-2550, 312-368-7800
www.steinroe.com

International Stock

PERFORMANCE — fund inception date: 3/1/94

	3yr Annual	5yr Annual	10yr Annual	Bull	Bear
Return (%)	2.7	2.5	na	51.2	-23.2
Differ from Category (+/-)	-6.2 low	-5.8 blw av	na	-39.7 blw av	0.8 av

Standard Deviation	Category Risk Index	Beta
17.9%—av	0.79—blw av	0.70

	2000	1999	1998	1997	1996	1995	1994	1993	1992	1991
Return (%)	-27.3	33.7	11.4	-3.5	8.3	3.8	—	—	—	—
Differ from Category (+/-)	-7.9	-27.0	5.6	-4.8	-6.2	-5.5	—	—	—	—
Return, Tax-Adjusted (%)	-27.4	32.9	11.0	-4.9	7.6	3.3	—	—	—	—

PER SHARE DATA

	2000	1999	1998	1997	1996	1995	1994	1993	1992	1991
Dividends, Net Income ($)	0.06	0.11	0.09	0.10	0.07	0.12	—	—	—	—
Distrib'ns, Cap Gain ($)	0.00	0.16	0.00	0.58	0.14	0.00	—	—	—	—
Net Asset Value ($)	10.10	13.99	10.69	9.68	10.76	10.14	—	—	—	—
Expense Ratio (%)	na	1.57	1.53	1.55	1.51	1.59	—	—	—	—
Yield (%)	0.59	0.77	0.84	0.97	0.64	1.18	—	—	—	—
Portfolio Turnover (%)	na	11	32	11	42	59	—	—	—	—
Total Assets (Millions $)	81	138	128	137	140	91	—	—	—	—

PORTFOLIO (as of 9/30/99)

Portfolio Manager: committee - 2000

Investm't Category: International Stock

- Domestic
- ✔ Foreign
- Asset Allocation
- Index
- Sector
- State Specific

Investment Style

- Large Cap
- Mid Cap
- Small Cap
- Growth
- Grth/Val
- Value

Portfolio

- 9.7% cash
- 87.6% stocks
- 2.3% pref/conv't pref
- 0.5% conv't bds/wrnts
- 0.0% corp bonds
- 0.0% gov't bonds
- 0.0% muni bonds
- 0.0% other

SHAREHOLDER INFORMATION

Minimum Investment
Initial: $2,500 Subsequent: $100

Minimum IRA Investment
Initial: $500 Subsequent: $50

Maximum Fees
Load: none 12b-1: none
Other: none

Services
- ✔ IRA
- ✔ Keogh
- ✔ Telephone Exchange

SteinRoe Inv: Young Invtr (SRYIX)

800-338-2550, 312-368-7800
www.steinroe.com

Growth

PERFORMANCE

fund inception date: 4/29/94

	3yr Annual	5yr Annual	10yr Annual	Bull	Bear
Return (%)	11.6	18.9	na	68.6	-20.6
Differ from Category (+/-)	0.6 av	2.8 abv av	na	18.9 abv av	-15.2 low

Standard Deviation	Category Risk Index	Beta
23.7%—abv av	1.22—high	1.15

	2000	1999	1998	1997	1996	1995	1994	1993	1992	1991
Return (%)	-10.0	31.6	17.6	26.2	35.0	39.7	—	—	—	—
Differ from Category (+/-)	-13.5	12.7	3.3	-0.9	12.7	9.3	—	—	—	—
Return, Tax-Adjusted (%)	-12.2	31.3	17.0	25.8	33.7	38.2	—	—	—	—

PER SHARE DATA

	2000	1999	1998	1997	1996	1995	1994	1993	1992	1991
Dividends, Net Income ($)	0.00	0.00	0.00	0.00	0.01	0.04	—	—	—	—
Distrib'ns, Cap Gain ($)	4.00	0.31	0.59	0.32	0.62	0.50	—	—	—	—
Net Asset Value ($)	27.33	34.87	26.74	23.29	18.71	14.34	—	—	—	—
Expense Ratio (%)	na	1.18	1.31	1.43	1.21	0.99	—	—	—	—
Yield (%)	0.00	0.00	0.00	0.00	0.05	0.26	—	—	—	—
Portfolio Turnover (%)	na	45	45	22	98	55	—	—	—	—
Total Assets (Millions $)	1,032	1,156	823	532	271	41	—	—	—	—

PORTFOLIO (as of 9/30/99)

Portfolio Manager: Erik Gustafson, David Brady - 1997

Investm't Category: Growth

✔ Domestic　　Index
✔ Foreign　　Sector
Asset Allocation　　State Specific

Investment Style

✔ Large Cap　　✔ Mid Cap　　Small Cap
✔ Growth　　Grth/Val　　Value

Portfolio

4.0%	cash	0.0%	corp bonds
96.0%	stocks	0.0%	gov't bonds
0.0%	pref/conv't pref	0.0%	muni bonds
0.0%	conv't bds/wrnts	0.0%	other

SHAREHOLDER INFORMATION

Minimum Investment

Initial: $2,500　　Subsequent: $100

Minimum IRA Investment

Initial: $500　　Subsequent: $50

Maximum Fees

Load: none　　12b-1: none
Other: none

Services

✔ IRA
✔ Keogh
✔ Telephone Exchange

Stratton Monthly Dvd REIT (STMDX)

800-634-5726, 610-941-0255

Growth & Income

PERFORMANCE

fund inception date: 5/30/80

	3yr Annual	5yr Annual	10yr Annual	Bull	Bear
Return (%)	-0.1	4.9	8.1	-1.8	12.9
Differ from Category (+/-)	-9.0 low	-9.4 low	-6.8 low	-35.3 low	13.0 high

Standard Deviation	Category Risk Index	Beta
13.5%—blw av	0.78—low	0.23

	2000	1999	1998	1997	1996	1995	1994	1993	1992	1991
Return (%)	20.1	-6.2	-11.7	18.0	8.5	23.4	-12.1	6.6	10.4	35.0
Differ from Category (+/-)	14.4	-17.0	-24.5	-8.9	-11.2	-6.1	-11.6	-7.2	-1.2	6.9
Return, Tax-Adjusted (%)	16.5	-9.4	-14.3	15.2	5.7	20.2	-14.7	3.9	8.2	32.3

PER SHARE DATA

	2000	1999	1998	1997	1996	1995	1994	1993	1992	1991
Dividends, Net Income ($)	1.92	2.04	2.06	1.92	1.92	1.92	1.92	1.95	1.94	1.95
Distrib'ns, Cap Gain ($)	0.00	0.00	0.00	0.00	0.00	0.00	0.00	0.00	0.00	0.00
Net Asset Value ($)	23.43	21.28	24.78	30.25	27.43	27.19	23.78	29.17	29.16	28.31
Expense Ratio (%)	na	1.09	1.02	1.02	1.02	1.08	0.99	1.10	1.23	1.27
Yield (%)	8.19	9.58	8.31	6.34	6.99	7.06	8.07	6.68	6.65	6.88
Portfolio Turnover (%)	na	13	18	42	69	39	19	35	44	14
Total Assets (Millions $)	56	59	79	101	103	128	121	176	88	43

PORTFOLIO (as of 6/30/00)

Portfolio Manager: James Stratton - 1980

Investm't Category: Growth & Income

✔ Domestic / Index
Foreign / ✔ Sector
Asset Allocation / State Specific

Investment Style

Large Cap / ✔ Mid Cap / ✔ Small Cap
Growth / Grth/Val / ✔ Value

Portfolio

3.9% cash / 2.5% corp bonds
91.9% stocks / 0.0% gov't bonds
1.7% pref/conv't pref / 0.0% muni bonds
0.0% conv't bds/wrnts / 0.0% other

SHAREHOLDER INFORMATION

Minimum Investment

Initial: $2,000 Subsequent: $100

Minimum IRA Investment

Initial: $1 Subsequent: $1

Maximum Fees

Load: none 12b-1: none
Other: none

Services

✔ IRA
✔ Keogh
✔ Telephone Exchange

Strong Adv Common Stock/Z (STCSX)

800-368-3863, 414-359-1400
www.strong-funds.com

Aggressive Growth

this fund is closed to new investors

PERFORMANCE

fund inception date: 12/29/89

	3yr Annual	5yr Annual	10yr Annual	Bull	Bear
Return (%)	13.9	17.1	21.3	75.4	-13.6
Differ from Category (+/-)	-2.3 av	2.5 av	5.5 abv av	-43.8 blw av	7.0 abv av

Standard Deviation	Category Risk Index	Beta
20.0%—abv av	0.62—low	0.97

	2000	1999	1998	1997	1996	1995	1994	1993	1992	1991
Return (%)	-1.2	40.3	6.6	24.0	20.4	32.4	-0.4	25.1	20.7	57.0
Differ from Category (+/-)	4.8	-17.2	-8.5	9.2	2.1	-2.2	0.4	-0.1	13.8	9.8
Return, Tax-Adjusted (%)	-4.7	36.4	5.3	20.1	15.4	28.4	-2.1	23.4	19.8	49.0

PER SHARE DATA

	2000	1999	1998	1997	1996	1995	1994	1993	1992	1991
Dividends, Net Income ($)	0.04	0.00	0.00	0.03	0.11	0.11	0.04	0.03	0.22	2.58
Distrib'ns, Cap Gain ($)	4.45	4.02	1.31	3.85	3.35	2.21	1.06	0.86	0.15	0.00
Net Asset Value ($)	20.16	25.21	21.06	21.02	20.24	19.77	16.74	17.94	15.07	12.84
Expense Ratio (%)	na	1.20	1.20	1.20	1.20	1.30	1.30	1.40	1.40	2.00
Yield (%)	0.16	0.00	0.00	0.12	0.46	0.50	0.22	0.15	1.44	20.09
Portfolio Turnover (%)	na	80	103	117	90	91	83	80	292	2,461
Total Assets (Millions $)	1,613	1,733	1,439	1,564	1,243	1,061	790	762	179	48

PORTFOLIO (as of 6/30/00)

Portfolio Manager: Richard Weiss - 1991

Investm't Category: Aggressive Growth

✔ Domestic
✔ Foreign
Asset Allocation
Index
Sector
State Specific

Investment Style

Large Cap ✔ Mid Cap Small Cap
Growth ✔ Grth/Val Value

Portfolio

7.8% cash
91.6% stocks
0.0% pref/conv't pref
0.0% conv't bds/wrnts
0.6% corp bonds
0.0% gov't bonds
0.0% muni bonds
0.0% other

SHAREHOLDER INFORMATION

Minimum Investment

Initial: $2,500 Subsequent: $50

Minimum IRA Investment

Initial: $250 Subsequent: $50

Maximum Fees

Load: none 12b-1: none
Other: none

Services

✔ IRA
✔ Keogh
✔ Telephone Exchange

Strong Adv US Value/Z

800-368-3863, 414-359-1400
www.strong-funds.com

(SEQIX)

Growth & Income

PERFORMANCE

fund inception date: 12/29/95

	3yr Annual	5yr Annual	10yr Annual	Bull	Bear
Return (%)	11.5	18.4	na	44.5	-7.1
Differ from Category (+/-)	2.6 abv av	4.1 high	na	11.0 abv av	-7.0 blw av

Standard Deviation	Category Risk Index	Beta
16.1%—av	0.93—blw av	0.88

	2000	1999	1998	1997	1996	1995	1994	1993	1992	1991
Return (%)	-1.7	15.0	22.6	31.3	28.1	—	—	—	—	—
Differ from Category (+/-)	-7.4	4.2	9.8	4.4	8.4	—	—	—	—	—
Return, Tax-Adjusted (%)	-2.2	14.4	22.3	29.8	27.5	—	—	—	—	—

PER SHARE DATA

	2000	1999	1998	1997	1996	1995	1994	1993	1992	1991
Dividends, Net Income ($)	0.07	0.04	0.09	0.12	0.15	—	—	—	—	—
Distrib'ns, Cap Gain ($)	0.46	0.48	0.00	0.68	0.00	—	—	—	—	—
Net Asset Value ($)	20.65	21.58	19.23	15.76	12.64	—	—	—	—	—
Expense Ratio (%)	na	1.10	1.10	1.10	1.30	—	—	—	—	—
Yield (%)	0.33	0.18	0.46	0.72	1.18	—	—	—	—	—
Portfolio Turnover (%)	na	32	83	152	158	—	—	—	—	—
Total Assets (Millions $)	240	190	186	145	38	—	—	—	—	—

PORTFOLIO (as of 6/30/00)

Portfolio Manager: Rimas Milaitis - 1995

Investm't Category: Growth & Income

✔ Domestic
✔ Foreign
Asset Allocation
Index
Sector
State Specific

Investment Style

✔ Large Cap
Growth
Mid Cap
✔ Grth/Val
Small Cap
Value

Portfolio

5.3% cash
92.4% stocks
2.1% pref/conv't pref
0.2% conv't bds/wrnts
0.0% corp bonds
0.0% gov't bonds
0.0% muni bonds
0.0% other

SHAREHOLDER INFORMATION

Minimum Investment

Initial: $2,500 Subsequent: $50

Minimum IRA Investment

Initial: $250 Subsequent: $50

Maximum Fees

Load: none 12b-1: none
Other: none

Services

✔ IRA
✔ Keogh
✔ Telephone Exchange

Strong American Utilities (SAMUX)

800-368-3863, 414-359-1400
www.strong-funds.com

Growth & Income

PERFORMANCE — fund inception date: 7/1/93

	3yr Annual	5yr Annual	10yr Annual	Bull	Bear
Return (%)	15.5	16.3	na	20.4	14.6
Differ from Category (+/-)	6.6 high	2.0 abv av	na	-13.1 blw av	14.7 high

Standard Deviation	Category Risk Index	Beta
15.7%—av	0.90—blw av	0.33

	2000	1999	1998	1997	1996	1995	1994	1993	1992	1991
Return (%)	27.3	0.5	20.3	27.5	8.3	36.9	-2.6	—	—	—
Differ from Category (+/-)	21.6	-10.3	7.5	0.6	-11.4	7.4	-2.1	—	—	—
Return, Tax-Adjusted (%)	25.2	-2.5	18.4	25.1	5.5	35.5	-4.3	—	—	—

PER SHARE DATA

	2000	1999	1998	1997	1996	1995	1994	1993	1992	1991
Dividends, Net Income ($)	0.35	0.40	0.38	0.36	0.40	0.32	0.46	—	—	—
Distrib'ns, Cap Gain ($)	0.82	1.76	0.61	0.76	0.67	0.00	0.00	—	—	—
Net Asset Value ($)	17.49	14.74	16.81	14.82	12.54	12.58	9.46	—	—	—
Expense Ratio (%)	na	1.00	1.00	1.10	1.20	1.30	0.50	—	—	—
Yield (%)	1.91	2.42	2.18	2.31	3.02	2.54	4.86	—	—	—
Portfolio Turnover (%)	na	69	69	61	84	56	105	—	—	—
Total Assets (Millions $)	268	216	245	187	134	118	37	—	—	—

PORTFOLIO (as of 6/30/00)

Portfolio Manager: Reaves, Ferer, Sorenson, Luftig - 1993

Investm't Category: Growth & Income

✔ Domestic | Index
Foreign | ✔ Sector
Asset Allocation | State Specific

Investment Style

✔ Large Cap | ✔ Mid Cap | Small Cap
Growth | Grth/Val | ✔ Value

Portfolio

4.3%	cash	0.0%	corp bonds
95.7%	stocks	0.0%	gov't bonds
0.0%	pref/conv't pref	0.0%	muni bonds
0.0%	conv't bds/wrnts	0.0%	other

SHAREHOLDER INFORMATION

Minimum Investment
Initial: $2,500 Subsequent: $50

Minimum IRA Investment
Initial: $250 Subsequent: $50

Maximum Fees
Load: none 12b-1: none
Other: none

Services
✔ IRA
✔ Keogh
✔ Telephone Exchange

Strong Asia Pacific (SASPX)

800-368-3863, 414-359-1400
www.strong-funds.com

International Stock

PERFORMANCE

fund inception date: 12/31/93

	3yr Annual	5yr Annual	10yr Annual	Bull	Bear
Return (%)	6.1	-3.3	na	171.3	-35.5
Differ from Category (+/-)	-2.8 blw av	-11.6 low	na	80.4 high	-11.5 low

Standard Deviation	Category Risk Index	Beta
30.1%—high	1.33—abv av	1.03

	2000	1999	1998	1997	1996	1995	1994	1993	1992	1991
Return (%)	-36.9	96.0	-3.1	-30.9	2.1	5.9	-5.2	—	—	—
Differ from Category (+/-)	-17.5	35.3	-8.9	-32.2	-12.4	-3.4	-2.1	—	—	—
Return, Tax-Adjusted (%)	-38.0	93.4	-3.3	-31.1	1.0	4.7	-5.5	—	—	—

PER SHARE DATA

	2000	1999	1998	1997	1996	1995	1994	1993	1992	1991
Dividends, Net Income ($)	0.35	0.40	0.04	0.07	0.17	0.28	0.00	—	—	—
Distrib'ns, Cap Gain ($)	0.00	0.00	0.00	0.00	0.11	0.00	0.11	—	—	—
Net Asset Value ($)	7.13	11.88	6.27	6.52	9.54	9.62	9.35	—	—	—
Expense Ratio (%)	na	1.70	2.00	2.00	2.30	2.00	2.00	—	—	—
Yield (%)	4.90	3.36	0.63	1.07	1.76	2.91	0.00	—	—	—
Portfolio Turnover (%)	na	206	192	96	91	104	103	—	—	—
Total Assets (Millions $)	53	139	26	24	70	57	57	—	—	—

PORTFOLIO (as of 6/30/00)

Portfolio Manager: Anthony Cragg - 1993

Investm't Category: International Stock

Domestic | Index
✔ Foreign | Sector
Asset Allocation | State Specific

Investment Style

Large Cap | Mid Cap | Small Cap
Growth | Grth/Val | Value

Portfolio

0.3% cash | 0.0% corp bonds
99.7% stocks | 0.0% gov't bonds
0.0% pref/conv't pref | 0.0% muni bonds
0.0% conv't bds/wrnts | 0.0% other

SHAREHOLDER INFORMATION

Minimum Investment
Initial: $2,500 | Subsequent: $50

Minimum IRA Investment
Initial: $250 | Subsequent: $50

Maximum Fees
Load: none | 12b-1: none
Other: none

Services
✔ IRA
✔ Keogh
✔ Telephone Exchange

Strong Balanced (STAAX)

800-368-3863, 414-359-1400
www.strong-funds.com

Balanced

PERFORMANCE — fund inception date: 12/30/81

	3yr Annual	5yr Annual	10yr Annual	Bull	Bear
Return (%)	9.4	11.0	11.1	38.8	-11.2
Differ from Category (+/-)	1.0 abv av	-0.4 av	-0.6 blw av	10.7 high	-8.0 low

Standard Deviation	Category Risk Index	Beta
13.3%—blw av	1.22—high	0.71

	2000	1999	1998	1997	1996	1995	1994	1993	1992	1991
Return (%)	-6.3	15.5	21.3	16.6	10.4	21.9	-1.5	14.5	3.2	19.6
Differ from Category (+/-)	-8.3	4.8	8.0	-2.2	-3.5	-3.6	-0.2	0.1	-5.2	-4.2
Return, Tax-Adjusted (%)	-8.5	13.5	20.2	13.1	6.4	18.2	-3.1	10.8	0.5	17.5

PER SHARE DATA

	2000	1999	1998	1997	1996	1995	1994	1993	1992	1991
Dividends, Net Income ($)	0.79	0.75	0.54	0.66	0.86	0.81	0.69	0.82	0.86	0.96
Distrib'ns, Cap Gain ($)	1.33	0.75	0.00	2.05	1.54	1.17	0.16	1.23	0.93	0.19
Net Asset Value ($)	21.83	25.55	23.48	19.83	19.40	19.78	17.91	19.06	18.49	19.68
Expense Ratio (%)	na	1.10	1.00	1.10	1.10	1.30	1.20	1.20	1.20	1.30
Yield (%)	3.41	2.85	2.29	3.01	4.10	3.86	3.81	4.04	4.42	4.83
Portfolio Turnover (%)	na	64	185	276	446	326	359	348	320	418
Total Assets (Millions $)	343	369	319	278	271	268	248	254	208	214

PORTFOLIO (as of 3/31/00)

Portfolio Manager: B. Tank, J. Koch, R. Milaitis - 1993

Investm't Category: Balanced

✔ Domestic	Index
✔ Foreign	Sector
✔ Asset Allocation	State Specific

Investment Style

Large Cap	Mid Cap	Small Cap
Growth	Grth/Val	Value

Portfolio

2.2%	cash	18.4%	corp bonds
62.9%	stocks	13.6%	gov't bonds
1.9%	pref/conv't pref	0.0%	muni bonds
0.4%	conv't bds/wrnts	0.6%	other

SHAREHOLDER INFORMATION

Minimum Investment
Initial: $250 — Subsequent: $50

Minimum IRA Investment
Initial: $250 — Subsequent: $50

Maximum Fees
Load: none — 12b-1: none
Other: none

Services
✔ IRA
✔ Keogh
✔ Telephone Exchange

Strong Discovery (STDIX)

800-368-3863, 414-359-1400
www.strong-funds.com

Aggressive Growth

PERFORMANCE

fund inception date: 12/31/87

	3yr Annual	5yr Annual	10yr Annual	Bull	Bear
Return (%)	5.4	5.6	13.3	31.0	-13.2
Differ from Category (+/-)	-10.8 blw av	-9.0 low	-2.5 blw av	-88.2 low	7.4 abv av

Standard Deviation	Category Risk Index	Beta
22.7%—abv av	0.70—low	0.83

	2000	1999	1998	1997	1996	1995	1994	1993	1992	1991
Return (%)	3.9	5.2	7.0	10.8	1.4	34.8	-5.6	22.2	1.9	67.6
Differ from Category (+/-)	9.9	-52.3	-8.1	-4.0	-16.9	0.2	-4.8	-3.0	-5.0	20.4
Return, Tax-Adjusted (%)	0.8	4.9	6.7	8.1	-1.7	30.9	-8.1	19.3	-0.9	59.7

PER SHARE DATA

	2000	1999	1998	1997	1996	1995	1994	1993	1992	1991
Dividends, Net Income ($)	0.03	0.00	0.00	0.00	1.11	0.10	0.69	0.49	1.49	0.83
Distrib'ns, Cap Gain ($)	2.77	0.21	0.24	2.29	0.59	2.04	0.68	0.92	0.15	2.59
Net Asset Value ($)	16.39	18.64	17.95	17.00	17.45	18.96	15.67	18.05	16.01	17.49
Expense Ratio (%)	na	1.40	1.30	1.40	1.40	1.46	1.50	1.50	1.50	1.60
Yield (%)	0.15	0.00	0.00	0.00	6.15	0.47	4.22	2.58	9.22	4.13
Portfolio Turnover (%)	na	214	186	169	792	516	408	668	1,259	1,060
Total Assets (Millions $)	152	187	321	383	513	599	388	301	193	162

PORTFOLIO (as of 6/30/00)

Portfolio Manager: Charles Paquelet - 1987

Investm't Category: Aggressive Growth

✔ Domestic | Index
✔ Foreign | Sector
Asset Allocation | State Specific

Investment Style

Large Cap | Mid Cap | ✔ Small Cap
✔ Growth | Grth/Val | Value

Portfolio

15.4% cash | 0.0% corp bonds
84.5% stocks | 0.0% gov't bonds
0.0% pref/conv't pref | 0.0% muni bonds
0.1% conv't bds/wrnts | 0.0% other

SHAREHOLDER INFORMATION

Minimum Investment
Initial: $2,500 | Subsequent: $50

Minimum IRA Investment
Initial: $250 | Subsequent: $50

Maximum Fees
Load: none | 12b-1: none
Other: none

Services
✔ IRA
✔ Keogh
✔ Telephone Exchange

Strong Growth (SGROX)

800-368-3863, 414-359-1400
www.strong-funds.com

Growth

PERFORMANCE — fund inception date: 12/31/93

	3yr Annual	5yr Annual	10yr Annual	Bull	Bear
Return (%)	26.3	23.4	na	132.7	-25.8
Differ from Category (+/-)	15.3 high	7.3 high	na	83.0 high	-20.4 low

Standard Deviation	Category Risk Index	Beta
34.5%—high	1.77—high	1.10

	2000	1999	1998	1997	1996	1995	1994	1993	1992	1991
Return (%)	-9.2	75.0	26.9	19.0	19.5	41.0	17.2	—	—	—
Differ from Category (+/-)	-12.7	56.1	12.6	-8.1	-2.8	10.6	17.4	—	—	—
Return, Tax-Adjusted (%)	-12.1	71.1	26.9	15.2	18.6	39.8	16.8	—	—	—

PER SHARE DATA

	2000	1999	1998	1997	1996	1995	1994	1993	1992	1991
Dividends, Net Income ($)	0.00	0.00	0.00	0.00	0.02	0.02	0.10	—	—	—
Distrib'ns, Cap Gain ($)	5.23	4.48	0.00	3.51	0.45	0.45	0.00	—	—	—
Net Asset Value ($)	27.05	35.66	23.25	18.31	18.50	15.88	11.61	—	—	—
Expense Ratio (%)	na	1.20	1.30	1.30	1.30	1.50	1.60	—	—	—
Yield (%)	0.00	0.00	0.00	0.00	0.10	0.12	0.86	—	—	—
Portfolio Turnover (%)	na	324	249	295	294	321	386	—	—	—
Total Assets (Millions $)	3,296	3,353	1,834	1,597	1,308	642	106	—	—	—

PORTFOLIO (as of 6/30/00)

Portfolio Manager: Ronald Ognar - 1993

Investm't Category: Growth

✔ Domestic — Index
✔ Foreign — Sector
Asset Allocation — State Specific

Investment Style

Large Cap — ✔ Mid Cap — ✔ Small Cap
✔ Growth — Grth/Val — Value

Portfolio

6.9%	cash	0.0%	corp bonds
93.1%	stocks	0.0%	gov't bonds
0.0%	pref/conv't pref	0.0%	muni bonds
0.0%	conv't bds/wrnts	0.0%	other

SHAREHOLDER INFORMATION

Minimum Investment

Initial: $2,500 — Subsequent: $50

Minimum IRA Investment

Initial: $250 — Subsequent: $50

Maximum Fees

Load: none — 12b-1: none
Other: none

Services

✔ IRA
✔ Keogh
✔ Telephone Exchange

Strong Growth & Inc/Inv (SGRIX)

800-368-3863, 414-359-1400
www.strong-funds.com

Growth

PERFORMANCE

fund inception date: 12/29/95

	3yr Annual	5yr Annual	10yr Annual	Bull	Bear
Return (%)	16.4	22.0	na	73.8	-17.9
Differ from Category (+/-)	5.4 high	5.9 high	na	24.1 abv av	-12.5 low

Standard Deviation	Category Risk Index	Beta
19.7%—abv av	1.01—av	1.03

	2000	1999	1998	1997	1996	1995	1994	1993	1992	1991
Return (%)	-10.2	32.2	32.9	30.3	31.9	—	—	—	—	—
Differ from Category (+/-)	-13.7	13.3	18.6	3.2	9.6	—	—	—	—	—
Return, Tax-Adjusted (%)	-10.4	32.1	32.8	29.0	31.6	—	—	—	—	—

PER SHARE DATA

	2000	1999	1998	1997	1996	1995	1994	1993	1992	1991
Dividends, Net Income ($)	0.00	0.00	0.01	0.07	0.06	—	—	—	—	—
Distrib'ns, Cap Gain ($)	0.32	0.02	0.00	0.69	0.01	—	—	—	—	—
Net Asset Value ($)	25.37	28.63	21.67	16.31	13.11	—	—	—	—	—
Expense Ratio (%)	na	1.10	1.10	1.20	1.90	—	—	—	—	—
Yield (%)	0.00	0.00	0.04	0.41	0.45	—	—	—	—	—
Portfolio Turnover (%)	na	52	107	237	2	—	—	—	—	—
Total Assets (Millions $)	1,110	997	482	246	48	—	—	—	—	—

PORTFOLIO (as of 6/30/00)

Portfolio Manager: Rimas Milaitis - 1995

Investm't Category: Growth

✔ Domestic
✔ Foreign
Asset Allocation
Index
Sector
State Specific

Investment Style

✔ Large Cap
✔ Growth
Mid Cap
Grth/Val
Small Cap
Value

Portfolio

7.1%	cash	0.0%	corp bonds
92.9%	stocks	0.0%	gov't bonds
0.0%	pref/conv't pref	0.0%	muni bonds
0.0%	conv't bds/wrnts	0.0%	other

SHAREHOLDER INFORMATION

Minimum Investment

Initial: $2,500 Subsequent: $50

Minimum IRA Investment

Initial: $250 Subsequent: $50

Maximum Fees

Load: none 12b-1: none
Other: none

Services

✔ IRA
✔ Keogh
✔ Telephone Exchange

Strong Growth 20/Inv (SGRTX)

800-368-3863, 414-359-1400
www.strong-funds.com

Aggressive Growth

PERFORMANCE

fund inception date: 6/30/97

	3yr Annual	5yr Annual	10yr Annual	Bull	Bear
Return (%)	36.8	na	na	187.2	-27.0
Differ from Category (+/-)	20.6 high	na	na	68.0 high	-6.4 av

Standard Deviation	Category Risk Index	Beta
34.4%—high	1.06—abv av	1.13

	2000	1999	1998	1997	1996	1995	1994	1993	1992	1991
Return (%)	-10.3	109.4	36.5	—	—	—	—	—	—	—
Differ from Category (+/-)	-4.3	51.9	21.4	—	—	—	—	—	—	—
Return, Tax-Adjusted (%)	-11.8	107.6	36.5	—	—	—	—	—	—	—

PER SHARE DATA

	2000	1999	1998	1997	1996	1995	1994	1993	1992	1991
Dividends, Net Income ($)	0.00	0.00	0.00	—	—	—	—	—	—	—
Distrib'ns, Cap Gain ($)	2.34	1.32	0.00	—	—	—	—	—	—	—
Net Asset Value ($)	25.13	30.63	15.44	—	—	—	—	—	—	—
Expense Ratio (%)	na	1.40	1.50	—	—	—	—	—	—	—
Yield (%)	0.00	0.00	0.00	—	—	—	—	—	—	—
Portfolio Turnover (%)	na	432	541	—	—	—	—	—	—	—
Total Assets (Millions $)	725	466	71	—	—	—	—	—	—	—

PORTFOLIO (as of 6/30/00)

Portfolio Manager: Ronald Ognar - 1997

Investm't Category: Aggressive Growth

✔ Domestic
Index
✔ Foreign
Sector
Asset Allocation
State Specific

Investment Style

Large Cap
✔ Mid Cap
✔ Small Cap
✔ Growth
Grth/Val
Value

Portfolio

0.1%	cash	0.0%	corp bonds
99.0%	stocks	0.0%	gov't bonds
0.0%	pref/conv't pref	0.0%	muni bonds
0.9%	conv't bds/wrnts	0.0%	other

SHAREHOLDER INFORMATION

Minimum Investment
Initial: $2,500 Subsequent: $50

Minimum IRA Investment
Initial: $250 Subsequent: $50

Maximum Fees
Load: none 12b-1: none
Other: none

Services
✔ IRA
✔ Keogh
✔ Telephone Exchange

Strong Index 500 (SINEX)

800-368-3863, 414-359-1400
www.strong-funds.com

Growth & Income

PERFORMANCE

fund inception date: 5/1/97

	3yr Annual	5yr Annual	10yr Annual	Bull	Bear
Return (%)	11.7	na	na	55.2	-11.8
Differ from Category (+/-)	2.8 abv av	na	na	21.7 abv av	-11.7 low

Standard Deviation	Category Risk Index	Beta
17.6%—av	1.02—abv av	1.00

	2000	1999	1998	1997	1996	1995	1994	1993	1992	1991
Return (%)	-9.5	20.3	28.1	—	—	—	—	—	—	—
Differ from Category (+/-)	-15.2	9.5	15.3	—	—	—	—	—	—	—
Return, Tax-Adjusted (%)	-10.4	19.4	27.7	—	—	—	—	—	—	—

PER SHARE DATA

	2000	1999	1998	1997	1996	1995	1994	1993	1992	1991
Dividends, Net Income ($)	0.13	0.14	0.12	—	—	—	—	—	—	—
Distrib'ns, Cap Gain ($)	0.62	0.37	0.00	—	—	—	—	—	—	—
Net Asset Value ($)	15.59	18.07	15.45	—	—	—	—	—	—	—
Expense Ratio (%)	na	0.45	0.45	—	—	—	—	—	—	—
Yield (%)	0.80	0.75	0.77	—	—	—	—	—	—	—
Portfolio Turnover (%)	na	11	—	—	—	—	—	—	—	—
Total Assets (Millions $)	185	185	109	—	—	—	—	—	—	—

PORTFOLIO (as of 6/30/00)

Portfolio Manager: committee - 1997

Investm't Category: Growth & Income

✔ Domestic ✔ Index
✔ Foreign Sector
Asset Allocation State Specific

Investment Style

✔ Large Cap Mid Cap Small Cap
Growth ✔ Grth/Val Value

Portfolio

3.5%	cash	0.0%	corp bonds
96.5%	stocks	0.0%	gov't bonds
0.0%	pref/conv't pref	0.0%	muni bonds
0.0%	conv't bds/wrnts	0.0%	other

SHAREHOLDER INFORMATION

Minimum Investment

Initial: $2,500 Subsequent: $50

Minimum IRA Investment

Initial: $500 Subsequent: $50

Maximum Fees

Load: 0.50% redemption 12b-1: none
Other: redemption fee applies for 6 months

Services

✔ IRA
✔ Keogh
✔ Telephone Exchange

Strong Int'l Stk (STISX)

800-368-3863, 414-359-1400
www.strong-funds.com

International Stock

PERFORMANCE

fund inception date: 3/4/92

	3yr Annual	5yr Annual	10yr Annual	Bull	Bear
Return (%)	4.3	1.0	na	88.6	-38.1
Differ from Category (+/-)	-4.6 blw av	-7.3 blw av	na	-2.3 abv av	-14.1 low

Standard Deviation	Category Risk Index	Beta
28.4%—high	1.25—abv av	0.74

	2000	1999	1998	1997	1996	1995	1994	1993	1992	1991
Return (%)	-36.6	92.6	-7.0	-14.2	8.1	7.8	-1.5	47.7	—	—
Differ from Category (+/-)	-17.2	31.9	-12.8	-15.5	-6.4	-1.5	1.6	7.5	—	—
Return, Tax-Adjusted (%)	-36.6	92.6	-7.7	-15.6	5.4	6.7	-4.0	46.9	—	—

PER SHARE DATA

	2000	1999	1998	1997	1996	1995	1994	1993	1992	1991
Dividends, Net Income ($)	0.00	0.00	0.20	0.36	0.33	0.35	0.00	0.02	—	—
Distrib'ns, Cap Gain ($)	0.00	0.00	0.00	0.26	0.80	0.00	1.30	0.22	—	—
Net Asset Value ($)	11.99	18.92	9.82	10.76	13.23	13.28	12.65	14.18	—	—
Expense Ratio (%)	na	1.80	1.90	1.60	1.70	1.80	1.70	1.90	—	—
Yield (%)	0.00	0.00	2.03	3.26	2.35	2.63	0.00	0.13	—	—
Portfolio Turnover (%)	na	84	228	143	108	102	137	140	—	—
Total Assets (Millions $)	106	177	95	147	296	214	257	128	—	—

PORTFOLIO (as of 6/30/00)

Portfolio Manager: David Lui - 1998

Investm't Category: International Stock

Domestic	Index
✔ Foreign	Sector
Asset Allocation	State Specific

Investment Style

Large Cap	Mid Cap	Small Cap
Growth	Grth/Val	Value

Portfolio

0.4%	cash	0.0%	corp bonds
99.6%	stocks	0.0%	gov't bonds
0.0%	pref/conv't pref	0.0%	muni bonds
0.0%	conv't bds/wrnts	0.0%	other

SHAREHOLDER INFORMATION

Minimum Investment

Initial: $2,500 Subsequent: $50

Minimum IRA Investment

Initial: $250 Subsequent: $50

Maximum Fees

Load: none 12b-1: none

Other: none

Services

✔ IRA

✔ Keogh

✔ Telephone Exchange

Strong Lrg Cap Growth (STRFX)

800-368-3863, 414-359-1400
www.strong-funds.com

Growth

PERFORMANCE — fund inception date: 12/30/81

	3yr Annual	5yr Annual	10yr Annual	Bull	Bear
Return (%)	22.3	21.0	18.2	109.6	-23.7
Differ from Category (+/-)	11.3 high	4.9 high	1.4 abv av	59.9 high	-18.3 low

Standard Deviation	Category Risk Index	Beta
28.8%—high	1.48—high	1.08

	2000	1999	1998	1997	1996	1995	1994	1993	1992	1991
Return (%)	-13.4	60.2	32.0	24.1	14.0	26.9	-1.3	22.5	0.5	33.5
Differ from Category (+/-)	-16.9	41.3	17.7	-3.0	-8.3	-3.5	-1.1	7.9	-12.1	-4.1
Return, Tax-Adjusted (%)	-15.9	55.6	31.6	18.6	8.7	24.8	-1.8	21.7	0.2	33.0

PER SHARE DATA

	2000	1999	1998	1997	1996	1995	1994	1993	1992	1991
Dividends, Net Income ($)	0.00	0.00	0.07	0.19	0.43	0.36	0.34	0.33	0.17	0.22
Distrib'ns, Cap Gain ($)	5.91	7.88	0.37	6.99	4.76	1.21	0.00	0.05	0.00	0.00
Net Asset Value ($)	34.77	47.10	34.48	26.46	27.23	28.38	23.62	24.30	20.17	20.24
Expense Ratio (%)	na	1.00	1.00	1.10	1.10	1.20	1.20	1.20	1.30	1.40
Yield (%)	0.00	0.00	0.20	0.56	1.34	1.21	1.43	1.35	0.84	1.08
Portfolio Turnover (%)	na	402	267	404	502	298	290	271	372	426
Total Assets (Millions $)	1,549	1,663	1,022	848	759	708	606	630	587	691

PORTFOLIO (as of 6/30/00)

Portfolio Manager: Ronald Ognar, Ian Rogers - 1993

Investm't Category: Growth

✔ Domestic　Index
✔ Foreign　Sector
Asset Allocation　State Specific

Investment Style

Large Cap　✔ Mid Cap　✔ Small Cap
✔ Growth　Grth/Val　Value

Portfolio

7.4%	cash	0.0%	corp bonds
91.0%	stocks	0.0%	gov't bonds
0.0%	pref/conv't pref	0.0%	muni bonds
1.6%	conv't bds/wrnts	0.0%	other

SHAREHOLDER INFORMATION

Minimum Investment
Initial: $2,500　Subsequent: $50

Minimum IRA Investment
Initial: $250　Subsequent: $50

Maximum Fees
Load: none　12b-1: none
Other: none

Services
✔ IRA
✔ Keogh
✔ Telephone Exchange

Strong Opportunity/Inv

800-368-3863, 414-359-1400
www.strong-funds.com

(SOPFX)

Growth

PERFORMANCE

fund inception date: 12/31/85

	3yr Annual	5yr Annual	10yr Annual	Bull	Bear
Return (%)	18.7	19.5	19.6	67.5	-6.3
Differ from Category (+/-)	7.7 high	3.4 abv av	2.8 high	17.8 abv av	-0.9 av

Standard Deviation	Category Risk Index	Beta
18.5%—av	0.95—blw av	0.94

	2000	1999	1998	1997	1996	1995	1994	1993	1992	1991
Return (%)	8.5	33.3	15.4	23.4	18.1	27.2	3.1	21.1	17.3	31.6
Differ from Category (+/-)	5.0	14.4	1.1	-3.7	-4.2	-3.2	3.3	6.5	4.7	-6.0
Return, Tax-Adjusted (%)	5.8	29.9	12.9	20.0	14.5	25.2	1.6	19.2	17.0	31.2

PER SHARE DATA

	2000	1999	1998	1997	1996	1995	1994	1993	1992	1991
Dividends, Net Income ($)	0.16	0.08	0.05	0.10	0.25	0.21	0.13	0.06	0.05	0.19
Distrib'ns, Cap Gain ($)	5.64	6.34	4.47	5.75	3.82	1.62	1.27	1.56	0.15	0.00
Net Asset Value ($)	42.35	44.69	38.62	37.41	35.26	33.35	27.71	28.23	24.70	21.24
Expense Ratio (%)	na	1.20	1.20	1.30	1.30	1.40	1.40	1.40	1.50	1.70
Yield (%)	0.33	0.15	0.11	0.23	0.63	0.60	0.44	0.20	0.20	0.89
Portfolio Turnover (%)	na	81	86	93	103	92	59	109	139	271
Total Assets (Millions $)	3,118	2,537	2,037	1,924	1,769	1,327	805	443	193	159

PORTFOLIO (as of 6/30/00)

Portfolio Manager: Richard Weiss - 1991

Investm't Category: Growth

✔ Domestic Index
✔ Foreign Sector
Asset Allocation State Specific

Investment Style

✔ Large Cap ✔ Mid Cap Small Cap
Growth Grth/Val ✔ Value

Portfolio

14.7%	cash	0.0%	corp bonds
85.3%	stocks	0.0%	gov't bonds
0.0%	pref/conv't pref	0.0%	muni bonds
0.0%	conv't bds/wrnts	0.0%	other

SHAREHOLDER INFORMATION

Minimum Investment

Initial: $2,500 Subsequent: $50

Minimum IRA Investment

Initial: $250 Subsequent: $50

Maximum Fees

Load: none 12b-1: none
Other: none

Services

✔ IRA
✔ Keogh
✔ Telephone Exchange

Strong Schafer Value

800-368-3863, 414-359-1400
www.strong-funds.com

(SCHVX)

Growth

PERFORMANCE — fund inception date: 10/22/85

	3yr Annual	5yr Annual	10yr Annual	Bull	Bear
Return (%)	-6.8	5.2	13.1	0.3	-0.5
Differ from Category (+/-)	-17.8 low	-10.9 low	-3.7 low	-49.4 low	4.9 abv av

Standard Deviation	Category Risk Index	Beta
21.0%—abv av	1.08—abv av	0.93

	2000	1999	1998	1997	1996	1995	1994	1993	1992	1991
Return (%)	3.5	-16.3	-6.6	29.3	23.2	34.1	-4.2	23.9	18.6	40.9
Differ from Category (+/-)	0.0	-35.2	-20.9	2.2	0.9	3.7	-4.0	9.3	6.0	3.3
Return, Tax-Adjusted (%)	3.5	-16.6	-6.8	28.3	21.8	32.5	-5.8	22.6	15.0	34.0

PER SHARE DATA

	2000	1999	1998	1997	1996	1995	1994	1993	1992	1991
Dividends, Net Income ($)	0.00	0.50	0.36	0.35	0.44	0.38	0.33	0.19	0.39	0.52
Distrib'ns, Cap Gain ($)	0.00	0.00	0.00	1.67	1.42	1.27	1.64	1.08	3.27	5.48
Net Asset Value ($)	50.83	49.07	59.29	63.90	51.02	42.92	33.23	36.78	30.70	28.98
Expense Ratio (%)	1.50	1.40	1.20	1.20	1.27	1.28	1.48	1.74	2.08	2.00
Yield (%)	0.00	1.01	0.60	0.53	0.83	0.85	0.94	0.50	1.14	1.50
Portfolio Turnover (%)	52	67	39	22	17	33	28	33	53	55
Total Assets (Millions $)	365	561	1,544	1,511	514	186	72	25	13	10

PORTFOLIO (as of 6/30/00)

Portfolio Manager: David Schafer - 1985

Investm't Category: Growth

✔ Domestic	Index
✔ Foreign	Sector
Asset Allocation	State Specific

Investment Style

✔ Large Cap	✔ Mid Cap	Small Cap
Growth	Grth/Val	✔ Value

Portfolio

4.7%	cash	0.0%	corp bonds
95.3%	stocks	0.0%	gov't bonds
0.0%	pref/conv't pref	0.0%	muni bonds
0.0%	conv't bds/wrnts	0.0%	other

SHAREHOLDER INFORMATION

Minimum Investment
Initial: $2,500 Subsequent: $50

Minimum IRA Investment
Initial: $250 Subsequent: $50

Maximum Fees
Load: none 12b-1: none
Other: none

Services
✔ IRA
✔ Keogh
✔ Telephone Exchange

Strong Value (STVAX)

800-368-3863, 414-359-1400
www.strong-funds.com

Growth

PERFORMANCE

fund inception date: 12/29/95

	3yr Annual	5yr Annual	10yr Annual	Bull	Bear
Return (%)	8.3	13.3	na	19.5	-3.3
Differ from Category (+/-)	-2.7 blw av	-2.8 blw av	na	-30.2 low	2.1 av

Standard Deviation	Category Risk Index	Beta
14.2%—blw av	0.73—low	0.66

	2000	1999	1998	1997	1996	1995	1994	1993	1992	1991
Return (%)	12.6	-1.9	15.1	25.9	16.8	—	—	—	—	—
Differ from Category (+/-)	9.1	-20.8	0.8	-1.2	-5.5	—	—	—	—	—
Return, Tax-Adjusted (%)	8.8	-5.0	13.7	24.4	16.3	—	—	—	—	—

PER SHARE DATA

	2000	1999	1998	1997	1996	1995	1994	1993	1992	1991
Dividends, Net Income ($)	0.01	0.05	0.06	0.10	0.12	—	—	—	—	—
Distrib'ns, Cap Gain ($)	2.28	2.28	0.79	0.64	0.00	—	—	—	—	—
Net Asset Value ($)	11.43	12.31	14.95	13.77	11.55	—	—	—	—	—
Expense Ratio (%)	na	1.40	1.30	1.50	1.50	—	—	—	—	—
Yield (%)	0.07	0.34	0.38	0.69	1.03	—	—	—	—	—
Portfolio Turnover (%)	na	104	93	103	89	—	—	—	—	—
Total Assets (Millions $)	48	58	91	93	55	—	—	—	—	—

PORTFOLIO (as of 6/30/00)

Portfolio Manager: Laura Sloate - 2000

Investm't Category: Growth

✔ Domestic | Index
Foreign | Sector
Asset Allocation | State Specific

Investment Style

Large Cap | ✔ Mid Cap | Small Cap
Growth | ✔ Grth/Val | Value

Portfolio

2.7%	cash	0.0%	corp bonds
97.3%	stocks	0.0%	gov't bonds
0.0%	pref/conv't pref	0.0%	muni bonds
0.0%	conv't bds/wrnts	0.0%	other

SHAREHOLDER INFORMATION

Minimum Investment
Initial: $2,500 Subsequent: $50

Minimum IRA Investment
Initial: $250 Subsequent: $50

Maximum Fees
Load: none 12b-1: none
Other: none

Services
✔ IRA
✔ Keogh
✔ Telephone Exchange

T Rowe Price Balanced (RPBAX)

800-638-5660, 410-547-2000
www.troweprice.com

Balanced

PERFORMANCE — fund inception date: 12/31/39

	3yr Annual	5yr Annual	10yr Annual	Bull	Bear
Return (%)	9.2	12.2	12.5	27.8	-2.6
Differ from Category (+/-)	0.8 av	0.8 av	0.8 abv av	-0.3 av	0.6 av

Standard Deviation	Category Risk Index	Beta
10.0%—blw av	0.91—blw av	0.55

	2000	1999	1998	1997	1996	1995	1994	1993	1992	1991
Return (%)	2.0	10.2	15.9	18.9	14.5	24.8	-2.0	13.8	7.7	21.9
Differ from Category (+/-)	0.0	-0.5	2.6	0.1	0.6	-0.7	-0.7	-0.6	-0.7	-1.9
Return, Tax-Adjusted (%)	0.5	8.8	14.6	17.2	12.7	22.7	-3.8	11.9	4.7	18.5

PER SHARE DATA

	2000	1999	1998	1997	1996	1995	1994	1993	1992	1991
Dividends, Net Income ($)	0.53	0.54	0.52	0.53	0.50	0.47	0.43	0.44	0.50	0.61
Distrib'ns, Cap Gain ($)	0.40	0.23	0.04	0.12	0.13	0.17	0.20	0.11	0.66	0.56
Net Asset Value ($)	19.17	19.69	18.59	16.54	14.48	13.22	11.14	12.02	11.07	11.42
Expense Ratio (%)	na	0.79	0.78	0.81	0.87	1.00	1.00	1.00	1.03	1.10
Yield (%)	2.70	2.71	2.79	3.18	3.42	3.51	3.79	3.62	4.26	5.09
Portfolio Turnover (%)	na	21	13	15	22	17	33	8	208	240
Total Assets (Millions $)	2,043	2,090	1,649	1,219	875	608	392	340	250	175

PORTFOLIO (as of 6/30/00)

Portfolio Manager: committee - 1991

Investm't Category: Balanced

✔ Domestic — Index
✔ Foreign — Sector
Asset Allocation — State Specific

Investment Style

Large Cap — Mid Cap — Small Cap
Growth — Grth/Val — Value

Portfolio

1.3%	cash	14.9%	corp bonds
62.5%	stocks	20.7%	gov't bonds
0.6%	pref/conv't pref	0.0%	muni bonds
0.0%	conv't bds/wrnts	0.0%	other

SHAREHOLDER INFORMATION

Minimum Investment
Initial: $2,500 — Subsequent: $100

Minimum IRA Investment
Initial: $1,000 — Subsequent: $50

Maximum Fees
Load: none — 12b-1: none
Other: none

Services
✔ IRA
Keogh
✔ Telephone Exchange

T Rowe Price Blue Chip Gr (TRBCX)

800-638-5660, 410-547-2000
www.troweprice.com

Growth

PERFORMANCE

fund inception date: 6/30/93

	3yr Annual	5yr Annual	10yr Annual	Bull	Bear
Return (%)	14.6	19.6	na	58.6	-10.3
Differ from Category (+/-)	3.6 abv av	3.5 high	na	8.9 abv av	-4.9 av

Standard Deviation	Category Risk Index	Beta
19.0%—av	0.98—blw av	1.05

	2000	1999	1998	1997	1996	1995	1994	1993	1992	1991
Return (%)	-2.5	19.9	28.8	27.5	27.7	37.8	0.8	—	—	—
Differ from Category (+/-)	-6.0	1.0	14.5	0.4	5.4	7.4	1.0	—	—	—
Return, Tax-Adjusted (%)	-3.3	19.6	28.2	27.2	27.1	37.0	0.1	—	—	—

PER SHARE DATA

	2000	1999	1998	1997	1996	1995	1994	1993	1992	1991
Dividends, Net Income ($)	0.00	0.03	0.11	0.12	0.14	0.15	0.11	—	—	—
Distrib'ns, Cap Gain ($)	1.62	0.33	0.39	0.02	0.08	0.08	0.11	—	—	—
Net Asset Value ($)	33.85	36.34	30.60	24.17	19.06	15.09	11.11	—	—	—
Expense Ratio (%)	na	0.91	0.91	0.95	1.12	1.25	1.25	—	—	—
Yield (%)	0.00	0.08	0.35	0.49	0.73	0.98	0.98	—	—	—
Portfolio Turnover (%)	na	41	35	23	26	43	75	—	—	—
Total Assets (Millions $)	7,154	6,708	4,330	2,344	539	146	38	—	—	—

PORTFOLIO (as of 6/30/00)

Portfolio Manager: committee - 1993

Investm't Category: Growth

✔ Domestic | Index
✔ Foreign | Sector
Asset Allocation | State Specific

Investment Style

✔ Large Cap | Mid Cap | Small Cap
✔ Growth | Grth/Val | Value

Portfolio

0.8%	cash	0.0%	corp bonds
99.2%	stocks	0.0%	gov't bonds
0.0%	pref/conv't pref	0.0%	muni bonds
0.0%	conv't bds/wrnts	0.0%	other

SHAREHOLDER INFORMATION

Minimum Investment

Initial: $2,500 Subsequent: $100

Minimum IRA Investment

Initial: $1,000 Subsequent: $50

Maximum Fees

Load: none 12b-1: none
Other: none

Services

✔ IRA
✔ Keogh
✔ Telephone Exchange

T Rowe Price Cap Apprec (PRWCX)

800-638-5660, 410-547-2000
www.troweprice.com

Balanced

PERFORMANCE — fund inception date: 6/30/86

	3yr Annual	5yr Annual	10yr Annual	Bull	Bear
Return (%)	11.4	13.4	13.8	14.8	13.4
Differ from Category (+/-)	3.0 high	2.0 abv av	2.1 high	-13.3 low	16.6 high

Standard Deviation	Category Risk Index	Beta
9.6%—blw av	0.88—blw av	0.29

	2000	1999	1998	1997	1996	1995	1994	1993	1992	1991
Return (%)	22.1	7.0	5.7	16.2	16.8	22.5	3.7	15.6	9.3	21.5
Differ from Category (+/-)	20.1	-3.7	-7.6	-2.6	2.9	-3.0	5.0	1.2	0.9	-2.3
Return, Tax-Adjusted (%)	19.3	3.7	1.8	12.6	13.2	19.3	1.0	14.1	7.4	18.3

PER SHARE DATA

	2000	1999	1998	1997	1996	1995	1994	1993	1992	1991
Dividends, Net Income ($)	0.45	0.50	0.50	0.50	0.60	0.44	0.35	0.18	0.50	0.43
Distrib'ns, Cap Gain ($)	0.82	1.13	1.82	1.58	0.90	0.72	0.69	0.33	0.16	0.64
Net Asset Value ($)	13.95	12.51	13.22	14.71	14.47	13.67	12.10	12.66	11.39	11.02
Expense Ratio (%)	na	0.88	0.62	0.64	0.76	1.05	1.10	1.09	1.08	1.20
Yield (%)	3.04	3.66	3.32	3.06	3.90	3.05	2.73	1.38	4.32	3.68
Portfolio Turnover (%)	na	28	53	48	44	49	43	39	30	51
Total Assets (Millions $)	848	855	1,003	1,059	959	864	653	536	359	215

PORTFOLIO (as of 6/30/00)

Portfolio Manager: committee - 1989

Investm't Category: Balanced

✔ Domestic	Index
✔ Foreign	Sector
Asset Allocation	State Specific

Investment Style

Large Cap	✔ Mid Cap	✔ Small Cap
Growth	Grth/Val	✔ Value

Portfolio

7.8%	cash	1.6%	corp bonds
58.1%	stocks	11.3%	gov't bonds
6.0%	pref/conv't pref	0.0%	muni bonds
15.2%	conv't bds/wrnts	0.0%	other

SHAREHOLDER INFORMATION

Minimum Investment
Initial: $2,500 — Subsequent: $100

Minimum IRA Investment
Initial: $1,000 — Subsequent: $50

Maximum Fees
Load: none — 12b-1: none
Other: none

Services
✔ IRA
✔ Keogh
✔ Telephone Exchange

T Rowe Price Cap Opport (PRCOX)

800-638-5660, 410-547-2000
www.troweprice.com

Growth

PERFORMANCE

fund inception date: 11/30/94

	3yr Annual	5yr Annual	10yr Annual	Bull	Bear
Return (%)	6.2	10.1	na	42.4	-11.8
Differ from Category (+/-)	-4.8 blw av	-6.0 low	na	-7.3 av	-6.4 blw av

Standard Deviation	Category Risk Index	Beta
19.6%—abv av	1.01—av	1.06

	2000	1999	1998	1997	1996	1995	1994	1993	1992	1991
Return (%)	-6.3	11.4	14.7	15.8	16.7	46.5	—	—	—	—
Differ from Category (+/-)	-9.8	-7.5	0.4	-11.3	-5.6	16.1	—	—	—	—
Return, Tax-Adjusted (%)	-8.1	6.6	13.6	13.7	15.2	43.4	—	—	—	—

PER SHARE DATA

	2000	1999	1998	1997	1996	1995	1994	1993	1992	1991
Dividends, Net Income ($)	0.00	0.00	0.00	0.00	0.00	0.01	—	—	—	—
Distrib'ns, Cap Gain ($)	1.48	4.27	0.88	1.59	0.74	1.13	—	—	—	—
Net Asset Value ($)	13.26	15.69	18.11	16.62	15.75	14.13	—	—	—	—
Expense Ratio (%)	na	1.26	1.35	1.35	1.35	1.35	—	—	—	—
Yield (%)	0.00	0.00	0.00	0.00	0.00	0.06	—	—	—	—
Portfolio Turnover (%)	na	133	74	85	107	137	—	—	—	—
Total Assets (Millions $)	93	109	124	109	125	61	—	—	—	—

PORTFOLIO (as of 6/30/00)

Portfolio Manager: committee - 1999

Investm't Category: Growth

✔ Domestic | Index
✔ Foreign | Sector
Asset Allocation | State Specific

Investment Style

✔ Large Cap | Mid Cap | Small Cap
Growth | ✔ Grth/Val | Value

Portfolio

2.4% cash | 0.0% corp bonds
97.6% stocks | 0.0% gov't bonds
0.0% pref/conv't pref | 0.0% muni bonds
0.0% conv't bds/wrnts | 0.0% other

SHAREHOLDER INFORMATION

Minimum Investment

Initial: $2,500 | Subsequent: $100

Minimum IRA Investment

Initial: $1,000 | Subsequent: $50

Maximum Fees

Load: none | 12b-1: none
Other: none

Services

✔ IRA
✔ Keogh
✔ Telephone Exchange

T Rowe Price Dividend Gr (PRDGX)

800-638-5660, 410-547-2000
www.troweprice.com

Growth & Income

PERFORMANCE — fund inception date: 12/31/92

	3yr Annual	5yr Annual	10yr Annual	Bull	Bear
Return (%)	7.1	15.0	na	15.7	5.9
Differ from Category (+/-)	-1.8 blw av	0.7 av	na	-17.8 blw av	6.0 abv av

Standard Deviation	Category Risk Index	Beta
13.4%—blw av	0.77—low	0.59

	2000	1999	1998	1997	1996	1995	1994	1993	1992	1991
Return (%)	10.0	-2.8	15.0	30.7	25.3	31.7	2.1	19.4	—	—
Differ from Category (+/-)	4.3	-13.6	2.2	3.8	5.6	2.2	2.6	5.6	—	—
Return, Tax-Adjusted (%)	9.3	-4.2	13.4	28.7	23.2	29.5	0.0	17.8	—	—

PER SHARE DATA

	2000	1999	1998	1997	1996	1995	1994	1993	1992	1991
Dividends, Net Income ($)	0.29	0.45	0.46	0.44	0.36	0.36	0.34	0.29	—	—
Distrib'ns, Cap Gain ($)	0.05	0.72	0.63	0.75	0.51	0.33	0.34	0.15	—	—
Net Asset Value ($)	21.88	20.21	22.01	20.13	16.37	13.81	11.04	11.48	—	—
Expense Ratio (%)	na	0.77	0.77	0.80	1.10	1.10	1.00	1.00	—	—
Yield (%)	1.32	2.15	2.03	2.10	2.13	2.54	2.98	2.49	—	—
Portfolio Turnover (%)	na	38	37	39	43	60	71	51	—	—
Total Assets (Millions $)	723	1,027	1,337	746	209	84	53	40	—	—

PORTFOLIO (as of 6/30/00)

Portfolio Manager: committee - 1992

Investm't Category: Growth & Income

✔ Domestic — Index
✔ Foreign — Sector
Asset Allocation — State Specific

Investment Style

✔ Large Cap — ✔ Mid Cap — Small Cap
Growth — Grth/Val — ✔ Value

Portfolio

3.5%	cash	0.0%	corp bonds
90.7%	stocks	3.0%	gov't bonds
0.3%	pref/conv't pref	0.0%	muni bonds
2.5%	conv't bds/wrnts	0.0%	other

SHAREHOLDER INFORMATION

Minimum Investment
Initial: $2,500 — Subsequent: $100

Minimum IRA Investment
Initial: $1,000 — Subsequent: $50

Maximum Fees
Load: none — 12b-1: none
Other: none

Services
✔ IRA
✔ Keogh
✔ Telephone Exchange

T Rowe Price Dvsfd Sm Cap (PRDSX)

800-638-5660, 410-547-2000
www.troweprice.com

Aggressive Growth

PERFORMANCE — fund inception date: 6/30/97

	3yr Annual	5yr Annual	10yr Annual	Bull	Bear
Return (%)	6.6	na	na	72.3	-27.1
Differ from Category (+/-)	-9.6 blw av	na	na	-46.9 blw av	-6.5 av

Standard Deviation	Category Risk Index	Beta
30.9%—high	0.95—av	1.18

	2000	1999	1998	1997	1996	1995	1994	1993	1992	1991
Return (%)	-8.2	27.6	3.5	—	—	—	—	—	—	—
Differ from Category (+/-)	-2.2	-29.9	-11.6	—	—	—	—	—	—	—
Return, Tax-Adjusted (%)	-8.7	27.6	3.4	—	—	—	—	—	—	—

PER SHARE DATA

	2000	1999	1998	1997	1996	1995	1994	1993	1992	1991
Dividends, Net Income ($)	0.00	0.00	0.00	—	—	—	—	—	—	—
Distrib'ns, Cap Gain ($)	0.40	0.00	0.03	—	—	—	—	—	—	—
Net Asset Value ($)	12.54	14.11	11.05	—	—	—	—	—	—	—
Expense Ratio (%)	na	1.25	1.25	—	—	—	—	—	—	—
Yield (%)	0.00	0.00	0.00	—	—	—	—	—	—	—
Portfolio Turnover (%)	na	49	40	—	—	—	—	—	—	—
Total Assets (Millions $)	76	74	70	—	—	—	—	—	—	—

PORTFOLIO (as of 6/30/00)

Portfolio Manager: committee - 1997

Investm't Category: Aggressive Growth

✔ Domestic	Index
✔ Foreign	Sector
Asset Allocation	State Specific

Investment Style

Large Cap	Mid Cap	✔ Small Cap
✔ Growth	Grth/Val	Value

Portfolio

2.9%	cash	0.0%	corp bonds
97.1%	stocks	0.0%	gov't bonds
0.0%	pref/conv't pref	0.0%	muni bonds
0.0%	conv't bds/wrnts	0.0%	other

SHAREHOLDER INFORMATION

Minimum Investment
Initial: $2,500 — Subsequent: $100

Minimum IRA Investment
Initial: $1,000 — Subsequent: $50

Maximum Fees
Load: 1.00% redemption — 12b-1: none
Other: redemption fee applies for 6 months

Services
✔ IRA
✔ Keogh
✔ Telephone Exchange

T Rowe Price Eq Index 500 (PREIX)

800-638-5660, 410-547-2000
www.troweprice.com

Growth & Income

PERFORMANCE — fund inception date: 3/30/90

	3yr Annual	5yr Annual	10yr Annual	Bull	Bear
Return (%)	11.9	18.0	16.9	55.7	-11.7
Differ from Category (+/-)	3.0 abv av	3.7 high	2.0 abv av	22.2 high	-11.6 blw av

Standard Deviation	Category Risk Index	Beta
17.6%—av	1.02—abv av	1.00

	2000	1999	1998	1997	1996	1995	1994	1993	1992	1991
Return (%)	-9.3	20.6	28.3	32.8	22.6	37.1	1.0	9.4	7.1	29.2
Differ from Category (+/-)	-15.0	9.8	15.5	5.9	2.9	7.6	1.5	-4.4	-4.5	1.1
Return, Tax-Adjusted (%)	-9.6	20.0	27.7	31.8	21.1	35.2	-0.3	8.3	6.3	27.8

PER SHARE DATA

	2000	1999	1998	1997	1996	1995	1994	1993	1992	1991
Dividends, Net Income ($)	0.33	0.34	0.34	0.34	0.38	0.40	0.36	0.32	0.30	0.34
Distrib'ns, Cap Gain ($)	0.08	0.31	0.09	0.25	0.34	0.30	0.16	0.01	0.01	0.08
Net Asset Value ($)	35.50	39.56	33.38	26.38	20.34	17.21	13.09	13.48	12.63	12.10
Expense Ratio (%)	na	0.40	0.40	0.40	0.40	0.45	0.45	0.45	0.45	0.45
Yield (%)	0.92	0.85	1.01	1.27	1.83	2.28	2.71	2.37	2.37	2.79
Portfolio Turnover (%)	na	5	5	0	1	1	1	0	0	5
Total Assets (Millions $)	4,123	5,049	3,347	1,908	807	457	270	166	128	22

PORTFOLIO (as of 6/30/00)

Portfolio Manager: committee - 1990

Investm't Category: Growth & Income

✔ Domestic
✔ Index
Foreign
Sector
Asset Allocation
State Specific

Investment Style

✔ Large Cap
Mid Cap
Small Cap
Growth
✔ Grth/Val
Value

Portfolio

0.0%	cash	0.0%	corp bonds
99.6%	stocks	0.0%	gov't bonds
0.0%	pref/conv't pref	0.0%	muni bonds
0.0%	conv't bds/wrnts	0.4%	other

SHAREHOLDER INFORMATION

Minimum Investment

Initial: $2,500 Subsequent: $100

Minimum IRA Investment

Initial: $1,000 Subsequent: $50

Maximum Fees

Load: 0.50% redemption 12b-1: none
Other: redemption fee applies for 6 months

Services

✔ IRA
Keogh
✔ Telephone Exchange

T Rowe Price Equity Inc (PRFDX)

800-638-5660, 410-547-2000
www.troweprice.com

Growth & Income

PERFORMANCE

fund inception date: 10/31/85

	3yr Annual	5yr Annual	10yr Annual	Bull	Bear
Return (%)	8.6	14.7	16.3	21.5	11.2
Differ from Category (+/-)	-0.3 av	0.4 av	1.4 abv av	-12.0 blw av	11.3 high

Standard Deviation	Category Risk Index	Beta
15.8%—av	0.91—blw av	0.58

	2000	1999	1998	1997	1996	1995	1994	1993	1992	1991
Return (%)	13.1	3.8	9.2	28.8	20.3	33.3	4.5	14.8	14.1	25.2
Differ from Category (+/-)	7.4	-7.0	-3.6	1.9	0.6	3.8	5.0	1.0	2.5	-2.9
Return, Tax-Adjusted (%)	10.1	1.5	7.1	25.7	17.8	30.7	1.7	12.1	12.0	23.4

PER SHARE DATA

	2000	1999	1998	1997	1996	1995	1994	1993	1992	1991
Dividends, Net Income ($)	0.51	0.53	0.61	0.66	0.65	0.65	0.59	0.54	0.63	0.61
Distrib'ns, Cap Gain ($)	2.64	1.97	1.49	2.14	0.84	0.54	0.81	0.72	0.39	0.10
Net Asset Value ($)	24.67	24.81	26.32	26.07	22.54	20.01	15.98	16.65	15.63	14.62
Expense Ratio (%)	na	0.77	0.77	0.79	0.81	0.85	0.88	0.91	0.97	1.05
Yield (%)	1.86	1.97	2.19	2.33	2.78	3.16	3.51	3.10	3.93	4.14
Portfolio Turnover (%)	na	22	23	23	25	28	36	31	30	34
Total Assets (Millions $)	10,294	12,321	13,495	12,771	7,818	5,214	3,203	2,851	2,091	1,335

PORTFOLIO (as of 6/30/00)

Portfolio Manager: committee - 1985

Investm't Category: Growth & Income

✔ Domestic
Index
✔ Foreign
Sector
Asset Allocation
State Specific

Investment Style

✔ Large Cap
✔ Mid Cap
Small Cap
Growth
Grth/Val
✔ Value

Portfolio

4.7% cash
95.3% stocks
0.0% pref/conv't pref
0.0% conv't bds/wrnts
0.0% corp bonds
0.0% gov't bonds
0.0% muni bonds
0.0% other

SHAREHOLDER INFORMATION

Minimum Investment

Initial: $2,500
Subsequent: $100

Minimum IRA Investment

Initial: $1,000
Subsequent: $50

Maximum Fees

Load: none
12b-1: none
Other: none

Services

✔ IRA
✔ Keogh
✔ Telephone Exchange

T Rowe Price Fincl Svc (PRISX)

800-638-5660, 410-547-2000
www.troweprice.com

Growth & Income

PERFORMANCE — fund inception date: 9/30/96

	3yr Annual	5yr Annual	10yr Annual	Bull	Bear
Return (%)	15.7	na	na	25.3	17.8
Differ from Category (+/-)	6.8 high	na	na	-8.2 blw av	17.9 high

Standard Deviation	Category Risk Index	Beta
25.1%—abv av	1.44—high	1.08

	2000	1999	1998	1997	1996	1995	1994	1993	1992	1991
Return (%)	36.7	1.7	11.5	41.4	—	—	—	—	—	—
Differ from Category (+/-)	31.0	-9.1	-1.3	14.5	—	—	—	—	—	—
Return, Tax-Adjusted (%)	35.7	0.4	10.6	40.4	—	—	—	—	—	—

PER SHARE DATA

	2000	1999	1998	1997	1996	1995	1994	1993	1992	1991
Dividends, Net Income ($)	0.09	0.10	0.16	0.10	—	—	—	—	—	—
Distrib'ns, Cap Gain ($)	0.55	0.85	0.34	0.33	—	—	—	—	—	—
Net Asset Value ($)	21.38	16.12	16.82	15.56	—	—	—	—	—	—
Expense Ratio (%)	na	1.14	1.19	1.25	—	—	—	—	—	—
Yield (%)	0.41	0.58	0.93	0.62	—	—	—	—	—	—
Portfolio Turnover (%)	na	37	47	46	—	—	—	—	—	—
Total Assets (Millions $)	286	159	224	177	—	—	—	—	—	—

PORTFOLIO (as of 6/30/00)

Portfolio Manager: committee - 1996

Investm't Category: Growth & Income

✔ Domestic — Index
✔ Foreign — ✔ Sector
Asset Allocation — State Specific

Investment Style

✔ Large Cap — Mid Cap — Small Cap
Growth — Grth/Val — ✔ Value

Portfolio

6.3%	cash	0.0%	corp bonds
93.7%	stocks	0.0%	gov't bonds
0.0%	pref/conv't pref	0.0%	muni bonds
0.0%	conv't bds/wrnts	0.0%	other

SHAREHOLDER INFORMATION

Minimum Investment
Initial: $2,500 — Subsequent: $100

Minimum IRA Investment
Initial: $1,000 — Subsequent: $50

Maximum Fees
Load: none — 12b-1: none
Other: none

Services
✔ IRA
✔ Keogh
✔ Telephone Exchange

T Rowe Price Growth Inc (PRGIX)

800-638-5660, 410-547-2000
www.troweprice.com

Growth & Income

PERFORMANCE — fund inception date: 12/21/82

	3yr Annual	5yr Annual	10yr Annual	Bull	Bear
Return (%)	7.5	14.0	15.7	22.5	3.1
Differ from Category (+/-)	-1.4 blw av	-0.3 av	0.8 av	-11.0 blw av	3.2 abv av

Standard Deviation	Category Risk Index	Beta
15.7%—av	0.90—blw av	0.74

	2000	1999	1998	1997	1996	1995	1994	1993	1992	1991
Return (%)	8.9	3.7	9.9	23.5	25.6	30.9	-0.1	12.9	15.3	31.5
Differ from Category (+/-)	3.2	-7.1	-2.9	-3.4	5.9	1.4	0.4	-0.9	3.7	3.4
Return, Tax-Adjusted (%)	6.8	1.2	7.4	21.6	23.2	28.3	-1.9	10.8	13.6	29.9

PER SHARE DATA

	2000	1999	1998	1997	1996	1995	1994	1993	1992	1991
Dividends, Net Income ($)	0.34	0.51	0.53	0.56	0.51	0.59	0.49	0.47	0.60	0.56
Distrib'ns, Cap Gain ($)	1.83	2.25	2.13	0.97	0.90	0.60	0.42	0.48	0.15	0.00
Net Asset Value ($)	24.44	24.44	26.25	26.36	22.63	19.18	15.63	16.57	15.53	14.16
Expense Ratio (%)	na	0.77	0.77	0.78	0.82	0.81	0.81	0.83	0.85	0.93
Yield (%)	1.29	1.91	1.86	2.04	2.16	2.98	3.05	2.75	3.82	3.95
Portfolio Turnover (%)	na	20	21	15	13	26	25	22	30	48
Total Assets (Millions $)	3,089	3,439	3,563	3,446	2,488	1,748	1,228	1,167	839	655

PORTFOLIO (as of 6/30/00)

Portfolio Manager: committee - 1987

Investm't Category: Growth & Income

✔ Domestic	Index
✔ Foreign	Sector
Asset Allocation	State Specific

Investment Style

✔ Large Cap	Mid Cap	Small Cap
Growth	Grth/Val	✔ Value

Portfolio

4.7% cash	0.0% corp bonds
92.9% stocks	0.0% gov't bonds
0.5% pref/conv't pref	0.0% muni bonds
1.9% conv't bds/wrnts	0.0% other

SHAREHOLDER INFORMATION

Minimum Investment
Initial: $2,500 Subsequent: $100

Minimum IRA Investment
Initial: $1,000 Subsequent: $50

Maximum Fees
Load: none 12b-1: none
Other: none

Services
✔ IRA
✔ Keogh
✔ Telephone Exchange

T Rowe Price Growth Stock (PRGFX)

800-638-5660, 410-547-2000
www.troweprice.com

Growth

PERFORMANCE — fund inception date: 4/11/50

	3yr Annual	5yr Annual	10yr Annual	Bull	Bear
Return (%)	15.9	19.1	17.9	59.1	-10.3
Differ from Category (+/-)	4.9 high	3.0 abv av	1.1 abv av	9.4 abv av	-4.9 av

Standard Deviation	Category Risk Index	Beta
18.8%—av	0.97—blw av	1.02

	2000	1999	1998	1997	1996	1995	1994	1993	1992	1991
Return (%)	0.2	22.1	27.4	26.5	21.7	30.9	0.8	15.5	5.9	33.7
Differ from Category (+/-)	-3.3	3.2	13.1	-0.6	-0.6	0.5	1.0	0.9	-6.7	-3.9
Return, Tax-Adjusted (%)	-3.6	18.5	24.1	23.2	18.9	28.9	-1.8	13.7	4.0	31.9

PER SHARE DATA

	2000	1999	1998	1997	1996	1995	1994	1993	1992	1991
Dividends, Net Income ($)	0.07	0.10	0.25	0.20	0.19	0.23	0.18	0.14	0.18	0.25
Distrib'ns, Cap Gain ($)	6.28	5.42	4.27	3.87	2.06	0.97	1.66	0.99	1.03	0.62
Net Asset Value ($)	27.20	33.27	32.07	28.99	26.18	23.35	18.75	20.42	18.66	18.75
Expense Ratio (%)	na	0.74	0.74	0.75	0.77	0.80	0.81	0.82	0.83	0.85
Yield (%)	0.20	0.25	0.68	0.60	0.67	0.94	0.88	0.65	0.91	1.29
Portfolio Turnover (%)	na	56	55	40	49	44	54	35	27	32
Total Assets (Millions $)	5,407	5,672	5,041	3,988	3,430	2,761	2,067	1,975	1,946	1,846

PORTFOLIO (as of 6/30/00)

Portfolio Manager: committee - 1997

Investm't Category: Growth

✔ Domestic	Index
✔ Foreign	Sector
Asset Allocation	State Specific

Investment Style

✔ Large Cap	Mid Cap	Small Cap
✔ Growth	Grth/Val	Value

Portfolio

3.0%	cash	0.0%	corp bonds
96.8%	stocks	0.0%	gov't bonds
0.0%	pref/conv't pref	0.0%	muni bonds
0.2%	conv't bds/wrnts	0.0%	other

SHAREHOLDER INFORMATION

Minimum Investment
Initial: $2,500 Subsequent: $100

Minimum IRA Investment
Initial: $1,000 Subsequent: $50

Maximum Fees
Load: none 12b-1: none
Other: none

Services
✔ IRA
✔ Keogh
✔ Telephone Exchange

T Rowe Price Hlth Science (PRHSX)

800-225-5660, 410-547-2000
www.troweprice.com

Aggressive Growth

PERFORMANCE — fund inception date: 12/29/95

	3yr Annual	5yr Annual	10yr Annual	Bull	Bear
Return (%)	26.2	24.9	na	45.2	23.5
Differ from Category (+/-)	10.0 abv av	10.3 high	na	-74.0 low	44.1 high

Standard Deviation	Category Risk Index	Beta
30.5%—high	0.94—av	0.52

	2000	1999	1998	1997	1996	1995	1994	1993	1992	1991
Return (%)	52.1	7.9	22.3	19.4	26.7	—	—	—	—	—
Differ from Category (+/-)	58.1	-49.6	7.2	4.6	8.4	—	—	—	—	—
Return, Tax-Adjusted (%)	48.9	6.3	21.3	17.8	25.5	—	—	—	—	—

PER SHARE DATA

	2000	1999	1998	1997	1996	1995	1994	1993	1992	1991
Dividends, Net Income ($)	0.00	0.00	0.00	0.00	0.00	—	—	—	—	—
Distrib'ns, Cap Gain ($)	2.48	1.26	0.66	0.97	0.40	—	—	—	—	—
Net Asset Value ($)	21.70	15.93	16.01	13.66	12.27	—	—	—	—	—
Expense Ratio (%)	na	1.11	1.16	1.18	1.35	—	—	—	—	—
Yield (%)	0.00	0.00	0.00	0.00	0.00	—	—	—	—	—
Portfolio Turnover (%)	na	82	86	104	133	—	—	—	—	—
Total Assets (Millions $)	863	302	316	271	193	—	—	—	—	—

PORTFOLIO (as of 6/30/00)

Portfolio Manager: committee - 1998

Investm't Category: Aggressive Growth

✔ Domestic
Foreign
Asset Allocation
Index
✔ Sector
State Specific

Investment Style

Large Cap
✔ Mid Cap
✔ Small Cap
✔ Growth
Grth/Val
Value

Portfolio

6.8%	cash	0.0%	corp bonds
93.4%	stocks	0.0%	gov't bonds
0.2%	pref/conv't pref	0.0%	muni bonds
0.0%	conv't bds/wrnts	-0.4%	other

SHAREHOLDER INFORMATION

Minimum Investment

Initial: $2,500 Subsequent: $100

Minimum IRA Investment

Initial: $1,000 Subsequent: $50

Maximum Fees

Load: none 12b-1: none
Other: none

Services

✔ IRA
✔ Keogh
✔ Telephone Exchange

T Rowe Price Intl: Discvr (PRIDX)

800-638-5660, 410-547-2000
www.troweprice.com

International Stock

PERFORMANCE — fund inception date: 12/30/88

	3yr Annual	5yr Annual	10yr Annual	Bull	Bear
Return (%)	31.6	19.6	12.6	166.0	-31.5
Differ from Category (+/-)	22.7 high	11.3 high	3.6 high	75.1 high	-7.5 blw av

Standard Deviation	Category Risk Index	Beta
29.0%—high	1.28—abv av	0.71

	2000	1999	1998	1997	1996	1995	1994	1993	1992	1991
Return (%)	-15.6	155.0	6.1	-5.6	13.8	-4.3	-7.6	49.8	-9.0	11.6
Differ from Category (+/-)	3.8	94.3	0.3	-6.9	-0.7	-13.6	-4.5	9.6	-5.5	-1.4
Return, Tax-Adjusted (%)	-18.7	151.4	5.6	-5.9	13.4	-4.5	-9.1	49.5	-9.3	11.2

PER SHARE DATA

	2000	1999	1998	1997	1996	1995	1994	1993	1992	1991
Dividends, Net Income ($)	0.00	0.00	0.01	0.00	0.07	0.10	0.06	0.07	0.13	0.13
Distrib'ns, Cap Gain ($)	5.83	2.81	0.30	0.25	0.06	0.02	0.87	0.02	0.00	0.00
Net Asset Value ($)	25.45	36.77	15.65	15.05	16.22	14.36	15.14	17.41	11.68	12.99
Expense Ratio (%)	na	1.42	1.47	1.41	1.45	1.50	1.50	1.50	1.50	1.50
Yield (%)	0.00	0.00	0.06	0.00	0.42	0.69	0.37	0.40	1.11	1.00
Portfolio Turnover (%)	na	98	34	72	52	43	57	72	38	56
Total Assets (Millions $)	800	686	193	228	322	302	437	392	166	166

PORTFOLIO (as of 6/30/00)

Portfolio Manager: committee - 1988

Investm't Category: International Stock

Domestic	Index
✔ Foreign	Sector
Asset Allocation	State Specific

Investment Style

Large Cap	Mid Cap	Small Cap
Growth	Grth/Val	Value

Portfolio

9.5%	cash	0.0%	corp bonds
90.5%	stocks	0.0%	gov't bonds
0.0%	pref/conv't pref	0.0%	muni bonds
0.0%	conv't bds/wrnts	0.0%	other

SHAREHOLDER INFORMATION

Minimum Investment

Initial: $2,500 Subsequent: $100

Minimum IRA Investment

Initial: $1,000 Subsequent: $50

Maximum Fees

Load: 2.00% redemption 12b-1: none

Other: redemption fee applies for 12 months

Services

✔ IRA

✔ Keogh

✔ Telephone Exchange

T Rowe Price Intl: Em Mk Stk (PRMSX)

800-638-5660, 410-547-2000
www.troweprice.com

International Stock

PERFORMANCE — fund inception date: 3/31/95

	3yr Annual	5yr Annual	10yr Annual	Bull	Bear
Return (%)	-0.5	2.1	na	120.9	-33.7
Differ from Category (+/-)	-9.4 low	-6.2 blw av	na	30.0 high	-9.7 blw av

Standard Deviation	Category Risk Index	Beta
33.0%—high	1.45—high	1.28

	2000	1999	1998	1997	1996	1995	1994	1993	1992	1991
Return (%)	-26.3	87.4	-28.7	1.2	11.8	—	—	—	—	—
Differ from Category (+/-)	-6.9	26.7	-34.5	-0.1	-2.7	—	—	—	—	—
Return, Tax-Adjusted (%)	-26.3	87.4	-28.8	0.9	10.8	—	—	—	—	—

PER SHARE DATA

	2000	1999	1998	1997	1996	1995	1994	1993	1992	1991
Dividends, Net Income ($)	0.00	0.00	0.04	0.00	0.04	—	—	—	—	—
Distrib'ns, Cap Gain ($)	0.00	0.00	0.00	0.15	0.30	—	—	—	—	—
Net Asset Value ($)	11.43	15.52	8.28	11.68	11.69	—	—	—	—	—
Expense Ratio (%)	na	1.75	1.75	1.75	1.75	—	—	—	—	—
Yield (%)	0.00	0.00	0.48	0.00	0.33	—	—	—	—	—
Portfolio Turnover (%)	na	59	54	84	41	—	—	—	—	—
Total Assets (Millions $)	139	162	72	123	73	—	—	—	—	—

PORTFOLIO (as of 6/30/00)

Portfolio Manager: committee - 1995

Investm't Category: International Stock

- Domestic
- ✔ Foreign
- Asset Allocation
- Index
- Sector
- State Specific

Investment Style

Large Cap, Mid Cap, Small Cap, Growth, Grth/Val, Value

Portfolio

4.0% cash	0.0% corp bonds
96.0% stocks	0.0% gov't bonds
0.0% pref/conv't pref	0.0% muni bonds
0.0% conv't bds/wrnts	0.0% other

SHAREHOLDER INFORMATION

Minimum Investment

Initial: $2,500 — Subsequent: $100

Minimum IRA Investment

Initial: $1,000 — Subsequent: $50

Maximum Fees

Load: 2.00% redemption — 12b-1: none

Other: redemption fee applies for 12 months

Services

- ✔ IRA
- ✔ Keogh
- ✔ Telephone Exchange

T Rowe Price Intl: Europn (PRESX)

800-638-5660, 410-547-2000
www.troweprice.com

International Stock

PERFORMANCE — fund inception date: 2/28/90

	3yr Annual	5yr Annual	10yr Annual	Bull	Bear
Return (%)	12.0	15.6	12.9	35.4	-12.7
Differ from Category (+/-)	3.1 abv av	7.3 high	3.9 high	-55.5 low	11.3 high

Standard Deviation	Category Risk Index	Beta
15.8%—av	0.70—low	0.57

	2000	1999	1998	1997	1996	1995	1994	1993	1992	1991
Return (%)	-6.6	19.7	25.8	17.0	25.8	21.8	4.0	27.2	-5.5	7.3
Differ from Category (+/-)	12.8	-41.0	20.0	15.7	11.3	12.5	7.1	-13.0	-2.0	-5.7
Return, Tax-Adjusted (%)	-8.0	17.6	22.9	15.2	24.6	20.5	3.4	27.0	-6.0	7.0

PER SHARE DATA

	2000	1999	1998	1997	1996	1995	1994	1993	1992	1991
Dividends, Net Income ($)	0.16	0.14	0.28	0.25	0.26	0.21	0.12	0.04	0.17	0.08
Distrib'ns, Cap Gain ($)	1.42	1.90	2.18	1.01	0.20	0.25	0.05	0.01	0.00	0.00
Net Asset Value ($)	20.64	23.86	21.77	19.36	17.62	14.37	12.17	11.86	9.36	10.09
Expense Ratio (%)	na	1.05	1.05	1.06	1.12	1.20	1.25	1.35	1.48	1.71
Yield (%)	0.72	0.54	1.16	1.22	1.45	1.43	0.98	0.33	1.81	0.79
Portfolio Turnover (%)	na	15	26	17	14	17	24	21	52	58
Total Assets (Millions $)	1,177	1,587	1,548	1,020	765	531	366	289	173	103

PORTFOLIO (as of 6/30/00)

Portfolio Manager: committee - 1990

Investm't Category: International Stock

Domestic	Index
✔ Foreign	Sector
Asset Allocation	State Specific

Investment Style

Large Cap	Mid Cap	Small Cap
Growth	Grth/Val	Value

Portfolio

7.0%	cash	0.0%	corp bonds
93.0%	stocks	0.0%	gov't bonds
0.0%	pref/conv't pref	0.0%	muni bonds
0.0%	conv't bds/wrnts	0.0%	other

SHAREHOLDER INFORMATION

Minimum Investment
Initial: $2,500 Subsequent: $100

Minimum IRA Investment
Initial: $1,000 Subsequent: $50

Maximum Fees
Load: none 12b-1: none
Other: none

Services
✔ IRA
✔ Keogh
✔ Telephone Exchange

T Rowe Price Intl: Japan (PRJPX)

800-638-5660, 410-547-2000
www.troweprice.com

International Stock

PERFORMANCE

fund inception date: 12/27/91

	3yr Annual	5yr Annual	10yr Annual	Bull	Bear
Return (%)	13.3	0.2	na	160.1	-28.3
Differ from Category (+/-)	4.4 abv av	-8.1 low	na	69.2 high	-4.3 blw av

Standard Deviation	Category Risk Index	Beta
24.9%—abv av	1.10—abv av	0.71

	2000	1999	1998	1997	1996	1995	1994	1993	1992	1991
Return (%)	-37.2	112.7	9.1	-22.0	-10.9	-3.1	15.0	20.6	-13.4	—
Differ from Category (+/-)	-17.8	52.0	3.3	-23.3	-25.4	-12.4	18.1	-19.6	-9.9	—
Return, Tax-Adjusted (%)	-38.7	112.5	9.1	-22.0	-10.9	-3.1	12.6	17.8	-13.4	—

PER SHARE DATA

	2000	1999	1998	1997	1996	1995	1994	1993	1992	1991
Dividends, Net Income ($)	0.00	0.00	0.00	0.00	0.00	0.00	0.00	0.00	0.00	—
Distrib'ns, Cap Gain ($)	1.20	0.05	0.00	0.00	0.00	0.00	0.81	0.85	0.00	—
Net Asset Value ($)	8.93	15.92	7.51	6.88	8.83	9.92	10.24	9.61	8.66	—
Expense Ratio (%)	na	1.14	1.32	1.24	1.32	1.50	1.50	1.50	1.50	—
Yield (%)	0.00	0.00	0.00	0.00	0.00	0.00	0.00	0.00	0.00	—
Portfolio Turnover (%)	na	58	66	32	29	62	61	61	42	—
Total Assets (Millions $)	280	595	181	152	146	207	169	70	45	—

PORTFOLIO (as of 6/30/00)

Portfolio Manager: committee - 1991

Investm't Category: International Stock

Domestic	Index
✔ Foreign	Sector
Asset Allocation	State Specific

Investment Style

Large Cap	Mid Cap	Small Cap
Growth	Grth/Val	Value

Portfolio

2.7%	cash	0.0%	corp bonds
97.3%	stocks	0.0%	gov't bonds
0.0%	pref/conv't pref	0.0%	muni bonds
0.0%	conv't bds/wrnts	0.0%	other

SHAREHOLDER INFORMATION

Minimum Investment
Initial: $2,500 Subsequent: $100

Minimum IRA Investment
Initial: $1,000 Subsequent: $50

Maximum Fees
Load: none 12b-1: none
Other: none

Services
✔ IRA
✔ Keogh
✔ Telephone Exchange

T Rowe Price Intl: Lat Am (PRLAX)

800-638-5660, 410-547-2000
www.troweprice.com

International Stock

PERFORMANCE

fund inception date: 12/29/93

	3yr Annual	5yr Annual	10yr Annual	Bull	Bear
Return (%)	-2.9	8.2	na	85.3	-22.3
Differ from Category (+/-)	-11.8 low	-0.1 av	na	-5.6 av	1.7 av

Standard Deviation	Category Risk Index	Beta
39.4%—high	1.74—high	1.43

	2000	1999	1998	1997	1996	1995	1994	1993	1992	1991
Return (%)	-11.1	59.3	-35.4	31.8	23.3	-18.7	-15.9	—	—	—
Differ from Category (+/-)	8.3	-1.4	-41.2	30.5	8.8	-28.0	-12.8	—	—	—
Return, Tax-Adjusted (%)	-11.2	59.0	-35.9	31.2	22.5	-18.9	-15.9	—	—	—

PER SHARE DATA

	2000	1999	1998	1997	1996	1995	1994	1993	1992	1991
Dividends, Net Income ($)	0.04	0.04	0.14	0.12	0.11	0.06	0.00	—	—	—
Distrib'ns, Cap Gain ($)	0.00	0.00	0.00	0.00	0.03	0.00	0.00	—	—	—
Net Asset Value ($)	9.56	10.81	6.81	10.77	8.26	6.81	8.45	—	—	—
Expense Ratio (%)	na	1.62	1.53	1.47	1.66	1.82	1.99	—	—	—
Yield (%)	0.41	0.37	2.05	1.11	1.32	0.88	0.00	—	—	—
Portfolio Turnover (%)	na	43	19	32	22	18	12	—	—	—
Total Assets (Millions $)	202	268	182	432	211	149	163	—	—	—

PORTFOLIO (as of 6/30/00)

Portfolio Manager: committee - 1993

Investm't Category: International Stock

Domestic	Index
✔ Foreign	Sector
Asset Allocation	State Specific

Investment Style

Large Cap	Mid Cap	Small Cap
Growth	Grth/Val	Value

Portfolio

2.8% cash	0.0% corp bonds
97.2% stocks	0.0% gov't bonds
0.0% pref/conv't pref	0.0% muni bonds
0.0% conv't bds/wrnts	0.0% other

SHAREHOLDER INFORMATION

Minimum Investment
Initial: $2,500 Subsequent: $100

Minimum IRA Investment
Initial: $1,000 Subsequent: $50

Maximum Fees
Load: 2.00% redemption 12b-1: none
Other: redemption fee applies for 12 months

Services
✔ IRA
✔ Keogh
✔ Telephone Exchange

T Rowe Price Intl: Nw Asia (PRASX)

800-638-5660, 410-547-2000
www.troweprice.com

International Stock

PERFORMANCE

fund inception date: 9/28/90

	3yr Annual	5yr Annual	10yr Annual	Bull	Bear
Return (%)	7.1	-2.5	5.7	155.5	-36.2
Differ from Category (+/-)	-1.8 blw av	-10.8 low	-3.3 low	64.6 high	-12.2 low

Standard Deviation	Category Risk Index	Beta
30.5%—high	1.35—abv av	0.99

	2000	1999	1998	1997	1996	1995	1994	1993	1992	1991
Return (%)	-30.7	99.8	-11.1	-37.1	13.5	3.7	-19.1	78.7	11.2	19.3
Differ from Category (+/-)	-11.3	39.1	-16.9	-38.4	-1.0	-5.6	-16.0	38.5	14.7	6.3
Return, Tax-Adjusted (%)	-30.7	99.4	-11.7	-37.4	13.1	3.2	-20.3	77.6	10.0	18.6

PER SHARE DATA

	2000	1999	1998	1997	1996	1995	1994	1993	1992	1991
Dividends, Net Income ($)	0.00	0.04	0.09	0.08	0.06	0.09	0.07	0.03	0.10	0.10
Distrib'ns, Cap Gain ($)	0.00	0.00	0.00	0.00	0.01	0.00	0.89	0.19	0.13	0.00
Net Asset Value ($)	6.90	9.97	5.01	5.74	9.26	8.22	8.01	11.10	6.34	5.91
Expense Ratio (%)	na	1.21	1.29	1.10	1.11	1.15	1.22	1.29	1.51	1.75
Yield (%)	0.00	0.40	1.79	1.39	0.64	1.09	0.78	0.31	1.54	1.69
Portfolio Turnover (%)	na	69	68	41	42	63	63	40	36	49
Total Assets (Millions $)	807	1,374	622	782	2,181	1,880	1,987	2,247	314	102

PORTFOLIO (as of 6/30/00)

Portfolio Manager: committee - 1990

Investm't Category: International Stock

Domestic	Index
✔ Foreign	Sector
Asset Allocation	State Specific

Investment Style

Large Cap	Mid Cap	Small Cap
Growth	Grth/Val	Value

Portfolio

7.8%	cash	0.0%	corp bonds
92.1%	stocks	0.0%	gov't bonds
0.0%	pref/conv't pref	0.0%	muni bonds
0.1%	conv't bds/wrnts	0.0%	other

SHAREHOLDER INFORMATION

Minimum Investment

Initial: $2,500 Subsequent: $100

Minimum IRA Investment

Initial: $1,000 Subsequent: $50

Maximum Fees

Load: none 12b-1: none

Other: none

Services

✔ IRA

✔ Keogh

✔ Telephone Exchange

T Rowe Price Intl: Stock (PRITX)

800-638-5660, 410-547-2000
www.troweprice.com

International Stock

PERFORMANCE — fund inception date: 5/9/80

	3yr Annual	5yr Annual	10yr Annual	Bull	Bear
Return (%)	9.0	9.0	10.3	55.5	-20.2
Differ from Category (+/-)	0.1 av	0.7 av	1.3 av	-35.4 blw av	3.8 abv av

Standard Deviation	Category Risk Index	Beta
17.6%—av	0.78—blw av	0.73

	2000	1999	1998	1997	1996	1995	1994	1993	1992	1991
Return (%)	-17.0	34.6	16.1	2.7	15.9	11.3	-0.7	40.1	-3.4	15.8
Differ from Category (+/-)	2.4	-26.1	10.3	1.4	1.4	2.0	2.4	-0.1	0.1	2.8
Return, Tax-Adjusted (%)	-18.4	33.0	14.9	1.3	14.8	10.1	-2.5	39.0	-4.3	13.7

PER SHARE DATA

	2000	1999	1998	1997	1996	1995	1994	1993	1992	1991
Dividends, Net Income ($)	0.09	0.13	0.22	0.20	0.18	0.18	0.12	0.09	0.16	0.15
Distrib'ns, Cap Gain ($)	1.18	0.91	0.35	0.55	0.20	0.20	0.62	0.20	0.16	0.49
Net Asset Value ($)	14.52	19.03	14.99	13.42	13.80	12.23	11.32	12.16	8.89	9.54
Expense Ratio (%)	na	0.85	0.85	0.85	0.88	0.91	0.97	1.01	1.05	1.10
Yield (%)	0.57	0.65	1.43	1.43	1.28	1.44	1.00	0.72	1.76	1.49
Portfolio Turnover (%)	na	17	12	15	11	17	22	29	38	45
Total Assets (Millions $)	9,796	12,673	10,141	9,720	9,340	6,703	5,786	4,296	1,949	1,476

PORTFOLIO (as of 6/30/00)

Portfolio Manager: committee - 1980

Investm't Category: International Stock

Domestic	Index
✔ Foreign	Sector
Asset Allocation	State Specific

Investment Style

Large Cap	Mid Cap	Small Cap
Growth	Grth/Val	Value

Portfolio

2.8% cash	0.0% corp bonds
95.3% stocks	0.0% gov't bonds
1.9% pref/conv't pref	0.0% muni bonds
0.0% conv't bds/wrnts	0.0% other

SHAREHOLDER INFORMATION

Minimum Investment
Initial: $2,500 — Subsequent: $100

Minimum IRA Investment
Initial: $1,000 — Subsequent: $50

Maximum Fees
Load: none — 12b-1: none
Other: none

Services
✔ IRA
✔ Keogh
✔ Telephone Exchange

T Rowe Price Media & Tele (PRMTX)

800-638-5660, 410-547-2000
www.troweprice.com

Aggressive Growth

PERFORMANCE — fund inception date: 7/28/97

	3yr Annual	5yr Annual	10yr Annual	Bull	Bear
Return (%)	25.0	na	na	168.9	-34.5
Differ from Category (+/-)	8.8 abv av	na	na	49.7 abv av	-13.9 blw av

Standard Deviation	Category Risk Index	Beta
31.1%—high	0.96—av	1.40

	2000	1999	1998	1997	1996	1995	1994	1993	1992	1991
Return (%)	-25.1	93.0	35.1	—	—	—	—	—	—	—
Differ from Category (+/-)	-19.1	35.5	20.0	—	—	—	—	—	—	—
Return, Tax-Adjusted (%)	-29.7	90.1	34.1	—	—	—	—	—	—	—

PER SHARE DATA

	2000	1999	1998	1997	1996	1995	1994	1993	1992	1991
Dividends, Net Income ($)	0.37	0.00	0.00	—	—	—	—	—	—	—
Distrib'ns, Cap Gain ($)	8.60	3.22	0.86	—	—	—	—	—	—	—
Net Asset Value ($)	21.65	39.99	22.54	—	—	—	—	—	—	—
Expense Ratio (%)	na	0.93	1.03	—	—	—	—	—	—	—
Yield (%)	1.22	0.00	0.00	—	—	—	—	—	—	—
Portfolio Turnover (%)	na	58	49	—	—	—	—	—	—	—
Total Assets (Millions $)	813	930	246	—	—	—	—	—	—	—

PORTFOLIO (as of 6/30/00)

Portfolio Manager: committee - 2000

Investm't Category: Aggressive Growth

✔ Domestic
Index
✔ Foreign
✔ Sector
Asset Allocation
State Specific

Investment Style

✔ Large Cap
✔ Mid Cap
✔ Small Cap
✔ Growth
Grth/Val
Value

Portfolio

3.8%	cash	0.0%	corp bonds
95.8%	stocks	0.0%	gov't bonds
0.4%	pref/conv't pref	0.0%	muni bonds
0.0%	conv't bds/wrnts	0.0%	other

SHAREHOLDER INFORMATION

Minimum Investment

Initial: $2,500 Subsequent: $100

Minimum IRA Investment

Initial: $1,000 Subsequent: $50

Maximum Fees

Load: none 12b-1: none
Other: none

Services

✔ IRA
✔ Keogh
✔ Telephone Exchange

T Rowe Price Mid-Cap Grth (RPMGX)

800-638-5660, 410-547-2000
www.troweprice.com

Growth

PERFORMANCE

fund inception date: 6/30/92

	3yr Annual	5yr Annual	10yr Annual	Bull	Bear
Return (%)	17.5	19.1	na	66.8	-9.5
Differ from Category (+/-)	6.5 high	3.0 abv av	na	17.1 abv av	-4.1 av

Standard Deviation	Category Risk Index	Beta
22.4%—abv av	1.15—abv av	1.10

	2000	1999	1998	1997	1996	1995	1994	1993	1992	1991
Return (%)	7.4	23.7	21.9	18.3	24.8	40.9	0.2	26.2	—	—
Differ from Category (+/-)	3.9	4.8	7.6	-8.8	2.5	10.5	0.4	11.6	—	—
Return, Tax-Adjusted (%)	5.7	22.5	21.3	18.0	23.8	39.4	-0.4	25.5	—	—

PER SHARE DATA

	2000	1999	1998	1997	1996	1995	1994	1993	1992	1991
Dividends, Net Income ($)	0.00	0.00	0.00	0.00	0.00	0.00	0.00	0.00	—	—
Distrib'ns, Cap Gain ($)	3.27	1.88	0.73	0.30	0.69	0.79	0.37	0.30	—	—
Net Asset Value ($)	39.79	40.13	34.08	28.60	24.43	20.13	14.85	15.18	—	—
Expense Ratio (%)	na	0.87	0.91	0.95	1.04	1.25	1.25	1.25	—	—
Yield (%)	0.00	0.00	0.00	0.00	0.00	0.00	0.00	0.00	—	—
Portfolio Turnover (%)	na	53	47	42	38	83	48	62	—	—
Total Assets (Millions $)	5,899	5,243	3,310	1,838	1,021	263	100	65	—	—

PORTFOLIO (as of 6/30/00)

Portfolio Manager: committee - 1992

Investm't Category: Growth

✔ Domestic — Index
✔ Foreign — Sector
Asset Allocation — State Specific

Investment Style

Large Cap — ✔ Mid Cap — Small Cap
✔ Growth — Grth/Val — Value

Portfolio

7.9% cash — 0.0% corp bonds
92.1% stocks — 0.0% gov't bonds
0.0% pref/conv't pref — 0.0% muni bonds
0.0% conv't bds/wrnts — 0.0% other

SHAREHOLDER INFORMATION

Minimum Investment
Initial: $2,500 — Subsequent: $100

Minimum IRA Investment
Initial: $1,000 — Subsequent: $50

Maximum Fees
Load: none — 12b-1: none
Other: none

Services
✔ IRA
✔ Keogh
✔ Telephone Exchange

T Rowe Price Mid-Cap Val

800-638-5660, 410-547-2000
www.troweprice.com

(TRMCX)

Growth

PERFORMANCE — fund inception date: 6/28/96

	3yr Annual	5yr Annual	10yr Annual	Bull	Bear
Return (%)	8.8	na	na	21.9	8.4
Differ from Category (+/-)	-2.2 blw av	na	na	-27.8 low	13.8 high

Standard Deviation	Category Risk Index	Beta
16.3%—av	0.84—low	0.66

	2000	1999	1998	1997	1996	1995	1994	1993	1992	1991
Return (%)	22.7	3.5	1.3	27.1	—	—	—	—	—	—
Differ from Category (+/-)	19.2	-15.4	-13.0	0.0	—	—	—	—	—	—
Return, Tax-Adjusted (%)	21.3	2.0	-0.2	26.5	—	—	—	—	—	—

PER SHARE DATA

	2000	1999	1998	1997	1996	1995	1994	1993	1992	1991
Dividends, Net Income ($)	0.17	0.23	0.19	0.08	—	—	—	—	—	—
Distrib'ns, Cap Gain ($)	0.56	0.51	0.76	0.14	—	—	—	—	—	—
Net Asset Value ($)	15.64	13.37	13.66	14.47	—	—	—	—	—	—
Expense Ratio (%)	na	1.04	1.08	1.25	—	—	—	—	—	—
Yield (%)	1.04	1.65	1.31	0.54	—	—	—	—	—	—
Portfolio Turnover (%)	na	27	32	16	—	—	—	—	—	—
Total Assets (Millions $)	252	211	221	217	—	—	—	—	—	—

PORTFOLIO (as of 6/30/00)

Portfolio Manager: committee - 1996

Investm't Category: Growth

✔ Domestic — Index
✔ Foreign — Sector
Asset Allocation — State Specific

Investment Style

Large Cap — ✔ Mid Cap — Small Cap
Growth — Grth/Val — ✔ Value

Portfolio

1.2%	cash	0.0%	corp bonds
97.8%	stocks	0.0%	gov't bonds
0.0%	pref/conv't pref	0.0%	muni bonds
1.0%	conv't bds/wrnts	0.0%	other

SHAREHOLDER INFORMATION

Minimum Investment
Initial: $2,500 — Subsequent: $100

Minimum IRA Investment
Initial: $1,000 — Subsequent: $50

Maximum Fees
Load: none — 12b-1: none
Other: none

Services
✔ IRA
✔ Keogh
✔ Telephone Exchange

T Rowe Price New Amer Gr (PRWAX)

800-638-5660, 410-547-2000
www.troweprice.com

Growth

PERFORMANCE — fund inception date: 9/30/85

	3yr Annual	5yr Annual	10yr Annual	Bull	Bear
Return (%)	5.9	11.5	17.0	49.5	-15.8
Differ from Category (+/-)	-5.1 blw av	-4.6 low	0.2 av	-0.2 av	-10.4 blw av

Standard Deviation	Category Risk Index	Beta
23.7%—abv av	1.22—high	1.23

	2000	1999	1998	1997	1996	1995	1994	1993	1992	1991
Return (%)	-10.5	12.7	17.8	21.0	20.0	44.3	-7.4	17.4	9.8	61.9
Differ from Category (+/-)	-14.0	-6.2	3.5	-6.1	-2.3	13.9	-7.2	2.8	-2.8	24.3
Return, Tax-Adjusted (%)	-13.6	10.4	16.0	19.8	17.2	42.3	-7.9	16.1	9.5	60.2

PER SHARE DATA

	2000	1999	1998	1997	1996	1995	1994	1993	1992	1991
Dividends, Net Income ($)	0.00	0.00	0.00	0.00	0.00	0.00	0.00	0.00	0.00	0.00
Distrib'ns, Cap Gain ($)	7.52	5.40	3.84	2.20	3.49	1.75	0.53	1.13	0.18	0.87
Net Asset Value ($)	35.77	48.06	47.79	44.19	38.37	34.91	25.42	28.04	24.86	22.79
Expense Ratio (%)	na	0.94	0.95	0.96	1.01	1.09	1.14	1.23	1.25	1.25
Yield (%)	0.00	0.00	0.00	0.00	0.00	0.00	0.00	0.00	0.00	0.00
Portfolio Turnover (%)	na	40	46	43	36	72	31	43	26	42
Total Assets (Millions $)	1,507	2,063	2,064	1,757	1,440	1,028	646	619	480	231

PORTFOLIO (as of 6/30/00)

Portfolio Manager: committee - 2000

Investm't Category: Growth

✔ Domestic — Index
Foreign — Sector
Asset Allocation — State Specific

Investment Style

✔ Large Cap — ✔ Mid Cap — Small Cap
✔ Growth — Grth/Val — Value

Portfolio

5.5%	cash	0.0%	corp bonds
94.5%	stocks	0.0%	gov't bonds
0.0%	pref/conv't pref	0.0%	muni bonds
0.0%	conv't bds/wrnts	0.0%	other

SHAREHOLDER INFORMATION

Minimum Investment
Initial: $2,500 — Subsequent: $100

Minimum IRA Investment
Initial: $1,000 — Subsequent: $50

Maximum Fees
Load: none — 12b-1: none
Other: none

Services
✔ IRA
✔ Keogh
✔ Telephone Exchange

T Rowe Price New Era (PRNEX)

800-638-5660, 410-547-2000
www.troweprice.com

Growth

PERFORMANCE

fund inception date: 5/28/69

	3yr Annual	5yr Annual	10yr Annual	Bull	Bear
Return (%)	9.5	12.6	12.0	41.2	4.2
Differ from Category (+/-)	-1.5 blw av	-3.5 blw av	-4.8 low	-8.5 av	9.6 abv av

Standard Deviation	Category Risk Index	Beta
24.2%—abv av	1.24—high	0.81

	2000	1999	1998	1997	1996	1995	1994	1993	1992	1991
Return (%)	20.3	21.2	-9.8	10.9	24.2	20.7	5.1	15.3	2.0	14.7
Differ from Category (+/-)	16.8	2.3	-24.1	-16.2	1.9	-9.7	5.3	0.7	-10.6	-22.9
Return, Tax-Adjusted (%)	18.3	18.7	-12.8	8.3	21.4	18.0	3.1	12.9	0.0	12.6

PER SHARE DATA

	2000	1999	1998	1997	1996	1995	1994	1993	1992	1991
Dividends, Net Income ($)	0.29	0.30	0.40	0.37	0.38	0.48	0.38	0.38	0.45	0.55
Distrib'ns, Cap Gain ($)	1.51	1.82	3.17	2.54	1.71	1.20	0.87	1.03	0.94	0.73
Net Asset Value ($)	24.30	21.80	19.78	25.95	26.06	22.65	20.15	20.35	18.88	19.86
Expense Ratio (%)	na	0.74	0.75	0.74	0.76	0.79	0.80	0.80	0.81	0.85
Yield (%)	1.12	1.27	1.74	1.29	1.36	2.01	1.80	1.77	2.27	2.67
Portfolio Turnover (%)	na	33	23	27	28	21	24	24	17	9
Total Assets (Millions $)	1,080	1,082	998	1,492	1,467	1,090	979	752	699	756

PORTFOLIO (as of 6/30/00)

Portfolio Manager: committee - 1997

Investm't Category: Growth

✔ Domestic — Index
✔ Foreign — ✔ Sector
Asset Allocation — State Specific

Investment Style

Large Cap — ✔ Mid Cap — Small Cap
Growth — Grth/Val — ✔ Value

Portfolio

3.5%	cash	0.0%	corp bonds
96.3%	stocks	0.0%	gov't bonds
0.0%	pref/conv't pref	0.0%	muni bonds
0.2%	conv't bds/wrnts	0.0%	other

SHAREHOLDER INFORMATION

Minimum Investment

Initial: $2,500 — Subsequent: $100

Minimum IRA Investment

Initial: $1,000 — Subsequent: $50

Maximum Fees

Load: none — 12b-1: none
Other: none

Services

✔ IRA
✔ Keogh
✔ Telephone Exchange

T Rowe Price New Horizons (PRNHX)

800-638-5660, 410-547-2000
www.troweprice.com

Aggressive Growth

this fund is closed to new investors

PERFORMANCE

fund inception date: 1/2/61

	3yr Annual	5yr Annual	10yr Annual	Bull	Bear
Return (%)	11.3	12.1	18.9	79.1	-22.1
Differ from Category (+/-)	-4.9 blw av	-2.5 blw av	3.1 av	-40.1 blw av	-1.5 av

Standard Deviation	Category Risk Index	Beta
31.5%—high	0.97—av	1.15

	2000	1999	1998	1997	1996	1995	1994	1993	1992	1991
Return (%)	-1.8	32.5	6.2	9.7	17.0	55.4	0.3	22.0	10.5	52.3
Differ from Category (+/-)	4.2	-25.0	-8.9	-5.1	-1.3	20.8	1.1	-3.2	3.6	5.1
Return, Tax-Adjusted (%)	-4.0	29.9	5.1	9.1	14.0	50.8	-2.1	17.1	7.3	51.1

PER SHARE DATA

	2000	1999	1998	1997	1996	1995	1994	1993	1992	1991
Dividends, Net Income ($)	0.00	0.00	0.00	0.00	0.00	0.00	0.00	0.00	0.00	0.05
Distrib'ns, Cap Gain ($)	3.14	3.02	1.27	0.58	2.19	2.41	1.43	2.70	1.76	0.39
Net Asset Value ($)	23.89	27.53	23.34	23.30	21.77	20.50	14.76	16.16	15.53	15.68
Expense Ratio (%)	na	0.90	0.89	0.88	0.90	0.92	0.93	0.93	0.93	0.92
Yield (%)	0.00	0.00	0.00	0.00	0.00	0.00	0.00	0.00	0.00	0.31
Portfolio Turnover (%)	na	45	41	45	41	58	44	49	50	33
Total Assets (Millions $)	5,836	6,021	5,228	5,103	4,363	2,854	1,648	1,627	1,547	1,470

PORTFOLIO (as of 6/30/00)

Portfolio Manager: committee - 1987

Investm't Category: Aggressive Growth

✔ Domestic | Index
✔ Foreign | Sector
Asset Allocation | State Specific

Investment Style

Large Cap | Mid Cap | ✔ Small Cap
✔ Growth | Grth/Val | Value

Portfolio

5.3%	cash	0.0%	corp bonds
94.5%	stocks	0.0%	gov't bonds
0.2%	pref/conv't pref	0.0%	muni bonds
0.0%	conv't bds/wrnts	0.0%	other

SHAREHOLDER INFORMATION

Minimum Investment
Initial: $2,500 Subsequent: $100

Minimum IRA Investment
Initial: $1,000 Subsequent: $50

Maximum Fees
Load: none 12b-1: none
Other: none

Services
✔ IRA
✔ Keogh
✔ Telephone Exchange

T Rowe Price Pers Str: Bal (TRPBX)

800-638-5660, 410-547-2000
www.troweprice.com

Balanced

PERFORMANCE

fund inception date: 7/29/94

	3yr Annual	5yr Annual	10yr Annual	Bull	Bear
Return (%)	9.0	11.7	na	23.8	0.0
Differ from Category (+/-)	0.6 av	0.3 av	na	-4.3 blw av	3.2 abv av

Standard Deviation	Category Risk Index	Beta
9.4%—blw av	0.86—blw av	0.49

	2000	1999	1998	1997	1996	1995	1994	1993	1992	1991
Return (%)	5.6	7.9	13.8	17.7	14.2	28.1	—	—	—	—
Differ from Category (+/-)	3.6	-2.8	0.5	-1.1	0.3	2.6	—	—	—	—
Return, Tax-Adjusted (%)	3.5	6.1	11.9	15.8	12.2	26.3	—	—	—	—

PER SHARE DATA

	2000	1999	1998	1997	1996	1995	1994	1993	1992	1991
Dividends, Net Income ($)	0.50	0.49	0.45	0.44	0.39	0.38	—	—	—	—
Distrib'ns, Cap Gain ($)	0.71	0.40	0.49	0.35	0.32	0.07	—	—	—	—
Net Asset Value ($)	15.92	16.24	15.90	14.82	13.29	12.29	—	—	—	—
Expense Ratio (%)	0.98	1.00	1.05	1.05	1.05	1.05	—	—	—	—
Yield (%)	3.00	2.94	2.74	2.90	2.86	3.07	—	—	—	—
Portfolio Turnover (%)	48	34	41	54	47	26	—	—	—	—
Total Assets (Millions $)	626	618	421	281	179	18	—	—	—	—

PORTFOLIO (as of 6/30/00)

Portfolio Manager: committee - 1998

Investm't Category: Balanced

✔ Domestic
✔ Foreign
✔ Asset Allocation
Index
Sector
State Specific

Investment Style

Large Cap / Mid Cap / Small Cap
Growth / Grth/Val / Value

Portfolio

1.9%	cash	13.5%	corp bonds
60.1%	stocks	24.5%	gov't bonds
0.0%	pref/conv't pref	0.0%	muni bonds
0.0%	conv't bds/wrnts	0.0%	other

SHAREHOLDER INFORMATION

Minimum Investment
Initial: $2,500 — Subsequent: $100

Minimum IRA Investment
Initial: $1,000 — Subsequent: $50

Maximum Fees
Load: none — 12b-1: none
Other: none

Services
✔ IRA
✔ Keogh
✔ Telephone Exchange

T Rowe Price Pers Str: Gr (TRSGX)

800-638-5660, 410-547-2000
www.troweprice.com

Balanced

PERFORMANCE — fund inception date: 7/29/94

	3yr Annual	5yr Annual	10yr Annual	Bull	Bear
Return (%)	10.4	13.8	na	31.4	-1.7
Differ from Category (+/-)	2.0 abv av	2.4 high	na	3.3 abv av	1.5 abv av

Standard Deviation	Category Risk Index	Beta
11.9%—blw av	1.09—abv av	0.63

	2000	1999	1998	1997	1996	1995	1994	1993	1992	1991
Return (%)	4.6	11.2	15.6	20.5	17.6	31.4	—	—	—	—
Differ from Category (+/-)	2.6	0.5	2.3	1.7	3.7	5.9	—	—	—	—
Return, Tax-Adjusted (%)	2.7	9.9	14.2	19.4	14.9	30.1	—	—	—	—

PER SHARE DATA

	2000	1999	1998	1997	1996	1995	1994	1993	1992	1991
Dividends, Net Income ($)	0.35	0.32	0.32	0.26	0.24	0.27	—	—	—	—
Distrib'ns, Cap Gain ($)	1.08	0.52	0.45	0.19	0.89	0.07	—	—	—	—
Net Asset Value ($)	18.95	19.48	18.30	16.52	14.08	12.92	—	—	—	—
Expense Ratio (%)	1.10	1.10	1.10	1.10	1.10	1.10	—	—	—	—
Yield (%)	1.74	1.60	1.70	1.55	1.60	2.07	—	—	—	—
Portfolio Turnover (%)	42	36	33	39	39	25	—	—	—	—
Total Assets (Millions $)	283	262	194	98	41	16	—	—	—	—

PORTFOLIO (as of 6/30/00)

Portfolio Manager: committee - 1998

Investm't Category: Balanced

✔ Domestic Index
✔ Foreign Sector
✔ Asset Allocation State Specific

Investment Style

Large Cap Mid Cap Small Cap
Growth Grth/Val Value

Portfolio

1.0%	cash	9.4%	corp bonds
79.0%	stocks	10.6%	gov't bonds
0.0%	pref/conv't pref	0.0%	muni bonds
0.0%	conv't bds/wrnts	0.0%	other

SHAREHOLDER INFORMATION

Minimum Investment
Initial: $2,500 Subsequent: $100

Minimum IRA Investment
Initial: $1,000 Subsequent: $50

Maximum Fees
Load: none 12b-1: none
Other: none

Services
✔ IRA
✔ Keogh
✔ Telephone Exchange

T Rowe Price Pers Str: Inc (PRSIX)

800-638-5660, 410-547-2000
www.troweprice.com

Balanced

PERFORMANCE

fund inception date: 7/29/94

	3yr Annual	5yr Annual	10yr Annual	Bull	Bear
Return (%)	7.7	9.9	na	16.6	1.5
Differ from Category (+/-)	-0.7 blw av	-1.5 blw av	na	-11.5 blw av	4.7 abv av

Standard Deviation	Category Risk Index	Beta
6.9%—blw av	0.63—low	0.35

	2000	1999	1998	1997	1996	1995	1994	1993	1992	1991
Return (%)	6.5	5.1	11.4	15.0	11.7	24.7	—	—	—	—
Differ from Category (+/-)	4.5	-5.6	-1.9	-3.8	-2.2	-0.8	—	—	—	—
Return, Tax-Adjusted (%)	4.6	2.9	9.6	12.7	7.7	22.4	—	—	—	—

PER SHARE DATA

	2000	1999	1998	1997	1996	1995	1994	1993	1992	1991
Dividends, Net Income ($)	0.53	0.53	0.49	0.53	0.47	0.48	—	—	—	—
Distrib'ns, Cap Gain ($)	0.16	0.37	0.10	0.28	0.98	0.10	—	—	—	—
Net Asset Value ($)	13.18	13.03	13.27	12.45	11.56	11.70	—	—	—	—
Expense Ratio (%)	0.90	0.90	0.95	0.95	0.95	0.95	—	—	—	—
Yield (%)	3.97	3.95	3.66	4.16	3.74	4.06	—	—	—	—
Portfolio Turnover (%)	45	48	30	44	34	51	—	—	—	—
Total Assets (Millions $)	221	206	213	66	33	25	—	—	—	—

PORTFOLIO (as of 6/30/00)

Portfolio Manager: committee - 1998

Investm't Category: Balanced

✔ Domestic
✔ Foreign
✔ Asset Allocation
Index
Sector
State Specific

Investment Style

Large Cap	Mid Cap	Small Cap
Growth	Grth/Val	Value

Portfolio

11.7%	cash	19.7%	corp bonds
42.4%	stocks	26.2%	gov't bonds
0.0%	pref/conv't pref	0.0%	muni bonds
0.0%	conv't bds/wrnts	0.0%	other

SHAREHOLDER INFORMATION

Minimum Investment
Initial: $2,500 Subsequent: $100

Minimum IRA Investment
Initial: $1,000 Subsequent: $50

Maximum Fees
Load: none 12b-1: none
Other: none

Services
✔ IRA
✔ Keogh
✔ Telephone Exchange

T Rowe Price Science & Tech (PRSCX)

800-638-5660, 410-547-2000
www.troweprice.com

Aggressive Growth

PERFORMANCE

fund inception date: 9/30/87

	3yr Annual	5yr Annual	10yr Annual	Bull	Bear
Return (%)	23.4	16.9	24.9	234.0	-41.7
Differ from Category (+/-)	7.2 abv av	2.3 av	9.1 high	114.8 high	-21.1 low

Standard Deviation	Category Risk Index	Beta
40.0%—high	1.23—abv av	1.72

	2000	1999	1998	1997	1996	1995	1994	1993	1992	1991
Return (%)	-34.1	100.9	42.3	1.7	14.2	55.5	15.7	24.2	18.7	60.1
Differ from Category (+/-)	-28.1	43.4	27.2	-13.1	-4.1	20.9	16.5	-1.0	11.8	12.9
Return, Tax-Adjusted (%)	-36.3	95.2	41.5	-0.2	10.7	49.6	15.2	20.1	16.6	58.7

PER SHARE DATA

	2000	1999	1998	1997	1996	1995	1994	1993	1992	1991
Dividends, Net Income ($)	0.00	0.00	0.00	0.00	0.00	0.00	0.00	0.00	0.00	0.00
Distrib'ns, Cap Gain ($)	7.28	10.72	0.99	2.87	3.60	4.54	0.30	2.51	1.12	0.48
Net Asset Value ($)	35.57	63.71	37.67	27.26	29.71	29.12	21.64	18.95	17.33	15.57
Expense Ratio (%)	na	0.87	0.94	0.94	0.97	1.06	1.11	1.25	1.25	1.25
Yield (%)	0.00	0.00	0.00	0.00	0.00	0.00	0.00	0.00	0.00	0.00
Portfolio Turnover (%)	na	128	109	133	125	136	113	163	144	148
Total Assets (Millions $)	8,906	12,270	4,695	3,538	3,291	2,285	915	501	281	166

PORTFOLIO (as of 6/30/00)

Portfolio Manager: committee - 1991

Investm't Category: Aggressive Growth

✔ Domestic
Index
✔ Foreign
✔ Sector
Asset Allocation
State Specific

Investment Style

Large Cap
✔ Mid Cap
✔ Small Cap
✔ Growth
Grth/Val
Value

Portfolio

1.9%	cash	0.0%	corp bonds
97.3%	stocks	0.0%	gov't bonds
0.8%	pref/conv't pref	0.0%	muni bonds
0.0%	conv't bds/wrnts	0.0%	other

SHAREHOLDER INFORMATION

Minimum Investment

Initial: $2,500 Subsequent: $100

Minimum IRA Investment

Initial: $1,000 Subsequent: $50

Maximum Fees

Load: none 12b-1: none
Other: none

Services

✔ IRA
✔ Keogh
✔ Telephone Exchange

T Rowe Price Sm Cap Stck (OTCFX)

800-638-5660, 410-547-2000
www.troweprice.com

Aggressive Growth

PERFORMANCE

fund inception date: 6/1/56

	3yr Annual	5yr Annual	10yr Annual	Bull	Bear
Return (%)	8.8	14.9	17.5	37.2	-3.8
Differ from Category (+/-)	-7.4 blw av	0.3 av	1.7 av	-82.0 low	16.8 high

Standard Deviation	Category Risk Index	Beta
20.2%—abv av	0.62—low	0.74

	2000	1999	1998	1997	1996	1995	1994	1993	1992	1991
Return (%)	16.4	14.6	-3.4	28.8	21.0	33.8	0.0	18.4	13.9	38.6
Differ from Category (+/-)	22.4	-42.9	-18.5	14.0	2.7	-0.8	0.8	-6.8	7.0	-8.6
Return, Tax-Adjusted (%)	13.9	13.5	-4.0	27.5	18.0	29.3	-2.9	15.3	6.0	36.8

PER SHARE DATA

	2000	1999	1998	1997	1996	1995	1994	1993	1992	1991
Dividends, Net Income ($)	0.14	0.08	0.10	0.04	0.09	0.12	0.03	0.00	0.07	0.09
Distrib'ns, Cap Gain ($)	2.46	0.89	0.50	1.01	1.58	2.01	1.56	1.58	4.64	0.68
Net Asset Value ($)	23.87	22.80	20.79	22.20	18.07	16.32	13.80	15.39	14.37	16.86
Expense Ratio (%)	na	0.96	1.01	1.02	1.07	1.13	1.11	1.20	1.32	1.34
Yield (%)	0.53	0.33	0.46	0.17	0.45	0.65	0.19	0.00	0.36	0.51
Portfolio Turnover (%)	na	42	26	22	31	72	41	40	31	31
Total Assets (Millions $)	2,076	1,740	1,152	816	415	278	196	204	186	268

PORTFOLIO (as of 6/30/00)

Portfolio Manager: committee - 1992

Investm't Category: Aggressive Growth

✔ Domestic
✔ Foreign
Asset Allocation
Index
Sector
State Specific

Investment Style

Large Cap
Mid Cap
✔ Small Cap
Growth
✔ Grth/Val
Value

Portfolio

7.8% cash
92.1% stocks
0.0% pref/conv't pref
0.1% conv't bds/wrnts
0.0% corp bonds
0.0% gov't bonds
0.0% muni bonds
0.0% other

SHAREHOLDER INFORMATION

Minimum Investment

Initial: $2,500 Subsequent: $100

Minimum IRA Investment

Initial: $1,000 Subsequent: $50

Maximum Fees

Load: none 12b-1: none
Other: none

Services

✔ IRA
✔ Keogh
✔ Telephone Exchange

T Rowe Price Sm Cap Value (PRSVX)

800-638-5660, 410-547-2000
www.troweprice.com

Growth

PERFORMANCE

fund inception date: 6/30/88

	3yr Annual	5yr Annual	10yr Annual	Bull	Bear
Return (%)	1.9	11.0	15.7	9.5	7.0
Differ from Category (+/-)	-9.1 low	-5.1 low	-1.1 blw av	-40.2 low	12.4 abv av

Standard Deviation	Category Risk Index	Beta
15.4%—av	0.79—low	0.48

	2000	1999	1998	1997	1996	1995	1994	1993	1992	1991
Return (%)	19.7	1.1	-12.4	27.9	24.6	29.2	-1.3	23.3	20.8	34.1
Differ from Category (+/-)	16.2	-17.8	-26.7	0.8	2.3	-1.2	-1.1	8.7	8.2	-3.5
Return, Tax-Adjusted (%)	17.3	-0.6	-13.8	26.0	22.6	27.3	-3.4	22.1	20.0	32.4

PER SHARE DATA

	2000	1999	1998	1997	1996	1995	1994	1993	1992	1991
Dividends, Net Income ($)	0.20	0.17	0.25	0.20	0.23	0.18	0.14	0.10	0.10	0.12
Distrib'ns, Cap Gain ($)	1.68	1.35	1.20	1.39	0.80	0.61	0.92	0.35	0.15	0.34
Net Asset Value ($)	19.14	17.62	18.97	23.40	19.56	16.53	13.40	14.68	12.28	10.37
Expense Ratio (%)	na	0.92	0.87	0.87	0.94	1.00	0.97	1.05	1.25	1.25
Yield (%)	0.96	0.89	1.23	0.80	1.12	1.05	0.97	0.66	0.80	1.12
Portfolio Turnover (%)	na	7	17	14	15	17	21	11	12	31
Total Assets (Millions $)	1,274	1,262	1,631	2,088	1,409	936	408	452	264	53

PORTFOLIO (as of 6/30/00)

Portfolio Manager: committee - 1991

Investm't Category: Growth

✔ Domestic — Index
✔ Foreign — Sector
Asset Allocation — State Specific

Investment Style

Large Cap — Mid Cap — ✔ Small Cap
Growth — Grth/Val — ✔ Value

Portfolio

3.0%	cash	0.3%	corp bonds
93.7%	stocks	0.0%	gov't bonds
2.7%	pref/conv't pref	0.0%	muni bonds
0.3%	conv't bds/wrnts	0.0%	other

SHAREHOLDER INFORMATION

Minimum Investment
Initial: $2,500 — Subsequent: $100

Minimum IRA Investment
Initial: $1,000 — Subsequent: $50

Maximum Fees
Load: 1.00% redemption — 12b-1: none
Other: redemption fee applies for 12 months

Services
✔ IRA
✔ Keogh
✔ Telephone Exchange

T Rowe Price Spect: Growth (PRSGX)

800-638-5660, 410-547-2000
www.troweprice.com

Growth

PERFORMANCE

fund inception date: 6/29/90

	3yr Annual	5yr Annual	10yr Annual	Bull	Bear
Return (%)	11.2	14.2	15.7	50.3	-9.7
Differ from Category (+/-)	0.2 av	-1.9 blw av	-1.1 blw av	0.6 av	-4.3 av

Standard Deviation	Category Risk Index	Beta
17.0%—av	0.87—low	0.86

	2000	1999	1998	1997	1996	1995	1994	1993	1992	1991
Return (%)	-0.1	21.1	13.6	17.3	20.5	29.9	1.3	20.9	7.2	29.8
Differ from Category (+/-)	-3.6	2.2	-0.7	-9.8	-1.8	-0.5	1.5	6.3	-5.4	-7.8
Return, Tax-Adjusted (%)	-2.4	18.3	11.4	14.6	17.9	27.2	-0.9	18.3	5.1	27.9

PER SHARE DATA

	2000	1999	1998	1997	1996	1995	1994	1993	1992	1991
Dividends, Net Income ($)	0.12	0.17	0.18	0.20	0.20	0.21	0.17	0.16	0.20	0.21
Distrib'ns, Cap Gain ($)	1.85	1.91	1.37	1.60	0.93	0.76	0.73	0.72	0.55	0.32
Net Asset Value ($)	15.72	17.71	16.45	15.93	15.13	13.49	11.13	11.87	10.54	10.53
Expense Ratio (%)	na	0.00	0.00	0.00	0.00	0.00	0.00	0.00	0.00	0.00
Yield (%)	0.68	0.86	1.01	1.14	1.24	1.47	1.43	1.27	1.80	1.93
Portfolio Turnover (%)	na	20	18	20	2	8	20	7	8	15
Total Assets (Millions $)	2,770	3,030	2,768	2,605	2,104	1,358	879	584	355	148

PORTFOLIO (as of 6/30/00)

Portfolio Manager: committee - 1990

Investm't Category: Growth

✔ Domestic — Index
✔ Foreign — Sector
Asset Allocation — State Specific

Investment Style

Large Cap — ✔ Mid Cap — Small Cap
✔ Growth — Grth/Val — Value

Portfolio

0.0%	cash	0.0%	corp bonds
0.0%	stocks	0.0%	gov't bonds
0.0%	pref/conv't pref	0.0%	muni bonds
0.0%	conv't bds/wrnts	100.0%	other

SHAREHOLDER INFORMATION

Minimum Investment

Initial: $2,500 — Subsequent: $100

Minimum IRA Investment

Initial: $1,000 — Subsequent: $50

Maximum Fees

Load: none — 12b-1: none
Other: none

Services

✔ IRA
✔ Keogh
✔ Telephone Exchange

T Rowe Price Spect: Income (RPSIX)

800-638-5660, 410-547-2000
www.troweprice.com

Balanced

PERFORMANCE — fund inception date: 6/29/90

	3yr Annual	5yr Annual	10yr Annual	Bull	Bear
Return (%)	4.6	6.7	8.9	6.0	2.9
Differ from Category (+/-)	-3.8 low	-4.7 low	-2.8 low	-22.1 low	6.1 high

Standard Deviation	Category Risk Index	Beta
4.3%—blw av	0.39—low	0.16

	2000	1999	1998	1997	1996	1995	1994	1993	1992	1991
Return (%)	7.4	0.2	6.5	12.1	7.6	19.4	-1.9	12.3	7.8	19.6
Differ from Category (+/-)	5.4	-10.5	-6.8	-6.7	-6.3	-6.1	-0.6	-2.1	-0.6	-4.2
Return, Tax-Adjusted (%)	4.8	-2.3	3.7	9.3	4.7	16.4	-4.5	9.2	5.3	16.8

PER SHARE DATA

	2000	1999	1998	1997	1996	1995	1994	1993	1992	1991
Dividends, Net Income ($)	0.69	0.68	0.72	0.70	0.71	0.71	0.68	0.69	0.76	0.82
Distrib'ns, Cap Gain ($)	0.00	0.13	0.18	0.15	0.15	0.06	0.10	0.19	0.08	0.06
Net Asset Value ($)	10.77	10.71	11.50	11.66	11.20	11.24	10.11	11.11	10.70	10.73
Expense Ratio (%)	na	0.00	0.00	0.00	0.00	0.00	0.00	0.00	0.00	0.00
Yield (%)	6.40	6.27	6.16	5.92	6.25	6.28	6.66	6.10	7.05	7.59
Portfolio Turnover (%)	na	19	13	14	17	12	23	14	14	19
Total Assets (Millions $)	2,370	2,548	2,574	2,022	1,355	986	624	587	376	147

PORTFOLIO (as of 6/30/00)

Portfolio Manager: committee - 1998

Investm't Category: Balanced

✔ Domestic — Index
✔ Foreign — Sector
✔ Asset Allocation — State Specific

Investment Style

Large Cap — Mid Cap — Small Cap
Growth — Grth/Val — Value

Portfolio

5.0%	cash	28.0%	corp bonds
13.0%	stocks	54.0%	gov't bonds
0.0%	pref/conv't pref	0.0%	muni bonds
0.0%	conv't bds/wrnts	0.0%	other

SHAREHOLDER INFORMATION

Minimum Investment
Initial: $2,500 — Subsequent: $100

Minimum IRA Investment
Initial: $1,000 — Subsequent: $50

Maximum Fees
Load: none — 12b-1: none
Other: none

Services
✔ IRA
✔ Keogh
✔ Telephone Exchange

T Rowe Price Spect: Intl (PSILX)

800-638-5660, 410-547-2000
www.troweprice.com

International Stock

PERFORMANCE

fund inception date: 12/31/96

	3yr Annual	5yr Annual	10yr Annual	Bull	Bear
Return (%)	10.1	na	na	62.4	-19.0
Differ from Category (+/-)	1.2 av	na	na	-28.5 blw av	5.0 abv av

Standard Deviation	Category Risk Index	Beta
17.3%—av	0.76—low	0.72

	2000	1999	1998	1997	1996	1995	1994	1993	1992	1991
Return (%)	-14.7	39.4	12.2	2.4	—	—	—	—	—	—
Differ from Category (+/-)	4.7	-21.3	6.4	1.1	—	—	—	—	—	—
Return, Tax-Adjusted (%)	-17.0	37.0	11.0	1.1	—	—	—	—	—	—

PER SHARE DATA

	2000	1999	1998	1997	1996	1995	1994	1993	1992	1991
Dividends, Net Income ($)	0.12	0.13	0.21	0.15	—	—	—	—	—	—
Distrib'ns, Cap Gain ($)	1.35	0.97	0.15	0.35	—	—	—	—	—	—
Net Asset Value ($)	10.08	13.53	10.56	9.74	—	—	—	—	—	—
Expense Ratio (%)	na	0.00	0.00	0.00	—	—	—	—	—	—
Yield (%)	1.04	0.89	1.96	1.48	—	—	—	—	—	—
Portfolio Turnover (%)	na	20	32	—	—	—	—	—	—	—
Total Assets (Millions $)	80	82	54	51	—	—	—	—	—	—

PORTFOLIO (as of 6/30/00)

Portfolio Manager: committee - 1997

Investm't Category: International Stock

Domestic	Index
✔ Foreign	Sector
✔ Asset Allocation	State Specific

Investment Style

Large Cap	Mid Cap	Small Cap
Growth	Grth/Val	Value

Portfolio

0.0%	cash	0.0%	corp bonds
100.0%	stocks	0.0%	gov't bonds
0.0%	pref/conv't pref	0.0%	muni bonds
0.0%	conv't bds/wrnts	0.0%	other

SHAREHOLDER INFORMATION

Minimum Investment
Initial: $2,500 Subsequent: $100

Minimum IRA Investment
Initial: $1,000 Subsequent: $50

Maximum Fees
Load: none 12b-1: none
Other: none

Services
✔ IRA
✔ Keogh
✔ Telephone Exchange

T Rowe Price Value (TRVLX)

800-638-5660, 410-547-2000
www.troweprice.com

Growth

PERFORMANCE

fund inception date: 9/30/94

	3yr Annual	5yr Annual	10yr Annual	Bull	Bear
Return (%)	10.5	17.5	na	31.2	8.4
Differ from Category (+/-)	-0.5 av	1.4 av	na	-18.5 blw av	13.8 high

Standard Deviation	Category Risk Index	Beta
19.1%—abv av	0.98—blw av	0.79

	2000	1999	1998	1997	1996	1995	1994	1993	1992	1991
Return (%)	15.7	9.1	6.8	29.2	28.5	39.8	—	—	—	—
Differ from Category (+/-)	12.2	-9.8	-7.5	2.1	6.2	9.4	—	—	—	—
Return, Tax-Adjusted (%)	14.2	6.2	5.3	26.3	25.7	36.5	—	—	—	—

PER SHARE DATA

	2000	1999	1998	1997	1996	1995	1994	1993	1992	1991
Dividends, Net Income ($)	0.23	0.21	0.20	0.21	0.26	0.26	—	—	—	—
Distrib'ns, Cap Gain ($)	0.84	2.20	0.96	1.83	0.91	0.82	—	—	—	—
Net Asset Value ($)	19.15	17.50	18.31	18.24	15.76	13.21	—	—	—	—
Expense Ratio (%)	na	0.92	0.98	1.05	1.10	1.10	—	—	—	—
Yield (%)	1.15	1.06	1.03	1.04	1.55	1.85	—	—	—	—
Portfolio Turnover (%)	na	68	72	67	68	90	—	—	—	—
Total Assets (Millions $)	908	851	774	546	197	46	—	—	—	—

PORTFOLIO (as of 6/30/00)

Portfolio Manager: committee - 1994

Investm't Category: Growth

✔ Domestic
Foreign
Asset Allocation
Index
Sector
State Specific

Investment Style

✔ Large Cap ✔ Mid Cap Small Cap
Growth Grth/Val ✔ Value

Portfolio

5.6% cash
94.4% stocks
0.0% pref/conv't pref
0.0% conv't bds/wrnts
0.0% corp bonds
0.0% gov't bonds
0.0% muni bonds
0.0% other

SHAREHOLDER INFORMATION

Minimum Investment
Initial: $2,500 Subsequent: $100

Minimum IRA Investment
Initial: $1,000 Subsequent: $50

Maximum Fees
Load: none 12b-1: none
Other: none

Services
✔ IRA
✔ Keogh
✔ Telephone Exchange

TIAA-CREF Growth & Income (TIGIX)

800-223-1200, 212-490-9000
www.tiaa-cref.org

Growth & Income

PERFORMANCE — fund inception date: 9/2/97

	3yr Annual	5yr Annual	10yr Annual	Bull	Bear
Return (%)	14.6	na	na	60.9	-11.6
Differ from Category (+/-)	5.7 high	na	na	27.4 high	-11.5 blw av

Standard Deviation	Category Risk Index	Beta
18.3%—av	1.05—abv av	1.03

	2000	1999	1998	1997	1996	1995	1994	1993	1992	1991
Return (%)	-7.3	24.4	30.5	—	—	—	—	—	—	—
Differ from Category (+/-)	-13.0	13.6	17.7	—	—	—	—	—	—	—
Return, Tax-Adjusted (%)	-8.3	23.2	30.0	—	—	—	—	—	—	—

PER SHARE DATA

	2000	1999	1998	1997	1996	1995	1994	1993	1992	1991
Dividends, Net Income ($)	0.11	0.11	0.10	—	—	—	—	—	—	—
Distrib'ns, Cap Gain ($)	0.61	0.53	0.02	—	—	—	—	—	—	—
Net Asset Value ($)	14.05	15.93	13.33	—	—	—	—	—	—	—
Expense Ratio (%)	na	0.43	0.43	—	—	—	—	—	—	—
Yield (%)	0.75	0.66	0.74	—	—	—	—	—	—	—
Portfolio Turnover (%)	na	39	71	—	—	—	—	—	—	—
Total Assets (Millions $)	647	541	232	—	—	—	—	—	—	—

PORTFOLIO (as of 6/30/00)

Portfolio Manager: committee - 1997

Investm't Category: Growth & Income
✔ Domestic
✔ Foreign
Asset Allocation
Index
Sector
State Specific

Investment Style
✔ Large Cap
Growth
Mid Cap
✔ Grth/Val
Small Cap
Value

Portfolio

0.6%	cash	0.0%	corp bonds
99.4%	stocks	0.0%	gov't bonds
0.0%	pref/conv't pref	0.0%	muni bonds
0.0%	conv't bds/wrnts	0.0%	other

SHAREHOLDER INFORMATION

Minimum Investment
Initial: $250 Subsequent: $25

Minimum IRA Investment
Initial: $250 Subsequent: $25

Maximum Fees
Load: none 12b-1: none
Other: none

Services
✔ IRA
Keogh
✔ Telephone Exchange

TIAA-CREF Growth Equity (TIGEX)

800-223-1200, 212-490-9000
www.tiaa-cref.org

Growth

PERFORMANCE — fund inception date: 9/2/97

	3yr Annual	5yr Annual	10yr Annual	Bull	Bear
Return (%)	12.9	na	na	83.9	-25.3
Differ from Category (+/-)	1.9 av	na	na	34.2 high	-19.9 low

Standard Deviation	Category Risk Index	Beta
24.1%—abv av	1.24—high	1.22

	2000	1999	1998	1997	1996	1995	1994	1993	1992	1991
Return (%)	-20.2	32.9	35.9	—	—	—	—	—	—	—
Differ from Category (+/-)	-23.7	14.0	21.6	—	—	—	—	—	—	—
Return, Tax-Adjusted (%)	-21.1	31.5	35.6	—	—	—	—	—	—	—

PER SHARE DATA

	2000	1999	1998	1997	1996	1995	1994	1993	1992	1991
Dividends, Net Income ($)	0.00	0.01	0.02	—	—	—	—	—	—	—
Distrib'ns, Cap Gain ($)	0.84	0.93	0.08	—	—	—	—	—	—	—
Net Asset Value ($)	12.87	17.19	13.65	—	—	—	—	—	—	—
Expense Ratio (%)	na	0.45	0.45	—	—	—	—	—	—	—
Yield (%)	0.00	0.05	0.14	—	—	—	—	—	—	—
Portfolio Turnover (%)	na	69	49	—	—	—	—	—	—	—
Total Assets (Millions $)	798	695	296	—	—	—	—	—	—	—

PORTFOLIO (as of 6/30/00)

Portfolio Manager: committee - 1999

Investm't Category: Growth

✔ Domestic — Index
✔ Foreign — Sector
Asset Allocation — State Specific

Investment Style

✔ Large Cap — Mid Cap — Small Cap
✔ Growth — Grth/Val — Value

Portfolio

0.8%	cash	0.0%	corp bonds
99.1%	stocks	0.1%	gov't bonds
0.0%	pref/conv't pref	0.0%	muni bonds
0.0%	conv't bds/wrnts	0.0%	other

SHAREHOLDER INFORMATION

Minimum Investment
Initial: $250 — Subsequent: $25

Minimum IRA Investment
Initial: $250 — Subsequent: $25

Maximum Fees
Load: none — 12b-1: none
Other: none

Services
✔ IRA
Keogh
✔ Telephone Exchange

TIAA-CREF Intl Equity

800-223-1200, 212-490-9000
www.tiaa-cref.org

(TIINX)

International Stock

PERFORMANCE

fund inception date: 9/2/97

	3yr Annual	5yr Annual	10yr Annual	Bull	Bear
Return (%)	14.1	na	na	82.1	-26.6
Differ from Category (+/-)	5.2 abv av	na	na	-8.8 av	-2.6 av

Standard Deviation	Category Risk Index	Beta
22.6%—abv av	1.00—av	0.67

	2000	1999	1998	1997	1996	1995	1994	1993	1992	1991
Return (%)	-19.9	55.8	19.2	—	—	—	—	—	—	—
Differ from Category (+/-)	-0.5	-4.9	13.4	—	—	—	—	—	—	—
Return, Tax-Adjusted (%)	-22.5	55.0	18.8	—	—	—	—	—	—	—

PER SHARE DATA

	2000	1999	1998	1997	1996	1995	1994	1993	1992	1991
Dividends, Net Income ($)	0.08	0.10	0.09	—	—	—	—	—	—	—
Distrib'ns, Cap Gain ($)	2.00	0.22	0.00	—	—	—	—	—	—	—
Net Asset Value ($)	10.75	16.08	10.54	—	—	—	—	—	—	—
Expense Ratio (%)	na	0.49	0.49	—	—	—	—	—	—	—
Yield (%)	0.62	0.61	0.85	—	—	—	—	—	—	—
Portfolio Turnover (%)	na	74	27	—	—	—	—	—	—	—
Total Assets (Millions $)	261	255	118	—	—	—	—	—	—	—

PORTFOLIO (as of 6/30/00)

Portfolio Manager: committee - 1997

Investm't Category: International Stock

Domestic	Index
✔ Foreign	Sector
Asset Allocation	State Specific

Investment Style

Large Cap	Mid Cap	Small Cap
Growth	Grth/Val	Value

Portfolio

0.2% cash	0.0% corp bonds
99.8% stocks	0.0% gov't bonds
0.0% pref/conv't pref	0.0% muni bonds
0.0% conv't bds/wrnts	0.0% other

SHAREHOLDER INFORMATION

Minimum Investment
Initial: $250 Subsequent: $25

Minimum IRA Investment
Initial: $250 Subsequent: $25

Maximum Fees
Load: none 12b-1: none
Other: none

Services
✔ IRA
Keogh
✔ Telephone Exchange

TIAA-CREF Managed Alloc (TIMAX)

800-223-1200, 212-490-9000
www.tiaa-cref.org

Balanced

PERFORMANCE

fund inception date: 9/2/97

	3yr Annual	5yr Annual	10yr Annual	Bull	Bear
Return (%)	11.1	na	na	40.5	-10.1
Differ from Category (+/-)	2.7 high	na	na	12.4 high	-6.9 low

Standard Deviation	Category Risk Index	Beta
11.8%—blw av	1.08—abv av	0.60

	2000	1999	1998	1997	1996	1995	1994	1993	1992	1991
Return (%)	-4.9	19.2	21.2	—	—	—	—	—	—	—
Differ from Category (+/-)	-6.9	8.5	7.9	—	—	—	—	—	—	—
Return, Tax-Adjusted (%)	-6.6	17.8	19.9	—	—	—	—	—	—	—

PER SHARE DATA

	2000	1999	1998	1997	1996	1995	1994	1993	1992	1991
Dividends, Net Income ($)	0.47	0.38	0.32	—	—	—	—	—	—	—
Distrib'ns, Cap Gain ($)	0.26	0.04	0.00	—	—	—	—	—	—	—
Net Asset Value ($)	12.20	13.59	11.79	—	—	—	—	—	—	—
Expense Ratio (%)	na	0.00	0.00	—	—	—	—	—	—	—
Yield (%)	3.77	2.78	2.71	—	—	—	—	—	—	—
Portfolio Turnover (%)	na	3	4	—	—	—	—	—	—	—
Total Assets (Millions $)	323	243	162	—	—	—	—	—	—	—

PORTFOLIO (as of 6/30/00)

Portfolio Manager: committee - 1997

Investm't Category: Balanced

✔ Domestic	Index
✔ Foreign	Sector
Asset Allocation	State Specific

Investment Style

Large Cap	Mid Cap	Small Cap
Growth	Grth/Val	Value

Portfolio

0.1%	cash	0.0%	corp bonds
0.0%	stocks	0.0%	gov't bonds
0.0%	pref/conv't pref	0.0%	muni bonds
0.0%	conv't bds/wrnts	99.9%	other

SHAREHOLDER INFORMATION

Minimum Investment

Initial: $250 Subsequent: $25

Minimum IRA Investment

Initial: $250 Subsequent: $25

Maximum Fees

Load: none 12b-1: none

Other: none

Services

✔ IRA

Keogh

✔ Telephone Exchange

Third Avenue Small Cap (TASCX)

800-443-1021, 212-888-6685
www.mjwhitman.com

Growth

PERFORMANCE — fund inception date: 4/1/97

	3yr Annual	5yr Annual	10yr Annual	Bull	Bear
Return (%)	8.2	na	na	26.8	2.8
Differ from Category (+/-)	-2.8 blw av	na	na	-22.9 blw av	8.2 abv av

Standard Deviation	Category Risk Index	Beta
17.8%—av	0.91—blw av	0.61

	2000	1999	1998	1997	1996	1995	1994	1993	1992	1991
Return (%)	17.1	11.2	-2.7	—	—	—	—	—	—	—
Differ from Category (+/-)	13.6	-7.7	-17.0	—	—	—	—	—	—	—
Return, Tax-Adjusted (%)	15.3	10.8	-2.9	—	—	—	—	—	—	—

PER SHARE DATA

	2000	1999	1998	1997	1996	1995	1994	1993	1992	1991
Dividends, Net Income ($)	0.21	0.09	0.08	—	—	—	—	—	—	—
Distrib'ns, Cap Gain ($)	0.68	0.00	0.00	—	—	—	—	—	—	—
Net Asset Value ($)	13.59	12.40	11.23	—	—	—	—	—	—	—
Expense Ratio (%)	na	1.28	1.28	—	—	—	—	—	—	—
Yield (%)	1.47	0.72	0.71	—	—	—	—	—	—	—
Portfolio Turnover (%)	na	10	6	—	—	—	—	—	—	—
Total Assets (Millions $)	141	127	144	—	—	—	—	—	—	—

PORTFOLIO (as of 6/30/00)

Portfolio Manager: Martin Whitman, Curtis Jensen - 1997

Investm't Category: Growth

✔ Domestic	Index
✔ Foreign	Sector
Asset Allocation	State Specific

Investment Style

Large Cap	Mid Cap	✔ Small Cap
Growth	✔ Grth/Val	Value

Portfolio

8.8%	cash	0.0%	corp bonds
91.5%	stocks	0.0%	gov't bonds
0.0%	pref/conv't pref	0.0%	muni bonds
0.0%	conv't bds/wrnts	-0.3%	other

SHAREHOLDER INFORMATION

Minimum Investment
Initial: $1,000 Subsequent: $1,000

Minimum IRA Investment
Initial: $500 Subsequent: $200

Maximum Fees
Load: none 12b-1: none
Other: none

Services
✔ IRA
Keogh
✔ Telephone Exchange

Third Avenue Value (TAVFX)

800-443-1021, 212-888-6685
www.mjwhitman.com

Growth

this fund is closed to new investors

PERFORMANCE

fund inception date: 10/9/90

	3yr Annual	5yr Annual	10yr Annual	Bull	Bear
Return (%)	12.2	16.4	18.7	35.3	-4.7
Differ from Category (+/-)	1.2 av	0.3 av	1.9 abv av	-14.4 blw av	0.7 av

Standard Deviation	Category Risk Index	Beta
16.5%—av	0.85—low	0.67

	2000	1999	1998	1997	1996	1995	1994	1993	1992	1991
Return (%)	20.7	12.8	3.9	23.8	21.9	31.7	-1.4	23.6	21.2	34.1
Differ from Category (+/-)	17.2	-6.1	-10.4	-3.3	-0.4	1.3	-1.2	9.0	8.6	-3.5
Return, Tax-Adjusted (%)	16.5	12.5	3.3	23.0	20.6	30.5	-2.1	22.4	20.1	28.8

PER SHARE DATA

	2000	1999	1998	1997	1996	1995	1994	1993	1992	1991
Dividends, Net Income ($)	0.68	0.00	0.40	0.41	0.57	0.40	0.24	0.26	0.20	0.14
Distrib'ns, Cap Gain ($)	6.15	0.42	0.00	0.16	0.14	0.14	0.14	0.24	0.24	1.89
Net Asset Value ($)	36.22	35.99	32.29	31.46	25.86	21.80	16.97	17.62	14.67	12.47
Expense Ratio (%)	na	1.10	1.08	1.13	1.21	1.25	1.16	1.42	2.32	2.50
Yield (%)	1.60	0.00	1.23	1.29	2.19	1.82	1.40	1.45	1.34	0.97
Portfolio Turnover (%)	na	5	24	10	14	15	5	17	31	67
Total Assets (Millions $)	1,782	1,379	1,600	1,676	644	328	180	137	38	18

PORTFOLIO (as of 6/30/00)

Portfolio Manager: Martin Whitman - 1990

Investm't Category: Growth

✔ Domestic	Index
Foreign	Sector
Asset Allocation	State Specific

Investment Style

Large Cap	✔ Mid Cap	✔ Small Cap
Growth	✔ Grth/Val	Value

Portfolio

4.6% cash	11.1% corp bonds
73.9% stocks	1.1% gov't bonds
1.4% pref/conv't pref	0.0% muni bonds
1.7% conv't bds/wrnts	6.2% other

SHAREHOLDER INFORMATION

Minimum Investment
Initial: $1,000 Subsequent: $1,000

Minimum IRA Investment
Initial: $500 Subsequent: $200

Maximum Fees
Load: none 12b-1: none
Other: none

Services
✔ IRA
✔ Keogh
✔ Telephone Exchange

Torray (TORYX)

800-443-3036, 301-493-4600
www.torray.com

Growth

PERFORMANCE

fund inception date: 12/17/90

	3yr Annual	5yr Annual	10yr Annual	Bull	Bear
Return (%)	9.0	18.0	18.5	53.4	-5.3
Differ from Category (+/-)	-2.0 blw av	1.9 abv av	1.7 abv av	3.7 av	0.1 av

Standard Deviation	Category Risk Index	Beta
20.3%—abv av	1.04—av	0.96

	2000	1999	1998	1997	1996	1995	1994	1993	1992	1991
Return (%)	-3.3	24.0	8.1	37.1	29.0	50.3	2.4	6.3	21.0	19.9
Differ from Category (+/-)	-6.8	5.1	-6.2	10.0	6.7	19.9	2.6	-8.3	8.4	-17.7
Return, Tax-Adjusted (%)	-4.7	23.4	7.9	36.4	27.9	49.0	0.5	5.5	20.5	18.5

PER SHARE DATA

	2000	1999	1998	1997	1996	1995	1994	1993	1992	1991
Dividends, Net Income ($)	0.25	0.07	0.13	0.12	0.18	0.21	0.21	0.12	0.18	0.23
Distrib'ns, Cap Gain ($)	2.80	0.78	0.00	0.57	0.53	0.31	0.64	0.21	0.00	0.21
Net Asset Value ($)	39.79	44.31	36.48	33.85	25.22	20.11	13.76	14.27	13.74	11.51
Expense Ratio (%)	na	1.07	1.09	1.13	1.25	1.25	1.25	1.25	1.25	1.25
Yield (%)	0.58	0.15	0.35	0.34	0.69	1.02	1.45	0.82	1.31	1.96
Portfolio Turnover (%)	na	32	25	11	20	22	36	29	37	21
Total Assets (Millions $)	1,788	1,845	1,460	603	116	50	23	19	10	4

PORTFOLIO (as of 6/30/00)

Portfolio Manager: Robert Torray - 1990

Investm't Category: Growth

✔ Domestic
Index
Foreign
Sector
Asset Allocation
State Specific

Investment Style

✔ Large Cap
Mid Cap
Small Cap
Growth
Grth/Val
✔ Value

Portfolio

0.2% cash
99.8% stocks
0.0% pref/conv't pref
0.0% conv't bds/wrnts
0.0% corp bonds
0.0% gov't bonds
0.0% muni bonds
0.0% other

SHAREHOLDER INFORMATION

Minimum Investment

Initial: $10,000 Subsequent: $500

Minimum IRA Investment

Initial: $2,000 Subsequent: $1

Maximum Fees

Load: none 12b-1: none
Other: none

Services

✔ IRA
Keogh
Telephone Exchange

Turner: Small Cap Grth (TSCEX)

800-224-6312, 610-251-0268
www.turner-invest.com

Aggressive Growth

this fund is closed to new investors

PERFORMANCE

fund inception date: 2/4/94

	3yr Annual	5yr Annual	10yr Annual	Bull	Bear
Return (%)	19.8	20.5	na	152.2	-33.4
Differ from Category (+/-)	3.6 av	5.9 abv av	na	33.0 abv av	-12.8 blw av

Standard Deviation	Category Risk Index	Beta
39.2%—high	1.21—abv av	1.31

	2000	1999	1998	1997	1996	1995	1994	1993	1992	1991
Return (%)	-14.3	85.0	8.5	14.7	28.8	68.1	—	—	—	—
Differ from Category (+/-)	-8.3	27.5	-6.6	-0.1	10.5	33.5	—	—	—	—
Return, Tax-Adjusted (%)	-19.3	79.6	8.5	14.3	27.9	65.4	—	—	—	—

PER SHARE DATA

	2000	1999	1998	1997	1996	1995	1994	1993	1992	1991
Dividends, Net Income ($)	0.00	0.00	0.00	0.00	0.00	0.00	—	—	—	—
Distrib'ns, Cap Gain ($)	10.47	7.18	0.00	0.43	0.51	1.03	—	—	—	—
Net Asset Value ($)	24.73	41.49	26.72	24.62	21.86	17.37	—	—	—	—
Expense Ratio (%)	1.25	1.27	1.28	1.24	1.25	1.25	—	—	—	—
Yield (%)	0.00	0.00	0.00	0.00	0.00	0.00	—	—	—	—
Portfolio Turnover (%)	203	223	167	130	149	183	—	—	—	—
Total Assets (Millions $)	368	379	188	153	74	16	—	—	—	—

PORTFOLIO (as of 6/30/00)

Portfolio Manager: McVail, McHugh, Sustersic - 1998

Investm't Category: Aggressive Growth

✔ Domestic
Foreign
Asset Allocation
Index
Sector
State Specific

Investment Style

Large Cap
Mid Cap
✔ Small Cap
✔ Growth
Grth/Val
Value

Portfolio

5.0%	cash	0.0%	corp bonds
95.0%	stocks	0.0%	gov't bonds
0.0%	pref/conv't pref	0.0%	muni bonds
0.0%	conv't bds/wrnts	0.0%	other

SHAREHOLDER INFORMATION

Minimum Investment

Initial: $2,500 Subsequent: $50

Minimum IRA Investment

Initial: $2,000 Subsequent: $50

Maximum Fees

Load: none 12b-1: none
Other: none

Services

✔ IRA
Keogh
✔ Telephone Exchange

Tweedy Browne Amer Value (TWEBX)

800-432-4789, 212-916-0600
www.tweedy.com

Growth

PERFORMANCE — fund inception date: 12/8/93

	3yr Annual	5yr Annual	10yr Annual	Bull	Bear
Return (%)	8.5	16.8	na	18.6	12.0
Differ from Category (+/-)	-2.5 blw av	0.7 av	na	-31.1 low	17.4 high

Standard Deviation	Category Risk Index	Beta
14.9%—av	0.77—low	0.62

	2000	1999	1998	1997	1996	1995	1994	1993	1992	1991
Return (%)	14.4	2.0	9.5	38.8	22.4	36.2	-0.5	—	—	—
Differ from Category (+/-)	10.9	-16.9	-4.8	11.7	0.1	5.8	-0.3	—	—	—
Return, Tax-Adjusted (%)	13.2	1.0	9.0	37.8	21.0	35.7	-0.7	—	—	—

PER SHARE DATA

	2000	1999	1998	1997	1996	1995	1994	1993	1992	1991
Dividends, Net Income ($)	0.10	0.27	0.14	0.16	0.17	0.10	0.06	—	—	—
Distrib'ns, Cap Gain ($)	1.07	0.53	0.25	0.43	0.41	0.02	0.00	—	—	—
Net Asset Value ($)	24.42	22.37	22.74	21.11	15.64	13.25	9.82	—	—	—
Expense Ratio (%)	1.37	1.39	1.39	1.39	1.39	1.74	2.26	—	—	—
Yield (%)	0.39	1.17	0.60	0.74	1.05	0.75	0.61	—	—	—
Portfolio Turnover (%)	19	16	6	16	9	4	0	—	—	—
Total Assets (Millions $)	915	1,025	1,160	721	277	168	35	—	—	—

PORTFOLIO (as of 6/30/00)

Portfolio Manager: C. Browne, W. Browne, J. Spears - 1993

Investm't Category: Growth

✔ Domestic — Index
✔ Foreign — Sector
Asset Allocation — State Specific

Investment Style

✔ Large Cap — ✔ Mid Cap — Small Cap
Growth — Grth/Val — ✔ Value

Portfolio

3.3%	cash	0.0%	corp bonds
96.7%	stocks	0.0%	gov't bonds
0.0%	pref/conv't pref	0.0%	muni bonds
0.0%	conv't bds/wrnts	0.0%	other

SHAREHOLDER INFORMATION

Minimum Investment
Initial: $2,500 — Subsequent: $250

Minimum IRA Investment
Initial: $500 — Subsequent: $250

Maximum Fees
Load: none — 12b-1: none
Other: none

Services
✔ IRA
Keogh
✔ Telephone Exchange

Tweedy Browne Global Val (TBGVX)

800-432-4789, 212-916-0600
www.tweedy.com

International Stock

PERFORMANCE — fund inception date: 6/15/93

	3yr Annual	5yr Annual	10yr Annual	Bull	Bear
Return (%)	16.0	18.2	na	39.9	6.1
Differ from Category (+/-)	7.1 high	9.9 high	na	-51.0 low	30.1 high

Standard Deviation	Category Risk Index	Beta
13.8%—blw av	0.61—low	0.52

	2000	1999	1998	1997	1996	1995	1994	1993	1992	1991
Return (%)	12.3	25.2	10.9	22.9	20.2	10.7	4.3	—	—	—
Differ from Category (+/-)	31.7	-35.5	5.1	21.6	5.7	1.4	7.4	—	—	—
Return, Tax-Adjusted (%)	9.4	23.9	8.7	19.8	17.3	10.2	3.9	—	—	—

PER SHARE DATA

	2000	1999	1998	1997	1996	1995	1994	1993	1992	1991
Dividends, Net Income ($)	0.20	0.25	0.37	0.87	0.55	0.00	0.00	—	—	—
Distrib'ns, Cap Gain ($)	2.51	0.58	0.99	0.48	0.56	0.20	0.16	—	—	—
Net Asset Value ($)	19.98	20.21	16.82	16.39	14.45	12.95	11.88	—	—	—
Expense Ratio (%)	1.38	1.41	1.42	1.58	1.60	1.65	1.73	—	—	—
Yield (%)	0.88	1.20	2.07	5.15	3.66	0.00	0.00	—	—	—
Portfolio Turnover (%)	16	23	16	20	17	16	143	—	—	—
Total Assets (Millions $)	3,520	3,141	2,492	1,985	1,211	801	565	—	—	—

PORTFOLIO (as of 6/30/00)

Portfolio Manager: C. Browne, W. Browne, J. Spears - 1993

Investm't Category: International Stock

✔ Domestic	Index
✔ Foreign	Sector
Asset Allocation	State Specific

Investment Style

Large Cap	Mid Cap	Small Cap
Growth	Grth/Val	Value

Portfolio

13.6%	cash	0.0%	corp bonds
85.3%	stocks	0.0%	gov't bonds
1.1%	pref/conv't pref	0.0%	muni bonds
0.0%	conv't bds/wrnts	0.0%	other

SHAREHOLDER INFORMATION

Minimum Investment
Initial: $2,500 — Subsequent: $250

Minimum IRA Investment
Initial: $500 — Subsequent: $250

Maximum Fees
Load: none — 12b-1: none
Other: none

Services
✔ IRA
✔ Keogh
✔ Telephone Exchange

UMB Scout Stock (UMBSX)

800-996-2862, 816-860-3714
www.umb.com

Growth & Income

PERFORMANCE

fund inception date: 11/18/82

	3yr Annual	5yr Annual	10yr Annual	Bull	Bear
Return (%)	6.8	10.6	11.6	33.3	-6.3
Differ from Category (+/-)	-2.1 blw av	-3.7 low	-3.3 low	-0.2 av	-6.2 blw av

Standard Deviation	Category Risk Index	Beta
14.1%—blw av	0.81—low	0.69

	2000	1999	1998	1997	1996	1995	1994	1993	1992	1991
Return (%)	0.1	13.3	7.6	21.0	12.2	19.6	2.7	10.6	7.1	24.7
Differ from Category (+/-)	-5.6	2.5	-5.2	-5.9	-7.5	-9.9	3.2	-3.2	-4.5	-3.4
Return, Tax-Adjusted (%)	-2.1	10.6	5.5	18.8	9.5	16.2	-0.4	8.3	5.7	23.5

PER SHARE DATA

	2000	1999	1998	1997	1996	1995	1994	1993	1992	1991
Dividends, Net Income ($)	0.20	0.30	0.41	0.42	0.43	0.51	0.46	0.33	0.38	0.47
Distrib'ns, Cap Gain ($)	1.80	1.88	1.13	1.03	0.91	1.08	1.19	0.82	0.31	0.00
Net Asset Value ($)	17.11	19.12	18.86	19.01	16.97	16.34	15.01	16.24	15.77	15.40
Expense Ratio (%)	0.87	0.87	0.86	0.86	0.85	0.86	0.87	0.87	0.86	0.85
Yield (%)	1.05	1.42	2.05	2.09	2.40	2.92	2.83	1.93	2.36	3.05
Portfolio Turnover (%)	30	14	10	16	28	52	22	21	12	8
Total Assets (Millions $)	148	165	186	198	179	146	120	113	85	65

PORTFOLIO (as of 3/31/00)

Portfolio Manager: David Anderson - 1982

Investm't Category: Growth & Income

✔ Domestic | Index
Foreign | Sector
Asset Allocation | State Specific

Investment Style

✔ Large Cap | ✔ Mid Cap | Small Cap
Growth | Grth/Val | ✔ Value

Portfolio

14.9% cash | 0.0% corp bonds
85.1% stocks | 0.0% gov't bonds
0.0% pref/conv't pref | 0.0% muni bonds
0.0% conv't bds/wrnts | 0.0% other

SHAREHOLDER INFORMATION

Minimum Investment
Initial: $1,000 | Subsequent: $100

Minimum IRA Investment
Initial: $250 | Subsequent: $100

Maximum Fees
Load: none | 12b-1: none
Other: none

Services
✔ IRA
✔ Keogh
✔ Telephone Exchange

UMB Scout Worldwide

800-996-2862, 816-860-3714
www.umb.com

(UMBWX)

International Stock

PERFORMANCE — fund inception date: 9/14/93

	3yr Annual	5yr Annual	10yr Annual	Bull	Bear
Return (%)	12.4	14.8	na	50.4	-12.3
Differ from Category (+/-)	3.5 abv av	6.5 high	na	-40.5 blw av	11.7 high

Standard Deviation	Category Risk Index	Beta
14.5%—av	0.64—low	0.64

	2000	1999	1998	1997	1996	1995	1994	1993	1992	1991
Return (%)	-8.1	31.4	17.9	18.3	18.3	14.6	3.8	—	—	—
Differ from Category (+/-)	11.3	-29.3	12.1	17.0	3.8	5.3	6.9	—	—	—
Return, Tax-Adjusted (%)	-8.6	30.5	17.1	17.3	17.3	13.4	2.9	—	—	—

PER SHARE DATA

	2000	1999	1998	1997	1996	1995	1994	1993	1992	1991
Dividends, Net Income ($)	0.04	0.21	0.31	0.24	0.23	0.22	0.22	—	—	—
Distrib'ns, Cap Gain ($)	0.56	0.36	0.01	0.22	0.10	0.12	0.02	—	—	—
Net Asset Value ($)	21.24	23.77	18.56	16.02	13.94	12.08	10.84	—	—	—
Expense Ratio (%)	0.91	0.86	0.87	0.86	0.85	0.85	0.85	—	—	—
Yield (%)	0.18	0.87	1.66	1.47	1.63	1.80	2.02	—	—	—
Portfolio Turnover (%)	8	8	3	18	5	27	24	—	—	—
Total Assets (Millions $)	238	267	107	57	42	23	17	—	—	—

PORTFOLIO (as of 3/31/00)

Portfolio Manager: James Moffett - 1993

Investm't Category: International Stock

✔ Domestic — Index
✔ Foreign — Sector
Asset Allocation — State Specific

Investment Style

Large Cap — Mid Cap — Small Cap
Growth — Grth/Val — Value

Portfolio

7.9%	cash	0.0%	corp bonds
92.1%	stocks	0.0%	gov't bonds
0.0%	pref/conv't pref	0.0%	muni bonds
0.0%	conv't bds/wrnts	0.0%	other

SHAREHOLDER INFORMATION

Minimum Investment

Initial: $1,000 — Subsequent: $100

Minimum IRA Investment

Initial: $250 — Subsequent: $100

Maximum Fees

Load: none — 12b-1: none
Other: none

Services

✔ IRA
✔ Keogh
✔ Telephone Exchange

US Glob Acc: Bonnel Growth (ACBGX)

800-873-8637, 210-308-1234
www.us-global.com

Aggressive Growth

PERFORMANCE

fund inception date: 10/17/94

	3yr Annual	5yr Annual	10yr Annual	Bull	Bear
Return (%)	24.0	21.9	na	142.0	-36.6
Differ from Category (+/-)	7.8 abv av	7.3 abv av	na	22.8 abv av	-16.0 low

Standard Deviation	Category Risk Index	Beta
36.0%—high	1.11—abv av	1.10

	2000	1999	1998	1997	1996	1995	1994	1993	1992	1991
Return (%)	-17.2	81.4	27.1	10.3	27.9	45.2	—	—	—	—
Differ from Category (+/-)	-11.2	23.9	12.0	-4.5	9.6	10.6	—	—	—	—
Return, Tax-Adjusted (%)	-21.4	77.5	26.0	6.2	27.5	43.3	—	—	—	—

PER SHARE DATA

	2000	1999	1998	1997	1996	1995	1994	1993	1992	1991
Dividends, Net Income ($)	0.00	0.00	0.15	0.00	0.06	0.00	—	—	—	—
Distrib'ns, Cap Gain ($)	6.48	3.74	0.58	3.56	0.10	0.65	—	—	—	—
Net Asset Value ($)	19.10	30.80	19.56	16.04	17.68	13.95	—	—	—	—
Expense Ratio (%)	na	1.77	1.84	1.72	1.83	2.48	—	—	—	—
Yield (%)	0.00	0.00	0.74	0.00	0.33	0.00	—	—	—	—
Portfolio Turnover (%)	na	197	190	52	212	145	—	—	—	—
Total Assets (Millions $)	183	240	107	103	98	36	—	—	—	—

PORTFOLIO (as of 6/30/00)

Portfolio Manager: Arthur Bonnel - 1994

Investm't Category: Aggressive Growth

✔ Domestic | Index
✔ Foreign | Sector
Asset Allocation | State Specific

Investment Style

Large Cap | Mid Cap | ✔ Small Cap
✔ Growth | Grth/Val | Value

Portfolio

1.7%	cash	0.0%	corp bonds
98.3%	stocks	0.0%	gov't bonds
0.0%	pref/conv't pref	0.0%	muni bonds
0.0%	conv't bds/wrnts	0.0%	other

SHAREHOLDER INFORMATION

Minimum Investment
Initial: $5,000 | Subsequent: $50

Minimum IRA Investment
Initial: none | Subsequent: none

Maximum Fees
Load: none | 12b-1: 0.25%
Other: none

Services
✔ IRA
✔ Keogh
✔ Telephone Exchange

US Global Leaders Growth (USGLX)

800-282-2340, 212-765-5350
www.usgloballeaders.com

Growth

PERFORMANCE — fund inception date: 9/29/95

	3yr Annual	5yr Annual	10yr Annual	Bull	Bear
Return (%)	14.0	20.7	na	43.2	3.3
Differ from Category (+/-)	3.0 abv av	4.6 high	na	-6.5 av	8.7 abv av

Standard Deviation	Category Risk Index	Beta
18.6%—av	0.96—blw av	0.88

	2000	1999	1998	1997	1996	1995	1994	1993	1992	1991
Return (%)	4.1	7.8	31.9	40.4	23.1	—	—	—	—	—
Differ from Category (+/-)	0.6	-11.1	17.6	13.3	0.8	—	—	—	—	—
Return, Tax-Adjusted (%)	4.1	7.8	31.9	40.4	22.5	—	—	—	—	—

PER SHARE DATA

	2000	1999	1998	1997	1996	1995	1994	1993	1992	1991
Dividends, Net Income ($)	0.00	0.00	0.00	0.00	0.14	—	—	—	—	—
Distrib'ns, Cap Gain ($)	0.00	0.00	0.00	0.00	0.00	—	—	—	—	—
Net Asset Value ($)	27.08	26.00	24.10	18.26	13.00	—	—	—	—	—
Expense Ratio (%)	1.31	1.31	1.42	1.48	1.48	—	—	—	—	—
Yield (%)	0.00	0.00	0.00	0.00	1.07	—	—	—	—	—
Portfolio Turnover (%)	24	14	4	21	4	—	—	—	—	—
Total Assets (Millions $)	87	118	104	44	10	—	—	—	—	—

PORTFOLIO (as of 6/30/00)

Portfolio Manager: George Yeager - 1995

Investm't Category: Growth

✔ Domestic — Index
✔ Foreign — Sector
Asset Allocation — State Specific

Investment Style

✔ Large Cap — Mid Cap — Small Cap
Growth — ✔ Grth/Val — Value

Portfolio

1.9% cash — 0.0% corp bonds
98.1% stocks — 0.0% gov't bonds
0.0% pref/conv't pref — 0.0% muni bonds
0.0% conv't bds/wrnts — 0.0% other

SHAREHOLDER INFORMATION

Minimum Investment
Initial: $2,000 — Subsequent: $1,000

Minimum IRA Investment
Initial: $1 — Subsequent: $1

Maximum Fees
Load: none — 12b-1: none
Other: none

Services
✔ IRA
✔ Keogh
Telephone Exchange

USAA First Start Growth (UFSGX)

800-531-8181, 210-456-7211
www.usaa.com

Growth

PERFORMANCE — fund inception date: 8/1/97

	3yr Annual	5yr Annual	10yr Annual	Bull	Bear
Return (%)	12.6	na	na	65.8	-23.4
Differ from Category (+/-)	1.6 av	na	na	16.1 abv av	-18.0 low

Standard Deviation	Category Risk Index	Beta
22.0%—abv av	1.13—abv av	1.13

	2000	1999	1998	1997	1996	1995	1994	1993	1992	1991
Return (%)	-16.4	21.8	40.4	—	—	—	—	—	—	—
Differ from Category (+/-)	-19.9	2.9	26.1	—	—	—	—	—	—	—
Return, Tax-Adjusted (%)	-16.4	21.7	40.2	—	—	—	—	—	—	—

PER SHARE DATA

	2000	1999	1998	1997	1996	1995	1994	1993	1992	1991
Dividends, Net Income ($)	0.00	0.00	0.00	—	—	—	—	—	—	—
Distrib'ns, Cap Gain ($)	0.00	0.05	0.08	—	—	—	—	—	—	—
Net Asset Value ($)	14.11	16.88	13.91	—	—	—	—	—	—	—
Expense Ratio (%)	1.65	1.65	1.52	—	—	—	—	—	—	—
Yield (%)	0.00	0.00	0.00	—	—	—	—	—	—	—
Portfolio Turnover (%)	52	26	52	—	—	—	—	—	—	—
Total Assets (Millions $)	213	205	74	—	—	—	—	—	—	—

PORTFOLIO (as of 6/30/00)

Portfolio Manager: Curt Rohrman - 1997

Investm't Category: Growth

✔ Domestic — Index
✔ Foreign — Sector
Asset Allocation — State Specific

Investment Style

✔ Large Cap — Mid Cap — Small Cap
✔ Growth — Grth/Val — Value

Portfolio

1.0%	cash	0.0%	corp bonds
99.0%	stocks	0.0%	gov't bonds
0.0%	pref/conv't pref	0.0%	muni bonds
0.0%	conv't bds/wrnts	0.0%	other

SHAREHOLDER INFORMATION

Minimum Investment
Initial: $3,000 — Subsequent: $20

Minimum IRA Investment
Initial: $250 — Subsequent: $20

Maximum Fees
Load: none — 12b-1: none
Other: none

Services
✔ IRA
✔ Keogh
✔ Telephone Exchange

USAA Inv: Balanced Stgy (USBSX)

800-531-8181, 210-456-7211
www.usaa.com

Balanced

PERFORMANCE

fund inception date: 9/1/95

	3yr Annual	5yr Annual	10yr Annual	Bull	Bear
Return (%)	7.2	10.7	na	39.6	-8.6
Differ from Category (+/-)	-1.2 blw av	-0.7 av	na	11.5 high	-5.4 low

Standard Deviation	Category Risk Index	Beta
12.1%—blw av	1.10—abv av	0.65

	2000	1999	1998	1997	1996	1995	1994	1993	1992	1991
Return (%)	-4.4	18.9	8.6	19.0	13.4	—	—	—	—	—
Differ from Category (+/-)	-6.4	8.2	-4.7	0.2	-0.5	—	—	—	—	—
Return, Tax-Adjusted (%)	-6.1	18.2	7.4	17.3	12.1	—	—	—	—	—

PER SHARE DATA

	2000	1999	1998	1997	1996	1995	1994	1993	1992	1991
Dividends, Net Income ($)	0.29	0.22	0.30	0.34	0.31	—	—	—	—	—
Distrib'ns, Cap Gain ($)	0.79	0.00	0.16	0.28	0.02	—	—	—	—	—
Net Asset Value ($)	13.92	15.64	13.36	12.74	11.26	—	—	—	—	—
Expense Ratio (%)	1.25	1.25	1.25	1.25	1.25	—	—	—	—	—
Yield (%)	1.97	1.40	2.21	2.61	2.74	—	—	—	—	—
Portfolio Turnover (%)	87	63	22	28	26	—	—	—	—	—
Total Assets (Millions $)	148	126	79	47	25	—	—	—	—	—

PORTFOLIO (as of 6/30/00)

Portfolio Manager: Parsons, Lundmark, Noble - 1998

Investm't Category: Balanced

✔ Domestic — Index
✔ Foreign — Sector
Asset Allocation — State Specific

Investment Style

Large Cap — Mid Cap — Small Cap
Growth — Grth/Val — Value

Portfolio

1.0%	cash	28.0%	corp bonds
65.0%	stocks	5.0%	gov't bonds
0.0%	pref/conv't pref	0.0%	muni bonds
0.0%	conv't bds/wrnts	1.0%	other

SHAREHOLDER INFORMATION

Minimum Investment
Initial: $3,000 — Subsequent: $50

Minimum IRA Investment
Initial: $250 — Subsequent: $50

Maximum Fees
Load: none — 12b-1: none
Other: none

Services
✔ IRA
✔ Keogh
✔ Telephone Exchange

USAA Inv: Crnrst Strategy (USCRX)

800-531-8181, 210-456-7211
www.usaa.com

Balanced

PERFORMANCE — fund inception date: 8/15/84

	3yr Annual	5yr Annual	10yr Annual	Bull	Bear
Return (%)	4.2	9.0	10.7	18.9	-3.1
Differ from Category (+/-)	-4.2 low	-2.4 blw av	-1.0 blw av	-9.2 blw av	0.1 av

Standard Deviation	Category Risk Index	Beta
10.3%—blw av	0.94—blw av	0.50

	2000	1999	1998	1997	1996	1995	1994	1993	1992	1991
Return (%)	2.7	8.1	2.0	15.6	17.8	18.3	-1.0	23.7	6.3	16.2
Differ from Category (+/-)	0.7	-2.6	-11.3	-3.2	3.9	-7.2	0.3	9.3	-2.1	-7.6
Return, Tax-Adjusted (%)	1.4	5.6	-0.2	13.0	15.5	16.4	-3.6	22.1	5.2	15.1

PER SHARE DATA

	2000	1999	1998	1997	1996	1995	1994	1993	1992	1991
Dividends, Net Income ($)	0.47	0.78	0.81	0.72	0.77	0.74	0.58	0.59	0.63	0.59
Distrib'ns, Cap Gain ($)	0.70	1.67	1.52	1.90	0.83	0.33	1.38	0.29	0.00	0.00
Net Asset Value ($)	25.53	25.98	26.33	28.06	26.59	24.03	21.24	23.46	19.69	19.12
Expense Ratio (%)	1.09	1.05	1.01	1.06	1.15	1.13	1.11	1.18	1.18	1.18
Yield (%)	1.79	2.82	2.90	2.40	2.80	3.03	2.56	2.48	3.19	3.08
Portfolio Turnover (%)	37	46	32	35	36	33	31	45	33	28
Total Assets (Millions $)	1,027	1,192	1,367	1,413	1,171	949	841	762	578	603

PORTFOLIO (as of 6/30/00)

Portfolio Manager: committee - 2000

Investm't Category: Balanced

✔ Domestic — Index
✔ Foreign — Sector
✔ Asset Allocation — State Specific

Investment Style

Large Cap — Mid Cap — Small Cap
Growth — Grth/Val — Value

Portfolio

2.0%	cash	0.0%	corp bonds
79.0%	stocks	19.0%	gov't bonds
0.0%	pref/conv't pref	0.0%	muni bonds
0.0%	conv't bds/wrnts	0.0%	other

SHAREHOLDER INFORMATION

Minimum Investment
Initial: $3,000 — Subsequent: $50

Minimum IRA Investment
Initial: $250 — Subsequent: $50

Maximum Fees
Load: none — 12b-1: none
Other: none

Services
✔ IRA
✔ Keogh
✔ Telephone Exchange

USAA Inv: Emerging Mrkts (USEMX)

800-531-8181, 210-456-7211
www.usaa.com

International Stock

PERFORMANCE — fund inception date: 11/7/94

	3yr Annual	5yr Annual	10yr Annual	Bull	Bear
Return (%)	-8.4	-2.9	na	96.9	-35.7
Differ from Category (+/-)	-17.3 low	-11.2 low	na	6.0 abv av	-11.7 low

Standard Deviation	Category Risk Index	Beta
32.3%—high	1.43—high	1.37

	2000	1999	1998	1997	1996	1995	1994	1993	1992	1991
Return (%)	-31.9	52.4	-26.1	-3.4	16.5	3.6	—	—	—	—
Differ from Category (+/-)	-12.5	-8.3	-31.9	-4.7	2.0	-5.7	—	—	—	—
Return, Tax-Adjusted (%)	-31.9	52.0	-26.3	-3.7	14.9	2.8	—	—	—	—

PER SHARE DATA

	2000	1999	1998	1997	1996	1995	1994	1993	1992	1991
Dividends, Net Income ($)	0.00	0.07	0.07	0.00	0.00	0.01	—	—	—	—
Distrib'ns, Cap Gain ($)	0.00	0.00	0.00	0.17	0.50	0.22	—	—	—	—
Net Asset Value ($)	7.38	10.85	7.17	9.79	10.29	9.26	—	—	—	—
Expense Ratio (%)	1.28	1.27	1.31	1.81	2.27	2.40	—	—	—	—
Yield (%)	0.00	0.64	0.97	0.00	0.00	0.10	—	—	—	—
Portfolio Turnover (%)	147	83	41	61	87	46	—	—	—	—
Total Assets (Millions $)	162	323	234	305	55	25	—	—	—	—

PORTFOLIO (as of 6/30/00)

Portfolio Manager: Kevin Moore - 1999

Investm't Category: International Stock

Domestic	Index
✔ Foreign	Sector
Asset Allocation	State Specific

Investment Style

Large Cap	Mid Cap	Small Cap
Growth	Grth/Val	Value

Portfolio

12.0%	cash	0.0%	corp bonds
83.0%	stocks	0.0%	gov't bonds
5.0%	pref/conv't pref	0.0%	muni bonds
0.0%	conv't bds/wrnts	0.0%	other

SHAREHOLDER INFORMATION

Minimum Investment
Initial: $3,000 — Subsequent: $50

Minimum IRA Investment
Initial: $250 — Subsequent: $50

Maximum Fees
Load: none — 12b-1: none
Other: none

Services
✔ IRA
✔ Keogh
✔ Telephone Exchange

USAA Inv: Gold (USAGX)

800-531-8181, 210-456-7211
www.usaa.com

Aggressive Growth

PERFORMANCE — fund inception date: 8/15/84

	3yr Annual	5yr Annual	10yr Annual	Bull	Bear
Return (%)	-2.7	-10.6	-2.8	62.0	-9.5
Differ from Category (+/-)	-18.9 low	-25.2 low	-18.6 low	-57.2 blw av	11.1 abv av

Standard Deviation	Category Risk Index	Beta
44.1%—high	1.36—high	0.90

	2000	1999	1998	1997	1996	1995	1994	1993	1992	1991
Return (%)	-14.9	7.1	1.0	-38.1	0.0	4.0	-9.3	58.3	-7.9	-4.4
Differ from Category (+/-)	-8.9	-50.4	-14.1	-52.9	-18.3	-30.6	-8.5	33.1	-14.8	-51.6
Return, Tax-Adjusted (%)	-15.0	7.1	1.0	-38.1	0.0	4.0	-9.3	58.2	-8.0	-4.7

PER SHARE DATA

	2000	1999	1998	1997	1996	1995	1994	1993	1992	1991
Dividends, Net Income ($)	0.02	0.00	0.00	0.00	0.00	0.00	0.01	0.01	0.04	0.08
Distrib'ns, Cap Gain ($)	0.00	0.00	0.00	0.00	0.00	0.00	0.00	0.00	0.00	0.00
Net Asset Value ($)	5.06	5.98	5.58	5.52	8.93	8.93	8.59	9.49	6.00	6.56
Expense Ratio (%)	1.58	1.52	1.46	1.31	1.33	1.28	1.26	1.41	1.43	1.45
Yield (%)	0.39	0.00	0.00	0.00	0.00	0.00	0.11	0.10	0.66	1.21
Portfolio Turnover (%)	27	33	19	26	16	34	34	81	19	13
Total Assets (Millions $)	65	88	91	84	129	143	158	181	109	118

PORTFOLIO (as of 6/30/00)

Portfolio Manager: Mark Johnson - 1994

Investm't Category: Aggressive Growth

✔ Domestic — Index
✔ Foreign — ✔ Sector
Asset Allocation — State Specific

Investment Style

Large Cap — Mid Cap — Small Cap
Growth — Grth/Val — Value

Portfolio

3.0%	cash	0.0%	corp bonds
97.0%	stocks	0.0%	gov't bonds
0.0%	pref/conv't pref	0.0%	muni bonds
0.0%	conv't bds/wrnts	0.0%	other

SHAREHOLDER INFORMATION

Minimum Investment

Initial: $3,000 — Subsequent: $50

Minimum IRA Investment

Initial: $250 — Subsequent: $50

Maximum Fees

Load: none — 12b-1: none
Other: none

Services

✔ IRA
✔ Keogh
✔ Telephone Exchange

USAA Inv: Growth & Tax (USBLX)

800-531-8181, 210-456-7211
www.usaa.com

Balanced

PERFORMANCE — fund inception date: 1/11/89

	3yr Annual	5yr Annual	10yr Annual	Bull	Bear
Return (%)	6.5	9.3	9.8	23.3	-6.9
Differ from Category (+/-)	-1.9 blw av	-2.1 blw av	-1.9 low	-4.8 blw av	-3.7 blw av

Standard Deviation	Category Risk Index	Beta
9.4%—blw av	0.86—blw av	0.49

	2000	1999	1998	1997	1996	1995	1994	1993	1992	1991
Return (%)	-0.6	9.2	11.5	16.1	11.1	22.7	-2.6	13.7	4.9	14.6
Differ from Category (+/-)	-2.6	-1.5	-1.8	-2.7	-2.8	-2.8	-1.3	-0.7	-3.5	-9.2
Return, Tax-Adjusted (%)	-1.7	8.0	9.4	13.9	8.9	20.9	-4.6	11.3	3.6	13.1

PER SHARE DATA

	2000	1999	1998	1997	1996	1995	1994	1993	1992	1991
Dividends, Net Income ($)	0.48	0.45	0.49	0.52	0.51	0.50	0.47	0.45	0.46	0.51
Distrib'ns, Cap Gain ($)	0.00	0.00	0.60	0.54	0.35	0.03	0.27	0.37	0.01	0.00
Net Asset Value ($)	16.63	17.21	16.18	15.51	14.31	13.70	11.64	12.71	11.92	11.82
Expense Ratio (%)	0.71	0.69	0.71	0.74	0.82	0.80	0.84	0.86	0.92	1.00
Yield (%)	2.88	2.61	2.92	3.23	3.47	3.64	3.94	3.44	3.85	4.31
Portfolio Turnover (%)	66	63	65	194	202	314	171	98	107	81
Total Assets (Millions $)	253	265	237	211	172	149	124	127	91	61

PORTFOLIO (as of 6/30/00)

Portfolio Manager: C. Gladson, P. O'Hare - 1999

Investm't Category: Balanced

✔ Domestic	Index
Foreign	Sector
✔ Asset Allocation	State Specific

Investment Style

Large Cap	Mid Cap	Small Cap
Growth	Grth/Val	Value

Portfolio

2.0%	cash	0.0%	corp bonds
51.0%	stocks	0.0%	gov't bonds
0.0%	pref/conv't pref	47.0%	muni bonds
0.0%	conv't bds/wrnts	0.0%	other

SHAREHOLDER INFORMATION

Minimum Investment
Initial: $3,000 — Subsequent: $50

Minimum IRA Investment
Initial: $250 — Subsequent: $50

Maximum Fees
Load: none — 12b-1: none
Other: none

Services
✔ IRA
Keogh
✔ Telephone Exchange

USAA Inv: Growth Stgy

800-531-8181, 210-456-7211
www.usaa.com

(USGSX)

Balanced

PERFORMANCE — fund inception date: 9/1/95

	3yr Annual	5yr Annual	10yr Annual	Bull	Bear
Return (%)	9.0	11.5	na	53.2	-13.9
Differ from Category (+/-)	0.6 av	0.1 av	na	25.1 high	-10.7 low

Standard Deviation	Category Risk Index	Beta
16.7%—av	1.52—high	0.85

	2000	1999	1998	1997	1996	1995	1994	1993	1992	1991
Return (%)	-6.8	20.9	14.9	9.1	22.1	—	—	—	—	—
Differ from Category (+/-)	-8.8	10.2	1.6	-9.7	8.2	—	—	—	—	—
Return, Tax-Adjusted (%)	-7.7	18.6	13.6	8.3	20.4	—	—	—	—	—

PER SHARE DATA

	2000	1999	1998	1997	1996	1995	1994	1993	1992	1991
Dividends, Net Income ($)	0.07	0.18	0.07	0.12	0.12	—	—	—	—	—
Distrib'ns, Cap Gain ($)	0.65	1.24	0.69	0.22	0.44	—	—	—	—	—
Net Asset Value ($)	14.10	15.82	14.33	13.15	12.38	—	—	—	—	—
Expense Ratio (%)	1.24	1.28	1.25	1.31	1.66	—	—	—	—	—
Yield (%)	0.47	1.05	0.46	0.89	0.93	—	—	—	—	—
Portfolio Turnover (%)	71	41	69	62	40	—	—	—	—	—
Total Assets (Millions $)	294	307	256	228	142	—	—	—	—	—

PORTFOLIO (as of 6/30/00)

Portfolio Manager: committee - 1995

Investm't Category: Balanced

✔ Domestic — Index
✔ Foreign — Sector
✔ Asset Allocation — State Specific

Investment Style

Large Cap — Mid Cap — Small Cap
Growth — Grth/Val — Value

Portfolio

2.0%	cash	14.0%	corp bonds
81.0%	stocks	3.0%	gov't bonds
0.0%	pref/conv't pref	0.0%	muni bonds
0.0%	conv't bds/wrnts	0.0%	other

SHAREHOLDER INFORMATION

Minimum Investment
Initial: $3,000 — Subsequent: $50

Minimum IRA Investment
Initial: $250 — Subsequent: $50

Maximum Fees
Load: none — 12b-1: none
Other: none

Services
✔ IRA
✔ Keogh
✔ Telephone Exchange

USAA Inv: Int'l (USIFX)

800-531-8181, 210-456-7211
www.usaa.com

International Stock

PERFORMANCE — fund inception date: 7/11/88

	3yr Annual	5yr Annual	10yr Annual	Bull	Bear
Return (%)	6.0	9.1	10.5	45.0	-16.8
Differ from Category (+/-)	-2.9 blw av	0.8 av	1.5 abv av	-45.9 low	7.2 abv av

Standard Deviation	Category Risk Index	Beta
17.2%—av	0.76—low	0.73

	2000	1999	1998	1997	1996	1995	1994	1993	1992	1991
Return (%)	-10.8	28.6	4.0	8.9	19.1	8.2	2.6	39.8	-0.1	13.4
Differ from Category (+/-)	8.6	-32.1	-1.8	7.6	4.6	-1.1	5.7	-0.4	3.4	0.4
Return, Tax-Adjusted (%)	-11.9	27.0	3.0	7.0	17.8	7.9	0.9	38.9	-0.4	13.1

PER SHARE DATA

	2000	1999	1998	1997	1996	1995	1994	1993	1992	1991
Dividends, Net Income ($)	0.11	0.18	0.19	0.12	0.19	0.06	0.00	0.00	0.13	0.09
Distrib'ns, Cap Gain ($)	1.09	1.13	0.54	1.56	0.50	0.08	0.97	0.35	0.00	0.00
Net Asset Value ($)	19.86	23.45	19.31	19.22	19.15	16.69	15.56	16.10	11.79	11.94
Expense Ratio (%)	1.11	1.12	1.05	1.09	1.19	1.17	1.31	1.50	1.69	1.82
Yield (%)	0.52	0.73	0.95	0.57	0.96	0.35	0.00	0.00	1.10	0.75
Portfolio Turnover (%)	39	37	42	46	70	64	44	52	34	64
Total Assets (Millions $)	460	608	531	575	513	351	337	131	43	31

PORTFOLIO (as of 6/30/00)

Portfolio Manager: Albert Sebastian, Kevin Moore - 1996

Investm't Category: International Stock

Domestic	Index
✔ Foreign	Sector
Asset Allocation	State Specific

Investment Style

Large Cap	Mid Cap	Small Cap
Growth	Grth/Val	Value

Portfolio

5.0% cash	0.0% corp bonds
95.0% stocks	0.0% gov't bonds
0.0% pref/conv't pref	0.0% muni bonds
0.0% conv't bds/wrnts	0.0% other

SHAREHOLDER INFORMATION

Minimum Investment
Initial: $3,000 — Subsequent: $50

Minimum IRA Investment
Initial: $250 — Subsequent: $50

Maximum Fees
Load: none — 12b-1: none
Other: none

Services
✔ IRA
✔ Keogh
✔ Telephone Exchange

USAA Inv: World Growth (USAWX)

800-531-8181, 210-456-7211
www.usaa.com

International Stock

PERFORMANCE fund inception date: 10/1/92

	3yr Annual	5yr Annual	10yr Annual	Bull	Bear
Return (%)	8.6	11.4	na	56.4	-17.7
Differ from Category (+/-)	-0.3 av	3.1 abv av	na	-34.5 blw av	6.3 abv av

Standard Deviation	Category Risk Index	Beta
17.9%—av	0.79—blw av	0.88

	2000	1999	1998	1997	1996	1995	1994	1993	1992	1991
Return (%)	-11.2	30.7	10.3	12.8	19.0	12.8	0.6	24.0	—	—
Differ from Category (+/-)	8.2	-30.0	4.5	11.5	4.5	3.5	3.7	-16.2	—	—
Return, Tax-Adjusted (%)	-12.2	28.9	9.4	11.2	16.7	12.0	0.0	23.8	—	—

PER SHARE DATA

	2000	1999	1998	1997	1996	1995	1994	1993	1992	1991
Dividends, Net Income ($)	0.07	0.06	0.10	0.07	0.13	0.08	0.00	0.01	—	—
Distrib'ns, Cap Gain ($)	1.01	1.43	0.51	1.01	0.91	0.23	0.28	0.05	—	—
Net Asset Value ($)	17.69	20.96	17.27	16.19	15.30	13.78	12.50	12.70	—	—
Expense Ratio (%)	1.12	1.16	1.13	1.20	1.27	1.28	1.28	1.70	—	—
Yield (%)	0.37	0.26	0.56	0.40	0.80	0.57	0.00	0.07	—	—
Portfolio Turnover (%)	39	51	45	50	60	58	38	45	—	—
Total Assets (Millions $)	353	399	327	321	266	223	185	95	—	—

PORTFOLIO (as of 6/30/00)

Portfolio Manager: Sebastian, Moore, Rohrman - 1992

Investm't Category: International Stock

✔ Domestic — Index
✔ Foreign — Sector
Asset Allocation — State Specific

Investment Style

Large Cap — Mid Cap — Small Cap
Growth — Grth/Val — Value

Portfolio

4.0%	cash	0.0%	corp bonds
93.0%	stocks	0.0%	gov't bonds
1.0%	pref/conv't pref	0.0%	muni bonds
1.0%	conv't bds/wrnts	1.0%	other

SHAREHOLDER INFORMATION

Minimum Investment
Initial: $3,000 — Subsequent: $50

Minimum IRA Investment
Initial: $250 — Subsequent: $50

Maximum Fees
Load: none — 12b-1: none
Other: none

Services
✔ IRA
✔ Keogh
✔ Telephone Exchange

USAA Mutual: Aggr Growth (USAUX)

800-531-8181, 210-456-7211
www.usaa.com

Aggressive Growth

PERFORMANCE — fund inception date: 10/19/81

	3yr Annual	5yr Annual	10yr Annual	Bull	Bear
Return (%)	23.1	18.5	19.4	190.8	-36.1
Differ from Category (+/-)	6.9 abv av	3.9 abv av	3.6 abv av	71.6 high	-15.5 blw av

Standard Deviation	Category Risk Index	Beta
42.9%—high	1.32—high	1.49

	2000	1999	1998	1997	1996	1995	1994	1993	1992	1991
Return (%)	-19.9	91.0	22.2	7.5	16.4	50.4	-0.8	8.1	-8.5	71.6
Differ from Category (+/-)	-13.9	33.5	7.1	-7.3	-1.9	15.8	0.0	-17.1	-15.4	24.4
Return, Tax-Adjusted (%)	-20.5	89.5	19.5	5.9	15.7	47.9	-2.9	6.3	-10.9	71.5

PER SHARE DATA

	2000	1999	1998	1997	1996	1995	1994	1993	1992	1991
Dividends, Net Income ($)	0.00	0.00	0.00	0.00	0.00	0.00	0.00	0.02	0.00	0.01
Distrib'ns, Cap Gain ($)	1.86	2.30	3.99	2.34	0.57	1.61	1.55	1.25	2.14	0.00
Net Asset Value ($)	42.78	55.15	30.69	29.73	29.81	26.09	18.46	20.22	19.93	24.42
Expense Ratio (%)	0.60	0.72	0.71	0.74	0.74	0.86	0.83	0.86	0.82	0.87
Yield (%)	0.00	0.00	0.00	0.00	0.00	0.00	0.00	0.09	0.00	0.04
Portfolio Turnover (%)	33	35	83	57	43	138	99	113	74	50
Total Assets (Millions $)	1,479	1,657	833	782	715	442	283	288	289	271

PORTFOLIO (as of 6/30/00)

Portfolio Manager: John Cabell, Eric Efron - 1995

Investm't Category: Aggressive Growth

✔ Domestic　　Index
Foreign　　Sector
Asset Allocation　　State Specific

Investment Style

Large Cap　　Mid Cap　　✔ Small Cap
✔ Growth　　Grth/Val　　Value

Portfolio

1.0%	cash	0.0%	corp bonds
99.0%	stocks	0.0%	gov't bonds
0.0%	pref/conv't pref	0.0%	muni bonds
0.0%	conv't bds/wrnts	0.0%	other

SHAREHOLDER INFORMATION

Minimum Investment
Initial: $3,000　　Subsequent: $50

Minimum IRA Investment
Initial: $250　　Subsequent: $50

Maximum Fees
Load: none　　12b-1: none
Other: none

Services
✔ IRA
✔ Keogh
✔ Telephone Exchange

USAA Mutual: Growth

800-531-8181, 210-456-7211
www.usaa.com

(USAAX)

Growth

PERFORMANCE — fund inception date: 4/5/71

	3yr Annual	5yr Annual	10yr Annual	Bull	Bear
Return (%)	9.1	9.7	12.6	64.3	-21.8
Differ from Category (+/-)	-1.9 blw av	-6.4 low	-4.2 low	14.6 abv av	-16.4 low

Standard Deviation	Category Risk Index	Beta
20.6%—abv av	1.06—av	1.10

	2000	1999	1998	1997	1996	1995	1994	1993	1992	1991
Return (%)	-19.0	21.6	32.1	3.6	17.8	32.1	3.3	7.4	9.9	27.8
Differ from Category (+/-)	-22.5	2.7	17.8	-23.5	-4.5	1.7	3.5	-7.2	-2.7	-9.8
Return, Tax-Adjusted (%)	-19.4	19.2	31.2	1.0	12.4	29.6	-1.2	4.0	8.8	26.8

PER SHARE DATA

	2000	1999	1998	1997	1996	1995	1994	1993	1992	1991
Dividends, Net Income ($)	0.00	0.04	0.02	0.08	0.34	0.29	0.27	0.16	0.32	0.41
Distrib'ns, Cap Gain ($)	0.51	2.51	0.74	2.22	3.21	0.97	2.51	1.99	0.27	0.00
Net Asset Value ($)	19.00	23.99	22.07	17.40	18.84	19.31	15.63	17.69	18.51	17.40
Expense Ratio (%)	0.96	0.97	0.96	0.97	1.01	1.04	1.04	1.07	1.07	1.11
Yield (%)	0.00	0.15	0.08	0.40	1.54	1.42	1.48	0.81	1.70	2.35
Portfolio Turnover (%)	133	39	68	75	62	70	118	96	39	37
Total Assets (Millions $)	1,502	1,866	1,546	1,356	1,316	1,067	677	617	503	365

PORTFOLIO (as of 6/30/00)

Portfolio Manager: Patrick O'Hare - 2000

Investm't Category: Growth

✔ Domestic	Index
Foreign	Sector
Asset Allocation	State Specific

Investment Style

✔ Large Cap	Mid Cap	Small Cap
✔ Growth	Grth/Val	Value

Portfolio

1.0%	cash	0.0%	corp bonds
99.0%	stocks	0.0%	gov't bonds
0.0%	pref/conv't pref	0.0%	muni bonds
0.0%	conv't bds/wrnts	0.0%	other

SHAREHOLDER INFORMATION

Minimum Investment
Initial: $3,000 — Subsequent: $50

Minimum IRA Investment
Initial: $250 — Subsequent: $50

Maximum Fees
Load: none — 12b-1: none
Other: none

Services
✔ IRA
✔ Keogh
✔ Telephone Exchange

USAA Mutual: Growth & Inc (USGRX)

800-531-8181, 210-456-7211
www.usaa.com

Growth & Income

PERFORMANCE — fund inception date: 6/1/93

	3yr Annual	5yr Annual	10yr Annual	Bull	Bear
Return (%)	7.8	14.2	na	38.8	-1.8
Differ from Category (+/-)	-1.1 blw av	-0.1 av	na	5.3 av	-1.7 av

Standard Deviation	Category Risk Index	Beta
17.0%—av	0.98—av	0.87

	2000	1999	1998	1997	1996	1995	1994	1993	1992	1991
Return (%)	2.9	14.3	6.4	26.0	23.0	31.5	1.2	—	—	—
Differ from Category (+/-)	-2.8	3.5	-6.4	-0.9	3.3	2.0	1.7	—	—	—
Return, Tax-Adjusted (%)	2.2	13.2	4.9	24.5	21.3	30.2	0.0	—	—	—

PER SHARE DATA

	2000	1999	1998	1997	1996	1995	1994	1993	1992	1991
Dividends, Net Income ($)	0.16	0.18	0.19	0.22	0.22	0.23	0.22	—	—	—
Distrib'ns, Cap Gain ($)	0.34	0.64	0.91	0.66	0.44	0.13	0.11	—	—	—
Net Asset Value ($)	20.03	19.96	18.23	18.31	15.26	13.00	10.18	—	—	—
Expense Ratio (%)	0.90	0.89	0.85	0.89	0.95	1.01	1.12	—	—	—
Yield (%)	0.78	0.87	0.99	1.15	1.40	1.75	2.13	—	—	—
Portfolio Turnover (%)	22	24	29	14	16	19	14	—	—	—
Total Assets (Millions $)	1,082	1,154	1,054	936	513	267	150	—	—	—

PORTFOLIO (as of 6/30/00)

Portfolio Manager: R. David Ullom - 1993

Investm't Category: Growth & Income

✔ Domestic — Index
Foreign — Sector
Asset Allocation — State Specific

Investment Style

✔ Large Cap — Mid Cap — Small Cap
Growth — Grth/Val — ✔ Value

Portfolio

3.9%	cash	0.0%	corp bonds
96.1%	stocks	0.0%	gov't bonds
0.0%	pref/conv't pref	0.0%	muni bonds
0.0%	conv't bds/wrnts	0.0%	other

SHAREHOLDER INFORMATION

Minimum Investment
Initial: $3,000 — Subsequent: $50

Minimum IRA Investment
Initial: $250 — Subsequent: $50

Maximum Fees
Load: none — 12b-1: none
Other: none

Services
✔ IRA
✔ Keogh
✔ Telephone Exchange

USAA Mutual: Income

800-531-8181, 210-456-7211
www.usaa.com

(USAIX)

Balanced

PERFORMANCE   fund inception date: 3/4/74

	3yr Annual	5yr Annual	10yr Annual	Bull	Bear
Return (%)	5.8	5.9	8.3	-1.4	7.5
Differ from Category (+/-)	-2.6 blw av	-5.5 low	-3.4 low	-29.5 low	10.7 high

Standard Deviation	Category Risk Index	Beta
3.2%—low	0.29—low	-0.01

	2000	1999	1998	1997	1996	1995	1994	1993	1992	1991
Return (%)	13.3	-3.8	8.7	11.0	1.3	24.4	-5.2	9.9	8.3	19.3
Differ from Category (+/-)	11.3	-14.5	-4.6	-7.8	-12.6	-1.1	-3.9	-4.5	-0.1	-4.5
Return, Tax-Adjusted (%)	10.5	-6.2	5.3	8.3	-1.2	21.4	-7.8	6.5	5.9	16.6

PER SHARE DATA

	2000	1999	1998	1997	1996	1995	1994	1993	1992	1991
Dividends, Net Income ($)	0.79	0.76	0.84	0.83	0.83	0.84	0.86	0.88	0.94	0.96
Distrib'ns, Cap Gain ($)	0.00	0.02	0.45	0.00	0.00	0.00	0.00	0.25	0.00	0.01
Net Asset Value ($)	11.96	11.30	12.56	12.78	12.31	13.00	11.19	12.71	12.61	12.55
Expense Ratio (%)	0.42	0.38	0.38	0.39	0.40	0.41	0.41	0.41	0.42	0.47
Yield (%)	6.60	6.71	6.45	6.49	6.74	6.46	7.68	6.79	7.45	7.64
Portfolio Turnover (%)	24	54	47	57	81	30	25	44	22	15
Total Assets (Millions $)	1,312	1,319	1,768	1,722	1,738	1,893	1,611	1,945	1,452	1,004

PORTFOLIO (as of 6/30/00)

Portfolio Manager: Didi Weinblatt - 2000

Investm't Category: Balanced

✔ Domestic	Index
Foreign	Sector
Asset Allocation	State Specific

Investment Style

Large Cap	Mid Cap	Small Cap
Growth	Grth/Val	Value

Portfolio

1.0% cash	24.0% corp bonds
0.0% stocks	66.0% gov't bonds
9.0% pref/conv't pref	0.0% muni bonds
0.0% conv't bds/wrnts	0.0% other

SHAREHOLDER INFORMATION

Minimum Investment

Initial: $3,000   Subsequent: $50

Minimum IRA Investment

Initial: $250   Subsequent: $50

Maximum Fees

Load: none   12b-1: none

Other: none

Services

✔ IRA

✔ Keogh

✔ Telephone Exchange

USAA Mutual: Income Stock (USISX)

800-531-8181, 210-456-7211
www.usaa.com

Growth & Income

PERFORMANCE — fund inception date: 5/4/87

	3yr Annual	5yr Annual	10yr Annual	Bull	Bear
Return (%)	6.8	12.9	13.6	19.6	4.2
Differ from Category (+/-)	-2.1 blw av	-1.4 blw av	-1.3 blw av	-13.9 blw av	4.3 abv av

Standard Deviation	Category Risk Index	Beta
15.0%—av	0.86—low	0.63

	2000	1999	1998	1997	1996	1995	1994	1993	1992	1991
Return (%)	10.8	1.9	8.0	27.8	17.8	28.6	-0.7	11.5	7.7	27.3
Differ from Category (+/-)	5.1	-8.9	-4.8	0.9	-1.9	-0.9	-0.2	-2.3	-3.9	-0.8
Return, Tax-Adjusted (%)	9.0	-0.6	5.8	24.7	14.5	25.6	-3.2	9.0	5.8	25.3

PER SHARE DATA

	2000	1999	1998	1997	1996	1995	1994	1993	1992	1991
Dividends, Net Income ($)	0.55	0.44	0.70	0.78	0.78	0.77	0.75	0.71	0.70	0.68
Distrib'ns, Cap Gain ($)	0.50	1.66	0.73	1.01	0.74	0.27	0.22	0.19	0.09	0.00
Net Asset Value ($)	18.63	17.83	19.57	19.55	16.83	15.67	13.06	14.13	13.48	13.27
Expense Ratio (%)	0.67	0.65	0.65	0.68	0.72	0.75	0.73	0.70	0.74	0.83
Yield (%)	2.87	2.25	3.44	3.79	4.43	4.83	5.64	4.95	5.15	5.12
Portfolio Turnover (%)	13	34	22	34	32	34	25	26	16	27
Total Assets (Millions $)	1,899	2,284	2,490	2,397	1,922	1,585	1,171	1,129	592	243

PORTFOLIO (as of 6/30/00)

Portfolio Manager: Stephan Klaffke - 1999

Investm't Category: Growth & Income

✔ Domestic — Index
Foreign — Sector
Asset Allocation — State Specific

Investment Style

✔ Large Cap — ✔ Mid Cap — Small Cap
Growth — Grth/Val — ✔ Value

Portfolio

6.0%	cash	0.0%	corp bonds
90.0%	stocks	0.0%	gov't bonds
0.0%	pref/conv't pref	0.0%	muni bonds
4.0%	conv't bds/wrnts	0.0%	other

SHAREHOLDER INFORMATION

Minimum Investment
Initial: $3,000 — Subsequent: $50

Minimum IRA Investment
Initial: $250 — Subsequent: $50

Maximum Fees
Load: none — 12b-1: none
Other: none

Services
✔ IRA
✔ Keogh
✔ Telephone Exchange

USAA S&P 500 Index

800-531-8181, 210-456-7211
www.usaa.com

(USSPX)

Growth & Income

PERFORMANCE — fund inception date: 5/1/96

	3yr Annual	5yr Annual	10yr Annual	Bull	Bear
Return (%)	12.0	na	na	55.8	-11.6
Differ from Category (+/-)	3.1 abv av	na	na	22.3 high	-11.5 blw av

Standard Deviation	Category Risk Index	Beta
17.6%—av	1.01—av	0.99

	2000	1999	1998	1997	1996	1995	1994	1993	1992	1991
Return (%)	-9.2	20.6	28.6	33.0	—	—	—	—	—	—
Differ from Category (+/-)	-14.9	9.8	15.8	6.1	—	—	—	—	—	—
Return, Tax-Adjusted (%)	-10.1	20.0	28.0	32.3	—	—	—	—	—	—

PER SHARE DATA

	2000	1999	1998	1997	1996	1995	1994	1993	1992	1991
Dividends, Net Income ($)	0.24	0.25	0.20	0.20	—	—	—	—	—	—
Distrib'ns, Cap Gain ($)	0.66	0.05	0.00	0.00	—	—	—	—	—	—
Net Asset Value ($)	19.91	22.92	19.27	15.16	—	—	—	—	—	—
Expense Ratio (%)	na	0.08	0.18	0.18	—	—	—	—	—	—
Yield (%)	1.16	1.08	1.03	1.31	—	—	—	—	—	—
Portfolio Turnover (%)	na	13	4	19	—	—	—	—	—	—
Total Assets (Millions $)	3,031	3,219	1,852	628	—	—	—	—	—	—

PORTFOLIO (as of 6/30/00)

Portfolio Manager: Frank Salerno - 1996

Investm't Category: Growth & Income

✔ Domestic ✔ Index
Foreign Sector
Asset Allocation State Specific

Investment Style

✔ Large Cap Mid Cap Small Cap
Growth ✔ Grth/Val Value

Portfolio

2.0%	cash	0.0%	corp bonds
98.0%	stocks	0.0%	gov't bonds
0.0%	pref/conv't pref	0.0%	muni bonds
0.0%	conv't bds/wrnts	0.0%	other

SHAREHOLDER INFORMATION

Minimum Investment

Initial: $3,000 Subsequent: $50

Minimum IRA Investment

Initial: $2,000 Subsequent: $50

Maximum Fees

Load: none 12b-1: none
Other: none

Services

✔ IRA
✔ Keogh
✔ Telephone Exchange

USAA Science & Technology (USSCX)

800-531-8181, 210-456-7211
www.usaa.com

Aggressive Growth

PERFORMANCE — fund inception date: 8/1/97

	3yr Annual	5yr Annual	10yr Annual	Bull	Bear
Return (%)	21.5	na	na	111.6	-29.8
Differ from Category (+/-)	5.3 abv av	na	na	-7.6 abv av	-9.2 blw av

Standard Deviation	Category Risk Index	Beta
30.4%—high	0.94—blw av	1.25

	2000	1999	1998	1997	1996	1995	1994	1993	1992	1991
Return (%)	-16.6	47.0	46.6	—	—	—	—	—	—	—
Differ from Category (+/-)	-10.6	-10.5	31.5	—	—	—	—	—	—	—
Return, Tax-Adjusted (%)	-16.6	46.6	46.6	—	—	—	—	—	—	—

PER SHARE DATA

	2000	1999	1998	1997	1996	1995	1994	1993	1992	1991
Dividends, Net Income ($)	0.00	0.00	0.00	—	—	—	—	—	—	—
Distrib'ns, Cap Gain ($)	0.00	0.25	0.00	—	—	—	—	—	—	—
Net Asset Value ($)	16.06	19.27	13.30	—	—	—	—	—	—	—
Expense Ratio (%)	1.22	1.33	1.42	—	—	—	—	—	—	—
Yield (%)	0.00	0.00	0.00	—	—	—	—	—	—	—
Portfolio Turnover (%)	69	44	76	—	—	—	—	—	—	—
Total Assets (Millions $)	499	415	159	—	—	—	—	—	—	—

PORTFOLIO (as of 6/30/00)

Portfolio Manager: Curt Rohrman - 1997

Investm't Category: Aggressive Growth

✔ Domestic　Index
Foreign　✔ Sector
Asset Allocation　State Specific

Investment Style

Large Cap　✔ Mid Cap　✔ Small Cap
✔ Growth　Grth/Val　Value

Portfolio

0.0%	cash	0.0%	corp bonds
100.0%	stocks	0.0%	gov't bonds
0.0%	pref/conv't pref	0.0%	muni bonds
0.0%	conv't bds/wrnts	0.0%	other

SHAREHOLDER INFORMATION

Minimum Investment
Initial: $3,000　Subsequent: $50

Minimum IRA Investment
Initial: $250　Subsequent: $50

Maximum Fees
Load: none　12b-1: none
Other: none

Services
✔ IRA
✔ Keogh
✔ Telephone Exchange

Value Line (VLIFX)

800-223-0818, 212-907-1500
www.valueline.com

Growth

PERFORMANCE — fund inception date: 3/1/50

	3yr Annual	5yr Annual	10yr Annual	Bull	Bear
Return (%)	8.8	13.9	14.9	71.1	-19.1
Differ from Category (+/-)	-2.2 blw av	-2.2 blw av	-1.9 blw av	21.4 abv av	-13.7 low

Standard Deviation	Category Risk Index	Beta
21.4%—abv av	1.10—abv av	1.11

	2000	1999	1998	1997	1996	1995	1994	1993	1992	1991
Return (%)	-15.3	26.7	20.2	21.5	22.5	32.1	-4.4	6.8	4.6	48.8
Differ from Category (+/-)	-18.8	7.8	5.9	-5.6	0.2	1.7	-4.2	-7.8	-8.0	11.2
Return, Tax-Adjusted (%)	-15.9	24.6	19.6	17.2	18.7	29.4	-8.6	4.5	0.5	46.5

PER SHARE DATA

	2000	1999	1998	1997	1996	1995	1994	1993	1992	1991
Dividends, Net Income ($)	0.00	0.00	0.05	0.14	0.11	0.12	0.09	0.07	0.16	0.23
Distrib'ns, Cap Gain ($)	0.86	2.35	0.47	3.79	2.21	1.19	2.61	1.39	2.73	0.92
Net Asset Value ($)	21.37	26.25	22.65	19.29	19.29	17.63	14.36	17.90	18.16	20.17
Expense Ratio (%)	na	0.76	0.77	0.78	0.80	0.85	0.82	0.80	0.84	0.71
Yield (%)	0.00	0.00	0.21	0.60	0.51	0.63	0.53	0.36	0.76	1.09
Portfolio Turnover (%)	na	36	98	68	54	78	150	120	129	109
Total Assets (Millions $)	388	494	418	382	348	317	272	331	327	320

PORTFOLIO (as of 6/30/00)

Portfolio Manager: committee - 1990

Investm't Category: Growth

✔ Domestic | Index
Foreign | Sector
Asset Allocation | State Specific

Investment Style

✔ Large Cap | Mid Cap | Small Cap
✔ Growth | Grth/Val | Value

Portfolio

3.5%	cash	0.0%	corp bonds
96.6%	stocks	0.0%	gov't bonds
0.0%	pref/conv't pref	0.0%	muni bonds
0.0%	conv't bds/wrnts	0.0%	other

SHAREHOLDER INFORMATION

Minimum Investment
Initial: $1,000 Subsequent: $100

Minimum IRA Investment
Initial: $1,000 Subsequent: $100

Maximum Fees
Load: none 12b-1: 0.25%
Other: none

Services
✔ IRA
✔ Keogh
✔ Telephone Exchange

Value Line Asset Alloc

800-223-0818, 212-907-1500
www.valueline.com

(VLAAX)

Balanced

PERFORMANCE

fund inception date: 8/24/93

	3yr Annual	5yr Annual	10yr Annual	Bull	Bear
Return (%)	14.8	18.3	na	61.0	-8.5
Differ from Category (+/-)	6.4 high	6.9 high	na	32.9 high	-5.3 low

Standard Deviation	Category Risk Index	Beta
19.7%—abv av	1.79—high	0.81

	2000	1999	1998	1997	1996	1995	1994	1993	1992	1991
Return (%)	0.4	19.8	25.7	20.9	26.6	36.1	3.4	—	—	—
Differ from Category (+/-)	-1.6	9.1	12.4	2.1	12.7	10.6	4.7	—	—	—
Return, Tax-Adjusted (%)	-0.6	17.8	25.2	17.5	20.1	32.2	2.9	—	—	—

PER SHARE DATA

	2000	1999	1998	1997	1996	1995	1994	1993	1992	1991
Dividends, Net Income ($)	0.32	0.24	0.02	0.25	0.25	0.12	0.06	—	—	—
Distrib'ns, Cap Gain ($)	0.40	1.24	0.25	1.82	2.69	1.29	0.10	—	—	—
Net Asset Value ($)	19.23	19.91	17.89	14.47	13.73	13.20	10.74	—	—	—
Expense Ratio (%)	1.03	1.08	1.15	1.23	1.38	1.76	0.47	—	—	—
Yield (%)	1.63	1.13	0.11	1.53	1.52	0.82	0.55	—	—	—
Portfolio Turnover (%)	72	129	139	192	244	211	—	—	—	—
Total Assets (Millions $)	295	289	178	101	69	49	22	—	—	—

PORTFOLIO (as of 6/30/00)

Portfolio Manager: committee - 1993

Investm't Category: Balanced

✔ Domestic	Index
Foreign	Sector
✔ Asset Allocation	State Specific

Investment Style

Large Cap	Mid Cap	Small Cap
Growth	Grth/Val	Value

Portfolio

8.1%	cash	0.6%	corp bonds
65.3%	stocks	31.7%	gov't bonds
0.0%	pref/conv't pref	0.0%	muni bonds
0.0%	conv't bds/wrnts	-5.7%	other

SHAREHOLDER INFORMATION

Minimum Investment
Initial: $1,000 Subsequent: $100

Minimum IRA Investment
Initial: $1,000 Subsequent: $100

Maximum Fees
Load: none 12b-1: 0.25%
Other: none

Services
✔ IRA
✔ Keogh
✔ Telephone Exchange

Value Line Convertible (VALCX)

800-223-0818, 212-907-1500
www.valueline.com

Growth & Income

PERFORMANCE — fund inception date: 6/3/85

	3yr Annual	5yr Annual	10yr Annual	Bull	Bear
Return (%)	7.4	11.7	13.0	44.7	-20.1
Differ from Category (+/-)	-1.5 blw av	-2.6 low	-1.9 low	11.2 abv av	-20.0 low

Standard Deviation	Category Risk Index	Beta
17.8%—av	1.03—abv av	0.62

	2000	1999	1998	1997	1996	1995	1994	1993	1992	1991
Return (%)	-7.5	33.3	0.5	17.0	20.2	22.7	-5.2	14.8	13.8	28.7
Differ from Category (+/-)	-13.2	22.5	-12.3	-9.9	0.5	-6.8	-4.7	1.0	2.2	0.6
Return, Tax-Adjusted (%)	-10.9	31.9	-2.2	13.8	14.7	20.2	-8.4	9.3	12.1	26.8

PER SHARE DATA

	2000	1999	1998	1997	1996	1995	1994	1993	1992	1991
Dividends, Net Income ($)	0.50	0.42	0.62	0.67	0.65	0.67	0.75	0.66	0.64	0.60
Distrib'ns, Cap Gain ($)	1.84	0.00	0.67	0.74	1.58	0.00	0.42	1.66	0.00	0.00
Net Asset Value ($)	12.65	16.29	12.61	13.86	13.10	12.79	11.01	12.85	13.25	12.25
Expense Ratio (%)	1.00	1.00	0.98	1.01	1.07	1.08	1.07	1.10	1.14	1.19
Yield (%)	3.45	2.57	4.66	4.58	4.42	5.23	6.56	4.54	4.83	4.89
Portfolio Turnover (%)	127	123	111	164	129	87	142	146	140	216
Total Assets (Millions $)	72	85	75	85	67	55	45	51	41	38

PORTFOLIO (as of 6/30/00)

Portfolio Manager: committee - 1985

Investm't Category: Growth & Income

✔ Domestic — Index
Foreign — Sector
Asset Allocation — State Specific

Investment Style

Large Cap — ✔ Mid Cap — ✔ Small Cap
✔ Growth — Grth/Val — Value

Portfolio

7.6%	cash	0.0%	corp bonds
4.1%	stocks	0.0%	gov't bonds
25.8%	pref/conv't pref	0.0%	muni bonds
62.6%	conv't bds/wrnts	0.0%	other

SHAREHOLDER INFORMATION

Minimum Investment
Initial: $1,000 — Subsequent: $250

Minimum IRA Investment
Initial: $1,000 — Subsequent: $100

Maximum Fees
Load: none — 12b-1: 0.25%
Other: none

Services
✔ IRA
✔ Keogh
✔ Telephone Exchange

Value Line Inc & Grth (VALIX)

800-233-0818, 212-907-1500
www.valueline.com

Balanced

PERFORMANCE — fund inception date: 10/1/52

	3yr Annual	5yr Annual	10yr Annual	Bull	Bear
Return (%)	16.3	17.0	14.1	69.0	-6.3
Differ from Category (+/-)	7.9 high	5.6 high	2.4 high	40.9 high	-3.1 blw av

Standard Deviation	Category Risk Index	Beta
17.3%—av	1.58—high	0.89

	2000	1999	1998	1997	1996	1995	1994	1993	1992	1991
Return (%)	-1.6	25.3	27.8	18.5	17.3	26.2	-4.3	8.8	1.7	28.5
Differ from Category (+/-)	-3.6	14.6	14.5	-0.3	3.4	0.7	-3.0	-5.6	-6.7	4.7
Return, Tax-Adjusted (%)	-3.7	21.3	26.0	16.1	12.0	23.7	-5.7	4.0	-0.8	26.9

PER SHARE DATA

	2000	1999	1998	1997	1996	1995	1994	1993	1992	1991
Dividends, Net Income ($)	0.13	0.11	0.10	0.15	0.24	0.25	0.21	0.21	0.27	0.31
Distrib'ns, Cap Gain ($)	0.81	1.67	0.52	0.57	1.03	0.20	0.05	0.93	0.41	0.00
Net Asset Value ($)	9.00	10.10	9.53	7.98	7.37	7.37	6.21	6.77	7.29	7.86
Expense Ratio (%)	na	0.83	0.87	0.87	0.93	0.94	0.90	0.88	0.89	0.74
Yield (%)	1.32	0.93	0.99	1.75	2.85	3.30	3.35	2.72	3.50	3.94
Portfolio Turnover (%)	na	64	99	54	83	76	56	165	85	67
Total Assets (Millions $)	218	229	188	160	147	144	131	162	163	172

PORTFOLIO (as of 6/30/00)

Portfolio Manager: committee - 1990

Investm't Category: Balanced

✔ Domestic — Index
Foreign — Sector
✔ Asset Allocation — State Specific

Investment Style

Large Cap — Mid Cap — Small Cap
Growth — Grth/Val — Value

Portfolio

10.4%	cash	3.6%	corp bonds
74.1%	stocks	11.8%	gov't bonds
0.0%	pref/conv't pref	0.0%	muni bonds
0.0%	conv't bds/wrnts	0.0%	other

SHAREHOLDER INFORMATION

Minimum Investment
Initial: $1,000 — Subsequent: $100

Minimum IRA Investment
Initial: $1,000 — Subsequent: $100

Maximum Fees
Load: none — 12b-1: 0.25%
Other: none

Services
✔ IRA
✔ Keogh
✔ Telephone Exchange

Value Line Lever Grth Inv (VALLX)

800-223-0818, 212-907-1500
www.valueline.com

Aggressive Growth

PERFORMANCE — fund inception date: 3/20/72

	3yr Annual	5yr Annual	10yr Annual	Bull	Bear
Return (%)	16.3	18.9	17.9	83.9	-18.4
Differ from Category (+/-)	0.1 av	4.3 abv av	2.1 av	-35.3 av	2.2 abv av

Standard Deviation	Category Risk Index	Beta
22.8%—abv av	0.70—low	1.21

	2000	1999	1998	1997	1996	1995	1994	1993	1992	1991
Return (%)	-13.9	30.9	39.6	23.7	22.3	37.0	-3.7	16.1	-2.4	46.3
Differ from Category (+/-)	-7.9	-26.6	24.5	8.9	4.0	2.4	-2.9	-9.1	-9.3	-0.9
Return, Tax-Adjusted (%)	-15.3	28.7	38.9	21.6	18.9	33.0	-4.3	14.7	-5.5	39.8

PER SHARE DATA

	2000	1999	1998	1997	1996	1995	1994	1993	1992	1991
Dividends, Net Income ($)	0.00	0.00	0.00	0.00	0.00	0.09	0.11	0.05	0.15	0.22
Distrib'ns, Cap Gain ($)	4.34	5.20	1.20	3.23	3.38	3.15	0.45	0.98	2.68	4.61
Net Asset Value ($)	45.63	57.98	48.42	35.58	31.51	28.50	23.18	24.67	22.15	25.64
Expense Ratio (%)	na	0.82	0.84	0.86	0.87	0.90	0.89	0.92	0.93	0.92
Yield (%)	0.00	0.00	0.00	0.00	0.00	0.28	0.46	0.19	0.60	0.72
Portfolio Turnover (%)	na	27	54	37	34	54	49	80	208	250
Total Assets (Millions $)	604	762	608	432	371	337	264	302	290	347

PORTFOLIO (as of 6/30/00)

Portfolio Manager: committee - 1990

Investm't Category: Aggressive Growth

✔ Domestic — Index
Foreign — Sector
Asset Allocation — State Specific

Investment Style

✔ Large Cap — Mid Cap — Small Cap
✔ Growth — Grth/Val — Value

Portfolio

2.4%	cash	0.0%	corp bonds
97.6%	stocks	0.0%	gov't bonds
0.0%	pref/conv't pref	0.0%	muni bonds
0.0%	conv't bds/wrnts	0.0%	other

SHAREHOLDER INFORMATION

Minimum Investment

Initial: $1,000 — Subsequent: $100

Minimum IRA Investment

Initial: $1,000 — Subsequent: $100

Maximum Fees

Load: none — 12b-1: none
Other: none

Services

✔ IRA
✔ Keogh
✔ Telephone Exchange

Value Line Specl Situatn (VALSX)

800-223-0818, 212-907-1500
www.valueline.com

Aggressive Growth

PERFORMANCE — fund inception date: 5/30/56

	3yr Annual	5yr Annual	10yr Annual	Bull	Bear
Return (%)	25.0	22.6	18.3	124.5	-21.9
Differ from Category (+/-)	8.8 abv av	8.0 abv av	2.5 av	5.3 abv av	-1.3 av

Standard Deviation	Category Risk Index	Beta
31.6%—high	0.97—av	1.18

	2000	1999	1998	1997	1996	1995	1994	1993	1992	1991
Return (%)	-6.7	61.6	29.8	32.0	7.2	28.9	1.0	12.9	-3.4	36.6
Differ from Category (+/-)	-0.7	4.1	14.7	17.2	-11.1	-5.7	1.8	-12.3	-10.3	-10.6
Return, Tax-Adjusted (%)	-7.9	60.0	28.3	27.5	0.1	20.9	-0.5	11.5	-3.6	34.6

PER SHARE DATA

	2000	1999	1998	1997	1996	1995	1994	1993	1992	1991
Dividends, Net Income ($)	0.00	0.00	0.00	0.00	0.26	0.06	0.00	0.00	0.00	0.05
Distrib'ns, Cap Gain ($)	1.71	1.39	1.04	2.98	3.75	4.49	0.96	0.74	0.14	0.85
Net Asset Value ($)	23.55	27.09	17.70	14.48	13.34	16.24	16.15	16.95	15.69	16.41
Expense Ratio (%)	na	0.89	1.02	1.08	1.08	1.10	1.10	1.06	1.09	1.04
Yield (%)	0.00	0.00	0.00	0.00	1.52	0.28	0.00	0.00	0.00	0.28
Portfolio Turnover (%)	na	85	183	240	146	10	37	39	43	37
Total Assets (Millions $)	370	419	190	116	89	98	90	91	101	129

PORTFOLIO (as of 6/30/00)

Portfolio Manager: committee - 1990

Investm't Category: Aggressive Growth

✔ Domestic　Index
Foreign　Sector
Asset Allocation　State Specific

Investment Style

Large Cap　Mid Cap　✔ Small Cap
✔ Growth　Grth/Val　Value

Portfolio

3.7%	cash	0.0%	corp bonds
96.3%	stocks	0.0%	gov't bonds
0.0%	pref/conv't pref	0.0%	muni bonds
0.0%	conv't bds/wrnts	0.0%	other

SHAREHOLDER INFORMATION

Minimum Investment

Initial: $1,000　Subsequent: $100

Minimum IRA Investment

Initial: $1,000　Subsequent: $100

Maximum Fees

Load: none　12b-1: 0.25%
Other: none

Services

✔ IRA
✔ Keogh
✔ Telephone Exchange

Van Wagoner Emerging Grth (VWEGX)

800-228-2121, 800-894-6694
www.vanwagoner.com

Aggressive Growth

this fund is closed to new investors

PERFORMANCE

fund inception date: 12/29/95

	3yr Annual	5yr Annual	10yr Annual	Bull	Bear
Return (%)	49.4	27.6	na	506.3	-35.7
Differ from Category (+/-)	33.2 high	13.0 high	na	387.1 high	-15.1 blw av

Standard Deviation	Category Risk Index	Beta
59.5%—high	1.83—high	1.70

	2000	1999	1998	1997	1996	1995	1994	1993	1992	1991
Return (%)	-20.9	291.1	7.9	-20.0	26.9	—	—	—	—	—
Differ from Category (+/-)	-14.9	233.6	-7.2	-34.8	8.6	—	—	—	—	—
Return, Tax-Adjusted (%)	-23.2	291.1	7.9	-20.0	26.9	—	—	—	—	—

PER SHARE DATA

	2000	1999	1998	1997	1996	1995	1994	1993	1992	1991
Dividends, Net Income ($)	0.00	0.00	0.00	0.00	0.00	—	—	—	—	—
Distrib'ns, Cap Gain ($)	4.98	0.00	0.00	0.00	0.00	—	—	—	—	—
Net Asset Value ($)	30.25	42.87	10.96	10.15	12.69	—	—	—	—	—
Expense Ratio (%)	na	1.79	1.95	1.88	1.95	—	—	—	—	—
Yield (%)	0.00	0.00	0.00	0.00	0.00	—	—	—	—	—
Portfolio Turnover (%)	na	353	668	333	159	—	—	—	—	—
Total Assets (Millions $)	801	1,474	189	313	638	—	—	—	—	—

PORTFOLIO (as of 6/30/00)

Portfolio Manager: Garrett Van Wagoner - 1995

Investm't Category: Aggressive Growth

✔ Domestic
Foreign
Asset Allocation
Index
Sector
State Specific

Investment Style

Large Cap
Mid Cap
✔ Small Cap
✔ Growth
Grth/Val
Value

Portfolio

0.0%	cash	0.0%	corp bonds
100.0%	stocks	0.0%	gov't bonds
0.0%	pref/conv't pref	0.0%	muni bonds
0.0%	conv't bds/wrnts	0.0%	other

SHAREHOLDER INFORMATION

Minimum Investment
Initial: $1,000 Subsequent: $50

Minimum IRA Investment
Initial: $500 Subsequent: $50

Maximum Fees
Load: none 12b-1: 0.19%
Other: none

Services
✔ IRA
✔ Keogh
✔ Telephone Exchange

Van Wagoner Micro-Cap Gr (VWMCX)

800-228-2121, 800-894-6694
www.vanwagoner.com

Aggressive Growth

this fund is closed to new investors

PERFORMANCE — fund inception date: 12/29/95

	3yr Annual	5yr Annual	10yr Annual	Bull	Bear
Return (%)	41.7	23.2	na	362.0	-36.9
Differ from Category (+/-)	25.5 high	8.6 abv av	na	242.8 high	-16.3 low

Standard Deviation	Category Risk Index	Beta
52.0%—high	1.60—high	1.58

	2000	1999	1998	1997	1996	1995	1994	1993	1992	1991
Return (%)	-18.2	207.8	13.1	-19.7	24.5	—	—	—	—	—
Differ from Category (+/-)	-12.2	150.3	-2.0	-34.5	6.2	—	—	—	—	—
Return, Tax-Adjusted (%)	-20.7	207.8	13.1	-19.7	24.5	—	—	—	—	—

PER SHARE DATA

	2000	1999	1998	1997	1996	1995	1994	1993	1992	1991
Dividends, Net Income ($)	0.00	0.00	0.00	0.00	0.00	—	—	—	—	—
Distrib'ns, Cap Gain ($)	4.50	0.00	0.00	0.00	0.00	—	—	—	—	—
Net Asset Value ($)	25.01	34.79	11.30	9.99	12.45	—	—	—	—	—
Expense Ratio (%)	na	1.95	1.95	1.95	1.95	—	—	—	—	—
Yield (%)	0.00	0.00	0.00	0.00	0.00	—	—	—	—	—
Portfolio Turnover (%)	na	180	367	232	153	—	—	—	—	—
Total Assets (Millions $)	157	296	46	71	140	—	—	—	—	—

PORTFOLIO (as of 6/30/00)

Portfolio Manager: Garrett Van Wagoner - 1995

Investm't Category: Aggressive Growth

✔ Domestic — Index
Foreign — Sector
Asset Allocation — State Specific

Investment Style

Large Cap — Mid Cap — ✔ Small Cap
✔ Growth — Grth/Val — Value

Portfolio

2.0%	cash	0.0%	corp bonds
98.0%	stocks	0.0%	gov't bonds
0.0%	pref/conv't pref	0.0%	muni bonds
0.0%	conv't bds/wrnts	0.0%	other

SHAREHOLDER INFORMATION

Minimum Investment

Initial: $1,000 — Subsequent: $50

Minimum IRA Investment

Initial: $500 — Subsequent: $50

Maximum Fees

Load: none — 12b-1: 0.20%
Other: none

Services

✔ IRA
✔ Keogh
✔ Telephone Exchange

Van Wagoner Mid-Cap Gr (VWMDX)

800-228-2121, 800-894-6694
www.vanwagoner.com

Aggressive Growth

PERFORMANCE — fund inception date: 12/29/95

	3yr Annual	5yr Annual	10yr Annual	Bull	Bear
Return (%)	26.5	16.6	na	234.5	-39.8
Differ from Category (+/-)	10.3 abv av	2.0 av	na	115.3 high	-19.2 low

Standard Deviation	Category Risk Index	Beta
52.5%—high	1.62—high	1.50

	2000	1999	1998	1997	1996	1995	1994	1993	1992	1991
Return (%)	-23.2	126.8	16.4	-13.8	23.9	—	—	—	—	—
Differ from Category (+/-)	-17.2	69.3	1.3	-28.6	5.6	—	—	—	—	—
Return, Tax-Adjusted (%)	-23.6	125.2	16.4	-13.8	23.9	—	—	—	—	—

PER SHARE DATA

	2000	1999	1998	1997	1996	1995	1994	1993	1992	1991
Dividends, Net Income ($)	0.00	0.00	0.00	0.00	0.00	—	—	—	—	—
Distrib'ns, Cap Gain ($)	0.64	0.95	0.00	0.00	0.00	—	—	—	—	—
Net Asset Value ($)	20.28	27.07	12.43	10.67	12.39	—	—	—	—	—
Expense Ratio (%)	na	1.85	1.95	1.80	2.05	—	—	—	—	—
Yield (%)	0.00	0.00	0.00	0.00	0.00	—	—	—	—	—
Portfolio Turnover (%)	na	589	787	304	173	—	—	—	—	—
Total Assets (Millions $)	181	141	45	73	137	—	—	—	—	—

PORTFOLIO (as of 6/30/00)

Portfolio Manager: Garrett Van Wagoner - 1995

Investm't Category: Aggressive Growth

✔ Domestic　Index
Foreign　Sector
Asset Allocation　State Specific

Investment Style

Large Cap　✔ Mid Cap　✔ Small Cap
✔ Growth　Grth/Val　Value

Portfolio

3.0%	cash	0.0%	corp bonds
97.0%	stocks	0.0%	gov't bonds
0.0%	pref/conv't pref	0.0%	muni bonds
0.0%	conv't bds/wrnts	0.0%	other

SHAREHOLDER INFORMATION

Minimum Investment
Initial: $1,000　Subsequent: $50

Minimum IRA Investment
Initial: $500　Subsequent: $50

Maximum Fees
Load: none　12b-1: 0.25%
Other: none

Services
✔ IRA
✔ Keogh
✔ Telephone Exchange

Vanguard Asset Allocation (VAAPX)

800-635-1511, 610-669-1000
www.vanguard.com

Balanced

PERFORMANCE — fund inception date: 11/3/88

	3yr Annual	5yr Annual	10yr Annual	Bull	Bear
Return (%)	11.4	15.3	15.2	26.9	-1.7
Differ from Category (+/-)	3.0 high	3.9 high	3.5 high	-1.2 av	1.5 abv av

Standard Deviation	Category Risk Index	Beta
10.6%—blw av	0.97—av	0.57

	2000	1999	1998	1997	1996	1995	1994	1993	1992	1991
Return (%)	4.9	5.2	25.3	27.3	15.7	35.4	-2.3	13.4	7.5	25.5
Differ from Category (+/-)	2.9	-5.5	12.0	8.5	1.8	9.9	-1.0	-1.0	-0.9	1.7
Return, Tax-Adjusted (%)	2.9	2.9	22.7	24.5	12.3	32.2	-3.8	10.9	5.7	23.4

PER SHARE DATA

	2000	1999	1998	1997	1996	1995	1994	1993	1992	1991
Dividends, Net Income ($)	1.02	0.88	0.76	0.74	0.72	0.66	0.57	0.48	0.59	0.59
Distrib'ns, Cap Gain ($)	0.27	0.96	1.18	1.01	1.05	0.61	0.00	0.53	0.17	0.19
Net Asset Value ($)	23.67	23.80	24.38	21.05	17.94	17.05	13.54	14.45	13.64	13.41
Expense Ratio (%)	0.44	0.49	0.49	0.49	0.47	0.49	0.50	0.49	0.52	0.44
Yield (%)	4.26	3.55	2.97	3.35	3.79	3.73	4.20	3.20	4.27	4.33
Portfolio Turnover (%)	29	11	60	10	47	34	51	31	18	44
Total Assets (Millions $)	8,626	8,597	6,974	4,099	2,596	1,791	1,125	1,125	587	341

PORTFOLIO (as of 6/30/00)

Portfolio Manager: William Fouse, Thomas Loeb - 1988

Investm't Category: Balanced

✔ Domestic | Index
Foreign | Sector
✔ Asset Allocation | State Specific

Investment Style

Large Cap | Mid Cap | Small Cap
Growth | Grth/Val | Value

Portfolio

10.0%	cash	0.0%	corp bonds
31.0%	stocks	59.0%	gov't bonds
0.0%	pref/conv't pref	0.0%	muni bonds
0.0%	conv't bds/wrnts	0.0%	other

SHAREHOLDER INFORMATION

Minimum Investment
Initial: $3,000 Subsequent: $100

Minimum IRA Investment
Initial: $1,000 Subsequent: $100

Maximum Fees
Load: none 12b-1: none
Other: none

Services
✔ IRA
✔ Keogh
✔ Telephone Exchange

Vanguard Balanced Index (VBINX)

800-635-1511, 610-669-1000
www.vanguard.com

Balanced

PERFORMANCE

fund inception date: 9/28/92

	3yr Annual	5yr Annual	10yr Annual	Bull	Bear
Return (%)	9.4	12.8	na	33.8	-6.8
Differ from Category (+/-)	1.0 abv av	1.4 abv av	na	5.7 abv av	-3.6 blw av

Standard Deviation	Category Risk Index	Beta
11.1%—blw av	1.01—av	0.60

	2000	1999	1998	1997	1996	1995	1994	1993	1992	1991
Return (%)	-2.0	13.6	17.8	22.2	13.9	28.6	-1.5	9.9	—	—
Differ from Category (+/-)	-4.0	2.9	4.5	3.4	0.0	3.1	-0.2	-4.5	—	—
Return, Tax-Adjusted (%)	-3.3	12.2	16.3	20.4	12.1	26.7	-2.9	8.3	—	—

PER SHARE DATA

	2000	1999	1998	1997	1996	1995	1994	1993	1992	1991
Dividends, Net Income ($)	0.64	0.58	0.54	0.53	0.49	0.45	0.40	0.39	—	—
Distrib'ns, Cap Gain ($)	0.10	0.14	0.14	0.14	0.12	0.05	0.00	0.03	—	—
Net Asset Value ($)	19.08	20.22	18.48	16.29	13.92	12.77	10.34	10.91	—	—
Expense Ratio (%)	na	0.20	0.21	0.20	0.20	0.20	0.20	0.20	—	—
Yield (%)	3.33	2.84	2.90	3.22	3.49	3.51	3.86	3.56	—	—
Portfolio Turnover (%)	na	29	25	18	37	14	16	25	—	—
Total Assets (Millions $)	3,588	3,128	2,003	1,260	826	590	402	367	—	—

PORTFOLIO (as of 6/30/00)

Portfolio Manager: George Sauter, Ian MacKinnon - 1992

Investm't Category: Balanced

✔ Domestic ✔ Index
Foreign Sector
Asset Allocation State Specific

Investment Style

Large Cap Mid Cap Small Cap
Growth Grth/Val Value

Portfolio

2.0%	cash	12.0%	corp bonds
59.0%	stocks	24.0%	gov't bonds
0.0%	pref/conv't pref	0.0%	muni bonds
0.0%	conv't bds/wrnts	3.0%	other

SHAREHOLDER INFORMATION

Minimum Investment
Initial: $3,000 Subsequent: $100

Minimum IRA Investment
Initial: $1,000 Subsequent: $100

Maximum Fees
Load: none 12b-1: none
Other: none

Services
✔ IRA
✔ Keogh
Telephone Exchange

Vanguard Capital Opport (VHCOX)

800-662-7447, 610-669-1000
www.vanguard.com

Aggressive Growth

this fund is closed to new investors

PERFORMANCE — fund inception date: 8/14/95

	3yr Annual	5yr Annual	10yr Annual	Bull	Bear
Return (%)	45.5	26.3	na	175.6	-13.6
Differ from Category (+/-)	29.3 high	11.7 high	na	56.4 abv av	7.0 abv av

Standard Deviation	Category Risk Index	Beta
25.9%—high	0.80—blw av	1.01

	2000	1999	1998	1997	1996	1995	1994	1993	1992	1991
Return (%)	18.0	97.7	31.9	-7.9	13.4	—	—	—	—	—
Differ from Category (+/-)	24.0	40.2	16.8	-22.7	-4.9	—	—	—	—	—
Return, Tax-Adjusted (%)	16.1	96.6	30.1	-8.0	13.4	—	—	—	—	—

PER SHARE DATA

	2000	1999	1998	1997	1996	1995	1994	1993	1992	1991
Dividends, Net Income ($)	0.16	0.03	0.01	0.04	0.00	—	—	—	—	—
Distrib'ns, Cap Gain ($)	1.92	0.59	0.89	0.00	0.00	—	—	—	—	—
Net Asset Value ($)	26.22	24.02	12.49	10.20	11.13	—	—	—	—	—
Expense Ratio (%)	na	0.75	0.94	0.49	0.50	—	—	—	—	—
Yield (%)	0.56	0.12	0.07	0.39	0.00	—	—	—	—	—
Portfolio Turnover (%)	na	22	103	195	128	—	—	—	—	—
Total Assets (Millions $)	4,887	2,366	206	63	117	—	—	—	—	—

PORTFOLIO (as of 6/30/00)

Portfolio Manager: committee - 1998

Investm't Category: Aggressive Growth

✔ Domestic
✔ Foreign
Asset Allocation
Index
Sector
State Specific

Investment Style

Large Cap ✔ Mid Cap ✔ Small Cap
✔ Growth Grth/Val Value

Portfolio

9.0%	cash	0.0%	corp bonds
91.0%	stocks	0.0%	gov't bonds
0.0%	pref/conv't pref	0.0%	muni bonds
0.0%	conv't bds/wrnts	0.0%	other

SHAREHOLDER INFORMATION

Minimum Investment
Initial: $25,000 Subsequent: $100

Minimum IRA Investment
Initial: $1,000 Subsequent: $100

Maximum Fees
Load: 1.00% redemption 12b-1: none
Other: redemption fee applies for 5 years

Services
✔ IRA
✔ Keogh
✔ Telephone Exchange

Vanguard Convertible Sec (VCVSX)

800-635-1511, 610-669-1000
www.vanguard.com

Growth & Income

PERFORMANCE

fund inception date: 6/17/86

	3yr Annual	5yr Annual	10yr Annual	Bull	Bear
Return (%)	10.9	12.9	13.8	46.8	-15.0
Differ from Category (+/-)	2.0 abv av	-1.4 blw av	-1.1 blw av	13.3 abv av	-14.9 low

Standard Deviation	Category Risk Index	Beta
18.4%—av	1.06—abv av	0.70

	2000	1999	1998	1997	1996	1995	1994	1993	1992	1991
Return (%)	4.2	30.3	0.5	16.3	15.4	16.7	-5.6	13.5	18.9	34.3
Differ from Category (+/-)	-1.5	19.5	-12.3	-10.6	-4.3	-12.8	-5.1	-0.3	7.3	6.2
Return, Tax-Adjusted (%)	1.7	27.3	-1.3	12.5	10.6	14.3	-7.7	9.5	17.3	32.2

PER SHARE DATA

	2000	1999	1998	1997	1996	1995	1994	1993	1992	1991
Dividends, Net Income ($)	0.57	0.50	0.54	0.54	0.47	0.54	0.51	0.53	0.53	0.54
Distrib'ns, Cap Gain ($)	0.51	0.70	0.00	1.12	1.29	0.14	0.18	0.91	0.00	0.00
Net Asset Value ($)	12.96	13.46	11.34	11.82	11.63	11.62	10.55	11.91	11.80	10.40
Expense Ratio (%)	na	0.55	0.73	0.67	0.69	0.77	0.73	0.71	0.85	0.81
Yield (%)	4.23	3.53	4.76	4.17	3.63	4.59	4.75	4.13	4.49	5.19
Portfolio Turnover (%)	na	162	186	182	98	51	52	81	55	57
Total Assets (Millions $)	323	197	177	186	166	167	170	204	135	60

PORTFOLIO (as of 6/30/00)

Portfolio Manager: Larry Keele - 1996

Investm't Category: Growth & Income

✔ Domestic — Index
Foreign — Sector
Asset Allocation — State Specific

Investment Style

Large Cap — ✔ Mid Cap — ✔ Small Cap
✔ Growth — Grth/Val — Value

Portfolio

4.0%	cash	0.0%	corp bonds
0.0%	stocks	0.0%	gov't bonds
22.0%	pref/conv't pref	0.0%	muni bonds
74.0%	conv't bds/wrnts	0.0%	other

SHAREHOLDER INFORMATION

Minimum Investment
Initial: $3,000 — Subsequent: $100

Minimum IRA Investment
Initial: $1,000 — Subsequent: $100

Maximum Fees
Load: none — 12b-1: none
Other: none

Services
✔ IRA
✔ Keogh
✔ Telephone Exchange

Vanguard Emg Mkt Stk Idx (VEIEX)

800-635-1511, 610-669-1000
www.vanguard.com

International Stock

PERFORMANCE

fund inception date: 5/4/94

	3yr Annual	5yr Annual	10yr Annual	Bull	Bear
Return (%)	-1.4	-1.5	na	110.2	-30.0
Differ from Category (+/-)	-10.3 low	-9.8 low	na	19.3 abv av	-6.0 blw av

Standard Deviation	Category Risk Index	Beta
30.4%—high	1.34—abv av	1.23

	2000	1999	1998	1997	1996	1995	1994	1993	1992	1991
Return (%)	-27.5	61.5	-18.2	-16.7	15.9	0.4	—	—	—	—
Differ from Category (+/-)	-8.1	0.8	-24.0	-18.0	1.4	-8.9	—	—	—	—
Return, Tax-Adjusted (%)	-28.1	60.1	-19.2	-17.4	15.2	-0.2	—	—	—	—

PER SHARE DATA

	2000	1999	1998	1997	1996	1995	1994	1993	1992	1991
Dividends, Net Income ($)	0.21	0.27	0.26	0.23	0.17	0.18	—	—	—	—
Distrib'ns, Cap Gain ($)	0.00	0.00	0.00	0.00	0.00	0.00	—	—	—	—
Net Asset Value ($)	8.84	12.50	7.91	9.99	12.28	10.74	—	—	—	—
Expense Ratio (%)	na	0.58	0.61	0.57	0.60	0.60	—	—	—	—
Yield (%)	2.37	2.16	3.28	2.30	1.38	1.67	—	—	—	—
Portfolio Turnover (%)	na	22	22	19	1	6	—	—	—	—
Total Assets (Millions $)	867	1,137	576	660	637	234	—	—	—	—

PORTFOLIO (as of 6/30/00)

Portfolio Manager: committee, George Sauter - 1994

Investm't Category: International Stock

Domestic	✔ Index
✔ Foreign	Sector
Asset Allocation	State Specific

Investment Style

Large Cap	Mid Cap	Small Cap
Growth	Grth/Val	Value

Portfolio

4.0% cash	0.0% corp bonds
96.0% stocks	0.0% gov't bonds
0.0% pref/conv't pref	0.0% muni bonds
0.0% conv't bds/wrnts	0.0% other

SHAREHOLDER INFORMATION

Minimum Investment

Initial: $3,000 Subsequent: $100

Minimum IRA Investment

Initial: $1,000 Subsequent: $100

Maximum Fees

Load: 0.50% redemption 12b-1: none
Other: redemption fee applies for 12 months

Services

✔ IRA
✔ Keogh
✔ Telephone Exchange

Vanguard Equity Income (VEIPX)

800-635-1511, 610-669-1000
www.vanguard.com

Growth & Income

PERFORMANCE

fund inception date: 3/21/88

	3yr Annual	5yr Annual	10yr Annual	Bull	Bear
Return (%)	9.9	15.4	15.8	20.9	9.8
Differ from Category (+/-)	1.0 av	1.1 av	0.9 av	-12.6 blw av	9.9 abv av

Standard Deviation	Category Risk Index	Beta
15.1%—av	0.87—blw av	0.61

	2000	1999	1998	1997	1996	1995	1994	1993	1992	1991
Return (%)	13.5	-0.1	17.3	31.1	17.3	37.3	-1.5	14.6	9.1	25.3
Differ from Category (+/-)	7.8	-10.9	4.5	4.2	-2.4	7.8	-1.0	0.8	-2.5	-2.8
Return, Tax-Adjusted (%)	11.4	-1.8	15.4	28.6	14.8	35.0	-3.3	11.6	7.6	23.1

PER SHARE DATA

	2000	1999	1998	1997	1996	1995	1994	1993	1992	1991
Dividends, Net Income ($)	0.61	0.65	0.64	0.67	0.64	0.60	0.58	0.61	0.59	0.65
Distrib'ns, Cap Gain ($)	1.14	0.87	0.83	0.89	0.58	0.17	0.09	0.52	0.00	0.10
Net Asset Value ($)	24.44	23.17	24.73	22.39	18.32	16.69	12.77	13.66	12.92	12.40
Expense Ratio (%)	0.43	0.41	0.39	0.45	0.42	0.47	0.43	0.40	0.44	0.46
Yield (%)	2.38	2.70	2.50	2.87	3.38	3.55	4.51	4.30	4.56	5.20
Portfolio Turnover (%)	36	18	23	22	21	31	18	15	13	9
Total Assets (Millions $)	2,448	2,874	2,938	2,099	1,424	1,102	869	1,067	835	569

PORTFOLIO (as of 6/30/00)

Portfolio Manager: committee - 1988

Investm't Category: Growth & Income

✔ Domestic
Foreign
Asset Allocation
Index
Sector
State Specific

Investment Style

✔ Large Cap
Growth
Mid Cap
Grth/Val
Small Cap
✔ Value

Portfolio

8.0% cash
91.0% stocks
0.0% pref/conv't pref
0.0% conv't bds/wrnts
1.0% corp bonds
0.0% gov't bonds
0.0% muni bonds
0.0% other

SHAREHOLDER INFORMATION

Minimum Investment

Initial: $3,000 Subsequent: $100

Minimum IRA Investment

Initial: $1,000 Subsequent: $100

Maximum Fees

Load: none 12b-1: none
Other: none

Services

✔ IRA
✔ Keogh
✔ Telephone Exchange

Vanguard Erpn Stock Index (VEURX)

800-662-2739, 610-669-1000
www.vanguard.com

International Stock

PERFORMANCE — fund inception date: 5/1/90

	3yr Annual	5yr Annual	10yr Annual	Bull	Bear
Return (%)	11.3	15.7	13.7	32.5	-14.2
Differ from Category (+/-)	2.4 abv av	7.4 high	4.7 high	-58.4 low	9.8 abv av

Standard Deviation	Category Risk Index	Beta
16.2%—av	0.71—low	0.65

	2000	1999	1998	1997	1996	1995	1994	1993	1992	1991
Return (%)	-8.2	16.6	28.8	24.2	21.2	22.2	1.8	29.1	-3.3	12.4
Differ from Category (+/-)	11.2	-44.1	23.0	22.9	6.7	12.9	4.9	-11.1	0.2	-0.6
Return, Tax-Adjusted (%)	-8.8	15.6	27.6	23.2	20.0	21.0	0.7	28.3	-4.1	11.5

PER SHARE DATA

	2000	1999	1998	1997	1996	1995	1994	1993	1992	1991
Dividends, Net Income ($)	0.42	0.50	0.52	0.37	0.36	0.32	0.28	0.17	0.26	0.26
Distrib'ns, Cap Gain ($)	0.05	0.15	0.14	0.08	0.06	0.04	0.06	0.00	0.00	0.00
Net Asset Value ($)	25.99	28.83	25.28	20.13	16.57	14.02	11.76	11.88	9.33	9.92
Expense Ratio (%)	na	0.29	0.29	0.31	0.35	0.32	0.32	0.32	0.32	0.33
Yield (%)	1.61	1.72	2.04	1.83	2.16	2.27	2.36	1.43	2.78	2.62
Portfolio Turnover (%)	na	7	7	3	4	3	6	4	1	15
Total Assets (Millions $)	5,266	6,106	4,479	2,432	1,594	1,017	715	600	256	160

PORTFOLIO (as of 6/30/00)

Portfolio Manager: committee, George Sauter - 1990

Investm't Category: International Stock

Domestic	✔ Index
✔ Foreign	Sector
Asset Allocation	State Specific

Investment Style

Large Cap	Mid Cap	Small Cap
Growth	Grth/Val	Value

Portfolio

0.0%	cash	0.0%	corp bonds
100.0%	stocks	0.0%	gov't bonds
0.0%	pref/conv't pref	0.0%	muni bonds
0.0%	conv't bds/wrnts	0.0%	other

SHAREHOLDER INFORMATION

Minimum Investment
Initial: $3,000 Subsequent: $100

Minimum IRA Investment
Initial: $1,000 Subsequent: $100

Maximum Fees
Load: none 12b-1: none
Other: none

Services
✔ IRA
✔ Keogh
✔ Telephone Exchange

Vanguard Explorer (VEXPX)

800-635-1511, 610-669-1000
www.vanguard.com

Aggressive Growth

PERFORMANCE

fund inception date: 12/11/67

	3yr Annual	5yr Annual	10yr Annual	Bull	Bear
Return (%)	15.7	15.1	18.0	83.9	-14.6
Differ from Category (+/-)	-0.5 av	0.5 av	2.2 av	-35.3 av	6.0 abv av

Standard Deviation	Category Risk Index	Beta
28.3%—high	0.87—blw av	1.01

	2000	1999	1998	1997	1996	1995	1994	1993	1992	1991
Return (%)	9.2	37.2	3.5	14.5	14.0	26.5	0.5	15.4	12.9	55.9
Differ from Category (+/-)	15.2	-20.3	-11.6	-0.3	-4.3	-8.1	1.3	-9.8	6.0	8.7
Return, Tax-Adjusted (%)	5.0	34.2	3.2	12.1	12.1	23.6	-1.0	11.9	12.2	55.5

PER SHARE DATA

	2000	1999	1998	1997	1996	1995	1994	1993	1992	1991
Dividends, Net Income ($)	0.25	0.23	0.20	0.25	0.27	0.24	0.17	0.14	0.13	0.26
Distrib'ns, Cap Gain ($)	13.91	8.03	0.30	5.85	2.83	4.00	2.26	5.17	0.78	0.00
Net Asset Value ($)	60.09	68.62	56.71	55.30	53.83	49.95	42.86	45.11	43.84	39.62
Expense Ratio (%)	na	0.74	0.62	0.62	0.63	0.68	0.70	0.73	0.69	0.56
Yield (%)	0.33	0.30	0.35	0.40	0.47	0.44	0.37	0.27	0.29	0.65
Portfolio Turnover (%)	na	79	72	84	51	60	82	51	43	49
Total Assets (Millions $)	4,046	3,136	2,463	2,541	2,263	1,647	1,121	847	620	429

PORTFOLIO (as of 6/30/00)

Portfolio Manager: committee - 1994

Investm't Category: Aggressive Growth

✔ Domestic　　Index
✔ Foreign　　Sector
Asset Allocation　　State Specific

Investment Style

Large Cap　　Mid Cap　　✔ Small Cap
✔ Growth　　Grth/Val　　Value

Portfolio

9.0%	cash	0.0%	corp bonds
91.0%	stocks	0.0%	gov't bonds
0.0%	pref/conv't pref	0.0%	muni bonds
0.0%	conv't bds/wrnts	0.0%	other

SHAREHOLDER INFORMATION

Minimum Investment

Initial: $3,000　　Subsequent: $100

Minimum IRA Investment

Initial: $1,000　　Subsequent: $100

Maximum Fees

Load: none　　12b-1: none
Other: none

Services

✔ IRA
✔ Keogh
✔ Telephone Exchange

Vanguard Global Asset All (VHAAX)

800-662-7447, 610-669-1000
www.vanguard.com

International Stock

PERFORMANCE — fund inception date: 8/14/95

	3yr Annual	5yr Annual	10yr Annual	Bull	Bear
Return (%)	10.2	10.0	na	23.5	-1.4
Differ from Category (+/-)	1.3 av	1.7 av	na	-67.4 low	22.6 high

Standard Deviation	Category Risk Index	Beta
5.7%—blw av	0.25—low	0.26

	2000	1999	1998	1997	1996	1995	1994	1993	1992	1991
Return (%)	4.1	11.8	15.1	9.2	9.9	—	—	—	—	—
Differ from Category (+/-)	23.5	-48.9	9.3	7.9	-4.6	—	—	—	—	—
Return, Tax-Adjusted (%)	1.5	8.5	11.7	5.3	6.7	—	—	—	—	—

PER SHARE DATA

	2000	1999	1998	1997	1996	1995	1994	1993	1992	1991
Dividends, Net Income ($)	0.54	0.52	0.62	0.75	0.58	—	—	—	—	—
Distrib'ns, Cap Gain ($)	0.32	0.73	0.48	0.54	0.34	—	—	—	—	—
Net Asset Value ($)	10.29	10.71	10.71	10.28	10.59	—	—	—	—	—
Expense Ratio (%)	na	0.58	0.54	0.54	0.79	—	—	—	—	—
Yield (%)	5.08	4.54	5.54	6.93	5.30	—	—	—	—	—
Portfolio Turnover (%)	na	188	182	162	191	—	—	—	—	—
Total Assets (Millions $)	110	103	77	80	77	—	—	—	—	—

PORTFOLIO (as of 6/30/00)

Portfolio Manager: Michael Duffy, Eric Bendickson - 1995

Investm't Category: International Stock

✔ Domestic — Index
✔ Foreign — Sector
✔ Asset Allocation — State Specific

Investment Style

Large Cap — Mid Cap — Small Cap
Growth — Grth/Val — Value

Portfolio

53.0%	cash	6.0%	corp bonds
5.0%	stocks	36.0%	gov't bonds
0.0%	pref/conv't pref	0.0%	muni bonds
0.0%	conv't bds/wrnts	0.0%	other

SHAREHOLDER INFORMATION

Minimum Investment
Initial: $3,000 — Subsequent: $100

Minimum IRA Investment
Initial: $1,000 — Subsequent: $100

Maximum Fees
Load: 1.00% redemption — 12b-1: none
Other: redemption fee applies for 5 years

Services
✔ IRA
✔ Keogh
✔ Telephone Exchange

Vanguard Global Equity (VHGEX)

800-662-7447, 610-669-1000
www.vanguard.com

International Stock

PERFORMANCE — fund inception date: 8/14/95

	3yr Annual	5yr Annual	10yr Annual	Bull	Bear
Return (%)	11.2	11.1	na	50.7	-3.5
Differ from Category (+/-)	2.3 abv av	2.8 abv av	na	-40.2 blw av	20.5 high

Standard Deviation	Category Risk Index	Beta
15.9%—av	0.70—low	0.76

	2000	1999	1998	1997	1996	1995	1994	1993	1992	1991
Return (%)	-0.1	25.9	9.3	6.9	15.5	—	—	—	—	—
Differ from Category (+/-)	19.3	-34.8	3.5	5.6	1.0	—	—	—	—	—
Return, Tax-Adjusted (%)	-2.4	23.9	7.1	5.3	14.4	—	—	—	—	—

PER SHARE DATA

	2000	1999	1998	1997	1996	1995	1994	1993	1992	1991
Dividends, Net Income ($)	0.26	0.18	0.26	0.23	0.14	—	—	—	—	—
Distrib'ns, Cap Gain ($)	1.17	0.84	0.75	0.44	0.19	—	—	—	—	—
Net Asset Value ($)	12.62	14.14	12.06	11.98	11.84	—	—	—	—	—
Expense Ratio (%)	na	0.71	0.68	0.71	0.85	—	—	—	—	—
Yield (%)	1.88	1.20	2.02	1.85	1.16	—	—	—	—	—
Portfolio Turnover (%)	na	36	34	24	29	—	—	—	—	—
Total Assets (Millions $)	137	144	128	126	106	—	—	—	—	—

PORTFOLIO (as of 6/30/00)

Portfolio Manager: Jeremy Hosking - 1995

Investm't Category: International Stock

✔ Domestic — Index
✔ Foreign — Sector
Asset Allocation — State Specific

Investment Style

Large Cap — Mid Cap — Small Cap
Growth — Grth/Val — Value

Portfolio

3.0%	cash	0.0%	corp bonds
97.0%	stocks	0.0%	gov't bonds
0.0%	pref/conv't pref	0.0%	muni bonds
0.0%	conv't bds/wrnts	0.0%	other

SHAREHOLDER INFORMATION

Minimum Investment
Initial: $3,000 — Subsequent: $100

Minimum IRA Investment
Initial: $1,000 — Subsequent: $100

Maximum Fees
Load: 1.00% redemption — 12b-1: none
Other: redemption fee applies for 5 years

Services
✔ IRA
✔ Keogh
✔ Telephone Exchange

Vanguard Growth & Income (VQNPX)

800-635-1511, 610-669-1000
www.vanguard.com

Growth & Income

PERFORMANCE — fund inception date: 12/10/86

	3yr Annual	5yr Annual	10yr Annual	Bull	Bear
Return (%)	12.4	18.8	17.6	59.2	-11.1
Differ from Category (+/-)	3.5 high	4.5 high	2.7 high	25.7 high	-11.0 blw av

Standard Deviation	Category Risk Index	Beta
18.2%—av	1.05—abv av	1.01

	2000	1999	1998	1997	1996	1995	1994	1993	1992	1991
Return (%)	-8.9	26.0	23.9	35.5	23.0	35.9	-0.6	13.8	7.0	30.2
Differ from Category (+/-)	-14.6	15.2	11.1	8.6	3.3	6.4	-0.1	0.0	-4.6	2.1
Return, Tax-Adjusted (%)	-10.0	24.7	22.4	31.8	19.6	33.4	-2.2	9.9	4.9	28.1

PER SHARE DATA

	2000	1999	1998	1997	1996	1995	1994	1993	1992	1991
Dividends, Net Income ($)	0.35	0.33	0.33	0.42	0.40	0.42	0.39	0.39	0.44	0.47
Distrib'ns, Cap Gain ($)	1.47	1.28	1.28	3.18	1.82	0.74	0.40	1.69	0.71	0.44
Net Asset Value ($)	32.06	37.08	30.76	26.19	22.23	19.95	15.56	16.45	16.30	16.32
Expense Ratio (%)	na	0.37	0.36	0.36	0.38	0.50	0.48	0.50	0.40	0.43
Yield (%)	1.04	0.86	1.02	1.43	1.66	2.02	2.44	2.14	2.58	2.80
Portfolio Turnover (%)	na	54	47	66	75	78	71	85	51	61
Total Assets (Millions $)	8,831	8,816	5,160	2,141	1,285	909	596	530	415	334

PORTFOLIO (as of 6/30/00)

Portfolio Manager: John Nagorniak - 1986

Investm't Category: Growth & Income

✔ Domestic — Index
Foreign — Sector
Asset Allocation — State Specific

Investment Style

✔ Large Cap — Mid Cap — Small Cap
Growth — ✔ Grth/Val — Value

Portfolio

1.0%	cash	0.0%	corp bonds
99.0%	stocks	0.0%	gov't bonds
0.0%	pref/conv't pref	0.0%	muni bonds
0.0%	conv't bds/wrnts	0.0%	other

SHAREHOLDER INFORMATION

Minimum Investment
Initial: $3,000 — Subsequent: $100

Minimum IRA Investment
Initial: $1,000 — Subsequent: $100

Maximum Fees
Load: none — 12b-1: none
Other: none

Services
✔ IRA
✔ Keogh
✔ Telephone Exchange

Vanguard Growth Equity (VGEQX)

800-224-6312, 610-669-1000
www.vanguard.com

Growth

PERFORMANCE

fund inception date: 3/11/92

	3yr Annual	5yr Annual	10yr Annual	Bull	Bear
Return (%)	17.7	20.6	na	114.6	-30.4
Differ from Category (+/-)	6.7 high	4.5 high	na	64.9 high	-25.0 low

Standard Deviation	Category Risk Index	Beta
29.1%—high	1.50—high	1.23

	2000	1999	1998	1997	1996	1995	1994	1993	1992	1991
Return (%)	-23.1	53.5	38.0	31.3	19.2	30.3	-6.7	15.3	—	—
Differ from Category (+/-)	-26.6	34.6	23.7	4.2	-3.1	-0.1	-6.5	0.7	—	—
Return, Tax-Adjusted (%)	-23.1	47.2	35.2	23.7	10.3	27.8	-7.0	15.0	—	—

PER SHARE DATA

	2000	1999	1998	1997	1996	1995	1994	1993	1992	1991
Dividends, Net Income ($)	0.00	0.00	0.00	0.00	0.00	0.13	0.10	0.08	—	—
Distrib'ns, Cap Gain ($)	0.00	4.51	1.59	4.81	4.59	0.84	0.00	0.00	—	—
Net Asset Value ($)	13.28	17.27	14.44	11.71	12.76	14.53	11.92	12.89	—	—
Expense Ratio (%)	0.74	0.92	1.04	1.02	1.06	0.95	0.95	1.00	—	—
Yield (%)	0.00	0.00	0.00	0.00	0.00	0.84	0.83	0.62	—	—
Portfolio Turnover (%)	303	328	249	178	147	96	164	88	—	—
Total Assets (Millions $)	897	203	123	89	90	105	112	71	—	—

PORTFOLIO (as of 6/30/00)

Portfolio Manager: committee - 2000

Investm't Category: Growth

✔ Domestic
Foreign
Asset Allocation
Index
Sector
State Specific

Investment Style

✔ Large Cap
✔ Mid Cap
Small Cap
✔ Growth
Grth/Val
Value

Portfolio

3.0% cash
97.0% stocks
0.0% pref/conv't pref
0.0% conv't bds/wrnts
0.0% corp bonds
0.0% gov't bonds
0.0% muni bonds
0.0% other

SHAREHOLDER INFORMATION

Minimum Investment

Initial: $10,000 Subsequent: $100

Minimum IRA Investment

Initial: $1,000 Subsequent: $100

Maximum Fees

Load: none 12b-1: none
Other: none

Services

✔ IRA
Keogh
✔ Telephone Exchange

Vanguard Idx: 500 Idx

800-635-1511, 610-669-1000
www.vanguard.com

(VFINX)

Growth & Income

PERFORMANCE

fund inception date: 8/31/76

	3yr Annual	5yr Annual	10yr Annual	Bull	Bear
Return (%)	12.2	18.3	17.3	56.3	-11.5
Differ from Category (+/-)	3.3 high	4.0 high	2.4 high	22.8 high	-11.4 blw av

Standard Deviation	Category Risk Index	Beta
17.6%—av	1.02—abv av	1.00

	2000	1999	1998	1997	1996	1995	1994	1993	1992	1991
Return (%)	-9.0	21.0	28.6	33.2	22.8	37.4	1.1	9.8	7.4	30.2
Differ from Category (+/-)	-14.7	10.2	15.8	6.3	3.1	7.9	1.6	-4.0	-4.2	2.1
Return, Tax-Adjusted (%)	-9.3	20.3	27.9	32.2	21.7	36.1	0.0	8.6	6.4	28.9

PER SHARE DATA

	2000	1999	1998	1997	1996	1995	1994	1993	1992	1991
Dividends, Net Income ($)	1.30	1.41	1.33	1.32	1.28	1.22	1.17	1.13	1.12	1.15
Distrib'ns, Cap Gain ($)	0.00	0.99	0.42	0.59	0.25	0.13	0.20	0.03	0.10	0.12
Net Asset Value ($)	121.86	135.33	113.95	90.07	69.16	57.60	42.97	43.83	40.97	39.32
Expense Ratio (%)	na	0.18	0.18	0.19	0.20	0.20	0.19	0.19	0.19	0.20
Yield (%)	1.06	1.03	1.16	1.45	1.84	2.11	2.71	2.57	2.72	2.91
Portfolio Turnover (%)	na	6	6	5	5	4	6	6	4	5
Total Assets (Millions $)	89,393	104,652	74,228	49,357	30,331	17,371	9,356	8,272	6,547	4,345

PORTFOLIO (as of 6/30/00)

Portfolio Manager: committee, George Sauter - 1987

Investm't Category: Growth & Income

✔ Domestic ✔ Index
Foreign Sector
Asset Allocation State Specific

Investment Style

✔ Large Cap Mid Cap Small Cap
Growth ✔ Grth/Val Value

Portfolio

4.0% cash
96.0% stocks
0.0% pref/conv't pref
0.0% conv't bds/wrnts
0.0% corp bonds
0.0% gov't bonds
0.0% muni bonds
0.0% other

SHAREHOLDER INFORMATION

Minimum Investment
Initial: $3,000 Subsequent: $100

Minimum IRA Investment
Initial: $1,000 Subsequent: $100

Maximum Fees
Load: none 12b-1: none
Other: none

Services
✔ IRA
✔ Keogh
✔ Telephone Exchange

Vanguard Idx: Ext Mkt/Inv (VEXMX)

800-635-1511, 610-669-1000
www.vanguard.com

Growth

PERFORMANCE

fund inception date: 12/21/87

	3yr Annual	5yr Annual	10yr Annual	Bull	Bear
Return (%)	7.6	13.1	16.1	78.2	-27.6
Differ from Category (+/-)	-3.4 blw av	-3.0 blw av	-0.7 av	28.5 high	-22.2 low

Standard Deviation	Category Risk Index	Beta
27.8%—high	1.43—high	1.11

	2000	1999	1998	1997	1996	1995	1994	1993	1992	1991
Return (%)	-15.5	36.2	8.3	26.7	17.6	33.7	-1.7	14.4	12.4	41.8
Differ from Category (+/-)	-19.0	17.3	-6.0	-0.4	-4.7	3.3	-1.5	-0.2	-0.2	4.2
Return, Tax-Adjusted (%)	-18.1	33.4	6.4	24.6	15.0	32.4	-2.6	13.5	11.5	40.6

PER SHARE DATA

	2000	1999	1998	1997	1996	1995	1994	1993	1992	1991
Dividends, Net Income ($)	0.26	0.31	0.37	0.36	0.34	0.30	0.28	0.23	0.25	0.25
Distrib'ns, Cap Gain ($)	4.43	3.64	2.17	1.91	1.72	0.40	0.29	0.20	0.18	0.20
Net Asset Value ($)	26.62	37.07	30.62	30.75	26.19	24.07	18.52	19.43	17.35	15.82
Expense Ratio (%)	na	0.25	0.23	0.23	0.25	0.20	0.20	0.20	0.20	0.19
Yield (%)	0.83	0.76	1.12	1.10	1.21	1.22	1.48	1.17	1.42	1.56
Portfolio Turnover (%)	na	26	27	15	22	14	19	13	9	11
Total Assets (Millions $)	3,752	4,221	2,938	2,722	2,098	1,523	967	927	584	372

PORTFOLIO (as of 6/30/00)

Portfolio Manager: committee, George Sauter - 1987

Investm't Category: Growth

✔ Domestic ✔ Index
Foreign Sector
Asset Allocation State Specific

Investment Style

Large Cap ✔ Mid Cap ✔ Small Cap
✔ Growth Grth/Val Value

Portfolio

2.0%	cash	0.0%	corp bonds
98.0%	stocks	0.0%	gov't bonds
0.0%	pref/conv't pref	0.0%	muni bonds
0.0%	conv't bds/wrnts	0.0%	other

SHAREHOLDER INFORMATION

Minimum Investment
Initial: $3,000 Subsequent: $100

Minimum IRA Investment
Initial: $1,000 Subsequent: $100

Maximum Fees
Load: none 12b-1: none
Other: none

Services
✔ IRA
✔ Keogh
✔ Telephone Exchange

Vanguard Idx: Growth/Inv (VIGRX)

800-635-1511, 610-669-1000
www.vanguard.com

Growth

PERFORMANCE

fund inception date: 11/2/92

	3yr Annual	5yr Annual	10yr Annual	Bull	Bear
Return (%)	12.5	19.1	na	71.2	-21.7
Differ from Category (+/-)	1.5 av	3.0 abv av	na	21.5 abv av	-16.3 low

Standard Deviation	Category Risk Index	Beta
21.0%—abv av	1.08—abv av	1.10

	2000	1999	1998	1997	1996	1995	1994	1993	1992	1991
Return (%)	-22.2	28.7	42.2	36.2	23.8	38.0	2.8	0.6	—	—
Differ from Category (+/-)	-25.7	9.8	27.9	9.1	1.5	7.6	3.0	-14.0	—	—
Return, Tax-Adjusted (%)	-22.3	27.7	41.7	35.3	22.8	37.2	1.9	-0.2	—	—

PER SHARE DATA

	2000	1999	1998	1997	1996	1995	1994	1993	1992	1991
Dividends, Net Income ($)	0.12	0.22	0.21	0.23	0.22	0.20	0.21	0.21	—	—
Distrib'ns, Cap Gain ($)	0.00	1.04	0.11	0.25	0.14	0.00	0.00	0.00	—	—
Net Asset Value ($)	30.57	39.43	31.67	22.53	16.91	13.97	10.28	10.20	—	—
Expense Ratio (%)	na	0.22	0.22	0.20	0.20	0.20	0.20	0.20	—	—
Yield (%)	0.39	0.54	0.66	1.00	1.29	1.43	2.04	2.05	—	—
Portfolio Turnover (%)	na	33	29	26	29	23	28	36	—	—
Total Assets (Millions $)	11,960	15,232	6,644	2,365	786	271	86	50	—	—

PORTFOLIO (as of 6/30/00)

Portfolio Manager: committee, George Sauter - 1992

Investm't Category: Growth

✔ Domestic
Foreign
Asset Allocation
✔ Index
Sector
State Specific

Investment Style

✔ Large Cap
Mid Cap
Small Cap
✔ Growth
Grth/Val
Value

Portfolio

0.0% cash
100.0% stocks
0.0% pref/conv't pref
0.0% conv't bds/wrnts
0.0% corp bonds
0.0% gov't bonds
0.0% muni bonds
0.0% other

SHAREHOLDER INFORMATION

Minimum Investment
Initial: $3,000 Subsequent: $100

Minimum IRA Investment
Initial: $1,000 Subsequent: $100

Maximum Fees
Load: none 12b-1: none
Other: none

Services
✔ IRA
✔ Keogh
✔ Telephone Exchange

Vanguard Idx: Sm Cap/Inv (NAESX)

800-635-1511, 610-669-1000
www.vanguard.com

Growth

PERFORMANCE

fund inception date: 1/31/74

	3yr Annual	5yr Annual	10yr Annual	Bull	Bear
Return (%)	5.2	11.4	16.1	54.3	-16.1
Differ from Category (+/-)	-5.8 low	-4.7 low	-0.7 av	4.6 av	-10.7 blw av

Standard Deviation	Category Risk Index	Beta
24.7%—abv av	1.27—high	0.88

	2000	1999	1998	1997	1996	1995	1994	1993	1992	1991
Return (%)	-2.6	23.1	-2.6	24.5	18.1	28.7	-0.5	18.7	18.2	45.2
Differ from Category (+/-)	-6.1	4.2	-16.9	-2.6	-4.2	-1.7	-0.3	4.1	5.6	7.6
Return, Tax-Adjusted (%)	-5.5	20.6	-4.4	22.8	15.3	27.2	-1.7	16.5	17.3	43.6

PER SHARE DATA

	2000	1999	1998	1997	1996	1995	1994	1993	1992	1991
Dividends, Net Income ($)	0.26	0.26	0.30	0.27	0.27	0.23	0.22	0.18	0.18	0.18
Distrib'ns, Cap Gain ($)	3.02	2.08	1.55	1.11	1.44	0.45	0.37	0.82	0.15	0.29
Net Asset Value ($)	19.44	23.60	21.20	23.75	20.23	18.61	14.99	15.67	14.07	12.19
Expense Ratio (%)	na	0.25	0.24	0.23	0.25	0.25	0.17	0.18	0.18	0.21
Yield (%)	1.15	1.01	1.31	1.08	1.24	1.20	1.43	1.09	1.26	1.44
Portfolio Turnover (%)	na	42	35	29	28	28	25	26	26	33
Total Assets (Millions $)	3,410	3,553	2,768	2,652	1,713	971	606	488	264	131

PORTFOLIO (as of 6/30/00)

Portfolio Manager: committee, George Sauter - 1989

Investm't Category: Growth

✔ Domestic
Foreign
Asset Allocation
✔ Index
Sector
State Specific

Investment Style

Large Cap
Mid Cap
✔ Small Cap
✔ Growth
Grth/Val
Value

Portfolio

0.0%	cash	0.0%	corp bonds
100.0%	stocks	0.0%	gov't bonds
0.0%	pref/conv't pref	0.0%	muni bonds
0.0%	conv't bds/wrnts	0.0%	other

SHAREHOLDER INFORMATION

Minimum Investment

Initial: $3,000 — Subsequent: $100

Minimum IRA Investment

Initial: $1,000 — Subsequent: $100

Maximum Fees

Load: none — 12b-1: none
Other: none

Services

✔ IRA
✔ Keogh
✔ Telephone Exchange

Vanguard Idx: Tot Stk/Inv (VTSMX)

800-635-1511, 610-669-1000
www.vanguard.com

Growth & Income

PERFORMANCE — fund inception date: 4/27/92

	3yr Annual	5yr Annual	10yr Annual	Bull	Bear
Return (%)	10.9	16.6	na	60.4	-15.3
Differ from Category (+/-)	2.0 abv av	2.3 abv av	na	26.9 high	-15.2 low

Standard Deviation	Category Risk Index	Beta
18.6%—av	1.07—high	1.01

	2000	1999	1998	1997	1996	1995	1994	1993	1992	1991
Return (%)	-10.5	23.8	23.2	30.9	20.9	35.7	-0.1	10.6	—	—
Differ from Category (+/-)	-16.2	13.0	10.4	4.0	1.2	6.2	0.4	-3.2	—	—
Return, Tax-Adjusted (%)	-10.9	23.0	22.5	29.8	19.9	34.5	-1.0	9.5	—	—

PER SHARE DATA

	2000	1999	1998	1997	1996	1995	1994	1993	1992	1991
Dividends, Net Income ($)	0.33	0.33	0.32	0.32	0.29	0.28	0.27	0.26	—	—
Distrib'ns, Cap Gain ($)	0.14	0.32	0.12	0.27	0.11	0.09	0.03	0.03	—	—
Net Asset Value ($)	29.26	33.22	27.42	22.64	17.77	15.04	11.37	11.69	—	—
Expense Ratio (%)	na	0.20	0.20	0.20	0.22	0.20	0.20	0.20	—	—
Yield (%)	1.12	0.98	1.16	1.39	1.62	1.85	2.36	2.21	—	—
Portfolio Turnover (%)	na	3	3	2	3	2	2	1	—	—
Total Assets (Millions $)	16,578	18,133	9,307	5,092	3,530	1,570	785	512	—	—

PORTFOLIO (as of 6/30/00)

Portfolio Manager: committee, George Sauter - 1992

Investm't Category: Growth & Income

✔ Domestic	✔ Index
Foreign	Sector
Asset Allocation	State Specific

Investment Style

✔ Large Cap	✔ Mid Cap	Small Cap
Growth	✔ Grth/Val	Value

Portfolio

3.0% cash	0.0% corp bonds
97.0% stocks	0.0% gov't bonds
0.0% pref/conv't pref	0.0% muni bonds
0.0% conv't bds/wrnts	0.0% other

SHAREHOLDER INFORMATION

Minimum Investment
Initial: $3,000 — Subsequent: $100

Minimum IRA Investment
Initial: $1,000 — Subsequent: $100

Maximum Fees
Load: none — 12b-1: none
Other: none

Services
✔ IRA
✔ Keogh
✔ Telephone Exchange

Vanguard Idx: Value/Inv (VIVAX)

800-635-1511, 610-669-1000
www.vanguard.com

Growth & Income

PERFORMANCE

fund inception date: 11/2/92

	3yr Annual	5yr Annual	10yr Annual	Bull	Bear
Return (%)	11.0	16.6	na	40.2	0.6
Differ from Category (+/-)	2.1 abv av	2.3 abv av	na	6.7 abv av	0.7 av

Standard Deviation	Category Risk Index	Beta
17.7%—av	1.02—abv av	0.88

	2000	1999	1998	1997	1996	1995	1994	1993	1992	1991
Return (%)	6.0	12.5	14.6	29.7	21.7	37.0	-0.6	18.2	—	—
Differ from Category (+/-)	0.3	1.7	1.8	2.8	2.0	7.5	-0.1	4.4	—	—
Return, Tax-Adjusted (%)	4.5	10.1	12.9	27.9	19.6	35.5	-2.2	16.5	—	—

PER SHARE DATA

	2000	1999	1998	1997	1996	1995	1994	1993	1992	1991
Dividends, Net Income ($)	0.35	0.36	0.36	0.37	0.38	0.40	0.38	0.38	—	—
Distrib'ns, Cap Gain ($)	0.98	1.95	0.99	0.75	0.57	0.00	0.16	0.06	—	—
Net Asset Value ($)	22.87	22.89	22.51	20.85	17.02	14.80	11.12	11.73	—	—
Expense Ratio (%)	na	0.22	0.22	0.20	0.20	0.20	0.20	0.20	—	—
Yield (%)	1.46	1.44	1.53	1.71	2.16	2.70	3.36	3.22	—	—
Portfolio Turnover (%)	na	41	33	26	29	26	32	30	—	—
Total Assets (Millions $)	3,316	3,377	2,420	1,795	1,015	496	296	190	—	—

PORTFOLIO (as of 6/30/00)

Portfolio Manager: committee, George Sauter - 1992

Investm't Category: Growth & Income

✔ Domestic ✔ Index
Foreign Sector
Asset Allocation State Specific

Investment Style

✔ Large Cap Mid Cap Small Cap
Growth Grth/Val ✔ Value

Portfolio

0.0%	cash	0.0%	corp bonds
100.0%	stocks	0.0%	gov't bonds
0.0%	pref/conv't pref	0.0%	muni bonds
0.0%	conv't bds/wrnts	0.0%	other

SHAREHOLDER INFORMATION

Minimum Investment

Initial: $3,000 Subsequent: $100

Minimum IRA Investment

Initial: $1,000 Subsequent: $100

Maximum Fees

Load: none 12b-1: none
Other: none

Services

✔ IRA
✔ Keogh
✔ Telephone Exchange

Vanguard Intl Value (VTRIX)

800-635-1511, 610-669-1000
www.vanguard.com

International Stock

PERFORMANCE — fund inception date: 5/16/83

	3yr Annual	5yr Annual	10yr Annual	Bull	Bear
Return (%)	10.4	7.2	7.9	45.5	-6.0
Differ from Category (+/-)	1.5 av	-1.1 blw av	-1.1 blw av	-45.4 low	18.0 high

Standard Deviation	Category Risk Index	Beta
17.5%—av	0.77—blw av	0.73

	2000	1999	1998	1997	1996	1995	1994	1993	1992	1991
Return (%)	-7.4	21.7	19.4	-4.5	10.2	9.6	5.2	30.4	-8.7	9.8
Differ from Category (+/-)	12.0	-39.0	13.6	-5.8	-4.3	0.3	8.3	-9.8	-5.2	-3.2
Return, Tax-Adjusted (%)	-8.5	20.0	16.7	-7.6	3.9	6.3	3.9	29.0	-9.7	8.2

PER SHARE DATA

	2000	1999	1998	1997	1996	1995	1994	1993	1992	1991
Dividends, Net Income ($)	0.73	0.66	1.06	0.69	0.82	0.79	0.56	0.81	0.67	0.77
Distrib'ns, Cap Gain ($)	0.19	0.73	0.90	2.95	5.77	2.51	0.63	0.00	0.28	0.61
Net Asset Value ($)	26.03	29.12	25.09	22.64	27.54	31.11	31.48	31.04	24.44	27.78
Expense Ratio (%)	na	0.59	0.52	0.49	0.50	0.38	0.34	0.40	0.42	0.38
Yield (%)	2.78	2.21	4.07	2.69	2.46	2.34	1.74	2.60	2.71	2.71
Portfolio Turnover (%)	na	41	39	37	82	43	40	39	51	46
Total Assets (Millions $)	821	1,044	806	776	916	988	1,053	982	678	878

PORTFOLIO (as of 6/30/00)

Portfolio Manager: Dayal, Holt, Foong - 2000

Investm't Category: International Stock

Domestic	Index
✔ Foreign	Sector
Asset Allocation	State Specific

Investment Style

Large Cap	Mid Cap	Small Cap
Growth	Grth/Val	Value

Portfolio

3.0% cash	0.0% corp bonds
96.0% stocks	0.0% gov't bonds
0.0% pref/conv't pref	0.0% muni bonds
0.0% conv't bds/wrnts	1.0% other

SHAREHOLDER INFORMATION

Minimum Investment
Initial: $3,000 — Subsequent: $100

Minimum IRA Investment
Initial: $1,000 — Subsequent: $100

Maximum Fees
Load: none — 12b-1: none
Other: none

Services
✔ IRA
✔ Keogh
✔ Telephone Exchange

Vanguard LifeStgy Cons Gr (VSCGX)

800-635-1511, 610-669-1000
www.vanguard.com

Balanced

PERFORMANCE

fund inception date: 7/18/94

	3yr Annual	5yr Annual	10yr Annual	Bull	Bear
Return (%)	8.8	10.6	na	21.3	-1.6
Differ from Category (+/-)	0.4 av	-0.8 blw av	na	-6.8 blw av	1.6 abv av

Standard Deviation	Category Risk Index	Beta
7.1%—blw av	0.65—low	0.38

	2000	1999	1998	1997	1996	1995	1994	1993	1992	1991
Return (%)	3.0	7.8	15.8	16.8	10.3	24.3	—	—	—	—
Differ from Category (+/-)	1.0	-2.9	2.5	-2.0	-3.6	-1.2	—	—	—	—
Return, Tax-Adjusted (%)	0.9	5.9	13.7	14.6	8.0	22.0	—	—	—	—

PER SHARE DATA

	2000	1999	1998	1997	1996	1995	1994	1993	1992	1991
Dividends, Net Income ($)	0.70	0.63	0.59	0.56	0.53	0.47	—	—	—	—
Distrib'ns, Cap Gain ($)	0.16	0.11	0.20	0.19	0.20	0.12	—	—	—	—
Net Asset Value ($)	14.70	15.10	14.71	13.40	12.14	11.68	—	—	—	—
Expense Ratio (%)	na	0.00	0.14	0.00	0.00	0.00	—	—	—	—
Yield (%)	4.71	4.14	3.95	4.12	4.29	3.98	—	—	—	—
Portfolio Turnover (%)	na	5	3	1	2	0	—	—	—	—
Total Assets (Millions $)	1,755	1,747	1,415	802	462	219	—	—	—	—

PORTFOLIO (as of 6/30/00)

Portfolio Manager: committee - 1994

Investm't Category: Balanced

✔ Domestic	Index
✔ Foreign	Sector
✔ Asset Allocation	State Specific

Investment Style

Large Cap	Mid Cap	Small Cap
Growth	Grth/Val	Value

Portfolio

0.0%	cash	0.0%	corp bonds
0.0%	stocks	0.0%	gov't bonds
0.0%	pref/conv't pref	0.0%	muni bonds
0.0%	conv't bds/wrnts	100.0%	other

SHAREHOLDER INFORMATION

Minimum Investment

Initial: $3,000 Subsequent: $100

Minimum IRA Investment

Initial: $1,000 Subsequent: $100

Maximum Fees

Load: none 12b-1: none

Other: none

Services

✔ IRA

✔ Keogh

✔ Telephone Exchange

Vanguard LifeStgy Grth

800-635-1511, 610-669-1000
www.vanguard.com

(VASGX)

Balanced

PERFORMANCE

fund inception date: 7/18/94

	3yr Annual	5yr Annual	10yr Annual	Bull	Bear
Return (%)	10.4	13.7	na	43.9	-10.4
Differ from Category (+/-)	2.0 abv av	2.3 high	na	15.8 high	-7.2 low

Standard Deviation	Category Risk Index	Beta
13.9%—blw av	1.27—high	0.76

	2000	1999	1998	1997	1996	1995	1994	1993	1992	1991
Return (%)	-5.4	17.3	21.4	22.2	15.4	29.2	—	—	—	—
Differ from Category (+/-)	-7.4	6.6	8.1	3.4	1.5	3.7	—	—	—	—
Return, Tax-Adjusted (%)	-6.5	16.1	20.0	20.6	13.7	27.5	—	—	—	—

PER SHARE DATA

	2000	1999	1998	1997	1996	1995	1994	1993	1992	1991
Dividends, Net Income ($)	0.51	0.45	0.41	0.38	0.35	0.31	—	—	—	—
Distrib'ns, Cap Gain ($)	0.17	0.16	0.26	0.29	0.23	0.15	—	—	—	—
Net Asset Value ($)	19.59	21.41	18.79	16.04	13.68	12.36	—	—	—	—
Expense Ratio (%)	na	0.00	0.14	0.00	0.00	0.00	—	—	—	—
Yield (%)	2.58	2.08	2.15	2.32	2.51	2.47	—	—	—	—
Portfolio Turnover (%)	na	1	2	1	0	1	—	—	—	—
Total Assets (Millions $)	3,376	3,177	1,924	1,183	628	217	—	—	—	—

PORTFOLIO (as of 6/30/00)

Portfolio Manager: committee - 1994

Investm't Category: Balanced

✔ Domestic
✔ Foreign
✔ Asset Allocation
Index
Sector
State Specific

Investment Style

Large Cap	Mid Cap	Small Cap
Growth	Grth/Val	Value

Portfolio

0.0%	cash	0.0%	corp bonds
0.0%	stocks	0.0%	gov't bonds
0.0%	pref/conv't pref	0.0%	muni bonds
0.0%	conv't bds/wrnts	100.0%	other

SHAREHOLDER INFORMATION

Minimum Investment
Initial: $3,000 Subsequent: $100

Minimum IRA Investment
Initial: $1,000 Subsequent: $100

Maximum Fees
Load: none 12b-1: none
Other: none

Services
✔ IRA
✔ Keogh
✔ Telephone Exchange

Vanguard LifeStgy Income (VASIX)

800-635-1511, 610-669-1000
www.vanguard.com

Balanced

PERFORMANCE

fund inception date: 7/18/94

	3yr Annual	5yr Annual	10yr Annual	Bull	Bear
Return (%)	7.9	9.0	na	10.8	3.2
Differ from Category (+/-)	-0.5 blw av	-2.4 blw av	na	-17.3 low	6.4 high

Standard Deviation	Category Risk Index	Beta
4.1%—blw av	0.37—low	0.18

	2000	1999	1998	1997	1996	1995	1994	1993	1992	1991
Return (%)	7.9	2.8	13.1	14.2	7.6	22.9	—	—	—	—
Differ from Category (+/-)	5.9	-7.9	-0.2	-4.6	-6.3	-2.6	—	—	—	—
Return, Tax-Adjusted (%)	5.4	0.6	10.7	11.8	4.8	20.6	—	—	—	—

PER SHARE DATA

	2000	1999	1998	1997	1996	1995	1994	1993	1992	1991
Dividends, Net Income ($)	0.74	0.69	0.63	0.63	0.64	0.49	—	—	—	—
Distrib'ns, Cap Gain ($)	0.08	0.07	0.19	0.10	0.21	0.09	—	—	—	—
Net Asset Value ($)	13.00	12.82	13.22	12.43	11.55	11.54	—	—	—	—
Expense Ratio (%)	na	0.00	0.14	0.00	0.00	0.00	—	—	—	—
Yield (%)	5.65	5.35	4.69	5.02	5.44	4.21	—	—	—	—
Portfolio Turnover (%)	na	11	3	6	22	1	—	—	—	—
Total Assets (Millions $)	620	555	448	243	151	120	—	—	—	—

PORTFOLIO (as of 6/30/00)

Portfolio Manager: committee - 1994

Investm't Category: Balanced

✔ Domestic
Foreign
✔ Asset Allocation
Index
Sector
State Specific

Investment Style

Large Cap Mid Cap Small Cap
Growth Grth/Val Value

Portfolio

0.0%	cash	0.0%	corp bonds
0.0%	stocks	0.0%	gov't bonds
0.0%	pref/conv't pref	0.0%	muni bonds
0.0%	conv't bds/wrnts	100.0%	other

SHAREHOLDER INFORMATION

Minimum Investment
Initial: $3,000 Subsequent: $100

Minimum IRA Investment
Initial: $1,000 Subsequent: $100

Maximum Fees
Load: none 12b-1: none
Other: none

Services
✔ IRA
✔ Keogh
✔ Telephone Exchange

Vanguard LifeStgy Mod Gr (VSMGX)

800-635-1511, 610-669-1000
www.vanguard.com

Balanced

PERFORMANCE — fund inception date: 7/18/94

	3yr Annual	5yr Annual	10yr Annual	Bull	Bear
Return (%)	9.7	12.2	na	31.7	-5.8
Differ from Category (+/-)	1.3 abv av	0.8 av	na	3.6 abv av	-2.6 blw av

Standard Deviation	Category Risk Index	Beta
10.4%—blw av	0.95—blw av	0.57

	2000	1999	1998	1997	1996	1995	1994	1993	1992	1991
Return (%)	-0.9	12.0	19.0	19.7	12.7	27.9	—	—	—	—
Differ from Category (+/-)	-2.9	1.3	5.7	0.9	-1.2	2.4	—	—	—	—
Return, Tax-Adjusted (%)	-2.4	10.5	17.3	17.8	10.7	26.0	—	—	—	—

PER SHARE DATA

	2000	1999	1998	1997	1996	1995	1994	1993	1992	1991
Dividends, Net Income ($)	0.64	0.55	0.51	0.49	0.44	0.36	—	—	—	—
Distrib'ns, Cap Gain ($)	0.14	0.13	0.24	0.21	0.23	0.13	—	—	—	—
Net Asset Value ($)	17.24	18.18	16.86	14.81	12.97	12.11	—	—	—	—
Expense Ratio (%)	na	0.00	0.14	0.00	0.00	0.00	—	—	—	—
Yield (%)	3.68	3.00	2.98	3.26	3.33	2.94	—	—	—	—
Portfolio Turnover (%)	na	3	5	2	3	1	—	—	—	—
Total Assets (Millions $)	3,628	3,440	2,201	1,358	825	234	—	—	—	—

PORTFOLIO (as of 6/30/00)

Portfolio Manager: committee - 1994

Investm't Category: Balanced

✔ Domestic — Index
✔ Foreign — Sector
✔ Asset Allocation — State Specific

Investment Style

Large Cap — Mid Cap — Small Cap
Growth — Grth/Val — Value

Portfolio

0.0%	cash	0.0%	corp bonds
0.0%	stocks	0.0%	gov't bonds
0.0%	pref/conv't pref	0.0%	muni bonds
0.0%	conv't bds/wrnts	100.0%	other

SHAREHOLDER INFORMATION

Minimum Investment
Initial: $3,000 — Subsequent: $100

Minimum IRA Investment
Initial: $1,000 — Subsequent: $100

Maximum Fees
Load: none — 12b-1: none
Other: none

Services
✔ IRA
✔ Keogh
✔ Telephone Exchange

Vanguard Morgan Growth (VMRGX)

800-635-1511, 610-669-1000
www.vanguard.com

Growth

PERFORMANCE — fund inception date: 12/31/68

	3yr Annual	5yr Annual	10yr Annual	Bull	Bear
Return (%)	12.7	18.2	16.7	78.6	-18.8
Differ from Category (+/-)	1.7 av	2.1 abv av	-0.1 av	28.9 high	-13.4 low

Standard Deviation	Category Risk Index	Beta
22.0%—abv av	1.13—abv av	1.16

	2000	1999	1998	1997	1996	1995	1994	1993	1992	1991
Return (%)	-12.5	34.1	22.2	30.8	23.3	35.9	-1.6	7.3	9.5	29.3
Differ from Category (+/-)	-16.0	15.2	7.9	3.7	1.0	5.5	-1.4	-7.3	-3.1	-8.3
Return, Tax-Adjusted (%)	-15.3	30.6	20.1	27.1	19.8	32.5	-2.7	3.7	7.8	26.1

PER SHARE DATA

	2000	1999	1998	1997	1996	1995	1994	1993	1992	1991
Dividends, Net Income ($)	0.15	0.15	0.18	0.16	0.14	0.15	0.14	0.18	0.18	0.29
Distrib'ns, Cap Gain ($)	2.95	3.08	1.43	2.52	1.53	1.16	0.31	1.35	0.52	0.86
Net Asset Value ($)	17.08	22.92	19.72	17.54	15.63	14.09	11.36	12.01	12.65	12.20
Expense Ratio (%)	na	0.42	0.44	0.48	0.51	0.47	0.50	0.49	0.48	0.46
Yield (%)	0.74	0.57	0.85	0.79	0.81	0.98	1.19	1.34	1.36	2.22
Portfolio Turnover (%)	na	65	81	76	73	72	84	72	64	52
Total Assets (Millions $)	4,931	5,066	3,555	2,795	2,053	1,471	1,074	1,135	1,116	956

PORTFOLIO (as of 6/30/00)

Portfolio Manager: committee - 1990

Investm't Category: Growth

✔ Domestic — Index
Foreign — Sector
Asset Allocation — State Specific

Investment Style

✔ Large Cap — ✔ Mid Cap — Small Cap
✔ Growth — Grth/Val — Value

Portfolio

8.0%	cash	0.0%	corp bonds
92.0%	stocks	0.0%	gov't bonds
0.0%	pref/conv't pref	0.0%	muni bonds
0.0%	conv't bds/wrnts	0.0%	other

SHAREHOLDER INFORMATION

Minimum Investment

Initial: $3,000 — Subsequent: $100

Minimum IRA Investment

Initial: $1,000 — Subsequent: $100

Maximum Fees

Load: none — 12b-1: none
Other: none

Services

✔ IRA
✔ Keogh
✔ Telephone Exchange

Vanguard PRIMECAP (VPMCX)

800-635-1511, 610-669-1000
www.vanguard.com

Growth

this fund is closed to new investors

PERFORMANCE

fund inception date: 11/1/84

	3yr Annual	5yr Annual	10yr Annual	Bull	Bear
Return (%)	22.8	24.5	22.7	91.2	-15.5
Differ from Category (+/-)	11.8 high	8.4 high	5.9 high	41.5 high	-10.1 blw av

Standard Deviation	Category Risk Index	Beta
20.9%—abv av	1.08—abv av	0.95

	2000	1999	1998	1997	1996	1995	1994	1993	1992	1991
Return (%)	4.4	41.3	25.4	36.8	18.3	35.4	11.4	18.0	8.9	33.1
Differ from Category (+/-)	0.9	22.4	11.1	9.7	-4.0	5.0	11.6	3.4	-3.7	-4.5
Return, Tax-Adjusted (%)	2.7	39.1	24.2	35.6	17.2	34.1	10.4	16.8	7.9	31.1

PER SHARE DATA

	2000	1999	1998	1997	1996	1995	1994	1993	1992	1991
Dividends, Net Income ($)	0.49	0.27	0.35	0.20	0.20	0.22	0.19	0.07	0.12	0.15
Distrib'ns, Cap Gain ($)	4.05	4.65	1.52	1.30	0.73	0.59	0.34	0.59	0.41	0.68
Net Asset Value ($)	60.38	62.07	47.66	39.57	30.08	26.23	19.98	18.42	16.19	15.36
Expense Ratio (%)	na	0.51	0.51	0.51	0.59	0.60	0.64	0.67	0.68	0.68
Yield (%)	0.76	0.40	0.71	0.48	0.64	0.82	0.93	0.36	0.72	0.93
Portfolio Turnover (%)	na	19	13	13	10	4	8	16	7	24
Total Assets (Millions $)	21,034	17,911	11,209	8,186	4,203	3,236	1,533	790	646	486

PORTFOLIO (as of 6/30/00)

Portfolio Manager: committee - 1984

Investm't Category: Growth

✔ Domestic   Index
Foreign   Sector
Asset Allocation   State Specific

Investment Style

✔ Large Cap   ✔ Mid Cap   Small Cap
✔ Growth   Grth/Val   Value

Portfolio

12.0%	cash	0.0%	corp bonds
88.0%	stocks	0.0%	gov't bonds
0.0%	pref/conv't pref	0.0%	muni bonds
0.0%	conv't bds/wrnts	0.0%	other

SHAREHOLDER INFORMATION

Minimum Investment

Initial: $3,000   Subsequent: $100

Minimum IRA Investment

Initial: $1,000   Subsequent: $100

Maximum Fees

Load: none   12b-1: none
Other: none

Services

✔ IRA
✔ Keogh
✔ Telephone Exchange

Vanguard Pacific Stk Idx (VPACX)

800-635-1511, 610-669-1000
www.vanguard.com

International Stock

PERFORMANCE — fund inception date: 5/1/90

	3yr Annual	5yr Annual	10yr Annual	Bull	Bear
Return (%)	6.1	-3.9	1.5	98.6	-22.5
Differ from Category (+/-)	-2.8 blw av	-12.2 low	-7.5 low	7.7 abv av	1.5 av

Standard Deviation	Category Risk Index	Beta
22.6%—abv av	1.00—av	0.86

	2000	1999	1998	1997	1996	1995	1994	1993	1992	1991
Return (%)	-25.7	57.0	2.4	-25.6	-7.8	2.8	12.9	35.4	-18.1	10.6
Differ from Category (+/-)	-6.3	-3.7	-3.4	-26.9	-22.3	-6.5	16.0	-4.8	-14.6	-2.4
Return, Tax-Adjusted (%)	-26.0	56.5	2.0	-25.9	-8.1	2.3	12.4	34.9	-18.5	10.4

PER SHARE DATA

	2000	1999	1998	1997	1996	1995	1994	1993	1992	1991
Dividends, Net Income ($)	0.12	0.09	0.06	0.09	0.09	0.12	0.08	0.06	0.05	0.05
Distrib'ns, Cap Gain ($)	0.00	0.00	0.00	0.00	0.00	0.00	0.06	0.05	0.10	0.00
Net Asset Value ($)	8.95	12.22	7.84	7.72	10.51	11.50	11.30	10.13	7.56	9.42
Expense Ratio (%)	na	0.37	0.40	0.35	0.35	0.32	0.32	0.32	0.32	0.32
Yield (%)	1.34	0.73	0.76	1.16	0.85	1.04	0.70	0.58	0.65	0.53
Portfolio Turnover (%)	na	6	4	8	9	1	4	7	3	21
Total Assets (Millions $)	1,910	2,526	1,032	827	977	830	697	492	206	84

PORTFOLIO (as of 6/30/00)

Portfolio Manager: committee, George Sauter - 2000

Investm't Category: International Stock

Domestic ✔ Index
✔ Foreign Sector
Asset Allocation State Specific

Investment Style

Large Cap Mid Cap Small Cap
Growth Grth/Val Value

Portfolio

0.0%	cash	1.0%	corp bonds
99.0%	stocks	0.0%	gov't bonds
0.0%	pref/conv't pref	0.0%	muni bonds
0.0%	conv't bds/wrnts	0.0%	other

SHAREHOLDER INFORMATION

Minimum Investment
Initial: $3,000 Subsequent: $100

Minimum IRA Investment
Initial: $1,000 Subsequent: $100

Maximum Fees
Load: none 12b-1: none
Other: none

Services
✔ IRA
✔ Keogh
✔ Telephone Exchange

Vanguard Preferred Stock (VQIIX)

800-635-1511, 610-669-1000
www.vanguard.com

Growth & Income

PERFORMANCE — fund inception date: 12/3/75

	3yr Annual	5yr Annual	10yr Annual	Bull	Bear
Return (%)	1.7	5.2	8.2	-5.8	2.7
Differ from Category (+/-)	-7.2 low	-9.1 low	-6.7 low	-39.3 low	2.8 av

Standard Deviation	Category Risk Index	Beta
3.4%—low	0.20—low	0.00

	2000	1999	1998	1997	1996	1995	1994	1993	1992	1991
Return (%)	4.7	-5.8	6.6	12.9	8.4	25.9	-7.9	13.0	8.4	20.9
Differ from Category (+/-)	-1.0	-16.6	-6.2	-14.0	-11.3	-3.6	-7.4	-0.8	-3.2	-7.2
Return, Tax-Adjusted (%)	2.1	-8.0	4.1	10.2	5.6	22.6	-10.5	9.5	5.9	18.2

PER SHARE DATA

	2000	1999	1998	1997	1996	1995	1994	1993	1992	1991
Dividends, Net Income ($)	0.58	0.59	0.58	0.65	0.66	0.67	0.65	0.71	0.73	0.72
Distrib'ns, Cap Gain ($)	0.00	0.00	0.12	0.00	0.00	0.00	0.00	0.14	0.00	0.00
Net Asset Value ($)	8.87	9.04	10.20	10.23	9.66	9.55	8.15	9.54	9.23	9.22
Expense Ratio (%)	na	0.36	0.36	0.37	0.39	0.52	0.51	0.53	0.58	0.63
Yield (%)	6.53	6.52	5.62	6.35	6.83	7.01	7.97	7.33	7.90	7.80
Portfolio Turnover (%)	na	11	39	34	31	15	27	45	33	18
Total Assets (Millions $)	201	282	372	329	297	311	278	386	186	100

PORTFOLIO (as of 6/30/00)

Portfolio Manager: Earl McEvoy - 1982

Investm't Category: Growth & Income

✔ Domestic — Index
Foreign — Sector
Asset Allocation — State Specific

Investment Style

Large Cap — Mid Cap — Small Cap
Growth — Grth/Val — Value

Portfolio

2.0%	cash	0.0%	corp bonds
0.0%	stocks	0.0%	gov't bonds
98.0%	pref/conv't pref	0.0%	muni bonds
0.0%	conv't bds/wrnts	0.0%	other

SHAREHOLDER INFORMATION

Minimum Investment
Initial: $3,000 — Subsequent: $100

Minimum IRA Investment
Initial: $1,000 — Subsequent: $100

Maximum Fees
Load: none — 12b-1: none
Other: none

Services
✔ IRA
✔ Keogh
✔ Telephone Exchange

Vanguard STAR (VGSTX)

800-635-1511, 610-669-1000
www.vanguard.com

Balanced

PERFORMANCE — fund inception date: 3/29/85

	3yr Annual	5yr Annual	10yr Annual	Bull	Bear
Return (%)	10.1	13.4	13.8	24.7	2.2
Differ from Category (+/-)	1.7 abv av	2.0 abv av	2.1 high	-3.4 av	5.4 high

Standard Deviation	Category Risk Index	Beta
11.1%—blw av	1.01—av	0.56

	2000	1999	1998	1997	1996	1995	1994	1993	1992	1991
Return (%)	10.9	7.1	12.3	21.1	16.1	28.6	-0.2	10.9	10.5	24.0
Differ from Category (+/-)	8.9	-3.6	-1.0	2.3	2.2	3.1	1.1	-3.5	2.1	0.2
Return, Tax-Adjusted (%)	7.6	5.3	9.8	18.1	12.7	25.5	-2.2	8.5	8.8	21.2

PER SHARE DATA

	2000	1999	1998	1997	1996	1995	1994	1993	1992	1991
Dividends, Net Income ($)	0.64	0.61	0.58	0.59	0.59	0.59	0.52	0.47	0.51	0.62
Distrib'ns, Cap Gain ($)	1.65	0.40	0.98	1.20	0.98	0.56	0.25	0.40	0.18	0.37
Net Asset Value ($)	17.81	18.21	17.96	17.38	15.86	15.02	12.60	13.41	12.88	12.29
Expense Ratio (%)	na	0.00	0.00	0.00	0.00	0.00	0.00	0.00	0.00	0.00
Yield (%)	3.28	3.27	3.06	3.17	3.50	3.78	4.04	3.40	3.90	4.89
Portfolio Turnover (%)	na	10	16	15	18	8	9	3	3	11
Total Assets (Millions $)	7,777	8,087	8,082	7,355	5,863	4,841	3,766	3,628	2,489	1,574

PORTFOLIO (as of 6/30/00)

Portfolio Manager: committee - 1985

Investm't Category: Balanced

✔ Domestic — Index
Foreign — Sector
Asset Allocation — State Specific

Investment Style

Large Cap — Mid Cap — Small Cap
Growth — Grth/Val — Value

Portfolio

0.0%	cash	0.0%	corp bonds
0.0%	stocks	0.0%	gov't bonds
0.0%	pref/conv't pref	0.0%	muni bonds
0.0%	conv't bds/wrnts	100.0%	other

SHAREHOLDER INFORMATION

Minimum Investment
Initial: $1,000 — Subsequent: $100

Minimum IRA Investment
Initial: $1,000 — Subsequent: $100

Maximum Fees
Load: none — 12b-1: none
Other: none

Services
✔ IRA
✔ Keogh
✔ Telephone Exchange

Vanguard Selected Value (VASVX)

800-662-7447, 610-669-1000
www.vanguard.com

Growth

PERFORMANCE — fund inception date: 2/15/96

	3yr Annual	5yr Annual	10yr Annual	Bull	Bear
Return (%)	0.6	na	na	17.2	10.4
Differ from Category (+/-)	-10.4 low	na	na	-32.5 low	15.8 high

Standard Deviation	Category Risk Index	Beta
23.4%—abv av	1.20—abv av	0.87

	2000	1999	1998	1997	1996	1995	1994	1993	1992	1991
Return (%)	17.3	-1.6	-11.7	17.3	—	—	—	—	—	—
Differ from Category (+/-)	13.8	-20.5	-26.0	-9.8	—	—	—	—	—	—
Return, Tax-Adjusted (%)	16.3	-2.4	-12.4	16.2	—	—	—	—	—	—

PER SHARE DATA

	2000	1999	1998	1997	1996	1995	1994	1993	1992	1991
Dividends, Net Income ($)	0.24	0.16	0.08	0.05	—	—	—	—	—	—
Distrib'ns, Cap Gain ($)	0.00	0.11	0.33	0.46	—	—	—	—	—	—
Net Asset Value ($)	11.42	9.94	10.39	12.28	—	—	—	—	—	—
Expense Ratio (%)	na	0.73	0.65	0.74	—	—	—	—	—	—
Yield (%)	2.10	1.59	0.74	0.39	—	—	—	—	—	—
Portfolio Turnover (%)	na	102	47	32	—	—	—	—	—	—
Total Assets (Millions $)	152	186	148	191	—	—	—	—	—	—

PORTFOLIO (as of 6/30/00)

Portfolio Manager: James Barrow - 1999

Investm't Category: Growth

✔ Domestic — Index
✔ Foreign — Sector
Asset Allocation — State Specific

Investment Style

Large Cap — ✔ Mid Cap — Small Cap
Growth — Grth/Val — ✔ Value

Portfolio

0.0%	cash	0.0%	corp bonds
100.0%	stocks	0.0%	gov't bonds
0.0%	pref/conv't pref	0.0%	muni bonds
0.0%	conv't bds/wrnts	0.0%	other

SHAREHOLDER INFORMATION

Minimum Investment

Initial: $3,000 — Subsequent: $100

Minimum IRA Investment

Initial: $1,000 — Subsequent: $100

Maximum Fees

Load: none — 12b-1: none
Other: none

Services

✔ IRA
✔ Keogh
✔ Telephone Exchange

Vanguard Specl: Energy (VGENX)

800-635-1511, 610-669-1000
www.vanguard.com

Growth

PERFORMANCE — fund inception date: 5/23/84

	3yr Annual	5yr Annual	10yr Annual	Bull	Bear
Return (%)	9.4	15.0	12.8	31.4	6.5
Differ from Category (+/-)	-1.6 blw av	-1.1 blw av	-4.0 low	-18.3 blw av	11.9 abv av

Standard Deviation	Category Risk Index	Beta
27.9%—high	1.44—high	0.81

	2000	1999	1998	1997	1996	1995	1994	1993	1992	1991
Return (%)	36.4	20.9	-20.5	14.8	33.9	25.3	-1.6	26.4	6.1	0.2
Differ from Category (+/-)	32.9	2.0	-34.8	-12.3	11.6	-5.1	-1.4	11.8	-6.5	-37.4
Return, Tax-Adjusted (%)	34.4	20.1	-21.4	13.0	32.7	23.9	-2.7	22.6	4.8	-1.5

PER SHARE DATA

	2000	1999	1998	1997	1996	1995	1994	1993	1992	1991
Dividends, Net Income ($)	0.36	0.35	0.35	0.32	0.24	0.28	0.24	0.29	0.36	0.42
Distrib'ns, Cap Gain ($)	1.38	0.00	0.42	1.33	0.40	0.30	0.29	1.38	0.18	0.42
Net Asset Value ($)	28.07	21.92	18.42	24.14	22.54	17.31	14.29	15.06	13.29	13.03
Expense Ratio (%)	0.48	0.41	0.38	0.39	0.51	0.30	0.17	0.21	0.30	0.35
Yield (%)	1.22	1.59	1.85	1.25	1.04	1.59	1.64	1.76	2.67	3.12
Portfolio Turnover (%)	18	22	19	15	21	13	41	37	42	40
Total Assets (Millions $)	1,189	1,018	819	1,181	847	506	445	269	155	116

PORTFOLIO (as of 6/30/00)

Portfolio Manager: Ernst Von Metzsch - 1984

Investm't Category: Growth

✔ Domestic
Index
✔ Foreign
✔ Sector
Asset Allocation
State Specific

Investment Style

Large Cap
✔ Mid Cap
Small Cap
Growth
Grth/Val
✔ Value

Portfolio

4.0%	cash	0.0%	corp bonds
96.0%	stocks	0.0%	gov't bonds
0.0%	pref/conv't pref	0.0%	muni bonds
0.0%	conv't bds/wrnts	0.0%	other

SHAREHOLDER INFORMATION

Minimum Investment

Initial: $3,000 Subsequent: $100

Minimum IRA Investment

Initial: $1,000 Subsequent: $100

Maximum Fees

Load: 1.00% redemption 12b-1: none
Other: redemption fee applies for 12 months

Services

✔ IRA
✔ Keogh
✔ Telephone Exchange

Vanguard Specl: Gold & PM (VGPMX)

800-635-1511, 610-669-1000
www.vanguard.com

Aggressive Growth

PERFORMANCE — fund inception date: 5/23/84

	3yr Annual	5yr Annual	10yr Annual	Bull	Bear
Return (%)	4.6	-7.0	0.2	70.4	4.4
Differ from Category (+/-)	-11.6 low	-21.6 low	-15.6 low	-48.8 blw av	25.0 high

Standard Deviation	Category Risk Index	Beta
37.9%—high	1.17—abv av	0.80

	2000	1999	1998	1997	1996	1995	1994	1993	1992	1991
Return (%)	-7.3	28.8	-3.9	-38.9	-0.7	-4.4	-5.4	93.3	-19.4	4.3
Differ from Category (+/-)	-1.3	-28.7	-19.0	-53.7	-19.0	-39.0	-4.6	68.1	-26.3	-42.9
Return, Tax-Adjusted (%)	-8.2	28.2	-4.4	-39.3	-1.5	-4.9	-6.2	92.1	-20.0	3.4

PER SHARE DATA

	2000	1999	1998	1997	1996	1995	1994	1993	1992	1991
Dividends, Net Income ($)	0.20	0.10	0.09	0.13	0.21	0.17	0.31	0.21	0.18	0.25
Distrib'ns, Cap Gain ($)	0.00	0.00	0.00	0.00	0.07	0.00	0.00	0.00	0.00	0.00
Net Asset Value ($)	7.58	8.41	6.61	6.97	11.63	11.98	12.72	13.78	7.24	9.21
Expense Ratio (%)	0.77	0.77	0.62	0.50	0.60	0.25	0.26	0.36	0.35	0.42
Yield (%)	2.63	1.18	1.36	1.86	1.79	1.41	2.43	1.52	2.48	2.71
Portfolio Turnover (%)	28	23	26	19	5	4	14	2	3	10
Total Assets (Millions $)	294	381	311	292	496	549	639	609	173	170

PORTFOLIO (as of 6/30/00)

Portfolio Manager: Graham French - 1996

Investm't Category: Aggressive Growth

✔ Domestic — Index
✔ Foreign — ✔ Sector
Asset Allocation — State Specific

Investment Style

Large Cap — Mid Cap — Small Cap
Growth — Grth/Val — Value

Portfolio

3.0%	cash	0.0%	corp bonds
96.0%	stocks	0.0%	gov't bonds
1.0%	pref/conv't pref	0.0%	muni bonds
0.0%	conv't bds/wrnts	0.0%	other

SHAREHOLDER INFORMATION

Minimum Investment
Initial: $3,000 — Subsequent: $100

Minimum IRA Investment
Initial: $1,000 — Subsequent: $100

Maximum Fees
Load: 1.00% redemption — 12b-1: none
Other: redemption fee applies for 12 months

Services
✔ IRA
✔ Keogh
✔ Telephone Exchange

Vanguard Specl: Health (VGHCX)

800-635-1511, 610-669-1000
www.vanguard.com

Growth

PERFORMANCE — fund inception date: 5/23/84

	3yr Annual	5yr Annual	10yr Annual	Bull	Bear
Return (%)	34.2	30.4	25.4	39.6	33.7
Differ from Category (+/-)	23.2 high	14.3 high	8.6 high	-10.1 av	39.1 high

Standard Deviation	Category Risk Index	Beta
14.2%—blw av	0.73—low	0.52

	2000	1999	1998	1997	1996	1995	1994	1993	1992	1991
Return (%)	60.5	7.0	40.8	28.5	21.3	45.1	9.5	11.8	-1.5	46.3
Differ from Category (+/-)	57.0	-11.9	26.5	1.4	-1.0	14.7	9.7	-2.8	-14.1	8.7
Return, Tax-Adjusted (%)	56.7	5.1	39.4	27.2	19.9	43.6	7.0	9.2	-3.0	45.0

PER SHARE DATA

	2000	1999	1998	1997	1996	1995	1994	1993	1992	1991
Dividends, Net Income ($)	1.07	0.97	0.84	0.78	0.74	0.57	0.57	0.76	0.70	0.53
Distrib'ns, Cap Gain ($)	15.93	7.14	3.08	2.14	1.29	1.02	2.31	1.97	1.20	0.53
Net Asset Value ($)	132.74	95.21	96.85	71.88	58.35	49.82	35.47	35.07	34.01	36.50
Expense Ratio (%)	0.41	0.36	0.40	0.38	0.46	0.40	0.19	0.22	0.30	0.36
Yield (%)	0.71	0.94	0.84	1.05	1.24	1.12	1.50	2.05	1.98	1.43
Portfolio Turnover (%)	27	11	10	7	13	25	19	15	7	17
Total Assets (Millions $)	17,507	10,420	9,268	4,466	2,661	1,473	708	609	607	547

PORTFOLIO (as of 6/30/00)

Portfolio Manager: Edward Owens - 1984

Investm't Category: Growth

✔ Domestic — Index
✔ Foreign — ✔ Sector
Asset Allocation — State Specific

Investment Style

Large Cap — ✔ Mid Cap — Small Cap
Growth — ✔ Grth/Val — Value

Portfolio

9.0%	cash	0.0%	corp bonds
91.0%	stocks	0.0%	gov't bonds
0.0%	pref/conv't pref	0.0%	muni bonds
0.0%	conv't bds/wrnts	0.0%	other

SHAREHOLDER INFORMATION

Minimum Investment
Initial: $10,000 — Subsequent: $100

Minimum IRA Investment
Initial: $1,000 — Subsequent: $100

Maximum Fees
Load: 1.00% redemption — 12b-1: none
Other: redemption fee applies for 5 years

Services
✔ IRA
✔ Keogh
✔ Telephone Exchange

Vanguard Specl: REIT Index (VGSIX)

800-662-7447, 610-669-1000
www.vanguard.com

Growth & Income

PERFORMANCE — fund inception date: 5/13/96

	3yr Annual	5yr Annual	10yr Annual	Bull	Bear
Return (%)	0.4	na	na	-0.3	15.2
Differ from Category (+/-)	-8.5 low	na	na	-33.8 low	15.3 high

Standard Deviation	Category Risk Index	Beta
14.2%—blw av	0.82—low	0.16

	2000	1999	1998	1997	1996	1995	1994	1993	1992	1991
Return (%)	26.3	-4.0	-16.3	18.7	—	—	—	—	—	—
Differ from Category (+/-)	20.6	-14.8	-29.1	-8.2	—	—	—	—	—	—
Return, Tax-Adjusted (%)	23.0	-6.7	-18.5	16.3	—	—	—	—	—	—

PER SHARE DATA

	2000	1999	1998	1997	1996	1995	1994	1993	1992	1991
Dividends, Net Income ($)	0.82	0.78	0.81	0.72	—	—	—	—	—	—
Distrib'ns, Cap Gain ($)	0.00	0.00	0.00	0.05	—	—	—	—	—	—
Net Asset Value ($)	11.56	9.85	11.08	14.16	—	—	—	—	—	—
Expense Ratio (%)	0.33	0.26	0.24	0.36	—	—	—	—	—	—
Yield (%)	7.09	7.91	7.31	5.06	—	—	—	—	—	—
Portfolio Turnover (%)	12	29	2	—	—	—	—	—	—	—
Total Assets (Millions $)	1,030	875	923	1,277	—	—	—	—	—	—

PORTFOLIO (as of 6/30/00)

Portfolio Manager: committee, George Sauter - 1996

Investm't Category: Growth & Income

✔ Domestic	✔ Index
Foreign	✔ Sector
Asset Allocation	State Specific

Investment Style

Large Cap	✔ Mid Cap	✔ Small Cap
Growth	Grth/Val	✔ Value

Portfolio

3.0%	cash	0.0%	corp bonds
97.0%	stocks	0.0%	gov't bonds
0.0%	pref/conv't pref	0.0%	muni bonds
0.0%	conv't bds/wrnts	0.0%	other

SHAREHOLDER INFORMATION

Minimum Investment
Initial: $3,000 Subsequent: $100

Minimum IRA Investment
Initial: $1,000 Subsequent: $100

Maximum Fees
Load: 1.00% redemption 12b-1: none
Other: redemption fee applies for 12 months

Services
✔ IRA
✔ Keogh
✔ Telephone Exchange

Vanguard Specl: Util Inc (VGSUX)

800-635-1511, 610-669-1000
www.vanguard.com

Growth & Income

PERFORMANCE — fund inception date: 5/15/92

	3yr Annual	5yr Annual	10yr Annual	Bull	Bear
Return (%)	11.9	13.0	na	15.3	4.7
Differ from Category (+/-)	3.0 abv av	-1.3 blw av	na	-18.2 blw av	4.8 abv av

Standard Deviation	Category Risk Index	Beta
12.9%—blw av	0.74—low	0.30

	2000	1999	1998	1997	1996	1995	1994	1993	1992	1991
Return (%)	18.7	-2.9	21.8	25.0	5.2	34.0	-8.5	15.0	—	—
Differ from Category (+/-)	13.0	-13.7	9.0	-1.9	-14.5	4.5	-8.0	1.2	—	—
Return, Tax-Adjusted (%)	16.2	-5.5	18.8	22.7	3.4	31.7	-10.7	11.9	—	—

PER SHARE DATA

	2000	1999	1998	1997	1996	1995	1994	1993	1992	1991
Dividends, Net Income ($)	0.53	0.51	0.59	0.60	0.56	0.56	0.59	0.56	—	—
Distrib'ns, Cap Gain ($)	0.73	1.20	1.01	0.26	0.02	0.00	0.12	0.40	—	—
Net Asset Value ($)	15.66	14.33	16.54	14.98	12.74	12.68	9.94	11.63	—	—
Expense Ratio (%)	0.40	0.38	0.44	0.40	0.44	0.50	0.42	0.45	—	—
Yield (%)	3.23	3.28	3.36	3.93	4.38	4.41	5.86	4.65	—	—
Portfolio Turnover (%)	47	55	41	38	35	35	46	20	—	—
Total Assets (Millions $)	906	840	951	684	658	757	560	774	—	—

PORTFOLIO (as of 6/30/00)

Portfolio Manager: Mark Beckwith, Earl McEvoy - 1996

Investm't Category: Growth & Income

✔ Domestic | Index
✔ Foreign | ✔ Sector
Asset Allocation | State Specific

Investment Style

✔ Large Cap | ✔ Mid Cap | Small Cap
Growth | ✔ Grth/Val | Value

Portfolio

4.0%	cash	0.0%	corp bonds
96.0%	stocks	0.0%	gov't bonds
0.0%	pref/conv't pref	0.0%	muni bonds
0.0%	conv't bds/wrnts	0.0%	other

SHAREHOLDER INFORMATION

Minimum Investment
Initial: $3,000 | Subsequent: $100

Minimum IRA Investment
Initial: $1,000 | Subsequent: $100

Maximum Fees
Load: none | 12b-1: none
Other: none

Services
✔ IRA
✔ Keogh
✔ Telephone Exchange

Vanguard Strategic Eqty (VSEQX)

800-662-7447, 610-669-1000
www.vanguard.com

Growth

PERFORMANCE — fund inception date: 8/14/95

	3yr Annual	5yr Annual	10yr Annual	Bull	Bear
Return (%)	8.8	15.2	na	50.7	-1.2
Differ from Category (+/-)	-2.2 blw av	-0.9 av	na	1.0 av	4.2 abv av

Standard Deviation	Category Risk Index	Beta
19.9%—abv av	1.02—av	0.97

	2000	1999	1998	1997	1996	1995	1994	1993	1992	1991
Return (%)	7.4	19.3	0.5	26.1	25.1	—	—	—	—	—
Differ from Category (+/-)	3.9	0.4	-13.8	-1.0	2.8	—	—	—	—	—
Return, Tax-Adjusted (%)	3.2	18.3	0.0	23.9	22.5	—	—	—	—	—

PER SHARE DATA

	2000	1999	1998	1997	1996	1995	1994	1993	1992	1991
Dividends, Net Income ($)	0.21	0.16	0.15	0.14	0.18	—	—	—	—	—
Distrib'ns, Cap Gain ($)	3.03	0.37	0.00	1.08	0.71	—	—	—	—	—
Net Asset Value ($)	14.58	16.76	14.52	14.60	12.57	—	—	—	—	—
Expense Ratio (%)	na	0.46	0.43	0.40	0.38	—	—	—	—	—
Yield (%)	1.19	0.93	1.03	0.89	1.35	—	—	—	—	—
Portfolio Turnover (%)	na	51	71	85	106	—	—	—	—	—
Total Assets (Millions $)	700	625	534	474	153	—	—	—	—	—

PORTFOLIO (as of 6/30/00)

Portfolio Manager: George Sauter - 1995

Investm't Category: Growth

✔ Domestic
Foreign
Asset Allocation
Index
Sector
State Specific

Investment Style

Large Cap
✔ Mid Cap
Small Cap
Growth
✔ Grth/Val
Value

Portfolio

3.0%	cash	0.0%	corp bonds
97.0%	stocks	0.0%	gov't bonds
0.0%	pref/conv't pref	0.0%	muni bonds
0.0%	conv't bds/wrnts	0.0%	other

SHAREHOLDER INFORMATION

Minimum Investment
Initial: $3,000 Subsequent: $100

Minimum IRA Investment
Initial: $1,000 Subsequent: $100

Maximum Fees
Load: 1.00% redemption 12b-1: none
Other: redemption fee applies for 5 years

Services
✔ IRA
✔ Keogh
✔ Telephone Exchange

Vanguard Tot Itl Stk Idx (VGTSX)

800-662-7447, 610-669-1000
www.vanguard.com

International Stock

PERFORMANCE — fund inception date: 4/29/96

	3yr Annual	5yr Annual	10yr Annual	Bull	Bear
Return (%)	8.2	na	na	53.2	-18.4
Differ from Category (+/-)	-0.7 av	na	na	-37.7 blw av	5.6 abv av

Standard Deviation	Category Risk Index	Beta
16.7%—av	0.74—low	0.75

	2000	1999	1998	1997	1996	1995	1994	1993	1992	1991
Return (%)	-15.6	29.9	15.6	-0.7	—	—	—	—	—	—
Differ from Category (+/-)	3.8	-30.8	9.8	-2.0	—	—	—	—	—	—
Return, Tax-Adjusted (%)	-16.2	29.1	14.7	-1.4	—	—	—	—	—	—

PER SHARE DATA

	2000	1999	1998	1997	1996	1995	1994	1993	1992	1991
Dividends, Net Income ($)	0.20	0.21	0.21	0.17	—	—	—	—	—	—
Distrib'ns, Cap Gain ($)	0.05	0.01	0.01	0.02	—	—	—	—	—	—
Net Asset Value ($)	11.83	14.31	11.19	9.87	—	—	—	—	—	—
Expense Ratio (%)	na	0.00	0.00	0.00	—	—	—	—	—	—
Yield (%)	1.68	1.46	1.87	1.71	—	—	—	—	—	—
Portfolio Turnover (%)	na	1	2	6	—	—	—	—	—	—
Total Assets (Millions $)	2,761	2,569	1,375	903	—	—	—	—	—	—

PORTFOLIO (as of 6/30/00)

Portfolio Manager: committee - 1996

Investm't Category: International Stock

- Domestic
- ✔ Foreign
- Asset Allocation
- ✔ Index
- Sector
- State Specific

Investment Style

- Large Cap
- Mid Cap
- Small Cap
- Growth
- Grth/Val
- Value

Portfolio

- 0.0% cash
- 0.0% stocks
- 0.0% pref/conv't pref
- 0.0% conv't bds/wrnts
- 0.0% corp bonds
- 0.0% gov't bonds
- 0.0% muni bonds
- 100.0% other

SHAREHOLDER INFORMATION

Minimum Investment
Initial: $3,000 Subsequent: $100

Minimum IRA Investment
Initial: $1,000 Subsequent: $100

Maximum Fees
Load: none 12b-1: none
Other: none

Services

- ✔ IRA
- ✔ Keogh
- Telephone Exchange

Vanguard Tx Mg Balanced (VTMFX)

800-635-1511, 610-669-1000
www.vanguard.com

Balanced

PERFORMANCE — fund inception date: 9/6/94

	3yr Annual	5yr Annual	10yr Annual	Bull	Bear
Return (%)	10.3	11.9	na	34.9	-6.4
Differ from Category (+/-)	1.9 abv av	0.5 av	na	6.8 abv av	-3.2 blw av

Standard Deviation	Category Risk Index	Beta
10.5%—blw av	0.96—blw av	0.56

	2000	1999	1998	1997	1996	1995	1994	1993	1992	1991
Return (%)	-0.5	15.4	16.9	16.5	12.2	24.5	—	—	—	—
Differ from Category (+/-)	-2.5	4.7	3.6	-2.3	-1.7	-1.0	—	—	—	—
Return, Tax-Adjusted (%)	-1.5	14.3	15.8	15.3	10.9	23.2	—	—	—	—

PER SHARE DATA

	2000	1999	1998	1997	1996	1995	1994	1993	1992	1991
Dividends, Net Income ($)	0.49	0.43	0.39	0.37	0.36	0.32	—	—	—	—
Distrib'ns, Cap Gain ($)	0.00	0.00	0.00	0.00	0.00	0.00	—	—	—	—
Net Asset Value ($)	18.30	18.87	16.74	14.67	12.92	11.85	—	—	—	—
Expense Ratio (%)	na	0.20	0.19	0.17	0.20	0.20	—	—	—	—
Yield (%)	2.67	2.27	2.32	2.52	2.78	2.70	—	—	—	—
Portfolio Turnover (%)	na	13	7	7	5	5	—	—	—	—
Total Assets (Millions $)	389	329	206	119	63	38	—	—	—	—

PORTFOLIO (as of 6/30/00)

Portfolio Manager: committee, George Sauter - 1994

Investm't Category: Balanced

✔ Domestic
Foreign
✔ Asset Allocation
Index
Sector
State Specific

Investment Style

Large Cap, Mid Cap, Small Cap
Growth, Grth/Val, Value

Portfolio

3.0%	cash	0.0%	corp bonds
47.0%	stocks	0.0%	gov't bonds
0.0%	pref/conv't pref	50.0%	muni bonds
0.0%	conv't bds/wrnts	0.0%	other

SHAREHOLDER INFORMATION

Minimum Investment

Initial: $10,000 — Subsequent: $100

Minimum IRA Investment

Initial: na — Subsequent: na

Maximum Fees

Load: 2.00% redemption — 12b-1: none

Other: redemption fee applies for 12 months

Services

IRA
Keogh
✔ Telephone Exchange

Vanguard Tx Mg Cap App (VMCAX)

800-635-1511, 610-669-1000
www.vanguard.com

Growth

PERFORMANCE — fund inception date: 9/6/94

	3yr Annual	5yr Annual	10yr Annual	Bull	Bear
Return (%)	15.3	18.7	na	79.9	-17.3
Differ from Category (+/-)	4.3 abv av	2.6 abv av	na	30.2 high	-11.9 blw av

Standard Deviation	Category Risk Index	Beta
21.2%—abv av	1.09—abv av	1.16

	2000	1999	1998	1997	1996	1995	1994	1993	1992	1991
Return (%)	-10.1	33.5	27.9	27.2	20.9	34.3	—	—	—	—
Differ from Category (+/-)	-13.6	14.6	13.6	0.1	-1.4	3.9	—	—	—	—
Return, Tax-Adjusted (%)	-10.2	33.3	27.6	26.9	20.5	33.9	—	—	—	—

PER SHARE DATA

	2000	1999	1998	1997	1996	1995	1994	1993	1992	1991
Dividends, Net Income ($)	0.11	0.12	0.13	0.12	0.11	0.09	—	—	—	—
Distrib'ns, Cap Gain ($)	0.00	0.00	0.00	0.00	0.00	0.00	—	—	—	—
Net Asset Value ($)	30.59	34.17	25.68	20.18	15.95	13.28	—	—	—	—
Expense Ratio (%)	na	0.19	0.19	0.17	0.20	0.20	—	—	—	—
Yield (%)	0.35	0.35	0.50	0.59	0.68	0.67	—	—	—	—
Portfolio Turnover (%)	na	12	5	4	12	7	—	—	—	—
Total Assets (Millions $)	2,577	2,378	1,478	892	517	254	—	—	—	—

PORTFOLIO (as of 6/30/00)

Portfolio Manager: committee, George Sauter - 1994

Investm't Category: Growth

✔ Domestic — Index
Foreign — Sector
Asset Allocation — State Specific

Investment Style

✔ Large Cap — Mid Cap — Small Cap
Growth — ✔ Grth/Val — Value

Portfolio

0.0%	cash	0.0%	corp bonds
100.0%	stocks	0.0%	gov't bonds
0.0%	pref/conv't pref	0.0%	muni bonds
0.0%	conv't bds/wrnts	0.0%	other

SHAREHOLDER INFORMATION

Minimum Investment
Initial: $10,000 — Subsequent: $100

Minimum IRA Investment
Initial: na — Subsequent: na

Maximum Fees
Load: 2.00% redemption — 12b-1: none
Other: redemption fee applies for 12 months

Services
IRA
Keogh
✔ Telephone Exchange

Vanguard Tx Mg Gr & Inc (VTGIX)

800-635-1511, 610-669-1000
www.vanguard.com

Growth & Income

PERFORMANCE — fund inception date: 9/6/94

	3yr Annual	5yr Annual	10yr Annual	Bull	Bear
Return (%)	12.3	18.3	na	56.3	-11.4
Differ from Category (+/-)	3.4 high	4.0 high	na	22.8 high	-11.3 blw av

Standard Deviation	Category Risk Index	Beta
17.6%—av	1.01—av	1.00

	2000	1999	1998	1997	1996	1995	1994	1993	1992	1991
Return (%)	-9.0	21.1	28.6	33.3	23.0	37.5	—	—	—	—
Differ from Category (+/-)	-14.7	10.3	15.8	6.4	3.3	8.0	—	—	—	—
Return, Tax-Adjusted (%)	-9.3	20.6	28.0	32.6	22.1	36.4	—	—	—	—

PER SHARE DATA

	2000	1999	1998	1997	1996	1995	1994	1993	1992	1991
Dividends, Net Income ($)	0.29	0.31	0.29	0.28	0.28	0.25	—	—	—	—
Distrib'ns, Cap Gain ($)	0.00	0.00	0.00	0.00	0.00	0.00	—	—	—	—
Net Asset Value ($)	28.66	31.81	26.55	20.88	15.89	13.16	—	—	—	—
Expense Ratio (%)	na	0.19	0.19	0.17	0.20	0.20	—	—	—	—
Yield (%)	1.01	0.97	1.09	1.34	1.76	1.89	—	—	—	—
Portfolio Turnover (%)	na	4	4	2	7	6	—	—	—	—
Total Assets (Millions $)	2,286	2,240	1,352	579	234	98	—	—	—	—

PORTFOLIO (as of 6/30/00)

Portfolio Manager: committee, George Sauter - 1994

Investm't Category: Growth & Income

✔ Domestic — Index
Foreign — Sector
Asset Allocation — State Specific

Investment Style

✔ Large Cap — Mid Cap — Small Cap
Growth — ✔ Grth/Val — Value

Portfolio

0.0%	cash	0.0%	corp bonds
100.0%	stocks	0.0%	gov't bonds
0.0%	pref/conv't pref	0.0%	muni bonds
0.0%	conv't bds/wrnts	0.0%	other

SHAREHOLDER INFORMATION

Minimum Investment

Initial: $10,000 — Subsequent: $100

Minimum IRA Investment

Initial: na — Subsequent: na

Maximum Fees

Load: 2.00% redemption — 12b-1: none
Other: redemption fee applies for 12 months

Services

IRA
Keogh
✔ Telephone Exchange

Vanguard US Growth

800-635-1511, 610-669-1000
www.vanguard.com

(VWUSX)

Growth

PERFORMANCE — fund inception date: 1/6/59

	3yr Annual	5yr Annual	10yr Annual	Bull	Bear
Return (%)	10.9	16.7	16.5	61.8	-21.9
Differ from Category (+/-)	-0.1 av	0.6 av	-0.3 av	12.1 abv av	-16.5 low

Standard Deviation	Category Risk Index	Beta
23.0%—abv av	1.18—abv av	1.18

	2000	1999	1998	1997	1996	1995	1994	1993	1992	1991
Return (%)	-20.1	22.2	39.9	25.9	26.0	38.4	3.8	-1.4	2.7	46.7
Differ from Category (+/-)	-23.6	3.3	25.6	-1.2	3.7	8.0	4.0	-16.0	-9.9	9.1
Return, Tax-Adjusted (%)	-23.5	20.9	38.0	24.6	23.2	36.6	3.3	-1.9	2.1	46.1

PER SHARE DATA

	2000	1999	1998	1997	1996	1995	1994	1993	1992	1991
Dividends, Net Income ($)	0.05	0.21	0.19	0.27	0.26	0.29	0.18	0.21	0.18	0.19
Distrib'ns, Cap Gain ($)	7.45	2.02	2.31	0.89	1.62	0.57	0.00	0.00	0.08	0.00
Net Asset Value ($)	27.65	43.53	37.49	28.70	23.74	20.35	15.33	14.93	15.36	15.20
Expense Ratio (%)	0.39	0.39	0.41	0.42	0.43	0.47	0.52	0.49	0.49	0.56
Yield (%)	0.14	0.46	0.47	0.91	1.02	1.38	1.17	1.40	1.16	1.25
Portfolio Turnover (%)	55	49	48	35	44	32	47	37	24	30
Total Assets (Millions $)	16,549	19,068	13,623	8,054	5,532	3,624	2,109	1,847	1,820	978

PORTFOLIO (as of 6/30/00)

Portfolio Manager: Parker, Hall, Fowler - 1987

Investm't Category: Growth

✔ Domestic	Index
Foreign	Sector
Asset Allocation	State Specific

Investment Style

✔ Large Cap	Mid Cap	Small Cap
✔ Growth	Grth/Val	Value

Portfolio

2.0%	cash	0.0%	corp bonds
98.0%	stocks	0.0%	gov't bonds
0.0%	pref/conv't pref	0.0%	muni bonds
0.0%	conv't bds/wrnts	0.0%	other

SHAREHOLDER INFORMATION

Minimum Investment

Initial: $3,000 Subsequent: $100

Minimum IRA Investment

Initial: $1,000 Subsequent: $100

Maximum Fees

Load: none 12b-1: none

Other: none

Services

✔ IRA
✔ Keogh
✔ Telephone Exchange

Vanguard Wellesley Income (VWINX)

800-635-1511, 610-669-1000
www.vanguard.com

Balanced

PERFORMANCE — fund inception date: 7/1/70

	3yr Annual	5yr Annual	10yr Annual	Bull	Bear
Return (%)	7.5	10.3	11.8	4.3	10.3
Differ from Category (+/-)	-0.9 blw av	-1.1 blw av	0.1 av	-23.8 low	13.5 high

Standard Deviation	Category Risk Index	Beta
6.9%—blw av	0.64—low	0.19

	2000	1999	1998	1997	1996	1995	1994	1993	1992	1991
Return (%)	16.1	-4.1	11.8	20.1	9.4	28.9	-4.4	14.6	8.7	21.4
Differ from Category (+/-)	14.1	-14.8	-1.5	1.3	-4.5	3.4	-3.1	0.2	0.3	-2.4
Return, Tax-Adjusted (%)	13.4	-7.2	8.7	16.3	6.3	25.7	-7.0	11.4	6.2	18.9

PER SHARE DATA

	2000	1999	1998	1997	1996	1995	1994	1993	1992	1991
Dividends, Net Income ($)	1.06	1.12	1.13	1.20	1.16	1.14	1.11	1.14	1.21	1.27
Distrib'ns, Cap Gain ($)	0.40	1.24	1.14	1.44	0.60	0.28	0.24	0.40	0.21	0.00
Net Asset Value ($)	20.34	18.85	22.12	21.86	20.51	20.44	17.05	19.24	18.16	18.07
Expense Ratio (%)	na	0.30	0.31	0.31	0.31	0.35	0.34	0.33	0.35	0.40
Yield (%)	5.11	5.57	4.85	5.15	5.49	5.50	6.41	5.80	6.58	7.02
Portfolio Turnover (%)	na	20	32	36	26	30	31	21	21	28
Total Assets (Millions $)	6,350	6,976	8,497	7,645	7,012	7,180	5,680	6,011	3,177	1,934

PORTFOLIO (as of 6/30/00)

Portfolio Manager: Earl McEvoy, John Ryan - 1982

Investm't Category: Balanced

✔ Domestic | Index
Foreign | Sector
Asset Allocation | State Specific

Investment Style

Large Cap | Mid Cap | Small Cap
Growth | Grth/Val | Value

Portfolio

3.0%	cash	40.0%	corp bonds
36.0%	stocks	21.0%	gov't bonds
0.0%	pref/conv't pref	0.0%	muni bonds
0.0%	conv't bds/wrnts	0.0%	other

SHAREHOLDER INFORMATION

Minimum Investment
Initial: $3,000 Subsequent: $100

Minimum IRA Investment
Initial: $1,000 Subsequent: $100

Maximum Fees
Load: none 12b-1: none
Other: none

Services
✔ IRA
✔ Keogh
✔ Telephone Exchange

Vanguard Wellington (VWELX)

800-635-1511, 610-669-1000
www.vanguard.com

Balanced

PERFORMANCE — fund inception date: 7/1/29

	3yr Annual	5yr Annual	10yr Annual	Bull	Bear
Return (%)	8.9	13.0	13.9	18.1	7.5
Differ from Category (+/-)	0.5 av	1.6 abv av	2.2 high	-10.0 blw av	10.7 high

Standard Deviation	Category Risk Index	Beta
10.8%—blw av	0.99—av	0.46

	2000	1999	1998	1997	1996	1995	1994	1993	1992	1991
Return (%)	10.4	4.4	12.0	23.2	16.1	32.9	-0.4	13.5	7.9	23.6
Differ from Category (+/-)	8.4	-6.3	-1.3	4.4	2.2	7.4	0.9	-0.9	-0.5	-0.2
Return, Tax-Adjusted (%)	7.8	1.8	8.8	20.3	13.1	30.5	-2.1	11.0	6.1	21.3

PER SHARE DATA

	2000	1999	1998	1997	1996	1995	1994	1993	1992	1991
Dividends, Net Income ($)	1.07	1.14	1.13	1.12	1.06	0.97	0.88	0.92	0.94	0.96
Distrib'ns, Cap Gain ($)	1.48	1.50	2.44	1.57	1.11	0.28	0.03	0.38	0.16	0.23
Net Asset Value ($)	28.21	27.96	29.35	29.45	26.15	24.43	19.39	20.40	19.16	18.81
Expense Ratio (%)	na	0.30	0.31	0.29	0.31	0.37	0.35	0.34	0.33	0.35
Yield (%)	3.60	3.86	3.55	3.61	3.88	3.92	4.53	4.42	4.86	5.04
Portfolio Turnover (%)	na	22	29	27	30	30	32	34	24	35
Total Assets (Millions $)	22,524	25,528	25,760	21,811	16,189	12,656	8,809	8,075	5,570	3,818

PORTFOLIO (as of 6/30/00)

Portfolio Manager: P. Kaplan, E. Von Metzsch - 1994

Investm't Category: Balanced

✔ Domestic	Index
✔ Foreign	Sector
Asset Allocation	State Specific

Investment Style

Large Cap	Mid Cap	Small Cap
Growth	Grth/Val	Value

Portfolio

4.0%	cash	24.0%	corp bonds
65.0%	stocks	7.0%	gov't bonds
0.0%	pref/conv't pref	0.0%	muni bonds
0.0%	conv't bds/wrnts	0.0%	other

SHAREHOLDER INFORMATION

Minimum Investment
Initial: $3,000 Subsequent: $100

Minimum IRA Investment
Initial: $1,000 Subsequent: $100

Maximum Fees
Load: none 12b-1: none
Other: none

Services
✔ IRA
✔ Keogh
✔ Telephone Exchange

Vanguard Windsor (VWNDX)

800-635-1511, 610-669-1000
www.vanguard.com

Growth & Income

PERFORMANCE — fund inception date: 10/23/58

	3yr Annual	5yr Annual	10yr Annual	Bull	Bear
Return (%)	9.2	14.9	16.6	34.7	6.3
Differ from Category (+/-)	0.3 av	0.6 av	1.7 abv av	1.2 av	6.4 abv av

Standard Deviation	Category Risk Index	Beta
21.6%—abv av	1.25—high	0.95

	2000	1999	1998	1997	1996	1995	1994	1993	1992	1991
Return (%)	15.8	11.5	0.8	21.9	26.3	30.1	-0.1	19.3	16.4	28.5
Differ from Category (+/-)	10.1	0.7	-12.0	-5.0	6.6	0.6	0.4	5.5	4.8	0.4
Return, Tax-Adjusted (%)	12.6	8.3	-1.2	17.6	22.6	25.5	-3.0	16.1	14.1	24.5

PER SHARE DATA

	2000	1999	1998	1997	1996	1995	1994	1993	1992	1991
Dividends, Net Income ($)	0.27	0.27	0.25	0.32	0.41	0.46	0.44	0.37	0.49	0.57
Distrib'ns, Cap Gain ($)	1.85	1.90	1.23	2.88	1.33	1.38	0.86	0.89	0.38	0.84
Net Asset Value ($)	15.29	15.17	15.57	16.98	16.59	14.53	12.59	13.91	12.74	11.72
Expense Ratio (%)	na	0.28	0.27	0.27	0.31	0.43	0.45	0.40	0.26	0.30
Yield (%)	1.57	1.58	1.48	1.61	2.28	2.89	3.27	2.50	3.73	4.53
Portfolio Turnover (%)	na	56	48	61	34	21	34	25	32	36
Total Assets (Millions $)	15,404	16,699	18,187	20,914	16,738	13,646	10,672	10,610	8,832	7,822

PORTFOLIO (as of 6/30/00)

Portfolio Manager: Freeman, Fedak, Pisarkiewicz - 1996

Investm't Category: Growth & Income

✔ Domestic	Index
Foreign	Sector
Asset Allocation	State Specific

Investment Style

✔ Large Cap	✔ Mid Cap	Small Cap
Growth	Grth/Val	✔ Value

Portfolio

3.0%	cash	0.0%	corp bonds
97.0%	stocks	0.0%	gov't bonds
0.0%	pref/conv't pref	0.0%	muni bonds
0.0%	conv't bds/wrnts	0.0%	other

SHAREHOLDER INFORMATION

Minimum Investment
Initial: $3,000 Subsequent: $100

Minimum IRA Investment
Initial: $1,000 Subsequent: $100

Maximum Fees
Load: none 12b-1: none
Other: none

Services
✔ IRA
✔ Keogh
✔ Telephone Exchange

Vanguard Windsor II

800-635-1511, 610-669-1000
www.vanguard.com

(VWNFX)

Growth & Income

PERFORMANCE — fund inception date: 6/24/85

	3yr Annual	5yr Annual	10yr Annual	Bull	Bear
Return (%)	8.6	16.0	16.8	14.6	8.9
Differ from Category (+/-)	-0.3 av	1.7 abv av	1.9 abv av	-18.9 blw av	9.0 abv av

Standard Deviation	Category Risk Index	Beta
18.1%—av	1.04—abv av	0.75

	2000	1999	1998	1997	1996	1995	1994	1993	1992	1991
Return (%)	16.8	-5.8	16.3	32.3	24.1	38.8	-1.1	13.6	11.9	28.6
Differ from Category (+/-)	11.1	-16.6	3.5	5.4	4.4	9.3	-0.6	-0.2	0.3	0.5
Return, Tax-Adjusted (%)	14.8	-8.3	13.5	29.3	21.3	36.1	-3.1	11.4	10.4	26.0

PER SHARE DATA

	2000	1999	1998	1997	1996	1995	1994	1993	1992	1991
Dividends, Net Income ($)	0.61	0.68	0.64	0.66	0.63	0.58	0.55	0.51	0.52	0.61
Distrib'ns, Cap Gain ($)	1.24	2.50	2.67	2.19	1.16	0.69	0.47	0.50	0.22	0.44
Net Asset Value ($)	27.20	24.97	29.85	28.62	23.83	20.66	15.82	17.04	15.91	14.89
Expense Ratio (%)	na	0.37	0.41	0.37	0.39	0.42	0.39	0.39	0.41	0.48
Yield (%)	2.14	2.47	1.96	2.14	2.52	2.71	3.37	2.90	3.22	3.97
Portfolio Turnover (%)	na	26	31	30	32	25	24	26	23	41
Total Assets (Millions $)	23,494	26,901	31,538	24,376	15,700	11,012	7,958	7,616	5,416	3,626

PORTFOLIO (as of 6/30/00)

Portfolio Manager: committee - 1985

Investm't Category: Growth & Income

✔ Domestic | Index
Foreign | Sector
Asset Allocation | State Specific

Investment Style

✔ Large Cap | ✔ Mid Cap | Small Cap
Growth | Grth/Val | ✔ Value

Portfolio

7.0%	cash	0.0%	corp bonds
93.0%	stocks	0.0%	gov't bonds
0.0%	pref/conv't pref	0.0%	muni bonds
0.0%	conv't bds/wrnts	0.0%	other

SHAREHOLDER INFORMATION

Minimum Investment

Initial: $3,000 | Subsequent: $100

Minimum IRA Investment

Initial: $1,000 | Subsequent: $100

Maximum Fees

Load: none | 12b-1: none
Other: none

Services

✔ IRA
✔ Keogh
✔ Telephone Exchange

Vanguard World: Intl Grth (VWIGX)

800-635-1511, 610-669-1000
www.vanguard.com

International Stock

PERFORMANCE — fund inception date: 9/30/85

	3yr Annual	5yr Annual	10yr Annual	Bull	Bear
Return (%)	10.5	10.0	10.2	46.2	-17.4
Differ from Category (+/-)	1.6 av	1.7 av	1.2 av	-44.7 low	6.6 abv av

Standard Deviation	Category Risk Index	Beta
16.3%—av	0.72—low	0.66

	2000	1999	1998	1997	1996	1995	1994	1993	1992	1991
Return (%)	-8.6	26.3	16.9	4.1	14.6	14.8	0.7	44.7	-5.7	4.7
Differ from Category (+/-)	10.8	-34.4	11.1	2.8	0.1	5.5	3.8	4.5	-2.2	-8.3
Return, Tax-Adjusted (%)	-10.2	24.7	16.1	2.9	13.0	13.7	0.1	44.2	-6.3	3.7

PER SHARE DATA

	2000	1999	1998	1997	1996	1995	1994	1993	1992	1991
Dividends, Net Income ($)	0.22	0.26	0.22	0.21	0.19	0.20	0.18	0.11	0.21	0.19
Distrib'ns, Cap Gain ($)	1.42	0.90	0.16	0.52	0.55	0.21	0.00	0.00	0.00	0.12
Net Asset Value ($)	18.87	22.49	18.77	16.39	16.46	15.02	13.43	13.51	9.41	10.21
Expense Ratio (%)	0.53	0.58	0.59	0.57	0.56	0.59	0.46	0.59	0.58	0.67
Yield (%)	1.08	1.11	1.16	1.24	1.11	1.31	1.34	0.81	2.23	1.83
Portfolio Turnover (%)	48	37	37	22	22	31	28	51	58	49
Total Assets (Millions $)	8,625	9,680	7,723	6,808	5,568	3,676	2,927	2,127	878	869

PORTFOLIO (as of 6/30/00)

Portfolio Manager: Richard Foulkes - 1981

Investm't Category: International Stock

Domestic	Index
✔ Foreign	Sector
Asset Allocation	State Specific

Investment Style

Large Cap	Mid Cap	Small Cap
Growth	Grth/Val	Value

Portfolio

8.0%	cash	0.0%	corp bonds
92.0%	stocks	0.0%	gov't bonds
0.0%	pref/conv't pref	0.0%	muni bonds
0.0%	conv't bds/wrnts	0.0%	other

SHAREHOLDER INFORMATION

Minimum Investment
Initial: $3,000 Subsequent: $100

Minimum IRA Investment
Initial: $1,000 Subsequent: $100

Maximum Fees
Load: none 12b-1: none
Other: none

Services
✔ IRA
✔ Keogh
✔ Telephone Exchange

Victory: Established Val/G (GETGX)

800-539-3863, 513-579-5000
www.victoryfunds.com

Growth

PERFORMANCE

fund inception date: 8/16/83

	3yr Annual	5yr Annual	10yr Annual	Bull	Bear
Return (%)	10.3	14.5	15.0	38.3	8.8
Differ from Category (+/-)	-0.7 av	-1.6 blw av	-1.8 blw av	-11.4 av	14.2 high

Standard Deviation	Category Risk Index	Beta
17.7%—av	0.91—blw av	0.76

	2000	1999	1998	1997	1996	1995	1994	1993	1992	1991
Return (%)	8.2	17.0	6.1	22.6	19.3	26.4	0.3	20.7	10.2	22.2
Differ from Category (+/-)	4.7	-1.9	-8.2	-4.5	-3.0	-4.0	0.5	6.1	-2.4	-15.4
Return, Tax-Adjusted (%)	6.4	14.2	4.4	20.0	16.1	24.3	-1.1	18.6	9.2	20.8

PER SHARE DATA

	2000	1999	1998	1997	1996	1995	1994	1993	1992	1991
Dividends, Net Income ($)	0.11	0.06	0.34	0.49	0.43	0.48	0.34	0.55	0.30	0.45
Distrib'ns, Cap Gain ($)	2.55	4.10	1.88	2.57	2.35	0.95	0.66	0.67	0.27	0.27
Net Asset Value ($)	31.87	32.00	31.02	31.37	28.19	26.00	21.77	22.71	19.87	18.60
Expense Ratio (%)	na	1.10	1.10	1.12	1.15	1.20	1.22	1.28	1.31	1.39
Yield (%)	0.31	0.16	1.03	1.44	1.40	1.78	1.51	2.35	1.48	2.38
Portfolio Turnover (%)	na	11	20	31	18	24	38	28	68	74
Total Assets (Millions $)	389	476	518	522	416	337	260	244	184	170

PORTFOLIO (as of 6/30/00)

Portfolio Manager: W. Leugers, D. Shick, G. Miller - 1983

Investm't Category: Growth

✔ Domestic	Index
Foreign	Sector
Asset Allocation	State Specific

Investment Style

✔ Large Cap	✔ Mid Cap	Small Cap
Growth	Grth/Val	✔ Value

Portfolio

0.8%	cash	0.0%	corp bonds
99.2%	stocks	0.0%	gov't bonds
0.0%	pref/conv't pref	0.0%	muni bonds
0.0%	conv't bds/wrnts	0.0%	other

SHAREHOLDER INFORMATION

Minimum Investment
Initial: $500 Subsequent: $25

Minimum IRA Investment
Initial: $100 Subsequent: $25

Maximum Fees
Load: none 12b-1: 0.50%
Other: none

Services
✔ IRA
✔ Keogh
✔ Telephone Exchange

Victory: Small Co Opp/G (GOGFX)

800-869-5999, 513-579-5000
www.victoryfunds.com

Growth

PERFORMANCE — fund inception date: 8/16/83

	3yr Annual	5yr Annual	10yr Annual	Bull	Bear
Return (%)	4.1	12.1	14.2	12.9	8.8
Differ from Category (+/-)	-6.9 low	-4.0 blw av	-2.6 blw av	-36.8 low	14.2 high

Standard Deviation	Category Risk Index	Beta
18.6%—av	0.96—blw av	0.78

	2000	1999	1998	1997	1996	1995	1994	1993	1992	1991
Return (%)	22.6	-1.0	-6.9	31.1	19.4	26.7	-2.1	11.0	14.3	35.9
Differ from Category (+/-)	19.1	-19.9	-21.2	4.0	-2.9	-3.7	-1.9	-3.6	1.7	-1.7
Return, Tax-Adjusted (%)	21.4	-1.0	-7.9	27.1	16.4	25.3	-3.1	9.5	12.9	33.6

PER SHARE DATA

	2000	1999	1998	1997	1996	1995	1994	1993	1992	1991
Dividends, Net Income ($)	0.00	0.00	0.14	0.78	0.16	0.18	0.25	0.07	0.10	0.42
Distrib'ns, Cap Gain ($)	1.37	0.00	1.08	3.05	2.04	0.57	0.31	0.80	0.64	0.52
Net Asset Value ($)	26.61	22.90	23.15	26.10	23.07	21.23	17.43	18.38	17.37	15.90
Expense Ratio (%)	na	1.29	1.31	1.36	1.41	1.37	1.38	1.44	1.49	1.61
Yield (%)	0.00	0.00	0.57	2.67	0.63	0.82	1.40	0.36	0.55	2.55
Portfolio Turnover (%)	na	16	42	34	23	31	40	39	64	64
Total Assets (Millions $)	90	108	151	157	115	97	82	83	60	39

PORTFOLIO (as of 6/30/00)

Portfolio Manager: W. Leugers, D. Shick, G. Miller - 1983

Investm't Category: Growth

✔ Domestic
Foreign
Asset Allocation
Index
Sector
State Specific

Investment Style

Large Cap
✔ Mid Cap
✔ Small Cap
Growth
Grth/Val
✔ Value

Portfolio

2.0% cash
98.1% stocks
0.0% pref/conv't pref
0.0% conv't bds/wrnts
0.0% corp bonds
0.0% gov't bonds
0.0% muni bonds
0.0% other

SHAREHOLDER INFORMATION

Minimum Investment
Initial: $500 — Subsequent: $25

Minimum IRA Investment
Initial: $100 — Subsequent: $25

Maximum Fees
Load: none — 12b-1: 0.50%
Other: none

Services
✔ IRA
✔ Keogh
✔ Telephone Exchange

Vintage Aggressive Growth (AVAGX)

800-438-6375, 515-244-5426
www.amcore.com

Aggressive Growth

PERFORMANCE

fund inception date: 9/29/95

	3yr Annual	5yr Annual	10yr Annual	Bull	Bear
Return (%)	11.5	15.8	na	59.3	-21.7
Differ from Category (+/-)	-4.7 blw av	1.2 av	na	-59.9 blw av	-1.1 av

Standard Deviation	Category Risk Index	Beta
24.6%—abv av	0.76—blw av	1.09

	2000	1999	1998	1997	1996	1995	1994	1993	1992	1991
Return (%)	-7.5	19.7	25.4	26.1	19.3	—	—	—	—	—
Differ from Category (+/-)	-1.5	-37.8	10.3	11.3	1.0	—	—	—	—	—
Return, Tax-Adjusted (%)	-11.2	16.7	23.9	25.7	19.3	—	—	—	—	—

PER SHARE DATA

	2000	1999	1998	1997	1996	1995	1994	1993	1992	1991
Dividends, Net Income ($)	0.00	0.00	0.00	0.00	0.00	—	—	—	—	—
Distrib'ns, Cap Gain ($)	3.43	2.58	1.14	0.24	0.00	—	—	—	—	—
Net Asset Value ($)	13.74	18.54	17.79	15.20	12.24	—	—	—	—	—
Expense Ratio (%)	0.14	1.42	1.56	1.63	1.57	—	—	—	—	—
Yield (%)	0.00	0.00	0.00	0.00	0.00	—	—	—	—	—
Portfolio Turnover (%)	156	61	86	45	—	—	—	—	—	—
Total Assets (Millions $)	125	146	117	85	41	—	—	—	—	—

PORTFOLIO (as of 6/30/00)

Portfolio Manager: committee - 1997

Investm't Category: Aggressive Growth

✔ Domestic
✔ Foreign
Asset Allocation
Index
Sector
State Specific

Investment Style

Large Cap
✔ Mid Cap
Small Cap
✔ Growth
Grth/Val
Value

Portfolio

2.0%	cash	0.0%	corp bonds
98.0%	stocks	0.0%	gov't bonds
0.0%	pref/conv't pref	0.0%	muni bonds
0.0%	conv't bds/wrnts	0.0%	other

SHAREHOLDER INFORMATION

Minimum Investment

Initial: $1,000 Subsequent: $50

Minimum IRA Investment

Initial: $25 Subsequent: $25

Maximum Fees

Load: none 12b-1: none
Other: none

Services

✔ IRA
✔ Keogh
✔ Telephone Exchange

Vintage Balanced (AMBFX)

800-438-6375, 515-244-5426
www.amcore.com

Balanced

PERFORMANCE — fund inception date: 6/15/95

	3yr Annual	5yr Annual	10yr Annual	Bull	Bear
Return (%)	9.2	11.8	na	34.0	-9.5
Differ from Category (+/-)	0.8 av	0.4 av	na	5.9 abv av	-6.3 low

Standard Deviation	Category Risk Index	Beta
12.2%—blw av	1.11—abv av	0.65

	2000	1999	1998	1997	1996	1995	1994	1993	1992	1991
Return (%)	-3.1	11.6	20.7	22.8	9.2	—	—	—	—	—
Differ from Category (+/-)	-5.1	0.9	7.4	4.0	-4.7	—	—	—	—	—
Return, Tax-Adjusted (%)	-5.2	9.0	18.8	21.9	8.6	—	—	—	—	—

PER SHARE DATA

	2000	1999	1998	1997	1996	1995	1994	1993	1992	1991
Dividends, Net Income ($)	0.32	0.26	0.25	0.18	0.16	—	—	—	—	—
Distrib'ns, Cap Gain ($)	1.05	1.50	0.81	0.17	0.00	—	—	—	—	—
Net Asset Value ($)	14.04	15.89	15.86	14.09	11.77	—	—	—	—	—
Expense Ratio (%)	1.20	1.28	1.38	1.55	1.32	—	—	—	—	—
Yield (%)	2.12	1.49	1.49	1.26	1.35	—	—	—	—	—
Portfolio Turnover (%)	64	48	101	38	—	—	—	—	—	—
Total Assets (Millions $)	80	95	75	47	17	—	—	—	—	—

PORTFOLIO (as of 6/30/00)

Portfolio Manager: committee - 1998

Investm't Category: Balanced

✔ Domestic	Index
✔ Foreign	Sector
Asset Allocation	State Specific

Investment Style

Large Cap	Mid Cap	Small Cap
Growth	Grth/Val	Value

Portfolio

2.0%	cash	16.0%	corp bonds
60.0%	stocks	21.0%	gov't bonds
0.0%	pref/conv't pref	1.0%	muni bonds
0.0%	conv't bds/wrnts	0.0%	other

SHAREHOLDER INFORMATION

Minimum Investment
Initial: $1,000 — Subsequent: $50

Minimum IRA Investment
Initial: $25 — Subsequent: $25

Maximum Fees
Load: none — 12b-1: none
Other: none

Services
✔ IRA
✔ Keogh
✔ Telephone Exchange

Vintage Equity/S (VEQSX)

800-438-6375, 515-244-5426
www.amcore.com

Growth

PERFORMANCE

fund inception date: 12/15/92

	3yr Annual	5yr Annual	10yr Annual	Bull	Bear
Return (%)	12.9	17.8	na	58.8	-12.6
Differ from Category (+/-)	1.9 abv av	1.7 av	na	9.1 abv av	-7.2 blw av

Standard Deviation	Category Risk Index	Beta
19.2%—abv av	0.99—av	1.03

	2000	1999	1998	1997	1996	1995	1994	1993	1992	1991
Return (%)	-7.0	21.7	27.4	30.1	21.3	35.7	2.0	5.4	—	—
Differ from Category (+/-)	-10.5	2.8	13.1	3.0	-1.0	5.3	2.2	-9.2	—	—
Return, Tax-Adjusted (%)	-8.5	18.3	25.4	27.4	20.1	34.5	1.3	4.6	—	—

PER SHARE DATA

	2000	1999	1998	1997	1996	1995	1994	1993	1992	1991
Dividends, Net Income ($)	0.00	0.00	0.01	0.01	0.06	0.14	0.15	0.20	—	—
Distrib'ns, Cap Gain ($)	1.80	3.65	1.83	2.14	0.50	0.23	0.02	0.00	—	—
Net Asset Value ($)	19.53	22.91	21.96	18.84	16.15	13.78	10.44	10.41	—	—
Expense Ratio (%)	1.36	1.40	1.31	1.33	1.09	1.07	0.54	0.23	—	—
Yield (%)	0.00	0.00	0.04	0.04	0.36	0.99	1.43	1.92	—	—
Portfolio Turnover (%)	89	59	72	37	33	21	4	0	—	—
Total Assets (Millions $)	265	318	229	384	252	194	130	118	—	—

PORTFOLIO (as of 6/30/00)

Portfolio Manager: committee - 1992

Investm't Category: Growth

✔ Domestic	Index
Foreign	Sector
Asset Allocation	State Specific

Investment Style

✔ Large Cap	Mid Cap	Small Cap
Growth	✔ Grth/Val	Value

Portfolio

1.0%	cash	0.0%	corp bonds
99.0%	stocks	0.0%	gov't bonds
0.0%	pref/conv't pref	0.0%	muni bonds
0.0%	conv't bds/wrnts	0.0%	other

SHAREHOLDER INFORMATION

Minimum Investment

Initial: $1,000 Subsequent: $50

Minimum IRA Investment

Initial: $25 Subsequent: $25

Maximum Fees

Load: none 12b-1: none

Other: none

Services

✔ IRA

✔ Keogh

✔ Telephone Exchange

Vontobel Intl Equity (VNEPX)

800-527-9500, 804-285-8211
www.vontobelfunds.com

International Stock

PERFORMANCE — fund inception date: 1/1/85

	3yr Annual	5yr Annual	10yr Annual	Bull	Bear
Return (%)	4.8	8.0	9.6	65.9	-33.2
Differ from Category (+/-)	-4.1 blw av	-0.3 av	0.6 av	-25.0 av	-9.2 blw av

Standard Deviation	Category Risk Index	Beta
22.4%—abv av	0.99—av	0.88

	2000	1999	1998	1997	1996	1995	1994	1993	1992	1991
Return (%)	-32.6	46.5	16.7	9.1	16.9	10.8	-5.3	40.8	-2.3	18.7
Differ from Category (+/-)	-13.2	-14.2	10.9	7.8	2.4	1.5	-2.2	0.6	1.2	5.7
Return, Tax-Adjusted (%)	-32.6	45.1	15.6	7.1	13.5	9.1	-5.4	40.8	-2.6	18.7

PER SHARE DATA

	2000	1999	1998	1997	1996	1995	1994	1993	1992	1991
Dividends, Net Income ($)	0.00	0.05	0.00	0.00	0.60	0.17	0.08	0.00	0.14	0.00
Distrib'ns, Cap Gain ($)	0.00	1.24	0.96	1.78	1.19	0.70	0.00	0.00	0.00	0.00
Net Asset Value ($)	18.86	28.01	20.18	18.15	18.22	17.13	16.23	17.22	12.23	12.67
Expense Ratio (%)	na	1.28	1.36	1.50	1.39	0.74	1.54	1.77	1.98	2.71
Yield (%)	0.00	0.17	0.00	0.00	3.09	0.95	0.49	0.00	1.14	0.00
Portfolio Turnover (%)	na	38	42	38	54	41	34	10	27	3
Total Assets (Millions $)	108	192	162	160	151	129	138	136	47	25

PORTFOLIO (as of 6/30/00)

Portfolio Manager: Fabrizio Pierallini - 1994

Investm't Category: International Stock

Domestic	Index
✔ Foreign	Sector
Asset Allocation	State Specific

Investment Style

Large Cap	Mid Cap	Small Cap
Growth	Grth/Val	Value

Portfolio

0.5% cash	0.0% corp bonds
99.5% stocks	0.0% gov't bonds
0.0% pref/conv't pref	0.0% muni bonds
0.0% conv't bds/wrnts	0.0% other

SHAREHOLDER INFORMATION

Minimum Investment
Initial: $200,000 Subsequent: $50

Minimum IRA Investment
Initial: $200,000 Subsequent: $50

Maximum Fees
Load: 2.00% redemption 12b-1: none
Other: redemption fee applies for 3 months

Services
✔ IRA
✔ Keogh
✔ Telephone Exchange

Vontobel US Value (VUSVX)

800-527-9500, 804-285-8211
www.vontobelfunds.com

Growth

PERFORMANCE

fund inception date: 3/30/90

	3yr Annual	5yr Annual	10yr Annual	Bull	Bear
Return (%)	10.0	16.7	17.7	2.7	27.6
Differ from Category (+/-)	-1.0 blw av	0.6 av	0.9 abv av	-47.0 low	33.0 high

Standard Deviation	Category Risk Index	Beta
20.1%—abv av	1.04—av	0.56

	2000	1999	1998	1997	1996	1995	1994	1993	1992	1991
Return (%)	35.1	-14.0	14.7	34.3	21.2	40.3	0.0	6.0	15.9	37.2
Differ from Category (+/-)	31.6	-32.9	0.4	7.2	-1.1	9.9	0.2	-8.6	3.3	-0.4
Return, Tax-Adjusted (%)	35.1	-14.2	12.0	31.2	16.1	37.1	-5.5	5.7	12.9	34.6

PER SHARE DATA

	2000	1999	1998	1997	1996	1995	1994	1993	1992	1991
Dividends, Net Income ($)	0.00	0.11	0.16	0.10	0.21	0.04	0.25	0.08	0.17	0.06
Distrib'ns, Cap Gain ($)	0.00	0.00	1.90	1.88	2.08	1.11	2.14	0.00	0.99	0.74
Net Asset Value ($)	19.29	14.27	16.73	16.51	13.78	13.25	10.26	12.64	12.00	11.36
Expense Ratio (%)	na	1.87	1.45	1.58	1.43	1.46	1.62	1.82	1.96	2.54
Yield (%)	0.00	0.77	0.85	0.54	1.32	0.27	2.01	0.63	1.30	0.49
Portfolio Turnover (%)	na	67	123	89	108	95	98	137	100	166
Total Assets (Millions $)	96	71	200	201	69	54	30	34	31	21

PORTFOLIO (as of 6/30/00)

Portfolio Manager: Edwin Walczak - 1990

Investm't Category: Growth

✔ Domestic — Index
Foreign — Sector
Asset Allocation — State Specific

Investment Style

✔ Large Cap — ✔ Mid Cap — Small Cap
Growth — Grth/Val — ✔ Value

Portfolio

5.5%	cash	0.0%	corp bonds
94.5%	stocks	0.0%	gov't bonds
0.0%	pref/conv't pref	0.0%	muni bonds
0.0%	conv't bds/wrnts	0.0%	other

SHAREHOLDER INFORMATION

Minimum Investment

Initial: $1,000 — Subsequent: $50

Minimum IRA Investment

Initial: $1,000 — Subsequent: $50

Maximum Fees

Load: none — 12b-1: none
Other: none

Services

✔ IRA
✔ Keogh
✔ Telephone Exchange

WPG Large Cap Growth (WPGFX)

800-223-3332, 212-908-9500
www.wpginvest.com

Growth

PERFORMANCE — fund inception date: 7/31/79

	3yr Annual	5yr Annual	10yr Annual	Bull	Bear
Return (%)	12.0	19.0	18.0	45.2	-11.4
Differ from Category (+/-)	1.0 av	2.9 abv av	1.2 abv av	-4.5 av	-6.0 blw av

Standard Deviation	Category Risk Index	Beta
19.1%—abv av	0.98—av	1.02

	2000	1999	1998	1997	1996	1995	1994	1993	1992	1991
Return (%)	-1.6	12.6	27.0	36.2	24.4	32.7	-5.4	9.5	13.8	40.7
Differ from Category (+/-)	-5.1	-6.3	12.7	9.1	2.1	2.3	-5.2	-5.1	1.2	3.1
Return, Tax-Adjusted (%)	-4.2	9.6	24.6	32.7	19.2	31.9	-6.5	5.7	8.1	40.3

PER SHARE DATA

	2000	1999	1998	1997	1996	1995	1994	1993	1992	1991
Dividends, Net Income ($)	0.00	0.16	0.13	0.26	0.55	0.36	0.62	0.89	0.51	0.22
Distrib'ns, Cap Gain ($)	5.35	5.65	3.85	4.51	4.37	0.03	0.09	1.93	4.68	0.00
Net Asset Value ($)	33.60	39.88	40.64	35.11	29.32	27.90	21.36	23.34	23.89	25.82
Expense Ratio (%)	na	1.03	1.04	1.06	1.15	1.24	1.23	1.26	1.34	1.48
Yield (%)	0.00	0.35	0.29	0.65	1.63	1.28	2.89	3.52	1.78	0.85
Portfolio Turnover (%)	na	68	65	69	75	73	71	86	76	89
Total Assets (Millions $)	107	139	160	117	82	67	61	62	49	42

PORTFOLIO (as of 6/30/00)

Portfolio Manager: A. Roy Knutsen - 1991

Investm't Category: Growth

✔ Domestic — Index
✔ Foreign — Sector
Asset Allocation — State Specific

Investment Style

✔ Large Cap — Mid Cap — Small Cap
✔ Growth — Grth/Val — Value

Portfolio

2.9%	cash	0.0%	corp bonds
97.1%	stocks	0.0%	gov't bonds
0.0%	pref/conv't pref	0.0%	muni bonds
0.0%	conv't bds/wrnts	0.0%	other

SHAREHOLDER INFORMATION

Minimum Investment

Initial: $2,500 — Subsequent: $100

Minimum IRA Investment

Initial: $250 — Subsequent: $100

Maximum Fees

Load: none — 12b-1: none
Other: none

Services

✔ IRA
✔ Keogh
✔ Telephone Exchange

WPG Tudor (TUDRX)

800-223-3332, 212-908-9500
www.wpginvest.com

Aggressive Growth

PERFORMANCE — fund inception date: 3/14/69

	3yr Annual	5yr Annual	10yr Annual	Bull	Bear
Return (%)	6.4	9.7	13.4	86.3	-21.4
Differ from Category (+/-)	-9.8 blw av	-4.9 blw av	-2.4 blw av	-32.9 av	-0.8 av

Standard Deviation	Category Risk Index	Beta
33.6%—high	1.04—av	1.06

	2000	1999	1998	1997	1996	1995	1994	1993	1992	1991
Return (%)	-5.1	63.2	-22.0	11.1	18.8	41.1	-9.8	13.3	5.1	45.8
Differ from Category (+/-)	0.9	5.7	-37.1	-3.7	0.5	6.5	-9.0	-11.9	-1.8	-1.4
Return, Tax-Adjusted (%)	-7.7	59.7	-23.1	7.7	11.0	39.6	-11.9	7.9	2.8	45.2

PER SHARE DATA

	2000	1999	1998	1997	1996	1995	1994	1993	1992	1991
Dividends, Net Income ($)	0.00	0.00	0.00	0.00	0.14	0.00	0.00	0.00	0.14	0.29
Distrib'ns, Cap Gain ($)	3.00	2.71	1.27	3.90	7.10	1.01	1.78	4.73	1.91	0.00
Net Asset Value ($)	18.41	22.91	15.74	21.90	23.28	26.24	19.34	23.40	24.85	25.68
Expense Ratio (%)	na	1.37	1.28	1.24	1.25	1.34	1.28	1.25	1.21	1.17
Yield (%)	0.00	0.00	0.00	0.00	0.46	0.00	0.00	0.00	0.52	1.12
Portfolio Turnover (%)	na	139	144	106	105	139	109	118	89	90
Total Assets (Millions $)	90	103	86	170	182	167	143	242	273	264

PORTFOLIO (as of 6/30/00)

Portfolio Manager: Lawrence Zuriff - 2000

Investm't Category: Aggressive Growth

✔ Domestic — Index
✔ Foreign — Sector
Asset Allocation — State Specific

Investment Style

Large Cap — Mid Cap — ✔ Small Cap
✔ Growth — Grth/Val — Value

Portfolio

8.9%	cash	0.0%	corp bonds
91.1%	stocks	0.0%	gov't bonds
0.0%	pref/conv't pref	0.0%	muni bonds
0.0%	conv't bds/wrnts	0.0%	other

SHAREHOLDER INFORMATION

Minimum Investment
Initial: $2,500 — Subsequent: $100

Minimum IRA Investment
Initial: $250 — Subsequent: $100

Maximum Fees
Load: none — 12b-1: none
Other: none

Services
✔ IRA
✔ Keogh
✔ Telephone Exchange

Warburg Cap App/Cmn (CUCAX)

800-927-2874, 212-878-0600
www.warburg.com

Growth

PERFORMANCE

fund inception date: 8/17/87

	3yr Annual	5yr Annual	10yr Annual	Bull	Bear
Return (%)	20.8	23.4	19.7	92.6	-18.5
Differ from Category (+/-)	9.8 high	7.3 high	2.9 high	42.9 high	-13.1 low

Standard Deviation	Category Risk Index	Beta
24.0%—abv av	1.23—high	1.06

	2000	1999	1998	1997	1996	1995	1994	1993	1992	1991
Return (%)	-5.2	48.3	25.6	31.3	23.2	38.1	-2.8	15.8	7.6	26.2
Differ from Category (+/-)	-8.7	29.4	11.3	4.2	0.9	7.7	-2.6	1.2	-5.0	-11.4
Return, Tax-Adjusted (%)	-8.1	45.6	24.6	26.6	19.6	33.4	-4.7	13.0	5.8	25.7

PER SHARE DATA

	2000	1999	1998	1997	1996	1995	1994	1993	1992	1991
Dividends, Net Income ($)	0.00	0.00	0.00	0.07	0.09	0.05	0.00	0.07	0.05	0.11
Distrib'ns, Cap Gain ($)	4.28	2.92	0.91	3.81	1.80	2.03	0.98	1.18	0.75	0.05
Net Asset Value ($)	23.65	29.34	21.96	18.27	16.94	15.32	12.66	14.06	13.24	13.06
Expense Ratio (%)	na	1.01	1.00	1.01	1.03	1.08	1.05	1.01	1.06	1.08
Yield (%)	0.00	0.00	0.00	0.31	0.48	0.28	0.00	0.45	0.35	0.83
Portfolio Turnover (%)	na	144	168	238	170	153	51	48	56	40
Total Assets (Millions $)	1,481	1,262	755	623	464	256	145	158	120	122

PORTFOLIO (as of 6/30/00)

Portfolio Manager: Susan Black - 1994

Investm't Category: Growth

✔ Domestic
✔ Foreign
Asset Allocation
Index
Sector
State Specific

Investment Style

✔ Large Cap
✔ Mid Cap
Small Cap
✔ Growth
Grth/Val
Value

Portfolio

8.2% cash	0.0% corp bonds
91.8% stocks	0.0% gov't bonds
0.0% pref/conv't pref	0.0% muni bonds
0.0% conv't bds/wrnts	0.0% other

SHAREHOLDER INFORMATION

Minimum Investment

Initial: $2,500 Subsequent: $100

Minimum IRA Investment

Initial: $500 Subsequent: $100

Maximum Fees

Load: none 12b-1: none

Other: none

Services

✔ IRA
Keogh
✔ Telephone Exchange

Warburg Emerg Grth/ Cmn (CUEGX)

800-927-2874, 212-878-0600
www.warburg.com

Aggressive Growth

PERFORMANCE

fund inception date: 1/22/88

	3yr Annual	5yr Annual	10yr Annual	Bull	Bear
Return (%)	9.7	11.9	18.0	82.4	-27.1
Differ from Category (+/-)	-6.5 blw av	-2.7 blw av	2.2 av	-36.8 av	-6.5 av

Standard Deviation	Category Risk Index	Beta
31.0%—high	0.96—av	1.16

	2000	1999	1998	1997	1996	1995	1994	1993	1992	1991
Return (%)	-12.0	41.8	5.8	21.2	9.8	46.2	-1.4	18.1	12.1	56.1
Differ from Category (+/-)	-6.0	-15.7	-9.3	6.4	-8.5	11.6	-0.6	-7.1	5.2	8.9
Return, Tax-Adjusted (%)	-15.4	38.6	5.8	19.7	9.7	43.9	-1.4	16.2	11.5	55.2

PER SHARE DATA

	2000	1999	1998	1997	1996	1995	1994	1993	1992	1991
Dividends, Net Income ($)	0.00	0.00	0.00	0.00	0.00	0.00	0.00	0.00	0.00	0.17
Distrib'ns, Cap Gain ($)	8.48	6.23	0.00	2.38	0.06	1.75	0.00	1.35	0.37	0.19
Net Asset Value ($)	35.90	49.86	39.97	37.77	33.22	30.30	21.99	22.31	20.07	18.23
Expense Ratio (%)	na	1.23	1.22	1.22	1.27	1.25	1.22	1.23	1.24	1.25
Yield (%)	0.00	0.00	0.00	0.00	0.00	0.00	0.00	0.00	0.00	0.92
Portfolio Turnover (%)	na	154	91	87	65	97	60	68	63	98
Total Assets (Millions $)	1,722	2,017	1,777	1,577	1,151	557	222	183	110	75

PORTFOLIO (as of 6/30/00)

Portfolio Manager: Elizabeth Dater, Stephen Lurito - 2000

Investm't Category: Aggressive Growth

✔ Domestic
✔ Foreign
Asset Allocation
Index
Sector
State Specific

Investment Style

Large Cap
Mid Cap
✔ Small Cap
✔ Growth
Grth/Val
Value

Portfolio

4.7% cash
94.4% stocks
0.4% pref/conv't pref
0.5% conv't bds/wrnts
0.0% corp bonds
0.0% gov't bonds
0.0% muni bonds
0.0% other

SHAREHOLDER INFORMATION

Minimum Investment

Initial: $100 Subsequent: $50

Minimum IRA Investment

Initial: $500 Subsequent: $50

Maximum Fees

Load: none 12b-1: none
Other: none

Services

✔ IRA
Keogh
✔ Telephone Exchange

Warburg Emerg Mkts/ Cmn (WPEMX)

800-927-2874, 212-878-0600
www.warburg.com

International Stock

PERFORMANCE — fund inception date: 1/3/95

	3yr Annual	5yr Annual	10yr Annual	Bull	Bear
Return (%)	-4.1	-5.0	na	113.4	-37.7
Differ from Category (+/-)	-13.0 low	-13.3 low	na	22.5 abv av	-13.7 low

Standard Deviation	Category Risk Index	Beta
32.5%—high	1.43—high	1.20

	2000	1999	1998	1997	1996	1995	1994	1993	1992	1991
Return (%)	-32.9	85.3	-29.2	-19.9	9.9	—	—	—	—	—
Differ from Category (+/-)	-13.5	24.6	-35.0	-21.2	-4.6	—	—	—	—	—
Return, Tax-Adjusted (%)	-32.9	85.3	-29.2	-20.6	9.7	—	—	—	—	—

PER SHARE DATA

	2000	1999	1998	1997	1996	1995	1994	1993	1992	1991
Dividends, Net Income ($)	0.02	0.00	0.00	0.00	0.02	—	—	—	—	—
Distrib'ns, Cap Gain ($)	0.00	0.00	0.00	0.47	0.05	—	—	—	—	—
Net Asset Value ($)	8.40	12.57	6.78	9.58	12.59	—	—	—	—	—
Expense Ratio (%)	na	1.66	1.65	1.66	1.61	—	—	—	—	—
Yield (%)	0.23	0.00	0.00	0.00	0.15	—	—	—	—	—
Portfolio Turnover (%)	na	196	125	92	61	—	—	—	—	—
Total Assets (Millions $)	51	108	61	116	212	—	—	—	—	—

PORTFOLIO (as of 6/30/00)

Portfolio Manager: R. Hrabchak, F. Laffan, J. Kim - 2000

Investm't Category: International Stock

Domestic	Index
✔ Foreign	Sector
Asset Allocation	State Specific

Investment Style

Large Cap	Mid Cap	Small Cap
Growth	Grth/Val	Value

Portfolio

6.4%	cash	0.0%	corp bonds
93.6%	stocks	0.0%	gov't bonds
0.1%	pref/conv't pref	0.0%	muni bonds
0.0%	conv't bds/wrnts	0.0%	other

SHAREHOLDER INFORMATION

Minimum Investment
Initial: $2,500 Subsequent: $100

Minimum IRA Investment
Initial: $500 Subsequent: $100

Maximum Fees
Load: none 12b-1: 0.25%
Other: none

Services
✔ IRA
Keogh
✔ Telephone Exchange

Warburg Glb Hlth Sci/ Cmn (WPHSX)

800-927-2874, 212-878-0600
www.warburg.com

Aggressive Growth

PERFORMANCE

fund inception date: 12/31/96

	3yr Annual	5yr Annual	10yr Annual	Bull	Bear
Return (%)	25.3	na	na	38.1	23.3
Differ from Category (+/-)	9.1 abv av	na	na	-81.1 low	43.9 high

Standard Deviation	Category Risk Index	Beta
26.2%—high	0.81—blw av	0.52

	2000	1999	1998	1997	1996	1995	1994	1993	1992	1991
Return (%)	38.9	6.3	33.1	27.3	—	—	—	—	—	—
Differ from Category (+/-)	44.9	-51.2	18.0	12.5	—	—	—	—	—	—
Return, Tax-Adjusted (%)	36.6	6.3	33.1	25.8	—	—	—	—	—	—

PER SHARE DATA

	2000	1999	1998	1997	1996	1995	1994	1993	1992	1991
Dividends, Net Income ($)	0.00	0.00	0.00	0.03	—	—	—	—	—	—
Distrib'ns, Cap Gain ($)	1.92	0.00	0.00	0.67	—	—	—	—	—	—
Net Asset Value ($)	21.71	16.99	15.97	11.99	—	—	—	—	—	—
Expense Ratio (%)	na	1.59	1.59	1.59	—	—	—	—	—	—
Yield (%)	0.00	0.00	0.00	0.23	—	—	—	—	—	—
Portfolio Turnover (%)	na	146	62	160	—	—	—	—	—	—
Total Assets (Millions $)	100	45	83	20	—	—	—	—	—	—

PORTFOLIO (as of 6/30/00)

Portfolio Manager: Susan Black, Peter Wen - 1996

Investm't Category: Aggressive Growth

✔ Domestic | Index
✔ Foreign | ✔ Sector
Asset Allocation | State Specific

Investment Style

Large Cap | Mid Cap | ✔ Small Cap
✔ Growth | Grth/Val | Value

Portfolio

1.4%	cash	0.0%	corp bonds
98.6%	stocks	0.0%	gov't bonds
0.0%	pref/conv't pref	0.0%	muni bonds
0.0%	conv't bds/wrnts	0.0%	other

SHAREHOLDER INFORMATION

Minimum Investment
Initial: $2,500 Subsequent: $100

Minimum IRA Investment
Initial: $500 Subsequent: $100

Maximum Fees
Load: none 12b-1: 0.25%
Other: none

Services
✔ IRA
Keogh
✔ Telephone Exchange

Warburg Intl Eqty/Cmn (CUIEX)

800-927-2874, 212-878-0600
www.warburg.com

International Stock

PERFORMANCE

fund inception date: 5/2/89

	3yr Annual	5yr Annual	10yr Annual	Bull	Bear
Return (%)	4.9	4.1	8.9	69.1	-30.0
Differ from Category (+/-)	-4.0 blw av	-4.2 blw av	-0.1 blw av	-21.8 av	-6.0 blw av

Standard Deviation	Category Risk Index	Beta
21.8%—abv av	0.96—av	0.76

	2000	1999	1998	1997	1996	1995	1994	1993	1992	1991
Return (%)	-29.5	56.9	4.5	-4.3	10.5	10.3	0.1	51.2	-4.3	20.6
Differ from Category (+/-)	-10.1	-3.8	-1.3	-5.6	-4.0	1.0	3.2	11.0	-0.8	7.6
Return, Tax-Adjusted (%)	-32.8	56.5	4.5	-7.3	9.0	8.9	-0.8	51.0	-4.6	19.7

PER SHARE DATA

	2000	1999	1998	1997	1996	1995	1994	1993	1992	1991
Dividends, Net Income ($)	0.14	0.15	0.00	0.29	0.47	0.62	0.10	0.03	0.05	0.32
Distrib'ns, Cap Gain ($)	4.32	0.00	0.00	2.56	0.37	0.00	0.52	0.03	0.12	0.00
Net Asset Value ($)	15.08	27.75	17.79	17.01	20.84	19.64	18.38	18.98	12.60	13.36
Expense Ratio (%)	na	1.44	1.36	1.33	1.37	1.38	1.44	1.48	1.49	1.50
Yield (%)	0.72	0.54	0.00	1.48	2.21	3.15	0.52	0.15	0.39	2.39
Portfolio Turnover (%)	na	116	95	61	32	22	17	22	53	54
Total Assets (Millions $)	610	1,150	1,172	1,956	2,953	2,220	1,551	506	99	76

PORTFOLIO (as of 6/30/00)

Portfolio Manager: Edwards, Ehrlich, Sharon, McBride - 1989

Investm't Category: International Stock

Domestic	Index
✔ Foreign	Sector
Asset Allocation	State Specific

Investment Style

Large Cap	Mid Cap	Small Cap
Growth	Grth/Val	Value

Portfolio

7.2%	cash	0.0%	corp bonds
90.4%	stocks	0.0%	gov't bonds
1.3%	pref/conv't pref	0.0%	muni bonds
1.1%	conv't bds/wrnts	0.0%	other

SHAREHOLDER INFORMATION

Minimum Investment
Initial: $2,500 Subsequent: $100

Minimum IRA Investment
Initial: $500 Subsequent: $50

Maximum Fees
Load: none 12b-1: none
Other: none

Services
✔ IRA
Keogh
✔ Telephone Exchange

Warburg Japan Growth/ Cmn (WPJGX)

800-927-2874, 212-878-0600
www.warburg.com

International Stock

PERFORMANCE — fund inception date: 12/29/95

	3yr Annual	5yr Annual	10yr Annual	Bull	Bear
Return (%)	5.0	2.1	na	250.5	-54.5
Differ from Category (+/-)	-3.9 blw av	-6.2 blw av	na	159.6 high	-30.5 low

Standard Deviation	Category Risk Index	Beta
43.4%—high	1.92—high	0.87

	2000	1999	1998	1997	1996	1995	1994	1993	1992	1991
Return (%)	-68.7	266.0	1.2	1.5	-5.4	—	—	—	—	—
Differ from Category (+/-)	-49.3	205.3	-4.6	0.2	-19.9	—	—	—	—	—
Return, Tax-Adjusted (%)	-71.9	265.7	1.2	1.5	-6.3	—	—	—	—	—

PER SHARE DATA

	2000	1999	1998	1997	1996	1995	1994	1993	1992	1991
Dividends, Net Income ($)	0.00	0.00	0.00	0.00	0.24	—	—	—	—	—
Distrib'ns, Cap Gain ($)	5.65	0.11	0.00	0.00	0.00	—	—	—	—	—
Net Asset Value ($)	6.96	34.53	9.47	9.35	9.21	—	—	—	—	—
Expense Ratio (%)	na	1.76	1.75	1.75	1.75	—	—	—	—	—
Yield (%)	0.00	0.00	0.00	0.00	2.60	—	—	—	—	—
Portfolio Turnover (%)	na	171	75	94	—	—	—	—	—	—
Total Assets (Millions $)	139	635	52	26	17	—	—	—	—	—

PORTFOLIO (as of 6/30/00)

Portfolio Manager: Nicholas Edwards, Todd Jacobson - 1995

Investm't Category: International Stock

Domestic	Index
✔ Foreign	Sector
Asset Allocation	State Specific

Investment Style

Large Cap	Mid Cap	Small Cap
Growth	Grth/Val	Value

Portfolio

6.3% cash	0.0% corp bonds
93.7% stocks	0.0% gov't bonds
0.0% pref/conv't pref	0.0% muni bonds
0.0% conv't bds/wrnts	0.0% other

SHAREHOLDER INFORMATION

Minimum Investment
Initial: $2,500 Subsequent: $100

Minimum IRA Investment
Initial: $500 Subsequent: $50

Maximum Fees
Load: none 12b-1: 0.25%
Other: none

Services
✔ IRA
Keogh
✔ Telephone Exchange

Warburg Japan Sm Co/ Cmn (WPJPX)

800-927-2874, 212-878-0600
www.warburg.com

International Stock

PERFORMANCE — fund inception date: 9/30/94

	3yr Annual	5yr Annual	10yr Annual	Bull	Bear
Return (%)	10.8	-2.4	na	346.6	-57.5
Differ from Category (+/-)	1.9 abv av	-10.7 low	na	255.7 high	-33.5 low

Standard Deviation	Category Risk Index	Beta
47.8%—high	2.11—high	0.86

	2000	1999	1998	1997	1996	1995	1994	1993	1992	1991
Return (%)	-71.8	328.6	12.7	-25.5	-13.0	-1.0	—	—	—	—
Differ from Category (+/-)	-52.4	267.9	6.9	-26.8	-27.5	-10.3	—	—	—	—
Return, Tax-Adjusted (%)	-78.6	328.4	12.7	-26.1	-13.2	-2.5	—	—	—	—

PER SHARE DATA

	2000	1999	1998	1997	1996	1995	1994	1993	1992	1991
Dividends, Net Income ($)	0.00	0.00	0.00	0.12	0.00	0.37	—	—	—	—
Distrib'ns, Cap Gain ($)	9.44	0.04	0.00	0.00	0.08	0.00	—	—	—	—
Net Asset Value ($)	2.23	27.59	6.45	5.72	7.85	9.13	—	—	—	—
Expense Ratio (%)	na	1.76	1.75	1.76	1.75	1.41	—	—	—	—
Yield (%)	0.00	0.00	0.00	2.09	0.00	4.05	—	—	—	—
Portfolio Turnover (%)	na	249	112	100	95	83	—	—	—	—
Total Assets (Millions $)	136	1,139	50	37	94	212	—	—	—	—

PORTFOLIO (as of 6/30/00)

Portfolio Manager: Nicholas Edwards, Todd Jacobson - 1994

Investm't Category: International Stock

Domestic — Index
✔ Foreign — Sector
Asset Allocation — State Specific

Investment Style

Large Cap — Mid Cap — Small Cap
Growth — Grth/Val — Value

Portfolio

2.5%	cash	0.0%	corp bonds
97.5%	stocks	0.0%	gov't bonds
0.0%	pref/conv't pref	0.0%	muni bonds
0.0%	conv't bds/wrnts	0.0%	other

SHAREHOLDER INFORMATION

Minimum Investment
Initial: $2,500 — Subsequent: $100

Minimum IRA Investment
Initial: $500 — Subsequent: $50

Maximum Fees
Load: 1.00% redemption — 12b-1: 0.25%
Other: redemption fee applies for 6 months

Services
✔ IRA
Keogh
✔ Telephone Exchange

Warburg Maj Frgn Mkt/ Cmn (WPMFX)

800-927-2874, 212-878-0600
www.warburg.com

International Stock

PERFORMANCE

fund inception date: 3/31/97

	3yr Annual	5yr Annual	10yr Annual	Bull	Bear
Return (%)	16.1	na	na	74.8	-20.0
Differ from Category (+/-)	7.2 high	na	na	-16.1 av	4.0 abv av

Standard Deviation	Category Risk Index	Beta
19.7%—abv av	0.87—blw av	0.62

	2000	1999	1998	1997	1996	1995	1994	1993	1992	1991
Return (%)	-16.3	61.5	15.9	—	—	—	—	—	—	—
Differ from Category (+/-)	3.1	0.8	10.1	—	—	—	—	—	—	—
Return, Tax-Adjusted (%)	-19.1	60.6	15.4	—	—	—	—	—	—	—

PER SHARE DATA

	2000	1999	1998	1997	1996	1995	1994	1993	1992	1991
Dividends, Net Income ($)	0.11	0.07	0.11	—	—	—	—	—	—	—
Distrib'ns, Cap Gain ($)	2.34	0.37	0.00	—	—	—	—	—	—	—
Net Asset Value ($)	12.51	17.96	11.43	—	—	—	—	—	—	—
Expense Ratio (%)	na	0.96	0.95	—	—	—	—	—	—	—
Yield (%)	0.74	0.38	0.96	—	—	—	—	—	—	—
Portfolio Turnover (%)	na	151	115	—	—	—	—	—	—	—
Total Assets (Millions $)	71	118	44	—	—	—	—	—	—	—

PORTFOLIO (as of 6/30/00)

Portfolio Manager: Edwards, Ehrlich - 1997

Investm't Category: International Stock

Domestic	Index
✔ Foreign	Sector
Asset Allocation	State Specific

Investment Style

Large Cap	Mid Cap	Small Cap
Growth	Grth/Val	Value

Portfolio

5.1%	cash	0.0%	corp bonds
94.0%	stocks	0.0%	gov't bonds
0.9%	pref/conv't pref	0.0%	muni bonds
0.0%	conv't bds/wrnts	0.0%	other

SHAREHOLDER INFORMATION

Minimum Investment
Initial: $2,500 Subsequent: $100

Minimum IRA Investment
Initial: $500 Subsequent: $50

Maximum Fees
Load: none 12b-1: none
Other: none

Services
✔ IRA
Keogh
✔ Telephone Exchange

Warburg Value/Cmn

800-927-2874, 212-878-0600
www.warburg.com

(RBEGX)

Growth & Income

PERFORMANCE — fund inception date: 10/6/88

	3yr Annual	5yr Annual	10yr Annual	Bull	Bear
Return (%)	9.1	10.8	13.7	27.0	4.0
Differ from Category (+/-)	0.2 av	-3.5 low	-1.2 blw av	-6.5 av	4.1 abv av

Standard Deviation	Category Risk Index	Beta
18.2%—av	1.05—abv av	0.79

	2000	1999	1998	1997	1996	1995	1994	1993	1992	1991
Return (%)	9.2	5.7	12.6	30.2	-1.1	20.4	7.5	35.7	8.5	13.0
Differ from Category (+/-)	3.5	-5.1	-0.2	3.3	-20.8	-9.1	8.0	21.9	-3.1	-15.1
Return, Tax-Adjusted (%)	6.0	0.8	11.6	25.8	-1.2	18.1	6.8	26.4	8.0	11.8

PER SHARE DATA

	2000	1999	1998	1997	1996	1995	1994	1993	1992	1991
Dividends, Net Income ($)	0.10	0.12	0.12	0.19	0.05	0.20	0.10	0.12	0.16	0.26
Distrib'ns, Cap Gain ($)	2.08	4.14	0.53	2.95	0.00	0.81	0.18	3.97	0.00	0.16
Net Asset Value ($)	13.62	14.60	17.88	16.48	15.15	15.39	13.64	12.95	12.56	11.73
Expense Ratio (%)	na	1.14	1.19	1.18	1.21	1.22	1.28	1.14	1.25	1.30
Yield (%)	0.63	0.64	0.65	0.97	0.33	1.23	0.72	0.70	1.27	2.18
Portfolio Turnover (%)	na	78	78	148	94	109	150	344	175	41
Total Assets (Millions $)	241	433	732	616	460	985	628	34	30	23

PORTFOLIO (as of 6/30/00)

Portfolio Manager: Scott Lewis, Stacey Dutton - 1998

Investm't Category: Growth & Income

✔ Domestic	Index
✔ Foreign	Sector
Asset Allocation	State Specific

Investment Style

✔ Large Cap	✔ Mid Cap	Small Cap
Growth	Grth/Val	✔ Value

Portfolio

0.7% cash	0.0% corp bonds
99.3% stocks	0.0% gov't bonds
0.0% pref/conv't pref	0.0% muni bonds
0.0% conv't bds/wrnts	0.0% other

SHAREHOLDER INFORMATION

Minimum Investment
Initial: $1,000 Subsequent: $100

Minimum IRA Investment
Initial: $500 Subsequent: $100

Maximum Fees
Load: none 12b-1: none
Other: none

Services
✔ IRA
Keogh
✔ Telephone Exchange

Wasatch: Core Growth (WGROX)

800-551-1700, 801-533-0778
www.wasatchfunds.com

Growth

PERFORMANCE

fund inception date: 12/19/86

	3yr Annual	5yr Annual	10yr Annual	Bull	Bear
Return (%)	18.5	19.8	19.3	51.8	19.8
Differ from Category (+/-)	7.5 high	3.7 high	2.5 high	2.1 av	25.2 high

Standard Deviation	Category Risk Index	Beta
22.7%—abv av	1.17—abv av	0.94

	2000	1999	1998	1997	1996	1995	1994	1993	1992	1991
Return (%)	37.3	19.3	1.5	27.5	16.5	40.4	2.6	11.1	4.7	40.8
Differ from Category (+/-)	33.8	0.4	-12.8	0.4	-5.8	10.0	2.8	-3.5	-7.9	3.2
Return, Tax-Adjusted (%)	35.2	18.8	0.7	25.5	14.0	39.5	-4.6	8.5	3.4	38.3

PER SHARE DATA

	2000	1999	1998	1997	1996	1995	1994	1993	1992	1991
Dividends, Net Income ($)	0.00	0.00	0.00	0.02	0.07	0.05	0.00	0.00	0.00	0.61
Distrib'ns, Cap Gain ($)	2.31	0.47	0.72	1.62	1.31	0.29	3.93	1.37	0.66	0.29
Net Asset Value ($)	28.71	22.80	19.57	20.22	17.19	15.96	11.61	15.14	14.90	14.87
Expense Ratio (%)	1.38	1.44	1.44	1.50	1.50	1.50	1.50	1.50	1.49	1.51
Yield (%)	0.00	0.00	0.00	0.09	0.37	0.30	0.00	0.00	0.00	4.02
Portfolio Turnover (%)	75	79	63	81	62	88	163	104	40	37
Total Assets (Millions $)	312	211	179	146	89	61	8	16	16	13

PORTFOLIO (as of 6/30/00)

Portfolio Manager: Samuel Stewart - 1997

Investm't Category: Growth

✔ Domestic — Index
✔ Foreign — Sector
Asset Allocation — State Specific

Investment Style

Large Cap — ✔ Mid Cap — ✔ Small Cap
Growth — Grth/Val — ✔ Value

Portfolio

10.1%	cash	0.0%	corp bonds
89.9%	stocks	0.0%	gov't bonds
0.0%	pref/conv't pref	0.0%	muni bonds
0.0%	conv't bds/wrnts	0.0%	other

SHAREHOLDER INFORMATION

Minimum Investment

Initial: $2,000 — Subsequent: $100

Minimum IRA Investment

Initial: $1,000 — Subsequent: $100

Maximum Fees

Load: none — 12b-1: none
Other: none

Services

✔ IRA
✔ Keogh
✔ Telephone Exchange

Wasatch: Micro Cap (WMICX)

800-551-1700, 801-533-0778
www.wasatchfunds.com

Aggressive Growth

this fund is closed to new investors

PERFORMANCE

fund inception date: 6/19/95

	3yr Annual	5yr Annual	10yr Annual	Bull	Bear
Return (%)	29.5	27.3	na	78.4	9.9
Differ from Category (+/-)	13.3 high	12.7 high	na	-40.8 blw av	30.5 high

Standard Deviation	Category Risk Index	Beta
25.1%—abv av	0.78—blw av	0.88

	2000	1999	1998	1997	1996	1995	1994	1993	1992	1991
Return (%)	37.5	32.8	18.9	35.3	13.6	—	—	—	—	—
Differ from Category (+/-)	43.5	-24.7	3.8	20.5	-4.7	—	—	—	—	—
Return, Tax-Adjusted (%)	31.0	30.7	17.0	33.1	11.8	—	—	—	—	—

PER SHARE DATA

	2000	1999	1998	1997	1996	1995	1994	1993	1992	1991
Dividends, Net Income ($)	0.00	0.00	0.00	0.00	0.00	—	—	—	—	—
Distrib'ns, Cap Gain ($)	1.54	0.41	0.35	0.33	0.18	—	—	—	—	—
Net Asset Value ($)	4.90	4.79	3.99	3.76	3.03	—	—	—	—	—
Expense Ratio (%)	2.38	2.46	2.50	2.50	2.50	—	—	—	—	—
Yield (%)	0.00	0.00	0.00	0.00	0.00	—	—	—	—	—
Portfolio Turnover (%)	69	57	81	99	84	—	—	—	—	—
Total Assets (Millions $)	213	167	154	120	82	—	—	—	—	—

PORTFOLIO (as of 6/30/00)

Portfolio Manager: Robert Gardiner - 1995

Investm't Category: Aggressive Growth

✔ Domestic
✔ Foreign
Asset Allocation
Index
Sector
State Specific

Investment Style

Large Cap
Mid Cap
✔ Small Cap
✔ Growth
Grth/Val
Value

Portfolio

18.0% cash
82.0% stocks
0.0% pref/conv't pref
0.0% conv't bds/wrnts
0.0% corp bonds
0.0% gov't bonds
0.0% muni bonds
0.0% other

SHAREHOLDER INFORMATION

Minimum Investment

Initial: $2,000 Subsequent: $100

Minimum IRA Investment

Initial: $1,000 Subsequent: $100

Maximum Fees

Load: none 12b-1: none
Other: none

Services

✔ IRA
Keogh
✔ Telephone Exchange

Wasatch: Small Cap Grth (WAAEX)

800-551-1700, 801-533-0778
www.wasatchfunds.com

Aggressive Growth

PERFORMANCE

fund inception date: 11/18/86

	3yr Annual	5yr Annual	10yr Annual	Bull	Bear
Return (%)	22.2	18.0	19.5	99.1	3.7
Differ from Category (+/-)	6.0 abv av	3.4 av	3.7 abv av	-20.1 av	24.3 high

Standard Deviation	Category Risk Index	Beta
28.2%—high	0.87—blw av	1.03

	2000	1999	1998	1997	1996	1995	1994	1993	1992	1991
Return (%)	16.8	40.8	11.1	19.2	5.1	28.1	5.4	22.4	4.7	50.4
Differ from Category (+/-)	22.8	-16.7	-4.0	4.4	-13.2	-6.5	6.2	-2.8	-2.2	3.2
Return, Tax-Adjusted (%)	12.7	38.4	8.6	16.1	3.6	27.3	3.2	20.3	3.6	48.0

PER SHARE DATA

	2000	1999	1998	1997	1996	1995	1994	1993	1992	1991
Dividends, Net Income ($)	0.00	0.00	0.00	0.00	0.00	0.00	0.00	0.00	0.00	0.72
Distrib'ns, Cap Gain ($)	5.84	2.71	3.07	3.69	1.22	0.54	1.51	1.22	0.66	0.18
Net Asset Value ($)	27.82	29.00	22.97	24.60	23.86	23.87	19.06	19.50	16.95	16.82
Expense Ratio (%)	1.38	1.44	1.48	1.50	1.50	1.37	1.50	1.50	1.51	1.51
Yield (%)	0.00	0.00	0.00	0.00	0.00	0.00	0.00	0.00	0.00	4.23
Portfolio Turnover (%)	72	46	56	48	73	29	64	70	32	41
Total Assets (Millions $)	214	181	156	172	219	294	55	29	15	9

PORTFOLIO (as of 6/30/00)

Portfolio Manager: Jeff Cardon - 1997

Investm't Category: Aggressive Growth

✔ Domestic
✔ Foreign
Asset Allocation
Index
Sector
State Specific

Investment Style

Large Cap
✔ Growth
Mid Cap
Grth/Val
✔ Small Cap
Value

Portfolio

10.0% cash
90.0% stocks
0.0% pref/conv't pref
0.0% conv't bds/wrnts
0.0% corp bonds
0.0% gov't bonds
0.0% muni bonds
0.0% other

SHAREHOLDER INFORMATION

Minimum Investment

Initial: $2,000 Subsequent: $100

Minimum IRA Investment

Initial: $1,000 Subsequent: $100

Maximum Fees

Load: none 12b-1: none
Other: none

Services

✔ IRA
✔ Keogh
✔ Telephone Exchange

Wasatch: Ultra Growth (WAMCX)

800-551-1700, 801-533-0778
www.wasatchfunds.com

Aggressive Growth

PERFORMANCE — fund inception date: 8/24/92

	3yr Annual	5yr Annual	10yr Annual	Bull	Bear
Return (%)	22.6	13.7	na	84.5	4.5
Differ from Category (+/-)	6.4 abv av	-0.9 blw av	na	-34.7 av	25.1 high

Standard Deviation	Category Risk Index	Beta
32.9%—high	1.01—av	1.10

	2000	1999	1998	1997	1996	1995	1994	1993	1992	1991
Return (%)	25.9	17.4	24.8	-0.5	3.5	58.7	8.1	-2.9	—	—
Differ from Category (+/-)	31.9	-40.1	9.7	-15.3	-14.8	24.1	8.9	-28.1	—	—
Return, Tax-Adjusted (%)	20.8	15.9	23.9	-2.6	3.5	58.2	8.0	-2.9	—	—

PER SHARE DATA

	2000	1999	1998	1997	1996	1995	1994	1993	1992	1991
Dividends, Net Income ($)	0.00	0.00	0.00	0.00	0.00	0.00	0.00	0.00	—	—
Distrib'ns, Cap Gain ($)	5.38	1.46	0.74	1.99	0.00	0.18	0.02	0.00	—	—
Net Asset Value ($)	21.41	21.48	19.77	16.71	18.94	18.29	11.64	10.79	—	—
Expense Ratio (%)	1.75	1.75	1.75	1.75	1.75	1.75	1.75	1.74	—	—
Yield (%)	0.00	0.00	0.00	0.00	0.00	0.00	0.00	0.00	—	—
Portfolio Turnover (%)	135	77	91	103	121	46	213	113	—	—
Total Assets (Millions $)	44	43	62	61	100	130	1	1	—	—

PORTFOLIO (as of 6/30/00)

Portfolio Manager: Karey Barker - 1993

Investm't Category: Aggressive Growth

✔ Domestic — Index
✔ Foreign — Sector
Asset Allocation — State Specific

Investment Style

Large Cap — Mid Cap — ✔ Small Cap
✔ Growth — Grth/Val — Value

Portfolio

15.3% cash	0.0% corp bonds
84.7% stocks	0.0% gov't bonds
0.0% pref/conv't pref	0.0% muni bonds
0.0% conv't bds/wrnts	0.0% other

SHAREHOLDER INFORMATION

Minimum Investment
Initial: $2,000 — Subsequent: $100

Minimum IRA Investment
Initial: $1,000 — Subsequent: $100

Maximum Fees
Load: none — 12b-1: none
Other: none

Services
✔ IRA
✔ Keogh
✔ Telephone Exchange

Wayne Hummer Growth (WHGRX)

800-621-4477, 312-431-1700
www.whummer.com

Growth

PERFORMANCE

fund inception date: 12/30/83

	3yr Annual	5yr Annual	10yr Annual	Bull	Bear
Return (%)	16.0	17.9	15.2	77.1	-6.7
Differ from Category (+/-)	5.0 high	1.8 av	-1.6 blw av	27.4 high	-1.3 av

Standard Deviation	Category Risk Index	Beta
19.6%—abv av	1.01—av	0.90

	2000	1999	1998	1997	1996	1995	1994	1993	1992	1991
Return (%)	-3.7	38.1	17.5	30.2	11.8	24.8	-0.9	3.5	10.3	28.8
Differ from Category (+/-)	-7.2	19.2	3.2	3.1	-10.5	-5.6	-0.7	-11.1	-2.3	-8.8
Return, Tax-Adjusted (%)	-5.5	35.8	16.3	28.0	10.2	23.5	-1.7	2.8	9.6	27.7

PER SHARE DATA

	2000	1999	1998	1997	1996	1995	1994	1993	1992	1991
Dividends, Net Income ($)	0.02	0.07	0.16	0.22	0.29	0.31	0.30	0.31	0.29	0.38
Distrib'ns, Cap Gain ($)	4.17	3.99	1.51	2.49	1.00	0.48	0.21	0.03	0.14	0.16
Net Asset Value ($)	40.09	45.97	36.81	32.80	27.50	25.81	21.34	22.06	21.64	20.02
Expense Ratio (%)	0.95	0.94	0.96	0.99	1.06	1.07	1.07	1.12	1.23	1.36
Yield (%)	0.04	0.14	0.41	0.62	1.01	1.17	1.39	1.40	1.33	1.88
Portfolio Turnover (%)	10	12	7	9	6	3	2	1	3	13
Total Assets (Millions $)	168	183	143	128	104	100	87	98	79	50

PORTFOLIO (as of 6/30/00)

Portfolio Manager: Thomas Rowland - 1987

Investm't Category: Growth

- ✔ Domestic
- Foreign
- Asset Allocation
- Index
- Sector
- State Specific

Investment Style

- ✔ Large Cap
- ✔ Mid Cap
- Small Cap
- ✔ Growth
- Grth/Val
- Value

Portfolio

3.9% cash	0.0% corp bonds
96.2% stocks	0.0% gov't bonds
0.0% pref/conv't pref	0.0% muni bonds
0.0% conv't bds/wrnts	0.0% other

SHAREHOLDER INFORMATION

Minimum Investment

Initial: $1,000 Subsequent: $500

Minimum IRA Investment

Initial: $500 Subsequent: $200

Maximum Fees

Load: 2.00% front 12b-1: none

Other: none

Services

- ✔ IRA
- ✔ Keogh
- ✔ Telephone Exchange

Weitz Partners Value

800-232-4161, 402-391-1980
www.weitzfunds.com

(WPVLX)

Growth

PERFORMANCE — fund inception date: 1/3/94

	3yr Annual	5yr Annual	10yr Annual	Bull	Bear
Return (%)	24.0	26.1	na	41.8	10.4
Differ from Category (+/-)	13.0 high	10.0 high	na	-7.9 av	15.8 high

Standard Deviation	Category Risk Index	Beta
15.2%—av	0.78—low	0.61

	2000	1999	1998	1997	1996	1995	1994	1993	1992	1991
Return (%)	21.0	22.0	29.1	40.6	19.0	38.6	—	—	—	—
Differ from Category (+/-)	17.5	3.1	14.8	13.5	-3.3	8.2	—	—	—	—
Return, Tax-Adjusted (%)	18.1	20.5	26.5	39.6	16.6	34.6	—	—	—	—

PER SHARE DATA

	2000	1999	1998	1997	1996	1995	1994	1993	1992	1991
Dividends, Net Income ($)	0.50	0.04	0.16	0.00	0.05	0.23	—	—	—	—
Distrib'ns, Cap Gain ($)	1.88	1.23	1.66	0.53	0.79	0.84	—	—	—	—
Net Asset Value ($)	21.51	20.02	17.68	15.45	11.52	10.39	—	—	—	—
Expense Ratio (%)	1.19	1.24	1.25	1.24	1.23	1.27	—	—	—	—
Yield (%)	2.13	0.18	0.82	0.00	0.40	2.04	—	—	—	—
Portfolio Turnover (%)	5	29	36	30	37	51	—	—	—	—
Total Assets (Millions $)	1,676	1,143	292	133	94	73	—	—	—	—

PORTFOLIO (as of 6/30/00)

Portfolio Manager: Wallace Weitz - 1994

Investm't Category: Growth

- ✔ Domestic
- ✔ Foreign
- Asset Allocation
- Index
- Sector
- State Specific

Investment Style

- ✔ Large Cap
- Growth
- Mid Cap
- Grth/Val
- Small Cap
- ✔ Value

Portfolio

- 18.4% cash
- 80.1% stocks
- 0.2% pref/conv't pref
- 0.0% conv't bds/wrnts
- 0.0% corp bonds
- 1.3% gov't bonds
- 0.0% muni bonds
- 0.0% other

SHAREHOLDER INFORMATION

Minimum Investment

Initial: $100,000 Subsequent: $5,000

Minimum IRA Investment

Initial: $100,000 Subsequent: $5,000

Maximum Fees

Load: none 12b-1: none

Other: none

Services

- ✔ IRA
- Keogh
- ✔ Telephone Exchange

Weitz Srs: Hickory (WEHIX)

800-232-4161, 402-391-1980
www.weitzfunds.com

Growth

this fund is closed to new investors

PERFORMANCE

fund inception date: 1/1/93

	3yr Annual	5yr Annual	10yr Annual	Bull	Bear
Return (%)	14.5	23.1	na	49.5	-15.0
Differ from Category (+/-)	3.5 abv av	7.0 high	na	-0.2 av	-9.6 blw av

Standard Deviation	Category Risk Index	Beta
21.1%—abv av	1.09—abv av	0.74

	2000	1999	1998	1997	1996	1995	1994	1993	1992	1991
Return (%)	-17.2	36.6	33.0	39.1	35.3	40.4	-17.2	—	—	—
Differ from Category (+/-)	-20.7	17.7	18.7	12.0	13.0	10.0	-17.0	—	—	—
Return, Tax-Adjusted (%)	-19.8	34.9	32.4	36.9	33.3	39.7	-18.3	—	—	—

PER SHARE DATA

	2000	1999	1998	1997	1996	1995	1994	1993	1992	1991
Dividends, Net Income ($)	0.00	0.01	0.09	0.07	0.00	0.13	0.28	—	—	—
Distrib'ns, Cap Gain ($)	5.29	2.55	0.44	1.90	1.03	0.06	0.17	—	—	—
Net Asset Value ($)	27.55	39.65	30.98	23.70	18.80	14.66	10.61	—	—	—
Expense Ratio (%)	1.23	1.30	1.46	1.50	1.50	1.50	1.50	—	—	—
Yield (%)	0.00	0.02	0.28	0.27	0.00	0.88	2.59	—	—	—
Portfolio Turnover (%)	46	40	29	28	28	20	29	—	—	—
Total Assets (Millions $)	440	913	538	21	10	5	3	—	—	—

PORTFOLIO (as of 6/30/00)

Portfolio Manager: Richard Lawson - 1993

Investm't Category: Growth

✔ Domestic	Index
✔ Foreign	Sector
Asset Allocation	State Specific

Investment Style

✔ Large Cap	Mid Cap	Small Cap
Growth	Grth/Val	✔ Value

Portfolio

4.3%	cash	0.0%	corp bonds
94.9%	stocks	0.0%	gov't bonds
0.8%	pref/conv't pref	0.0%	muni bonds
0.0%	conv't bds/wrnts	0.0%	other

SHAREHOLDER INFORMATION

Minimum Investment
Initial: $25,000 Subsequent: $1

Minimum IRA Investment
Initial: $25,000 Subsequent: $1

Maximum Fees
Load: none 12b-1: none
Other: none

Services
✔ IRA
Keogh
✔ Telephone Exchange

Weitz Srs: Value (WVALX)

800-232-4161, 402-391-1980
www.weitzfunds.com

Growth

PERFORMANCE

fund inception date: 5/9/86

	3yr Annual	5yr Annual	10yr Annual	Bull	Bear
Return (%)	23.1	25.2	20.9	37.7	10.4
Differ from Category (+/-)	12.1 high	9.1 high	4.1 high	-12.0 blw av	15.8 high

Standard Deviation	Category Risk Index	Beta
14.9%—av	0.77—low	0.57

	2000	1999	1998	1997	1996	1995	1994	1993	1992	1991
Return (%)	19.6	20.9	28.9	38.9	18.7	38.3	-9.8	19.9	13.5	27.6
Differ from Category (+/-)	16.1	2.0	14.6	11.8	-3.6	7.9	-9.6	5.3	0.9	-10.0
Return, Tax-Adjusted (%)	16.9	19.2	26.2	35.7	16.7	35.0	-10.9	18.7	11.7	25.7

PER SHARE DATA

	2000	1999	1998	1997	1996	1995	1994	1993	1992	1991
Dividends, Net Income ($)	0.48	0.36	0.17	0.31	0.12	0.41	0.02	0.02	0.27	0.32
Distrib'ns, Cap Gain ($)	3.42	1.67	3.01	2.60	1.10	1.08	0.69	0.58	0.54	0.39
Net Asset Value ($)	35.22	33.08	29.07	25.15	20.59	18.38	14.43	16.80	14.54	13.58
Expense Ratio (%)	1.19	1.26	1.27	1.29	1.35	1.42	1.41	1.35	1.40	1.49
Yield (%)	1.24	1.03	0.52	1.11	0.55	2.10	0.13	0.11	1.79	2.29
Portfolio Turnover (%)	31	36	39	39	40	28	23	23	35	28
Total Assets (Millions $)	2,910	2,679	1,196	365	260	149	107	106	49	32

PORTFOLIO (as of 6/30/00)

Portfolio Manager: Wallace Weitz - 1986

Investm't Category: Growth

✔ Domestic
Foreign
Asset Allocation
Index
Sector
State Specific

Investment Style

✔ Large Cap
✔ Mid Cap
Small Cap
Growth
Grth/Val
✔ Value

Portfolio

9.7%	cash	0.1%	corp bonds
85.9%	stocks	3.6%	gov't bonds
0.5%	pref/conv't pref	0.0%	muni bonds
0.2%	conv't bds/wrnts	0.0%	other

SHAREHOLDER INFORMATION

Minimum Investment

Initial: $25,000 Subsequent: $1

Minimum IRA Investment

Initial: $25,000 Subsequent: $1

Maximum Fees

Load: none 12b-1: none
Other: none

Services

✔ IRA
✔ Keogh
✔ Telephone Exchange

Westcore: Blue Chip (WTMVX)

800-392-2673, 303-623-2577
www.westcore.com

Growth & Income

PERFORMANCE

fund inception date: 6/1/88

	3yr Annual	5yr Annual	10yr Annual	Bull	Bear
Return (%)	7.5	14.5	15.3	32.6	-5.9
Differ from Category (+/-)	-1.4 blw av	0.2 av	0.4 av	-0.9 av	-5.8 blw av

Standard Deviation	Category Risk Index	Beta
18.0%—av	1.03—abv av	0.92

	2000	1999	1998	1997	1996	1995	1994	1993	1992	1991
Return (%)	0.5	4.9	17.8	30.9	21.2	36.4	0.3	12.4	1.9	34.4
Differ from Category (+/-)	-5.2	-5.9	5.0	4.0	1.5	6.9	0.8	-1.4	-9.7	6.3
Return, Tax-Adjusted (%)	-2.2	1.8	14.4	25.5	15.5	32.7	-0.6	8.6	-0.1	32.8

PER SHARE DATA

	2000	1999	1998	1997	1996	1995	1994	1993	1992	1991
Dividends, Net Income ($)	0.04	0.00	0.08	0.15	0.22	0.26	0.19	0.40	0.23	0.35
Distrib'ns, Cap Gain ($)	1.98	2.52	2.61	3.98	2.87	1.30	0.19	1.17	0.74	0.21
Net Asset Value ($)	12.87	14.90	16.77	16.70	15.96	15.69	12.67	13.01	13.01	13.73
Expense Ratio (%)	1.15	1.15	1.15	1.15	1.10	1.01	1.06	0.99	0.91	0.84
Yield (%)	0.26	0.00	0.41	0.72	1.16	1.53	1.47	2.82	1.67	2.51
Portfolio Turnover (%)	73	73	48	43	65	61	41	85	123	142
Total Assets (Millions $)	50	60	72	62	56	62	40	33	32	32

PORTFOLIO (as of 9/30/99)

Portfolio Manager: T. Quinlisk, C. Petersen - 2000

Investm't Category: Growth & Income

✔ Domestic　　Index
✔ Foreign　　Sector
Asset Allocation　　State Specific

Investment Style

✔ Large Cap　　Mid Cap　　Small Cap
Growth　　Grth/Val　　✔ Value

Portfolio

1.4%	cash	0.0%	corp bonds
98.6%	stocks	0.0%	gov't bonds
0.0%	pref/conv't pref	0.0%	muni bonds
0.0%	conv't bds/wrnts	0.0%	other

SHAREHOLDER INFORMATION

Minimum Investment
Initial: $2,500　　Subsequent: $100

Minimum IRA Investment
Initial: $1,000　　Subsequent: $100

Maximum Fees
Load: none　　12b-1: none
Other: none

Services
✔ IRA
✔ Keogh
✔ Telephone Exchange

Westcore: MIDCO Growth (WTMGX)

800-392-2673, 303-623-2577
www.westcore.com

Aggressive Growth

PERFORMANCE

fund inception date: 8/1/86

	3yr Annual	5yr Annual	10yr Annual	Bull	Bear
Return (%)	13.2	14.2	17.7	115.5	-33.3
Differ from Category (+/-)	-3.0 av	-0.4 av	1.9 av	-3.7 abv av	-12.7 blw av

Standard Deviation	Category Risk Index	Beta
34.3%—high	1.06—abv av	1.21

	2000	1999	1998	1997	1996	1995	1994	1993	1992	1991
Return (%)	-17.5	59.3	10.4	14.8	16.9	27.4	-1.0	17.4	6.4	67.0
Differ from Category (+/-)	-11.5	1.8	-4.7	0.0	-1.4	-7.2	-0.2	-7.8	-0.5	19.8
Return, Tax-Adjusted (%)	-27.4	49.9	7.8	11.5	12.6	26.1	-1.8	15.5	4.3	62.7

PER SHARE DATA

	2000	1999	1998	1997	1996	1995	1994	1993	1992	1991
Dividends, Net Income ($)	0.00	0.00	0.00	0.00	0.00	0.00	0.00	0.00	0.00	0.33
Distrib'ns, Cap Gain ($)	9.96	8.84	2.50	3.24	3.01	0.71	0.52	1.03	1.10	1.20
Net Asset Value ($)	6.41	20.06	18.92	19.66	20.06	19.76	16.08	16.79	15.20	15.35
Expense Ratio (%)	1.15	1.15	1.13	1.14	1.08	0.94	0.84	0.83	0.80	0.78
Yield (%)	0.00	0.00	0.00	0.00	0.00	0.00	0.00	0.00	0.00	1.99
Portfolio Turnover (%)	117	116	75	60	62	50	52	56	48	75
Total Assets (Millions $)	168	300	491	602	569	547	362	279	215	178

PORTFOLIO (as of 9/30/99)

Portfolio Manager: Todger Anderson - 1986

Investm't Category: Aggressive Growth

✔ Domestic
✔ Foreign
Asset Allocation
Index
Sector
State Specific

Investment Style

Large Cap
✔ Mid Cap
✔ Small Cap
✔ Growth
Grth/Val
Value

Portfolio

2.4%	cash	0.0%	corp bonds
97.6%	stocks	0.0%	gov't bonds
0.0%	pref/conv't pref	0.0%	muni bonds
0.0%	conv't bds/wrnts	0.0%	other

SHAREHOLDER INFORMATION

Minimum Investment

Initial: $2,500 Subsequent: $100

Minimum IRA Investment

Initial: $1,000 Subsequent: $100

Maximum Fees

Load: none 12b-1: none
Other: none

Services

✔ IRA
✔ Keogh
✔ Telephone Exchange

Weston: New Century Bal

888-639-0102, 781-239-0445

(NCIPX)

Balanced

PERFORMANCE

fund inception date: 2/1/89

	3yr Annual	5yr Annual	10yr Annual	Bull	Bear
Return (%)	8.8	11.3	11.6	36.0	-10.0
Differ from Category (+/-)	0.4 av	-0.1 av	-0.1 av	7.9 abv av	-6.8 low

Standard Deviation	Category Risk Index	Beta
12.4%—blw av	1.13—abv av	0.54

	2000	1999	1998	1997	1996	1995	1994	1993	1992	1991
Return (%)	-3.7	18.2	13.1	18.5	12.2	22.8	-2.4	15.5	2.8	22.9
Differ from Category (+/-)	-5.7	7.5	-0.2	-0.3	-1.7	-2.7	-1.1	1.1	-5.6	-0.9
Return, Tax-Adjusted (%)	-5.5	15.7	10.5	13.5	9.4	20.0	-4.7	14.6	-0.5	21.5

PER SHARE DATA

	2000	1999	1998	1997	1996	1995	1994	1993	1992	1991
Dividends, Net Income ($)	0.43	0.40	0.30	0.79	0.29	0.34	0.39	0.23	0.37	0.38
Distrib'ns, Cap Gain ($)	0.44	0.77	0.99	1.55	0.80	0.58	0.47	0.00	1.00	0.05
Net Asset Value ($)	12.45	13.85	12.72	12.40	12.61	12.32	10.94	12.08	10.67	11.72
Expense Ratio (%)	na	1.46	1.46	1.41	1.61	1.61	1.60	1.54	1.58	1.76
Yield (%)	3.33	2.73	2.18	5.66	2.16	2.63	3.41	1.90	3.17	3.22
Portfolio Turnover (%)	na	60	59	80	172	206	107	133	224	156
Total Assets (Millions $)	75	73	60	48	41	31	22	23	17	19

PORTFOLIO (as of 6/30/00)

Portfolio Manager: Wayne Grzecki - 1995

Investm't Category: Balanced

✔ Domestic   Index
✔ Foreign   Sector
✔ Asset Allocation   State Specific

Investment Style

Large Cap   Mid Cap   Small Cap
Growth   Grth/Val   Value

Portfolio

0.7%	cash	0.0%	corp bonds
0.0%	stocks	0.0%	gov't bonds
0.0%	pref/conv't pref	0.0%	muni bonds
0.0%	conv't bds/wrnts	99.3%	other

SHAREHOLDER INFORMATION

Minimum Investment

Initial: $5,000   Subsequent: $100

Minimum IRA Investment

Initial: na   Subsequent: na

Maximum Fees

Load: none   12b-1: 0.19%
Other: none

Services

IRA
✔ Keogh
✔ Telephone Exchange

Weston: New Century Cap (NCCPX)

888-639-0102, 781-239-0445

Growth

PERFORMANCE — fund inception date: 1/31/89

	3yr Annual	5yr Annual	10yr Annual	Bull	Bear
Return (%)	12.7	15.6	15.2	68.3	-18.1
Differ from Category (+/-)	1.7 av	-0.5 av	-1.6 blw av	18.6 abv av	-12.7 low

Standard Deviation	Category Risk Index	Beta
19.4%—abv av	1.00—av	0.86

	2000	1999	1998	1997	1996	1995	1994	1993	1992	1991
Return (%)	-10.8	34.3	19.6	26.0	14.5	28.0	0.0	13.8	0.5	36.4
Differ from Category (+/-)	-14.3	15.4	5.3	-1.1	-7.8	-2.4	0.2	-0.8	-12.1	-1.2
Return, Tax-Adjusted (%)	-12.2	32.6	17.3	20.5	11.5	24.7	-2.3	13.8	-3.2	35.3

PER SHARE DATA

	2000	1999	1998	1997	1996	1995	1994	1993	1992	1991
Dividends, Net Income ($)	0.00	0.02	0.00	0.35	0.08	0.28	0.22	0.00	0.16	0.11
Distrib'ns, Cap Gain ($)	1.37	1.14	1.53	3.13	1.33	1.01	0.76	0.00	1.56	0.26
Net Asset Value ($)	15.23	18.63	14.74	13.59	13.99	13.63	11.94	12.93	11.36	13.02
Expense Ratio (%)	na	1.39	1.44	1.43	1.47	1.38	1.60	1.54	1.58	1.76
Yield (%)	0.00	0.10	0.00	2.09	0.52	1.91	1.73	0.00	1.23	0.82
Portfolio Turnover (%)	na	64	102	93	214	108	107	133	224	156
Total Assets (Millions $)	140	144	104	79	64	51	36	38	32	39

PORTFOLIO (as of 6/30/00)

Portfolio Manager: Wayne Grzecki - 1995

Investm't Category: Growth

✔ Domestic — Index
✔ Foreign — Sector
Asset Allocation — State Specific

Investment Style

✔ Large Cap — ✔ Mid Cap — Small Cap
✔ Growth — Grth/Val — Value

Portfolio

0.6%	cash	0.0%	corp bonds
0.0%	stocks	0.0%	gov't bonds
0.0%	pref/conv't pref	0.0%	muni bonds
0.0%	conv't bds/wrnts	99.4%	other

SHAREHOLDER INFORMATION

Minimum Investment
Initial: $5,000 — Subsequent: $100

Minimum IRA Investment
Initial: na — Subsequent: na

Maximum Fees
Load: none — 12b-1: 0.17%
Other: none

Services
IRA
✔ Keogh
✔ Telephone Exchange

White Oak Growth (WOGSX)

888-462-5386
www.oakassociates.com

Aggressive Growth

PERFORMANCE — fund inception date: 8/3/92

	3yr Annual	5yr Annual	10yr Annual	Bull	Bear
Return (%)	29.4	28.9	na	117.8	-11.1
Differ from Category (+/-)	13.2 high	14.3 high	na	-1.4 abv av	9.5 abv av

Standard Deviation	Category Risk Index	Beta
29.3%—high	0.90—blw av	1.41

	2000	1999	1998	1997	1996	1995	1994	1993	1992	1991
Return (%)	3.5	50.1	39.5	24.2	32.2	52.7	6.2	-0.2	—	—
Differ from Category (+/-)	9.5	-7.4	24.4	9.4	13.9	18.1	7.0	-25.4	—	—
Return, Tax-Adjusted (%)	3.4	50.1	39.5	24.1	31.9	52.5	6.1	-0.3	—	—

PER SHARE DATA

	2000	1999	1998	1997	1996	1995	1994	1993	1992	1991
Dividends, Net Income ($)	0.00	0.00	0.00	0.02	0.05	0.03	0.02	0.05	—	—
Distrib'ns, Cap Gain ($)	0.27	0.00	0.00	0.06	0.07	0.00	0.00	0.00	—	—
Net Asset Value ($)	63.07	61.12	40.71	29.18	23.55	17.90	11.75	11.08	—	—
Expense Ratio (%)	0.96	1.00	1.00	0.98	0.95	0.97	0.97	0.97	—	—
Yield (%)	0.00	0.00	0.00	0.06	0.21	0.16	0.17	0.45	—	—
Portfolio Turnover (%)	13	6	6	7	8	22	37	27	—	—
Total Assets (Millions $)	5,485	2,725	1,092	391	40	10	5	5	—	—

PORTFOLIO (as of 6/30/00)

Portfolio Manager: Oelschlager, Barton, MacKay - 1992

Investm't Category: Aggressive Growth

✔ Domestic — Index
✔ Foreign — Sector
Asset Allocation — State Specific

Investment Style

✔ Large Cap — Mid Cap — Small Cap
✔ Growth — Grth/Val — Value

Portfolio

2.2%	cash	0.0%	corp bonds
97.8%	stocks	0.0%	gov't bonds
0.0%	pref/conv't pref	0.0%	muni bonds
0.0%	conv't bds/wrnts	0.0%	other

SHAREHOLDER INFORMATION

Minimum Investment
Initial: $2,000 — Subsequent: $50

Minimum IRA Investment
Initial: $2,000 — Subsequent: $50

Maximum Fees
Load: none — 12b-1: none
Other: none

Services
✔ IRA
Keogh
✔ Telephone Exchange

Williamsburg: Gov't St Eqty (GVEQX)

800-443-4249, 513-629-2000
www.tleavell.com

Growth

PERFORMANCE — fund inception date: 6/3/91

	3yr Annual	5yr Annual	10yr Annual	Bull	Bear
Return (%)	11.6	16.6	na	52.4	-8.0
Differ from Category (+/-)	0.6 av	0.5 av	na	2.7 av	-2.6 av

Standard Deviation	Category Risk Index	Beta
16.2%—av	0.83—low	0.90

	2000	1999	1998	1997	1996	1995	1994	1993	1992	1991
Return (%)	-4.5	17.7	23.7	27.8	21.4	27.4	-2.7	3.1	6.0	—
Differ from Category (+/-)	-8.0	-1.2	9.4	0.7	-0.9	-3.0	-2.5	-11.5	-6.6	—
Return, Tax-Adjusted (%)	-4.6	17.2	22.8	26.7	19.5	26.4	-3.2	2.6	5.3	—

PER SHARE DATA

	2000	1999	1998	1997	1996	1995	1994	1993	1992	1991
Dividends, Net Income ($)	0.15	0.19	0.30	0.32	0.36	0.41	0.35	0.24	0.43	—
Distrib'ns, Cap Gain ($)	0.00	0.62	1.08	1.08	1.32	0.20	0.00	0.00	0.00	—
Net Asset Value ($)	52.32	54.96	47.48	39.63	32.16	27.95	22.45	23.46	22.98	—
Expense Ratio (%)	0.83	0.85	0.80	0.89	0.94	0.91	1.00	1.00	1.00	—
Yield (%)	0.28	0.34	0.61	0.78	1.07	1.45	1.55	1.02	1.87	—
Portfolio Turnover (%)	17	22	18	20	31	55	63	59	—	—
Total Assets (Millions $)	110	109	86	66	48	38	29	26	19	—

PORTFOLIO (as of 6/30/00)

Portfolio Manager: Tom Leavell, Stephen Simmons - 1991

Investm't Category: Growth

✔ Domestic	Index
✔ Foreign	Sector
Asset Allocation	State Specific

Investment Style

✔ Large Cap	Mid Cap	Small Cap
Growth	✔ Grth/Val	Value

Portfolio

2.4%	cash	0.0%	corp bonds
97.6%	stocks	0.0%	gov't bonds
0.0%	pref/conv't pref	0.0%	muni bonds
0.0%	conv't bds/wrnts	0.0%	other

SHAREHOLDER INFORMATION

Minimum Investment
Initial: $5,000 — Subsequent: $500

Minimum IRA Investment
Initial: $1,000 — Subsequent: $500

Maximum Fees
Load: none — 12b-1: none
Other: none

Services
✔ IRA
✔ Keogh
Telephone Exchange

Wm Blair: Growth/N (WBGSX)

800-742-7272, 312-364-8000
www.wmblair.com

Growth

PERFORMANCE — fund inception date: 3/20/46

	3yr Annual	5yr Annual	10yr Annual	Bull	Bear
Return (%)	12.1	14.8	17.3	58.6	-13.8
Differ from Category (+/-)	1.1 av	-1.3 blw av	0.5 av	8.9 abv av	-8.4 blw av

Standard Deviation	Category Risk Index	Beta
21.0%—abv av	1.08—abv av	1.07

	2000	1999	1998	1997	1996	1995	1994	1993	1992	1991
Return (%)	-7.4	19.9	27.1	20.0	17.9	29.1	6.4	15.5	7.6	44.3
Differ from Category (+/-)	-10.9	1.0	12.8	-7.1	-4.4	-1.3	6.6	0.9	-5.0	6.7
Return, Tax-Adjusted (%)	-13.1	18.3	25.1	18.8	16.5	27.6	4.2	12.2	5.2	42.1

PER SHARE DATA

	2000	1999	1998	1997	1996	1995	1994	1993	1992	1991
Dividends, Net Income ($)	0.00	0.00	0.00	0.00	0.01	0.03	0.02	0.03	0.04	0.07
Distrib'ns, Cap Gain ($)	5.78	1.43	1.50	0.80	0.54	0.45	0.71	1.04	0.76	0.45
Net Asset Value ($)	12.73	20.10	17.97	15.35	13.48	11.90	9.60	9.73	9.39	9.49
Expense Ratio (%)	na	0.86	0.84	0.84	0.79	0.63	0.71	0.78	0.83	0.90
Yield (%)	0.00	0.00	0.00	0.00	0.07	0.24	0.19	0.27	0.39	0.70
Portfolio Turnover (%)	na	52	37	34	43	40	46	55	27	33
Total Assets (Millions $)	106	220	742	591	501	362	182	149	111	91

PORTFOLIO (as of 6/30/00)

Portfolio Manager: R. Barber, M. Fuller, G. Lash - 1993

Investm't Category: Growth

- ✔ Domestic
- Foreign
- Asset Allocation
- Index
- Sector
- State Specific

Investment Style

- ✔ Large Cap
- ✔ Mid Cap
- Small Cap
- ✔ Growth
- Grth/Val
- Value

Portfolio

4.7%	cash	0.0%	corp bonds
93.5%	stocks	0.0%	gov't bonds
1.3%	pref/conv't pref	0.0%	muni bonds
0.5%	conv't bds/wrnts	0.0%	other

SHAREHOLDER INFORMATION

Minimum Investment

Initial: $5,000 Subsequent: $1,000

Minimum IRA Investment

Initial: $2,000 Subsequent: $1,000

Maximum Fees

Load: 1.00% redemption 12b-1: 0.25%

Other: redemption fee applies for 6 months

Services

- ✔ IRA
- ✔ Keogh
- ✔ Telephone Exchange

Wm Blair: Intl Grth/N

800-742-7272, 312-364-8000
www.wmblair.com

(WBIGX)

International Stock

PERFORMANCE — fund inception date: 10/1/92

	3yr Annual	5yr Annual	10yr Annual	Bull	Bear
Return (%)	26.2	19.1	na	122.1	-18.1
Differ from Category (+/-)	17.3 high	10.8 high	na	31.2 high	5.9 abv av

Standard Deviation	Category Risk Index	Beta
22.6%—abv av	1.00—av	0.77

	2000	1999	1998	1997	1996	1995	1994	1993	1992	1991
Return (%)	-8.1	96.2	11.4	8.3	10.2	7.2	0.0	33.8	—	—
Differ from Category (+/-)	11.3	35.5	5.6	7.0	-4.3	-2.1	3.1	-6.4	—	—
Return, Tax-Adjusted (%)	-11.5	90.0	11.3	5.4	9.1	6.7	-1.7	32.7	—	—

PER SHARE DATA

	2000	1999	1998	1997	1996	1995	1994	1993	1992	1991
Dividends, Net Income ($)	0.07	0.00	0.02	0.07	0.06	0.13	0.02	0.03	—	—
Distrib'ns, Cap Gain ($)	3.97	4.49	0.00	1.86	0.42	0.00	0.78	0.32	—	—
Net Asset Value ($)	17.93	24.03	14.62	13.14	13.95	13.12	12.36	13.18	—	—
Expense Ratio (%)	na	1.35	1.36	1.43	1.44	1.50	1.51	1.71	—	—
Yield (%)	0.31	0.00	0.13	0.46	0.41	0.99	0.15	0.22	—	—
Portfolio Turnover (%)	na	122	98	102	89	72	40	83	—	—
Total Assets (Millions $)	104	38	139	128	105	89	71	40	—	—

PORTFOLIO (as of 6/30/00)

Portfolio Manager: W. George Greig - 1996

Investm't Category: International Stock

Domestic	Index
✔ Foreign	Sector
Asset Allocation	State Specific

Investment Style

Large Cap	Mid Cap	Small Cap
Growth	Grth/Val	Value

Portfolio

8.9%	cash	0.0%	corp bonds
87.0%	stocks	0.0%	gov't bonds
4.1%	pref/conv't pref	0.0%	muni bonds
0.0%	conv't bds/wrnts	0.0%	other

SHAREHOLDER INFORMATION

Minimum Investment
Initial: $5,000 Subsequent: $1,000

Minimum IRA Investment
Initial: $2,000 Subsequent: $1,000

Maximum Fees
Load: 1.00% redemption 12b-1: 0.25%
Other: redemption fee applies for 6 months

Services
✔ IRA
✔ Keogh
✔ Telephone Exchange

Wright Eq: Intl Blue Chip (WIBCX)

800-888-9471, 203-330-5000
www.wisi.com

International Stock

PERFORMANCE — fund inception date: 9/14/89

	3yr Annual	5yr Annual	10yr Annual	Bull	Bear
Return (%)	5.5	7.5	8.8	55.2	-22.1
Differ from Category (+/-)	-3.4 blw av	-0.8 blw av	-0.2 blw av	-35.7 blw av	1.9 av

Standard Deviation	Category Risk Index	Beta
20.0%—abv av	0.88—blw av	0.79

	2000	1999	1998	1997	1996	1995	1994	1993	1992	1991
Return (%)	-18.1	35.1	6.1	1.5	20.7	13.6	-1.6	28.4	-3.9	17.2
Differ from Category (+/-)	1.3	-25.6	0.3	0.2	6.2	4.3	1.5	-11.8	-0.4	4.2
Return, Tax-Adjusted (%)	-18.5	32.2	4.8	0.2	18.5	13.2	-1.8	28.0	-4.1	16.8

PER SHARE DATA

	2000	1999	1998	1997	1996	1995	1994	1993	1992	1991
Dividends, Net Income ($)	0.00	0.00	0.07	0.16	0.10	0.10	0.10	0.07	0.09	0.11
Distrib'ns, Cap Gain ($)	0.40	2.29	0.87	0.74	1.01	0.00	0.00	0.02	0.00	0.00
Net Asset Value ($)	15.18	19.02	16.02	16.02	16.69	14.77	13.09	13.41	10.52	11.04
Expense Ratio (%)	na	1.49	1.35	1.31	1.30	1.29	1.31	1.46	1.51	1.67
Yield (%)	0.00	0.00	0.41	0.95	0.56	0.67	0.76	0.52	0.85	0.99
Portfolio Turnover (%)	na	105	66	37	29	12	12	30	15	12
Total Assets (Millions $)	109	148	193	212	268	237	201	100	75	51

PORTFOLIO (as of 6/30/00)

Portfolio Manager: committee - 1989

Investm't Category: International Stock

Domestic	Index
✔ Foreign	Sector
Asset Allocation	State Specific

Investment Style

Large Cap	Mid Cap	Small Cap
Growth	Grth/Val	Value

Portfolio

8.3%	cash	0.0%	corp bonds
91.7%	stocks	0.0%	gov't bonds
0.0%	pref/conv't pref	0.0%	muni bonds
0.0%	conv't bds/wrnts	0.0%	other

SHAREHOLDER INFORMATION

Minimum Investment
Initial: $1,000 Subsequent: $1

Minimum IRA Investment
Initial: $1,000 Subsequent: $1

Maximum Fees
Load: none 12b-1: 0.25%
Other: none

Services
✔ IRA
✔ Keogh
✔ Telephone Exchange

Wright Eq: Major Blue Chip (WQCEX)

800-888-9471, 203-330-5000
www.wisi.com

Growth

PERFORMANCE — fund inception date: 7/22/85

	3yr Annual	5yr Annual	10yr Annual	Bull	Bear
Return (%)	9.3	15.5	14.8	58.3	-14.1
Differ from Category (+/-)	-1.7 blw av	-0.6 av	-2.0 blw av	8.6 abv av	-8.7 blw av

Standard Deviation	Category Risk Index	Beta
17.9%—av	0.92—blw av	0.96

	2000	1999	1998	1997	1996	1995	1994	1993	1992	1991
Return (%)	-12.4	23.8	20.4	33.8	17.6	28.9	-0.7	0.9	8.0	38.9
Differ from Category (+/-)	-15.9	4.9	6.1	6.7	-4.7	-1.5	-0.5	-13.7	-4.6	1.3
Return, Tax-Adjusted (%)	-13.1	22.8	19.0	27.1	12.1	23.8	-3.5	-0.8	3.2	38.3

PER SHARE DATA

	2000	1999	1998	1997	1996	1995	1994	1993	1992	1991
Dividends, Net Income ($)	0.01	0.04	0.05	0.08	0.12	0.16	0.16	0.16	0.16	0.19
Distrib'ns, Cap Gain ($)	0.58	0.57	0.71	3.96	2.27	1.84	1.05	0.63	2.32	0.00
Net Asset Value ($)	13.70	16.28	13.67	12.02	12.45	12.65	11.39	12.71	13.38	14.73
Expense Ratio (%)	na	1.05	1.05	1.08	1.05	1.05	0.99	0.97	1.01	1.03
Yield (%)	0.07	0.23	0.34	0.50	0.81	1.10	1.28	1.19	1.01	1.28
Portfolio Turnover (%)	na	59	36	89	45	83	55	53	70	9
Total Assets (Millions $)	138	145	50	27	25	49	51	88	80	79

PORTFOLIO (as of 6/30/00)

Portfolio Manager: committee - 1985

Investm't Category: Growth

✔ Domestic	Index
Foreign	Sector
Asset Allocation	State Specific

Investment Style

✔ Large Cap	Mid Cap	Small Cap
Growth	Grth/Val	✔ Value

Portfolio

0.0%	cash	0.0%	corp bonds
100.0%	stocks	0.0%	gov't bonds
0.0%	pref/conv't pref	0.0%	muni bonds
0.0%	conv't bds/wrnts	0.0%	other

SHAREHOLDER INFORMATION

Minimum Investment

Initial: $1,000 Subsequent: $1

Minimum IRA Investment

Initial: $1,000 Subsequent: $1

Maximum Fees

Load: none 12b-1: 0.25%

Other: none

Services

✔ IRA

Keogh

✔ Telephone Exchange

Wright Eq: Sel Blue Chip (WSBEX)

800-888-9471, 203-330-5000
www.wisi.com

Growth

PERFORMANCE — fund inception date: 1/4/83

	3yr Annual	5yr Annual	10yr Annual	Bull	Bear
Return (%)	5.4	13.0	12.9	29.3	-4.5
Differ from Category (+/-)	-5.6 low	-3.1 blw av	-3.9 low	-20.4 blw av	0.9 av

Standard Deviation	Category Risk Index	Beta
20.6%—abv av	1.06—av	0.93

	2000	1999	1998	1997	1996	1995	1994	1993	1992	1991
Return (%)	10.7	5.7	0.1	32.6	18.5	30.3	-3.5	2.0	4.7	35.9
Differ from Category (+/-)	7.2	-13.2	-14.2	5.5	-3.8	-0.1	-3.3	-12.6	-7.9	-1.7
Return, Tax-Adjusted (%)	6.3	1.8	-1.5	28.1	14.7	27.8	-4.6	1.5	-0.4	32.8

PER SHARE DATA

	2000	1999	1998	1997	1996	1995	1994	1993	1992	1991
Dividends, Net Income ($)	0.00	0.05	0.09	0.14	0.20	0.20	0.18	0.17	0.20	0.25
Distrib'ns, Cap Gain ($)	3.29	3.26	1.43	3.69	1.99	0.95	0.36	0.00	2.91	1.23
Net Asset Value ($)	13.43	15.13	17.63	19.20	17.73	16.83	13.85	14.92	14.79	17.18
Expense Ratio (%)	na	1.16	1.11	1.08	1.04	1.04	1.03	1.03	1.02	1.35
Yield (%)	0.00	0.27	0.47	0.61	1.01	1.12	1.26	1.13	1.12	1.35
Portfolio Turnover (%)	na	106	78	28	43	44	72	28	77	72
Total Assets (Millions $)	49	74	221	259	205	217	187	175	153	167

PORTFOLIO (as of 6/30/00)

Portfolio Manager: committee - 1983

Investm't Category: Growth

✔ Domestic — Index
Foreign — Sector
Asset Allocation — State Specific

Investment Style

Large Cap — ✔ Mid Cap — Small Cap
Growth — ✔ Grth/Val — Value

Portfolio

-0.9% cash — 0.0% corp bonds
100.9% stocks — 0.0% gov't bonds
0.0% pref/conv't pref — 0.0% muni bonds
0.0% conv't bds/wrnts — 0.0% other

SHAREHOLDER INFORMATION

Minimum Investment
Initial: $1,000 — Subsequent: $1

Minimum IRA Investment
Initial: $1,000 — Subsequent: $1

Maximum Fees
Load: none — 12b-1: 0.25%
Other: none

Services
✔ IRA
Keogh
✔ Telephone Exchange

Yacktman (YACKX)

800-525-8258, 312-201-9480
www.yacktman.com

Growth

PERFORMANCE — fund inception date: 7/2/92

	3yr Annual	5yr Annual	10yr Annual	Bull	Bear
Return (%)	-1.7	7.1	na	-0.5	21.0
Differ from Category (+/-)	-12.7 low	-9.0 low	na	-50.2 low	26.4 high

Standard Deviation	Category Risk Index	Beta
19.3%—abv av	0.99—av	0.67

	2000	1999	1998	1997	1996	1995	1994	1993	1992	1991
Return (%)	13.4	-16.9	0.6	18.2	26.0	30.4	8.7	-6.5	—	—
Differ from Category (+/-)	9.9	-35.8	-13.7	-8.9	3.7	0.0	8.9	-21.1	—	—
Return, Tax-Adjusted (%)	11.4	-17.4	-3.1	15.2	21.4	27.3	7.4	-7.0	—	—

PER SHARE DATA

	2000	1999	1998	1997	1996	1995	1994	1993	1992	1991
Dividends, Net Income ($)	0.06	0.09	0.13	0.22	0.23	0.22	0.21	0.14	—	—
Distrib'ns, Cap Gain ($)	0.81	0.15	2.37	1.50	1.64	0.77	0.12	0.00	—	—
Net Asset Value ($)	9.80	9.40	11.61	14.05	13.34	12.09	10.05	9.56	—	—
Expense Ratio (%)	na	0.71	1.14	0.86	0.90	0.89	1.07	1.18	—	—
Yield (%)	0.56	0.94	0.92	1.41	1.53	1.71	2.06	1.46	—	—
Portfolio Turnover (%)	na	4	14	69	58	55	49	61	—	—
Total Assets (Millions $)	80	109	307	1,082	755	566	295	143	—	—

PORTFOLIO (as of 6/30/00)

Portfolio Manager: Donald Yacktman - 1992

Investm't Category: Growth

✔ Domestic	Index
✔ Foreign	Sector
Asset Allocation	State Specific

Investment Style

✔ Large Cap	✔ Mid Cap	✔ Small Cap
Growth	Grth/Val	✔ Value

Portfolio

7.9%	cash	0.0%	corp bonds
92.2%	stocks	0.0%	gov't bonds
0.0%	pref/conv't pref	0.0%	muni bonds
0.0%	conv't bds/wrnts	0.0%	other

SHAREHOLDER INFORMATION

Minimum Investment
Initial: $2,500 Subsequent: $100

Minimum IRA Investment
Initial: $500 Subsequent: $100

Maximum Fees
Load: none 12b-1: none
Other: none

Services
✔ IRA
✔ Keogh
✔ Telephone Exchange

Individual Fund Listings

Bond Funds

1838 Fixed Income (ETFIX)

877-367-1838, 610-293-4300
www.1838ia.com

General Bond

PERFORMANCE AND PER SHARE DATA — fund inception date: 9/2/97

	3yr Annual	5yr Annual	10yr Annual	Category Risk Index
Return (%)	5.4	na	na	1.01—av
Differ from Category (+/-)	-0.1 av	na	na	**Avg Mat** 7.6 yrs

	2000	1999	1998	1997	1996	1995	1994	1993	1992	1991
Return (%)	10.4	-0.7	7.0	—	—	—	—	—	—	—
Differ from Category (+/-)	0.7	-0.7	-0.3	—	—	—	—	—	—	—
Return, Tax-Adjusted (%)	7.8	-2.7	4.6	—	—	—	—	—	—	—
Dividends, Net Income ($)	0.63	0.53	0.59	—	—	—	—	—	—	—
Expense Ratio (%)	na	0.61	0.75	—	—	—	—	—	—	—
Yield (%)	6.31	5.49	5.75	—	—	—	—	—	—	—

SHAREHOLDER INFORMATION

Minimum Investment
Initial: $1,000 IRA: $1
Subsequent: $1 IRA: $1

Maximum Fees
Load: none 12b-1: none
Other: none

ABN AMRO: Fxd Inc/Cmn (RTFTX)

800-443-4725, 312-855-3350
www.abnamrofunds-usa.com

General Bond

PERFORMANCE AND PER SHARE DATA — fund inception date: 1/4/93

	3yr Annual	5yr Annual	10yr Annual	Category Risk Index
Return (%)	5.0	5.5	na	1.04—av
Differ from Category (+/-)	-0.5 low	-0.1 blw av	na	**Avg Mat** 8.2 yrs

	2000	1999	1998	1997	1996	1995	1994	1993	1992	1991
Return (%)	10.6	-2.1	7.1	9.2	3.4	17.7	-3.8	—	—	—
Differ from Category (+/-)	0.9	-2.1	-0.2	0.8	-0.1	1.5	-1.1	—	—	—
Return, Tax-Adjusted (%)	8.1	-4.2	4.6	6.8	1.1	15.2	-5.8	—	—	—
Dividends, Net Income ($)	0.59	0.56	0.58	0.60	0.59	0.58	0.54	—	—	—
Expense Ratio (%)	na	0.69	0.72	0.71	0.98	0.99	0.98	—	—	—
Yield (%)	5.92	5.85	5.53	5.79	5.86	5.62	5.80	—	—	—

SHAREHOLDER INFORMATION

Minimum Investment
Initial: $2,000 IRA: $1,000
Subsequent: $100 IRA: $100

Maximum Fees
Load: none 12b-1: none
Other: none

AMF Adjust Rate Mortgage (ASARX)

800-527-3713, 312-573-9354
www.amffunds.com

Mortgage-Backed Bond

PERFORMANCE AND PER SHARE DATA **fund inception date: 9/18/91**

	3yr Annual	5yr Annual	10yr Annual	Category Risk Index	
Return (%)	5.6	5.8	na	0.23—low	
Differ from Category (+/-)	0.0 blw av	-0.1 av	na	**Avg Mat**	4.0 yrs

	2000	1999	1998	1997	1996	1995	1994	1993	1992	1991
Return (%)	7.1	4.6	5.1	6.5	5.9	9.1	1.9	4.7	4.4	—
Differ from Category (+/-)	-2.8	3.6	-1.1	-2.0	1.7	-5.8	3.2	-1.7	-2.1	—
Return, Tax-Adjusted (%)	4.6	2.4	2.9	4.1	3.5	6.6	0.0	3.0	2.8	—
Dividends, Net Income ($)	0.62	0.53	0.55	0.60	0.59	0.61	0.46	0.42	0.49	—
Expense Ratio (%)	na	0.48	0.49	0.50	0.47	0.48	0.47	0.46	0.44	—
Yield (%)	6.26	5.38	5.54	6.01	5.92	6.11	4.73	4.20	4.92	—

SHAREHOLDER INFORMATION

Minimum Investment
Initial: $10,000 IRA: na
Subsequent: $1 IRA: na

Maximum Fees
Load: none 12b-1: 0.15%
Other: none

AMF Interm Mortgage Sec (ASCPX)

800-527-3713, 312-573-9354
www.amffunds.com

Mortgage-Backed Bond

PERFORMANCE AND PER SHARE DATA **fund inception date: 12/1/86**

	3yr Annual	5yr Annual	10yr Annual	Category Risk Index	
Return (%)	5.9	5.8	7.1	0.90—blw av	
Differ from Category (+/-)	0.3 high	-0.1 blw av	0.0 av	**Avg Mat**	4.9 yrs

	2000	1999	1998	1997	1996	1995	1994	1993	1992	1991
Return (%)	9.7	1.4	6.8	8.3	2.8	13.8	-1.6	6.8	7.8	16.1
Differ from Category (+/-)	-0.2	0.4	0.6	-0.2	-1.4	-1.1	-0.3	0.4	1.3	1.4
Return, Tax-Adjusted (%)	7.2	-0.8	4.4	5.5	0.3	11.1	-3.7	4.4	5.6	13.4
Dividends, Net Income ($)	0.58	0.54	0.58	0.65	0.61	0.62	0.55	0.58	0.69	0.79
Expense Ratio (%)	na	0.48	0.49	0.49	0.44	0.38	0.39	0.37	0.43	0.63
Yield (%)	6.09	5.84	6.01	6.77	6.43	6.30	5.97	5.84	7.01	8.06

SHAREHOLDER INFORMATION

Minimum Investment
Initial: $10,000 IRA: na
Subsequent: $1 IRA: na

Maximum Fees
Load: none 12b-1: 0.15%
Other: none

AMF Short US Gov't Sec (ASITX)

800-527-3713, 312-573-9354
www.amffunds.com

Government Bond

PERFORMANCE AND PER SHARE DATA **fund inception date: 11/26/82**

	3yr Annual	5yr Annual	10yr Annual	Category Risk Index
Return (%)	5.5	5.3	6.1	0.43—low
Differ from Category (+/-)	-0.7 blw av	-0.6 blw av	-1.5 low	**Avg Mat** 1.5 yrs

	2000	1999	1998	1997	1996	1995	1994	1993	1992	1991
Return (%)	7.7	2.3	6.6	6.2	3.6	11.3	0.3	5.7	6.5	11.8
Differ from Category (+/-)	-6.1	5.3	-2.5	-3.6	1.5	-7.5	3.9	-4.9	-0.1	-3.1
Return, Tax-Adjusted (%)	5.3	0.2	4.3	3.8	1.2	8.7	-1.7	3.5	4.3	9.3
Dividends, Net Income ($)	0.61	0.55	0.60	0.62	0.63	0.66	0.57	0.58	0.74	0.82
Expense Ratio (%)	na	0.49	0.50	0.49	0.48	0.49	0.47	0.48	0.50	0.51
Yield (%)	5.83	5.34	5.66	5.88	5.98	6.12	5.52	5.35	6.84	7.54

SHAREHOLDER INFORMATION

Minimum Investment
Initial: $10,000 IRA: na
Subsequent: $1 IRA: na

Maximum Fees
Load: none 12b-1: 0.15%
Other: none

AMF US Gov't Mortgage Sec (ASMTX)

800-527-3713, 312-573-9354
www.amffunds.com

Mortgage-Backed Bond

PERFORMANCE AND PER SHARE DATA **fund inception date: 1/23/84**

	3yr Annual	5yr Annual	10yr Annual	Category Risk Index
Return (%)	5.9	6.0	7.1	1.04—av
Differ from Category (+/-)	0.3 abv av	0.1 abv av	0.0 av	**Avg Mat** 8.1 yrs

	2000	1999	1998	1997	1996	1995	1994	1993	1992	1991
Return (%)	10.4	0.5	7.0	9.6	2.8	16.1	-2.3	6.8	6.4	14.7
Differ from Category (+/-)	0.5	-0.5	0.8	1.1	-1.4	1.2	-1.0	0.4	-0.1	0.0
Return, Tax-Adjusted (%)	7.7	-1.8	4.4	6.7	0.1	13.1	-4.9	3.6	4.0	12.0
Dividends, Net Income ($)	0.67	0.64	0.68	0.76	0.74	0.76	0.73	0.80	0.88	0.94
Expense Ratio (%)	na	0.52	0.53	0.53	0.52	0.53	0.51	0.51	0.53	0.54
Yield (%)	6.39	6.31	6.34	7.12	7.08	6.96	7.22	7.13	7.80	8.20

SHAREHOLDER INFORMATION

Minimum Investment
Initial: $10,000 IRA: na
Subsequent: $1 IRA: na

Maximum Fees
Load: none 12b-1: 0.15%
Other: none

Alleghany: Chicago Bd/N (CHTBX)

800-992-8151, 312-223-2000
www.alleghanyfunds.com

General Bond

PERFORMANCE AND PER SHARE DATA **fund inception date: 12/13/93**

	3yr Annual	5yr Annual	10yr Annual	Category Risk Index
Return (%)	5.9	6.1	na	0.94—blw av
Differ from Category (+/-)	0.4 abv av	0.5 high	na	**Avg Mat** 9.1 yrs

	2000	1999	1998	1997	1996	1995	1994	1993	1992	1991
Return (%)	10.8	-0.4	7.6	8.9	3.8	17.5	-2.8	—	—	—
Differ from Category (+/-)	1.1	-0.4	0.3	0.5	0.3	1.3	-0.1	—	—	—
Return, Tax-Adjusted (%)	8.1	-2.7	5.1	6.4	1.5	14.8	-5.0	—	—	—
Dividends, Net Income ($)	0.64	0.61	0.60	0.60	0.58	0.60	0.58	—	—	—
Expense Ratio (%)	na	0.80	0.80	0.80	0.80	0.80	0.80	—	—	—
Yield (%)	6.45	6.38	5.84	5.93	5.88	5.95	6.35	—	—	—

SHAREHOLDER INFORMATION

Minimum Investment
Initial: $2,500 IRA: $500
Subsequent: $1 IRA: $1

Maximum Fees
Load: none 12b-1: 0.25%
Other: none

Amer Cent: AZ Intm Muni/Inv (BEAMX)

800-345-2021, 816-531-5575
www.americancentury.com

Tax-Exempt Bond

PERFORMANCE AND PER SHARE DATA **fund inception date: 4/11/94**

	3yr Annual	5yr Annual	10yr Annual	Category Risk Index
Return (%)	4.7	4.9	na	0.85—blw av
Differ from Category (+/-)	0.9 abv av	0.0 av	na	**Avg Mat** 9.7 yrs

	2000	1999	1998	1997	1996	1995	1994	1993	1992	1991
Return (%)	9.7	-0.9	5.8	6.8	3.7	13.1	—	—	—	—
Differ from Category (+/-)	0.3	1.7	0.2	-1.4	0.0	-2.0	—	—	—	—
Return, Tax-Adjusted (%)	9.7	-0.9	5.6	6.7	3.7	13.1	—	—	—	—
Dividends, Net Income ($)	0.49	0.46	0.46	0.45	0.47	0.52	—	—	—	—
Expense Ratio (%)	0.51	0.51	0.54	0.79	0.14	0.00	—	—	—	—
Yield (%)	4.60	4.50	4.24	4.19	4.48	4.91	—	—	—	—

SHAREHOLDER INFORMATION

Minimum Investment
Initial: $2,500 IRA: na
Subsequent: $50 IRA: na

Maximum Fees
Load: none 12b-1: none
Other: none

Amer Cent: Bond/Inv (TWLBX)

800-345-2021, 816-531-5575
www.americancentury.com

Corporate Bond

PERFORMANCE AND PER SHARE DATA **fund inception date: 3/2/87**

	3yr Annual	5yr Annual	10yr Annual	Category Risk Index
Return (%)	4.5	4.9	7.1	1.12—abv av
Differ from Category (+/-)	-0.5 blw av	-0.8 low	-1.0 blw av	**Avg Mat** 8.1 yrs

	2000	1999	1998	1997	1996	1995	1994	1993	1992	1991
Return (%)	9.7	-2.1	6.5	8.7	2.4	20.2	-4.5	10.1	5.5	17.4
Differ from Category (+/-)	1.7	-3.4	0.6	-0.4	-3.1	2.3	-2.2	-1.7	-3.8	-0.3
Return, Tax-Adjusted (%)	7.1	-4.2	4.2	6.2	-0.1	17.4	-6.8	9.7	3.0	14.9
Dividends, Net Income ($)	0.57	0.54	0.56	0.59	0.59	0.60	0.58	0.62	0.63	0.73
Expense Ratio (%)	na	0.80	0.80	0.80	0.79	0.78	0.88	1.00	0.98	0.96
Yield (%)	6.15	6.00	5.74	6.07	6.14	6.01	6.55	6.16	6.39	7.26

SHAREHOLDER INFORMATION

Minimum Investment
Initial: $2,500 IRA: $1,000
Subsequent: $250 IRA: $250

Maximum Fees
Load: none 12b-1: none
Other: none

Amer Cent: CA Hi Yield (BCHYX)

800-345-2021, 816-531-5575
www.americancentury.com

Tax-Exempt Bond

PERFORMANCE AND PER SHARE DATA **fund inception date: 12/30/86**

	3yr Annual	5yr Annual	10yr Annual	Category Risk Index
Return (%)	5.1	6.3	7.6	1.12—abv av
Differ from Category (+/-)	1.3 high	1.4 high	1.1 high	**Avg Mat** 19.3 yrs

	2000	1999	1998	1997	1996	1995	1994	1993	1992	1991
Return (%)	12.7	-3.3	6.7	10.5	5.8	18.2	-5.3	13.1	9.1	10.9
Differ from Category (+/-)	3.3	-0.7	1.1	2.3	2.1	3.1	-0.4	1.4	0.7	-0.4
Return, Tax-Adjusted (%)	12.7	-3.3	6.4	10.2	5.8	18.2	-5.3	12.7	9.1	10.9
Dividends, Net Income ($)	0.52	0.49	0.50	0.53	0.55	0.56	0.55	0.57	0.57	0.59
Expense Ratio (%)	0.54	0.54	0.54	0.50	0.51	0.51	0.51	0.55	0.56	0.50
Yield (%)	5.41	5.43	5.04	5.35	5.80	5.89	6.44	5.86	6.25	6.62

SHAREHOLDER INFORMATION

Minimum Investment
Initial: $5,000 IRA: na
Subsequent: $1 IRA: na

Maximum Fees
Load: none 12b-1: none
Other: none

Amer Cent: CA Ins TF/Inv (BCINX)

800-345-2021, 816-531-5575
www.americancentury.com

Tax-Exempt Bond

PERFORMANCE AND PER SHARE DATA **fund inception date: 12/30/86**

	3yr Annual	5yr Annual	10yr Annual	Category Risk Index
Return (%)	5.1	5.6	7.2	1.34—high
Differ from Category (+/-)	1.3 high	0.7 high	0.7 high	**Avg Mat** 16.6 yrs

	2000	1999	1998	1997	1996	1995	1994	1993	1992	1991
Return (%)	14.5	-4.4	6.0	9.3	3.7	19.0	-6.5	13.4	9.1	11.2
Differ from Category (+/-)	5.1	-1.8	0.4	1.1	0.0	3.9	-1.6	1.7	0.7	-0.1
Return, Tax-Adjusted (%)	14.5	-4.4	5.9	9.0	3.7	19.0	-6.5	12.6	9.1	11.2
Dividends, Net Income ($)	0.49	0.49	0.50	0.52	0.53	0.53	0.52	0.54	0.66	0.57
Expense Ratio (%)	0.51	0.51	0.51	0.48	0.49	0.50	0.49	0.52	0.55	0.59
Yield (%)	4.68	5.10	4.72	4.89	5.17	5.09	5.63	5.04	6.63	5.85

SHAREHOLDER INFORMATION

Minimum Investment
Initial: $5,000 IRA: na
Subsequent: $1 IRA: na

Maximum Fees
Load: none 12b-1: none
Other: none

Amer Cent: CA Intm TF/Inv (BCITX)

800-345-2021, 816-531-5575
www.americancentury.com

Tax-Exempt Bond

PERFORMANCE AND PER SHARE DATA **fund inception date: 11/9/83**

	3yr Annual	5yr Annual	10yr Annual	Category Risk Index
Return (%)	4.7	5.2	6.3	0.90—blw av
Differ from Category (+/-)	0.9 abv av	0.3 av	-0.2 blw av	**Avg Mat** 8.4 yrs

	2000	1999	1998	1997	1996	1995	1994	1993	1992	1991
Return (%)	10.1	-1.1	5.5	7.9	4.2	13.5	-3.7	10.6	7.0	10.3
Differ from Category (+/-)	0.7	1.5	-0.1	-0.3	0.5	-1.6	1.2	-1.1	-1.4	-1.0
Return, Tax-Adjusted (%)	10.1	-1.1	5.3	7.6	4.1	13.5	-3.7	10.3	6.9	10.3
Dividends, Net Income ($)	0.50	0.48	0.51	0.57	0.54	0.54	0.53	0.55	0.57	0.59
Expense Ratio (%)	0.51	0.51	0.51	0.48	0.48	0.48	0.48	0.50	0.52	0.55
Yield (%)	4.45	4.49	4.47	4.98	4.82	4.79	5.08	4.79	5.23	5.49

SHAREHOLDER INFORMATION

Minimum Investment
Initial: $5,000 IRA: na
Subsequent: $1 IRA: na

Maximum Fees
Load: none 12b-1: none
Other: none

Amer Cent: CA Long Tm/Inv (BCLTX)

800-345-2021, 816-531-5575
www.americancentury.com

Tax-Exempt Bond

PERFORMANCE AND PER SHARE DATA **fund inception date: 11/9/83**

	3yr Annual	5yr Annual	10yr Annual	Category Risk Index
Return (%)	4.9	5.6	7.3	1.38—high
Differ from Category (+/-)	1.1 high	0.7 high	0.8 high	**Avg Mat** 17.0 yrs

	2000	1999	1998	1997	1996	1995	1994	1993	1992	1991
Return (%)	14.9	-5.2	6.2	9.7	3.5	19.7	-6.5	13.7	8.1	11.7
Differ from Category (+/-)	5.5	-2.6	0.6	1.5	-0.2	4.6	-1.6	2.0	-0.3	0.4
Return, Tax-Adjusted (%)	14.9	-5.2	6.0	9.3	3.4	19.7	-6.6	12.6	7.4	11.7
Dividends, Net Income ($)	0.55	0.55	0.57	0.60	0.61	0.61	0.61	0.65	0.68	0.69
Expense Ratio (%)	0.51	0.51	0.51	0.48	0.48	0.49	0.48	0.49	0.52	0.55
Yield (%)	4.81	5.25	4.86	5.09	5.38	5.27	5.94	5.38	5.92	6.11

SHAREHOLDER INFORMATION

Minimum Investment
Initial: $5,000 IRA: na
Subsequent: $1 IRA: na

Maximum Fees
Load: none 12b-1: none
Other: none

Amer Cent: CA Ltd TF/Inv (BCSTX)

800-345-2021, 816-531-5575
www.americancentury.com

Tax-Exempt Bond

PERFORMANCE AND PER SHARE DATA **fund inception date: 6/1/92**

	3yr Annual	5yr Annual	10yr Annual	Category Risk Index
Return (%)	4.3	4.4	na	0.50—low
Differ from Category (+/-)	0.5 av	-0.5 low	na	**Avg Mat** 3.5 yrs

	2000	1999	1998	1997	1996	1995	1994	1993	1992	1991
Return (%)	7.0	1.0	4.9	5.3	3.9	8.3	-0.6	5.9	—	—
Differ from Category (+/-)	-2.4	3.6	-0.7	-2.9	0.2	-6.8	4.3	-5.8	—	—
Return, Tax-Adjusted (%)	7.0	1.0	4.9	5.3	3.9	8.3	-0.6	5.8	—	—
Dividends, Net Income ($)	0.42	0.39	0.40	0.42	0.43	0.42	0.38	0.37	—	—
Expense Ratio (%)	na	0.51	0.52	0.49	0.49	0.51	0.51	0.36	—	—
Yield (%)	4.01	3.83	3.82	4.05	4.19	4.08	3.83	3.56	—	—

SHAREHOLDER INFORMATION

Minimum Investment
Initial: $5,000 IRA: na
Subsequent: $1 IRA: na

Maximum Fees
Load: none 12b-1: none
Other: none

Amer Cent: FL Intm Muni/Inv (ACBFX)

800-345-2021, 816-531-5575
www.americancentury.com

Tax-Exempt Bond

PERFORMANCE AND PER SHARE DATA **fund inception date: 4/11/94**

	3yr Annual	5yr Annual	10yr Annual	Category Risk Index
Return (%)	5.1	5.4	na	0.86—blw av
Differ from Category (+/-)	1.3 high	0.5 abv av	na	**Avg Mat** 9.8 yrs

	2000	1999	1998	1997	1996	1995	1994	1993	1992	1991
Return (%)	9.9	-0.6	6.4	8.1	3.6	13.5	—	—	—	—
Differ from Category (+/-)	0.5	2.0	0.8	-0.1	-0.1	-1.6	—	—	—	—
Return, Tax-Adjusted (%)	9.9	-0.6	6.1	7.8	3.5	13.4	—	—	—	—
Dividends, Net Income ($)	0.47	0.43	0.44	0.45	0.48	0.53	—	—	—	—
Expense Ratio (%)	0.51	0.51	0.54	0.54	0.13	0.00	—	—	—	—
Yield (%)	4.42	4.24	4.09	4.21	4.63	5.04	—	—	—	—

SHAREHOLDER INFORMATION

Minimum Investment
Initial: $2,500 IRA: na
Subsequent: $50 IRA: na

Maximum Fees
Load: none 12b-1: none
Other: none

Amer Cent: GNMA/Inv (BGNMX)

800-345-2021, 816-531-5575
www.americancentury.com

Mortgage-Backed Bond

PERFORMANCE AND PER SHARE DATA **fund inception date: 9/23/85**

	3yr Annual	5yr Annual	10yr Annual	Category Risk Index
Return (%)	5.8	6.2	7.4	0.98—blw av
Differ from Category (+/-)	0.2 abv av	0.3 high	0.3 high	**Avg Mat** 23.3 yrs

	2000	1999	1998	1997	1996	1995	1994	1993	1992	1991
Return (%)	10.5	0.8	6.3	8.7	5.2	15.8	-1.6	6.5	7.6	15.5
Differ from Category (+/-)	0.6	-0.2	0.1	0.2	1.0	0.9	-0.3	0.1	1.1	0.8
Return, Tax-Adjusted (%)	7.8	-1.5	3.9	6.0	2.5	12.8	-4.0	3.9	5.2	12.8
Dividends, Net Income ($)	0.68	0.64	0.64	0.69	0.71	0.74	0.67	0.70	0.81	0.86
Expense Ratio (%)	0.59	0.59	0.58	0.55	0.58	0.58	0.54	0.56	0.62	0.72
Yield (%)	6.48	6.31	5.98	6.46	6.76	6.92	6.76	6.49	7.51	7.96

SHAREHOLDER INFORMATION

Minimum Investment
Initial: $2,500 IRA: $1,000
Subsequent: $50 IRA: $50

Maximum Fees
Load: none 12b-1: none
Other: none

Amer Cent: Intl Bond/Inv (BEGBX)

800-345-2021, 816-531-5575
www.americancentury.com

International Bond

PERFORMANCE AND PER SHARE DATA **fund inception date: 1/7/92**

	3yr Annual	5yr Annual	10yr Annual	Category Risk Index
Return (%)	1.4	0.8	na	1.16—high
Differ from Category (+/-)	-1.8 blw av	-4.4 low	na	**Avg Mat** 6.2 yrs

	2000	1999	1998	1997	1996	1995	1994	1993	1992	1991
Return (%)	-1.1	-10.3	17.8	-5.8	6.3	24.4	1.5	11.7	—	—
Differ from Category (+/-)	-5.6	-14.1	14.2	-9.7	-7.8	7.5	8.7	-3.5	—	—
Return, Tax-Adjusted (%)	-1.5	-11.9	16.7	-6.1	3.5	20.9	-0.7	10.5	—	—
Dividends, Net Income ($)	0.10	0.42	0.17	0.03	0.72	0.90	0.60	0.11	—	—
Expense Ratio (%)	na	0.85	0.84	0.84	0.83	0.72	0.86	0.85	—	—
Yield (%)	0.96	3.90	1.34	0.27	6.03	7.53	5.78	0.99	—	—

SHAREHOLDER INFORMATION

Minimum Investment
Initial: $2,500 IRA: $1,000
Subsequent: $100 IRA: $100

Maximum Fees
Load: none 12b-1: none
Other: none

Amer Cent: Intm Tax-Free/Inv (TWTIX)

800-345-2021, 816-531-5575
www.americancentury.com

Tax-Exempt Bond

PERFORMANCE AND PER SHARE DATA **fund inception date: 3/2/87**

	3yr Annual	5yr Annual	10yr Annual	Category Risk Index
Return (%)	4.8	5.1	6.1	0.85—blw av
Differ from Category (+/-)	1.0 high	0.2 av	-0.4 blw av	**Avg Mat** 10.2 yrs

	2000	1999	1998	1997	1996	1995	1994	1993	1992	1991
Return (%)	9.9	-1.0	5.8	7.4	3.9	11.9	-2.0	9.0	7.1	10.0
Differ from Category (+/-)	0.5	1.6	0.2	-0.8	0.2	-3.2	2.9	-2.7	-1.3	-1.3
Return, Tax-Adjusted (%)	9.9	-1.0	5.6	7.2	3.8	11.7	-2.2	8.9	6.8	10.0
Dividends, Net Income ($)	0.49	0.46	0.48	0.48	0.48	0.48	0.47	0.47	0.47	0.52
Expense Ratio (%)	0.91	0.51	0.51	0.58	0.60	0.60	0.60	0.72	0.98	0.96
Yield (%)	4.68	4.59	4.50	4.51	4.61	4.54	4.71	4.35	4.53	5.14

SHAREHOLDER INFORMATION

Minimum Investment
Initial: $5,000 IRA: na
Subsequent: $50 IRA: na

Maximum Fees
Load: none 12b-1: none
Other: none

Amer Cent: Intm Trs/Inv (CPTNX)

800-345-2021, 816-531-5575
www.americancentury.com

Government Bond

PERFORMANCE AND PER SHARE DATA **fund inception date: 5/16/80**

	3yr Annual	5yr Annual	10yr Annual	Category Risk Index
Return (%)	6.2	6.2	6.9	1.19—abv av
Differ from Category (+/-)	0.0 abv av	0.3 abv av	-0.7 av	**Avg Mat** 5.7 yrs

	2000	1999	1998	1997	1996	1995	1994	1993	1992	1991
Return (%)	12.6	-2.1	8.8	8.3	4.0	13.7	-2.3	7.9	6.5	13.7
Differ from Category (+/-)	-1.2	0.9	-0.3	-1.5	1.9	-5.1	1.3	-2.7	-0.1	-1.2
Return, Tax-Adjusted (%)	10.4	-3.9	6.3	6.0	1.8	11.3	-4.1	5.3	3.6	11.5
Dividends, Net Income ($)	0.55	0.49	0.56	0.58	0.57	0.58	0.50	0.49	0.59	0.71
Expense Ratio (%)	0.51	0.51	0.51	0.51	0.53	0.53	0.51	0.53	0.59	0.73
Yield (%)	5.19	4.91	5.13	5.49	5.52	5.53	5.12	4.54	5.39	6.54

SHAREHOLDER INFORMATION

Minimum Investment
Initial: $2,500 IRA: $1,000
Subsequent: $50 IRA: $50

Maximum Fees
Load: none 12b-1: none
Other: none

Amer Cent: Long Tm TF/Inv (TWTLX)

800-345-2021, 816-531-5575
www.americancentury.com

Tax-Exempt Bond

PERFORMANCE AND PER SHARE DATA **fund inception date: 3/2/87**

	3yr Annual	5yr Annual	10yr Annual	Category Risk Index
Return (%)	4.2	5.0	6.7	1.30—high
Differ from Category (+/-)	0.4 blw av	0.1 av	0.2 av	**Avg Mat** 16.5 yrs

	2000	1999	1998	1997	1996	1995	1994	1993	1992	1991
Return (%)	12.7	-5.0	5.9	9.5	3.1	18.4	-5.5	12.1	7.6	11.1
Differ from Category (+/-)	3.3	-2.4	0.3	1.3	-0.6	3.3	-0.6	0.4	-0.8	-0.2
Return, Tax-Adjusted (%)	12.7	-5.0	5.5	9.0	3.1	18.4	-5.6	12.0	7.1	11.0
Dividends, Net Income ($)	0.53	0.51	0.53	0.54	0.53	0.53	0.51	0.52	0.52	0.57
Expense Ratio (%)	0.51	0.51	0.51	0.58	0.59	0.60	0.60	0.73	0.98	0.96
Yield (%)	5.10	5.25	4.85	4.88	4.98	4.88	5.26	4.66	4.90	5.46

SHAREHOLDER INFORMATION

Minimum Investment
Initial: $5,000 IRA: na
Subsequent: $50 IRA: na

Maximum Fees
Load: none 12b-1: none
Other: none

Amer Cent: Long Trsy/Inv (BLAGX)

800-345-2021, 816-531-5575
www.americancentury.com

Government Bond

PERFORMANCE AND PER SHARE DATA **fund inception date: 9/8/92**

	3yr Annual	5yr Annual	10yr Annual	Category Risk Index
Return (%)	7.1	6.8	na	2.02—high
Differ from Category (+/-)	0.9 high	0.9 high	na	**Avg Mat** 19.1 yrs

	2000	1999	1998	1997	1996	1995	1994	1993	1992	1991
Return (%)	19.4	-8.7	12.7	14.7	-1.3	29.2	-9.2	17.6	—	—
Differ from Category (+/-)	5.6	-5.7	3.6	4.9	-3.4	10.4	-5.6	7.0	—	—
Return, Tax-Adjusted (%)	16.9	-10.6	9.3	12.3	-3.5	26.4	-11.4	13.2	—	—
Dividends, Net Income ($)	0.56	0.54	0.60	0.59	0.60	0.60	0.59	0.65	—	—
Expense Ratio (%)	0.51	0.51	0.54	0.60	0.67	0.67	0.57	0.00	—	—
Yield (%)	5.37	5.85	5.32	5.58	6.13	5.68	6.78	6.01	—	—

SHAREHOLDER INFORMATION

Minimum Investment
Initial: $2,500 IRA: $1,000
Subsequent: $50 IRA: $50

Maximum Fees
Load: none 12b-1: none
Other: none

Amer Cent: Premium Bond/ Inv (ACBPX)

800-345-2021, 816-531-5575
www.americancentury.com

General Bond

PERFORMANCE AND PER SHARE DATA **fund inception date: 4/1/93**

	3yr Annual	5yr Annual	10yr Annual	Category Risk Index
Return (%)	5.7	5.7	na	1.05—abv av
Differ from Category (+/-)	0.2 av	0.1 av	na	**Avg Mat** 8.0 yrs

	2000	1999	1998	1997	1996	1995	1994	1993	1992	1991
Return (%)	11.0	-1.2	7.8	8.8	2.7	20.0	-4.1	—	—	—
Differ from Category (+/-)	1.3	-1.2	0.5	0.4	-0.8	3.8	-1.4	—	—	—
Return, Tax-Adjusted (%)	8.4	-3.4	5.3	6.2	0.3	17.4	-6.2	—	—	—
Dividends, Net Income ($)	0.62	0.58	0.59	0.60	0.61	0.60	0.56	—	—	—
Expense Ratio (%)	0.45	0.45	0.45	0.45	0.43	0.45	0.45	—	—	—
Yield (%)	6.21	6.06	5.71	5.87	6.11	5.81	6.12	—	—	—

SHAREHOLDER INFORMATION

Minimum Investment
Initial: $100,000 IRA: $100,000
Subsequent: $50 IRA: $50

Maximum Fees
Load: none 12b-1: none
Other: none

Amer Cent: Sht Tm Gov't/Inv (TWUSX)

800-345-2021, 816-531-5575
www.americancentury.com

Government Bond

PERFORMANCE AND PER SHARE DATA **fund inception date: 12/15/82**

	3yr Annual	5yr Annual	10yr Annual	Category Risk Index
Return (%)	5.1	5.1	5.5	0.51—blw av
Differ from Category (+/-)	-1.1 low	-0.8 low	-2.1 low	**Avg Mat** 2.4 yrs

	2000	1999	1998	1997	1996	1995	1994	1993	1992	1991
Return (%)	7.8	1.7	6.0	5.9	4.1	10.4	-0.4	4.1	4.3	11.6
Differ from Category (+/-)	-6.0	4.7	-3.1	-3.9	2.0	-8.4	3.2	-6.5	-2.3	-3.3
Return, Tax-Adjusted (%)	5.4	-0.2	3.9	3.7	1.9	8.1	-2.2	3.9	2.9	9.5
Dividends, Net Income ($)	0.54	0.48	0.49	0.51	0.51	0.51	0.44	0.33	0.42	0.60
Expense Ratio (%)	0.59	0.59	0.59	0.68	0.70	0.70	0.81	1.00	0.99	0.99
Yield (%)	5.76	5.20	5.13	5.37	5.39	5.32	4.80	3.41	4.38	6.23

SHAREHOLDER INFORMATION

Minimum Investment
Initial: $2,500 IRA: $1,000
Subsequent: $50 IRA: $50

Maximum Fees
Load: none 12b-1: none
Other: none

Amer Cent: Sht Tm Trsy/Inv (BSTAX)

800-345-2021, 816-531-5575
www.americancentury.com

Government Bond

PERFORMANCE AND PER SHARE DATA **fund inception date: 9/8/92**

	3yr Annual	5yr Annual	10yr Annual	Category Risk Index
Return (%)	5.2	5.1	na	0.43—low
Differ from Category (+/-)	-1.0 low	-0.8 low	na	**Avg Mat** 1.4 yrs

	2000	1999	1998	1997	1996	1995	1994	1993	1992	1991
Return (%)	7.1	2.1	6.4	6.0	4.1	9.9	0.1	5.3	—	—
Differ from Category (+/-)	-6.7	5.1	-2.7	-3.8	2.0	-8.9	3.7	-5.3	—	—
Return, Tax-Adjusted (%)	5.0	0.3	4.3	3.8	1.8	7.6	-1.6	3.6	—	—
Dividends, Net Income ($)	0.51	0.45	0.50	0.52	0.51	0.54	0.44	0.38	—	—
Expense Ratio (%)	0.51	0.51	0.55	0.61	0.67	0.67	0.58	0.00	—	—
Yield (%)	5.19	4.65	5.04	5.30	5.18	5.42	4.59	3.78	—	—

SHAREHOLDER INFORMATION

Minimum Investment
Initial: $2,500 IRA: $1,000
Subsequent: $50 IRA: $50

Maximum Fees
Load: none 12b-1: none
Other: none

Amer Cent: Target 2005/Inv (BTFIX)

800-345-2021, 816-531-5575
www.americancentury.com

Government Bond

PERFORMANCE AND PER SHARE DATA **fund inception date: 3/25/85**

	3yr Annual	5yr Annual	10yr Annual	Category Risk Index
Return (%)	8.1	6.8	10.5	2.26—high
Differ from Category (+/-)	1.9 high	0.9 high	2.9 high	**Avg Mat** 5.3 yrs

	2000	1999	1998	1997	1996	1995	1994	1993	1992	1991
Return (%)	19.9	-6.3	12.5	11.6	-1.2	32.6	-8.9	21.5	9.5	21.4
Differ from Category (+/-)	6.1	-3.3	3.4	1.8	-3.3	13.8	-5.3	10.9	2.9	6.5
Return, Tax-Adjusted (%)	17.3	-8.9	10.0	8.9	-3.9	30.1	-11.6	11.5	6.7	19.3
Dividends, Net Income ($)	0.00	0.00	0.00	0.00	0.00	0.00	0.00	0.00	0.00	0.00
Expense Ratio (%)	0.59	0.59	0.59	0.57	0.58	0.70	0.64	0.62	0.63	0.70
Yield (%)	0.00	0.00	0.00	0.00	0.00	0.00	0.00	0.00	0.00	0.00

SHAREHOLDER INFORMATION

Minimum Investment
Initial: $2,500 IRA: $1,000
Subsequent: $50 IRA: $50

Maximum Fees
Load: none 12b-1: none
Other: none

Amer Cent: Target 2010/Inv (BTTNX)

800-345-2021, 816-531-5575
www.americancentury.com

Government Bond

PERFORMANCE AND PER SHARE DATA **fund inception date: 3/25/85**

	3yr Annual	5yr Annual	10yr Annual	Category Risk Index
Return (%)	9.0	7.8	11.9	2.99—high
Differ from Category (+/-)	2.8 high	1.9 high	4.3 high	**Avg Mat** 10.3 yrs

	2000	1999	1998	1997	1996	1995	1994	1993	1992	1991
Return (%)	28.8	-12.1	14.5	16.7	-3.5	42.0	-11.5	26.2	9.7	21.0
Differ from Category (+/-)	15.0	-9.1	5.4	6.9	-5.6	23.2	-7.9	15.6	3.1	6.1
Return, Tax-Adjusted (%)	26.3	-14.3	11.6	14.2	-6.8	40.0	-13.8	18.5	6.3	19.1
Dividends, Net Income ($)	0.00	0.00	0.00	0.00	0.00	0.00	0.00	0.00	0.00	0.00
Expense Ratio (%)	0.59	0.59	0.59	0.62	0.67	0.70	0.68	0.66	0.70	0.70
Yield (%)	0.00	0.00	0.00	0.00	0.00	0.00	0.00	0.00	0.00	0.00

SHAREHOLDER INFORMATION

Minimum Investment
Initial: $2,500 IRA: $1,000
Subsequent: $50 IRA: $50

Maximum Fees
Load: none 12b-1: none
Other: none

Amer Cent: Target 2015/Inv (BTFTX)

800-345-2021, 816-531-5575
www.americancentury.com

Government Bond

PERFORMANCE AND PER SHARE DATA **fund inception date: 9/1/86**

	3yr Annual	5yr Annual	10yr Annual	Category Risk Index
Return (%)	9.1	8.4	13.0	3.34—high
Differ from Category (+/-)	2.9 high	2.5 high	5.4 high	**Avg Mat** 15.4 yrs

	2000	1999	1998	1997	1996	1995	1994	1993	1992	1991
Return (%)	33.5	-14.9	14.4	22.9	-6.0	52.7	-14.0	30.5	7.7	22.4
Differ from Category (+/-)	19.7	-11.9	5.3	13.1	-8.1	33.9	-10.4	19.9	1.1	7.5
Return, Tax-Adjusted (%)	30.8	-17.0	12.3	19.3	-8.6	47.9	-15.0	12.6	5.3	20.3
Dividends, Net Income ($)	0.00	0.00	0.00	0.00	0.00	0.00	0.00	0.00	0.00	0.00
Expense Ratio (%)	0.59	0.59	0.59	0.61	0.65	0.70	0.68	0.63	0.62	0.61
Yield (%)	0.00	0.00	0.00	0.00	0.00	0.00	0.00	0.00	0.00	0.00

SHAREHOLDER INFORMATION

Minimum Investment
Initial: $2,500 IRA: $1,000
Subsequent: $50 IRA: $50

Maximum Fees
Load: none 12b-1: none
Other: none

Amer Cent: Target 2020/Inv (BTTTX)

800-345-2021, 816-531-5575
www.americancentury.com

Government Bond

PERFORMANCE AND PER SHARE DATA **fund inception date: 12/29/89**

	3yr Annual	5yr Annual	10yr Annual	Category Risk Index
Return (%)	9.5	9.1	13.4	5.00—high
Differ from Category (+/-)	3.3 high	3.2 high	5.8 high	**Avg Mat** 20.2 yrs

	2000	1999	1998	1997	1996	1995	1994	1993	1992	1991
Return (%)	48.0	-20.7	12.0	28.6	-8.4	61.3	-17.6	35.6	8.3	17.3
Differ from Category (+/-)	34.2	-17.7	2.9	18.8	-10.5	42.5	-14.0	25.0	1.7	2.4
Return, Tax-Adjusted (%)	43.4	-25.3	4.5	21.9	-10.7	59.9	-18.1	25.7	5.4	15.5
Dividends, Net Income ($)	0.00	0.00	0.00	0.00	0.00	0.00	0.00	0.00	0.00	0.00
Expense Ratio (%)	0.59	0.59	0.59	0.53	0.61	0.70	0.70	0.70	0.66	0.67
Yield (%)	0.00	0.00	0.00	0.00	0.00	0.00	0.00	0.00	0.00	0.00

SHAREHOLDER INFORMATION

Minimum Investment
Initial: $2,500 IRA: $1,000
Subsequent: $50 IRA: $50

Maximum Fees
Load: none 12b-1: none
Other: none

Amer Cent: Target 2025/Inv (BTTRX)

800-345-2021, 816-531-5575
www.americancentury.com

Government Bond

PERFORMANCE AND PER SHARE DATA **fund inception date: 2/15/96**

	3yr Annual	5yr Annual	10yr Annual	Category Risk Index
Return (%)	11.1	na	na	4.80—high
Differ from Category (+/-)	4.9 high	na	na	**Avg Mat** 25.0 yrs

	2000	1999	1998	1997	1996	1995	1994	1993	1992	1991
Return (%)	42.6	-20.8	21.6	32.0	—	—	—	—	—	—
Differ from Category (+/-)	28.8	-17.8	12.5	22.2	—	—	—	—	—	—
Return, Tax-Adjusted (%)	39.0	-22.2	19.2	30.0	—	—	—	—	—	—
Dividends, Net Income ($)	1.99	1.16	1.34	0.72	—	—	—	—	—	—
Expense Ratio (%)	0.59	0.59	0.59	0.62	—	—	—	—	—	—
Yield (%)	6.00	4.70	4.26	2.76	—	—	—	—	—	—

SHAREHOLDER INFORMATION

Minimum Investment
Initial: $2,500 IRA: $1,000
Subsequent: $50 IRA: $50

Maximum Fees
Load: none 12b-1: none
Other: none

Aon: Gov't Securities (AGSYX)

800-266-3637, 804-281-6049

Government Bond

PERFORMANCE AND PER SHARE DATA **fund inception date: 9/3/96**

	3yr Annual	5yr Annual	10yr Annual	Category Risk Index
Return (%)	6.1	na	na	1.30—abv av
Differ from Category (+/-)	-0.1 abv av	na	na	**Avg Mat** 10.3 yrs

	2000	1999	1998	1997	1996	1995	1994	1993	1992	1991
Return (%)	13.2	-4.4	10.5	9.9	—	—	—	—	—	—
Differ from Category (+/-)	-0.6	-1.4	1.4	0.1	—	—	—	—	—	—
Return, Tax-Adjusted (%)	10.7	-6.6	7.6	7.5	—	—	—	—	—	—
Dividends, Net Income ($)	0.58	0.56	0.58	0.60	—	—	—	—	—	—
Expense Ratio (%)	na	0.22	0.23	0.46	—	—	—	—	—	—
Yield (%)	5.69	5.79	5.24	5.68	—	—	—	—	—	—

SHAREHOLDER INFORMATION

Minimum Investment
Initial: $1,000 IRA: $1,000
Subsequent: $100 IRA: $100

Maximum Fees
Load: none 12b-1: none
Other: none

BB&K Int'l Bd (BBIFX)

800-882-8383, 650-571-5800
www.bailard.com

International Bond

PERFORMANCE AND PER SHARE DATA **fund inception date: 10/4/90**

	3yr Annual	5yr Annual	10yr Annual	Category Risk Index
Return (%)	2.5	3.6	5.0	0.57—blw av
Differ from Category (+/-)	-0.7 av	-1.6 av	-0.4 av	**Avg Mat** 6.4 yrs

	2000	1999	1998	1997	1996	1995	1994	1993	1992	1991
Return (%)	1.3	-4.6	11.5	2.6	8.4	20.6	-19.2	14.7	6.9	13.9
Differ from Category (+/-)	-3.2	-8.4	7.9	-1.3	-5.7	3.7	-12.0	-0.5	3.3	-0.8
Return, Tax-Adjusted (%)	-3.3	-5.8	10.3	-1.5	5.0	14.4	-21.6	10.3	3.6	10.7
Dividends, Net Income ($)	0.88	0.25	0.22	0.86	0.70	1.21	0.65	1.11	1.10	1.03
Expense Ratio (%)	1.22	1.26	1.26	1.35	1.22	1.16	1.12	0.42	0.64	0.53
Yield (%)	13.15	3.33	2.70	11.48	8.58	14.79	8.32	10.62	10.89	9.83

SHAREHOLDER INFORMATION

Minimum Investment
Initial: $5,000 IRA: $5,000
Subsequent: $100 IRA: $100

Maximum Fees
Load: none 12b-1: none
Other: none

Babson Bond Tr: Port L (BABIX)

800-422-2766, 816-751-5900
www.babsonfunds.com

General Bond

PERFORMANCE AND PER SHARE DATA **fund inception date: 1/1/45**

	3yr Annual	5yr Annual	10yr Annual	Category Risk Index
Return (%)	5.2	5.5	7.3	1.12—abv av
Differ from Category (+/-)	-0.3 blw av	-0.1 av	0.1 av	**Avg Mat** 8.9 yrs

	2000	1999	1998	1997	1996	1995	1994	1993	1992	1991
Return (%)	9.9	-1.3	7.3	9.2	3.1	15.9	-3.2	11.1	7.9	14.9
Differ from Category (+/-)	0.2	-1.3	0.0	0.8	-0.4	-0.3	-0.5	1.4	1.1	-0.6
Return, Tax-Adjusted (%)	7.4	-3.2	5.0	6.8	0.6	13.2	-5.6	7.5	5.4	12.2
Dividends, Net Income ($)	0.09	0.08	0.09	0.09	0.10	0.10	0.10	0.11	0.12	0.13
Expense Ratio (%)	0.98	0.97	0.97	0.97	0.97	0.97	0.97	0.98	0.99	0.98
Yield (%)	5.88	5.40	5.66	5.73	6.53	6.28	6.80	6.54	7.36	7.97

SHAREHOLDER INFORMATION

Minimum Investment
Initial: $1,000 IRA: $250
Subsequent: $100 IRA: $50

Maximum Fees
Load: none 12b-1: none
Other: none

Bremer Inv: Bond (BBNDX)

800-595-5552, 800-595-5552
www.bremer.com

General Bond

PERFORMANCE AND PER SHARE DATA **fund inception date: 1/27/97**

	3yr Annual	5yr Annual	10yr Annual	Category Risk Index
Return (%)	5.1	na	na	0.85—blw av
Differ from Category (+/-)	-0.4 low	na	na	**Avg Mat** 8.4 yrs

	2000	1999	1998	1997	1996	1995	1994	1993	1992	1991
Return (%)	9.2	-0.4	6.7	—	—	—	—	—	—	—
Differ from Category (+/-)	-0.5	-0.4	-0.6	—	—	—	—	—	—	—
Return, Tax-Adjusted (%)	6.8	-2.4	4.5	—	—	—	—	—	—	—
Dividends, Net Income ($)	0.58	0.54	0.55	—	—	—	—	—	—	—
Expense Ratio (%)	0.91	0.90	0.89	—	—	—	—	—	—	—
Yield (%)	5.81	5.56	5.32	—	—	—	—	—	—	—

SHAREHOLDER INFORMATION

Minimum Investment
Initial: $2,000 IRA: $500
Subsequent: $100 IRA: $100

Maximum Fees
Load: none 12b-1: 0.01%
Other: none

CA Inv: CA Tax-Free Income (CFNTX)

800-225-8778, 415-398-2727
www.caltrust.com

Tax-Exempt Bond

PERFORMANCE AND PER SHARE DATA **fund inception date: 12/4/85**

	3yr Annual	5yr Annual	10yr Annual	Category Risk Index
Return (%)	4.8	5.3	7.1	1.22—high
Differ from Category (+/-)	1.0 high	0.4 abv av	0.6 abv av	**Avg Mat** 11.2 yrs

	2000	1999	1998	1997	1996	1995	1994	1993	1992	1991
Return (%)	12.4	-3.5	6.3	9.2	3.1	20.6	-8.6	14.7	8.8	12.1
Differ from Category (+/-)	3.0	-0.9	0.7	1.0	-0.6	5.5	-3.7	3.0	0.4	0.8
Return, Tax-Adjusted (%)	12.3	-3.5	6.1	8.9	3.1	20.6	-9.0	14.0	8.6	12.1
Dividends, Net Income ($)	0.54	0.56	0.57	0.59	0.61	0.61	0.62	0.67	0.71	0.73
Expense Ratio (%)	0.64	0.61	0.61	0.59	0.60	0.62	0.60	0.60	0.60	0.60
Yield (%)	4.16	4.62	4.31	4.47	4.82	4.73	5.42	4.97	5.70	6.01

SHAREHOLDER INFORMATION

Minimum Investment
Initial: $10,000 IRA: na
Subsequent: $250 IRA: na

Maximum Fees
Load: none 12b-1: none
Other: none

Calvert Tax-Free Rsv: Ltd/A (CTFLX)

800-368-2750, 301-951-4800
www.calvertgroup.com

Tax-Exempt Bond

PERFORMANCE AND PER SHARE DATA **fund inception date: 3/31/81**

	3yr Annual	5yr Annual	10yr Annual	Category Risk Index	
Return (%)	3.7	3.8	4.2	0.11—low	
Differ from Category (+/-)	-0.1 low	-1.1 low	-2.3 low	**Avg Mat**	0.9 yrs

	2000	1999	1998	1997	1996	1995	1994	1993	1992	1991
Return (%)	4.5	2.8	3.8	4.0	3.9	5.5	2.4	4.0	4.9	6.4
Differ from Category (+/-)	-4.9	5.4	-1.8	-4.2	0.2	-9.6	7.3	-7.7	-3.5	-4.9
Return, Tax-Adjusted (%)	4.5	2.8	3.8	4.0	3.9	5.5	2.4	4.0	4.9	6.4
Dividends, Net Income ($)	0.45	0.37	0.39	0.41	0.44	0.44	0.38	0.38	0.49	0.62
Expense Ratio (%)	na	0.70	0.70	0.69	0.70	0.70	0.66	0.67	0.71	0.73
Yield (%)	4.22	3.47	3.64	3.83	4.11	4.10	3.58	3.54	4.58	5.82

SHAREHOLDER INFORMATION

Minimum Investment
Initial: $2,000 IRA: na
Subsequent: $250 IRA: na

Maximum Fees
Load: 1.00% front 12b-1: none
Other: none

Citizens: Income (WAIMX)

800-223-7010, 603-436-5152
www.citizensfunds.com

Corporate Bond

PERFORMANCE AND PER SHARE DATA **fund inception date: 6/11/92**

	3yr Annual	5yr Annual	10yr Annual	Category Risk Index	
Return (%)	4.0	5.4	na	0.91—av	
Differ from Category (+/-)	-1.0 blw av	-0.3 blw av	na	**Avg Mat**	7.5 yrs

	2000	1999	1998	1997	1996	1995	1994	1993	1992	1991
Return (%)	7.2	-0.8	5.8	10.4	4.8	17.3	-3.0	9.9	—	—
Differ from Category (+/-)	-0.8	-2.1	-0.1	1.3	-0.7	-0.6	-0.7	-1.9	—	—
Return, Tax-Adjusted (%)	4.5	-2.9	3.6	7.9	2.3	14.6	-5.2	7.7	—	—
Dividends, Net Income ($)	0.68	0.59	0.58	0.65	0.65	0.66	0.60	0.55	—	—
Expense Ratio (%)	1.45	1.45	1.74	1.41	1.38	1.35	1.25	1.42	—	—
Yield (%)	6.62	5.75	5.29	5.94	6.17	6.17	6.17	5.16	—	—

SHAREHOLDER INFORMATION

Minimum Investment
Initial: $2,500 IRA: $1,000
Subsequent: $1 IRA: $50

Maximum Fees
Load: none 12b-1: 0.25%
Other: none

Columbia Fixed Income Sec (CFISX)

800-547-1707, 503-222-3606
www.columbiafunds.com

General Bond

PERFORMANCE AND PER SHARE DATA **fund inception date: 1/6/83**

	3yr Annual	5yr Annual	10yr Annual	Category Risk Index
Return (%)	5.8	6.0	7.9	1.11—abv av
Differ from Category (+/-)	0.3 abv av	0.4 abv av	0.7 high	**Avg Mat** 6.1 yrs

	2000	1999	1998	1997	1996	1995	1994	1993	1992	1991
Return (%)	11.2	-0.7	7.4	9.5	3.3	18.9	-3.3	10.3	7.9	16.9
Differ from Category (+/-)	1.5	-0.7	0.1	1.1	-0.2	2.7	-0.6	0.6	1.1	1.4
Return, Tax-Adjusted (%)	8.6	-3.2	4.7	6.9	0.8	16.0	-5.7	7.0	4.9	14.0
Dividends, Net Income ($)	0.81	0.87	0.83	0.84	0.85	0.88	0.83	0.84	0.95	0.99
Expense Ratio (%)	na	0.64	0.65	0.66	0.64	0.65	0.66	0.66	0.66	0.69
Yield (%)	6.24	6.99	6.12	6.25	6.49	6.51	6.82	6.08	6.93	7.18

SHAREHOLDER INFORMATION

Minimum Investment
Initial: $1,000 IRA: $1,000
Subsequent: $100 IRA: $100

Maximum Fees
Load: none 12b-1: none
Other: none

Columbia OR Muni Bond (CMBFX)

800-547-1707, 503-222-3606
www.columbiafunds.com

Tax-Exempt Bond

PERFORMANCE AND PER SHARE DATA **fund inception date: 5/23/84**

	3yr Annual	5yr Annual	10yr Annual	Category Risk Index
Return (%)	4.1	4.8	6.1	1.00—av
Differ from Category (+/-)	0.3 blw av	-0.1 blw av	-0.4 blw av	**Avg Mat** 13.5 yrs

	2000	1999	1998	1997	1996	1995	1994	1993	1992	1991
Return (%)	9.8	-2.6	5.5	8.3	3.7	14.1	-4.6	10.5	6.5	11.8
Differ from Category (+/-)	0.4	0.0	-0.1	0.1	0.0	-1.0	0.3	-1.2	-1.9	0.5
Return, Tax-Adjusted (%)	9.8	-2.6	5.3	8.1	3.5	13.9	-4.6	10.3	6.2	11.7
Dividends, Net Income ($)	0.53	0.56	0.57	0.59	0.60	0.63	0.64	0.66	0.69	0.72
Expense Ratio (%)	na	0.57	0.58	0.57	0.56	0.57	0.57	0.58	0.59	0.59
Yield (%)	4.36	4.84	4.53	4.70	4.91	5.06	5.57	5.16	5.60	5.87

SHAREHOLDER INFORMATION

Minimum Investment
Initial: $1,000 IRA: na
Subsequent: $100 IRA: na

Maximum Fees
Load: none 12b-1: none
Other: none

Dodge & Cox Income (DODIX)

800-621-3979, 415-981-1710
www.dodgeandcox.com

General Bond

PERFORMANCE AND PER SHARE DATA **fund inception date: 1/2/89**

	3yr Annual	5yr Annual	10yr Annual	Category Risk Index
Return (%)	5.8	6.2	8.3	1.03—av
Differ from Category (+/-)	0.3 abv av	0.6 high	1.1 high	**Avg Mat** 11.1 yrs

	2000	1999	1998	1997	1996	1995	1994	1993	1992	1991
Return (%)	10.7	-0.8	8.0	10.0	3.6	20.2	-2.8	11.3	7.7	17.9
Differ from Category (+/-)	1.0	-0.8	0.7	1.6	0.1	4.0	-0.1	1.6	0.9	2.4
Return, Tax-Adjusted (%)	7.9	-3.1	5.5	7.5	1.1	17.1	-5.4	8.2	5.2	15.4
Dividends, Net Income ($)	0.78	0.71	0.72	0.73	0.74	0.81	0.76	0.78	0.82	0.82
Expense Ratio (%)	na	0.46	0.47	0.49	0.50	0.54	0.54	0.60	0.62	0.64
Yield (%)	6.61	6.20	5.84	6.04	6.33	6.72	7.04	6.46	7.04	7.05

SHAREHOLDER INFORMATION

Minimum Investment
Initial: $2,500 IRA: $1,000
Subsequent: $100 IRA: $100

Maximum Fees
Load: none 12b-1: none
Other: none

Dreyfus A Bonds Plus (DRBDX)

800-645-6561, 516-794-5452
www.dreyfus.com

General Bond

PERFORMANCE AND PER SHARE DATA **fund inception date: 6/25/76**

	3yr Annual	5yr Annual	10yr Annual	Category Risk Index
Return (%)	4.8	5.3	8.0	1.15—high
Differ from Category (+/-)	-0.7 low	-0.3 blw av	0.8 high	**Avg Mat** 10.1 yrs

	2000	1999	1998	1997	1996	1995	1994	1993	1992	1991
Return (%)	10.2	1.7	2.6	9.5	2.6	20.3	-6.1	14.9	8.2	18.7
Differ from Category (+/-)	0.5	1.7	-4.7	1.1	-0.9	4.1	-3.4	5.2	1.4	3.2
Return, Tax-Adjusted (%)	7.7	-0.6	0.0	6.8	0.2	17.5	-8.6	11.0	5.5	16.1
Dividends, Net Income ($)	0.83	0.83	0.85	0.88	0.87	0.93	0.94	1.00	1.07	1.10
Expense Ratio (%)	1.00	0.96	0.95	0.96	0.93	0.99	0.90	0.93	0.88	0.85
Yield (%)	5.97	6.19	5.98	5.92	6.03	6.23	7.06	6.34	7.21	7.46

SHAREHOLDER INFORMATION

Minimum Investment
Initial: $2,500 IRA: $750
Subsequent: $100 IRA: $1

Maximum Fees
Load: none 12b-1: none
Other: none

Dreyfus BASIC GNMA (DIGFX)

800-645-6561, 516-794-5452
www.dreyfus.com

Mortgage-Backed Bond

PERFORMANCE AND PER SHARE DATA — **fund inception date: 8/5/87**

	3yr Annual	5yr Annual	10yr Annual	Category Risk Index
Return (%)	6.1	6.5	7.6	1.38—high
Differ from Category (+/-)	0.5 high	0.6 high	0.5 high	**Avg Mat** 8.5 yrs

	2000	1999	1998	1997	1996	1995	1994	1993	1992	1991
Return (%)	11.0	2.8	4.7	9.5	4.8	16.6	-0.9	8.7	7.0	13.2
Differ from Category (+/-)	1.1	1.8	-1.5	1.0	0.6	1.7	0.4	2.3	0.5	-1.5
Return, Tax-Adjusted (%)	8.4	0.1	2.1	6.6	2.2	13.7	-3.6	5.8	4.6	10.9
Dividends, Net Income ($)	0.91	0.95	0.97	0.98	0.98	1.02	1.07	1.11	1.16	1.05
Expense Ratio (%)	na	0.65	0.65	0.65	0.65	0.34	0.06	0.00	0.00	0.00
Yield (%)	6.07	6.56	6.44	6.30	6.47	6.61	7.55	7.21	7.63	6.84

SHAREHOLDER INFORMATION

Minimum Investment
Initial: $10,000 IRA: $5,000
Subsequent: $1,000 IRA: $1,000

Maximum Fees
Load: none 12b-1: none
Other: none

Dreyfus BASIC Intm Muni (DBIMX)

800-645-6561, 516-794-5452
www.dreyfus.com

Tax-Exempt Bond

PERFORMANCE AND PER SHARE DATA — **fund inception date: 5/4/94**

	3yr Annual	5yr Annual	10yr Annual	Category Risk Index
Return (%)	5.0	5.7	na	1.09—av
Differ from Category (+/-)	1.2 high	0.8 high	na	**Avg Mat** 9.1 yrs

	2000	1999	1998	1997	1996	1995	1994	1993	1992	1991
Return (%)	11.4	-2.4	6.7	8.7	4.8	13.8	—	—	—	—
Differ from Category (+/-)	2.0	0.2	1.1	0.5	1.1	-1.3	—	—	—	—
Return, Tax-Adjusted (%)	11.3	-2.4	6.5	8.4	4.7	13.8	—	—	—	—
Dividends, Net Income ($)	0.61	0.60	0.61	0.64	0.66	0.67	—	—	—	—
Expense Ratio (%)	0.45	0.45	0.45	0.24	0.39	0.11	—	—	—	—
Yield (%)	4.56	4.76	4.48	4.73	5.04	5.10	—	—	—	—

SHAREHOLDER INFORMATION

Minimum Investment
Initial: $10,000 IRA: na
Subsequent: $1,000 IRA: na

Maximum Fees
Load: none 12b-1: none
Other: none

Dreyfus BASIC Muni Bond (DRMBX)

800-645-6561, 516-794-5452
www.dreyfus.com

Tax-Exempt Bond

PERFORMANCE AND PER SHARE DATA — fund inception date: 5/6/94

	3yr Annual	5yr Annual	10yr Annual	Category Risk Index
Return (%)	4.6	5.8	na	1.40—high
Differ from Category (+/-)	0.8 abv av	0.9 high	na	**Avg Mat** 18.5 yrs

	2000	1999	1998	1997	1996	1995	1994	1993	1992	1991
Return (%)	13.9	-5.7	6.7	10.9	4.5	19.2	—	—	—	—
Differ from Category (+/-)	4.5	-3.1	1.1	2.7	0.8	4.1	—	—	—	—
Return, Tax-Adjusted (%)	13.9	-5.7	6.4	10.6	4.3	19.1	—	—	—	—
Dividends, Net Income ($)	0.66	0.65	0.67	0.71	0.73	0.74	—	—	—	—
Expense Ratio (%)	0.45	0.45	0.45	0.26	0.39	0.20	—	—	—	—
Yield (%)	4.90	5.22	4.78	5.08	5.45	5.45	—	—	—	—

SHAREHOLDER INFORMATION

Minimum Investment
Initial: $10,000 IRA: na
Subsequent: $1,000 IRA: na

Maximum Fees
Load: none 12b-1: none
Other: none

Dreyfus CA Interm Muni Bd (DCIMX)

800-645-6561, 516-794-5452
www.dreyfus.com

Tax-Exempt Bond

PERFORMANCE AND PER SHARE DATA — fund inception date: 4/20/92

	3yr Annual	5yr Annual	10yr Annual	Category Risk Index
Return (%)	4.4	4.8	na	0.87—blw av
Differ from Category (+/-)	0.6 av	-0.1 av	na	**Avg Mat** 9.2 yrs

	2000	1999	1998	1997	1996	1995	1994	1993	1992	1991
Return (%)	9.4	-1.6	5.7	7.6	3.6	13.4	-5.5	14.4	—	—
Differ from Category (+/-)	0.0	1.0	0.1	-0.6	-0.1	-1.7	-0.6	2.7	—	—
Return, Tax-Adjusted (%)	9.4	-1.6	5.7	7.6	3.6	13.4	-5.5	14.4	—	—
Dividends, Net Income ($)	0.58	0.58	0.58	0.59	0.60	0.63	0.67	0.73	—	—
Expense Ratio (%)	0.79	0.80	0.79	0.78	0.65	0.32	0.04	0.00	—	—
Yield (%)	4.18	4.38	4.13	4.26	4.46	4.64	5.34	5.22	—	—

SHAREHOLDER INFORMATION

Minimum Investment
Initial: $2,500 IRA: na
Subsequent: $100 IRA: na

Maximum Fees
Load: 1.00% redemption 12b-1: none
Other: redemption fee applies for 15 days

Dreyfus CA Tax-Exempt Bd (DRCAX)

800-645-6561, 516-794-5452
www.dreyfus.com

Tax-Exempt Bond

PERFORMANCE AND PER SHARE DATA — fund inception date: 7/26/83

	3yr Annual	5yr Annual	10yr Annual	Category Risk Index
Return (%)	5.2	5.4	6.1	1.35—high
Differ from Category (+/-)	1.4 high	0.5 abv av	-0.4 blw av	**Avg Mat** 23.3 yrs

	2000	1999	1998	1997	1996	1995	1994	1993	1992	1991
Return (%)	15.2	-4.4	5.8	8.2	3.4	14.0	-7.1	11.8	6.6	10.3
Differ from Category (+/-)	5.8	-1.8	0.2	0.0	-0.3	-1.1	-2.2	0.1	-1.8	-1.0
Return, Tax-Adjusted (%)	15.2	-4.4	5.7	8.2	3.4	14.0	-7.1	11.4	6.3	10.2
Dividends, Net Income ($)	0.70	0.68	0.68	0.71	0.73	0.79	0.82	0.86	0.90	0.95
Expense Ratio (%)	0.73	0.72	0.71	0.73	0.69	0.71	0.70	0.69	0.68	0.69
Yield (%)	4.69	4.98	4.52	4.77	5.05	5.37	6.00	5.47	5.99	6.33

SHAREHOLDER INFORMATION

Minimum Investment
Initial: $2,500 IRA: na
Subsequent: $100 IRA: na

Maximum Fees
Load: 0.10% redemption 12b-1: none
Other: redemption fee applies for 15 days

Dreyfus CT Interm Muni Bd (DCTIX)

800-645-6561, 516-794-5452
www.dreyfus.com

Tax-Exempt Bond

PERFORMANCE AND PER SHARE DATA — fund inception date: 6/26/92

	3yr Annual	5yr Annual	10yr Annual	Category Risk Index
Return (%)	3.8	4.5	na	0.73—low
Differ from Category (+/-)	0.0 low	-0.4 blw av	na	**Avg Mat** 6.3 yrs

	2000	1999	1998	1997	1996	1995	1994	1993	1992	1991
Return (%)	7.5	-1.1	5.4	7.5	3.7	14.2	-4.6	12.7	—	—
Differ from Category (+/-)	-1.9	1.5	-0.2	-0.7	0.0	-0.9	0.3	1.0	—	—
Return, Tax-Adjusted (%)	7.5	-1.1	5.4	7.5	3.7	14.2	-4.6	12.7	—	—
Dividends, Net Income ($)	0.59	0.57	0.58	0.59	0.59	0.60	0.66	0.68	—	—
Expense Ratio (%)	0.79	0.80	0.78	0.78	0.72	0.34	0.01	0.00	—	—
Yield (%)	4.30	4.27	4.12	4.24	4.36	4.40	5.29	4.93	—	—

SHAREHOLDER INFORMATION

Minimum Investment
Initial: $2,500 IRA: na
Subsequent: $100 IRA: na

Maximum Fees
Load: 1.00% redemption 12b-1: none
Other: redemption fee applies for 15 days

Dreyfus FL Interm Muni Bd (DFLIX)

800-645-6561, 516-794-5452
www.dreyfus.com

Tax-Exempt Bond

PERFORMANCE AND PER SHARE DATA **fund inception date: 1/21/92**

	3yr Annual	5yr Annual	10yr Annual	Category Risk Index
Return (%)	3.7	4.1	na	0.76—low
Differ from Category (+/-)	-0.1 low	-0.8 low	na	**Avg Mat** 6.9 yrs

	2000	1999	1998	1997	1996	1995	1994	1993	1992	1991
Return (%)	7.5	-1.1	4.9	6.3	3.3	13.9	-4.9	12.8	—	—
Differ from Category (+/-)	-1.9	1.5	-0.7	-1.9	-0.4	-1.2	0.0	1.1	—	—
Return, Tax-Adjusted (%)	7.5	-1.1	4.7	6.2	3.3	13.9	-4.9	12.7	—	—
Dividends, Net Income ($)	0.58	0.58	0.59	0.59	0.61	0.62	0.65	0.70	—	—
Expense Ratio (%)	na	0.81	0.81	0.80	0.80	0.64	0.48	0.20	—	—
Yield (%)	4.39	4.51	4.30	4.31	4.53	4.55	5.19	5.05	—	—

SHAREHOLDER INFORMATION

Minimum Investment
Initial: $2,500 IRA: na
Subsequent: $100 IRA: na

Maximum Fees
Load: 1.00% redemption 12b-1: none
Other: redemption fee applies for 15 days

Dreyfus GNMA (DRGMX)

800-645-6561, 516-794-5452
www.dreyfus.com

Mortgage-Backed Bond

PERFORMANCE AND PER SHARE DATA **fund inception date: 5/29/85**

	3yr Annual	5yr Annual	10yr Annual	Category Risk Index
Return (%)	5.2	5.7	6.8	1.26—high
Differ from Category (+/-)	-0.4 low	-0.2 blw av	-0.3 blw av	**Avg Mat** 8.4 yrs

	2000	1999	1998	1997	1996	1995	1994	1993	1992	1991
Return (%)	10.5	1.3	4.1	8.8	4.4	15.1	-2.7	7.1	6.3	14.4
Differ from Category (+/-)	0.6	0.3	-2.1	0.3	0.2	0.2	-1.4	0.7	-0.2	-0.3
Return, Tax-Adjusted (%)	7.9	-1.1	1.6	6.3	1.9	12.3	-5.1	4.4	4.0	11.7
Dividends, Net Income ($)	0.89	0.89	0.91	0.90	0.93	0.97	0.94	1.03	1.12	1.23
Expense Ratio (%)	0.92	0.94	0.96	0.96	0.96	0.97	0.95	0.94	0.95	0.97
Yield (%)	6.19	6.42	6.25	6.05	6.40	6.53	6.81	6.79	7.40	8.02

SHAREHOLDER INFORMATION

Minimum Investment
Initial: $2,500 IRA: $750
Subsequent: $100 IRA: $1

Maximum Fees
Load: none 12b-1: 0.20%
Other: none

Dreyfus Gen CA Muni Bond (GCABX)

800-645-6561, 516-794-5452
www.dreyfus.com

Tax-Exempt Bond

PERFORMANCE AND PER SHARE DATA **fund inception date: 10/11/89**

	3yr Annual	5yr Annual	10yr Annual	Category Risk Index
Return (%)	4.5	5.3	6.9	1.44—high
Differ from Category (+/-)	0.7 abv av	0.4 abv av	0.4 abv av	**Avg Mat** 22.2 yrs

	2000	1999	1998	1997	1996	1995	1994	1993	1992	1991
Return (%)	15.1	-5.9	5.4	8.8	4.2	18.0	-7.0	13.6	8.6	10.9
Differ from Category (+/-)	5.7	-3.3	-0.2	0.6	0.5	2.9	-2.1	1.9	0.2	-0.4
Return, Tax-Adjusted (%)	15.1	-5.9	5.1	8.6	3.7	17.6	-7.1	13.4	8.4	10.9
Dividends, Net Income ($)	0.64	0.64	0.66	0.69	0.68	0.71	0.76	0.80	0.84	0.88
Expense Ratio (%)	0.77	0.78	0.77	0.76	0.76	0.76	0.76	0.64	0.37	0.21
Yield (%)	4.84	5.27	4.81	5.02	5.02	5.14	6.10	5.61	6.28	6.71

SHAREHOLDER INFORMATION

Minimum Investment
Initial: $2,500 IRA: na
Subsequent: $100 IRA: na

Maximum Fees
Load: 0.10% redemption 12b-1: 0.25%
Other: redemption fee applies for 15 days

Dreyfus Gen Muni Bond (GMBDX)

800-645-6561, 516-794-5452
www.dreyfus.com

Tax-Exempt Bond

PERFORMANCE AND PER SHARE DATA **fund inception date: 3/21/84**

	3yr Annual	5yr Annual	10yr Annual	Category Risk Index
Return (%)	3.3	4.2	6.6	1.10—abv av
Differ from Category (+/-)	-0.5 low	-0.7 low	0.1 av	**Avg Mat** 20.7 yrs

	2000	1999	1998	1997	1996	1995	1994	1993	1992	1991
Return (%)	10.9	-5.2	4.9	8.0	3.1	17.2	-7.3	13.3	9.8	14.6
Differ from Category (+/-)	1.5	-2.6	-0.7	-0.2	-0.6	2.1	-2.4	1.6	1.4	3.3
Return, Tax-Adjusted (%)	10.9	-5.3	4.5	7.9	2.6	17.1	-7.5	12.8	9.5	14.5
Dividends, Net Income ($)	0.72	0.72	0.75	0.77	0.79	0.81	0.86	0.91	0.99	1.06
Expense Ratio (%)	0.87	0.86	0.87	0.88	0.88	0.87	0.82	0.41	0.01	0.00
Yield (%)	5.25	5.47	5.03	5.15	5.32	5.32	6.21	5.66	6.53	7.16

SHAREHOLDER INFORMATION

Minimum Investment
Initial: $2,500 IRA: na
Subsequent: $100 IRA: na

Maximum Fees
Load: 0.10% redemption 12b-1: 0.20%
Other: redemption fee applies for 15 days

Dreyfus Gen NY Muni Bond (GNYMX)

800-645-6561, 516-794-5452
www.dreyfus.com

Tax-Exempt Bond

PERFORMANCE AND PER SHARE DATA **fund inception date: 11/19/84**

	3yr Annual	5yr Annual	10yr Annual	Category Risk Index
Return (%)	4.3	5.1	7.1	1.14—abv av
Differ from Category (+/-)	0.5 av	0.2 av	0.6 abv av	**Avg Mat** 18.5 yrs

	2000	1999	1998	1997	1996	1995	1994	1993	1992	1991
Return (%)	11.9	-4.6	6.3	9.5	3.0	16.5	-7.1	14.1	10.0	14.0
Differ from Category (+/-)	2.5	-2.0	0.7	1.3	-0.7	1.4	-2.2	2.4	1.6	2.7
Return, Tax-Adjusted (%)	11.9	-4.6	6.0	9.3	2.8	16.3	-7.2	13.6	9.6	14.0
Dividends, Net Income ($)	0.92	0.93	0.95	0.98	1.00	1.04	1.12	1.16	1.21	1.29
Expense Ratio (%)	0.91	0.92	0.90	0.91	0.91	0.81	0.76	0.69	0.62	0.36
Yield (%)	4.67	5.02	4.60	4.78	5.05	5.11	6.05	5.41	6.01	6.63

SHAREHOLDER INFORMATION

Minimum Investment
Initial: $2,500 IRA: na
Subsequent: $100 IRA: na

Maximum Fees
Load: 0.10% redemption 12b-1: 0.20%
Other: redemption fee applies for 15 days

Dreyfus Insured Muni Bond (DTBDX)

800-645-6561, 516-794-5452
www.dreyfus.com

Tax-Exempt Bond

PERFORMANCE AND PER SHARE DATA **fund inception date: 6/25/85**

	3yr Annual	5yr Annual	10yr Annual	Category Risk Index
Return (%)	4.5	4.8	6.0	1.22—high
Differ from Category (+/-)	0.7 av	-0.1 blw av	-0.5 low	**Avg Mat** 23.8 yrs

	2000	1999	1998	1997	1996	1995	1994	1993	1992	1991
Return (%)	13.2	-4.7	5.8	8.3	2.2	15.5	-8.6	12.5	7.7	11.3
Differ from Category (+/-)	3.8	-2.1	0.2	0.1	-1.5	0.4	-3.7	0.8	-0.7	0.0
Return, Tax-Adjusted (%)	13.2	-4.7	5.8	8.3	2.2	15.5	-8.6	11.4	7.3	11.3
Dividends, Net Income ($)	0.85	0.84	0.84	0.86	0.87	0.91	0.95	1.02	1.08	1.10
Expense Ratio (%)	0.85	0.85	0.85	0.80	0.85	0.94	0.93	0.94	0.96	0.96
Yield (%)	4.72	5.03	4.57	4.72	4.93	5.02	5.75	5.15	5.76	5.95

SHAREHOLDER INFORMATION

Minimum Investment
Initial: $2,500 IRA: na
Subsequent: $100 IRA: na

Maximum Fees
Load: 0.10% redemption 12b-1: 0.20%
Other: redemption fee applies for 15 days

Dreyfus Interm Muni Bond (DITEX)

800-782-6620, 516-794-5452
www.dreyfus.com

Tax-Exempt Bond

PERFORMANCE AND PER SHARE DATA **fund inception date: 8/11/83**

	3yr Annual	5yr Annual	10yr Annual	Category Risk Index
Return (%)	3.8	4.5	6.2	0.79—low
Differ from Category (+/-)	0.0 low	-0.4 low	-0.3 blw av	**Avg Mat** 7.8 yrs

	2000	1999	1998	1997	1996	1995	1994	1993	1992	1991
Return (%)	7.7	-1.5	5.5	7.6	3.8	14.2	-4.5	11.5	8.7	11.1
Differ from Category (+/-)	-1.7	1.1	-0.1	-0.6	0.1	-0.9	0.4	-0.2	0.3	-0.2
Return, Tax-Adjusted (%)	7.7	-1.6	5.3	7.4	3.5	14.1	-4.6	11.1	8.0	10.9
Dividends, Net Income ($)	0.64	0.66	0.67	0.69	0.72	0.72	0.75	0.77	0.84	0.90
Expense Ratio (%)	0.75	0.75	0.74	0.73	0.71	0.73	0.70	0.71	0.70	0.69
Yield (%)	4.75	5.00	4.71	4.84	5.13	5.05	5.68	5.21	5.88	6.41

SHAREHOLDER INFORMATION

Minimum Investment
Initial: $2,500 IRA: na
Subsequent: $100 IRA: na

Maximum Fees
Load: 0.10% redemption 12b-1: none
Other: redemption fee applies for 15 days

Dreyfus Inv Grd Bd: Sh Inc (DSTIX)

800-645-6561, 516-794-5452
www.dreyfus.com

Corporate Bond

PERFORMANCE AND PER SHARE DATA **fund inception date: 8/18/92**

	3yr Annual	5yr Annual	10yr Annual	Category Risk Index
Return (%)	6.4	6.7	na	0.75—blw av
Differ from Category (+/-)	1.4 high	1.0 high	na	**Avg Mat** 3.0 yrs

	2000	1999	1998	1997	1996	1995	1994	1993	1992	1991
Return (%)	8.9	6.2	4.2	8.2	6.1	11.1	0.1	9.1	—	—
Differ from Category (+/-)	0.9	4.9	-1.7	-0.9	0.6	-6.8	2.4	-2.7	—	—
Return, Tax-Adjusted (%)	6.2	3.6	1.6	5.3	3.4	8.4	-2.5	6.1	—	—
Dividends, Net Income ($)	0.77	0.77	0.79	0.85	0.82	0.79	0.83	0.91	—	—
Expense Ratio (%)	0.84	0.87	0.87	0.80	0.80	0.61	0.24	0.00	—	—
Yield (%)	6.46	6.59	6.72	7.05	6.86	6.55	7.15	7.32	—	—

SHAREHOLDER INFORMATION

Minimum Investment
Initial: $2,500 IRA: $750
Subsequent: $100 IRA: $1

Maximum Fees
Load: none 12b-1: none
Other: none

Dreyfus MA Interm Muni Bd (DMAIX)

800-645-6561, 516-794-5452
www.dreyfus.com

Tax-Exempt Bond

PERFORMANCE AND PER SHARE DATA — fund inception date: 6/26/92

	3yr Annual	5yr Annual	10yr Annual	Category Risk Index
Return (%)	4.2	4.7	na	0.88—blw av
Differ from Category (+/-)	0.4 blw av	-0.2 blw av	na	**Avg Mat** 7.7 yrs

	2000	1999	1998	1997	1996	1995	1994	1993	1992	1991
Return (%)	8.9	-1.4	5.6	7.5	3.4	14.6	-6.4	12.5	—	—
Differ from Category (+/-)	-0.5	1.2	0.0	-0.7	-0.3	-0.5	-1.5	0.8	—	—
Return, Tax-Adjusted (%)	8.9	-1.4	5.6	7.5	3.4	14.6	-6.4	12.5	—	—
Dividends, Net Income ($)	0.59	0.57	0.58	0.59	0.58	0.58	0.62	0.67	—	—
Expense Ratio (%)	0.80	0.80	0.80	0.80	0.75	0.49	0.06	0.00	—	—
Yield (%)	4.34	4.37	4.19	4.32	4.37	4.33	5.06	4.88	—	—

SHAREHOLDER INFORMATION

Minimum Investment
Initial: $2,500 IRA: na
Subsequent: $100 IRA: na

Maximum Fees
Load: 1.00% redemption 12b-1: none
Other: redemption fee applies for 15 days

Dreyfus MA Tax-Exempt Bd (DMEBX)

800-645-6561, 516-794-5452
www.dreyfus.com

Tax-Exempt Bond

PERFORMANCE AND PER SHARE DATA — fund inception date: 6/11/85

	3yr Annual	5yr Annual	10yr Annual	Category Risk Index
Return (%)	4.2	5.1	6.6	1.13—abv av
Differ from Category (+/-)	0.4 blw av	0.2 av	0.1 av	**Avg Mat** 21.5 yrs

	2000	1999	1998	1997	1996	1995	1994	1993	1992	1991
Return (%)	11.8	-4.5	6.0	9.0	4.0	15.5	-6.0	12.4	7.4	12.6
Differ from Category (+/-)	2.4	-1.9	0.4	0.8	0.3	0.4	-1.1	0.7	-1.0	1.3
Return, Tax-Adjusted (%)	11.8	-4.5	5.8	9.0	4.0	15.5	-6.0	11.6	7.4	12.6
Dividends, Net Income ($)	0.82	0.81	0.82	0.84	0.86	0.89	0.90	0.93	0.97	1.03
Expense Ratio (%)	0.85	0.82	0.81	0.79	0.79	0.80	0.80	0.81	0.84	0.81
Yield (%)	5.00	5.23	4.77	4.94	5.24	5.35	5.91	5.29	5.87	6.31

SHAREHOLDER INFORMATION

Minimum Investment
Initial: $2,500 IRA: na
Subsequent: $100 IRA: na

Maximum Fees
Load: 1.00% redemption 12b-1: none
Other: redemption fee applies for 15 days

Dreyfus Muni Bond (DRTAX)

800-645-6561, 516-794-5452
www.dreyfus.com

Tax-Exempt Bond

PERFORMANCE AND PER SHARE DATA — fund inception date: 10/4/76

	3yr Annual	5yr Annual	10yr Annual	Category Risk Index
Return (%)	3.6	4.5	6.2	1.23—high
Differ from Category (+/-)	-0.2 low	-0.4 low	-0.3 blw av	**Avg Mat** 22.3 yrs

	2000	1999	1998	1997	1996	1995	1994	1993	1992	1991
Return (%)	11.9	-5.9	5.6	7.9	3.8	15.6	-6.9	12.7	8.4	11.9
Differ from Category (+/-)	2.5	-3.3	0.0	-0.3	0.1	0.5	-2.0	1.0	0.0	0.6
Return, Tax-Adjusted (%)	11.9	-5.9	5.2	7.8	3.8	15.6	-7.0	11.9	7.8	11.9
Dividends, Net Income ($)	0.59	0.61	0.63	0.66	0.68	0.70	0.73	0.77	0.82	0.85
Expense Ratio (%)	0.76	0.73	0.73	0.71	0.71	0.69	0.68	0.69	0.68	0.67
Yield (%)	4.94	5.43	4.92	5.16	5.44	5.50	6.23	5.62	6.24	6.57

SHAREHOLDER INFORMATION

Minimum Investment
Initial: $2,500 IRA: na
Subsequent: $100 IRA: na

Maximum Fees
Load: 0.10% redemption 12b-1: none
Other: redemption fee applies for 15 days

Dreyfus NJ Interm Mu Bond (DNJIX)

800-645-6561, 516-794-5452
www.dreyfus.com

Tax-Exempt Bond

PERFORMANCE AND PER SHARE DATA — fund inception date: 6/26/92

	3yr Annual	5yr Annual	10yr Annual	Category Risk Index
Return (%)	3.9	4.4	na	0.70—low
Differ from Category (+/-)	0.1 low	-0.5 low	na	**Avg Mat** 6.3 yrs

	2000	1999	1998	1997	1996	1995	1994	1993	1992	1991
Return (%)	7.2	-0.6	5.4	6.9	3.3	14.1	-5.2	12.4	—	—
Differ from Category (+/-)	-2.2	2.0	-0.2	-1.3	-0.4	-1.0	-0.3	0.7	—	—
Return, Tax-Adjusted (%)	7.2	-0.6	5.4	6.9	3.3	14.1	-5.2	12.4	—	—
Dividends, Net Income ($)	0.58	0.58	0.58	0.59	0.59	0.61	0.65	0.68	—	—
Expense Ratio (%)	0.79	0.80	0.78	0.78	0.72	0.45	0.06	0.00	—	—
Yield (%)	4.24	4.35	4.14	4.25	4.36	4.45	5.17	4.88	—	—

SHAREHOLDER INFORMATION

Minimum Investment
Initial: $2,500 IRA: na
Subsequent: $100 IRA: na

Maximum Fees
Load: 1.00% redemption 12b-1: none
Other: redemption fee applies for 15 days

Dreyfus NJ Mu Bond (DRNJX)

800-782-6620, 516-794-5452
www.dreyfus.com

Tax-Exempt Bond

PERFORMANCE AND PER SHARE DATA **fund inception date: 11/6/87**

	3yr Annual	5yr Annual	10yr Annual	Category Risk Index
Return (%)	4.0	4.8	6.5	1.08—av
Differ from Category (+/-)	0.2 blw av	-0.1 blw av	0.0 av	**Avg Mat** 16.1 yrs

	2000	1999	1998	1997	1996	1995	1994	1993	1992	1991
Return (%)	11.2	-4.2	5.8	8.8	3.4	15.2	-6.0	12.9	8.7	11.9
Differ from Category (+/-)	1.8	-1.6	0.2	0.6	-0.3	0.1	-1.1	1.2	0.3	0.6
Return, Tax-Adjusted (%)	11.2	-4.2	5.6	8.6	2.9	15.2	-6.0	12.8	8.2	11.8
Dividends, Net Income ($)	0.63	0.63	0.65	0.68	0.71	0.74	0.77	0.78	0.79	0.80
Expense Ratio (%)	na	0.89	0.90	0.80	0.80	0.80	0.77	0.72	0.73	0.75
Yield (%)	4.90	5.17	4.83	5.05	5.36	5.47	6.19	5.55	5.90	6.10

SHAREHOLDER INFORMATION

Minimum Investment
Initial: $2,500 IRA: na
Subsequent: $100 IRA: na

Maximum Fees
Load: 1.00% redemption 12b-1: 0.25%
Other: redemption fee applies for 15 days

Dreyfus NY Interm Tx Ex (DRNIX)

800-645-6561, 516-794-5452
www.dreyfus.com

Tax-Exempt Bond

PERFORMANCE AND PER SHARE DATA **fund inception date: 6/12/87**

	3yr Annual	5yr Annual	10yr Annual	Category Risk Index
Return (%)	4.3	5.0	6.5	0.94—blw av
Differ from Category (+/-)	0.5 av	0.1 av	0.0 blw av	**Avg Mat** 8.7 yrs

	2000	1999	1998	1997	1996	1995	1994	1993	1992	1991
Return (%)	9.5	-2.2	6.0	8.2	4.1	14.0	-5.1	11.5	9.3	11.1
Differ from Category (+/-)	0.1	0.4	0.4	0.0	0.4	-1.1	-0.2	-0.2	0.9	-0.2
Return, Tax-Adjusted (%)	9.5	-2.3	5.7	8.1	3.8	14.0	-5.1	11.4	9.1	10.9
Dividends, Net Income ($)	0.79	0.79	0.81	0.82	0.84	0.84	0.85	0.89	0.97	1.02
Expense Ratio (%)	0.80	0.80	0.80	0.80	0.84	0.96	0.89	0.85	0.85	0.60
Yield (%)	4.34	4.51	4.28	4.38	4.60	4.57	5.03	4.75	5.47	5.91

SHAREHOLDER INFORMATION

Minimum Investment
Initial: $2,500 IRA: na
Subsequent: $100 IRA: na

Maximum Fees
Load: 1.00% redemption 12b-1: 0.25%
Other: redemption fee applies for 15 days

Dreyfus NY Tax Ex Bond (DRNYX)

800-645-6561, 516-794-5452
www.dreyfus.com

Tax-Exempt Bond

PERFORMANCE AND PER SHARE DATA **fund inception date: 7/26/83**

	3yr Annual	5yr Annual	10yr Annual	Category Risk Index
Return (%)	4.4	4.9	6.6	1.09—abv av
Differ from Category (+/-)	0.6 av	0.0 av	0.1 av	**Avg Mat** 17.1 yrs

	2000	1999	1998	1997	1996	1995	1994	1993	1992	1991
Return (%)	11.1	-3.8	6.7	9.1	2.4	16.2	-6.9	12.6	8.8	12.4
Differ from Category (+/-)	1.7	-1.2	1.1	0.9	-1.3	1.1	-2.0	0.9	0.4	1.1
Return, Tax-Adjusted (%)	11.1	-3.9	6.5	8.9	2.2	16.1	-7.0	11.9	8.4	12.4
Dividends, Net Income ($)	0.71	0.73	0.74	0.75	0.77	0.80	0.85	0.90	0.98	1.02
Expense Ratio (%)	0.75	0.75	0.73	0.74	0.71	0.72	0.71	0.70	0.69	0.70
Yield (%)	4.75	5.12	4.71	4.82	5.11	5.15	5.99	5.44	6.23	6.62

SHAREHOLDER INFORMATION

Minimum Investment
Initial: $2,500 IRA: na
Subsequent: $100 IRA: na

Maximum Fees
Load: 0.10% redemption 12b-1: none
Other: redemption fee applies for 15 days

Dreyfus PA Interm Muni Bd (DPABX)

800-645-6561, 516-794-5452
www.dreyfus.com

Tax-Exempt Bond

PERFORMANCE AND PER SHARE DATA **fund inception date: 12/16/93**

	3yr Annual	5yr Annual	10yr Annual	Category Risk Index
Return (%)	4.6	5.2	na	1.02—av
Differ from Category (+/-)	0.8 abv av	0.3 abv av	na	**Avg Mat** 9.3 yrs

	2000	1999	1998	1997	1996	1995	1994	1993	1992	1991
Return (%)	11.0	-2.1	5.5	8.3	4.1	15.2	-1.5	—	—	—
Differ from Category (+/-)	1.6	0.5	-0.1	0.1	0.4	0.1	3.4	—	—	—
Return, Tax-Adjusted (%)	10.9	-2.1	5.3	8.3	4.1	15.2	-1.5	—	—	—
Dividends, Net Income ($)	0.60	0.58	0.59	0.59	0.59	0.62	0.63	—	—	—
Expense Ratio (%)	na	0.80	0.80	0.80	0.80	0.48	—	—	—	—
Yield (%)	4.46	4.55	4.30	4.34	4.50	4.70	5.25	—	—	—

SHAREHOLDER INFORMATION

Minimum Investment
Initial: $2,500 IRA: na
Subsequent: $100 IRA: na

Maximum Fees
Load: 1.00% redemption 12b-1: none
Other: redemption fee applies for 5 months

Dreyfus Short Int Gov't (DSIGX)

800-554-4611, 516-794-5452
www.dreyfus.com

Government Bond

PERFORMANCE AND PER SHARE DATA **fund inception date: 4/6/87**

	3yr Annual	5yr Annual	10yr Annual	Category Risk Index
Return (%)	5.7	5.4	6.6	0.64—blw av
Differ from Category (+/-)	-0.5 blw av	-0.5 blw av	-1.0 av	**Avg Mat** 2.4 yrs

	2000	1999	1998	1997	1996	1995	1994	1993	1992	1991
Return (%)	8.9	1.8	6.4	6.1	3.9	12.6	-0.7	7.3	7.0	13.4
Differ from Category (+/-)	-4.9	4.8	-2.7	-3.7	1.8	-6.2	2.9	-3.3	0.4	-1.5
Return, Tax-Adjusted (%)	6.6	-0.4	3.6	3.6	1.5	9.8	-3.3	4.4	4.2	10.6
Dividends, Net Income ($)	0.60	0.61	0.74	0.67	0.65	0.72	0.75	0.77	0.81	0.83
Expense Ratio (%)	na	0.71	0.70	0.74	0.74	0.62	0.47	0.40	0.35	0.49
Yield (%)	5.63	5.88	6.86	6.18	5.97	6.48	7.12	6.74	6.94	6.98

SHAREHOLDER INFORMATION

Minimum Investment
Initial: $2,500 IRA: $750
Subsequent: $100 IRA: $1

Maximum Fees
Load: none 12b-1: none
Other: none

Dreyfus Short Int Muni Bd (DSIBX)

800-554-4611, 516-794-5452
www.dreyfus.com

Tax-Exempt Bond

PERFORMANCE AND PER SHARE DATA **fund inception date: 4/30/87**

	3yr Annual	5yr Annual	10yr Annual	Category Risk Index
Return (%)	3.8	4.1	4.9	0.24—low
Differ from Category (+/-)	0.0 low	-0.8 low	-1.6 low	**Avg Mat** 2.3 yrs

	2000	1999	1998	1997	1996	1995	1994	1993	1992	1991
Return (%)	4.9	2.0	4.4	5.1	4.2	7.1	-0.3	6.6	6.7	8.2
Differ from Category (+/-)	-4.5	4.6	-1.2	-3.1	0.5	-8.0	4.6	-5.1	-1.7	-3.1
Return, Tax-Adjusted (%)	4.9	2.0	4.4	5.1	4.2	7.1	-0.3	6.5	6.6	8.2
Dividends, Net Income ($)	0.54	0.53	0.54	0.54	0.57	0.57	0.56	0.58	0.65	0.71
Expense Ratio (%)	0.73	0.73	0.76	0.80	0.68	0.70	0.74	0.75	0.72	0.59
Yield (%)	4.17	4.12	4.11	4.12	4.39	4.38	4.40	4.35	4.97	5.51

SHAREHOLDER INFORMATION

Minimum Investment
Initial: $2,500 IRA: na
Subsequent: $100 IRA: na

Maximum Fees
Load: 0.10% redemption 12b-1: 0.10%
Other: redemption fee applies for 1 month

Dreyfus US Treasury Intm (DRGIX)

800-554-4611, 516-794-5452
www.dreyfus.com

Government Bond

PERFORMANCE AND PER SHARE DATA **fund inception date: 3/27/87**

	3yr Annual	5yr Annual	10yr Annual	Category Risk Index
Return (%)	5.4	5.3	7.0	1.30—abv av
Differ from Category (+/-)	-0.8 blw av	-0.6 blw av	-0.6 av	**Avg Mat** 6.9 yrs

	2000	1999	1998	1997	1996	1995	1994	1993	1992	1991
Return (%)	12.8	-3.4	7.6	7.6	3.0	15.7	-3.9	11.0	7.1	15.2
Differ from Category (+/-)	-1.0	-0.4	-1.5	-2.2	0.9	-3.1	-0.3	0.4	0.5	0.3
Return, Tax-Adjusted (%)	10.1	-5.7	5.1	4.7	0.5	12.8	-6.5	8.1	4.7	12.5
Dividends, Net Income ($)	0.77	0.75	0.78	0.91	0.82	0.89	0.91	0.94	1.00	1.06
Expense Ratio (%)	na	0.80	0.80	0.80	0.80	0.88	0.89	0.73	0.52	0.62
Yield (%)	6.24	6.43	6.07	7.16	6.46	6.77	7.48	6.91	7.62	8.01

SHAREHOLDER INFORMATION

Minimum Investment
Initial: $2,500 IRA: $750
Subsequent: $100 IRA: $1

Maximum Fees
Load: none 12b-1: none
Other: none

Dreyfus US Treasury Long (DRGBX)

800-554-4611, 516-794-5452
www.dreyfus.com

Government Bond

PERFORMANCE AND PER SHARE DATA **fund inception date: 3/27/87**

	3yr Annual	5yr Annual	10yr Annual	Category Risk Index
Return (%)	6.2	6.1	8.5	2.01—abv av
Differ from Category (+/-)	0.0 abv av	0.2 abv av	0.9 high	**Avg Mat** 19.3 yrs

	2000	1999	1998	1997	1996	1995	1994	1993	1992	1991
Return (%)	17.7	-8.1	10.8	11.6	0.8	24.9	-9.1	16.5	7.5	18.2
Differ from Category (+/-)	3.9	-5.1	1.7	1.8	-1.3	6.1	-5.5	5.9	0.9	3.3
Return, Tax-Adjusted (%)	15.4	-10.0	8.7	9.0	-1.7	22.0	-11.6	13.6	5.1	15.5
Dividends, Net Income ($)	0.81	0.81	0.79	0.93	0.98	0.96	1.00	1.02	1.07	1.13
Expense Ratio (%)	na	0.80	0.80	0.80	0.80	0.93	0.98	0.78	0.56	0.25
Yield (%)	5.19	5.78	4.90	6.07	6.70	6.19	7.54	6.50	7.44	7.83

SHAREHOLDER INFORMATION

Minimum Investment
Initial: $2,500 IRA: $750
Subsequent: $100 IRA: $1

Maximum Fees
Load: none 12b-1: none
Other: none

Dreyfus US Treasury Short (DRTSX)

800-554-4611, 516-794-5452
www.dreyfus.com

Government Bond

PERFORMANCE AND PER SHARE DATA **fund inception date: 9/10/87**

	3yr Annual	5yr Annual	10yr Annual	Category Risk Index
Return (%)	5.3	5.2	6.3	0.62—blw av
Differ from Category (+/-)	-0.9 blw av	-0.7 blw av	-1.3 blw av	**Avg Mat** 2.2 yrs

	2000	1999	1998	1997	1996	1995	1994	1993	1992	1991
Return (%)	8.7	1.3	6.1	6.1	4.0	11.3	-0.3	7.0	7.0	12.9
Differ from Category (+/-)	-5.1	4.3	-3.0	-3.7	1.9	-7.5	3.3	-3.6	0.4	-2.0
Return, Tax-Adjusted (%)	6.4	-0.8	3.7	3.6	1.6	8.5	-3.1	3.8	4.4	10.6
Dividends, Net Income ($)	0.82	0.82	0.87	0.92	0.90	1.02	1.14	1.25	1.35	1.12
Expense Ratio (%)	na	0.80	0.79	0.70	0.70	0.62	0.35	0.11	0.03	0.00
Yield (%)	5.63	5.79	5.88	6.22	6.07	6.74	7.83	7.93	8.48	6.92

SHAREHOLDER INFORMATION

Minimum Investment
Initial: $2,500 IRA: $750
Subsequent: $100 IRA: $1

Maximum Fees
Load: none 12b-1: none
Other: none

Dupree: KY Tax-Free Income (KYTFX)

800-866-0614, 606-254-7741
www.dupree-funds.com

Tax-Exempt Bond

PERFORMANCE AND PER SHARE DATA **fund inception date: 7/2/79**

	3yr Annual	5yr Annual	10yr Annual	Category Risk Index
Return (%)	3.9	4.7	6.6	0.98—av
Differ from Category (+/-)	0.1 blw av	-0.2 blw av	0.1 av	**Avg Mat** 16.5 yrs

	2000	1999	1998	1997	1996	1995	1994	1993	1992	1991
Return (%)	8.0	-1.4	5.6	8.0	3.6	14.8	-2.9	12.6	9.0	10.6
Differ from Category (+/-)	-1.4	1.2	0.0	-0.2	-0.1	-0.3	2.0	0.9	0.6	-0.7
Return, Tax-Adjusted (%)	8.0	-1.4	5.6	8.0	3.6	14.6	-2.9	12.4	9.0	10.6
Dividends, Net Income ($)	0.37	0.37	0.38	0.39	0.39	0.44	0.40	0.41	0.43	0.44
Expense Ratio (%)	0.61	0.61	0.62	0.63	0.62	0.63	0.69	0.67	0.71	0.75
Yield (%)	4.97	5.11	4.92	5.07	5.20	5.74	5.64	5.28	5.90	6.20

SHAREHOLDER INFORMATION

Minimum Investment
Initial: $100 IRA: na
Subsequent: $100 IRA: na

Maximum Fees
Load: none 12b-1: none
Other: none

Dupree: KY Tax-Free Short-Med (KYSMX)

800-866-0614, 606-254-7741
www.dupree-funds.com

Tax-Exempt Bond

PERFORMANCE AND PER SHARE DATA **fund inception date: 9/15/87**

	3yr Annual	5yr Annual	10yr Annual	Category Risk Index	
Return (%)	3.4	3.8	4.6	0.39—low	
Differ from Category (+/-)	-0.4 low	-1.1 low	-1.9 low	**Avg Mat**	5.5 yrs

	2000	1999	1998	1997	1996	1995	1994	1993	1992	1991
Return (%)	5.4	0.2	4.6	5.1	3.9	6.2	1.0	5.6	6.8	7.2
Differ from Category (+/-)	-4.0	2.8	-1.0	-3.1	0.2	-8.9	5.9	-6.1	-1.6	-4.1
Return, Tax-Adjusted (%)	5.4	0.2	4.6	5.1	3.9	6.2	1.0	5.6	6.8	7.2
Dividends, Net Income ($)	0.22	0.20	0.21	0.21	0.21	0.20	0.20	0.21	0.24	0.26
Expense Ratio (%)	0.69	0.72	0.74	0.72	0.75	0.72	0.72	0.76	0.76	0.76
Yield (%)	4.24	3.89	3.94	3.96	4.00	3.80	3.88	3.96	4.58	5.06

SHAREHOLDER INFORMATION

Minimum Investment
Initial: $100 IRA: na
Subsequent: $100 IRA: na

Maximum Fees
Load: none 12b-1: none
Other: none

Empire Bldr Tax-Free Bd/Bldr (EMBTX)

800-847-5886, 212-953-7800

Tax-Exempt Bond

PERFORMANCE AND PER SHARE DATA **fund inception date: 6/1/84**

	3yr Annual	5yr Annual	10yr Annual	Category Risk Index	
Return (%)	4.3	4.7	6.4	1.31—high	
Differ from Category (+/-)	0.5 av	-0.2 blw av	-0.1 blw av	**Avg Mat**	8.0 yrs

	2000	1999	1998	1997	1996	1995	1994	1993	1992	1991
Return (%)	13.6	-4.8	4.9	7.9	3.0	14.5	-4.4	12.2	8.0	11.6
Differ from Category (+/-)	4.2	-2.2	-0.7	-0.3	-0.7	-0.6	0.5	0.5	-0.4	0.3
Return, Tax-Adjusted (%)	13.6	-4.8	4.4	7.8	2.8	14.5	-4.7	11.8	7.7	11.0
Dividends, Net Income ($)	0.74	0.75	0.74	0.80	0.86	0.87	0.85	0.92	0.93	0.99
Expense Ratio (%)	1.08	1.05	0.81	1.07	1.01	0.93	0.98	1.03	1.07	1.27
Yield (%)	4.17	4.59	4.02	4.36	4.82	4.78	5.03	4.88	5.21	5.58

SHAREHOLDER INFORMATION

Minimum Investment
Initial: $1,000 IRA: na
Subsequent: $100 IRA: na

Maximum Fees
Load: none 12b-1: none
Other: none

Empire Bldr Tax-Free Bd/ Prem (EMTPX)

800-847-5886, 212-953-7800

Tax-Exempt Bond

PERFORMANCE AND PER SHARE DATA **fund inception date: 4/15/96**

	3yr Annual	5yr Annual	10yr Annual	Category Risk Index
Return (%)	4.6	na	na	1.31—high
Differ from Category (+/-)	0.8 abv av	na	na	**Avg Mat** 8.0 yrs

	2000	1999	1998	1997	1996	1995	1994	1993	1992	1991
Return (%)	14.0	-4.5	5.2	8.1	—	—	—	—	—	—
Differ from Category (+/-)	4.6	-1.9	-0.4	-0.1	—	—	—	—	—	—
Return, Tax-Adjusted (%)	14.0	-4.5	4.7	8.0	—	—	—	—	—	—
Dividends, Net Income ($)	0.79	0.80	0.80	0.84	—	—	—	—	—	—
Expense Ratio (%)	0.79	0.82	0.81	0.93	—	—	—	—	—	—
Yield (%)	4.45	4.90	4.35	4.58	—	—	—	—	—	—

SHAREHOLDER INFORMATION

Minimum Investment
Initial: $20,000 IRA: na
Subsequent: $5,000 IRA: na

Maximum Fees
Load: none 12b-1: none
Other: none

Excelsior CA Tx Ex Income (UMCAX)

800-446-1012
www.excelsiorfunds.com

Tax-Exempt Bond

PERFORMANCE AND PER SHARE DATA **fund inception date: 10/1/96**

	3yr Annual	5yr Annual	10yr Annual	Category Risk Index
Return (%)	4.0	na	na	0.59—low
Differ from Category (+/-)	0.2 blw av	na	na	**Avg Mat** 4.8 yrs

	2000	1999	1998	1997	1996	1995	1994	1993	1992	1991
Return (%)	6.9	0.1	5.2	5.7	—	—	—	—	—	—
Differ from Category (+/-)	-2.5	2.7	-0.4	-2.5	—	—	—	—	—	—
Return, Tax-Adjusted (%)	6.9	0.1	5.2	5.7	—	—	—	—	—	—
Dividends, Net Income ($)	0.26	0.25	0.26	0.27	—	—	—	—	—	—
Expense Ratio (%)	0.50	0.50	0.50	0.66	—	—	—	—	—	—
Yield (%)	3.60	3.57	3.58	3.77	—	—	—	—	—	—

SHAREHOLDER INFORMATION

Minimum Investment
Initial: $500 IRA: na
Subsequent: $50 IRA: na

Maximum Fees
Load: none 12b-1: none
Other: none

Excelsior Intm Mgd Inc (UIMIX)

800-446-1012
www.excelsiorfunds.com

General Bond

PERFORMANCE AND PER SHARE DATA — fund inception date: 12/31/92

	3yr Annual	5yr Annual	10yr Annual	Category Risk Index
Return (%)	5.7	5.4	na	1.05—abv av
Differ from Category (+/-)	0.2 av	-0.2 blw av	na	**Avg Mat** 11.8 yrs

	2000	1999	1998	1997	1996	1995	1994	1993	1992	1991
Return (%)	10.6	-1.5	8.4	8.4	1.9	19.2	-3.7	8.4	—	—
Differ from Category (+/-)	0.9	-1.5	1.1	0.0	-1.6	3.0	-1.0	-1.3	—	—
Return, Tax-Adjusted (%)	8.1	-3.5	5.8	6.1	-0.3	16.5	-5.7	6.2	—	—
Dividends, Net Income ($)	0.42	0.38	0.39	0.40	0.41	0.43	0.36	0.31	—	—
Expense Ratio (%)	0.58	0.60	0.61	0.63	0.64	0.66	0.69	0.72	—	—
Yield (%)	5.96	5.61	5.26	5.54	5.82	5.86	5.49	4.26	—	—

SHAREHOLDER INFORMATION

Minimum Investment
Initial: $500 IRA: $250
Subsequent: $50 IRA: $50

Maximum Fees
Load: none 12b-1: none
Other: none

Excelsior Intm Tax Exmpt (UMITX)

800-446-1012
www.excelsiorfunds.com

Tax-Exempt Bond

PERFORMANCE AND PER SHARE DATA — fund inception date: 12/2/85

	3yr Annual	5yr Annual	10yr Annual	Category Risk Index
Return (%)	4.5	5.0	6.4	0.91—blw av
Differ from Category (+/-)	0.7 abv av	0.1 av	-0.1 blw av	**Avg Mat** 8.1 yrs

	2000	1999	1998	1997	1996	1995	1994	1993	1992	1991
Return (%)	9.4	-1.7	6.3	7.3	4.1	15.0	-4.1	10.7	8.5	10.1
Differ from Category (+/-)	0.0	0.9	0.7	-0.9	0.4	-0.1	0.8	-1.0	0.1	-1.2
Return, Tax-Adjusted (%)	9.4	-1.7	6.0	7.2	4.1	15.0	-4.1	9.1	7.5	9.9
Dividends, Net Income ($)	0.38	0.36	0.38	0.40	0.40	0.40	0.35	0.35	0.43	0.52
Expense Ratio (%)	0.57	0.58	0.58	0.58	0.60	0.61	0.64	0.64	0.64	0.66
Yield (%)	4.02	4.00	3.93	4.22	4.33	4.32	4.16	3.62	4.59	5.70

SHAREHOLDER INFORMATION

Minimum Investment
Initial: $500 IRA: na
Subsequent: $50 IRA: na

Maximum Fees
Load: none 12b-1: none
Other: none

Excelsior Long-Term Tx Ex (UMLTX)

800-446-1012
www.excelsiorfunds.com

Tax-Exempt Bond

PERFORMANCE AND PER SHARE DATA **fund inception date: 2/5/86**

	3yr Annual	5yr Annual	10yr Annual	Category Risk Index
Return (%)	4.2	5.1	7.9	1.70—high
Differ from Category (+/-)	0.4 blw av	0.2 av	1.4 high	**Avg Mat** 18.1 yrs

	2000	1999	1998	1997	1996	1995	1994	1993	1992	1991
Return (%)	17.2	-8.9	6.3	9.4	3.6	23.4	-5.7	15.6	10.0	12.7
Differ from Category (+/-)	7.8	-6.3	0.7	1.2	-0.1	8.3	-0.8	3.9	1.6	1.4
Return, Tax-Adjusted (%)	17.2	-9.0	5.7	9.1	3.2	22.9	-5.9	13.3	8.5	12.0
Dividends, Net Income ($)	0.41	0.40	0.42	0.44	0.46	0.46	0.41	0.42	0.46	0.52
Expense Ratio (%)	0.75	0.76	0.74	0.74	0.77	0.80	0.85	0.86	0.85	0.86
Yield (%)	4.25	4.61	4.10	4.33	4.68	4.55	4.72	4.03	4.65	5.38

SHAREHOLDER INFORMATION

Minimum Investment
Initial: $500 IRA: na
Subsequent: $50 IRA: na

Maximum Fees
Load: none 12b-1: none
Other: none

Excelsior Managed Income (UMMGX)

800-446-1012
www.excelsiorfunds.com

General Bond

PERFORMANCE AND PER SHARE DATA **fund inception date: 1/9/86**

	3yr Annual	5yr Annual	10yr Annual	Category Risk Index
Return (%)	5.9	5.6	7.7	1.17—high
Differ from Category (+/-)	0.4 abv av	0.0 av	0.5 abv av	**Avg Mat** 13.3 yrs

	2000	1999	1998	1997	1996	1995	1994	1993	1992	1991
Return (%)	12.4	-2.5	8.5	9.7	0.5	22.4	-5.5	12.6	5.8	16.6
Differ from Category (+/-)	2.7	-2.5	1.2	1.3	-3.0	6.2	-2.8	2.9	-1.0	1.1
Return, Tax-Adjusted (%)	10.0	-4.5	5.9	7.4	-1.6	19.7	-7.5	8.0	3.0	13.6
Dividends, Net Income ($)	0.50	0.45	0.46	0.50	0.51	0.54	0.47	0.50	0.58	0.65
Expense Ratio (%)	0.88	0.90	0.90	0.90	0.96	1.00	0.90	0.89	1.05	1.11
Yield (%)	5.56	5.29	4.87	5.45	5.77	5.80	5.80	5.07	6.09	6.60

SHAREHOLDER INFORMATION

Minimum Investment
Initial: $500 IRA: $250
Subsequent: $50 IRA: $50

Maximum Fees
Load: none 12b-1: none
Other: none

Excelsior NY Intm Tx Ex (UMNYX)

800-446-1012
www.excelsiorfunds.com

Tax-Exempt Bond

PERFORMANCE AND PER SHARE DATA **fund inception date: 5/31/90**

	3yr Annual	5yr Annual	10yr Annual	Category Risk Index
Return (%)	4.5	4.9	5.8	0.97—av
Differ from Category (+/-)	0.7 abv av	0.0 av	-0.7 low	**Avg Mat** 8.6 yrs

	2000	1999	1998	1997	1996	1995	1994	1993	1992	1991
Return (%)	9.7	-2.1	6.3	6.6	4.3	13.6	-4.2	9.2	6.5	9.5
Differ from Category (+/-)	0.3	0.5	0.7	-1.6	0.6	-1.5	0.7	-2.5	-1.9	-1.8
Return, Tax-Adjusted (%)	9.7	-2.3	6.0	6.6	4.3	13.6	-4.4	8.2	6.1	9.2
Dividends, Net Income ($)	0.33	0.31	0.33	0.35	0.35	0.35	0.31	0.31	0.35	0.42
Expense Ratio (%)	0.73	0.73	0.71	0.72	0.75	0.78	0.87	0.89	0.88	0.86
Yield (%)	3.78	3.71	3.68	4.00	4.09	4.09	3.90	3.48	4.08	4.97

SHAREHOLDER INFORMATION

Minimum Investment
Initial: $500 IRA: na
Subsequent: $50 IRA: na

Maximum Fees
Load: none 12b-1: none
Other: none

Excelsior Sh Tm Gov't Sec (UMGVX)

800-446-1012
www.excelsiorfunds.com

Government Bond

PERFORMANCE AND PER SHARE DATA **fund inception date: 12/31/92**

	3yr Annual	5yr Annual	10yr Annual	Category Risk Index
Return (%)	5.3	5.2	na	0.43—low
Differ from Category (+/-)	-0.9 low	-0.7 low	na	**Avg Mat** 2.3 yrs

	2000	1999	1998	1997	1996	1995	1994	1993	1992	1991
Return (%)	7.6	2.3	6.3	5.8	3.9	10.2	1.0	4.3	—	—
Differ from Category (+/-)	-6.2	5.3	-2.8	-4.0	1.8	-8.6	4.6	-6.3	—	—
Return, Tax-Adjusted (%)	5.4	0.4	4.3	3.7	1.7	7.8	-0.6	2.8	—	—
Dividends, Net Income ($)	0.38	0.33	0.35	0.36	0.38	0.40	0.29	0.24	—	—
Expense Ratio (%)	0.54	0.58	0.62	0.61	0.61	0.61	0.62	0.62	—	—
Yield (%)	5.42	4.78	4.94	5.14	5.45	5.64	4.26	3.40	—	—

SHAREHOLDER INFORMATION

Minimum Investment
Initial: $500 IRA: $250
Subsequent: $50 IRA: $50

Maximum Fees
Load: none 12b-1: none
Other: none

Fidelity Capital & Inc (FAGIX)

800-544-8888, 801-534-1910
www.fidelity.com

Corporate High-Yield Bond

PERFORMANCE AND PER SHARE DATA **fund inception date: 11/1/77**

	3yr Annual	5yr Annual	10yr Annual	Category Risk Index
Return (%)	2.4	6.5	12.2	1.45—high
Differ from Category (+/-)	2.4 high	1.1 high	2.4 high	**Avg Mat** 5.4 yrs

	2000	1999	1998	1997	1996	1995	1994	1993	1992	1991
Return (%)	-9.4	13.2	4.7	14.7	11.4	16.7	-4.6	24.9	28.0	29.8
Differ from Category (+/-)	-2.5	7.6	2.8	0.1	-4.3	-0.7	-2.4	5.5	11.8	2.3
Return, Tax-Adjusted (%)	-12.5	9.0	0.4	11.8	7.9	12.7	-7.7	21.0	25.1	26.1
Dividends, Net Income ($)	0.74	0.72	0.94	0.67	0.79	0.87	0.79	0.83	0.66	0.73
Expense Ratio (%)	0.82	0.81	0.82	0.86	0.98	0.96	0.97	0.91	0.80	0.81
Yield (%)	9.57	7.36	9.85	6.69	8.44	9.49	9.15	8.41	7.66	10.02

SHAREHOLDER INFORMATION

Minimum Investment
Initial: $2,500 IRA: $500
Subsequent: $250 IRA: $250

Maximum Fees
Load: 1.50% redemption 12b-1: none
Other: redemption fee applies for 12 months

Fidelity Ginnie Mae (FGMNX)

800-544-8544, 801-534-1910
www.fidelity.com

Mortgage-Backed Bond

PERFORMANCE AND PER SHARE DATA **fund inception date: 11/8/85**

	3yr Annual	5yr Annual	10yr Annual	Category Risk Index
Return (%)	6.0	6.3	7.1	1.00—av
Differ from Category (+/-)	0.4 high	0.4 high	0.0 abv av	**Avg Mat** 7.8 yrs

	2000	1999	1998	1997	1996	1995	1994	1993	1992	1991
Return (%)	10.7	1.2	6.3	8.7	4.8	16.6	-1.9	6.1	6.6	13.5
Differ from Category (+/-)	0.8	0.2	0.1	0.2	0.6	1.7	-0.6	-0.3	0.1	-1.2
Return, Tax-Adjusted (%)	8.0	-1.2	3.8	6.1	2.2	13.7	-4.2	3.2	4.5	11.0
Dividends, Net Income ($)	0.70	0.66	0.67	0.70	0.69	0.71	0.63	0.62	0.74	0.83
Expense Ratio (%)	0.63	0.64	0.72	0.75	0.75	0.75	0.82	0.80	0.80	0.83
Yield (%)	6.52	6.37	6.15	6.42	6.44	6.51	6.29	5.58	6.68	7.47

SHAREHOLDER INFORMATION

Minimum Investment
Initial: $2,500 IRA: $500
Subsequent: $250 IRA: $250

Maximum Fees
Load: none 12b-1: none
Other: none

Fidelity Gov't Inc (FGOVX)

800-544-8544, 801-534-1910
www.fidelity.com

Government Bond

PERFORMANCE AND PER SHARE DATA **fund inception date: 4/4/79**

	3yr Annual	5yr Annual	10yr Annual	Category Risk Index
Return (%)	6.1	5.8	7.6	1.12—av
Differ from Category (+/-)	-0.1 abv av	-0.1 av	0.0 abv av	**Avg Mat** 9.2 yrs

	2000	1999	1998	1997	1996	1995	1994	1993	1992	1991
Return (%)	12.6	-2.2	8.5	8.9	2.0	18.0	-5.2	12.3	7.9	15.9
Differ from Category (+/-)	-1.2	0.8	-0.6	-0.9	-0.1	-0.8	-1.6	1.7	1.3	1.0
Return, Tax-Adjusted (%)	10.0	-4.3	6.1	6.4	-0.6	15.3	-7.5	8.8	5.0	13.3
Dividends, Net Income ($)	0.61	0.56	0.60	0.61	0.67	0.61	0.61	0.67	0.73	0.80
Expense Ratio (%)	0.66	0.67	0.68	0.73	0.72	0.71	0.69	0.69	0.70	0.70
Yield (%)	6.18	5.98	5.91	6.15	6.91	5.99	6.63	6.29	7.05	7.76

SHAREHOLDER INFORMATION

Minimum Investment
Initial: $2,500 IRA: $500
Subsequent: $250 IRA: $250

Maximum Fees
Load: none 12b-1: none
Other: none

Fidelity High Income (SPHIX)

800-544-8888, 801-534-1910
www.fidelity.com

Corporate High-Yield Bond

PERFORMANCE AND PER SHARE DATA **fund inception date: 8/29/90**

	3yr Annual	5yr Annual	10yr Annual	Category Risk Index
Return (%)	-1.1	5.0	12.0	1.38—high
Differ from Category (+/-)	-1.1 blw av	-0.4 blw av	2.2 high	**Avg Mat** 7.1 yrs

	2000	1999	1998	1997	1996	1995	1994	1993	1992	1991
Return (%)	-14.2	8.9	3.3	15.9	14.1	18.5	3.2	21.8	21.5	34.3
Differ from Category (+/-)	-7.3	3.3	1.4	1.3	-1.6	1.1	5.4	2.4	5.3	6.8
Return, Tax-Adjusted (%)	-17.2	5.0	-0.3	11.9	10.0	14.1	-0.2	16.0	17.0	29.1
Dividends, Net Income ($)	0.92	1.16	1.06	1.11	1.06	1.17	0.99	1.12	1.25	1.29
Expense Ratio (%)	0.74	0.80	0.80	0.80	0.80	0.80	0.75	0.70	0.70	0.70
Yield (%)	9.73	9.65	8.54	8.32	8.28	9.48	8.57	8.64	10.39	11.39

SHAREHOLDER INFORMATION

Minimum Investment
Initial: $2,500 IRA: $500
Subsequent: $250 IRA: $250

Maximum Fees
Load: 1.00% redemption 12b-1: none
Other: redemption fee applies for 9 months

Fidelity Instl Sh Int Gvt (FFXSX)

800-522-7297, 801-534-1910
www.fidelity.com

Government Bond

PERFORMANCE AND PER SHARE DATA **fund inception date: 11/10/86**

	3yr Annual	5yr Annual	10yr Annual	Category Risk Index
Return (%)	5.9	5.7	6.4	0.57—blw av
Differ from Category (+/-)	-0.3 av	-0.2 av	-1.2 blw av	**Avg Mat** 3.8 yrs

	2000	1999	1998	1997	1996	1995	1994	1993	1992	1991
Return (%)	9.0	2.0	6.9	6.3	4.7	12.4	-0.8	5.8	6.3	12.7
Differ from Category (+/-)	-4.8	5.0	-2.2	-3.5	2.6	-6.4	2.8	-4.8	-0.3	-2.2
Return, Tax-Adjusted (%)	6.3	-0.3	4.3	3.9	2.0	9.5	-3.2	3.4	4.3	10.2
Dividends, Net Income ($)	0.60	0.56	0.60	0.57	0.64	0.65	0.61	0.58	0.62	0.75
Expense Ratio (%)	na	0.44	0.45	0.44	0.41	0.45	0.45	0.45	0.45	0.45
Yield (%)	6.48	6.17	6.34	6.05	6.79	6.74	6.64	5.86	6.25	7.55

SHAREHOLDER INFORMATION

Minimum Investment		**Maximum Fees**	
Initial: $100,000	IRA: $1	Load: none	12b-1: none
Subsequent: $2,500	IRA: $1	Other: none	

Fidelity Interm Bond (FTHRX)

800-544-8888, 801-534-1910
www.fidelity.com

General Bond

PERFORMANCE AND PER SHARE DATA **fund inception date: 5/23/75**

	3yr Annual	5yr Annual	10yr Annual	Category Risk Index
Return (%)	5.9	5.8	7.1	0.81—blw av
Differ from Category (+/-)	0.4 abv av	0.2 av	-0.1 av	**Avg Mat** 6.1 yrs

	2000	1999	1998	1997	1996	1995	1994	1993	1992	1991
Return (%)	9.7	0.9	7.3	7.5	3.6	12.8	-2.0	11.9	6.0	14.4
Differ from Category (+/-)	0.0	0.9	0.0	-0.9	0.1	-3.4	0.7	2.2	-0.8	-1.1
Return, Tax-Adjusted (%)	7.1	-1.4	4.8	4.9	1.0	10.2	-4.5	8.8	3.6	12.0
Dividends, Net Income ($)	0.63	0.60	0.62	0.64	0.65	0.64	0.64	0.75	0.76	0.76
Expense Ratio (%)	0.66	0.65	0.65	0.71	0.71	0.68	0.64	0.61	0.63	0.66
Yield (%)	6.27	6.14	6.03	6.29	6.42	6.14	6.45	6.89	7.25	7.15

SHAREHOLDER INFORMATION

Minimum Investment		**Maximum Fees**	
Initial: $2,500	IRA: $500	Load: none	12b-1: none
Subsequent: $250	IRA: $250	Other: none	

Fidelity Interm Gvt Inc (FSTGX)

800-544-8544, 801-534-1910
www.fidelity.com

Government Bond

PERFORMANCE AND PER SHARE DATA **fund inception date: 5/2/88**

	3yr Annual	5yr Annual	10yr Annual	Category Risk Index
Return (%)	6.0	5.8	6.5	0.78—av
Differ from Category (+/-)	-0.2 av	-0.1 av	-1.1 blw av	**Avg Mat** 5.5 yrs

	2000	1999	1998	1997	1996	1995	1994	1993	1992	1991
Return (%)	10.3	0.6	7.4	7.1	4.1	13.9	-0.9	6.4	5.7	11.9
Differ from Category (+/-)	-3.5	3.6	-1.7	-2.7	2.0	-4.9	2.7	-4.2	-0.9	-3.0
Return, Tax-Adjusted (%)	7.7	-1.7	4.8	4.5	1.5	11.3	-3.0	3.5	3.7	9.2
Dividends, Net Income ($)	0.61	0.59	0.63	0.63	0.65	0.61	0.55	0.57	0.60	0.81
Expense Ratio (%)	0.61	0.53	0.38	0.54	0.62	0.65	0.65	0.65	0.61	0.50
Yield (%)	6.34	6.33	6.39	6.44	6.67	6.10	5.88	5.57	5.87	7.85

SHAREHOLDER INFORMATION

Minimum Investment
Initial: $2,500 IRA: $500
Subsequent: $250 IRA: $250

Maximum Fees
Load: none 12b-1: none
Other: none

Fidelity Intl Bond (FGBDX)

800-544-6666, 801-534-1910
www.fidelity.com

International Bond

PERFORMANCE AND PER SHARE DATA **fund inception date: 12/30/86**

	3yr Annual	5yr Annual	10yr Annual	Category Risk Index
Return (%)	2.7	2.0	3.5	0.99—av
Differ from Category (+/-)	-0.5 av	-3.2 blw av	-1.9 blw av	**Avg Mat** 8.9 yrs

	2000	1999	1998	1997	1996	1995	1994	1993	1992	1991
Return (%)	1.4	0.5	6.2	-1.3	3.4	6.6	-16.3	21.9	4.4	12.7
Differ from Category (+/-)	-3.1	-3.3	2.6	-5.2	-10.7	-10.3	-9.1	6.7	0.8	-2.0
Return, Tax-Adjusted (%)	-0.5	-1.5	3.9	-3.2	1.2	4.3	-18.5	18.3	1.5	10.2
Dividends, Net Income ($)	0.42	0.48	0.52	0.49	0.54	0.57	0.69	0.85	1.08	0.72
Expense Ratio (%)	na	1.27	1.26	1.27	1.22	1.17	1.14	1.17	1.23	1.35
Yield (%)	5.02	5.53	5.70	5.39	5.55	5.73	6.96	6.60	9.52	5.96

SHAREHOLDER INFORMATION

Minimum Investment
Initial: $2,500 IRA: $500
Subsequent: $250 IRA: $250

Maximum Fees
Load: none 12b-1: none
Other: none

Fidelity Invest Grade Bd (FBNDX)

800-544-8888, 801-534-1910
www.fidelity.com

General Bond

PERFORMANCE AND PER SHARE DATA — fund inception date: 8/6/71

	3yr Annual	5yr Annual	10yr Annual	Category Risk Index
Return (%)	5.8	5.8	8.0	1.01—av
Differ from Category (+/-)	0.3 abv av	0.2 abv av	0.8 high	**Avg Mat** 9.7 yrs

	2000	1999	1998	1997	1996	1995	1994	1993	1992	1991
Return (%)	10.8	-1.0	7.9	8.9	3.0	15.5	-5.3	16.2	8.3	18.9
Differ from Category (+/-)	1.1	-1.0	0.6	0.5	-0.5	-0.7	-2.6	6.5	1.5	3.4
Return, Tax-Adjusted (%)	8.2	-3.2	5.5	6.3	0.5	12.7	-8.2	13.1	5.9	16.1
Dividends, Net Income ($)	0.44	0.42	0.42	0.45	0.46	0.46	0.50	0.56	0.55	0.59
Expense Ratio (%)	0.69	0.70	0.72	0.76	0.76	0.75	0.74	0.68	0.70	0.67
Yield (%)	6.14	6.09	5.66	6.18	6.46	6.20	7.17	7.09	7.53	8.10

SHAREHOLDER INFORMATION

Minimum Investment
Initial: $2,500 IRA: $500
Subsequent: $250 IRA: $250

Maximum Fees
Load: none 12b-1: none
Other: none

Fidelity New Markets Inc (FNMIX)

800-544-6666, 801-534-1910
www.fidelity.com

International Bond

PERFORMANCE AND PER SHARE DATA — fund inception date: 5/4/93

	3yr Annual	5yr Annual	10yr Annual	Category Risk Index
Return (%)	6.6	14.8	na	3.34—high
Differ from Category (+/-)	3.4 high	9.6 high	na	**Avg Mat** 11.6 yrs

	2000	1999	1998	1997	1996	1995	1994	1993	1992	1991
Return (%)	14.3	36.7	-22.3	16.4	41.3	7.8	-16.4	—	—	—
Differ from Category (+/-)	9.8	32.9	-25.9	12.5	27.2	-9.1	-9.2	—	—	—
Return, Tax-Adjusted (%)	9.7	32.2	-25.9	11.4	37.5	4.2	-18.5	—	—	—
Dividends, Net Income ($)	1.29	1.01	1.21	1.19	0.93	0.91	0.56	—	—	—
Expense Ratio (%)	na	1.07	1.13	1.08	1.09	1.20	1.28	—	—	—
Yield (%)	11.32	9.07	13.45	8.59	7.17	9.14	5.38	—	—	—

SHAREHOLDER INFORMATION

Minimum Investment
Initial: $2,500 IRA: $500
Subsequent: $250 IRA: $250

Maximum Fees
Load: 1.00% redemption 12b-1: none
Other: redemption fee applies for 6 months

Fidelity Short Tm Bond (FSHBX)

800-544-8888, 801-534-1910
www.fidelity.com

Corporate Bond

PERFORMANCE AND PER SHARE DATA **fund inception date: 9/15/86**

	3yr Annual	5yr Annual	10yr Annual	Category Risk Index
Return (%)	5.7	5.6	6.3	0.40—low
Differ from Category (+/-)	0.7 abv av	-0.1 blw av	-1.8 low	**Avg Mat** 2.4 yrs

	2000	1999	1998	1997	1996	1995	1994	1993	1992	1991
Return (%)	7.8	3.2	6.1	6.2	4.7	9.8	-4.0	9.1	7.3	14.0
Differ from Category (+/-)	-0.2	1.9	0.2	-2.9	-0.8	-8.1	-1.7	-2.7	-2.0	-3.7
Return, Tax-Adjusted (%)	5.3	1.0	3.7	3.7	2.2	7.3	-6.3	6.3	4.8	11.2
Dividends, Net Income ($)	0.52	0.48	0.51	0.54	0.56	0.54	0.57	0.66	0.74	0.81
Expense Ratio (%)	0.63	0.65	0.70	0.70	0.68	0.69	0.80	0.77	0.86	0.83
Yield (%)	6.03	5.64	5.85	6.20	6.42	6.08	6.62	6.91	7.88	8.57

SHAREHOLDER INFORMATION

Minimum Investment
Initial: $2,500 IRA: $500
Subsequent: $250 IRA: $250

Maximum Fees
Load: none 12b-1: none
Other: none

Fidelity Spart CA Muni (FCTFX)

800-544-8888, 801-534-1910
www.fidelity.com

Tax-Exempt Bond

PERFORMANCE AND PER SHARE DATA **fund inception date: 7/3/84**

	3yr Annual	5yr Annual	10yr Annual	Category Risk Index
Return (%)	5.2	6.0	7.0	1.11—abv av
Differ from Category (+/-)	1.4 high	1.1 high	0.5 abv av	**Avg Mat** 14.6 yrs

	2000	1999	1998	1997	1996	1995	1994	1993	1992	1991
Return (%)	12.5	-2.7	6.5	9.8	4.7	19.1	-8.8	13.4	8.7	10.1
Differ from Category (+/-)	3.1	-0.1	0.9	1.6	1.0	4.0	-3.9	1.7	0.3	-1.2
Return, Tax-Adjusted (%)	12.5	-2.7	6.3	9.8	4.7	19.1	-9.1	12.7	8.7	10.1
Dividends, Net Income ($)	0.57	0.55	0.57	0.59	0.60	0.62	0.69	0.72	0.74	0.74
Expense Ratio (%)	0.49	0.52	0.53	0.59	0.58	0.56	0.57	0.60	0.59	0.58
Yield (%)	4.63	4.77	4.55	4.79	5.09	5.23	6.47	5.67	6.23	6.36

SHAREHOLDER INFORMATION

Minimum Investment
Initial: $10,000 IRA: na
Subsequent: $1,000 IRA: na

Maximum Fees
Load: none 12b-1: none
Other: none

Fidelity Spart CT Muni (FICNX)

800-544-8888, 801-534-1910
www.fidelity.com

Tax-Exempt Bond

PERFORMANCE AND PER SHARE DATA **fund inception date: 10/27/87**

	3yr Annual	5yr Annual	10yr Annual	Category Risk Index
Return (%)	4.7	5.5	6.7	1.00—av
Differ from Category (+/-)	0.9 abv av	0.6 abv av	0.2 av	**Avg Mat** 14.0 yrs

	2000	1999	1998	1997	1996	1995	1994	1993	1992	1991
Return (%)	10.9	-2.0	5.8	9.1	4.2	17.1	-7.0	12.9	8.2	10.5
Differ from Category (+/-)	1.5	0.6	0.2	0.9	0.5	2.0	-2.1	1.2	-0.2	-0.8
Return, Tax-Adjusted (%)	10.9	-2.0	5.7	8.9	4.2	17.1	-7.2	12.0	8.2	10.5
Dividends, Net Income ($)	0.55	0.52	0.53	0.55	0.56	0.61	0.63	0.67	0.69	0.68
Expense Ratio (%)	na	0.49	0.54	0.55	0.52	0.55	0.55	0.55	0.55	0.55
Yield (%)	4.85	4.83	4.58	4.75	5.03	5.42	6.14	5.56	6.11	6.13

SHAREHOLDER INFORMATION

Minimum Investment
Initial: $10,000 IRA: na
Subsequent: $1,000 IRA: na

Maximum Fees
Load: 0.50% redemption 12b-1: none
Other: redemption fee applies for 6 months

Fidelity Spart FL Income (FFLIX)

800-544-8888, 801-534-1910
www.fidelity.com

Tax-Exempt Bond

PERFORMANCE AND PER SHARE DATA **fund inception date: 3/16/92**

	3yr Annual	5yr Annual	10yr Annual	Category Risk Index
Return (%)	4.6	5.3	na	1.00—av
Differ from Category (+/-)	0.8 abv av	0.4 abv av	na	**Avg Mat** 14.3 yrs

	2000	1999	1998	1997	1996	1995	1994	1993	1992	1991
Return (%)	10.8	-2.7	6.2	8.7	3.9	18.6	-6.7	14.8	—	—
Differ from Category (+/-)	1.4	-0.1	0.6	0.5	0.2	3.5	-1.8	3.1	—	—
Return, Tax-Adjusted (%)	10.8	-2.7	6.0	8.6	3.9	18.6	-6.7	14.2	—	—
Dividends, Net Income ($)	0.53	0.51	0.52	0.53	0.54	0.56	0.58	0.61	—	—
Expense Ratio (%)	na	0.55	0.55	0.55	0.55	0.55	0.54	0.25	—	—
Yield (%)	4.68	4.74	4.45	4.59	4.85	4.98	5.80	5.29	—	—

SHAREHOLDER INFORMATION

Minimum Investment
Initial: $10,000 IRA: na
Subsequent: $1,000 IRA: na

Maximum Fees
Load: 0.50% redemption 12b-1: none
Other: redemption fee applies for 6 months

Fidelity Spart Gov't Inc (SPGVX)

800-544-8888, 801-534-1910
www.fidelity.com

Government Bond

PERFORMANCE AND PER SHARE DATA — fund inception date: 12/20/88

	3yr Annual	5yr Annual	10yr Annual	Category Risk Index
Return (%)	6.2	6.0	7.3	1.16—av
Differ from Category (+/-)	0.0 abv av	0.1 abv av	-0.3 abv av	**Avg Mat** 9.6 yrs

	2000	1999	1998	1997	1996	1995	1994	1993	1992	1991
Return (%)	12.7	-2.5	9.0	9.2	2.6	18.1	-3.5	7.3	7.1	15.1
Differ from Category (+/-)	-1.1	0.5	-0.1	-0.6	0.5	-0.7	0.1	-3.3	0.5	0.2
Return, Tax-Adjusted (%)	10.1	-4.6	6.6	6.7	0.1	15.3	-6.0	4.3	3.9	12.5
Dividends, Net Income ($)	0.65	0.58	0.62	0.64	0.67	0.66	0.70	0.61	0.76	0.83
Expense Ratio (%)	0.50	0.51	0.60	0.60	0.65	0.65	0.65	0.65	0.65	0.53
Yield (%)	6.20	5.85	5.76	6.11	6.56	6.21	7.29	5.57	6.78	7.37

SHAREHOLDER INFORMATION

Minimum Investment
Initial: $25,000 IRA: $25,000
Subsequent: $1,000 IRA: $1,000

Maximum Fees
Load: none 12b-1: none
Other: none

Fidelity Spart Int Muni (FLTMX)

800-544-8888, 801-534-1910
www.fidelity.com

Tax-Exempt Bond

PERFORMANCE AND PER SHARE DATA — fund inception date: 4/15/77

	3yr Annual	5yr Annual	10yr Annual	Category Risk Index
Return (%)	4.6	5.2	6.6	0.81—blw av
Differ from Category (+/-)	0.8 abv av	0.3 abv av	0.1 av	**Avg Mat** 8.2 yrs

	2000	1999	1998	1997	1996	1995	1994	1993	1992	1991
Return (%)	9.2	-1.0	5.8	8.3	4.3	14.8	-4.7	12.2	8.1	11.1
Differ from Category (+/-)	-0.2	1.6	0.2	0.1	0.6	-0.3	0.2	0.5	-0.3	-0.2
Return, Tax-Adjusted (%)	9.2	-1.0	5.6	8.1	4.2	14.8	-4.7	11.5	7.8	10.6
Dividends, Net Income ($)	0.47	0.46	0.47	0.48	0.48	0.49	0.51	0.51	0.57	0.60
Expense Ratio (%)	na	0.48	0.50	0.55	0.56	0.58	0.56	0.57	0.64	0.68
Yield (%)	4.80	4.88	4.68	4.80	4.93	5.00	5.66	4.98	5.87	6.20

SHAREHOLDER INFORMATION

Minimum Investment
Initial: $10,000 IRA: na
Subsequent: $1,000 IRA: na

Maximum Fees
Load: none 12b-1: none
Other: none

Fidelity Spart Inv Grade (FSIBX)

800-544-8544, 801-534-1910
www.fidelity.com

General Bond

PERFORMANCE AND PER SHARE DATA — fund inception date: 9/30/92

	3yr Annual	5yr Annual	10yr Annual	Category Risk Index
Return (%)	6.2	6.1	na	1.04—av
Differ from Category (+/-)	0.7 high	0.5 high	na	**Avg Mat** 9.7 yrs

	2000	1999	1998	1997	1996	1995	1994	1993	1992	1991
Return (%)	11.0	-0.7	8.7	9.2	3.1	18.6	-5.1	15.7	—	—
Differ from Category (+/-)	1.3	-0.7	1.4	0.8	-0.4	2.4	-2.4	6.0	—	—
Return, Tax-Adjusted (%)	8.3	-3.0	6.1	6.6	0.7	15.8	-7.7	12.5	—	—
Dividends, Net Income ($)	0.65	0.62	0.63	0.64	0.63	0.65	0.70	0.78	—	—
Expense Ratio (%)	0.50	0.47	0.38	0.48	0.65	0.65	0.65	0.65	—	—
Yield (%)	6.35	6.30	5.93	6.17	6.23	6.22	7.42	7.29	—	—

SHAREHOLDER INFORMATION

Minimum Investment
Initial: $25,000 IRA: $25,000
Subsequent: $1,000 IRA: $1,000

Maximum Fees
Load: none 12b-1: none
Other: none

Fidelity Spart MA Muni (FDMMX)

800-544-8888, 801-534-1910
www.fidelity.com

Tax-Exempt Bond

PERFORMANCE AND PER SHARE DATA — fund inception date: 11/10/83

	3yr Annual	5yr Annual	10yr Annual	Category Risk Index
Return (%)	4.9	5.5	7.1	1.02—av
Differ from Category (+/-)	1.1 high	0.6 abv av	0.6 abv av	**Avg Mat** 17.0 yrs

	2000	1999	1998	1997	1996	1995	1994	1993	1992	1991
Return (%)	11.8	-2.1	5.6	9.3	3.5	18.0	-6.0	12.9	9.2	11.3
Differ from Category (+/-)	2.4	0.5	0.0	1.1	-0.2	2.9	-1.1	1.2	0.8	0.0
Return, Tax-Adjusted (%)	11.8	-2.1	5.5	9.3	3.5	18.0	-6.5	12.2	9.0	11.0
Dividends, Net Income ($)	0.56	0.55	0.57	0.59	0.60	0.65	0.70	0.71	0.72	0.75
Expense Ratio (%)	0.49	0.49	0.53	0.56	0.54	0.55	0.54	0.55	0.57	0.56
Yield (%)	4.73	4.93	4.75	4.95	5.23	5.56	6.53	5.73	6.14	6.52

SHAREHOLDER INFORMATION

Minimum Investment
Initial: $10,000 IRA: na
Subsequent: $1,000 IRA: na

Maximum Fees
Load: none 12b-1: none
Other: none

Fidelity Spart MD Income (SMDMX)

800-544-8888, 801-534-1910
www.fidelity.com

Tax-Exempt Bond

PERFORMANCE AND PER SHARE DATA **fund inception date: 4/22/93**

	3yr Annual	5yr Annual	10yr Annual	Category Risk Index
Return (%)	4.7	5.4	na	0.97—blw av
Differ from Category (+/-)	0.9 abv av	0.5 abv av	na	**Avg Mat** 14.1 yrs

	2000	1999	1998	1997	1996	1995	1994	1993	1992	1991
Return (%)	11.0	-2.1	5.9	8.8	3.8	17.7	-7.5	—	—	—
Differ from Category (+/-)	1.6	0.5	0.3	0.6	0.1	2.6	-2.6	—	—	—
Return, Tax-Adjusted (%)	11.0	-2.1	5.9	8.8	3.8	17.7	-7.5	—	—	—
Dividends, Net Income ($)	0.48	0.45	0.45	0.46	0.47	0.52	0.55	—	—	—
Expense Ratio (%)	0.55	0.55	0.55	0.55	0.39	0.15	0.03	—	—	—
Yield (%)	4.58	4.54	4.25	4.41	4.68	5.13	6.06	—	—	—

SHAREHOLDER INFORMATION

Minimum Investment
Initial: $10,000 IRA: na
Subsequent: $1,000 IRA: na

Maximum Fees
Load: 0.50% redemption 12b-1: none
Other: redemption fee applies for 6 months

Fidelity Spart MI Muni (FMHTX)

800-544-8888, 801-534-1910
www.fidelity.com

Tax-Exempt Bond

PERFORMANCE AND PER SHARE DATA **fund inception date: 11/12/85**

	3yr Annual	5yr Annual	10yr Annual	Category Risk Index
Return (%)	4.6	5.1	6.7	1.01—av
Differ from Category (+/-)	0.8 abv av	0.2 av	0.2 av	**Avg Mat** 13.7 yrs

	2000	1999	1998	1997	1996	1995	1994	1993	1992	1991
Return (%)	11.1	-2.6	5.7	8.5	3.3	15.4	-7.5	13.8	9.5	12.0
Differ from Category (+/-)	1.7	0.0	0.1	0.3	-0.4	0.3	-2.6	2.1	1.1	0.7
Return, Tax-Adjusted (%)	11.1	-2.6	5.7	8.3	3.3	15.4	-7.8	13.2	9.4	12.0
Dividends, Net Income ($)	0.56	0.55	0.55	0.52	0.63	0.61	0.68	0.70	0.73	0.74
Expense Ratio (%)	na	0.52	0.55	0.56	0.59	0.60	0.57	0.59	0.61	0.62
Yield (%)	4.87	5.05	4.69	4.43	5.57	5.27	6.32	5.56	6.22	6.48

SHAREHOLDER INFORMATION

Minimum Investment
Initial: $10,000 IRA: na
Subsequent: $1,000 IRA: na

Maximum Fees
Load: none 12b-1: none
Other: none

Fidelity Spart MN Muni (FIMIX)

800-544-8888, 801-534-1910
www.fidelity.com

Tax-Exempt Bond

PERFORMANCE AND PER SHARE DATA fund inception date: 11/21/85

	3yr Annual	5yr Annual	10yr Annual	Category Risk Index
Return (%)	4.4	5.1	6.2	0.94—blw av
Differ from Category (+/-)	0.6 av	0.2 av	-0.3 blw av	**Avg Mat** 14.4 yrs

	2000	1999	1998	1997	1996	1995	1994	1993	1992	1991
Return (%)	10.6	-2.4	5.5	8.8	3.7	15.8	-5.9	12.4	7.6	8.4
Differ from Category (+/-)	1.2	0.2	-0.1	0.6	0.0	0.7	-1.0	0.7	-0.8	-2.9
Return, Tax-Adjusted (%)	10.6	-2.4	5.5	8.8	3.7	15.8	-6.0	12.4	7.6	8.4
Dividends, Net Income ($)	0.52	0.51	0.53	0.55	0.56	0.61	0.63	0.64	0.67	0.68
Expense Ratio (%)	na	0.51	0.55	0.56	0.60	0.55	0.59	0.61	0.67	0.72
Yield (%)	4.64	4.79	4.64	4.85	5.11	5.49	6.16	5.55	6.17	6.33

SHAREHOLDER INFORMATION

Minimum Investment
Initial: $10,000 IRA: na
Subsequent: $1,000 IRA: na

Maximum Fees
Load: none 12b-1: none
Other: none

Fidelity Spart Muni Inc (FHIGX)

800-544-8888, 801-534-1910
www.fidelity.com

Tax-Exempt Bond

PERFORMANCE AND PER SHARE DATA fund inception date: 11/30/77

	3yr Annual	5yr Annual	10yr Annual	Category Risk Index
Return (%)	5.1	5.8	6.7	1.07—av
Differ from Category (+/-)	1.3 high	0.9 high	0.2 av	**Avg Mat** 16.1 yrs

	2000	1999	1998	1997	1996	1995	1994	1993	1992	1991
Return (%)	12.2	-2.4	6.0	8.7	4.9	16.1	-7.4	13.1	8.3	10.1
Differ from Category (+/-)	2.8	0.2	0.4	0.5	1.2	1.0	-2.5	1.4	-0.1	-1.2
Return, Tax-Adjusted (%)	12.2	-2.4	6.0	8.5	4.8	16.1	-7.4	11.9	7.8	9.7
Dividends, Net Income ($)	0.62	0.59	0.60	0.55	0.64	0.66	0.75	0.76	0.80	0.83
Expense Ratio (%)	na	0.49	0.53	0.55	0.56	0.57	0.56	0.56	0.57	0.56
Yield (%)	4.88	4.95	4.68	4.31	5.20	5.33	6.66	5.65	6.25	6.51

SHAREHOLDER INFORMATION

Minimum Investment
Initial: $10,000 IRA: na
Subsequent: $1,000 IRA: na

Maximum Fees
Load: none 12b-1: none
Other: none

Fidelity Spart NJ Muni (FNJHX)

800-544-8888, 801-534-1910
www.fidelity.com

Tax-Exempt Bond

PERFORMANCE AND PER SHARE DATA — fund inception date: 12/31/87

	3yr Annual	5yr Annual	10yr Annual	Category Risk Index
Return (%)	5.1	5.5	6.9	0.97—av
Differ from Category (+/-)	1.3 high	0.6 abv av	0.4 abv av	**Avg Mat** 16.8 yrs

	2000	1999	1998	1997	1996	1995	1994	1993	1992	1991
Return (%)	11.3	-1.4	5.7	8.3	4.0	15.3	-5.7	13.0	8.7	12.3
Differ from Category (+/-)	1.9	1.2	0.1	0.1	0.3	0.2	-0.8	1.3	0.3	1.0
Return, Tax-Adjusted (%)	11.3	-1.4	5.5	8.1	3.6	15.2	-5.7	12.6	8.2	12.0
Dividends, Net Income ($)	0.56	0.52	0.54	0.55	0.58	0.61	0.63	0.63	0.69	0.69
Expense Ratio (%)	na	0.55	0.55	0.55	0.52	0.55	0.55	0.55	0.51	0.52
Yield (%)	4.90	4.81	4.67	4.78	5.12	5.31	5.99	5.26	6.08	6.17

SHAREHOLDER INFORMATION

Minimum Investment
Initial: $10,000 IRA: na
Subsequent: $1,000 IRA: na

Maximum Fees
Load: 0.50% redemption 12b-1: none
Other: redemption fee applies for 6 months

Fidelity Spart NY Muni In (FTFMX)

800-544-8888, 801-534-1910
www.fidelity.com

Tax-Exempt Bond

PERFORMANCE AND PER SHARE DATA — fund inception date: 7/10/84

	3yr Annual	5yr Annual	10yr Annual	Category Risk Index
Return (%)	5.0	5.7	7.3	1.20—abv av
Differ from Category (+/-)	1.2 high	0.8 high	0.8 high	**Avg Mat** 15.8 yrs

	2000	1999	1998	1997	1996	1995	1994	1993	1992	1991
Return (%)	12.8	-3.2	6.3	9.7	3.7	19.5	-8.0	12.8	8.9	13.3
Differ from Category (+/-)	3.4	-0.6	0.7	1.5	0.0	4.4	-3.1	1.1	0.5	2.0
Return, Tax-Adjusted (%)	12.8	-3.2	6.0	9.6	3.7	19.5	-8.5	11.7	8.9	13.3
Dividends, Net Income ($)	0.60	0.58	0.60	0.62	0.63	0.63	0.67	0.72	0.77	0.77
Expense Ratio (%)	0.49	0.53	0.55	0.59	0.58	0.58	0.58	0.61	0.61	0.59
Yield (%)	4.70	4.88	4.60	4.81	5.10	5.03	5.93	5.36	6.12	6.27

SHAREHOLDER INFORMATION

Minimum Investment
Initial: $10,000 IRA: na
Subsequent: $1,000 IRA: na

Maximum Fees
Load: none 12b-1: none
Other: none

Fidelity Spart OH Muni (FOHFX)

800-544-8888, 801-534-1910
www.fidelity.com

Tax-Exempt Bond

PERFORMANCE AND PER SHARE DATA **fund inception date: 11/15/85**

	3yr Annual	5yr Annual	10yr Annual	Category Risk Index
Return (%)	4.7	5.4	6.9	1.07—av
Differ from Category (+/-)	0.9 abv av	0.5 abv av	0.4 abv av	**Avg Mat** 15.2 yrs

	2000	1999	1998	1997	1996	1995	1994	1993	1992	1991
Return (%)	11.6	-2.8	5.7	8.7	4.2	16.3	-5.5	12.5	8.6	11.4
Differ from Category (+/-)	2.2	-0.2	0.1	0.5	0.5	1.2	-0.6	0.8	0.2	0.1
Return, Tax-Adjusted (%)	11.6	-2.8	5.5	8.4	4.0	16.3	-5.9	11.8	8.6	11.4
Dividends, Net Income ($)	0.55	0.53	0.53	0.55	0.56	0.61	0.65	0.69	0.71	0.71
Expense Ratio (%)	na	0.51	0.55	0.56	0.59	0.58	0.57	0.57	0.61	0.64
Yield (%)	4.76	4.87	4.47	4.64	4.86	5.26	6.06	5.62	6.14	6.27

SHAREHOLDER INFORMATION

Minimum Investment
Initial: $10,000 IRA: na
Subsequent: $1,000 IRA: na

Maximum Fees
Load: none 12b-1: none
Other: none

Fidelity Spart PA Muni (FPXTX)

800-544-8888, 801-534-1910
www.fidelity.com

Tax-Exempt Bond

PERFORMANCE AND PER SHARE DATA **fund inception date: 8/6/86**

	3yr Annual	5yr Annual	10yr Annual	Category Risk Index
Return (%)	4.7	5.2	7.2	0.97—av
Differ from Category (+/-)	0.9 abv av	0.3 abv av	0.7 abv av	**Avg Mat** 13.3 yrs

	2000	1999	1998	1997	1996	1995	1994	1993	1992	1991
Return (%)	10.9	-2.1	5.7	8.3	4.0	17.4	-5.0	13.1	9.1	12.4
Differ from Category (+/-)	1.5	0.5	0.1	0.1	0.3	2.3	-0.1	1.4	0.7	1.1
Return, Tax-Adjusted (%)	10.9	-2.2	5.5	8.2	3.8	17.4	-5.7	12.7	9.1	12.4
Dividends, Net Income ($)	0.49	0.48	0.48	0.50	0.52	0.59	0.65	0.67	0.69	0.70
Expense Ratio (%)	na	0.50	0.55	0.55	0.53	0.55	0.55	0.55	0.55	0.55
Yield (%)	4.60	4.74	4.39	4.61	4.92	5.52	6.54	5.94	6.51	6.75

SHAREHOLDER INFORMATION

Minimum Investment
Initial: $10,000 IRA: na
Subsequent: $1,000 IRA: na

Maximum Fees
Load: 0.50% redemption 12b-1: none
Other: redemption fee applies for 6 months

Fidelity Spart Sh Int Mun (FSTFX)

800-544-8888, 801-534-1910
www.fidelity.com

Tax-Exempt Bond

PERFORMANCE AND PER SHARE DATA **fund inception date: 12/24/86**

	3yr Annual	5yr Annual	10yr Annual	Category Risk Index
Return (%)	4.1	4.3	5.2	0.40—low
Differ from Category (+/-)	0.3 blw av	-0.6 low	-1.3 low	**Avg Mat** 3.3 yrs

	2000	1999	1998	1997	1996	1995	1994	1993	1992	1991
Return (%)	6.2	1.6	4.6	5.4	3.8	8.4	0.0	7.1	6.1	8.8
Differ from Category (+/-)	-3.2	4.2	-1.0	-2.8	0.1	-6.7	4.9	-4.6	-2.3	-2.5
Return, Tax-Adjusted (%)	6.2	1.6	4.6	5.4	3.8	8.4	0.0	7.0	6.1	8.8
Dividends, Net Income ($)	0.41	0.38	0.41	0.42	0.42	0.42	0.43	0.45	0.49	0.55
Expense Ratio (%)	0.51	0.55	0.55	0.55	0.54	0.55	0.47	0.55	0.55	0.55
Yield (%)	4.05	3.82	4.03	4.15	4.19	4.18	4.45	4.44	4.95	5.62

SHAREHOLDER INFORMATION

Minimum Investment
Initial: $10,000 IRA: na
Subsequent: $1,000 IRA: na

Maximum Fees
Load: none 12b-1: none
Other: none

First Hawaii Muni Bond (SURFX)

808-988-8088

Tax-Exempt Bond

PERFORMANCE AND PER SHARE DATA **fund inception date: 11/30/88**

	3yr Annual	5yr Annual	10yr Annual	Category Risk Index
Return (%)	3.7	4.4	6.0	0.79—low
Differ from Category (+/-)	-0.1 low	-0.5 low	-0.5 low	**Avg Mat** 18.7 yrs

	2000	1999	1998	1997	1996	1995	1994	1993	1992	1991
Return (%)	8.4	-1.9	4.8	7.1	4.1	14.4	-4.8	10.6	8.7	10.6
Differ from Category (+/-)	-1.0	0.7	-0.8	-1.1	0.4	-0.7	0.1	-1.1	0.3	-0.7
Return, Tax-Adjusted (%)	8.4	-1.9	4.8	7.1	4.1	14.4	-4.9	10.4	8.6	10.6
Dividends, Net Income ($)	0.51	0.53	0.54	0.54	0.54	0.55	0.55	0.57	0.61	0.61
Expense Ratio (%)	0.98	0.94	0.89	0.98	0.98	0.97	0.95	0.95	0.95	0.91
Yield (%)	4.73	5.08	4.83	4.83	4.92	4.96	5.36	4.98	5.59	5.74

SHAREHOLDER INFORMATION

Minimum Investment
Initial: $1,000 IRA: na
Subsequent: $100 IRA: na

Maximum Fees
Load: none 12b-1: none
Other: none

Fremont: Bond
(FBDFX)

800-548-4539, 415-284-8900
www.fremontfunds.com

General Bond

PERFORMANCE AND PER SHARE DATA — fund inception date: 4/30/93

	3yr Annual	5yr Annual	10yr Annual	Category Risk Index
Return (%)	6.6	6.9	na	1.20—high
Differ from Category (+/-)	1.1 high	1.3 high	na	**Avg Mat** 7.3 yrs

	2000	1999	1998	1997	1996	1995	1994	1993	1992	1991
Return (%)	11.7	-1.2	9.8	9.7	5.2	21.2	-4.0	—	—	—
Differ from Category (+/-)	2.0	-1.2	2.5	1.3	1.7	5.0	-1.3	—	—	—
Return, Tax-Adjusted (%)	9.1	-3.4	6.9	6.9	2.5	17.6	-6.1	—	—	—
Dividends, Net Income ($)	0.62	0.58	0.60	0.64	0.68	0.67	0.55	—	—	—
Expense Ratio (%)	na	0.60	0.60	0.61	0.68	0.60	0.66	—	—	—
Yield (%)	6.21	6.09	5.71	6.25	6.83	6.46	6.01	—	—	—

SHAREHOLDER INFORMATION

Minimum Investment
Initial: $2,000 IRA: $1,000
Subsequent: $100 IRA: $100

Maximum Fees
Load: none 12b-1: none
Other: none

Fremont: CA Interm Tax-Free
(FCATX)

800-548-4539, 415-284-8900
www.fremontfunds.com

Tax-Exempt Bond

PERFORMANCE AND PER SHARE DATA — fund inception date: 7/2/90

	3yr Annual	5yr Annual	10yr Annual	Category Risk Index
Return (%)	4.4	4.8	6.0	0.80—blw av
Differ from Category (+/-)	0.6 av	-0.1 blw av	-0.5 blw av	**Avg Mat** 8.6 yrs

	2000	1999	1998	1997	1996	1995	1994	1993	1992	1991
Return (%)	8.7	-0.9	5.7	7.2	3.6	14.8	-4.8	9.9	7.3	10.7
Differ from Category (+/-)	-0.7	1.7	0.1	-1.0	-0.1	-0.3	0.1	-1.8	-1.1	-0.6
Return, Tax-Adjusted (%)	8.7	-0.9	5.7	7.2	3.6	14.7	-4.8	9.6	7.2	10.5
Dividends, Net Income ($)	0.49	0.50	0.50	0.51	0.48	0.53	0.52	0.55	0.56	0.60
Expense Ratio (%)	na	0.45	0.47	0.49	0.51	0.53	0.51	0.50	0.54	0.36
Yield (%)	4.45	4.72	4.46	4.59	4.42	4.83	5.18	4.92	5.22	5.66

SHAREHOLDER INFORMATION

Minimum Investment
Initial: $2,000 IRA: na
Subsequent: $100 IRA: na

Maximum Fees
Load: none 12b-1: none
Other: none

Galaxy II: US/Ret A (IUTIX)

877-289-4252, 508-871-9908
www.galaxyfunds.com

Government Bond

PERFORMANCE AND PER SHARE DATA **fund inception date: 6/4/91**

	3yr Annual	5yr Annual	10yr Annual	Category Risk Index	
Return (%)	6.5	6.2	na	1.17—av	
Differ from Category (+/-)	0.3 abv av	0.3 abv av	na	**Avg Mat**	9.0 yrs

	2000	1999	1998	1997	1996	1995	1994	1993	1992	1991
Return (%)	13.1	-2.4	9.7	9.2	2.2	18.0	-3.7	10.2	6.7	—
Differ from Category (+/-)	-0.7	0.6	0.6	-0.6	0.1	-0.8	-0.1	-0.4	0.1	—
Return, Tax-Adjusted (%)	10.6	-4.8	7.3	6.7	-0.1	15.2	-6.3	7.1	4.5	—
Dividends, Net Income ($)	0.61	0.68	0.62	0.63	0.64	0.66	0.61	0.58	0.63	—
Expense Ratio (%)	0.41	0.41	0.40	0.40	0.40	0.40	0.40	0.40	0.40	—
Yield (%)	5.76	6.84	5.69	5.99	6.25	6.19	6.21	5.19	5.82	—

SHAREHOLDER INFORMATION

Minimum Investment
Initial: $2,500 IRA: $500
Subsequent: $100 IRA: $100

Maximum Fees
Load: none 12b-1: none
Other: none

Galaxy: CT Intm Muni/Tr (SCTEX)

877-289-4252, 508-871-9908
www.1784funds.com

Tax-Exempt Bond

PERFORMANCE AND PER SHARE DATA **fund inception date: 8/1/94**

	3yr Annual	5yr Annual	10yr Annual	Category Risk Index	
Return (%)	4.5	5.1	na	1.02—av	
Differ from Category (+/-)	0.7 abv av	0.2 av	na	**Avg Mat**	7.5 yrs

	2000	1999	1998	1997	1996	1995	1994	1993	1992	1991
Return (%)	10.1	-2.8	6.6	8.5	3.7	14.6	—	—	—	—
Differ from Category (+/-)	0.7	-0.2	1.0	0.3	0.0	-0.5	—	—	—	—
Return, Tax-Adjusted (%)	10.1	-2.8	6.4	8.4	3.7	14.6	—	—	—	—
Dividends, Net Income ($)	0.45	0.46	0.48	0.50	0.51	0.51	—	—	—	—
Expense Ratio (%)	0.80	0.80	0.80	0.76	0.75	0.52	—	—	—	—
Yield (%)	4.24	4.54	4.38	4.65	4.90	4.83	—	—	—	—

SHAREHOLDER INFORMATION

Minimum Investment
Initial: $1,000 IRA: na
Subsequent: $1 IRA: na

Maximum Fees
Load: none 12b-1: 0.25%
Other: none

Galaxy: FL Muni/Tr (SFTEX)

877-289-4252, 508-871-9908
www.1784funds.com

Tax-Exempt Bond

PERFORMANCE AND PER SHARE DATA **fund inception date: 6/27/97**

	3yr Annual	5yr Annual	10yr Annual	Category Risk Index
Return (%)	4.0	na	na	0.98—av
Differ from Category (+/-)	0.2 blw av	na	na	**Avg Mat** 7.4 yrs

	2000	1999	1998	1997	1996	1995	1994	1993	1992	1991
Return (%)	9.0	-2.7	6.3	—	—	—	—	—	—	—
Differ from Category (+/-)	-0.4	-0.1	0.7	—	—	—	—	—	—	—
Return, Tax-Adjusted (%)	9.0	-2.7	6.0	—	—	—	—	—	—	—
Dividends, Net Income ($)	0.42	0.43	0.45	—	—	—	—	—	—	—
Expense Ratio (%)	0.80	0.80	0.80	—	—	—	—	—	—	—
Yield (%)	4.18	4.47	4.30	—	—	—	—	—	—	—

SHAREHOLDER INFORMATION

Minimum Investment
Initial: $1,000 IRA: na
Subsequent: $250 IRA: na

Maximum Fees
Load: none 12b-1: 0.25%
Other: none

Galaxy: Intm TE Bond/Tr (SETMX)

877-289-4252, 508-871-9908
www.1784funds.com

Tax-Exempt Bond

PERFORMANCE AND PER SHARE DATA **fund inception date: 6/14/93**

	3yr Annual	5yr Annual	10yr Annual	Category Risk Index
Return (%)	4.5	5.3	na	1.08—av
Differ from Category (+/-)	0.7 av	0.4 abv av	na	**Avg Mat** 8.2 yrs

	2000	1999	1998	1997	1996	1995	1994	1993	1992	1991
Return (%)	10.5	-2.9	6.4	9.1	4.2	14.3	-3.0	—	—	—
Differ from Category (+/-)	1.1	-0.3	0.8	0.9	0.5	-0.8	1.9	—	—	—
Return, Tax-Adjusted (%)	10.5	-3.0	6.0	8.9	4.0	14.1	-3.0	—	—	—
Dividends, Net Income ($)	0.44	0.44	0.46	0.49	0.50	0.49	0.47	—	—	—
Expense Ratio (%)	0.80	0.80	0.80	0.80	0.79	0.80	0.32	—	—	—
Yield (%)	4.31	4.51	4.31	4.63	4.87	4.71	4.91	—	—	—

SHAREHOLDER INFORMATION

Minimum Investment
Initial: $1,000 IRA: na
Subsequent: $100 IRA: na

Maximum Fees
Load: none 12b-1: 0.25%
Other: none

Galaxy: MA Intm Muni/Tr (SEMAX)

877-289-4252, 508-871-9908
www.1784funds.com

Tax-Exempt Bond

PERFORMANCE AND PER SHARE DATA — fund inception date: 6/14/93

	3yr Annual	5yr Annual	10yr Annual	Category Risk Index
Return (%)	4.4	5.1	na	1.00—av
Differ from Category (+/-)	0.6 av	0.2 av	na	**Avg Mat** 7.8 yrs

	2000	1999	1998	1997	1996	1995	1994	1993	1992	1991
Return (%)	9.9	-2.0	5.8	8.8	3.3	13.7	-5.4	—	—	—
Differ from Category (+/-)	0.5	0.6	0.2	0.6	-0.4	-1.4	-0.5	—	—	—
Return, Tax-Adjusted (%)	9.9	-2.0	5.8	8.8	3.3	13.7	-5.4	—	—	—
Dividends, Net Income ($)	0.44	0.44	0.46	0.46	0.47	0.46	0.47	—	—	—
Expense Ratio (%)	0.80	0.80	0.80	0.79	0.80	0.80	0.33	—	—	—
Yield (%)	4.24	4.46	4.37	4.42	4.70	4.53	5.02	—	—	—

SHAREHOLDER INFORMATION

Minimum Investment
Initial: $1,000 — IRA: na
Subsequent: $100 — IRA: na

Maximum Fees
Load: none — 12b-1: 0.25%
Other: none

Harbor: Bond (HABDX)

800-422-1050, 419-247-2477
www.harborfund.com

General Bond

PERFORMANCE AND PER SHARE DATA — fund inception date: 12/29/87

	3yr Annual	5yr Annual	10yr Annual	Category Risk Index
Return (%)	6.3	6.6	8.8	1.14—abv av
Differ from Category (+/-)	0.8 high	1.0 high	1.6 high	**Avg Mat** 8.9 yrs

	2000	1999	1998	1997	1996	1995	1994	1993	1992	1991
Return (%)	10.2	-0.3	9.5	9.3	4.9	19.1	-3.7	12.4	9.1	19.6
Differ from Category (+/-)	0.5	-0.3	2.2	0.9	1.4	2.9	-1.0	2.7	2.3	4.1
Return, Tax-Adjusted (%)	8.4	-2.2	6.4	6.5	2.4	16.0	-5.8	8.8	6.4	16.3
Dividends, Net Income ($)	0.44	0.56	0.63	0.66	0.70	0.78	0.60	0.64	0.74	0.86
Expense Ratio (%)	na	0.61	0.65	0.67	0.70	0.76	0.77	0.72	0.77	0.86
Yield (%)	3.89	5.24	5.34	5.68	6.22	6.83	5.83	5.41	6.52	7.57

SHAREHOLDER INFORMATION

Minimum Investment
Initial: $1,000 — IRA: $500
Subsequent: $100 — IRA: $100

Maximum Fees
Load: none — 12b-1: none
Other: none

Harbor: Short Duration (HASDX)

800-422-1050, 419-247-2477
www.harborfund.com

General Bond

PERFORMANCE AND PER SHARE DATA **fund inception date: 1/2/92**

	3yr Annual	5yr Annual	10yr Annual	Category Risk Index
Return (%)	5.8	6.0	na	0.32—low
Differ from Category (+/-)	0.3 abv av	0.4 abv av	na	**Avg Mat** 4.6 yrs

	2000	1999	1998	1997	1996	1995	1994	1993	1992	1991
Return (%)	7.4	3.7	6.3	6.2	6.3	7.4	2.7	4.4	—	—
Differ from Category (+/-)	-2.3	3.7	-1.0	-2.2	2.8	-8.8	5.4	-5.3	—	—
Return, Tax-Adjusted (%)	4.8	1.5	4.0	3.7	3.1	4.8	-0.6	-0.1	—	—
Dividends, Net Income ($)	0.54	0.46	0.48	0.54	0.69	0.56	0.78	1.15	—	—
Expense Ratio (%)	na	0.28	0.36	0.62	0.33	0.39	0.38	0.43	—	—
Yield (%)	6.30	5.41	5.54	6.27	8.00	6.37	8.95	12.43	—	—

SHAREHOLDER INFORMATION

Minimum Investment		**Maximum Fees**	
Initial: $1,000	IRA: $500	Load: none	12b-1: none
Subsequent: $100	IRA: $100	Other: none	

Heartland Grp: WI Tax-Free (HRWIX)

800-432-7856, 414-289-7000
www.heartlandfunds.com

Tax-Exempt Bond

PERFORMANCE AND PER SHARE DATA **fund inception date: 4/3/92**

	3yr Annual	5yr Annual	10yr Annual	Category Risk Index
Return (%)	3.0	4.2	na	0.92—blw av
Differ from Category (+/-)	-0.8 low	-0.7 low	na	**Avg Mat** 14.3 yrs

	2000	1999	1998	1997	1996	1995	1994	1993	1992	1991
Return (%)	7.4	-3.2	5.4	8.0	3.8	17.7	-6.4	10.5	—	—
Differ from Category (+/-)	-2.0	-0.6	-0.2	-0.2	0.1	2.6	-1.5	-1.2	—	—
Return, Tax-Adjusted (%)	7.4	-3.2	5.4	8.0	3.8	17.7	-6.4	10.5	—	—
Dividends, Net Income ($)	0.50	0.51	0.51	0.51	0.51	0.51	0.50	0.49	—	—
Expense Ratio (%)	na	0.82	0.78	0.81	0.80	0.86	0.85	0.84	—	—
Yield (%)	5.08	5.29	4.86	4.88	5.01	4.95	5.42	4.72	—	—

SHAREHOLDER INFORMATION

Minimum Investment		**Maximum Fees**	
Initial: $1,000	IRA: na	Load: none	12b-1: none
Subsequent: $100	IRA: na	Other: none	

Homestead: Sht Tm Bond (HOSBX)

800-258-3030, 703-907-6039
www.nreca.org/homestead

General Bond

PERFORMANCE AND PER SHARE DATA **fund inception date: 11/5/91**

	3yr Annual	5yr Annual	10yr Annual	Category Risk Index
Return (%)	5.7	5.8	na	0.39—low
Differ from Category (+/-)	0.2 av	0.2 av	na	**Avg Mat** 2.9 yrs

	2000	1999	1998	1997	1996	1995	1994	1993	1992	1991
Return (%)	7.8	3.2	6.4	6.6	5.1	10.7	0.0	6.6	6.3	—
Differ from Category (+/-)	-1.9	3.2	-0.9	-1.8	1.6	-5.5	2.7	-3.1	-0.5	—
Return, Tax-Adjusted (%)	5.5	1.0	4.2	4.3	2.8	8.5	-1.8	4.7	4.7	—
Dividends, Net Income ($)	0.29	0.28	0.28	0.29	0.29	0.27	0.24	0.24	0.26	—
Expense Ratio (%)	na	0.75	0.75	0.75	0.75	0.75	0.75	0.75	0.75	—
Yield (%)	5.59	5.50	5.37	5.59	5.63	5.20	4.84	4.62	5.09	—

SHAREHOLDER INFORMATION

Minimum Investment
Initial: $500 IRA: $200
Subsequent: $1 IRA: $1

Maximum Fees
Load: none 12b-1: none
Other: none

INVESCO High Yield/Inv (FHYPX)

800-525-8085, 303-930-6300
www.invesco.com

Corporate High-Yield Bond

PERFORMANCE AND PER SHARE DATA **fund inception date: 3/1/84**

	3yr Annual	5yr Annual	10yr Annual	Category Risk Index
Return (%)	-1.2	5.1	8.9	1.29—abv av
Differ from Category (+/-)	-1.2 blw av	-0.3 av	-0.9 blw av	**Avg Mat** 7.0 yrs

	2000	1999	1998	1997	1996	1995	1994	1993	1992	1991
Return (%)	-12.0	9.2	0.0	17.0	14.0	17.9	-4.9	15.7	14.6	23.5
Differ from Category (+/-)	-5.1	3.6	-1.9	2.4	-1.7	0.5	-2.7	-3.7	-1.6	-4.0
Return, Tax-Adjusted (%)	-15.6	5.6	-3.9	12.3	10.3	13.9	-8.4	12.2	11.7	19.9
Dividends, Net Income ($)	0.60	0.58	0.63	0.63	0.61	0.64	0.65	0.60	0.62	0.68
Expense Ratio (%)	1.00	0.99	0.86	1.00	0.99	1.00	0.97	0.97	1.00	1.05
Yield (%)	11.76	9.02	9.53	8.26	8.55	9.37	10.14	8.07	8.89	10.21

SHAREHOLDER INFORMATION

Minimum Investment
Initial: $1,000 IRA: $250
Subsequent: $50 IRA: $50

Maximum Fees
Load: none 12b-1: 0.25%
Other: none

INVESCO Select Income/Inv (FBDSX)

800-525-8085, 303-930-6300
www.invesco.com

Corporate Bond

PERFORMANCE AND PER SHARE DATA **fund inception date: 1/11/77**

	3yr Annual	5yr Annual	10yr Annual	Category Risk Index
Return (%)	3.5	5.3	8.4	1.12—abv av
Differ from Category (+/-)	-1.5 low	-0.4 blw av	0.3 abv av	**Avg Mat** 11.1 yrs

	2000	1999	1998	1997	1996	1995	1994	1993	1992	1991
Return (%)	5.1	-1.4	7.0	11.7	4.8	20.6	-1.1	11.3	10.3	18.6
Differ from Category (+/-)	-2.9	-2.7	1.1	2.6	-0.7	2.7	1.2	-0.5	1.0	0.9
Return, Tax-Adjusted (%)	2.2	-3.8	4.1	8.5	2.0	17.4	-3.8	7.5	7.4	15.8
Dividends, Net Income ($)	0.44	0.41	0.42	0.44	0.46	0.46	0.45	0.49	0.52	0.52
Expense Ratio (%)	1.06	1.06	1.06	1.03	1.01	1.00	1.11	1.15	1.14	1.15
Yield (%)	7.41	6.75	6.26	6.44	7.00	6.80	7.46	7.25	7.85	8.00

SHAREHOLDER INFORMATION

Minimum Investment		**Maximum Fees**	
Initial: $1,000	IRA: $250	Load: none	12b-1: 0.25%
Subsequent: $50	IRA: $50	Other: none	

INVESCO Tax-Free Bond/Inv (FTIFX)

800-525-8085, 303-930-6300
www.invesco.com

Tax-Exempt Bond

PERFORMANCE AND PER SHARE DATA **fund inception date: 8/14/81**

	3yr Annual	5yr Annual	10yr Annual	Category Risk Index
Return (%)	4.2	4.7	6.5	1.10—abv av
Differ from Category (+/-)	0.4 blw av	-0.2 blw av	0.0 av	**Avg Mat** 16.5 yrs

	2000	1999	1998	1997	1996	1995	1994	1993	1992	1991
Return (%)	12.0	-3.3	4.6	8.6	2.3	15.6	-5.5	12.0	8.7	12.5
Differ from Category (+/-)	2.6	-0.7	-1.0	0.4	-1.4	0.5	-0.6	0.3	0.3	1.2
Return, Tax-Adjusted (%)	12.0	-3.3	4.0	8.3	1.9	15.2	-6.0	11.3	8.1	12.2
Dividends, Net Income ($)	0.65	0.61	0.63	0.63	0.69	0.78	0.81	0.85	0.90	0.93
Expense Ratio (%)	0.91	0.90	0.91	0.90	0.91	0.92	1.00	1.03	1.02	0.93
Yield (%)	4.29	4.30	4.00	3.97	4.47	4.89	5.46	5.02	5.54	5.82

SHAREHOLDER INFORMATION

Minimum Investment		**Maximum Fees**	
Initial: $1,000	IRA: na	Load: none	12b-1: 0.25%
Subsequent: $50	IRA: na	Other: none	

INVESCO US Gov't Secur/Inv (FBDGX)

800-525-8085, 303-930-6300
www.invesco.com

Government Bond

PERFORMANCE AND PER SHARE DATA **fund inception date: 1/2/86**

	3yr Annual	5yr Annual	10yr Annual	Category Risk Index
Return (%)	6.0	6.1	7.4	1.47—abv av
Differ from Category (+/-)	-0.2 av	0.2 abv av	-0.2 abv av	**Avg Mat** 21.4 yrs

	2000	1999	1998	1997	1996	1995	1994	1993	1992	1991
Return (%)	14.6	-5.4	10.0	12.2	0.4	22.1	-7.1	10.2	5.7	15.4
Differ from Category (+/-)	0.8	-2.4	0.9	2.4	-1.7	3.3	-3.5	-0.4	-0.9	0.5
Return, Tax-Adjusted (%)	12.4	-7.5	6.4	9.5	-1.7	19.5	-9.2	7.4	3.8	13.2
Dividends, Net Income ($)	0.36	0.40	0.38	0.42	0.43	0.44	0.42	0.42	0.45	0.49
Expense Ratio (%)	1.02	1.01	1.01	1.01	1.02	1.00	1.32	1.40	1.27	1.27
Yield (%)	4.95	5.98	4.70	5.34	5.79	5.61	6.16	5.28	5.91	6.40

SHAREHOLDER INFORMATION

Minimum Investment
Initial: $1,000 IRA: $250
Subsequent: $50 IRA: $50

Maximum Fees
Load: none 12b-1: 0.25%
Other: none

Janus Inv: Federal Tx Ex (JATEX)

800-525-8983, 303-333-3863
www.janus.com

Tax-Exempt Bond

PERFORMANCE AND PER SHARE DATA **fund inception date: 5/3/93**

	3yr Annual	5yr Annual	10yr Annual	Category Risk Index
Return (%)	3.1	4.5	na	1.04—av
Differ from Category (+/-)	-0.7 low	-0.4 blw av	na	**Avg Mat** 12.0 yrs

	2000	1999	1998	1997	1996	1995	1994	1993	1992	1991
Return (%)	8.9	-4.3	5.2	8.9	4.7	15.8	-7.7	—	—	—
Differ from Category (+/-)	-0.5	-1.7	-0.4	0.7	1.0	0.7	-2.8	—	—	—
Return, Tax-Adjusted (%)	8.9	-4.3	5.2	8.9	4.7	15.8	-7.7	—	—	—
Dividends, Net Income ($)	0.33	0.34	0.34	0.34	0.36	0.36	0.36	—	—	—
Expense Ratio (%)	na	0.65	0.65	0.65	0.65	0.65	0.65	—	—	—
Yield (%)	4.81	5.13	4.67	4.69	5.15	5.12	5.63	—	—	—

SHAREHOLDER INFORMATION

Minimum Investment
Initial: $2,500 IRA: na
Subsequent: $100 IRA: na

Maximum Fees
Load: none 12b-1: none
Other: none

Janus Inv: Flexible Income (JAFIX)

800-525-8983, 303-333-3863
www.janus.com

Corporate Bond

PERFORMANCE AND PER SHARE DATA **fund inception date: 7/7/87**

	3yr Annual	5yr Annual	10yr Annual	Category Risk Index
Return (%)	4.4	6.3	10.0	1.09—av
Differ from Category (+/-)	-0.6 blw av	0.6 high	1.9 high	**Avg Mat** 5.8 yrs

	2000	1999	1998	1997	1996	1995	1994	1993	1992	1991
Return (%)	4.8	0.4	8.2	11.4	6.8	21.1	-2.9	15.6	11.8	25.9
Differ from Category (+/-)	-3.2	-0.9	2.3	2.3	1.3	3.2	-0.6	3.8	2.5	8.2
Return, Tax-Adjusted (%)	2.0	-2.1	5.4	8.2	3.8	17.8	-5.7	11.7	9.0	22.4
Dividends, Net Income ($)	0.64	0.64	0.66	0.67	0.73	0.72	0.71	0.75	0.79	0.89
Expense Ratio (%)	na	0.81	0.82	0.86	0.87	0.96	0.93	1.00	1.00	1.00
Yield (%)	7.00	6.84	6.60	6.65	7.52	7.33	8.11	7.53	8.46	9.79

SHAREHOLDER INFORMATION

Minimum Investment
Initial: $2,500 IRA: $500
Subsequent: $100 IRA: $100

Maximum Fees
Load: none 12b-1: none
Other: none

Janus Inv: High Yield (JAHYX)

800-525-3713, 303-333-3863
www.janus.com

Corporate High-Yield Bond

PERFORMANCE AND PER SHARE DATA **fund inception date: 12/29/95**

	3yr Annual	5yr Annual	10yr Annual	Category Risk Index
Return (%)	3.0	9.3	na	0.83—blw av
Differ from Category (+/-)	3.0 high	3.9 high	na	**Avg Mat** 4.1 yrs

	2000	1999	1998	1997	1996	1995	1994	1993	1992	1991
Return (%)	2.4	5.5	1.1	15.4	24.0	—	—	—	—	—
Differ from Category (+/-)	9.3	-0.1	-0.8	0.8	8.3	—	—	—	—	—
Return, Tax-Adjusted (%)	-0.8	2.1	-2.0	11.1	19.8	—	—	—	—	—
Dividends, Net Income ($)	0.84	0.89	0.92	0.94	0.97	—	—	—	—	—
Expense Ratio (%)	na	1.00	0.96	1.00	1.00	—	—	—	—	—
Yield (%)	8.66	8.65	8.67	7.87	8.55	—	—	—	—	—

SHAREHOLDER INFORMATION

Minimum Investment
Initial: $2,500 IRA: $500
Subsequent: $100 IRA: $100

Maximum Fees
Load: none 12b-1: none
Other: none

Janus Inv: Short-Term Bond (JASBX)

800-525-3713, 303-333-3863
www.janus.com

Corporate Bond

PERFORMANCE AND PER SHARE DATA **fund inception date: 9/1/92**

	3yr Annual	5yr Annual	10yr Annual	Category Risk Index
Return (%)	5.7	6.0	na	0.47—blw av
Differ from Category (+/-)	0.7 high	0.3 abv av	na	**Avg Mat** 1.4 yrs

	2000	1999	1998	1997	1996	1995	1994	1993	1992	1991
Return (%)	7.7	2.9	6.7	6.6	6.1	7.9	0.3	6.1	—	—
Differ from Category (+/-)	-0.3	1.6	0.8	-2.5	0.6	-10.0	2.6	-5.7	—	—
Return, Tax-Adjusted (%)	5.4	0.7	4.3	4.2	3.8	5.5	-2.0	4.1	—	—
Dividends, Net Income ($)	0.16	0.16	0.17	0.17	0.16	0.17	0.18	0.14	—	—
Expense Ratio (%)	na	0.65	0.65	0.65	0.65	0.65	0.65	0.83	—	—
Yield (%)	5.55	5.65	5.84	5.88	5.55	5.92	6.36	4.65	—	—

SHAREHOLDER INFORMATION

Minimum Investment
Initial: $2,500 IRA: $500
Subsequent: $100 IRA: $100

Maximum Fees
Load: none 12b-1: none
Other: none

Legg Mason Gl: Gl Gov't/P (LMGGX)

800-822-5544, 410-539-0000
www.leggmason.com

International Bond

PERFORMANCE AND PER SHARE DATA **fund inception date: 4/15/93**

	3yr Annual	5yr Annual	10yr Annual	Category Risk Index
Return (%)	0.6	1.6	na	1.01—av
Differ from Category (+/-)	-2.6 low	-3.6 blw av	na	**Avg Mat** 11.1 yrs

	2000	1999	1998	1997	1996	1995	1994	1993	1992	1991
Return (%)	-5.0	-3.2	11.0	-1.6	8.2	21.0	-1.6	—	—	—
Differ from Category (+/-)	-9.5	-7.0	7.4	-5.5	-5.9	4.1	5.6	—	—	—
Return, Tax-Adjusted (%)	-7.3	-5.0	9.1	-3.8	5.5	16.1	-3.8	—	—	—
Dividends, Net Income ($)	0.56	0.44	0.43	0.53	0.62	1.16	0.58	—	—	—
Expense Ratio (%)	na	1.90	1.87	1.86	1.86	1.80	1.30	—	—	—
Yield (%)	6.78	4.70	4.21	5.46	5.89	11.24	6.09	—	—	—

SHAREHOLDER INFORMATION

Minimum Investment
Initial: $1,000 IRA: $1,000
Subsequent: $100 IRA: $100

Maximum Fees
Load: none 12b-1: 0.75%
Other: none

Legg Mason Inc: Gov't Int/P (LGINX)

800-822-5544, 410-539-0000
www.leggmason.com

Government Bond

PERFORMANCE AND PER SHARE DATA **fund inception date: 8/7/87**

	3yr Annual	5yr Annual	10yr Annual	Category Risk Index
Return (%)	5.0	5.3	6.4	0.85—av
Differ from Category (+/-)	-1.2 low	-0.6 blw av	-1.2 blw av	**Avg Mat** 9.2 yrs

	2000	1999	1998	1997	1996	1995	1994	1993	1992	1991
Return (%)	9.6	-0.7	6.5	6.9	4.4	13.8	-1.9	6.6	6.2	14.3
Differ from Category (+/-)	-4.2	2.3	-2.6	-2.9	2.3	-5.0	1.7	-4.0	-0.4	-0.6
Return, Tax-Adjusted (%)	7.2	-2.6	4.4	4.5	2.1	11.5	-3.8	3.4	4.2	11.5
Dividends, Net Income ($)	0.59	0.51	0.55	0.60	0.60	0.56	0.51	0.54	0.60	0.71
Expense Ratio (%)	na	1.00	1.00	1.00	0.98	0.90	0.90	0.90	0.90	0.80
Yield (%)	5.75	5.14	5.23	5.76	5.81	5.34	5.24	4.96	5.54	6.46

SHAREHOLDER INFORMATION

Minimum Investment
Initial: $1,000 IRA: $1,000
Subsequent: $100 IRA: $100

Maximum Fees
Load: none 12b-1: 0.50%
Other: none

Legg Mason Inc: Hi Yld/P (LMHYX)

800-822-5544, 410-539-0000
www.leggmason.com

Corporate High-Yield Bond

PERFORMANCE AND PER SHARE DATA **fund inception date: 2/1/94**

	3yr Annual	5yr Annual	10yr Annual	Category Risk Index
Return (%)	-3.6	3.5	na	1.43—high
Differ from Category (+/-)	-3.6 low	-1.9 blw av	na	**Avg Mat** 9.9 yrs

	2000	1999	1998	1997	1996	1995	1994	1993	1992	1991
Return (%)	-16.5	9.4	-2.0	15.8	14.9	18.0	—	—	—	—
Differ from Category (+/-)	-9.6	3.8	-3.9	1.2	-0.8	0.6	—	—	—	—
Return, Tax-Adjusted (%)	-21.6	6.5	-5.2	12.2	11.2	14.2	—	—	—	—
Dividends, Net Income ($)	1.27	1.04	1.32	1.34	1.34	1.28	—	—	—	—
Expense Ratio (%)	na	1.31	1.30	1.30	1.35	1.50	—	—	—	—
Yield (%)	10.95	6.92	8.98	8.18	8.71	8.75	—	—	—	—

SHAREHOLDER INFORMATION

Minimum Investment
Initial: $1,000 IRA: $1,000
Subsequent: $100 IRA: $100

Maximum Fees
Load: none 12b-1: 0.50%
Other: none

Legg Mason Inc: Inv Grd/P (LMIGX)

800-822-5544, 410-539-0000
www.leggmason.com

General Bond

PERFORMANCE AND PER SHARE DATA **fund inception date: 8/7/87**

	3yr Annual	5yr Annual	10yr Annual	Category Risk Index
Return (%)	4.8	5.7	7.6	1.26—high
Differ from Category (+/-)	-0.7 low	0.1 av	0.4 abv av	**Avg Mat** 11.9 yrs

	2000	1999	1998	1997	1996	1995	1994	1993	1992	1991
Return (%)	8.8	-1.1	7.0	10.3	4.3	20.1	-4.8	11.2	6.7	15.9
Differ from Category (+/-)	-0.9	-1.1	-0.3	1.9	0.8	3.9	-2.1	1.5	-0.1	0.4
Return, Tax-Adjusted (%)	6.2	-3.3	4.4	7.8	1.8	17.3	-7.1	6.6	4.6	13.4
Dividends, Net Income ($)	0.64	0.58	0.60	0.64	0.64	0.64	0.59	0.62	0.66	0.75
Expense Ratio (%)	na	1.00	1.00	1.00	0.97	0.87	0.85	0.85	0.85	0.71
Yield (%)	6.41	5.91	5.60	6.04	6.26	6.13	6.33	5.51	6.13	6.98

SHAREHOLDER INFORMATION

Minimum Investment
Initial: $1,000 IRA: $1,000
Subsequent: $100 IRA: $100

Maximum Fees
Load: none 12b-1: 0.50%
Other: none

Legg Mason Tax-Free: Int In/P (LTITX)

800-822-5544, 410-539-0000
www.leggmason.com

Tax-Exempt Bond

PERFORMANCE AND PER SHARE DATA **fund inception date: 11/9/92**

	3yr Annual	5yr Annual	10yr Annual	Category Risk Index
Return (%)	4.0	4.3	na	0.75—low
Differ from Category (+/-)	0.2 blw av	-0.6 low	na	**Avg Mat** 7.1 yrs

	2000	1999	1998	1997	1996	1995	1994	1993	1992	1991
Return (%)	8.1	-0.9	5.2	6.0	3.4	11.9	-1.9	9.9	—	—
Differ from Category (+/-)	-1.3	1.7	-0.4	-2.2	-0.3	-3.2	3.0	-1.8	—	—
Return, Tax-Adjusted (%)	8.1	-0.9	5.2	6.0	3.4	11.9	-1.9	9.8	—	—
Dividends, Net Income ($)	0.65	0.63	0.66	0.67	0.66	0.70	0.70	0.69	—	—
Expense Ratio (%)	0.70	0.70	0.70	0.66	0.56	0.34	0.30	0.20	—	—
Yield (%)	4.18	4.19	4.17	4.27	4.28	4.49	4.80	4.42	—	—

SHAREHOLDER INFORMATION

Minimum Investment
Initial: $1,000 IRA: na
Subsequent: $100 IRA: na

Maximum Fees
Load: none 12b-1: 0.25%
Other: none

Loomis Sayles Bond/Ist (LSBDX)

800-633-3330, 617-482-2450
www.loomissayles.com

Corporate Bond

PERFORMANCE AND PER SHARE DATA **fund inception date: 5/10/91**

	3yr Annual	5yr Annual	10yr Annual	Category Risk Index
Return (%)	4.5	7.2	na	2.53—high
Differ from Category (+/-)	-0.5 blw av	1.5 high	na	**Avg Mat** 17.5 yrs

	2000	1999	1998	1997	1996	1995	1994	1993	1992	1991
Return (%)	4.3	4.5	4.6	12.6	10.2	31.9	-4.0	22.2	14.2	—
Differ from Category (+/-)	-3.7	3.2	-1.3	3.5	4.7	14.0	-1.7	10.4	4.9	—
Return, Tax-Adjusted (%)	1.0	1.3	0.8	9.4	6.8	28.4	-6.9	17.9	10.4	—
Dividends, Net Income ($)	0.94	0.95	0.95	0.86	0.86	0.82	0.86	0.80	0.76	—
Expense Ratio (%)	0.75	0.75	0.75	0.75	0.75	0.83	0.84	0.94	1.00	—
Yield (%)	8.49	8.24	7.62	6.59	6.80	6.62	8.55	6.76	6.97	—

SHAREHOLDER INFORMATION

Minimum Investment
Initial: $25,000 IRA: $5,000
Subsequent: $50 IRA: $50

Maximum Fees
Load: none 12b-1: none
Other: none

Marshall: Gov't Inc/Inv (MRGIX)

800-236-8554, 412-288-1900
www.marshallfunds.com

Government Bond

PERFORMANCE AND PER SHARE DATA **fund inception date: 12/11/92**

	3yr Annual	5yr Annual	10yr Annual	Category Risk Index
Return (%)	5.4	5.5	na	0.76—av
Differ from Category (+/-)	-0.8 blw av	-0.4 blw av	na	**Avg Mat** 6.3 yrs

	2000	1999	1998	1997	1996	1995	1994	1993	1992	1991
Return (%)	9.6	0.4	6.5	8.4	3.0	16.9	-2.7	5.9	—	—
Differ from Category (+/-)	-4.2	3.4	-2.6	-1.4	0.9	-1.9	0.9	-4.7	—	—
Return, Tax-Adjusted (%)	7.1	-1.8	4.1	5.8	0.5	14.1	-5.1	2.8	—	—
Dividends, Net Income ($)	0.56	0.54	0.58	0.62	0.61	0.61	0.60	0.67	—	—
Expense Ratio (%)	0.85	0.86	0.87	0.86	0.86	0.86	0.86	0.85	—	—
Yield (%)	5.96	5.92	6.03	6.46	6.45	6.23	6.71	6.74	—	—

SHAREHOLDER INFORMATION

Minimum Investment
Initial: $1,000 IRA: $1,000
Subsequent: $50 IRA: $50

Maximum Fees
Load: none 12b-1: none
Other: none

Marshall: Intm Bond/Inv (MAIBX)

800-236-8554, 412-288-1900
www.marshallfunds.com

General Bond

PERFORMANCE AND PER SHARE DATA **fund inception date: 11/20/92**

	3yr Annual	5yr Annual	10yr Annual	Category Risk Index
Return (%)	5.4	5.1	na	0.69—blw av
Differ from Category (+/-)	-0.1 av	-0.5 low	na	**Avg Mat** 4.4 yrs

	2000	1999	1998	1997	1996	1995	1994	1993	1992	1991
Return (%)	8.7	1.4	6.3	7.1	2.4	15.4	-3.0	6.8	—	—
Differ from Category (+/-)	-1.0	1.4	-1.0	-1.3	-1.1	-0.8	-0.3	-2.9	—	—
Return, Tax-Adjusted (%)	6.2	-0.8	3.9	4.6	0.0	12.7	-5.3	3.8	—	—
Dividends, Net Income ($)	0.57	0.55	0.56	0.58	0.57	0.60	0.59	0.62	—	—
Expense Ratio (%)	0.70	0.71	0.71	0.72	0.72	0.70	0.71	0.70	—	—
Yield (%)	6.12	6.03	5.87	6.09	6.03	6.12	6.52	6.13	—	—

SHAREHOLDER INFORMATION

Minimum Investment
Initial: $1,000 IRA: $1,000
Subsequent: $50 IRA: $50

Maximum Fees
Load: none 12b-1: none
Other: none

Marshall: Intm Tax-Free/Inv (MITFX)

800-236-8554, 412-288-1900
www.marshallfunds.com

Tax-Exempt Bond

PERFORMANCE AND PER SHARE DATA **fund inception date: 2/1/94**

	3yr Annual	5yr Annual	10yr Annual	Category Risk Index
Return (%)	4.1	4.6	na	0.88—blw av
Differ from Category (+/-)	0.3 blw av	-0.3 blw av	na	**Avg Mat** 7.3 yrs

	2000	1999	1998	1997	1996	1995	1994	1993	1992	1991
Return (%)	9.1	-1.9	5.6	6.7	3.8	11.5	—	—	—	—
Differ from Category (+/-)	-0.3	0.7	0.0	-1.5	0.1	-3.6	—	—	—	—
Return, Tax-Adjusted (%)	9.1	-1.9	5.4	6.7	3.8	11.5	—	—	—	—
Dividends, Net Income ($)	0.43	0.41	0.42	0.43	0.43	0.42	—	—	—	—
Expense Ratio (%)	0.60	0.61	0.61	0.61	0.61	0.61	—	—	—	—
Yield (%)	4.25	4.23	4.05	4.20	4.30	4.17	—	—	—	—

SHAREHOLDER INFORMATION

Minimum Investment
Initial: $1,000 IRA: na
Subsequent: $50 IRA: na

Maximum Fees
Load: none 12b-1: none
Other: none

Marshall: Short Tm Inc/Inv (MSINX)

800-236-8554, 412-288-1900
www.marshallfunds.com

General Bond

PERFORMANCE AND PER SHARE DATA **fund inception date: 10/30/92**

	3yr Annual	5yr Annual	10yr Annual	Category Risk Index
Return (%)	5.3	5.4	na	0.55—low
Differ from Category (+/-)	-0.2 blw av	-0.2 blw av	na	**Avg Mat** 2.6 yrs

	2000	1999	1998	1997	1996	1995	1994	1993	1992	1991
Return (%)	6.7	4.5	4.9	6.3	4.9	8.9	1.8	3.6	—	—
Differ from Category (+/-)	-3.0	4.5	-2.4	-2.1	1.4	-7.3	4.5	-6.1	—	—
Return, Tax-Adjusted (%)	4.1	2.2	2.4	3.7	2.4	6.4	0.0	1.7	—	—
Dividends, Net Income ($)	0.61	0.53	0.60	0.61	0.61	0.59	0.47	0.47	—	—
Expense Ratio (%)	0.50	0.51	0.50	0.49	0.51	0.51	0.50	0.50	—	—
Yield (%)	6.51	5.65	6.32	6.33	6.32	6.02	4.91	4.76	—	—

SHAREHOLDER INFORMATION

Minimum Investment
Initial: $1,000 IRA: $1,000
Subsequent: $50 IRA: $50

Maximum Fees
Load: none 12b-1: none
Other: none

McM Interm Fixed Income (MCMNX)

800-788-9485, 415-616-9320
www.mcmfunds.com

General Bond

PERFORMANCE AND PER SHARE DATA **fund inception date: 7/14/94**

	3yr Annual	5yr Annual	10yr Annual	Category Risk Index
Return (%)	5.6	5.8	na	0.96—av
Differ from Category (+/-)	0.1 av	0.2 av	na	**Avg Mat** 4.3 yrs

	2000	1999	1998	1997	1996	1995	1994	1993	1992	1991
Return (%)	9.8	-0.3	7.8	7.9	4.1	14.9	—	—	—	—
Differ from Category (+/-)	0.1	-0.3	0.5	-0.5	0.6	-1.3	—	—	—	—
Return, Tax-Adjusted (%)	7.4	-2.4	5.5	5.6	1.8	12.3	—	—	—	—
Dividends, Net Income ($)	0.59	0.56	0.58	0.59	0.59	0.55	—	—	—	—
Expense Ratio (%)	0.50	0.50	0.50	0.50	0.50	0.50	—	—	—	—
Yield (%)	5.71	5.60	5.44	5.65	5.75	5.21	—	—	—	—

SHAREHOLDER INFORMATION

Minimum Investment
Initial: $5,000 IRA: $5,000
Subsequent: $250 IRA: $250

Maximum Fees
Load: none 12b-1: none
Other: none

Mercury Low Dur/I (MLOIX)

800-236-4479, 609-282-2800
www.mercuryfunds.com

General Bond

PERFORMANCE AND PER SHARE DATA **fund inception date: 5/19/93**

	3yr Annual	5yr Annual	10yr Annual	Category Risk Index	
Return (%)	5.2	5.9	na	0.50—low	
Differ from Category (+/-)	-0.3 blw av	0.3 abv av	na	**Avg Mat**	2.7 yrs

	2000	1999	1998	1997	1996	1995	1994	1993	1992	1991
Return (%)	7.0	3.1	5.6	7.6	6.2	12.7	5.2	—	—	—
Differ from Category (+/-)	-2.7	3.1	-1.7	-0.8	2.7	-3.5	7.9	—	—	—
Return, Tax-Adjusted (%)	4.2	0.8	3.0	4.8	3.5	9.5	2.4	—	—	—
Dividends, Net Income ($)	0.67	0.56	0.65	0.68	0.67	0.75	0.69	—	—	—
Expense Ratio (%)	na	0.58	0.58	0.58	0.58	0.58	0.58	—	—	—
Yield (%)	6.82	5.70	6.44	6.64	6.57	7.28	7.00	—	—	—

SHAREHOLDER INFORMATION

Minimum Investment
Initial: $10,000 IRA: $10,000
Subsequent: $1 IRA: $1

Maximum Fees
Load: none 12b-1: none
Other: none

Mercury Tot Ret/I (MTOIX)

800-236-4479, 609-282-2800
www.mercuryfunds.com

General Bond

PERFORMANCE AND PER SHARE DATA **fund inception date: 12/6/94**

	3yr Annual	5yr Annual	10yr Annual	Category Risk Index	
Return (%)	4.8	5.9	na	1.07—abv av	
Differ from Category (+/-)	-0.7 low	0.3 abv av	na	**Avg Mat**	7.6 yrs

	2000	1999	1998	1997	1996	1995	1994	1993	1992	1991
Return (%)	7.7	-1.6	8.7	10.7	4.3	21.4	—	—	—	—
Differ from Category (+/-)	-2.0	-1.6	1.4	2.3	0.8	5.2	—	—	—	—
Return, Tax-Adjusted (%)	5.0	-3.8	5.9	7.6	1.3	18.1	—	—	—	—
Dividends, Net Income ($)	0.83	0.76	0.89	1.00	0.92	0.90	—	—	—	—
Expense Ratio (%)	na	0.65	0.65	0.65	0.68	0.80	—	—	—	—
Yield (%)	6.61	6.09	6.56	7.51	7.03	6.62	—	—	—	—

SHAREHOLDER INFORMATION

Minimum Investment
Initial: $10,000 IRA: $10,000
Subsequent: $1 IRA: $1

Maximum Fees
Load: none 12b-1: none
Other: none

Metropolitan West Lw Dr/M (MWLDX)

800-241-4671, 310-966-8900
www.mws.com

Corporate Bond

PERFORMANCE AND PER SHARE DATA **fund inception date: 3/31/97**

	3yr Annual	5yr Annual	10yr Annual	Category Risk Index	
Return (%)	6.8	na	na	0.49—blw av	
Differ from Category (+/-)	1.8 high	na	na	**Avg Mat**	4.8 yrs

	2000	1999	1998	1997	1996	1995	1994	1993	1992	1991
Return (%)	7.5	6.2	6.6	—	—	—	—	—	—	—
Differ from Category (+/-)	-0.5	4.9	0.7	—	—	—	—	—	—	—
Return, Tax-Adjusted (%)	4.2	3.3	4.0	—	—	—	—	—	—	—
Dividends, Net Income ($)	0.83	0.71	0.66	—	—	—	—	—	—	—
Expense Ratio (%)	0.58	0.58	0.58	—	—	—	—	—	—	—
Yield (%)	8.37	7.05	6.49	—	—	—	—	—	—	—

SHAREHOLDER INFORMATION

Minimum Investment
Initial: $5,000 IRA: $1,000
Subsequent: $1 IRA: $1

Maximum Fees
Load: none 12b-1: 0.19%
Other: none

Metropolitan West TR Bd/M (MWTRX)

800-241-4671, 310-966-8900
www.mws.com

Corporate Bond

PERFORMANCE AND PER SHARE DATA **fund inception date: 3/31/97**

	3yr Annual	5yr Annual	10yr Annual	Category Risk Index	
Return (%)	7.3	na	na	0.93—av	
Differ from Category (+/-)	2.3 high	na	na	**Avg Mat**	8.4 yrs

	2000	1999	1998	1997	1996	1995	1994	1993	1992	1991
Return (%)	10.4	1.7	9.9	—	—	—	—	—	—	—
Differ from Category (+/-)	2.4	0.4	4.0	—	—	—	—	—	—	—
Return, Tax-Adjusted (%)	6.7	-1.1	6.9	—	—	—	—	—	—	—
Dividends, Net Income ($)	0.93	0.75	0.71	—	—	—	—	—	—	—
Expense Ratio (%)	0.65	0.65	0.65	—	—	—	—	—	—	—
Yield (%)	9.19	7.44	6.58	—	—	—	—	—	—	—

SHAREHOLDER INFORMATION

Minimum Investment
Initial: $5,000 IRA: $1,000
Subsequent: $1 IRA: $1

Maximum Fees
Load: none 12b-1: 0.21%
Other: none

Montgomery Sht Dur Gvt/R (MNSGX)

800-572-3863, 415-248-6000
www.montgomeryfunds.com

Government Bond

PERFORMANCE AND PER SHARE DATA **fund inception date: 12/18/92**

	3yr Annual	5yr Annual	10yr Annual	Category Risk Index
Return (%)	5.9	6.0	na	0.48—low
Differ from Category (+/-)	-0.3 av	0.1 abv av	na	**Avg Mat** 2.9 yrs

	2000	1999	1998	1997	1996	1995	1994	1993	1992	1991
Return (%)	8.1	2.5	7.3	6.9	5.1	11.5	1.1	8.0	—	—
Differ from Category (+/-)	-5.7	5.5	-1.8	-2.9	3.0	-7.3	4.7	-2.6	—	—
Return, Tax-Adjusted (%)	5.7	0.3	5.0	4.6	2.8	8.9	-1.1	5.3	—	—
Dividends, Net Income ($)	0.59	0.55	0.56	0.57	0.57	0.62	0.58	0.64	—	—
Expense Ratio (%)	0.63	1.35	0.70	0.60	0.60	1.38	0.71	0.22	—	—
Yield (%)	5.84	5.54	5.45	5.64	5.69	6.15	6.02	6.29	—	—

SHAREHOLDER INFORMATION

Minimum Investment
Initial: $1,000 IRA: $1,000
Subsequent: $100 IRA: $100

Maximum Fees
Load: none 12b-1: none
Other: none

Neuberger Ltd Mat Bond (NLMBX)

800-877-9700, 212-476-8800
www.nbfunds.com

General Bond

PERFORMANCE AND PER SHARE DATA **fund inception date: 6/9/86**

	3yr Annual	5yr Annual	10yr Annual	Category Risk Index
Return (%)	4.3	4.8	5.7	0.55—low
Differ from Category (+/-)	-1.2 low	-0.8 low	-1.5 low	**Avg Mat** 3.0 yrs

	2000	1999	1998	1997	1996	1995	1994	1993	1992	1991
Return (%)	6.6	1.6	4.6	6.8	4.5	10.5	-0.3	6.7	5.1	11.8
Differ from Category (+/-)	-3.1	1.6	-2.7	-1.6	1.0	-5.7	2.4	-3.0	-1.7	-3.7
Return, Tax-Adjusted (%)	4.0	-0.7	2.2	4.3	2.1	8.0	-2.4	4.3	3.1	9.6
Dividends, Net Income ($)	0.60	0.59	0.59	0.63	0.60	0.61	0.56	0.56	0.61	0.69
Expense Ratio (%)	0.70	0.70	0.70	0.70	0.70	0.70	0.69	0.65	0.65	0.65
Yield (%)	6.36	6.25	5.97	6.29	6.01	6.00	5.73	5.37	5.89	6.60

SHAREHOLDER INFORMATION

Minimum Investment
Initial: $2,000 IRA: $250
Subsequent: $100 IRA: $100

Maximum Fees
Load: none 12b-1: none
Other: none

Nicholas Income (NCINX)

800-227-5987, 414-272-6133
www.nicholasfunds.com

Corporate High-Yield Bond

PERFORMANCE AND PER SHARE DATA — fund inception date: 1/1/29

	3yr Annual	5yr Annual	10yr Annual	Category Risk Index
Return (%)	-3.4	2.7	7.3	1.04—av
Differ from Category (+/-)	-3.4 blw av	-2.7 low	-2.5 low	**Avg Mat** 6.3 yrs

	2000	1999	1998	1997	1996	1995	1994	1993	1992	1991
Return (%)	-10.3	0.0	0.4	13.1	12.3	16.1	-0.1	12.9	10.3	23.0
Differ from Category (+/-)	-3.4	-5.6	-1.5	-1.5	-3.4	-1.3	2.1	-6.5	-5.9	-4.5
Return, Tax-Adjusted (%)	-14.1	-3.8	-2.9	9.8	8.9	12.5	-3.4	9.6	7.6	19.4
Dividends, Net Income ($)	0.30	0.33	0.31	0.29	0.29	0.29	0.30	0.28	0.29	0.34
Expense Ratio (%)	na	0.50	0.48	0.50	0.55	0.60	0.59	0.62	0.69	0.76
Yield (%)	12.24	10.78	9.14	7.85	8.21	8.47	9.34	7.95	8.57	10.17

SHAREHOLDER INFORMATION

Minimum Investment
Initial: $500 IRA: $500
Subsequent: $100 IRA: $100

Maximum Fees
Load: none 12b-1: none
Other: none

Northeast Investors Tr (NTHEX)

800-225-6704, 617-523-3588
www.northeastinvestors.com

Corporate High-Yield Bond

PERFORMANCE AND PER SHARE DATA — fund inception date: 3/1/50

	3yr Annual	5yr Annual	10yr Annual	Category Risk Index
Return (%)	-1.0	5.8	11.3	1.00—av
Differ from Category (+/-)	-1.0 av	0.4 abv av	1.5 abv av	**Avg Mat** 7.0 yrs

	2000	1999	1998	1997	1996	1995	1994	1993	1992	1991
Return (%)	-6.0	3.5	-0.2	13.8	20.1	17.2	2.2	23.5	17.4	26.3
Differ from Category (+/-)	0.9	-2.1	-2.1	-0.8	4.4	-0.2	4.4	4.1	1.2	-1.2
Return, Tax-Adjusted (%)	-10.2	-0.5	-3.8	10.3	16.2	13.0	-1.5	19.2	13.5	21.3
Dividends, Net Income ($)	1.06	1.06	1.00	0.96	1.00	0.99	0.98	1.00	1.11	1.30
Expense Ratio (%)	0.61	0.61	0.61	0.64	0.66	0.67	0.70	0.73	0.79	0.88
Yield (%)	12.97	10.84	9.39	8.24	8.99	9.74	10.26	9.71	12.05	14.72

SHAREHOLDER INFORMATION

Minimum Investment
Initial: $1,000 IRA: $500
Subsequent: $50 IRA: $50

Maximum Fees
Load: none 12b-1: none
Other: none

Northern CA Tax-Exempt (NCATX)

800-595-9111
www.northernfunds.com

Tax-Exempt Bond

PERFORMANCE AND PER SHARE DATA **fund inception date: 4/8/97**

	3yr Annual	5yr Annual	10yr Annual	Category Risk Index
Return (%)	5.1	na	na	1.28—high
Differ from Category (+/-)	1.3 high	na	na	**Avg Mat** 15.2 yrs

	2000	1999	1998	1997	1996	1995	1994	1993	1992	1991
Return (%)	13.9	-3.9	6.4	—	—	—	—	—	—	—
Differ from Category (+/-)	4.5	-1.3	0.8	—	—	—	—	—	—	—
Return, Tax-Adjusted (%)	13.9	-3.9	6.2	—	—	—	—	—	—	—
Dividends, Net Income ($)	0.45	0.43	0.42	—	—	—	—	—	—	—
Expense Ratio (%)	0.85	0.85	0.85	—	—	—	—	—	—	—
Yield (%)	4.10	4.27	3.81	—	—	—	—	—	—	—

SHAREHOLDER INFORMATION

Minimum Investment
Initial: $2,500 IRA: na
Subsequent: $50 IRA: na

Maximum Fees
Load: none 12b-1: none
Other: none

Northern Fixed Income (NOFIX)

800-595-9111
www.northernfunds.com

General Bond

PERFORMANCE AND PER SHARE DATA **fund inception date: 4/4/94**

	3yr Annual	5yr Annual	10yr Annual	Category Risk Index
Return (%)	5.1	5.4	na	1.16—high
Differ from Category (+/-)	-0.4 blw av	-0.2 blw av	na	**Avg Mat** 10.2 yrs

	2000	1999	1998	1997	1996	1995	1994	1993	1992	1991
Return (%)	10.9	-2.8	7.9	9.3	2.5	18.7	—	—	—	—
Differ from Category (+/-)	1.2	-2.8	0.6	0.9	-1.0	2.5	—	—	—	—
Return, Tax-Adjusted (%)	8.5	-4.8	5.3	6.9	0.1	15.6	—	—	—	—
Dividends, Net Income ($)	0.56	0.53	0.54	0.59	0.56	0.61	—	—	—	—
Expense Ratio (%)	0.90	0.90	0.90	0.90	0.90	0.90	—	—	—	—
Yield (%)	5.60	5.53	5.06	5.66	5.48	5.70	—	—	—	—

SHAREHOLDER INFORMATION

Minimum Investment
Initial: $2,500 IRA: $500
Subsequent: $50 IRA: $50

Maximum Fees
Load: none 12b-1: none
Other: none

Northern Intm Tax-Exempt (NOITX)

800-595-9111
www.northernfunds.com

Tax-Exempt Bond

PERFORMANCE AND PER SHARE DATA **fund inception date: 4/4/94**

	3yr Annual	5yr Annual	10yr Annual	Category Risk Index
Return (%)	3.9	4.2	na	0.75—low
Differ from Category (+/-)	0.1 blw av	-0.7 low	na	**Avg Mat** 7.3 yrs

	2000	1999	1998	1997	1996	1995	1994	1993	1992	1991
Return (%)	7.9	-0.9	5.1	5.8	3.3	11.9	—	—	—	—
Differ from Category (+/-)	-1.5	1.7	-0.5	-2.4	-0.4	-3.2	—	—	—	—
Return, Tax-Adjusted (%)	7.9	-0.9	4.9	5.8	3.0	11.6	—	—	—	—
Dividends, Net Income ($)	0.40	0.39	0.38	0.39	0.40	0.40	—	—	—	—
Expense Ratio (%)	0.85	0.85	0.85	0.85	0.85	0.85	—	—	—	—
Yield (%)	3.89	3.93	3.61	3.76	3.89	3.83	—	—	—	—

SHAREHOLDER INFORMATION

Minimum Investment
Initial: $2,500 IRA: na
Subsequent: $50 IRA: na

Maximum Fees
Load: none 12b-1: none
Other: none

Northern Tax-Exempt (NOTEX)

800-595-9111
www.northernfunds.com

Tax-Exempt Bond

PERFORMANCE AND PER SHARE DATA **fund inception date: 4/4/94**

	3yr Annual	5yr Annual	10yr Annual	Category Risk Index
Return (%)	4.4	4.9	na	1.19—abv av
Differ from Category (+/-)	0.6 av	0.0 av	na	**Avg Mat** 15.3 yrs

	2000	1999	1998	1997	1996	1995	1994	1993	1992	1991
Return (%)	12.2	-4.1	5.7	8.7	2.8	17.3	—	—	—	—
Differ from Category (+/-)	2.8	-1.5	0.1	0.5	-0.9	2.2	—	—	—	—
Return, Tax-Adjusted (%)	12.2	-4.1	5.2	8.5	2.6	17.2	—	—	—	—
Dividends, Net Income ($)	0.47	0.44	0.44	0.48	0.50	0.47	—	—	—	—
Expense Ratio (%)	0.85	0.85	0.85	0.85	0.85	0.85	—	—	—	—
Yield (%)	4.48	4.48	4.03	4.43	4.77	4.38	—	—	—	—

SHAREHOLDER INFORMATION

Minimum Investment
Initial: $2,500 IRA: na
Subsequent: $50 IRA: na

Maximum Fees
Load: none 12b-1: none
Other: none

Northern US Gov't (NOUGX)

800-595-9111
www.northernfunds.com

Government Bond

PERFORMANCE AND PER SHARE DATA **fund inception date: 4/4/94**

	3yr Annual	5yr Annual	10yr Annual	Category Risk Index
Return (%)	5.6	5.4	na	0.82—av
Differ from Category (+/-)	-0.6 blw av	-0.5 blw av	na	**Avg Mat** 5.2 yrs

	2000	1999	1998	1997	1996	1995	1994	1993	1992	1991
Return (%)	9.4	0.3	7.4	7.2	3.0	12.6	—	—	—	—
Differ from Category (+/-)	-4.4	3.3	-1.7	-2.6	0.9	-6.2	—	—	—	—
Return, Tax-Adjusted (%)	7.4	-1.5	4.9	5.1	0.9	10.5	—	—	—	—
Dividends, Net Income ($)	0.48	0.47	0.49	0.53	0.50	0.51	—	—	—	—
Expense Ratio (%)	0.90	0.90	0.90	0.90	0.90	0.90	—	—	—	—
Yield (%)	4.73	4.82	4.69	5.20	4.95	4.95	—	—	—	—

SHAREHOLDER INFORMATION

Minimum Investment
Initial: $2,500 IRA: $500
Subsequent: $50 IRA: $50

Maximum Fees
Load: none 12b-1: none
Other: none

Payden & Rygel Glbl Fix/R (PYGFX)

800-572-9336, 213-625-1900
www.payden.com

International Bond

PERFORMANCE AND PER SHARE DATA **fund inception date: 9/1/92**

	3yr Annual	5yr Annual	10yr Annual	Category Risk Index
Return (%)	7.9	7.7	na	0.50—blw av
Differ from Category (+/-)	4.7 high	2.5 high	na	**Avg Mat** 8.4 yrs

	2000	1999	1998	1997	1996	1995	1994	1993	1992	1991
Return (%)	13.1	-0.5	11.6	9.0	5.7	17.9	-3.0	13.1	—	—
Differ from Category (+/-)	8.6	-4.3	8.0	5.1	-8.4	1.0	4.2	-2.1	—	—
Return, Tax-Adjusted (%)	10.0	-2.7	8.3	5.3	2.8	14.3	-4.4	10.4	—	—
Dividends, Net Income ($)	0.74	0.58	0.67	0.95	0.76	0.88	0.38	0.50	—	—
Expense Ratio (%)	na	0.49	0.49	0.49	0.53	0.50	0.55	0.70	—	—
Yield (%)	7.24	5.94	6.24	9.27	7.37	8.38	3.91	4.69	—	—

SHAREHOLDER INFORMATION

Minimum Investment
Initial: $5,000 IRA: $2,000
Subsequent: $1,000 IRA: $1,000

Maximum Fees
Load: none 12b-1: none
Other: none

Payden & Rygel Glbl Sht/R (PYGSX)

800-572-9336, 213-625-1900
www.payden.com

International Bond

PERFORMANCE AND PER SHARE DATA **fund inception date: 9/18/96**

	3yr Annual	5yr Annual	10yr Annual	Category Risk Index
Return (%)	5.6	na	na	0.17—low
Differ from Category (+/-)	2.4 high	na	na	**Avg Mat** 2.0 yrs

	2000	1999	1998	1997	1996	1995	1994	1993	1992	1991
Return (%)	6.9	2.2	7.8	6.5	—	—	—	—	—	—
Differ from Category (+/-)	2.4	-1.6	4.2	2.6	—	—	—	—	—	—
Return, Tax-Adjusted (%)	5.4	-0.8	4.0	4.0	—	—	—	—	—	—
Dividends, Net Income ($)	0.35	0.77	0.97	0.64	—	—	—	—	—	—
Expense Ratio (%)	na	0.50	0.44	0.45	—	—	—	—	—	—
Yield (%)	3.61	8.20	9.75	6.31	—	—	—	—	—	—

SHAREHOLDER INFORMATION

Minimum Investment
Initial: $100,000 IRA: $100,000
Subsequent: $1,000 IRA: $1,000

Maximum Fees
Load: none 12b-1: none
Other: none

Payden & Rygel High Inc/R (PYHRX)

800-572-9336, 213-625-1900
www.payden.com

Corporate High-Yield Bond

PERFORMANCE AND PER SHARE DATA **fund inception date: 12/30/97**

	3yr Annual	5yr Annual	10yr Annual	Category Risk Index
Return (%)	2.5	na	na	0.71—low
Differ from Category (+/-)	2.5 high	na	na	**Avg Mat** 7.9 yrs

	2000	1999	1998	1997	1996	1995	1994	1993	1992	1991
Return (%)	-1.7	3.1	6.3	—	—	—	—	—	—	—
Differ from Category (+/-)	5.2	-2.5	4.4	—	—	—	—	—	—	—
Return, Tax-Adjusted (%)	-5.1	0.0	3.9	—	—	—	—	—	—	—
Dividends, Net Income ($)	0.83	0.79	0.60	—	—	—	—	—	—	—
Expense Ratio (%)	na	0.55	0.54	—	—	—	—	—	—	—
Yield (%)	9.77	8.33	6.01	—	—	—	—	—	—	—

SHAREHOLDER INFORMATION

Minimum Investment
Initial: $5,000 IRA: $2,000
Subsequent: $1,000 IRA: $1,000

Maximum Fees
Load: none 12b-1: none
Other: none

Payden & Rygel Inv Qual/R (PYOPX)

800-572-9336, 213-625-1900
www.payden.com

General Bond

PERFORMANCE AND PER SHARE DATA **fund inception date: 12/30/93**

	3yr Annual	5yr Annual	10yr Annual	Category Risk Index
Return (%)	5.2	5.2	na	1.16—high
Differ from Category (+/-)	-0.3 blw av	-0.4 low	na	**Avg Mat** 9.5 yrs

	2000	1999	1998	1997	1996	1995	1994	1993	1992	1991
Return (%)	10.3	-2.2	8.0	9.0	1.7	19.7	-4.6	—	—	—
Differ from Category (+/-)	0.6	-2.2	0.7	0.6	-1.8	3.5	-1.9	—	—	—
Return, Tax-Adjusted (%)	7.6	-4.5	5.4	6.5	-0.7	17.2	-6.4	—	—	—
Dividends, Net Income ($)	0.62	0.59	0.59	0.58	0.62	0.56	0.47	—	—	—
Expense Ratio (%)	na	0.50	0.44	0.45	0.00	0.45	0.49	—	—	—
Yield (%)	6.49	6.37	5.81	5.78	6.35	5.47	5.18	—	—	—

SHAREHOLDER INFORMATION

Minimum Investment
Initial: $5,000 IRA: $2,000
Subsequent: $1,000 IRA: $1,000

Maximum Fees
Load: none 12b-1: none
Other: none

Payden & Rygel Ltd Mat/R (PYLMX)

800-572-9336, 213-625-1900
www.payden.com

General Bond

PERFORMANCE AND PER SHARE DATA **fund inception date: 5/2/94**

	3yr Annual	5yr Annual	10yr Annual	Category Risk Index
Return (%)	5.6	5.5	na	0.19—low
Differ from Category (+/-)	0.1 av	-0.1 blw av	na	**Avg Mat** 0.7 yrs

	2000	1999	1998	1997	1996	1995	1994	1993	1992	1991
Return (%)	7.0	4.2	5.8	5.4	5.1	7.0	—	—	—	—
Differ from Category (+/-)	-2.7	4.2	-1.5	-3.0	1.6	-9.2	—	—	—	—
Return, Tax-Adjusted (%)	4.6	2.1	3.5	3.3	3.0	4.7	—	—	—	—
Dividends, Net Income ($)	0.60	0.52	0.56	0.53	0.52	0.57	—	—	—	—
Expense Ratio (%)	na	0.38	0.29	0.30	0.30	0.33	—	—	—	—
Yield (%)	5.98	5.22	5.56	5.27	5.17	5.66	—	—	—	—

SHAREHOLDER INFORMATION

Minimum Investment
Initial: $100,000 IRA: $2,000
Subsequent: $100,000 IRA: $1,000

Maximum Fees
Load: none 12b-1: none
Other: none

Payden & Rygel Sht Bond/R (PYSBX)

800-572-9336, 213-625-1900
www.payden.com

General Bond

this fund is closed to new investors

PERFORMANCE AND PER SHARE DATA **fund inception date: 12/30/93**

	3yr Annual	5yr Annual	10yr Annual	Category Risk Index
Return (%)	5.8	5.4	na	0.50—low
Differ from Category (+/-)	0.3 abv av	-0.2 blw av	na	**Avg Mat** 1.8 yrs

	2000	1999	1998	1997	1996	1995	1994	1993	1992	1991
Return (%)	8.5	2.6	6.4	5.8	3.6	11.4	0.3	—	—	—
Differ from Category (+/-)	-1.2	2.6	-0.9	-2.6	0.1	-4.8	3.0	—	—	—
Return, Tax-Adjusted (%)	6.0	0.4	3.8	3.4	1.5	9.1	-1.3	—	—	—
Dividends, Net Income ($)	0.59	0.55	0.63	0.58	0.53	0.55	0.42	—	—	—
Expense Ratio (%)	na	0.40	0.30	0.40	0.40	0.40	0.48	—	—	—
Yield (%)	6.01	5.72	6.35	5.84	5.33	5.43	4.37	—	—	—

SHAREHOLDER INFORMATION

Minimum Investment
Initial: $100,000 IRA: $2,000
Subsequent: $100,000 IRA: $1,000

Maximum Fees
Load: none 12b-1: none
Other: none

Payden & Rygel Tot Ret/R (PYTRX)

800-572-9336, 213-625-1900
www.payden.com

General Bond

PERFORMANCE AND PER SHARE DATA **fund inception date: 12/9/96**

	3yr Annual	5yr Annual	10yr Annual	Category Risk Index
Return (%)	5.3	na	na	1.22—high
Differ from Category (+/-)	-0.2 blw av	na	na	**Avg Mat** 9.2 yrs

	2000	1999	1998	1997	1996	1995	1994	1993	1992	1991
Return (%)	10.1	-2.5	8.8	8.8	—	—	—	—	—	—
Differ from Category (+/-)	0.4	-2.5	1.5	0.4	—	—	—	—	—	—
Return, Tax-Adjusted (%)	7.2	-4.6	6.1	6.2	—	—	—	—	—	—
Dividends, Net Income ($)	0.67	0.56	0.65	0.60	—	—	—	—	—	—
Expense Ratio (%)	na	0.50	0.44	0.45	—	—	—	—	—	—
Yield (%)	6.90	5.91	6.29	5.89	—	—	—	—	—	—

SHAREHOLDER INFORMATION

Minimum Investment
Initial: $100,000 IRA: $100,000
Subsequent: $1,000 IRA: $1,000

Maximum Fees
Load: none 12b-1: none
Other: none

Payden & Rygel US Gov't/R (PYUSX)

800-572-9336, 213-625-1900
www.payden.com

Government Bond

PERFORMANCE AND PER SHARE DATA **fund inception date: 12/30/94**

	3yr Annual	5yr Annual	10yr Annual	Category Risk Index
Return (%)	6.1	5.5	na	0.67—blw av
Differ from Category (+/-)	-0.1 abv av	-0.4 blw av	na	**Avg Mat** 2.4 yrs

	2000	1999	1998	1997	1996	1995	1994	1993	1992	1991
Return (%)	8.8	1.7	7.7	6.5	2.9	14.7	—	—	—	—
Differ from Category (+/-)	-5.0	4.7	-1.4	-3.3	0.8	-4.1	—	—	—	—
Return, Tax-Adjusted (%)	6.5	-0.4	5.4	4.3	0.7	12.1	—	—	—	—
Dividends, Net Income ($)	0.58	0.57	0.57	0.57	0.58	0.62	—	—	—	—
Expense Ratio (%)	na	0.40	0.34	0.45	0.45	0.45	—	—	—	—
Yield (%)	5.44	5.49	5.26	5.37	5.52	5.74	—	—	—	—

SHAREHOLDER INFORMATION

Minimum Investment
Initial: $5,000 IRA: $2,000
Subsequent: $1,000 IRA: $1,000

Maximum Fees
Load: none 12b-1: none
Other: none

Permanent Port: Treas Bill (PRTBX)

800-531-5142, 512-453-7558

Government Bond

PERFORMANCE AND PER SHARE DATA **fund inception date: 9/21/87**

	3yr Annual	5yr Annual	10yr Annual	Category Risk Index
Return (%)	4.2	4.2	3.9	0.07—low
Differ from Category (+/-)	-2.0 low	-1.7 low	-3.7 low	**Avg Mat** 0.2 yrs

	2000	1999	1998	1997	1996	1995	1994	1993	1992	1991
Return (%)	4.9	3.7	4.1	4.0	4.2	4.9	3.3	2.2	2.8	5.2
Differ from Category (+/-)	-8.9	6.7	-5.0	-5.8	2.1	-13.9	6.9	-8.4	-3.8	-9.7
Return, Tax-Adjusted (%)	3.5	2.1	2.7	2.3	2.3	3.7	2.8	1.5	1.6	4.5
Dividends, Net Income ($)	2.38	2.59	2.34	2.74	3.14	1.84	0.67	1.08	2.41	1.30
Expense Ratio (%)	1.02	0.96	1.20	0.90	0.82	0.82	0.72	0.73	0.73	0.83
Yield (%)	3.46	3.82	3.45	4.06	4.66	2.72	1.01	1.67	3.74	2.00

SHAREHOLDER INFORMATION

Minimum Investment
Initial: $1,000 IRA: $1,000
Subsequent: $100 IRA: $100

Maximum Fees
Load: none 12b-1: none
Other: none

Preferred Fixed Income (PFXIX)

800-662-4769, 309-675-5123
www.preferredgroup.com

General Bond

PERFORMANCE AND PER SHARE DATA **fund inception date: 7/1/92**

	3yr Annual	5yr Annual	10yr Annual	Category Risk Index
Return (%)	5.4	5.5	na	1.05—abv av
Differ from Category (+/-)	-0.1 av	-0.1 blw av	na	**Avg Mat** 17.6 yrs

	2000	1999	1998	1997	1996	1995	1994	1993	1992	1991
Return (%)	10.5	-0.7	6.9	8.4	2.9	17.6	-2.3	10.2	—	—
Differ from Category (+/-)	0.8	-0.7	-0.4	0.0	-0.6	1.4	0.4	0.5	—	—
Return, Tax-Adjusted (%)	8.0	-2.9	4.1	5.7	0.6	15.0	-4.2	7.5	—	—
Dividends, Net Income ($)	0.59	0.58	0.61	0.64	0.59	0.59	0.51	0.47	—	—
Expense Ratio (%)	0.68	0.65	0.67	0.74	0.93	0.95	0.97	1.05	—	—
Yield (%)	5.94	6.06	5.85	6.14	5.74	5.55	5.32	4.41	—	—

SHAREHOLDER INFORMATION

Minimum Investment
Initial: $1,000 IRA: $250
Subsequent: $50 IRA: $50

Maximum Fees
Load: none 12b-1: none
Other: none

Preferred Short-Term Gov't (PFSGX)

800-662-4769, 309-675-5123
www.preferredgroup.com

Government Bond

PERFORMANCE AND PER SHARE DATA **fund inception date: 7/1/92**

	3yr Annual	5yr Annual	10yr Annual	Category Risk Index
Return (%)	5.0	5.2	na	0.40—low
Differ from Category (+/-)	-1.2 low	-0.7 low	na	**Avg Mat** 1.9 yrs

	2000	1999	1998	1997	1996	1995	1994	1993	1992	1991
Return (%)	8.1	2.3	4.7	6.1	4.7	9.0	-0.6	5.5	—	—
Differ from Category (+/-)	-5.7	5.3	-4.4	-3.7	2.6	-9.8	3.0	-5.1	—	—
Return, Tax-Adjusted (%)	5.7	0.3	2.6	3.8	2.6	6.7	-2.2	3.9	—	—
Dividends, Net Income ($)	0.56	0.47	0.51	0.55	0.52	0.54	0.42	0.38	—	—
Expense Ratio (%)	0.57	0.55	0.60	0.63	0.66	0.71	0.74	0.78	—	—
Yield (%)	5.77	4.93	5.22	5.59	5.30	5.47	4.38	3.76	—	—

SHAREHOLDER INFORMATION

Minimum Investment
Initial: $1,000 IRA: $250
Subsequent: $50 IRA: $50

Maximum Fees
Load: none 12b-1: none
Other: none

SAFECO CA Tax-Free Inc (SFCAX)

800-624-5711, 206-545-7319
www.safecofunds.com

Tax-Exempt Bond

PERFORMANCE AND PER SHARE DATA **fund inception date: 10/5/83**

	3yr Annual	5yr Annual	10yr Annual	Category Risk Index
Return (%)	4.6	5.5	7.5	1.78—high
Differ from Category (+/-)	0.8 abv av	0.6 high	1.0 high	**Avg Mat** 24.8 yrs

	2000	1999	1998	1997	1996	1995	1994	1993	1992	1991
Return (%)	18.7	-9.1	6.1	11.5	2.5	26.1	-9.1	13.2	7.9	12.5
Differ from Category (+/-)	9.3	-6.5	0.5	3.3	-1.2	11.0	-4.2	1.5	-0.5	1.2
Return, Tax-Adjusted (%)	18.7	-9.1	5.5	11.4	2.2	26.1	-9.3	12.4	7.5	12.3
Dividends, Net Income ($)	0.56	0.56	0.59	0.60	0.61	0.62	0.63	0.66	0.68	0.70
Expense Ratio (%)	na	0.74	0.68	0.69	0.69	0.70	0.68	0.66	0.67	0.67
Yield (%)	4.48	5.07	4.50	4.62	4.94	4.89	5.90	5.16	5.65	5.89

SHAREHOLDER INFORMATION

Minimum Investment
Initial: $1,000 IRA: na
Subsequent: $100 IRA: na

Maximum Fees
Load: none 12b-1: none
Other: none

SAFECO High Yld Bd (SAFHX)

800-624-5711, 206-545-7319
www.safecofunds.com

Corporate High-Yield Bond

PERFORMANCE AND PER SHARE DATA **fund inception date: 9/7/88**

	3yr Annual	5yr Annual	10yr Annual	Category Risk Index
Return (%)	0.9	5.0	9.1	1.01—av
Differ from Category (+/-)	0.9 av	-0.4 blw av	-0.7 av	**Avg Mat** 6.5 yrs

	2000	1999	1998	1997	1996	1995	1994	1993	1992	1991
Return (%)	-5.4	3.8	4.9	12.7	10.3	15.5	-2.2	16.9	13.8	24.2
Differ from Category (+/-)	1.5	-1.8	3.0	-1.9	-5.4	-1.9	0.0	-2.5	-2.4	-3.3
Return, Tax-Adjusted (%)	-8.5	0.5	1.5	9.2	6.8	11.9	-5.7	13.0	10.5	20.7
Dividends, Net Income ($)	0.67	0.72	0.78	0.76	0.77	0.75	0.84	0.85	0.88	0.85
Expense Ratio (%)	na	0.95	0.92	0.90	0.90	1.01	1.03	1.09	1.05	1.11
Yield (%)	9.22	8.59	8.88	8.32	8.73	8.59	10.18	9.13	10.08	10.02

SHAREHOLDER INFORMATION

Minimum Investment
Initial: $1,000 IRA: $1,000
Subsequent: $100 IRA: $100

Maximum Fees
Load: none 12b-1: none
Other: none

SAFECO Muni Bond (SFCOX)

800-624-5711, 206-545-7319
www.safecofunds.com

Tax-Exempt Bond

PERFORMANCE AND PER SHARE DATA **fund inception date: 11/18/81**

	3yr Annual	5yr Annual	10yr Annual	Category Risk Index
Return (%)	4.3	5.3	7.2	1.36—high
Differ from Category (+/-)	0.5 av	0.4 abv av	0.7 abv av	**Avg Mat** 24.1 yrs

	2000	1999	1998	1997	1996	1995	1994	1993	1992	1991
Return (%)	14.1	-6.2	6.3	10.6	3.1	20.9	-8.2	12.6	8.7	13.7
Differ from Category (+/-)	4.7	-3.6	0.7	2.4	-0.6	5.8	-3.3	0.9	0.3	2.4
Return, Tax-Adjusted (%)	14.1	-6.2	5.9	10.3	3.1	20.9	-8.2	11.9	8.3	13.5
Dividends, Net Income ($)	0.69	0.68	0.73	0.74	0.75	0.70	0.76	0.78	0.82	0.85
Expense Ratio (%)	na	0.60	0.51	0.53	0.53	0.56	0.52	0.53	0.54	0.56
Yield (%)	4.94	5.27	4.96	5.04	5.36	4.89	6.08	5.29	5.85	6.18

SHAREHOLDER INFORMATION

Minimum Investment		**Maximum Fees**	
Initial: $1,000	IRA: na	Load: none	12b-1: none
Subsequent: $100	IRA: na	Other: none	

SSgA: Bond Market (SSBMX)

800-647-7327, 253-572-9500
www.ssgafunds.com

General Bond

PERFORMANCE AND PER SHARE DATA **fund inception date: 2/7/96**

	3yr Annual	5yr Annual	10yr Annual	Category Risk Index
Return (%)	5.8	na	na	1.05—abv av
Differ from Category (+/-)	0.3 abv av	na	na	**Avg Mat** 9.3 yrs

	2000	1999	1998	1997	1996	1995	1994	1993	1992	1991
Return (%)	10.8	-1.3	8.3	8.9	—	—	—	—	—	—
Differ from Category (+/-)	1.1	-1.3	1.0	0.5	—	—	—	—	—	—
Return, Tax-Adjusted (%)	8.3	-3.3	5.7	6.6	—	—	—	—	—	—
Dividends, Net Income ($)	0.59	0.53	0.56	0.55	—	—	—	—	—	—
Expense Ratio (%)	0.48	0.50	0.48	0.50	—	—	—	—	—	—
Yield (%)	6.01	5.62	5.44	5.46	—	—	—	—	—	—

SHAREHOLDER INFORMATION

Minimum Investment		**Maximum Fees**	
Initial: $1,000	IRA: $250	Load: none	12b-1: 0.06%
Subsequent: $100	IRA: $100	Other: none	

SSgA: Interm (SSINX)

800-647-7327, 253-572-9500
www.ssgafunds.com

General Bond

PERFORMANCE AND PER SHARE DATA **fund inception date: 9/1/93**

	3yr Annual	5yr Annual	10yr Annual	Category Risk Index
Return (%)	5.8	5.7	na	0.92—blw av
Differ from Category (+/-)	0.3 abv av	0.1 av	na	**Avg Mat** 5.4 yrs

	2000	1999	1998	1997	1996	1995	1994	1993	1992	1991
Return (%)	10.0	0.0	7.9	7.4	3.6	16.6	-4.4	—	—	—
Differ from Category (+/-)	0.3	0.0	0.6	-1.0	0.1	0.4	-1.7	—	—	—
Return, Tax-Adjusted (%)	7.7	-2.0	5.4	5.1	1.4	14.1	-6.3	—	—	—
Dividends, Net Income ($)	0.53	0.52	0.52	0.54	0.54	0.54	0.49	—	—	—
Expense Ratio (%)	0.60	0.60	0.60	0.60	0.60	0.60	0.60	—	—	—
Yield (%)	5.49	5.60	5.21	5.53	5.62	5.51	5.51	—	—	—

SHAREHOLDER INFORMATION

Minimum Investment
Initial: $1,000 IRA: $250
Subsequent: $100 IRA: $100

Maximum Fees
Load: none 12b-1: 0.10%
Other: none

SSgA: Yield Plus (SSYPX)

800-647-7327, 253-572-9500
www.ssgafunds.com

Corporate Bond

PERFORMANCE AND PER SHARE DATA **fund inception date: 11/9/92**

	3yr Annual	5yr Annual	10yr Annual	Category Risk Index
Return (%)	5.6	5.6	na	0.16—low
Differ from Category (+/-)	0.6 abv av	-0.1 blw av	na	**Avg Mat** na

	2000	1999	1998	1997	1996	1995	1994	1993	1992	1991
Return (%)	6.6	5.5	4.8	5.5	5.4	6.5	4.1	3.4	—	—
Differ from Category (+/-)	-1.4	4.2	-1.1	-3.6	-0.1	-11.4	6.4	-8.4	—	—
Return, Tax-Adjusted (%)	4.1	3.4	2.5	3.3	3.2	4.1	2.3	2.0	—	—
Dividends, Net Income ($)	0.61	0.52	0.56	0.55	0.54	0.58	0.43	0.34	—	—
Expense Ratio (%)	0.42	0.41	0.41	0.38	0.36	0.38	0.35	0.38	—	—
Yield (%)	6.13	5.24	5.65	5.50	5.40	5.79	4.31	3.40	—	—

SHAREHOLDER INFORMATION

Minimum Investment
Initial: $1,000 IRA: $250
Subsequent: $100 IRA: $100

Maximum Fees
Load: none 12b-1: 0.09%
Other: none

Schwab Inv: CA Lg Tm TF Bd (SWCAX)

800-435-4000, 800-266-5623
www.schwab.com

Tax-Exempt Bond

PERFORMANCE AND PER SHARE DATA **fund inception date: 2/24/92**

	3yr Annual	5yr Annual	10yr Annual	Category Risk Index
Return (%)	4.8	5.7	na	1.40—high
Differ from Category (+/-)	1.0 abv av	0.8 high	na	**Avg Mat** 20.8 yrs

	2000	1999	1998	1997	1996	1995	1994	1993	1992	1991
Return (%)	15.2	-6.1	6.4	10.0	4.3	19.8	-8.9	12.8	—	—
Differ from Category (+/-)	5.8	-3.5	0.8	1.8	0.6	4.7	-4.0	1.1	—	—
Return, Tax-Adjusted (%)	15.2	-6.1	6.4	10.0	4.3	19.8	-8.9	12.4	—	—
Dividends, Net Income ($)	0.55	0.54	0.53	0.56	0.56	0.56	0.55	0.56	—	—
Expense Ratio (%)	0.49	0.49	0.49	0.49	0.49	0.58	0.60	0.60	—	—
Yield (%)	4.85	5.21	4.57	4.91	5.13	5.08	5.67	4.93	—	—

SHAREHOLDER INFORMATION

Minimum Investment
Initial: $2,500 IRA: na
Subsequent: $500 IRA: na

Maximum Fees
Load: none 12b-1: none
Other: none

Schwab Inv: CA Sh Int TF Bd (SWCSX)

800-435-4000, 800-266-5623
www.schwab.com

Tax-Exempt Bond

PERFORMANCE AND PER SHARE DATA **fund inception date: 4/20/93**

	3yr Annual	5yr Annual	10yr Annual	Category Risk Index
Return (%)	4.2	4.3	na	0.52—low
Differ from Category (+/-)	0.4 blw av	-0.6 low	na	**Avg Mat** 4.3 yrs

	2000	1999	1998	1997	1996	1995	1994	1993	1992	1991
Return (%)	7.2	0.6	4.8	5.1	3.9	10.4	-2.0	—	—	—
Differ from Category (+/-)	-2.2	3.2	-0.8	-3.1	0.2	-4.7	2.9	—	—	—
Return, Tax-Adjusted (%)	7.2	0.6	4.8	5.1	3.9	10.4	-2.0	—	—	—
Dividends, Net Income ($)	0.39	0.38	0.40	0.42	0.42	0.42	0.38	—	—	—
Expense Ratio (%)	0.49	0.49	0.49	0.49	0.49	0.50	0.48	—	—	—
Yield (%)	3.79	3.81	3.88	4.11	4.15	4.13	3.95	—	—	—

SHAREHOLDER INFORMATION

Minimum Investment
Initial: $2,500 IRA: na
Subsequent: $500 IRA: na

Maximum Fees
Load: none 12b-1: none
Other: none

Schwab Inv: Lg Tm TF (SWNTX)

800-435-4000, 800-266-5623
www.schwab.com

Tax-Exempt Bond

PERFORMANCE AND PER SHARE DATA **fund inception date: 9/11/92**

	3yr Annual	5yr Annual	10yr Annual	Category Risk Index
Return (%)	4.3	5.4	na	1.51—high
Differ from Category (+/-)	0.5 av	0.5 abv av	na	**Avg Mat** 20.6 yrs

	2000	1999	1998	1997	1996	1995	1994	1993	1992	1991
Return (%)	15.6	-7.3	6.1	9.8	4.1	18.1	-7.0	13.6	—	—
Differ from Category (+/-)	6.2	-4.7	0.5	1.6	0.4	3.0	-2.1	1.9	—	—
Return, Tax-Adjusted (%)	15.6	-7.3	6.0	9.8	4.1	18.1	-7.0	13.3	—	—
Dividends, Net Income ($)	0.50	0.50	0.51	0.52	0.51	0.52	0.51	0.54	—	—
Expense Ratio (%)	0.49	0.49	0.49	0.49	0.49	0.54	0.51	0.45	—	—
Yield (%)	4.69	5.16	4.63	4.78	4.89	4.94	5.44	5.04	—	—

SHAREHOLDER INFORMATION

Minimum Investment
Initial: $2,500 IRA: na
Subsequent: $500 IRA: na

Maximum Fees
Load: none 12b-1: none
Other: none

Schwab Inv: Sh Tm Bd Mkt (SWBDX)

800-435-4000, 800-266-5623
www.schwab.com

Government Bond

PERFORMANCE AND PER SHARE DATA **fund inception date: 11/5/91**

	3yr Annual	5yr Annual	10yr Annual	Category Risk Index
Return (%)	5.8	5.6	na	0.64—blw av
Differ from Category (+/-)	-0.4 av	-0.3 av	na	**Avg Mat** 3.3 yrs

	2000	1999	1998	1997	1996	1995	1994	1993	1992	1991
Return (%)	9.1	1.5	6.9	6.8	4.0	10.9	-2.7	7.8	6.0	—
Differ from Category (+/-)	-4.7	4.5	-2.2	-3.0	1.9	-7.9	0.9	-2.8	-0.6	—
Return, Tax-Adjusted (%)	6.6	-0.4	4.7	4.4	1.6	8.4	-4.7	5.3	4.1	—
Dividends, Net Income ($)	0.59	0.50	0.53	0.58	0.59	0.60	0.54	0.55	0.59	—
Expense Ratio (%)	0.35	0.35	0.46	0.49	0.49	0.58	0.60	0.60	0.43	—
Yield (%)	5.99	5.21	5.32	5.90	6.05	6.02	5.65	5.23	5.73	—

SHAREHOLDER INFORMATION

Minimum Investment
Initial: $2,500 IRA: $500
Subsequent: $500 IRA: $100

Maximum Fees
Load: none 12b-1: none
Other: none

Schwab Inv: Sh/Int TF (SWITX)

800-435-4000, 800-266-5623
www.schwab.com

Tax-Exempt Bond

PERFORMANCE AND PER SHARE DATA **fund inception date: 4/21/93**

	3yr Annual	5yr Annual	10yr Annual	Category Risk Index
Return (%)	3.9	4.1	na	0.54—low
Differ from Category (+/-)	0.1 blw av	-0.8 low	na	**Avg Mat** 4.1 yrs

	2000	1999	1998	1997	1996	1995	1994	1993	1992	1991
Return (%)	6.6	0.5	4.7	5.1	3.5	9.2	-1.1	—	—	—
Differ from Category (+/-)	-2.8	3.1	-0.9	-3.1	-0.2	-5.9	3.8	—	—	—
Return, Tax-Adjusted (%)	6.6	0.5	4.7	5.1	3.5	9.2	-1.1	—	—	—
Dividends, Net Income ($)	0.40	0.40	0.40	0.41	0.41	0.40	0.37	—	—	—
Expense Ratio (%)	0.49	0.49	0.49	0.49	0.49	0.49	0.48	—	—	—
Yield (%)	3.92	4.02	3.88	4.00	4.04	3.92	3.81	—	—	—

SHAREHOLDER INFORMATION

Minimum Investment
Initial: $2,500 IRA: na
Subsequent: $500 IRA: na

Maximum Fees
Load: none 12b-1: none
Other: none

Schwab Inv: Tot Bd Mkt Ix (SWLBX)

800-435-4000, 800-266-5623
www.schwab.com

General Bond

PERFORMANCE AND PER SHARE DATA **fund inception date: 3/5/93**

	3yr Annual	5yr Annual	10yr Annual	Category Risk Index
Return (%)	6.0	5.7	na	1.13—abv av
Differ from Category (+/-)	0.5 abv av	0.1 av	na	**Avg Mat** 11.3 yrs

	2000	1999	1998	1997	1996	1995	1994	1993	1992	1991
Return (%)	11.0	-1.0	8.4	9.9	1.0	22.4	-5.7	—	—	—
Differ from Category (+/-)	1.3	-1.0	1.1	1.5	-2.5	6.2	-3.0	—	—	—
Return, Tax-Adjusted (%)	8.4	-3.1	5.9	7.3	-1.5	19.4	-8.1	—	—	—
Dividends, Net Income ($)	0.62	0.55	0.58	0.63	0.65	0.67	0.63	—	—	—
Expense Ratio (%)	0.35	0.35	0.31	0.20	0.00	0.00	0.00	—	—	—
Yield (%)	6.25	5.77	5.66	6.29	6.69	6.51	7.00	—	—	—

SHAREHOLDER INFORMATION

Minimum Investment
Initial: $2,500 IRA: $500
Subsequent: $500 IRA: $100

Maximum Fees
Load: none 12b-1: none
Other: none

Scudder CA Tax-Free (SCTFX)

800-225-2470, 312-781-1121
www.scudder.com

Tax-Exempt Bond

PERFORMANCE AND PER SHARE DATA **fund inception date: 7/22/83**

	3yr Annual	5yr Annual	10yr Annual	Category Risk Index
Return (%)	5.0	5.7	7.4	1.19—abv av
Differ from Category (+/-)	1.2 high	0.8 high	0.9 high	**Avg Mat** 11.5 yrs

	2000	1999	1998	1997	1996	1995	1994	1993	1992	1991
Return (%)	12.5	-2.8	6.0	10.2	3.5	18.9	-7.2	13.8	9.3	12.6
Differ from Category (+/-)	3.1	-0.2	0.4	2.0	-0.2	3.8	-2.3	2.1	0.9	1.3
Return, Tax-Adjusted (%)	12.5	-2.8	6.0	10.1	3.5	18.9	-7.4	12.0	8.0	11.8
Dividends, Net Income ($)	0.52	0.50	0.51	0.51	0.51	0.50	0.50	0.55	0.59	0.62
Expense Ratio (%)	0.76	0.76	0.78	0.78	0.77	0.80	0.78	0.79	0.81	0.84
Yield (%)	4.66	4.80	4.54	4.59	4.82	4.65	5.23	4.77	5.29	5.61

SHAREHOLDER INFORMATION

Minimum Investment
Initial: $2,500 IRA: na
Subsequent: $100 IRA: na

Maximum Fees
Load: none 12b-1: none
Other: none

Scudder Emerg Mkts Inc (SCEMX)

800-225-2470, 312-781-1121
www.scudder.com

International Bond

PERFORMANCE AND PER SHARE DATA **fund inception date: 12/31/93**

	3yr Annual	5yr Annual	10yr Annual	Category Risk Index
Return (%)	-2.0	7.4	na	3.41—high
Differ from Category (+/-)	-5.2 low	2.2 abv av	na	**Avg Mat** 15.4 yrs

	2000	1999	1998	1997	1996	1995	1994	1993	1992	1991
Return (%)	10.0	22.7	-30.3	13.1	34.5	19.4	-8.0	—	—	—
Differ from Category (+/-)	5.5	18.9	-33.9	9.2	20.4	2.5	-0.8	—	—	—
Return, Tax-Adjusted (%)	5.7	18.9	-33.6	7.2	27.1	15.0	-10.5	—	—	—
Dividends, Net Income ($)	0.85	0.67	0.95	1.06	1.20	1.13	0.76	—	—	—
Expense Ratio (%)	na	1.75	1.56	1.49	1.44	1.50	1.50	—	—	—
Yield (%)	10.91	8.50	13.51	8.30	8.91	10.27	7.40	—	—	—

SHAREHOLDER INFORMATION

Minimum Investment
Initial: $2,500 IRA: $1,000
Subsequent: $100 IRA: $50

Maximum Fees
Load: none 12b-1: none
Other: none

Scudder GNMA/AARP (AGNMX)

800-253-2277, 617-295-1000
aarp.scudder.com

Mortgage-Backed Bond

PERFORMANCE AND PER SHARE DATA **fund inception date: 1/31/85**

	3yr Annual	5yr Annual	10yr Annual	Category Risk Index
Return (%)	5.7	5.9	6.7	1.03—av
Differ from Category (+/-)	0.1 av	0.0 av	-0.4 low	**Avg Mat** 8.6 yrs

	2000	1999	1998	1997	1996	1995	1994	1993	1992	1991
Return (%)	10.2	0.5	6.7	7.9	4.4	12.8	-1.6	5.9	6.5	14.3
Differ from Category (+/-)	0.3	-0.5	0.5	-0.6	0.2	-2.1	-0.3	-0.5	0.0	-0.4
Return, Tax-Adjusted (%)	7.6	-1.8	4.1	5.3	1.8	10.0	-3.9	3.1	4.1	11.7
Dividends, Net Income ($)	0.91	0.92	0.98	0.98	0.97	1.01	0.94	1.09	1.21	1.25
Expense Ratio (%)	0.73	0.65	0.61	0.65	0.64	0.67	0.66	0.70	0.72	0.74
Yield (%)	6.10	6.38	6.43	6.43	6.44	6.57	6.45	6.91	7.59	7.74

SHAREHOLDER INFORMATION

Minimum Investment
Initial: $1,000 IRA: $500
Subsequent: $50 IRA: $1

Maximum Fees
Load: none 12b-1: none
Other: none

Scudder Global Bond/S (SSTGX)

800-225-2470, 312-781-1121
www.scudder.com

International Bond

PERFORMANCE AND PER SHARE DATA **fund inception date: 3/1/91**

	3yr Annual	5yr Annual	10yr Annual	Category Risk Index
Return (%)	3.7	2.9	na	0.64—av
Differ from Category (+/-)	0.5 abv av	-2.3 av	na	**Avg Mat** 7.9 yrs

	2000	1999	1998	1997	1996	1995	1994	1993	1992	1991
Return (%)	4.3	-4.0	11.4	0.3	3.1	7.7	-1.1	6.7	5.4	—
Differ from Category (+/-)	-0.2	-7.8	7.8	-3.6	-11.0	-9.2	6.1	-8.5	1.8	—
Return, Tax-Adjusted (%)	2.4	-5.8	9.0	-2.0	0.7	4.7	-4.0	3.5	2.6	—
Dividends, Net Income ($)	0.43	0.47	0.58	0.61	0.63	0.79	0.86	0.93	1.05	—
Expense Ratio (%)	na	1.16	1.00	1.00	1.00	1.00	1.00	1.00	1.00	—
Yield (%)	4.69	5.10	5.75	6.34	6.17	7.50	8.15	8.06	8.95	—

SHAREHOLDER INFORMATION

Minimum Investment
Initial: $2,500 IRA: $1,000
Subsequent: $100 IRA: $50

Maximum Fees
Load: none 12b-1: none
Other: none

Scudder High Yield Bond/S (SHBDX)

800-225-2470, 312-781-1121
www.scudder.com

Corporate High-Yield Bond

PERFORMANCE AND PER SHARE DATA **fund inception date: 6/28/96**

	3yr Annual	5yr Annual	10yr Annual	Category Risk Index
Return (%)	0.2	na	na	0.96—av
Differ from Category (+/-)	0.2 av	na	na	**Avg Mat** 6.6 yrs

	2000	1999	1998	1997	1996	1995	1994	1993	1992	1991
Return (%)	-6.7	3.4	4.5	14.8	—	—	—	—	—	—
Differ from Category (+/-)	0.2	-2.2	2.6	0.2	—	—	—	—	—	—
Return, Tax-Adjusted (%)	-10.5	-0.2	0.7	10.9	—	—	—	—	—	—
Dividends, Net Income ($)	1.13	1.14	1.20	1.16	—	—	—	—	—	—
Expense Ratio (%)	0.75	0.44	0.03	0.00	—	—	—	—	—	—
Yield (%)	11.69	9.87	9.70	8.83	—	—	—	—	—	—

SHAREHOLDER INFORMATION

Minimum Investment
Initial: $2,500 IRA: $1,000
Subsequent: $100 IRA: $50

Maximum Fees
Load: 1.00% redemption 12b-1: none
Other: redemption fee applies for 12 months

Scudder High Yld Tax-Free/S (SHYTX)

800-225-2470, 312-781-1121
www.scudder.com

Tax-Exempt Bond

PERFORMANCE AND PER SHARE DATA **fund inception date: 1/22/87**

	3yr Annual	5yr Annual	10yr Annual	Category Risk Index
Return (%)	4.3	5.8	7.5	0.94—blw av
Differ from Category (+/-)	0.5 av	0.9 high	1.0 high	**Avg Mat** 13.8 yrs

	2000	1999	1998	1997	1996	1995	1994	1993	1992	1991
Return (%)	9.1	-2.2	6.3	12.0	4.4	19.2	-8.3	13.8	10.8	13.4
Differ from Category (+/-)	-0.3	0.4	0.7	3.8	0.7	4.1	-3.4	2.1	2.4	2.1
Return, Tax-Adjusted (%)	9.1	-2.2	6.3	12.0	4.4	19.2	-8.3	13.1	10.1	12.8
Dividends, Net Income ($)	0.68	0.64	0.64	0.66	0.66	0.71	0.66	0.67	0.72	0.75
Expense Ratio (%)	0.87	0.83	0.84	0.90	0.91	0.80	0.80	0.92	0.98	1.00
Yield (%)	5.49	5.32	4.94	5.16	5.48	5.82	6.07	5.22	5.92	6.31

SHAREHOLDER INFORMATION

Minimum Investment
Initial: $2,500 IRA: na
Subsequent: $100 IRA: na

Maximum Fees
Load: none 12b-1: none
Other: none

Scudder Income/S (SCSBX)

800-225-2470, 312-781-1121
www.scudder.com

General Bond

PERFORMANCE AND PER SHARE DATA **fund inception date: 4/24/28**

	3yr Annual	5yr Annual	10yr Annual	Category Risk Index
Return (%)	4.6	5.2	7.4	1.07—abv av
Differ from Category (+/-)	-0.9 low	-0.4 low	0.2 av	**Avg Mat** 9.0 yrs

	2000	1999	1998	1997	1996	1995	1994	1993	1992	1991
Return (%)	9.7	-1.4	6.0	8.7	3.4	18.5	-4.4	12.6	6.7	17.3
Differ from Category (+/-)	0.0	-1.4	-1.3	0.3	-0.1	2.3	-1.7	2.9	-0.1	1.8
Return, Tax-Adjusted (%)	6.9	-3.7	3.3	6.3	0.8	15.5	-6.6	8.8	3.8	14.7
Dividends, Net Income ($)	0.85	0.80	0.78	0.79	0.81	0.86	0.76	0.87	0.93	0.94
Expense Ratio (%)	0.95	0.95	0.99	1.18	0.98	1.01	0.97	0.92	0.93	0.97
Yield (%)	6.77	6.53	5.78	5.86	6.11	6.28	6.15	6.08	6.70	6.70

SHAREHOLDER INFORMATION

Minimum Investment
Initial: $2,500 IRA: $1,000
Subsequent: $100 IRA: $50

Maximum Fees
Load: none 12b-1: none
Other: none

Scudder MA Tax-Free/S (SCMAX)

800-225-2470, 312-781-1121
www.scudder.com

Tax-Exempt Bond

PERFORMANCE AND PER SHARE DATA **fund inception date: 5/28/87**

	3yr Annual	5yr Annual	10yr Annual	Category Risk Index
Return (%)	4.8	5.3	7.4	1.02—av
Differ from Category (+/-)	1.0 abv av	0.4 abv av	0.9 high	**Avg Mat** 9.2 yrs

	2000	1999	1998	1997	1996	1995	1994	1993	1992	1991
Return (%)	10.9	-2.2	6.2	8.5	4.0	17.8	-6.1	14.2	10.8	12.2
Differ from Category (+/-)	1.5	0.4	0.6	0.3	0.3	2.7	-1.2	2.5	2.4	0.9
Return, Tax-Adjusted (%)	10.9	-2.2	6.1	8.5	4.0	17.8	-6.1	13.9	10.4	12.0
Dividends, Net Income ($)	0.69	0.68	0.69	0.70	0.70	0.71	0.76	0.82	0.83	0.80
Expense Ratio (%)	0.74	0.73	0.76	0.76	0.75	0.47	0.07	0.00	0.48	0.60
Yield (%)	4.86	5.04	4.75	4.87	5.03	5.04	6.04	5.72	6.16	6.13

SHAREHOLDER INFORMATION

Minimum Investment
Initial: $2,500 IRA: na
Subsequent: $100 IRA: na

Maximum Fees
Load: none 12b-1: none
Other: none

Scudder Managed Muni Bd/S (SCMBX)

800-225-2470, 312-781-1121
www.scudder.com

Tax-Exempt Bond

PERFORMANCE AND PER SHARE DATA **fund inception date: 10/14/76**

	3yr Annual	5yr Annual	10yr Annual	Category Risk Index
Return (%)	4.9	5.6	7.2	1.06—av
Differ from Category (+/-)	1.1 high	0.7 high	0.7 abv av	**Avg Mat** 9.7 yrs

	2000	1999	1998	1997	1996	1995	1994	1993	1992	1991
Return (%)	10.9	-1.9	6.2	9.2	4.1	17.1	-6.0	13.3	8.9	12.2
Differ from Category (+/-)	1.5	0.7	0.6	1.0	0.4	2.0	-1.1	1.6	0.5	0.9
Return, Tax-Adjusted (%)	10.9	-1.9	6.0	9.0	4.1	17.1	-6.0	12.4	7.8	11.8
Dividends, Net Income ($)	0.44	0.44	0.45	0.45	0.45	0.47	0.45	0.47	0.50	0.52
Expense Ratio (%)	0.65	0.62	0.62	0.64	0.63	0.64	0.63	0.63	0.63	0.64
Yield (%)	4.89	5.14	4.87	4.90	5.09	5.25	5.56	5.01	5.52	5.83

SHAREHOLDER INFORMATION

Minimum Investment
Initial: $2,500 IRA: na
Subsequent: $100 IRA: na

Maximum Fees
Load: none 12b-1: none
Other: none

Scudder Medium Tm Tax-Free/S (SCMTX)

800-225-2470, 312-781-1121
www.scudder.com

Tax-Exempt Bond

PERFORMANCE AND PER SHARE DATA **fund inception date: 4/12/83**

	3yr Annual	5yr Annual	10yr Annual	Category Risk Index
Return (%)	4.2	4.8	6.6	0.80—low
Differ from Category (+/-)	0.4 blw av	-0.1 blw av	0.1 av	**Avg Mat** 6.0 yrs

	2000	1999	1998	1997	1996	1995	1994	1993	1992	1991
Return (%)	8.4	-1.1	5.5	7.6	4.0	14.3	-3.4	10.9	8.9	12.1
Differ from Category (+/-)	-1.0	1.5	-0.1	-0.6	0.3	-0.8	1.5	-0.8	0.5	0.8
Return, Tax-Adjusted (%)	8.4	-1.1	5.4	7.5	3.9	14.1	-3.4	10.7	8.8	12.1
Dividends, Net Income ($)	0.51	0.51	0.51	0.52	0.52	0.53	0.55	0.60	0.64	0.66
Expense Ratio (%)	na	0.72	0.72	0.74	0.72	0.70	0.63	0.14	0.00	0.00
Yield (%)	4.56	4.70	4.43	4.53	4.65	4.68	5.28	5.25	5.87	6.21

SHAREHOLDER INFORMATION

Minimum Investment
Initial: $2,500 IRA: na
Subsequent: $100 IRA: na

Maximum Fees
Load: none 12b-1: none
Other: none

Scudder NY TF (SCYTX)

800-225-2470, 312-781-1121
www.scudder.com

Tax-Exempt Bond

PERFORMANCE AND PER SHARE DATA **fund inception date: 7/22/83**

	3yr Annual	5yr Annual	10yr Annual	Category Risk Index
Return (%)	4.6	5.4	7.3	1.13—abv av
Differ from Category (+/-)	0.8 abv av	0.5 abv av	0.8 high	**Avg Mat** 10.6 yrs

	2000	1999	1998	1997	1996	1995	1994	1993	1992	1991
Return (%)	11.4	-2.8	5.8	9.8	3.2	17.9	-7.1	12.9	10.2	14.4
Differ from Category (+/-)	2.0	-0.2	0.2	1.6	-0.5	2.8	-2.2	1.2	1.8	3.1
Return, Tax-Adjusted (%)	11.4	-2.8	5.8	9.7	3.1	17.9	-7.2	11.0	8.7	13.7
Dividends, Net Income ($)	0.51	0.50	0.50	0.51	0.53	0.52	0.51	0.56	0.61	0.65
Expense Ratio (%)	0.83	0.82	0.83	0.83	0.82	0.82	0.82	0.82	0.87	0.91
Yield (%)	4.50	4.69	4.36	4.50	4.89	4.72	5.17	4.70	5.22	5.67

SHAREHOLDER INFORMATION

Minimum Investment
Initial: $2,500 IRA: na
Subsequent: $100 IRA: na

Maximum Fees
Load: none 12b-1: none
Other: none

Scudder Sh Term Bd/S (SCSTX)

800-225-2470, 312-781-1121
www.scudder.com

General Bond

PERFORMANCE AND PER SHARE DATA **fund inception date: 4/2/84**

	3yr Annual	5yr Annual	10yr Annual	Category Risk Index
Return (%)	4.4	4.6	5.8	0.54—low
Differ from Category (+/-)	-1.1 low	-1.0 low	-1.4 low	**Avg Mat** 2.6 yrs

	2000	1999	1998	1997	1996	1995	1994	1993	1992	1991
Return (%)	7.5	1.5	4.3	6.1	3.8	10.7	-2.8	8.1	5.5	14.2
Differ from Category (+/-)	-2.2	1.5	-3.0	-2.3	0.3	-5.5	-0.1	-1.6	-1.3	-1.3
Return, Tax-Adjusted (%)	5.1	-0.6	2.0	3.6	1.3	8.1	-5.2	5.2	3.0	11.3
Dividends, Net Income ($)	0.63	0.59	0.63	0.67	0.71	0.70	0.75	0.80	0.95	1.08
Expense Ratio (%)	na	0.85	0.86	1.25	0.80	0.76	0.73	0.68	0.75	0.44
Yield (%)	5.96	5.65	5.79	6.06	6.42	6.16	6.86	6.62	7.96	8.82

SHAREHOLDER INFORMATION

Minimum Investment
Initial: $2,500 IRA: $1,000
Subsequent: $100 IRA: $50

Maximum Fees
Load: none 12b-1: none
Other: none

Sit Minnesota Tax-Free Inc (SMTFX)

800-332-5580, 612-334-5888
www.sitfunds.com

Tax-Exempt Bond

PERFORMANCE AND PER SHARE DATA **fund inception date: 12/1/93**

	3yr Annual	5yr Annual	10yr Annual	Category Risk Index
Return (%)	3.3	4.7	na	0.76—low
Differ from Category (+/-)	-0.5 low	-0.2 blw av	na	**Avg Mat** 17.1 yrs

	2000	1999	1998	1997	1996	1995	1994	1993	1992	1991
Return (%)	8.1	-3.8	6.1	8.1	5.8	11.8	0.6	—	—	—
Differ from Category (+/-)	-1.3	-1.2	0.5	-0.1	2.1	-3.3	5.5	—	—	—
Return, Tax-Adjusted (%)	8.1	-3.8	6.1	8.1	5.8	11.8	0.6	—	—	—
Dividends, Net Income ($)	0.52	0.50	0.52	0.55	0.57	0.56	0.55	—	—	—
Expense Ratio (%)	0.80	0.80	0.80	0.80	0.80	0.80	0.80	—	—	—
Yield (%)	5.23	5.15	4.90	5.23	5.56	5.47	5.68	—	—	—

SHAREHOLDER INFORMATION

Minimum Investment
Initial: $2,000 IRA: na
Subsequent: $100 IRA: na

Maximum Fees
Load: none 12b-1: none
Other: none

Sit Tax-Free Income (SNTIX)

800-332-5580, 612-334-5888
www.sitfunds.com

Tax-Exempt Bond

PERFORMANCE AND PER SHARE DATA **fund inception date: 9/29/88**

	3yr Annual	5yr Annual	10yr Annual	Category Risk Index
Return (%)	3.3	5.1	6.4	0.91—blw av
Differ from Category (+/-)	-0.5 low	0.2 av	-0.1 blw av	**Avg Mat** 16.5 yrs

	2000	1999	1998	1997	1996	1995	1994	1993	1992	1991
Return (%)	8.3	-4.0	6.2	9.8	5.6	12.8	-0.6	10.4	7.7	9.2
Differ from Category (+/-)	-1.1	-1.4	0.6	1.6	1.9	-2.3	4.3	-1.3	-0.7	-2.1
Return, Tax-Adjusted (%)	8.3	-4.0	6.1	9.6	5.6	12.8	-0.6	10.1	7.5	9.2
Dividends, Net Income ($)	0.50	0.50	0.52	0.55	0.56	0.55	0.56	0.58	0.64	0.70
Expense Ratio (%)	0.70	0.71	0.76	0.79	0.80	0.79	0.77	0.80	0.80	0.80
Yield (%)	5.09	5.23	4.95	5.26	5.57	5.46	5.92	5.70	6.53	7.20

SHAREHOLDER INFORMATION

Minimum Investment
Initial: $2,000 IRA: na
Subsequent: $100 IRA: na

Maximum Fees
Load: none 12b-1: none
Other: none

Sit US Gov't Sec (SNGVX)

800-332-5580, 612-334-5888
www.sitfunds.com

Government Bond

PERFORMANCE AND PER SHARE DATA **fund inception date: 6/2/87**

	3yr Annual	5yr Annual	10yr Annual	Category Risk Index
Return (%)	5.6	6.0	6.8	0.50—low
Differ from Category (+/-)	-0.6 blw av	0.1 av	-0.8 av	**Avg Mat** 15.0 yrs

	2000	1999	1998	1997	1996	1995	1994	1993	1992	1991
Return (%)	9.1	1.3	6.5	8.1	4.9	11.5	1.7	7.3	5.4	12.8
Differ from Category (+/-)	-4.7	4.3	-2.6	-1.7	2.8	-7.3	5.3	-3.3	-1.2	-2.1
Return, Tax-Adjusted (%)	6.6	-0.7	4.2	5.7	2.4	8.7	-0.6	4.6	3.0	10.0
Dividends, Net Income ($)	0.64	0.56	0.56	0.63	0.65	0.70	0.64	0.67	0.70	0.79
Expense Ratio (%)	0.80	0.80	0.80	0.80	0.80	0.80	0.86	0.89	0.80	0.90
Yield (%)	6.10	5.47	5.21	5.92	6.22	6.60	6.29	6.27	6.51	7.14

SHAREHOLDER INFORMATION

Minimum Investment		**Maximum Fees**	
Initial: $2,000	IRA: $1	Load: none	12b-1: none
Subsequent: $100	IRA: $1	Other: none	

SteinRoe Inc: Income (SRINX)

800-338-2550, 312-368-7800
www.steinroe.com

Corporate Bond

PERFORMANCE AND PER SHARE DATA **fund inception date: 3/5/86**

	3yr Annual	5yr Annual	10yr Annual	Category Risk Index
Return (%)	4.9	5.8	8.2	1.16—abv av
Differ from Category (+/-)	-0.1 av	0.1 abv av	0.1 av	**Avg Mat** 11.3 yrs

	2000	1999	1998	1997	1996	1995	1994	1993	1992	1991
Return (%)	9.8	1.2	4.0	9.5	4.8	19.7	-3.8	13.3	9.1	17.1
Differ from Category (+/-)	1.8	-0.1	-1.9	0.4	-0.7	1.8	-1.5	1.5	-0.2	-0.6
Return, Tax-Adjusted (%)	6.7	-1.5	1.3	6.7	2.0	16.5	-6.4	10.3	6.6	14.4
Dividends, Net Income ($)	0.70	0.67	0.68	0.69	0.70	0.71	0.69	0.71	0.76	0.77
Expense Ratio (%)	0.86	0.84	0.83	0.84	0.82	0.82	0.82	0.82	0.90	0.95
Yield (%)	7.48	7.29	6.97	6.87	7.12	7.04	7.61	7.00	7.91	8.07

SHAREHOLDER INFORMATION

Minimum Investment		**Maximum Fees**	
Initial: $2,500	IRA: $500	Load: none	12b-1: none
Subsequent: $100	IRA: $50	Other: none	

SteinRoe Inc: Interm Bond (SRBFX)

800-338-2550, 312-368-7800
www.steinroe.com

General Bond

PERFORMANCE AND PER SHARE DATA **fund inception date: 12/5/78**

	3yr Annual	5yr Annual	10yr Annual	Category Risk Index
Return (%)	6.0	6.3	7.7	1.03—av
Differ from Category (+/-)	0.5 high	0.7 high	0.5 abv av	**Avg Mat** 9.3 yrs

	2000	1999	1998	1997	1996	1995	1994	1993	1992	1991
Return (%)	10.7	1.2	6.3	9.2	4.5	16.8	-2.5	9.1	7.6	15.0
Differ from Category (+/-)	1.0	1.2	-1.0	0.8	1.0	0.6	0.2	-0.6	0.8	-0.5
Return, Tax-Adjusted (%)	7.8	-1.3	3.7	6.5	1.8	13.9	-4.9	5.7	5.2	12.5
Dividends, Net Income ($)	0.60	0.58	0.58	0.58	0.60	0.58	0.56	0.59	0.68	0.68
Expense Ratio (%)	0.72	0.72	0.72	0.73	0.70	0.70	0.70	0.67	0.70	0.73
Yield (%)	6.91	6.88	6.52	6.50	6.88	6.48	6.83	6.40	7.55	7.53

SHAREHOLDER INFORMATION

Minimum Investment
Initial: $2,500 IRA: $500
Subsequent: $100 IRA: $50

Maximum Fees
Load: none 12b-1: none
Other: none

SteinRoe Muni: High Yield (SRHMX)

800-338-2550, 312-368-7800
www.steinroe.com

Tax-Exempt Bond

PERFORMANCE AND PER SHARE DATA **fund inception date: 3/5/84**

	3yr Annual	5yr Annual	10yr Annual	Category Risk Index
Return (%)	3.3	4.8	6.2	0.77—low
Differ from Category (+/-)	-0.5 low	-0.1 blw av	-0.3 blw av	**Avg Mat** 17.5 yrs

	2000	1999	1998	1997	1996	1995	1994	1993	1992	1991
Return (%)	7.0	-2.0	5.2	9.6	4.5	17.6	-4.0	10.6	5.3	9.8
Differ from Category (+/-)	-2.4	0.6	-0.4	1.4	0.8	2.5	0.9	-1.1	-3.1	-1.5
Return, Tax-Adjusted (%)	7.0	-2.0	5.2	9.6	4.5	17.6	-4.0	10.0	4.8	9.3
Dividends, Net Income ($)	0.61	0.64	0.63	0.69	0.70	0.66	0.65	0.68	0.74	0.81
Expense Ratio (%)	0.78	0.77	0.75	0.77	0.85	0.86	0.76	0.73	0.69	0.71
Yield (%)	5.42	5.76	5.25	5.75	6.02	5.58	6.10	5.67	6.34	6.76

SHAREHOLDER INFORMATION

Minimum Investment
Initial: $2,500 IRA: na
Subsequent: $100 IRA: na

Maximum Fees
Load: none 12b-1: none
Other: none

SteinRoe Muni: Interm (SRIMX)

800-338-2550, 312-368-7800
www.steinroe.com

Tax-Exempt Bond

PERFORMANCE AND PER SHARE DATA **fund inception date: 10/9/85**

	3yr Annual	5yr Annual	10yr Annual	Category Risk Index
Return (%)	4.3	4.9	6.2	0.88—blw av
Differ from Category (+/-)	0.5 av	0.0 av	-0.3 blw av	**Avg Mat** 9.3 yrs

	2000	1999	1998	1997	1996	1995	1994	1993	1992	1991
Return (%)	9.4	-1.4	5.4	7.5	4.1	12.9	-3.3	11.0	7.6	10.6
Differ from Category (+/-)	0.0	1.2	-0.2	-0.7	0.4	-2.2	1.6	-0.7	-0.8	-0.7
Return, Tax-Adjusted (%)	9.4	-1.4	5.3	7.4	3.9	12.9	-3.3	10.5	7.2	10.1
Dividends, Net Income ($)	0.53	0.53	0.53	0.54	0.54	0.54	0.53	0.53	0.55	0.59
Expense Ratio (%)	0.70	0.70	0.70	0.70	0.70	0.74	0.71	0.72	0.79	0.80
Yield (%)	4.66	4.84	4.53	4.63	4.72	4.69	4.95	4.49	4.88	5.29

SHAREHOLDER INFORMATION

Minimum Investment		**Maximum Fees**	
Initial: $2,500	IRA: na	Load: none	12b-1: none
Subsequent: $100	IRA: na	Other: none	

SteinRoe Muni: Managed (SRMMX)

800-338-2550, 312-368-7800
www.steinroe.com

Tax-Exempt Bond

PERFORMANCE AND PER SHARE DATA **fund inception date: 2/23/77**

	3yr Annual	5yr Annual	10yr Annual	Category Risk Index
Return (%)	4.6	5.3	6.8	1.17—abv av
Differ from Category (+/-)	0.8 abv av	0.4 abv av	0.3 av	**Avg Mat** 16.5 yrs

	2000	1999	1998	1997	1996	1995	1994	1993	1992	1991
Return (%)	12.4	-3.4	5.4	9.3	3.7	16.6	-5.3	11.2	8.2	11.8
Differ from Category (+/-)	3.0	-0.8	-0.2	1.1	0.0	1.5	-0.4	-0.5	-0.2	0.5
Return, Tax-Adjusted (%)	12.2	-3.6	5.4	9.3	3.7	16.6	-5.3	10.7	7.7	11.1
Dividends, Net Income ($)	0.44	0.47	0.47	0.48	0.48	0.49	0.50	0.50	0.53	0.55
Expense Ratio (%)	0.69	0.72	0.72	0.73	0.72	0.65	0.65	0.64	0.64	0.66
Yield (%)	4.81	5.43	4.97	5.10	5.29	5.31	5.98	5.25	5.76	5.97

SHAREHOLDER INFORMATION

Minimum Investment		**Maximum Fees**	
Initial: $2,500	IRA: na	Load: none	12b-1: none
Subsequent: $100	IRA: na	Other: none	

Strong Adv Short Dur Bd/Z (STGBX)

800-368-1683, 414-359-1400
www.strong-funds.com

International Bond

PERFORMANCE AND PER SHARE DATA — fund inception date: 3/31/94

	3yr Annual	5yr Annual	10yr Annual	Category Risk Index
Return (%)	5.4	6.5	na	0.22—low
Differ from Category (+/-)	2.2 high	1.3 abv av	na	**Avg Mat** 1.4 yrs

	2000	1999	1998	1997	1996	1995	1994	1993	1992	1991
Return (%)	6.4	5.7	4.0	6.6	10.0	10.4	—	—	—	—
Differ from Category (+/-)	1.9	1.9	0.4	2.7	-4.1	-6.5	—	—	—	—
Return, Tax-Adjusted (%)	3.8	3.3	1.7	3.1	7.2	7.4	—	—	—	—
Dividends, Net Income ($)	0.66	0.62	0.60	0.89	0.72	0.76	—	—	—	—
Expense Ratio (%)	na	1.10	0.90	0.70	0.00	0.00	—	—	—	—
Yield (%)	6.49	6.08	5.85	8.47	6.72	7.29	—	—	—	—

SHAREHOLDER INFORMATION

Minimum Investment
Initial: $2,500 IRA: $250
Subsequent: $50 IRA: $50

Maximum Fees
Load: none 12b-1: none
Other: none

Strong Advantage/Inv (STADX)

800-368-3863, 414-359-1400
www.strong-funds.com

General Bond

PERFORMANCE AND PER SHARE DATA — fund inception date: 11/25/88

	3yr Annual	5yr Annual	10yr Annual	Category Risk Index
Return (%)	5.5	5.9	6.7	0.25—low
Differ from Category (+/-)	0.0 av	0.3 abv av	-0.5 blw av	**Avg Mat** 0.8 yrs

	2000	1999	1998	1997	1996	1995	1994	1993	1992	1991
Return (%)	6.7	5.2	4.7	6.5	6.6	7.5	3.5	7.8	8.4	10.6
Differ from Category (+/-)	-3.0	5.2	-2.6	-1.9	3.1	-8.7	6.2	-1.9	1.6	-4.9
Return, Tax-Adjusted (%)	4.1	2.8	2.3	4.0	4.1	4.8	1.3	5.4	6.2	8.1
Dividends, Net Income ($)	0.63	0.58	0.59	0.62	0.61	0.66	0.54	0.59	0.70	0.75
Expense Ratio (%)	0.80	0.70	0.80	0.80	0.80	0.80	0.80	0.90	1.00	1.20
Yield (%)	6.37	5.87	5.92	6.15	6.05	6.57	5.40	5.78	6.99	7.57

SHAREHOLDER INFORMATION

Minimum Investment
Initial: $2,500 IRA: $250
Subsequent: $50 IRA: $50

Maximum Fees
Load: none 12b-1: none
Other: none

Strong Corporate Bd/Inv (STCBX)

800-368-3863, 414-359-1400
www.strong-funds.com

Corporate Bond

PERFORMANCE AND PER SHARE DATA — fund inception date: 12/12/85

	3yr Annual	5yr Annual	10yr Annual	Category Risk Index
Return (%)	4.9	6.3	9.4	1.22—high
Differ from Category (+/-)	-0.1 av	0.6 high	1.3 high	**Avg Mat** 10.3 yrs

	2000	1999	1998	1997	1996	1995	1994	1993	1992	1991
Return (%)	7.8	-0.2	7.2	11.8	5.5	25.3	-1.3	16.7	9.3	14.8
Differ from Category (+/-)	-0.2	-1.5	1.3	2.7	0.0	7.4	1.0	4.9	0.0	-2.9
Return, Tax-Adjusted (%)	4.9	-2.7	4.5	9.0	2.8	22.0	-4.1	13.7	6.6	12.1
Dividends, Net Income ($)	0.75	0.73	0.74	0.75	0.72	0.76	0.73	0.69	0.81	0.76
Expense Ratio (%)	na	0.80	0.90	1.00	1.00	1.10	1.10	1.10	1.30	1.50
Yield (%)	7.12	6.95	6.57	6.69	6.71	6.97	7.79	6.73	8.61	8.11

SHAREHOLDER INFORMATION

Minimum Investment
Initial: $2,500 IRA: $250
Subsequent: $50 IRA: $50

Maximum Fees
Load: none 12b-1: none
Other: none

Strong Gov't Sec/Inv (STVSX)

800-368-3863, 414-359-1400
www.strong-funds.com

General Bond

PERFORMANCE AND PER SHARE DATA — fund inception date: 10/29/86

	3yr Annual	5yr Annual	10yr Annual	Category Risk Index
Return (%)	5.9	5.9	8.3	1.00—av
Differ from Category (+/-)	0.4 abv av	0.3 abv av	1.1 high	**Avg Mat** 5.7 yrs

	2000	1999	1998	1997	1996	1995	1994	1993	1992	1991
Return (%)	11.3	-1.0	8.1	9.0	2.8	19.9	-3.3	12.7	9.2	16.6
Differ from Category (+/-)	1.6	-1.0	0.8	0.6	-0.7	3.7	-0.6	3.0	2.4	1.1
Return, Tax-Adjusted (%)	8.9	-3.0	5.4	6.5	0.4	17.1	-5.6	9.1	5.6	13.8
Dividends, Net Income ($)	0.59	0.56	0.61	0.64	0.63	0.66	0.62	0.65	0.80	0.76
Expense Ratio (%)	na	0.80	0.80	0.80	0.90	0.90	0.90	0.80	0.70	0.80
Yield (%)	5.57	5.55	5.55	5.95	6.01	6.09	6.43	5.89	7.35	6.95

SHAREHOLDER INFORMATION

Minimum Investment
Initial: $2,500 IRA: $250
Subsequent: $50 IRA: $50

Maximum Fees
Load: none 12b-1: none
Other: none

Strong Hi Yld Bond/Inv (STHYX)

800-368-3863, 414-359-1400
www.strong-funds.com

Corporate High-Yield Bond

PERFORMANCE AND PER SHARE DATA **fund inception date: 12/28/95**

	3yr Annual	5yr Annual	10yr Annual	Category Risk Index
Return (%)	1.0	8.7	na	1.14—abv av
Differ from Category (+/-)	1.0 abv av	3.3 high	na	**Avg Mat** 6.7 yrs

	2000	1999	1998	1997	1996	1995	1994	1993	1992	1991
Return (%)	-7.0	7.8	3.0	15.9	26.8	—	—	—	—	—
Differ from Category (+/-)	-0.1	2.2	1.1	1.3	11.1	—	—	—	—	—
Return, Tax-Adjusted (%)	-11.1	3.9	-0.6	11.7	22.4	—	—	—	—	—
Dividends, Net Income ($)	1.14	1.08	1.05	1.04	1.02	—	—	—	—	—
Expense Ratio (%)	na	0.80	0.80	0.60	0.00	—	—	—	—	—
Yield (%)	12.72	10.00	9.42	8.55	8.80	—	—	—	—	—

SHAREHOLDER INFORMATION

Minimum Investment
Initial: $2,500 IRA: $250
Subsequent: $50 IRA: $50

Maximum Fees
Load: none 12b-1: none
Other: none

Strong Hi Yld Muni Bd (SHYLX)

800-368-1683, 414-359-1400
www.strong-funds.com

Tax-Exempt Bond

PERFORMANCE AND PER SHARE DATA **fund inception date: 10/1/93**

	3yr Annual	5yr Annual	10yr Annual	Category Risk Index
Return (%)	-0.6	3.2	na	1.01—av
Differ from Category (+/-)	-4.4 low	-1.7 low	na	**Avg Mat** 15.0 yrs

	2000	1999	1998	1997	1996	1995	1994	1993	1992	1991
Return (%)	-1.4	-5.4	5.2	13.8	5.1	14.6	-0.9	—	—	—
Differ from Category (+/-)	-10.8	-2.8	-0.4	5.6	1.4	-0.5	4.0	—	—	—
Return, Tax-Adjusted (%)	-1.4	-5.4	5.1	13.7	5.1	14.6	-0.9	—	—	—
Dividends, Net Income ($)	0.58	0.57	0.58	0.60	0.64	0.69	0.71	—	—	—
Expense Ratio (%)	0.70	0.70	0.70	0.70	0.70	0.00	0.00	—	—	—
Yield (%)	6.82	6.18	5.59	5.74	6.57	6.96	7.64	—	—	—

SHAREHOLDER INFORMATION

Minimum Investment
Initial: $2,500 IRA: na
Subsequent: $50 IRA: na

Maximum Fees
Load: none 12b-1: none
Other: none

Strong Muni Advtg (SMUAX)

800-368-3863, 414-359-1400
www.strong-funds.com

Tax-Exempt Bond

PERFORMANCE AND PER SHARE DATA **fund inception date: 11/30/95**

	3yr Annual	5yr Annual	10yr Annual	Category Risk Index
Return (%)	3.8	4.2	na	0.17—low
Differ from Category (+/-)	0.0 low	-0.7 low	na	**Avg Mat** 0.9 yrs

	2000	1999	1998	1997	1996	1995	1994	1993	1992	1991
Return (%)	3.9	2.9	4.5	5.1	4.8	—	—	—	—	—
Differ from Category (+/-)	-5.5	5.5	-1.1	-3.1	1.1	—	—	—	—	—
Return, Tax-Adjusted (%)	3.9	2.9	4.5	5.1	4.8	—	—	—	—	—
Dividends, Net Income ($)	0.23	0.20	0.21	0.23	0.24	—	—	—	—	—
Expense Ratio (%)	0.60	0.50	0.40	0.70	0.00	—	—	—	—	—
Yield (%)	4.65	4.01	4.16	4.57	4.79	—	—	—	—	—

SHAREHOLDER INFORMATION

Minimum Investment		**Maximum Fees**	
Initial: $2,500	IRA: na	Load: none	12b-1: none
Subsequent: $50	IRA: na	Other: none	

Strong Muni Bond (SXFIX)

800-368-3863, 414-359-1400
www.strong-funds.com

Tax-Exempt Bond

PERFORMANCE AND PER SHARE DATA **fund inception date: 10/23/86**

	3yr Annual	5yr Annual	10yr Annual	Category Risk Index
Return (%)	1.0	3.4	5.9	1.17—abv av
Differ from Category (+/-)	-2.8 low	-1.5 low	-0.6 low	**Avg Mat** 10.1 yrs

	2000	1999	1998	1997	1996	1995	1994	1993	1992	1991
Return (%)	3.3	-6.4	6.6	12.1	2.4	11.3	-4.5	11.7	12.1	13.2
Differ from Category (+/-)	-6.1	-3.8	1.0	3.9	-1.3	-3.8	0.4	0.0	3.7	1.9
Return, Tax-Adjusted (%)	3.3	-6.4	6.6	12.1	2.4	11.3	-4.5	10.8	11.3	13.2
Dividends, Net Income ($)	0.48	0.49	0.51	0.50	0.49	0.73	0.55	0.58	0.65	0.64
Expense Ratio (%)	0.80	0.70	0.70	0.80	0.80	0.90	0.80	0.70	0.10	0.10
Yield (%)	5.56	5.54	5.12	5.09	5.30	7.66	5.95	5.49	6.34	6.55

SHAREHOLDER INFORMATION

Minimum Investment		**Maximum Fees**	
Initial: $2,500	IRA: na	Load: none	12b-1: none
Subsequent: $50	IRA: na	Other: none	

Strong Sht Tm Bond/Inv (SSTBX)

800-368-3863, 414-359-1400
www.strong-funds.com

General Bond

PERFORMANCE AND PER SHARE DATA **fund inception date: 8/31/87**

	3yr Annual	5yr Annual	10yr Annual	Category Risk Index
Return (%)	5.4	6.0	7.0	0.43—low
Differ from Category (+/-)	-0.1 blw av	0.4 abv av	-0.2 blw av	**Avg Mat** 1.7 yrs

	2000	1999	1998	1997	1996	1995	1994	1993	1992	1991
Return (%)	7.2	4.2	4.8	7.1	6.7	11.9	-1.6	9.3	6.6	14.6
Differ from Category (+/-)	-2.5	4.2	-2.5	-1.3	3.2	-4.3	1.1	-0.4	-0.2	-0.9
Return, Tax-Adjusted (%)	4.5	1.6	2.1	4.3	3.9	9.0	-4.0	6.6	4.2	12.1
Dividends, Net Income ($)	0.63	0.61	0.65	0.68	0.68	0.67	0.64	0.66	0.78	0.74
Expense Ratio (%)	na	0.80	0.80	0.90	0.90	1.00	0.90	0.80	0.60	1.00
Yield (%)	6.70	6.50	6.77	6.95	6.94	6.80	6.79	6.45	7.80	7.31

SHAREHOLDER INFORMATION

Minimum Investment
Initial: $2,500 IRA: $250
Subsequent: $50 IRA: $50

Maximum Fees
Load: none 12b-1: none
Other: none

Strong Sht Tm HY Bond/Inv (STHBX)

800-368-3863, 414-359-1400
www.strong-funds.com

Corporate High-Yield Bond

PERFORMANCE AND PER SHARE DATA **fund inception date: 6/30/97**

	3yr Annual	5yr Annual	10yr Annual	Category Risk Index
Return (%)	6.2	na	na	0.35—low
Differ from Category (+/-)	6.2 high	na	na	**Avg Mat** 2.1 yrs

	2000	1999	1998	1997	1996	1995	1994	1993	1992	1991
Return (%)	.5.0	5.3	8.3	—	—	—	—	—	—	—
Differ from Category (+/-)	11.9	-0.3	6.4	—	—	—	—	—	—	—
Return, Tax-Adjusted (%)	1.8	2.2	5.2	—	—	—	—	—	—	—
Dividends, Net Income ($)	0.80	0.80	0.77	—	—	—	—	—	—	—
Expense Ratio (%)	na	0.80	0.90	—	—	—	—	—	—	—
Yield (%)	8.17	7.92	7.39	—	—	—	—	—	—	—

SHAREHOLDER INFORMATION

Minimum Investment
Initial: $2,500 IRA: $250
Subsequent: $50 IRA: $50

Maximum Fees
Load: none 12b-1: none
Other: none

Strong Sht Tm HY Mu/Inv (SSHMX)

800-368-3863, 414-359-1400
www.strong-funds.com

Tax-Exempt Bond

PERFORMANCE AND PER SHARE DATA **fund inception date: 11/28/97**

	3yr Annual	5yr Annual	10yr Annual	Category Risk Index
Return (%)	3.7	na	na	0.43—low
Differ from Category (+/-)	-0.1 low	na	na	**Avg Mat** 2.3 yrs

	2000	1999	1998	1997	1996	1995	1994	1993	1992	1991
Return (%)	4.2	0.8	6.1	—	—	—	—	—	—	—
Differ from Category (+/-)	-5.2	3.4	0.5	—	—	—	—	—	—	—
Return, Tax-Adjusted (%)	4.2	0.8	6.1	—	—	—	—	—	—	—
Dividends, Net Income ($)	0.50	0.49	0.51	—	—	—	—	—	—	—
Expense Ratio (%)	0.60	0.40	0.40	—	—	—	—	—	—	—
Yield (%)	5.19	5.03	5.02	—	—	—	—	—	—	—

SHAREHOLDER INFORMATION

Minimum Investment
Initial: $2,500 IRA: na
Subsequent: $50 IRA: na

Maximum Fees
Load: none 12b-1: none
Other: none

Strong Sht Tm Mu Bond/Inv (STSMX)

800-368-3863, 414-359-1400
www.strong-funds.com

Tax-Exempt Bond

PERFORMANCE AND PER SHARE DATA **fund inception date: 12/31/91**

	3yr Annual	5yr Annual	10yr Annual	Category Risk Index
Return (%)	3.9	4.6	na	0.39—low
Differ from Category (+/-)	0.1 low	-0.3 blw av	na	**Avg Mat** 2.3 yrs

	2000	1999	1998	1997	1996	1995	1994	1993	1992	1991
Return (%)	5.0	1.1	5.5	6.9	4.8	5.3	-1.6	6.7	7.1	—
Differ from Category (+/-)	-4.4	3.7	-0.1	-1.3	1.1	-9.8	3.3	-5.0	-1.3	—
Return, Tax-Adjusted (%)	5.0	1.1	5.5	6.9	4.8	5.3	-1.6	6.5	7.0	—
Dividends, Net Income ($)	0.46	0.45	0.48	0.47	0.49	0.47	0.45	0.44	0.48	—
Expense Ratio (%)	0.60	0.60	0.60	0.70	0.70	0.80	0.70	0.60	0.20	—
Yield (%)	4.77	4.67	4.81	4.73	5.03	4.81	4.62	4.21	4.70	—

SHAREHOLDER INFORMATION

Minimum Investment
Initial: $2,500 IRA: na
Subsequent: $50 IRA: na

Maximum Fees
Load: none 12b-1: none
Other: none

T Rowe Price CA TF: Bond (PRXCX)

800-638-5660, 410-547-2000
www.troweprice.com

Tax-Exempt Bond

PERFORMANCE AND PER SHARE DATA **fund inception date: 9/15/86**

	3yr Annual	5yr Annual	10yr Annual	Category Risk Index
Return (%)	5.1	5.7	7.2	1.15—abv av
Differ from Category (+/-)	1.3 high	0.8 high	0.7 abv av	**Avg Mat** 17.2 yrs

	2000	1999	1998	1997	1996	1995	1994	1993	1992	1991
Return (%)	12.8	-3.3	6.4	9.0	4.5	17.3	-5.7	12.4	8.9	12.1
Differ from Category (+/-)	3.4	-0.7	0.8	0.8	0.8	2.2	-0.8	0.7	0.5	0.8
Return, Tax-Adjusted (%)	12.8	-3.3	6.3	9.0	4.5	17.3	-5.7	11.7	8.9	12.1
Dividends, Net Income ($)	0.52	0.51	0.52	0.54	0.54	0.55	0.54	0.55	0.58	0.58
Expense Ratio (%)	0.56	0.58	0.58	0.62	0.63	0.60	0.60	0.60	0.60	0.73
Yield (%)	4.80	5.04	4.72	4.97	5.15	5.20	5.66	5.04	5.67	5.83

SHAREHOLDER INFORMATION

Minimum Investment
Initial: $2,500 IRA: na
Subsequent: $100 IRA: na

Maximum Fees
Load: none 12b-1: none
Other: none

T Rowe Price Corp Income (PRPIX)

800-638-5660, 410-547-2000
www.troweprice.com

Corporate Bond

PERFORMANCE AND PER SHARE DATA **fund inception date: 10/31/95**

	3yr Annual	5yr Annual	10yr Annual	Category Risk Index
Return (%)	3.0	5.2	na	1.70—high
Differ from Category (+/-)	-2.0 low	-0.5 low	na	**Avg Mat** 11.4 yrs

	2000	1999	1998	1997	1996	1995	1994	1993	1992	1991
Return (%)	7.9	-0.8	2.2	12.5	4.6	—	—	—	—	—
Differ from Category (+/-)	-0.1	-2.1	-3.7	3.4	-0.9	—	—	—	—	—
Return, Tax-Adjusted (%)	4.9	-3.4	-0.6	9.5	1.7	—	—	—	—	—
Dividends, Net Income ($)	0.68	0.66	0.73	0.75	0.73	—	—	—	—	—
Expense Ratio (%)	0.80	0.80	0.80	0.80	0.80	—	—	—	—	—
Yield (%)	7.45	7.24	7.38	7.21	7.33	—	—	—	—	—

SHAREHOLDER INFORMATION

Minimum Investment
Initial: $2,500 IRA: $1,000
Subsequent: $100 IRA: $50

Maximum Fees
Load: none 12b-1: none
Other: none

T Rowe Price GNMA (PRGMX)

800-638-5660, 410-547-2000
www.troweprice.com

Mortgage-Backed Bond

PERFORMANCE AND PER SHARE DATA **fund inception date: 11/26/85**

	3yr Annual	5yr Annual	10yr Annual	Category Risk Index	
Return (%)	5.8	5.9	7.2	1.19—high	
Differ from Category (+/-)	0.2 av	0.0 abv av	0.1 abv av	**Avg Mat**	8.6 yrs

	2000	1999	1998	1997	1996	1995	1994	1993	1992	1991
Return (%)	10.9	0.2	6.5	9.4	3.1	17.8	-1.6	6.1	6.4	15.0
Differ from Category (+/-)	1.0	-0.8	0.3	0.9	-1.1	2.9	-0.3	-0.3	-0.1	0.3
Return, Tax-Adjusted (%)	8.3	-2.2	3.9	6.6	0.4	14.8	-4.3	3.3	4.0	12.3
Dividends, Net Income ($)	0.59	0.59	0.62	0.64	0.65	0.67	0.67	0.69	0.76	0.80
Expense Ratio (%)	0.71	0.71	0.70	0.74	0.74	0.76	0.77	0.79	0.86	0.85
Yield (%)	6.31	6.56	6.47	6.68	6.93	6.87	7.54	7.09	7.73	8.02

SHAREHOLDER INFORMATION

Minimum Investment
Initial: $2,500 IRA: $1,000
Subsequent: $100 IRA: $50

Maximum Fees
Load: none 12b-1: none
Other: none

T Rowe Price High Yield (PRHYX)

800-638-5660, 410-547-2000
www.troweprice.com

Corporate High-Yield Bond

PERFORMANCE AND PER SHARE DATA **fund inception date: 12/31/84**

	3yr Annual	5yr Annual	10yr Annual	Category Risk Index	
Return (%)	1.7	6.1	10.1	0.82—blw av	
Differ from Category (+/-)	1.7 abv av	0.7 abv av	0.3 av	**Avg Mat**	8.8 yrs

	2000	1999	1998	1997	1996	1995	1994	1993	1992	1991
Return (%)	-3.2	4.1	4.4	14.4	11.5	15.7	-7.9	21.8	14.7	30.8
Differ from Category (+/-)	3.7	-1.5	2.5	-0.2	-4.2	-1.7	-5.7	2.4	-1.5	3.3
Return, Tax-Adjusted (%)	-6.9	0.5	0.9	10.8	7.8	11.9	-11.1	17.9	11.5	26.7
Dividends, Net Income ($)	0.76	0.75	0.76	0.75	0.75	0.74	0.75	0.81	0.82	0.89
Expense Ratio (%)	0.83	0.82	0.81	0.84	0.85	0.88	0.85	0.89	0.97	1.03
Yield (%)	10.95	9.44	9.09	8.58	8.99	9.03	9.67	8.78	9.89	11.15

SHAREHOLDER INFORMATION

Minimum Investment
Initial: $2,500 IRA: $1,000
Subsequent: $100 IRA: $50

Maximum Fees
Load: 1.00% redemption 12b-1: none
Other: redemption fee applies for 12 months

T Rowe Price Intl: Bd (RPIBX)

800-638-5660, 410-547-2000
www.troweprice.com

International Bond

PERFORMANCE AND PER SHARE DATA **fund inception date: 9/10/86**

	3yr Annual	5yr Annual	10yr Annual	Category Risk Index
Return (%)	0.8	1.2	6.1	1.07—abv av
Differ from Category (+/-)	-2.4 blw av	-4.0 low	0.7 abv av	**Avg Mat** 7.8 yrs

	2000	1999	1998	1997	1996	1995	1994	1993	1992	1991
Return (%)	-3.1	-7.8	15.0	-3.1	7.1	20.3	-1.8	20.0	2.3	17.7
Differ from Category (+/-)	-7.6	-11.6	11.4	-7.0	-7.0	3.4	5.4	4.8	-1.3	3.0
Return, Tax-Adjusted (%)	-4.7	-9.4	12.8	-5.1	4.5	17.3	-4.6	15.8	-0.5	15.1
Dividends, Net Income ($)	0.39	0.38	0.51	0.52	0.60	0.62	0.59	0.68	0.83	0.77
Expense Ratio (%)	na	0.90	0.88	0.86	0.87	0.92	0.98	0.99	1.08	1.24
Yield (%)	4.60	4.09	4.87	5.41	5.67	5.86	6.17	6.29	8.50	7.43

SHAREHOLDER INFORMATION

Minimum Investment
Initial: $2,500 IRA: $1,000
Subsequent: $100 IRA: $50

Maximum Fees
Load: none 12b-1: none
Other: none

T Rowe Price Intl: Em Mk Bd (PREMX)

800-638-5660, 410-547-2000
www.troweprice.com

International Bond

PERFORMANCE AND PER SHARE DATA **fund inception date: 12/30/94**

	3yr Annual	5yr Annual	10yr Annual	Category Risk Index
Return (%)	2.9	11.7	na	3.23—high
Differ from Category (+/-)	-0.3 av	6.5 high	na	**Avg Mat** 14.1 yrs

	2000	1999	1998	1997	1996	1995	1994	1993	1992	1991
Return (%)	15.2	22.9	-23.0	16.8	36.7	22.8	—	—	—	—
Differ from Category (+/-)	10.7	19.1	-26.6	12.9	22.6	5.9	—	—	—	—
Return, Tax-Adjusted (%)	11.1	18.2	-27.0	12.9	31.8	17.8	—	—	—	—
Dividends, Net Income ($)	1.04	1.08	1.31	1.14	1.01	0.75	—	—	—	—
Expense Ratio (%)	na	1.25	1.25	1.25	1.25	1.25	—	—	—	—
Yield (%)	9.86	10.68	13.90	8.17	7.54	6.58	—	—	—	—

SHAREHOLDER INFORMATION

Minimum Investment
Initial: $2,500 IRA: $1,000
Subsequent: $100 IRA: $50

Maximum Fees
Load: none 12b-1: none
Other: none

T Rowe Price New Income (PRCIX)

800-638-5660, 410-547-2000
www.troweprice.com

General Bond

PERFORMANCE AND PER SHARE DATA **fund inception date: 10/15/73**

	3yr Annual	5yr Annual	10yr Annual	Category Risk Index
Return (%)	4.7	5.1	7.0	1.21—high
Differ from Category (+/-)	-0.8 low	-0.5 low	-0.2 blw av	**Avg Mat** 9.9 yrs

	2000	1999	1998	1997	1996	1995	1994	1993	1992	1991
Return (%)	11.1	-1.5	5.0	9.3	2.3	18.3	-2.2	9.5	4.9	15.5
Differ from Category (+/-)	1.4	-1.5	-2.3	0.9	-1.2	2.1	0.5	-0.2	-1.9	0.0
Return, Tax-Adjusted (%)	8.5	-3.7	2.2	6.6	-0.2	15.4	-4.8	6.9	2.9	13.0
Dividends, Net Income ($)	0.53	0.51	0.56	0.57	0.59	0.60	0.57	0.53	0.59	0.67
Expense Ratio (%)	0.73	0.72	0.71	0.74	0.75	0.78	0.82	0.84	0.87	0.88
Yield (%)	6.23	6.25	6.25	6.25	6.63	6.46	6.73	5.69	6.55	7.30

SHAREHOLDER INFORMATION

Minimum Investment
Initial: $2,500 IRA: $100
Subsequent: $100 IRA: $50

Maximum Fees
Load: none 12b-1: none
Other: none

T Rowe Price Sht Tm Bond (PRWBX)

800-638-5660, 410-547-2000
www.troweprice.com

General Bond

PERFORMANCE AND PER SHARE DATA **fund inception date: 3/2/84**

	3yr Annual	5yr Annual	10yr Annual	Category Risk Index
Return (%)	5.6	5.4	5.6	0.53—low
Differ from Category (+/-)	0.1 av	-0.2 blw av	-1.6 low	**Avg Mat** 2.2 yrs

	2000	1999	1998	1997	1996	1995	1994	1993	1992	1991
Return (%)	8.4	2.2	6.1	6.2	3.9	9.7	-2.9	6.6	5.0	11.2
Differ from Category (+/-)	-1.3	2.2	-1.2	-2.2	0.4	-6.5	-0.2	-3.1	-1.8	-4.3
Return, Tax-Adjusted (%)	6.0	0.0	3.8	3.9	1.6	7.2	-5.0	4.1	3.0	9.0
Dividends, Net Income ($)	0.27	0.25	0.26	0.27	0.27	0.29	0.27	0.31	0.33	0.35
Expense Ratio (%)	0.72	0.73	0.72	0.74	0.72	0.79	0.74	0.76	0.88	0.93
Yield (%)	5.80	5.49	5.53	5.76	5.78	6.07	5.83	6.13	6.54	6.82

SHAREHOLDER INFORMATION

Minimum Investment
Initial: $2,500 IRA: $1,000
Subsequent: $100 IRA: $50

Maximum Fees
Load: none 12b-1: none
Other: none

T Rowe Price Sum: Muni Inc (PRINX)

800-638-5660, 410-547-2000
www.troweprice.com

Tax-Exempt Bond

PERFORMANCE AND PER SHARE DATA **fund inception date: 10/29/93**

	3yr Annual	5yr Annual	10yr Annual	Category Risk Index
Return (%)	4.4	5.9	na	1.14—abv av
Differ from Category (+/-)	0.6 av	1.0 high	na	**Avg Mat** 16.0 yrs

	2000	1999	1998	1997	1996	1995	1994	1993	1992	1991
Return (%)	11.9	-4.0	6.1	11.6	5.0	17.8	-4.5	—	—	—
Differ from Category (+/-)	2.5	-1.4	0.5	3.4	1.3	2.7	0.4	—	—	—
Return, Tax-Adjusted (%)	11.9	-4.0	6.0	11.6	5.0	17.8	-4.5	—	—	—
Dividends, Net Income ($)	0.52	0.49	0.51	0.54	0.54	0.54	0.50	—	—	—
Expense Ratio (%)	na	0.50	0.50	0.50	0.50	0.50	0.50	—	—	—
Yield (%)	4.99	5.00	4.73	5.07	5.37	5.34	5.51	—	—	—

SHAREHOLDER INFORMATION

Minimum Investment
Initial: $25,000 IRA: na
Subsequent: $1,000 IRA: na

Maximum Fees
Load: none 12b-1: none
Other: none

T Rowe Price Sum: Muni Int (PRSMX)

800-638-5660, 410-547-2000
www.troweprice.com

Tax-Exempt Bond

PERFORMANCE AND PER SHARE DATA **fund inception date: 10/29/93**

	3yr Annual	5yr Annual	10yr Annual	Category Risk Index
Return (%)	4.3	5.2	na	0.81—blw av
Differ from Category (+/-)	0.5 av	0.3 av	na	**Avg Mat** 7.0 yrs

	2000	1999	1998	1997	1996	1995	1994	1993	1992	1991
Return (%)	8.7	-1.2	5.7	8.4	4.6	13.7	-1.6	—	—	—
Differ from Category (+/-)	-0.7	1.4	0.1	0.2	0.9	-1.4	3.3	—	—	—
Return, Tax-Adjusted (%)	8.7	-1.2	5.6	8.3	4.6	13.7	-1.6	—	—	—
Dividends, Net Income ($)	0.48	0.46	0.47	0.48	0.48	0.48	0.44	—	—	—
Expense Ratio (%)	na	0.50	0.50	0.50	0.50	0.50	0.50	—	—	—
Yield (%)	4.58	4.55	4.39	4.51	4.67	4.66	4.63	—	—	—

SHAREHOLDER INFORMATION

Minimum Investment
Initial: $25,000 IRA: na
Subsequent: $1,000 IRA: na

Maximum Fees
Load: none 12b-1: none
Other: none

T Rowe Price TF: FL Int (FLTFX)

800-638-5660, 410-547-2000
www.troweprice.com

Tax-Exempt Bond

PERFORMANCE AND PER SHARE DATA **fund inception date: 3/31/93**

	3yr Annual	5yr Annual	10yr Annual	Category Risk Index
Return (%)	4.3	4.6	na	0.85—blw av
Differ from Category (+/-)	0.5 av	-0.3 blw av	na	**Avg Mat** 7.5 yrs

	2000	1999	1998	1997	1996	1995	1994	1993	1992	1991
Return (%)	8.6	-1.1	5.6	6.7	3.6	13.1	-2.6	—	—	—
Differ from Category (+/-)	-0.8	1.5	0.0	-1.5	-0.1	-2.0	2.3	—	—	—
Return, Tax-Adjusted (%)	8.6	-1.1	5.6	6.7	3.5	13.1	-2.6	—	—	—
Dividends, Net Income ($)	0.46	0.45	0.46	0.46	0.45	0.46	0.42	—	—	—
Expense Ratio (%)	0.60	0.60	0.60	1.65	0.60	0.60	0.60	—	—	—
Yield (%)	4.30	4.36	4.23	4.28	4.27	4.33	4.27	—	—	—

SHAREHOLDER INFORMATION

Minimum Investment
Initial: $2,500 IRA: na
Subsequent: $100 IRA: na

Maximum Fees
Load: none 12b-1: none
Other: none

T Rowe Price TF: GA Bond (GTFBX)

800-225-5132, 410-547-2000
www.troweprice.com

Tax-Exempt Bond

PERFORMANCE AND PER SHARE DATA **fund inception date: 3/31/93**

	3yr Annual	5yr Annual	10yr Annual	Category Risk Index
Return (%)	4.5	5.4	na	1.10—abv av
Differ from Category (+/-)	0.7 av	0.5 abv av	na	**Avg Mat** 17.7 yrs

	2000	1999	1998	1997	1996	1995	1994	1993	1992	1991
Return (%)	11.6	-3.6	6.1	9.6	3.9	17.7	-5.9	—	—	—
Differ from Category (+/-)	2.2	-1.0	0.5	1.4	0.2	2.6	-1.0	—	—	—
Return, Tax-Adjusted (%)	11.6	-3.6	6.1	9.6	3.9	17.7	-6.0	—	—	—
Dividends, Net Income ($)	0.51	0.49	0.50	0.51	0.51	0.52	0.50	—	—	—
Expense Ratio (%)	0.65	0.65	0.65	0.65	0.65	0.65	0.65	—	—	—
Yield (%)	4.72	4.82	4.52	4.67	4.88	4.92	5.27	—	—	—

SHAREHOLDER INFORMATION

Minimum Investment
Initial: $2,500 IRA: na
Subsequent: $100 IRA: na

Maximum Fees
Load: none 12b-1: none
Other: none

T Rowe Price TF: High Yld (PRFHX)

800-225-5132, 410-547-2000
www.troweprice.com

Tax-Exempt Bond

PERFORMANCE AND PER SHARE DATA **fund inception date: 3/1/85**

	3yr Annual	5yr Annual	10yr Annual	Category Risk Index
Return (%)	2.7	4.6	6.8	1.00—av
Differ from Category (+/-)	-1.1 low	-0.3 blw av	0.3 av	**Avg Mat** 20.3 yrs

	2000	1999	1998	1997	1996	1995	1994	1993	1992	1991
Return (%)	8.1	-5.1	5.5	10.1	4.9	16.5	-4.3	12.9	9.5	11.7
Differ from Category (+/-)	-1.3	-2.5	-0.1	1.9	1.2	1.4	0.6	1.2	1.1	0.4
Return, Tax-Adjusted (%)	8.1	-5.1	5.4	10.1	4.9	16.5	-4.3	12.3	9.2	11.4
Dividends, Net Income ($)	0.66	0.65	0.67	0.69	0.70	0.72	0.72	0.74	0.79	0.81
Expense Ratio (%)	0.71	0.71	0.72	0.74	0.75	0.79	0.79	0.81	0.83	0.85
Yield (%)	5.72	5.75	5.30	5.46	5.77	5.88	6.42	5.83	6.56	6.84

SHAREHOLDER INFORMATION

Minimum Investment
Initial: $2,500 IRA: na
Subsequent: $100 IRA: na

Maximum Fees
Load: none 12b-1: none
Other: none

T Rowe Price TF: Income (PRTAX)

800-638-5660, 410-547-2000
www.troweprice.com

Tax-Exempt Bond

PERFORMANCE AND PER SHARE DATA **fund inception date: 10/26/76**

	3yr Annual	5yr Annual	10yr Annual	Category Risk Index
Return (%)	4.5	5.2	7.1	1.12—abv av
Differ from Category (+/-)	0.7 abv av	0.3 av	0.6 abv av	**Avg Mat** 15.7 yrs

	2000	1999	1998	1997	1996	1995	1994	1993	1992	1991
Return (%)	12.2	-3.9	5.9	9.3	3.2	17.6	-5.4	12.7	9.3	12.1
Differ from Category (+/-)	2.8	-1.3	0.3	1.1	-0.5	2.5	-0.5	1.0	0.9	0.8
Return, Tax-Adjusted (%)	12.2	-3.9	5.8	9.3	3.2	17.6	-5.5	12.1	9.3	12.1
Dividends, Net Income ($)	0.49	0.49	0.50	0.51	0.51	0.52	0.52	0.53	0.56	0.56
Expense Ratio (%)	0.55	0.55	0.55	0.57	0.58	0.59	0.59	0.61	0.62	0.63
Yield (%)	5.06	5.38	4.99	5.13	5.31	5.30	5.88	5.25	5.93	6.10

SHAREHOLDER INFORMATION

Minimum Investment
Initial: $2,500 IRA: na
Subsequent: $100 IRA: na

Maximum Fees
Load: none 12b-1: none
Other: none

T Rowe Price TF: Int (PTIBX)

800-638-5660, 410-547-2000
www.troweprice.com

Tax-Exempt Bond

PERFORMANCE AND PER SHARE DATA **fund inception date: 11/30/92**

	3yr Annual	5yr Annual	10yr Annual	Category Risk Index
Return (%)	4.3	4.8	na	0.86—blw av
Differ from Category (+/-)	0.5 av	-0.1 av	na	**Avg Mat** 7.9 yrs

	2000	1999	1998	1997	1996	1995	1994	1993	1992	1991
Return (%)	8.9	-1.2	5.7	7.2	4.1	13.0	-2.6	12.6	—	—
Differ from Category (+/-)	-0.5	1.4	0.1	-1.0	0.4	-2.1	2.3	0.9	—	—
Return, Tax-Adjusted (%)	8.9	-1.2	5.6	7.1	4.1	13.0	-2.6	12.4	—	—
Dividends, Net Income ($)	0.49	0.47	0.48	0.48	0.47	0.48	0.45	0.48	—	—
Expense Ratio (%)	0.63	0.65	0.65	0.65	0.65	0.65	0.33	0.00	—	—
Yield (%)	4.49	4.46	4.29	4.33	4.35	4.43	4.47	4.41	—	—

SHAREHOLDER INFORMATION

Minimum Investment
Initial: $2,500 IRA: na
Subsequent: $100 IRA: na

Maximum Fees
Load: none 12b-1: none
Other: none

T Rowe Price TF: MD Bond (MDXBX)

800-225-5132, 410-547-2000
www.troweprice.com

Tax-Exempt Bond

PERFORMANCE AND PER SHARE DATA **fund inception date: 3/31/87**

	3yr Annual	5yr Annual	10yr Annual	Category Risk Index
Return (%)	4.6	5.2	6.8	1.01—av
Differ from Category (+/-)	0.8 abv av	0.3 av	0.3 av	**Avg Mat** 18.9 yrs

	2000	1999	1998	1997	1996	1995	1994	1993	1992	1991
Return (%)	11.4	-3.1	6.1	8.6	3.7	16.4	-5.0	12.6	8.5	11.2
Differ from Category (+/-)	2.0	-0.5	0.5	0.4	0.0	1.3	-0.1	0.9	0.1	-0.1
Return, Tax-Adjusted (%)	11.4	-3.1	6.1	8.6	3.7	16.4	-5.0	12.3	8.3	11.0
Dividends, Net Income ($)	0.53	0.53	0.55	0.55	0.55	0.56	0.56	0.56	0.57	0.59
Expense Ratio (%)	0.51	0.51	0.51	0.54	0.54	0.57	0.57	0.61	0.64	0.68
Yield (%)	5.07	5.35	5.11	5.15	5.31	5.31	5.84	5.19	5.62	5.93

SHAREHOLDER INFORMATION

Minimum Investment
Initial: $2,500 IRA: na
Subsequent: $100 IRA: na

Maximum Fees
Load: none 12b-1: none
Other: none

T Rowe Price TF: MD Short (PRMDX)

800-225-5132, 410-547-2000
www.troweprice.com

Tax-Exempt Bond

PERFORMANCE AND PER SHARE DATA **fund inception date: 1/29/93**

	3yr Annual	5yr Annual	10yr Annual	Category Risk Index
Return (%)	3.9	3.8	na	0.38—low
Differ from Category (+/-)	0.1 low	-1.1 low	na	**Avg Mat** 6.6 yrs

	2000	1999	1998	1997	1996	1995	1994	1993	1992	1991
Return (%)	5.5	1.5	4.7	4.1	3.4	7.5	0.6	—	—	—
Differ from Category (+/-)	-3.9	4.1	-0.9	-4.1	-0.3	-7.6	5.5	—	—	—
Return, Tax-Adjusted (%)	5.5	1.5	4.7	4.1	3.4	7.5	0.6	—	—	—
Dividends, Net Income ($)	0.19	0.18	0.19	0.19	0.20	0.21	0.17	—	—	—
Expense Ratio (%)	0.60	0.65	0.65	0.65	0.65	0.65	0.65	—	—	—
Yield (%)	3.70	3.56	3.68	3.71	3.91	4.08	3.41	—	—	—

SHAREHOLDER INFORMATION

Minimum Investment
Initial: $2,500 IRA: na
Subsequent: $100 IRA: na

Maximum Fees
Load: none 12b-1: none
Other: none

T Rowe Price TF: NJ Bond (NJTFX)

800-638-5660, 410-547-2000
www.troweprice.com

Tax-Exempt Bond

PERFORMANCE AND PER SHARE DATA **fund inception date: 4/30/91**

	3yr Annual	5yr Annual	10yr Annual	Category Risk Index
Return (%)	4.3	5.0	na	1.11—abv av
Differ from Category (+/-)	0.5 av	0.1 av	na	**Avg Mat** 17.3 yrs

	2000	1999	1998	1997	1996	1995	1994	1993	1992	1991
Return (%)	11.4	-4.1	6.2	9.1	3.2	16.9	-6.0	13.9	9.6	—
Differ from Category (+/-)	2.0	-1.5	0.6	0.9	-0.5	1.8	-1.1	2.2	1.2	—
Return, Tax-Adjusted (%)	11.4	-4.1	6.2	9.1	3.2	16.9	-6.0	13.5	9.4	—
Dividends, Net Income ($)	0.54	0.53	0.55	0.57	0.56	0.58	0.56	0.55	0.58	—
Expense Ratio (%)	0.65	0.65	0.65	0.65	0.65	0.65	0.65	0.65	0.65	—
Yield (%)	4.79	4.98	4.72	4.96	5.05	5.13	5.49	4.74	5.39	—

SHAREHOLDER INFORMATION

Minimum Investment
Initial: $2,500 IRA: na
Subsequent: $100 IRA: na

Maximum Fees
Load: none 12b-1: none
Other: none

T Rowe Price TF: NY Bond (PRNYX)

800-225-5132, 410-547-2000
www.troweprice.com

Tax-Exempt Bond

PERFORMANCE AND PER SHARE DATA **fund inception date: 8/28/86**

	3yr Annual	5yr Annual	10yr Annual	Category Risk Index
Return (%)	4.5	5.3	7.2	1.25—high
Differ from Category (+/-)	0.7 abv av	0.4 abv av	0.7 high	Avg Mat 19.0 yrs

	2000	1999	1998	1997	1996	1995	1994	1993	1992	1991
Return (%)	12.8	-4.7	6.4	9.5	3.7	17.2	-5.8	13.3	10.3	12.4
Differ from Category (+/-)	3.4	-2.1	0.8	1.3	0.0	2.1	-0.9	1.6	1.9	1.1
Return, Tax-Adjusted (%)	12.8	-4.7	6.1	9.5	3.7	17.2	-5.9	12.8	10.3	12.4
Dividends, Net Income ($)	0.53	0.52	0.54	0.56	0.57	0.57	0.58	0.59	0.62	0.62
Expense Ratio (%)	0.58	0.59	0.61	0.65	0.65	0.60	0.60	0.60	0.60	0.73
Yield (%)	4.84	5.09	4.73	4.98	5.27	5.18	5.81	5.18	5.85	6.08

SHAREHOLDER INFORMATION

Minimum Investment
Initial: $2,500 IRA: na
Subsequent: $100 IRA: na

Maximum Fees
Load: none 12b-1: none
Other: none

T Rowe Price TF: Short Int (PRFSX)

800-638-5660, 410-547-2000
www.troweprice.com

Tax-Exempt Bond

PERFORMANCE AND PER SHARE DATA **fund inception date: 12/23/83**

	3yr Annual	5yr Annual	10yr Annual	Category Risk Index
Return (%)	4.2	4.3	5.0	0.50—low
Differ from Category (+/-)	0.4 blw av	-0.6 low	-1.5 low	Avg Mat 4.2 yrs

	2000	1999	1998	1997	1996	1995	1994	1993	1992	1991
Return (%)	6.7	0.9	4.9	5.3	4.0	8.1	0.3	6.3	6.0	7.8
Differ from Category (+/-)	-2.7	3.5	-0.7	-2.9	0.3	-7.0	5.2	-5.4	-2.4	-3.5
Return, Tax-Adjusted (%)	6.7	0.8	4.8	5.1	4.0	8.1	0.3	6.3	6.0	7.8
Dividends, Net Income ($)	0.22	0.21	0.22	0.22	0.22	0.23	0.21	0.22	0.24	0.28
Expense Ratio (%)	0.53	0.53	0.54	0.56	0.57	0.59	0.60	0.63	0.67	0.74
Yield (%)	4.12	4.02	4.07	4.08	4.11	4.29	4.05	4.08	4.54	5.36

SHAREHOLDER INFORMATION

Minimum Investment
Initial: $2,500 IRA: na
Subsequent: $100 IRA: na

Maximum Fees
Load: none 12b-1: none
Other: none

T Rowe Price TF: VA Bond (PRVAX)

800-638-5660, 410-547-2000
www.troweprice.com

Tax-Exempt Bond

PERFORMANCE AND PER SHARE DATA **fund inception date: 4/30/91**

	3yr Annual	5yr Annual	10yr Annual	Category Risk Index
Return (%)	4.7	5.4	na	1.12—abv av
Differ from Category (+/-)	0.9 abv av	0.5 abv av	na	**Avg Mat** 15.4 yrs

	2000	1999	1998	1997	1996	1995	1994	1993	1992	1991
Return (%)	11.9	-3.4	6.1	8.9	4.1	16.8	-5.0	12.5	9.1	—
Differ from Category (+/-)	2.5	-0.8	0.5	0.7	0.4	1.7	-0.1	0.8	0.7	—
Return, Tax-Adjusted (%)	11.9	-3.4	5.8	8.9	4.1	16.8	-5.0	12.1	9.0	—
Dividends, Net Income ($)	0.55	0.53	0.56	0.57	0.57	0.57	0.56	0.56	0.57	—
Expense Ratio (%)	0.55	0.57	0.58	0.65	0.65	0.65	0.65	0.65	0.65	—
Yield (%)	4.90	5.02	4.83	4.97	5.15	5.09	5.53	4.91	5.33	—

SHAREHOLDER INFORMATION

Minimum Investment
Initial: $2,500 IRA: na
Subsequent: $100 IRA: na

Maximum Fees
Load: none 12b-1: none
Other: none

T Rowe Price Treas Interm (PRTIX)

800-638-5660, 410-547-2000
www.troweprice.com

Government Bond

PERFORMANCE AND PER SHARE DATA **fund inception date: 9/28/89**

	3yr Annual	5yr Annual	10yr Annual	Category Risk Index
Return (%)	6.0	5.7	7.0	1.35—abv av
Differ from Category (+/-)	-0.2 av	-0.2 av	-0.6 av	**Avg Mat** 5.8 yrs

	2000	1999	1998	1997	1996	1995	1994	1993	1992	1991
Return (%)	11.6	-3.2	10.2	8.1	2.3	15.8	-2.2	7.9	6.2	14.7
Differ from Category (+/-)	-2.2	-0.2	1.1	-1.7	0.2	-3.0	1.4	-2.7	-0.4	-0.2
Return, Tax-Adjusted (%)	9.5	-5.2	7.8	5.8	0.0	13.2	-4.5	5.6	3.6	12.3
Dividends, Net Income ($)	0.26	0.26	0.28	0.30	0.31	0.32	0.30	0.29	0.32	0.35
Expense Ratio (%)	0.64	0.62	0.61	0.64	0.65	0.69	0.79	0.80	0.80	0.80
Yield (%)	4.94	5.18	5.07	5.68	5.98	5.94	6.04	5.38	5.92	6.43

SHAREHOLDER INFORMATION

Minimum Investment
Initial: $2,500 IRA: $1,000
Subsequent: $100 IRA: $50

Maximum Fees
Load: none 12b-1: none
Other: none

T Rowe Price Treas Long (PRULX)

800-638-5660, 410-547-2000
www.troweprice.com

Government Bond

PERFORMANCE AND PER SHARE DATA **fund inception date: 9/28/89**

	3yr Annual	5yr Annual	10yr Annual	Category Risk Index
Return (%)	7.0	6.5	8.7	2.06—high
Differ from Category (+/-)	0.8 high	0.6 high	1.1 high	**Avg Mat** 15.6 yrs

	2000	1999	1998	1997	1996	1995	1994	1993	1992	1991
Return (%)	19.1	-8.7	12.8	14.7	-2.3	28.5	-5.7	12.9	5.8	16.2
Differ from Category (+/-)	5.3	-5.7	3.7	4.9	-4.4	9.7	-2.1	2.3	-0.8	1.3
Return, Tax-Adjusted (%)	16.7	-10.9	10.4	12.3	-4.4	25.7	-8.2	9.5	3.0	13.8
Dividends, Net Income ($)	0.61	0.62	0.62	0.63	0.63	0.65	0.68	0.67	0.72	0.77
Expense Ratio (%)	0.64	0.66	0.67	0.80	0.80	0.80	0.80	0.80	0.80	0.80
Yield (%)	5.30	6.00	5.14	5.59	6.04	5.72	7.21	6.09	6.76	7.14

SHAREHOLDER INFORMATION

Minimum Investment
Initial: $2,500 IRA: $1,000
Subsequent: $100 IRA: $50

Maximum Fees
Load: none 12b-1: none
Other: none

TIAA-CREF Bond Plus (TIPBX)

800-223-1200, 212-490-9000
www.tiaa-cref.org

General Bond

PERFORMANCE AND PER SHARE DATA **fund inception date: 9/2/97**

	3yr Annual	5yr Annual	10yr Annual	Category Risk Index
Return (%)	6.3	na	na	1.05—abv av
Differ from Category (+/-)	0.8 high	na	na	**Avg Mat** 28.1 yrs

	2000	1999	1998	1997	1996	1995	1994	1993	1992	1991
Return (%)	11.6	-1.0	8.9	—	—	—	—	—	—	—
Differ from Category (+/-)	1.9	-1.0	1.6	—	—	—	—	—	—	—
Return, Tax-Adjusted (%)	9.0	-3.1	6.5	—	—	—	—	—	—	—
Dividends, Net Income ($)	0.62	0.56	0.56	—	—	—	—	—	—	—
Expense Ratio (%)	na	0.30	0.30	—	—	—	—	—	—	—
Yield (%)	6.14	5.81	5.38	—	—	—	—	—	—	—

SHAREHOLDER INFORMATION

Minimum Investment
Initial: $250 IRA: $250
Subsequent: $25 IRA: $25

Maximum Fees
Load: none 12b-1: none
Other: none

UMB Scout Bond (UMBBX)

800-996-2862, 816-860-3714
www.umb.com

General Bond

PERFORMANCE AND PER SHARE DATA **fund inception date: 11/18/82**

	3yr Annual	5yr Annual	10yr Annual	Category Risk Index
Return (%)	5.4	5.4	6.5	0.84—blw av
Differ from Category (+/-)	-0.1 blw av	-0.2 blw av	-0.7 blw av	**Avg Mat** 4.9 yrs

	2000	1999	1998	1997	1996	1995	1994	1993	1992	1991
Return (%)	9.2	0.1	7.1	7.2	3.5	14.0	-3.0	8.3	6.6	13.2
Differ from Category (+/-)	-0.5	0.1	-0.2	-1.2	0.0	-2.2	-0.3	-1.4	-0.2	-2.3
Return, Tax-Adjusted (%)	6.9	-1.9	4.9	4.9	1.3	11.6	-5.1	5.9	4.6	11.1
Dividends, Net Income ($)	0.60	0.60	0.61	0.62	0.62	0.62	0.63	0.63	0.71	0.71
Expense Ratio (%)	0.87	0.87	0.87	0.87	0.86	0.86	0.87	0.87	0.87	0.87
Yield (%)	5.41	5.58	5.38	5.55	5.62	5.50	6.02	5.49	6.33	6.34

SHAREHOLDER INFORMATION

Minimum Investment
Initial: $1,000 IRA: $250
Subsequent: $100 IRA: $100

Maximum Fees
Load: none 12b-1: none
Other: none

USAA Inv: GNMA (USGNX)

800-531-8181, 210-456-7211
www.usaa.com

Mortgage-Backed Bond

PERFORMANCE AND PER SHARE DATA **fund inception date: 2/1/91**

	3yr Annual	5yr Annual	10yr Annual	Category Risk Index
Return (%)	5.3	5.7	na	1.67—high
Differ from Category (+/-)	-0.3 blw av	-0.2 low	na	**Avg Mat** 8.1 yrs

	2000	1999	1998	1997	1996	1995	1994	1993	1992	1991
Return (%)	12.1	-3.5	8.2	9.5	2.9	16.7	0.0	7.1	6.0	—
Differ from Category (+/-)	2.2	-4.5	2.0	1.0	-1.3	1.8	1.3	0.7	-0.5	—
Return, Tax-Adjusted (%)	9.3	-5.8	5.6	6.8	0.2	13.7	-2.6	4.1	3.6	—
Dividends, Net Income ($)	0.65	0.63	0.65	0.67	0.69	0.72	0.70	0.78	0.80	—
Expense Ratio (%)	0.32	0.31	0.30	0.30	0.32	0.32	0.31	0.32	0.38	—
Yield (%)	6.60	6.70	6.25	6.54	6.90	6.92	7.31	7.58	7.73	—

SHAREHOLDER INFORMATION

Minimum Investment
Initial: $3,000 IRA: $250
Subsequent: $50 IRA: $50

Maximum Fees
Load: none 12b-1: none
Other: none

USAA Inv: Income Stgy (USICX)

800-531-8181, 210-456-7211
www.usaa.com

General Bond

PERFORMANCE AND PER SHARE DATA **fund inception date: 9/1/95**

	3yr Annual	5yr Annual	10yr Annual	Category Risk Index
Return (%)	6.3	7.2	na	1.66—high
Differ from Category (+/-)	0.8 high	1.6 high	na	**Avg Mat** 9.3 yrs

	2000	1999	1998	1997	1996	1995	1994	1993	1992	1991
Return (%)	6.0	2.1	11.2	15.2	2.5	—	—	—	—	—
Differ from Category (+/-)	-3.7	2.1	3.9	6.8	-1.0	—	—	—	—	—
Return, Tax-Adjusted (%)	3.8	0.2	9.5	13.2	0.7	—	—	—	—	—
Dividends, Net Income ($)	0.55	0.48	0.43	0.49	0.47	—	—	—	—	—
Expense Ratio (%)	1.01	0.97	1.00	1.00	1.00	—	—	—	—	—
Yield (%)	4.54	3.95	3.44	4.19	4.43	—	—	—	—	—

SHAREHOLDER INFORMATION

Minimum Investment
Initial: $3,000 IRA: $250
Subsequent: $50 IRA: $50

Maximum Fees
Load: none 12b-1: none
Other: none

USAA Mutual: Short-Term Bd (USSBX)

800-531-8181, 210-456-7211
www.usaa.com

Corporate Bond

PERFORMANCE AND PER SHARE DATA **fund inception date: 6/1/93**

	3yr Annual	5yr Annual	10yr Annual	Category Risk Index
Return (%)	5.3	5.9	na	0.47—low
Differ from Category (+/-)	0.3 abv av	0.2 abv av	na	**Avg Mat** 2.4 yrs

	2000	1999	1998	1997	1996	1995	1994	1993	1992	1991
Return (%)	7.1	4.0	5.0	7.1	6.3	11.2	0.0	—	—	—
Differ from Category (+/-)	-0.9	2.7	-0.9	-2.0	0.8	-6.7	2.3	—	—	—
Return, Tax-Adjusted (%)	4.4	1.6	2.5	4.6	3.9	8.5	-1.9	—	—	—
Dividends, Net Income ($)	0.64	0.59	0.60	0.61	0.60	0.64	0.50	—	—	—
Expense Ratio (%)	0.48	0.50	0.50	0.50	0.50	0.50	0.50	—	—	—
Yield (%)	6.61	6.10	6.07	6.10	6.04	6.44	5.24	—	—	—

SHAREHOLDER INFORMATION

Minimum Investment
Initial: $3,000 IRA: $250
Subsequent: $50 IRA: $50

Maximum Fees
Load: none 12b-1: none
Other: none

USAA State TF: FL TF Inc (UFLTX)

800-531-8181, 210-456-7211
www.usaa.com

Tax-Exempt Bond

PERFORMANCE AND PER SHARE DATA **fund inception date: 10/1/93**

	3yr Annual	5yr Annual	10yr Annual	Category Risk Index
Return (%)	4.1	5.5	na	1.29—high
Differ from Category (+/-)	0.3 blw av	0.6 high	na	**Avg Mat** 20.0 yrs

	2000	1999	1998	1997	1996	1995	1994	1993	1992	1991
Return (%)	12.8	-5.9	6.3	11.1	4.3	18.9	-10.0	—	—	—
Differ from Category (+/-)	3.4	-3.3	0.7	2.9	0.6	3.8	-5.1	—	—	—
Return, Tax-Adjusted (%)	12.8	-5.9	6.3	11.1	4.3	18.9	-10.0	—	—	—
Dividends, Net Income ($)	0.48	0.53	0.49	0.51	0.51	0.51	0.48	—	—	—
Expense Ratio (%)	0.48	0.47	0.50	0.50	0.50	0.50	0.50	—	—	—
Yield (%)	5.00	5.90	4.86	5.12	5.39	5.32	5.64	—	—	—

SHAREHOLDER INFORMATION

Minimum Investment
Initial: $3,000 IRA: na
Subsequent: $50 IRA: na

Maximum Fees
Load: none 12b-1: none
Other: none

USAA Tax Ex: CA Bond (USCBX)

800-531-8181, 210-456-7211
www.usaa.com

Tax-Exempt Bond

PERFORMANCE AND PER SHARE DATA **fund inception date: 8/1/89**

	3yr Annual	5yr Annual	10yr Annual	Category Risk Index
Return (%)	5.0	6.1	7.2	1.26—high
Differ from Category (+/-)	1.2 high	1.2 high	0.7 abv av	**Avg Mat** 20.2 yrs

	2000	1999	1998	1997	1996	1995	1994	1993	1992	1991
Return (%)	14.3	-5.2	6.8	10.4	5.3	21.8	-9.3	12.7	8.2	10.9
Differ from Category (+/-)	4.9	-2.6	1.2	2.2	1.6	6.7	-4.4	1.0	-0.2	-0.4
Return, Tax-Adjusted (%)	14.3	-5.2	6.8	10.4	5.3	21.8	-9.3	12.1	7.9	10.9
Dividends, Net Income ($)	0.56	0.58	0.59	0.61	0.60	0.59	0.58	0.59	0.63	0.66
Expense Ratio (%)	0.39	0.39	0.40	0.41	0.42	0.44	0.44	0.46	0.48	0.50
Yield (%)	5.07	5.69	5.20	5.45	5.60	5.48	6.19	5.30	5.97	6.37

SHAREHOLDER INFORMATION

Minimum Investment
Initial: $3,000 IRA: na
Subsequent: $50 IRA: na

Maximum Fees
Load: none 12b-1: none
Other: none

USAA Tax Ex: Interm-Term (USATX)

800-531-8181, 210-456-7211
www.usaa.com

Tax-Exempt Bond

PERFORMANCE AND PER SHARE DATA **fund inception date: 3/19/82**

	3yr Annual	5yr Annual	10yr Annual	Category Risk Index
Return (%)	4.4	5.4	6.8	0.88—blw av
Differ from Category (+/-)	0.6 av	0.5 abv av	0.3 av	**Avg Mat** 8.6 yrs

	2000	1999	1998	1997	1996	1995	1994	1993	1992	1991
Return (%)	9.8	-2.5	6.3	9.3	4.4	15.0	-4.0	11.4	8.4	11.1
Differ from Category (+/-)	0.4	0.1	0.7	1.1	0.7	-0.1	0.9	-0.3	0.0	-0.2
Return, Tax-Adjusted (%)	9.8	-2.5	6.3	9.3	4.4	15.0	-4.0	11.1	8.4	11.1
Dividends, Net Income ($)	0.69	0.69	0.70	0.71	0.72	0.71	0.68	0.70	0.75	0.80
Expense Ratio (%)	0.36	0.36	0.37	0.37	0.38	0.40	0.40	0.42	0.44	0.43
Yield (%)	5.31	5.53	5.18	5.30	5.57	5.42	5.64	5.22	5.91	6.44

SHAREHOLDER INFORMATION

Minimum Investment
Initial: $3,000 IRA: na
Subsequent: $50 IRA: na

Maximum Fees
Load: none 12b-1: none
Other: none

USAA Tax Ex: Long-Term (USTEX)

800-531-8181, 210-456-7211
www.usaa.com

Tax-Exempt Bond

PERFORMANCE AND PER SHARE DATA **fund inception date: 3/19/82**

	3yr Annual	5yr Annual	10yr Annual	Category Risk Index
Return (%)	4.1	5.4	6.9	1.13—abv av
Differ from Category (+/-)	0.3 blw av	0.5 abv av	0.4 abv av	**Avg Mat** 20.1 yrs

	2000	1999	1998	1997	1996	1995	1994	1993	1992	1991
Return (%)	12.1	-5.0	5.9	10.3	4.4	18.5	-7.9	12.5	8.6	12.3
Differ from Category (+/-)	2.7	-2.4	0.3	2.1	0.7	3.4	-3.0	0.8	0.2	1.0
Return, Tax-Adjusted (%)	12.1	-5.0	5.9	10.3	4.4	18.5	-8.0	11.3	8.4	12.3
Dividends, Net Income ($)	0.74	0.76	0.76	0.77	0.78	0.80	0.77	0.84	0.89	0.92
Expense Ratio (%)	0.36	0.36	0.36	0.37	0.37	0.38	0.38	0.39	0.40	0.40
Yield (%)	5.55	6.03	5.41	5.50	5.81	5.86	6.26	5.70	6.37	6.70

SHAREHOLDER INFORMATION

Minimum Investment
Initial: $3,000 IRA: na
Subsequent: $50 IRA: na

Maximum Fees
Load: none 12b-1: none
Other: none

USAA Tax Ex: NY Bond (USNYX)

800-531-8181, 210-456-7211
www.usaa.com

Tax-Exempt Bond

PERFORMANCE AND PER SHARE DATA — fund inception date: 10/15/90

	3yr Annual	5yr Annual	10yr Annual	Category Risk Index
Return (%)	5.1	5.9	7.2	1.24—high
Differ from Category (+/-)	1.3 high	1.0 high	0.7 high	**Avg Mat** 17.8 yrs

	2000	1999	1998	1997	1996	1995	1994	1993	1992	1991
Return (%)	14.8	-5.0	6.6	10.6	3.7	18.0	-8.9	13.4	8.9	13.7
Differ from Category (+/-)	5.4	-2.4	1.0	2.4	0.0	2.9	-4.0	1.7	0.5	2.4
Return, Tax-Adjusted (%)	14.8	-5.0	6.6	10.6	3.7	18.0	-8.9	12.7	8.6	13.7
Dividends, Net Income ($)	0.59	0.60	0.61	0.63	0.63	0.63	0.61	0.62	0.65	0.69
Expense Ratio (%)	0.50	0.50	0.50	0.50	0.50	0.50	0.50	0.50	0.50	0.50
Yield (%)	5.13	5.68	5.19	5.43	5.68	5.56	5.99	5.11	5.71	6.22

SHAREHOLDER INFORMATION

Minimum Investment
Initial: $3,000 — IRA: na
Subsequent: $50 — IRA: na

Maximum Fees
Load: none — 12b-1: none
Other: none

USAA Tax Ex: Short-Term (USSTX)

800-531-8181, 210-456-7211
www.usaa.com

Tax-Exempt Bond

PERFORMANCE AND PER SHARE DATA — fund inception date: 3/19/82

	3yr Annual	5yr Annual	10yr Annual	Category Risk Index
Return (%)	4.2	4.5	5.0	0.33—low
Differ from Category (+/-)	0.4 blw av	-0.4 blw av	-1.5 low	**Avg Mat** 2.7 yrs

	2000	1999	1998	1997	1996	1995	1994	1993	1992	1991
Return (%)	6.0	1.6	4.9	5.8	4.4	8.1	0.8	5.5	5.9	7.7
Differ from Category (+/-)	-3.4	4.2	-0.7	-2.4	0.7	-7.0	5.7	-6.2	-2.5	-3.6
Return, Tax-Adjusted (%)	6.0	1.6	4.9	5.8	4.4	8.1	0.8	5.5	5.9	7.7
Dividends, Net Income ($)	0.48	0.47	0.49	0.48	0.49	0.50	0.45	0.46	0.52	0.61
Expense Ratio (%)	0.38	0.38	0.39	0.41	0.42	0.42	0.43	0.43	0.48	0.50
Yield (%)	4.52	4.48	4.54	4.46	4.61	4.69	4.35	4.29	4.91	5.80

SHAREHOLDER INFORMATION

Minimum Investment
Initial: $3,000 — IRA: na
Subsequent: $50 — IRA: na

Maximum Fees
Load: none — 12b-1: none
Other: none

USAA Tax Ex: Virginia Bond (USVAX)

800-531-8181, 210-456-7211
www.usaa.com

Tax-Exempt Bond

PERFORMANCE AND PER SHARE DATA **fund inception date: 10/15/90**

	3yr Annual	5yr Annual	10yr Annual	Category Risk Index
Return (%)	4.6	5.6	7.0	1.12—abv av
Differ from Category (+/-)	0.8 abv av	0.7 high	0.5 abv av	**Avg Mat** 19.2 yrs

	2000	1999	1998	1997	1996	1995	1994	1993	1992	1991
Return (%)	13.1	-4.6	6.0	9.4	5.0	17.0	-6.3	12.6	8.4	11.7
Differ from Category (+/-)	3.7	-2.0	0.4	1.2	1.3	1.9	-1.4	0.9	0.0	0.4
Return, Tax-Adjusted (%)	13.1	-4.6	6.0	9.4	5.0	17.0	-6.3	12.2	8.2	11.7
Dividends, Net Income ($)	0.58	0.59	0.60	0.62	0.63	0.63	0.61	0.62	0.64	0.68
Expense Ratio (%)	0.43	0.43	0.44	0.46	0.48	0.50	0.49	0.50	0.50	0.50
Yield (%)	5.16	5.63	5.18	5.38	5.67	5.62	6.01	5.34	5.83	6.33

SHAREHOLDER INFORMATION

Minimum Investment
Initial: $3,000 IRA: na
Subsequent: $50 IRA: na

Maximum Fees
Load: none 12b-1: none
Other: none

Value Line Aggressive Inc (VAGIX)

800-223-0818, 212-907-1500
www.valueline.com

Corporate High-Yield Bond

PERFORMANCE AND PER SHARE DATA **fund inception date: 2/19/86**

	3yr Annual	5yr Annual	10yr Annual	Category Risk Index
Return (%)	-7.6	1.5	7.6	1.31—high
Differ from Category (+/-)	-7.6 low	-3.9 low	-2.2 blw av	**Avg Mat** 6.7 yrs

	2000	1999	1998	1997	1996	1995	1994	1993	1992	1991
Return (%)	-23.6	9.0	-5.2	14.0	19.7	20.0	-4.0	19.0	12.1	26.6
Differ from Category (+/-)	-16.7	3.4	-7.1	-0.6	4.0	2.6	-1.8	-0.4	-4.1	-0.9
Return, Tax-Adjusted (%)	-27.2	5.0	-8.7	10.5	15.7	16.0	-7.3	15.3	9.1	22.8
Dividends, Net Income ($)	0.67	0.73	0.77	0.72	0.74	0.69	0.67	0.66	0.68	0.75
Expense Ratio (%)	0.82	0.81	0.95	1.10	1.22	1.27	1.20	1.15	1.18	1.43
Yield (%)	13.50	10.08	10.49	8.44	9.06	9.21	9.73	8.38	9.43	10.62

SHAREHOLDER INFORMATION

Minimum Investment
Initial: $1,000 IRA: $1,000
Subsequent: $250 IRA: $250

Maximum Fees
Load: none 12b-1: 0.25%
Other: none

Value Line Tx Ex Natl Bd (VLHYX)

800-223-0818, 212-907-1500
www.valueline.com

Tax-Exempt Bond

PERFORMANCE AND PER SHARE DATA **fund inception date: 3/27/84**

	3yr Annual	5yr Annual	10yr Annual	Category Risk Index
Return (%)	4.0	4.8	6.3	1.07—av
Differ from Category (+/-)	0.2 blw av	-0.1 blw av	-0.2 blw av	**Avg Mat** 18.9 yrs

	2000	1999	1998	1997	1996	1995	1994	1993	1992	1991
Return (%)	12.1	-4.8	5.4	8.7	3.5	16.6	-6.9	11.4	7.8	12.2
Differ from Category (+/-)	2.7	-2.2	-0.2	0.5	-0.2	1.5	-2.0	-0.3	-0.6	0.9
Return, Tax-Adjusted (%)	12.1	-4.8	4.9	8.5	3.5	16.6	-6.9	10.8	7.8	12.2
Dividends, Net Income ($)	0.49	0.48	0.52	0.54	0.55	0.55	0.56	0.60	0.63	0.69
Expense Ratio (%)	0.64	0.63	0.63	0.60	0.62	0.61	0.58	0.60	0.58	0.60
Yield (%)	4.68	4.87	4.68	4.84	5.10	5.02	5.63	5.23	5.80	6.46

SHAREHOLDER INFORMATION

Minimum Investment
Initial: $1,000 IRA: na
Subsequent: $250 IRA: na

Maximum Fees
Load: none 12b-1: 0.25%
Other: none

Value Line US Gov't Sec (VALBX)

800-223-0818, 212-907-1500
www.valueline.com

Government Bond

PERFORMANCE AND PER SHARE DATA **fund inception date: 9/2/81**

	3yr Annual	5yr Annual	10yr Annual	Category Risk Index
Return (%)	5.8	6.1	6.4	1.09—av
Differ from Category (+/-)	-0.4 blw av	0.2 abv av	-1.2 blw av	**Avg Mat** 8.2 yrs

	2000	1999	1998	1997	1996	1995	1994	1993	1992	1991
Return (%)	11.3	-1.1	7.6	9.2	3.9	14.4	-10.6	9.7	6.3	16.4
Differ from Category (+/-)	-2.5	1.9	-1.5	-0.6	1.8	-4.4	-7.0	-0.9	-0.3	1.5
Return, Tax-Adjusted (%)	8.9	-3.1	5.2	6.5	1.1	11.6	-13.0	6.0	3.9	13.9
Dividends, Net Income ($)	0.63	0.60	0.66	0.72	0.77	0.73	0.78	0.94	0.88	0.95
Expense Ratio (%)	0.73	0.67	0.66	0.65	0.65	0.66	0.63	0.61	0.64	0.64
Yield (%)	5.64	5.64	5.80	6.44	7.04	6.47	7.41	7.25	6.88	7.37

SHAREHOLDER INFORMATION

Minimum Investment
Initial: $1,000 IRA: $1,000
Subsequent: $250 IRA: $250

Maximum Fees
Load: none 12b-1: 0.25%
Other: none

Vanguard Admrl: Int Treas (VAITX)

800-635-1511, 610-669-1000
www.vanguard.com

Government Bond

PERFORMANCE AND PER SHARE DATA **fund inception date: 12/14/92**

	3yr Annual	5yr Annual	10yr Annual	Category Risk Index
Return (%)	6.9	6.3	na	1.45—abv av
Differ from Category (+/-)	0.7 high	0.4 high	na	**Avg Mat** 7.5 yrs

	2000	1999	1998	1997	1996	1995	1994	1993	1992	1991
Return (%)	14.1	-3.4	10.8	9.0	2.0	20.5	-4.2	11.3	—	—
Differ from Category (+/-)	0.3	-0.4	1.7	-0.8	-0.1	1.7	-0.6	0.7	—	—
Return, Tax-Adjusted (%)	11.5	-5.6	8.4	6.5	-0.3	17.7	-6.3	8.6	—	—
Dividends, Net Income ($)	0.64	0.60	0.62	0.64	0.64	0.66	0.58	0.58	—	—
Expense Ratio (%)	0.15	0.15	0.15	0.15	0.15	0.15	0.15	0.15	—	—
Yield (%)	6.02	6.03	5.67	6.11	6.26	6.18	6.13	5.47	—	—

SHAREHOLDER INFORMATION

Minimum Investment
Initial: $50,000 IRA: $50,000
Subsequent: $100 IRA: $100

Maximum Fees
Load: none 12b-1: none
Other: none

Vanguard Admrl: Long Treas (VALGX)

800-635-1511, 610-669-1000
www.vanguard.com

Government Bond

PERFORMANCE AND PER SHARE DATA **fund inception date: 12/14/92**

	3yr Annual	5yr Annual	10yr Annual	Category Risk Index
Return (%)	7.2	6.8	na	2.09—high
Differ from Category (+/-)	1.0 high	0.9 high	na	**Avg Mat** 18.6 yrs

	2000	1999	1998	1997	1996	1995	1994	1993	1992	1991
Return (%)	19.8	-9.0	13.2	13.9	-1.0	30.0	-6.8	16.6	—	—
Differ from Category (+/-)	6.0	-6.0	4.1	4.1	-3.1	11.2	-3.2	6.0	—	—
Return, Tax-Adjusted (%)	17.2	-11.1	10.7	11.3	-3.4	26.7	-9.4	13.0	—	—
Dividends, Net Income ($)	0.64	0.58	0.65	0.67	0.68	0.69	0.66	0.71	—	—
Expense Ratio (%)	0.15	0.15	0.15	0.15	0.89	0.15	0.15	0.15	—	—
Yield (%)	5.70	5.77	5.55	6.11	6.60	6.16	7.08	6.46	—	—

SHAREHOLDER INFORMATION

Minimum Investment
Initial: $50,000 IRA: $50,000
Subsequent: $100 IRA: $100

Maximum Fees
Load: none 12b-1: none
Other: none

Vanguard Admrl: Sh Treas (VASTX)

800-635-1511, 610-669-1000
www.vanguard.com

Government Bond

PERFORMANCE AND PER SHARE DATA **fund inception date: 12/14/92**

	3yr Annual	5yr Annual	10yr Annual	Category Risk Index
Return (%)	6.0	5.8	na	0.60—blw av
Differ from Category (+/-)	-0.2 av	-0.1 av	na	**Avg Mat** 2.7 yrs

	2000	1999	1998	1997	1996	1995	1994	1993	1992	1991
Return (%)	8.9	1.8	7.5	6.4	4.4	12.0	-0.3	6.4	—	—
Differ from Category (+/-)	-4.9	4.8	-1.6	-3.4	2.3	-6.8	3.3	-4.2	—	—
Return, Tax-Adjusted (%)	6.5	-0.2	5.2	4.0	2.1	9.5	-2.2	4.5	—	—
Dividends, Net Income ($)	0.59	0.52	0.55	0.59	0.58	0.60	0.50	0.45	—	—
Expense Ratio (%)	0.15	0.15	0.15	0.15	0.15	0.15	0.15	0.15	—	—
Yield (%)	5.82	5.26	5.35	5.84	5.77	5.88	5.15	4.39	—	—

SHAREHOLDER INFORMATION

Minimum Investment
Initial: $50,000 IRA: $50,000
Subsequent: $100 IRA: $100

Maximum Fees
Load: none 12b-1: none
Other: none

Vanguard Bd Idx: Interm Tm (VBIIX)

800-635-1511, 610-669-1000
www.vanguard.com

General Bond

PERFORMANCE AND PER SHARE DATA **fund inception date: 3/1/94**

	3yr Annual	5yr Annual	10yr Annual	Category Risk Index
Return (%)	6.3	6.2	na	1.43—high
Differ from Category (+/-)	0.8 high	0.6 high	na	**Avg Mat** 7.8 yrs

	2000	1999	1998	1997	1996	1995	1994	1993	1992	1991
Return (%)	12.7	-3.0	10.0	9.4	2.5	21.0	—	—	—	—
Differ from Category (+/-)	3.0	-3.0	2.7	1.0	-1.0	4.8	—	—	—	—
Return, Tax-Adjusted (%)	9.9	-5.4	7.3	6.7	0.0	18.0	—	—	—	—
Dividends, Net Income ($)	0.65	0.62	0.64	0.66	0.64	0.66	—	—	—	—
Expense Ratio (%)	na	0.20	0.20	0.20	0.20	0.20	—	—	—	—
Yield (%)	6.48	6.49	6.06	6.47	6.42	6.35	—	—	—	—

SHAREHOLDER INFORMATION

Minimum Investment
Initial: $3,000 IRA: $1,000
Subsequent: $100 IRA: $100

Maximum Fees
Load: none 12b-1: none
Other: none

Vanguard Bd Idx: Long-Term (VBLTX)

800-635-1511, 610-669-1000
www.vanguard.com

General Bond

PERFORMANCE AND PER SHARE DATA **fund inception date: 3/1/94**

	3yr Annual	5yr Annual	10yr Annual	Category Risk Index
Return (%)	6.3	6.4	na	1.98—high
Differ from Category (+/-)	0.8 high	0.8 high	na	**Avg Mat** 22.9 yrs

	2000	1999	1998	1997	1996	1995	1994	1993	1992	1991
Return (%)	16.4	-7.8	11.9	14.2	-0.2	29.7	—	—	—	—
Differ from Category (+/-)	6.7	-7.8	4.6	5.8	-3.7	13.5	—	—	—	—
Return, Tax-Adjusted (%)	13.7	-10.1	9.4	11.5	-2.6	26.5	—	—	—	—
Dividends, Net Income ($)	0.66	0.66	0.66	0.67	0.67	0.69	—	—	—	—
Expense Ratio (%)	na	0.20	0.20	0.20	0.20	0.18	—	—	—	—
Yield (%)	6.19	6.74	5.80	6.21	6.64	6.36	—	—	—	—

SHAREHOLDER INFORMATION

Minimum Investment
Initial: $3,000 IRA: $1,000
Subsequent: $100 IRA: $100

Maximum Fees
Load: none 12b-1: none
Other: none

Vanguard Bd Idx: Short Trm (VBISX)

800-635-1511, 610-669-1000
www.vanguard.com

General Bond

PERFORMANCE AND PER SHARE DATA **fund inception date: 3/1/94**

	3yr Annual	5yr Annual	10yr Annual	Category Risk Index
Return (%)	6.1	6.0	na	0.62—blw av
Differ from Category (+/-)	0.6 high	0.4 abv av	na	**Avg Mat** 2.8 yrs

	2000	1999	1998	1997	1996	1995	1994	1993	1992	1991
Return (%)	8.9	2.0	7.6	7.0	4.5	12.8	—	—	—	—
Differ from Category (+/-)	-0.8	2.0	0.3	-1.4	1.0	-3.4	—	—	—	—
Return, Tax-Adjusted (%)	6.4	-0.1	5.2	4.6	2.2	10.2	—	—	—	—
Dividends, Net Income ($)	0.60	0.53	0.57	0.59	0.58	0.62	—	—	—	—
Expense Ratio (%)	na	0.20	0.20	0.20	0.20	0.20	—	—	—	—
Yield (%)	6.01	5.43	5.61	5.90	5.84	6.15	—	—	—	—

SHAREHOLDER INFORMATION

Minimum Investment
Initial: $3,000 IRA: $1,000
Subsequent: $100 IRA: $100

Maximum Fees
Load: none 12b-1: none
Other: none

Vanguard Bd Idx: Tot Bd (VBMFX)

800-635-1511, 610-669-1000
www.vanguard.com

General Bond

PERFORMANCE AND PER SHARE DATA **fund inception date: 12/9/86**

	3yr Annual	5yr Annual	10yr Annual	Category Risk Index
Return (%)	6.2	6.3	7.8	1.02—av
Differ from Category (+/-)	0.7 high	0.7 high	0.6 abv av	**Avg Mat** 9.0 yrs

	2000	1999	1998	1997	1996	1995	1994	1993	1992	1991
Return (%)	11.4	-0.7	8.5	9.4	3.5	18.1	-2.6	9.6	7.1	15.2
Differ from Category (+/-)	1.7	-0.7	1.2	1.0	0.0	1.9	0.1	-0.1	0.3	-0.3
Return, Tax-Adjusted (%)	8.7	-3.0	6.0	6.8	1.0	15.3	-5.0	6.7	4.7	12.6
Dividends, Net Income ($)	0.64	0.61	0.62	0.64	0.64	0.64	0.62	0.63	0.69	0.76
Expense Ratio (%)	na	0.20	0.20	0.20	0.20	0.20	0.18	0.18	0.20	0.16
Yield (%)	6.42	6.37	6.01	6.34	6.50	6.31	6.76	6.19	6.92	7.59

SHAREHOLDER INFORMATION

Minimum Investment
Initial: $3,000 IRA: $1,000
Subsequent: $100 IRA: $100

Maximum Fees
Load: none 12b-1: none
Other: none

Vanguard CA: Ins Intm TE (VCAIX)

800-635-1511, 610-669-1000
www.vanguard.com

Tax-Exempt Bond

PERFORMANCE AND PER SHARE DATA **fund inception date: 3/4/94**

	3yr Annual	5yr Annual	10yr Annual	Category Risk Index
Return (%)	5.3	5.8	na	0.92—blw av
Differ from Category (+/-)	1.5 high	0.9 high	na	**Avg Mat** 7.5 yrs

	2000	1999	1998	1997	1996	1995	1994	1993	1992	1991
Return (%)	11.0	-0.5	6.0	7.6	5.4	13.1	—	—	—	—
Differ from Category (+/-)	1.6	2.1	0.4	-0.6	1.7	-2.0	—	—	—	—
Return, Tax-Adjusted (%)	11.0	-0.5	6.0	7.6	5.3	13.1	—	—	—	—
Dividends, Net Income ($)	0.51	0.48	0.48	0.50	0.50	0.51	—	—	—	—
Expense Ratio (%)	na	0.17	0.19	0.18	0.19	0.21	—	—	—	—
Yield (%)	4.64	4.62	4.39	4.64	4.75	4.87	—	—	—	—

SHAREHOLDER INFORMATION

Minimum Investment
Initial: $3,000 IRA: na
Subsequent: $100 IRA: na

Maximum Fees
Load: none 12b-1: none
Other: none

Vanguard CA: Ins Long Tm (VCITX)

800-635-1511, 610-669-1000
www.vanguard.com

Tax-Exempt Bond

PERFORMANCE AND PER SHARE DATA **fund inception date: 4/7/86**

	3yr Annual	5yr Annual	10yr Annual	Category Risk Index
Return (%)	7.2	7.1	8.0	1.47—high
Differ from Category (+/-)	3.4 high	2.2 high	1.5 high	**Avg Mat** 13.2 yrs

	2000	1999	1998	1997	1996	1995	1994	1993	1992	1991
Return (%)	19.4	-3.1	6.6	8.9	4.9	18.5	-5.6	12.8	9.3	11.0
Differ from Category (+/-)	10.0	-0.5	1.0	0.7	1.2	3.4	-0.7	1.1	0.9	-0.3
Return, Tax-Adjusted (%)	19.4	-3.1	6.4	8.7	4.6	18.5	-5.6	12.4	8.8	11.0
Dividends, Net Income ($)	0.99	0.56	0.57	0.59	0.59	0.60	0.60	0.60	0.63	0.64
Expense Ratio (%)	na	0.18	0.19	0.16	0.19	0.21	0.19	0.19	0.24	0.25
Yield (%)	8.47	5.24	4.87	5.09	5.21	5.27	5.92	5.20	5.74	6.01

SHAREHOLDER INFORMATION

Minimum Investment
Initial: $3,000 IRA: na
Subsequent: $100 IRA: na

Maximum Fees
Load: none 12b-1: none
Other: none

Vanguard FL Ins Lg Tm TE (VFLTX)

800-635-1511, 610-669-1000
www.vanguard.com

Tax-Exempt Bond

PERFORMANCE AND PER SHARE DATA **fund inception date: 8/31/92**

	3yr Annual	5yr Annual	10yr Annual	Category Risk Index
Return (%)	5.5	5.9	na	1.24—high
Differ from Category (+/-)	1.7 high	1.0 high	na	**Avg Mat** 12.4 yrs

	2000	1999	1998	1997	1996	1995	1994	1993	1992	1991
Return (%)	13.2	-2.7	6.6	8.9	4.1	17.7	-4.7	13.4	—	—
Differ from Category (+/-)	3.8	-0.1	1.0	0.7	0.4	2.6	0.2	1.7	—	—
Return, Tax-Adjusted (%)	13.2	-2.7	6.4	8.9	4.1	17.7	-4.7	13.2	—	—
Dividends, Net Income ($)	0.55	0.54	0.54	0.56	0.55	0.55	0.55	0.53	—	—
Expense Ratio (%)	na	0.18	0.20	0.19	0.19	0.20	0.22	0.21	—	—
Yield (%)	4.82	5.09	4.67	4.93	5.01	4.96	5.54	4.80	—	—

SHAREHOLDER INFORMATION

Minimum Investment
Initial: $3,000 IRA: na
Subsequent: $100 IRA: na

Maximum Fees
Load: none 12b-1: none
Other: none

Vanguard Fxd: GNMA (VFIIX)

800-662-7447, 610-669-1000
www.vanguard.com

Mortgage-Backed Bond

PERFORMANCE AND PER SHARE DATA **fund inception date: 6/27/80**

	3yr Annual	5yr Annual	10yr Annual	Category Risk Index
Return (%)	6.2	6.7	7.7	1.12—abv av
Differ from Category (+/-)	0.6 high	0.8 high	0.6 high	**Avg Mat** 8.0 yrs

	2000	1999	1998	1997	1996	1995	1994	1993	1992	1991
Return (%)	11.2	0.7	7.1	9.4	5.2	17.0	-0.9	5.8	6.8	16.7
Differ from Category (+/-)	1.3	-0.3	0.9	0.9	1.0	2.1	0.4	-0.6	0.3	2.0
Return, Tax-Adjusted (%)	8.4	-1.8	4.4	6.6	2.4	13.9	-3.4	3.3	4.5	14.0
Dividends, Net Income ($)	0.68	0.66	0.69	0.71	0.72	0.73	0.68	0.65	0.78	0.83
Expense Ratio (%)	0.27	0.30	0.31	0.27	0.29	0.30	0.28	0.29	0.29	0.34
Yield (%)	6.64	6.69	6.59	6.80	7.04	6.99	7.09	6.26	7.48	7.88

SHAREHOLDER INFORMATION

Minimum Investment
Initial: $3,000 IRA: $1,000
Subsequent: $100 IRA: $100

Maximum Fees
Load: none 12b-1: none
Other: none

Vanguard Fxd: Hi Yld Corp (VWEHX)

800-635-1511, 610-669-1000
www.vanguard.com

Corporate High-Yield Bond

PERFORMANCE AND PER SHARE DATA **fund inception date: 12/27/78**

	3yr Annual	5yr Annual	10yr Annual	Category Risk Index
Return (%)	2.3	5.6	10.3	0.72—low
Differ from Category (+/-)	2.3 abv av	0.2 av	0.5 abv av	**Avg Mat** 6.9 yrs

	2000	1999	1998	1997	1996	1995	1994	1993	1992	1991
Return (%)	-0.8	2.5	5.6	11.9	9.5	19.1	-1.7	18.2	14.2	29.0
Differ from Category (+/-)	6.1	-3.1	3.7	-2.7	-6.2	1.7	0.5	-1.2	-2.0	1.5
Return, Tax-Adjusted (%)	-4.1	-0.6	2.3	8.4	6.0	15.4	-5.0	14.5	11.0	25.1
Dividends, Net Income ($)	0.63	0.63	0.66	0.68	0.68	0.67	0.67	0.69	0.73	0.77
Expense Ratio (%)	0.28	0.29	0.28	0.29	0.34	0.34	0.32	0.34	0.34	0.40
Yield (%)	9.41	8.52	8.40	8.41	8.64	8.53	9.30	8.60	9.85	10.75

SHAREHOLDER INFORMATION

Minimum Investment
Initial: $3,000 IRA: $1,000
Subsequent: $100 IRA: $100

Maximum Fees
Load: 1.00% redemption 12b-1: none
Other: redemption fee applies for 12 months

Vanguard Fxd: Interm Corp (VFICX)

800-662-7447, 610-669-1000
www.vanguard.com

Corporate Bond

PERFORMANCE AND PER SHARE DATA **fund inception date: 11/1/93**

	3yr Annual	5yr Annual	10yr Annual	Category Risk Index
Return (%)	5.6	5.7	na	1.22—abv av
Differ from Category (+/-)	0.6 abv av	0.0 av	na	**Avg Mat** 7.3 yrs

	2000	1999	1998	1997	1996	1995	1994	1993	1992	1991
Return (%)	10.7	-1.5	8.3	8.9	2.7	21.3	-4.2	—	—	—
Differ from Category (+/-)	2.7	-2.8	2.4	-0.2	-2.8	3.4	-1.9	—	—	—
Return, Tax-Adjusted (%)	7.8	-4.0	5.6	6.3	0.2	18.4	-6.4	—	—	—
Dividends, Net Income ($)	0.66	0.62	0.62	0.63	0.63	0.65	0.57	—	—	—
Expense Ratio (%)	0.25	0.27	0.26	0.25	0.28	0.28	0.25	—	—	—
Yield (%)	6.95	6.70	6.13	6.33	6.45	6.40	6.36	—	—	—

SHAREHOLDER INFORMATION

Minimum Investment
Initial: $3,000 IRA: $1,000
Subsequent: $100 IRA: $100

Maximum Fees
Load: none 12b-1: none
Other: none

Vanguard Fxd: Interm Treas (VFITX)

800-662-7447, 610-669-1000
www.vanguard.com

Government Bond

PERFORMANCE AND PER SHARE DATA **fund inception date: 10/28/91**

	3yr Annual	5yr Annual	10yr Annual	Category Risk Index
Return (%)	6.7	6.2	na	1.44—abv av
Differ from Category (+/-)	0.5 abv av	0.3 abv av	na	**Avg Mat** 7.5 yrs

	2000	1999	1998	1997	1996	1995	1994	1993	1992	1991
Return (%)	14.0	-3.5	10.6	8.9	1.9	20.4	-4.3	11.4	7.7	—
Differ from Category (+/-)	0.2	-0.5	1.5	-0.9	-0.2	1.6	-0.7	0.8	1.1	—
Return, Tax-Adjusted (%)	11.4	-5.7	8.2	6.4	-0.4	17.6	-6.5	7.9	5.6	—
Dividends, Net Income ($)	0.64	0.62	0.63	0.64	0.64	0.66	0.59	0.62	0.67	—
Expense Ratio (%)	0.27	0.27	0.27	0.25	0.28	0.28	0.26	0.26	0.26	—
Yield (%)	5.89	6.12	5.65	5.99	6.14	6.06	6.11	5.57	6.33	—

SHAREHOLDER INFORMATION

Minimum Investment
Initial: $3,000 IRA: $1,000
Subsequent: $100 IRA: $100

Maximum Fees
Load: none 12b-1: none
Other: none

Vanguard Fxd: Long Tm Corp (VWESX)

800-662-7447, 610-669-1000
www.vanguard.com

Corporate Bond

PERFORMANCE AND PER SHARE DATA **fund inception date: 6/29/73**

	3yr Annual	5yr Annual	10yr Annual	Category Risk Index
Return (%)	4.6	5.6	9.1	1.59—high
Differ from Category (+/-)	-0.4 av	-0.1 av	1.0 abv av	**Avg Mat** 18.7 yrs

	2000	1999	1998	1997	1996	1995	1994	1993	1992	1991
Return (%)	11.7	-6.2	9.2	13.7	1.1	26.4	-5.2	14.4	9.7	20.9
Differ from Category (+/-)	3.7	-7.5	3.3	4.6	-4.4	8.5	-2.9	2.6	0.4	3.2
Return, Tax-Adjusted (%)	8.9	-8.6	6.2	10.7	-1.8	23.3	-8.0	10.7	6.8	18.1
Dividends, Net Income ($)	0.57	0.56	0.58	0.61	0.61	0.62	0.61	0.63	0.68	0.70
Expense Ratio (%)	0.30	0.30	0.32	0.28	0.31	0.32	0.30	0.31	0.31	0.37
Yield (%)	6.74	6.86	6.11	6.53	6.82	6.54	7.51	6.65	7.54	7.89

SHAREHOLDER INFORMATION

Minimum Investment
Initial: $3,000 IRA: $1,000
Subsequent: $100 IRA: $100

Maximum Fees
Load: none 12b-1: none
Other: none

Vanguard Fxd: Long Tm Trea (VUSTX)

800-662-7447, 610-669-1000
www.vanguard.com

Government Bond

PERFORMANCE AND PER SHARE DATA **fund inception date: 5/19/86**

	3yr Annual	5yr Annual	10yr Annual	Category Risk Index
Return (%)	7.3	6.8	9.5	2.08—high
Differ from Category (+/-)	1.1 high	0.9 high	1.9 high	**Avg Mat** 18.5 yrs

	2000	1999	1998	1997	1996	1995	1994	1993	1992	1991
Return (%)	19.7	-8.6	13.0	13.9	-1.2	30.0	-7.0	16.7	7.4	17.4
Differ from Category (+/-)	5.9	-5.6	3.9	4.1	-3.3	11.2	-3.4	6.1	0.8	2.5
Return, Tax-Adjusted (%)	17.1	-10.9	10.6	11.3	-3.6	26.3	-9.7	13.4	3.4	14.9
Dividends, Net Income ($)	0.62	0.61	0.63	0.64	0.65	0.67	0.66	0.68	0.73	0.76
Expense Ratio (%)	0.28	0.27	0.27	0.25	0.27	0.28	0.26	0.27	0.26	0.30
Yield (%)	5.68	6.23	5.54	6.01	6.51	6.08	7.20	6.33	6.94	7.21

SHAREHOLDER INFORMATION

Minimum Investment
Initial: $3,000 IRA: $1,000
Subsequent: $100 IRA: $100

Maximum Fees
Load: none 12b-1: none
Other: none

Vanguard Fxd: Sh Tm Corp (VFSTX)

800-662-7447, 610-669-1000
www.vanguard.com

Corporate Bond

PERFORMANCE AND PER SHARE DATA **fund inception date: 10/29/82**

	3yr Annual	5yr Annual	10yr Annual	Category Risk Index
Return (%)	5.9	5.9	6.9	0.53—blw av
Differ from Category (+/-)	0.9 high	0.2 abv av	-1.2 blw av	**Avg Mat** 2.5 yrs

	2000	1999	1998	1997	1996	1995	1994	1993	1992	1991
Return (%)	8.1	3.3	6.5	6.9	4.7	12.7	0.0	6.9	7.2	13.0
Differ from Category (+/-)	0.1	2.0	0.6	-2.2	-0.8	-5.2	2.3	-4.9	-2.1	-4.7
Return, Tax-Adjusted (%)	5.4	0.9	4.0	4.4	2.3	10.1	-2.1	4.4	4.8	10.6
Dividends, Net Income ($)	0.70	0.65	0.66	0.66	0.66	0.66	0.58	0.61	0.70	0.81
Expense Ratio (%)	0.25	0.27	0.28	0.25	0.27	0.28	0.26	0.27	0.26	0.31
Yield (%)	6.57	6.17	6.08	6.10	6.13	6.04	5.63	5.55	6.34	7.38

SHAREHOLDER INFORMATION

Minimum Investment
Initial: $3,000 IRA: $1,000
Subsequent: $100 IRA: $100

Maximum Fees
Load: none 12b-1: none
Other: none

Vanguard Fxd: Sh Tm Fed (VSGBX)

800-662-7447, 610-669-1000
www.vanguard.com

Government Bond

PERFORMANCE AND PER SHARE DATA **fund inception date: 12/28/87**

	3yr Annual	5yr Annual	10yr Annual	Category Risk Index
Return (%)	6.1	5.9	6.5	0.58—blw av
Differ from Category (+/-)	-0.1 abv av	0.0 av	-1.1 blw av	**Avg Mat** 2.8 yrs

	2000	1999	1998	1997	1996	1995	1994	1993	1992	1991
Return (%)	9.1	2.0	7.2	6.4	4.7	12.3	-0.9	7.0	6.1	12.2
Differ from Category (+/-)	-4.7	5.0	-1.9	-3.4	2.6	-6.5	2.7	-3.6	-0.5	-2.7
Return, Tax-Adjusted (%)	6.7	-0.1	4.9	4.0	2.3	9.8	-2.9	4.6	3.8	9.7
Dividends, Net Income ($)	0.60	0.56	0.58	0.61	0.61	0.61	0.54	0.52	0.61	0.72
Expense Ratio (%)	0.27	0.27	0.27	0.25	0.27	0.28	0.26	0.27	0.26	0.30
Yield (%)	5.89	5.65	5.65	6.02	6.03	5.95	5.56	4.97	5.84	6.85

SHAREHOLDER INFORMATION

Minimum Investment
Initial: $3,000 IRA: $1,000
Subsequent: $100 IRA: $100

Maximum Fees
Load: none 12b-1: none
Other: none

Vanguard Fxd: Sh Tm Treas (VFISX)

800-662-7447, 610-669-1000
www.vanguard.com

Government Bond

PERFORMANCE AND PER SHARE DATA **fund inception date: 10/28/91**

	3yr Annual	5yr Annual	10yr Annual	Category Risk Index
Return (%)	5.9	5.7	na	0.62—blw av
Differ from Category (+/-)	-0.3 av	-0.2 av	na	**Avg Mat** 2.7 yrs

	2000	1999	1998	1997	1996	1995	1994	1993	1992	1991
Return (%)	8.8	1.8	7.3	6.3	4.3	12.1	-0.4	6.3	6.7	—
Differ from Category (+/-)	-5.0	4.8	-1.8	-3.5	2.2	-6.7	3.2	-4.3	0.1	—
Return, Tax-Adjusted (%)	6.4	-0.2	5.1	4.0	2.0	9.5	-2.3	4.2	5.0	—
Dividends, Net Income ($)	0.59	0.52	0.55	0.59	0.58	0.62	0.51	0.49	0.52	—
Expense Ratio (%)	0.27	0.27	0.27	0.25	0.27	0.28	0.26	0.26	0.26	—
Yield (%)	5.74	5.18	5.29	5.77	5.70	6.00	5.19	4.68	5.02	—

SHAREHOLDER INFORMATION

Minimum Investment
Initial: $3,000 IRA: $1,000
Subsequent: $100 IRA: $100

Maximum Fees
Load: none 12b-1: none
Other: none

Vanguard Muni: High Yield (VWAHX)

800-635-1511, 610-669-1000
www.vanguard.com

Tax-Exempt Bond

PERFORMANCE AND PER SHARE DATA **fund inception date: 12/27/78**

	3yr Annual	5yr Annual	10yr Annual	Category Risk Index
Return (%)	4.4	5.3	7.5	1.07—av
Differ from Category (+/-)	0.6 av	0.4 abv av	1.0 high	**Avg Mat** 12.1 yrs

	2000	1999	1998	1997	1996	1995	1994	1993	1992	1991
Return (%)	10.7	-3.3	6.4	9.2	4.4	18.1	-5.0	12.6	9.8	14.7
Differ from Category (+/-)	1.3	-0.7	0.8	1.0	0.7	3.0	-0.1	0.9	1.4	3.4
Return, Tax-Adjusted (%)	10.7	-3.3	6.2	9.1	4.4	18.1	-5.4	12.0	9.1	14.4
Dividends, Net Income ($)	0.58	0.57	0.57	0.59	0.58	0.61	0.62	0.65	0.70	0.73
Expense Ratio (%)	na	0.18	0.20	0.19	0.20	0.22	0.20	0.20	0.23	0.25
Yield (%)	5.52	5.67	5.16	5.37	5.45	5.66	6.30	5.79	6.46	6.86

SHAREHOLDER INFORMATION

Minimum Investment
Initial: $3,000 IRA: na
Subsequent: $100 IRA: na

Maximum Fees
Load: none 12b-1: none
Other: none

Vanguard Muni: Ins Long Tm (VILPX)

800-635-1511, 610-669-1000
www.vanguard.com

Tax-Exempt Bond

PERFORMANCE AND PER SHARE DATA **fund inception date: 10/1/84**

	3yr Annual	5yr Annual	10yr Annual	Category Risk Index
Return (%)	5.4	5.7	7.4	1.23—high
Differ from Category (+/-)	1.6 high	0.8 high	0.9 high	**Avg Mat** 11.7 yrs

	2000	1999	1998	1997	1996	1995	1994	1993	1992	1991
Return (%)	13.6	-2.9	6.1	8.6	4.0	18.5	-5.5	13.0	9.1	12.4
Differ from Category (+/-)	4.2	-0.3	0.5	0.4	0.3	3.4	-0.6	1.3	0.7	1.1
Return, Tax-Adjusted (%)	13.6	-2.9	6.0	8.4	3.8	18.5	-5.8	12.6	8.6	12.2
Dividends, Net Income ($)	0.64	0.64	0.65	0.67	0.67	0.67	0.70	0.70	0.74	0.77
Expense Ratio (%)	na	0.19	0.21	0.19	0.20	0.22	0.20	0.20	0.23	0.25
Yield (%)	5.10	5.49	5.11	5.27	5.39	5.31	6.14	5.39	5.99	6.36

SHAREHOLDER INFORMATION

Minimum Investment
Initial: $3,000 IRA: na
Subsequent: $100 IRA: na

Maximum Fees
Load: none 12b-1: none
Other: none

Vanguard Muni: Interm Tm (VWITX)

800-635-1511, 610-669-1000
www.vanguard.com

Tax-Exempt Bond

PERFORMANCE AND PER SHARE DATA **fund inception date: 9/1/77**

	3yr Annual	5yr Annual	10yr Annual	Category Risk Index
Return (%)	4.7	5.1	6.8	0.84—blw av
Differ from Category (+/-)	0.9 abv av	0.2 av	0.3 av	**Avg Mat** 6.7 yrs

	2000	1999	1998	1997	1996	1995	1994	1993	1992	1991
Return (%)	9.2	-0.5	5.7	7.0	4.1	13.6	-2.1	11.5	8.8	12.1
Differ from Category (+/-)	-0.2	2.1	0.1	-1.2	0.4	-1.5	2.8	-0.2	0.4	0.8
Return, Tax-Adjusted (%)	9.2	-0.5	5.6	6.9	4.1	13.6	-2.4	11.3	8.5	11.9
Dividends, Net Income ($)	0.64	0.64	0.65	0.66	0.66	0.67	0.68	0.69	0.73	0.78
Expense Ratio (%)	na	0.18	0.21	0.19	0.20	0.22	0.20	0.20	0.23	0.25
Yield (%)	4.82	5.01	4.81	4.89	4.98	5.01	5.42	5.07	5.63	6.15

SHAREHOLDER INFORMATION

Minimum Investment
Initial: $3,000 IRA: na
Subsequent: $100 IRA: na

Maximum Fees
Load: none 12b-1: none
Other: none

Vanguard Muni: Limited Tm (VMLTX)

800-662-2739, 610-669-1000
www.vanguard.com

Tax-Exempt Bond

PERFORMANCE AND PER SHARE DATA **fund inception date: 8/31/87**

	3yr Annual	5yr Annual	10yr Annual	Category Risk Index
Return (%)	4.2	4.4	5.2	0.43—low
Differ from Category (+/-)	0.4 blw av	-0.5 low	-1.3 low	**Avg Mat** 3.0 yrs

	2000	1999	1998	1997	1996	1995	1994	1993	1992	1991
Return (%)	6.3	1.4	5.1	5.1	4.0	8.5	0.0	6.3	6.3	9.4
Differ from Category (+/-)	-3.1	4.0	-0.5	-3.1	0.3	-6.6	4.9	-5.4	-2.1	-1.9
Return, Tax-Adjusted (%)	6.3	1.4	5.1	5.1	4.0	8.5	0.0	6.2	6.1	9.2
Dividends, Net Income ($)	0.47	0.45	0.45	0.47	0.47	0.48	0.45	0.46	0.51	0.59
Expense Ratio (%)	na	0.18	0.21	0.19	0.21	0.22	0.20	0.20	0.23	0.25
Yield (%)	4.38	4.26	4.14	4.36	4.38	4.46	4.33	4.24	4.77	5.55

SHAREHOLDER INFORMATION

Minimum Investment
Initial: $3,000 IRA: na
Subsequent: $100 IRA: na

Maximum Fees
Load: none 12b-1: none
Other: none

Vanguard Muni: Long-Term (VWLTX)

800-635-1511, 610-669-1000
www.vanguard.com

Tax-Exempt Bond

PERFORMANCE AND PER SHARE DATA **fund inception date: 9/1/77**

	3yr Annual	5yr Annual	10yr Annual	Category Risk Index
Return (%)	5.0	5.7	7.6	1.21—high
Differ from Category (+/-)	1.2 high	0.8 high	1.1 high	**Avg Mat** 12.4 yrs

	2000	1999	1998	1997	1996	1995	1994	1993	1992	1991
Return (%)	13.4	-3.5	6.0	9.2	4.4	18.7	-5.7	13.4	9.3	13.5
Differ from Category (+/-)	4.0	-0.9	0.4	1.0	0.7	3.6	-0.8	1.7	0.9	2.2
Return, Tax-Adjusted (%)	13.4	-3.5	5.8	9.1	4.3	18.7	-6.0	12.8	8.5	12.9
Dividends, Net Income ($)	0.58	0.56	0.57	0.58	0.58	0.59	0.61	0.62	0.68	0.73
Expense Ratio (%)	na	0.18	0.21	0.19	0.20	0.23	0.20	0.20	0.23	0.25
Yield (%)	5.23	5.43	5.01	5.11	5.28	5.32	6.08	5.39	6.18	6.69

SHAREHOLDER INFORMATION

Minimum Investment
Initial: $3,000 IRA: na
Subsequent: $100 IRA: na

Maximum Fees
Load: none 12b-1: none
Other: none

Vanguard Muni: Short-Term (VWSTX)

800-635-1511, 610-669-1000
www.vanguard.com

Tax-Exempt Bond

PERFORMANCE AND PER SHARE DATA **fund inception date: 9/1/77**

	3yr Annual	5yr Annual	10yr Annual	Category Risk Index
Return (%)	3.9	3.9	4.2	0.17—low
Differ from Category (+/-)	0.1 low	-1.0 low	-2.3 low	**Avg Mat** 1.1 yrs

	2000	1999	1998	1997	1996	1995	1994	1993	1992	1991
Return (%)	4.9	2.5	4.3	4.0	3.6	5.9	1.6	3.8	4.7	7.1
Differ from Category (+/-)	-4.5	5.1	-1.3	-4.2	-0.1	-9.2	6.5	-7.9	-3.7	-4.2
Return, Tax-Adjusted (%)	4.9	2.5	4.3	4.0	3.6	5.9	1.6	3.7	4.6	6.9
Dividends, Net Income ($)	0.63	0.57	0.60	0.61	0.60	0.61	0.54	0.57	0.66	0.82
Expense Ratio (%)	na	0.18	0.20	0.19	0.20	0.22	0.20	0.20	0.23	0.25
Yield (%)	4.04	3.68	3.83	3.91	3.85	3.90	3.52	3.64	4.20	5.22

SHAREHOLDER INFORMATION

Minimum Investment
Initial: $3,000 IRA: na
Subsequent: $100 IRA: na

Maximum Fees
Load: none 12b-1: none
Other: none

Vanguard NJ Ins Lg Tm TE (VNJTX)

800-635-1511, 610-669-1000
www.vanguard.com

Tax-Exempt Bond

PERFORMANCE AND PER SHARE DATA **fund inception date: 2/3/88**

	3yr Annual	5yr Annual	10yr Annual	Category Risk Index
Return (%)	5.3	5.5	7.2	1.12—abv av
Differ from Category (+/-)	1.5 high	0.6 abv av	0.7 abv av	**Avg Mat** 11.1 yrs

	2000	1999	1998	1997	1996	1995	1994	1993	1992	1991
Return (%)	12.4	-2.3	6.3	8.5	3.1	17.3	-5.2	13.3	9.3	11.2
Differ from Category (+/-)	3.0	0.3	0.7	0.3	-0.6	2.2	-0.3	1.6	0.9	-0.1
Return, Tax-Adjusted (%)	12.4	-2.3	6.2	8.4	3.0	17.1	-5.2	13.1	8.9	11.2
Dividends, Net Income ($)	0.59	0.58	0.59	0.60	0.61	0.62	0.62	0.63	0.65	0.67
Expense Ratio (%)	na	0.19	0.20	0.18	0.20	0.22	0.21	0.20	0.25	0.24
Yield (%)	4.99	5.23	4.92	5.05	5.28	5.23	5.81	5.26	5.76	6.11

SHAREHOLDER INFORMATION

Minimum Investment
Initial: $3,000 IRA: na
Subsequent: $100 IRA: na

Maximum Fees
Load: none 12b-1: none
Other: none

Vanguard NY Ins Lg Tm TE (VNYTX)

800-635-1511, 610-669-1000
www.vanguard.com

Tax-Exempt Bond

PERFORMANCE AND PER SHARE DATA — fund inception date: 4/7/86

	3yr Annual	5yr Annual	10yr Annual	Category Risk Index
Return (%)	5.3	5.7	7.4	1.25—high
Differ from Category (+/-)	1.5 high	0.8 high	0.9 high	**Avg Mat** 12.8 yrs

	2000	1999	1998	1997	1996	1995	1994	1993	1992	1991
Return (%)	13.7	-3.3	6.2	8.7	4.0	17.7	-5.6	13.0	9.7	12.8
Differ from Category (+/-)	4.3	-0.7	0.6	0.5	0.3	2.6	-0.7	1.3	1.3	1.5
Return, Tax-Adjusted (%)	13.7	-3.3	6.0	8.6	3.8	17.5	-5.6	12.9	9.3	12.8
Dividends, Net Income ($)	0.55	0.54	0.56	0.57	0.56	0.57	0.59	0.59	0.62	0.63
Expense Ratio (%)	na	0.20	0.21	0.20	0.20	0.23	0.22	0.19	0.23	0.27
Yield (%)	4.95	5.24	4.96	5.09	5.14	5.14	5.93	5.28	5.87	6.15

SHAREHOLDER INFORMATION

Minimum Investment
Initial: $3,000 IRA: na
Subsequent: $100 IRA: na

Maximum Fees
Load: none 12b-1: none
Other: none

Vanguard OH Ins Lg Tm TE (VOHIX)

800-635-1511, 610-669-1000
www.vanguard.com

Tax-Exempt Bond

PERFORMANCE AND PER SHARE DATA — fund inception date: 6/18/90

	3yr Annual	5yr Annual	10yr Annual	Category Risk Index
Return (%)	5.1	5.6	7.2	1.16—abv av
Differ from Category (+/-)	1.3 high	0.7 high	0.7 abv av	**Avg Mat** 11.8 yrs

	2000	1999	1998	1997	1996	1995	1994	1993	1992	1991
Return (%)	12.8	-2.9	6.2	8.4	4.2	16.8	-5.1	12.7	9.4	11.9
Differ from Category (+/-)	3.4	-0.3	0.6	0.2	0.5	1.7	-0.2	1.0	1.0	0.6
Return, Tax-Adjusted (%)	12.8	-2.9	6.1	8.4	4.0	16.8	-5.1	12.6	9.0	11.9
Dividends, Net Income ($)	0.59	0.58	0.59	0.59	0.60	0.60	0.60	0.60	0.62	0.64
Expense Ratio (%)	na	0.19	0.20	0.17	0.20	0.21	0.23	0.21	0.31	0.27
Yield (%)	4.98	5.24	4.91	4.97	5.18	5.12	5.67	5.08	5.55	5.92

SHAREHOLDER INFORMATION

Minimum Investment
Initial: $3,000 IRA: na
Subsequent: $100 IRA: na

Maximum Fees
Load: none 12b-1: none
Other: none

Vanguard PA Tx Ex Ins LT (VPAIX)

800-635-1511, 610-669-1000
www.vanguard.com

Tax-Exempt Bond

PERFORMANCE AND PER SHARE DATA **fund inception date: 4/7/86**

	3yr Annual	5yr Annual	10yr Annual	Category Risk Index
Return (%)	5.2	5.6	7.3	1.12—abv av
Differ from Category (+/-)	1.4 high	0.7 high	0.8 high	**Avg Mat** 11.6 yrs

	2000	1999	1998	1997	1996	1995	1994	1993	1992	1991
Return (%)	12.7	-2.6	6.1	8.2	4.3	16.4	-4.5	12.7	10.1	12.3
Differ from Category (+/-)	3.3	0.0	0.5	0.0	0.6	1.3	0.4	1.0	1.7	1.0
Return, Tax-Adjusted (%)	12.7	-2.6	5.9	8.2	4.1	16.3	-4.5	12.5	9.5	12.2
Dividends, Net Income ($)	0.58	0.57	0.59	0.59	0.60	0.61	0.62	0.62	0.66	0.67
Expense Ratio (%)	na	0.19	0.20	0.18	0.19	0.22	0.20	0.20	0.24	0.25
Yield (%)	5.15	5.41	5.13	5.17	5.37	5.37	6.01	5.38	5.98	6.27

SHAREHOLDER INFORMATION

Minimum Investment
Initial: $3,000 IRA: na
Subsequent: $100 IRA: na

Maximum Fees
Load: none 12b-1: none
Other: none

Victory: Fund for Income/G (GGIFX)

800-539-3863, 513-579-5000
www.victoryfunds.com

Mortgage-Backed Bond

PERFORMANCE AND PER SHARE DATA **fund inception date: 9/16/87**

	3yr Annual	5yr Annual	10yr Annual	Category Risk Index
Return (%)	5.9	5.9	7.0	1.00—blw av
Differ from Category (+/-)	0.3 abv av	0.0 av	-0.1 blw av	**Avg Mat** 8.0 yrs

	2000	1999	1998	1997	1996	1995	1994	1993	1992	1991
Return (%)	9.9	0.7	7.3	8.3	3.5	17.2	-3.3	7.5	6.2	14.0
Differ from Category (+/-)	0.0	-0.3	1.1	-0.2	-0.7	2.3	-2.0	1.1	-0.3	-0.7
Return, Tax-Adjusted (%)	7.2	-1.6	5.0	5.9	1.2	14.5	-5.8	4.9	3.8	11.3
Dividends, Net Income ($)	0.83	0.78	0.75	0.77	0.76	0.78	0.75	0.73	0.86	0.94
Expense Ratio (%)	na	0.88	1.00	0.90	0.90	0.92	0.90	0.90	0.94	0.99
Yield (%)	6.38	6.18	5.63	5.85	5.90	5.89	6.16	5.37	6.37	6.85

SHAREHOLDER INFORMATION

Minimum Investment
Initial: $500 IRA: $100
Subsequent: $25 IRA: $25

Maximum Fees
Load: none 12b-1: 0.25%
Other: none

Vintage Income (AVINX)

800-438-6375, 515-244-5426
www.amcore.com

General Bond

PERFORMANCE AND PER SHARE DATA **fund inception date: 12/15/92**

	3yr Annual	5yr Annual	10yr Annual	Category Risk Index
Return (%)	5.1	5.0	na	0.90—blw av
Differ from Category (+/-)	-0.4 blw av	-0.6 low	na	**Avg Mat** 7.7 yrs

	2000	1999	1998	1997	1996	1995	1994	1993	1992	1991
Return (%)	9.4	-0.7	7.0	7.1	2.8	14.4	-3.1	9.0	—	—
Differ from Category (+/-)	-0.3	-0.7	-0.3	-1.3	-0.7	-1.8	-0.4	-0.7	—	—
Return, Tax-Adjusted (%)	6.9	-2.8	4.7	5.0	0.6	11.8	-5.1	6.5	—	—
Dividends, Net Income ($)	0.59	0.56	0.57	0.51	0.55	0.61	0.52	0.61	—	—
Expense Ratio (%)	0.99	1.01	1.15	1.20	0.97	0.94	0.51	0.29	—	—
Yield (%)	6.02	5.88	5.61	5.07	5.57	6.00	5.51	5.92	—	—

SHAREHOLDER INFORMATION

Minimum Investment
Initial: $1,000 IRA: $25
Subsequent: $50 IRA: $25

Maximum Fees
Load: none 12b-1: none
Other: none

Vintage Limited Term Bond (AFTRX)

800-438-6375, 515-244-5426
www.amcore.com

General Bond

PERFORMANCE AND PER SHARE DATA **fund inception date: 6/15/95**

	3yr Annual	5yr Annual	10yr Annual	Category Risk Index
Return (%)	4.4	4.3	na	0.61—blw av
Differ from Category (+/-)	-1.1 low	-1.3 low	na	**Avg Mat** 3.0 yrs

	2000	1999	1998	1997	1996	1995	1994	1993	1992	1991
Return (%)	6.7	0.5	6.1	6.7	1.7	—	—	—	—	—
Differ from Category (+/-)	-3.0	0.5	-1.2	-1.7	-1.8	—	—	—	—	—
Return, Tax-Adjusted (%)	4.5	-1.4	4.1	4.6	-0.2	—	—	—	—	—
Dividends, Net Income ($)	0.52	0.49	0.48	0.50	0.51	—	—	—	—	—
Expense Ratio (%)	0.92	1.05	1.35	1.40	1.18	—	—	—	—	—
Yield (%)	5.32	5.07	4.75	5.01	5.18	—	—	—	—	—

SHAREHOLDER INFORMATION

Minimum Investment
Initial: $1,000 IRA: $25
Subsequent: $50 IRA: $25

Maximum Fees
Load: none 12b-1: none
Other: none

WPG Tr: Core Bond (WPGVX)

800-223-3332, 212-908-9500
www.wpginvest.com

General Bond

PERFORMANCE AND PER SHARE DATA **fund inception date: 2/20/86**

	3yr Annual	5yr Annual	10yr Annual	Category Risk Index
Return (%)	6.4	6.1	6.1	1.12—abv av
Differ from Category (+/-)	0.9 high	0.5 high	-1.1 low	**Avg Mat** 9.4 yrs

	2000	1999	1998	1997	1996	1995	1994	1993	1992	1991
Return (%)	10.6	-0.1	9.2	7.3	3.8	13.3	-8.8	8.9	5.4	13.9
Differ from Category (+/-)	0.9	-0.1	1.9	-1.1	0.3	-2.9	-6.1	-0.8	-1.4	-1.6
Return, Tax-Adjusted (%)	8.0	-2.3	6.9	5.1	1.5	10.6	-11.2	5.4	2.7	11.5
Dividends, Net Income ($)	0.59	0.55	0.54	0.50	0.53	0.58	0.64	0.79	0.77	0.79
Expense Ratio (%)	na	0.50	0.50	0.50	0.81	0.85	0.80	0.81	0.78	0.81
Yield (%)	6.27	6.06	5.60	5.35	5.76	6.18	7.24	7.50	7.29	7.32

SHAREHOLDER INFORMATION

Minimum Investment
Initial: $25,000 IRA: $25,000
Subsequent: $5,000 IRA: $5,000

Maximum Fees
Load: none 12b-1: none
Other: none

Warburg Fixed Inc/Cmn (CUFIX)

800-927-2874, 212-878-0600
www.warburg.com

General Bond

PERFORMANCE AND PER SHARE DATA **fund inception date: 8/17/87**

	3yr Annual	5yr Annual	10yr Annual	Category Risk Index
Return (%)	5.1	6.0	7.8	0.95—av
Differ from Category (+/-)	-0.4 blw av	0.4 abv av	0.6 abv av	**Avg Mat** 18.0 yrs

	2000	1999	1998	1997	1996	1995	1994	1993	1992	1991
Return (%)	9.1	0.0	6.5	8.8	6.1	15.1	-0.6	11.1	6.7	16.8
Differ from Category (+/-)	-0.6	0.0	-0.8	0.4	2.6	-1.1	2.1	1.4	-0.1	1.3
Return, Tax-Adjusted (%)	6.5	-2.2	4.2	6.2	3.6	12.2	-3.1	8.5	4.5	14.4
Dividends, Net Income ($)	0.63	0.58	0.57	0.61	0.63	0.68	0.67	0.56	0.67	0.70
Expense Ratio (%)	na	0.76	0.75	0.75	0.75	0.75	0.75	0.75	0.75	0.75
Yield (%)	6.30	5.93	5.48	5.86	6.20	6.67	7.06	5.42	6.82	7.09

SHAREHOLDER INFORMATION

Minimum Investment
Initial: $2,500 IRA: $500
Subsequent: $100 IRA: $50

Maximum Fees
Load: none 12b-1: none
Other: none

Warburg Glbl Fxd Inc/Cmn (CGFIX)

800-927-2874, 212-878-0600
www.warburg.com

International Bond

PERFORMANCE AND PER SHARE DATA **fund inception date: 11/1/90**

	3yr Annual	5yr Annual	10yr Annual	Category Risk Index
Return (%)	5.2	5.5	7.2	0.44—blw av
Differ from Category (+/-)	2.0 abv av	0.3 av	1.8 high	**Avg Mat** 11.3 yrs

	2000	1999	1998	1997	1996	1995	1994	1993	1992	1991
Return (%)	7.2	0.3	8.4	2.1	9.9	16.0	-5.4	19.6	2.1	14.7
Differ from Category (+/-)	2.7	-3.5	4.8	-1.8	-4.2	-0.9	1.8	4.4	-1.5	0.0
Return, Tax-Adjusted (%)	3.4	-2.1	6.0	-1.0	6.5	12.6	-6.6	16.3	-0.7	12.8
Dividends, Net Income ($)	0.94	0.66	0.62	0.88	0.93	0.85	0.36	0.74	0.88	0.59
Expense Ratio (%)	na	0.96	0.95	0.96	0.95	0.95	0.95	0.49	0.45	1.09
Yield (%)	9.68	6.61	5.84	8.48	8.44	7.79	3.54	6.57	8.64	5.44

SHAREHOLDER INFORMATION

Minimum Investment
Initial: $2,500 IRA: $500
Subsequent: $100 IRA: $50

Maximum Fees
Load: none 12b-1: none
Other: none

Warburg Intm Mat Gv/Cmn (CUIGX)

800-927-2874, 212-878-0600
www.warburg.com

Government Bond

PERFORMANCE AND PER SHARE DATA **fund inception date: 8/22/88**

	3yr Annual	5yr Annual	10yr Annual	Category Risk Index
Return (%)	5.7	5.4	6.9	0.90—av
Differ from Category (+/-)	-0.5 blw av	-0.5 blw av	-0.7 av	**Avg Mat** 12.2 yrs

	2000	1999	1998	1997	1996	1995	1994	1993	1992	1991
Return (%)	9.8	-0.4	8.1	7.5	2.2	16.2	-1.7	7.3	6.6	14.9
Differ from Category (+/-)	-4.0	2.6	-1.0	-2.3	0.1	-2.6	1.9	-3.3	0.0	0.0
Return, Tax-Adjusted (%)	7.5	-2.4	5.8	5.2	-0.2	13.5	-3.8	3.7	3.3	12.6
Dividends, Net Income ($)	0.54	0.53	0.55	0.57	0.57	0.59	0.55	0.52	0.85	0.75
Expense Ratio (%)	na	0.61	0.60	0.61	0.60	0.60	0.60	0.60	0.60	0.57
Yield (%)	5.38	5.48	5.33	5.66	5.68	5.64	5.75	4.76	7.72	6.72

SHAREHOLDER INFORMATION

Minimum Investment
Initial: $2,500 IRA: $500
Subsequent: $100 IRA: $50

Maximum Fees
Load: none 12b-1: none
Other: none

Warburg NY Intm Muni/Cmn (CNMBX)

800-927-2874, 212-878-0600
www.warburg.com

Tax-Exempt Bond

PERFORMANCE AND PER SHARE DATA **fund inception date: 4/1/87**

	3yr Annual	5yr Annual	10yr Annual	Category Risk Index
Return (%)	4.5	4.7	5.9	0.80—blw av
Differ from Category (+/-)	0.7 abv av	-0.2 blw av	-0.6 low	**Avg Mat** 7.3 yrs

	2000	1999	1998	1997	1996	1995	1994	1993	1992	1991
Return (%)	8.9	-0.4	5.4	5.8	4.3	9.5	-0.5	9.8	7.5	9.4
Differ from Category (+/-)	-0.5	2.2	-0.2	-2.4	0.6	-5.6	4.4	-1.9	-0.9	-1.9
Return, Tax-Adjusted (%)	8.9	-0.4	5.3	5.8	3.9	9.1	-0.5	9.4	7.3	9.4
Dividends, Net Income ($)	0.42	0.41	0.43	0.44	0.45	0.45	0.45	0.46	0.49	0.56
Expense Ratio (%)	na	0.61	0.60	0.60	0.59	0.60	0.60	0.58	0.55	0.55
Yield (%)	4.02	4.09	4.09	4.23	4.33	4.28	4.48	4.30	4.80	5.61

SHAREHOLDER INFORMATION

Minimum Investment
Initial: $2,500 IRA: na
Subsequent: $100 IRA: na

Maximum Fees
Load: none 12b-1: none
Other: none

Wasatch-Hoisington: US Trs (WHOSX)

800-551-1700, 801-533-0778
www.wasatchfunds.com

Government Bond

PERFORMANCE AND PER SHARE DATA **fund inception date: 12/19/86**

	3yr Annual	5yr Annual	10yr Annual	Category Risk Index
Return (%)	7.0	8.8	7.9	2.55—high
Differ from Category (+/-)	0.8 high	2.9 high	0.3 abv av	**Avg Mat** 25.1 yrs

	2000	1999	1998	1997	1996	1995	1994	1993	1992	1991
Return (%)	21.9	-12.3	14.6	13.5	9.8	11.4	1.5	3.9	4.7	13.6
Differ from Category (+/-)	8.1	-9.3	5.5	3.7	7.7	-7.4	5.1	-6.7	-1.9	-1.3
Return, Tax-Adjusted (%)	19.8	-14.5	13.5	11.4	7.8	9.5	-0.7	2.0	1.6	11.0
Dividends, Net Income ($)	0.55	0.72	0.28	0.56	0.51	0.45	0.58	0.46	0.53	0.69
Expense Ratio (%)	0.75	0.75	0.75	0.75	0.93	1.00	1.00	1.00	1.00	1.01
Yield (%)	4.44	6.79	2.15	4.83	4.77	4.40	6.06	4.59	4.96	6.33

SHAREHOLDER INFORMATION

Minimum Investment
Initial: $2,000 IRA: $1,000
Subsequent: $100 IRA: $100

Maximum Fees
Load: none 12b-1: none
Other: none

Wright Inc: Current Income (WCIFX)

800-888-9471, 203-330-5000
www.wisi.com

Mortgage-Backed Bond

PERFORMANCE AND PER SHARE DATA **fund inception date: 4/30/87**

	3yr Annual	5yr Annual	10yr Annual	Category Risk Index
Return (%)	5.7	6.0	7.1	1.05—abv av
Differ from Category (+/-)	0.1 av	0.1 abv av	0.0 av	**Avg Mat** 7.6 yrs

	2000	1999	1998	1997	1996	1995	1994	1993	1992	1991
Return (%)	10.2	0.5	6.6	8.5	4.3	17.4	-3.2	6.5	6.7	15.3
Differ from Category (+/-)	0.3	-0.5	0.4	0.0	0.1	2.5	-1.9	0.1	0.2	0.6
Return, Tax-Adjusted (%)	7.7	-1.8	4.1	5.9	1.8	14.5	-5.7	3.8	4.5	12.8
Dividends, Net Income ($)	0.63	0.62	0.65	0.66	0.67	0.69	0.68	0.72	0.76	0.79
Expense Ratio (%)	na	0.91	0.90	0.89	0.90	0.90	0.80	0.80	0.90	0.90
Yield (%)	6.02	6.14	6.09	6.20	6.42	6.46	7.00	6.69	7.05	7.28

SHAREHOLDER INFORMATION

Minimum Investment
Initial: $1,000 IRA: $1,000
Subsequent: $1 IRA: $1

Maximum Fees
Load: none 12b-1: 0.25%
Other: none

Wright Inc: Total Ret Bd (WTRBX)

800-888-9471, 203-330-5000
www.wisi.com

General Bond

PERFORMANCE AND PER SHARE DATA **fund inception date: 7/25/83**

	3yr Annual	5yr Annual	10yr Annual	Category Risk Index
Return (%)	5.2	5.1	7.2	1.30—high
Differ from Category (+/-)	-0.3 blw av	-0.5 low	0.0 av	**Avg Mat** 8.4 yrs

	2000	1999	1998	1997	1996	1995	1994	1993	1992	1991
Return (%)	10.6	-3.8	9.5	9.2	0.8	21.9	-6.5	11.0	7.1	15.3
Differ from Category (+/-)	.0.9	-3.8	2.2	0.8	-2.7	5.7	-3.8	1.3	0.3	-0.2
Return, Tax-Adjusted (%)	.8.3	-5.8	7.1	7.0	-1.3	19.3	-8.7	8.1	5.0	13.0
Dividends, Net Income ($)	0.70	0.67	0.69	0.68	0.71	0.75	0.73	0.78	0.82	0.85
Expense Ratio (%)	na	0.90	0.90	0.90	0.80	0.80	0.80	0.80	0.80	0.80
Yield (%)	5.54	5.53	5.13	5.25	5.68	5.71	6.38	5.91	6.50	6.75

SHAREHOLDER INFORMATION

Minimum Investment
Initial: $1,000 IRA: $1,000
Subsequent: $1 IRA: $1

Maximum Fees
Load: none 12b-1: 0.25%
Other: none

Appendix A

Special Types of Funds

ASSET ALLOCATION FUNDS

ABN AMRO: Balanced/Cmn (Bal: RBTCX)
Alleghany: Chicago Bal/N (Bal: CHTAX)
Alleghany: Mntg & Cldwl Bl/N (Bal: MOBAX)
Amer Cent: Stg Al Agg/Inv (Bal: TWSAX)
Amer Cent: Stg Al Cnsrv/Inv (Bal: TWSCX)
Amer Cent: Stg Al Mod/Inv (Bal: TWSMX)
Aon: Asset Allocation (Bal: AONAX)
Boston Balanced (Bal: BMGFX)
CGM Mutual (Bal: LOMMX)
Columbia Balanced (Bal: CBALX)
Dreyfus Life: Gr & Inc/R (Bal: DGIRX)
Fidelity Asset Mgr (Bal: FASMX)
Fidelity Asset Mgr Growth (Bal: FASGX)
Fidelity Asset Mgr Income (Bal: FASIX)
Fidelity Balanced (Bal: FBALX)
Fidelity Global Balanced (IntlS: FGBLX)
Flex-fund: Muirfield (GI: FLMFX)
Fremont: Global (IntlS: FMAFX)
Gabelli Westwood Bal/AAA (Bal: WEBAX)
INVESCO Equity Income/Inv (Bal: FIIIX)
INVESCO Total Return/Inv (Bal: FSFLX)
Markman Aggressive Alloc (AG: MMAGX)
Markman Moderate Alloc (GI: MMMGX)
Montgomery Balanced/R (Bal: MNAAX)
Northeast Investors Tr (B-CHY: NTHEX)
Permanent Port: Perm Port (Bal: PRPFX)
Preferred Asset Allocatn (Bal: PFAAX)
Rainier: Balanced (Bal: RIMBX)
Schwab MarketMgr: Bal (Bal: SWOBX)
Schwab MarketMgr: Growth (Bal: SWOGX)
Schwab MarketMgr: Intl (IntlS: SWOIX)
Schwab MarketMgr: Sm Cp (AG: SWOSX)
Schwab MarketTrack: Bal (Bal: SWBGX)
Schwab MarketTrack: Cnsrv (Bal: SWCGX)
Schwab MarketTrack: Growth (Bal: SWHGX)
Scudder Pathway: Balanced (Bal: SPBAX)
Scudder Pathway: Growth/S (GI: SPGRX)

SteinRoe Inv: Balanced (Bal: SRFBX)
Strong Balanced (Bal: STAAX)
T Rowe Price Pers Str: Bal (Bal: TRPBX)
T Rowe Price Pers Str: Gr (Bal: TRSGX)
T Rowe Price Pers Str: Inc (Bal: PRSIX)
T Rowe Price Spect: Income (Bal: RPSIX)
T Rowe Price Spect: Intl (IntlS: PSILX)
TIAA-CREF Managed Alloc (Bal: TIMAX)
USAA Inv: Balanced Stgy (Bal: USBSX)
USAA Inv: Crnrst Strategy (Bal: USCRX)
USAA Inv: Growth & Tax (Bal: USBLX)
USAA Inv: Growth Stgy (Bal: USGSX)
USAA Inv: Income Stgy (B-Gen: USICX)
Value Line Asset Alloc (Bal: VLAAX)
Value Line Inc & Grth (Bal: VALIX)
Vanguard Asset Allocation (Bal: VAAPX)
Vanguard Global Asset All (IntlS: VHAAX)
Vanguard LifeStgy Cons Gr (Bal: VSCGX)
Vanguard LifeStgy Grth (Bal: VASGX)
Vanguard LifeStgy Income (Bal: VASIX)
Vanguard LifeStgy Mod Gr (Bal: VSMGX)
Vanguard Tx Mg Balanced (Bal: VTMFX)
Weston: New Century Bal (Bal: NCIPX)

FUNDS INVESTING IN FUNDS

Fidelity Freedom 2000 (Bal: FFFBX)
Fidelity Freedom 2010 (Bal: FFFCX)
Fidelity Freedom 2020 (Bal: FFFDX)
Fidelity Freedom 2030 (GI: FFFEX)
Fidelity Freedom Income (Bal: FFFAX)
Flex-fund: Muirfield (GI: FLMFX)
Markman Aggressive Alloc (AG: MMAGX)
Markman Moderate Alloc (GI: MMMGX)
Montgomery Balanced/R (Bal: MNAAX)
Rightime: Fund (GI: RTFDX)
Schwab MarketMgr: Bal (Bal: SWOBX)
Schwab MarketMgr: Growth (Bal: SWOGX)
Schwab MarketMgr: Intl (IntlS: SWOIX)
Schwab MarketMgr: Sm Cp (AG: SWOSX)
Schwab MarketTrack: Bal (Bal: SWBGX)
Schwab MarketTrack: Cnsrv (Bal: SWCGX)
Schwab MarketTrack: Growth (Bal: SWHGX)
Scudder Pathway: Balanced (Bal: SPBAX)
Scudder Pathway: Growth/S (GI: SPGRX)
SSgA Life Sol: Balanced (Bal: SSLBX)
T Rowe Price Spect: Growth (Grth: PRSGX)

T Rowe Price Spect: Income (Bal: RPSIX)
T Rowe Price Spect: Intl (IntlS: PSILX)
TIAA-CREF Managed Alloc (Bal: TIMAX)
Vanguard LifeStgy Cons Gr (Bal: VSCGX)
Vanguard LifeStgy Grth (Bal: VASGX)
Vanguard LifeStgy Income (Bal: VASIX)
Vanguard LifeStgy Mod Gr (Bal: VSMGX)
Vanguard STAR (Bal: VGSTX)
Vanguard Tot Itl Stk Idx (IntlS: VGTSX)
Weston: New Century Bal (Bal: NCIPX)
Weston: New Century Cap (Grth: NCCPX)

GLOBAL FUNDS

Amer Cent: Global Ntrl/Inv (IntlS: BGRIX)
Columbia Intl Stock (IntlS: CMISX)
Dreyfus Founders: Wld Gr/F (IntlS: FWWGX)
Dreyfus Global Growth (IntlS: DSWIX)
Fidelity Global Balanced (IntlS: FGBLX)
Fidelity Intl Bond (IntlB: FGBDX)
Fidelity Intl Grth & Inc (IntlS: FIGRX)
Fidelity New Markets Inc (IntlB: FNMIX)
Fidelity Worldwide (IntlS: FWWFX)
Fremont: Global (IntlS: FMAFX)
Gabelli Gl Growth/AAA (IntlS: GICPX)
Gabelli Gl Telecomm/AAA (IntlS: GABTX)
INVESCO Telcom/Inv (IntlS: ISWCX)
Janus Inv: Worldwide (IntlS: JAWWX)
Legg Mason Gl: Gl Gov't/P (IntlB: LMGGX)
Montgomery Glbl Commun/R (IntlS: MNGCX)
Montgomery Glbl Oppor/R (IntlS: MNGOX)
Montgomery Global 20/R (IntlS: MNSFX)
Payden & Rygel Glbl Fix/R (IntlB: PYGFX)
Payden & Rygel Glbl Sht/R (IntlB: PYGSX)
RS: Contrarian/A (IntlS: RSCOX)
Scudder Global Bond/S (IntlB: SSTGX)
Scudder Global/S (IntlS: SCOBX)
SSgA: Emerging Markets (IntlS: SSEMX)
Strong Adv Short Dur Bd/Z (IntlB: STGBX)
Tweedy Browne Global Val (IntlS: TBGVX)
UMB Scout Worldwide (IntlS: UMBWX)
USAA Inv: World Growth (IntlS: USAWX)
Vanguard Global Asset All (IntlS: VHAAX)
Vanguard Global Equity (IntlS: VHGEX)
Warburg Glbl Fxd Inc/Cmn (IntlB: CGFIX)

INDEX MUTUAL FUNDS

American Gas Association
American Gas Index (GI: GASFX)

FTSE Gold Mines
Amer Cent: Global Gold/Inv (AG: BGEIX)

Galaxy U.S. Treasury
Galaxy II: US/Ret A (B-Gov: IUTIX)

Lehman Brothers Aggregate Bond
Schwab Inv: Tot Bd Mkt Ix (B-Gen: SWLBX)
Vanguard Bd Idx: Tot Bd (B-Gen: VBMFX)

Lehman Brothers Mutual Fund Intermediate (5-10) Gov't/Corporate
Vanguard Bd Idx: Interm Tm (B-Gen: VBIIX)

Lehman Brothers Mutual Fund Long (10+) Gov't/Corporate
Vanguard Bd Idx: Long-Term (B-Gen: VBLTX)

Lehman Brothers Mutual Fund Short (1-5) Gov't/Corporate
Schwab Inv: Sh Tm Bd Mkt (B-Gov: SWBDX)
Vanguard Bd Idx: Short Trm (B-Gen: VBISX)

Morgan Stanley REIT
Vanguard Specl: REIT Index (GI: VGSIX)

MSCI EAFE + MSCI Emerging Markets Free
Vanguard Tot Itl Stk Idx (IntlS: VGTSX)

MSCI Emerging Markets Free
Vanguard Emg Mkt Stk Idx (IntlS: VEIEX)

MSCI Europe
Vanguard Erpn Stock Index (IntlS: VEURX)

MSCI Pacific
Vanguard Pacific Stk Idx (IntlS: VPACX)

Nasdaq 100
Rydex: OTC/Inv (AG: RYOCX)

Russell 2000

Vanguard Idx: Sm Cap/Inv (Grth: NAESX)

S&P 500

CA Inv: S&P 500 Index (GI: SPFIX)
Dreyfus Index: S&P 500 Idx (GI: PEOPX)
Fidelity Spart 500 Index (GI: FSMKX)
Galaxy II: Large Co (GI: ILCIX)
Northern Stock Index (GI: NOSIX)
Schwab Cap Tr: S&P 500/I (GI: SWPIX)
Scudder S&P 500 Index/S (GI: SCPIX)
SSgA: S&P 500 Index (GI: SVSPX)
Strong Index 500 (GI: SINEX)
T Rowe Price Eq Index 500 (GI: PREIX)
USAA S&P 500 Index (GI: USSPX)
Vanguard Idx: 500 Idx (GI: VFINX)

S&P 500/BARRA Growth

Vanguard Idx: Growth/Inv (Grth: VIGRX)

S&P 500/BARRA Value

Vanguard Idx: Value/Inv (GI: VIVAX)

S&P Midcap 400

CA Inv: S&P Mid Cap Index (Grth: SPMIX)
Dreyfus Index: Midcap Idx (Grth: PESPX)

S&P SmallCap 600

Galaxy II: Small Co (AG: ISCIX)

S&P Utilities

Galaxy II: Utility (GI: IUTLX)

Schwab 1000

Schwab Inv: 1000/I (GI: SNXFX)

Schwab International

Schwab Intl Index/I (IntlS: SWINX)

Schwab Small Cap 1000

Schwab Cap Tr: Sm Cp Ix/I (AG: SWSMX)

Wilshire 4500

Vanguard Idx: Ext Mkt/Inv (Grth: VEXMX)

Wilshire 5000
Fidelity Spart Total Mkt (GI: FSTMX)
Vanguard Idx: Tot Stk/Inv (GI: VTSMX)

Wilshire 5000 (60%)/Lehman Aggregate Bond (40%)
Vanguard Balanced Index (Bal: VBINX)

SECTOR FUNDS

Amer Cent: Global Gold/Inv (AG: BGEIX)
Amer Cent: Real Estate/Inv (GI: REACX)
Amer Cent: Utilities/Inv (GI: BULIX)
American Gas Index (GI: GASFX)
Brazos Real Estate/Y (GI: BJRSX)
Century Shares (GI: CENSX)
CGM Realty (GI: CGMRX)
Cohen & Steers Realty Shs (GI: CSRSX)
Columbia Real Estate Eqty (GI: CREEX)
Fidelity Real Estate Inv (GI: FRESX)
Fidelity Sel Air Trans (AG: FSAIX)
Fidelity Sel Banking (Grth: FSRBX)
Fidelity Sel Biotech (AG: FBIOX)
Fidelity Sel Brokerage (AG: FSLBX)
Fidelity Sel Computers (AG: FDCPX)
Fidelity Sel Defense (Grth: FSDAX)
Fidelity Sel Develop Comm (AG: FSDCX)
Fidelity Sel Electronics (AG: FSELX)
Fidelity Sel Energy (Grth: FSENX)
Fidelity Sel Energy Serv (AG: FSESX)
Fidelity Sel Financl Serv (Grth: FIDSX)
Fidelity Sel Food & Agri (GI: FDFAX)
Fidelity Sel Gold Port (AG: FSAGX)
Fidelity Sel Health Care (Grth: FSPHX)
Fidelity Sel Home Finance (Grth: FSVLX)
Fidelity Sel Insurance (Grth: FSPCX)
Fidelity Sel Leisure (AG: FDLSX)
Fidelity Sel Med Dlvry (AG: FSHCX)
Fidelity Sel Multimedia (AG: FBMPX)
Fidelity Sel Natural Gas (Grth: FSNGX)
Fidelity Sel Retailing (Grth: FSRPX)
Fidelity Sel Software (AG: FSCSX)
Fidelity Sel Technology (AG: FSPTX)
Fidelity Sel Telecomm (AG: FSTCX)
Fidelity Sel Utilities Gr (GI: FSUTX)
Fidelity Utilities (GI: FIUIX)
Firsthand: Tech Value (AG: TVFQX)
Gabelli Gl Telecomm/AAA (IntlS: GABTX)

Galaxy II: Utility (GI: IUTLX)
ICON Leisure & Consumer (Grth: ICLEX)
INVESCO Energy/Inv (AG: FSTEX)
INVESCO Financial Svc/Inv (Grth: FSFSX)
INVESCO Gold/Inv (AG: FGLDX)
INVESCO Health Sci/Inv (AG: FHLSX)
INVESCO Leisure/Inv (Grth: FLISX)
INVESCO Tech/Inv (AG: FTCHX)
INVESCO Telcom/Inv (IntlS: ISWCX)
INVESCO Utilities/Inv (GI: FSTUX)
Longleaf Partners Realty (GI: LLREX)
Montgomery Glbl Commun/R (IntlS: MNGCX)
Northern Technology (AG: NTCHX)
PBHG Tech & Comm (AG: PBTCX)
RS: Information Age/A (AG: RSIFX)
Scudder Gold (AG: SCGDX)
Stratton Monthly Dvd REIT (GI: STMDX)
Strong American Utilities (GI: SAMUX)
T Rowe Price Fincl Svc (GI: PRISX)
T Rowe Price Hlth Science (AG: PRHSX)
T Rowe Price Media & Tele (AG: PRMTX)
T Rowe Price New Era (Grth: PRNEX)
T Rowe Price Science & Tech (AG: PRSCX)
USAA Inv: Gold (AG: USAGX)
USAA Science & Technology (AG: USSCX)
Vanguard Specl: Energy (Grth: VGENX)
Vanguard Specl: Gold & PM (AG: VGPMX)
Vanguard Specl: Health (Grth: VGHCX)
Vanguard Specl: REIT Index (GI: VGSIX)
Vanguard Specl: Util Inc (GI: VGSUX)
Warburg Glb Hlth Sci/Cmn (AG: WPHSX)

SOCIALLY CONSCIOUS FUNDS

Aquinas Value (GI: AQEIX)
Citizens: Core Gr/R (Grth: WAIDX)
Citizens: Emg Gr/R (AG: WAEGX)
Citizens: Income (B-Cor: WAIMX)
Domini Social Equity (Grth: DSEFX)
Dreyfus Premier Third/Z (Grth: DRTHX)
Neuberger Soc Respv (Grth: NBSRX)
Pax World Balanced (Bal: PAXWX)
USAA First Start Growth (Grth: UFSGX)

STATE-SPECIFIC TAX-EXEMPT BOND FUNDS

Arizona

Amer Cent: AZ Intm Muni/Inv (BEAMX)

California

Amer Cent: CA Hi Yield (BCHYX)
Amer Cent: CA Ins TF/Inv (BCINX)
Amer Cent: CA Intm TF/Inv (BCITX)
Amer Cent: CA Long Tm/Inv (BCLTX)
Amer Cent: CA Ltd TF/Inv (BCSTX)
CA Inv: CA Tax-Free Income (CFNTX)
Dreyfus CA Interm Muni Bd (DCIMX)
Dreyfus CA Tax-Exempt Bd (DRCAX)
Dreyfus Gen CA Muni Bond (GCABX)
Excelsior CA Tx Ex Income (UMCAX)
Fidelity Spart CA Muni (FCTFX)
Fremont: CA Interm Tax-Free (FCATX)
Northern CA Tax-Exempt (NCATX)
SAFECO CA Tax-Free Inc (SFCAX)
Schwab Inv: CA Lg Tm TF Bd (SWCAX)
Schwab Inv: CA Sh Int TF Bd (SWCSX)
Scudder CA Tax-Free (SCTFX)
T Rowe Price CA TF: Bond (PRXCX)
USAA Tax Ex: CA Bond (USCBX)
Vanguard CA: Ins Intm TE (VCAIX)
Vanguard CA: Ins Long Tm (VCITX)

Connecticut

Dreyfus CT Interm Muni Bd (DCTIX)
Fidelity Spart CT Muni (FICNX)
Galaxy: CT Intm Muni/Tr (SCTEX)

Florida

Amer Cent: FL Intm Muni/Inv (ACBFX)
Dreyfus FL Interm Muni Bd (DFLIX)
Fidelity Spart FL Income (FFLIX)
Galaxy: FL Muni/Tr (SFTEX)
T Rowe Price TF: FL Int (FLTFX)
USAA State TF: FL TF Inc (UFLTX)
Vanguard FL Ins Lg Tm TE (VFLTX)

Georgia

T Rowe Price TF: GA Bond (GTFBX)

Hawaii
First Hawaii Muni Bond (SURFX)

Kentucky
Dupree: KY Tax-Free Income (KYTFX)
Dupree: KY Tax-Free Short-Med (KYSMX)

Massachusetts
Dreyfus MA Interm Muni Bd (DMAIX)
Dreyfus MA Tax-Exempt Bd (DMEBX)
Fidelity Spart MA Muni (FDMMX)
Galaxy: MA Intm Muni/Tr (SEMAX)
Scudder MA Tax-Free/S (SCMAX)

Maryland
Fidelity Spart MD Income (SMDMX)
T Rowe Price TF: MD Bond (MDXBX)
T Rowe Price TF: MD Short (PRMDX)

Michigan
Fidelity Spart MI Muni (FMHTX)

Minnesota
Fidelity Spart MN Muni (FIMIX)
Sit Minnesota Tax-Free Inc (SMTFX)

New Jersey
Dreyfus NJ Interm Mu Bond (DNJIX)
Dreyfus NJ Mu Bond (DRNJX)
Fidelity Spart NJ Muni (FNJHX)
T Rowe Price TF: NJ Bond (NJTFX)
Vanguard NJ Ins Lg Tm TE (VNJTX)

New York
Dreyfus Gen NY Muni Bond (GNYMX)
Dreyfus NY Interm Tx Ex (DRNIX)
Dreyfus NY Tax Ex Bond (DRNYX)
Empire Bldr Tax-Free Bd/Bldr (EMBTX)
Empire Bldr Tax-Free Bd/Prem (EMTPX)
Excelsior NY Intm Tx Ex (UMNYX)
Fidelity Spart NY Muni In (FTFMX)
Scudder NY TF (SCYTX)
T Rowe Price TF: NY Bond (PRNYX)
USAA Tax Ex: NY Bond (USNYX)
Vanguard NY Ins Lg Tm TE (VNYTX)
Warburg NY Intm Muni/Cmn (CNMBX)

Ohio

Fidelity Spart OH Muni (FOHFX)
Vanguard OH Ins Lg Tm TE (VOHIX)

Oregon

Columbia OR Muni Bond (CMBFX)

Pennsylvania

Dreyfus PA Interm Muni Bd (DPABX)
Fidelity Spart PA Muni (FPXTX)
Vanguard PA Tx Ex Ins LT (VPAIX)

Virginia

T Rowe Price TF: VA Bond (PRVAX)
USAA Tax Ex: Virginia Bond (USVAX)

Wisconsin

Heartland Grp: WI Tax-Free (HRWIX)

Appendix B

Changes to the Funds

FUND NAME CHANGES

Former	*Current*
AARP Growth: Capital Growth	Scudder Capital Grth/AARP
AARP GNMA & US Treasury	Scudder GNMA/AARP
ABN AMRO: Small Cap Growth—Cmn	ABN AMRO: Sm Cap/Cmn
Acorn Inv: Acorn	Liberty Acorn/Z
Acorn Inv: Acorn USA	Liberty Acorn USA/Z
Acorn Inv: Int'l	Liberty Acorn Internatl/Z
Aquinas Equity Income	Aquinas Value
Berger One Hundred	Berger Growth
Boston 1784 CT Tax Exempt	Galaxy: CT Intm Muni/Tr
Boston 1784 Growth	Galaxy: Growth II/Tr
Boston 1784 MA Tax-Exempt Income	Galaxy: MA Intm Muni/Tr
Boston 1784 Tax-Exempt Medium Income	Galaxy: Intm TE Bond/Tr
Citizens: Index—Ret	Citizens: Core Gr/R
FAM Value	Fenimore: Value
Fidelity Hong Kong & China	Fidelity China Region
Fidelity Int'l Value	Fidelity Aggressive Intl
Fidelity Spart Market Index	Fidelity Spart 500 Index
Dreyfus Founders: Growth	Founders: Large Cap Gr
Guinness Flight China & Hong Kong	Investec China & HK
Hotchkis & Wiley Equity Income	Mercury HW Lrge Cap Val/I
Hotchkis & Wiley Int'l	Mercury HW Intl Val/I
Hotchkis & Wiley Low Duration	Mercury Low Dur/I
Hotchkis & Wiley Total Return	Mercury Tot Ret/I
IAA Growth	Country Growth
Lexington Corp Leaders	Pilgrim Corp Leaders/A
Lexington Worldwide Emerging Mkt	Pilgrim Wldwd Emerg Mkt/A
Montgomery Select 50—R	Montgomery Global 20/R
Northern Small Cap	Northern Small Cap Value
O'Shaughnessy Cornerstone Growth	Hennessy Crnst Grth
Pax World	Pax World Balanced
SAFECO Income	SAFECO Div Income
Smith Breeden US Equity Market +	Managers: US Stk Mkt Plus
Strong Asset Allocation	Strong Balanced
Strong Equity Income	Strong Adv US Value/Z
Strong Short-Term Global Bond	Strong Adv Short Dur Bd/Z

Strong Total Return	Strong Lrg Cap Growth
Turner: Growth Equity	Vanguard Growth Equity
Van Wagoner Micro Cap	Van Wagoner Micro-Cap Gr
Van Wagoner Mid Cap	Van Wagoner Mid-Cap Gr
Vanguard Aggressive Growth	Vanguard Strategic Eqty
Vanguard STAR: LifeStrategy Conserv Growth	Vanguard LifeStgy Cons Gr
Vanguard STAR: LifeStrategy Growth	Vanguard LifeStgy Grth
Vanguard STAR: LifeStrategy Income	Vanguard LifeStgy Income
Vanguard STAR: LifeStrategy Moderate Growth	Vanguard LifeStgy Mod Gr
Vanguard STAR: Total Int'l	Vanguard Tot Itl Stk Idx
Warburg Pincus Growth & Income—Cmn	Warburg Value/Cmn
WPG Growth & Income	WPG Large Cap Growth
Wasatch Aggressive Equity	Wasatch: Small Cap Grth
Wasatch Growth	Wasatch: Core Growth
Wasatch Mid-Cap	Wasatch: Ultra Growth

FUNDS DROPPED FROM THE GUIDE

Fund	*Reason Eliminated*
AARP Growth: Bal Stk & Bond	Merged into Scudder Balanced Fund
AARP Growth: Global Growth	Merged into Scudder Global Fund/S
AARP Growth: Growth & Inc	Merged into Scudder Growth & Income
AARP Income: Hi Qlty ST Bond	Merged into Scudder Short Term Bond
AARP Tax-Free: Ins General	Merged into Scudder Managed Muni Bond
ABN AMRO: Asian Tigers—Cmn	Low asset size
ABN AMRO: TxEx Fxd Inc—Cmn	Low asset size
Amer Cent Ltd Tax-Free	Low asset size
Amer Cent Target 2000—Inv	Matured 12/00
API Growth	Not tracked by Standard & Poor's Micropal
Aquinas Balanced	Low asset size
Aquinas Fixed Income	Low asset size
Babson Bond: Port S	Low asset size
Babson Tax-Free Inc: Port L	Low asset size
Baron Growth	Low asset size
BB&K Diversa	Low asset size
Berwyn	Low asset size
Berwyn Income	Low asset size
BNY Hamilton: Eqty Inc—Inv	Low asset size
Boston 1784 Asset Alloc	Merged into Galaxy: Asset Allocation Fund
Boston 1784 Growth & Inc	Merged into Galaxy: Growth & Income Fund
Boston 1784 Income	Merged into Galaxy: High Quality Bond
Boston 1784 Int'l Equity	Merged into Galaxy: International Equity
Boston 1784 RI Tax-Exempt	Merged into Galaxy: RI Muni Bond Fund
Boston 1784 Short-Term Income	Merged into Galaxy: Short Term Bond Fund
Boston 1784 US Gvt Med-Term	Merged into Galaxy: Interm Gov't
Bundage Story & Rose Sh Int Fxd Inc	Low asset size
Buffalo Balanced	Low asset size

Buffalo High Yield....................Low asset size
CGM Fixed Income....................Low asset size
Clover Equity Value....................Low asset size
Columbia US Gov't Sec....................Low asset size
Crabbe Huson Special....................Imposed a 5.75% front end load
Dreyfus Core Bond....................Imposed a 4.5% front end load
Dreyfus Growth & Value: Agg Grth....................Low asset size
Dreyfus High Yield Sec....................Imposed a 5.75% front end load
Dreyfus Short-Term Hi Yld....................Merged into Premier Ltd Term Hi Inc Fund/A
Evergreen Amer Utility....................Merged into Evergreen Utility Fund/A
Excelsior Latin America....................Low asset size
Fidelity Sel Automotive....................Low asset size
Fidelity Sel Chemicals....................Low asset size
Fidelity Sel Consmr Ind....................Low asset size
Fidelity Sel Construction....................Low asset size
Fidelity Sel Indust Equip....................Low asset size
Fidelity Sel Prec Metals....................Merged into Fidelity Sel Gold Port
Fiduciary Capital Growth....................Low asset size
First Eagle Int'l—Y....................Low asset size
Govett Small Companies—A....................Merged into ARK Funds: Small Cap Equity
Greenspring....................Low asset size
Heartland Grp: Gov't....................Liquidated
Heartland Grp: Value Plus....................Low asset size
Hotchkis & Wiley Balanced....................Low asset size
IAI Balanced....................Merged into Federated Stock & Bond Fund/A
IAI Bond....................Merged into Federated Investment Bond
IAI Emerging Growth....................Merged into Federated Aggressive Grth/A
IAI Growth & Income....................Merged into Federated American Leaders/A
IAI Int'l....................Merged into Federated Int'l Equity/A
IAI Midcap Growth....................Merged into Federated Growth Strategies/A
IAI Regional....................Merged into Federated Capital Appreciation
INVESCO Int'l: Pacific Bas....................Liquidated
INVESCO Splty: Latin Amer....................Liquidated
Jurika & Voyles Balance—J....................Low asset size
Lexington Glbl Inc....................Low asset size
Lexington GNMA Income....................Imposed a 5.75% front-end load
Lexington Goldfund....................Low asset size
Lexington Growth & Income....................Imposed a 5.75% front-end load
Lindner Mrkt Neutral—Inv....................Low asset size
Lindner Utility—Inv....................Low asset size
Loomis Sayles Core Vl—Ist....................Low asset size
Loomis Sayles Glbl Bond—Ist....................Low asset size
Loomis Sayles Growth—Ist....................Low asset size
Maxus Equity—Inv....................Low asset size
Maxus Income—Inv....................Low asset size
Midas....................Low asset size

Fund	Status
Montgomery Emg Asia—R	Low asset size
Montgomery Int'l Sm Cap—R	Merged into Montgomery Intl Gr/R
Mosaic Tax-Free: National	Low asset size
Mosaic Tax-Free: Virginia	Low asset size
Neuberger Muni Sec	Low asset size
O'Shaughnessy Crnrst Val	Low asset size
Oakmark Int'l Small Cap	Low asset size
Reich & Tang Equity	Merged into Delafield Fund
RS Glbl Natural Res—A	Low asset size
RS Partners—A	Low asset size
Rushmore Tax-Free Inv: MD	Low asset size
Rushmore Tax-Free Inv: VA	Low asset size
Rydex URSA	Low asset size
SAFECO GNMA	Low asset size
Schroder Lrg Cap Eqty—Inv	Merged into Schroder US Diversified Grth/Inv
Schwartz Value	Low asset size
Scudder GNMA	Merged into Scudder GNMA/AARP Shares
Scudder Int'l Bond	Merged into Scudder Global Bond Fund
Scudder Limited-Term Tax-Free	Merged into Scudder Medium Term Tax Free
Scudder MA Lmtd term Tax-Free	Merged into Scudder MA Tax Free Fund
Scudder Micro Cap	Merged into Scudder Small Co Stock Fund
Scudder Ohio Tax-Free	Merged into Scudder Managed Muni Bond
Shelby	Low asset size
Skyline Sm Cap Value Plus	Merged into Skyline: Special Equities
Smith Breeden Int Dur Gv	Low asset size
Smith Breeden Sh Dur Gvt	Low asset size
Stonebridge Growth	Low asset size
Stratton Growth	Low asset size
T. Rowe Price Int'l: Gl Bond	Merged into T. Rowe Price Intl Fund: Bond
T. Rowe Price Short-Term Gov't	Merged into T. Rowe Price Short Term Bond
T. Rowe Price Sum: Ltd-Term	Merged into T. Rowe Price Short Term Bond
UMB Scout Regional	Low asset size
US Glob Inv: Gold Shares	Low asset size
US Glob Inv: World Gold	Low asset size
US Gov't Securities	Low asset size
Value Line NY Tax-Exempt	Low asset size
Warburg Balanced—Cmn	Low asset size
Warburg Post-Vent—Cmn	Merged into Warburg Global Post-Vent/Cmn
Warburg Small Co Val—Cmn	Low asset size
Westcore Small Cap Opport	Low asset size
William Blair Income	Low asset size
WPG Quantitative Eqty	Low asset size
Wright US Gov Near-Term	Low asset size

Index

B

C

D

E

F

G

H

I

J

N

O

P

R

S

T

U

V

Y